APA Handbook of

Forensic Neuropsychology

APA Handbooks in Psychology® Series

APA Addiction Syndrome Handbook—two volumes
Howard J. Shaffer, Editor-in-Chief
APA Educational Psychology Handbook—three volumes
Karen R. Harris, Steve Graham, and Tim Urdan, Editors-in-Chief
APA Handbook of Behavior Analysis—two volumes
Gregory J. Madden, Editor-in-Chief
APA Handbook of Career Intervention—two volumes
Paul J. Hartung, Mark L. Savickas, and W. Bruce Walsh, Editors-in-Chief
APA Handbook of Clinical Geropsychology—two volumes
Peter A. Lichtenberg and Benjamin T. Mast, Editors-in-Chief
APA Handbook of Clinical Psychology—five volumes
John C. Norcross, Gary R. VandenBos, and Donald K. Freedheim, Editors-in-Chief
APA Handbook of Community Psychology—two volumes
Meg A. Bond, Irma Serrano-García, and Christopher B. Keys, Editors-in-Chief
APA Handbook of Comparative Psychology—two volumes
Josep Call, Editor-in-Chief
APA Handbook of Counseling Psychology—two volumes
Nadya A. Fouad, Editor-in-Chief
APA Handbook of Ethics in Psychology—two volumes
Samuel J. Knapp, Editor-in-Chief
APA Handbook of Forensic Neuropsychology—one volume
Shane S. Bush, Editor-in-Chief
APA Handbook of Forensic Psychology—two volumes
Brian L. Cutler and Patricia A. Zapf, Editors-in-Chief
APA Handbook of Human Systems Integration—one volume
Deborah A. Boehm-Davis, Francis T. Durso, and John D. Lee, Editors-in-Chief
APA Handbook of Industrial and Organizational Psychology—three volumes
Sheldon Zedeck, Editor-in-Chief
APA Handbook of Men and Masculinities—one volume
Y. Joel Wong and Stephen R. Wester, Editors-in-Chief
APA Handbook of Multicultural Psychology—two volumes
Frederick T. L. Leong, Editor-in-Chief
APA Handbook of Nonverbal Communication—one volume
David Matsumoto, Hyisung C. Hwang, and Mark G. Frank, Editors-in-Chief
APA Handbook of Personality and Social Psychology—four volumes
Mario Mikulincer and Phillip R. Shaver, Editors-in-Chief
APA Handbook of Psychology and Juvenile Justice—one volume
Kirk Heilbrun, Editor-in-Chief
APA Handbook of Psychology, Religion, and Spirituality—two volumes
Kenneth I. Pargament, Editor-in-Chief
APA Handbook of Research Methods in Psychology—three volumes
Harris Cooper, Editor-in-Chief
APA Handbook of Sexuality and Psychology—two volumes
Deborah L. Tolman and Lisa M. Diamond, Editors-in-Chief
APA Handbook of Testing and Assessment in Psychology—three volumes
Kurt F. Geisinger, Editor-in-Chief
APA Handbook of Trauma Psychology—two volumes
Steven N. Gold, Editor-in-Chief

APA Handbooks in Psychology

APA Handbook of Forensic Neuropsychology

Shane S. Bush, *Editor-in-Chief*
George J. Demakis and Martin L. Rohling, *Associate Editors*

American Psychological Association • Washington, DC

Published by
American Psychological Association
750 First Street, NE
Washington, DC 20002-4242
www.apa.org

To order
APA Order Department
P.O. Box 92984
Washington, DC 20090-2984
Tel: (800) 374-2721; Direct: (202) 336-5510
Fax: (202) 336-5502; TDD/TTY: (202) 336-6123
Online: www.apa.org/pubs/books/
E-mail: order@apa.org

In the U.K., Europe, Africa, and the Middle East, copies may be ordered from
American Psychological Association
3 Henrietta Street
Covent Garden, London
WC2E 8LU England

American Psychological Association Staff
Jasper Simons, *Executive Publisher*
Brenda Carter, *Publisher, APA Books*
Patricia D. Mathis, *Reference Editorial Manager, APA Books*
Lisa T. Corry, *Project Editor, APA Books*

Typeset in Berkeley by Cenveo Publisher Services, Columbia, MD

Printer: Sheridan Books, Chelsea, MI
Cover Designer: Naylor Design, Washington, DC

Library of Congress Cataloging-in-Publication Data
Names: Bush, Shane S., 1965– editor. | Demakis, George J., editor. | Rohling, Martin L., editor.
Title: APA handbook of forensic neuropsychology / Shane S. Bush, editor-in-chief ; George J. Demakis and Martin L. Rohling, associate editors.
Other titles: Handbook of forensic neuropsychology
Description: Washington, DC : American Psychological Association, [2017] | Series: APA handbooks in psychology series | Includes bibliographical references and index.
Identifiers: LCCN 2017001679| ISBN 9781433826948 | ISBN 1433826941
Subjects: LCSH: Forensic neuropsychology—Handbooks, manuals, etc. | Clinical neuropsychology—Handbooks, manuals, etc.
Classification: LCC RA1147.5 .A63 2017 | DDC 614/.15—dc23
LC record available at https://lccn.loc.gov/2017001679

British Library Cataloguing-in-Publication Data
A CIP record is available from the British Library.

Printed in the United States of America
First Edition

http://dx.doi.org/10.1037/0000032-000

Contents

Editorial Board

About the Editor-in-Chief

Shane S. Bush, PhD, ABPP, is director of Long Island Neuropsychology, PC. He is also a neuropsychologist with the VA New York Harbor Healthcare System. He is board certified in clinical neuropsychology, rehabilitation psychology, clinical psychology, and geropsychology. He has been awarded fellow status by the American Psychological Association (APA; Divisions 12, 18, 20, 22, 40, and 42). He is a past president and fellow of the National Academy of Neuropsychology. He has also held elected positions or served as a committee member for the American Academy of Clinical Neuropsychology, American Board of Professional Neuropsychology, American Board of Geropsychology, and multiple APA divisions. He has served as an editorial board member of *Applied Neuropsychology, Archives of Clinical Neuropsychology, Clinical Gerontologist, Ethics and Behavior, Journal of Forensic Neuropsychology, Journal of Head Trauma Rehabilitation, Journal of Pediatric Neuropsychology, Psychological Injury and Law,* and *The Clinical Neuropsychologist.* He has presented on issues relevant to forensic neuropsychology at national and international conferences. He has over 130 publications, including more than 15 books; six special issues of journals; 90 articles, book chapters, and encyclopedia entries; and 13 position papers for professional organizations, many of which are directly relevant to the practice of forensic neuropsychology. In 2014, he was presented with the Outstanding Supervisor of the Year Award by the Department of Psychiatry at Stony Brook University Medical School. He is a veteran of both the U.S. Marine Corps and Naval Reserve.

Contributors

Beth Caillouet Arredondo, PhD, ABPP-CN, Neuropsychology Lab, Western State Hospital, Staunton, VA, and Department of Psychiatry and Neurobehavioral Sciences, University of Virginia School of Medicine, Charlottesville

Bradley N. Axelrod, PhD, ABN, John D. Dingell Department of Veterans Affairs Medical Center, Detroit, MI

Shane S. Bush, PhD, ABPP, Long Island Neuropsychology, PC, Lake Ronkonkoma, NY

Desiree A. Byrd, PhD, ABPP-CN, Department of Neurology and Department of Psychiatry, Icahn School of Medicine at Mount Sinai, New York, NY

Joshua E. Caron, PhD, ABPP-CN, Neuropsychology Section, VA Maine Healthcare System, Lewiston

Jeremy J. Davis, PsyD, ABPP-CN, Division of Physical Medicine and Rehabilitation, University of Utah School of Medicine, Salt Lake City

George J. Demakis, PhD, Department of Psychology, University of North Carolina, Charlotte

Joseph W. Fink, PhD, ABPP-CN, Department of Psychiatry and Behavioral Neuroscience, University of Chicago, Chicago, IL

R. Brock Frost, PhD, Department of Psychiatry and Behavioral Sciences, Center for Neuropsychological Services, University of New Mexico School of Medicine, Albuquerque

Michelle R. Guyton, PhD, ABPP, Northwest Forensic Institute, Portland, OR

David E. Hartman, PhD, MS, ABN, ABPP, Medical and Forensic Neuropsychology, Chicago, IL

Robert L. Heilbronner, PhD, ABPP-CN, Chicago Neuropsychology Group and Northwestern University Feinberg School of Medicine, Chicago, IL

Michelle Hoy-Watkins, PsyD, Department of Forensic Psychology, Chicago School of Professional Psychology, Chicago, IL

John H. King, PhD, ABPP-CN, Department of Psychiatry and Behavioral Sciences, Center for Neuropsychological Services, University of New Mexico School of Medicine, Albuquerque

Jennifer Langhinrichsen-Rohling, PhD, Department of Psychology and Gulf Coast Behavioral Health and Resiliency Center, University of South Alabama, Mobile

Glenn J. Larrabee, PhD, ABPP-CN, Independent Practice, Sarasota, FL

Cutter A. Lindbergh, MA, Department of Psychology, University of Georgia, Athens

Loren E. Mallory, PhD, ABPP, Willamette Falls Neuropsychology, Oregon City, OR

Eric G. Mart, PhD, ABPP (Forensic), Independent Practice, Portsmouth, NH

Stephen S. Meharg, PhD, ABN, Independent Practice, Longview, WA

John E. Meyers, PsyD, ABN, ABPdN, Comprehensive MedPsych Systems, Sarasota, FL
Justin B. Miller, PhD, ABPP-CN, Cleveland Clinic Lou Ruvo Center for Brain Health, Las Vegas, NV
L. Stephen Miller, PhD, Department of Psychology, University of Georgia, Athens
Joel E. Morgan, PhD, ABPP-CN, Neuropsychology Associates of New Jersey, Morristown
Shelley Peery, PhD, San Francisco Neuropsychology PC, San Francisco, CA
Emalee J. W. Quickel, PhD, Department of Psychology, Loyola University Maryland, Baltimore
Paul M. Richards, PhD, Independent Practice, Louisville, CO
Martin L. Rohling, PhD, Department of Psychology, University of South Alabama, Mobile
Summer N. Rolin, PsyD, Division of Physical Medicine and Rehabilitation, University of Utah School of Medicine, Salt Lake City
Christian Schutte, PhD, ABPP-CN, Henry Ford Allegiance Health, Jackson, MI
Joseph J. Sesta, PhD, MP, Department of Forensic Psychology, Chicago School of Professional Psychology, Chicago, IL, and Suncoast Neuropsychology, LLC, Apollo Beach, FL
Adriana M. Strutt, PhD, ABPP-CN, Department of Neurology and Department of Psychiatry and Behavioral Sciences, Baylor College of Medicine, Houston, TX
Chriscelyn M. Tussey, PsyD, ABPP, Metropolitan Forensic and Neuropsychological Consultation, PLLC, and Department of Psychiatry, New York University School of Medicine, New York
Dustin Wahlstrom, PhD, Pearson Clinical Assessments, San Antonio, TX
Gerald Young, PhD, CPsych, Department of Psychology, Glendon College, York University, Toronto, Ontario, Canada

Series Preface

The *APA Handbook of Forensic Neuropsychology* is the 24th publication to be released in the American Psychological Association's *APA Handbooks in Psychology®* series, instituted in 2010. The series comprehends both single volumes and multivolume sets focused on core subfields or on highly focused content areas and emerging subfields. A complete listing of the series titles to date can be found on p. ii.

Each publication in the series is primarily formulated to address the reference interests and needs of researchers, clinicians, and practitioners in psychology. Each also addresses the needs of graduate students for well-organized and highly detailed supplementary texts, whether to "fill in" their own specialty areas or to acquire solid familiarity with other specialties and emerging trends across the breadth of psychology. Many of the sets additionally bear strong interest for professionals in pertinent complementary fields (i.e., depending on content area), be they corporate executives and human resources personnel; psychiatrists; doctors, nurses, and other health personnel; teachers and school administrators; counselors; legal professionals; and so forth.

Under the direction of small and select editorial boards consisting of top scholars in the field, with chapters authored by both senior and rising researchers and practitioners, each reference commits to a steady focus on best science and best practice. Coverage converges on what is currently known in the particular topical area (including basic historical reviews) and the identification of the most pertinent sources of information in both the core and evolving literature. Volumes and chapters alike pinpoint practical issues; probe unresolved and controversial topics; and highlight future theoretical, research, and practice trends. The editors provide guidance to the "dialogue" among chapters through internal cross-referencing that demonstrates a robust integration of topics. The user is thus offered a clear understanding of the complex interrelationships within each field.

With the imprimatur of the largest scientific and professional organization representing psychology in the United States and the largest association of psychologists in the world, and with content edited and authored by some of its most respected members, the *APA Handbooks in Psychology* series is an indispensable and authoritative reference resource for researchers, instructors, practitioners, and field leaders alike.

Jasper Simons
Executive Publisher

Foreword

The field of clinical neuropsychology is not static, and neither is the application of clinical neuropsychology to forensic matters. The *APA Handbook of Forensic Neuropsychology* is a welcome addition to the literature and will be of benefit not only to clinical neuropsychologists who work in the forensic arena but also to attorneys whose work involves clinical neuropsychology.

This volume is organized into six major sections. Part I covers basic statistical issues that go beyond what many of us learned in graduate school. This excellent update covers both basic issues and current challenges that cannot be ignored. The chapter on ethical practice focuses on commonly encountered dilemmas and offers proposed solutions.

Part II addresses the methods and procedures in the clinical neuropsychology assessment process. This section begins with a chapter devoted to a review of records, clinical interviewing, and behavioral observations. The next chapter deals with neuropsychological tests and neuropsychological batteries and is followed by a chapter on symptom and performance validity. In the latter chapter, the authors recommend the use of the term *performance validity measure* to encompass all methods of validity assessment (i.e., performance validity tests, symptom validity tests, and embedded validity indices). Part II concludes with a chapter on neuroimaging techniques that provides a historical perspective and delineates commonly used techniques and, most important, discusses their current limitations.

Part III deals with the assessment of traumatic brain injury across the severity spectrum, as well as co-occurring psychological disorders such as posttraumatic stress disorder, depression, and anxiety. Also included are chapters on the role of chronic pain and somatic and cogniform disorders.

Part IV includes chapters on population-specific issues, including veterans compensation and pension evaluation, disability determination, civil capacities, criminal responsibility, and competency to stand trial. The section concludes with a chapter on cultural diversity issues.

Part V focuses on forensic neuropsychological reports, issues associated with the admissibility of neuropsychological evidence, and testimony in neuropsychological cases. This section concludes with a unique chapter on the consumers of forensic neuropsychological services.

Part VI addresses two future issues for forensic neuropsychology: (a) the role of technology and the use of computerized assessments as more instruments become digitally based and (b) the educational and training needs of the next generation of clinical neuropsychologists.

This handbook would be an excellent text for an advanced graduate-level seminar in forensic clinical neuropsychology, and it would serve as a reference for general psychological and neuropsychological assessment seminars. Moreover, given the breadth and scope of the topics covered, it is recommended reading for not only early career neuropsychologists but also seasoned neuropsychologists.

Finally, writing this Foreword to the *APA Handbook of Forensic Neuropsychology* has been an educational experience for me as a scientist–practitioner. This truly is a handbook in every respect of that word and definitely deserves a place in your practice's library.

Robert J. McCaffrey, PhD, ABN, ABPdN
Past President, National Academy of Neuropsychology
Past President, American Board of Professional Neuropsychology
Professor, University at Albany, State University of New York
President, American Board of Pediatric Neuropsychology
Editor-in-Chief, *Developmental Neuropsychology*

Introduction

Individuals with known or suspected cognitive problems interact with legal and administrative decision makers for a variety of purposes. Whether in the context of civil litigation, the criminal justice system, or determination of benefits, triers of fact and administrative decision makers rely on experts to provide information about the individual that bears on the decision to be made. Neuropsychologists, as experts in understanding neurocognitive disorders, psychological functioning, and veracity of presentation, are particularly well qualified to advise forensic decision makers about these issues. Practitioners answer forensic questions and inform decision makers by applying neuropsychological principles, knowledge, and practices. Use of an empirically based multimethod approach allows neuropsychologists to provide forensic opinions that are based on scientific evidence, thereby satisfying legal admissibility standards and promoting objectivity.

Despite its tremendous growth in recent years, forensic neuropsychology remains a relatively young subspecialty. The American Psychological Association Commission for the Recognition of Specialties and Proficiencies in Professional Psychology (APA CRSPPP; 2010a, 2010b) provided formal specialty recognition of clinical neuropsychology in 1996 and recognition of forensic psychology in 2001. APA CRSPPP (2010a) described the specialty of clinical neuropsychology as follows:

> Clinical neuropsychology is a specialty in professional psychology that applies principles of assessment and intervention based upon the scientific study of human behavior as it relates to normal and abnormal functioning of the central nervous system. The specialty is dedicated to enhancing the understanding of brain-behavior relationships and the application of such knowledge to human problems. (para. 1)

APA CRSPPP (2010b) described forensic psychology as follows:

> Forensic psychology is the professional practice by psychologists within the areas of clinical psychology, counseling psychology, school psychology or another specialty recognized by the American Psychological Association, when they are engaged as experts and represent themselves as such, in an activity primarily intended to provide professional psychological expertise to the judicial system. (para. 1)

On the basis of these definitions, forensic neuropsychology can be considered a subspecialty within neuropsychology whereby neuropsychological knowledge and services, including testimony and trial consultation, are provided to inform legal or administrative decisions. Beginning in the early 1990s, books with *forensic neuropsychology* in the title began emerging, defining the scope of practice of this subspecialty and providing information for practitioners to apply in this rapidly growing area of practice (Doerr & Carlin, 1991; Horton & Hartlage, 2003; McCaffrey, Williams, Fisher, & Laing, 1997; Sweet, 1999; Valciukas, 1995). Since the publication of those early volumes, new editions and books have been published, reflecting the continued growth and evolving nature of the science and practices that underlie this subspecialty. Kaufmann (2009) quantified the rapid growth of forensic neuropsychology. At that time, he conducted a Lexis search and found 4,358 cases using the root *neuropsycholo-* during the prior 70 years, 71% of which were adjudicated in the decade preceding his search. He further reported, "The growth of legal cases referencing neuropsychology is outpacing every related area of brain–behavior expertise and this growth is accelerating" (p. 1131).

Differences exist between clinical and forensic neuropsychological practices. Because neuropsychologists are traditionally trained in clinical contexts, the differences between clinical and forensic practices are typically learned after the completion of formal training but ideally before engaging in forensic activities. Sometimes, however, clinical reports are used by attorneys, administrative decision makers, or others to help support a legal position or inform forensic decisions. In such instances, clinical neuropsychologists find themselves drawn into a forensic context and need to learn, sometimes quickly, what to expect from the process and how professional behaviors may need to be altered.

A position paper from the National Academy of Neuropsychology (Bush & NAN Policy and Planning Committee, 2005) is particularly useful and describes some of the primary distinctions between clinical and forensic neuropsychological evaluations. Some of the general differences, as described in this resource and the forensic neuropsychology literature more broadly, include (a) the nature of the neuropsychologist's roles with the retaining party and examinee; (b) the importance of striving for objectivity despite perceived or overt encouragement or incentive to do otherwise; (c) the nature of privacy, confidentiality, feedback, and dissemination of results; (d) requests for third-party observers; (e) the evaluation process, including the extent of records reviewed, selection of measures that conform to admissibility requirements, and the extent of validity assessment performed; (f) the need to opine about the relationship between the neuropsychological findings and the legal issue; and (g) the adversarial nature of the process in general.

There are currently a number of books on forensic neuropsychology (e.g., Boone, 2013; Hall, 2008; Heilbronner, 2008; Larrabee, 2012; Sweet, 1999) and one handbook of forensic neuropsychology (Horton & Hartlage, 2010). Additional books are also available on various aspects of forensic neuropsychology, such as criminal populations (e.g., Denney & Sullivan, 2008; Sherman & Brooks, 2012), and topics of considerable relevance to forensic neuropsychology, such as independent medical examinations, malingering, and decision-making capacity (e.g., Bush & Iverson, 2012; Carone & Bush, 2013; Demakis, 2012; Larrabee, 2007; Morgan & Sweet, 2009; Oakes, Lovejoy, & Bush, 2017). The primary difference between this handbook and previous texts involves breadth and depth of coverage. This handbook comprehensively reviews the foundation and current best practices of forensic neuropsychology and provides vision and direction for the future of the specialty. The handbook also provides considerable depth of coverage from theoretical, empirical, and applied perspectives. In addition, unlike single-author volumes, this book draws on the knowledge and experiences of numerous neuropsychology practitioners and scholars. With this handbook, we inform practitioners who desire advanced and contemporary reviews of the topics making up this specialty.

EDITORIAL VISION

Clinical neuropsychology is a constantly evolving specialty, with important and exciting advances in many aspects of practice, and the application of clinical neuropsychology to forensic questions and issues is growing at a tremendous rate. We envisioned a handbook that covered the scientific and clinical neuropsychological advances and their application in forensic contexts. To accomplish this goal, the handbook (a) presents the theoretical, statistical, and ethical foundations of forensic neuropsychology; (b) describes current assessment measures and procedures used in forensic neuropsychology, with an emphasis on their empirical evidence base; (c) integrates recently published empirical literature involving commonly encountered disorders and special populations; (d) describes reporting, admissibility, and testimony issues involving neuropsychology in forensic matters; and (e) describes future directions involving the intersection of clinical neuropsychology and legal matters.

Part I: Theoretical, Statistical, and Ethical Foundations

A strong foundation for competent practice of forensic neuropsychology requires an understanding of its theoretical underpinnings, its empirical and statistical base, and the ethical issues and challenges inherent in this type of practice. Understanding the origin and development of forensic neuropsychology provides practitioners a context from which to make informed practice decisions. Familiarity with trends and lasting changes allows practitioners to best understand current practices. Such understanding allows for well-reasoned decisions about the applied aspects of neuropsychological practice in general, as well as how these aspects are applied in specific cases.

Knowledge of statistical concepts and formulas is essential to interpreting neuropsychological test results. Essential decisions, such as how to determine whether a score or pattern of scores reflects impaired cognitive abilities, require at least a basic understanding of base rates of low scores, the nature and frequency of various test performances or outcomes for different disorders, the amount of test score change expected across test administrations, standard errors of measurement, positive and negative predictive values, and other statistical issues and procedures. The strength of conclusions that can be generated and presented to a trier of fact often depends on such statistics.

Many challenges to ethical practice exist in forensic contexts. There are strong incentives in forensic contexts for neuropsychologists to practice outside of their areas of competence, compromise their methods, and sway their opinions and statements in favor of the retaining party. Practitioners must be aware of common pitfalls, develop and maintain ethical practices, and strive for high standards of ethical behavior. Additionally, relevant laws and court cases influence the practice of forensic neuropsychology.

Part II: Assessment Measures and Procedures

The appropriate selection and use of assessment measures and procedures is necessary for practitioners to arrive at accurate and meaningful conclusions that assist forensic decision makers. Reviewing records, observing behavior, and interviewing collateral sources provide valuable information. Knowing what to review, what questions to ask, and how to integrate the information best positions practitioners to arrive at accurate conclusions.

Psychometric assessment options include fixed batteries, co-normed tests, and flexible approaches. A process-based approach can also be informative. Understanding the strengths and weaknesses of various tests and procedures is essential for practitioners when selecting and using the measures with a given examinee. Publication of new tests and new versions of traditional tests is an ongoing process. Similarly, publication of new normative data for existing tests occurs regularly and can be valuable to practitioners. Of considerable importance is the continued rapid growth of validity assessment measures and indicators. In addition, neuroimaging continues to evolve and to offer neuropsychologists another important piece of information for understanding the neurological functioning of examinees.

Part III: Disorders and Special Populations

The neuropsychological knowledge base and methods used differ with various medical, psychiatric, and neurological disorders and vary across examinee populations and examination settings. It is not possible to cover all disorders or populations encountered in forensic contexts by neuropsychologists. As a result, we selected a sample of disorders that, based on our familiarity with published literature and our clinical experiences, are most commonly encountered in forensic neuropsychology. Traumatic brain injury (TBI) in its various severities is clearly the most commonly encountered neurological disorder in personal injury cases. We provide separate chapters for mild and moderate to severe TBI because of their different pathologies, presenting problems, and outcomes.

We considered including additional types of injuries, such as toxic exposure and electrical injury, but concluded that, despite their importance for many individuals, they were not encountered with sufficient frequency to warrant inclusion. In some civil forensic contexts, dementias are commonly encountered. Because questions of decision-making capacity are primarily relevant for people with dementia, the dementias are covered in the civil capacities chapter in Part IV rather than with the other disorders in Part III. Psychiatric disorders and pain, rather than additional acquired brain disorders, are included in Part III because they commonly underlie or coexist with perceived or actual cognitive problems.

Part IV: Special Topics and Populations

A chapter in this section is devoted to neuropsychological assessment of veterans, given the large number of veterans of the recent wars who report neuropsychological problems and the unique context (Veterans Affairs system) in which most veterans are evaluated and pursue benefits. Because of unique issues encountered with disability evaluations and decision-making capacity evaluations, chapters are devoted to those topics. A chapter is also devoted to diversity issues. Although diversity is addressed when relevant in chapters throughout the handbook, we believe that a separate chapter is needed because of the significance of factors, particularly race, in neuropsychological performance. Coverage of diversity includes (a) examinee perception of, and response to, the evaluation process, such as stereotype threat; (b) selection and use of appropriate tests and norms; and (c) best practices in use of interpreters.

Part V: Neuropsychology in the Courtroom

Practitioners of forensic neuropsychology must understand differences between clinical and forensic reports, including use of various legal terms (e.g., *reasonable degree of certainty*). Understanding what legal consumers want, admissibility requirements, and how to present neuropsychological data and conclusions to triers of fact are important practical matters that are often not taught in training programs. Information and recommendations provided by experienced practitioners will help readers improve their services to forensic clients and reduce error in the all-too-common trial-and-error learning process.

Part VI: Future Directions

Technology will likely play an increasingly important part in forensic neuropsychology. Examples include computerized test administration, scoring, and interpretation; increased reliance on complex statistical methods; and more sophisticated and readily available neuroimaging. Also, with the increase in ethnic diversity and the aging population occurring across the United States, there is a need for continued advancements in the reliable and valid assessment of diverse populations. Designing educational programs that account for the rapid changes in forensic neuropsychological assessment is critically important for integrating new graduates into this specialty practice. These issues and additional changes are addressed in this final section.

ACKNOWLEDGMENTS

An endeavor of this magnitude requires a team of collaborators with shared vision and investment of energy working together to bring the project to fruition, and we are grateful to everyone who helped make this publication possible. Specifically, we thank our contributing authors for sharing their knowledge and experience and donating their time to provide state-of-the-art-and-science coverage of important aspects of forensic neuropsychology. We are also grateful to our friends at APA Books, particularly Susan Reynolds, Theodore J. Baroody, and Lisa Corry, for recognizing the importance of this topic, embracing this project, and providing guidance and support throughout the process.

References

American Psychological Association, Commission for the Recognition of Specialties and Proficiencies in Professional Psychology. (2010a). *Clinical neuropsychology*. Retrieved from http://www.apa.org/ed/graduate/specialize/neuro.aspx

American Psychological Association, Commission for the Recognition of Specialties and Proficiencies in Professional Psychology. (2010b). *Forensic psychology*. Retrieved from http://www.apa.org/ed/graduate/specialize/forensic.aspx

Boone, K. B. (2013). *Clinical practice of forensic neuropsychology: An evidence-based approach*. New York, NY: Guilford Press.

Bush, S. S., & Iverson, G. L. (Eds.). (2012). *Neuropsychological assessment of work-related injuries*. New York, NY: Guilford Press.

Bush, S. S., & NAN Policy and Planning Committee. (2005). Independent and court-ordered forensic neuropsychological examinations: Official statement of the National Academy of Neuropsychology. *Archives of Clinical Neuropsychology, 20*, 997–1007. http://dx.doi.org/10.1016/j.acn.2005.06.003

Carone, D., & Bush, S. S. (Eds.). (2013). *Mild traumatic brain injury: Symptom validity assessment and malingering*. New York, NY: Springer.

Demakis, G. J. (Ed.). (2012). *Civil capacities in clinical neuropsychology: Research findings and practical applications*. New York, NY: Oxford University Press.

Denney, R. L., & Sullivan, J. P. (2008). *Clinical neuropsychology in the criminal forensic setting*. New York, NY: Guilford Press.

Doerr, H. O., & Carlin, A. S. (Eds.). (1991). *Forensic neuropsychology: Legal and scientific bases*. New York, NY: Guilford Press.

Hall, H. V. (Ed.). (2008). *Forensic psychology and neuropsychology for criminal and civil cases*. Boca Raton, FL: CRC Press.

Heilbronner, R. L. (Ed.). (2008). *Neuropsychology in the courtroom: Expert analysis of reports and testimony*. New York, NY: Guilford Press.

Horton, A. M., & Hartlage, L. C. (Eds.). (2003). *Handbook of forensic neuropsychology*. New York, NY: Springer.

Horton, A. M., & Hartlage, L. C. (Eds.). (2010). *Handbook of forensic neuropsychology* (2nd ed.). New York, NY: Springer.

Kaufmann, P. M. (2009). Protecting raw data and psychological tests from wrongful disclosure: A primer on the law and other persuasive strategies. *Clinical Neuropsychology, 23,* 1130–1159. http://dx.doi.org/10.1080/13854040903107809

Larrabee, G. J. (Ed.). (2007). *Assessment of malingered neuropsychological deficits*. New York, NY: Oxford University Press.

Larrabee, G. J. (Ed.). (2012). *Forensic neuropsychology: A scientific approach* (2nd ed.). New York, NY: Oxford University Press.

McCaffrey, R. J., Williams, A. D., Fisher, J. M., & Laing, L. C. (1997). *The practice of forensic neuropsychology: Meeting challenges in the courtroom*. New York, NY: Plenum Press.

Morgan, J. E., & Sweet, J. J. (Eds.). (2009). *Neuropsychology of malingering casebook*. New York, NY: Psychology Press.

Oakes, H., Lovejoy, D., & Bush, S. S. (2017). *The independent neuropsychological evaluation*. New York, NY: Oxford University Press.

Sherman, E. M. S., & Brooks, B. L. (Eds.). (2012). *Pediatric forensic neuropsychology*. New York, NY: Oxford University Press.

Sweet, J. J. (Ed.). (1999). *Forensic neuropsychology: Fundamentals and practice*. Lisse, the Netherlands: Swets & Zeitlinger.

Valciukas, J. A. (1995). *Forensic neuropsychology: Conceptual foundations and clinical practice*. New York, NY: Haworth Press.

Part I

THEORETICAL, STATISTICAL, AND ETHICAL FOUNDATIONS

CHAPTER 1

FUNDAMENTAL FORENSIC STATISTICS: STATISTICS EVERY FORENSIC NEUROPSYCHOLOGIST MUST KNOW

Martin L. Rohling, Bradley N. Axelrod, and Jennifer Langhinrichsen-Rohling

> The fear of statistics will keep you average.
>
> —Albert Einstein (as cited in Isaacson, 2007)

The epigraph highlights essential characteristics of statistics in the area of forensic neuropsychological practice. Excellent practice needs to be objective. Through the use of appropriate statistics, the expert promotes a more objective stance and minimizes bias. However, to accomplish this task, the expert must be knowledgeable about statistics. Without this knowledge, the chance of being seen as biased or actually being biased increases.

We know of many statistical commentaries that have been written by authors who for the most part point to the errors made by researchers and practitioners alike (e.g., Millis, 2003). Monahan (2008) and others have commented on the poor use of evidence-based practice in the health care professions. Neal and Grisso (2014) expressed concern over the wide diversity in forensic cases, which has resulted in clinicians, who face many choices about a wide variety of instruments, needing a great deal of knowledge about a host of instruments. Neal and Grisso noted,

> The lack of any standardized approach to various referral questions might contribute to lower interrater rates of agreement in forensic opinions, as major variation in methods may substantially influence the outcome of evaluations. Moreover, attorneys and courts that use our information are required to become familiar with a bewilderingly wide range of tools, rather than becoming consumer-wise regarding a more limited number. The question these observations raise is whether the "typical training" of forensic evaluators to use a flexible approach to each case is the best approach to training. (p. 1417)

Another problem forensic neuropsychologists must face is that the statistical reasoning in which they engage is not well known or understood by judges, juries, or mediators (Greiffenstein & Kaufmann, 2012). These stakeholders have neither been trained in nor are they aware of the mathematical manipulations that must be comprehended for them to come to "fair" judgments. The statistical reasoning of the expert in forensic contexts may seem, at times, to be simple arithmetic. This is rarely the case. It is not simple for the layman to appreciate the statistical logic used by the forensic neuropsychologist. Therefore, it is incumbent on the expert to translate complicated mathematical concepts into layman's terms.

The influence of neuropsychologists in forensic settings is ever increasing (Sweet & Meyers, 2012). Several reviews have demonstrated the value that clinical neuropsychology brings to the forensic arena. For example, reviews by Serafim et al. (2015) and Neal and Grisso (2014) have shown how neuropsychology has had an ever increasing influence on

http://dx.doi.org/10.1037/0000032-001
APA Handbook of Forensic Neuropsychology, S. S. Bush (Editor-in-Chief)

society through its influence on forensic outcomes. Thus, it is critical for forensic neuropsychologists to maintain their credibility if they want to continue to have such a positive influence. Appropriate use of statistics improves one's credibility.

IMPORTANCE OF BASE RATES

Detecting a rare event is often considered evidence of a person's intellect; in fact, it is the basis of many popular movies and television shows, such as *House M.D.* (Shore & Singer, 2004–2012). However, it is also important to recognize that neuropsychologists will likely be accurate in their diagnoses more of the time by concluding that the patient has the more common of conditions. Furthermore, Dawes, Faust, and Meehl (1989), as well as Garb (2005), have demonstrated that clinical judgment is often less accurate than is an automated, actuarial, or mechanical decision process. Humans all too often allow emotion to influence their judgment; emotions are also associated with limitations in working memory, causing a reduction in accuracy. Thus, people tend to use decision heuristics that may be faster and easier to apply but that can cause them to focus on more salient or dramatic facts, rather than using statistics and probabilities, which are more accurate and tend to examine the most relevant data (Klayman & Ha, 1987; Trope, Gervey, & Liberman, 1997). For example, it does not take much, if any, neuropsychological testing to determine whether an individual has severe dementia, has Down's syndrome, or has had a large left hemisphere middle cerebral artery stroke (i.e., suffers from expressive aphasia). Yet rare and exceptional conditions do occur, and they need to be considered. The toughest cases to handle are those conditions that have a low base rate of occurrence.

Most expert witnesses expect to exceed the base rate of percentage of accuracy. Nevertheless, there are times when experts must provide diagnostic impressions that likely cause them, on average, to fall well below the base rate estimate. That is because the court may set a degree of certainty that exceeds what the expert is capable of achieving. For example, a reasonable degree of medical certainty might translate to mean "more likely than not," which is considered a probability just above 50%. However, "beyond a reasonable doubt" is often considered to be more consistent with a Type I error rate typically used for scientific publishing (i.e., $p \leq .05$; Stoffelmayr & Diamond, 2000). Using more common language, the courts would rather allow 19 guilty people to go free than unjustly imprison one innocent person. These "preconditions" on levels of certainty may cause the expert to present diagnostic conclusions that fall, on average, lower than a base rate guess. "More likely than not" is more consistent with a more than 50% to 92% likelihood (Engel, 2009), and "preponderance of evidence" might be considered to be better than a 75% to 92% chance of occurring (Calfree & Craswell, 1984; Engel, 2009). The preponderance of the evidence is most consistent with the phrase "reasonable medical certainty" (Diamond, 1985). The level of certainty can vary from one context to another, and experts should be aware of the criteria to which they are expected to adhere, so as to remain consistent with that criteria.

One issue to address when addressing levels of certainty is statistical power. Cohen (1988) recommended for common research questions that a beta-to-alpha ratio should be 4:1. This means that it is 4 times more likely that a Type II error will be made (i.e., assume a condition is not present when in fact it actually exists) than it is that a Type I error will be made (i.e., assume a condition is present when in fact it is not). Although the inherent meaning of the terms *Type I error* and *Type II error* apply in the forensic setting, the ratios recommended by Cohen (1988) may not. Obviously, if one is asked to apply the standard of "to a reasonable degree of medical certainty," this is more consistent with a beta-to-alpha ratio of 1:1. However, if the standard is "beyond a reasonable doubt," then the ratio between these two might need to be greater than 4:1.

To provide the best statistical information in a forensic context, the forensic neuropsychologist must know not just the base rates of the various conditions (i.e., epidemiology) but also the base rates of the referral conditions. Specifically, what are the diagnostic groups most commonly referred to neuropsychologists?

Population base rates, referral base rates, forensic referral base rates, and practice-specific base rates may all vary across time, geographic regions, and practice settings. One should not conclude that the base rate of a disorder in North America is the same as the base rate of neuropsychological referrals or the base rate of forensic referrals. Although related, these base rates can vary substantially from one another. According to Rabin, Barr, and Burton (2005), the most common referrals for assessment in the United States, based on the number of providers who are asked to assess individuals for adult neuropsychological impairment, are mild head trauma (90%), dementia (78%), stroke and vascular disorders (77%), seizure disorders (77%), severe head trauma (69%), central nervous system tumors (60%), multiple sclerosis (53%), toxic and metabolic concerns (49%), and AIDS (25%). It is helpful to keep statistics on the rates of referral for various disorders within a given practice to aid in the diagnostic process. Of course, caution should be taken to avoid confirmatory bias when it has been established that most referrals reflect a certain type of disorder. Despite the estimated base rates for the occurrence and assessment of various disorders, one has to take the context of the referrals into account to get the most useful base rates.

CHOOSING THE MOST SENSITIVE TESTS

In our opinion, most clinicians select instruments on the basis of what they learned to administer during their graduate training. However, competent practice requires that neuropsychologists remain up to date on instrument development and revisions of published instruments; at some point, neuropsychologists are forced to go beyond what they learned in graduate school, often quickly after graduation. For example, for a number of years, clinicians examined the Verbal IQ–Performance IQ split to aid in the diagnosis of a neurological disorder and the localization of function (e.g., Iverson, Turner, & Green, 1999; Matarazzo & Herman, 1984). However, Verbal IQ and Performance IQ scores are no longer calculated in the Wechsler batteries, and the domain structure of the batteries has been modified. In fact, the Wechsler Intelligence Scale for Children—Fifth Edition now requires only seven subtest scores to generate a Full Scale IQ (FSIQ), and the battery has expanded from four to five cognitive domains. The names of the subtests have been changed as well. For example, Digit Symbol is now universally referred to as Coding (Lezak, Howieson, Bigler, & Tranel, 2012). Several older constructs have been discarded and replaced by newer ones. For example, Freedom From Distractibility is now called Working Memory, which is further split into verbal and nonverbal components (Weiss, Saklofske, Holdnack, & Prifitera, 2015). Perceptual Reasoning is no longer a domain name in the fifth edition (Weiss et al. 2015); it has been replaced by Fluid Reasoning and Visual Reasoning.

Some have argued that publishers are encouraged to revise tests for market reasons (Loring & Bauer, 2010). It would seem, however, that science has provided an ever more complex understanding of what makes up the core domains of human cognition (Benson, Hulac, & Kranzler, 2010; Tulsky & Price, 2003). At some point, normative data, based on a particular cohort, becomes too old for use, such as the Wechsler Adult Intelligence Scale (WAIS). Publishers try to keep up with changes in cognitive models, which can present a challenge if one uses older batteries that do not include subtests designed to assess newly developed cognitive constructs. Some terms that are more commonly used by the public have fallen out of favor in the professional community (e.g., *concentration*) and are not found as often in the professional vernacular of the contemporary clinical neuropsychologist (Strauss, Sherman, & Spreen, 2006). Yet, some constructs have remained stable over time, such as vocabulary (defining words) and tests of reading recognition or word reading (Weiss et al., 2015). However, even if the names of batteries, domains, and subtests do not change and consistency is maintained in terms of the items to which an examinee is exposed, norms for the instrument might need updating in response to the Flynn effect (Trahan, Stuebing, Fletcher, & Hiscock, 2014), as well as to increase sensitivity and specificity when testing ethnically diverse patients (Manly et al., 2011). In fact, this expanding and updating of normative data has become a necessity as the population of the United States grows in diversity.

Staying up to date while using the most appropriate research-based instruments is challenging. Yet, when communicating with attorneys, judges, and juries, the forensic neuropsychologist must use language that allows them to understand what is being discussed (Greiffenstein & Kaufmann, 2012). There is little reason to use the term *visuospatial reasoning* if it comes across as Latin to the audience. Terms that might be frowned on when communicating with colleagues might remain the terms of choice when presenting results in a forensic context. Neuropsychologists have even invented terms to replace professional jargon. Martin L. Rohling has referred to a function of the frontal lobes as "applying the brakes" when the more technical term might be "response inhibition" or "impulse control." When presenting more obscure diagnostic labels, such as dyscalculia, a practitioner is more likely to get a point across by noting that the examinee has trouble with mathematics because of an inability to appreciate the concepts and symbols used to represent quantities and mathematical operators or has lost the ability to appreciate the reasoning behind these symbols.

Core Test Batteries

When a neuropsychologist is selecting tests that will be included in a battery, several issues should be taken into consideration. Frequency of test use (Rabin et al., 2005) is important, because one has to rely on the literature to support an opinion, and there has to be sufficient literature available to adequately determine its meaning. As a result, contemporary instruments, because of their relatively limited research base, may not always be the best choice. Tests that measure the construct of interest with the greatest purity (e.g., Figure Weights; Holdnack, Zhou, Larrabee, Millis, & Salthouse, 2011) are preferred over those that are contaminated with variance from multiple domains (e.g., Picture Completion). Ease of interpretation is also important. Trying to present in a concise and meaningful manner all of the data that is generated from the California Verbal Learning Test—Second Edition (CVLT–II; Delis, Kramer, Kaplan, & Ober, 2000) is prone to failure, but simple summary scores, such as those provided by the Finger Tapping Test (Reitan & Wolfson, 1985) or total time when completing the Trail Making Test (Reitan & Wolfson, 1985), make the job of the forensic evaluator easier and more effective.

Tests that have high face validity, by definition, are easier for nonprofessionals to appreciate than tests without it. Although face validity is not required for competent professional assessment, it allows the expert to explain results with less confusion. For neuropsychologists attempting to communicate the meaning of test scores to a lay audience, it can be more difficult to describe such terms as *perseverative responding* from the Wisconsin Card Sorting Test (Heaton, Chelune, Talley, Kay, & Curtiss, 1981). In contrast, descriptions of tests with cognitive domains included in their names, such as the Wechsler Memory Scale—Fourth Edition (Wechsler, 2008b) and the CVLT–II (Delis et al., 2000) can facilitate the audience's comprehension of the scores. An extensive review of the best instruments for use in a core battery is beyond the scope of this chapter. The reader is referred to Chapter 4 of this handbook for details. Knowing what others have included in their ability-focused batteries is often a good place to start (Larrabee, Millis, & Meyers, 2008).

Caution is warranted when selecting tests administered via computer with canned computerized interpretations (Rabin, Spadaccini, Brodale, Elbulok-Charcape, & Barr, 2014). There are times when clinicians administer computerized batteries designed for a particular purpose to examinees who have been referred for another purpose. For example, relying on computerized interpretation does not absolve the clinician from knowing what the programmer used to generate the printout. If the norms of a battery were developed using college athletes, it is inappropriate to use this battery with higher functioning individuals who might have a dementing illness. The practitioner is responsible for everything said and written in a report. If the practitioner does not understand why the printout reads the way it does, the instrument should not be used. If neuropsychologists do not know how the normative scores that have been printed out were generated, they should not use the test in a forensic context. They may well be asked how they reached their diagnostic conclusions, and without detailed knowledge, they will be unable to answer.

Most important, neuropsychologists must keep abreast of the topics of performance validity and symptom validity assessment (Larrabee, 2012), which are critical when conducting evaluations in forensic settings (Heilbronner, Sweet, Morgan, Larrabee, & Millis, 2009). These measures provide scores that have distributional properties that are non-normal and require specialized statistical analyses (i.e., nonparametric) for competent analysis (Millis, 2003; Osborne & Costello, 2004).

Using the right instrument to assess performance in the various cognitive domains. All too often, neuropsychologists rely on outdated tests with which they have had extensive personal experience and for which they believe they know what is being measured. However, wiser neuropsychologists must stay current not just with test revisions but with test and battery factor structures (Holdnack et al., 2011; Larrabee et al., 2008). They must ensure that the tests that have been selected represent the constructs of interest. Neuropsychologists should not select tests or batteries on the basis of their familiarity with the test or the test's popularity within their community. For example, measures of verbal memory that do not include a delayed component load on a working memory factor (Engle, Kane, & Tuholski, 2003; Holdnack et al., 2011) rather than on a verbal memory factors (Tulsky & Price, 2003).

Matching tests to referral questions. Neuropsychology as a science makes it possible to make diagnostic decisions on the basis of test score patterns that demonstrate strengths and weaknesses across domains. However, this requires that the tests administered in a battery sufficiently measure the domains of interest, so that known patterns are revealed. Diagnostic conclusions based on pattern analysis exist for such disorders as Alzheimer's disease (AD; Jacobs et al., 1994), traumatic brain injury (TBI; Arciniegas, Anderson, Topkoff, & McAllister, 2005; Meyers, Miller, & Tuita, 2014; Meyers & Rohling, 2004), Parkinson's disease (Braun et al., 2011; Muslimovi´c, Post, Speelman, & Schmand, 2005), cerebrovascular accidents (Nyenhuis et al., 2004), and neurotoxicity (Rohling & Demakis, 2006, 2007). Deficits caused by these disorders are well known, and score pattern predictions can be made as long as a core battery of well-validated tests with representative norms has been used.

Test battery power: How much is needed? Moderate to severe dementia does not require the neuropsychologist to administer a lengthy test battery to reach a valid diagnosis. The impairments associated with dementia are generally obvious. When test scores are combined with results from neuroimaging, an accurate diagnosis is relatively easy to reach. However, more subtle deficits exist in the early stages of the disorder. At the outset of the disorder, the chance that clinicians will incorrectly conclude that examinees do not have dementia when in fact they do is much greater than that they will conclude that examinees have dementia when in fact they do not. This is particularly true when examinees have functioned at a high level premorbidly. To avoid making such errors with examinees who have mild dementia, a longer and more powerful test battery is necessary.

To help a less statistically minded audience appreciate the meaning of the power of a test battery, Martin L. Rohling has used the analogy of finding a needle in a haystack: It might take a long time to search the entire haystack. Achieving a high degree of certainty in the context of cognitive assessment requires longer and more sensitive test batteries, which in turn are more powerful. This analogy also applies to the assessment of patients who have had a mild TBI (Rohling et al., 2011) or who have been exposed to low levels of neurotoxins (Rohling & Demakis, 2006). However, if one is asked to find an automobile in a haystack, the time required to achieve the same degree of certainty is much shorter and the power of the test battery can be much lower.

Paradoxically, many neuropsychologists receive referrals that simply state "screen for early dementia." This is equivalent to having 10 minutes to look (i.e., screen) for a needle (i.e., small amount of visible deficit) in a rather large haystack (i.e., all of cognition). There is not enough time to adequately complete the task. Furthermore, most test batteries do not possess sufficient power to determine whether there is, or is not, a needle in the haystack.

Average time required per test and the number of scores needed for accuracy. Understanding the time associated with test administration in forensic settings is important for practitioners. We used three different methods to estimate the average length of time it takes to obtain a test score within a battery. First, we examined subtests of the fourth edition of the WAIS (WAIS–IV). On the basis of the manual, it takes an average of 75 minutes to administer the 11 subtests that are necessary to calculate a FSIQ, which averages to 6.8 minutes per score. Second, we examined the Meyers Neuropsychological Battery (Meyers, 2015), which takes, on average, 170 minutes to administer to obtain 26 separate scores, with a mean of 6.5 minutes per score. Finally, Camara, Nathan, and Puente (2000) reported results of a survey of a large number of psychologists to identify the most commonly administered instruments as well as the amount of time it takes to administer them. We examined the reported data for the top 20 instruments, which would take 915 minutes to administer and would result in 143 test scores, with an average of 6.4 minutes per score. Each of these methods converges on an average of 6.5 minutes per score. Camara et al. (2000) also reported that the average assessment battery takes a psychologist 390 minutes to administer, resulting in an average of 60 scores obtain per test battery. Using the traditional *p* value equal to .05 and a one-tailed *t* test, the typical effect size that can be reliably detected with such a battery is −0.32. Practically speaking, using the WAIS–IV FSIQ as a summary measure, such an effect size represents a drop in score of close to 5 points. Using the 95% confidence interval for the FSIQ, the FSIQ can vary from the estimated calculated FSIQ by ±4.0 points (Wechsler, 2008a). Thus, the detectable deficit that can be reliably detected by the typical battery is just beyond the typical confidence interval used for the FSIQ. If an examinee's expected degree of impairment is greater than this, fewer tests would be needed to reliably detect such a deficit. If an examinee's expected degree of impairment is less than this estimate, the test battery may need to be lengthened to reliably detect such a deficit.

Using data reported by Rohling, Meyers, and Millis (2003), an effect size of a magnitude of −0.32 can be expected for a patient who has residual cognitive impairment from a TBI that caused a loss of consciousness of between 1 and 6 days, with a median of 2 days, which would have an average time of posttraumatic amnesia of 7 days. Unfortunately, because the majority of TBI patients have a loss of consciousness that is less than this (and thus less obvious deficits are likely), the typical test battery does not have sufficient power to detect the expected degree of cognitive loss. In fact, if the effect size of impairment is as small as −0.22, which is consistent with a median loss of consciousness of 2 hours, it would take 120 test scores and 2 days of assessment time to reliably detect impairment. It would also mean that the average FSIQ of such a patient, who had a premorbid FSIQ of 100, would drop 3 points to a 97.

One has to wonder whether such a small effect size is detectable by the patients themselves or by significant others who interact with them on a day-to-day basis. Using the WAIS–IV manual (Wechsler, 2008a), a drop of this magnitude is consistent with the normal aging process of 33 years, meaning that a typical 27-year-old's raw scores will fall this amount by around age 60. The point we are trying to make is not about age's influence on cognitive ability; rather, small reductions in cognitive ability may not warrant increases in test battery power to improve detection. Such an increase may be impractical and essentially unnecessary when the deficits that might actually exist will have a negligible effect on everyday functioning. Furthermore, if practitioners chose not to amend their test batteries to increase their sensitivity, there will be a concomitant increase in the number of false negatives, or the conclusion that no impairment exists when it actually does (even though the existing impairment is quite small and may have few functional implications). On the basis of the estimated reliability of the average test battery and the representative sample size (i.e., number of test scores per battery), the typical neuropsychologist using such a battery whose base rate of impairment in referred patients is 50%, will have a sensitivity of .67 and a specificity of .67, with an overall correct classification rate of 67%. One third of the patients will be misclassified, with the number of misdiagnosed individuals being classified as normal when they are not equal to the number of normal individuals who are misdiagnosed as being impaired.

Understanding Effect Sizes of Deficits on the Basis of Premorbid and Postassessment Scores

Many people do not appreciate how it is impossible to have "no child left behind" (Bush, 2001) or "zero tolerance" for just about anything (Skiba, 2000). Statistically, such comments suggest that a distribution of scores can be one tailed and positively skewed, with an average score that is the same as the minimum score. Many clinicians implicitly make this assumption by not taking premorbid functioning into account when generating a diagnosis. They are essentially assuming that everyone comes to the assessment with a premorbid level of ability that is at the population average of 100.

Furthermore, to have zero tolerance, there is a commitment to avoiding any and all Type II errors (i.e., ensuring that a single incident of a disorder is not missed). To do this, one has to drastically increase the time and resources committed to the task. Such an increase often results in social costs that exceed the proposed benefits it might provide. All neuropsychologists must practice with limited resources and imperfect assessment instruments. As a result, it is impossible to avoid erring when diagnosing disorders. The question neuropsychologists should ask themselves is "Under the current set of conditions, what percentage of error is acceptable?"

As noted in our example of age's effect on cognitive ability, there are plenty of cases in which deficits are detected with a reasonable degree of statistical certainty, but the clinical meaningfulness of such deficits is minimal. For example, how much cognitive ability must an individual possess to competently practice medicine? Research by Hauser (2002) demonstrated that for a job with a high cognitive demand, such as practicing medicine, the sample's 80% confidence interval for FSIQ has a low of 104 and a high of 129. For jobs with a low cognitive demand, such as a maintenance worker, the sample's confidence interval for FSIQ has a low of 76 and a high of 115. Such a wide range of cognitive abilities within the various job categories listed demonstrates how small of an effect minor changes in cognitive ability, such as 3 to 5 IQ points, might have on competency on the job. In essence, many people can lose some IQ and still be well within the parameters of what the job might require.

This argument is designed to highlight the need to understand the effect sizes of impairment and to consider them in the context of the patient's premorbid life. Small effect sizes, such as that associated with mild TBI, require high-powered test batteries to facilitate detection (see the Test Battery Power section of this chapter). Yet, when the effect size is applied back to the individual, not all detected deficits are of equal significance. Some may not even be noticed by the examinee, significant others, or the employer.

DIAGNOSTIC STATISTICS

Test Properties

After completing a basic graduate course in psychometrics, some students seem to believe that they have sufficient knowledge of reliability and validity to competently practice. Yet, these two terms are often confused with one another. Sometimes making the distinction is not as simple as some might think. Additional education and experience with these constructs is needed for successful forensic neuropsychological practice.

Reliability. This section on reliability is likely rather different from other texts or sources covering this material. Common terms for each type of reliability, as well as the general definition of each, are listed in Table 1.1. More detailed descriptions are available from several other sources (e.g., Gignac, 2009). In this chapter, we have chosen to address conceptual issues related to reliability, which we believe are more often encountered in the forensic arena. These issues are also detailed in Table 1.1, along with examples of how such problems are often manifested.

First, we reiterate what we think has been drilled into all graduate students during their training, which is that validity is bounded by reliability (Markus & Borsboom, 2013). More specifically, one cannot have a valid measure that is unreliable. In other words, reliability is a necessary but not sufficient condition for validity. However, a measure

TABLE 1.1

Types of Reliability and Potential Problems With Reported Estimates, Including Examples of Each Type of Problem

Type of reliability	Definition	Potential problems	Examples
Test–retest (T-RT)	Used to assess the degree of stability of measurement over longer periods of time	The time span on which a test's T-RT was calculated does not reflect that which is typically used by clinicians.	T-RT reliability of an instrument is published on the basis of a difference in time that is not commonly seen in clinical practice. *Examples:* • A computerized concussion battery reported a T-RT based on a 1-month difference in time, but actual baseline assessments typically occur across a 2-year difference. • A memory test used with older adults reported a T-RT difference in time of 1 month, but actual assessments are conducted only once a year.
Internal consistency (IC)	Used to determine whether the items included in an instrument are associated with one another, that is, the consistency of results across items within a test	A test of a multidimensional constructs (e.g., depression) publishes an IC that is generated across domains, but the IC of the items within a domain was not calculated	IC is mistaken for a measurement of a multidimensional instrument's construct validity, but when the test's IC is generated from items applied at the domain level, it is significantly different from the reported overall IC. *Examples:* • A memory test includes items of verbal, visual, and working memory. The IC reported is for the entire battery, not for the items of a domain. • A test's reported IC was based on the measurement of a multidimensional construct, but the domains are intercorrelated (e.g., height and weight). The high IC suggested the construct was unitary, which is misleading.
Interrater (IR)	Used to assess the degree to which different raters give consistent estimates of the same event	The construct measured is influenced by rater demographics, but the effect was undetected because the IR reliability was generated from raters and examinees who did not differ in terms of demographics	IR reliability is influenced by traits possessed by raters (i.e., age, gender, and ethnicity). The IR reliability was generated from raters whose demographics were the same. *Examples:* • A test is designed to assess trauma severity after a rape. The IR reliability was generated using female raters, but this is uncommon in a clinical setting. • A test is designed to assess IQ, but the published IR reliability was generated from raters of ethnic backgrounds that are incongruent with the examinee's.
Parallel forms (PF)	Used to assess the consistency of the results of two tests constructed in the same way from the same content	The PF reliability of a test uses items thought to measure a single construct, but the items vary in terms of degree of difficulty.	PF reliabilities reported are inaccurate because they were generated from items that are not of the same construct. *Example:* • The PF reliability include measures of verbal and nonverbal skills, but these are proportioned differently across the forms.

may be reliable and yet invalid for the purposes of the assessment in which it is used. Moreover, instruments do not possess a "trait" of reliability or validity. Each of these statistics is generated within a distinct context. More specifically, the normative sample and the set of conditions under which the instrument's reliability and validity have been developed may not reflect the set of circumstances for which an assessment is being conducted. If the context listed in an instrument's technical manual does not reflect the circumstances in which an assessment is conducted, the reported statistics may not apply to the examinee being evaluated. However, because of limits on the amount of information that might be available on an instrument across contexts, practitioners are often left with limited choices and must decide when to apply or ignore an instrument's documented reliability and validity. Nevertheless, forensic neuropsychologists should be aware of the assumptions they are making and be prepared to defend them, as well as prepared to estimate the degree of error that might have been introduced as a result of their choices.

Conceptually, reliability might best be considered to be measurements of the same thing across two points in time. However, if the construct being measured is a state (i.e., mood) and not a trait (e.g., personality), it will by definition change more rapidly over time. To obtain a reliable estimate of a construct that is a statelike variable, the difference between the two points in time of measurement has to be shorter than what might be acceptable if the construct was considered a trait. Thus, the method used to assess the reliability of an instrument that is used to measure a trait might best be test–retest. The interval of time between the two assessments can be days, weeks, months, or even years. In fact, such an analysis is often referred to as *stability*.

However, when the construct of interest is a state, then one can expect changes to occur more rapidly over time. Therefore, the interval between assessments should be substantially shorter. In fact, test–retest reliability might be inappropriate under these sets of conditions. A more reasonable method of determining an instrument's reliability under such circumstances is internal consistency. The most common type of method used for this type of reliability is coefficient alpha (Peterson, 1994). We consider internal consistency to be equivalent to shrinking the difference between the two times of assessment to zero. Similarly, when conducting a parallel forms estimate of reliability, it is common for the two forms to be administered within a small timeframe, thus making the difference from Time 1 to Time 2 quite small.

Peterson (1994) recommended a minimal internal consistency reliability of .70. Examining the reliability index, Peterson's recommendation of .70 equates to a correlation between observed and true scores of .84. Consequently, a recommendation of .70 is associated with a minimum of 70% of the observed score variance being attributable to true score variance. Nunnally and Bernstein (1994) recommended a minimum reliability of .70 for research purposes and instrument development. They also recommended a minimum reliability of .80 for basic research and .90 for clinical decision making. Some have argued that setting such a high bar for an instrument's reliability in clinical practice will result in clinicians avoiding the use of instruments that fall below this mark. Yet, many of these instruments are more effective than alternative methods, such as clinical judgment. In summary, the clinician should not throw the baby out with the bathwater (Calamia, Markon, & Tranel, 2013) by not using a reasonable instrument in favor of using clinical judgment, even if the instrument's internal consistency is not as high as the clinician would optimally prefer.

Another concern we have regarding measures of reliability is whether the measurement method used involves parametric or nonparametric statistics. For example, when measuring mood with the Beck Depression Inventory–II (Beck, Steer, & Brown, 1996), the test developer must decide whether the scores obtained from an instrument have the properties of an ordinal, interval, or ratio scale. Specifically, are the differences between points on the scale of an equal magnitude across the scores obtained and can an examinee be without any amount of the construct (i.e., does zero mean the complete absence of the construct)? Practically speaking, this means that the practitioners must decide whether the difference between 7 and 8 points on the inventory is equivalent to the difference between 21 and 22 points. Furthermore, if the examinee scores a 0 on the Beck Depression Inventory–II, this implies that the examinee is without mood. This clarification is important because reliability and validity estimates of interval and ratio scales are best generated using parametric methods, whereas reliability and validity estimates of nominal and ordinal scales are best generated from nonparametric methods.

When using instruments that vary in terms of scale properties, practitioners have to take into account the degree to which chance might influence measurements from the instrument. An interval scale with four measurement levels (e.g., 0 to 3) should be corrected for chance agreement. That is, even when the two scores are acquired at separate times, it is likely that, by chance alone, the scores will be in agreement because there are so few options in question. Such chance agreements inflate estimates of reliability because a portion of the variance is attributable to chance and not to some quantifiable amount of the construct being measured. Test developers should apply corrections to their reported estimates of interrater reliability so this does not have to be considered by every clinician in practice.

The main point here is that the forensic neuropsychologist must be able to understand the statistical properties of tests used as well as determine the examinees to which the instrument's psychometric qualities apply. Selecting instruments that do not possess sufficient reliabilities, generated from samples that are not representative of the case examined, will result in considerably more errors in diagnosis. It is worth repeating that validity is bounded by reliability. Using tests that have undemonstrated reliability in the case examined will result in invalid assessment and diagnostic errors (Essig, Mittenberg, Petersen, Strauman, & Cooper, 2001).

Validity. Just as the reliability of a test is sample specific, so too is its validity. Just because a test has demonstrated reliability with a particular sample of individuals who might have similar demographics does not mean that the test scores that are obtained from the assessment validly measured the construct in a forensic or diagnostic context (Gignac, 2009).

For instance, the WAIS–IV might be a reliable measure of general intellectual ability when used with older adults, but it might not be a valid measure for tracking the progression of a condition such as early AD. The hallmark of AD is memory impairment (Jacobs et al., 1994). Demonstrating retention of the cognitive abilities typically measured by the WAIS–IV is not a valid way to rule out AD. A more valid measure would be a test of memory, which includes a scale that detects rapid forgetting (Attali, De Anna, Dubois, & Dalla Barba, 2009; Cullum, Butters, Tröster, & Salmon, 1990). Scores on the WAIS–IV may remain reasonably stable even though the disease has progressed and storage rates are decreasing at a more rapid rate than scores on the WAIS–IV subtests such as Digit Span might suggest.

Standardization and norms. Determining whether a test has sufficient reliability and validity for use with a specific case requires the neuropsychologist to be aware of the normative sample from which scores reported in the test manual are derived. Much has been made about the need to co-norm a battery of tests for the comparisons among test scores across constructs, such as is available in the Neuropsychological Assessment Battery (Stern & White, 2003), WAIS–IV, Wechsler Memory Scale—Fourth Edition, and Advanced Clinical Solutions system, or what might be similarly available in the Heaton, Miller, Taylor, and Grant (2004) system. However, Rohling et al. (2015) recently demonstrated that if the test developers adequately sampled the demographics of the population of concern, competent practice does not require that all tests were given to the same normative sample. That does not mean that a co-normed system does not have benefits that make the comparison of scores across domains easier and more accurate, just that the overall results of an assessment are not clinically and meaningfully different when scores are from a non–co-normed set of samples. This minor difference is primarily due to the fact that the correlations among tests are more accurate in a co-normed system than when generated from various samples that are demographically similar but not identical. Yet, when examining results on a case-by-case basis, clinicians can reliably determine deficits from normality with adequate norms, even if they are not able to make as accurate a comparison among test scores. Thus, when a neuropsychologist is selecting tests and norms, it is important that the various normative databases are capable of adequately adjusting scores for the examinee's demographic background, taking into account the influence of age, education, gender, ethnicity, and primary or first language.

Domain of interest and assessment quality. This section only briefly covers the domains of interest here, as more comprehensive coverage of this topic is provided in Chapter 4 of this handbook. As Larrabee et al. (2009), Flanagan, Ortiz, and Alfonso (2013), and Rohling, Miller, and Langhinrichsen-Rohling (2004) have shown, there are core domains of human cognition that are likely universal, which should include measures of verbal reasoning, visuospatial or fluid reasoning, verbal memory, visual memory, processing speed, psychomotor skills, and sensory–perceptual skills. When generating a battery of tests, administering it to the examinee, and interpreting the resulting scores, neuropsychologists should ensure that they have assessed each of these domains at some level, while assessing an examinee's skills in more depth for the domains thought to be affected by the disease or disorder for which the examinee has been referred. Practitioners need to assess the domains both broadly and, when addressing aspects relating to the specific referral problem, in depth. To accomplish this task, wise forensic examiners must own and be familiar with the test manuals and published findings of those tests they administer. In addition, examiners should also own and frequently check the major compendiums of neuropsychological tests and norms (e.g., Strauss et al., 2006).

Differential Diagnosis Using Evidence-Based Practice Statistics

Differential diagnosis is frequently the most important task the forensic neuropsychologist is asked to complete. It can be conceptualized as a statistical question, analogous to what is done when conducting a multiple regression analysis, with a number of standardized beta weights that reflect the percentage of variance for which scores within a cognitive domain are able to account (e.g., tests scores from verbal and visual memory tests when considering a diagnosis of AD). The impairment that is caused by the incident, accident, or disease may not entirely account for the cognitive, behavioral, and emotional problems exhibited by the examinee. Premorbid issues and concurrent factors (e.g., anxiety or compensation) may explain more variance than the injury or disorder in question. Thus, the examiner is asked to decide not only whether there is an impairment but which percentage of the impairment is likely due to a particular disease, experience, or traumatic event.

Diagnostic statistics that have been developed for use by evidence-based practitioners are not the typical statistics that have been traditionally taught in graduate courses in psychometrics. Rather, they are a particular kind of statistics that require more sophistication on the examiner's part for proper utilization when determining an examinee's diagnosis. The guidelines published in the literature for evidence-based practice in medicine have pushed many other health care professions, as well as neuropsychologists, to know and use more complicated analyses on a day-to-day basis (Monahan, 2008). A list of these statistics is provided in Table 1.2. Some of these are most likely familiar to readers (e.g., base rate, true positive, and specificity); others may be recognized but are not typically used by many readers (e.g., positive likelihood ratio and odds ratio).

Sensitivity. A test's sensitivity is defined as how likely it is to detect a disorder in cases who have the disorder. Sensitivities can vary on the basis of the normative sample being examined. For example, the Mini-Mental State Examination (Folstein, Folstein, & McHugh et al., 1975) may be sensitive to changes in older adults who progress from moderate to severe dementia, but it may be insensitive to recovery of younger adults who have had a mild traumatic brain injury. Thus, the forensic neuropsychologist must know more about a test's sensitivity than what is reported in a manual. This additional information is often found in neuropsychological compendiums or in the peer-reviewed literature. The variability found in a test's sensitivity to different disorders and samples is an example of how tests do not possess traits such as sensitivity and specificity. Sensitivity is an example of a statistic that is context specific. A common error many neuropsychologists make is to use the sensitivity published in a test's manual, which was generated from a normative sample whose demographic background does not reflect that of the examinee (e.g., native English speakers when the examinee's primary language is Spanish) or with an examinee whose disease-specific concerns expressed in a referral (e.g., neurotoxicity) were never addressed when the test was being developed.

Specificity. The specificities published in a test's manual are often specific to the samples examined

TABLE 1.2

Common Types of Validity Cited in the Literature

Validity labels	Brief definitions	Example
Construct	The degree to which a test measures the thing it is supposed to measure. Psychological constructs are often referred to as *latent traits*. As noted by Trochim (2006), essentially all validity is construct validity. Without construct validity, there is nothing to measure and nothing to be reliably measured. Furthermore, construct validity is determined by how well one translates or operationally defines through methods of measurement the thing one wants to measure.	When someone says a person has a good memory, they are referring to a latent trait that they believe people possess in varying amounts. They are also, at an intuitive level, measuring people, using their own behavioral observations. Structuring those observations leads one to operationally define a construct and engage in rigorous and experimental ways, attempting to verify the construct's existence. In practical terms, memory might be operationally defined by scores on the Wechsler Memory Scale.
Face	At an intuitive level, most people who look at an instrument and believe it to be measuring what it is purported to measure (i.e., the construct of interest).	When assessing a latent construct such as depression, the typical person will expect to see questions on the test that require the person to quantify the degree of sadness or lack of pleasure.
Content	The test items sample the hypothesized content of the construct.	When a construct is multidimensional—for example, intelligence—the test includes items that measure the various domains of the construct, such as verbal reasoning, visuospatial reasoning, and processing speed. If the test is designed to measure mathematical ability, it will include both math operations and quantitative reasoning.
Predictive	The value of an instrument is quantified by how well it can predict future events. If a latent trait is being reliably assessed by the instrument, then the value of the instrument will depend on its ability to predict future events.	Measures of the latent trait of intelligence should be able to predict future events that require one to be intelligent, such as success in school, future earnings, or ability to problem solve in the real world.
Incremental predictive	The test scores are able to account for additional variance in a construct over and above that explained by another test's scores.	The instrument, if new, must improve on the predictive power of instruments that preceded it in development. If it does no better or worse in explaining behavior, it has no incremental validity.
Criterion related	The instrument measures varying degrees of the construct, such that if a sufficient amount exists, then other events should be achievable.	If a score on a test is used to determine who is admitted into a training program, then the instrument must be shown to be an accurate predictor of success or failure in the program. For example, scores on the GRE subject tests should be associated with success and failure of students in the program, as measured by graduation rates, passing of the licensing exam, and the quality of the work product once on the job after training has been completed.
Concurrent	An instrument has concurrent validity if the scores on the instrument can be shown to be associated with previously established measures of performance.	Immediately after graduating with an undergraduate degree in psychology, scores on the GRE psychology subject test are associated with one's undergraduate GPA, calculated from the grades one has obtained in his or her psychology courses.
Convergent	An instrument has convergent validity if it can be shown that scores on the instrument converge on measures shown to be associated with the latent trait being measured.	As a measure's scores change, scores on other measures of similar constructs similarly change. For example, as scores on a measure of depression increase, scores on a measure of euphoria decrease.

Discriminant	An instrument possesses discriminant validity if it can be shown that examinees' scores are not associated with measures of other constructs that are not believed to be associated with the latent trait being measured.	Scores on a reading test are not predictive of scores of athletic ability, such as gross motor speed, agility, and strength.
Factorial	There are strong associations between measures that are meant to be in common and weak or small associations between measures that are intended to be independent.	A measure has factorial validity if it can be shown that scores on the measure are associated with scores on other measures that are associated with the construct and are not associated with scores on measures that are thought to be different from the ability. For example, as scores on the Matrix Reasoning subtest change, scores on the Figure Weights subtest change similarly, and both scores are unrelated to scores from the Coding subtest, scores on the Digit Span subtest, or both.

during stages of test development. For example, a test of letter fluency (FAS; Benton & Hamsher, 1978) may be sensitive to language dysfunction but not specific to it. Letter fluency tasks may also be affected by executive dysfunction. A test of verbal memory, such as the CVLT–II (Delis et al., 2000), may be sensitive to verbal memory impairment caused by AD (Jacobs et al., 1994), but low scores are not specific to AD (Holdnack & Drozdick, 2009); various individual difference factors also influence verbal memory.

A common error described in the literature covering decision heuristics in human judgment is the confirmation bias (Klayman & Ha, 1987). Many neuropsychologists engage in confirmation bias without being cognizant of doing so. This bias occurs when the neuropsychologist does not consider or seek evidence that is incongruent with the referral diagnosis. Avoiding the confirmation bias requires the examiner to be aware of a test's specificity. If the practitioner does not seek disconfirming evidence for the referred diagnosis, then he or she is more likely to misdiagnose the examinee (i.e.., false positive). For example, if a 24-year-old man who was in involved in an auto accident 1 year earlier and incurred a mild TBI obtains low scores on the CVLT–II, it might be erroneous to interpret these low scores as evidence of impairment resulting from mild TBI. The fact that his primary language is Spanish might have caused him to obtain lower scores than he would have obtained if the test had been administered in Spanish (Peña-Casanova et al., 2009). The impact of being tested in a language that is not one's primary or first language might account for more variance than the influence of mild TBI. Thus, the English version of the CVLT–II might be sensitive to verbal memory impairment caused by TBI, but it is not specific to verbal memory impairment in native Spanish speakers. This example highlights the need for clinicians to assess both for the presence of a disorder and for the possibility that a low score might have been caused by factors other than those for which the examinee has been referred. If a similarly low score is not also found on other measures of the same construct, the neuropsychologist should be more cautious when considering the assumed caused of impairment implied by the referral. In fact, Hill, Rohling, Boettcher, and Meyers (2013) have shown that excessive variability in test scores designed to measure a similar construct is evidence of invalid or feigned performance and not of neuropathology.

Positive predictive value. The positive predictive value (PPV) is a ratio of the actual number of cases who have a disorder divided by the total number of cases whom the instrument detected as having the disorder. At times, low PPVs are acceptable if the consequence of increasing the PPV is a concomitant increase in false negatives. For example, a PPV that is low when applied to the rate of hospitalization of examinees who are thought to be at risk for suicide might be acceptable if the consequence of raising the PPV would likely result in more false negatives or failing to hospitalize an examinee who eventually goes on to commit suicide but who scored in the range that was thought to evidence a lack of suicidal intent. The social cost of a low PPV is less than that associated with a higher PPV.

Negative predictive value. The Negative predictive value (NPV) is the ratio of the number of examinees without the disorder whose scores fell below the cutoff set for detecting the existence of a disorder, divided by the total number of cases who scored below the cutoff, some of whom are false negatives. A low NPV might be acceptable if the consequence of increasing it is an unacceptable increase in false positives. For example, when considering the scores obtained from a performance validity test, which is designed to detect invalid performance across the test battery, some practitioners believe that more harm is done by misidentifying examinees who are truly impaired as feigning than is done by misidentifying feigning examinees as having performed validly. Such a belief might lead some examiners to accept lower NPVs because they are more concerned about the costs of too many false positives (i.e., a person with deficits caused by TBI is wrongly identified as performing invalidly) than about the costs of too many false negatives (i.e., a person is identified as suffering from cognitive deficits caused by TBI who actually engaged in invalid responding).

Positive and negative likelihood ratios. We have sometimes found these statistics more difficult to calculate than they are to appreciate once calculated. Likelihood ratios are calculated by dividing the probability of one event by the probability of another event. For example, the positive likelihood ratio is calculated by dividing the probability that an examinee has a disorder divided by the probability that the examinee does not have a disorder. More specifically, a positive likelihood ratio of 10.0 for a brain tumor means that the examinee's obtained score (e.g., radiologist's measurement of volume of the hippocampus using an MRI) is 10 times higher than the scores obtained by those who do not have a brain tumor. The equations used to calculate the PPV, NPV, and positive and negative likelihood ratios are provided in Table 1.3.

Frequency of low scores occurring by chance alone. Recently, a number of papers and professional presentations by various authors have demonstrated that a large number of low scores obtained by examinees on test batteries occur by chance alone (e.g., Binder, Iverson, & Brooks, 2009; Brooks, 2010; Brooks, Holdnack, & Iverson, 2011; Brooks, Iverson, Holdnack, & Feldman, 2008; Iverson, 2015; Schretlen, Testa, Winicki, Pearlson, & Gordon, 2008). These analyses are typically conducted on the normative sample of a particular battery of tests (e.g., WISC–IV and Wechsler Memory Scale—Fourth Edition), showing the frequency of scores falling below some cut score (e.g., 1.0, 1.5, or 2.0 standard deviations below the mean) that are obtained by normal individuals. The purpose of demonstrating this phenomenon is to help clinicians to avoid misdiagnosing individuals with neuropsychological impairment when none exists. These researchers have demonstrated that low scores are relatively common for normal individuals and that the frequency of a particular individual's obtaining low scores is influenced by premorbid factors, such as his or her age, education, and intelligence.

The problem with this methodology, as highlighted by Iverson (2015), is that such findings do not give clinicians much guidance as to how they should interpret low scores when they are found. Rohling and colleagues (e.g., Hill et al., 2013; Rohling, 2012; Rohling, Larrabee, & Millis, 2012) have demonstrated that a more reliable method of determining whether low scores reflect normal variability, neuropathology, or invalid performance is to examine the intraindividual variability (IIV) of an examinee's scores, which is independent of the premorbid factors that cause variations in the frequency of low scores falling below a cut score. IIV is obtained by averaging the cognitive test scores obtained during an assessment (i.e., overall test battery mean), which have been converted to a common metric (*T* scores, standard scores, or *z* scores), and calculating the standard deviation of the individual's scores. The resulting distribution is typically normal and has a mean IIV that is equal to the standard deviation of the common metric (*T* score IIV = 10, standard score IIV = 15, *z* score IIV = 0). IIVs that are between 30% and 100%

TABLE 1.3

Equations for Statistics Associated With Evidence-Based Practice

Evidence-based medicine statistic	Abbreviations, ratios, or equations	Definition of terms
True positive	TP = No. of cases with disorder detected as w/disorder	TP (n_{d+a+}) is the number of cases in a sample that are detected by the test as having the disorder that have the disorder; "hit."
True negative	TN = no. of cases without disorder detected as without disorder	TN (n_{d-a-}) is the number of cases in a sample that are detected by the test as not having the disorder that do not have the disorder; "correct rejection."
False positive	FP = No. of cases without disorder detected as with disorder	FP (n_{d+a-}) is the number of cases in a sample that are detected by the test as having the disorder that do not have the disorder; Type I error.
False negative	FN = No. of cases with disorder detected as without disorder	FN (n_{d-a+}) is the number of cases in a sample that are detected by the test as not having the disorder that have the disorder; Type II error.
Base rate	$BR = \frac{(TP+FN)}{(TP+TN+FP+FN)}$	BR (N_{a+}/N) is the proportion of cases in a sample that have the disorder.
Sensitivity	$SN = \frac{TP}{(TP+FN)}$	SN (n_{d+a+}/N_{a+}) is the proportion of cases in a sample that actually have the disorder that are detected by the test as having the disorder.
Specificity	$SP = \frac{TN}{(TN+FP)}$	SP (n_{d-a-}/N_{a-}) is the proportion of cases in a sample that actually do not have the disorder that are detected by the test as not having the disorder.
Positive predictive value	$PPV = \frac{TP}{(TP+FP)}$	PPV (n_{d+a+}/N_{d+}) is the proportion of cases in a sample detected by the test that have the disorder that are detected by the test as having the disorder.
Negative predictive value	$NPV = \frac{TN}{(TN+FN)}$	NPV (n_{d-a-}/N_{d-}) is the proportion of cases in a sample that actually do not have the disorder that are detected by the test as not having the disorder.
Correct classification rate	$CCR = \frac{(TP+TN)}{(TP+TN+FP+FN)}$	CCR [($n_{d+a+} + n_{d-a-})/N_t$] is the proportion of cases in a sample that are correctly classified as having and not having the disorder.
Positive likelihood ratio	$+LR = \frac{SN}{1-SN}$	+LR is the probability of a case that has the disorder being detected by the test as having the disorder divided by the probability of a case that does not have the disorder being detected by the test as having the disorder.
Negative likelihood ratio	$-LR = \frac{SP}{(1-SP)}$	−LR is the probability of a case that has the disorder being detected by the test as not having the disorder divided by the probability of a case that does not have the disorder being detected by the test as not having the disorder.
Odds ratio	$OR = \frac{(TP/TN)}{(FP/FN)}$	OR [($n_{d+a+} + n_{d-a-}$)/([($n_{d-a+} + n_{d+a-}$)] is a measure of association between the probability of a test correctly identifying whether a disorder exists divided by the probability of a test incorrectly identifying if a disorder exists.

Note. a = actual; d = detected; + = have; − = don't have: *t* = total.

greater than expected in normal individuals are more commonly obtained by patients who have neuropathology. IIVs that are more than twice the expected scores are more common in individuals who have failed performance validity tests. Furthermore, IIVs that are negatively skewed (i.e., thus come from non-normal distributions) are also more likely to come from examinees that have performed invalidly on cognitive tests. The IIV statistic addresses concerns expressed by Iverson (2015) as to how clinicians might use these scores diagnostically, because it provides guidance to clinicians as to how to interpret the frequency of low scores obtained across a test battery.

DETERMINING CAUSALITY WITH POINT IN TIME MEASUREMENT

Forensic neuropsychologists do not typically review an examinee's life history as though it were a movie. Rather, snapshots in time are provided to them that must then be used to project both forward and backward in time to create a movie of the examinee's life. Being accurate in predicting an examinee's past, present, and future experiences and behavior is difficult. Often, the snapshots of the present are scores that fall in the impaired range on tests of cognitive ability as well as of emotional or personality functioning. Statistically, the task of the examiner is to determine the answers to the following three questions:

1. What percentage of variance in the examinee's scores can be explained by a preexisting condition (e.g., developmental dyslexia or a history of substance abuse)?
2. What percentage of variance in the examinee's scores can be explained by the event or events detailed in the referral question (e.g., cognitive impairment caused by a TBI suffered in an auto accident)?
3. What percentage of the variance in an examinee's scores can be explained by a third variable that may be interacting with the first two variables (e.g., depression, feigning, or infection after the auto accident)?

Such causal inferences are inherently challenging. Many neuropsychologists likely recall learning the old adage "correlation does not imply causation." Some may further recall that there are three options to consider under these conditions: (a) A caused B, (b) B caused A, or (c) C caused both A and B. To put this adage into an assessment context, we must consider how our assessments are based not on experimental designs but are quasi experimental in nature. Assume for the sake of this example that A is defined as an elderly woman involved in a serious automobile accident. B is defined as low cognitive ability as quantified by test scores obtained during an assessment. C is defined as evidence of severe depression, as quantified by emotional or personality test scores obtained during the assessment. The elderly woman's impaired cognition might have been caused by a brain injury she suffered during the auto accident (i.e., A caused B). Alternatively, it is also possible that woman caused the auto accident because her cognition is impaired (i.e., B caused A). Finally, a third possibility is that the third variable, that is, major depressive disorder, caused both the cognitive impairment and the auto accident (i.e., C caused both A and B). A fourth explanation is that a TBI suffered in the auto accident accounts for 25% of the variance in test scores, with 50% of the variance accounted for by the examinee's dementia. The remaining 25% of the variance might be explained by the preexisting condition of major depressive disorder. Parsing out causal variance is not an easy task. It requires the neuropsychologist to be up to date with the literature regarding the amount of variance different conditions account for in test scores. Although this task is complicated, and at times impossible to complete on the basis of available data, it is implied that forensic neuropsychologists will at a minimum attempt to engage in such parsing when they receive a referral in a forensic context.

CONCLUSION

Statistical literacy is a necessary but not sufficient condition for competent practice as a forensic neuropsychologist. But statistical literacy requires more than just knowledge of the psychometric properties of the instruments used for an evaluation. Psychometric data are never gathered in a vacuum. The needed data must allow for generalization from the psychometric facts to each examinee's unique set of circumstances. Using data that were generated from a normative sample that is not sufficiently similar to the case being examined is likely to cause diagnostic errors.

Furthermore, as noted by Briggs (2013), statistics are not so much about math as they are tools used to develop knowledge and communicate that knowledge coherently to others. Thus, practitioners must not just understand the math involved, they must also fully appreciate what it is that the data show and be able to translate that appreciation into laymen's terms. If they are unable to do those things successfully, practitioners may waste much time, money, and energy. Failure to obtain and apply essential statistics in forensic neuropsychology might be analogous to what happens in American football when a player runs a kickoff out of his own end zone, travels 99 yards down field, but fumbles the ball just before scoring a touchdown. Similarly, a well-conceived test battery, with exceptional instruments, administered in an expert manner, scored meticulously, interpreted using the latest models of cognition and the most up-to-date statistical models and computer packages, will be of no value if the neuropsychologist is not able to convey his or her knowledge to others working in a forensic context. In fact, we have all too often seen the arrogant statistician turn jurors off by speaking in tongues, seemingly disrespectful and interpreted by jurors as condescending. Such behavior is like fumbling the ball before scoring the touchdown. We have found that the best defense against such an outcome is to fully understand the nature of the instruments that have been included in the battery and the meaning of the scores that have been obtained. Once mastered, translating these ideas into another mode of communication is much easier. This allows one to adeptly translate what has been learned from the statistical manipulation of data to those who might be less knowledgeable about psychometrics and diagnostic statistics.

References

Arciniegas, D. B., Anderson, C. A., Topkoff, J., & McAllister, T. W. (2005). Mild traumatic brain injury: A neuropsychiatric approach to diagnosis, evaluation, and treatment. *Neuropsychiatric Disease and Treatment, 1*, 311–327.

Attali, E., De Anna, F., Dubois, B., & Dalla Barba, G. (2009). Confabulation in Alzheimer's disease: Poor encoding and retrieval of over-learned information. *Brain: A Journal of Neurology, 132*, 204–212. http://dx.doi.org/10.1093/brain/awn241

Beck, A. T., Steer, R. A., & Brown, G. K. (1996). *Beck Depression Inventory–II manual*. San Antonio, TX: Psychological Corporation.

Benson, N., Hulac, D. M., & Kranzler, J. H. (2010). Independent examination of the Wechsler Adult Intelligence Scale—Fourth Edition (WAIS–IV): What does the WAIS–IV measure? *Psychological Assessment, 22*, 121–130. http://dx.doi.org/10.1037/a0017767

Benton, A., & Hamsher, K. (1978). *Multilingual Aphasia Examination manual*. Iowa City: University of Iowa.

Binder, L. M., Iverson, G. L., & Brooks, B. L. (2009). To err is human: "Abnormal" neuropsychological scores and variability are common in healthy adults. *Archives of Clinical Neuropsychology, 24*, 31–46. http://dx.doi.org/10.1093/arclin/acn001

Braun, M., Tupper, D., Kaufmann, P., McCrea, M., Postal, K., Westerveld, M., . . . Deer, T. (2011). Neuropsychological assessment: A valuable tool in the diagnosis and management of neurological, neurodevelopmental, medical, and psychiatric disorders. *Cognitive and Behavioral Neurology, 24*, 107–114. http://dx.doi.org/10.1097/WNN.0b013e3182351289

Briggs, W. (2013, January 24). *Statistics is not math: Update to allow new comments* [Weblog message]. Retrieved from http://wmbriggs.com/post/3169

Brooks, B. L. (2010). Seeing the forest for the trees: Prevalence of low scores on the Wechsler Intelligence Scale for Children, fourth edition (WISC–IV). *Psychological Assessment, 22*, 650–656.

Brooks, B. L., Holdnack, J. A., & Iverson, G. L. (2011). Advanced clinical interpretation of the WAIS–IV and WMS–IV: Prevalence of low scores varies by level of intelligence and years of education. *Assessment, 18*, 156–167. http://dx.doi.org/10.1177/1073191110385316

Brooks, B. L., Iverson, G. L., Holdnack, J. A., & Feldman, H. H. (2008). Potential for misclassification of mild cognitive impairment: A study of memory scores on the Wechsler Memory Scale–III in healthy older adults. *Journal of the International Neuropsychological Society, 14*, 463–478. http://dx.doi.org/10.1017/S1355617708080521

Bush, G. W. (2001). *No child left behind*. Washington, DC: U.S. Department of Education.

Calamia, M., Markon, K., & Tranel, D. (2013). The robust reliability of neuropsychological measures: Meta-analyses of test–retest correlations. *Clinical Neuropsychologist, 27*, 1077–1105. http://dx.doi.org/10.1080/13854046.2013.809795

Calfee, J. E., & Craswell, R. (1984). Some effects of uncertainty on compliance with legal standards. *Virginia Law Review, 70*, 965–1003. http://dx.doi.org/10.2307/1072946

Camara, W. J., Nathan, J. S., & Puente, A. E. (2000). Psychological test usage: Implications. *Professional Psychology: Research and Practice, 31*, 141–154. http://dx.doi.org/10.1037/0735-7028.31.2.141

Cohen, J. (1988). *Statistical power analysis for the behavioral sciences* (2nd ed.). Hillsdale, NJ: Erlbaum.

Cullum, C. M., Butters, N., Tröster, A. I., & Salmon, D. P. (1990). Normal aging and forgetting rates on the Wechsler Memory Scale-Revised. *Archives of Clinical Neuropsychology*, *5*, 23–30. http://dx.doi.org/10.1016/0887-6177(90)90004-9

Dawes, R. M., Faust, D., & Meehl, P. E. (1989). Clinical versus actuarial judgment. *Science*, *243*, 1668–1674. http://dx.doi.org/10.1126/science.2648573

Delis, D. C., Kramer, J. H., Kaplan, E., & Ober, B. A. (2000). *California Verbal Learning Test adult version: Manual* (2nd ed.). San Antonio, TX: Psychological Corporation.

Diamond, B. L. (1985). Reasonable medical certainty, diagnostic thresholds, and definitions of mental illness in the legal context. *Bulletin of the American Academy of Psychiatry and the Law*, *13*, 121–128.

Engel, C. (2009). Preponderance of the evidence versus in-time conviction: A behavioral perspective on a conflict between American and Continental European law. *Vermont Law Review*, *333*, 435–468.

Engle, R. W., Kane, M. J., & Tuholski, S. W. (2003). Individual differences in working memory capacity and what they tell us about controlled attention, general fluid intelligence, and functions of the prefrontal cortex. In A. Miyake & P. Shah (Eds.), *Models of working memory: Mechanisms and active maintenance an executive control* (pp. 102–134). New York, NY: Cambridge University Press.

Essig, S. M., Mittenberg, W., Petersen, R. S., Strauman, S., & Cooper, J. T. (2001). Practices in forensic neuropsychology: Perspectives of neuropsychologists and trial attorneys. *Archives of Clinical Neuropsychology*, *16*, 271–291. http://dx.doi.org/10.1093/arclin/16.3.271

Flanagan, D. P., Ortiz, S. O., & Alfonso, V. C. (2013). *Essentials of cross-battery assessment*. New York, NY: Wiley.

Folstein, M. F., Folstein, S. E., & McHugh, P. R. (1975). "Mini-mental state": A practical method for grading the cognitive state of patients for the clinician. *Journal of Psychiatric Research*, *12*, 189–198. http://dx.doi.org/10.1016/0022-3956(75)90026-6

Garb, H. N. (2005). Clinical judgment and decision making. *Annual Review of Clinical Psychology*, *1*, 67–89. http://dx.doi.org/10.1146/annurev.clinpsy.1.102803.143810

Gignac, G. E. (2009). Psychometrics and the measurement of emotional intelligence. In C. Stough, D. H. Saklofske, & J. D. A. Parker (Eds.), *Assessing emotional intelligence* (pp. 9–40). http://dx.doi.org/10.1007/978-0-387-88370-0_2

Greiffenstein, M. F., & Kaufmann, P. (2012). Neuropsychology and law: Principles of productive attorney-neuropsychologist relations. In G. J. Larrabee (Ed.), *Forensic neuropsychology: A scientific approach* (2nd ed., pp. 23–69). New York, NY: Oxford University Press.

Hauser, R. M. (2002). *Meritocracy, cognitive ability, and the sources of occupational success*. Madison: University of Wisconsin Press.

Heaton, R. K., Chelune, G. J., Talley, J. L., Kay, G. G., & Curtiss, G. (1981). *The professional manual for the Wisconsin Card Sort Test (WCST)*. Los Angeles, CA: Western Psychological Services.

Heaton, R. K., Miller, W., Taylor, M. J., & Grant, I. (2004). *Revised comprehensive norms for an expanded Halstead–Reitan Battery: Demographically adjusted neuropsychological norms for African American and Caucasian adults*. Lutz, FL: Psychological Assessment Resources.

Heilbronner, R. L., Sweet, J. J., Morgan, J. E., Larrabee, G. J., & Millis, S. R. (2009). American Academy of Clinical Neuropsychology Consensus Conference Statement on the neuropsychological assessment of effort, response bias, and malingering. *Clinical Neuropsychologist*, *23*, 1093–1129. http://dx.doi.org/10.1080/13854040903155063

Hill, B. D., Rohling, M. L., Boettcher, A. C., & Meyers, J. E. (2013). Cognitive intra-individual variability has a positive association with traumatic brain injury severity and suboptimal effort. *Archives of Clinical Neuropsychology*, *28*, 640–648. http://dx.doi.org/10.1093/arclin/act045

Holdnack, J. A., & Drozdick, L. W. (2009). *Advanced Clinical Solutions: Clinical and interpretive manual*. San Antonio, TX: Pearson.

Holdnack, J. A., Zhou, X., Larrabee, G. J., Millis, S. R., & Salthouse, T. A. (2011). Confirmatory factor analysis of the WAIS–IV/WMS–IV. *Assessment*, *18*, 178–191. http://dx.doi.org/10.1177/1073191110393106

Isaacson, W. (2007). *Einstein: His life and universe*. New York, NY: Simon & Schuster.

Iverson, G. L. (2015). *Improving the methodology for assessing mild cognitive impairment across the lifespan*. Presidential address presented at the 35th annual meeting of the National Academy of Neuropsychology, Austin, TX.

Iverson, G. L., Turner, R. A., & Green, P. (1999). Predictive validity of WAIS–R VIQ-PIQ splits in persons with major depression. *Journal of Clinical Psychology*, *55*, 519–524. http://dx.doi.org/10.1002/(SICI)1097-4679(199904)55:4<519::AID-JCLP14>3.0.CO;2-B

Jacobs, D., Sano, M., Marder, K., Bell, K., Bylsma, F., Lafleche, G., . . . Stern, Y. (1994). Age at onset of Alzheimer's disease: Relation to pattern of cognitive dysfunction and rate of decline. *Neurology*,

44, 1215–1220. http://dx.doi.org/10.1212/WNL.44.7.1215

Klayman, J., & Ha, Y.-W. (1987). Confirmation, disconfirmation, and information in hypothesis testing. *Psychological Review, 94*, 211–228. http://dx.doi.org/10.1037/0033-295X.94.2.211

Larrabee, G. J. (2012). Performance validity and symptom validity in neuropsychological assessment. *Journal of the International Neuropsychological Society, 18*, 625–630. http://dx.doi.org/10.1017/S1355617712000240

Larrabee, G. J., Millis, S. R., & Meyers, J. E. (2008). Sensitivity to brain dysfunction of the Halstead–Reitan vs. an ability-focused neuropsychological battery. *Clinical Neuropsychologist, 22*, 813–825. http://dx.doi.org/10.1080/13854040701625846

Lezak, M. D., Howieson, D. B., Bigler, E. D., & Tranel, D. (2012). *Neuropsychological assessment* (5th ed.). New York, NY: Oxford University Press.

Loring, D. W., & Bauer, R. M. (2010). Testing the limits: Cautions and concerns regarding the new Wechsler IQ and Memory scales. *Neurology, 74*, 685–690. http://dx.doi.org/10.1212/WNL.0b013e3181d0cd12

Manly, J. J., Smith, C., Crystal, H. A., Richardson, J., Golub, E. T., Greenblatt, R., . . . Young, M. (2011). Relationship of ethnicity, age, education, and reading level to speed and executive function among HIV+ and HIV− women: The Women's Interagency HIV Study (WIHS) Neurocognitive Substudy. *Journal of Clinical and Experimental Neuropsychology, 33*, 853–863. http://dx.doi.org/10.1080/13803395.2010.547662

Markus, K. A., & Borsboom, D. (2013). *Frontiers of test validity theory: Measurement, causation, and meaning.* New York, NY: Routledge.

Matarazzo, J. D., & Herman, D. O. (1984). Base rate data for the WAIS–R: Test–retest stability and VIQ-PIQ differences. *Journal of Clinical Neuropsychology, 6*, 351–366. http://dx.doi.org/10.1080/01688638408401227

Meyers, J. E. (2015). *Manual for the Meyers Neuropsychological Battery (MNB)*. Retrieved from http://meyersneuropsychological.com

Meyers, J. E., Miller, R. M., & Tuita, A. R. (2014). Using pattern analysis matching to differentiate TBI and PTSD in a military sample. *Applied Neuropsychology: Adult, 21*, 60–68. http://dx.doi.org/10.1080/09084282.2012.737881

Meyers, J. E., & Rohling, M. L. (2004). Validation of the Meyers Short Battery on mild TBI patients. *Archives of Clinical Neuropsychology, 19*, 637–651. http://dx.doi.org/10.1016/j.acn.2003.08.007

Millis, S. (2003). Statistical practices: The seven deadly sins. *Child Neuropsychology, 9*, 221–233. http://dx.doi.org/10.1076/chin.9.3.221.16455

Monahan, J. (2008). Statistical literacy: A prerequisite for evidence-based medicine. *Psychological Science in the Public Interest, 21*(9), i–ii.

Muslimović, D., Post, B., Speelman, J. D., & Schmand, B. (2005). Cognitive profile of patients with newly diagnosed Parkinson disease. *Neurology, 65*, 1239–1245. http://dx.doi.org/10.1212/01.wnl.0000180516.69442.95

Neal, T. M. S., & Grisso, T. (2014). The cognitive underpinnings of bias in forensic mental health evaluations. *Psychology, Public Policy, and Law, 20*, 200–211. http://dx.doi.org/10.1037/a0035824

Nunnally, J. C., & Bernstein, I. H. (1994). *Psychometric theory* (3rd ed.). New York, NY: McGraw-Hill.

Nyenhuis, D. L., Gorelick, P. B., Geenen, E. J., Smith, C. A., Gencheva, E., Freels, S., & deToledo-Morrell, L. (2004). The pattern of neuropsychological deficits in vascular cognitive impairment-no dementia (vascular CIND). *Clinical Neuropsychologist, 18*, 41–49. http://dx.doi.org/10.1080/13854040490507145

Osborne, J. W., & Costello, A. B. (2004). Sample size and subject to item ratio in principal components analysis. *Practical Assessment, Research, and Evaluation, 9*(11). Retrieved from http://pareonline.net/getvn.asp?v=9&n=11

Peña-Casanova, J., Quiñones-Ubeda, S., Quintana-Aparicio, M., Aguilar, M., Badenes, D., Molinuevo, J. L., . . . Blesa, R. (2009). Spanish Multicenter Normative Studies (NEURONORMA Project): Norms for verbal span, visuospatial span, letter and number sequencing, trail making test, and symbol digit modalities test. *Archives of Clinical Neuropsychology, 24*, 321–341. http://dx.doi.org/10.1093/arclin/acp038

Peterson, R. A. (1994). A meta-analysis of Cronbach's coefficient alpha. *Journal of Consumer Research, 21*, 381–391. http://dx.doi.org/10.1086/209405

Rabin, L. A., Barr, W. B., & Burton, L. A. (2005). Assessment practices of clinical neuropsychologists in the United States and Canada: A survey of INS, NAN, and APA Division 40 members. *Archives of Clinical Neuropsychology, 20*, 33–65. http://dx.doi.org/10.1016/j.acn.2004.02.005

Rabin, L. A., Spadaccini, A. T., Brodale, D. L., Elbulok-Charcape, M. M., & Barr, W. B. (2014). Utilization rates of computerized tests and test batteries among clinical neuropsychologists in the United States and Canada. *Professional Psychology: Research and Practice, 45*, 368–377. http://dx.doi.org/10.1037/a0037987

Reitan, R. M., & Wolfson, D. (1985). *The Halstead–Reitan Neuropsychological Test Battery: Theory and interpretation*. Tucson, AZ: Neuropsychology Press.

Rohling, M. L. (2012, June). *Does meta-analysis help or obscure diagnosis of low base rate conditions? Implications for forensic applications*. Paper presented at the 12th annual meeting of the American Academy of Clinical Neuropsychology, Chicago, IL.

Rohling, M. L., Binder, L. M., Demakis, G. J., Larrabee, G. J., Ploetz, D. M., & Langhinrichsen-Rohling, J. (2011). A meta-analysis of neuropsychological outcome after mild traumatic brain injury: Re-analyses and reconsiderations of Binder et al. (1997), Frencham et al. (2005), and Pertab et al. (2009). *Clinical Neuropsychologist, 25*, 608–623. http://dx.doi.org/10.1080/13854046.2011.565076

Rohling, M. L., & Demakis, G. J. (2006). A meta-analysis of the neuropsychological effects of occupational exposure to mercury. *Clinical Neuropsychologist, 20*, 108–132. http://dx.doi.org/10.1080/13854040500203324

Rohling, M. L., & Demakis, G. J. (2007). Potential neuropsychological profiles in welders occupationally exposed to manganese: An examination of effect size patterns. *Journal of Clinical and Experimental Neuropsychology, 29*, 813–822. http://dx.doi.org/10.1080/13803390601087072

Rohling, M. L., Larrabee, G. J., & Millis, S. R. (2012). The "Miserable Minority" following mild traumatic brain injury: Who are they and do meta-analyses hide them? *Clinical Neuropsychologist, 26*, 197–213. http://dx.doi.org/10.1080/13854046.2011.647085

Rohling, M. L., Meyers, J. E., & Millis, S. (2003). Neuropsychological impairment following traumatic brain injury: A dose–response analysis. *Clinical Neuropsychologist, 17*, 289–302. http://dx.doi.org/10.1076/clin.17.3.289.18086

Rohling, M. L., Miller, L. S., & Langhinrichsen-Rohling, J. (2004). Rohling's Interpretive Method for neuropsychological data analysis: A response to critics. *Neuropsychology Review, 14*, 155–169. http://dx.doi.org/10.1023/B:NERV.0000048182.55980.4b

Rohling, M. L., Miller, R. M., Axelrod, B. N., Wall, J. R., Lee, J. H., & Kinikini, D. T. (2015). Is co-norming required? *Archives of Clinical Neuropsychology, 30*, 611–633.

Schretlen, D. J., Testa, S. M., Winicki, J. M., Pearlson, G. D., & Gordon, B. (2008). Frequency and bases of abnormal performance by healthy adults on neuropsychological testing. *Journal of the International Neuropsychological Society, 14*, 436–445. http://dx.doi.org/10.1017/S1355617708080387

Serafim, A. D. P., Saffi, F., Barbosa da Silva, T. G., de Almeida, C. V., Hokama, E., de Barros, D. M., & Dias, A. M. (2015). Forensic neuropsychological assessment: A review of its scope. *Archives of Clinical Psychiatry, 42*, 63–67.

Shore, D. (Writer), & Singer, B. (Director). (2004–2012). *House M.D.* [Television series]. Los Angeles, CA: Shore Z Productions.

Skiba, R. J. (2000). *Zero tolerance, zero evidence: An analysis of school disciplinary practice policy* (Policy Research Report SRS2). Bloomington: Indiana Education Policy Center.

Stern, R. A., & White, T. (2003). *Neuropsychological Assessment Battery—Manual*. Lutz, FL: Psychological Assessment Resources.

Stoffelmayr, E., & Diamond, S. S. (2000). The conflict between precision and flexibility in explaining "beyond a reasonable doubt." *Psychology, Public Policy, and Law, 6*, 769–787. http://dx.doi.org/10.1037/1076-8971.6.3.769

Strauss, E., Sherman, E. M., & Spreen, O. (2006). *A compendium of neuropsychological tests: Administration, norms, and commentary* (3rd ed.). New York, NY: Oxford University Press.

Sweet, J. J., & Meyers, D. G. (2012). Trends in forensic practice and research. In G. J. Larrabee (Ed.), *Forensic neuropsychology: A scientific approach* (2nd ed., pp. 501–516). New York, NY: Oxford University Press.

Trahan, L. H., Stuebing, K. K., Fletcher, J. M., & Hiscock, M. (2014). The Flynn effect: A meta-analysis. *Psychological Bulletin, 140*, 1332–1360. http://dx.doi.org/10.1037/a0037173

Trochim, W. M. K. (2006). *The research methods knowledge base* (2nd ed.). Retrieved from http://www.socialresearchmethods.net/kb

Trope, Y., Gervey, B., & Liberman, B. (1997). Wishful thinking from a pragmatic hypothesis-testing perspective. In M. S. Myslobodsky (Ed.), *The mythomanias: The nature of deception and self-deception* (pp. 105–131). Mahwah, NJ: Erlbaum.

Tulsky, D. S., & Price, L. R. (2003). The joint WAIS–III and WMS–III factor structure: Development and cross-validation of a six-factor model of cognitive functioning. *Psychological Assessment, 15*, 149–162. http://dx.doi.org/10.1037/1040-3590.15.2.149

Wechsler, D. (2008a). *Manual for the Wechsler Adult Intelligence Scale* (4th ed.). San Antonio, TX: Pearson.

Wechsler, D. (2008b). *Manual for the Wechsler Memory Scale* (4th ed.). San Antonio, TX: Pearson.

Weiss, L. G., Saklofske, D. H., Holdnack, J. A., & Prifitera, A. (2015). *WISC–V assessment and interpretation: Scientist-practitioner perspectives*. New York, NY: Academic Press.

CHAPTER 2

ETHICAL PRACTICE IN FORENSIC NEUROPSYCHOLOGY

Shane S. Bush and Joel E. Morgan

Neuropsychologists serve important functions in the assessment and treatment of individuals who are involved in civil, criminal, and administrative forensic contexts. They apply scientific methods and neuropsychological knowledge to inform triers of fact about individuals involved in legal matters to facilitate judicious resolutions. Neuropsychologists also provide clinical services to individuals who are involved in litigation or are pursuing disability benefits. Forensic practice provides neuropsychologists the opportunity to apply and demonstrate their knowledge and skills at the highest level of professional and ethical practice. In their interactions with legal and administrative systems, neuropsychologists encounter ethical issues and dilemmas that differ in important ways from those encountered in purely clinical contexts. Each decision, action, and conclusion is subject to critical examination by knowledgeable colleagues, aggressive attorneys, and triers of fact. Although forensic practitioners may escape such scrutiny for some time, eventually all forensic practitioners are called to answer for their actions. For those aspiring to high standards of practice, such answers are easy to come by and difficult for opposing counsel or experts to attack. Of course, there may, and likely over the course of a career will, be times when highly qualified, ethically minded, and well-intentioned neuropsychologists arrive at inaccurate diagnoses and conclusions or use idiosyncratic methodology. However, forensic contexts often allow for redress of such inaccuracies. Combining a strong forensic neuropsychology foundation with a personal commitment to high standards of ethical practice allows neuropsychologists to make meaningful contributions in forensic contexts. In this chapter, examples of ethical challenges are presented and then addressed in the context of ethics resources and ethical decision making.

Although most ethical requirements and professional guidelines are relevant to the practice of forensic neuropsychology, we have provided a list of 12 issues that experience and empirical literature indicate are of particular relevance (see Exhibit 2.1). It is understood that the order of importance of the ethical and professional issues covered in the list will vary depending on the forensic practice context, and issues not on this list may well be of critical importance to some forensic neuropsychologists.

RESOURCE-BASED AND EXPERIENCE-INFORMED DECISION MAKING

Neuropsychological decision making is data driven, with reliance on statistical information and empirical research. Qualitative data and clinical experience also contribute valuable information to the diagnostic, causal, prognostic, and other decisions that neuropsychologists make in the contexts of both clinical and forensic practice. Such quantitative and qualitative information also serves as the foundation for ethical practice and decision making. Ethical decisions are not based solely on the practitioner's subjective impressions, and ethical behavior does not occur, at least consistently, by chance. Ethical decision making, like clinical decision making, is informed by multiple resources, including empirical

http://dx.doi.org/10.1037/0000032-002
APA Handbook of Forensic Neuropsychology, S. S. Bush (Editor-in-Chief)

Exhibit 2.1
Twelve Important Ethical and Professional Issues in Forensic Neuropsychology

1. Professional competence
2. Third-party requests for services
3. Multiple relationships and conflicts of interest
4. Informed consent and notification of purpose (including privacy and confidentiality)
5. Bases for assessments and scientific and professional judgment
6. Use of assessments and interpreting assessment results
7. Test security and release of test data
8. Contingency fees
9. Impartiality and bias
10. Third-party observers
11. Accuracy and truthfulness in public statements (reports and testimony)
12. Addressing ethical misconduct

studies. Professional ethics codes, practice guidelines, jurisdictional statutes and related case law, scholarly publications, and related resources help neuropsychologists anticipate, avoid, and address ethical challenges. Although the ethical aspects of some forensic activities have been addressed with empirical research (e.g., impact of third-party presence on test performance; see McCaffrey, Lynch, & Yantz, 2005, for a review), other aspects are informed by widely accepted ethical principles. Awareness of both the research and the scholarly discussions of ethical principles arms neuropsychologists with the information necessary to maintain high standards of ethical forensic practice. Exhibit 2.2 provides a list of selected resources for ethical decision making in forensic neuropsychology. In addition to awareness and understanding of relevant resources, a structured decision-making model facilitates sound decision making. Numerous ethical decision-making models have been proposed to assist practitioners (e.g., Bush, 2007; Bush, Connell, & Denney, 2006).

Exhibit 2.2
Selected Position Statements for Ethical Decision Making in Forensic Neuropsychology

- "Specialty Guidelines for Forensic Psychology" (American Psychological Association [APA], 2013)
- "Policy Statement on the Presence of Third Party Observers in Neuropsychological Assessment" (American Academy of Clinical Neuropsychology [AACN], 2001)
- "Statement on Third Party Observers in Psychological Testing and Assessment: A Framework for Decision Making" (APA, 2007b)
- "Presence of Third Party Observers During Neuropsychological Testing" (National Academy of Neuropsychology [NAN], 2000a)
- "Official Position of the American Academy of Clinical Neuropsychology on Ethical Complaints Made Against Clinical Neuropsychologists During Adversarial Proceedings" (AACN, 2003)
- "Strategies for Private Practitioners Coping With Subpoenas or Compelled Testimony for Client Records or Test Data" (APA, 2006)
- "Record Keeping Guidelines" (APA, 2007a)
- "Test Security: Official Statement of the National Academy of Neuropsychology" (NAN, 2000b)
- "Test Security: An Update" (NAN Policy and Planning Committee, 2003)
- *Handling Requests to Release Test Data, Recording and/or Reproductions of Test Data* (NAN Policy and Planning Committee, 2000)
- "Symptom Validity Assessment: Practice Issues and Medical Necessity" (Bush, Ruff, et al., 2005)
- "American Academy of Clinical Neuropsychology Consensus Conference Statement on the Neuropsychological Assessment of Effort, Response Bias, and Malingering" (Heilbronner et al., 2009)
- "Independent and Court-Ordered Forensic Neuropsychological Examinations" (Bush & NAN Policy and Planning Committee, 2005)
- "Secretive Recording of Neuropsychological Testing and Interviewing" (Bush et al., 2009)
- "Conflict of Interest Inherent in Contingency Fee Arrangements" (Binder et al., 2012)

ROLES AND RELATIONSHIPS

The following vignette illustrates ethical challenges involving roles and relationships in forensic neuropsychology. The importance of clarifying roles is emphasized.

Vignette

An adult patient is referred to a neuropsychologist for evaluation and treatment because of postconcussive symptoms that emerged after a motor vehicle collision. The other driver's automobile insurance company is the payer for the services. A neuropsychological evaluation is performed, and the report is written in the form of a letter to the insurance claim representative rather than to the neurologist who made the referral. The report is titled "Initial Neuropsychological Report," but no plans for additional evaluation are offered. A course of treatment is initiated to address the cognitive and emotional problems identified by the evaluation. Six months later, the neuropsychologist is contacted by the patient's attorney asking for copies of records. During a brief discussion, the neuropsychologist explains that a more conclusive forensic report can be generated, if desired, for a fee to be paid by the attorney. The attorney agrees. The neuropsychologist obtains and reviews relevant records; interviews the patient's spouse; administers additional tests, including multiple symptom and performance validity measures; and generates the new report.

Discussion

Neuropsychologists serve in a variety of roles in the evaluation and treatment of persons involved in litigation; however, serving in conflicting roles for the same person compromises ethical principles and threatens the value of the services provided and the interests of all involved parties. Serving as both a treating doctor and a forensic expert for the same person is an example of assuming conflicting roles that threaten to harm patient care and the legal system's pursuit of justice. This does not mean that clinicians cannot or should not testify about the facts of a patient's treatment and any evaluations on which such treatment is based. Treating doctors, when basing their opinions and conclusions on the information they have obtained and limiting the confidence placed in their conclusions accordingly, provide a valuable service to triers of fact. However, treating doctors, who often do not have all relevant records or access to important collateral sources of information or perform extensive testing, do a disservice to justice by overstating their opinions and conclusions.

In contrast to a treating doctor, a forensic expert often gathers extensive records, including police reports, medical records, and other records of the immediate aftermath of the event in question, as well as surveillance videos when available; performs a comprehensive evaluation, including thorough validity assessment; and interviews collateral sources of information as needed. On the basis of such information, forensic experts can offer opinions and conclusions about proximate causes of the presenting problems, presence of and degree of impairment, and prognosis or permanency, often with a greater degree of accuracy and thus certainty than most treating doctors are in a position to offer. On the surface, obtaining such information and performing such an evaluation, which can improve the clinician's understanding of the patient and thus accuracy in testimony, seems like a good way to help the patient, but that is the problem. A forensic expert, wanting to be helpful, must only be helpful to the trier of fact, not to the examinee. Thus, the forensic expert strives to be as objective as possible. The wish to be helpful to the patient or the defense introduces bias into the forensic evaluation process, which can color opinions and contribute to unjust legal decisions. In this regard, forensic neuropsychologists should be aware of the nonverbal or implicit pull to be part of the patient's team.

Treating clinicians who perform forensic evaluations of, or generate forensic reports for, their patients also threaten the treating relationship. Evaluation findings that are unhelpful to the patient, such as suboptimal effort, a normal mental status, or a lack of cognitive deficits, can adversely affect the therapeutic alliance and harm the patient's trust in psychology in general. As a result, much-needed mental health services may be terminated and avoided in the future.

Much has been written about clinical and forensic roles and relationships and their blending, with most forensic psychology publications at least touching on the topic (e.g., Bush, 2005; Bush et al., 2006; L. R. Greenberg & Gould, 2001; S. Greenberg & Shuman, 1997; Iverson, 2000; Macartney-Filgate & Snow, 2004; Malina, Nelson, & Sweet, 2005; Morgan & Bush, 2005; Strasburger, Gutheil, & Brodsky, 1997; Sweet, Grote, & van Gorp, 2002). The American Psychological Association's (APA; 2017) *Ethical Principles of Psychologists and Code of Conduct* (hereinafter referred to as the Ethics Code) defines multiple relationships (Standard 3.05), in part, as a psychologist having a professional relationship with a person and at the same time having another type of relationship (e.g., nonprofessional) with the person. On the basis of this definition, a psychologist who is both a treating doctor and a forensic expert for the same person does not have multiple relationships with the person because both relationships are professional. However, Standard 3.06 (Conflicts of Interest) is relevant because having a professional relationship (i.e., treating doctor) with a patient and then taking on another professional role (i.e., forensic expert) with the person could reasonably be expected to affect objectivity or effectiveness in performing professional functions. Such situations are to be avoided. In addition, it could reasonably be argued that providing an initial or preliminary report with the goal of offering a final or forensic report at a later date for an additional fee to be paid by the patient's counsel is exploitative (Standard 3.08, Exploitative Relationships).

In contrast to the Ethics Code, the Specialty Guidelines for Forensic Psychology (APA, 2013) include the provision of both treatment and forensic services to the same person as a multiple relationship. Guideline 4.01.01 (Therapeutic-Forensic Role Conflicts) states,

> Providing forensic and therapeutic psychological services to the same individual or closely related individuals involves multiple relationships that may impair objectivity and/or cause exploitation or other harm. Therefore, when requested or ordered to provide either concurrent or sequential forensic and therapeutic services, forensic practitioners are encouraged to disclose the potential risk and make reasonable efforts to refer the request to another qualified provider. If referral is not possible, the forensic practitioner is encouraged to consider the risks and benefits to all parties and to the legal system or entity likely to be impacted, the possibility of separating each service widely in time, seeking judicial review and direction, and consulting with knowledgeable colleagues. When providing both forensic and therapeutic services, forensic practitioners seek to minimize the potential negative effects of this circumstance. (p. 11)

By initiating a role change in a manner that could be exploitative and harmful to the patient and the pursuit of a just legal decision, the neuropsychologist's practices in this vignette were inconsistent with appropriate practices according to both the Ethics Code and the Specialty Guidelines for Forensic Psychology. Reports should be considered final for the purpose for which they are written and submitted. When additional records have been requested or additional testing is needed, an addendum to the original report typically satisfies the needs of all parties and eliminates the need for multiple versions of a report. For readers in the early stages of their career in forensic neuropsychology, this case scenario is a common one, where a seemingly clinical referral morphs into a forensic case. Knowledge of this in advance can go a long way toward preventing troublesome ethical issues.

BASES FOR OPINIONS

The following vignette illustrates ethical challenges that emerge when forming opinions and arriving at conclusions in forensic cases. An appropriate evidence-based approach is emphasized.

Vignette

A 65-year-old African American woman with 12 years of education is referred for a neuropsychological evaluation to determine financial decision-making capacity. The neuropsychologist performs a comprehensive evaluation, including an interview of the patient and her adult daughter and administration of an extensive test battery, which is completed over the course of 7 hours in 1 day. The patient performed 1 standard deviation below the mean on four measures, the Wechsler Adult Intelligence Scale—Fourth Edition Arithmetic and Vocabulary subtests, the Wide Range Achievement Test 4 Math Computation subtest, and the Trail Making Test Part B. Demographically corrected norms were used for the Wechsler Adult Intelligence Scale—Fourth Edition and Trail Making Test, but not for others, such as the Wide Range Achievement Test 4. Although education level was taken into account with the demographically corrected norms, quality of education could not be accounted for with the norms and was not considered by the neuropsychologist. On the basis of the test results and the daughter's report that the patient has experienced cognitive decline and can no longer manage her own finances, the neuropsychologist provided a *Diagnostic and Statistical Manual of Mental Disorders* (5th ed.; American Psychiatric Association, 2013) diagnosis of unspecified mild neurocognitive disorder and concluded that the patient lacked the cognitive capacity to independently manage her finances.

Discussion

The evaluation performed by the neuropsychologist appears more than adequate to address the referral question. In fact, it could easily be argued that the evaluation was too extensive for this patient, particularly for completion in 1 day. However, the neuropsychologist evidenced a lack of understanding of how to use the information and data that were obtained. According to the Ethics Code (Standard 2.04, Bases for Scientific and Professional Judgments), "Psychologists' work is based upon established scientific and professional knowledge of the discipline." The neuropsychologist failed to consider that it is common and in fact normal for four test scores from a comprehensive battery of tests to fall 1 standard deviation below the mean (Binder, Iverson, & Brooks, 2009; Brooks, Iverson, & White, 2007; Iverson, Brooks, & Holdnack, 2008).

In addition, failure to consider quality of education, particularly among older adult minorities, can result in overpathologizing findings (e.g., Byrd & Manly, 2012). These authors, citing prior scholars, noted,

> Factors such as whether African Americans attended school before or after the Supreme Court's 1954 *Brown v. Board of Education* decision banning segregation in public schools, unequal distribution of educational funds, variable teacher education, shorter length of school year, and lower attendance due to required work had a profound effect on the quality of education received by African Americans. (p. 126)

Limitations in academic achievement skills would not be unexpected for such individuals and, in the absence of other patterns of deficits, would likely not reflect an acquired neurocognitive disorder. Thus, because of a lack of scientific and professional knowledge, the neuropsychologist in this case likely arrived at incorrect conclusions about the examinee, which will have the effect of limiting the examinee's autonomy and potentially adversely affecting her emotional state.

Neuropsychologists assessing older adults, children, or others for whom input or pressure from involved family members or other interested parties is present should consider the input of such persons in the context of information provided by the examinee, available records, and test data, aware that involved parties may have considerable incentive to present information that favors their interests. In such cases, a bit of professional suspicion is important. Consideration of objective data, interpreted according to the prevailing and most current science of the discipline, serves both examiners and judicial or administrative decision makers well in such situations.

TEST SELECTION

The following vignette illustrates ethical challenges that emerge when choosing assessment measures in forensic cases. Issues surrounding filing complaints against colleagues are also explored.

Vignette

As part of his legal defense, a 45-year-old man undergoes a neuropsychological evaluation to determine whether developmentally based limitations with intellectual functioning or other cognitive abilities may have contributed to his committing the crime for which he has been arrested and charged. The man had undergone intelligence testing 10 years before as part of a vocational rehabilitation program. Having obtained the prior test results, the neuropsychologist, wanting to make direct comparisons between prior and current test results, decides to use the older version of the intelligence test, as well as the memory test with which the intelligence test was co-normed. The rest of his test battery consists of the same measures that he usually uses for similar cases. A neuropsychology colleague retained by the district attorney's office notices that the older version of the intelligence test was used instead of the current edition of the test which has been available for nearly 10 years. Citing the Ethics Code (Standard 9.08, Obsolete Tests and Outdated Test Results), the neuropsychologist files a complaint with the APA Ethics Committee.

Discussion

Forensic neuropsychologists have many measures to choose from when performing evaluations. Test selection depends on many factors, including (a) the purpose of the evaluation; (b) the available normative data and their relevance to the examinee's demographics and known or suspected neuropathology; (c) other characteristics of the examinee, such as sensory or motor impairments or lack of fluency in English; (d) the setting in which the evaluation will be performed; (e) the examinee's prior experience with psychological or neuropsychological measures; and (f) the availability of prior test results. Most neuropsychologists maintain a flexible battery approach to testing (Rabin, Barr, & Burton, 2005; Sweet, Meyer, Nelson, & Moberg, 2011), which affords them the freedom to tailor their usual core battery of tests to meet the needs of a given examination on the basis of various test selection factors. Such flexibility includes making determinations about which version or edition of a given test to use.

In addition to the availability of new tests, new versions of established tests are frequently published, leaving practitioners to decide whether or when to adopt the newest version of the test. Ethical Standard 9.08, Section b, states that psychologists do not base "decisions or recommendations on tests and measures that are obsolete and not useful for the current purpose." Simply having a new version of a test become available does not necessarily render prior versions of the test obsolete for all patient populations or evaluations. A variety of factors, including serial evaluations of the same person, should be considered when making such determinations (Bush, 2010).

In the case described, the neuropsychologist for the defense chose to use prior versions of the intelligence and memory tests because he believed that doing so would best serve the purposes of the evaluation. The ability to directly compare scores, having considered psychometric issues such as practice effects, can be valuable for some types of evaluations, particularly when improvement or decline is expected on the basis of the person's injury or illness. However, in this case, which involves suspicion of developmentally based limitations with intelligence, there is little reason to expect meaningful change in intellectual or cognitive functioning during the middle adult years. The ability to determine current functioning in the most reliable and accurate manner is of primary importance for this evaluation. Direct comparison of current scores to prior scores is less important. Thus, the most recently published version of the tests may have been preferred. Nevertheless, the prior version of the test is not obsolete; it can still be useful for the purpose of the evaluation. Therefore, the decision of the neuropsychologist for the prosecution to file a complaint seems unsubstantiated and may have been a tactic to try to discredit the opposing expert.

Frivolous complaints are unnecessarily harmful to the practitioner against whom the complaint is made, potentially misleading to the triers of fact, and possibly harmful to the pursuit of justice. The Ethics Code (Standard 1.07, Improper Complaints) states that psychologists should not file, or encourage the filing of, complaints "with reckless disregard for or willful ignorance of facts that would disprove the allegation." To eliminate the perception that an ethics complaint is frivolous and serves only to intimidate or discredit a colleague, practitioners who have detected unethical or other inappropriate behavior by a colleague are advised to wait until the forensic matter at hand has been completed, and then, if the ethical issue still seems to need addressing, file a complaint or otherwise address the issue at that time (American Academy of Clinical Neuropsychology, 2003; Grote, Lewin, Sweet, & van Gorp, 2000). Some states forbid the filing of an ethical complaint during the course of litigation. Of course, if there is evidence that a colleague's behavior will likely result in direct, imminent, and significant harm to someone, an immediate ethical or legal response would be necessary. Although the stakes can be high in both civil and criminal cases, an undesirable verdict for an examinee should not be considered as something harmful caused by a competent neuropsychologist practicing in good faith. Thus, in this case, it was the neuropsychologist retained by the prosecution who engaged in inappropriate behavior by filing an inappropriate complaint during a legal case.

SYMPTOM, PERFORMANCE, AND RESPONSE VALIDITY

The following vignette illustrates ethical challenges that emerge when assessing the validity of an examinee's responses and presentation. Ethical issues involved in basing decisions solely on record review are also addressed.

Vignette

"I can tell when older adults aren't trying their best, and besides, they almost never malinger." This deposition testimony was used to defend a neuropsychologist's decision to forego any formal symptom or performance validity assessment in the evaluation of a 65-year-old man who sustained a mild traumatic brain injury when he was hit by a slow-moving mail truck while walking his dog. The neuropsychologist retained by the defense to review the report and test data from the plaintiff's neuropsychologist opined that the plaintiff's (a) inability to repeat more than three digits forward and two digits in reverse sequence, (b) inability to correctly identify more than 10 words on the California Verbal Learning Test—Second Edition Forced Choice Recognition Trial, (c) incorrect responses to four Wisconsin Card Sorting Test perfect matches, and (d) atypical pattern of scores on the Stroop Color-Word Test (10 more color naming responses than word reading responses in a man with no history of verbal learning disability) was clear evidence of suboptimal performance, invalidating the data. Furthermore, the defense-retained neuropsychologist stated that given the relatively mild injury, which had been sustained 18 months before the neuropsychological evaluation, could not possibly be resulting in the low and atypical test scores; therefore, the plaintiff must be malingering.

Discussion

Older adults are not immune to inaccurate reporting of history, fabrication or embellishment of current symptoms, or suboptimal performance. Clinicians who believe they can tell, solely on the basis of subjective impressions and clinical judgment, whether an examinee is approaching an examination in a valid manner are very likely overestimating their abilities (Guilmette, 2013). Psychometric assessment of symptom and performance validity is an essential component of forensic neuropsychological examinations (Bush et al., 2005; Heilbronner, Sweet, Morgan, Larrabee, & Millis, 2009), and response validity (i.e., accuracy of self-reported history) can be assessed by comparing self-reported background information with educational, vocational, military, medical, and other records. Failure to use psychometric validity assessment measures in forensic neuropsychological examinations is inconsistent with prevailing standards of practice and fails to satisfy Ethical Standards 2.04 (Bases for Scientific and Professional Judgments) and 9.01 (Bases for Assessments).

There are many reasons why plaintiffs, including older adults, provide invalid responses and poor effort (Iverson, 2005); malingering is one such reason and must be considered. However, failure to consider other possible reasons for invalid presentations reflects inappropriate practice. Determinations of malingering, based in part on objective, psychometric evidence, can be made using probabilistic language on the basis of delineated criteria such as those proposed by Slick, Sherman, and Iverson (1999) and Slick and Sherman (2013). Thus, in this case, the plaintiff's neuropsychologist failed to practice in an ethical manner by relying solely on clinical judgment to make determinations about symptom and performance validity, but the defense's neuropsychologist may have inappropriately neglected consideration of possible reasons for suboptimal performance other than malingering. Incompetent practice is unethical practice.

Regarding the defense's expert relying on peer or record review to make determinations about the plaintiff, rather than performing his own examination, the Ethics Code (Standard 9.01, Bases for Assessments, Section C) states, "When psychologists conduct a record review or provide consultation or supervision and an individual examination is not warranted or necessary for the opinion, psychologists explain this and the sources of information on which they based their conclusions and recommendations." Having received recent examination results from the plaintiff's neuropsychologist, the defense expert made an apparently appropriate determination that he did not need to perform his own examination. As long as his reasoning is explained and the information on which he arrived at his conclusions is described (and both are sound, reasonable, and appropriate), he has acted in an ethical manner.

THIRD-PARTY OBSERVERS

The following vignette illustrates ethical issues that apply when considering requests to have third parties observe forensic neuropsychological evaluations. The empirical evidence of the impact of third parties on examinee performance can help guide decisions.

Vignette

A neuropsychologist is retained by the defense in a personal injury case. At the scheduled time of the examination, the plaintiff arrives with a registered nurse who consults with, and has been hired by, the plaintiff's attorney. The nurse, a very pleasant woman, informs the neuropsychologist that she is there to observe the examination. She assures the neuropsychologist that she will sit quietly, out of sight of the plaintiff, and be as unobtrusive as possible. The neuropsychologist informs her, respectfully, that she will be doing no such thing. He explains the ethical issues and position of the profession (American Academy of Clinical Neuropsychology, 2001; National Academy of Neuropsychology, 2000a) that such practices are inappropriate and unacceptable. He states that she can be present for the clinical interview but not the testing. The nurse reminds the neuropsychologist that the plaintiff has the legal right in that jurisdiction to have a third party present during the examination and that the examination cannot go forward without her being in the room. The neuropsychologist replies that he understands but cannot be flexible on the issue. The nurse informs him that she frequently observes neuropsychological examinations performed by other practitioners in the area, including having observed two such examinations that month performed by a neuropsychologist who is just a few miles away. The neuropsychologist realizes that he will likely lose the income from this examination just to have the local colleague perform the examination without concern for appropriate practices. The neuropsychologist and nurse agree to contact their respective retaining parties to see whether something can be done to satisfy all parties. After 30 minutes, during which time the retaining parties speak by phone to address the issue, the examination is cancelled.

Discussion

The willingness of local colleagues to engage in unethical or otherwise inappropriate professional behavior does not provide justification for engaging in such behavior. Neuropsychologists sometimes consider a variety of factors when deciding whether to engage in a professional behavior that they know is inconsistent with acceptable standards of practice. Such factors include the amount of income that can be made or lost or the belief that one is better qualified than others to provide the service being considered. However, neither loss of income nor the belief that one is better qualified than a local colleague to perform a given examination is justification for engaging in unethical or otherwise unprofessional behavior.

With the knowledge that third-party presence can affect test results and that test security can be compromised (Howe & McCaffrey, 2010), sacrificing one's principles by allowing a third party to observe neuropsychological testing can be harmful to the examinee, the pursuit of just legal decisions, neuropsychology as a profession, and society in general. Therefore, allowing observers of forensic neuropsychological evaluations fails to satisfy the first General Principle (Beneficence and Nonmaleficence) and should not occur. Of course, there are situations in which the benefits of a third party being present outweigh the negative aspects, such as use of an interpreter when a neuropsychologist who is a native speaker of the language is not available.

TEST SECURITY

Forensic neuropsychology practitioners frequently receive requests for records, including raw test data, from attorneys and other involved parties. The following vignette illustrates ethical issues that apply when considering requests for raw test data.

Vignette

A neuropsychologist who performed a clinical neuropsychological evaluation of a patient who is involved in litigation receives a subpoena *duces tecum* requiring the reproduction of all original documents in the possession of the neuropsychologist (see Appendix 2.1 for a sample subpoena), threatening a contempt of court charge if the records are not made available by a date just 3 days from the day on which the subpoena was received. The subpoena, signed by the patient's attorney, is accompanied by a signed release from the patient and a check for $15. The neuropsychologist, committed to maintaining test security, does not immediately send the requested records. Instead, he responds promptly with a letter that describes the neuropsychologist's ethical, professional, and legal obligations and offers solutions to meet the needs of all parties (see sample letter in Appendix 2.2).

Discussion

It is not uncommon for neuropsychologists who evaluate and treat patients who have been in accidents and are involved in litigation to receive subpoenas. Receipt of such subpoenas need not be a source of stress. Professional materials exist to assist practitioners in negotiating subpoenas and compelled testimony (APA, 2006, 2008; Zur, 2015). Neuropsychologists need to respond to, but not necessarily comply with, valid subpoenas signed by attorneys. In the interests of safeguarding test materials and protecting patients from possible harm, neuropsychologists can use subpoenas as an opportunity to educate attorneys and courts about neuropsychological services, the unique measures and procedures used, and the importance of safeguarding the measures. Often, a negotiated agreement that provides test scores to attorneys or provides their neuropsychological experts with all test data can satisfy the needs of all parties. Thus, the neuropsychologist in this case acted appropriately by responding promptly with the letter to the attorney.

GETTING IT RIGHT AFTER GETTING IT WRONG

Despite appropriate training and best efforts, it is unrealistic to believe that a neuropsychologist can get every diagnosis correct over the course of career. The following vignette illustrates the ethical issues that apply when a neuropsychologist receives convincing evidence that a prior diagnosis was incorrect.

Vignette

A neuropsychologist, retained by a disability insurance carrier, performs an independent medical examination of a person who has applied for disability benefits. The examinee's cognitive profile reveals some relative strengths and weaknesses but is interpreted as being within expectations on the basis of estimates of optimal functioning. Minnesota Multiphasic Personality Inventory–2 scales reveal no emotional distress; however, some mild but vocationally meaningful personality changes are missed. The neuropsychologist concludes that there is no neurocognitive disorder and no evidence of disability. Less than a year later, the neuropsychologist receives from the disability insurance carrier records of a recent neuropsychological evaluation performed by a colleague who was retained by the examinee's counsel. The neuropsychologist is asked to comment on the colleague's opinions. The neuropsychologist finds that the relative weaknesses observed during the independent medical examination are now much more pronounced, and the examinee's functioning in multiple settings has reportedly declined substantially. There is no evidence of suboptimal performance or invalid symptom reporting. The colleague diagnosed the examinee with major neurocognitive disorder due to Pick disease and concluded that the examinee is unable to perform essential work responsibilities. The neuropsychologist reviews the colleague's data and agrees with the colleague's opinions. Given the rapid disease progression and the updated evaluation results, the neuropsychologist realizes that he missed the condition at the time of the independent medical examination and welcomes the opportunity to correct his original opinion.

Discussion

Competent, well-intentioned practitioners make mistakes. Such mistakes can range from the very minor, such as a scoring error that does not affect the interpretation of the test, to the more significant, such as misdiagnosis. Of course, there is often room for disagreement among colleagues on matters large and small. Some disorders can be particularly difficult to detect or accurately diagnose, particularly in the early stages or mild forms. Pick disease is one such condition, particularly early in the disease process when the presenting symptoms often involve behavior change and cognition remains intact, although overlap with Alzheimer's disease is often evident as the disease progresses (LaMarre & Kramer, 2013; Lezak, Howieson, & Loring, 2004; Wittenberg et al., 2008).

The opportunity to correct a mistake in clinical or forensic practice is both uncommon and a gift. Most mistakes probably remain unknown by the practitioners who made them, either because they go undetected or because they are never brought to the practitioner's attention. Once the mistake has been identified by another person, the manner in which the mistake is revealed to the practitioner can range from private and sensitive to public and hostile. Although no neuropsychologist likes to learn that she or he made a mistake, how one handles the mistake after becoming aware of it has more direct ethical implications than whether the mistake was made. It can be natural to take a defensive position and try to justify the prior thinking that led to the alleged or identified mistake. Such defensiveness may be appropriate; the other person's opinion, rather than the original, may be incorrect. However, when persuasive evidence becomes available, whether in written form or during testimony, that one's prior stance was incorrect, the neuropsychologist practicing with integrity acknowledges and strives to correct the mistake.

General Principle C (Integrity) states, "Psychologists seek to promote accuracy, honesty, and truthfulness in the science, teaching, and practice of psychology." The Specialty Guidelines for Forensic Psychology, emphasizing the importance of integrity by addressing it in the first guideline, reinforces the wording of General Principle C and adds that psychologists "resist partisan pressures to provide services in any ways that might tend to be misleading or inaccurate." Maintaining a position once its inaccuracy has been revealed is inconsistent with ethical practice (Standard 5.01, Avoidance of False or Deceptive Statements). Thus, the neuropsychologist in this case, by welcoming the opportunity to revisit and change the original diagnosis, is practicing with integrity and in an ethically appropriate manner.

CONCLUSION

Forensic practice, with an understanding that one's work will be scrutinized and challenged, often publicly, by attorneys and knowledgeable colleagues, provides neuropsychologists extra incentive to maintain current knowledge and sharp skills. An essential aspect of successful practice is maintaining awareness of ethical issues and challenges commonly encountered in forensic practice. Consistent with the 4 A's of ethical practice (Bush, 2009), Anticipating ethical challenges helps practitioners Avoid pitfalls and Address dilemmas when encountered, because the practitioner Aspires to the highest standards of professional behavior. Well-prepared neuropsychologists practicing in good faith provide valuable services to a legal system charged with providing just decisions for persons who are often experiencing very complex neurological and psychiatric problems.

APPENDIX 2.1

SAMPLE SUBPOENA *DUCES TECUM*

COURT
COUNTY OF

....

Index No.:
Calendar No.:
Plaintiff(s):
-against-
Defendant(s):

....

THE PEOPLE OF THE STATE OF NEW YORK
TO: Dr. X, Ph.D.
GREETINGS:
WE COMMAND YOU, that all business and excuses being laid aside, you and each of you (check one box):

- ☐ make available, by the 10th day of June 2015 and permit the party seeking discovery, or someone acting on his or her behalf, to inspect, copy, test or photograph the following:
- ☐ deliver to, by the 10th day of June 2015 complete and accurate copies of the following: All records in your possession.

All papers or other items delivered pursuant to this subpoena shall be accompanied by a copy of this subpoena.

IF THIS SUBPOENA IS ADDRESSED TO A NON-PARTY: The reason this disclosure is necessary is:

IF THIS SUBPOENA IS ADDRESSED TO A NON-PARTY MEDICAL PROVIDER FOR PATIENT'S RECORDS: Written authorization from the patient is attached. (Records shall not be provided unless this subpoena is accompanied by a written authorization by the patient.)

1. Per CPLR §3120, parties must be given no less than 20 days after the service of this subpoena.
2. Per CPLR §3122(d), "Unless the subpoena duces tecum directs the production of original documents for inspection and copying at the place where such items are usually maintained, it shall be sufficient for the custodian or other qualified person to deliver complete and accurate copies of the items to be produced. The reasonable production expenses of a non-party witness shall be defrayed by the party seeking discovery."
3. Stated per CPLR §3101(a)(4).
4. Per CPLR §3122(a): "Any subpoena served upon a medical provider requesting the medical records of a patient shall state in conspicuous bold faced type that the records shall not be provided unless the subpoena is accompanied by a written authorization by the patient."

Your failure to comply with this subpoena is punishable as a contempt of court.

Attorney name: typed and signed
Attorney(s) for (firm)
Office and P.O. Address
Telephone No.

APPENDIX 2.2

SAMPLE RESPONSE TO SUBPOENA *DUCES TECUM*

DATE:
TO:
RE: Subpoena of records
Patient:
SSN (last 4):

Dear Ms. ____________:

Today I received your Subpoena Duces Tecum dated June 7, 2015, for records for the above named patient, and I am glad to comply with the subpoena. The neuropsychological records include office intake forms, reports, invoices, letters, a list of all tests and scores, and computerized test results. I have 94 pages of such records and request $0.75 per page for reproducing the records, plus the cost of shipping, for a total of $80.50. If that will be a problem, please let me know.

Please be aware that the records described above do not include raw neuropsychological test data (e.g., test forms). I appreciate the importance of disclosure of important information in litigated matters; however, as detailed in this letter, neuropsychologists have conflicting legal and ethical obligations when asked/ordered to release raw test data to anyone other than another neuropsychologist. The 2 primary issues of concern are as follows:

1. The security of neuropsychological test materials and data is necessary to ensure the validity of future examinations. Through the dissemination of test forms and responses, potential examinees may familiarize themselves with the materials and then provide answers that do not reflect their true neuropsychological status. This situation is analogous to making the LSAT questions and answers widely available.
2. Providing raw test data to persons who are not trained to interpret them can result in misuse and misinterpretation of the information and

> ultimately result in harm. As a result, psychologists have an ethical obligation to release raw test data only to other psychologists who have the education and training to use and interpret the information appropriately.

Both legal and ethical obligations to maintain test security are presented in more detail below.

Legal Considerations

In the case of *Detroit Edison Co. v. National Labor Relations Board* (NLRB) 440 U.S. 301 (1979), the U.S. Supreme Court determined that psychologists should not release raw data and psychological test materials to nonpsychologists.

Additionally, when psychologists purchase tests and test forms, they agree to comply with federal copyright law. For example, when purchasing test materials from Pearson Assessments, the Terms & Conditions of Purchase state, "Pearson Products are protected by various intellectual property laws, including trade secrets, copyright and trademarks. Printing or reproducing copyright-protected materials or content . . . is prohibited by law and by these Ts & Cs. Pearson software outputs, including but not limited to reports, are protected as trade secrets. Trade secrets are not permitted to be disclosed in response to requests made pursuant to HIPAA or to any other data disclosure law that exempts disclosure of information or documents protected as trade secrets. . . . *The Customer may not, under any circumstance, copy or reproduce the text or graphic image of any test item* [italics added]."

Professional Ethics

The Ethics Code of the American Psychological Association (2017) states in Standard 9.04, "Psychologists may refrain from releasing test data to protect a client/patient or others from substantial harm or misuse or misrepresentation of the data or the test, recognizing that in many instances release of confidential information under these circumstances is regulated by law." In Standard 9.11, the Ethics Code further states, "Psychologists make reasonable efforts to maintain the integrity and security of test materials and other assessment techniques consistent with law and contractual obligations, and in a manner that permits adherence to this Ethics Code."

Additionally, the Standards for Educational and Psychological Testing (American Educational Research Association, American Psychological Association, & National Council on Measurement in Education, 2014) state in Standard 10.18 that professionals have a responsibility to maintain the security of testing materials and respect copyright laws. In litigation, inspection of the instruments should be restricted, to the extent permitted by law, to those who are legally or ethically obligated to safeguard test security (i.e., other psychologists) or should occur in a controlled environment.

Professional Position Papers

Guidelines published by neuropsychological professional organizations emphasize the importance of maintaining test security and releasing raw test data to persons who are qualified by education and training to understand the information and who are also bound by ethical and legal requirements to maintain test security.

- Attix, D. K., Donders, J., Johnson-Greene, D., Grote, C. L., Harris, J. G., & Bauer, R. M. (2007). Disclosure of neuropsychological test data: Official position of Division 40 (Clinical Neuropsychology) of the American Psychological Association, Association of Postdoctoral Programs in Clinical Neuropsychology, and American Academy of Clinical Neuropsychology. *Clinical Neuropsychologist, 21,* 232–238.
- National Academy of Neuropsychology. (2000). Test security: Official statement of the National Academy of Neuropsychology. *Archives of Clinical Neuropsychology, 15,* 383–386.
- National Academy of Neuropsychology Policy and Planning Committee. (2003). *Test security: An update. Official statement of the National Academy of Neuropsychology.* Retrieved from http://nanonline.org/paio/security_update.shtm

Proposed Solutions

1. A summary sheet listing standardized scores for all tests that were administered is appended to the neuropsychological report. This summary sheet should suffice for most purposes and will be included with other records upon receipt of the copying and shipping fee.

2. Forward the name and contact information of a neuropsychologist to whom the materials can be released (an additional $30.00 copying fee is requested for reproducing raw test data).
3. Provide a court order stipulating that the test materials and data will be protected in the following ways:
   - no broad circulation
   - no unauthorized copies are made
   - minimize presentation in court
   - protect/seal exhibits and court records related to the test materials and raw test data
   - destroy or return test materials following conclusion of the matter.

I appreciate your consideration of these issues and your understanding of the importance for the general public of maintaining the security of neuropsychological test materials and raw test data. I look forward to working with you to resolve this issue in a manner that is consistent with my legal, ethical, and professional obligations.

If you have any questions, please let me know.

Sincerely,

Dr. X, PhD, ABPP

References

American Academy of Clinical Neuropsychology. (2001). Special presentation: Policy statement on the presence of third party observers in neuropsychological assessments. *Clinical Neuropsychologist, 15*, 433–439. http://dx.doi.org/10.1076/clin.15.4.433.1888

American Academy of Clinical Neuropsychology. (2003). From the academy: Official position of the American Academy of Clinical Neuropsychology on ethical complaints made against clinical neuropsychologists during adversarial proceedings. *Clinical Neuropsychologist, 17*, 443–445. http://dx.doi.org/10.1076/clin.17.4.443.27943

American Educational Research Association, American Psychological Association, & National Council on Measurement in Education. (2014). *Standards for educational and psychological testing*. Washington, DC: American Educational Research Association.

American Psychiatric Association. (2013). *Diagnostic and statistical manual of mental disorders* (5th ed.). Washington, DC: Author.

American Psychological Association. (2006). Strategies for private practitioners coping with subpoenas or compelled testimony for client records or test data. *Professional Psychology: Research and Practice, 37*, 215–222. http://dx.doi.org/10.1037/0735-7028.37.2.215

American Psychological Association. (2007a). Record keeping guidelines. *American Psychologist, 62*, 993–1004. http://dx.doi.org/10.1037/0003-066X.62.9.993

American Psychological Association. (2007b). *Statement on third party observers in psychological testing and assessment: A framework for decision making*. Retrieved from http://www.apa.org/science/programs/testing/third-party-observers.pdf

American Psychological Association. (2008). *How to deal with a subpoena*. Retrieved from http://www.apapracticecentral.org/update/2008/12-17/subpoena.aspx

American Psychological Association. (2013). Specialty guidelines for forensic psychology. *American Psychologist, 68*, 7–19. http://dx.doi.org/10.1037/a0029889

American Psychological Association. (2017). *Ethical principles of psychologists and code of conduct* (2002, Amended June 1, 2010 and January 1, 2017). Retrieved from http://www.apa.org/ethics/code/index.aspx

Binder, L. M., Iverson, G. L., & Brooks, B. L. (2009). To err is human: "Abnormal" neuropsychological scores and variability are common in healthy adults. *Archives of Clinical Neuropsychology, 24*, 31–46. http://dx.doi.org/10.1093/arclin/acn001

Binder, L. M., Ruff, R. M., Iverson, G. L., Bush, S. S., MacAllister, W. S., Richards, P. M., & Stutts, M. (2012). *Conflict of interest inherent in contingency fee arrangements: National Academy of Neuropsychology position statement*. Retrieved from https://www.nanonline.org/docs/ResearchandPublications/PositionPapers /Position%20Statement%20on%20Contingency%20fee.pdf

Brooks, B. L., Iverson, G. L., & White, T. (2007). Substantial risk of "accidental MCI" in healthy older adults: Base rates of low memory scores in neuropsychological assessment. *Journal of the International Neuropsychological Society, 13*, 490–500. http://dx.doi.org/10.1017/S1355617707070531

Bush, S. S. (2005). Introduction to ethical challenges in forensic neuropsychology. In S. S. Bush (Ed.), *A casebook of ethical challenges in neuropsychology* (pp. 10–14). New York, NY: Psychology Press.

Bush, S. S. (2007). *Ethical decision making in clinical neuropsychology*. New York, NY: Oxford University Press.

Bush, S. S. (2009). *Geriatric mental health ethics: A casebook*. New York, NY: Springer.

Bush, S. S. (2010). Determining whether or when to adopt new versions of psychological and neuropsychological tests: Ethical and professional considerations. *Clinical Neuropsychologist*, *24*, 7–16. http://dx.doi.org/10.1080/13854040903313589

Bush, S. S., Connell, M. A., & Denney, R. L. (2006). *Ethical issues in forensic psychology: A systematic model for decision making*. http://dx.doi.org/10.1037/11469-000

Bush, S. S., & NAN Policy and Planning Committee. (2005). Independent and court-ordered forensic neuropsychological examinations: Official statement of the National Academy of Neuropsychology. *Archives of Clinical Neuropsychology*, *20*, 997–1007. http://dx.doi.org/10.1016/j.acn.2005.06.003

Bush, S. S., Pimental, P. A., Ruff, R. M., Iverson, G. L., Barth, J. T., Broshek, D. K., & National Academy of Neuropsychology. (2009). Secretive recording of neuropsychological testing and interviewing: Official position of the National Academy of Neuropsychology. *Archives of Clinical Neuropsychology*, *24*, 1–2. http://dx.doi.org/10.1093/arclin/acp002

Bush, S. S., Ruff, R. M., Tröster, A. I., Barth, J. T., Koffler, S. P., Pliskin, N. H., . . . Silver, C. H. (2005). Symptom validity assessment: Practice issues and medical necessity. *Archives of Clinical Neuropsychology*, *20*, 419–426. http://dx.doi.org/10.1016/j.acn.2005.02.002

Byrd, D. A., & Manly, J. J. (2012). Cultural considerations in the neuropsychological assessment of older adults. In S. S. Bush & T. A. Martin (Eds.), *Geriatric neuropsychology: Practice essentials* (pp. 115–139). New York, NY: Psychology Press.

Greenberg, L. R., & Gould, J. W. (2001). The treating expert: A hybrid role with firm boundaries. *Professional Psychology: Research and Practice*, *32*, 469–478. http://dx.doi.org/10.1037/0735-7028.32.5.469

Greenberg, S., & Shuman, D. (1997). Irreconcilable conflict between therapeutic and forensic roles. *Professional Psychology: Research and Practice*, *28*, 50–57. http://dx.doi.org/10.1037/0735-7028.28.1.50

Grote, C. L., Lewin, J. L., Sweet, J. J., & van Gorp, W. G. (2000). Responses to perceived unethical practices in clinical neuropsychology: Ethical and legal considerations. *Clinical Neuropsychologist*, *14*, 119–134. http:// dx.doi.org/10.1076/1385-4046(200002)14:1;1-8;FT119

Guilmette, T. J. (2013). The role of clinical judgment in symptom validity assessment. In D. A. Carone & S. S. Bush (Eds.), *Mild traumatic brain injury: Symptom validity assessment and malingering* (pp. 31–43). New York, NY: Springer.

Heilbronner, R. L., Sweet, J. J., Morgan, J. E., Larrabee, G. J., & Millis, S. R. (2009). American Academy of Clinical Neuropsychology Consensus Conference Statement on the neuropsychological assessment of effort, response bias, and malingering. *Clinical Neuropsychologist*, *23*, 1093–1129. http://dx.doi.org/10.1080/13854040903155063

Howe, L. L., & McCaffrey, R. J. (2010). Third party observation during neuropsychological evaluation: An update on the literature, practical advice for practitioners, and future directions. *Clinical Neuropsychologist*, *24*, 518–537. http://dx.doi.org/10.1080/13854041003775347

Iverson, G. L. (2000). Dual relationships in psycholegal evaluations: Treating psychologists service as expert witnesses. *American Journal of Forensic Psychology*, *18*, 79–87.

Iverson, G. L. (2005). Outcome from mild traumatic brain injury. *Current Opinion in Psychiatry*, *18*, 301–317. http://dx.doi.org/10.1097/01.yco.0000165601.29047.ae

Iverson, G. L., Brooks, B. L., & Holdnack, J. A. (2008). Misdiagnosis of cognitive impairment in forensic neuropsychology. In R. L. Heilbronner (Ed.), *Neuropsychology in the courtroom: Expert analysis of reports and testimony* (pp. 243–287). New York, NY: Guilford Press.

LaMarre, A., & Kramer, J. H. (2013). Accurate assessment of behavioral variant of frontotemporal dementia. In L. D. Ravdin & H. L. Katzen (Eds.), *Handbook on the neuropsychology of aging and dementia* (pp. 313–332). http://dx.doi.org/10.1007/978-1-4614-3106-0_21

Lezak, M. D., Howieson, D. B., & Loring, D. W. (2004). *Neuropsychological assessment* (4th ed.). New York, NY: Oxford University Press.

Macartney-Filgate, M. S., & Snow, W. G. (2004). The practitioner as expert witness. In D. R. Evans (Ed.), *The law, standards, and ethics in the practice of psychology* (2nd ed., pp. 397–429). Toronto, Ontario, Canada: Emond Montgomery.

Malina, A. C., Nelson, N. W., & Sweet, J. J. (2005). Framing the relationships in forensic neuropsychology: Ethical issues. *Journal of Forensic Neuropsychology*, *4*(3), 21–44. http://dx.doi.org/10.1300/J151v04n03_03

McCaffrey, R. J., Lynch, J. K., & Yantz, C. L. (2005). Third party observers: Why all the fuss? *Journal of Forensic Neuropsychology*, *4*(2), 1–15. http://dx.doi.org/10.1300/J151v04n02_01

Morgan, J. E., & Bush, S. S. (2005). Anticipating forensic involvement: Ethical considerations for clinical neuropsychologists. *Journal of Forensic*

Neuropsychology, *4*(3), 11–20. http://dx.doi.org/10.1300/J151v04n03_02

National Academy of Neuropsychology. (2000a). Presence of third party observers during neuropsychological testing: Official statement of the National Academy of Neuropsychology. *Archives of Clinical Neuropsychology*, *15*, 379–380. http://dx.doi.org/10.1093/arclin/15.5.379

National Academy of Neuropsychology. (2000b). Test security: Official statement of the National Academy of Neuropsychology. *Archives of Clinical Neuropsychology*, *15*, 383–386.

National Academy of Neuropsychology Policy and Planning Committee. (2000). *Handling requests to release test data, recording and/or reproductions of test data: Official statement of the National Academy of Neuropsychology*. Retrieved from http://nanonline.org/docs/ResearchandPublications/PositionPapers/Test%20Security%20Appendix%2003.pdf

National Academy of Neuropsychology Policy and Planning Committee. (2003). *Test security: An update. Official statement of the National Academy of Neuropsychology*. Retrieved from http://nanonline.org/paio/security_update.shtm

Rabin, L. A., Barr, W. B., & Burton, L. A. (2005). Assessment practices of clinical neuropsychologists in the United States and Canada: A survey of INS, NAN, and APA Division 40 members. *Archives of Clinical Neuropsychology*, *20*, 33–65. http://dx.doi.org/10.1016/j.acn.2004.02.005

Slick, D. J., & Sherman, E. M. (2013). Differential diagnosis of malingering. In D. A. Carone & S. S. Bush (Eds.), *Mild traumatic brain injury: Symptom validity assessment and malingering* (pp. 57–72). New York, NY: Springer.

Slick, D. J., Sherman, E. M., & Iverson, G. L. (1999). Diagnostic criteria for malingered neurocognitive dysfunction: Proposed standards for clinical practice and research. *Clinical Neuropsychologist*, *13*, 545–561. http://dx.doi.org/10.1076/1385-4046(199911)13:04;1-Y;FT545

Strasburger, L. H., Gutheil, T. G., & Brodsky, A. (1997). On wearing two hats: Role conflict in serving as both psychotherapist and expert witness. *American Journal of Psychiatry*, *154*, 448–456. http://dx.doi.org/10.1176/ajp.154.4.448

Sweet, J. J., Grote, C., & van Gorp, W. G. (2002). Ethical issues in forensic neuropsychology. In S. S. Bush & M. L. Drexler (Eds.), *Ethical issues in clinical neuropsychology* (pp. 103–133). Lisse, the Netherlands: Swets & Zeitlinger.

Sweet, J. J., Meyer, D. G., Nelson, N. W., & Moberg, P. J. (2011). The TCN/AACN 2010 "salary survey": Professional practices, beliefs, and incomes of U.S. neuropsychologists. *Clinical Neuropsychologist*, *25*, 12–61. http://dx.doi.org/10.1080/13854046.2010.544165

Wittenberg, D., Possin, K. L., Rascovsky, K., Rankin, K. P., Miller, B. L., & Kramer, J. H. (2008). The early neuropsychological and behavioral characteristics of frontotemporal dementia. *Neuropsychology Review*, *18*, 91–102. http://dx.doi.org/10.1007/s11065-008-9056-z

Zur, O. (2015). *Subpoenas and how to handle them: Guidelines for psychotherapists and counselors*. Retrieved from http://www.zurinstitute.com/subpoena.html

Part II

ASSESSMENT MEASURES AND PROCEDURES

CHAPTER 3

BEYOND THE TESTS: RECORD REVIEW, INTERVIEW, AND OBSERVATIONS IN FORENSIC NEUROPSYCHOLOGY

Joseph W. Fink

Testing is but one part of the forensic neuropsychological (FN) evaluation process. Psychometric testing indeed offers a powerful lens through which human behavior can be systematically sampled and measured. The forensic interview, behavioral observations, and record review represent additional lenses through which behavior is sampled and assayed. Like a compound microscope, the emergent resolving power of analysis is greatly magnified when all of these lenses are brought together and focused in a concerted fashion.

This chapter examines the FN interview, observations, and record review and explores how these information sources complement test results to assist the trier of fact. Before reviewing each of these lenses, the critical need to account for bias, which cuts across all of these modes of data analysis, is highlighted. The chapter is pitched toward the neuropsychologist's role in civil, administrative, and probate forensic cases, though many elements are likewise germane to criminal cases. The review is framed by the common goal of striving for "accuracy, impartiality, fairness, and independence" (American Psychological Association [APA], 2013, p. 8) in FN evaluations.

THROUGH A LENS, DARKLY: ACCOUNTING FOR BIAS

"When conducting forensic examinations, forensic practitioners strive to be unbiased and impartial, and avoid partisan presentation of unrepresentative, incomplete, or inaccurate evidence that might mislead finders of fact" (APA, 2013, p. 9). A major task in focusing the lenses of FN assessment (testing, interview, observations, records) to produce a view of a case that is high in resolution and fidelity is to ensure each lens is not clouded or otherwise distorted. Thus, distorting bias must be accounted for and minimized. With respect to neuropsychological testing, the art and science of bias detection has undergone a momentous paradigm shift with the advent and refinement of symptom and performance validity techniques (Boone, 2007; Larrabee, 2007). However, bias detection in the interview, record review, and observations draws heavily on subfields of psychological sciences such as social psychology (Snyder, 1981) and the cognitive science of heuristics (Kahneman, 2011). For example, the work of Tversky and Kahneman (1981) has shed light on the mental shortcuts (heuristics) that people tend to use in seeking to understand complex and ambiguous information. This research illustrates that the potential for bias is endemic and to a certain extent inherent to human cognition, judgment, and decision making.

In the quest for truth in the forensic realm, the neuropsychologist must have knowledge and tools to reckon with potential sources of both overt and covert bias in both examinee and examiner. The neuropsychologist's toolbox includes psychometric instruments for detecting and characterizing performance and response bias in testing behavior. For detecting and characterizing bias in the records, interview, and observable behavior, not only a solid foundation in the functional neuroanatomical

http://dx.doi.org/10.1037/0000032-003
APA Handbook of Forensic Neuropsychology, S. S. Bush (Editor-in-Chief)

underpinning of cognition but also the social and heuristic factors influencing human cognition place the neuropsychologist in a unique position to assist the trier of fact. Although an exhaustive review of bias research is beyond the scope of this chapter, some sources of bias that tend to be uniquely affiliated with each of these lenses are reviewed later, but first some overarching and cross-cutting themes related to bias are considered.

Examinee Bias

Before considering a particular examinee's idiographic biases, a sensitivity to and consideration of a range of nomothetic human diversity issues should inform the neuropsychologist's approach. The Specialty Guidelines for Forensic Psychology (APA, 2013) stress the importance of understanding

> how factors associated with age, gender, gender identity, race, ethnicity, culture, national origin, religion, sexual orientation, disability, language, socioeconomic status, or other relevant individual and cultural differences may affect and be related to the basis for people's contact and involvement in the legal system. (p. 10)

Thus, training in diversity issues can help the neuropsychologist avoid pitfalls of group attribution error, self-referencing, and stereotyping biases.

In its most overt form, examinee bias may take the form of malingering, an intentional form of information distortion in which symptoms are falsely produced or grossly exaggerated for external incentives (American Psychiatric Association, 2013). However, a wide range of examinee biases are by degrees much less overt or consciously intentional yet may become evident on careful review of records, interview, and observations. For instance, the so-called "good old days bias," also deemed the *rosy retrospection bias* (Shermer, 2011), refers to the tendency for individuals to inflate premorbid abilities, health, and well-being, such as has been identified among individuals with persisting complaints after mild traumatic brain injury (Hilsabeck, Gouvier, & Bolter, 1998; Iverson, Lange, Brooks, & Ashton Rennison, 2010). Such biased recall may in turn heighten distress and breed misattribution of subsequent commonplace problems as manifestations of permanent dysfunction, leading to expectation as etiology (Mittenberg, DiGiulio, Perrin, & Bass, 1992).

The potency of expectancy effects, such as are typically observed in placebo phenomena in clinical research, is important as a potential biasing influence for patients participating in the rituals, symbols, and interactions of medical or psychological treatment. In reviewing social psychological factors that can influence examinee perception and reporting of persisting symptoms after mild traumatic brain injury, Iverson and Lange (2012) identified biasing factors that may arise from involvement in treatment. Among these factors are iatrogenesis (e.g., an increased sense of ill health and adverse effect caused by medical professionals labeling and treating the patient as having brain damage) and, relatedly, nocebo effect (i.e., causation of sickness by the expectations of sickness engendered by medical treatment).

Neuropsychologist, Know Thyself

Research on bias from cognitive and social psychology has informed the ways in which not only examinee bias but also examiner bias can affect the collection, analysis, and interpretation of data from the interview, observations, and record review. The recent work of Murrie, Boccaccini, Guarnera, and Rufino (2013), for instance, indicated a tendency for a partisan allegiance bias, in which forensic psychologists in an experiment tended to form opinions that clearly inclined toward the adversarial side that hired them. In practice, such bias may, for a very small subset of examiners, one hopes, be overtly driven by unethical financial self-interest, yet there are likewise a host of covert, unintentional cognitive biases that have been identified as potential factors influencing evaluators' judgments (Neal & Grisso, 2014; Richards, Geiger, & Tussey, 2015).

> We see what we look for, and we look for what we know. (Goethe, as cited in Roberts, 1999, p. 209)

Shermer (2011) deemed confirmation bias the "mother of all cognitive biases" (p. 259), because a great many other biases arise from or are related to confirmation bias, the tendency to seek and find confirmatory evidence in support of an already existing hypothesis or latent belief while ignoring or reinterpreting disconfirming evidence. Although a complete review of evaluator biases is beyond the scope of this chapter, following is a sampling (based on Shermer, 2011) of some key biases that can influence appraisals and judgments in the FN interview, observations, and review of records:

Hindsight bias. Hindsight bias is the tendency to reconstruct the past to fit present knowledge, much as a Monday morning quarterback devastated by his team's defeat is overconfident about how he would have called a critical play in the game differently. For example, in a medical malpractice case, an evaluator with hindsight knowledge of an outcome may be similarly overconfident that a patient with a cognitive impairment who mistakenly took a near-fatal overdose should not have been prescribed a cardiac medication that was to be self-administered.

Framing effects. A framing effect is the tendency to draw different conclusions on the basis of how data are presented. For example, the framing effect of a neuropsychological evaluation context may lead an evaluator to observe the examinee wearing sunglasses into the office as a sign of symptom amplification, which it can often be (Bengtzen, Woodward, Lynn, Newman, & Biousse. 2008). However, some individuals may have genuine ophthalmologic photosensitivity, which should also be considered.

Anchoring effect. The anchoring effect is the tendency to rely too heavily on a past reference or on one piece of information when making decisions. A subtype is the halo effect, a tendency to generalize one positive trait of an individual to all other traits of that person. For example, when told by an attorney on an initial phone consultation that her client is a pillar of the community, a volunteer advocate for children's rights who was injured in an auto accident caused by a trucker with a past felony, the evaluator may subsequently tend to ignore or explain away symptoms that are neurologically implausible.

Availability heuristic. The availability heuristic is the tendency to assign probabilities of potential outcomes on the basis of examples (particularly those that are vivid, unusual, or emotionally charged) that are immediately available. For instance, awash in media attention to chronic traumatic encephalopathy and putative associations between sports concussions and risk for suicidality, a neuropsychologist paints a dire prognosis for an otherwise healthy young litigant with a single uncomplicated sports concussion.

Inattentional blindness. Inattentional blindness bias is the tendency to miss something obvious or general while attending to something special and specific, classically illustrated in the Simons and Chabris (1999) experiment in which participants viewing a video often failed to see a "gorilla" walking through a room of people playing a ball game. For example, during an interview a neuropsychologist directing questions to a litigant's spouse about her husband's accident fails to see the husband become diaphoretic, tremulous, and tachypneic during her hackneyed recounting.

Approaches to Debiasing

> The first principle is that you must not fool yourself—and you are the easiest person to fool. (Feynman, 1974, p. 12)

The bias blind spot is a meta-bias consisting of the tendency to recognize the operation of cognitive biases in other people but to be blind to their influence on one's own judgments and beliefs. Shermer (2011) argued that science is the "ultimate bias-detection machine" (p. 278), with mechanisms for systematic skepticism, peer review, questioning of evidence, valuing replication and converging data, and seeking out disconfirming evidence. Understanding the cognitive bias literature should lead the forensic neuropsychologist to appreciate the difficulty of apprehending one's own bias and compel a process of debiasing that models in microcosm the scientific process of review, systematic doubt, questioning, and replication with multiple sources of convergent data. In a seminal article that has stimulated a great deal of discussion (e.g., Greiffenstein & Kaufmann, 2012; Lees-Haley, 1999), Sweet and Moulthrop (1999) introduced a set of self-examination questions aimed at stimulating the neuropsychologist to objectively consider possible bias. A sampling of these questions includes the following:

Do I receive referrals from only plaintiff attorneys or only defense attorneys?
Do I almost always reach conclusions favorable to the side that has retained me?
Have I moved away from being an expert witness to being an advocate?
Do I routinely apply the same decision rules for establishing brain dysfunction no matter which side retains me?
Have I been reaching the same diagnostic conclusion at a much higher base rate than my colleagues or at a higher rate than described in the literature?

Such questions are important guideposts for sober self-examination, though as some authors have pointed out there can be important caveats, such as scenarios in which simple ratio tallies of defense to plaintiff referrals may not necessarily denote lack of objectivity (Greiffenstein & Kaufmann, 2012). Nonetheless, self-review as well as candid feedback from professional peers can be used to reflect on one's overall practice patterns, also inviting a wider set of meta-cognitive questions that can help increase awareness of bias in particular forensic cases through continual self-examination. Exhibit 3.1 provides a sample of such questions.

Exhibit 3.1
Sample Meta-Cognitive Questions to Increase Awareness of Bias in Particular Cases

- Do my political or religious commitments or beliefs influence my view of this examinee's behavior?
- How does my level of comfort with corporate or adversarial processes influence my understanding of the litigant's claims?
- Because of my background and formation, do I tend to be a champion for the misunderstood, thus biasing my view of a litigant as a victimized pawn to larger self-interested forces?
- Am I a champion for those trying to root out unjust claims for undeserved benefits and rewards?
- Have I or a loved one experienced an event (e.g., injury, misdiagnosis, unfounded lawsuit) that colors my view or even sense of allegiance in the case at hand?
- To what extent does my sense of teamwork and duty feel allied with the trier of fact versus the hiring attorney?
- Can I afford a loss of pride that may come with changing my mind when I encounter information that disconfirms my initial hypotheses?

Because a forensic neuropsychologist is by training first a psychologist, such self-reflection should be deeply inculcated by one's formative clinical training, including supervision that helps uncover one's so-called countertransferences that are elicited by various types of patients. Viewing videotapes of one's interviews in a supervisory or peer consultation context can be particularly helpful in obtaining insight about one's own reactions, both deep seated (e.g., "Do I smile when uncomfortable with emotional content?") and more mundane (e.g., "Are my lapses in eye contact and facial expression while writing notes reflecting more sternness than intended?"). Such training followed by ample clinical experience should increase awareness of one's particular response to examinee behaviors such as hostility, neediness, victimization, and entitlement. Expertise with the methods of cognitive–behavioral therapeutic work can offer yet another means of skilled uncovering of one's underlying beliefs, assumptions, and automatic thoughts that are elicited when evaluating others' behavior as revealed in the interview, observations, and record review. Thus, a solid grounding in clinical competency is an important foundation for appreciating one's own biases.

A variety of other debiasing strategies have been developed. A critical awareness of the initial hypotheses one forms is particularly important to guard against confirmation bias. There is an understandable tendency, which is in part inherent to human cognition, to begin forming hypotheses even early in one's involvement in a case when initial summary information is presented. It is important to hold open a wide range of potential hypotheses from the earliest explorations of the case, perhaps at no time more important than in the opening salvo when the case is being presented by a potential referral source, when primacy, framing, and anchoring effect biases are particularly potent.

Once a hypothesis is born in the mind of the neuropsychologist, human cognition tends toward confirmatory rather than disconfirmatory evidence. A deliberate and ongoing search for disconfirmatory evidence for initial hypotheses is recommended to counter the tendency for confirmatory searching (Wedding & Faust, 1989). Establishing at least two competing hypotheses can be helpful in reducing confirmation bias (Richards et al., 2015). A related mental habit that has been recommended, dating to Sir Francis Bacon, is to consider the opposite during the ongoing process of judgment formation (Lord, Lepper, & Preston, 1984), keeping alive a wide range of interpretations during data gathering by considering possibilities at odds with working hypotheses. In Kahneman's (2011) heuristic framework, much of the work of avoiding bias involves active engagement of the effortful and "slow" thinking system to critically review the more automatic, rapid, and intuitive impressions of the "fast" thinking system. Considering how rapidly the fast thinking system begins forming appraisals and judgments about complex and ambiguous information, it is important to enable a process of slow thinking from the very earliest considerations of case information. For the majority of FN evaluations, the first encounters between evaluator and case data come with the presentation of the case by the referring party and review of records.

RECORD REVIEW

Use of collateral records, what Huss (2009) referred to as "archival and third-party information" (p. 34), is recognized as integral to the FN evaluation, because the Specialty Guidelines for Forensic Psychology (APA, 2013) specify the need to "strive to access information or records from collateral sources" (p. 14) and "avoid relying solely on one source of data" (p. 15).

In approaching a record review, the work of the forensic neuropsychologist can be likened to that of an archeologist or a historian. As with the work of an archeologist conducting a field excavation, delving into case records is not a headlong plowing or random digging process but instead a careful and systematic process of uncovering, preserving, and documenting. Careful tagging of the temporal strata and attention to the context from which data or relics are extracted is critical, with a premium placed on avoiding contamination or comingling of material from disparate strata. As with the work of a historian attempting to learn the truth about a historical event, it is important to distinguish primary from secondary sources, to seek information that is independently attested to by multiple observers, and to prioritize information from neutral sources closest to the event in space and time, before the elaborations of oral transmission and faulty recall distort primary witness accounts. Similarly, for the FN record review, it is important to carefully track the source and context of information.

Practical Issues in Record Reviews

Perhaps more than any other factor, the volume of records reviewed often contributes to the length of many FN reports, owing to the importance of documenting the information on which the expert has relied in forming opinions. Whereas in clinical reports an interleaving and integration of history gathered from both patient interview and records may be desirable to cogently unfold a succinct clinical story, in forensic reports it is recommended that sources of information be clearly distinguished. Thus, entirely separate, delineated report sections (e.g., History According to Interview of Mr. X, Behavioral Observations, Collateral Record Review) help to clearly preserve the provenance of information. Mention of key information should clearly cite the source document and, for material already indexed for the court, page references can be given (e.g., Bates number, deposition transcript page). Verbatim quotations from primary source material should be used judiciously for descriptions in which the precise phrasing is critical. As a rule of thumb, anything weighted as significant to one's expert opinion should be summarized.

To the extent that Chekhov's playwriting axiom is true, that the dramatist should not place a gun on the fireplace mantel in an early act that does not fire by the last act, so too in FN evaluation reports the obverse holds, that expert opinions in the last act should be buttressed by prior clear presentation of the data from which opinions are formed. The report should include all key data, both pro and con, for the eventual carefully weighed opinion. The neuropsychologist should seek to ensure that all critical records have been obtained whenever possible. In addition to medical and psychological records, other records such as pharmacy and work records, as well as deposition transcripts, may be important for one's opinion. If the review of provided records reveals the existence of other additional pertinent records, these should be requested through the referring attorney. Preinjury records (e.g., school records, standardized test scores, military records) are likely to be useful in establishing patterns and levels of premorbid functioning. It is recommended that early in one's involvement in a case, a list of key types of records be discussed with the referring party. If review of provided records reveals references to additional important records, these should be requested as well. If critical records cannot be obtained, such missing data points should be cited in one's report.

The project of taking a banker's box or more of voluminous case records and rendering an objective, scientifically informed analysis distilled into the FN report is no small feat. Records may arrive as a welter of poorly organized information that comes in multiple shipments. One should be wary of early bias formation from primacy effects if only material advantageous to the referring party is sent first. To guard against confirmation bias that may flow from initial hypotheses, one's review should start with primary source material from independent reporters close in time and space to the key events, such as first responder and emergency department records (Richards et al., 2015). It is helpful to organize the review chronologically to assist in developing a clear timeline that reveals both how symptoms and clinical themes unfold over time and the temporal relationship among key events. In the case of an injury or other discrete event (e.g., alleged traumatic brain injury, anoxia during surgery, work-related carbon monoxide exposure), the report can segregate sections reviewing preinjury, acute injury, and postinjury records. Indeed, for some cases it may be helpful to include a timeline figure in the forensic report that demarcates landmark events in the examinee's history, to provide an overview map of chronologies that may be quite complex.

Reviewing Multidisciplinary Records

The forensic neuropsychologist should have broad-based training and experience interacting with multiple professional disciplines. In keeping with the Houston Conference Guidelines on training in clinical neuropsychology (Hannay et al., 1998), the neuropsychologist training model includes extensive education in a range of knowledge domains including psychopathology, psychometrics, functional neuroanatomy, neurological and non-neurological medical conditions, neuroimaging, and psychopharmacology. Broad clinical experience in multidisciplinary medical settings is particularly valuable to understanding the medical chart, including its nomenclature, abbreviations, multidisciplinary practice patterns, and record formats. Lerner and Schoenberg (2011) and Harel, Steinberg, and Snyder (2006) have offered primers for neuropsychological analysis of the medical chart.

In weighing the value of information in the medical records, it is important to both consider the source and separate the wheat from the chaff (Murray, 1965). In considering the source, for example, much has been written about the potential for advocacy bias in treaters who have developed a close, empathic therapeutic alliance with their patient (Richards et al., 2015). Additionally, caution may be necessary in accepting assessments or diagnoses at face value. For example, though a set of records may include nursing notes with checkmarks for "alert and oriented times three" after a head injury, it is not always clear whether orientation has actually been tested in a systematic fashion as opposed to a global, untested impression. Diagnoses of conditions such as posttraumatic stress disorder based on intuitive impression rather than criteria-based review can set up a propagating bias that has been labeled *diagnosis momentum*, in which a provisional or working diagnosis gets passed from clinician to clinician in such a way that it becomes virtually reified without careful evidence-based reconsideration (Richards et al., 2015).

As is discussed later, risk for this propagating error is increased with the advent of electronic health records (EHRs), wherein not only is sharing of information among providers made easier, but entries into the records gain a "stickiness" as they are automatically imported from older to newer notes. This can lead to errors of both over- and underpathologizing because not only unsupported clinical diagnoses but also unfounded references to malingering can stick with a claimant and subsequently bias later evaluators' impressions (Richards et al., 2015). The forensic neuropsychologist must therefore engage in critical, evidence-based scrutiny of labels and diagnoses.

Separating the wheat from the chaff in cross-disciplinary records can likewise pose challenges. For example, extended treatment with physical, occupational, or speech-language therapies may generate a large volume of session records, many of which may reflect a boilerplate format approach that leads to repetitious chaff from which it may be difficult to separate out the wheat. Summary documents (e.g., initial assessment, discharge report) are typically most helpful in providing an overall view through other professionals' eyes, but one should not take for granted that such documents fully capture all of the relevant data. Preinjury records in particular may be laden with chaff, in the sense that there are often many health care contacts for minor, commonplace medical issues (e.g., coughs, sore throats, ingrown toenails). The neuropsychologist should become efficient in review of such material, making sure one is not, to use another metaphor, missing nuggets of gold in the ore.

Special Considerations

Case synopsis. The referring party may include with the primary source records a prepared summary of the records. Such secondary material should be regarded cautiously. Although it may serve as an initial bird's-eye glimpse of the case that allows a broad view of the lay of the land, the neuropsychologist should be alert for biases that might stem from a case advocacy viewpoint or unintentional layperson's (e.g., paralegal's) limitations in selecting and abstracting complex medical and psychological information.

Electronic health records. As the era of handwritten records is entering its twilight, it is with good riddance that the decipherer's task of trying to make the illegible legible can be relinquished. In its current state, however, the EHR brings its own unique pitfalls. For all the potential and real benefits of the EHR, template-assisted electronic records increase the risk for propagation of error because elements such as the past medical history and social history may be automatically autopopulated into subsequent encounter notes, including those of multiple treatment providers. Thus, an early inadvertent error can be passed along and take on the *prima facie* appearance of a multiply attested fact. In addition, lengthy problem or diagnosis lists may be ported into serial progress notes in a way that makes the original provenance of the items unclear. Moreover, as already noted, disorders and diagnoses that may have been ruled out can become ensconced on such problem lists as though they have been verified through a thorough review of clinical evidence rather than suggested tentatively (i.e., diagnosis momentum).

Surveillance video and social media. Neuropsychologists are increasingly being provided with video footage of litigants. Review of surveillance video warrants careful consideration for potential bias. The selected footage is often edited or otherwise taken out of context, though sometimes the footage may stand alone and speak for itself (e.g., an examinee with claimed left hemiparesis shown pitching southpaw in a softball game). More often, for establishing a naturalistic view of cognitive functioning, the video may be of more limited or ambiguous value. Such footage is unlikely to be a completely random sampling of behavior because it is typically filmed in a public space. Often wordless footage depicting quotidian activities in public (pumping gas, going in and out of retail businesses) may be of greater value to medical experts analyzing movement patterns and physical functioning claimed to have been affected as opposed to neurocognitive functioning. Also, such surveillance video is most likely obtained by the defense in civil cases, though plaintiff's counsel may produce material such as pre- and postinjury home videos that should be considered with the same cautions mentioned above. Finally, the neuropsychologist may be provided social media content (e.g., Facebook entries, blog postings, website comment section posts) that likewise must be carefully regarded as to their actual authorship, context, and date. The neuropsychologist should consult with the referring party before actively seeking out information on his or her own from social media venues.

INTERVIEW

From a practical standpoint, the interview and behavioral observations are inextricably intertwined, but for expository purposes they are discussed as separate facets of the FN assessment process. Whereas the record review largely represents an encounter with others' written accounts of a litigant, the interview is a live and dynamic human encounter, and as such a forum in which interviewer and examinee biases and their potential interactions must be carefully considered. The examinee's verbal responses represent self-report par excellence, which comes with strengths and limitations.

> Everything is held together by stories.
> (Lopez, as cited in Evans, 1994, p. 62)

An obvious strength of interview self-reporting is the opportunity to gather unmediated firsthand accounts of history and subjective accounts of current functioning. In the same way that the tangle of records must be organized and brought to order in the record review, the interview is an opportunity to glean a narrative structure from the examinee's viewpoint. It is an opportunity to delve deeper than disjointed lists of symptom complaints and decontextualized endorsements on psychological measures and to uncover the examinee's subjective story. The examinee's account should reveal the narrative threads that hold together his or her understanding of what has happened, how symptoms have evolved and interact, causal attributions, which symptoms are weighted as most troubling or perceived as disabling, and how it all fits into overall biographical context. Along the way, the neuropsychologist should seek to ascertain the examinee's beliefs, assumptions, and reasoning patterns that underlie his or her narrative recounting. To the extent possible in a potentially adversarial context, rapport should be established generally through an approach that is straightforward, genuine, and professional. A broad and deep base of clinical experience can help prepare the neuropsychologist for the challenges of gaining adequate rapport with various presentations (e.g., the rambling, the laconic, the hostile, the ingratiating, the overwhelmed, the psychotic, the suicidal, the disingenuous).

Important time points in the symptom history should be explored (e.g., did a subjective increase in symptoms correspond to starting medication with cognitive side effects? Was the claimant informed by a physician at a certain point that there was permanent brain damage?). What are the examinee's sources of information (e.g., websites, online support groups, family members, books) about the condition and, in turn, what might be the framing effects of these sources? As in a good clinical interview, a tremendous amount of focus should be placed on listening, with intense curiosity as a guide to help thoroughly explore relevant areas of the examinee's experience. The neuropsychologist should strive to use language and terminology that the examinee will understand. For example, terms such as *cognitive, visuospatial,* and *executive* are largely terms of art with no guarantee that the examinee will understand them as intended.

In gathering such self-report data, the neuropsychologist is well poised to take into account the research findings that bear on self-report and its limitations. For example, given the reconstructive nature of human memory, the reliability and accuracy of first-hand reports of events can be influenced by a variety of factors that affect acquisition and retrieval of information (Loftus, 2003). Expectations, stress, memory decay over time, and influence of questioning by multiple prior evaluators are examples of factors that can influence event reporting (Castelli et al., 2006). Research, including meta-analytic studies, has indicated that the correlation between eyewitness reporters' confidence in their recall and accuracy of recall can vary widely (Castelli et al., 2006). For example, the accuracy of self-reported medical history has been found to vary significantly (Ruchinskas, 2012). In a comparison of self-reported and actual academic performance as revealed by academic records, Greiffenstein, Baker, and Johnson-Greene (2002) found that a group of litigants inflated past academic performance more than nonlitigating controls. Considering more subjective symptom reports, even among nonlitigating individuals, the literature examining correlations between self-reported and actual neuropsychological symptoms has indicated that self-report tends to be more closely associated with mood than with neuropsychological test performance (e.g., Otto et al., 1994). Thus, part of the task of the FN interview is to accurately capture the claimant's story while considering potential biasing factors.

Although the FN interview should be more like a conversation than an interrogation in its tone and flow, unlike a completely open-ended casual conversation, the FN interview is guided by the mission of reconnoitering and mapping the terrain of an individual's experience related to the current issue and how it fits into the larger context of his or her life story. In this sense, it should thus be a pointed conversation. However, the sharp contrast that is sometimes categorically drawn between unstructured and structured interview approaches tends to represent a false dichotomy. As in the aftermath of the increasingly bygone "test battery wars," which starkly counter posed fixed batteries versus process approaches to neuropsychological testing, the skilled neuropsychologist can pursue an interview approach that in the end may be regarded as a semistructured process, generally moving from less to more structure as it unfolds to reduce confirmation bias and responder bias. As such, a general pattern of starting with more open-ended queries before proceeding to more specific questions will help guard against the possibility of not looking for evidence that may disconfirm initial working hypotheses. This approach is reminiscent of Harry Stack Sullivan's (1970) notion of a reconnaissance phase of the interview occurring before detailed inquiry ensues. If more structured interview protocols are used (e.g., broad-band instruments such as the Structured Clinical Interview for DSM–5 [First, Williams, Karg, & Spitzer, 2015] or narrow-band instruments such as posttraumatic stress disorder–specific structured interviews), it is recommended that they be used after the less structured portions of the interview.

The elements covered in the FN interview largely overlap with and follow the contours of a good clinical history interview (see Exhibit 3.2), and gathering this breadth of information for every case

Exhibit 3.2
General Elements of the Forensic Neuropsychological Interview

Preamble: informed consent

- Clarification of reasons for evaluation and explanation of evaluation process
- Limits of confidentiality, lack of doctor–patient treatment relationship
- Importance of candor and full effort

Account of event or situation in litigation
History of symptoms

- Onset and course of cognitive, psychological, and physical symptoms
- Intensity, duration, frequency, variability, examples
- Preexisting versus new, relationship to events in litigation
- Exacerbating and ameliorating factors

Daily functioning

- Current living situation and typical daily routines
- Basic and higher level activities of daily living
- Functioning in work, school, and social settings
- Sources of stress
- Roles of pain, sleep issues, medications, and caffeine
- Physical exercise

Medical history

- Chronic and acute conditions across life history
- Neurological symptoms and history of traumatic head injuries
- Treatment history: outpatient, inpatient, and surgeries
- Alcohol and drug, nicotine, and other substance use history
- Prescription medication history, nonprescription remedies or supplements
- Family medical history

Psychiatric history

- Current and lifelong history of psychological problems
- Treatment history: psychotherapy, medications, and hospitalizations
- History of suicidal or homicidal thoughts and behaviors
- Family psychiatric history

(*continues*)

Exhibit 3.2 (*Continued*)
General Elements of the Forensic Neuropsychological Interview

Social history

- Perinatal and early development
- Family constellation and relationship history
- Trauma and abuse history
- Educational history: academic performance and attainment, strengths and weaknesses
- Employment and military history, performance reviews, and vocational goals
- Legal history: criminal charges and prior litigation
- Hobbies, activities, and interests and levels of social support

is another guard against confirmation bias. Even if the natural flow of a particular interview results in these interview elements not being addressed in lockstep sequence, a comprehensive outline of areas to be covered serves as a mental template to guide the overall inquiry, rather than it being exclusively guided by questions selected to investigate preformed hypotheses. However, it is not uncommon for the FN interview to be lengthier than a standard clinical history interview because several areas typically require more detailed coverage.

First, before the interview proper can commence, and certainly before neuropsychological testing can take place, a set of "preamble" consent and procedural issues must be addressed to ensure that the examinee is fully informed about the examination. Sweet, Ecklund-Johnson, and Malina (2008) described a number of points that must be discussed, including clarification of the reasons for the evaluation; identification of the referral source and any relationship with the examiner; a description of the types of information that will be gathered; a description of the limits of confidentiality, differentiating it from a normal doctor–patient relationship; clarification that no treatment will be offered; the intent of the examiner to maintain objectivity without acting as an interested party regarding the outcome of the claim; and the importance of the examinee's being honest and putting forth full effort in testing. Although these key points generally do need to be covered, rather than being presented as a barrage of opening legalistic provisos and disclaimers that may undercut rapport before it has formed, these points can be conveyed in a dialogue that may start with the question "What is your understanding of why you are here and the nature of this evaluation?" In most settings, the examinee's oral and written consent to proceed should be obtained after this dialogue. A sample written consent form can be found in Bush (2005).

A second element of the FN interview that tends to require more detailed inquiry compared with a standard clinical interview is establishing the examinee's precise understanding of how symptoms are or are not related to the event or issues in litigation. A third area of detailed inquiry is the examinee's daily activities and functional status. As such, it may be helpful to ask the examinee to walk through a typical day, probing for fine-grained rather than broad and impressionistic accounts of what the examinee can and cannot do and why. The interview is thus an opportunity to carefully dissect and understand symptom reports, anchoring them in concrete, operationalized terms that can later be cross-checked against neuropsychological test results, behavioral observations, and depictions in the case records. A fourth area that warrants particularly detailed inquiry is the examinee's current status on the day of the evaluation with respect to any factors (e.g., fatigue, pain, medication effects) that could reasonably influence the data being gathered via interview, observations, and testing.

Finally, to ensure that key interview information is being understood and gathered accurately, checks can be built into the interview. For instance, at appropriate junctures during the interview, and particularly when the interview is wrapping up, it can be helpful for the neuropsychologist to recap and summarize an account of the key facts and narrative that have been gleaned from the interview ("Let me see if I have understood what you have been telling me, you said. . . ."). This process provides an opportunity for the examinee to (a) correct or edit any misunderstandings, (b) further elucidate key points, and (c) provide endorsement that the neuropsychologist is not distorting the interviewee's account. As a further guard against confirmation bias, as the interview is wrapping up the examinee can be asked whether any areas of importance were missed and whether he or she would like to add anything else.

Collateral Informants in the Interview

It is fairly common to include collateral informants (e.g., spouse or other family member) in clinical evaluations during the interview phase. It is likewise often desirable in FN evaluations to have input from a collateral person during the interview to gather additional perspective on the case. However, several cautionary issues must be considered. The neuropsychologist should be mindful that a potential collateral informant may not only be an emotionally interested party at heightened risk for biased reporting but may also actually be a literal party to the lawsuit (e.g., a spouse with coplaintiff loss of consortium claims); therefore, the legal ramifications of including such a person in the interview should be discussed with the referring attorney.

The presence of a third party in the evaluation process has been more extensively studied for its potential effects on testing rather than on the interview process. If a collateral informant is included in the interview, the joint interview calls on many of the neuropsychologist's skills honed by clinical experience in order to orchestrate the session so as to facilitate optimal yield of relevant information while preserving the sources of information. In general, for a given line of inquiry, it is advisable to have the examinee answer first and then to have the collateral person follow up with any additional information that may qualify or expand on the examinee's perspective. It is important to document the exact nature and duration of the examinee's relationship with the collateral informant and to carefully record who offers what information.

Use of History Questionnaires

Whether a commercially available background or intake form or a history questionnaire uniquely developed by the neuropsychologist, use of a history questionnaire as a complement to the clinical interview has potential risks and benefits. Arguably the chief risk of having the examinee fill out such a form before the interview is the potential for "leading the witness" by posing areas of inquiry in advance that could allow a shaping of responses or perhaps inadvertent response bias because the examinee may endorse a wide range of symptoms that may not have been spontaneously recalled. The benefits of using a history questionnaire before an interview include increases in thoroughness and efficiency. As a guard against confirmation bias, particularly if using an omnibus questionnaire that is also customarily used for diverse clinical cases, the questionnaire can allow for a broad canvassing of symptoms and history that can elicit important information that has not already been captured by the records or included in case formulations by other evaluators or attorneys. A history questionnaire can also expedite the interview process by (a) efficiently gathering granular details of past medical and social history that might take up inordinate amounts of precious interview time, (b) priming the examinee for what topics need to be covered, and (c) providing a forum in which the examinee can put responses in his or her own words in a way that eliminates the risk of being inadvertently misquoted.

BEHAVIORAL OBSERVATIONS

> It is alertness to such things as intonation, rate of speech, difficulty with enunciation, rather than preoccupation with the words spoken, that the psychiatric interview becomes meaningful. (Sullivan, 1954, p. 39)

It has long been appreciated that there are modes and levels of communication that go beyond an examinee's declarative verbal statements. The neuropsychologist's observation of nonverbal behaviors represents a parallel process that occurs during the interview simultaneously with the gathering of the examinee's declarative verbal accounts. A robust foundation of clinical experience with varied patient populations can help calibrate one's perceptions and appraisals of what behaviors are clinically relevant. Careful observation of behaviors is a crucial component of the interview, but observations throughout testing as well as before and after the evaluation are likewise germane. An examinee's behavior during telephone interactions in setting up the appointment, during initial interactions with office staff, during breaks in the evaluation, and while leaving the appointment may be potentially significant. As such, it is important that testing technicians, and other staff who may interact with examinees, have training in reliably communicating these observations to the neuropsychologist. As in clinical sessions with patients, the opening salvo and concluding moments of an FN session may be particularly rich in terms of behavioral observations.

Although observations alone may not be of final probative value, they can seed hypotheses that can be tested in the multimethod matrix of other data sources. For instance, the behavior of an examinee who enters the office suite and immediately seeks to control the room temperature and lighting, computer screen saver, and whether staff wear perfume or cologne might be interpreted in different ways (e.g., bids to assert power and control in the interview, demonstrative exaggeration of symptoms, an expression of vulnerability, or a proactive approach to ensuring optimal conditions for maximal effort toward testing). The behaviors can be noted and hypotheses tested via convergence with other evidence. Because observations are typically made as part of a dynamic interactive social exchange, the potential for biasing factors must again be considered. Just as the FN evaluation process provides a set of opportunities to explore the signal value of examinee behaviors, neuropsychologists should cultivate, via self-examination and feedback from others, an awareness of the potential signal value of their own behavioral presentation, office environment, and procedures. Do you sit behind a desk during the interview? Do you wear a lab coat, business suit, or casual clothing? Do others generally regard you as aloof and pensive or as warm and gregarious? Do you address the examinee by first name or more formally? Although there are not necessarily right or wrong answers to such questions, by training the neuropsychologist should be aware that social psychology has identified a variety of factors (e.g., authority, likability, attractiveness) that can influence what behaviors are elicited in an interaction (Taylor, Peplau, & Sears, 2005).

Systematic observations of behavior, affect, and cognition traditionally fall under the rubric of the mental status examination. A range of typical dimensions of behavior is observed and assayed, including appearance, motor activity, level of consciousness, orientation, language, memory, mood and affect, perceptual processes, thought content and process, insight, interpersonal manner, and level of rapport with the examiner. The mental status examination is a mainstay component of mental health (Groth-Marnat, 2009; Trzepacz & Baker, 1993) and neurological mental status and behavioral assessment (Strub & Black, 2000) and is not explicated in fine detail in this chapter. Vanderploeg (2000) offered an excellent outline (pp. 16–17) for behavioral observations and mental status evaluation specific to the neuropsychological evaluation. In the FN evaluation, most of these dimensions of behavior are assessed qualitatively during the interview or are subsumed under the more comprehensive, quantitative findings from formal neuropsychological testing. Description of the examinee's behavior should be detailed and highly specific, painting a picture that Greiffenstein and Kaufmann (2012) called "a vivid description of the examinee as part of a mental status examination that leaps from the page in three dimensions" (p. 48).

Observations should be described in objective, specific, behavioral terms rather than in conclusory statements. For example, the conclusory "mind-reading" observation that "the examinee felt upset at times" might be rendered as "When his current employment situation was discussed, Mr. X became tearful, his voice volume and rate of speech increased, and his accounts became laced with expletives for the only time in the lengthy interview." As another example, the observation that "the examinee was defensive" might better be rendered as "Mr. X's affect became particularly constricted, eye contact became sporadic, and he twice changed the topic to his current symptom complaints when his prior injury lawsuit was discussed." Behavioral observations should thus be rendered in terms of what can reliably be perceived.

CONCLUSION

To return to the analogy of a compound microscope, the resolving power of the FN evaluation process is enhanced when all of the methodological lenses are focused together on a case in an integrated fashion. Invoking a different metaphor for the interdependence of these methods, Lally (2003) described the FN evaluation as resting on a stable and valid foundation because of its "legs" of tests, interview and observations, and collateral record sources. In this sense, neuropsychological test results stand most stably when placed within an integrated and interdependent system of multiple data sources. Integration of these data sources involves a consistency analysis. Larrabee (2012) suggested a four-component consistency analysis for neuropsychological decision making that considers the following:

1. Are the test data consistent within and between neuropsychological domains?
2. Is the neuropsychological profile consistent with the suspected etiologic condition?
3. Are the neuropsychological data consistent with the documented severity of injury?
4. Are the neuropsychological data consistent with the examinee's behavioral presentation?

Thus, the FN evaluation offers a unique opportunity to assist the trier of fact in a forensic case by providing test data, the meaning of which is illuminated by the contextual matrix of information derived from the record review, clinical interview, and behavioral observations.

References

American Psychiatric Association. (2013). *Diagnostic and statistical manual of mental disorders* (5th ed.). Washington, DC: Author.

American Psychological Association. (2013). Specialty guidelines for forensic psychology. *American Psychologist*, *68*, 7–19. http://dx.doi.org/10.1037/a0029889

Bengtzen, R., Woodward, M., Lynn, M. J., Newman, N. J., & Biousse, V. (2008). The "sunglasses sign" predicts nonorganic visual loss in neuro-ophthalmologic practice. *Neurology*, *70*, 218–221. http://dx.doi.org/10.1212/01.wnl.0000287090.98555.56

Boone, K. B. (Ed.). (2007). *Assessment of feigned cognitive impairment: A neuropsychological perspective*. New York, NY: Guilford Press.

Bush, S. S., & NAN Policy and Planning Committee. (2005). Independent and court-ordered forensic neuropsychological examinations: Official statement of the National Academy of Neuropsychology. *Archives of Clinical Neuropsychology*, *20*, 997–1007. http://dx.doi.org/10.1016/j.acn.2005.06.003

Castelli, P., Goodman, G. S., Edelstein, R. S., Mitchell, E. B., Paz Alonso, P. M., Lyons, K. E., & Newton, J. W. (2006). Evaluating eyewitness testimony in adults and children. In I. B. Weiner & A. K. Hess (Eds.), *The handbook of forensic psychology* (3rd ed., pp. 243–304). Hoboken, NJ: Wiley.

Evans, A. (1994). Leaning into the light: An interview with Barry Lopez. *Poets and Writers*, 22, 62–79.

Feynman, R. P. (1974). Cargo cult science (1974 CalTech Commencement Address). *Engineering and Science*, *37*(7), 10–13.

First, M. B., Williams, J. B. W., Karg, R. S., & Spitzer, R. L. (2015). *Structured Clinical Interview for DSM–5: Clinician version*. Arlington, VA: American Psychiatric Publishing.

Greiffenstein, M. F., Baker, W. J., & Johnson-Greene, D. (2002). Actual versus self-reported scholastic achievement of litigating postconcussion and severe closed head injury claimants. *Psychological Assessment*, *14*, 202–208. http://dx.doi.org/10.1037/1040-3590.14.2.202

Greiffenstein, M. F., & Kaufmann, P. M. (2012). Neuropsychology and law: Principles of productive attorney-neuropsychologist relations. In G. J. Larrabee (Ed.), *Forensic neuropsychology: A scientific approach* (pp. 23–69). New York, NY: Oxford University Press.

Groth-Marnat, G. (2009). *Handbook of psychological assessment*. Hoboken, NJ: Wiley.

Hannay, H. J., Bieliasuskas, L. A., Crosson, B., Hammeke, T., deS. Hamsher, K., & Koffler, S. (Eds.). (1998). Proceedings of the Houston conference on specialty education and training in clinical neuropsychology [Special issue]. *Archives of Clinical Neuropsychology*, *13*(2). http://dx.doi.org/10.1093/arclin/13.2.160

Harel, B. T., Steinberg, B. A., & Snyder, P. J. (2006). The medical chart: Efficient information gathering strategies and proper chart noting. In P. J. Snyder, P. D. Nussbaum, & D. L. Robins (Eds.), *Clinical neuropsychology: A pocket handbook for assessment* (pp. 9–16). http://dx.doi.org/10.1037/11299-001

Hilsabeck, R. C., Gouvier, W. D., & Bolter, J. F. (1998). Reconstructive memory bias in recall of neuropsychological symptomatology. *Journal of Clinical and Experimental Neuropsychology*, *20*, 328–338. http://dx.doi.org/10.1076/jcen.20.3.328.813

Huss, M. T. (2009). *Forensic psychology: Research, clinical practice, and application*. Malden, MA: Wiley-Blackwell.

Iverson, G. L., & Lange, R. T. (2012). Post-concussion syndrome. In M. R. Schoenberg & J. G. Scott (Eds.), *The little black book of neuropsychology: A syndrome-based approach* (pp. 745–764). New York, NY: Springer.

Iverson, G. L., Lange, R. T., Brooks, B. L., & Ashton Rennison, V. L. (2010). "Good old days" bias following mild traumatic brain injury. *Clinical Neuropsychologist*, *24*, 17–37. http://dx.doi.org/10.1080/13854040903190797

Kahneman, D. (2011). *Thinking, fast and slow*. New York, NY: Farrar, Straus & Giroux.

Lally, S. J. (2003). What tests are acceptable for use in forensic evaluations? A survey of experts. *Professional Psychology: Research and Practice*, *34*, 491–498. http://dx.doi.org/10.1037/0735-7028.34.5.491

Larrabee, G. J. (2007). Assessment of malingering. In G. J. Larrabee (Ed.), *Forensic neuropsychology: A scientific approach* (pp. 116–159). New York, NY: Oxford University Press.

Larrabee, G. J. (2012). A scientific approach to forensic neuropsychology. In G. J. Larrabee (Ed.), *Forensic neuropsychology: A scientific approach* (pp. 3–22). New York, NY: Oxford University Press.

Lees-Haley, P. R. (1999). Commentary on Sweet and Moulthrop's debiasing procedures. *Journal of Forensic Neuropsychology*, *1*, 43–47. http://dx.doi.org/10.1300/J151v01n03_04

Lerner, A. J., & Schoenberg, M. R. (2011). Deconstructing the medical chart. In M. R. Schoenberg & J. G. Scott (Eds.), *The little black book of neuropsychology: A syndrome-based approach* (pp. 39–58). http://dx.doi.org/10.1007/978-0-387-76978-3_2

Loftus, E. (2003). Our changeable memories: Legal and practical implications. *Nature Reviews Neuroscience*, *4*, 231–234. http://dx.doi.org/10.1038/nrn1054

Lord, C. G., Lepper, M. R., & Preston, E. (1984). Considering the opposite: A corrective strategy for social judgment. *Journal of Personality and Social Psychology*, *47*, 1231–1243. http://dx.doi.org/10.1037/0022-3514.47.6.1231

Mittenberg, W., DiGiulio, D. V., Perrin, S., & Bass, A. E. (1992). Symptoms following mild head injury: Expectation as aetiology. *Journal of Neurology, Neurosurgery, and Psychiatry*, *55*, 200–204. http://dx.doi.org/10.1136/jnnp.55.3.200

Murray, H. A. (1965). Uses of the Thematic Apperception Test. In B. I. Murstein (Ed.), *Handbook of projective techniques* (pp. 425–432). New York, NY: Basic Books.

Murrie, D. C., Boccaccini, M. T., Guarnera, L. A., & Rufino, K. A. (2013). Are forensic experts biased by the side that retained them? *Psychological Science*, *24*, 1889–1897. http://dx.doi.org/10.1177/0956797613481812

Neal, T. M. S., & Grisso, T. (2014). The cognitive underpinnings of bias in forensic mental health evaluations. *Psychology, Public Policy, and Law*, *20*, 200–211. http://dx.doi.org/10.1037/a0035824

Otto, M. W., Bruder, G. E., Fava, M., Delis, D. C., Quitkin, F. M., & Rosenbaum, J. F. (1994). Norms for depressed patients for the California Verbal Learning Test: Associations with depression severity and self-report of cognitive difficulties. *Archives of Clinical Neuropsychology*, *9*, 81–88. http://dx.doi.org/10.1093/arclin/9.1.81

Richards, P. M., Geiger, J. A., & Tussey, C. M. (2015). The dirty dozen: 12 sources of bias in forensic neuropsychology with ways to mitigate. *Psychological Injury and Law*, *8*, 265–280. http://dx.doi.org/10.1007/s12207-015-9235-1

Roberts, R. J. (1999). Epilepsy spectrum disorder in the context of mild traumatic brain injury. In N. R. Varney & R. J. Roberts (Eds.), *Evaluation and treatment of mild traumatic brain injury* (pp. 209–248). Mahwah, NJ: Erlbaum.

Ruchinskas, R. (2012). Other aspects of data collection in capacity evaluations. In G. J. Demakis (Ed.), *Civil capacities in clinical neuropsychology: Research findings and practical applications* (pp. 228–241). New York, NY: Oxford University Press.

Shermer, M. (2011). *The believing brain*. New York, NY: Times Books.

Simons, D. J., & Chabris, C. F. (1999). Gorillas in our midst: Sustained inattentional blindness for dynamic events. *Perception*, *28*, 1059–1074. http://dx.doi.org/10.1068/p281059

Snyder, M. (1981). Seek and ye shall find: Testing hypotheses about other people. In E. T. Higgins (Ed.), *Social cognition: The Ontario symposium on personality and social psychology* (pp. 277–303). Hillsdale, NJ: Erlbaum.

Strub, R. L., & Black, F. W. (2000). *The mental status examination in neurology* (4th ed.). Philadelphia, PA: Davis.

Sullivan, H. S. (1954). Basic concepts in the psychiatric interview. *Pastoral Psychology*, *5*, 39–46. http://dx.doi.org/10.1007/BF01564923

Sullivan, H. S. (1970). *The psychiatric interview*. New York, NY: Norton.

Sweet, J. J., Ecklund-Johnson, E., & Malina, A. (2008). Forensic neuropsychology: An overview of issues and directions. In J. E. Morgan & J. H. Ricker (Eds.), *Textbook of clinical neuropsychology* (pp. 869–890). New York, NY: Taylor & Francis.

Sweet, J. J., & Moulthrop, M. A. (1999). Self-examination questions as a means of identifying bias in adversarial assessments. *Journal of Forensic Neuropsychology*, *1*, 73–88. http://dx.doi.org/10.1300/J151v01n01_06

Taylor, S. E., Peplau, L. A., & Sears, D. O. (2005). *Social psychology* (12th ed.). New York, NY: Pearson.

Trzepacz, P. T., & Baker, R. W. (1993). *The psychiatric mental status examination.* Oxford, England: Oxford University Press.

Tversky, A., & Kahneman, D. (1981). The framing of decisions and the psychology of choice. *Science, 211*, 453–458. http://dx.doi.org/10.1126/science.7455683

Vanderploeg, R. D. (2000). Interview and testing: The data collection phase of neuropsychological evaluations. In R. D. Vanderploeg (Ed.), *Clinician's guide to neuropsychological assessment* (2nd ed., pp. 3–38). New York, NY: Routledge.

Wedding, D., & Faust, D. (1989). Clinical judgment and decision making in neuropsychology. *Archives of Clinical Neuropsychology, 4*, 233–265. http://dx.doi.org/10.1016/0887-6177(89)90016-4

CHAPTER 4

SELECTION OF TESTS AND BATTERIES FOR FORENSIC NEUROPSYCHOLOGICAL EVALUATIONS

Glenn J. Larrabee

The forensic neuropsychological evaluation relies on direct examination of the person involved in a legal action, such as personal injury litigation, criminal proceedings, or civil competency, as well as integration of the direct examination results with the relevant preexisting records of the case. The direct portion of the examination involves a comprehensive clinical interview, as well as detailed neuropsychological testing. The results of direct examination must also be integrated and interpreted within the context of the relevant records of the case such as medical records in a personal injury action, arrest records in a criminal action, or relevant financial records in an older person undergoing examination for competency. The most direct connection of the neuropsychological evaluation results to a specific legal issue is in a personal injury case, wherein the examination results are directly relevant to establishing the damages in the case. Less direct connections exist in establishing criminal responsibility and competencies and civil capacities. In these matters, the neuropsychological findings may play a secondary or even a minor role because the person being evaluated may simultaneously show both neuropsychological impairment and preserved competency to stand trial or preserved testamentary capacity. In other words, the neuropsychological test findings do not always fully address the legal issue that is in contention. The special demands of assessing criminal competencies and responsibility are discussed in Chapter 15 of this handbook; assessment of civil capacities is discussed in Chapter 14 of this handbook.

GENERAL DEFINITIONS OF NEUROPSYCHOLOGY AND TESTING APPROACHES

The American Academy of Clinical Neuropsychology practice guidelines for neuropsychological assessment and consultation define clinical neuropsychology as "an applied science that examines the impact of both normal and abnormal brain functioning on a broad range of cognitive, emotional, and behavioral functions" (Board of Directors, 2007, p. 211). In this document, the academy further specifies the areas of testing as including intellectual and achievement testing, language skills, simple and complex attention, learning and memory, visuospatial skills, executive functions, problem solving and reasoning, sensorimotor skills, social–emotional functioning, and adaptive behavior.

Bauer (2000) has described three general approaches to neuropsychological testing: (a) the fixed battery approach, in which every person examined is administered the same battery of tests, exemplified by the Halstead–Reitan Neuropsychological Test Battery (HRB); (b) the flexible core battery, in which every examinee is administered a core set of tests with flexible, adjustable testing to further evaluate problems identified by the core tests; and (c) the completely flexible approach wherein test selection is dependent on the specific clinical presentation of the particular examinee. Surveys have shown that the most widely used approach over the past several years has been the flexible battery approach (Rabin, Barr, & Burton, 2005; Sweet,

http://dx.doi.org/10.1037/0000032-004
APA Handbook of Forensic Neuropsychology, S. S. Bush (Editor-in-Chief)

Meyer, Nelson, & Moberg, 2011). Sweet et al. (2011) described a decreasing percentage of use of the fixed battery approach from 1989 through 2010, with the 2010 results showing that 78% used a flexible battery, 18% used a completely flexible approach, and 5% used a fixed battery such as the HRB. The most commonly used tests in the Rabin et al. (2005) survey were the revised or third editions of the Wechsler Adult Intelligence Scale (WAIS), revised or third editions of the Wechsler Memory Scale (WMS), Trail Making Test, and the first or second editions of the California Verbal Learning Test.

Sweet et al. (2011) provided additional information about how neuropsychological testing is conducted. Approximately 50% of neuropsychologists use nonpsychologist test technicians and psychometricians for test administration. The average length of a forensic neuropsychological evaluation is 12.7 hours (*SD* = 6.4), with a median of 12.0 and an interquartile range from 9 hours at the 25th percentile to 16 hours at the 75th percentile.

NEUROPSYCHOLOGICAL TESTS: ADMISSIBILITY AS EVIDENCE

Admissibility is discussed in depth in Chapter 18 of this handbook. The older Frye standard (*Frye vs. United States,* 1923) required a procedure to be generally accepted by the profession in order to be admissible. At the battery level, this older standard would support the use of the flexible battery approach but not fixed battery approaches such as the HRB or the Luria–Nebraska Neuropsychological Battery as per the recent survey of Sweet et al. (2011). The *Frye* standard is also potentially insensitive to the scientific merit of more recently developed test batteries such as the Neuropsychological Assessment Battery (Stern & White, 2003) because more novel procedures have not yet reached the level of general acceptance. The Daubert standard (*Daubert vs. Merrell Dow Pharmaceuticals, Inc.,* 1993) assigned a gatekeeper role to judges and is more open to the admissibility of newer, novel procedures, because it advises consideration of (a) whether the procedure can be, and has been, submitted to empirical test; (b) whether the procedure has been submitted to peer review; (c) whether the error rate of the procedure is known and how large the error rate is; and (d) whether the procedure is generally accepted in the scientific community (Sweet, Ecklund-Johnson, & Malina, 2008). As noted by Sweet et al. (2008), the trial judge is not required to consider the presence of all of these factors in every case, and it is up to the judge to determine how the factors are to be applied in a specific case.

Despite the survey evidence for test usage showing the flexible battery approach to be predominant, the completely flexible approach faced a Daubert challenge in *Baxter vs. Temple* (2008). The testimony of the neuropsychologist who relied on the flexible Boston process approach was excluded at the trial court level in this case. The American Academy of Clinical Neuropsychology filed an amicus brief supporting the use of flexible approaches such as the Boston process approach, drawing a parallel between this type of practice and the practice of clinical neurology, and the New Hampshire Supreme Court reversed the trial court's decision that excluded the Boston process approach from testimony (see Kaufmann, 2012, for more detailed discussion of this case, as well as Chapter 18, this handbook).

SELECTING THE APPROPRIATE TEST BATTERY

References for the tests to be discussed in the remainder of the chapter can be found in Lezak, Howieson, Bigler, and Tranel (2012). Despite the widespread use of a core flexible battery (Sweet et al., 2011), there is no common core battery used by all. As shown in the survey by Rabin et al. (2005), certain procedures are commonly administered in adult neuropsychological evaluations, for example, the Wechsler Scales of Intelligence, the Minnesota Multiphasic Personality Inventory, and the Trail Making Test. In a recent review article (Larrabee, 2014c), I presented a framework for developing the core of a flexible battery, based on considerations of construct validity and various aspects of criterion validity. In addition, I advised including tests that contained embedded or derived measures of performance validity (PVTs; Larrabee, 2012a).

Last, I recommended using criterion groups of moderate and severe traumatic brain injury (TBI), mild cognitive impairment (MCI), early Alzheimer's disease (AD), and unilateral stroke. Candidate tests were to be evaluated on the following basis:

1. Are they a measure of a core ability?
2. Are they sensitive to presence of impairment?
3. Are they sensitive to the severity of impairment?
4. Are they affected by unilateral stroke, aphasia, or neglect?
5. Do they predict functional capacities?
6. Do they contain an embedded or derived measure of performance validity?

Review of several factor analyses in Larrabee (2014c) established the following six core domains of ability: (a) Verbal Symbolic Ability, (b) Visuoperceptual–Visuospatial Judgment and Problem Solving, (c) Sensorimotor Skills, (d) Attention–Working Memory, (e) Processing Speed, and (f) Learning and Memory. The last domain, learning and memory, can be subdivided into verbal and visual learning and memory. There was no Executive Function factor, because tests that are typically thought of as measures of executive function loaded on other factors; for example, Controlled Oral Word Association loaded on Verbal Symbolic Ability and Processing Speed (Larrabee, 2000; Larrabee & Curtiss, 1992), Trail Making B loaded on Processing Speed, and the Category Test and Wisconsin Card Sorting Test loaded on the Visuoperceptual–Visuospatial Judgment and Problem Solving factor (Leonberger, Nicks, Larrabee, & Goldfader, 1992). In my review (Larrabee, 2014c), the domains of ability most sensitive to presence of impairment due to any cause were memory and processing speed. Domains most sensitive to both severity of impairment and impairment in functional capacities were Verbal Symbolic Abilities, Visuoperceptual–Visuospatial Judgment and Problem Solving, Attention–Working Memory, and Processing Speed.

In Larrabee (2014c), I suggested a hypothetical battery, including 27 tests covering the six domains of ability, with 10 of these tests also providing information on performance validity (Larrabee, 2012a). The first domain is Verbal Symbolic Ability, including Controlled Oral Word Association, Animal Naming, WAIS—Fourth Edition (WAIS–IV) Information and Similarities, and Wide Range Achievement Text 4 (WRAT4) Reading and Arithmetic. Controlled Oral Word Association was shown to be sensitive to the capacity to make informed medical decisions (Marson, Ingram, Cody, & Harrell, 1995). Semantic fluency (i.e., the ability to name things in a semantic category, e.g., animal naming) predicted conversion from amnestic MCI to AD (Griffith et al., 2006). By contrast, the Hopkins Verbal Learning Test, sensitive to discriminating those subjects with MCI, was insensitive to conversion of MCI to AD (Griffith et al., 2006). WAIS Information was correlated with the severity of AD (Larrabee, Largen, & Levin, 1985), in contrast to Verbal Selective Reminding, which was the most sensitive discriminator of AD from normal subjects but was unrelated to severity of AD. Historically, the Similarities subtest has been the WAIS verbal subtest most sensitive to acquired brain dysfunction (Loring & Larrabee, 2006), although more recently the Information and Vocabulary subtests have shown larger Cohen's *d*s in contrasts of the WAIS–IV performance of normal subjects and persons with MCI, AD, or TBI (Wechsler, 2008). WRAT4 Reading provides a quick screen for presence of sufficient reading skills for completion of the Minnesota Multiphasic Personality Inventory–2 Restructured Form (MMPI–2–RF) and has also been used in prediction of premorbid intellectual abilities (Lezak et al., 2012). WRAT4 Arithmetic has been found to predict financial capacity in older adults (Sherod et al., 2009).

The second domain, Visuoperceptual–Visuospatial Judgment and Problem Solving, includes Benton Visual Form Discrimination, WAIS–IV Block Design and Visual Puzzles, and the Wisconsin Card Sorting Test. Visual Form Discrimination is sensitive to both unilateral and bilateral brain disease, with the highest percentage of impaired performances in bilateral-diffuse and right posterior brain injuries (Benton, Sivan, de S. Hamsher, Varney, & Spreen, 1994). I also reported utility for Visual Form Discrimination as a measure of embedded or derived performance validity (Larrabee, 2003a). On the WAIS–IV, both Block Design and Visual Puzzles produce effect sizes in the range of 0.70 to 1.07 in discriminating subjects with TBI and AD from normative subjects (Wechsler, 2008). The Wisconsin Card Sorting Test is a measure of problem solving under conditions of limited feedback that is sensitive to a variety of lesion locations, including frontal, diffuse, and nonfrontal areas of the brain (Heaton, Miller, Taylor, & Grant, 2004). Select scores from the Wisconsin Card Sorting Test inform performance validity, including Failure to Maintain Set and Other responses (Greve, Bianchini, Mathias, Houston, & Crouch, 2002; Larrabee, 2003a; Suhr & Boyer, 1999).

The third domain, Sensorimotor Skills, includes the Finger Tapping Test, Grip Strength, and the Grooved Pegboard Test. As a group, these three tests can be sensitive to unilateral brain damage, given the known contralateral representation of the motor system (i.e., the left side of the brain controls the right side of the body; Lezak et al., 2012). In one investigation, the Grooved Pegboard Test was more sensitive for discriminating neurological from pseudoneurological cases than any other neuropsychological test, including the seven primary scores from the HRB; word fluency; Trail Making Test; WAIS–Revised Digit Symbol, Block Design, and Similarities; and WMS Delayed Logical Memory and Visual Reproduction (Larrabee, Millis, & Meyers, 2008). Atypically low performance on the Finger Tapping Test yields information on performance validity (Arnold et al., 2005; Axelrod, Meyers, & Davis, 2014; Larrabee, 2003a).

The fourth domain is Attention–Working Memory, including WAIS–IV Digit Span, Arithmetic, and Letter Number Sequencing, plus WMS—Fourth Edition (WMS–IV) Symbol Span. The first three tests define verbal working memory, with Symbol Span defining visual working memory. Earnst et al. (2001) found predictive relationships between performance on Digit Span, Arithmetic, and Letter Number Sequencing and various aspects of financial competency. Both the Digit Span scaled score and a derivative score known as Reliable Digit Span (Greiffenstein, Baker, & Gola, 1994) yield information on performance validity (Jasinski, Berry, Shandera, & Clark, 2011).

The fifth domain is Processing Speed, defined by the Trail Making Test, WAIS–IV Symbol Search and Coding, and the Stroop Color and Word Test. Measures of processing speed, in combination with memory tests, are among the most sensitive measures for detecting the presence of impairment. For example, J. B. Miller, Fichtenberg, and Millis (2010) found that discrimination of brain-damaged and pseudoneurological controls was as accurate, based on the California Verbal Learning Test—Second Edition and WAIS—Third Edition (WAIS–III) Processing Speed Index in tandem (area under the receiver operating characteristic curve of .90), as discrimination based on these measures as well as on *T* scores for language (average *T* score for the Boston Naming Test and Animal Naming), WAIS–III Perceptual Organization Index, and WAIS–III Working Memory Index (area under receiver operating characteristic curve of .89). In addition to being sensitive to presence of AD, the WAIS Digit Symbol subtest was sensitive to the severity of AD, as contrasted with the Verbal Selective Reminding test, which was sensitive only to the presence of AD, not to the severity of this disorder (Larrabee, Largen, & Levin, 1985). Trail Making Test Parts A and B, along with the Grooved Pegboard Test and Symbol Digit Modalities Test (a processing speed task), predicted return to work and activities of daily living, contrasted with the California Verbal Learning Test and Rey Auditory Verbal Learning (AVLT) test, which did not predict functional status (Williams, Rapport, Hanks, Millis, & Greene, 2013). Driving ability has been correlated with performance on the Trail Making Test Part B for both severe TBI (Novack et al., 2006) and questionable dementia (Whelihan, DiCarlo, & Paul, 2005).

As noted, Learning and Memory can be divided into two subcategories, Verbal Learning and Memory and Visual Learning and Memory. Verbal Learning and Memory is represented by tests of text recall, such as WMS–IV Logical Memory, by measures of paired associate learning such as WMS–IV Verbal Paired Associates, and by measures of verbal supraspan learning such as the AVLT. Both Logical Memory and Verbal Paired associates contain PVTs based on poor performance on delayed recognition (*Advanced Clinical Solutions*, 2009). Both show varying degrees of sensitivity to the presence of a variety of clinical disorders (Wechsler, 2009). The AVLT words recalled on Trial 5 provided the single best score in a comprehensive battery of tests, including the HRB, for discriminating between a group of patients with brain dysfunction and normal controls (Powell, Cripe, & Dodrill, 1991). Loring et al. (2008) found a Cohen's *d* of 0.47 associated with AVLT differences between patients with left and right temporal lobe epilepsy, which was significantly larger than the value of 0.29 for discriminating between patients with left and right temporal lobe epilepsy on the basis of their California Verbal Learning Test scores. Several PVTs exist for the AVLT. Barrash, Suhr, and Manzel (2004) expanded the AVLT to include an additional 60-minute delayed recall and recognition trial, and they have derived an Exaggeration Index based on seven atypical patterns of performance on the test. Boone, Lu, and Wen (2005) derived a PVT for the AVLT based on poor recognition scores, with particular emphasis on the first third of the word list. Davis, Millis, and Axelrod (2012) used logistic regression to derive a PVT formula based on total words learned and delayed recognition.

Visual Learning and Memory can be assessed by WMS–IV Visual Reproduction, the Continuous Visual Memory Test, and the Hannay, Levin, and Grossman (1979) Continuous Recognition Memory Test. Visual Reproduction has a long history in neuropsychological assessment dating to the original WMS. The immediate reproduction trials appear to be more closely associated with performance on WAIS Block Design and Object Assembly subtests (spatial–constructional tasks) than with memory; however, a delayed reproduction administration mitigates this effect, showing a stronger association with memory than with spatial ability (Larrabee & Curtiss, 1995; Larrabee, Kane, et al., 1985). The WMS–IV Visual Reproduction delayed recognition trial yielded PVT information (*Advanced Clinical Solutions,* 2009). The Continuous Visual Memory Test assesses recognition memory for detection of recurring abstract geometric forms, whereas the Continuous Recognition Memory Test measures detection of recurring meaningful pictures such as insects and seashells. Both have been found to be sensitive to acquired brain impairment (Hannay et al., 1979; Trahan & Larrabee, 1988), and both contain embedded PVTs (Larrabee, 2009).

In summary, this hypothetical battery contains 27 measures requiring a total administration time of about 4.5 hours. As reviewed, the tests making up this hypothetical battery include measures that are sensitive to the presence and severity of disorder and predict important activities of daily living. Moreover, the battery includes 10 embedded or derived PVTs. In a forensic (as well as a general clinical) setting, the MMPI–2–RF should also be administered, adding another hour to this core battery, but also adding five symptom validity scales: Infrequent Responses (F-r), Infrequent Psychopathology Responses (Fp-r), Infrequent Somatic Responses (Fs), Symptom Validity (FBS-r), and Response Bias (RBS).

The above hypothetical battery, as is characteristic of most core flexible battery approaches, is not based on co-normed tests. This is not a significant issue in interpretation, because L. S. Miller and Rohling (2001) developed a statistical procedure derived from meta-analytic methods for combining and analyzing individually normed tests. In a recent article, Rohling et al. (2015) demonstrated essentially identical Overall Test Battery Mean *T* scores for a common set of tests scored using (a) the Mitrushina, Boone, Razani, and D'Elia (2005) meta-analytically derived norms; (b) Heaton et al. (2004) co-normed data; and (c) Meyers Neuropsychological Battery norms (which are a composite of aggregated individually normed tests, with regression smoothing for age, gender, and education based on a large patient database; Meyers, 1995). Statistical bases for data interpretation are further discussed in Chapter 1 of this handbook.

PRACTICE OF FORENSIC NEUROPSYCHOLOGICAL EVALUATION

In my opinion, the practice of forensic neuropsychological evaluation represents the highest level of practice, demanding the greatest expertise. One must be up to date on the neuropsychological literature, as well as on the literature in related fields (e.g., neurology, neuroradiology), and have a current understanding of rules governing admissibility of evidence in one's jurisdiction. Each forensic neuropsychological evaluation is akin to preparing an individual case study for publication.

Although the hypothetical core battery that I have proposed requires approximately 5.5 hours (neuropsychological testing plus MMPI–2–RF) as reviewed in the preceding section, the amount of testing that is conducted is significantly greater in actual forensic practice. It is important to perform redundant assessments in each of the core ability areas to evaluate for consistency of performance. Moreover, I have not provided a detailed discussion of the importance of assessing both performance validity and symptom validity (Larrabee, 2012a), because this material is covered in Chapter 5 of this handbook. As with assessment of the core ability areas, testing of performance and symptom validity should be redundant, with multiple PVTs that evaluate validity of perception, motor function, working memory, processing speed, verbal and visual memory abilities, and problem-solving skills.

As noted earlier in this chapter, the Sweet et al. (2011) survey showed an average time per forensic evaluation of 12.7 hours, with a median of 12.0 hours and an interquartile range (middle 50%) of 9 to 16 hours. At the time of preparation of this chapter, the forensic evaluations that I conduct typically take, on average, 12 hours scheduled over a 2-day period. This examination includes open-ended and structured interviews and a brief follow-up interview, with the bulk of the time involving direct examination. In addition to conducting the clinical interview, structured interview, and follow-up interview, I also do about 1.5 hours of testing myself, including two PVTs, Controlled Oral Word Association, Animal Naming, Trail Making Test, WMS–IV Logical Memory, and the AVLT. My bachelor's-level assistant does the remainder of the testing and scores all of the tests. In addition to the 10 embedded–derived PVTs described earlier, the litigant–claimant is administered six freestanding PVTs that mimic measures of verbal and visual memory and processing speed. I also administer a complete WAIS–IV including Letter Number Sequencing and add the Purdue Pegboard to my sensorimotor testing to provide a fine motor test in addition to the Grooved Pegboard Test. Because most of my forensic work involves claimants in automobile accidents, pain is a frequent complaint, so I also administer three self-report pain scales: the McGill Pain Questionnaire (Melzack, 1975), Pain Disability Index (Tait, Chibnall, & Krause, 1990), and Modified Somatic Perception Questionnaire (Main, 1983). In Larrabee (2003b), I reported symptom validity test cutoffs for all three of these scales. Bianchini et al. (2014) replicated these findings for the Pain Disability Index and Modified Somatic Perception Questionnaire, refined the cutoffs, and demonstrated that item endorsement on the Pain Disability Index and Modified Somatic Perception Questionnaire is not related to the degree of actual physical pathology in pain patients with or without malingered pain-related disability.

The first step in analyzing the neuropsychological test data is to determine whether the data are valid, which is accomplished by considering scores on freestanding and embedded or derived PVTs as well as self-report on measures containing symptom validity tests (Larrabee, 2012a). Berthelson, Mulchan, Odland, Miller, and Mittenberg (2013) raised concerns about the risk of obtaining an elevated false alarm rate associated with the use of multiple PVTs, based on Monte Carlo simulation, using a criterion of failure of two or more PVTs. Davis and Millis (2014) and I (Larrabee, 2014a) demonstrated that this was not a significant concern, based on analysis of actual clinical data; that is, the Monte Carlo simulations overestimate false positive error, likely because PVTs form skewed distributions, with performance commonly at the ceiling, whereas the accuracy of Monte Carlo simulation is dependent on normally distributed scores. In Larrabee (2014a, 2014b), I offered interpretive guidelines for minimizing the chances of false positive error, including determining the characteristics of patients identified as false positives in past research; if examinees do not show these characteristics (e.g., severe TBI, AD, or schizophrenia), they are likely not a false positive, as a result of the failure of two or more PVTs. For examinees showing histories associated with false positive scores, one can adjust cutoffs on the individual PVT for the clinical condition with elevated false positive rates or adjust the number of PVT failures required to reach a conclusion of invalid performance. Other strategies include demonstration of preserved performance on standard tests of memory and processing speed for people failing PVTs that mimic memory and processing speed. This particular pattern shows that examinees possessed sufficient native ability to pass the PVTs that they actually failed.

Typically, if an examinee fails two or more PVTs (or one at worse-than-chance performance) and there are no viable explanations for PVT failure, there is a high probability of invalid test performance. In this circumstance, the remainder of the test results may be an inaccurate measure of actual ability. Normal-range performances, in and of themselves, may actually be underestimates of the actual level of ability. The information obtained is helpful only in ruling out acquired impairment, for example, when the examinee shows normal memory and processing speed. Poor performances, by contrast, are more likely due to intentional underperformance rather than acquired impairment, particularly when there are no risk factors for false positive errors on PVTs. More detailed discussion of PVTs and symptom validity tests appears in Chapter 5 of this handbook.

I have proposed an interpretive method for analyzing neuropsychological data in forensic settings based on analysis of four types of consistency (Larrabee, 1990, 2012b). The first type of consistency requires determination of whether the data are consistent within and between neuropsychological domains. For an example of within-domain consistency, if an examinee fails an easier task of motor function such as Finger Tapping, the examinee should not perform at average or above-average levels on the Grooved Pegboard (Greiffenstein, Baker, & Gola, 1996). Between domains, if an examinee demonstrates very poor attention or working memory, he or she should not show evidence of average or above-average memory performance (Mittenberg, Azrin, Millsaps, & Heilbronner, 1993). The second type of consistency concerns whether the neuropsychological profile is consistent with the suspected etiology of brain dysfunction. For example, gross impairment in verbal symbolic functioning and visuoperceptual–visuospatial judgment and problem solving, accompanied by normal verbal and visual learning and memory, is inconsistent with the presence of dementia. The third type of consistency is whether the neuropsychological data are consistent with the medically documented severity of injury. That is, a claimant–litigant with a history consistent with mild TBI should not perform at the level of impairment characteristic of severe TBI (Rohling, Meyers, & Millis, 2003). Finally, the neuropsychological data should be consistent with the examinee's behavioral presentation. A claimant with impaired memory performance should not be able to present a detailed history of providers seen and treatments received or a detailed account of the automobile accident that was experienced.

CONCLUSION

The current chapter presents a hypothetical core ability–focused neuropsychological battery that covers the six core domains of neuropsychological abilities and is sensitive to the presence of disorder, severity of disorder, and the consequences of impairment of capacities for effective daily living. The proposed core battery also incorporates embedded–derived measures of performance and symptom validity, so that the clinician can directly evaluate the validity of the examinee's clinical presentation, which is always the first step in evaluating the data collected from direct neuropsychological examination. A general model is described for interpretation of test results that relies on the consistency or inconsistency of test results.

References

Advanced clinical solutions for use with WAIS–IV and WMS–IV. (2009). San Antonio, TX: Pearson Education.

Arnold, G., Boone, K. B., Lu, P., Dean, A., Wen, J., Nitch, S., & McPherson, S. (2005). Sensitivity and specificity of finger tapping test scores for the detection of suspect effort. *Clinical Neuropsychologist, 19,* 105–120. http://dx.doi.org/10.1080/13854040490888567

Axelrod, B. N., Meyers, J. E., & Davis, J. J. (2014). Finger Tapping Test performance as a measure of performance validity. *Clinical Neuropsychologist, 28,* 876–888. http://dx.doi.org/10.1080/13854046.2014.907583

Barrash, J., Suhr, J., & Manzel, K. (2004). Detecting poor effort and malingering with an expanded version of the Auditory Verbal Learning Test (AVLTX): Validation with clinical samples. *Journal of Clinical and Experimental Neuropsychology*, *26*, 125–140. http://dx.doi.org/10.1076/jcen.26.1.125.23928

Bauer, R. M. (2000). The flexible battery approach to neuropsychological assessment. In R. D. Vanderploeg (Ed.), *Clinician's guide to neuropsychological assessment* (2nd ed., pp. 419–448). Mahwah, NJ: Erlbaum.

Baxter v. Temple, 949 A. 2d 167 (NH, 2008).

Benton, A. L., Sivan, A. B., & deS. Hamsher, K., Varney, N. R., & Spreen, O. (1994). *Contributions to neuropsychological assessment: A clinical manual* (2nd ed.). New York, NY: Oxford University Press.

Berthelson, L., Mulchan, S. S., Odland, A. P., Miller, L. J., & Mittenberg, W. (2013). False positive diagnosis of malingering due to the use of multiple effort tests. *Brain Injury*, *27*, 909–916. http://dx.doi.org/10.3109/02699052.2013.793400

Bianchini, K. J., Aguerrevere, L. E., Guise, B. J., Ord, J. S., Etherton, J. L., Meyers, J. E., . . . Bui, J. (2014). Accuracy of the Modified Somatic Perception Questionnaire and Pain Disability Index in the detection of malingered pain-related disability in chronic pain. *Clinical Neuropsychologist*, *28*, 1376–1394. http://dx.doi.org/10.1080/13854046.2014.9861990

Board of Directors. (2007). American Academy of Clinical Neuropsychology (AACN) practice guidelines for neuropsychological assessment and consultation. *Clinical Neuropsychologist*, *21*, 209–231. http://dx.doi.org/10.1080/13825580601025932

Boone, K. B., Lu, P., & Wen, J. (2005). Comparison of various RAVLT scores in the detection of noncredible memory performance. *Archives of Clinical Neuropsychology*, *20*, 301–319. http://dx.doi.org/10.1016/j.acn.2004.08.001

Daubert v. Merrell Dow Pharmaceuticals, Inc., 509 U.S. 579 (1993).

Davis, J. J., & Millis, S. R. (2014). Examination of performance validity test failure in relation to number of tests administered. *Clinical Neuropsychologist*, *28*, 199–214. http://dx.doi.org/10.1080/13854046.2014.884633

Davis, J. J., Millis, S. R., & Axelrod, B. N. (2012). Derivation of an embedded Rey Auditory Verbal Learning Test performance validity indicator. *Clinical Neuropsychologist*, *26*, 1397–1408. http://dx.doi.org/10.1080/13854046.2012.728627

Earnst, K. S., Wadley, V. G., Aldridge, T. M., Steenwyk, A. B., Hammond, A. E., Harrell, L. E., & Marson, D. C. (2001). Loss of financial capacity in Alzheimer's disease: The role of working memory. *Aging, Neuropsychology, and Cognition*, *8*, 109–119. http://dx.doi.org/10.1076/anec.8.2.109.839

Frye v. United States, 293 F. 1013 (D.C. Cir. 1923).

Greiffenstein, M. F., Baker, W. J., & Gola, T. (1994). Validation of malingered amnesia measures with a large clinical sample. *Psychological Assessment*, *6*, 218–224.

Greiffenstein, M. F., Baker, W. J., & Gola, T. (1996). Motor dysfunction profiles in traumatic brain injury and postconcussion syndrome. *Journal of the International Neuropsychological Society*, *2*, 477–485. http://dx.doi.org/10.1017/S1355617700001648

Greve, K. W., Bianchini, K. J., Mathias, C. W., Houston, R. J., & Crouch, J. A. (2002). Detecting malingered performance with the Wisconsin Card Sorting Test: A preliminary investigation in traumatic brain injury. *Clinical Neuropsychologist*, *16*, 179–191. http://dx.doi.org/10.1076/clin.16.2.179.13241

Griffith, H. R., Netson, K. L., Harrell, L. E., Zamrini, E. Y., Brockington, J. C., & Marson, D. C. (2006). Amnestic mild cognitive impairment: Diagnostic outcomes and clinical prediction over a two-year time period. *Journal of the International Neuropsychological Society*, *12*, 166–175. http://dx.doi.org/10.1017/S1355617706060267

Hannay, H. J., Levin, H. S., & Grossman, R. G. (1979). Impaired recognition memory after head injury. *Cortex*, *15*, 269–283. http://dx.doi.org/10.1016/S0010-9452(79)80031-3

Heaton, R. K., Miller, S. W., Taylor, M. J., & Grant, I. (2004). *Revised comprehensive norms for an expanded Halstead–Reitan Battery: Demographically adjusted norms for African American and Caucasian adults (HRB)*. Lutz, FL: Psychological Assessment Resources.

Jasinski, L. J., Berry, D. T. R., Shandera, A. L., & Clark, J. A. (2011). Use of the Wechsler Adult Intelligence Scale Digit Span subtest for malingering detection: A meta-analytic review. *Journal of Clinical and Experimental Neuropsychology*, *33*, 300–314. http://dx.doi.org/10.1080/13803395.2010.516743

Kaufmann, P. M. (2012). Admissibility of expert opinions based on neuropsychological evidence. In G. J. Larrabee (Ed.), *Forensic neuropsychology: A scientific approach* (2nd ed., pp. 70–100). New York, NY: Oxford University Press.

Larrabee, G. J. (1990). Cautions in the use of neuropsychological evaluation in legal settings. *Neuropsychology*, *4*, 239–247. http://dx.doi.org/10.1037/0894-4105.4.4.239

Larrabee, G. J. (2000). Association between IQ and neuropsychological test performance: Commentary on Tremont, Hoffman, Scott, and Adams (1998). *Clinical Neuropsychologist*, *14*, 139–145. http://dx.doi.org/10.1076/1385-4046(200002)14:1;1-8;FT139

Larrabee, G. J. (2003a). Detection of malingering using atypical performance patterns on standard neuropsychological tests. *Clinical Neuropsychologist*, *17*, 410–425. http://dx.doi.org/10.1076/clin.17.3.410.18089

Larrabee, G. J. (2003b). Exaggerated pain report in litigants with malingered neurocognitive dysfunction. *Clinical Neuropsychologist*, *17*, 395–401. http://dx.doi.org/10.1076/clin.17.3.395.18087

Larrabee, G. J. (2009). Malingering Scales for the Continuous Recognition Memory Test and the Continuous Visual Memory Test. *Clinical Neuropsychologist*, *23*, 167–180. http://dx.doi.org/10.1080/13854040801968443

Larrabee, G. J. (2012a). Performance validity and symptom validity in neuropsychological assessment. *Journal of the International Neuropsychological Society*, *18*, 625–630. http://dx.doi.org/10.1017/S1355617712000240

Larrabee, G. J. (2012b). A scientific approach to forensic neuropsychology. In G. J. Larrabee (Ed.), *Forensic neuropsychology: A scientific approach* (2nd ed., pp. 3–22). New York, NY: Oxford University Press.

Larrabee, G. J. (2014a). False-positive rates associated with the use of multiple performance and symptom validity tests. *Archives of Clinical Neuropsychology*, *29*, 364–373. http://dx.doi.org/10.1093/arclin/acu019

Larrabee, G. J. (2014b). Minimizing false positive error with multiple performance validity tests: Response to Bilder, Sugar, and Hellemann (2014 this issue). *Clinical Neuropsychologist*, *28*, 1230–1242. http://dx.doi.org/10.1080/13854046.2014.988754

Larrabee, G. J. (2014c). Test validity and performance validity: Considerations in providing a framework for development of an ability-focused neuropsychological test battery. *Archives of Clinical Neuropsychology*, *29*, 695–714. http://dx.doi.org/10.1093/arclin/acu049

Larrabee, G. J., & Curtiss, G. (1992). Factor structure of an ability-focused neuropsychological battery [Abstract]. *Journal of Clinical and Experimental Neuropsychology*, *14*, 65.

Larrabee, G. J., & Curtiss, G. (1995). Construct validity of various verbal and visual memory tests. *Journal of Clinical and Experimental Neuropsychology*, *17*, 536–547. http://dx.doi.org/10.1080/01688639508405144

Larrabee, G. J., Kane, R. L., Schuck, J. R., & Francis, D. J. (1985). Construct validity of various memory testing procedures. *Journal of Clinical and Experimental Neuropsychology*, *7*, 239–250. http://dx.doi.org/10.1080/01688638508401257

Larrabee, G. J., Largen, J. W., & Levin, H. S. (1985). Sensitivity of age-decline resistant ("hold") WAIS subtests to Alzheimer's disease. *Journal of Clinical and Experimental Neuropsychology*, *7*, 497–504. http://dx.doi.org/10.1080/01688638508401281

Larrabee, G. J., Millis, S. R., & Meyers, J. E. (2008). Sensitivity to brain dysfunction of the Halstead–Reitan vs. an ability-focused neuropsychological battery. *Clinical Neuropsychologist*, *22*, 813–825. http://dx.doi.org/10.1080/13854040701625846

Leonberger, F. T., Nicks, S. D., Larrabee, G. J., & Goldfader, P. R. (1992). Factor structure of the Wechsler Memory Scale—Revised within a neuropsychological battery. *Neuropsychology*, *6*, 239–249. http://dx.doi.org/10.1037/0894-4105.6.3.239

Lezak, M. D., Howieson, D. B., Bigler, E. D., & Tranel, D. (2012). *Neuropsychological assessment* (5th ed.). New York, NY: Oxford University Press.

Loring, D. W., & Larrabee, G. J. (2006). Sensitivity of the Halstead and Wechsler Test Batteries to brain damage: Evidence from Reitan's original validation sample. *Clinical Neuropsychologist*, *20*, 221–229. http://dx.doi.org/10.1080/13854040590947443

Loring, D. W., Strauss, E., Hermann, B. P., Barr, W. B., Perrine, K., Trenerry, M. R., . . . Bowden, S. C. (2008). Differential neuropsychological test sensitivity to left temporal lobe epilepsy. *Journal of the International Neuropsychological Society*, *14*, 394–400. http://dx.doi.org/10.1017/S1355617708080582

Main, C. J. (1983). The Modified Somatic Perception Questionnaire (MSPQ). *Journal of Psychosomatic Research*, *27*, 503–514. http://dx.doi.org/10.1016/0022-3999(83)90040-5

Marson, D. C., Ingram, K. K., Cody, H. A., & Harrell, L. E. (1995). Assessing the competency of patients with Alzheimer's disease under different legal standards: A prototype instrument. *Archives of Neurology*, *52*, 949–954. http://dx.doi.org/10.1001/archneur.1995.00540340029010

Melzack, R. (1975). The McGill Pain Questionnaire: Major properties and scoring methods. *Pain*, *1*, 277–299. http://dx.doi.org/10.1016/0304-3959(75)90044-5

Meyers, J. E. (1995). *Manual for the Meyers Neuropsychological Battery (MNB)*. Retrieved from http://www.meyersneuropsychological.com

Miller, J. B., Fichtenberg, N. L., & Millis, S. R. (2010). Diagnostic efficiency of an ability-focused battery. *Clinical Neuropsychologist*, *24*, 678–688. http://dx.doi.org/10.1080/13854041003601493

Miller, L. S., & Rohling, M. L. (2001). A statistical interpretive method for neuropsychological test data. *Neuropsychology Review*, *11*, 143–169. http://dx.doi.org/10.1023/A:1016602708066

Mitrushina, M., Boone, K. B., Razani, J., & D'Elia, L. F. (2005). *Handbook of normative data for neuropsychological assessment* (2nd ed.). New York, NY: Oxford University Press.

Mittenberg, W., Azrin, R., Millsaps, C., & Heilbronner, R. L. (1993). Identification of malingered head injury on the Wechsler Memory Scale—Revised. *Psychological Assessment*, *5*, 34–40. http://dx.doi.org/10.1037/1040-3590.5.1.34

Novack, T. A., Baños, J. H., Alderson, A. L., Schneider, J. J., Weed, W., Blankenship, J., & Salisbury, D. (2006). UFOV performance and driving ability following traumatic brain injury. *Brain Injury*, *20*, 455–461. http://dx.doi.org/10.1080/02699050600664541

Powell, J. B., Cripe, L. I., & Dodrill, C. B. (1991). Assessment of brain impairment with the Rey Auditory Verbal Learning Test: A comparison with other neuropsychological measures. *Archives of Clinical Neuropsychology*, *6*, 241–249. http://dx.doi.org/10.1093/arclin/6.4.241

Rabin, L. A., Barr, W. B., & Burton, L. A. (2005). Assessment practices of clinical neuropsychologists in the United States and Canada: A survey of INS, NAN, and APA Division 40 members. *Archives of Clinical Neuropsychology*, *20*, 33–65. http://dx.doi.org/10.1016/j.acn.2004.02.005

Rohling, M. L., Meyers, J. E., & Millis, S. R. (2003). Neuropsychological impairment following traumatic brain injury: A dose-response analysis. *Clinical Neuropsychologist*, *17*, 289–302. http://dx.doi.org/10.1076/clin.17.3.289.18086

Rohling, M. L., Miller, R. M., Axelrod, B. N., Wall, J. R., Lee, A. J., & Kinikini, D. T. (2015). Is co-norming required? *Archives of Clinical Neuropsychology, 30*, 611–633. http://dx.doi.org/10.1093/arclin/acv039

Sherod, M. G., Griffith, H. R., Copeland, J., Belue, K., Kryzwanski, S., Zamrini, E. Y., . . . Marson, D. C. (2009). Neurocognitive predictors of financial capacity across the dementia spectrum: Normal aging, MCI, and Alzheimer's disease. *Journal of the International Neuropsychological Society*, *15*, 258–267. http://dx.doi.org/10.1017/S1355617709090365

Stern, R. A., & White, T. R. (2003). *Neuropsychological assessment battery: Manual*. Lutz, FL: Psychological Assessment Resources.

Suhr, J. A., & Boyer, D. (1999). Use of the Wisconsin Card Sorting Test in the detection of malingering in student simulator and patient samples. *Journal of Clinical and Experimental Neuropsychology*, *21*, 701–708. http://dx.doi.org/10.1076/jcen.21.5.701.868

Sweet, J. J., Ecklund-Johnson, E., & Malina, A. (2008). Forensic neuropsychology: An overview of issues and directions. In J. E. Morgan & J. R. Ricker (Eds.), *Textbook of clinical neuropsychology* (pp. 869–890). New York, NY: Taylor & Francis.

Sweet, J. J., Meyer, D. G., Nelson, N. W., & Moberg, P. J. (2011). The TCN/AACN 2010 "salary survey": Professional practices, beliefs, and incomes of U.S. neuropsychologists. *Clinical Neuropsychologist*, *25*, 12–61. http://dx.doi.org/10.1080/13854046.2010.544165

Tait, R. C., Chibnall, J. T., & Krause, S. (1990). The Pain Disability Index: Psychometric properties. *Pain*, *40*, 171–182. http://dx.doi.org/10.1016/0304-3959(90)90068-O

Trahan, D. E., & Larrabee, G. J. (1988). *The Continuous Visual Memory Test*. Lutz, FL: Psychological Assessment Resources.

Wechsler, D. (2008). *WAIS–IV: Technical and interpretive manual*. San Antonio, TX: Pearson.

Wechsler, D. (2009). *WMS–IV: Technical and interpretive manual*. San Antonio, TX: Pearson.

Whelihan, W. M., DiCarlo, M. A., & Paul, R. H. (2005). The relationship of neuropsychological functioning to driving competence in older persons with early cognitive decline. *Archives of Clinical Neuropsychology*, *20*, 217–228. http://dx.doi.org/10.1016/j.acn.2004.07.002

Williams, M. W., Rapport, L. J., Hanks, R. A., Millis, S. R., & Greene, H. A. (2013). Incremental validity of neuropsychological evaluations to computed tomography in predicting long-term outcomes after traumatic brain injury. *Clinical Neuropsychologist*, *27*, 356–375. http://dx.doi.org/10.1080/13854046.2013.765507

CHAPTER 5

SYMPTOM AND PERFORMANCE VALIDITY ASSESSMENT IN FORENSIC NEUROPSYCHOLOGY

Justin B. Miller, Bradley N. Axelrod, Christian Schutte, and Jeremy J. Davis

Objective assessment of data validity has become a ubiquitous practice in neuropsychological assessment. Historically prominent in medicolegal contexts, with clearly articulated consensus statements regarding use of formal validity measures (Bush et al., 2005; Heilbronner, Sweet, Morgan, Larrabee, & Millis, 2009), validity assessment has increasingly been recognized as having an important role in clinical and research settings as well. The aims of the current chapter are twofold. The first portion discusses several facets of practical implementation of validity measures, including psychometric considerations, test selection, and clinical decision making, that can all be applied in forensic, clinical, and academic practice. Several theoretical points of consideration that are specific to validity measures are also reviewed. Later portions of the chapter are intended to provide a more focused discussion of specific methods of assessing validity, including behavioral observation, and formal stand-alone and embedded measures of both symptom and performance validity.

Although this chapter is written with an emphasis on utilization within a forensic context, much of the information should be applicable to clinical and research settings as well. Regardless of the context (e.g., medicolegal, clinical diagnosis, treatment planning, research), assessment of neuropsychological function and the utility of obtained findings is predicated on effortful task engagement (Lezak, Howieson, Loring, Hannay, & Fischer, 2004). Beyond typical secondary gain factors (e.g., financial remuneration), individuals may demonstrate limited engagement for a multitude of reasons. For example, Morra, Gold, Sullivan, and Strauss (2015) examined performance validity in those diagnosed with schizophrenia. Although the participants in their study were not under any clear influence from secondary gain, approximately 10% of them were likely offering inadequate effort, which Morra et al. attributed to other factors, stating that "negative symptoms and psychological processes may be core to diminished effort during neuropsychological testing" (p. 206).

Similarly, Erdodi et al. (2014) reported that approximately 40% of their mixed clinical psychiatric sample was suspected of offering suboptimal effort despite no "credible evidence of neuropsychological impairment" (p. 572), and DeRight and Jorgensen (2015) found that approximately 10% of their undergraduate research sample demonstrated evidence of poor effort. Nonfinancial secondary gain issues have also been identified in clinical settings, such as cases of attention deficit/hyperactivity disorder in which desirable stimulant medications and academic accommodation may lead to misrepresentation of cognitive dysfunction (Williamson et al., 2014). Although not the focus of this chapter, these data are presented here to highlight that the validity of neuropsychological data is of paramount importance across all settings, and formal assessment of validity should be a standard component of cognitive testing.

PRACTICAL MATTERS OF VALIDITY ASSESSMENT

The terminology surrounding validity testing has evolved over the years. Historically, measures used to

http://dx.doi.org/10.1037/0000032-005
APA Handbook of Forensic Neuropsychology, S. S. Bush (Editor-in-Chief)

detect feigned cognitive and psychiatric presentation have been referred to as *malingering tests, effort tests,* and generically as *symptom validity tests* (SVTs; Boone, 2007). A recent distinction has been made between performance and symptom validity, with the former referring to the validity of cognitive findings and exaggeration or fabrication of cognitive symptoms. *Symptom validity* refers to exaggeration or fabrication of psychiatric symptoms (Larrabee, 2012). The terms *performance validity test* (PVT) or *symptom validity test* suggest that there are specific tests to evaluate validity of cognitive test results and self-reported subjective answers. Although the field has adopted these terms as shorthand for all validity measures, it is important to recognize that assessing symptom and performance validity is not exclusive to formal tests, and the widespread use of PVT and SVT should not be the only basis for minimizing inferences regarding the utility of qualitative, observational methods in determining validity. As such, some have advocated for the use of the terms *performance validity measure* (PVM) and *symptom validity measure* (SVM), which we use interchangeably throughout this chapter in recognition that validity assessment may use information extracted from a test that was not primarily designed for measuring validity in addition to measures explicitly designed for that purpose.

Performance on validity measures typically results in a classification of performance as either valid or invalid. However, the underlying construct (i.e., effort and motivation) may not be an all-or-none phenomenon (Iverson, 2006). Several classification schemes have been developed by practicing clinicians and researchers to facilitate communication, classification, and research on malingering (e.g., Greiffenstein, Gola, & Baker, 1995; Rogers, 1990). Developed specifically for use in neuropsychology, one of the most commonly used schemata is the diagnostic criteria for malingered neurocognitive deficit proposed by Slick, Sherman, and Iverson (1999). Diagnosis of malingered neurocognitive deficit is a multifaceted assessment method that takes into consideration behavioral self-report, observations of behavior, medical records, and neuropsychological test performance.

Slick et al. (1999) defined *malingered neurocognitive deficit* as follows:

> The volitional exaggeration or fabrication of cognitive dysfunction for the purpose of obtaining substantial material gain, or avoiding or escaping formal duty or responsibility. Substantial material gain includes money, goods, or services of nontrivial value (e.g., financial compensation for personal injury) and formal duties are defined as actions that people are legally obligated to perform (e.g., prison, military, or public service, or child support payments or other financial obligations). Formal responsibilities are those that involve accountability or liability within legal proceedings (e.g., competency to stand trial). (p. 552)

Three levels of classification are articulated in the Slick et al. (1999) criteria—definite malingering, probable malingering, and possible malingering—and objectively defined criteria are provided for each level. Common across all three levels of classification is the presence of a substantial external incentive, and that the presentation is not fully accounted for by other factors such as psychiatric, neurological, or developmental causes. Further distinction is based on the level of certainty and the nature and amount of clinical data suggestive of malingering. The major distinction between definite malingering and probable malingering is the absence of clear evidence indicating a definite bias toward incorrect responding for probable malingering.

The lowest level of certainty in the Slick et al. criteria (1999) is possible malingering, which is considered if the evidence suggests symptom exaggeration but is less convincing than in probable or definite malingering. Possible malingering is also considered in cases in which criteria for definite or probable malingering are met, but alternative explanations cannot be ruled out. These criteria have been informally adopted by much of the neuropsychology community as a way to objectively classify suboptimal test performance; however, there have been no studies of these three different groupings to determine whether these classifications are empirically supported.

A core tenet of the Slick et al. (1999) criteria is the intent of the test taker. Although it is perfectly reasonable to assume that a test taker may try hard to perform poorly (i.e., intentional underperformance), it is equally reasonable for someone to put forth poor effort (i.e., not try his or her best) while intending to perform well; this distinction is neglected by the Slick et al. criteria. Frederick and Bowden (2009) proposed a dual-axis model incorporating intent (i.e., to provide correct or incorrect responses) along one axis, ranging from positive (i.e., perform well) to negative (i.e., perform poorly), and effort on the other axis, ranging from good to poor. They defined *effort* as "intensity of application toward a goal on a continuum from low to high" (p. 112). The resulting cross-tabulation of these axes results in four categories: (a) "high effort to respond correctly," (b) "low effort to respond correctly," (c) "low effort with no intent to respond correctly," and (d) "high effort with no intent to respond correctly." Frederick and Bowden contrasted this conceptualization of validity with other uses of *effort* that conflate it with malingering and provide the example that performing below cutoff on a validity measure is often interpreted as malingering when other explanations might warrant consideration.

A significant limitation of this model is that, except for significantly below-chance performance, symptom and PVMs do not under most circumstances provide indication of effort or intent. They merely provide indication that a test taker has performed in a way that is different from the normal population of test takers, which is a vastly distinct concept. At a fundamental level, there is no other neuropsychological measure available that is reliable and valid that allows for inferences to be drawn about the population of membership based solely on exclusion from another population. More succinctly, when an examinee does not fall in the normal population on symptom or PVMs (i.e., performs below clinical cutoff), it is difficult to make inferences about the population to which they belong without evidence of intent. This is a small but significant distinction to keep in mind, and it is for specifically this reason that performance on validity measures should not be used in isolation to make determinations of malingering, which by definition requires knowledge of intent. In the absence of below-chance performance, current validity measures do not provide such information.

If a distinction can be made between intentional exaggeration and malingering, it is clearly a very fine line, as is the distinction between poor effort and intentional feigning. Although intentional exaggeration provides a very important piece of information that can be used when considering the presence of malingering, conflating validity with effort is highly ill advised. Although they are closely related in the context of a neuropsychological evaluation, they are most certainly not synonymous or interchangeable. It is entirely plausible to obtain a valid profile that reflects poor effort (e.g., lackadaisical approach), just as much as it is possible to obtain a cognitive profile that is deemed invalid despite an examinee's best effort (e.g., dementia). It is for that reason some neuropsychologists use validity measures to determine whether the examinee was engaged in the evaluation process. For example, a person who is falling asleep as a result of too much medication would not provide a valid self-presentation of an underaroused state, even though that individual is not intentionally performing poorly.

PSYCHOMETRIC CONSIDERATIONS OF VALIDITY MEASURES

No chapter on neuropsychological assessment would be complete without discussion of psychometrics. Validity testing is no different. In addition to fundamentals such as reliability and validity, those that are of utmost concern for validity measures are related to classification accuracy. Specifically, sensitivity, specificity, positive predictive power, and negative predictive power warrant particularly careful scrutiny and should be readily available in any well-reported publication or test manual. Given the risk of harm associated with falsely accusing a test taker of putting forth poor effort (i.e., a false-positive error), most PVMs and SVMs place a premium on specificity, often at the expense of sensitivity. Maintaining a high negative predictive power is also preferred, in a similar effort to minimize risk of falsely labeling performance as invalid. Most cut scores attempt to achieve an optimal balance between classification accuracy statistics, and these values will vary as a function of the chosen criterion. Selecting the optimal cut value for use in a given setting requires careful consideration of relevant contextual factors (e.g., costs associated with false-positive vs. false-negative errors) and prevalence data. Although these are certainly valuable indices of diagnostic ability, it is important to remember that positive predictive power and negative predictive power values represent overall performance at the group level. Moreover, positive predictive power and negative predictive power may not be the same in an individual practitioner's setting, where base rates (BRs) may differ from that in a published study.

Maintaining a local database can be useful in establishing local prevalence estimates, as well as local normative data that can be used to determine the frequency of low scores. By integrating prevalence statistics and using odds ratios, clinicians can also make empirically informed decisions. For this reason, new studies of PVMs and SVMs often incorporate classification rates for varying BRs so the classification rates can be adjusted for clinics with different levels of prevalence. Larrabee (2008) demonstrated how a test with the same likelihood ratio (0.5) of detecting invalid performance can result in an odds ratio of 0.55 when the BR is 10% but an odds ratio of 20.0 when the BR of deficient effort is 80%.

As with any neuropsychological measure, proper implementation that is consistent with standardization is critical to retain the test's psychometric properties and maximize its clinical utility as per the intended and validated use. Several key differences, however, differentiate PVMs and traditional measures of cognitive ability, which require careful consideration during use and interpretation. Unlike traditional cognitive measures, which are used to formulate clinical impressions of cognitive ability and thus make inferences about underlying brain functioning or functional abilities, validity measures are intended to guide decision making regarding the credibility of an obtained cognitive profile and the individual's approach to cognitive testing (i.e., PVTs) or his or her report of psychological symptoms (i.e., SVTs). Although this may seem obvious, there are subtleties to this distinction that are quite significant and must not be overlooked.

Fundamentally, neuropsychological tests are designed to measure facets of cognitive ability, the results of which are then typically used to make inferences about underlying brain functioning. PVMs, however, are purportedly so simple as to be devoid of significant cognitive demand and thus do not allow for valid inferences about brain functioning. In theory, to serve their purpose as an indication of validity, PVMs should thus be unrelated to brain function. This is particularly true for stand-alone measures, and studies have demonstrated that even individuals who are neurologically compromised are capable of performing normally on these measures (e.g., Carone, Green, & Drane, 2014; Eichstaedt et al., 2014; Ploetz, Mazur-Mosiewicz, Kirkwood, Sherman, & Brooks, 2016). Certainly, this is not the case for embedded measures of performance validity (e.g., Reliable Digit Span; Greiffenstein et al., 1995; Holdnack & Drozdick, 2009), which by definition are contained within standard neuropsychological measures and thus more susceptible to neurological dysfunction. However, the methods used to validate embedded PVTs seek to demonstrate concurrent validity with established stand-alone measures, as well as to identify levels of performance that have very low prevalence in clinical populations (e.g., traumatic brain injury [TBI], dementia).

There is evidence that suggests that some of the stand-alone PVTs do correlate with validated measures of cognitive ability, though. For example, several indices obtained from administration of the Word Memory Test (WMT; i.e., multiple choice, paired associates, free recall) are described as "memory" indices by the author (Green, 2003), leading to development of the Genuine Memory Impairment Profile. Although independent research has questioned the utility of the WMT memory indices in a sample with TBI (Donders & Strong, 2013), Armistead-Jehle, Green, Gervais, and Hungerford (2015) reported significant relationships among indices of TBI severity and WMT memory subtests in clinical examinees who passed WMT validity subtests. Moderate to strong positive correlations were also reported between California Verbal Learning Test—Second Edition (CVLT–II; Delis, Kramer, Kaplan, & Ober, 2000) subtests and WMT subtests in examinees who passed WMT validity subtests. Most PVTs, however, are instead used to make inferences about an individual's approach to cognitive testing, the results of which are then used to contextualize and interpret the remainder of a cognitive profile obtained from standard neuropsychological measures. This is in stark contrast to traditional cognitive measures.

Another significant distinguishing characteristic of PVMs is that with traditional cognitive measures, poor performance is often correlated with reliable measures of neurological functioning (e.g., MRI, computerized tomography, electroencephalogram), which is one method of validating a test's sensitivity to brain dysfunction; this is a hallmark of neuropsychological testing and harkens back to the roots of the field. There is no such standard for PVMs or SVMs. Though some research has demonstrated a distributed network of functional recruitment, including frontal and parietal cortices during performance on the WMT (Allen, Bigler, Larsen, Goodrich-Hunsaker, & Hopkins, 2007; Allen, Wu, & Bigler, 2011), limited data have pointed to a specific cortical region associated with effortful performance. Fox (2011) reported significant associations between measures of cerebral insult (e.g., positive neuroimaging findings) and neuropsychological test data in participants who passed PVTs and noted nonsignificant relationships in participants who failed PVTs. Moreover, the fact that patients with significant neurological compromise can accurately complete measures of performance validity with ease further weakens any association with specific pathology.

Interpretation of PVTs is also very different from that of standard measures of cognitive functioning. Unlike many traditional cognitive measures, for which obtained scores are typically continuous and normally distributed, yielding a range of possible values and performance classifications, the simplicity of most stand-alone PVTs typically generates a distribution of scores that is highly skewed with narrow dispersion. Given that the cognitive construct underlying the parent task of embedded indices is more likely to be normally distributed, this is less of a concern for embedded measures. As such, statistical analysis of PVT data also warrants a careful review of assumptions, because many PVT scores grossly violate the assumption of normality, and equal variances should not be readily assumed. This is particularly important to consider when evaluating empirical validity research, because application of parametric tests to nonnormal or heteroscedastic data may increase the probability of false-positive statistical findings.

Although the individual scores used to make determinations of credibility can usually assume a range of possible values for either stand-alone or embedded measures, these values are typically used to inform a binary classification decision (i.e., pass or fail) and do not have inherent interpretive value in and of themselves. For example, a score that is 10 points above cutoff is no more indicative of normal performance than a score that is 1 point above cutoff. Conversely, a score of 34 correct out of 50 possible items is no different from a score of 44 or 24; they are all simply classified as "below cutoff." An exception to this is when scores from forced-choice measures are statistically below chance performance, though even then the classification is still binary; it is either valid or invalid. Although performance that is statistically worse than chance has been argued as "the smoking gun of intent" (Pankratz & Erickson, 1990, p. 385) and as "persuasive evidence of response bias" (Millis, 2004, p. 1083), and it is often considered a gold-standard criterion for validation purposes, in reality this is a rare phenomenon. As revealed in a study by Greve, Binder, and Bianchini (2009), only about 12% of a litigating population in private practice performed below chance on any one measure, far below estimated BRs for poor effort in mild TBI (mTBI). Consequently, cutoff scores have been established for most validity measures through empirical research studying patterns of performance among individuals suspected of putting forth poor effort (e.g., known-groups designs; simulator studies).

Research Methods

Several approaches to effort testing research exist, including case study, differential prevalence designs, simulation studies, and known-group designs. Although a comprehensive review of research methods is beyond the scope of this chapter and well documented elsewhere (e.g., Rogers, 1997), each validation method has its strengths and weaknesses, and knowing these limitations is important when evaluating the validity literature. Several of the primary paradigms are briefly reviewed here to introduce readers to the major research methods.

Because individuals who are attempting to feign cognitive dysfunction in a clinical or forensic setting are likely to be quite reluctant to admit to feigning or malingering, simulation designs attempt to artificially establish a group of individuals who have been instructed to underperform in an attempt to feign cognitive impairment. These simulators are then typically compared with a sample of healthy adults without the same instruction or with a well-defined clinical group without incentive to underperform. Although this is useful during early development of a new validity measure, simulation designs suffer from limited external validity or generalizability. Given the artificial nature of the design, it is not clear whether the simulator samples match individuals underperforming in a clinical setting or a medicolegal setting; there may be significant differences in familiarity with the feigned condition, exposure to coaching, motivation, or use of strategy in feigning or in other factors, such as psychological distress resulting from the injury or involvement in litigation. It is also difficult to assess participants' willingness to feign poor performance, and some research has shown that even coached individuals find it difficult to simulate plausible deficits (Wall & Davis, 2013).

As with any diagnostic test, it is essential to carefully review both the empirical literature and the test manual for specific information about how a particular cut score was derived, the populations studied, the study design, and the comparison standards to ensure that the intended test operating characteristics are retained when used in practice. As when selecting normative references for cognitive measures, when selecting an appropriate criterion to establish invalidity for an individual measure, it is important to understand the characteristics of the reference group, as well as the criterion group, to evaluate comparability between the study sample and an individual test taker. For example, a measure validated on a sample of people with a history of mTBI seeking compensation may not retain the same psychometric properties when applied to individuals with learning disability who are attempting to obtain academic accommodations, and thus may not be appropriate.

Understanding how a cutoff score was derived is also essential. One approach is to evaluate the BR of an obtained score in a well-characterized reference group to determine whether a test taker's level of performance is statistically rare in the documented clinical reference group (Backhaus, Fichtenberg, & Hanks, 2004; Larrabee, 2008). These floor effect models are useful, particularly with disorders that have been well researched and defined. For example, it has been well established that there is a dose–response relationship between the severity of TBI and the outcome (Carroll et al., 2004; Dikmen, Machamer, Winn, & Temkin, 1995; Rohling, Meyers, & Millis, 2003) and that individuals who have sustained a mTBI are very unlikely to have any neurologically based cognitive deficits at 1 year postinjury (Dikmen et al., 1995). Thus, if an individual with a history of mTBI generates a score that is statistically infrequent among those with more severe injuries, it should raise concerns about the validity of performance, particularly if observed in a context with secondary gain. This approach is exemplified by the Advanced Clinical Solutions (ACS; Holdnack & Drozdick, 2009) supplement available for the Wechsler tests (Wechsler, 2008a, 2008b), in which the BRs of scores for several measures are reported for a number of clinical subgroups.

A point of caution regarding relying on floor effect models is that some clinical disorders, such as dementia, show a high false-positive rate using embedded indices (Bortnik, Horner, & Bachman, 2013). Therefore, the development of embedded indices should be carefully evaluated so that they are used in appropriate populations to avoid false-positive identification of invalid test performance. Floor effect models may also have limited utility in progressive disorders, where the floor of performance moves over time (e.g., dementia), though they work well in more stable disorders (e.g., postacute TBI).

Another approach to performance validity assessment uses traditional methods of establishing concurrent validity by comparing the classification accuracy of a new measure with that of a well-validated gold standard (e.g., Test of Memory Malingering [TOMM], WMT), often in a known-group design format. This approach may well be one of the most commonly used methods, but it relies heavily on the validity of the criterion. Sometimes referred to as *criterion variable designs*, known-groups studies are especially useful in clinical situations in which archival research in mixed clinical samples may be collected over a period of time. One can use a well-validated measure, such as the TOMM or the Medical Symptom Validity Test (MSVT; Green, 2005), to define valid versus invalid performance and compare its classification accuracy with that of additional stand-alone or embedded measures. One strength of this method is sheer convenience, as exemplified by the proliferation of studies reporting on embedded indices of performance validity. These types of samples are readily available to researchers who archive data obtained as a part of clinical practice, which leads to efficient data collection, larger samples, and samples that may be more generalizable to common clinical populations. Practitioners must keep in mind that no measure is a perfect predictor of suboptimal performance, and when evaluating a validity measure that has been validated using this method, being equally familiar with the criterion is essential because any shortcomings of the criterion measure may similarly limit the classification accuracy of the new measure.

Another key distinction between validity testing and cognitive testing is that effort or test engagement may vacillate over the course of an evaluation, which is also theoretically different from most other cognitive abilities (Heilbronner et al., 2009). As a result, some have suggested that validity be assessed routinely throughout an evaluation (Boone, 2009) to ensure adequate sampling over the course of testing. This approach is further supported by Axelrod, Meyers, and Davis (2014) in their examination of validity issues on motor testing.

Practical Implementation of Performance and Symptom Validity Measures

As with any neuropsychological test battery, selecting which measures to include and how many are necessary to provide an adequate assessment of validity requires careful consideration. Although the number of available stand-alone validity measures to draw from is generally less than what is available for most cognitive domains, and many of the PVMs are presented as memory tests, there is some degree of diversity among measures that allows for customization of a PVT battery. Similar to when one is selecting cognitive measures, the purpose of the evaluation and the primary complaints are critical factors to consider when choosing validity measures. In a litigation or disability context in which an individual may be attempting to gain financial remuneration for an injury, the presence of a financial incentive can be a very powerful motivating force that may compel exaggeration. Evasion of criminal culpability, avoidance of responsibility, and even obtaining controlled substances (e.g., narcotic pain medications) can similarly provide sufficient motivation to alter an individual's response style or symptom presentation and should not be overlooked as motivators for exaggeration.

Although research on the approaches used by individuals feigning cognitive impairment is sparse, bearing in mind the nature of complaints is critical when selecting PVTs. Claims of memory impairment are quite common, which is likely one of the reasons why many PVTs use a memory-based format with high face-validity as a memory test. When encountering such complaints, integrating PVTs that target memory is prudent. Some examinees may identify attention as a primary problem and feign distractibility, and others may attempt to demonstrate severely slowed processing speed. Comparatively few stand-alone PVTs target cognitive functioning other than memory; however, several good examples exist and should be readily available to clinicians working regularly in the forensic arena. The Victoria Symptom Validity Test (Slick, Hopp, Strauss, & Thompson, 1997) and Portland Digit Recognition Test (Binder & Willis, 1991) both require examinees to pay attention initially; for an individual attempting to dissimulate problems with attention, abnormally poor initial attention may be a prime target for validity assessment. The b Test (Boone, Lu, & Herzberg, 2002) is a measure that requires sustained attention and uses both errors (i.e., inattention) and processing speed in calculating the error score used in determination of credibility. As a result, this measure is likely sensitive to individuals feigning slowed processing as well as inattention. The Dot Counting Test (Boone, Lu, & Herzberg, 2002) is another exemplar of a non–memory validity measure.

To broaden the scope of domain coverage, numerous embedded PVTs have been validated and are sensitive to feigned cognitive impairment in domains other than memory. Dozens of indices across cognitive, sensory, and motor domains are available for use as psychometrically based indicators of performance validity. For example, the Reliable Digit Span (RDS; Greiffenstein et al., 1995) provides a measure of validity contained within an attention task. The Picture Completion Most Discrepant Index (Solomon et al., 2010) has been validated as a measure sensitive to feigned visuospatial impairment. Sugarman and Axelrod (2015) found word list generation to be helpful in discriminating good effort from poor effort. Different versions of the finger-tapping test have all demonstrated sensitivity to feigned performance (cf. Axelrod et al., 2014).

Rather than providing a criterion of invalidity, the embedded validity indices contained within the ACS provide BRs of scores for multiple clinical samples (e.g., people with TBI, mild intellectual disability, schizophrenia, attention deficit/hyperactivity disorder) for the recognition trials of Verbal Paired Associations, Logical Memory, and Visual Reproduction subtests from the Wechsler Memory Scale—Fourth Edition (Wechsler, 2008b), as well as the RDS. The ACS also contains a stand-alone measure, the Word Choice Test, which is a forced-choice task similar to the Recognition Memory Test (Warrington, 1984) and TOMM. Unlike the TOMM, however, it contains only a single learning trial and one recognition trial. Scores for the ACS are obtained as part of routine administration of the Wechsler Memory Scale—Fourth Edition and the Digit Span subtest from the Wechsler Adult Intelligence Scale—Fourth Edition (Wechsler, 2008a). Tables provided in the Clinical and Interpretive manual report the relative frequency of an obtained score in a clinical group.

Maintenance of a local database facilitates determination of the frequency of an obtained score in a relevant clinical sample. In the absence of a local dataset, BR comparisons can still be made with published literature by finding a study whose participants are similar to a clinical patient in terms of demographic factors and clinical characteristics. Using measures of central tendency and dispersion reported in the literature, where an individual's obtained score falls in the reported distribution can be calculated for normally distributed tasks (e.g., a *z* score). It is noteworthy that most embedded measures have a normal distribution, whereas stand-alone measures of performance validity are negatively skewed, with the majority of individuals obtaining scores near the ceiling. The BR method can also be used with standard cognitive measures. For example, if a test taker who claims to have persisting deficits from a mTBI obtains a raw score of 30 on the Boston Naming Test (Kaplan, Goodglass, & Weintraub, 2001) and a large-sample study of people with a history of mTBI reports a mean score of 55 and a standard deviation of 5, the test taker's obtained score is thus 5 standard deviations below the mean of a comparable group, which would warrant careful consideration of alternative explanations, including the possibility of poor effort or symptom exaggeration.

Selecting a battery of validity measures. When it comes to performance and SVMs, selecting a battery of measures to include requires careful attention. Over time, most practitioners will develop personal preferences as to which validity measures they prefer and thus integrate into regular clinical practice, essentially adopting somewhat of a fixed battery approach to validity testing. One advantage of this approach is increased familiarity with the unique test operating characteristics of the most frequently used measures and learning how well a particular set of measures performs both individually and collectively when used together. Using the same set of validity measures also facilitates establishment of a local normative reference, as well as a repository of data for research purposes. A potential downside to such an approach is that the practitioner may develop a reputation among referral sources for administering a particular set of PVTs, which may increase vulnerability to coaching to avoid detection.

Alternatively, many practitioners prefer a flexible approach, which parallels the flexible or ability-focused concept commonly used in developing a cognitive battery (Sweet, Meyer, Nelson, & Moberg, 2011). Clinicians are likely to have several PVMs and SVMs available at their disposal and will vary test selection for an individual case on the basis of the presenting complaints and context of the evaluation (e.g., criminal, civil, personal injury). Some practitioners may also choose to use a gating method—one or two measures of performance validity are deployed and if performance is satisfactory, then no further validity testing is completed. If the individual fails one of the gate measures, then more validity measures can be added to generate additional evidence. Although such an approach may be efficient because it reduces the number of tests administered and the time required for an evaluation, it may, depending on the gate measures, increase false-negative rates (i.e., the chances of an individual putting forth poor effort going undetected). It may therefore be beneficial to choose a gate measure with high sensitivity, so long as there is an a priori intention that positive findings will be followed up with additional validity measures.

When developing a battery, integrating both stand-alone and embedded measures helps to minimize the risk of false-negative errors and broadens the scope of domain coverage in an effort to capture individuals targeting domains other than memory. Embedded measures have an added potential benefit of providing useful clinical data for valid responding, and they are typically less vulnerable to coaching, particularly classification models that are derived from multiple scores (e.g., Miller et al., 2011; Sugarman & Axelrod, 2015; Wolfe et al., 2010).

Coaching—providing sufficient information to assist examinees in portraying themselves in a disingenuous way (Suhr & Gunstad, 2007)—is still highly prevalent in forensic practice and can take multiple forms. In addition to information available on the Internet and from attorneys, undergoing multiple neuropsychological evaluations, which is common for individuals involved in litigation, can provide clients with information on how to take cognitive tests, especially when they are provided feedback on their performance (Suhr & Gunstad, 2007). The three most common methods of coaching include providing information related to injury symptoms, test-taking strategies (e.g., "if you see a test where you have to choose between two pictures, do your best"), and warning clients of the use of PVTs within the assessment (Suhr & Gunstad, 2007). Coaching is especially a concern with stand-alone measures, which necessarily limits their utility and sensitivity. Given that a substantial portion of stand-alone measures use some form of forced-choice paradigm, the savvy (i.e., coached) test taker may be able to easily identify them. Suhr and Gunstad (2000) found that although coached simulators performed more poorly than a good effort group, they still performed better than the noncoached group. They concluded that performance on forced-choice measures is easily altered by coaching, which is similar to findings from DiCarlo, Gfeller, and Oliveri (2000). Embedded indices have the potential benefit of avoiding this pitfall, particularly when more sophisticated methods of pattern analysis and statistical approaches are used.

Ultimately, the decision of which validity measures incorporate into a clinical inventory will be multifactorial and guided by individual practice parameters. Carefully balancing the risk of false-positive and false-negative errors should be at the core of validity test selection decisions. Choosing a set of both embedded and stand-alone measures to assess for overall test battery invalidity should also be done judiciously, because using multiple measures from the same cognitive domain may be redundant and lead to an overly confident conclusion regarding invalidity. Thus, selecting measures with low intercorrelations is critical to reduce the likelihood of false-positive classification errors as a result of shared instead of unique variance when aggregating findings across validity measures.

How many measures should be administered? With numerous stand-alone measures and even more embedded measures to choose from, the topic of how many to include in an assessment has been debated, and no definitive answer has been reached. Without question, assessment of performance and symptom validity throughout the course of an evaluation is recommended because of the possibility of varying levels of effort (Heilbronner et al., 2009). Although it may be tempting for some practitioners to include every stand-alone measure and only cognitive measures with embedded validity indicators, doing so may increase the risk of false-positive findings as a result of high intercorrelations among measures. With highly intercorrelated validity measures, the number of failed validity measures may increase as a result of shared variance in test performance that cuts across measures instead of measuring unique variance.

Despite recommendations for continuous sampling for evidence of invalidity throughout cognitive evaluations, concerns have been raised that the probability of false-positive findings may increase as a function of the number of validity measures administered (Bilder, Sugar, & Hellemann, 2014; Odland, Lammy, Martin, Grote, & Mittenberg, 2015). It has been well established that the probability that a normal, healthy test taker will obtain a deficient score on normally distributed cognitive tests increases when more tests are administered (Axelrod, Wall, & Estes, 2008; Binder, Iverson, & Brooks, 2009; Brooks, Strauss, Sherman, Iverson, & Slick, 2009). It therefore seems plausible that similar patterns of normal variability in performance may arise for validity measures. To explore this empirically, Berthelson, Mulchan, Odland, Miller, and Mittenberg (2013) conducted a Monte Carlo simulation and found that when failure on two PVTs was used as the criterion for poor effort, 38% of test takers putting forth good effort would be classified incorrectly when 10 PVTs were administered. However, in an archival review of clinical data collected from a sample of neurological patients without incentive to underperform, Davis and Millis (2014) found that education and functional status—not the number of PVTs administered—were related to the incidence of false-positive errors. Moreover, the actual failure rates reported by Davis and Millis were lower than predictions made by Berthelson et al. One possible explanation is that most cognitive measures are normally distributed, and thus obtained scores can more readily assume a wider range of possible outcomes. As previously noted, however, validity measures generate a much narrower dispersion of scores in a highly skewed distribution, which limits the possibility of chance findings based on normal variability.

At this point in time, continual sampling of performance and symptom validity is still recommended to ensure adequate domain coverage, as well as sufficient sampling over the course of an evaluation. As long as the intercorrelations among measures remain adequately low, there currently are no empirical data to support a ceiling on the number of validity measures to administer; however, ongoing research in this area is certainly warranted.

Implementation in Clinical Practice

Once a set of appropriate measures has been selected, the manner in which they are implemented in forensic practice also requires careful consideration. Before beginning an evaluation, clinicians have to decide whether to inform individuals that validity measures will be used. This decision is delicate and highly personal, and it ultimately boils down to personal preference and situational demands. Although many clinicians believe that full transparency regarding validity assessment is the best policy (i.e., explicitly informing test takers that performance validity will be evaluated objectively throughout testing), other providers prefer to limit disclosures about validity testing. There is little systematic research on the relative effects of each approach on test performance, but there is some evidence that suggests that informing patients about the use of validity measures increases sophistication of response patterns (Youngjohn, Lees-Haley, & Binder, 1999), which may in turn facilitate avoidance of detection.

One approach, and perhaps the most common, is to simply encourage test takers to perform their best without providing any information that validity will be evaluated. Some clinicians believe that this allows examinees to approach testing in a way that is congruent with their natural interests. The belief may be that an examinee who is intent on feigning cognitive impairment or underperforming on a test should be allowed do so with minimal influence from the examiner, thus preserving the individual's natural behavioral predisposition. Others believe that this approach is unnecessarily and arguably intentionally deceptive, preventing a test taker from making a fully informed decision about how to proceed during testing.

Alternatively, some providers prefer to inform test takers that full effort is paramount and that their approach to testing and the validity of data will be evaluated throughout the assessment. One advantage of this approach is that a test taker is afforded the opportunity to make an informed decision; however, the individual who is intent on underperforming may not be swayed from his or her intentions with such nonspecific information and may in fact become vigilant for potential validity measures.

Another option is to inform test takers that specific tests will be used to evaluate the credibility of their approach to testing. Although informing test takers which tests are specifically designed to measure validity is highly inappropriate (and doing so ultimately undermines the clinical utility of the validity measures by breaching test security), informing an individual that some measures or indices of a battery are intended to provide information about their approach to testing provides the most transparency. It affords examinees an opportunity to make a fully informed decision about their approach to and engagement with testing. Such information may deter examinees from prior considerations of underperformance, although it also increases the risk that examinees will increase the sophistication of dissimulation strategies. Whether this increased sophistication increases their chances of avoiding detection remains unclear.

Responding to performance validity failures during testing. Determinations about the credibility of an examinee's presentation can be readily made throughout the evaluation. Although some methods of assessing validity require more careful consideration and reference to external criteria (e.g., base rate determinations, probability models), information regarding validity classification is immediately available on test completion when using a cut score as a criterion of effort. When there is clear evidence of suboptimal performance, the question then arises as to what to do and, more important, how to shape the remainder of the evaluation. There is unlikely to be a one-size-fits-all process or response that can be applied universally. The nature of the evaluation, the context of testing, the preferences of the referral source, and relevant case characteristics should all be integrated into decision making.

The simplest approach is to note the poor performance and continue testing as planned, without altering the battery or testing approach and without providing any indication to the test taker about the abnormal performance. One significant advantage to this approach is that it does not provide information to the test taker that may influence his or her approach to subsequent testing. Much like the decision to refrain from informing a test taker about the use of validity measures, proceeding with an evaluation as planned despite failed validity measures essentially ensures the evaluation will capture an entirely endogenously driven approach to test taking. It also affords the clinician an opportunity to observe performance across a variety of cognitive domains, which although of limited clinical validity, can still provide useful information.

Continuing as planned with testing also limits the test taker's ability to identify which measures were used to measure validity, which could be used in a future evaluation to guide response patterns. Clearly, a major disadvantage, particularly in the face of multiple failures, is that the remainder of data collection will generate data of limited utility regarding actual cognitive functioning, squandering both time and clinical resources. Proceeding with testing despite failed validity measures also exposes patients to tests, which creates familiarity and increases practice effects that may lead to more sophisticated dissimulation efforts in the future. It may be wise to avoid measures that are particularly prone to practice effects in such situations (e.g., Wisconsin Card Sorting Test; Basso, Lowery, Ghormley, & Bornstein, 2001; Heaton, Chelune, Talley, Kay, & Curtiss, 1993).

Another option is to interrupt testing and discuss the patient's approach to testing after a validity measure has yielded positive findings. One possibility is to reiterate the importance of putting forth a good effort on cognitive testing to generate useful information. Some clinicians prefer to take this opportunity to explicitly inform test takers about their failed validity performance and to then reiterate the importance of good effort; however, doing so provides information to the savvy test taker as to which measures were used as markers of performance validity. Depending on the context of the evaluation, it may be prudent to discuss possible reasons why an individual may not be performing at an optimal level and explore any factors that are potentially interfering with test performance. Doing so may elicit useful information and potentially identify transient situational factors that can be mitigated to increase motivation to perform well. For many individuals, however, no amount of discussion or exploration will sway their intentions, and in some instances confronting an individual about poor validity test performance may lead to more defensive behavior.

Alternatively, some clinicians choose to immediately discontinue testing when SVTs or PVTs are failed, which in certain circumstances may be an appropriate course of action. Doing so limits exposure to cognitive measures and helps preserve limited resources. One notable drawback is that it increases the chances of revealing which measures are the validity indicators. It may be difficult for a test taker to know when an examination is discontinued prematurely, but the test taker may have some insight that testing was stopped early if he or she was prepared for a lengthy evaluation (as is often the case in forensic settings).

Given that SVMs are self-contained in a questionnaire, symptom inventory, or other form of symptom report, there is less decision making on the part of the clinician during test administration. Rather, decisions regarding the validity of assessments are made on completion of testing.

Interpretation of performance and symptom validity measures. Interpreting a profile of symptom and performance data is a complex, multifaceted process that requires conscientious review. Current classifications for most individual measures of performance validity, either embedded or stand-alone, generate a binary outcome (e.g., pass–fail, valid–invalid); however, the likelihood that effort itself is binary is quite low. Just as it would be poor practice to make a clinical inference about overall language functioning on the basis of a word reading test, it would similarly be imprudent to make a determination about the validity of an entire neuropsychological profile on the basis of one validity measure. For embedded measures, a score falling below the cutoff raises sufficient question about the validity of performance on the parent measure, though such determinations cannot be made with the same degree of precision for stand-alone measures. Rather, the overall pattern of performance across both embedded and stand-alone validity measures requires careful review, including the proportion of validity measures failed, the context of the evaluation, the intercorrelations among validity measures, and the penalty for misclassification errors.

A major point of consideration is that results of PVMs and SVMs may not necessarily generalize across both domains, and factor analysis has supported a distinction between performance and symptom validity (Van Dyke, Millis, Axelrod, & Hanks, 2013). For example, if an individual completes multiple measures of personality functioning and generates invalid profiles, this does not necessarily imply that measures of cognitive functioning are similarly invalid, and vice versa. An individual seeking financial compensation for emotional trauma may have significant incentive to exaggerate emotional distress but little to no motivation to simultaneously feign cognitive dysfunction. To assume that cognitive data are invalid as a result of failed SVMs goes beyond the appropriate use of the measures. This is just one specific example of how the individual context of a case must always be accounted for in clinical and forensic decision making.

Occasionally, a test taker will generate a profile of validity findings that is so egregious that there is little room for interpretation. For example, obtaining multiple scores that are statistically below chance levels (e.g., 17 or less on a forced-choice test with 50 trials) is typically an extremely strong indication of response bias. Although it is rare to encounter below-chance performance in clinical practice, when it occurs it is important to ensure that the respondent correctly understood the task demands. A simple misunderstanding of instructions could easily lead to a significantly abnormal score, which if interpreted without subsequent inquiry could lead to erroneous conclusions.

Proper adherence to test protocols should minimize such instances, though it remains important for neuropsychologists to critically evaluate alternative explanations for aberrant scores, particularly infrequent scores such as statistically below-chance performance.

Attempting to establish intent to perform poorly can be a particularly challenging but important part of the diagnostic process. Assuming that the examinee correctly understood the task and response options, performance that is statistically below chance strongly suggests an intentional effort to perform poorly, because the implication is that the test taker was required to recall the correct response and consciously respond incorrectly. Binomial theorem can be used to determine whether an examinee's performance was statistically worse than chance. Numerous online calculators exist that allow for simple determination of the probability of obtaining a given score on the number of trials, the number of items correct, and the probability of success on any given trial (which for any forced-choice test will equal 0.5).

Even without formal measures, practitioners can create a simple forced-choice task that can be used during an interview or brief bedside exam. An examiner can present an item, such as a coin or a pencil eraser, to an examinee and then show the examinee that the examiner is holding it in one of his or her hands. A forced-choice paradigm can be created by asking the examinee in which hand the item was placed. To integrate a face-valid cognitive demand, a distracter task can be integrated, such as asking the examinee to count backward by sevens. This coin-in-hand test or eraser test can be evaluated using the binomial theorem. For example, if one gave an examinee 20 trials of a forced-choice recognition memory task (i.e., was the item in this hand or that hand?), binomial theory would note that obtaining a score of 8 correct is no different from chance performance ($p = .12$). However, a raw score of 6 correct out of 20 is significant ($p = .04$). Assuming task demands were understood correctly, one has to be intentionally underperforming to obtain a score that is statistically worse than chance performance.

Presented differently, if one were to correctly respond to 10 out of 25 trials, the resulting score would not be significantly below chance ($p = .10$). However, if one were to correctly respond to only 10 items out of 40 trials, the resulting score would be statistically worse than chance ($p < .001$). It is important to note that although a score of 40% correct is well below cutoffs for most (if not all) validity measures and is below the odds predicted for an individual forced-choice trial, this level of performance is not statistically below chance. In other words, statistically below-chance performance does not equate to less than 50% correct (Binder, Larrabee, & Millis, 2014).

Forced-choice recognition memory research has demonstrated that few individuals actually perform significantly worse than chance (Binder, 2003; Grote et al., 2000), and there are few published studies that report below-chance performance. Recognizing the infrequency of below-chance performance, clinical cutoffs have been derived that are typically well above chance yet still capable of identifying suboptimal performance while retaining adequate specificity. In practice, it is much more common to encounter performance that is below these empirically derived cutoffs for valid responding. Most published stand-alone measures use the cutoff approach and present data in the test manual to use in determining invalid performance. Subsequent studies often help to fine-tune optimal cutoff scores for various patient populations. Establishing criterion scores for embedded measures is frequently accomplished through empirical research, and some indices may have multiple cut points suggested (e.g., RDS, CVLT–II Forced Choice Recognition, TOMM). Selecting which cut points to use as a criterion of poor effort varies as a function of the testing context and the characteristics of the evaluation. It is essential that pass–fail criteria be objectively established a priori and that they are not manipulated as a matter of convenience post hoc to advance or support a particular position.

It is commonly understood that clinical impressions should never be made on the basis of a single score or test, and determinations of validity are no different. No measure of performance or symptom validity should be viewed as a litmus test. Although some evidence has suggested that failure of even one validity measure is associated with sizable performance decrements on cognitive measures (Constantinou, Bauer, Ashendorf, Fisher, & McCaffrey, 2005; Fox, 2011; Proto et al., 2014), failure on one measure (unless below chance) is not uncommon (Dean, Victor, Boone, & Arnold, 2008; Meyers & Volbrecht, 2003). Thus, caution is warranted to avoid overinterpreting a single failed PVT. To reduce the risk of inaccurate classification, no measure should be used in isolation to identify poor performance (Bush et al., 2005; Heilbronner et al., 2009), and ruling an entire profile invalid on the basis of one failed validity indicator, especially when several PVTs have been administered, is inappropriate. The findings of Proto et al. (2014), however, suggest that a single below-criterion performance should not be overlooked. This is just one of many reasons why multiple SVTs and PVTs should be an integral part of any comprehensive assessment battery, whether for forensic, clinical, or research purposes.

Assuming that the intercorrelations of selected validity measures are sufficiently low, frequently accepted interpretive guidelines have suggested that failed performance on two or more PVTs is consistent with invalid performance (Larrabee, 2008; Meyers & Volbrecht, 2003), and additional research has suggested diminishing increases in classification accuracy with guidelines that require more than two failed validity measures (Bashem et al., 2014). Being mindful of the individual test operating characteristics, however, is crucial when using such a rule because classification accuracy may vary as a function of the number of tests given (Berthelson et al., 2013; Odland et al., 2015), as well as specific combinations of tests (Bashem et al., 2014). Moreover, independence of validity measures cannot be readily assumed with PVTs (Berthelson et al., 2013; Schutte & Axelrod, 2013). Creation of local data repositories for both PVMs and SVMs will greatly facilitate precise, context-specific correlations and local test operating characteristics because the intercorrelations reported among PVTs in the literature may not readily translate to individual practice settings with different parameters.

One important point of consideration is that it may not be appropriate to aggregate across both SVMs and PVMs because they may not measure the same constructs equally. For example, exaggeration of posttraumatic stress disorder (PTSD) symptoms is likely distinct from feigned memory loss. Thus, when using a decision rule of "two or more failures," one should not count across both PVMs and SVMs or use multiple indices from the same measure. Simply using the number of failed PVTs on a test battery is practical and intuitive, such as that suggested by Larrabee (2003a, 2008), but issues of multicollinearity (the strength of the relationships between variables in the model), differing likelihood ratios (the likelihood a test result would be present among those with and without the condition of interest), and the different test batteries that are used among clinicians may limit generalization of such criteria across settings. In addition, there may be legitimate reasons for failure on validity indices (e.g., dementia), which can change the meaning of obtained results. Although combinations of specific measures and cut scores for multiple failures published by Larrabee (2008) and Victor, Boone, Serpa, Buehler, and Ziegler (2009) perform well, one should not conclude that any combination of validity indices is adequate to identify suboptimal effort across settings. Thus, when using multiple PVTs to assess for overall test battery validity, it is useful to empirically study the test operating characteristics in the local (or similar) setting, to ensure that the relationship between validity measures is low and that classification accuracy is comparable to published empirical studies.

As an alternative to examining the absolute number of failed validity measures, it has recently been suggested that the proportion of validity measures failed out of the number administered be considered in determinations of profile validity to minimize the cumulative false-positive rate (Odland et al., 2015). Aggregating findings from published clinical samples reporting symptom and performance validity data, Odland et al. (2015) reported a strong inverse relationship between the proportion of validity indices failed and the cumulative false-positive rate ($r_s = -.83$). Several recommendations were offered, most notably that the cumulative false-positive rate is dependent on (a) the number of validity measures interpreted, (b) the psychometric properties of each validity measure, and (c) the association between each measure. This reinforces the idea that adopting a generic rule of "two or more failures" may not generalize (e.g., Bilder et al., 2014) and that false-positive rates are sensitive to the specific combination of PVTs interpreted (e.g., Bashem et al., 2014). More important, the inverse could also be argued; if one were asked to perform a series of simple, independent tasks (e.g., count to three, clap your hands), it seems improbable that an increase in the number of those tasks would increase the possibility of a false positive. More research in this area is certainly warranted.

Interpretation of cognitive and symptom report data in light of validity data. Once a combination of validity measures has been selected, and a criterion for invalidity has been established, the clinician is next faced with the decision of how to interpret the remaining data. In cases of normal SVT and PVT performance, it can minimally be assumed that the obtained cognitive profile is valid and that symptom inventories reflect an approximation of psychiatric functioning. Making assumptions about effort on cognitive testing, however, may be tenuous. Even knowing that the person put forth sufficient effort to perform normally on validity measures, one should not infer that the person performed his or her best. Such profiles can create quite the interpretive quandary when the remaining cognitive data are inconsistent with additional sources of information (e.g., multiple scores in the severely impaired range for someone who continues to work) or the nature of the injury (e.g., severe memory impairment after isolated concussion). Such discrepancies may satisfy Criteria B from the Slick et al. (1999) guidelines in which subjective judgments evaluating performance and patterns of performance are evaluated. Thus, even in the absence of PVT failures, the person's presentation may still be consistent with possible or probable malingering classifications, as discussed previously.

When some or all validity measures are failed, interpretation can be similarly complicated, and decisions about how to proceed will depend on the case's individual circumstances. Assuming that testing was completed, generating a profile of cognitive data despite failed validity measures, it is certainly possible to interpret the remaining data as a valid reflection of actual ability, despite clear indication of underperformance. Although false-positive findings can and do occur, this approach will most certainly be met with strong criticism and require the clinician to be prepared with a very strong defense as to why validity indicators were ignored. Given that none of the commonly used SVMs or PVMs to date have reliably been able to establish cutoff scores associated with clinically acceptable sensitivity and perfect specificity, false positives are expected. Most validity measures are created in attempts to aim for specificity of at least 0.90 and sensitivity of at least 0.50. The onus of responsibility is therefore on the clinician to present convincing evidence supporting the notion that the obtained PVT findings are wrong. Much more research systematically evaluating the nuances of false-positive findings from an empirical standpoint is needed; however, a substantial amount of data available to date have provided strong support for the rarity of false-positives.

In most circumstances, it is very difficult to generate a convincing argument that validity measure findings are inaccurate, forcing the clinician to decide how to proceed. When there is a convincing pattern of symptom exaggeration and performance validity failures, perhaps the most conservative approach is to generalize across the entire obtained cognitive and symptom profile, deeming it invalid and thus uninterpretable. In a high-stakes context such as a forensic setting, this is certainly reasonable and, depending on the extent of validity measure failure, may be most appropriate. The assumption is that if performance on validity measures is convincingly below cutoffs, there is enough doubt about performance on the remainder of the obtained profile to question the rest of the findings. One counterargument is that this approach relies heavily on generalizations of performance on only a few tests across a much larger set of measures.

Alternatively, it may be appropriate to interpret obtained cognitive findings as reflecting a minimum level of functioning. For example, scores falling within normative expectation despite multiple failed validity measures are a clear indication that the individual is minimally capable of performing at a level consistent with peers. Unless an individual has considerable familiarity with the tests (i.e., was coached or had prior exposure), it would be very difficult to "fake good" and obtain scores that overestimate ability. However, there is certainly the potential to underestimate ability, which may be the case when validity measures are sufficiently failed.

When an examinee generates an equivocal profile of performance and validity findings (e.g., one of six validity measures is below criterion, or one PVT and one SVT are below criterion), interpretation can be much less straightforward, particularly when the indicator falling below criterion is an embedded measure. As has been reiterated repeatedly throughout this chapter, remaining cognizant of the contextual factors surrounding testing is critical. In situations in which the penalty for false-positive errors is high (e.g., denial of medical benefits for legitimate injury), it may be appropriate to view the validity profile from the perspective that the majority of measures were passed, comment on the anomaly, but ultimately proceed with interpretation. Alternatively, it may be more prudent to adopt a conservative approach and interpret the cognitive profile as an underestimate of functioning. Given recent research suggesting that even a single failed validity measure may be associated with significantly lower scores on cognitive measures (Proto et al., 2014), this approach could be supported. In the case of a single failed embedded validity measure, being mindful of plausible alternative reasons to account for the abnormal performance is especially critical (e.g., is RDS performance low because of bona fide cognitive impairment?).

Alternative explanations for validity measure failure. As clearly stated by Slick et al. (1999), "To conclude that a person is malingering, one must rule out the alternatives" (p. 558). Although poor effort is probably the most common reason an individual would fail a validity measure, it is important to consider alternative reasons that may provide insight into an individual's performance. It is worth reiterating that only significantly below-chance performance is capable of providing an indication of intent, and to ascribe below-cutoff but above-chance scores to intentional misrepresentation reaches beyond the capability of any currently available validity measure.

As with many diagnostic criteria, Criteria D from Slick et al. (1999) stipulates, "Behaviors meeting necessary criteria from groups B or C are not fully accounted for by Psychiatric, Neurological, or Developmental Factors" (p. 554). This is an essential point of consideration when making determinations about validity profiles. In cases in which there is reasonable suspicion of dementia, for example, the risk of false-positive findings is increased (Burton, Enright, O'Connell, Lanting, & Morgan, 2015; Dean, Victor, Boone, Philpott, & Hess, 2009). For this reason, some measures have developed a paradigm of within-test pattern performance intended to parse out those with genuine cognitive impairment (Eichstaedt et al., 2014; Green, Montijo, & Brockhaus, 2011; M. Henry, Merten, Wolf, & Harth, 2010). There is also evidence to suggest that medication side effects have the potential to influence performance on validity measures leading to increased false-positive errors. In a placebo-controlled, double-blind, randomized crossover design, Loring et al. (2011) found significant detrimental effects of acute benzodiazepine use on two of three clinical criteria for the WMT. Validity measures, especially embedded measures, are also subject to cultural and linguistic influences. For example, RDS has shown lower specificity among those who speak English as a second language across a number of cutoffs (Schroeder, Twumasi-Ankrah, Baade, & Marshall, 2012). Although it has been suggested that some of the available validity measures can be effectively implemented with non–English speakers, doing so may require manipulating the criterion for failure in some populations, which remains poorly studied. Caution is certainly warranted when implementing PVMs and SVMs in non–English-speaking populations and those for whom English is a second language.

Several nonneurological factors, including expectations, diagnosis threat, psychiatric disorders, and low IQ have been suggested as alternative factors to consider as contributing to performance validity failures for some test takers (Larrabee & Rohling, 2013; Silver, 2012). For example, the very nature of a litigating context is inherently adversarial, and a number of studies, including meta-analytic reviews, have suggested that involvement in litigation can be associated with worse outcomes, particularly among individuals with a history of mTBI (Binder & Rohling, 1996; Carroll et al., 2004; Tsanadis et al., 2008). Being examined in a high-stakes environment in which reports of cognitive difficulties and emotional symptoms are questioned, scrutinized, and challenged may introduce stress and a threat sufficient to interfere with performance on cognitive testing, including validity testing (Inzlicht, 2011; Suhr & Gunstad, 2002, 2005). Although the effects of these factors likely vary among individuals and none may universally lead to poor performance on validity measures, mindfulness about alternative explanations is critical to avoid treating validity measures as a hammer capable only of pounding nails.

Ethical Considerations

As with all psychological measures, ethical and legal considerations are important factors in guiding behavior and practice with regard to validity assessment. Issues of test security, interpretation and explanation of assessment results, and release of test data are among the most salient, in addition to remaining cognizant of the legal rights of test publishers (e.g., copyright laws). Maintenance of test security is extremely important because any significant breach has the potential to undermine the clinical utility of that measure. Given that many individuals examined in a forensic setting have a high likelihood of being examined more than once in a short period of time, any knowledge gained about validity testing can be used to circumvent future detection.

Standard 9.11 (Maintaining Test Security) of the American Psychological Association's (2017) *Ethical Principles of Psychologists and Code of Conduct* states, "Psychologists make reasonable efforts to maintain the integrity and security of test materials and other assessment techniques consistent with law and contractual obligations, and in a manner that permits adherence to this Ethics Code" (p. 11). Being mindful of test security during administration, when writing reports and providing depositions, and in courtroom testimony is incredibly important. During testing, exposure to test stimuli is obviously unavoidable; however, maintenance of good assessment practices includes keeping materials hidden when not in use, limiting exposure to record forms during testing, and refraining from revealing the names of tests to examinees.

Clinicians who enlist the assistance of a psychometrician are responsible for ensuring that they too are equally informed and sensitive to test security. Including the names of both stand-alone and embedded validity indicators in written reports may be good clinical practice (Heilbronner et al., 2009), though doing so may provide sufficient information to test takers and attorneys to facilitate coaching. A preference may be to indicate generically that formal validity measures were administered without referring to them by name. Adopting a conservative approach (e.g., providing only enough detail to allow another neuropsychologist to infer the specific measure) may be best when writing reports. Nevertheless, in deposition and court testimony, it is likely that tests will be explicitly referred to by name. Providing feedback directly to referral sources should be guided by similar principles. Ultimately, the level of detail to include in written work products, deposition and testimony, and verbal feedback to attorneys is left to the discretion of the clinician, but maintenance of test security should serve as a guiding principle.

Interpreting and explaining test results should similarly be guided by codes of ethical conduct, which also present unique challenges for validity testing. Standard 9.06 of the *Ethical Principles* states,

> When interpreting assessment results, including automated interpretations, psychologists take into account the purpose of the assessment as well as the various test factors, test-taking abilities and other characteristics of the person being assessed, such as situational, personal, linguistic and cultural differences, that might affect psychologists' judgments or reduce the accuracy of their interpretations. They indicate any significant limitations of their interpretations. (APA, 2017, p. 13)

Of particular relevance in this standard is accounting for individual difference factors (e.g., personal, linguistic, and cultural differences) that may influence interpretation. At present, the validity literature is lacking robust scientific exploration of how these factors may influence performance on validity measures. The effects of demographic factors on standard cognitive measures are well studied at this point, and a sizable literature exists on how individual differences such as language, culture, ethnicity, and education can influence test performance. For many cognitive tests, use of appropriate, demographically specific normative references effectively accounts for these differences, but the same cannot be said for validity testing. Thus, when working with individuals from populations different from those reported in the empirical studies, caution is warranted when interpreting validity results, and any limitations should be appropriately acknowledged.

QUALITATIVE INFORMATION

Behavioral Observations

Early evaluations of effort and motivation made significant use of examinees' behavioral presentation and atypical responses. From these behavioral data points, more formalized testing eventually developed. Despite the proliferation of various tests and methods of examining validity from a quantitative perspective, however, it is important that the value of behavioral observations are not forgotten. Qualitative data can be incredibly useful in identifying uncommon response styles and behavioral shenanigans that examinees may engage in, which may raise concerns about the accuracy and credibility of data obtained from a neuropsychological evaluation.

Neuropsychologists who regularly work in forensics have borne witness to many instances of blatantly feigned behavior. In one of few studies examining the qualitative presentation of feigned cognitive impairment, Iverson (1995) found that the most common presentation was to feign complete amnesia, including for autobiographical information, as well as being uncooperative and slow and acting confused. Some examinees may be more sophisticated than others, going to great lengths to maintain their charade (e.g., atypical speech patterns). Others may be so oblivious that they impeach themselves with their own malarkey without even trying. For example, a practitioner working in a Veterans Affairs hospital was called into an interview by a colleague to provide a second opinion. The patient was asked, "Mr. X, can you please show [the doctor] what you can't do with your arm?" to which the patient responded with "I can't do this, or this, or this," demonstrating complete range of motion in the purportedly affected limb (Glenn Larrabee, personal communication, May 12, 2015). Examples like this highlight the utility of having several brief behavioral exams available at the ready.

Although clinicians may have their own collection of significant qualitative errors and unusual behaviors, some researchers have provided guidelines that may be useful when considering the credibility of some behaviors. It is worth reiterating that neurological changes can lead to some incredibly peculiar presentations, and none should be considered in isolation; however, implausible, bizarre, and inconsistent behaviors should be thoroughly vetted, particularly when there is potential for secondary gain. For example, expressively aphasic responses in individuals who otherwise sustained minimal injury in a concussive event cast doubt on honesty.

One example of a cluster of unusual behavior is Ganser syndrome, which is an intentional production of symptoms used to simulate serious mental illness often characterized by nonsensical, approximate answers to simplistic questions. In many cases, the presentation is considered a factitious disorder, using current nomenclature. The quality of Ganser responses can be incorporated into behavior observed and answers provided during clinical evaluations. A pattern of near-miss answers is a telltale sign of some type of diminished cooperation. Poorly educated individuals can make valid errors on some seemingly easy tasks. Ganser responses are the rarely occurring errors that are not reported in poorly educated individuals, and they raise concern as to the examinee's honesty. For example, when asked how many weeks are in a year, a less educated individual might not know the correct response of 52. However, they may simply estimate that there are 4 weeks in 1 month and 12 months in 1 year and determine that 48 is a reasonable (though incorrect) response. A poor incorrect response would include near-miss answers such as "51 weeks" or "53 weeks."

Other atypical responses, such as "29 weeks," are infrequent even for those who are most cognitively limited and suggest an intentional misrepresentation of true ability. Similarly, if a patient is asked what 5 − 1 equals, a patient can respond "6" if he or she is not careful, but atypical answers such as 17 or 3.75 occur so rarely that they cannot be viewed as anything but intentionally incorrect.

Consistency Across Settings

There is an old adage that when one lies, it is difficult to keep the information straight, and with the myriad health providers and appointments a litigant is likely to be involved with, spanning months to years, it may be harder for the litigant to recall who was told what. However, if one always tells the truth, there is only one thing to remember. Although subtle inconsistencies in symptom reporting across providers are inevitable to some degree, major inconsistencies should raise concern.

With that premise, it is important to evaluate the consistency of patients' subjective reports when reviewing what is recalled, or told, to various clinicians. There is also evidence that suggests that symptom reports can also vary as a function of the measures used (Kondiles, Starr, Larson, & Zollman, 2015). Most professionals will offer an initial assessment that incorporates a history of a specific event, and comparing what is recalled from session to session can be enlightening. According to classification standards published in 1993 by the American Congress of Rehabilitation Medicine for people who sustain a mTBI (i.e., concussive injury), the natural course of amnesia, if present, involves onset soon after the accident, with gradual abatement within a 24-hour period. Therefore, when one reads ambulance and emergency department reports in which the examinee denies a loss of consciousness but 3 months later reports that the first postaccident memory was resting on the couch 2 weeks later, increased suspicion is warranted. Likewise, an individual who reports continuous memory after an incident to some clinicians but claims loss of consciousness to others appears a questionable historian.

Although some degree of variability in symptom reports between providers may be normal, in other cases the presenting complaints and reported symptoms may vary to such a significant degree that, in the absence of any medical explanation, the forensic examiner must question whether attempts at dissimulation were made. For example, if headaches and shoulder pain are reported at some appointments, but low back pain and neck pain are primary symptoms reported at other appointments, one plausible explanation is that the examinee may be intentionally trying to mislead the interviewers. Clinicians must, however, also consider plausible reasons for variable symptom reporting. For example, an orthopedic surgeon's records may have no mention of head trauma or posttraumatic stress because the patient did not think to mention those problems to a doctor being seen for physical injuries unrelated to the brain, and the orthopedic surgeon did not ask about such problems.

Another qualitative method for evaluating inconsistencies speaks to the person seen for evaluation whose behavior differs from self-report. One individual who was being treated at an outpatient facility claimed that her only residual deficiency was related to her inability to accurately count money and change. When surreptitiously observed by one of her treating therapists at a nearby convenience store, the patient was heard to say, "You did not give me the correct change." After she looked up to see the therapist witnessing the exchange, the patient continued by saying, "or maybe you did . . . whatever." Along the same lines, a clinician will sometimes see a patient who claims disorientation, confusion, and poor memory, but despite these concerns, the patient was able to arrive to the appointment on time and unaccompanied. For that reason, asking specifically how an individual remembered the appointment and got to the clinic is important.

SYMPTOM VALIDITY TESTS

Validity testing began with a simple model referencing only the credibility of symptoms generically. Recent literature in validity assessment, however, has distinguished between PVTs and SVTs (Larrabee, 2012), with SVTs referring to methods of evaluating the veracity or accuracy of symptoms endorsed on self-report measures. This section focuses specifically on SVTs and is organized by embedded and free-standing measures, with the section on embedded measures further divided into sections discussing comprehensive personality inventories (e.g., the Minnesota Multiphasic Personality Inventory—2—Restructured Form [MMPI–2–RF]; Ben-Porath & Tellegen, 2008) and brief, disorder- or syndrome-focused instruments.

Embedded Symptom Validity Tests

Embedded SVTs are scales or combinations of items that have been developed and studied as a means of establishing whether self-report data provided by an examinee are interpretable. One of the simplest strategies involves tallying the number of nonscorable items (i.e., omitted, multiple, or illegible responses). Test manuals often provide a cutoff for the maximum number of nonscorable items that can be obtained and still allow meaningful interpretation of the results. Additional strategies involve the use of specific scales to identify response styles that might affect or limit the interpretability of the profile. Common response styles identified by such scales include inattention or disregard for item content (i.e., random responding), symptom underreporting, and symptom overreporting.

Comprehensive Personality Inventories

Use of comprehensive personality inventories is common practice in forensic neuropsychological settings (Sharland & Gfeller, 2007). They provide information on psychopathology and personality traits that can be used to contextualize obtained cognitive data. In addition, information from personality inventories is useful in identifying the presence of psychiatric conditions or personality traits that can be an important component of the differential diagnosis (Boone & Lu, 1999). Most multiscale inventories also contain embedded indices of symptom validity. Several of the most commonly used inventories are briefly reviewed here, with specific attention to validity scales contained within the measures that are used to establish the validity and interpretability of the obtained profile.

Millon Clinical Multiaxial Inventory. The Millon Clinical Multiaxial Inventory (MCMI; Millon, Millon, Davis, & Grossman, 2006), currently in its third edition (MCMI–III), is a 175-item self-report measure based on Millon's personality theory that has scales developed to identify psychopathology and clinically relevant personality styles. The MCMI–III norm-referenced scores are reported as base rates (BR) rather than other commonly used metrics (e.g., *T* scores). Scales relevant to data validity include two indicators of random responding—Invalidity (Scale V) and Inconsistency (Scale W)—and three scales, termed *modifying indices,* to detect potentially invalidating response styles. Modifying indices include Disclosure (X), intended to measure open responding; Desirability (Y), intended to measure defensive responding; and Debasement (Z), intended to measure overpathologizing responses. Interpretive guidelines include cutoffs indicating protocol invalidity for the modifying indices in isolation: X raw scores less than 34 or more than 178; Y BR more than 74; and Z BR more than 85. In addition, patterns across the modifying indices are associated with symptom underreporting (low scores on X and Z; high score on Y) and overreporting (high scores on X and Z; low score on Y).

Daubert and Metzler (2000) used a simulation design study with psychiatric outpatients to examine cutoffs on individual scales in addition to the profile across modifying indices. In differentiating among participants with standard and fake-bad instructions, the standard cutoffs on X (BR ≥ 85), Y (BR ≤ 35), and Z (BR ≥ 85) demonstrated adequate sensitivity (X = .61, Y = .58, and Z = .55) but low specificity (X = .81, Y = .76, and Z = .79). Optimal cutoffs improved overall classification accuracy, but specificity remained low (X = .71, Y = .74, and Z = .78).

Schoenberg, Dorr, and Morgan (2003) differentiated psychiatric inpatients from student simulators randomized to fake-bad or standard instruction groups on the basis of MCMI–III modifying indices. Significant group differences were observed on all three modifying indices. Receiver operating characteristic analyses, however, did not appear promising. The published cutoff performed very poorly, and optimal cutoffs demonstrated low specificity: X BR more than 89 (sensitivity = .35; specificity = .88); Y BR less than 21 (sensitivity = .33; specificity = .85);

and Z BR more than 82 (sensitivity = .59; specificity = .66). In a follow-up study, Schoenberg, Dorr, and Morgan (2006) reported improved classification accuracy for two discriminant functions based on combinations of modifying indices and clinical scales. The first function included modifying index X and clinical scales 8A (Negativisitic), C (Borderline), P (Paranoid), SS (Thought Disorder), and PP (Delusional Disorder). In a validation sample subset, the first function identified 45% of simulators instructed to fake-bad while maintaining an acceptable false-positive rate (specificity = .90). The second function included modifying indices X and Y and clinical scales PP (Delusional Disorder) and 7 (Compulsive). In a validation sample subset, the second function identified 71% of fake-bad simulators, but the false-positive rate was elevated (specificity = .83).

Ruocco, Swirsky-Sacchetti, and Choca (2007) compared MCMI–III profiles of psychiatric patients with a demographically matched group of individuals reporting a history of TBI. The TBI group mainly involved cases of mTBI (84%), and the majority of participants were evaluated in the context of disability claims or litigation (92%). Significant differences were observed on X and Y modifying indices, with TBI patients scoring higher on X and lower on Y than psychiatric patients. The groups were not significantly different on Z, but a trend toward higher scores was observed in the TBI group. Data on the number of protocols involving invalidating response styles or evidence of impression management were not reported.

A number of criticisms of the MCMI–III validity scales have been offered. Berry and Schipper (2007) noted that the scale intended to capture random responding (Scale V) may be prone to false-negative errors given that it contains only three items interspersed throughout the scale. They also raised concern that the recommended cutoffs on modifying indices X, Y, and Z were based on infrequently observed scores in normative samples without a consideration of independent response-style criteria. An additional concern raised by Berry and Schipper and other authors (e.g., Groth-Marnat, 2003) is a lag between new versions of the instrument and the empirical basis for interpreting the scales. Thus, the evidence base necessary to support admissibility in forensic proceedings might be lacking. After reviewing the MCMI literature, Sellbom and Bagby (2008) concluded that extreme scores might identify an invalid protocol but asserted that "under no circumstances should practitioners use this measure in forensic evaluations to determine response styles" (p. 205).

Minnesota Multiphasic Personality Inventory—2—Restructured Form. The MMPI family of instruments has long been one of the most commonly used group of personality and psychopathology inventories (Camara, Nathan, & Puente, 2000; Lees-Haley, Smith, Williams, & Dunn, 1996; Rabin, Barr, & Burton, 2005), and it also ranks high among commonly used measures of symptom validity (Sharland & Gfeller, 2007). The importance of scales to determine the validity of the obtained profile was recognized early in the history of the instrument (Graham, 2000; McKinley, Hathaway, & Meehl, 1948), and independent research led to the development of additional scales that were initially not part of the standard scoring protocols (Lees-Haley, English, & Glenn, 1991). The combination of early consideration of methods to establish the validity of the profile, the growth of independent research on the measure, and the number of validity approaches used make the MMPI a prototypical example of an embedded SVT. Versions of the MMPI in current use with adults include the second edition (MMPI–2; Butcher, Dahlstrom, Graham, Tellegen, & Kaemmer, 1989) and the restructured form (MMPI–2–RF; Ben-Porath & Tellegen, 2008). Given the focus and limitations of the current review, only the MMPI–2–RF is discussed here.

Per the test manual, MMPI–2–RF protocol validity can be classified into three areas: content nonresponsiveness, underreporting, and overreporting. *Content nonresponsiveness* refers to inferences regarding the examinee's understanding of test items and patterns of response including either excessive variability or invariability. Three scales contributing to a determination regarding content nonresponsiveness include the Cannot Say (CNS), Variable Response Inconsistency (VRIN-r), and True Response Inconsistency (TRIN-r) scales. The CNS scale is the sum of nonscorable responses that can represent omissions or double-endorsed items (i.e., marked both true and false). The manual provides cutoffs for CNS and indicates that scales are not interpretable if more than 10% of the items are unscorable. An elevated CNS score thus precludes interpretation of the lack of an elevation on the affected scales. The VRIN-r scale is determined from 53 pairs of items with similar content. An inconsistent response to one of the pairs of items raises the VRIN-r raw score by 1 point, and a VRIN-r *T* score of 80 or higher indicates protocol invalidity due to excessive response variability. Possible explanations for invalidating VRIN-r elevations provided by the test manual include poor understanding of item content (e.g., reduced reading comprehension) or an intentional approach to the test (e.g., being uncooperative).

The TRIN-r scale is determined from 26 pairs of items that are worded so that consistent responding will result in opposite responses (i.e., true–false or false–true). The TRIN-r raw score is calculated to represent a tendency toward acquiescent (true) or nonacquiescent (false) responding that is inconsistent with item content. TRIN-r scores are accompanied by an indication of the direction of fixed responding, and a TRIN-r *T* score of 80 or more in either direction (i.e., true or false) is indicative of an invalid protocol due to fixed responding. According to the manual, the probable interpretation of an invalidating TRIN-r elevation is an uncooperative response to the test (Ben-Porath & Tellegen, 2008).

Symptom underreporting scales on the MMPI–2–RF include the Uncommon Virtues (L-r) and Adjustment Validity (K-r) scales. The Uncommon Virtues scale is based on 14 items with content about minor foibles that many people are quick to acknowledge. Elevations on L-r indicate a response style associated with favorable self-presentation. Interpretive guidelines recommend consideration of possible underreporting for L-r *T* scores in the 70 to 79 range. Scores falling above this range increase concern for the possibility of protocol invalidity. When L-r is significantly elevated, clinical scales falling in the normal range may not necessarily indicate the absence of psychopathology.

The Adjustment Validity scale involves 14 items with content related to adjustment. Higher scores indicate self-presentation as being well adjusted, which requires corroboration from additional data sources. Interpretive guidelines recommend consideration of possible underreporting for K-r T scores in the 66 to 69 range. *T* scores of 70 or higher indicate underreporting due to self-presentation as exceptionally well adjusted. Elevations on K-r may also preclude interpretation of normal-range clinical scales as evidence of no psychopathology.

MMPI–2–RF scales that are useful in identification of symptom overreporting include the Infrequent Responses (F-r), Infrequent Psychopathology Responses (Fp-r), Infrequent Somatic Responses (Fs), Symptom Validity (FBS-r), Response Bias (RBS), and the Henry–Heilbronner Index (HHI-r) scales. The F-r scale is based on 32 items that were infrequently endorsed in the normative sample, and elevations are associated with possible overreporting of psychological difficulty covering a wide assortment of symptoms. A caveat with F-r is that individuals in considerable emotional distress or with substantial psychopathology can produce valid elevations on F-r. The manual recommends an F-r cutoff of 120 or higher for protocol invalidity and consideration of additional clinical and historical data for determining whether elevations below the threshold for invalidity represent overreporting versus significant distress or psychopathology. The Fp-r scale includes 21 items that were rarely endorsed by respondents with established diagnoses of severe psychopathology. Fp-r scores of 100 or higher indicate an invalid protocol. The manual recommends consideration of F-r and Fp-r scores together: Concurrent F-r and Fp-r elevations indicate greater probability of overreporting; F-r elevation in the context of nonelevated Fp-r indicates greater probability of significant emotional distress or psychopathology.

The Fs scale is derived from 16 items that were infrequently endorsed by patients under treatment for medical conditions. Fs *T* scores of 100 or higher indicate possible invalidity of scores on somatic complaints scales as a result of symptom overreporting. FBS-r (Ben-Porath & Tellegen, 2008) is also sensitive to symptom overreporting and includes 30 items that are associated with noncredible complaints. The scale represents a portion of items from a 45-item scale initially derived from MMPI–2 items referred to as the Fake Bad Scale (FBS; Lees-Haley et al., 1991) and was developed to identify noncredible symptom reporting in personal injury litigants and disability claimants and has been the subject of numerous empirical studies to date (Greiffenstein, Fox, & Lees-Haley, 2007). The MMPI–2–RF manual recommends interpretation of FBS-r T scores in the 80–99 range as evidence of possible over-reporting of somatic symptoms and/or cognitive difficulty and FBS-r T scores of 100 or higher as an indication of invalidity on Somatic Scales.

The RBS was also initially developed for the MMPI–2 (Gervais, Ben-Porath, Wygant, & Green, 2007) and was based on items that differentiated disability claimants grouped by PVMs. All 28 items from the original scale have been retained in the MMPI–2–RF. The MMPI–2–RF manual recommends interpretation of RBS *T* scores in the 80 to 99 range as evidence of possible overreporting of memory difficulty and RBS *T* scores of 100 or higher as evidence that the Cognitive Complaints scale may be invalid.

The Henry–Heilbronner Index (G. K. Henry, Heilbronner, Mittenberg, & Enders, 2006) was developed for the MMPI–2 from items originally included in FBS and a Pseudoneurologic Scale that had been developed for the MMPI (Shaw & Matthews, 1965). G. K. Henry et al. (2006) empirically selected 15 of the items from the original scales that were identified as showing the greatest discrimination between head injury litigants identified as probable malingerers on the basis of PVT findings and a nonlitigating clinical group with a history of TBI. G. K. Henry, Heilbronner, Algina, and Kaya (2013) subsequently reported preliminary findings on the HHI-r, which includes 11 items retained in the MMPI–2–RF, in the same sample used to derive the original scale.

Personality Assessment Inventory. The Personality Assessment Inventory (PAI; Morey, 1991) is a 344-item measure that includes eight scales developed to assess validity of the results. Four of the scales were initially included in an earlier version of the measure, and four scales added later are included in interpretive reports from the current version of the test. Similar to the validity scales for other measures, the PAI validity scales identify content nonresponsive responding (Inconsistency and Infrequency), denial or underreporting of symptoms (Positive Impression Management, Defensiveness Index, and Cashel Discriminant Function), and symptom overreporting (Negative Impression Management [NIM], Malingering Index, and Rogers Discriminant Function).

The Inconsistency scale is based on 10 pairs of items with similar content developed to assess random responses. The Infrequency scale is based on eight items that were infrequently endorsed by normative samples and is intended to capture inappropriate responses due to inattention, randomness, or reading difficulty. *T* scores of 73 or higher on the Inconsistency scale indicate an invalid profile, and *T* scores of 75 or higher on the Infrequency scale are indicative of an invalid profile.

The NIM scale is derived from nine items that were endorsed by individuals who were instructed to complete the measure with "fake-bad" instructions and is designed to capture symptom overreporting. The Positive Impression Management scale was similarly developed and is based on nine items that were endorsed by individuals who were instructed to complete the measure with "fake-good" instructions. *T* scores of 91 or higher on the NIM scale indicate an invalid protocol, and *T* scores of 68 or higher on the Positive Impression Management indicate an invalid profile.

Several composite indexes have also been developed with the intention of detecting symptom invalidity. The Defensiveness Index is determined on the basis of scores on 12 other clinical scales and subscales. These scores are combined to assess the presence of eight attributes associated with defensiveness. The Defensiveness Index is thought to possibly capture more sophisticated denial of difficulties, but it may also show an association with psychological status. The Cashel Discriminant Function scale, developed by Cashel, Rogers, Sewell, and Martin-Cannici (1995) is a discriminant function that distinguishes PAI profiles obtained from standard instructions and coached instructions that included discussion of standard validity indices on the measure. Variables included in the

Cashel Discriminant Function scale were from the following PAI scales: Borderline Features, Positive Impression Management, Mania, Treatment Rejection, Alcohol Problems, and Stress. It is thought to reflect defensiveness with less association with actual psychopathology than the Defensiveness Index. The Malingering Index is also derived from scores on other PAI scales (i.e., NIM and 11 clinical scales and subscales) that were empirically found to differentiate simulators from clinical respondents who completed the measure with standard instructions. Rogers, Sewel, Morey, and Ulstad (1996) developed the Rogers Discriminant Function scale from PAI scales and subscales that differentiated simulators feigning disorders from genuine respondents. Several of these independently developed measures have been incorporated into the standard PAI score report (e.g., Malingering Index and Rogers Discriminant Function scale) and are described in detail in the manual and reference texts (Morey, 1991, 1996, 2003).

Disorder- and Symptom-Specific Scales

The previously reviewed embedded SVMs are derived from larger inventories of personality functioning and psychological functioning without specificity to a particular syndrome. Those inventories can be incredibly informative tools, though they may be too lengthy and impractical for use with some patients. In many circumstances, administering scales that are specific to particular disorders may also be of interest. The need to evaluate the credibility of responses is no different for these measures. Although not an exhaustive list, several examples are described here.

Mild Brain Injury Atypical Symptoms Scale. The Mild Brain Injury Atypical Symptoms Scale (mBIAS; Cooper, Nelson, Armistead-Jehle, & Bowles, 2011) is a five-item scale of symptom overreporting that was designed to be embedded in postconcussive and PTSD symptom checklists. The authors developed items that would reflect highly unusual symptoms and placed them within the items of the Neurobehavioral Symptom Inventory (Cicerone & Kalmar, 1995) and the Posttraumatic Stress Disorder Checklist—Military (PCL-M; Blanchard, Jones-Alexander, Buckley, & Forneris, 1996) in a computer-administered format. The combined measures were administered to a sample of active-duty service members ($N = 403$) categorized according to medical history. Cooper et al. (2011) reported factor-analytic results that supported an overreporting factor on which the mBIAS items loaded. With overreporting criteria defined as total scores on the Neurobehavioral Symptom Inventory (NSI; Cicerone & Kalmar, 1995) and PCL–M more than 1.5 standard deviations above normative mean, an mBIAS cutoff of 8 or more demonstrated a sensitivity of .94 and a specificity of .92. Lange, Edmed, Sullivan, French, and Cooper (2013) examined the mBIAS in a simulation design using undergraduates and the civilian version of the PCL. Using an mBIAS cutoff of 8 or more was associated with sensitivity of .34 and perfect specificity. Lowering the cutoff to 6 or more demonstrated improved sensitivity of .72 with a specificity of .88. These preliminary findings provide promising support for practitioners who routinely use the PCL and NSI and wish to incorporate an embedded measure of symptom overreporting. Additional research is necessary to validate the use of the measure in other populations using a known-groups design.

Modified Somatic Perception Questionnaire. The Modified Somatic Perception Questionnaire (MSPQ; Main, 1983) is a 13-item self-report measure developed for use with chronic pain patients involving four-point ratings of symptoms. Larrabee (2003b) reported MSPQ findings in a sample ($N = 29$) of litigants who met criteria for probable or definite malingered neurocognitive dysfunction. In comparison with other pain questionnaires, the MSPQ showed the largest effect size between the total scores of litigants and clinical data from chronic pain patients ($d = 2.92$). An MSPQ cutoff (>10) showed excellent sensitivity (.90) and specificity (.90) in discriminating participants from published data for chronic pain patients. Although the study sample size was small, these findings provided very strong initial support for use of the MSPQ in identifying symptom embellishment among individuals reporting chronic pain.

Bianchini et al. (2014) studied the MSPQ in a retrospective sample of pain patients grouped according to criteria for malingered pain-related disability (Bianchini, Greve, & Glynn, 2005). The MSPQ was used to differentiate patients with and without incentive (n = 74) from patients identified as showing probable and definite malingered pain-related disability (n = 105). The previously identified MSPQ cutoff (>10) showed a high false-positive rate (32%), but higher cutoffs showed improved specificity: MSPQ score more than 15 (sensitivity = .55; specificity = .89) and MSPQ score more than 17 (sensitivity = .39; specificity = .95). The authors provided interpretative guidelines for MSPQ scores: A MSPQ score of less than 10 indicates minimal psychosocial complications; a MSPQ score from 10 to 16, malingering or somatoform presentation possible but not reliably differentiated; and a MSPQ score of 17 or more, malingering likely.

Neurobehavioral Symptom Inventory. The NSI (Cicerone & Kalmar, 1995) is a 22-item self-report measure of postconcussive items. It has been studied fairly extensively among veterans (Benge, Pastorek, & Thornton, 2009; Soble et al., 2014) after being included in the measures implemented across Veterans Affairs Medical Centers and clinics. Vanderploeg et al. (2014) reported on the development and cross-validation of embedded validity measures within the NSI. In the derivation study, they described scales based on unusual items (NIM-5), items that were infrequently endorsed (Low-6), and nonoverlapping items from those two measures combined (Validity-10). Derivation study participants included active-duty service members presenting for workup for possible TBI and rehabilitation patients (n = 443), personnel from the Florida National Guard who completed an online postdeployment survey (n = 3,127), and national data from the Veterans Affairs TBI evaluation process (n = 48,175). Optimal cutoffs were identified for the three embedded scales, as well as the total NSI score. These various methods generated the following classifications: NIM-5 score, more than 12 (sensitivity = .74; specificity = .93); Low-6 score, more than 13 (sensitivity = .66; specificity = .91); Validity-10, more than 22 (sensitivity = .81; specificity = .94); and NSI total score, more than 58 (sensitivity = .79; specificity = .93).

In the cross-validation study, participants were active-duty service members (N = 206) presenting for outpatient neuropsychological evaluation subsequent to reported TBI (69% mild), and the external criterion measure was the NIM scale on the PAI (T > 75). The classification accuracy of the previously identified cutoffs as reported in the validation sample were marginally lower, with specificity above .80 and sensitivity above .48: NIM-5 score, more than 12 (sensitivity = .48; specificity = .82); Low-6 score, more than 13 (sensitivity = .62; specificity = .83); Validity-10 score, more than 22 (sensitivity = .61; specificity = .85); and NSI total score, more than 58 (sensitivity = .59; specificity = .84). Although promising, subsequent research on these scales was not identified.

Postconcussive Symptom Questionnaire. The Postconcussive Symptom Questionnaire (PCSQ; Lees-Haley, 1992) was developed as a 44-item symptom checklist with dichotomous scoring. Confirmatory factor and internal consistency analyses of a 44-item version of the measure were reported to support a four-factor model capturing psychological, cognitive, somatic, and infrequently endorsed symptoms (Axelrod et al., 1996). Subsequent research supported the factor structure and implemented a 5-point rating scale rather than dichotomous scoring (Axelrod, Fox, Lees-Haley, Earnest, & Dolezal-Wood, 1998). Axelrod and Lees-Haley (2002) later found higher PCSQ total scores to be associated with elevations on overreporting scales on the MMPI–2. Additional analyses revealed a relationship between PCSQ factors and MMPI–2 scales, including correspondences between the psychological factor and MMPI–2 items reflecting dysphoria and unhappiness and between the somatic factor and MMPI–2 items related to health concerns and physical symptoms. Tsanadis et al. (2008) examined the PCSQ in a sample with a reported history of TBI. Compared with individuals in litigation with a history of moderate to severe TBI, participants in litigation with reported questionable performance validity produced significantly higher elevations on three of the four factors with medium to large effect sizes observed on psychological (d = 0.84), cognitive (d = .69), and somatic factors (d = .83).

Two shorter versions of the PCSQ have been developed on the basis of Rasch analysis, including the Postconcussive Symptom Questionnaire 19-item short form (PCSQ–19; Millis, Hanks, Fichtenberg, & Axelrod, 2007), and on receiver operating characteristic curve analysis to identify items discriminating individuals with questionable performance validity (i.e., PCSQ Negative Impression Management [PCSQ–NIM]; Tsanadis et al., 2007). Van Dyke, Axelrod, and Schutte (2010) compared the PCSQ, PCSQ–19, and PCSQ–NIM in a sample of veterans (N = 112) with neurologic and psychiatric complaints. Participants were grouped on the basis of overreporting identified by elevations on the MMPI–2's RBS and FBS scales. Receiver operating characteristic analyses revealed "excellent" (Hosmer & Lemeshow, 2000) overall classification accuracy based on area under the curve (AUC) values for all three PCSQ versions, with a slight advantage for the PCSQ–19 (AUC = .86) over the PCSQ (AUC = .85) and PCSQ–NIM (AUC = .84). Optimal cutoffs were reported: PCSQ score of more than 27 (sensitivity = .36; specificity =.94), PCSQ–19 score of more than 15 (sensitivity = .36; specificity = .91), and PCSQ–NIM score of more than 16 (sensitivity = .28; specificity = .91).

Freestanding Symptom Validity Tests

Although the embedded and specific symptoms scales mentioned above provide information in the context of a parent scale or inventory designed primarily to assess psychopathology, symptom endorsement, or personality traits, freestanding SVTs serve only to identify invalid or noncredible response styles. A benefit of freestanding measures is that they can be developed to target noncredible symptoms with less concern for overlapping items (i.e., items that might represent valid symptom reporting at one level of endorsement and symptom overreporting at another, higher level). Limitations of freestanding measures include additional time for test administration and the possibility of greater susceptibility to coaching.

Memory Complaints Inventory. The Memory Complaints Inventory (MCI; Green, 2004) is a computer-administered measure of subjective memory complaints. Examinees respond to 58 questions grouped into nine scales: General Memory Problems, Numeric Information Problems, Visuospatial Memory Problems, Verbal Memory Problems, Pain Interferes With Memory, Memory Interferes With Work, Impairment of Remote Memory, Amnesia for Complex Behavior, and Amnesia for Antisocial Behavior. The first six scales identify memory complaints that can be consistent with memory difficulty that has a neurological basis; the last three scales identify nonneurological memory complaints that may be psychogenic or the result of symptom magnification. Comparison group data are provided for a range of diagnoses and presentations based on the clinical datasets of the author and colleagues.

Rohling, Green, Allen, and Iverson (2002) explored associations among depressive symptoms, subjective cognitive complaints, and objective cognitive performance in a sample of individuals who passed validity measures and were grouped according to high and low endorsement of depressive symptoms. Significant differences were observed across all MCI subtests and total scores between high and low depression groups with large effect sizes (g = 0.82–1.34). In contrast, cognitive measures of attention, memory, and executive function did not show significant differences across high and low depression groups. These findings demonstrate that although individuals with more severe depression are likely to have more complaints about cognitive functioning, they perform comparably to individuals with less severe depression on objective cognitive testing.

Gervais, Ben-Porath, Wygant, and Sellbom (2010) examined relationships among MMPI–2–RF validity scales and the MCI in a sample (N = 1,550) of consecutive referrals for evaluation in the context of disability claims not related to head injury. MCI scales showed moderate correlations with many of the MMPI–2–RF's overreporting scales, with RBS showing higher correlations with MCI scales than most other MMPI–2–RF overreporting scales: F-r (rs = .37–.61), Fp-r (rs = .18–.45),

Fs (*rs* = .29–.56), FBS-r (*rs* = .33–.54), and RBS (*rs* = .43–.69). In addition, RBS incrementally added to prediction of MCI scores with other MMPI–2–RF overreporting scales.

Armistead-Jehle, Gervais, and Green (2012b) reported MCI results in large samples of disability claimants with neurological (*n* = 1,597) or non-neurological (*n* = 2,118) presenting conditions grouped by separate freestanding and embedded PVTs. Across several PVTs, a consistent inverse relationship was observed between subjective memory complaints and PVT scores: As PVT scores decreased, MCI scales increased, with the largest elevations observed in groups scoring near or below chance level on forced-choice PVTs. In a follow-up study, Armistead-Jehle, Gervais, and Green (2012a) examined MCI and PVT relationships in a sample of current and former military personnel and their family members without known compensation seeking. Similar to the earlier study, MCI scores increased as PVT scores decreased. A difference from the prior study was observed in that an embedded PVT showed lower correlations with MCI scales than the associations among freestanding PVTs and MCI scales.

Morel Emotional Numbing Test. The Morel Emotional Numbing Test (MENT; Morel, 1998, 2013) is a 60-item forced-choice measure designed to detect feigned PTSD symptoms. The examinee is instructed to match emotional labels (e.g., *happy, sad*) with photographs of faces after being provided with information that affect recognition may be reduced in individuals diagnosed with PTSD. The error rate across all trials is the measure of interest. The development sample included 34 veterans diagnosed with schizophrenia or receiving inpatient substance abuse treatment and 68 veterans seeking compensation for combat-related PTSD grouped into valid responders diagnosed with PTSD, valid responders not diagnosed with PTSD, older valid responders, and veterans with questionable symptom validity determined on the basis of clinical interview data and the MMPI–2 F-K index. The patient groups and valid PTSD claimants showed low mean error rates that ranged from 1.8 (*SD* = 2.0) to 5.5 (*SD* = 3.3) and were not significantly different. In contrast, the group of PTSD claimants with questionable validity demonstrated 17.8 mean errors (*SD* = 8.5). A cutoff of 9 or higher was recommended.

Morel (2008a) examined the MENT in a follow-up study of 37 veterans separated by performance on the WMT (Green, 2003; Green, Allen, & Astner, 1996) into credible (*n* = 15) and questionable validity (*n* = 22) groups. Veterans in the credible group showed significantly lower MENT errors (*M* = 2.0, *SD* = 2.1) than those in the questionable validity group (*M* = 14.5, *SD* = 11.8) with a large effect size (*d* = 1.5). A significant negative correlation was reported between MENT and WMT scores, and receiver operating characteristic analysis of the MENT in differentiating participant groups was reported to show AUC of .86.

Morel and Shepherd (2008) conducted a meta-analytic review on the MENT. They aggregated findings across five published studies on the measure and reported mean error rates for credible (*M* = 4.1; 95% CI [2.7, 5.4]) and questionably valid (*M* = 14.9; 95% CI [10.5, 19.3]) examinees. Pooled values for sensitivity (.79) and specificity (.96) were also reported. The MENT has also been studied in European research (e.g., Geraerts et al., 2009), but changes to test stimuli and instructions necessary for use in other countries may limit comparability with earlier studies (Boone, 2013). Also, there appears to be some variation regarding cutoffs compared with the original study (cf. Zimmermann et al., 2013). Other reviewers noted concerns arising from variability in instructions provided to different groups in the original study (Guriel & Fremouw, 2003). Although the MENT appears promising, additional research on the measure is needed given the limited cross-validation data and concerns related to differences in versions of the measure.

Quick Test for Posttraumatic Stress Disorder. The Quick Test for Posttraumatic Stress Disorder (Q-PTSD; Morel, 2008b) is an eight-item self-report measure involving 5-point rating scales on content thought to be unrelated to actual PTSD symptoms. The initial study involved a simulation design of college student volunteers randomized to control (*n* = 39) or symptom-feigning (*n* = 39) groups.

The simulator group was instructed to feign combat-related PTSD and provided with an informational handout that is freely available online. Feigning participants scored significantly higher on the Q-PTSD (*M* = 24.2, *SD* = 6.5) than control participants (*M* = 8.8, *SD* = 1.6) with a very large effect size (*d* = 3.3). The Q-PTSD demonstrated excellent sensitivity (.99) and adequate specificity (.92), and a cutoff of 17 or higher was recommended. In a follow-up study, veteran compensation claimants for service-connected PSTD were examined using the Q-PTSD with the MENT serving as a criterion validity measure. The Q-PTSD demonstrated a sensitivity of .67 and a specificity of .92 in differentiating veterans classified by the MENT. A strong positive correlation was reported between the Q-PTSD score and MENT errors (*r* = .73). A literature review did not identify subsequent research using the Q-PTSD. Cross-validation research appears to be needed before the measure is used clinically.

Structured Inventory of Malingered Symptomatology. The Structured Inventory of Malingered Symptomatology (Widows & Smith, 2005) is a 75-item true–false instrument developed as a screening instrument for identification of feigned psychopathology and neuropsychological complaints. Its five scales target symptoms or conditions thought to be common targets of feigned symptomatology: Low Intelligence, Affective Disorders, Neurologic Impairment, Psychosis, and Amnesia. A total score cutoff (>14) indicates a need for further assessment of malingering. Initial development and validation studies (Smith & Burger, 1997) were conducted using a simulation design with evidence of adequate scale reliability (.80–.88), factor-analytic results supporting a five-factor model, and promising classification accuracy for the total score (sensitivity = .96, specificity = .88).

The Structured Inventory of Malingered Symptomatology has been widely studied in clinical and forensic groups and in additional simulation studies. A recent meta-analysis of the measure summarized findings from 31 studies (van Impelen, Merckelbach, Jelicic, & Merten, 2014) and noted support for accurate discrimination of feigners and honest responders, resilience to coaching, and concern for elevated false-positive rates in some populations (e.g., schizophrenia, intellectual disability). Across different reviews (Boone, 2013; Smith, 2008), a consistent concern has been the elevated false-positive rate using the original total score cutoff (>14). Boone (2013) recommended a much higher cutoff (≥23) and also noted concern over low specificity in specific clinical conditions including intellectual disability and functional neurological symptoms.

PERFORMANCE VALIDITY TESTS

Stand-Alone Performance Validity Measures

Free-standing measures of validity were initially developed as a way to explicitly detect intentionally deficient performance and functional neurological symptoms (e.g., Grosz & Zimmermann, 1965). It was later understood that by using clinical cases of bona fide neurological injury or patients with diagnoses of dementia, one could compare an examinee's performance with that of these other samples. If an individual with a history of mTBI performed worse than an individual with a severe brain injury or worse than an individual with severe dementia, then that individual's impaired test performance could be considered intentional. Similarly, some new PVMs used older measures to validate the test, demonstrating that the newer PVM was able to detect at the same level as a previously used PVM. The newer tasks may do so in fewer trials, with improved test operating characteristics (e.g., sensitivity, specificity) with a different method, or by addressing the same issue in a different manner.

Forced-choice methods for assessing effort have been well established by using convenient statistical properties, such as potential identification of a statistically below-chance performance. They are also convenient because several already well-developed and commonly used ability measures contain forced-choice tasks, such as new learning and memory (including the CVLT–II [Delis et al., 2000], Rey Auditory Verbal Learning Test [Schmidt, 1996], Rey–Osterrieth Complex Figure [Osterrieth, 1944; Rey, 1941], and Warrington's Recognition Memory Test [Warrington, 1984]), and sensory–perceptual functioning (e.g., Speech Sounds Perception Test,

Seashore Rhythm Test; Reitan & Wolfson, 1993). Although these measures are useful, they are often limited because of their low number of items, such as on the CVLT–II Forced Choice that has 16 items. It is preferable to have at least 25 items and desirable to have 50 because a statistically below-chance performance is difficult to obtain with fewer items (Millis, 2004).

Dot Counting Test. The Dot Counting Test (Boone, Lu, Back, et al., 2002) presents 12 cards with from 6 to 28 dots per card. The examinee is asked to count the number of dots on each card as quickly as possible. Half of the cards show the dots in a random array, and the other half present stimuli in a more organized fashion. Primary measures of interest include the length of time to count grouped and ungrouped numbers, as well as the total number of errors. Early studies found that individuals putting forth adequate effort counted dots presented in a readily apparent organization more quickly than they counted dots presented in a random array. Those demonstrating questionable effort, however, showed smaller discrepancies such that the effects washed out (e.g., Lezak et al., 2004). Boone, Lu, Back, et al. (2002) created a total score including time for completion as well as number of errors identified, which differentiated individuals seeking disability from nonpatient controls with sensitivity of .79 and specificity of .90.

Test of Memory Malingering. The TOMM (Tombaugh, 1996) is one of the earlier freestanding forced-choice tests of validity and has been the subject of a considerable amount of research (e.g., Barhon, Batchelor, Meares, Chekaluk, & Shores, 2015; Perna & Loughan, 2014; Stenclik, Miele, Silk-Eglit, Lynch, & McCaffrey, 2013; Teichner, Wagner, & Newman, 2000; Whitney, Shepard, & Davis, 2013). It consists of two learning trials and an optional retention trial. Initially, it was determined that Trial 2 and Retention scores of 45 or better (90% correct) were indicative of adequate effort (Rees, Tombaugh, Gansler, & Moczynski, 1998), which is consistent with guidelines reported in the test manual. When using these cutoff scores in samples of patients with brain injury versus those otherwise found to be demonstrating invalid performance, the TOMM generated sensitivity of .64 and specificity of .93 (Haber & Fichtenberg, 2006).

Several alternative scoring paradigms have been created since the TOMM's publication. For example, scores used to detect poor effort in Trial 1 (80% correct or lower) have been effective at distinguishing intact from impaired validity with sensitivity of .77 and specificity of .92 (Denning, 2012). Denning (2012) also introduced an additional method of detecting invalidity on the TOMM by examining the number of consecutively correct items within the first 10 responses on Trial 1 (TOMMe10). His preliminary study in which any error within the first 10 items was considered invalid performance resulted in sensitivity of .71 and a specificity of .93 (Denning, 2012). Kulas, Axelrod, and Rinaldi (2014) offered a validation study of these multiple methods in a sample of veterans otherwise classified as passing all other validity tasks ($n = 52$) or failing two or more validity tasks ($n = 12$). Setting specificity to at least .90, adequate classification accuracy was found for the following cutoffs: (a) TOMMe10 of 2 or more errors, (b) Trial 1 < 84% correct, (c) Trial 2 < 98% correct, and (d) Retention < 98% correct. The overall hit rates for these four derived cutoff scores were .83, .84, .92, and .91, respectively, and sensitivity was at least .5 for all four scores.

The Albany Consistency Index (Gunner, Miele, Lynch, & McCaffrey, 2012) is a supplemental index that can be derived from standard administration of the TOMM by calculating the number of items consistently incorrect, the number consistently correct, and the number of inconsistent responses across trials. Using the WMT as an external criterion, 10 or more inconsistent responses across all three TOMM trials increased sensitivity to poor performance to .71 over standard TOMM failure criteria while maintaining excellent specificity (Gunner et al., 2012). In an independent cross-validation study, Schroeder et al. (2013) found that the Albany Consistency Index demonstrated the highest sensitivity (.81) of any of the individual TOMM trials, with the best overall performance (AUC = .93), providing independent support for this index. A cross-validation of this method with a different sample found that the same cutoff had adequate sensitivity (.75) and specificity (.89), with an AUC of .94 (Kulas et al., 2014).

Victoria Symptom Validity Test. The Victoria Symptom Validity Test (Slick et al., 1997) is another forced-choice recognition memory test that uses a computer interface. In this task, the examinee is initially shown a multidigit number and is then presented with two multidigit numbers after a brief delay and asked to identify which of the two was presented initially. The task has high face validity as a memory task and is presented as seemingly difficult, with the time delay between the initial presentation and the target presentations increasing over the course of the test. Early studies found that the Victoria Symptom Validity Test had 100% specificity and 59% sensitivity (Grote et al., 2000). Loring, Lee, and Meador (2005), however, later revealed an unacceptably high number of false positives in a clinical sample, noting that more than 60% of cases obtained scores of more than six errors on the difficult items, which is thought to be indicative of suboptimal performance.

Word Memory Test. The WMT was initially introduced and researched as an orally administered, pencil-and-paper test (Green et al., 1996) and was later adapted for computer administration (Green, 2003). On this task, the examinee views two learning trials of 20 semantically related word pairs. He or she is then shown 20 pairs of words and selects the true word previously presented from the foil for each pair. After a 30-minute delay, recognition memory is again evaluated using the same format. In addition to determining whether the words identified after the delay are comparable those identified on the initial task, the WMT further evaluates memory using multiple-choice, paired-associate, and free-recall modalities.

Results on the WMT are compared with a variety of patient samples that are used as comparison groups. Individual pass–fail criteria have also been provided by the publisher. A sizable body of literature provides robust support for use of the WMT in multiple contexts and with numerous patient populations (e.g., Armistead-Jehle & Buican, 2013; Carone, 2014; Davis & Wall, 2014; Donders & Strong, 2013; Fazio, Sanders, & Denney, 2015; Hall, Worthington, & Venables, 2014; Heyanka et al., 2015). Clinicians choosing to integrate the WMT into regular practice would be well served by maintaining at least a minimum level of familiarity with this literature.

Medical Symptom Validity Test. The MSVT (Green, 2005) is a shortened version of the WMT with fewer items, shorter delay, and omission of the multiple-choice aspect of the task. Different cutoff scores were developed for the MSVT in comparison with the WMT in light of the varied difficulty levels between the tasks. Studies have demonstrated the clinical utility of the MSVT in terms of sensitivity in samples of compensation-seeking individuals (Richman et al., 2006) and simulators (Armistead-Jehle & Denney, 2015). At the same time, reports of high specificity are provided for adults with low intelligence (Green & Flaro, 2015), children with a history of mTBI (Kirkwood & Kirk, 2010), and children with moderate to severe brain injury (Carone, 2008). The MSVT has also been shown to be relatively robust to coaching (Weinborn, Woods, Nulsen, & Leighton, 2012). Although some studies found some performance patterns more indicative of significant cognitive impairment than invalidity (Howe & Loring, 2009; Howe, Anderson, Kaufman, Sachs, & Loring, 2007), subsequent studies did not support the notion that the initial patterns generated were indicative of a true cognitive disorder in examinees who failed easy portions of the test (e.g., Axelrod & Schutte, 2010).

Nonverbal Medical Symptom Validity Test. The Nonverbal MSVT (NV–MSVT; Green, 2008b) presents stimuli in a manner similar to the WMT and MSVT, using two obviously related pictures. Studies have found 72% sensitivity in simulators and specificities of more than 95% for individuals with dementia and good-effort controls (M. Henry et al., 2010), and Singhal, Green, Ashaye, Shankar, and Gill (2009) found specificity of 100% in a dementia sample relative to a simulation group. In their comparison of the WMT, MSVT, and NV–MSVT, Armistead-Jehle and Denney (2015) found the NV–MSVT to be the most sensitive measure in a sample of psychology graduate students coached to simulate dementia. One important point of note is that standard administration requires participants to say out loud the names of pictures presented. Thus, although the program presents visual stimuli, it is not a purely nonverbal task.

The Advanced Interpretation program (Green, 2008a) allows clinicians to evaluate test results of existing groups using both quantitative data and qualitative performance patterns. More important, the Advanced Interpretation program not only compares results for each of the measures published by Green's with existing patient samples, it also compares results of the three validity tests with each other, providing additional information pertaining to performance validity. Despite some concerns raised regarding the influence of genuine cognitive impairment on the MSVT (M. Henry et al., 2010), the NV–MSVT and WMT offer rich information in terms of both overall scores and patterns of scores when used in conjunction with the Advanced Interpretation Program.

Embedded Performance Validity Tasks

Embedded measures of performance validity offer several advantages not available in stand-alone measures. Although stand-alone measures often offer stronger sensitivity to suboptimal effort, embedded indices added to a battery of stand-alone validity measures can enhance neuropsychological evaluations in both clinical and medicolegal contexts; they offer added efficiency because they are already being administered in the clinical battery. There are limitations to the amount of time and tolerance patients have for testing, and extended demands on their attention places an upper limit on the number of measures that can realistically be administered. Embedded indices allow for efficient assessment of effort without placing further time constraints on the examination, which is one of the stronger arguments for their use. Use of embedded indices also allows for assessment of effort in multiple domains and multiple measures over time, such as attention span, processing speed, motor functions, executive functioning, and memory, which may increase diagnostic certainty with regard to overall test battery suboptimal effort or the potential for variability in the examinee's engagement over the course of the examination. Although stand-alone PVMs can be used at multiple time points across the evaluation, use of several embedded indices more easily allows for this to occur, which is suggested by Heilbronner et al. (2009) as a best practice.

With the abundance of embedded validity measures available, many of which have not been independently validated after their initial publication, it would be inefficient to review each measure reported in the literature. The practicing clinician is encouraged to review their cognitive test battery and consult the literature to identify potential measures of performance validity contained within their chosen cognitive measures, and, using the methods outlined throughout this chapter, select those that will provide the greatest clinical utility. Moreover, although some commonalities are sure to exist across clinical test batteries, variability in cognitive test selection is a certainty, and attempting to provide a single chapter covering the breadth of measures available is sure to be less than comprehensive for all clinicians. Indices from a number of standard measures have been shown to be potentially sensitive to poor effort, including the Rey Complex Figure Test (Lu, Boone, Cozolino, & Mitchell, 2003), Wisconsin Card Sorting Test (Greve, Heinly, Bianchini, & Love, 2009), Trail Making Test (Iverson, Lange, Green, & Franzen, 2002), Children's CVLT (Baker, Connery, Kirk, & Kirkwood, 2014), Comalli Stroop Test (Arentsen et al., 2013), and Boston Naming Test (Whiteside et al., 2015), among many others. Several approaches and embedded measures that are commonly used are briefly reviewed here.

It is important to note that in addition to using individual indices that are thought to be sensitive to poor effort, several non–test-based methods of identifying performance invalidity are available. For example, the pattern of an examinee's performance may be inconsistent with known patterns of cognitive dysfunction. Informally comparing measures thought to be either sensitive or resilient to a particular disorder or disease process is often useful. Such is the case with TBI. With the exception of patients who have a history of certain neurological or neurodevelopmental comorbidities (e.g., various learning disorders) or specific pathology (e.g., frontal hemorrhage causing tissue damage), verbal functioning and academic abilities are likely to be relatively resilient to the sequelae of TBI in comparison to performance on tasks known to be sensitive to the sequelae of TBI, such as processing speed, complex attention, executive functioning, or new learning and memory. This is the foundation of using word-reading tasks to estimate premorbid functioning. For example, if one's general intellectual functioning performance was in the borderline impaired range, say a Full Scale IQ of 70 on the Wechsler Adult Intelligence Scale—Fourth Edition, with performances on the Wide Range Achievement Test 4 of 70 for reading and 70 for spelling, it can be reasonably concluded on the basis of consistency that the examinee likely has long-standing cognitive skills in the borderline impaired range, because these abilities are generally thought to be robust to neurological compromise. In contrast, given similar levels of performance observed in a formerly high-functioning individual in the context of secondary gain with evidence of suboptimal effort, the examiner may be inclined to consider the possibility that the overall test battery is invalid.

In some instances, there are formal methods of comparing patterns of performance, such as contrasting Digit Span performance and Vocabulary on the Wechsler Adult Intelligence Scale—Third Edition (Wechsler, 1997), which are both subtests that are unlikely to be strongly affected by TBI or other disorders. For example, Millis, Ross, and Ricker (1998) replicated Mittenberg, Azrin, Millsaps, and Heilbronner's (1993) Vocabulary minus Digit Span (V − DS) scaled score difference using the Wechsler Adult Intelligence Scale—Revised and found that using a cut score of V − DS of 2 or greater resulted in a sensitivity of .72 and a specificity of .89 when comparing those with a history of mTBI who had the potential of financial compensation with those with documented moderate to severe TBI. However, a subsequent examination by Axelrod, Fichtenberg, Millis and Wertheimer (2006) found that V − DS was unable to differentiate poor effort among three groups of patients (those with TBI, probable malingerers, and those with mTBI who were not involved in litigation). The authors found that a cut score (≤7) for the Digit Span age-corrected scaled score was the best discriminator compared with other Digit Span measures (i.e., V − DS, RDS, raw score for Digit Span forward and backward) with classification rates of 69%, 75%, and 77%, respectively, in the above groups.

Discriminant function analysis another alternative method of assessing validity that uses not a formal test but rather a statistical model for predicting group membership using one or a linear combination of continuous or binary independent variables. In the case of evaluating effort, good versus poor effort can be predicted using a combination of multiple measures on a battery of cognitive tests. This allows clinicians to identify group membership for an individual case by multiplying the individual variables by the beta weights in the model. There are limitations, because discriminant function analysis assumes that variables are normally distributed and groups have equal variances, which is often an assumption that is violated in embedded PVTs, which often have skewed distributions.

Multiple regression and, more commonly, logistic regression that examines one or more linear variables, such as cognitive measures, has increasingly been used in the classification of effort. In contrast to other methods, one benefit of logistical regression is that it is more robust to unequal variances and nonnormal distributions. Additional diagnostics can examine multicollinearity issues and other model fit statistics, which is important given the potential for strong relationships between embedded PVTs. One of the most prominent benefits of this approach is that measures across a test battery can be included in a single model to identify patterns of performance on cognitive testing at multiple time points while controlling for multicollinearity issues.

Two examples of such an approach use a logistic regression model, which calculates the probability of group membership on the basis of data obtained from known groups. Wolfe et al. (2010) generated a predictive algorithm from variables contained within the CVLT–II using Bayesian model averaging to identify a parsimonious set of predictor variables capable of differentiating valid from invalid neuropsychological profiles. Using the regression weights from the logistic regression to generate a linear model and exponentiating the function, a probability value is calculated. Probabilities exceeding .50 can be considered as having a higher-than-chance probability of belonging to the criterion group, in this case individuals classified as exerting poor effort. Miller et al. (2011) generated a similar prediction model for the five variables contained within the ACS for Wechsler tests.

Caution is warranted when deploying such formulas in clinical or forensic practice, however, because the models are highly sensitive to the unique characteristics of the validation sample, and any nuances may limit generalization to other groups. For example, Donders and Strong (2011) attempted to cross-validate the findings of Wolfe et al. (2010), found an unacceptably high false-positive rate, and urged strong caution if the formula were used in clinical settings. An additional weakness of this approach is that it requires large samples (more than 200), or there is a risk that the model will be overly optimistic, which can be addressed using techniques such as bootstrapping. In addition, Greve and Bianchini (2002) pointed out that regression assumes that individuals tend to exert poor effort or malinger in a uniform fashion, and they may not. Relying on regression-based methods also reduces flexibility in administration of a battery of measures, because the function requires all predictors to be entered. Nevertheless, the regression method is attractive because of its multiple benefits, although more empirical validation of regression-based formula in other samples needs to be done.

Conclusion

Although the utility of embedded measures is clear, they also come with a warning, because they have several significant limitations. Many of these measures were developed with well-defined samples that were stable in nature, such as people with mTBI versus moderate to severe TBI, which allows for identification of suboptimal effort; however, people with other disorders may not share the same properties. For example, embedded measures are often too sensitive in populations with dementia, and the development of some embedded measures is not consistent with the known progressive pathology in dementia (e.g., floor effect models). With appropriate care and understanding of the development and psychometrics of embedded measures chosen for a test battery, embedded measures offer significant clinical utility to assure valid data that aid in accurate differential diagnosis in neuropsychological evaluations. Given their strengths, it is likely that embedded indices will continue to gain more prominence in neuropsychological evaluations, and the use of formal statistical combinations of embedded indices (e.g., logistic regression) will also likely continue to gain a place in neuropsychological evaluations.

FINAL CONCLUSIONS

By this point, there should be little doubt about the importance of objectively assessing the credibility of an examinee's presentation in any clinical context using formal PVMs and SVMs, but nowhere is validity assessment more important than in a forensic setting. As with traditional measures of cognitive functioning, effective use of validity measures requires a solid foundation of clinical skill and psychometric knowledge. Unlike traditional cognitive measures, however, validity measures present significant differences in interpretation that have direct implications for clinical and forensic practice in both real-time and subsequent formulation.

This chapter has provided insight into some of these distinctions, but it is by no means intended for use as an isolated reference. Empirical research in validity assessment has accelerated exponentially, and it is anticipated to continue along this trajectory because there is still much to learn. False-positive findings are particularly problematic for validity testing, and the recent flurry of articles on this topic is likely a foreshadowing of future work in the area. Further disentanglement of effort from intent from validity is also warranted, because at present the methods of parsing these contributions have established an incredibly high bar (i.e., significantly below-chance performance). Additional study should be given to better operationally defining what is meant by *invalid* performance so future studies evaluating performance validity can prospectively use a specific criterion. Once such a clear criterion can be determined, the criteria initially set forth by Slick et al. (1999) could be explicitly and objectively evaluated.

References

Allen, M. D., Bigler, E. D., Larsen, J., Goodrich-Hunsaker, N. J., & Hopkins, R. O. (2007). Functional neuroimaging evidence for high cognitive effort on the Word Memory Test in the absence of external incentives. *Brain Injury, 21,* 1425–1428. http://dx.doi.org/10.1080/02699050701769819

Allen, M. D., Wu, T. C., & Bigler, E. D. (2011). Traumatic brain injury alters Word Memory Test performance by slowing response time and increasing cortical activation: An fMRI study of a symptom validity test. *Psychological Injury and Law, 4,* 140–146. http://dx.doi.org/10.1007/s12207-011-9105-4

American Congress of Rehabilitation Medicine, Head Injury Interdisciplinary Special Interest Group, Committee on Mild Traumatic Brain Injury. (1993). Definition of mild traumatic brain injury. *Journal of Head Trauma Rehabilitation, 8,* 86–87. http://dx.doi.org/10.1097/00001199-199309000-00010

American Psychological Association. (2017). *Ethical principles of psychologists and code of conduct* (2002, Amended June 1, 2010 and January 1, 2017). Retrieved from http://www.apa.org/ethics/code/index.aspx

Arentsen, T. J., Boone, K. B., Lo, T. T., Goldberg, H. E., Cottingham, M. E., Victor, T. L., . . . Zeller, M. A. (2013). Effectiveness of the Comalli Stroop Test as a measure of negative response bias. *Clinical Neuropsychologist, 27,* 1060–1076. http://dx.doi.org/10.1080/13854046.2013.803603

Armistead-Jehle, P., & Buican, B. (2013). Comparison of select Advanced Clinical Solutions embedded effort measures to the Word Memory Test in the detection of suboptimal effort. *Archives of Clinical Neuropsychology, 28,* 297–301. http://dx.doi.org/10.1093/arclin/act017

Armistead-Jehle, P., & Denney, R. L. (2015). The detection of feigned impairment using the WMT, MSVT, and NV-MSVT. *Applied Neuropsychology: Adult, 22,* 147–155. http://dx.doi.org/10.1080/23279095.2014.880842

Armistead-Jehle, P., Gervais, R. O., & Green, P. (2012a). Memory Complaints Inventory and Symptom Validity Test performance in a clinical sample. *Archives of Clinical Neuropsychology, 27,* 725–734. http://dx.doi.org/10.1093/arclin/acs071

Armistead-Jehle, P., Gervais, R. O., & Green, P. (2012b). Memory Complaints Inventory results as a function of symptom validity test performance. *Archives of Clinical Neuropsychology, 27,* 101–113. http://dx.doi.org/10.1093/arclin/acr081

Armistead-Jehle, P., Green, P., Gervais, R. O., & Hungerford, L. D. (2015). An examination of the Word Memory Test as a measure of memory. *Applied Neuropsychology: Adult, 22,* 415–426. http://dx.doi.org/10.1080/23279095.2014.953678

Axelrod, B. N., Fichtenberg, N. L., Millis, S. R., & Wertheimer, J. C. (2006). Detecting incomplete effort with Digit Span from the Wechsler Adult Intelligence Scale—Third Edition. *Clinical Neuropsychologist, 20,* 513–523. http://dx.doi.org/10.1080/13854040590967117

Axelrod, B. N., Fox, D. D., Lees-Haley, P. R., Earnest, K., & Dolezal-Wood, S. (1998). Application of the Postconcussive Syndrome Questionnaire with medical and psychiatric outpatients. *Archives of Clinical Neuropsychology, 13,* 543–548. http://dx.doi.org/10.1093/arclin/13.6.543

Axelrod, B. N., Fox, D. D., Lees-Haley, P. R., Earnest, K., Dolezal-Wood, S., & Goldman, R. S. (1996). Latent structure of the Postconcussion Syndrome Questionnaire. *Psychological Assessment, 8,* 422–427. http://dx.doi.org/10.1037/1040-3590.8.4.422

Axelrod, B. N., & Lees-Haley, P. (2002). Construct validity of the PCSQ as related to the MMPI–2. *Archives of Clinical Neuropsychology, 17,* 343–350. http://dx.doi.org/10.1093/arclin/17.4.343

Axelrod, B. N., Meyers, J. E., & Davis, J. J. (2014). Finger Tapping Test performance as a measure of performance validity. *Clinical Neuropsychologist, 28,* 876–888. http://dx.doi.org/10.1080/13854046.2014.907583

Axelrod, B. N., & Schutte, C. (2010). Analysis of the dementia profile on the Medical Symptom Validity Test. *Clinical Neuropsychologist, 24,* 873–881. http://dx.doi.org/10.1080/13854040903527295

Axelrod, B. N., Wall, J. R., & Estes, B. W. (2008). Use of the binomial distribution to predict impairment: Application in a nonclinical sample. *Applied Neuropsychology, 15,* 170–175. http://dx.doi.org/10.1080/09084280802324184

Backhaus, S. L., Fichtenberg, N. L., & Hanks, R. A. (2004). Detection of sub-optimal performance using a floor effect strategy in patients with traumatic brain injury. *Clinical Neuropsychologist, 18,* 591–603. http://dx.doi.org/10.1080/13854040490888558

Baker, D. A., Connery, A. K., Kirk, J. W., & Kirkwood, M. W. (2014). Embedded performance validity indicators within the California Verbal Learning Test, Children's Version. *Clinical Neuropsychologist, 28,* 116–127. http://dx.doi.org/10.1080/13854046.2013.858184

Barhon, L. I., Batchelor, J., Meares, S., Chekaluk, E., & Shores, E. A. (2015). A comparison of the degree of effort involved in the TOMM and the ACS Word Choice Test using a dual-task paradigm. *Applied Neuropsychology: Adult, 22,* 114–123. http://dx.doi.org/10.1080/23279095.2013.863775

Bashem, J. R., Rapport, L. J., Miller, J. B., Hanks, R. A., Axelrod, B. N., & Millis, S. R. (2014). Comparisons of five performance validity indices in bona fide and simulated traumatic brain injury. *Clinical Neuropsychologist, 28,* 851–875. http://dx.doi.org/10.1080/13854046.2014.927927

Basso, M. R., Lowery, N., Ghormley, C., & Bornstein, R. A. (2001). Practice effects on the Wisconsin Card Sorting Test–64 Card version across 12 months. *Clinical Neuropsychologist, 15,* 471–478. http://dx.doi.org/10.1076/clin.15.4.471.1883

Benge, J. F., Pastorek, N. J., & Thornton, G. M. (2009). Postconcussive symptoms in OEF-OIF veterans: Factor structure and impact of posttraumatic stress. *Rehabilitation Psychology, 54,* 270–278. http://dx.doi.org/10.1037/a0016736

Ben-Porath, Y. S., & Tellegen, A. (2008). *MMPI–2–RF: Manual for administration, scoring, and interpretation.* Minneapolis: University of Minnesota Press.

Berry, D. T. R., & Schipper, L. J. (2007). Detection of feigned psychiatric symptoms during forensic neuropsychological evaluations. In G. J. Larrabee (Ed.), *Assessment of malingered neuropsychological deficits* (pp. 226–263). New York, NY: Oxford University Press.

Berthelson, L., Mulchan, S. S., Odland, A. P., Miller, L. J., & Mittenberg, W. (2013). False positive diagnosis of malingering due to the use of multiple effort tests. *Brain Injury, 27,* 909–916. http://dx.doi.org/10.3109/02699052.2013.793400

Bianchini, K. J., Aguerrevere, L. E., Guise, B. J., Ord, J. S., Etherton, J. L., Meyers, J. E., . . . Bui, J. (2014). Accuracy of the Modified Somatic Perception Questionnaire and Pain Disability Index in the detection of malingered pain-related disability in chronic pain. *Clinical Neuropsychologist, 28,* 1376–1394. http://dx.doi.org/10.1080/13854046.2014.986199

Bianchini, K. J., Greve, K. W., & Glynn, G. (2005). On the diagnosis of malingered pain-related disability: Lessons from cognitive malingering research. *Spine Journal, 5,* 404–417. http://dx.doi.org/10.1016/j.spinee.2004.11.016

Bilder, R. M., Sugar, C. A., & Hellemann, G. S. (2014). Cumulative false positive rates given multiple performance validity tests: Commentary on Davis and Millis (2014) and Larrabee (2014). *Clinical Neuropsychologist, 28,* 1212–1223. http://dx.doi.org/10.1080/13854046.2014.969774

Binder, L. M. (2003). The Portland Digit Recognition Test: A review of validation data and clinical use. *Journal of Forensic Neuropsychology, 2,* 27–41. http://dx.doi.org/10.1300/J151v02n03_02

Binder, L. M., Iverson, G. L., & Brooks, B. L. (2009). To err is human: "Abnormal" neuropsychological scores and variability are common in healthy adults. *Archives of Clinical Neuropsychology, 24,* 31–46. http://dx.doi.org/10.1093/arclin/acn001

Binder, L. M., Larrabee, G. J., & Millis, S. R. (2014). Intent to fail: Significance testing of forced choice test results. *Clinical Neuropsychologist, 28,* 1366–1375. http://dx.doi.org/10.1080/13854046.2014.978383

Binder, L. M., & Rohling, M. L. (1996). Money matters: A meta-analytic review of the effects of financial incentives on recovery after closed-head injury. *American Journal of Psychiatry, 153,* 7–10. http://dx.doi.org/10.1176/ajp.153.1.7

Binder, L. M., & Willis, S. C. (1991). Assessment of motivation after financially compensable minor head trauma. *Psychological Assessment: Journal of Consulting and Clinical Psychology, 3,* 175–181. http://dx.doi.org/10.1037/1040-3590.3.2.175

Blanchard, E. B., Jones-Alexander, J., Buckley, T. C., & Forneris, C. A. (1996). Psychometric properties of the PTSD Checklist (PCL). *Behaviour Research and Therapy, 34,* 669–673. http://dx.doi.org/10.1016/0005-7967(96)00033-2

Boone, K. B. (2007). *Assessment of feigned cognitive impairment: A neuropsychological perspective.* New York, NY: Guilford Press.

Boone, K. B. (2009). The need for continuous and comprehensive sampling of effort/response bias during neuropsychological examinations. *Clinical Neuropsychologist, 23,* 729–741. http://dx.doi.org/10.1080/13854040802427803

Boone, K. B. (2013). *Clinical practice of forensic neuropsychology: An evidence-based approach.* New York, NY: Guilford Press.

Boone, K. B., Lu, P., Back, C., King, C., Lee, A., Philpott, L., . . . Warner-Chacon, K. (2002). Sensitivity and specificity of the Rey Dot Counting Test in patients with suspect effort and various clinical samples. *Archives of Clinical Neuropsychology, 17,* 625–642. http://dx.doi.org/10.1093/arclin/17.7.625

Boone, K. B., Lu, P., & Herzberg, D. S. (2002). *The Dot Counting Test Manual.* Los Angeles, CA: Western Psychological Services.

Boone, K. B., & Lu, P. H. (1999). Impact of somatoform symptomatology on credibility of cognitive performance. *Clinical Neuropsychologist, 13,* 414–419. http://dx.doi.org/10.1076/1385-4046(199911)13:04;1-Y;FT414

Bortnik, K. E., Horner, M. D., & Bachman, D. L. (2013). Performance on standard indexes of effort among patients with dementia. *Applied Neuropsychology: Adult, 20,* 233–242. http://dx.doi.org/10.1080/09084282.2012.695757

Brooks, B. L., Strauss, E., Sherman, E. M., Iverson, G. L., & Slick, D. J. (2009). Developments in neuropsychological assessment: Refining psychometric and clinical interpretive methods. *Canadian Psychology, 50,* 196–209. http://dx.doi.org/10.1037/a0016066

Burton, R. L., Enright, J., O'Connell, M. E., Lanting, S., & Morgan, D. (2015). RBANS embedded measures of suboptimal effort in dementia: Effort scale has a lower failure rate than the effort index. *Archives of Clinical Neuropsychology, 30,* 1–6. http://dx.doi.org/10.1093/arclin/acu070

Bush, S. S., Ruff, R. M., Tröster, A. I., Barth, J. T., Koffler, S. P., Pliskin, N. H., . . . Silver, C. H. (2005). Symptom validity assessment: Practice issues and medical necessity. *Archives of Clinical Neuropsychology, 20,* 419–426. http://dx.doi.org/10.1016/j.acn.2005.02.002

Butcher, J. N., Dahlstrom, W. G., Graham, J. R., Tellegen, A., & Kaemmer, B. (1989). *Minnesota Multiphasic Personality Inventory—2 (MMPI–2): Manual for administration and scoring*. Minneapolis: University of Minnesota Press.

Camara, W. J., Nathan, J. S., & Puente, A. E. (2000). Psychological test usage: Implications in professional psychology. *Professional Psychology: Research and Practice, 31,* 141–154. http://dx.doi.org/10.1037/0735-7028.31.2.141

Carone, D. A. (2008). Children with moderate/severe brain damage/dysfunction outperform adults with mild-to-no brain damage on the Medical Symptom Validity Test. *Brain Injury,* 22, 960–971. http://dx.doi.org/10.1080/02699050802491297

Carone, D. A. (2014). Young child with severe brain volume loss easily passes the word memory test and medical symptom validity test: Implications for mild TBI. *Clinical Neuropsychologist,* 28, 146–162. http://dx.doi.org/10.1080/13854046.2013.861019

Carone, D. A., Green, P., & Drane, D. L. (2014). Word memory test profiles in two cases with surgical removal of the left anterior hippocampus and parahippocampal gyrus. *Applied Neuropsychology: Adult, 21,* 155–160. http://dx.doi.org/10.1080/09084282.2012.755533

Carroll, L. J., Cassidy, J. D., Peloso, P. M., Borg, J., von Holst, H., Holm, L., . . . Pépin, M. (2004). Prognosis for mild traumatic brain injury: Results of the WHO Collaborating Centre Task Force on Mild Traumatic Brain Injury. *Journal of Rehabilitation Medicine, 36*(Suppl.), 84–105. http://dx.doi.org/10.1080/16501960410023859

Cashel, M. L., Rogers, R., Sewell, K., & Martin-Cannici, C. (1995). The Personality Assessment Inventory (PAI) and the detection of defensiveness. *Assessment,* 2, 333–342. http://dx.doi.org/10.1177/1073191195002004004

Cicerone, K. D., & Kalmar, K. (1995). Persistent postconcussion syndrome: The structure of subjective complaints after mild traumatic brain injury. *Journal of Head Trauma Rehabilitation, 10,* 1–17. http://dx.doi.org/10.1097/00001199-199510030-00002

Constantinou, M., Bauer, L., Ashendorf, L., Fisher, J. M., & McCaffrey, R. J. (2005). Is poor performance on recognition memory effort measures indicative of generalized poor performance on neuropsychological tests? *Archives of Clinical Neuropsychology, 20,* 191–198. http://dx.doi.org/10.1016/j.acn.2004.06.002

Cooper, D. B., Nelson, L., Armistead-Jehle, P., & Bowles, A. O. (2011). Utility of the Mild Brain Injury Atypical Symptoms Scale as a screening measure for symptom over-reporting in Operation Enduring Freedom/Operation Iraqi Freedom service members with post-concussive complaints. *Archives of Clinical Neuropsychology, 26,* 718–727. http://dx.doi.org/10.1093/arclin/acr070

Daubert, S. D., & Metzler, A. E. (2000). The detection of fake-bad and fake-good responding on the Millon Clinical Multiaxial Inventory III. *Psychological Assessment, 12,* 418–424. http://dx.doi.org/10.1037/1040-3590.12.4.418

Davis, J. J., & Millis, S. R. (2014). Examination of performance validity test failure in relation to number of tests administered. *Clinical Neuropsychologist,* 28, 199–214. http://dx.doi.org/10.1080/13854046.2014.884633

Davis, J. J., & Wall, J. R. (2014). Examining verbal memory on the Word Memory Test and California Verbal Learning Test-Second Edition. *Archives of Clinical Neuropsychology, 29,* 747–753. http://dx.doi.org/10.1093/arclin/acu030

Dean, A. C., Victor, T. L., Boone, K. B., & Arnold, G. (2008). The relationship of IQ to effort test performance. *Clinical Neuropsychologist, 22,* 705–722. http://dx.doi.org/10.1080/13854040701440493

Dean, A. C., Victor, T. L., Boone, K. B., Philpott, L. M., & Hess, R. A. (2009). Dementia and effort test performance. *Clinical Neuropsychologist, 23,* 133–152. http://dx.doi.org/10.1080/13854040701819050

Delis, D., Kramer, J., Kaplan, E., & Ober, B. (2000). *The California Verbal Learning Test* (2nd ed.). Lutz, FL: Psychological Assessment Resources.

Denning, J. H. (2012). The efficiency and accuracy of the Test of Memory Malingering Trial 1, errors on the first 10 items of the Test of Memory Malingering, and five embedded measures in predicting invalid test performance. *Archives of Clinical Neuropsychology,* 27, 417–432. http://dx.doi.org/10.1093/arclin/acs044

DeRight, J., & Jorgensen, R. S. (2015). I just want my research credit: Frequency of suboptimal effort in a nonclinical healthy undergraduate sample. *Clinical Neuropsychologist, 29,* 101–117. http://dx.doi.org/10.1080/13854046.2014.989267

DiCarlo, M. A., Gfeller, J. D., & Oliveri, M. V. (2000). Effects of coaching on detecting feigned cognitive impairment with the Category Test. *Archives of Clinical Neuropsychology, 15,* 399–413. http://dx.doi.org/10.1093/arclin/15.5.399

Dikmen, S. S., Machamer, J. E., Winn, H. R., & Temkin, N. R. (1995). Neuropsychological outcome at 1-year post head-injury. *Neuropsychology, 9,* 80–90. http://dx.doi.org/10.1037/0894-4105.9.1.80

Donders, J., & Strong, C. A. (2011). Embedded effort indicators on the California Verbal Learning Test—Second Edition (CVLT–II): An attempted cross-validation. *Clinical Neuropsychologist, 25,* 173–184. http://dx.doi.org/10.1080/13854046.2010.536781

Donders, J., & Strong, C. A. (2013). Does Green's Word Memory Test really measure memory? *Journal of Clinical and Experimental Neuropsychology, 35,* 827–834. http://dx.doi.org/10.1080/13803395.2013.824557

Eichstaedt, K. E., Clifton, W. E., Vale, F. L., Benbadis, S. R., Bozorg, A. M., Rodgers-Neame, N. T., & Schoenberg, M. R. (2014). Sensitivity of Green's Word Memory Test genuine memory impairment profile to temporal pathology: A study in patients with temporal lobe epilepsy. *Clinical Neuropsychologist, 28,* 941–953. http://dx.doi.org/10.1080/13854046.2014.942374

Erdodi, L., Pelletier, C., Tyson, B., Lichtenstein, J., Holcomb, M., Condiracci, C., & Roth, R. (2014). Embedded validity indicators in Conners' Continuous Performance Test, Second Edition (CPT–II) discriminate valid from invalid profiles more accurately during the repeat administration in a psychiatric sample. *Archives of Clinical Neuropsychology, 29,* 572–573. http://dx.doi.org/10.1093/arclin/acu038.184

Fazio, R. L., Sanders, J. F., & Denney, R. L. (2015). Comparison of performance of the Test of Memory Malingering and Word Memory Test in a criminal forensic sample. *Archives of Clinical Neuropsychology, 30,* 293–301. http://dx.doi.org/10.1093/arclin/acv024

Fox, D. D. (2011). Symptom validity test failure indicates invalidity of neuropsychological tests. *Clinical Neuropsychologist, 25,* 488–495. http://dx.doi.org/10.1080/13854046.2011.554443

Frederick, R. I., & Bowden, S. C. (2009). Evaluating constructs represented by symptom validity tests in forensic neuropsychological assessment of traumatic brain injury. *Journal of Head Trauma Rehabilitation, 24,* 105–122. http://dx.doi.org/10.1097/HTR.0b013e31819b1210

Geraerts, E., Kozaric-Kovacic, D., Merckelbach, H., Peraica, T., Jelicic, M., & Candel, I. (2009). Detecting deception of war-related posttraumatic stress disorder. *Journal of Forensic Psychiatry and Psychology, 20,* 278–285. http://dx.doi.org/10.1080/14789940802340906

Gervais, R. O., Ben-Porath, Y. S., Wygant, D. B., & Green, P. (2007). Development and validation of a Response Bias Scale (RBS) for the MMPI–2. *Assessment, 14,* 196–208. http://dx.doi.org/10.1177/1073191106295861

Gervais, R. O., Ben-Porath, Y. S., Wygant, D. B., & Sellbom, M. (2010). Incremental validity of the MMPI–2–RF over-reporting scales and RBS in assessing the veracity of memory complaints. *Archives of Clinical Neuropsychology, 25,* 274–284. http://dx.doi.org/10.1093/arclin/acq018

Graham, J. R. (2000). *MMPI–2: Assessing personality and psychopathology.* New York, NY: Oxford University Press.

Green, P. (2003). *Word Memory Test for Windows: User's manual.* Edmonton, Alberta, Canada: Green's Publishing.

Green, P. (2004). *Memory Complaints Inventory.* Edmonton, Alberta, Canada: Green's Publishing.

Green, P. (2005). *Medical Symptom Validity Test.* Edmonton, Alberta, Canada: Green's Publishing.

Green, P. (2008a). *The Advanced Interpretation Computer Program.* Edmonton, Alberta, Canada: Green's Publishing.

Green, P. (2008b). *Nonverbal Medical Symptom Validity Test.* Edmonton, Alberta, Canada: Green's Publishing.

Green, P., Allen, L. M., & Astner, K. (1996). *The Word Memory Test: A user's guide to the oral and computer-administered forms, U.S. Version 1.1.* Durham, NC: CogniSyst.

Green, P., & Flaro, L. (2015). Results from three performance validity tests (PVTs) in adults with intellectual deficits. *Applied Neuropsychology: Adult, 22,* 293–303.

Green, P., Montijo, J., & Brockhaus, R. (2011). High specificity of the Word Memory Test and Medical Symptom Validity Test in groups with severe verbal memory impairment. *Applied Neuropsychology, 18,* 86–94. http://dx.doi.org/10.1080/09084282.2010.523389

Greiffenstein, M. F., Fox, D. D., & Lees-Haley, P. R. (2007). The MMPI–2 Fake Bad Scale in detection of noncredible brain injury claims. In K. B. Boone (Ed.), *Assessment of feigned cognitive impairment:*

a neuropsychological perspective (pp. 210–235). New York, NY: Guilford Press.

Greiffenstein, M. F., Gola, T., & Baker, W. J. (1995). MMPI–2 validity scales versus domain specific measures in detection of factitious traumatic brain injury. *Clinical Neuropsychologist, 9,* 230–240. http://dx.doi.org/10.1080/13854049508400485

Greve, K. W., & Bianchini, K. J. (2002). Using the Wisconsin Card Sorting Test to detect malingering: An analysis of the specificity of two methods in nonmalingering normal and patient samples. *Journal of Clinical and Experimental Neuropsychology, 24,* 48–54. http://dx.doi.org/10.1076/jcen.24.1.48.968

Greve, K. W., Binder, L. M., & Bianchini, K. J. (2009). Rates of below-chance performance in forced-choice symptom validity tests. *Clinical Neuropsychologist, 23,* 534–544. http://dx.doi.org/10.1080/13854040802232690

Greve, K. W., Heinly, M. T., Bianchini, K. J., & Love, J. M. (2009). Malingering detection with the Wisconsin Card Sorting Test in mild traumatic brain injury. *Clinical Neuropsychologist, 23,* 343–362. http://dx.doi.org/10.1080/13854040802054169

Grosz, H. J., & Zimmerman, J. (1965). Experimental analysis of hysterical blindness: A follow-up report and new experimental data. *Archives of General Psychiatry, 13,* 255–260. http://dx.doi.org/10.1001/archpsyc.1965.01730030061008

Grote, C. L., Kooker, E. K., Garron, D. C., Nyenhuis, D. L., Smith, C. A., & Mattingly, M. L. (2000). Performance of compensation seeking and noncompensation seeking samples on the Victoria symptom validity test: Cross-validation and extension of a standardization study. *Journal of Clinical and Experimental Neuropsychology,* 22, 709–719. http://dx.doi.org/10.1076/jcen.22.6.709.958

Groth-Marnat, G. (2003). *Handbook of psychological assessment* (4th ed.). Hoboken, NJ: Wiley.

Gunner, J. H., Miele, A. S., Lynch, J. K., & McCaffrey, R. J. (2012). The Albany Consistency Index for the Test of Memory Malingering. *Archives of Clinical Neuropsychology,* 27, 1–9. http://dx.doi.org/10.1093/arclin/acr089

Guriel, J., & Fremouw, W. (2003). Assessing malingered posttraumatic stress disorder: A critical review. *Clinical Psychology Review, 23,* 881–904. http://dx.doi.org/10.1016/j.cpr.2003.07.001

Haber, A. H., & Fichtenberg, N. L. (2006). Replication of the Test of Memory Malingering (TOMM) in a traumatic brain injury and head trauma sample. *Clinical Neuropsychologist, 20,* 524–532. http://dx.doi.org/10.1080/13854040590967595

Hall, V. L., Worthington, A., & Venables, K. (2014). A UK pilot study: The specificity of the Word Memory Test effort sub-tests in acute minimal to mild head injury. *Journal of Neuropsychology, 8,* 216–230. http://dx.doi.org/10.1111/jnp.12021

Heaton, R. K., Chelune, G. J., Talley, J. L., Kay, G. G., & Curtiss, G. (1993). *Wisconsin Card Sorting Test manual: Revised and expanded.* Lutz, FL: Psychological Assessment Resources.

Heilbronner, R. L., Sweet, J. J., Morgan, J. E., Larrabee, G. J., & Millis, S. R. (2009). American Academy of Clinical Neuropsychology Consensus Conference Statement on the neuropsychological assessment of effort, response bias, and malingering. *Clinical Neuropsychologist, 23,* 1093–1129. http://dx.doi.org/10.1080/13854040903155063

Henry, G. K., Heilbronner, R. L., Algina, J., & Kaya, Y. (2013). Derivation of the MMPI–2–RF Henry–Heilbronner Index-r (HHI-r) scale. *Clinical Neuropsychologist, 27,* 509–515. http://dx.doi.org/10.1080/13854046.2012.739644

Henry, G. K., Heilbronner, R. L., Mittenberg, W., & Enders, C. (2006). The Henry–Heilbronner Index: A 15-item empirically derived MMPI–2 subscale for identifying probable malingering in personal injury litigants and disability claimants. *Clinical Neuropsychologist, 20,* 786–797. http://dx.doi.org/10.1080/13854040500287749

Henry, M., Merten, T., Wolf, S. A., & Harth, S. (2010). Nonverbal Medical Symptom Validity Test performance of elderly healthy adults and clinical neurology patients. *Journal of Clinical and Experimental Neuropsychology, 32,* 19–27. http://dx.doi.org/10.1080/13803390902791653

Heyanka, D. J., Thaler, N. S., Linck, J. F., Pastorek, N. J., Miller, B., Romesser, J., & Sim, A. H. (2015). A factor analytic approach to the validation of the Word Memory Test and Test of Memory Malingering as measures of effort and not memory. *Archives of Clinical Neuropsychology, 30,* 369–376. http://dx.doi.org/10.1093/arclin/acv025

Holdnack, J. A., & Drozdick, L. W. (2009). *Advanced clinical solutions for the WAIS–IV and WMS–IV: Clinical and interpretive manual.* San Antonio, TX: Pearson.

Hosmer, D. W., & Lemeshow, S. (2000). *Applied logistic regression* (2nd ed.). http://dx.doi.org/10.1002/0471722146

Howe, L. L., Anderson, A. M., Kaufman, D. A., Sachs, B. C., & Loring, D. W. (2007). Characterization of the Medical Symptom Validity Test in evaluation of clinically referred memory disorders clinic patients. *Archives of Clinical Neuropsychology, 22,* 753–761. http://dx.doi.org/10.1016/j.acn.2007.06.003

Howe, L. L., & Loring, D. W. (2009). Classification accuracy and predictive ability of the Medical

Symptom Validity Test's dementia profile and general memory impairment profile. *Clinical Neuropsychologist, 23,* 329–342. http://dx.doi.org/10.1080/13854040801945060

Inzlicht, M. (2011). *Stereotype threat: Theory, process, and application.* http://dx.doi.org/10.1093/acprof:oso/9780199732449.001.0001

Iverson, G. L. (1995). Qualitative aspects of malingered memory deficits. *Brain Injury, 9,* 35–40. http://dx.doi.org/10.3109/02699059509004569

Iverson, G. L. (2006). Ethical issues associated with the assessment of exaggeration, poor effort, and malingering. *Applied Neuropsychology, 13,* 77–90. http://dx.doi.org/10.1207/s15324826an1302_3

Iverson, G. L., Lange, R. T., Green, P., & Franzen, M. D. (2002). Detecting exaggeration and malingering with the Trail Making Test. *Clinical Neuropsychologist, 16,* 398–406. http://dx.doi.org/10.1076/clin.16.3.398.13861

Kaplan, E., Goodglass, H., & Weintraub, S. (2001). *Boston Naming Test* (2nd ed.). Philadelphia, PA: Lippincott Williams & Wilkins.

Kirkwood, M. W., & Kirk, J. W. (2010). The base rate of suboptimal effort in a pediatric mild TBI sample: Performance on the Medical Symptom Validity Test. *Clinical Neuropsychologist, 24,* 860–872. http://dx.doi.org/10.1080/13854040903527287

Kondiles, B. R., Starr, C. R., Larson, E. B., & Zollman, F. (2015). Method of assessment and symptom reporting in veterans with mild traumatic brain injury. *Health Psychology and Behavioral Medicine, 3,* 1–11. http://dx.doi.org/10.1080/21642850.2014.966717

Kulas, J. F., Axelrod, B. N., & Rinaldi, A. (2014). Cross-validation of supplemental Test of Memory Malingering scores as performance validity measures. *Psychological Injury and Law, 7,* 236–244. http://dx.doi.org/10.1007/s12207-014-9200-4

Lange, R. T., Edmed, S. L., Sullivan, K. A., French, L. M., & Cooper, D. B. (2013). Utility of the Mild Brain Injury Atypical Symptoms Scale to detect symptom exaggeration: An analogue simulation study. *Journal of Clinical and Experimental Neuropsychology, 35,* 192–209. http://dx.doi.org/10.1080/13803395.2012.761677

Larrabee, G. J. (2003a). Detection of malingering using atypical performance patterns on standard neuropsychological tests. *Clinical Neuropsychologist, 17,* 410–425. http://dx.doi.org/10.1076/clin.17.3.410.18089

Larrabee, G. J. (2003b). Exaggerated pain report in litigants with malingered neurocognitive dysfunction. *Clinical Neuropsychologist, 17,* 395–401. http://dx.doi.org/10.1076/clin.17.3.395.18087

Larrabee, G. J. (2008). Aggregation across multiple indicators improves the detection of malingering: Relationship to likelihood ratios. *Clinical Neuropsychologist, 22,* 666–679. http://dx.doi.org/10.1080/13854040701494987

Larrabee, G. J. (2012). Performance validity and symptom validity in neuropsychological assessment. *Journal of the International Neuropsychological Society, 18,* 625–630. http://dx.doi.org/10.1017/S1355617712000240

Larrabee, G. J., & Rohling, M. L. (2013). Neuropsychological differential diagnosis of mild traumatic brain injury. *Behavioral Sciences and the Law, 31,* 686–701. http://dx.doi.org/10.1002/bsl.2087

Lees-Haley, P. R. (1992). Neuropsychological complaint base rates of personal injury claimants. *Forensic Reports, 5,* 385–391.

Lees-Haley, P. R., English, L. T., & Glenn, W. J. (1991). A Fake Bad Scale on the MMPI–2 for personal injury claimants. *Psychological Reports, 68,* 203–210. http://dx.doi.org/10.2466/pr0.1991.68.1.203

Lees-Haley, P. R., Smith, H. H., Williams, C. W., & Dunn, J. T. (1996). Forensic neuropsychological test usage: An empirical study. *Archives of Clinical Neuropsychology, 11,* 45–51. http://dx.doi.org/10.1093/arclin/11.1.45

Lezak, M. D., Howieson, D. B., Loring, D. W., Hannay, J., & Fischer, J. S. (2004). *Neuropsychological assessment* (4th ed.). New York, NY: Oxford University Press.

Loring, D. W., Lee, G. P., & Meador, K. J. (2005). Victoria Symptom Validity Test Performance in nonlitigating epilepsy surgery candidates. *Journal of Clinical and Experimental Neuropsychology, 27,* 610–617. http://dx.doi.org/10.1080/13803390490918471

Loring, D. W., Marino, S. E., Drane, D. L., Parfitt, D., Finney, G. R., & Meador, K. J. (2011). Lorazepam effects on Word Memory Test performance: A randomized, double-blind, placebo-controlled, crossover trial. *Clinical Neuropsychologist, 25,* 799–811. http://dx.doi.org/10.1080/13854046.2011.583279

Lu, P. H., Boone, K. B., Cozolino, L., & Mitchell, C. (2003). Effectiveness of the Rey–Osterrieth Complex Figure Test and the Meyers and Meyers recognition trial in the detection of suspect effort. *Clinical Neuropsychologist, 17,* 426–440. http://dx.doi.org/10.1076/clin.17.3.426.18083

Main, C. J. (1983). The Modified Somatic Perception Questionnaire (MSPQ). *Journal of Psychosomatic Research, 27,* 503–514. http://dx.doi.org/10.1016/0022-3999(83)90040-5

McKinley, J. C., Hathaway, S. R., & Meehl, P. E. (1948). The Minnesota Multiphasic Personality Inventory: VI. The K scale. *Journal of Consulting Psychology, 12,* 20–31. http://dx.doi.org/10.1037/h0061377

Meyers, J. E., & Volbrecht, M. E. (2003). A validation of multiple malingering detection methods in a large clinical sample. *Archives of Clinical Neuropsychology, 18,* 261–276. http://dx.doi.org/10.1093/arclin/18.3.261

Miller, J. B., Millis, S. R., Rapport, L. J., Bashem, J. R., Hanks, R. A., & Axelrod, B. N. (2011). Detection of insufficient effort using the advanced clinical solutions for the Wechsler Memory Scale, Fourth Edition. *Clinical Neuropsychologist, 25,* 160–172. https://dx.doi.org/10.1080/13854046.2010.533197

Millis, S. R. (2004). Evaluation of malingered neurocognitive disorders. In M. Rizzo & P. Eslinger (Eds.), *Principals and practice of behavioral neurology and neuropsychology* (pp. 1077–1089). Philadelphia, PA: Saunders.

Millis, S. R., Hanks, R. A., Fichtenberg, N. L., & Axelrod, B. N. (2007, February). *Rasch analysis of the PCSQ: Measuring the core construct of head injury symptomatology.* Paper presented at the 35th Annual Meeting of the International Neuropsychological Society, Portland, OR.

Millis, S. R., Ross, S. R., & Ricker, J. H. (1998). Detection of incomplete effort on the Wechsler Adult Intelligence Scale-Revised: A cross-validation. *Journal of Clinical and Experimental Neuropsychology, 20,* 167–173. http://dx.doi.org/10.1076/jcen.20.2.167.1171

Millon, T., Millon, C., Davis, R., & Grossman, S. (2006). *MCMI–III manual* (3rd ed.). Minneapolis, MN: Pearson Assessments.

Mittenberg, W., Azrin, R., Millsaps, C., & Heilbronner, R. L. (1993). Identification of malingered head injury on the Wechsler Memory Scale—Revised. *Psychological Assessment, 5,* 34–40. http://dx.doi.org/10.1037/1040-3590.5.1.34

Morel, K. R. (1998). Development and preliminary validation of a forced-choice test of response bias for posttraumatic stress disorder. *Journal of Personality Assessment, 70,* 299–314. http://dx.doi.org/10.1207/s15327752jpa7002_8

Morel, K. R. (2008a). Comparison of the Morel Emotional Numbing Test for Posttraumatic Stress Disorder to the Word Memory Test in neuropsychological evaluations. *Clinical Neuropsychologist, 22,* 350–362. http://dx.doi.org/10.1080/13854040701300531

Morel, K. R. (2008b). Development of a validity scale for combat-related posttraumatic stress disorder: Evidence from simulated malingerers and actual disability claimants. *Journal of Forensic Psychiatry and Psychology, 19,* 52–63. http://dx.doi.org/10.1080/14789940701594645

Morel, K. R. (2013). Cutoff scores for the Morel Emotional Numbing Test for PTSD: Considerations for use in VA mental health examinations. *Psychological Injury and Law, 6,* 138–143. http://dx.doi.org/10.1007/s12207-013-9151-1

Morel, K. R., & Shepherd, B. E. (2008). Meta-analysis of the Morel Emotional Numbing Test for PTSD: Comment on Singh, Avasthi, and Grover. *German Journal of Psychiatry, 11,* 128–131.

Morey, L. C. (1991). *Personality Assessment Inventory professional manual.* Odessa, FL: Psychological Assessment Resources.

Morey, L. C. (1996). *An interpretive guide to the Personality Assessment Inventory.* Odessa, FL: Psychological Assessment Resources.

Morey, L. C. (2003). *Essentials of PAI assessment.* New York, NY: Wiley.

Morra, L. F., Gold, J. M., Sullivan, S. K., & Strauss, G. P. (2015). Predictors of neuropsychological effort test performance in schizophrenia. *Schizophrenia Research, 162,* 205–210. http://dx.doi.org/10.1016/j.schres.2014.12.033

Odland, A. P., Lammy, A. B., Martin, P. K., Grote, C. L., & Mittenberg, W. (2015). Advanced administration and interpretation of multiple validity tests. *Psychological Injury and Law, 8,* 46–63. http://dx.doi.org/10.1007/s12207-015-9216-4

Osterrieth, P. A. (1944). The test of copying a complex figure: A contribution to the study of perception and memory. *Archives de Psychologie, 30,* 286–356.

Pankratz, L., & Erickson, R. C. (1990). Two views of malingering. *Clinical Neuropsychologist, 4,* 379–389. http://dx.doi.org/10.1080/13854049008401832

Perna, R., & Loughan, A. R. (2014). The influence of effort on neuropsychological performance in children: Is performance on the TOMM indicative of neuropsychological ability? *Applied Neuropsychology: Child, 3,* 31–37. http://dx.doi.org/10.1080/21622965.2012.686339

Ploetz, D. M., Mazur-Mosiewicz, A., Kirkwood, M. W., Sherman, E. M., & Brooks, B. L. (2016). Performance on the Test of Memory Malingering in children with neurological conditions. *Child Neuropsychology, 22,* 133–142. http://dx.doi.org/10.1080/09297049.2014.986446

Proto, D. A., Pastorek, N. J., Miller, B. I., Romesser, J. M., Sim, A. H., & Linck, J. F. (2014). The dangers of failing one or more performance validity tests in individuals claiming mild traumatic brain injury-related postconcussive symptoms. *Archives of Clinical Neuropsychology, 29,* 614–624. http://dx.doi.org/10.1093/arclin/acu044

Rabin, L. A., Barr, W. B., & Burton, L. A. (2005). Assessment practices of clinical neuropsychologists in the United States and Canada: A survey of INS, NAN, and APA Division 40 members. *Archives of Clinical Neuropsychology, 20,* 33–65. http://dx.doi.org/10.1016/j.acn.2004.02.005

Rees, L. M., Tombaugh, T. N., Gansler, D. A., & Moczynski, N. P. (1998). Five validation experiments on the Test of Memory Malingering. *Psychological Assessment, 10,* 10–20. http://dx.doi.org/10.1037/1040-3590.10.1.10

Reitan, R. M., & Wolfson, D. (1993). *The Halstead–Reitan Neuropsychological Test Battery: Theory and clinical interpretation* (2nd ed.). Tucson, AZ: Neuropsychology Press.

Rey, A. (1941). The psychological examination in cases of traumatic encephalopathy. Problems. *Archives de Psychologie, 28,* 215–285.

Richman, J., Green, P., Gervais, R., Flaro, L., Merten, T., Brockhaus, R., & Ranks, D. (2006). Objective tests of symptom exaggeration in independent medical examinations. *Journal of Occupational and Environmental Medicine, 48,* 303–311. http://dx.doi.org/10.1097/01.jom.0000183482.41957.c3

Rogers, R. (1990). Models of feigned mental illness. *Professional Psychology: Research and Practice, 21,* 182–188. http://dx.doi.org/10.1037/0735-7028.21.3.182

Rogers, R. (1997). Researching dissimulation. In R. Rogers (Ed.), *Clinical assessment of malingering and deception* (2nd ed., pp. 398–426). New York, NY: Guilford Press.

Rogers, R., Sewell, K. W., Morey, L. C., & Ulstad, K. L. (1996). Detection of feigned mental disorders on the Personality Assessment Inventory: A discriminant analysis. *Journal of Personality Assessment, 67,* 629–640. http://dx.doi.org/10.1207/s15327752jpa6703_15

Rohling, M. L., Green, P., Allen, L. M., III, & Iverson, G. L. (2002). Depressive symptoms and neurocognitive test scores in patients passing symptom validity tests. *Archives of Clinical Neuropsychology, 17,* 205–222. http://dx.doi.org/10.1093/arclin/17.3.205

Rohling, M. L., Meyers, J. E., & Millis, S. R. (2003). Neuropsychological impairment following traumatic brain injury: A dose-response analysis. *Clinical Neuropsychologist, 17,* 289–302. http://dx.doi.org/10.1076/clin.17.3.289.18086

Ruocco, A. C., Swirsky-Sacchetti, T., & Choca, J. P. (2007). Assessing personality and psychopathology after traumatic brain injury with the Millon Clinical Multiaxial Inventory–III. *Brain Injury, 21,* 1233–1244. http://dx.doi.org/10.1080/02699050701716919

Schmidt, M. (1996). *Rey Auditory and Verbal Learning Test: A handbook.* Los Angeles, CA: Western Psychological Services.

Schoenberg, M. R., Dorr, D., & Morgan, C. D. (2003). The ability of the Millon Clinical Multiaxial Inventory—Third Edition to detect malingering. *Psychological Assessment, 15,* 198–204. http://dx.doi.org/10.1037/1040-3590.15.2.198

Schoenberg, M. R., Dorr, D., & Morgan, C. D. (2006). Development of discriminant functions to detect dissimulation for the Millon Clinical Multiaxial Inventory (3rd edition). *Journal of Forensic Psychiatry and Psychology, 17,* 405–416.

Schroeder, R. W., Buddin, W. H., Jr., Hargrave, D. D., VonDran, E. J., Campbell, E. B., Brockman, C. J., . . . Baade, L. E. (2013). Efficacy of Test of Memory Malingering Trial 1, Trial 2, the Retention Trial, and the Albany Consistency Index in a criterion group forensic neuropsychological sample. *Archives of Clinical Neuropsychology, 28,* 21–29. http://dx.doi.org/10.1093/arclin/acs094

Schroeder, R. W., Twumasi-Ankrah, P., Baade, L. E., & Marshall, P. S. (2012). Reliable Digit Span: A systematic review and cross-validation study. *Assessment, 19,* 21–30. http://dx.doi.org/10.1177/1073191111428764

Schutte, C., & Axelrod, B. N. (2013). Use of embedded cognitive symptom validity measures in mild traumatic brain injury cases. In D. A. Carone & S. S. Bush (Eds.), *Mild traumatic brain injury: Symptom validity assessment and malingering* (pp. 159–181). New York, NY: Springer.

Sellbom, M., & Bagby, R. M. (2008). Response styles on multiscale inventories. In R. Rogers (Ed.), *Clinical assessment of malingering and deception* (3rd ed., pp. 182–206). New York, NY: Guilford Press.

Sharland, M. J., & Gfeller, J. D. (2007). A survey of neuropsychologists' beliefs and practices with respect to the assessment of effort. *Archives of Clinical Neuropsychology, 22,* 213–223. http://dx.doi.org/10.1016/j.acn.2006.12.004

Shaw, D. J., & Matthews, C. G. (1965). Differential MMPI performance of brain-damaged vs. pseudo-neurologic groups. *Journal of Clinical Psychology, 21,* 405–408. http://dx.doi.org/10.1002/1097-4679(196510)21:4<405::AID-JCLP2270210416>3.0.CO;2-I

Silver, J. M. (2012). Effort, exaggeration and malingering after concussion. *Journal of Neurology, Neurosurgery, and Psychiatry, 83,* 836–841. http://dx.doi.org/10.1136/jnnp-2011-302078

Singhal, A., Green, P., Ashaye, K., Shankar, K., & Gill, D. (2009). High specificity of the Medical Symptom Validity Test in patients with very severe memory impairment. *Archives of Clinical Neuropsychology, 24,* 721–728. http://dx.doi.org/10.1093/arclin/acp074

Slick, D. J., Hopp, G., Strauss, E., & Thompson, G. (1997). *Victoria Symptoms Validity Test: Professional manual*. Odessa, FL: Psychological Assessment Resources.

Slick, D. J., Sherman, E. M. S., & Iverson, G. L. (1999). Diagnostic criteria for malingered neurocognitive dysfunction: Proposed standards for clinical practice and research. *Clinical Neuropsychologist, 13,* 545–561. http://dx.doi.org/10.1076/1385-4046(199911)13:04;1-Y;FT545

Smith, G. (2008). Brief screening measures of the detection of feigned psychopathology. In R. Rogers (Ed.), *Clinical assessment of malingering and deception* (3rd ed., pp. 323–342). New York, NY: Guilford Press.

Smith, G. P., & Burger, G. K. (1997). Detection of malingering: Validation of the Structured Inventory of Malingered Symptomatology (SIMS). *Journal of the American Academy of Psychiatry and the Law, 25,* 183–189.

Soble, J. R., Silva, M. A., Vanderploeg, R. D., Curtiss, G., Belanger, H. G., Donnell, A. J., & Scott, S. G. (2014). Normative data for the Neurobehavioral Symptom Inventory (NSI) and post-concussion symptom profiles among TBI, PTSD, and nonclinical samples. *Clinical Neuropsychologist, 28,* 614–632. http://dx.doi.org/10.1080/13854046.2014.894576

Solomon, R. E., Boone, K. B., Miora, D., Skidmore, S., Cottingham, M., Victor, T., . . . Zeller, M. (2010). Use of the WAIS–III picture completion subtest as an embedded measure of response bias. *Clinical Neuropsychologist, 24,* 1243–1256. http://dx.doi.org/10.1080/13854046.2010.514864

Stenclik, J. H., Miele, A. S., Silk-Eglit, G., Lynch, J. K., & McCaffrey, R. J. (2013). Can the sensitivity and specificity of the TOMM be increased with differential cutoff scores? *Applied Neuropsychology: Adult, 20,* 243–248. http://dx.doi.org/10.1080/09084282.2012.704603

Sugarman, M. A., & Axelrod, B. N. (2015). Embedded measures of performance validity using verbal fluency tests in a clinical sample. *Applied Neuropsychology: Adult, 22,* 141–146. http://dx.doi.org/10.1080/23279095.2013.873439

Suhr, J. A., & Gunstad, J. (2000). The effects of coaching on the sensitivity and specificity of malingering measures. *Archives of Clinical Neuropsychology, 15,* 415–424. http://dx.doi.org/10.1093/arclin/15.5.415

Suhr, J. A., & Gunstad, J. (2002). "Diagnosis threat": The effect of negative expectations on cognitive performance in head injury. *Journal of Clinical and Experimental Neuropsychology, 24,* 448–457. http://dx.doi.org/10.1076/jcen.24.4.448.1039

Suhr, J. A., & Gunstad, J. (2005). Further exploration of the effect of "diagnosis threat" on cognitive performance in individuals with mild head injury. *Journal of the International Neuropsychological Society, 11,* 23–29. http://dx.doi.org/10.1017/S1355617705050010

Suhr, J. A., & Gunstad, J. (2007). Coaching and malingering: A review. In G. J. Larrabee (Ed.), *Assessment of malingered neurocognitive deficits* (pp. 287–311). New York, NY: Oxford University Press.

Sweet, J. J., Meyer, D. G., Nelson, N. W., & Moberg, P. J. (2011). The TCN/AACN 2010 "salary survey": Professional practices, beliefs, and incomes of U.S. neuropsychologists. *Clinical Neuropsychologist, 25,* 12–61. http://dx.doi.org/10.1080/13854046.2010.544165

Teichner, G., Wagner, M. T., & Newman, S. A. (2000). Psychometric validation and clinical application of the Test of Memory Malingering (TOMM). *Archives of Clinical Neuropsychology, 15,* 673–674. http://dx.doi.org/10.1093/arclin/15.8.673a

Tombaugh, T. (1996). *Test of Memory Malingering*. North Tonawanda, NY: Multi-Health Systems.

Tsanadis, J., Montoya, E., Hanks, R. A., Millis, S. R., Fichtenberg, N. L., & Axelrod, B. N. (2008). Brain injury severity, litigation status, and self-report of postconcussive symptoms. *Clinical Neuropsychologist, 22,* 1080–1092. http://dx.doi.org/10.1080/13854040701796928

Tsanadis, J., Montoya, E., Millis, S. R., Hanks, R. A., Fichtenberg, N. L., & Axelrod, B. N. (2007, February). *A negative impression management scale for the postconcussive syndrome questionnaire*. Paper presented at the 35th Annual Meeting of the International Neuropsychological Society, Portland, OR.

Vanderploeg, R. D., Cooper, D. B., Belanger, H. G., Donnell, A. J., Kennedy, J. E., Hopewell, C. A., & Scott, S. G. (2014). Screening for postdeployment conditions: Development and cross-validation of an embedded validity scale in the neurobehavioral symptom inventory. *Journal of Head Trauma Rehabilitation, 29,* 1–10. http://dx.doi.org/10.1097/HTR.0b013e318281966e

Van Dyke, S. A., Axelrod, B. N., & Schutte, C. (2010). The utility of the post-concussive symptom questionnaire. *Archives of Clinical Neuropsychology, 25,* 634–639. http://dx.doi.org/10.1093/arclin/acq063

Van Dyke, S. A., Millis, S. R., Axelrod, B. N., & Hanks, R. A. (2013). Assessing effort: Differentiating performance and symptom validity. *Clinical Neuropsychologist, 27,* 1234–1246. http://dx.doi.org/10.1080/13854046.2013.835447

van Impelen, A., Merckelbach, H., Jelicic, M., & Merten, T. (2014). The Structured Inventory of Malingered Symptomatology (SIMS): A systematic review and meta-analysis. *Clinical Neuropsychologist, 28,*

1336–1365. http://dx.doi.org/10.1080/13854046.2014.984763

Victor, T. L., Boone, K. B., Serpa, J. G., Buehler, J., & Ziegler, E. A. (2009). Interpreting the meaning of multiple symptom validity test failure. *Clinical Neuropsychologist, 23,* 297–313. http://dx.doi.org/10.1080/13854040802232682

Wall, J. R., & Davis, J. J. (2013, August). *Examining protocol adherence in simulation research.* Paper presented at the 121st Annual Convention of the American Psychological Association, Honolulu, HI.

Warrington, E. K. (1984). *Recognition Memory Test.* Lutz, FL: Psychological Assessment Resources.

Wechsler, D. (1997). *Wechsler Adult Intelligence Scale* (3rd ed.). San Antonio, TX: Psychological Corporation.

Wechsler, D. (2008a). *Wechsler Adult Intelligence Scale* (4th ed.). San Antonio, TX: Psychological Corporation.

Wechsler, D. (2008b). *Wechsler Memory Scale* (4th ed.). San Antonio, TX: Pearson.

Weinborn, M., Woods, S. P., Nulsen, C., & Leighton, A. (2012). The effects of coaching on the verbal and nonverbal Medical Symptom Validity Tests. *Clinical Neuropsychologist, 26,* 832–849. http://dx.doi.org/10.1080/13854046.2012.686630

Whiteside, D. M., Kogan, J., Wardin, L., Phillips, D., Franzwa, M. G., Rice, L., . . . Roper, B. (2015). Language-based embedded performance validity measures in traumatic brain injury. *Journal of Clinical and Experimental Neuropsychology, 37,* 220–227. http://dx.doi.org/10.1080/13803395.2014.1002758

Whitney, K. A., Shepard, P. H., & Davis, J. J. (2013). WAIS–IV Digit Span variables: Are they valuable for use in predicting TOMM and MSVT failure? *Applied Neuropsychology: Adult, 20,* 83–94. http://dx.doi.org/10.1080/09084282.2012.670167

Widows, M. R., & Smith, G. P. (2005). *Structured Inventory of Malingered Symptomatology professional manual.* Odessa, FL: Psychological Assessment Resources.

Williamson, K. D., Combs, H. L., Berry, D. T., Harp, J. P., Mason, L. H., & Edmundson, M. (2014). Discriminating among ADHD alone, ADHD with a comorbid psychological disorder, and feigned ADHD in a college sample. *Clinical Neuropsychologist, 28,* 1182–1196. http://dx.doi.org/10.1080/13854046.2014.956674

Wolfe, P. L., Millis, S. R., Hanks, R., Fichtenberg, N., Larrabee, G. J., & Sweet, J. J. (2010). Effort indicators within the California Verbal Learning Test—II (CVLT–II). *Clinical Neuropsychologist, 24,* 153–168. http://dx.doi.org/10.1080/13854040903107791

Youngjohn, J. R., Lees-Haley, P. R., & Binder, L. M. (1999). Comment: Warning malingerers produces more sophisticated malingering. *Archives of Clinical Neuropsychology, 14,* 511–515.

Zimmermann, P., Kowalski, J. T., Alliger-Horn, C., Danker-Hopfe, H., Engers, A., Meermann, R., & Hellweg, R. (2013). Detection of malingering in the assessment of occupational disability in the military. *German Journal of Psychiatry, 16,* 54–60.

CHAPTER 6

NEUROIMAGING TECHNIQUES IN THE COURTROOM

L. Stephen Miller and Cutter A. Lindbergh

Given advances in noninvasive imaging tools in neuroscience and understanding of the brain over the years, it is natural to see their appeal as scientific evidence and, subsequently, their rise in the courtroom setting. Although neuroimaging techniques have been applied in a wide range of capacities, such as to discern factual truth from deception and establish neurological competence for criminal behavior, we focus our review on brain insult and mild traumatic brain injury (mTBI) in particular. This focus is largely because of new interest in elucidating objective evidence of subtle brain injury in the courtroom and greater agreement on the use of neuroimaging techniques to identify major TBI.

Our goals are to present current neuroimaging techniques and review their use in forensic settings. We present descriptions of X-ray, computed tomography (CT), positron emission tomography (PET), single-photon emission computed tomography (SPECT), electroencephalography (EEG), magnetoencephalography (MEG), and of course magnetic resonance imaging (MRI) and functional MRI (fMRI) and provide brief historical backgrounds for each. We arbitrarily divide these techniques and their use in the forensic arena into measures of structure and measures of function. Although both of these broad measurement types sometimes use similar technical processes, they are different in their approaches in that structural measures focus on anatomy, and functional measures focus on activity of an anatomical area. We provide both supportive and cautionary evidence regarding the use of these methods in a legal context and opinion regarding the veracity of their current and future use as sensitive markers of developed or acquired change in the brain. We begin by reviewing methods of evaluating structural brain changes and their current use and likelihood of future use in the courtroom, followed by a similar treatise on functional brain imaging methods.

STRUCTURAL NEUROIMAGING

Common neuroimaging modalities to assess brain structure include X-ray and CT, as well as a variety of MRI-based techniques. We discuss each of these approaches in turn, including a basic description of the underlying technology and an overview of relevance to the courtroom.

Radiography

Description and uses. X-ray technology (radiography), discovered in 1895 by Wilhelm Konrad Roentgen (Khoshbin & Khoshbin, 2007; Nitzke, 1971), works by producing short wavelength electromagnetic energy beams (0.1–1,000 angstroms) made of high-energy photons that can penetrate solids (Zillmer, Spiers, & Culbertson, 2008). Images are possible because these "Roentgen rays" travel through different tissues at different rates on the basis of degree of absorption, which varies according to tissue density. Using X-rays provides high-quality information about bone structure and trauma (see Figure 6.1), including certain tissue abnormalities, tumors, and other disease states. The addition of

http://dx.doi.org/10.1037/0000032-006
APA Handbook of Forensic Neuropsychology, S. S. Bush (Editor-in-Chief)

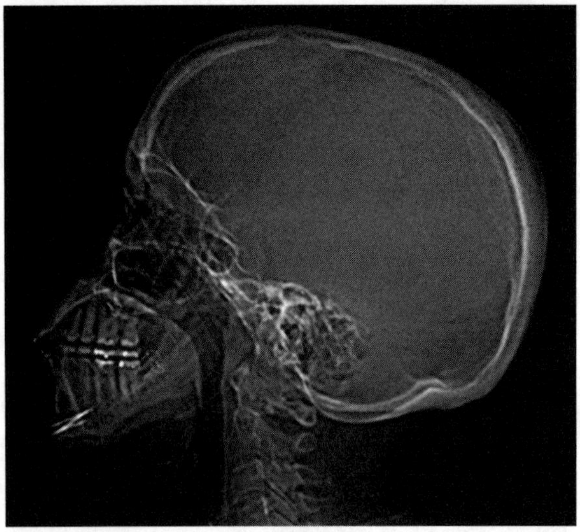

FIGURE 6.1. Skull X-ray: Lateral (sagittal) high-resolution view. Credit: Aaron Filler, MD, PhD. Used with permission. Licensed under Creative Commons (http://creativecommons.org/licenses/by-sa/3.0).

injectable agents used together with X-rays enhances the contrast between tissue types.

There is, of course, some risk of radiation damage. When photons are beamed through the body, most are absorbed in the cellular tissue, and the energy can negatively affect that tissue. Thus, X-ray exposure is regulated, and radiation exposure should be limited.

Research and applicability to the courtroom. *Smith v. Grant* (1896) marked the first medical malpractice case in the United States in which X-ray evidence was used in the courtroom (Goldberg, 2013). James Smith, a 23-year-old law clerk, admitted an X-ray image of his fractured left thigh to show that his treating physician, W. W. Grant, should have immobilized his leg rather than recommending physical exercise (Goldberg, 2013; *Smith v. Grant*, 1896). X-ray images have since been used in countless court cases (e.g., *Dillon v. Evanston Hospital*, 2002; *Hunt v. Bradshaw*, 1955; *Levitsky v. Garden Time, Inc*, 2015). X-ray has the advantage of being painless and relatively inexpensive, and it is often available or easily obtained after medical evaluation. In the study of brain trauma, X-ray offers good visualization of skull integrity including porosity, bone fractures, and certain foreign bodies such as bullets or material fragments (Zillmer et al., 2008). With the help of contrast agents, it can show arterial blockage, some large tumors, hydrocephalus, and evidence for certain disease states such as meningitis. However, the resolution of X-ray is not nearly as high as that of newer techniques, including CT and MRI, which limits its use as a measure of brain anatomy or changes in that anatomy (Shenton et al., 2012). Although brain tissue does vary somewhat in density, it is generally too uniform for standard X-ray to show significant differences in subtypes of tissue. Therefore, X-ray in its traditional format, including contrast based, is not likely to have significant impact in the court setting as evidence for most types of brain trauma independent of skull fracture or the presence of radio-opaque foreign bodies.

Computed Tomography

Description and uses. Developed in the early 1970s (Haeger, 1998), CT is essentially a very specialized radiography method. CT is a computer-based assembly of multiple X-ray images. Rather than a single exposure taken through a large area of tissue, CT uses pairs of X-ray sources—detectors—that allow images of multiple thin planar slices of tissue to be taken at or near the same time from a variety of angles around the head to create two- and three-dimensional image sets (O. D. Jones, Buckholtz, Schall, & Marois, 2014). A significant advantage is the large reduction in the amount of tissues superimposed on each other, reducing the signal scattering effect of conventional X-ray.

Because of the reduction in tissue overlap and use of multiple planes of data, CT resolution is vastly better than that of conventional X-ray when imaging soft tissue, and contrasts have a much finer grain (Khoshbin & Khoshbin, 2007; see Figure 6.2). Brain anatomy can be imaged with modest clarity, and gross differences between gray and white matter and between brain and nonbrain tissue can usually be seen. CT imaging is often used to detect and differentiate tumor types, which tend to show up as hyperdensities. In regard to trauma identification, blood clots are readily seen, and blood vessels can be imaged quite well, allowing the identification of defects within vessels. One of the most important

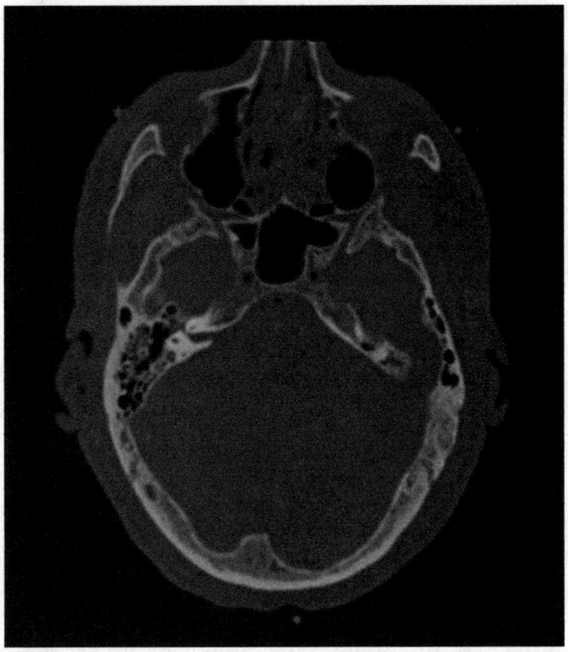

FIGURE 6.2. Mid-axial computed tomography scan of adult female brain. From the National Library of Medicine Visible Human Project. Printed with permission.

uses of CT has been its ability to detect blood hemorrhages. CT has a nearly 100% detection rate for brain hemorrhaging, a common sequela of brain trauma or injury.

As with X-ray, CT remains relatively inexpensive, is quick and efficient, and is readily available in most medical settings (Simpson, 2012). The presence of ferromagnetic objects is not a dangerous issue as it is with MRI, so it is easier to use with life support or monitoring equipment (Shenton et al., 2012). CT still includes exposure to radiographic photons, which can negatively affect cellular tissue, although to a lesser extent than conventional X-ray.

Research and applicability to the courtroom. CT is the standard imaging modality for assessing closed-head injury in the emergency department (Johnston, Ptito, Chankowsky, & Chen, 2001) and is the most used imaging modality within the first 24 hours of neurotrauma (e.g., Coles, 2007). Thus, it is not surprising that it is commonly proffered in the courtroom as evidence for or against brain insult. Perhaps the most notable use of CT in the courtroom was to provide evidence that John Hinckley, who shot President Ronald Reagan in 1981, had schizophrenia in support of an insanity ruling (Simpson, 2012). More specifically, the defense pointed out that Hinckley had "widened sulci," which were argued to be present in roughly one in three individuals with schizophrenia but only one in 50 individuals in the general population (Lincoln, 1987).

Because CT scanning has been around for quite some time, research is available regarding its efficacy in delineating brain damage in a legal setting. As with X-ray, CT can provide compelling evidence of damage from open-head injuries because of its ability to show detail of bone fractures and skull fragments relative to nervous tissue. The relatively high level of accuracy with which CT can identify major head injuries involving skull fractures, intracranial hemorrhage, and gross brain structural abnormalities (e.g., Johnston et al., 2001; Le & Gean, 2009; Shenton et al., 2012) renders it a viable imaging modality for court cases involving these conditions, particularly given that CT abnormalities are readily apparent and understandable to jurors and judges. A recent study ($N = 658$) demonstrated that CT scan abnormalities were evident in 81% of severe TBI patients (Glasgow Coma Scale score ≤ 8), though this dropped to 60% in moderate TBI patients (Glasgow Coma Scale score = 9–12; B. Jacobs et al., 2013).

Other studies have suggested that CT is similar or perhaps even superior in some cases to MRI for identifying skull fractures as well as acute epidural and subdural hematoma (Gentry, Godersky, Thompson, & Dunn, 1988; Le & Gean, 2009; Orrison et al., 1994). For example, CT scans have demonstrated significantly higher sensitivity than MRI scans with respect to fracture (94% and 36%, respectively), and the two modalities are comparable with respect to scalp swelling (56% and 60%, respectively; Orrison et al., 1994). In a sample of 40 patients with acute closed-head trauma, the sensitivity of CT to hemorrhagic lesions was 89.8%, which was comparable to the sensitivities of both T_1- and T_2-weighted MRI (87.1% and 92.5%, respectively; Gentry et al., 1988).

On the basis of these findings and others, the American College of Radiology Appropriateness Criteria recommend CT as the preferred imaging technique for moderate to severe acute closed-head injury (American College of Radiology, 2012). In addition, a number of studies have supported the predictive utility of CT classification for outcome after moderate to severe head injury, both as a stand-alone tool and in combination with other predictive variables (e.g., age, motor impairment, pupillary reactivity, and Glasgow Coma Scale score; Hukkelhoven et al., 2005; Lobato et al., 1983; Ono, Yamaura, Kubota, Okimura, & Isobe, 2001). For example, CT findings such as subarachnoid hemorrhage and multiplicity of parenchymal lesions in patients with severe head injury, when incorporated into algorithms with other patient characteristics, predicted 6-month outcomes with accuracy as high as 92.1% (Ono et al., 2001). However, the ability of CT to distinguish between different brain structures and tissue types (i.e., contrast resolution; Simpson, 2012) remains controversial. It is also rather insensitive to the small nonhemorrhagic lesions typically seen in mild to moderate brain trauma and is of little value in determining smaller white matter disturbances.

Even with severe TBI, CT findings of brain tissue trauma can be equivocal. On the basis of comparison of emergency department premortem CT scans with postmortem pathology reports, Molina, Nichols, and Dimaio (2007) demonstrated that of 111 head CT scans corresponding to 295 injuries, only 24 CT scans correlated completely with autopsy findings, 66 scans correlated partially, and 21 scans did not correlate at all. Overall, CT scans demonstrated reasonable sensitivity for identifying subdural hematomas (66%) but were poor at identifying basilar skull fractures (only 19%; Molina et al., 2007). Because of poor sensitivity, CT seems inadequate when used alone for courtroom testimony when attempting to delineate brain tissue trauma (Molina et al., 2007).

Several studies have shown the inadequacy of CT to identify milder TBI (e.g., Mac Donald et al., 2011). Only 30% of patients with a Glasgow Coma Scale score of 13, 20% with a score of 14, and 5% with a score of 15 were found to have an abnormal CT scan (Borg et al., 2004). Even the relation between positive CT scans and cognitive changes can be equivocal. For example, when comparing mTBI patients with abnormal CT scans with patients with normal CT scans, the effects were too small for groups to be reliably differentiated on the basis of corresponding neuropsychological performance (Iverson, 2006).

Taken together, the danger of concluding that an individual has not suffered a TBI based solely on a negative CT scan is probably real (as discussed by Bazarian, Blyth, & Cimpello, 2006). Unfortunately, it has historically been concluded that a normal CT scan is evidence for a lack of brain injury (e.g., Palchak et al., 2003) or a nonclinically important brain injury (e.g., Stiell et al., 2001). This is clearly not the case.

Magnetic Resonance Imaging (T_1- and T_2-Weighted, Proton Density)

Description and uses. Along with CT, MRI makes up the majority of brain imaging technologies in use today (Organisation for Economic Co-operation and Development, 2013). MRI is a noninvasive imaging technique that uses magnetic fields and radiofrequency (RF) energy to affect atomic nuclei. As with CT, the object is to produce a series of cross-sectional planar images that show contrast differences across tissue types. Unlike CT scanning, MRI has the advantage of not using any ionizing radiation. Instead, MRI passes a strong magnetic field through the tissue of interest and detects spin phenomena of subatomic particles (protons). Hydrogen is most often targeted because it is so abundant in biological tissue and its nucleus is a single proton. Using a RF field applied to the tissue, proton orientations are temporarily moved (the "flip angle"). Once this RF field is removed, the protons return to their normal orientation within the external magnetic field ("relaxing") while releasing the energy they absorbed while under the RF field. This released RF energy and subsequent relaxation of the proton from the resultant flip angle can be detected by an RF receiver as a signal change. Differences in the temporal gradient (duration) of this relaxation suggest different proportions of the hydrogen protons, and thus differing tissue. MRI has no equal in terms of spatial resolution, routinely producing images at the submillimeter level.

As in CT scanning, collections of planar images are combined via a computer program to "reconstruct" tissue in two- and three-dimensional space. The final result is a very fine, detailed picture of tissue anatomy that varies according to the type of MRI image acquired (see Figure 6.3). Because of its high resolution, it is often the neuroimaging technique of choice when looking for tumors or abnormal tissue in the brain, though it can be applied to a variety of other pathological processes. These processes include subtle atrophy or degeneration of brain volume, smaller metastatic tumors, certain kinds of intracranial vascular lesions, protein disturbances (e.g., plaques) specific to multiple sclerosis and features of Parkinson's disease (and germane to recent questions regarding chronic traumatic encephalopathy) and tissue scarring from earlier lesions.

Another great advantage of MRI is its flexibility. MRI technologies have been adapted to measure the dispersion of a range of chemicals (e.g., neurotransmitter substances) in the central nervous system (magnetic resonance spectroscopy) or to gather detailed images of the entire blood system (magnetic resonance angiography). Finally, MRI measures have been developed to obtain indirect measures of functional brain activity (fMRI, discussed in a later section of this chapter).

All available evidence suggests that the magnetic field exposure in MRI is generally harmless to body tissue. However, the process has some risks. Because of the strong magnetic field, ferrous-based objects must be kept outside of the scanning environment, including medical equipment and materials within the patient's soft tissue (e.g., aneurysm clips), as well as closed-circuit electroconductive devices (e.g., pacemakers). In addition, RF pulses can

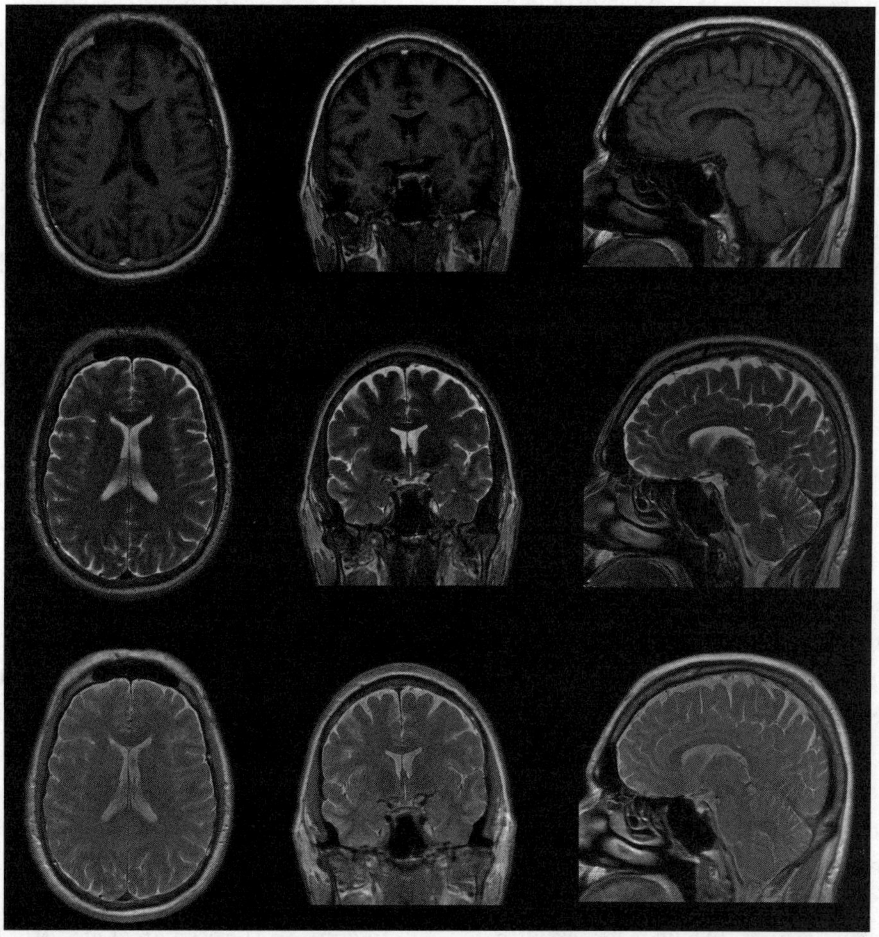

FIGURE 6.3. Common types and views of structural human brain MRI scans: axial, coronal, and sagittal views, respectively, from T_1-weighted scan (first row), T_2-weighted scan (second row), and proton density–weighted scan (third row).

generate localized heat within body tissue if unregulated, causing tissue damage in extreme cases.

Research and applicability to the courtroom. Conventional MRI techniques are frequently used in forensic settings, and they are well established as being generally more sensitive and specific for detecting brain injury abnormalities than CT, particularly when the injury is of a milder nature such as small intracranial blood collections and axonal injury (Bazarian et al., 2006; Gentry et al., 1988; Johnston et al., 2001; Mittl et al., 1994; Shenton et al., 2012). For example, MRI has been demonstrated to be capable of identifying structural abnormalities in 30% of patients who present with negative CT scans after mild head injury (Mittl et al., 1994). Similarly, in a sample of patients with closed-head trauma of varying severity, T_2-weighted MRI was far more sensitive to nonhemorrhagic lesions than CT (sensitivities = 93.3% and 17.7%, respectively; Gentry et al., 1988).

When samples exclude mild head injury cases and are restricted to patients with only moderate to severe head injury, some form of brain abnormality is apparent in virtually every case (Skandsen et al., 2010). Relative to CT, MRI has been found to be equal or superior at identifying brain abnormalities in 95% of cases with moderate to severe head injuries (Kelly et al., 1988). Brain injury profile as revealed through MRI has long demonstrated prognostic value as well (Weiss, Galanaud, Carpentier, Naccache, & Puybasset, 2007). In particular, the presence and extent of diffuse axonal injury and level of lesion burden predict patient outcome, including postinjury functioning on the Glasgow Outcome Scale, neuropsychological performance, and mortality (Carpentier et al., 2006; Paterakis, Karantanas, Komnos, & Volikas, 2000; Wedekind, Hesselmann, Lippert-Grüner, & Ebel, 2002).

Despite its greater sensitivity compared with other structural imaging techniques, measurement of brain damage after mTBI remains challenging, likely because of both technological limitations and the heterogeneity of this disorder. As with CT, conventional MRI often appears negative after mTBI (Bigler, Deibert, & Filley, 2013; Shenton et al., 2012). Overall, the prevalence of abnormal MRI scan after mTBI is quite variable, with 43% to 90% of cases presenting with negative scans (Hofman et al., 2001; Hughes et al., 2004; Voller et al., 1999). In addition, MRI abnormalities in mTBI patients appear to be only weakly correlated with neuropsychological functioning in the acute phase and uncorrelated with postconcussion syndrome and return-to-work status at 6 months (Hughes et al., 2004). Thus, MRI techniques may not be predictive of mTBI patients with ongoing complications.

It should be reiterated that different structural imaging techniques may confer advantage depending on the presenting injury. For instance, although MRI is more sensitive than CT scans for brain injuries involving contusion, shearing, subdural hematoma, and epidural hematoma, CT may be more sensitive than MRI for skull fractures (Orrison et al., 1994). Issues of specificity should also be considered when MRI scans suggest the presence of brain abnormalities after injury. For example, it is difficult to distinguish small lobar white matter lesions adjacent to gray matter, which are commonly interpreted as axonal damage after head injury, from nonspecific hyperintensities in patients who have never been injured (Katzman, Dagher, & Patronas, 1999).

Other (Advanced) MRI Techniques

Over the past 25 years, MRI technology has been refined and advanced, producing a variety of approaches that hold potential in the context of assessing brain injury. Perfusion-weighted imaging is a technique used to assess abnormal blood supply and abnormal perfusion. Arterial spin labeling is a newer measure of cerebral blood flow that has been used to identify reduced cerebral blood flow in pediatric mTBI patients (primarily in the bilateral frontotemporal regions), even when traditional MRI scans and neuropsychological performance are normal (Wang et al., 2015). Adults with a history of mTBI have also been shown to exhibit significant differences in arterial spin labeling measures relative to controls (Grossman et al., 2013).

On the basis of the principle of Brownian motion of water molecules (i.e., random motion), diffusion-weighted imaging is a good technique for assessing the presence of edema (Le & Gean, 2009; Shenton et al., 2012). A similar procedure, susceptibility-weighted imaging, measures hypointensities related to byproducts of blood degradation (hemosiderin; Bigler et al., 2013) and has shown good sensitivity to microhemorrhages (Park et al., 2009). Indeed, susceptibility-weighted imaging may be up to 6 times more sensitive to hemorrhagic diffuse axonal injuries than conventional MRI (Tong et al., 2004).

Fluid-attenuated inversion recovery sequences have been applied to evaluate white matter hyperintensities in the context of brain insult (Marquez de la Plata et al., 2007). These researchers found white matter lesion volume (resulting from diffuse axonal injury) to be reliably quantifiable using fluid-attenuation inversion recovery–weighted MRI and predictive of worse functional outcomes in a sample of moderate to severe TBI patients.

Magnetization transfer ratio, which is considered an indirect assessment of myelin integrity (Mottershead et al., 2003), is reduced in some white matter regions after mTBI (McGowan et al., 2000) and may hold promise in assessing traumatic lesions (see Le & Gean, 2009, for a review).

Magnetic resonance spectroscopy, which assesses brain metabolites reflective of neuronal integrity (Narayana, 2005), provides a candidate measure of metabolic disturbance after mTBI, though findings have been somewhat inconsistent (see Gardner, Iverson, & Stanwell, 2014, and Lin et al., 2012, for recent reviews). Nevertheless, spectroscopy offers more direct assessment of neurotransmitter levels and cell death (Vagnozzi et al., 2010; Yeo et al., 2011), which may be particularly relevant to mTBI.

Diffusion Tensor Imaging

Description and uses. A special use of diffusion-weighted imaging is diffusion tensor imaging (DTI). DTI is thought to measure white matter integrity not immediately visible from inspection of conventional MRI (Nusbaum, Tang, Buchsbaum, Wei, & Atlas, 2001). DTI uses the diffusion of water molecules to estimate the orientation and coherence of white matter fiber tracts and infer integrity of white matter microstructure. Diffusivity exists on a continuum from isotropic movement (water moves uniformly in all directions) to anisotropic movement (water moves primarily in one direction; see Figure 6.4). In the brain, isotropic movement is greater in areas of cerebrospinal fluid and gray matter because water is less constrained by physical boundaries, whereas anisotropic movement is greater in white matter, where structures such as myelin sheaths and microtubules constrain water movement (Chanraud, Zahr, Sullivan, & Pfefferbaum, 2010). With DTI, diffusion-weighted images are acquired along multiple orientations and analyzed to calculate a tensor, which quantifies diffusion along three primary axes: v1, v2, and v3 (Melhem et al., 2002). Three eigenvalues (λ_1, λ_2, and λ_3) describe the strength of diffusion along the corresponding axes and can be combined to describe different properties of white matter.

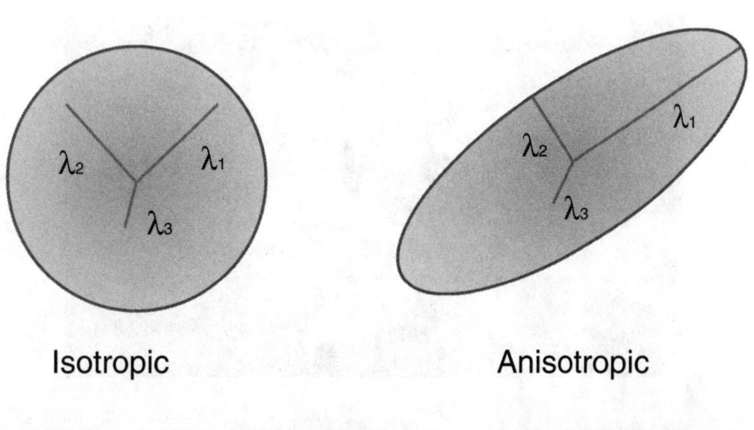

FIGURE 6.4. Isotropy and anisotropy. λ_1 = longitudinal (axial) diffusivity; $(\lambda_2 + \lambda_3) / 2$ = radial diffusivity; $\lambda_1 + \lambda_2 + \lambda_3 / 3$ = mean diffusivity.

Four primary measures of diffusivity are used in research. Mean diffusivity is the average diffusivity along all three axes within a particular white matter region (Bennett, Madden, Vaidya, Howard, & Howard, 2010). Fractional anisotropy (FA) is the diffusivity of water along the primary axis (λ_1) relative to the other two axes (λ_2 and λ_3); it measures the degree of orientational diffusion within a white matter region (Chanraud et al., 2010). Axial diffusivity is the diffusivity of water along the primary axis (λ_1); it is thought to reflect axonal integrity and may relate to axonal degradation (Alexander, Lee, Lazar, & Field, 2007) or shrinkage (Bennett et al., 2010). Finally, radial diffusivity is the average diffusivity along the two secondary axes (λ_2 and λ_3); it is thought to be a measure of myelin integrity (Chanraud et al., 2010). Association of axial diffusivity with axonal integrity and radial diffusivity with myelination is supported by nonhuman animal models (Beaulieu, 2002). These DTI-derived diffusivity measures provide the data most commonly presented as evidence of change or trauma, essentially reflecting high or low diffusivity. Another highly visual format is to present MRI diffusion-weighted derived images of the diffusivity measures directly, showing the relative size and directionality of the white matter tracts they are thought to represent (see Figure 6.5).

Research and applicability to the courtroom. DTI may be the most "hopeful" neuroimaging technique for identification of underlying structural damage in TBI, particularly mTBI, so its use in the courtroom has much potential. This perspective is supported by a number of recent comprehensive reviews of the literature (e.g., Bigler, 2013; Kou & Haacke, 2014; Niogi & Mukherjee, 2010), that have consistently suggested greater sensitivity and predictive power than any other MRI modality in the assessment of mTBI. In many ways, this is consistent with conceptions of mTBI as damage to white matter networks (e.g., Pandit et al., 2013) and the notion that DTI measures microstructural changes in white matter (e.g., Pierpaoli & Basser, 1996).

The sensitivity of DTI to brain injury has been demonstrated across a number of studies. On the basis of a review of 100 published studies, Hulkower, Poliak, Rosenbaum, Zimmerman, and Lipton (2013) concluded that DTI represents an "extremely useful and robust tool" (p. 2071) for evaluating brain abnormalities after TBI and "effectively differentiates patients with TBI and controls" (p. 2064). More important, this review consistently observed that reduced white matter FA was associated with TBI despite the fact that the included studies had considerable heterogeneity in terms of injury severity level, patient demographics, and data analysis techniques. Reduced FA has been found in various brain structures, including centrum semiovale, corpus callosum, and internal capsule in both acute (within 1 week postinjury) and chronic (up to 9 years postinjury) patients relative to controls (e.g., Inglese et al., 2005; Kraus et al., 2007; Miles et al., 2008). More important, white matter change has

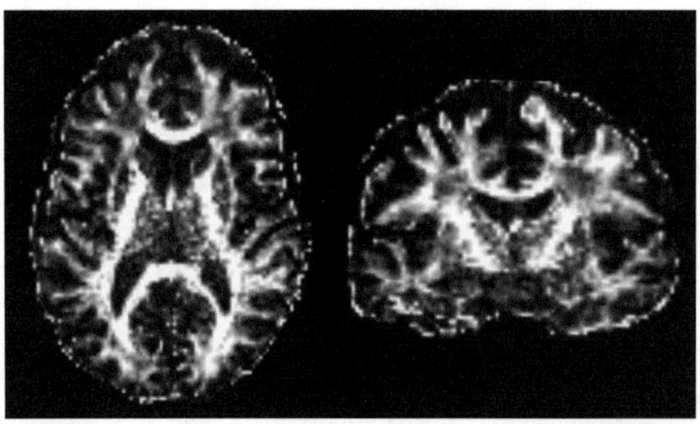

FIGURE 6.5. Diffusion tensor MRI scan illustrating fractional anisotropy–derived data: axial view (left) and coronal view (right).

been evident in all severities of TBI (ranging from mild to severe) even when conventional structural techniques (e.g., CT and MRI) appear normal (Abe et al., 2008; Chanraud et al., 2010; O'Sullivan et al., 2001; Toth et al., 2013), and these changes exist on a spectrum such that worse injury is associated with more pronounced changes (Kraus et al., 2007). Although FA is by far the most common DTI metric used in TBI research, alternative metrics (e.g., mean diffusivity) may provide unique information and have shown promise in distinguishing TBI patients from controls (Bazarian, Zhu, Blyth, Borrino, & Zhong, 2012; Narayana et al., 2015).

DTI findings after brain injury correlate with clinically meaningful functional outcomes, as well. For example, white matter integrity has been demonstrated to correlate with neuropsychological performance, including executive functions, memory, and attention, both within the first few days after injury and at 6-month follow-up assessments (Kraus et al., 2007; Miles et al., 2008). DTI findings have also been found to predict other clinically relevant outcomes, including TBI severity (i.e., Glasgow Coma Scale scores; e.g., Bendlin et al., 2008), postconcussive symptoms (e.g., Bazarian et al., 2007), mood symptoms (Chu et al., 2010), and outcome more globally, such as Glasgow Outcome Scale scores (e.g., Levin et al., 2008).

However, as Silver (2012) pointed out, discrepant findings are not uncommon. In contrast to the results previously presented, several studies have found elevated FA after brain injury (e.g., Mayer et al., 2010; Yallampalli et al., 2013), areas of both high and low FA (e.g., Lipton et al., 2012), or an absence of white matter injury (e.g., Lange, Iverson, Brubacher, Mädler, & Heran, 2012; Levin et al., 2010). The relationship of DTI metrics to clinical outcomes has similarly been contradictory. For example, some research findings have suggested that FA is positively correlated with neuropsychological functioning, global outcome, TBI severity, and postconcussive symptoms, whereas other findings have suggested no correlation or even a negative correlation (Hulkower et al., 2013).

Recent meta-analyses of the use of DTI in assessing neural changes post-TBI have helped to clarify some of the discrepancies in the literature. Perhaps most notably, there is considerable variability in brain regions evaluated despite observations that reductions in FA appear in certain regions post-mTBI (e.g., splenium of the corpus callosum) but not in others (e.g., genu of the corpus callosum; Aoki, Inokuchi, Gunshin, Yahagi, & Suwa, 2012). In addition, Eierud et al. (2014) provided evidence for elevated white matter anisotropy values in acute mTBI but depressed anisotropy values in chronic mTBI. This temporal difference in direction of findings may help to clarify inconsistent findings in the literature by "time resolving the results," because studies vary considerably in when imaging data are collected, from hours to years postinjury. Nevertheless, it is important to note that when examined independently, individual DTI studies appear to show sporadic white matter differences, and it is only when integrating across studies that these systematic distributions emerge.

A variety of other factors likely contribute to the observed variability in DTI findings after brain insult, such as the manner in which data are collected and then analyzed, the variables chosen for anisotropy, the uncontrolled impact of third-factor variables, the misinterpretation of data, and so forth. The lack of established best-practice guidelines for acquiring and analyzing DTI data has been noted in reviews as a major problem in the use of DTI findings in the courtroom, because different approaches—ranging from magnetic field strength to registration and smoothing processes—can lead to dramatically different results (Papinutto, Maule, & Jovicich, 2013; Wortzel, Tsiouris, & Filippi, 2014). For instance, hardware differences have been shown to result in different findings with the same subject (Vollmar et al., 2010). Similarly, when the same DTI data set was distributed to nine research groups for voxel-based analyses, nine different results were reported (D. K. Jones et al., 2007).

A variety of psychiatric conditions (e.g., depressive disorders, anxiety disorders, personality disorders), which are common among litigants, have been shown to have an impact on DTI findings (White, Nelson, & Lim, 2008). More important, heterogeneity related to these conditions was found in particular in brain regions that are often identified in mTBI suggesting the possibility that they, rather than the mTBI, could be the source of DTI differences. Other factors that can contribute to individual variability in white matter integrity include cigarette smoking (Paul, Grieve, et al., 2008), early life stressors (Paul, Henry, et al., 2008), and childhood verbal abuse (Choi, Jeong, Rohan, Polcari, & Teicher, 2009). Thus, regardless of presence or extent of TBI, a variety of factors might lead to variation in white matter integrity, potentially confounding results (Wortzel et al., 2014).

As noted by Wortzel et al. (2014), one of the major problems with DTI, and in fact with many of the current advanced neuroimaging techniques, is the discrepancy between positive imaging findings and functional findings. Several systematic reviews (e.g., Carroll et al., 2004; Dikmen et al., 2009) and meta-analyses (e.g., Belanger, Curtiss, Demery, Lebowitz, & Vanderploeg, 2005; Rohling et al., 2011) have all suggested good prognosis after mTBI, with complete recovery generally representing the norm (it should be noted this is not the case for repeated mTBI; e.g., McKee et al., 2013). In the smaller number of mTBI sufferers who do not recover, it has been difficult to determine whether their functional impairments are due to the injury or to other factors or conditions (e.g., comorbidities).

In light of the many factors contributing to variability in the literature and contradictory findings, it is not surprising that experts in the field have concluded that DTI, although a potentially informative and powerful tool, has a high potential for medicolegal abuse. As pointed out by Wortzel et al. (2014), the remarkable science and dazzling images can be very persuasive in the courtroom and tempt conclusions that exceed the limitations of the technology. Unfortunately, not only is medicocolegal abuse of DTI findings a possibility, but it may occur with some regularity, particularly in cases involving mild head injury (Wortzel et al., 2014). The need for a "healthy skepticism" (Wortzel et al., 2014, p. 5) surrounding the implementation of this advanced neuroimaging technique in forensic settings seems highly appropriate.

It should be noted that there are ways to improve DTI reliability and accuracy, such as using a greater number of diffusion directions (Mukherjee, Chung, Berman, Hess, & Henry, 2008), using higher field strength (Alexander, Lee, Wu, & Field, 2006), and decreasing the thickness of slices (Papinutto et al., 2013). However, as pointed out by the American Society of Functional Neuroradiology (2012) DTI Standards and Practice Subcommittee, in the absence of widely accepted guidelines for acquiring and analyzing DTI data, a number of choices must be made that can have a profound impact on the end results and resulting conclusions. The subcommittee ultimately concluded that individuals who are charged with making clinical decisions on the basis of DTI findings must be aware of the many limitations, pitfalls, assumptions, and approximations associated with this technique and advised interpretation of the data "in conjunction with conventional anatomical imaging as well as other clinical data" (p. 5). Accordingly, open dialogue and clear understanding about the many issues that can contribute to different results and interpretations are strongly recommended in the courtroom, and DTI findings should always be taken in context with a variety of other data sources.

FUNCTIONAL NEUROIMAGING

All of the previously described techniques can be considered, in one form or another, to be aimed at assessing the anatomy of brain tissue and changes in that anatomy as a result of some sort of brain insult. Functional neuroimaging techniques are fundamentally different in their approach in that the focus is on the physiological or metabolic activity occurring within an anatomical area, and they thus provide unique and complementary information. This is particularly important to consider given that brain injury, whether mild or more severe, is a dynamic process with evolving sequelae that unfold across multiple levels of analysis, ranging from the individual neuron to interactions among neural networks, to ultimately affect cognition and behavior (Bigler & Maxwell, 2012; Johnston et al., 2001). Brain insult initiates a complex metabolic cascade of events involving alterations in neurotransmitter systems, cerebral blood flow, and protein synthesis, much of which is invisible or only indirectly visible using conventional structural imaging methods, particularly in the acute phase (Lin et al., 2012).

Functional techniques provide a window into these clinically meaningful processes and are reviewed in the following sections.

Positron Emission Tomography

Description and uses. PET is a technique in which naturally occurring chemicals, most often glucose or oxygen or sometimes analogs of those compounds, can be labeled or tagged with a radioactive component. This radiotracer is then injected into the bloodstream and becomes distributed to areas of the body in which that compound is normally distributed or metabolized. Sensors of the PET scanner are able to detect the radioactivity as the compound is distributed to different tissues on the basis of decay properties of positively charged particles called positrons. These data are used to reconstruct the distribution of the compound via computer software, resulting in two- and three-dimensional images of that distribution. In the case of glucose, sensors detect the radioactive labeled glucose as it moves from the injection site through the arterial system of the brain. Areas that accumulate larger amounts of labeled glucose are presumably using more glucose, a proxy measure of brain activity.

The advent of PET neuroimaging has opened up a whole new set of methodologies for understanding the functions of the brain in real time. Because it measures chemical processes such as blood flow or glucose metabolism, PET allows inspection of changes in the chemical processes of the brain as a result of both normal and abnormal functioning. Hence, one can view normal metabolic processes during cognitive activities (e.g., remembering a string of words) to assess brain areas using energy during those activities. Also, one can assess change that occurs while engaged in a cognitive task after brain disease or insult. Spatial resolution of PET is moderate, with perfusion study resolution down to the order of 2 to 5 cubic millimeters.

The use of fast-decaying radioactive tracers in PET has advantages and disadvantages. The advantages are that they allow fairly rapid measurement, and thus brain function that occurs in this short time frame can be measured. The disadvantage is the need for expensive and highly specialized equipment to prepare these tracers, such as a cyclotron, designed to accelerate and then capture hydrogen ions for radioisotope production. PET neuroimaging is also not without some risks. These risks include exposure to small amounts of radioactivity as well as small risks of infection because of the introduction of a foreign substance to the blood stream.

Research and applicability to the courtroom. Although PET scans have been introduced as evidence in a number of court cases (e.g., *California v. Carrizalez,* 2011; *People v. Weinstein,* 1992; *United States v. Gigante,* 1997), interpretations of the implications of identified brain abnormalities have varied widely in forensic settings (Rushing, 2014). For example, in one of the most prominent court cases to date involving PET (*People v. Weinstein,* 1992), a PET scan showing reduced glucose metabolism in frontal regions related to an arachnoid cyst was presented as evidence that Herbert Weinstein, who had admitted to murdering his wife, suffered cognitive impairments that reduced culpability for his actions. This evidence was found to be persuasive, and sentencing was reduced to manslaughter. By contrast, the ruling was not as favorable for the mafia leader Vincent Gigante, charged with conspiracy and racketeering, whose defense team introduced a PET scan as evidence for dementia-related brain pathology (Rushing, 2014; *United States v. Gigante,* 1997). The prosecution countered by pointing out that Gigante's regimen of psychotropic medication could have been responsible for the observed PET abnormalities and that the comparison group differed on a number of important characteristics (e.g., age). Consequently, Gigante was judged to be competent to stand trial and was sentenced accordingly.

In brain insult (e.g., trauma, tumors, epileptic foci), hypometabolism is frequently seen, as was the case for Herbert Weinstein. In degenerative diseases, it has been seen in a variety of cortical and subcortical regions (Mazziotta, 1989; Mazziotta, Frackowiak, & Phelps, 1992). This hypometabolism is presumed to reflect synaptic loss, deficits in energy metabolism, or a reduction in glucose transport. Interestingly, PET has been used somewhat less in studies involving mTBI (Eiereud et al., 2014).

Nevertheless, PET offers excellent sensitivity for molecular processes and is thus well suited to detect changes in brain metabolism after TBI. For example, depressed glucose metabolism, which correlates with behavioral and cognitive functioning postinjury, has been found after TBI (Giza & Hovda, 2001).

After excluding complicated mTBI cases (in which abnormalities were observable on CT or standard MRI scans), Byrnes et al. (2014) identified 10 published studies evaluating PET and mTBI, many of which were conducted with military populations. To provide a few recent examples, Peskind et al. (2011) studied postconcussive symptoms in a sample of war veterans with blast injuries and found correlations with reductions in metabolic rate for glucose consumption in infratentorial structures (i.e., cerebellum, vermis, pons) and medial temporal cortex. Mendez et al. (2013) evaluated blunt force mTBI versus blast force mTBI. Hypometabolism was observed in 15 a priori regions of interest in both groups. Relative to the blunt force–injured group, the blast group showed decreased uptake in right superior parietal regions. Decreased uptake in the left medial frontal area in the blast group was also related to cognitive functioning (possibly indicative of parietal–frontal network disruption). Petrie et al. (2014) found decreased labeled glucose (FDG) uptake in parietal cortex, somatosensory cortex, and visual cortex, as well as lower uptake in parahippocampal gyrus for veterans who had been subject to more than 20 blast mTBIs relative to those who had been exposed to fewer than 20 blasts mTBIs.

Challenges with the PET and mTBI literature include notable inconsistencies in techniques used to assess glucose uptake and metabolism, coupled with limited information in many studies regarding the quantification methods used to analyze PET images. The literature has little consensus regarding standards for PET acquisition parameters or postprocessing analyses. Furthermore, there is little consensus about the best parameters to use as injury biomarkers (e.g., in FDG-PET, parameters include standardized uptake value, relative uptake value, metabolic rate for glucose consumption, FDG uptake, and others). Additionally, little work has evaluated variables such as injury type, age, time postinjury, or injury history. Despite this variability in methodology, however, there appears to be fairly consistent observations in the literature of hypometabolism and depressed uptake of FDG, both globally and in specific brain regions, after mTBI. In turn, hypometabolism is correlated with cognitive and functional deficits, such as attentional problems, irritability, social withdrawal, sleep disturbance, memory difficulties, and depressive symptoms (Gross, Kling, Henry, Herndon, & Lavretsky, 1996; Mendez et al., 2013). These data suggest that PET may be a relatively strong indicator of functional brain disturbance and is sensitive to brain dysfunction that might not otherwise be found, but it may not be overly specific.

Single-Photon Emission Computed Tomography

Description and uses. SPECT is similar to PET in that it uses radioactive tracers with a similar detection system to reconstruct images of activity occurring in the brain. However, the images are less detailed, and rapid changes in brain function cannot be observed because of the tracers used.

Unlike PET, which measures positron emission, SPECT uses specialized detectors or gamma cameras to record photon emission from radioactive tracers injected into the blood supply to the brain. Thus, it can be a measure of cerebral blood perfusion, or regional cerebral blood flow. However, SPECT also takes advantage of special tracers that are absorbed into the brain tissue itself via the blood supply system. SPECT uses radioactive tracers that have a longer shelf life than typical PET tracers, and several are commercially available. Most of these tracers (e.g., iodine 123-IMP) quickly move across the blood–brain barrier and over time accumulate in brain regions in relation to the rate of blood flow to that brain region. A specialized type of SPECT scanning sometimes used is an inhalation method of the radioactive tracer Xenon-133 to measure regional cerebral blood flow. Unlike other tracers, Xenon-133 clears the brain very rapidly, allowing multiple independent studies to be performed in succession. SPECT images are collected over many angles, which can then be computer reconstructed in any two-dimensional or three-dimensional space.

This allows for SPECT images to be "coregistered" with CT or MRI scans to give information about structural morphology and functional activity in the brain.

Advantages of SPECT include reduced expense and expertise needed to conduct the studies compared with PET or fMRI, discussed later. Also, longer lasting radioactive tracers are used, making them better products for storage without specialized manufacturing procedures. Limitations include a somewhat lower level of resolution than PET, although the newer multidetector systems used in research settings have spatial resolution approaching PET-quality systems. In addition, SPECT has a reduced ability to image deeper brain structures because photons are attenuated as they pass through tissue. SPECT has been used for some time in the study of brain function. It has proven especially useful in measuring dopamine distribution and identifying ischemic insult (Donnemiller et al., 2000).

Research and applicability to the courtroom. SPECT has potential advantages for use in the courtroom, especially with mTBI. Practically speaking, it is available at many major hospitals, and there is a fairly extensive body of literature involving SPECT and brain injury. It is sensitive to metabolic disturbances after mTBI, given associated alterations in blood flow. This has been borne out in some research because SPECT shows good sensitivity and negative predictive power in terms of predicting clinical outcomes, such as postconsussive symptoms and neuropsychological functioning, particularly if abnormalities remain evident with increasing time postinjury (A. Jacobs, Put, Ingels, & Bossuyt, 1994; A. Jacobs, Put, Ingels, Put, & Bossuyt, 1996). Also, absence of SPECT abnormalities provides good evidence of a positive prognosis after brain injury. Raji et al. (2014) completed a recent systematic review of more than 70 SPECT studies, both longitudinal and cross-sectional, in the diagnosis and treatment of brain injury. Overall, positive predictive power ranged from 59% to 95%, increasing as time postinjury increased. Both longitudinal and cross-sectional studies have indicated that SPECT identified lesions that were not shown in traditional CT or MRI scans, and SPECT was superior to CT and MRI for both acute and chronic brain injury (particularly mTBI). Brain abnormalities were most commonly found in the frontal lobe (49 of 52 cross-sectional studies [94%]) and the temporal lobe (40 of 52 cross-sectional studies [77%]). Finally, SPECT abnormalities correlated with neuropsychological and neurological outcomes in 13 of the 14 longitudinal studies and 18 of the 22 cross-sectional studies that included neuropsychological data.

Difficulties with using the SPECT TBI literature base in the medicolegal arena include the multiple techniques used for conducting the imaging (e.g., whether subjects are in a resting state or performing tasks) and the use of different tracer types with different biokinetics. Nevertheless, SPECT has considerable potential in diagnosing mTBI and appears to have clear advantages over CT and MRI in terms of sensitivity (Davis et al., 2000). A significant criticism however, is that specificity is not great; SPECT abnormalities could be the product of a variety of different factors (e.g., migraines, chronic pain, drug abuse, psychological disorders; Wortzel, Filley, Anderson, Oster, & Arciniegas, 2008). The bottom line is that expert testimony involving SPECT should only be considered in the context of clinical history, neuropsychological functioning, structural brain images, and other data and should not be a stand-alone diagnostic method. This view is consistent with correspondence between Adinoff and Devous (2010) and Amen (2010), who agreed that the evidence base to support the application of SPECT for diagnosis and treatment without the consideration of other sources of data is insufficient. As noted by Amen (2010), "Thoughtful clinicians would never use SPECT in isolation.... That is not how imaging is or should be practiced." (p. 1125).

Electromagnetophysiological Techniques

Description and uses. EEG, its complement event-related potentials, and MEG are all functional imaging technologies based on summative information of very large aggregates of neurons. They have the advantage of high temporal resolution, on the order of a few milliseconds, but relatively less spatial resolution. Both EEG and event-related potentials measure electrical activity associated with neuronal firing characteristics, whereas MEG measures very small magnetic field changes occurring during neuronal activity. Because of the high temporal resolution, these techniques provide information concerning the relative timing of events and can provide important data regarding brain region connectivity and direction of neuronal activity. They have been somewhat limited by the poor depth of signal detection, because electrodes are placed on the scalp and thus signals must pass through tissue and bone. EEG assesses spontaneous neuronal activity, and event-related potentials measure the electrical potentials elicited by presented stimuli (e.g., motor, sensory, or cognitive information; Nidal & Malik, 2015). They are thought to reflect dendritic activity within upper cortical cell layers (G. H. Glaser, 1963). MEG provides similar temporal resolution with somewhat greater spatial resolution. MEG is unique in that it provides a direct measurement of magnetic signal resulting from neuronal activity in gray matter. In many respects, MEG represents the most direct measurement of neuronal activity of any of the functional neuroimaging methods.

EEG and event-related potential data have primarily been used to quantify neuronal processing changes by defining architectural changes in the major frequency bands—alpha, beta, theta, and delta. They have also been used to assess changes in functional independence of cortical areas. A more thorough discussion of these functional techniques is beyond the scope of this chapter, but interested readers are directed to a number of comprehensive reviews in the literature (e.g., Leiser, Dunlop, Bowlby, & Devilbiss, 2011; McLoughlin, Makeig, & Tsuang, 2014; Michel & Murray, 2012).

Unlike conventional EEG, which generally entails visual analysis of raw data by an electroencephalographer, quantitative EEG (qEEG) uses software-assisted statistical analysis to quantitatively assess EEG data for abnormalities (Arciniegas, 2011). Similar to the advantages afforded by traditional EEG, qEEG provides high temporal resolution (millisecond range), offers a more direct measure of excitatory and inhibitory cortical neuronal activity than hemodynamic-based signals such as fMRI, and does not involve radiation exposure (Coburn et al., 2006). In addition, it is portable and relatively inexpensive, and spatial resolution has been improved dramatically with increases in channel capacity from 20 to 512. As discussed in the following section, however, this technique faces serious challenges regarding issues surrounding specificity and reliability.

Research and applicability to the courtroom. Perhaps the most notable forensic application of EEG data was in the defense of Jack Ruby, who was charged with murdering President John F. Kennedy's assassin, Lee Harvey Oswald. Dr. Frederick Gibbs testified that brief bursts of notched six-per-second wave activity measured at right temporal electrode sites provided evidence for a psychomotor variant of epilepsy and various forms of personality instability, such as difficulties with emotional control (Gutmann, 2007). In addition to routine use in the assessment and monitoring of epilepsy (Maganti & Rutecki, 2013), the potential for EEG to inform diagnosis and treatment of a variety of other clinical conditions, such as mood disorders, learning disabilities, schizophrenia, chronic pain, and Alzheimer's disease, has shown promise (Leiser et al., 2011) and is an active area of investigation.

EEG (as well as MEG) may be particularly relevant to TBI cases given its superior temporal resolution and ability to more directly assess neural activity relative to other functional imaging techniques, such as fMRI (Gosselin et al., 2011). EEG is the first neurodiagnostic tool to evaluate changes in brain functioning after TBI (M. A. Glaser & Sjaardema, 1940), and its applications have been advanced and refined considerably over the years (Arciniegas, 2011). Although EEG is not routinely administered immediately after TBI, some studies have reported generalized or focal slow wave activity and attenuated posterior alpha within several hours postinjury (Nuwer, Hovda, Schrader, & Vespa, 2005). Findings have been somewhat inconsistent, however, with different research groups finding different forms of EEG abnormalities postinjury (e.g., generalized bursts) or even an absence of EEG abnormalities altogether (Arciniegas, 2011). This may in part be attributable to observations that different severities of TBI appear to produce different patterns of EEG abnormalities, such as lower frequency wave activity in more severe cases (Thatcher et al., 2001).

It is important to note that EEG abnormalities have evidenced some predictive utility, with one study demonstrating an association between pathological EEG within 24 hours after TBI and clinical outcomes 23 years later when incorporated into an algorithm with posttraumatic amnesia (Hessen & Nestvold, 2009). More recent and sophisticated EEG analyses have demonstrated abnormalities in the optimal ratio of local to distal functional connectivity in the cerebral cortex following TBI (Tsirka et al., 2011). More specifically, mTBI patients evidence reduced theta band "clustering," a proxy for local neural network organization and synchrony, during cognitive task performance in underlying brain regions, which is consistent with neuronal disorganization resulting from insult (Tsirka et al., 2011). Although EEG alterations associated with mTBI tend to normalize within a few months in the majority of mTBI cases, abnormalities such as diffuse intermixed slowing may persist in some patients, though it is unclear whether such abnormalities are a product of the injury itself or of other potential confounds such as anxiety or medication use (see Arciniegas, 2011, and Nuwer et al., 2005, for reviews). One factor that may predict persistent abnormalities in brain electrical activity is the extent to which waveforms deviate from normality in the acute phase (Rapp et al., 2015). For example, ongoing alterations in EEG alpha power dynamics were observed in 85% of mTBI patients who demonstrated greater than 20% alpha power suppression 7 days postinjury (Slobounov, Sebastianelli, & Hallett, 2012).

qEEG has shown some promise in the detection of neurological dysfunction (Prichep et al., 2012), though significant research is still needed before it can confidently be implemented in the courtroom, and caution is recommended. This is consistent with conclusions reached by the Committee on Research of the American Neuropsychiatric Association (Coburn et al., 2006), which noted a number of serious methodological problems in qEEG research, including considerable heterogeneity in hardware and software; data processing strategies; and quality, size, and generalizability of normative databases used for comparison.

With respect to TBI, and mTBI in particular, the available qEEG literature has suggested considerable variability in the specific expression of qEEG abnormalities across studies (Arciniegas, 2011). In a recent review evaluating the evidence for the use of qEEG as a detection tool for mTBI, Rapp et al. (2015) concluded that, at best, qEEG offers an imperfect assessment of mTBI, and its sole use is not currently supported. In short, although abnormal activity has been observed after head injury, qEEG faces serious issues surrounding its specificity and reliability.

In light of seminal findings in animal and human models that axonal injuries associated with brain injury are related to pathological slow-wave activity in gray matter (Ball, Gloor, & Schaul, 1977), MEG is a good candidate measure of head trauma given well-established sensitivity to abnormal delta-band (1–4 Hz) and theta-band (5–7 Hz) signals (Lewine, Davis, Sloan, Kodituwakku, & Orrison, 1999). Several studies have indicated that patients who have had mild brain injury display abnormal low-frequency magnetic field activity as measured with resting-state MEG, which has evidenced greater sensitivity than conventional MRI or EEG (e.g., Lewine et al., 1999, 2007).

Recently, Huang et al. (2014) used a voxel-based whole-brain MEG slow-wave technique to evaluate abnormalities in 84 patients who had mTBI and presented with ongoing postconcussive symptoms. Although positive conventional MRI scans were observed in fewer than 10% of the sample, MEG delta-wave abnormalities appeared in more than 80% of blast brain-injured patients and nonblast brain-injured patients. The brain regions most affected were prefrontal, posterior parietal, inferior temporal, hippocampus, and cerebellum, with slow-wave activity in prefrontal areas correlating with personality changes, attentional difficulties, affective lability, and depressive symptomatology. A recent review of the literature (Huang, Risling, & Baker, 2016) suggested that, on average, MEG detects abnormalities in 87% of mTBI cases, with higher sensitivity for blast-induced mTBI (96%) relative to non–blast-induced mTBI (77%). Although the sensitivity of MEG to mTBI suggests potential for courtroom use, specificity is problematic given that a variety of other conditions (brain tumors, stroke, epilepsy, etc.) can also result in abnormal slow waves (Huang et al., 2016). Accordingly, it is advisable to supplement MEG evidence in forensic settings with structural imaging (e.g., CT and MRI), neuropsychological test results, medical history, and other sources of clinically relevant information. Although MEG appears to be used far less frequently in the courtroom than other imaging modalities, it is interesting to note that in one recent case, the plaintiff's counsel's failure to admit MEG findings was used to support conclusions of an absence of neural changes posttrauma (*Grange Insurance Company v. Sawmiller*, 2014).

Functional MRI

Description and uses. Probably no neuroimaging technique has received as much attention as fMRI. fMRI uses many of the same principles of standard MRI. However, rather than focusing on the magnetization properties of hydrogen protons, fMRI uses measurement of the magnetic properties of oxygen during times of brain activity. Images are based on the indirect measurement of activity in the brain through comparisons of magnetization changes resulting from blood flow, blood volume, and oxygen saturation. This is known as the blood-oxygen-level–dependent (BOLD) method (Ogawa et al., 1993). The typical BOLD fMRI strategy is to measure the amount of oxygenated hemoglobin in the microvascular system in specific brain regions during a particular brain activity compared with inactivity. When a brain area is activated, there are proportional increases of oxygenated blood in the microvasculature and associated changes in magnetic properties.

fMRI has a multitude of advantages over other functional imaging techniques. Compared with PET and SPECT, its spatial resolution is much greater, with accurate resolution now below 1 cubic millimeter. Thus, the image clarity is far superior. Because the data are collected using MRI techniques and equipment, concomitant MRI structural images can be collected, giving very precise coregistering capabilities. Together, fMRI and MRI provide exquisitely sensitive images of the brain's functional activity and precise placement of that activity on the morphological MRI images (see Figure 6.6). fMRI, like MRI, is viewed as a safe, noninvasive method of in vivo assessment of the workings of the brain. However, the same risks inherent in MRI are also inherent in fMRI.

Research and applicability to the courtroom. The potential for fMRI to serve as a tool in civil and criminal litigation has been studied and applied in a wide range of capacities, such as discerning truth telling from lying, evaluating whether an individual

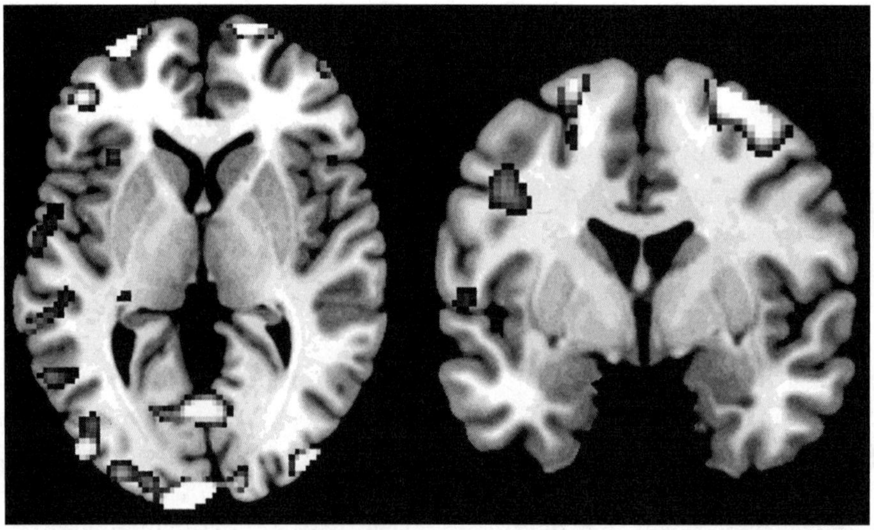

FIGURE 6.6. **Functional MRI (grayscale). Data overlaid on a T_1-weighted MRI showing task-dependent activation during a verbal memory task: axial view (left) and coronal view (right).**

has knowledge or memory of a particular event or piece of information, and determining neurological capacity for competence and culpability (Ganis, Rosenfeld, Meixner, Kievit, & Schendan, 2011; Kozel et al., 2005; Langleben et al., 2005; Somerville, Hare, & Casey, 2011). Given its diverse range of applications, it is not surprising that fMRI findings have been used as evidence in numerous court cases.

With respect to brain trauma, the literature supports findings of altered or adapted activation of brain regions while engaging in cognitive tasks in brain-injured compared with non–brain-injured persons. Although findings have largely been consistent in demonstrating increased BOLD signal (i.e., hyperactivation) in moderate to severe TBI cases relative to controls, findings have been more inconsistent for mild head injury (Bryer, Medaglia, Rostami, & Hillary, 2013). As illustrated in a recent review of fMRI and TBI (Mayer, Bellgowan, & Hanlon, 2015), some studies have found hypoactivation post-mTBI relative to controls (e.g., Talavage et al., 2014), and others have found hyperactivation (e.g., Scheibel et al., 2012), a combination of hypo- and hyperactivation (e.g., Witt, Lovejoy, Pearlson, & Stevens, 2010), or no differences in brain activity (e.g., Elbin et al., 2012). These inconsistencies are difficult to reconcile from a theoretical perspective given evidence-based rationales for both hypoactivation (e.g., damage to neural systems, failed engagement of compensatory processes) and hyperactivation (e.g., reorganization of neural networks, compensatory processes, or poor regulation of neural systems) after insult (Bryer et al., 2013).

A likely explanation for inconsistent fMRI findings associated with mTBI involves the numerous methodological differences between studies, such as cognitive task modality, population (e.g., civilian vs. military), type of injury, patient age, time postinjury, setting, level of trauma severity, presence of comorbidities, and so forth (Mayer et al., 2015). For example, Fischer et al. (2014) found hyperactivation during response inhibition failure in military TBI patients relative to military controls but interestingly found hypoactivation in the same regions in civilian TBI patients, which may indicate different neuropathologies (e.g., blast-induced vs. acceleration–deceleration or blunt-force trauma). In another set of studies, decreased amygdala activity was observed in concussed veterans with depressive symptoms relative to concussed veterans without depressive symptoms in response to emotional faces, suggesting the importance of considering patient variables even when injury etiologies are shared (Matthews, Simmons, & Strigo, 2011; Matthews, Strigo, et al., 2011). The same research group demonstrated that injury severity has a differential impact on patterns of brain activation. A recent meta-analysis (Bryer et al., 2013) suggested the importance of considering the specific type of task used, even when the same general cognitive skill is being assessed.

Meta-analytic findings have revealed a "frontal vulnerability" associated with mTBI, specifically characterized by reduced signaling primarily in anterior regions (i.e., right and left middle frontal gyrus, right anterior cingulate, right middle temporal gyrus, right precentral gyrus, and right and left dorsolateral prefrontal cortex) and increased activity primarily in posterior regions (i.e., right cerebellar tonsil, right inferior parietal lobule, left culmen, right inferior frontal gyrus, right insula, and right supramarginal gyrus) relative to control groups (Eierud et al., 2014). As Eierud et al. (2014) noted, this pattern of activity is consistent with the anterior to posterior gradient observed in white matter FA values described earlier, though unfortunately the fMRI analysis had insufficient power to evaluate time postinjury as a potential moderating variable. Of note, the observed frontal vulnerability maps onto, and likely underlies, cognitive difficulties that are frequently associated with mTBI, particularly those related to executive dysfunction and processing speed and other higher order cognitive abilities.

fMRI abnormalities after brain insult have been shown to correlate with clinical outcomes, including cognitive functioning, mood symptoms, and recovery profile more globally (Mayer et al., 2015). However, there appears to be heterogeneity in the type of fMRI abnormalities that correlate with outcome. As examples, hyperactivation in various regions has been shown to predict self-reported symptom severity, presence of postconcussive symptoms, impulse control difficulties, and overall worse recovery profiles (Fischer et al., 2014; Lovell et al., 2007; Smits et al., 2009). Yet, hypoactivation has been correlated with negative outcomes as well, such as magnitude of postconcussive symptoms, depressive symptomatology, length of posttraumatic amnesia, and injury severity (Chen, Johnston, Collie, McCrory, & Ptito, 2007; Matthews, Simmons, & Strigo, 2011; Matthews, Strigo, et al., 2011; Stulemeijer et al., 2010). Still other findings have suggested underlying differences in patterns of neural activity in mTBI patients relative to noninjured controls despite equivalent cognitive performance between groups (Ford, Giovanello, & Guskiewicz, 2013).

In short, task-dependent fMRI holds promise in the courtroom as a marker of brain injury and predictor of clinical outcome, though caution is warranted. Relative to other imaging modalities that assess structural integrity, fMRI sheds light on dynamic changes associated with brain dysfunction during performance of cognitive and emotional tasks, which provides an analogue to real-world settings (Mayer et al., 2015). It is also capable of identifying changes in relatively deeper gray matter structures, where shearing associated with TBI has been shown to occur, that may not be revealed through other techniques (L. Zhang, Yang, & King, 2004). Despite these advantages, findings have been largely inconsistent, particularly in mTBI, as to the nature of brain activation that can be expected postinjury and its relationship to functional outcomes. In essence, the functional significance of observed alterations in neural activity after brain insult remains to be fully elucidated (McDonald, Saykin, & McAllister, 2012). As noted by Mayer et al. (2015), adequately powered clinical studies with the same inclusionary and exclusionary criteria are required before conclusions can confidently be drawn regarding the nature and significance of fMRI findings in mTBI. Until then, fMRI is recommended only as a supplement to other assessment procedures and patient history in the courtroom.

Resting-state functional MRI. In contrast to task-dependent fMRI, which entails participant engagement in a task that draws on higher order cognitive functions, resting-state scans generally require participants to passively lie in the scanner with eyes closed or fixated on a set visual stimulus (e.g., a fixation cross). Rather than evaluating evoked BOLD activity, the interest is on intrinsic activity or functional connectivity, consisting of synchronous neuronal fluctuations across spatially distributed networks (Mayer et al., 2015). Such activity consumes significant amounts of the brain's energy resources, given that as much as 60% to 80% of the brain's metabolic load is estimated to be related to maintaining homeostasis (Raichle & Mintun, 2006). In light of findings noted previously that TBI is associated with changes in baseline metabolism, resting-state fMRI has received increased attention as a potential candidate in assessing brain injury. Although promising in theory, the application of resting-state fMRI to mTBI is relatively new, and thus only a small (but growing) number of studies exist on the topic.

Most of the available literature has focused on connectivity involving the "default mode network" that includes nodes in the posterior cingulate cortex, ventral anterior cingulate cortex, and supramarginal gyrus (McDonald et al., 2012). This network is conceptualized as those brain regions that are active when the participant is not focused on any particular stimulus and the brain is in a wakeful rest. Several studies have demonstrated that mTBI patients demonstrate abnormal functional connectivity relative to control groups (Johnson et al., 2012; Mayer, Mannell, Ling, Gasparovic, & Yeo, 2011; Tang et al., 2011). As an example, Mayer et al. (2011) found that mTBI patients displayed reduced functional connectivity within the default mode network and hyperconnectivity between DMN and lateral prefrontal cortex relative to controls, despite normal T_1 and T_2 imaging and neuropsychological test results. Functional connectivity abnormalities classified patients and controls with good accuracy (84.3%) and significantly predicted cognitive complaints in the semiacute phase (i.e., <3 weeks postinjury). The observed alterations in connectivity persisted into the late recovery phase (i.e., 3–5 months postinjury), suggesting sensitivity to enduring effects of brain dysfunction. Tang et al. (2011) observed hyperconnectivity in cingulate, temporal, and frontal regions in mTBI patients relative to controls, as well as increased activity and greater asymmetry in thalamic resting state networks. In turn, abnormalities in thalamocortical connectivity were associated with worse neurocognitive performance and clinical outcomes, including depressive and postconcussive symptoms. Alterations in connectivity after head injury have also been correlated with the number of previous concussions sustained (Johnson et al., 2012) and postconcussive syndrome (Stevens et al., 2012) and have demonstrated sensitivity to blast-induced TBI (Vakhtin et al., 2013). It should be noted that functional connectivity abnormalities associated with brain injury have been observed in a variety of regions beyond those mentioned thus far, such as visual cortex, hippocampus, and motor-striatal network (Shumskaya, Andriessen, Norris, & Vos, 2012; Slobounov et al., 2011; Zhou et al., 2014).

Resting-state findings in mTBI patients have been complicated by observations that functional connectivity is increased in some connective groups (hubs) but decreased in others or appears relatively normal compared with non-injured controls (K. Zhang et al., 2012). Longitudinal studies have also been mixed, with some findings suggesting increased connectivity in the acute phase and decreased connectivity in the chronic phase and other findings suggesting relative stability across time (Mayer et al., 2011; Messé et al., 2013). Unfortunately, as the literature currently stands, the relatively small number of studies on the topic and variability in methodologies between studies limit the identification of a reliable mTBI resting-state signature.

In addition to complexities and inconsistencies in the literature, as well as variability in procedures for acquiring and analyzing resting-state data (Mannell et al., 2010), common criticisms of this technique include a lack of control over cognitive activities of the patient (Mayer et al., 2015). Another disadvantage of resting-state studies is that random influences or fluctuations of the data, referred to as "noise," have more of an impact relative to task-dependent studies (Saad et al., 2012). Despite these limitations, resting-state fMRI also comes with a number of advantages over task-based fMRI (Mayer et al., 2015), such as minimized impact of various confounds related to poor effort, fatigue, and the like, which may be particularly relevant in a litigant population. It is also applicable to a wide range of TBI severity, from mild injury to limited consciousness (Sharp, Scott, & Leech, 2014). Along these lines, resting state may be most advantageous during the acute phase when cognitive and other deficits (which may interfere with task performance) are most pronounced. Finally, there is a reduced need for resources relative to task-dependent paradigms that require presentation software, MRI-compatible goggles, and response boxes. However, until a more thorough evidence base accumulates, resting-state fMRI should only be used with great caution in forensic settings and never as a stand-alone diagnostic.

UTILITY AND CHALLENGES IN FORENSIC SETTINGS

Although the use of advanced forms of neuroimaging in the courtroom is a relatively new phenomenon, with legal scholarship only recently beginning to incorporate discussions of the importance of these technologies (Shen, 2010), it is becoming increasingly mainstream. For example, neuroscientific research was recently admitted in a landmark Supreme Court case to demonstrate that regions subserving cognitive control in the adolescent brain are still developing and thus juveniles should not be sentenced to life without parole for nonhomicide offenses (*Graham v. Florida,* 2010). This trend is not surprising given that the basic function of the law is to regulate behavior, and neuroimaging methods are among the most powerful, robust, and objective tools available to shed light on the biological mechanisms underlying behavior (Meixner, 2015). As with any emerging technology, however, the potential for good must be carefully weighed against the potential for harm. To this end, a summary of the advantages and disadvantages of each imaging modality reviewed in this chapter in the courtroom setting is provided in Table 6.1.

In addition to considering strengths and weaknesses specific to each technique, a number of common challenges have emerged in the literature that must be kept in mind when applying neuroimaging findings to forensic settings. Perhaps the most significant challenge is what has been described as the "group-to-individual problem," whereby there

TABLE 6.1

Summary of Common Imaging Techniques and Uses

Technique	Description	Potential courtroom uses	Advantages	Cautions and disadvantages
Structural				
X-ray	Uses short-wavelength electromagnetic beams that pass through tissues at different rates on the basis of density and associated absorption properties	• Can be used in head injury involving trauma to bone or radio-opaque foreign bodies (e.g., bullets) • Contrast agents may identify arterial blockage, large tumors, hydrocephalus, some disease states (e.g., meningitis)	• Good visualization of skull integrity and radio-opaque foreign materials • Quick, inexpensive, widely available • Damage readily interpretable	• Poor resolution of CNS tissue and tissue subtypes • Single plane, tissue superimposed on image • Risk of radiation damage to tissue
CT	Uses computer-assisted assembly of multiple X-ray images from multiple angles around head	• CT is standard for closed-head injury, particularly in the acute phase • Identifies tumors, blood clots, blood hemorrhages, old lesions (hypodensities), brain swelling, herniation, and radio-opaque foreign bodies • Contrast agents may increase visualization of normal versus abnormal tissue	• Soft-tissue resolution better than X-ray • Multiplane, three-dimensional image reconstruction • High accuracy for major head injury, including skull fractures, intracranial hemorrhage, and gross abnormality • Abnormalities readily apparent and understandable to jurors and judges • Inexpensive, quick, widely available	• Radiographic photon exposure can affect cellular tissue (though less than X-ray) • Sensitivity to brain injury decreases substantially from major to moderate severity • Inadequate sensitivity for mild head injury cases
MRI	Uses strong magnetic fields and radiofrequency pulses to evaluate spin phenomena of atomic particles (hydrogen) to provide information about tissue	• Used for many types and severities of brain injury • Identifies tumors, brain atrophy, intracranial vascular lesions, protein disturbances (e.g., plaques), tissue scarring, cerebral contusions, subdural and epidural hematoma, and hemorrhages • Offers information about macroscopic white matter damage and shearing	• With CT, most common used brain imaging technology • No ionizing radiation • High resolution of CNS tissue, including superior contrast between tissue classes • Imaging in multiple planes • Reduced artifact from bone • More sensitive and specific than CT scans for all severities of brain injury and edema • High accuracy for moderate and severe head injury	• Incompatible with ferromagnetic materials and objects • Poor sensitivity to mild brain injury • Presence of abnormalities may not be specific to head injury
DTI	Uses MRI technology to evaluate diffusion of water molecules in white matter	• Assesses abnormalities in white matter integrity associated with head injury and disease processes	• Provides information about microstructural neuroanatomical changes after insult, including assessment of fiber tracts • Has the greatest sensitivity and predictive power relative to other MR modalities in mTBI assessment	• Considerable heterogeneity in pattern of DTI findings after head injury, which appears to depend on factors such as brain region evaluated, time since injury, data acquisition and analysis procedures • Multiple factors can impact DTI findings (e.g., psychiatric conditions, lifestyle choices), thus specificity is questionable • A number of choices made during acquisition and analysis, can influence results

Functional				
PET	Uses a radioactive tracer injected into the bloodstream to tag naturally occurring chemicals (e.g., glucose or oxygen) or their analogs (e.g., FDG); decay properties involving positron emission measured as proxy of brain activity	• Shows changes in chemical processes in the brain (e.g., metabolism) associated with head injury and neurodegenerative diseases	• Sensitive to brain abnormalities in mild head injury cases not seen with CT or MRI • Potential specificity for blunt-force versus blast-induced mTBI • Consistent observation of hypometabolism and depressed FDG uptake after brain injury • Rapid measure of brain function	• Moderate spatial resolution • Exposure to small amounts of radioactivity, mild risks of injecting foreign substance into bloodstream • Little consensus about acquisition and analysis procedures, including optimal parameters to serve as an injury biomarker • Expensive and specialized equipment (e.g., cyclotron) and procedures required to prepare radioactive tracers
SPECT	Evaluates decay properties of radioactive tracers, similar to PET; records photon emission rather than positron emission	• Shows changes in rates of cerebral blood flow, metabolic processes, and neurotransmitter activity resulting from head injury or neurological disease (e.g., dementia)	• Less expense and expertise required relative to PET or fMRI • Available in most major hospitals • Good sensitivity to brain injury, including milder forms that return negative results on CT or conventional MR scans	• Modest resolution, less detailed images • Tracers do not allow assessment of rapid changes in brain function • Limited capability to image deep brain structures • Poor specificity to brain injury, variety of conditions lead to similar SPECT findings (e.g., migraines, drug abuse, psychiatric conditions) • Heterogeneity of chosen tracers and acquisition techniques
EEG	Measures summed electrical activity associated with neuronal firing via electrodes placed on scalp, includes spontaneous neuronal activity and electrical potentials elicited by presented stimuli	• Assesses architectural abnormalities in brain-wave activity (e.g., pathological slow-wave activity) resulting from neurological injury or disease	• High temporal resolution • Relatively direct assessment of neural activity • Portable and relatively inexpensive	• Modest spatial resolution, improves with increases in channel capacity • Poor depth of signal detection • Wide variety of EEG abnormalities observed postinsult • Some concern about specificity given many conditions can lead to abnormalities (e.g., anxiety and medication use) • Not routinely administered after TBI
qEEG	Uses software-assisted statistical analysis to quantify EEG data for abnormalities	• May possibly be incorporated (e.g., discriminant functions) into assessment batteries for head injury, pending accumulation of sufficient research base	• Similar advantages to traditional EEG	• Heterogeneity in patterns of qEEG abnormalities postinjury • Poor specificity • Reliability remains to be established • Variability in data acquisition and analysis procedures • Comparison groups overly pure; generalizability unclear

(*continues*)

TABLE 6.1 (*Continued*)

Summary of Common Imaging Techniques and Uses

Technique	Description	Potential courtroom uses	Advantages	Cautions and disadvantages
		Functional		
MEG	Measures small changes in magnetic fields associated with direct neuronal activity in gray matter	• Evaluates abnormalities in low-frequency magnetic field activity resulting from brain insult and other neurological conditions	• High temporal resolution • Arguably most direct assessment of neuronal activity relative to other techniques • Better spatial resolution relative to EEG • Pathological slow-wave activity more sensitive to mild brain injury than conventional MRI • Sensitive to blast-induced TBI	• Specificity poor, variety of other conditions (e.g., brain tumors, epilepsy) associated with abnormal slow-wave activity; recommended to supplement MEG findings with structural imaging (CT or MRI) and medical history • Has been used less frequently in the courtroom relative to other imaging techniques
Task-dependent fMRI	Has similar principles to structural MRI; focuses on magnetic properties of oxygenated relative to deoxygenated hemoglobin in cerebral blood to provide index of brain activity; the BOLD signal is measured while patients perform cognitive tasks	• Evaluates the extent to which the BOLD signal deviates from normality during cognitive performance after brain trauma or other neurobiological processes • fMRI has been applied in other capacities, such as to determine truthfulness, prior knowledge or memory of information, and competence	• High spatial resolution, image clarity • Easily coregistered with structural MRI images • Consistent pattern of hyperactivation observed in moderate to severe head injury • Identifies brain dysfunction in deep gray matter structures	• Incompatible with ferromagnetic materials/objects • Inconsistent pattern of fMRI abnormalities in mild head injury (e.g., hyperactivation, hypoactivation, hyper- and hypoactivation, normal activation) • Hemodynamic signal is indirect measure of brain dysfunction • Rarely administered after TBI
Resting-state fMRI	Assesses intrinsic activity or functional connectivity involving synchronous fluctuations in neuronal activity across identified networks of brain regions; patient lies passively in scanner	• Examines abnormalities in functional connectivity (in default mode as well as other networks) associated with baseline metabolic and homeostatic changes resulting from head injury	• Early findings show promise in assessing TBI, including mTBI • Sensitive to blast-induced TBI • Minimal impact of confounds of poor effort and fatigue • Applicable to range of TBI severity, including severe cases with limited consciousness • Reduced need for resources (e.g., presentation software) relative to task-dependent approaches	• Limited evidence base given application to brain insult is relatively new • Complex pattern of decreased connectivity in some hubs and increased connectivity in others after brain insult • Some findings have suggested lack of sensitivity to mild head injury • Appear to be postinjury changes in connectivity patterns across time; remains to be clarified • Variability in methods for acquiring and analyzing data • Lack of control over cognitive activities of the patient • More affected by “noise” relative to task-dependent fMRI • Not routinely administered after TBI

Note. BOLD = blood-oxygen-level–dependent; CNS = central nervous system; CT = computed tomography; DTI = diffusion tensor imaging; EEG = electroencephalography; fMRI = functional MRI; MEG = magnetoencephalography; MRI = magnetic resonance imaging; mTBI = mild traumatic brain injury; PET = positron emission tomography; qEEG = quantitative electroencephalography; SPECT = single-photon emission computed tomography; TBI = traumatic brain injury.

exists a fundamental discrepancy between the goals of scientists to generalize findings to the larger population and the goals of courts to particularize findings to individual cases (see Faigman, Monahan, & Slobogin, 2014, for a discussion). The neuroimaging studies described in this chapter provide information based on statistical averages across groups of individuals; they do not provide specific information about any one individual. Unfortunately, there is inconsistency in courts with respect to how this gap is bridged; some judges permit expert witnesses to formulate conclusions specific to the case at hand, whereas others restrict conclusions to more general, population-level inferences and leave decision making regarding applicability to the jurors (Faigman et al., 2014). As noted by Wortzel, Kraus, Filley, Anderson, and Arciniegas (2011), there is also inconsistency in how neuroscientists describe findings with respect to the degree of relevance to patient- versus group-level inferences, which can further contribute to confusion in the courtroom.

Misinterpretations regarding null hypothesis significance testing, in both the scientific and the legal communities, similarly muddy the waters. As elaborated by Trafimow (2014), the null hypothesis significance testing procedure, as applied in the present context, evaluates whether the difference in a parameter of interest (e.g., diffusivity-derived FA values) between two populations (e.g., brain-injured and non-injured individuals) can be said to be "significant." If the resulting *p* value from the test does not exceed some cutoff, which is set rather arbitrarily at .05 by convention, the difference is described as statistically significant, and the conclusion is generally reached that "something is there." Unfortunately, *p* is often interpreted to represent the probability that the null hypothesis (e.g., there is no difference in white matter integrity between brain-injured and non–brain-injured individuals) is true. In reality, however, *p* represents the probability of a given finding relative to the null hypothesis being true, which ultimately means that a small *p* value provides far less convincing evidence that the null hypothesis is false than is commonly interpreted (for an excellent review of this concept, see Nickerson, 2000).

Although general patterns can be identified, woven throughout this chapter are examples of how the literature base for each neuroimaging modality is rife with inconsistent and even contradictory findings. These discrepancies are due to a number of factors, some of which remain to be identified, but among the most probable culprits include markedly heterogeneous data acquisition and analysis approaches that are compounded by the failure of many authors to provide sufficient information regarding exactly what procedures were followed to allow for meaningful interpretation and the opportunity to replicate. A second culprit is that brain injury is an extremely broad construct. There is considerable variability in the literature in terms of injury type, amount of time since injury, injury severity, operationalization of injury, and so on. In turn, these factors likely interact in complex ways with patient variables, such as age and presence of comorbidities. In many ways, it is understandable that such variability would exist when one considers the inherent difficulties associated with studying brain-injured populations. The consequence has been small and underpowered sample sizes and thus poor estimates of effect size (Mayer et al., 2015). Despite these challenges, large and well-designed studies with equivalent exclusionary and inclusionary criteria, as well as homologous data acquisition and analysis procedures, are required before reliable conclusions can be drawn at the group level, let alone the individual level.

Finally, the relationship between brain abnormalities identified through neuroimaging in head-injured patients and functional outcomes remains to be fully elucidated. This is problematic given that abnormalities across virtually all of the imaging techniques discussed thus far can be attributable to a variety of factors that may be largely unrelated to the brain insult, such as lifestyle choices, personality variables, or comorbid psychiatric conditions, which in many cases provide statistically more probable explanations. For example, as noted by Wortzel et al. (2014), chronic microvascular ischemia is very prevalent in the general population (Vermeer et al., 2003), particularly in older adults, and thus represents a more likely source of subcortical T_2 hyperintensities than a traumatic brain event. Relatedly, it is difficult to determine whether persisting neural abnormalities after injury are due to the injury itself or to the many conditions that tend to coincide with brain injury, such as mood dysregulation (Covassin, Elbin, Larson, & Kontos, 2012), which could represent either direct or indirect consequences of injury (or some combination) or perhaps even risk factors for the injury. Even if a reliable brain injury signature were to be identified, the functional implications of the neural signature would need to be clarified, particularly in light of findings reviewed previously of neuroanatomical alterations in brain-injured patients in the absence of cognitive or other observable symptoms (Bigler & Maxwell, 2012). It is unclear whether this speaks to a lack of sensitivity of available behavior measures or—perhaps just as likely—to hypersensitivity of neuroimaging methods to clinically meaningless abnormalities that do not confer functional limitations.

The prospect of routinely using neuroimaging techniques in the courtroom is alluring, and for good reason; these tools hold potential to offer objective windows into the mind. This concept is particularly appealing in litigant-seeking populations where the veracity of self-report is questionable and the stakes are high. Yet the sexiness of neuroimaging measures has understandably elicited concern that judges and jurors may be seduced into drawing conclusions based on spectacular imagery without adequate consideration of their many limitations. Indeed, the persuasive power of brain images has been demonstrated empirically, even when used in conjunction with illogical scientific text (McCabe & Castel, 2008). Although the rapid evolution of neuroimaging methodologies renders it difficult to predict their future course in the courtroom, one thing seems certain: Premature application not only risks harming or unjustly benefiting litigants, but it will also foster widespread societal distrust that could undermine future use even if sufficient empirical evidence eventually accumulates (Adinoff & Devous, 2010).

Although society is often enamored of "silver bullet" solutions to problems, the use of neuroimaging findings in the courtroom holds greatest promise when systematically considered alongside a variety of other data sources. For example, the accuracy of CT in mTBI assessment can be increased tremendously by incorporating other variables into the diagnostic process, such as presence of headache, vomiting, short-term memory deficits, seizure, and physical evidence of trauma above the shoulders, as well as patient age and substance-induced intoxication when injured (Haydel et al., 2000). Findings have indicated that various combinations of these variables with CT findings can lead to sensitivities as high as 95% and specificities as high as 100% (Sharif-Alhoseini, Khodadadi, Chardoli, & Rahimi-Movaghar, 2011). The use of optimally weighted algorithms incorporating imaging results has demonstrated long-term prognostic value as well (Hessen & Nestvold, 2009).

There is also exciting potential to combine multiple imaging modalities in medicolegal assessment of brain insult, because each approach provides unique information and offers complementary advantage. A small but growing number of studies (Grossman et al., 2012, 2013; Lewine et al., 2007; Matthews, Strigo, et al., 2011; Narayana et al., 2015) have suggested that integrative consideration of data across neuroimaging techniques notably improves sensitivity and specificity, not only to presence of brain injury in general but also with respect to specific profiles of brain injury (e.g., with or without loss of consciousness) and functional outcomes (e.g., mood and cognitive symptoms). It has been noted that techniques that assess particularly disparate features of neuropathology, such as EEG and fMRI, are optimal candidates for combination (Mayer et al., 2015). Considering forming a multimodal battery based on which techniques are most complementary in terms of sensitivity and specificity to brain insult (e.g., concerns regarding sensitivity of conventional MR techniques to mild head injury could be countered by superior sensitivity of SPECT), using the information presented in Table 6.1, is further recommended. Despite initial promise, it should be emphasized that research on multimodal imaging is still in its early stages, and until a more sturdy empirical foundation is established, the same cautions apply for courtroom use as with single-modality imaging.

References

Abe, O., Yamasue, H., Aoki, S., Suga, M., Yamada, H., Kasai, K., . . . Ohtomo, K. (2008). Aging in the CNS: Comparison of gray/white matter volume and diffusion tensor data. *Neurobiology of Aging, 29,* 102–116. http://dx.doi.org/10.1016/j.neurobiolaging.2006.09.003

Adinoff, B., & Devous, M. (2010). Scientifically unfounded claims in diagnosing and treating patients. *American Journal of Psychiatry, 167,* 598–598. http://dx.doi.org/10.1176/appi.ajp.2010.10020157

Alexander, A. L., Lee, J. E., Lazar, M., & Field, A. S. (2007). Diffusion tensor imaging of the brain. *Neurotherapeutics, 4,* 316–329. http://dx.doi.org/10.1016/j.nurt.2007.05.011

Alexander, A. L., Lee, J. E., Wu, Y.-C., & Field, A. S. (2006). Comparison of diffusion tensor imaging measurements at 3.0 T versus 1.5 T with and without parallel imaging. *Neuroimaging Clinics of North America, 16,* 299–309. http://dx.doi.org/10.1016/j.nic.2006.02.006

Amen, D. (2010). Brain SPECT imaging in clinical practice. *American Journal of Psychiatry, 167,* 1125–1126. http://dx.doi.org/10.1176/appi.ajp.2010.10060814

American College of Radiology. (2012). *ACR appropriateness criteria.* Retrieved from http://www.acr.org/Quality-Safety/Appropriateness-Criteria

American Society of Functional Neuroradiology. (2012). *ASFNR guidelines for clinical application of diffusion tensor imaging.* Retrieved from http://www.asfnr.org/clinical_stds.html

Aoki, Y., Inokuchi, R., Gunshin, M., Yahagi, N., & Suwa, H. (2012). Diffusion tensor imaging studies of mild traumatic brain injury: A meta-analysis. *Journal of Neurology, Neurosurgery, and Psychiatry, 83,* 870–876. http://dx.doi.org/10.1136/jnnp-2012-302742

Arciniegas, D. B. (2011). Clinical electrophysiologic assessments and mild traumatic brain injury: State-of-the-science and implications for clinical practice. *International Journal of Psychophysiology, 82,* 41–52. http://dx.doi.org/10.1016/j.ijpsycho.2011.03.004

Ball, G. J., Gloor, P., & Schaul, N. (1977). The cortical electromicrophysiology of pathological delta waves in the electroencephalogram of cats. *Electroencephalography and Clinical Neurophysiology, 43,* 346–361. http://dx.doi.org/10.1016/0013-4694(77)90258-9

Bazarian, J. J., Blyth, B., & Cimpello, L. (2006). Bench to bedside: Evidence for brain injury after concussion—Looking beyond the computed tomography scan. *Academic Emergency Medicine, 13,* 199–214. http://dx.doi.org/10.1197/j.aem.2005.07.031

Bazarian, J. J., Zhong, J., Blyth, B., Zhu, T., Kavcic, V., & Peterson, D. (2007). Diffusion tensor imaging detects clinically important axonal damage after mild traumatic brain injury: A pilot study. *Journal of Neurotrauma, 24,* 1447–1459. http://dx.doi.org/10.1089/neu.2007.0241

Bazarian, J. J., Zhu, T., Blyth, B., Borrino, A., & Zhong, J. (2012). Subject-specific changes in brain white matter on diffusion tensor imaging after sports-related concussion. *Magnetic Resonance Imaging, 30,* 171–180. http://dx.doi.org/10.1016/j.mri.2011.10.001

Beaulieu, C. (2002). The basis of anisotropic water diffusion in the nervous system—a technical review. *NMR in Biomedicine, 15,* 435–455. http://dx.doi.org/10.1002/nbm.782

Belanger, H. G., Curtiss, G., Demery, J. A., Lebowitz, B. K., & Vanderploeg, R. D. (2005). Factors moderating neuropsychological outcomes following mild traumatic brain injury: A meta-analysis. *Journal of the International Neuropsychological Society, 11,* 215–227. http://dx.doi.org/10.1017/S1355617705050277

Bendlin, B. B., Ries, M. L., Lazar, M., Alexander, A. L., Dempsey, R. J., Rowley, H. A., . . . Johnson, S. C. (2008). Longitudinal changes in patients with traumatic brain injury assessed with diffusion tensor and volumetric imaging. *NeuroImage, 42,* 503–514. http://dx.doi.org/10.1016/j.neuroimage.2008.04.254

Bennett, I. J., Madden, D. J., Vaidya, C. J., Howard, D. V., & Howard, J. H., Jr. (2010). Age-related differences in multiple measures of white matter integrity: A diffusion tensor imaging study of healthy aging. *Human Brain Mapping, 31,* 378–390.

Bigler, E. D. (2013). Neuroimaging biomarkers in mild traumatic brain injury (mTBI). *Neuropsychology Review, 23,* 169–209. http://dx.doi.org/10.1007/s11065-013-9237-2

Bigler, E. D., Deibert, E., & Filley, C. M. (2013). When is a concussion no longer a concussion? *Neurology, 81,* 14–15. http://dx.doi.org/10.1212/WNL.0b013e318299cd0e

Bigler, E. D., & Maxwell, W. L. (2012). Neuropathology of mild traumatic brain injury: Relationship to neuroimaging findings. *Brain Imaging and Behavior, 6,* 108–136. http://dx.doi.org/10.1007/s11682-011-9145-0

Borg, J., Holm, L., Cassidy, J. D., Peloso, P. M., Carroll, L. J., von Holst, H., & Ericson, K. (2004). Diagnostic procedures in mild traumatic brain injury: Results of the WHO Collaborating Centre Task Force on Mild Traumatic Brain Injury. *Journal of Rehabilitation Medicine, 43* (Suppl.), 61–75. http://dx.doi.org/10.1080/16501960410023822

Bryer, E. J., Medaglia, J. D., Rostami, S., & Hillary, F. G. (2013). Neural recruitment after mild traumatic brain injury is task dependent: A meta-analysis. *Journal of the International Neuropsychological Society, 19,* 751–762. http://dx.doi.org/10.1017/S1355617713000490

Byrnes, K. R., Wilson, C. M., Brabazon, F., von Leden, R., Jurgens, J. S., Oakes, T. R., & Selwyn, R. G. (2014). FDG-PET imaging in mild traumatic brain injury: A critical review. *Frontiers in Neuroenergetics, 5,* 13. http://dx.doi.org/10.3389/fnene.2013.00013

California v. Carrizalez, Transcript of Kelly-Frye Hearing at 1-267, No. VCF 169926C (2011).

Carpentier, A., Galanaud, D., Puybasset, L., Muller, J.-C., Lescot, T., Boch, A.-L., . . . van Effenterre, R. (2006). Early morphologic and spectroscopic magnetic resonance in severe traumatic brain injuries can detect "invisible brain stem damage" and predict "vegetative states." *Journal of Neurotrauma, 23,* 674–685. http://dx.doi.org/10.1089/neu.2006.23.674

Carroll, L. J., Cassidy, J. D., Peloso, P. M., Borg, J., von Holst, H., Holm, L., . . . Pépin, M. (2004). Prognosis for mild traumatic brain injury: Results of the WHO Collaborating Centre Task Force on Mild Traumatic Brain Injury. *Journal of Rehabilitation Medicine, 43* (Suppl.), 84–105. http://dx.doi.org/10.1080/16501960410023859

Chanraud, S., Zahr, N., Sullivan, E. V., & Pfefferbaum, A. (2010). MR diffusion tensor imaging: A window into white matter integrity of the working brain. *Neuropsychology Review, 20,* 209–225. http://dx.doi.org/10.1007/s11065-010-9129-7

Chen, J.-K., Johnston, K. M., Collie, A., McCrory, P., & Ptito, A. (2007). A validation of the post concussion symptom scale in the assessment of complex concussion using cognitive testing and functional MRI. *Journal of Neurology, Neurosurgery, and Psychiatry, 78,* 1231–1238. http://dx.doi.org/10.1136/jnnp.2006.110395

Choi, J., Jeong, B., Rohan, M. L., Polcari, A. M., & Teicher, M. H. (2009). Preliminary evidence for white matter tract abnormalities in young adults exposed to parental verbal abuse. *Biological Psychiatry, 65,* 227–234. http://dx.doi.org/10.1016/j.biopsych.2008.06.022

Chu, Z., Wilde, E. A., Hunter, J. V., McCauley, S. R., Bigler, E. D., Troyanskaya, M., . . . Levin, H. S. (2010). Voxel-based analysis of diffusion tensor imaging in mild traumatic brain injury in adolescents. *American Journal of Neuroradiology, 31,* 340–346. http://dx.doi.org/10.3174/ajnr.A1806

Coburn, K. L., Lauterbach, E. C., Boutros, N. N., Black, K. J., Arciniegas, D. B., & Coffey, C. E. (2006). The value of quantitative electroencephalography in clinical psychiatry: A report by the Committee on Research of the American Neuropsychiatric Association. *Journal of Neuropsychiatry and Clinical Neurosciences, 18,* 460–500. http://dx.doi.org/10.1176/jnp.2006.18.4.460

Coles, J. P. (2007). Imaging after brain injury. *British Journal of Anaesthesia, 99,* 49–60. http://dx.doi.org/10.1093/bja/aem141

Covassin, T., Elbin, R. J., III, Larson, E., & Kontos, A. P. (2012). Sex and age differences in depression and baseline sport-related concussion neurocognitive performance and symptoms. *Clinical Journal of Sport Medicine, 22,* 98–104. http://dx.doi.org/10.1097/JSM.0b013e31823403d2

Davis, P. C., Drayer, B. P., Anderson, R. E., Braffman, B., Deck, M. D., Hasso, A. N., . . . Masdeu, J. C. (2000). Head trauma. American College of Radiology. ACR Appropriateness Criteria. *Radiology, 215*(Suppl.), 507–524.

Dikmen, S. S., Corrigan, J. D., Levin, H. S., Machamer, J., Stiers, W., & Weisskopf, M. G. (2009). Cognitive outcome following traumatic brain injury. *Journal of Head Trauma Rehabilitation, 24,* 430–438. http://dx.doi.org/10.1097/HTR.0b013e3181c133e9

Dillon v. Evanston Hosp., 771 N.E.2d 357 (Illinois 2002).

Donnemiller, E., Brenneis, C., Wissel, J., Scherfler, C., Poewe, W., Riccabona, G., & Wenning, G. K. (2000). Impaired dopaminergic neurotransmission in patients with traumatic brain injury: A SPECT study using 123I-β-CIT and 123I-IBZM. *European Journal of Nuclear Medicine, 27,* 1410–1414. http://dx.doi.org/10.1007/s002590000308

Eierud, C., Craddock, R. C., Fletcher, S., Aulakh, M., King-Casas, B., Kuehl, D., & LaConte, S. M. (2014). Neuroimaging after mild traumatic brain injury: Review and meta-analysis. *NeuroImage: Clinical, 4,* 283–294. http://dx.doi.org/10.1016/j.nicl.2013.12.009

Elbin, R. J., Covassin, T., Hakun, J., Kontos, A. P., Berger, K., Pfeiffer, K., & Ravizza, S. (2012). Do brain activation changes persist in athletes with a history of multiple concussions who are asymptomatic? *Brain Injury, 26,* 1217–1225. http://dx.doi.org/10.3109/02699052.2012.672788

Faigman, D. L., Monahan, J., & Slobogin, C. (2014). Group to individual (G2i) inference in scientific expert testimony. *University of Chicago Law Review, 81,* 417–480.

Fischer, B. L., Parsons, M., Durgerian, S., Reece, C., Mourany, L., Lowe, M. J., . . . Rao, S. M. (2014). Neural activation during response inhibition differentiates blast from mechanical causes of mild to moderate traumatic brain injury. *Journal of Neurotrauma, 31,* 169–179. http://dx.doi.org/10.1089/neu.2013.2877

Ford, J. H., Giovanello, K. S., & Guskiewicz, K. M. (2013). Episodic memory in former professional football players with a history of concussion: An event-related functional neuroimaging study. *Journal of Neurotrauma, 30,* 1683–1701. http://dx.doi.org/10.1089/neu.2012.2535

Ganis, G., Rosenfeld, J. P., Meixner, J., Kievit, R. A., & Schendan, H. E. (2011). Lying in the scanner: Covert countermeasures disrupt deception detection by functional magnetic resonance imaging. *NeuroImage, 55,* 312–319. http://dx.doi.org/10.1016/j.neuroimage.2010.11.025

Gardner, A., Iverson, G. L., & Stanwell, P. (2014). A systematic review of proton magnetic resonance spectroscopy findings in sport-related concussion. *Journal of Neurotrauma, 31,* 1–18. http://dx.doi.org/10.1089/neu.2013.3079

Gentry, L. R., Godersky, J. C., Thompson, B., & Dunn, V. D. (1988). Prospective comparative study of intermediate-field MR and CT in the evaluation of closed head trauma. *American Journal of Neuroradiology, 9,* 91–100.

Giza, C. C., & Hovda, D. A. (2001). The neurometabolic cascade of concussion. *Journal of Athletic Training, 36,* 228–235.

Glaser, G. H. (1963). The normal electroencephalogram and its reactivity. In G. H. Glaser (Ed.), *EEG and behavior* (pp. 3–23). New York, NY: Basic Books.

Glaser, M. A., & Sjaardema, H. (1940). The value of the electroencephalograph in craniocerebral injuries. *West Journal of Surgery, 48,* 689–696.

Goldberg, D. S. (2013). The transformative power of X-rays in U.S. scientific and medical litigation: Mechanical objectivity in *Smith v. Grant* (1896). *Perspectives on Science, 21,* 23–57. http://dx.doi.org/10.1162/POSC_a_00085

Gosselin, N., Bottari, C., Chen, J.-K., Petrides, M., Tinawi, S., de Guise, E., & Ptito, A. (2011). Electrophysiology and functional MRI in post-acute mild traumatic brain injury. *Journal of Neurotrauma, 28,* 329–341. http://dx.doi.org/10.1089/neu.2010.1493

Graham v. Florida, 130 S. Ct. 2011, 560 U.S. 48, 176 L. Ed. 2d 825 (2010).

Grange Insurance Company v. Sawmiller, 140 Ohio St. 3d 1417 (Ct. App. 2014).

Gross, H., Kling, A., Henry, G., Herndon, C., & Lavretsky, H. (1996). Local cerebral glucose metabolism in patients with long-term behavioral and cognitive deficits following mild traumatic brain injury. *Journal of Neuropsychiatry and Clinical Neurosciences, 8,* 324–334. http://dx.doi.org/10.1176/jnp.8.3.324

Grossman, E. J., Ge, Y., Jensen, J. H., Babb, J. S., Miles, L., Reaume, J., . . . Inglese, M. (2012). Thalamus and cognitive impairment in mild traumatic brain injury: A diffusional kurtosis imaging study. *Journal of Neurotrauma, 29,* 2318–2327. http://dx.doi.org/10.1089/neu.2011.1763

Grossman, E. J., Jensen, J. H., Babb, J. S., Chen, Q., Tabesh, A., Fieremans, E., . . . Grossman, R. I. (2013). Cognitive impairment in mild traumatic brain injury: A longitudinal diffusional kurtosis and perfusion imaging study. *American Journal of Neuroradiology, 34,* 951–957, S1–S3. http://dx.doi.org/10.3174/ajnr.A3358

Gutmann, L. (2007). Jack Ruby. *Neurology, 68,* 707–708. http://dx.doi.org/10.1212/01.wnl.0000256034.72576.13

Haeger, K. (1998). *The illustrated history of surgery.* London, England: Canadian Medical Association.

Haydel, M. J., Preston, C. A., Mills, T. J., Luber, S., Blaudeau, E., & DeBlieux, P. M. C. (2000). Indications for computed tomography in patients with minor head injury. *New England Journal of Medicine, 343,* 100–105. http://dx.doi.org/10.1056/NEJM200007133430204

Hessen, E., & Nestvold, K. (2009). Indicators of complicated mild TBI predict MMPI-2 scores after 23 years. *Brain Injury, 23,* 234–242. http://dx.doi.org/10.1080/02699050902748349

Hofman, P. A., Stapert, S. Z., van Kroonenburgh, M. J., Jolles, J., de Kruijk, J., & Wilmink, J. T. (2001). MR imaging, single-photon emission CT, and neurocognitive performance after mild traumatic brain injury. *American Journal of Neuroradiology, 22,* 441–449.

Huang, M., Risling, M., & Baker, D. G. (2016). The role of biomarkers and MEG-based imaging markers in the diagnosis of post-traumatic stress disorder and blast-induced mild traumatic brain injury. *Psychoneuroendocrinology, 63,* 398–409. http://dx.doi.org/10.1016/j.psyneuen.2015.02.008

Huang, M.-X., Nichols, S., Baker, D. G., Robb, A., Angeles, A., Yurgil, K. A., . . . Lee, R. R. (2014). Single-subject-based whole-brain MEG slow-wave imaging approach for detecting abnormality in patients with mild traumatic brain injury. *NeuroImage: Clinical, 5,* 109–119. http://dx.doi.org/10.1016/j.nicl.2014.06.004

Hughes, D. G., Jackson, A., Mason, D. L., Berry, E., Hollis, S., & Yates, D. W. (2004). Abnormalities on magnetic resonance imaging seen acutely following mild traumatic brain injury: Correlation with neuropsychological tests and delayed recovery. *Neuroradiology, 46,* 550–558. http://dx.doi.org/10.1007/s00234-004-1227-x

Hukkelhoven, C. W. P. M., Steyerberg, E. W., Habbema, J. D. F., Farace, E., Marmarou, A., Murray, G. D., . . . Maas, A. I. R. (2005). Predicting outcome after traumatic brain injury: Development and validation of a prognostic score based on admission characteristics. *Journal of Neurotrauma, 22,* 1025–1039. http://dx.doi.org/10.1089/neu.2005.22.1025

Hulkower, M. B., Poliak, D. B., Rosenbaum, S. B., Zimmerman, M. E., & Lipton, M. L. (2013). A decade of DTI in traumatic brain injury: 10 years and 100 articles later. *American Journal of Neuroradiology, 34,* 2064–2074. http://dx.doi.org/10.3174/ajnr.A3395

Hunt v. Bradshaw, 242 NC 517, 88 S.E.2d 762 (1955).

Inglese, M., Makani, S., Johnson, G., Cohen, B. A., Silver, J. A., Gonen, O., & Grossman, R. I. (2005). Diffuse axonal injury in mild traumatic brain injury: A diffusion tensor imaging study. *Journal of Neurosurgery, 103,* 298–303. http://dx.doi.org/10.3171/jns.2005.103.2.0298

Iverson, G. L. (2006). Complicated vs uncomplicated mild traumatic brain injury: Acute neuropsychological outcome. *Brain Injury, 20,* 1335–1344. http://dx.doi.org/10.1080/02699050601082156

Jacobs, A., Put, E., Ingels, M., & Bossuyt, A. (1994). Prospective evaluation of technetium-99m-HMPAO SPECT in mild and moderate traumatic brain injury. *Journal of Nuclear Medicine, 35,* 942–947.

Jacobs, A., Put, E., Ingels, M., Put, T., & Bossuyt, A. (1996). One-year follow-up of technetium-99m-HMPAO SPECT in mild head injury. *Journal of Nuclear Medicine, 37,* 1605–1609.

Jacobs, B., Beems, T., van der Vliet, T. M., van Vugt, A. B., Hoedemaekers, C., Horn, J., . . . Vos, P. E. (2013). Outcome prediction in moderate and severe traumatic brain injury: A focus on computed tomography variables. *Neurocritical Care, 19,* 79–89. http://dx.doi.org/10.1007/s12028-012-9795-9

Johnson, B., Zhang, K., Gay, M., Horovitz, S., Hallett, M., Sebastianelli, W., & Slobounov, S. (2012). Alteration of brain default network in subacute phase of injury in concussed individuals: Resting-state fMRI study. *NeuroImage, 59,* 511–518. http://dx.doi.org/10.1016/j.neuroimage.2011.07.081

Johnston, K. M., Ptito, A., Chankowsky, J., & Chen, J. K. (2001). New frontiers in diagnostic imaging in concussive head injury. *Clinical Journal of Sport Medicine, 11,* 166–175. http://dx.doi.org/10.1097/00042752-200107000-00007

Jones, D. K., Chitnis, X. A., Job, D., Khong, P. L., Leung, L. T., Marenco, S. M., . . . Symms, M. R. (2007). What happens when nine different groups analyze the same DT-MRI data set 590 using voxel-based methods? *Proceedings of the International Society for Magnetic Resonance in Medicine, 15,* 74.

Jones, O. D., Buckholtz, J. W., Schall, J. D., & Marois, R. (2014). Brain imaging for judges: An introduction to law and neuroscience. *Court Review, 50,* 44.

Katzman, G. L., Dagher, A. P., & Patronas, N. J. (1999). Incidental findings on brain magnetic resonance imaging from 1000 asymptomatic volunteers. *JAMA, 282,* 36–39. http://dx.doi.org/10.1001/jama.282.1.36

Kelly, A. B., Zimmerman, R. D., Snow, R. B., Gandy, S. E., Heier, L. A., & Deck, M. D. (1988). Head trauma: Comparison of MR and CT—experience in 100 patients. *American Journal of Neuroradiology, 9,* 699–708.

Khoshbin, L. S., & Khoshbin, S. (2007). Imaging the mind, minding the image: An historical introduction to brain imaging and the law. *American Journal of Law and Medicine, 33,* 171–192.

Kou, Z., & Haacke, E. M. (2014). Advanced neuroimaging of mild traumatic brain injury. In S. M. Slobounov & W. J. Sebastianelli (Eds.), *Concussions in athletics* (pp. 217–234). http://dx.doi.org/10.1007/978-1-4939-0295-8_12

Kozel, F. A., Johnson, K. A., Mu, Q., Grenesko, E. L., Laken, S. J., & George, M. S. (2005). Detecting deception using functional magnetic resonance imaging. *Biological Psychiatry, 58,* 605–613. http://dx.doi.org/10.1016/j.biopsych.2005.07.040

Kraus, M. F., Susmaras, T., Caughlin, B. P., Walker, C. J., Sweeney, J. A., & Little, D. M. (2007). White matter integrity and cognition in chronic traumatic brain injury: A diffusion tensor imaging study. *Brain: A Journal of Neurology, 130,* 2508–2519. http://dx.doi.org/10.1093/brain/awm216

Lange, R. T., Iverson, G. L., Brubacher, J. R., Mädler, B., & Heran, M. K. (2012). Diffusion tensor imaging findings are not strongly associated with postconcussional disorder 2 months following mild traumatic brain injury. *Journal of Head Trauma Rehabilitation, 27,* 188–198. http://dx.doi.org/10.1097/HTR.0b013e318217f0ad

Langleben, D. D., Loughead, J. W., Bilker, W. B., Ruparel, K., Childress, A. R., Busch, S. I., & Gur, R. C. (2005). Telling truth from lie in individual subjects with fast event-related fMRI. *Human Brain Mapping, 26,* 262–272. http://dx.doi.org/10.1002/hbm.20191

Le, T. H., & Gean, A. D. (2009). Neuroimaging of traumatic brain injury. *Mount Sinai Journal of Medicine: A Journal of Translational and Personalized Medicine, 76,* 145–162. http://dx.doi.org/10.1002/msj.20102

Leiser, S. C., Dunlop, J., Bowlby, M. R., & Devilbiss, D. M. (2011). Aligning strategies for using EEG as a surrogate biomarker: A review of preclinical and clinical research. *Biochemical Pharmacology, 81,* 1408–1421. http://dx.doi.org/10.1016/j.bcp.2010.10.002

Levin, H. S., Wilde, E., Troyanskaya, M., Petersen, N. J., Scheibel, R., Newsome, M., . . . Li, X. (2010). Diffusion tensor imaging of mild to moderate blast-related traumatic brain injury and its sequelae. *Journal of Neurotrauma, 27,* 683–694. http://dx.doi.org/10.1089/neu.2009.1073

Levin, H. S., Wilde, E. A., Chu, Z., Yallampalli, R., Hanten, G. R., Li, X., . . . Hunter, J. V. (2008). Diffusion tensor imaging in relation to cognitive and functional outcome of traumatic brain injury in children. *Journal of Head Trauma Rehabilitation, 23,* 197–208. http://dx.doi.org/10.1097/01.HTR.0000327252.54128.7c

Levitsky v. Garden Time, Inc., 126 A.D.3d 1264, 6 N.Y.S.3d 697 (App. Div. 2015).

Lewine, J. D., Davis, J. T., Bigler, E. D., Thoma, R., Hill, D., Funke, M., . . . Orrison, W. W. (2007). Objective documentation of traumatic brain injury subsequent to mild head trauma: Multimodal brain imaging with MEG, SPECT, and MRI. *Journal of Head Trauma Rehabilitation, 22,* 141–155. http://dx.doi.org/10.1097/01.HTR.0000271115.29954.27

Lewine, J. D., Davis, J. T., Sloan, J. H., Kodituwakku, P. W., & Orrison, W. W., Jr. (1999). Neuromagnetic assessment of pathophysiologic brain activity induced by minor head trauma. *American Journal of Neuroradiology, 20,* 857–866.

Lin, A. P., Liao, H. J., Merugumala, S. K., Prabhu, S. P., Meehan, W. P., III, & Ross, B. D. (2012). Metabolic imaging of mild traumatic brain injury. *Brain Imaging and Behavior, 6,* 208–223. http://dx.doi.org/10.1007/s11682-012-9181-4

Lincoln, C. (1987). *The insanity defense and the trial of John W. Hinckley Jr.* New York, NY: Laurel.

Lipton, M. L., Kim, N., Park, Y. K., Hulkower, M. B., Gardin, T. M., Shifteh, K., . . . Branch, C. A. (2012). Robust detection of traumatic axonal injury in individual mild traumatic brain injury patients: Intersubject variation, change over time and bidirectional changes in anisotropy. *Brain Imaging and Behavior, 6,* 329–342. http://dx.doi.org/10.1007/s11682-012-9175-2

Lobato, R. D., Cordobes, F., Rivas, J. J., de la Fuente, M., Montero, A., Barcena, A., . . . Lamas, E. (1983). Outcome from severe head injury related to the type of intracranial lesion: A computerized tomography study. *Journal of Neurosurgery, 59,* 762–774. http://dx.doi.org/10.3171/jns.1983.59.5.0762

Lovell, M. R., Pardini, J. E., Welling, J., Collins, M. W., Bakal, J., Lazar, N., . . . Becker, J. T. (2007). Functional brain abnormalities are related to clinical recovery and time to return-to-play in athletes. *Neurosurgery, 61,* 352–359. http://dx.doi.org/10.1227/01.NEU.0000279985.94168.7F

Mac Donald, C. L., Johnson, A. M., Cooper, D., Nelson, E. C., Werner, N. J., Shimony, J. S., . . . Brody, D. L. (2011). Detection of blast-related traumatic brain injury in U.S. military personnel. *New England Journal of Medicine, 364,* 2091–2100. http://dx.doi.org/10.1056/NEJMoa1008069

Maganti, R. K., & Rutecki, P. (2013). EEG and epilepsy monitoring. *Continuum, 19,* 598–622. http://dx.doi.org/10.1212/01.CON.0000431378.51935.d8

Mannell, M. V., Franco, A. R., Calhoun, V. D., Cañive, J. M., Thoma, R. J., & Mayer, A. R. (2010). Resting state and task-induced deactivation: A methodological comparison in patients with schizophrenia and healthy controls. *Human Brain Mapping, 31,* 424–437.

Marquez de la Plata, C., Ardelean, A., Koovakkattu, D., Srinivasan, P., Miller, A., Phuong, V., . . . Devous, M., Sr. (2007). Magnetic resonance imaging of diffuse axonal injury: Quantitative assessment of white matter lesion volume. *Journal of Neurotrauma, 24,* 591–598. http://dx.doi.org/10.1089/neu.2006.0214

Matthews, S., Simmons, A., & Strigo, I. (2011). The effects of loss versus alteration of consciousness on inhibition-related brain activity among individuals with a history of blast-related concussion. *Psychiatry Research: Neuroimaging, 191,* 76–79. http://dx.doi.org/10.1016/j.pscychresns.2010.09.013

Matthews, S. C., Strigo, I. A., Simmons, A. N., O'Connell, R. M., Reinhardt, L. E., & Moseley, S. A. (2011). A multimodal imaging study in U.S. veterans of Operations Iraqi and Enduring Freedom with and without major depression after blast-related concussion. *NeuroImage, 54*(Suppl. 1), S69–S75. http://dx.doi.org/10.1016/j.neuroimage.2010.04.269

Mayer, A. R., Bellgowan, P. S. F., & Hanlon, F. M. (2015). Functional magnetic resonance imaging of mild traumatic brain injury. *Neuroscience and Biobehavioral Reviews, 49,* 8–18. http://dx.doi.org/10.1016/j.neubiorev.2014.11.016

Mayer, A. R., Ling, J., Mannell, M. V., Gasparovic, C., Phillips, J. P., Doezema, D., . . . Yeo, R. A. (2010). A prospective diffusion tensor imaging study in mild traumatic brain injury. *Neurology, 74,* 643–650. http://dx.doi.org/10.1212/WNL.0b013e3181d0ccdd

Mayer, A. R., Mannell, M. V., Ling, J., Gasparovic, C., & Yeo, R. A. (2011). Functional connectivity in mild traumatic brain injury. *Human Brain Mapping, 32,* 1825–1835. http://dx.doi.org/10.1002/hbm.21151

Mazziotta, J. C. (1989). Huntington's disease: Studies with structural imaging techniques and positron emission tomography. *Seminars in Neurology, 9,* 360–369. http://dx.doi.org/10.1055/s-2008-1041346

Mazziotta, J. C., Frackowiak, R. S. J., & Phelps, M. E. (1992). The use of positron emission tomography in the clinical assessment of dementia. *Seminars in*

Nuclear Medicine, 22, 233–246. http://dx.doi.org/10.1016/S0001-2998(05)80118-7

McCabe, D. P., & Castel, A. D. (2008). Seeing is believing: The effect of brain images on judgments of scientific reasoning. *Cognition, 107,* 343–352. http://dx.doi.org/10.1016/j.cognition.2007.07.017

McDonald, B. C., Saykin, A. J., & McAllister, T. W. (2012). Functional MRI of mild traumatic brain injury (mTBI): Progress and perspectives from the first decade of studies. *Brain Imaging and Behavior, 6,* 193–207. http://dx.doi.org/10.1007/s11682-012-9173-4

McGowan, J. C., Yang, J. H., Plotkin, R. C., Grossman, R. I., Umile, E. M., Cecil, K. M., & Bagley, L. J. (2000). Magnetization transfer imaging in the detection of injury associated with mild head trauma. *American Journal of Neuroradiology, 21,* 875–880.

McKee, A. C., Stein, T. D., Nowinski, C. J., Stern, R. A., Daneshvar, D. H., Alvarez, V. E., . . . Cantu, R. C. (2013). The spectrum of disease in chronic traumatic encephalopathy. *Brain: A Journal of Neurology, 136,* 43–64. http://dx.doi.org/10.1093/brain/aws307

McLoughlin, G., Makeig, S., & Tsuang, M. T. (2014). In search of biomarkers in psychiatry: EEG-based measures of brain function. *American Journal of Medical Genetics: Part B. Neuropsychiatric Genetics, 165,* 111–121. http://dx.doi.org/10.1002/ajmg.b.32208

Meixner, J. B. (2015). Applications of neuroscience in criminal law: Legal and methodological issues. *Current Neurology and Neuroscience Reports, 15,* 513. http://dx.doi.org/10.1007/s11910-014-0513-1

Melhem, E. R., Mori, S., Mukundan, G., Kraut, M. A., Pomper, M. G., & van Zijl, P. C. M. (2002). Diffusion tensor MR imaging of the brain and white matter tractography. *American Journal of Roentgenology, 178,* 3–16. http://dx.doi.org/10.2214/ajr.178.1.1780003

Mendez, M. F., Owens, E. M., Reza Berenji, G., Peppers, D. C., Liang, L.-J., & Licht, E. A. (2013). Mild traumatic brain injury from primary blast vs. blunt forces: Post-concussion consequences and functional neuroimaging. *NeuroRehabilitation, 32,* 397–407.

Messé, A., Caplain, S., Pélégrini-Issac, M., Blancho, S., Lévy, R., Aghakhani, N., . . . Lehéricy, S. (2013). Specific and evolving resting-state network alterations in post-concussion syndrome following mild traumatic brain injury. *PLoS One, 8,* e65470. http://dx.doi.org/10.1371/journal.pone.0065470

Michel, C. M., & Murray, M. M. (2012). Towards the utilization of EEG as a brain imaging tool. *NeuroImage, 61,* 371–385. http://dx.doi.org/10.1016/j.neuroimage.2011.12.039

Miles, L., Grossman, R. I., Johnson, G., Babb, J. S., Diller, L., & Inglese, M. (2008). Short-term DTI predictors of cognitive dysfunction in mild traumatic brain injury. *Brain Injury, 22,* 115–122. http://dx.doi.org/10.1080/02699050801888816

Mittl, R. L., Grossman, R. I., Hiehle, J. F., Hurst, R. W., Kauder, D. R., Gennarelli, T. A., & Alburger, G. W. (1994). Prevalence of MR evidence of diffuse axonal injury in patients with mild head injury and normal head CT findings. *American Journal of Neuroradiology, 15,* 1583–1589.

Molina, D. K., Nichols, J. J., & Dimaio, V. J. M. (2007). The sensitivity of computed tomography (CT) scans in detecting trauma: Are CT scans reliable enough for courtroom testimony? *Journal of Trauma, 63,* 625–629. http://dx.doi.org/10.1097/01.ta.0000236055.33085.77

Mottershead, J. P., Schmierer, K., Clemence, M., Thornton, J. S., Scaravilli, F., Barker, G. J., . . . Miller, D. H. (2003). High field MRI correlates of myelin content and axonal density in multiple sclerosis—a post-mortem study of the spinal cord. *Journal of Neurology, 250,* 1293–1301. http://dx.doi.org/10.1007/s00415-003-0192-3

Mukherjee, P., Chung, S. W., Berman, J. I., Hess, C. P., & Henry, R. G. (2008). Diffusion tensor MR imaging and fiber tractography: Technical considerations. *American Journal of Neuroradiology, 29,* 843–852. http://dx.doi.org/10.3174/ajnr.A1052

Narayana, P. A. (2005). Magnetic resonance spectroscopy in the monitoring of multiple sclerosis. *Journal of Neuroimaging, 15*(Suppl.), 46S–57S. http://dx.doi.org/10.1177/1051228405284200

Narayana, P. A., Yu, X., Hasan, K. M., Wilde, E. A., Levin, H. S., Hunter, J. V., . . . McCarthy, J. J. (2015). Multi-modal MRI of mild traumatic brain injury. *NeuroImage: Clinical, 7,* 87–97. http://dx.doi.org/10.1016/j.nicl.2014.07.010

Nickerson, R. S. (2000). Null hypothesis significance testing: A review of an old and continuing controversy. *Psychological Methods, 5,* 241–301. http://dx.doi.org/10.1037/1082-989X.5.2.241

Nidal, K., & Malik, A. S. (2015). *EEG/ERP analysis: Methods and applications.* Boca Raton, FL: CRC Press.

Niogi, S. N., & Mukherjee, P. (2010). Diffusion tensor imaging of mild traumatic brain injury. *Journal of Head Trauma Rehabilitation, 25,* 241–255. http://dx.doi.org/10.1097/HTR.0b013e3181e52c2a

Nitzke, R. W. (1971). *The life of Wilhelm Conrad Roentgen, discoverer of the X-ray.* Tucson: University of Arizona Press.

Nusbaum, A. O., Tang, C. Y., Buchsbaum, M. S., Wei, T. C., & Atlas, S. W. (2001). Regional and global changes in cerebral diffusion with normal aging. *American Journal of Neuroradiology, 22,* 136–142.

Nuwer, M. R., Hovda, D. A., Schrader, L. M., & Vespa, P. M. (2005). Routine and quantitative EEG in mild traumatic brain injury. *Clinical Neurophysiology, 116,* 2001–2025. http://dx.doi.org/10.1016/j.clinph.2005.05.008

Ogawa, S., Menon, R. S., Tank, D. W., Kim, S. G., Merkle, H., Ellermann, J. M., & Ugurbil, K. (1993). Functional brain mapping by blood oxygenation level-dependent contrast magnetic resonance imaging: A comparison of signal characteristics with a biophysical model. *Biophysical Journal, 64,* 803–812. http://dx.doi.org/10.1016/S0006-3495(93)81441-3

Ono, J., Yamaura, A., Kubota, M., Okimura, Y., & Isobe, K. (2001). Outcome prediction in severe head injury: Analyses of clinical prognostic factors. *Journal of Clinical Neuroscience, 8,* 120–123. http://dx.doi.org/10.1054/jocn.2000.0732

Organisation for Economic Co-operation and Development. (2013). *Health at a glance 2013: OECD indicators.* http://dx.doi.org/10.1787/health_glance-2013-en

Orrison, W. W., Gentry, L. R., Stimac, G. K., Tarrel, R. M., Espinosa, M. C., & Cobb, L. C. (1994). Blinded comparison of cranial CT and MR in closed head injury evaluation. *American Journal of Neuroradiology, 15,* 351–356.

O'Sullivan, M., Jones, D. K., Summers, P. E., Morris, R. G., Williams, S. C. R., & Markus, H. S. (2001). Evidence for cortical "disconnection" as a mechanism of age-related cognitive decline. *Neurology, 57,* 632–638. http://dx.doi.org/10.1212/WNL.57.4.632

Palchak, M. J., Holmes, J. F., Vance, C. W., Gelber, R. E., Schauer, B. A., Harrison, M. J., . . . Kuppermann, N. (2003). A decision rule for identifying children at low risk for brain injuries after blunt head trauma. *Annals of Emergency Medicine, 42,* 492–506. http://dx.doi.org/10.1067/S0196-0644(03)00425-6

Pandit, A. S., Expert, P., Lambiotte, R., Bonnelle, V., Leech, R., Turkheimer, F. E., & Sharp, D. J. (2013). Traumatic brain injury impairs small-world topology. *Neurology, 80,* 1826–1833. http://dx.doi.org/10.1212/WNL.0b013e3182929f38

Papinutto, N. D., Maule, F., & Jovicich, J. (2013). Reproducibility and biases in high field brain diffusion MRI: An evaluation of acquisition and analysis variables. *Magnetic Resonance Imaging, 31,* 827–839. http://dx.doi.org/10.1016/j.mri.2013.03.004

Park, J.-H., Park, S.-W., Kang, S.-H., Nam, T.-K., Min, B.-K., & Hwang, S.-N. (2009). Detection of traumatic cerebral microbleeds by susceptibility-weighted image of MRI. *Journal of Korean Neurosurgical Society, 46,* 365–369. http://dx.doi.org/10.3340/jkns.2009.46.4.365

Paterakis, K., Karantanas, A. H., Komnos, A., & Volikas, Z. (2000). Outcome of patients with diffuse axonal injury: The significance and prognostic value of MRI in the acute phase. *Journal of Trauma, 49,* 1071–1075. http://dx.doi.org/10.1097/00005373-200012000-00016

Paul, R., Henry, L., Grieve, S. M., Guilmette, T. J., Niaura, R., Bryant, R., . . . Gordon, E. (2008). The relationship between early life stress and microstructural integrity of the corpus callosum in a non-clinical population. *Neuropsychiatric Disease and Treatment, 4,* 193–201. http://dx.doi.org/10.2147/NDT.S1549

Paul, R. H., Grieve, S. M., Niaura, R., David, S. P., Laidlaw, D. H., Cohen, R., . . . Gordon, E. (2008). Chronic cigarette smoking and the microstructural integrity of white matter in healthy adults: A diffusion tensor imaging study. *Nicotine and Tobacco Research, 10,* 137–147. http://dx.doi.org/10.1080/14622200701767829

People v. Weinstein, 591 N.Y.S.2d 715 (N.Y. Sup. Ct. 1992).

Peskind, E. R., Petrie, E. C., Cross, D. J., Pagulayan, K., McCraw, K., Hoff, D., . . . Minoshima, S. (2011). Cerebrocerebellar hypometabolism associated with repetitive blast exposure mild traumatic brain injury in 12 Iraq war veterans with persistent post-concussive symptoms. *NeuroImage, 54*(Suppl. 1), S76–S82. http://dx.doi.org/10.1016/j.neuroimage.2010.04.008

Petrie, E. C., Cross, D. J., Yarnykh, V. L., Richards, T., Martin, N. M., Pagulayan, K., . . . Peskind, E. R. (2014). Neuroimaging, behavioral, and psychological sequelae of repetitive combined blast/impact mild traumatic brain injury in Iraq and Afghanistan war veterans. *Journal of Neurotrauma, 31,* 425–436. http://dx.doi.org/10.1089/neu.2013.2952

Pierpaoli, C., & Basser, P. J. (1996). Toward a quantitative assessment of diffusion anisotropy. *Magnetic Resonance in Medicine, 36,* 893–906. http://dx.doi.org/10.1002/mrm.1910360612

Prichep, L. S., Jacquin, A., Filipenko, J., Dastidar, S. G., Zabele, S., Vodencarević, A., & Rothman, N. S. (2012). Classification of traumatic brain injury severity using informed data reduction in a series of binary classifier algorithms. *IEEE Transactions on Neural Systems and Rehabilitation Engineering, 20,* 806–822. http://dx.doi.org/10.1109/TNSRE.2012.2206609

Raichle, M. E., & Mintun, M. A. (2006). Brain work and brain imaging. *Annual Review of Neuroscience, 29,* 449–476. http://dx.doi.org/10.1146/annurev.neuro.29.051605.112819

Raji, C. A., Tarzwell, R., Pavel, D., Schneider, H., Uszler, M., Thornton, J., . . . Henderson, T. (2014). Clinical utility of SPECT neuroimaging in the diagnosis and treatment of traumatic brain injury: A systematic review. *PLoS One*, *9*, e91088. http://dx.doi.org/10.1371/journal.pone.0091088

Rapp, P. E., Keyser, D. O., Albano, A., Hernandez, R., Gibson, D. B., Zambon, R. A., . . . Nichols, A. S. (2015). Traumatic brain injury detection using electrophysiological methods. *Frontiers in Human Neuroscience*, *9*, 11. http://dx.doi.org/10.3389/fnhum.2015.00011

Rohling, M. L., Binder, L. M., Demakis, G. J., Larrabee, G. J., Ploetz, D. M., & Langhinrichsen-Rohling, J. (2011). A meta-analysis of neuropsychological outcome after mild traumatic brain injury: Re-analyses and reconsiderations of Binder et al. (1997), Frencham et al. (2005), and Pertab et al. (2009). *Clinical Neuropsychologist*, *25*, 608–623. http://dx.doi.org/10.1080/13854046.2011.565076

Rushing, S. E. (2014). Admissibility of brain scans in criminal trials: The case of positron emission tomography. *Court Review*, *50*, 62.

Saad, Z. S., Gotts, S. J., Murphy, K., Chen, G., Jo, H. J., Martin, A., & Cox, R. W. (2012). Trouble at rest: How correlation patterns and group differences become distorted after global signal regression. *Brain Connectivity*, *2*, 25–32. http://dx.doi.org/10.1089/brain.2012.0080

Scheibel, R. S., Newsome, M. R., Troyanskaya, M., Lin, X., Steinberg, J. L., Radaideh, M., & Levin, H. S. (2012). Altered brain activation in military personnel with one or more traumatic brain injuries following blast. *Journal of the International Neuropsychological Society*, *18*, 89–100. http://dx.doi.org/10.1017/S1355617711001433

Sharif-Alhoseini, M., Khodadadi, H., Chardoli, M., & Rahimi-Movaghar, V. (2011). Indications for brain computed tomography scan after minor head injury. *Journal of Emergencies, Trauma, and Shock*, *4*, 472–476.

Sharp, D. J., Scott, G., & Leech, R. (2014). Network dysfunction after traumatic brain injury. *Nature Reviews Neurology*, *10*, 156–166. http://dx.doi.org/10.1038/nrneurol.2014.15

Shen, F. X. (2010). Law and neuroscience bibliography: Navigating the emerging field of neurolaw. *International Journal of Legal Information*, *38*, 352–399.

Shenton, M. E., Hamoda, H. M., Schneiderman, J. S., Bouix, S., Pasternak, O., Rathi, Y., . . . Zafonte, R. (2012). A review of magnetic resonance imaging and diffusion tensor imaging findings in mild traumatic brain injury. *Brain Imaging and Behavior*, *6*, 137–192. http://dx.doi.org/10.1007/s11682-012-9156-5

Shumskaya, E., Andriessen, T. M. J. C., Norris, D. G., & Vos, P. E. (2012). Abnormal whole-brain functional networks in homogeneous acute mild traumatic brain injury. *Neurology*, *79*, 175–182. http://dx.doi.org/10.1212/WNL.0b013e31825f04fb

Silver, J. M. (2012). Diffusion tensor imaging and mild traumatic brain injury in soldiers: Abnormal findings, uncertain implications. *American Journal of Psychiatry*, *169*, 1230–1232. http://dx.doi.org/10.1176/appi.ajp.2012.12091230

Simpson, J. R. (Ed.). (2012). *Neuroimaging in forensic psychiatry: From the clinic to the courtroom*. http://dx.doi.org/10.1002/9781119968900

Skandsen, T., Kvistad, K. A., Solheim, O., Strand, I. H., Folvik, M., & Vik, A. (2010). Prevalence and impact of diffuse axonal injury in patients with moderate and severe head injury: A cohort study of early magnetic resonance imaging findings and 1-year outcome. *Journal of Neurosurgery*, *113*, 556–563. http://dx.doi.org/10.3171/2009.9.JNS09626

Slobounov, S., Sebastianelli, W., & Hallett, M. (2012). Residual brain dysfunction observed one year post-mild traumatic brain injury: Combined EEG and balance study. *Clinical Neurophysiology*, *123*, 1755–1761. http://dx.doi.org/10.1016/j.clinph.2011.12.022

Slobounov, S. M., Gay, M., Zhang, K., Johnson, B., Pennell, D., Sebastianelli, W., . . . Hallett, M. (2011). Alteration of brain functional network at rest and in response to YMCA physical stress test in concussed athletes: RsFMRI study. *NeuroImage*, *55*, 1716–1727. http://dx.doi.org/10.1016/j.neuroimage.2011.01.024

Smith v. Grant, "First Amended Complaint," No. 24,159 (Arapahoe County), Colorado State Archives (1896).

Smits, M., Dippel, D. W. J., Houston, G. C., Wielopolski, P. A., Koudstaal, P. J., Hunink, M. G. M., & van der Lugt, A. (2009). Postconcussion syndrome after minor head injury: Brain activation of working memory and attention. *Human Brain Mapping*, *30*, 2789–2803. http://dx.doi.org/10.1002/hbm.20709

Somerville, L. H., Hare, T., & Casey, B. J. (2011). Frontostriatal maturation predicts cognitive control failure to appetitive cues in adolescents. *Journal of Cognitive Neuroscience*, *23*, 2123–2134. http://dx.doi.org/10.1162/jocn.2010.21572

Stevens, M. C., Lovejoy, D., Kim, J., Oakes, H., Kureshi, I., & Witt, S. T. (2012). Multiple resting state network functional connectivity abnormalities in mild traumatic brain injury. *Brain Imaging and Behavior*, *6*, 293–318. http://dx.doi.org/10.1007/s11682-012-9157-4

Stiell, I. G., Wells, G. A., Vandemheen, K., Clement, C., Lesiuk, H., Laupacis, A., . . . Worthington, J. (2001). The Canadian CT Head Rule for patients with minor head injury. *Lancet*, *357*, 1391–1396. http://dx.doi.org/10.1016/S0140-6736(00)04561-X

Stulemeijer, M., Vos, P. E., van der Werf, S., van Dijk, G., Rijpkema, M., & Fernández, G. (2010). How mild traumatic brain injury may affect declarative memory performance in the post-acute stage. *Journal of Neurotrauma, 27,* 1585–1595. http://dx.doi.org/10.1089/neu.2010.1298

Talavage, T. M., Nauman, E. A., Breedlove, E. L., Yoruk, U., Dye, A. E., Morigaki, K. E., . . . Leverenz, L. J. (2014). Functionally-detected cognitive impairment in high school football players without clinically-diagnosed concussion. *Journal of Neurotrauma, 31,* 327–338. http://dx.doi.org/10.1089/neu.2010.1512

Tang, L., Ge, Y., Sodickson, D. K., Miles, L., Zhou, Y., Reaume, J., & Grossman, R. I. (2011). Thalamic resting-state functional networks: Disruption in patients with mild traumatic brain injury. *Radiology, 260,* 831–840. http://dx.doi.org/10.1148/radiol.11110014

Thatcher, R. W., North, D. M., Curtin, R. T., Walker, R. A., Biver, C. J., Gomez, J. F., & Salazar, A. M. (2001). An EEG severity index of traumatic brain injury. *Journal of Neuropsychiatry and Clinical Neurosciences, 13,* 77–87. http://dx.doi.org/10.1176/jnp.13.1.77

Tong, K. A., Ashwal, S., Holshouser, B. A., Nickerson, J. P., Wall, C. J., Shutter, L. A., . . . Kido, D. (2004). Diffuse axonal injury in children: Clinical correlation with hemorrhagic lesions. *Annals of Neurology, 56,* 36–50. http://dx.doi.org/10.1002/ana.20123

Toth, A., Kovacs, N., Perlaki, G., Orsi, G., Aradi, M., Komaromy, H., . . . Schwarcz, A. (2013). Multi-modal magnetic resonance imaging in the acute and sub-acute phase of mild traumatic brain injury: Can we see the difference? *Journal of Neurotrauma, 30,* 2–10. http://dx.doi.org/10.1089/neu.2012.2486

Trafimow, D. (2014). More reasons why diffuse tensor imaging is problematic in medicolegal settings. *AJOB Neuroscience, 5,* 39–41. http://dx.doi.org/10.1080/21507740.2014.884187

Tsirka, V., Simos, P. G., Vakis, A., Kanatsouli, K., Vourkas, M., Erimaki, S., . . . Micheloyannis, S. (2011). Mild traumatic brain injury: Graph-model characterization of brain networks for episodic memory. *International Journal of Psychophysiology, 79,* 89–96. http://dx.doi.org/10.1016/j.ijpsycho.2010.09.006

United States v. Gigante, 982 F. Supp. 140 (E.D.N.Y. 1997).

Vagnozzi, R., Signoretti, S., Cristofori, L., Alessandrini, F., Floris, R., Isgrò, E., . . . Lazzarino, G. (2010). Assessment of metabolic brain damage and recovery following mild traumatic brain injury: A multicentre, proton magnetic resonance spectroscopic study in concussed patients. *Brain: A Journal of Neurology, 133,* 3232–3242. http://dx.doi.org/10.1093/brain/awq200

Vakhtin, A. A., Calhoun, V. D., Jung, R. E., Prestopnik, J. L., Taylor, P. A., & Ford, C. C. (2013). Changes in intrinsic functional brain networks following blast-induced mild traumatic brain injury. *Brain Injury, 27,* 1304–1310. http://dx.doi.org/10.3109/02699052.2013.823561

Vermeer, S. E., Hollander, M., van Dijk, E. J., Hofman, A., Koudstaal, P. J., & Breteler, M. M. B. (2003). Silent brain infarcts and white matter lesions increase stroke risk in the general population: The Rotterdam Scan Study. *Stroke, 34,* 1126–1129. http://dx.doi.org/10.1161/01.STR.0000068408.82115.D2

Voller, B., Benke, T., Benedetto, K., Schnider, P., Auff, E., & Aichner, F. (1999). Neuropsychological, MRI and EEG findings after very mild traumatic brain injury. *Brain Injury, 13,* 821–827. http://dx.doi.org/10.1080/026990599121214

Vollmar, C., O'Muircheartaigh, J., Barker, G. J., Symms, M. R., Thompson, P., Kumari, V., . . . Koepp, M. J. (2010). Identical, but not the same: Intra-site and inter-site reproducibility of fractional anisotropy measures on two 3.0T scanners. *NeuroImage, 51,* 1384–1394. http://dx.doi.org/10.1016/j.neuroimage.2010.03.046

Wang, Y., West, J. D., Bailey, J. N., Westfall, D. R., Xiao, H., Arnold, T. W., . . . McDonald, B. C. (2015). Decreased cerebral blood flow in chronic pediatric mild TBI: An MRI perfusion study. *Developmental Neuropsychology, 40,* 40–44. http://dx.doi.org/10.1080/87565641.2014.979927

Wedekind, C., Hesselmann, V., Lippert-Grüner, M., & Ebel, M. (2002). Trauma to the pontomesencephalic brainstem—a major clue to the prognosis of severe traumatic brain injury. *British Journal of Neurosurgery, 16,* 256–260. http://dx.doi.org/10.1080/02688690220148842

Weiss, N., Galanaud, D., Carpentier, A., Naccache, L., & Puybasset, L. (2007). Clinical review: Prognostic value of magnetic resonance imaging in acute brain injury and coma. *Critical Care, 11,* 230–242. http://dx.doi.org/10.1186/cc6107

White, T., Nelson, M., & Lim, K. O. (2008). Diffusion tensor imaging in psychiatric disorders. *Topics in Magnetic Resonance Imaging, 19,* 97–109. http://dx.doi.org/10.1097/RMR.0b013e3181809f1e

Witt, S. T., Lovejoy, D. W., Pearlson, G. D., & Stevens, M. C. (2010). Decreased prefrontal cortex activity in mild traumatic brain injury during performance of an auditory oddball task. *Brain Imaging and Behavior, 4,* 232–247. http://dx.doi.org/10.1007/s11682-010-9102-3

Wortzel, H. S., Filley, C. M., Anderson, C. A., Oster, T., & Arciniegas, D. B. (2008). Forensic applications of cerebral single photon emission computed tomography in mild traumatic brain injury. *Journal of the American Academy of Psychiatry and the Law, 36,* 310–322.

Wortzel, H. S., Kraus, M. F., Filley, C. M., Anderson, C. A., & Arciniegas, D. B. (2011). Diffusion tensor imaging in mild traumatic brain injury litigation. *Journal of the American Academy of Psychiatry and the Law, 39,* 511–523.

Wortzel, H. S., Tsiouris, A. J., & Filippi, C. G. (2014). The potential for medicolegal abuse: Diffusion tensor imaging in traumatic brain injury. *AJOB Neuroscience, 5,* 9–15. http://dx.doi.org/10.1080/21507740.2014.880088

Yallampalli, R., Wilde, E. A., Bigler, E. D., McCauley, S. R., Hanten, G., Troyanskaya, M., . . . Levin, H. S. (2013). Acute white matter differences in the fornix following mild traumatic brain injury using diffusion tensor imaging. *Journal of Neuroimaging, 23,* 224–227. http://dx.doi.org/10.1111/j.1552-6569.2010.00537.x

Yeo, R. A., Gasparovic, C., Merideth, F., Ruhl, D., Doezema, D., & Mayer, A. R. (2011). A longitudinal proton magnetic resonance spectroscopy study of mild traumatic brain injury. *Journal of Neurotrauma, 28,* 1–11. http://dx.doi.org/10.1089/neu.2010.1578

Zhang, K., Johnson, B., Gay, M., Horovitz, S. G., Hallett, M., Sebastianelli, W., & Slobounov, S. (2012). Default mode network in concussed individuals in response to the YMCA physical stress test. *Journal of Neurotrauma, 29,* 756–765. http://dx.doi.org/10.1089/neu.2011.2125

Zhang, L., Yang, K. H., & King, A. I. (2004). A proposed injury threshold for mild traumatic brain injury. *Journal of Biomechanical Engineering, 126,* 226–236. http://dx.doi.org/10.1115/1.1691446

Zhou, Y., Lui, Y. W., Zuo, X.-N., Milham, M. P., Reaume, J., Grossman, R. I., & Ge, Y. (2014). Characterization of thalamo-cortical association using amplitude and connectivity of functional MRI in mild traumatic brain injury. *Journal of Magnetic Resonance Imaging, 39,* 1558–1568. http://dx.doi.org/10.1002/jmri.24310

Zillmer, E. A., Spiers, M. V., & Culbertson, W. (2008). *Principles of neuropsychology* (2nd ed.). Belmont, CA: Thomson Wadsworth.

Part III

DISORDERS AND SPECIAL POPULATIONS

CHAPTER 7

MILD TRAUMATIC BRAIN INJURY

Martin L. Rohling, Jennifer Langhinrichsen-Rohling, and Bradley N. Axelrod

One of the more common referrals for neuropsychological evaluation involves individuals who have sustained a mild traumatic brain injury (mTBI). The sheer prevalence of this diagnosis in the forensic clinical domain requires a careful discussion and analysis of the diagnosis, its definition, anticipated duration of recovery, and expected potential long-term sequelae, if any. Potentially concurrent non-neurocognitive factors, such as psychiatric symptoms or intentional misrepresentation, must also be carefully considered. Reliable and valid methods for evaluating and interpreting all symptoms and conclusions are essential. This chapter leads the practicing neuropsychologist through the relevant issues associated with cases of mTBI and provides two case examples that constitute a step-by-step guide for those performing such evaluations in a forensic context.

MULTIPLE DEFINITIONS AND RISK FACTORS FOR MILD TRAUMATIC BRAIN INJURY

Several organizations, associations, and researchers have developed different definitions of mTBI, and noteworthy authors of books and reviews, such as McCrea (2008) and Carone and Bush (2013), have lamented the excessive and differing criteria used to diagnose the presence, severity, and long-term outcomes associated with mTBI (also commonly referred to as *concussion*). For example, McCrea's chapter "Challenges in Defining and Diagnosing MTBI" captures the wide variety of definitions in eight separate tables (pp. 13–42). This lack of consensus across the field creates a substantial challenge for the forensic neuropsychologist, who is asked to assess individuals who have allegedly experienced an mTBI and subsequently find themselves in a legal context.

Fortunately, Larrabee and Rohling (2013) summarized some of the commonalities across mTBI diagnostic systems, which include loss of consciousness (LOC), posttraumatic amnesia (PTA), and mental confusion or disorientation. Some consensus has emerged. Most of the accepted definitions for mTBI require an LOC of 30 minutes or less and PTA of less than 24 hours. Furthermore, an initial Glasgow Coma Scale (GCS) score has to be no lower than 13 (out of 15). Typically, there can be no or only minor, nonspecific abnormalities found on, such as computed tomography (CT) or MRI scans. When detected, abnormalities are likely to have existed before the injury but to have previously gone undetected. When injury-specific contusions are identified in the context of characteristics that would otherwise indicate mTBI, the injury is commonly referred to as a *complicated mTBI,* and the outcome tends to be more similar to that of brain injuries of greater severity.

In terms of common usage, Stein (1996, as cited in McCrea, 2008) developed diagnostic criteria for all levels of traumatic brain injury (TBI). These criteria are listed in the first two columns of Table 7.1. The American Congress of Rehabilitation Medicine (Mild Traumatic Brain Injury Committee, 1993) developed the most generally accepted diagnostic

http://dx.doi.org/10.1037/0000032-007
APA Handbook of Forensic Neuropsychology, S. S. Bush (Editor-in-Chief)

TABLE 7.1

Acute Indices of Severity of Traumatic Brain Injury

TBI severity measure and criteria score	Severity label	Mr. Eyer (case study)
Glasgow Coma Scale		
13–15	Mild	14 days
9–12	Moderate	
6–8	Severe	
3–5	Very severe	
Loss of consciousness		
<30 min	Mild	<1 min
30 min–24 hr	Moderate	
>1 day	Severe	
<24 hr	Mild	
Posttraumatic amnesia		
24 hr	Moderate	
>1 day	Severe	10 days
None	Mild	
Neuroimaging Abnormal		
Mild	Complicated mild	Yes
Obvious–moderate	Moderate	
Obvious–large	Severe	

Data from Stein (1996).

criteria for mTBI, which are listed in Table 7.2. The criteria listed in this table are very similar to those developed by the World Health Organization's (WHO) Collaborating Centre Task Force on Mild Traumatic Brain Injury (Holm, Cassidy, Carroll, & Borg, 2005). Finally, in the sports concussion literature, the American Academy of Neurology has developed criteria for classifying the severity of concussion (Giza et al., 2013), which divides mTBI or concussion into Class I, Class II, and Class III. These criteria are listed in Table 7.3.

Cassidy et al. (2004) systematically reviewed the incidence of and risk factors for mTBI. They noted,

> There is no universally accepted definition of MTBI, and the studies are so

TABLE 7.2

Definition of Mild Traumatic Brain Injury

An individual with an mild traumatic brain injury has had a traumatically induced physiological disruption of brain function, as manifested by ≥1 of the following 7 criteria

1 Any loss of consciousness <30 min
2 Any loss of memory for events immediately before or after accident ≤24 hr
3 Any alteration of mental state at the time of the accident (e.g., feeling dazed, disoriented, or confused)
4 Focal neurologic deficits that might or might not be transient

But where the severity of the injury does not exceed the following:

5 Loss of consciousness ≥30 min
6 Posttraumatic amnesia >24 hr
7 Glasgow Coma Scale <13 after 30 min

Data from Mild Traumatic Brain Injury Committee (1993).

TABLE 7.3

Indices of Concussion Severity Developed by Giza et al. (2013) for the American Academy of Neurology

Concussion symptoms and criteria score	Class
Confusion	
Transient	Class I
Transient	Class II
Extended	Class III
Mental status abnormalities	
<15 min	Class I
≥15 min	Class II
≥15 min	Class III
Concussion symptoms	
<15 min	Class I
≥15 min	Class II
≥15 min	Class III
Loss of consciousness	
None	Class I
None	Class II
Brief (seconds)	Class III

> heterogeneous that it is difficult to compare incidence rates and risk factors. One major problem is the lack of a standard definition of the lower range of severity for MTBI. Those studies that use the common criteria of GCS 13–15 to define MTBI also do not specify the mildest end of the severity spectrum. (pp. 47–48)

Some of the risk factors for mTBI that Cassidy et al. (2004) highlighted are (a) being male, (b) falling in the late adolescent–young adult age range, (c) being a member of an ethnic minority group, and (d) being of lower socioeconomic status. Cassidy et al. were not able to characterize risk factors for pediatric mTBI cases because the published data available for this age group were insufficient. Nevertheless, they thought the data were robust enough to suggest that girls are at greater risk of sports-related mTBI than are boys, particularly when they are playing the same sport (e.g., soccer). Thus, girls appear to have a greater relative risk of sustaining an mTBI, although boys are at greater overall risk of mTBI than are girls because of their differential, and higher, rate of participation in contact sports.

Regarding the causes of all severity of TBI, the Centers for Disease Control and Prevention (2003, 2015; Faul, Xu, Wald, & Coronado, 2010) has stated that falls cause 35.2% of all TBIs. Motor vehicle accidents (MVAs) are the second most common cause, accounting for 17.3% of TBIs; however, MVAs account for 31.8% of deaths resulting from TBI. Having an object fall or strike a person (e.g., tree branch or baseball bat) is the third most common cause, accounting for 16.5% of all TBIs. Assaults, the fourth most common cause of TBI, account for 10%. The remaining 21% of TBIs are due to other or unknown causes. Children and elderly adults are the most likely victims of falls that cause TBI; the majority of TBIs that are due to MVAs occur to individuals between ages 16 and 25 years.

Challenges and Solutions Associated With Severity Indices for Traumatic Brain Injury

The main problem neuropsychologists face when trying to generate valid diagnostic criteria for mTBI is that there is a significant range restriction, making ratio comparisons invalid. Hypothetically, if one was to measure the severity of TBI using a yardstick, the end representing mTBI would be just one-tenth of an inch. The next segment of the yardstick, spanning moderate TBI, would cover approximately

5 inches and account for 14% of the yardstick's total length. The remaining 31 inches of the yardstick, 86% of its entire length, would represent severe TBI.

As our example illustrates, many indices of TBI severity are not a ratio scale. In fact, it would be better to consider our yardstick to be a quadratic, logarithmic, or exponential scale. If our yardstick were transformed into a curvilinear (e.g., quadratic or logarithmic) scale, the length covering mTBI would be converted into a ratio scale with mTBI equal to 1, moderate TBI equal to 3, and severe TBI equal to 5. Such a transformation results in an equal distance between the various severity groups.

Appropriately using the concept of range restriction and on the basis of patients' responses to verbal commands, Dikmen, Machamer, Winn, and Temkin (1995) divided TBI severity into six groups: (a) less than 1 hour with a mean PTA of 3.9 days; (b) 1 to 23 hours with a mean PTA of 9.1 days; (c) 1 to 6 days with a mean PTA of 17.3 days; (d) 7 to 13 days with a mean PTA of 36.7 days; (e) 14 to 28 days with a mean PTA of 44.0 days; and (f) more than 28 days with a mean PTA of 97.3 days. As shown by Rohling, Meyers, and Millis (2003), these six groups suffered residual cognitive deficits 1 year postinjury that had effect sizes of −0.02, −0.22, −0.45, −0.68, −1.33, and −2.33, respectively. The *x*-axis was defined as time spent unconscious (i.e., LOC) and the *y*-axis as the effect size of cognitive deficits. The regression equation that best fits these types of data is logarithmic and is shown in the left panel of Figure 7.1. The *r* value generated equals .983 ($p < .0001$).

Schretlen and Shapiro (2003) also found the relationship between TBI severity and cognitive deficits to be logarithmic, lending support to our own model. The strength of this relationship means it can be used rather simply by clinicians. Knowing the duration of a patient's LOC with a sufficient degree of certainty allows a clinician to predict, with slightly less certainty, the degree of cognitive impairment that can be expected. Vice versa, a case that presents with a certain level of impairment should have a documented LOC that makes that impairment reasonable. If not, other factors for the impairment (e.g., feigning) should not only be considered, but should be fully assessed.

Interestingly, however, when the hours of PTA define TBI severity, the regression equation that best models these data is linear. The right panel of Figure 7.1 shows this association. The *r* value generated in this case is equal to .993 ($p < .0001$), which is nearly a perfect fit. Thus, the neuropsychologist can, with confidence, prospectively

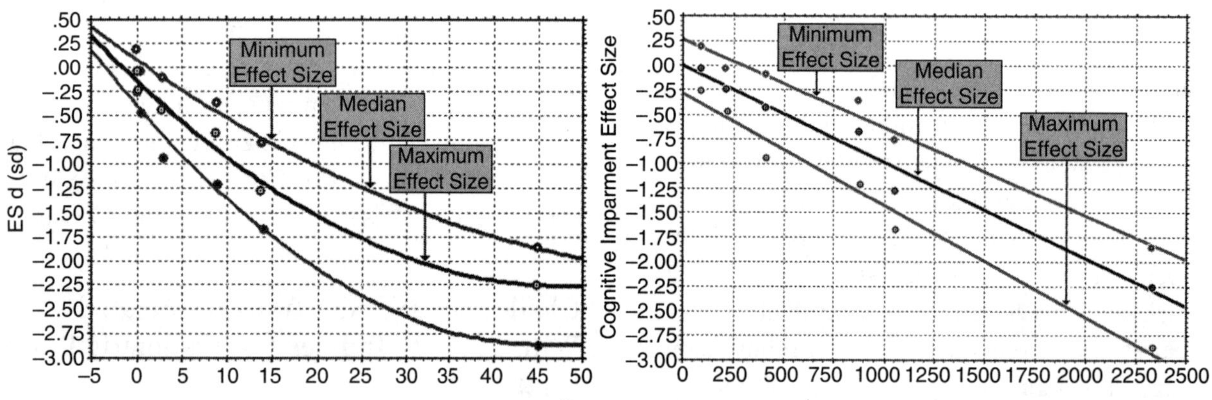

FIGURE 7.1. Left panel: logarithmic regression with TBI severity measured by LOC on the *x*-axis and cognitive deficit effect size on the *y*-axis. Right panel: Results of linear regression with TBI severity measured by PTA on the *x*-axis and cognitive deficit effect size on the *y*-axis. Data are from Dikmen, Machamer, Winn, and Temkin (1995) and Rohling, Meyers, and Millis (2003). Eq. = equation; ES = effect size; LOC = loss of consciousness; PTA = posttraumatic amnesia; TBI = traumatic brain injury.

determine the degree of deficit expected for examinees on the basis of their known PTA. Alternatively, this same relationship can be used, retrospectively, to determine whether the examinee has achieved maximum cognitive recovery (i.e., PTA and cognitive deficits fall on the regression line) or whether the individual might be exaggerating deficits beyond what is expected on the basis of the person's PTA (i.e., cognitive deficits are substantially below expectation on the basis of the regression line). Given the strength of this relationship, forensic neuropsychologists should exhaustively search the medical records to find an estimate of PTA. It is also typically worthwhile to estimate PTA from interviews with the examinee or collateral sources, although such estimates may contain a substantial amount of error variance. Furthermore, the field of neuropsychology should continue to advocate for standardized PTA assessment as a routine part of hospital care for those who have sustained a TBI (e.g., Novak, 2004; Sherer, Struchen, Yablon, Wang, & Nick, 2008).

Returning to the yardstick analogy, one can imagine the distance between the end of the yardstick and the first inch being further divided, but the statistical relationship previously found may not be as stable in this subsection compared with the entire length of the yardstick. In fact, the association between severity of TBI and cognitive deficits for the mildest severity group has a restricted range, in terms of both the independent variable and the dependent measure. Minimizing the problem of range restriction is accomplished by considering the signs and symptoms of mTBI that typically occur within hours to days after the event rather than waiting a year before attempting to retrospectively determine these injury characteristics.

Another method of handling the range restriction problem is to identify which cognitive domain is the most sensitive to the effects of an mTBI (i.e., the canary in the coal mine). Rohling et al. (2011) showed that the acute influence of mTBI is most clear-cut on measures of verbal, visual, and working memory. Adequately assessing these domains can assist the examiner in determining the severity of the examinee's injury. It is also important to choose the most precise method for quantifying injury severity, such as LOC, GCS, PTA, or balance. Of these, we find that LOC is the most objective and predictive, followed by GCS, PTA, and balance. Less exacting methods create more error variance in both the independent and the dependent variables during the period for which associations have been generated. Conversely, the more precise the data gathered from records are (e.g., LOC to the minute in cases of mTBI), the more accurate the prediction of cognitive performance will be postinjury. Unfortunately, the data in the records are, at times, not listed in the medical file or there is insufficient documentation of detail for the forensic neuropsychologist, making determinations more challenging. A case that illustrates these concerns and how to make important determinations by means of what chart notes do exist is presented later in this chapter (i.e., Case Example 2).

Returning to Rohling et al. (2011), these researchers conducted a meta-analysis of the association between cognitive deficits and time post-mTBI. They divided the group studied into four groups on the basis of postinjury time: (a) less than 8 days, with a median of 3 days; (b) 8 to 30 days, with a median of 14 days; (c) 31 to 92 days, with a median of 42 days; and (d) more than 92 days, with a median of 175 days. The associated levels of cognitive deficits across these four groups were, respectively, −0.39, −0.32, −0.14, and −0.07. The most severe deficits were seen closest in time to the mTBI, with few, if any, deficits persisting past 3 months. When logarithmic regression was conducted on these two variables, with the *x*-axis defined as the amount of time since the mTBI and the *y*-axis defined as cognitive deficit, the resulting *r* value was .989. The regression line is presented in Figure 7.2.

The curvilinear relationship accounted for 98% of the variance among the scores [$y = .550 + 0.101 * \ln(x)$]. Of course, the resulting correlation was generated using group data. Thus, the standard error of the estimate from Rohling et al.'s (2011) meta-analysis tends to be narrower than what is typically calculated with individual subject's data, making a direct inference from the equation overly precise. Nevertheless, the correlation generated by Rohling et al.'s meta-analysis provides the forensic neuropsychologist with an easy-to-use rubric for generating

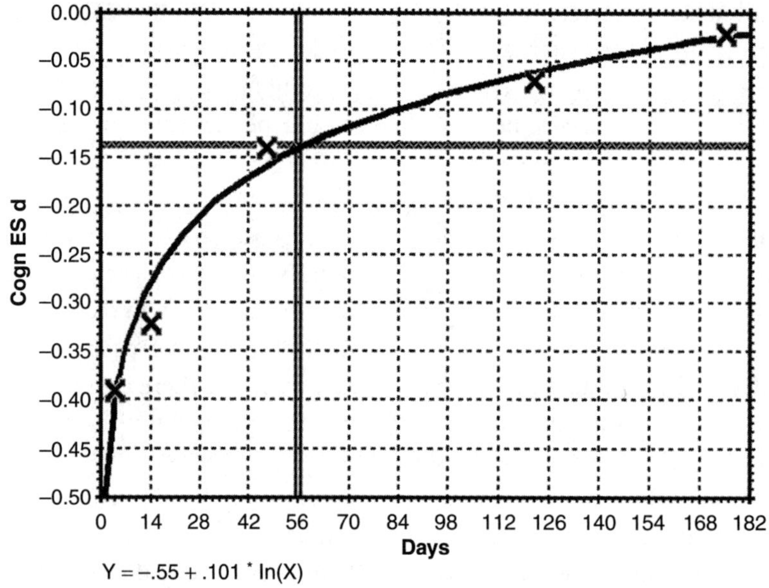

FIGURE 7.2. Logarithmic regression showing the relationship between time postinjury and cognitive deficits for mTBI patients. The effect sizes shown come from an mTBI meta-analysis by Rohling et al. (2011). Data are mean effect sizes for all cognitive domains assessed. Cogn. = cognitive; ES = effect size; mTBI = mild traumatic brain injury.

an expected rate of recovery for mTBI examinees. Moreover, a full consideration of the resulting relationship illustrates an important point: The nature of cognitive recovery from mTBI is curvilinear, such that the largest percentage of recovered cognitive ability occurs early, and there is a diminishing rate of recovery later (Rohling et al., 2011).

The severity of mTBI may have some relevance for acute management or treatment planning. However, Rohling and colleagues (Binder, Rohling, & Larrabee, 1997; Rohling et al., 2011) have shown that individuals should expect to return to their premorbid level of functioning within 3 months or less postinjury. It is worth noting that the meta-analysis conducted by Binder et al. (1997) used the most broad and inclusive definition of mTBI (i.e., LOC of 60 minutes or less). Thus, their analysis included the most severely injured of the mTBI sample. Yet, their postinjury results remained quite similar to premorbid ability. Even individuals who lost consciousness for up to 1 hour, as a group, showed no lasting deficits beyond 3 months. These data strongly suggest that if examinees who have experienced an mTBI have continued complaints of a somatic nature past 3 months, these complaints are most likely caused by the effects of litigation (Belanger, Curtiss, Demery, Lebowitz, & Vanderploeg, 2005) or by problems that existed premorbidly (Iverson, Lange, Brooks, & Rennison, 2010), rather than by the neurological injury.

Outcomes From a Mild Traumatic Brain Injury and Expected Rates of Recovery

The most likely outcome from a single uncomplicated mTBI is recovery to baseline by 3 months postinjury. Several meta-analytic studies (Belanger et al., 2005; Binder et al., 1997; Frencham, Fox, & Maybery, 2005; Rohling et al., 2011; Schretlen & Shapiro, 2003) have examined cognitive outcomes after an mTBI. Rohling et al. (2011) examined outcome data as a function of cognitive domains as well as time posttrauma. They found that the domains that had the largest effect sizes during the 1st week postinjury were verbal memory (−0.35), visual memory (−0.31), and working memory (−0.32). These domains are most associated with the early impact of an mTBI and can be detectable by a neuropsychologist who is assessing an individual immediately posttrauma. They can be thought of as the signature cognitive triad of mTBI in the early postinjury period. Worth noting is that processing speed (−0.17) was not in the top group of affected domains during this period and should not be considered the canary in the coal mine. Although forensic neuropsychological evaluations do not occur in the 1st week postinjury, the existence of neuropsychological results from evaluations performed in clinical contexts during this period can later inform forensic examiners.

By 93 days postinjury, only working memory, of all the cognitive domains, demonstrated a significant effect size (i.e., −0.19); however, an effect size of this magnitude is too small to be diagnostically reliable or clinically meaningful and is equivalent to a Wechsler Adult Intelligence Scale—Fourth Edition (Wechsler, 2008a) Working Memory Index reduction of just under 3 points, which is essentially the same magnitude of the measurement error (6 points) for this index. These findings indicate that competent forensic neuropsychologists, using the measurement devices that currently exist, will by and large be unable to reliably detect cognitive deficits associated with an mTBI at any time point past 3 months postinjury.

Although the majority of the meta-analytic research has examined residual cognitive effects, Mathias and Coats (1999), as well as Levin et al. (2001), found a favorable post-mTBI outcome regarding psychological problems as well. More recently, Panayiotou, Jackson, and Crowe (2010) conducted a meta-analysis that assessed psychiatric symptoms such as depression, anxiety, coping skills, and psychosocial disability that were present post-mTBI. The overall effect size was −0.05, and no domain was significantly different from zero. The best psychological outcome was found in children age 16 years and younger as well as in adults older than age 65 years (Babikian et al., 2011; Goldstein & Levin, 2001).

Thus, as we have reviewed, state-of-the-art research has definitively demonstrated that a person with a single mTBI has no long-term cognitive or psychological deficits. This was also the conclusion reached by the Committee on Traumatic Brain Injury: Board of Health Care Services (Institute of Medicine, 2006), the WHO (Carroll, Cassidy, Holm, Kraus, & Coronado, 2004), the American Medical Association (Giza et al., 2013), the Department of Veterans Affairs, and the Department of Defense (Research Advisory Committee on Gulf War Veterans' Illnesses, 2008), as well as six meta-analyses (Belanger et al., 2005; Belanger, Spiegel, & Vanderploeg, 2010; Binder et al., 2007; Frencham et al., 2005; Rohling et al., 2011; Schretlen & Shapiro, 2003), which represents hundreds of studies and thousands of individuals.

Specifically, the Institute of Medicine (2009), in a publication related to the consequences associated with TBI and the Gulf War, collected more than 30,000 articles related to mTBI. It systematically reviewed 1,900 of the articles considered relevant. After an exhaustive review, the committee concluded, "The evidence was inadequate and insufficient with respect to the long-term adverse social functioning, including unemployment, diminished social relationships, and decrease in the ability to live independently" (p. 7).

Using a similar process, the WHO Collaborating Centre Task Force on Mild Traumatic Brain Injury (Carroll, Cassidy, Peloso, et al., 2004) identified 38,806 citations, of which 743 directly focused on mTBI. Of these, 313 (42%) were accepted on scientific merit and formed the basis of the task force's synthesis of best evidence. The task force concluded that children's prognosis after an mTBI is good, with resolution of symptoms within 2 to 3 months. They found little, if any, evidence of residual cognitive, behavioral, or academic deficits related to children's experience of mTBI. The task force noted that both adults and children experienced similar symptoms shortly after an mTBI. These symptoms include headache, dizziness, and fatigue, among others. Children's symptoms in particular resolved quickly. According to the WHO review (Carroll, Cassidy, Peloso, et al., 2004), cognitive deficits and symptoms are common for adults in the acute stage post-mTBI, but injured individuals should expect full recovery to occur within 3 months, with the same pattern of expectation for symptom resolution observed in the majority of studies.

However, studies have demonstrated persistent symptoms in people post-mTBI who are involved in compensation or litigation, which appears to be a potential precipitating or maintaining factor (e.g., Rohling, Binder, & Langhinrichsen-Rohling, 1995). Binder et al. (1997) noted that researchers have not consistently found other predictors for this finding. However, preexisting persistent headaches, anxious or depressed mood, and inattentive symptoms might contribute to any long-standing postconcussion symptoms. The methodologically strongest studies of mTBI, in that they included appropriate control groups and considered the effects of other non-mTBI factors, showed symptom resolution within weeks to 3 months.

Expected Sequelae After an Mild Traumatic Brain Injury

The percentage of those with an mTBI who are expected to have prolonged symptoms is often cited as 15%. Ruff and colleagues (Ruff, Camenzuli, & Mueller, 1996; Ruff et al., 1994) were the first to refer to this group of individuals as the "miserable minority." The 15% statistic has typically been attributed to Alexander (1995), although many sources have cited Guerrero, Thurman, and Sniezek (2000) or Kushner (1998). Of note, Alexander generated his 15% estimate from Rutherford, Merrett, and McDonald (1979) and McLean, Temkin, Dikmen, and Wyler (1983). The Rutherford et al. article relied on patient self-report, and they noted,

> Of the 19 patients who had symptoms at one year, eight were involved in lawsuits and six had been suspected of malingering six weeks after their accident. Five of these patients were both involved in lawsuits and suspected of malingering. (p. 228)

McLean et al. also documented symptoms based on self-report. Therefore, the estimated percentage of mTBI patients with prolonged or persistent symptoms (the miserable minority) came from patients' self-report, not from objective assessments or prospective research designs. Moreover, many of these subjects had documented in their records other factors that are known to be associated with motivation to exaggerate their symptoms. Recently, Rohling, Larrabee, and Millis (2012) statistically demonstrated that the miserable minority is unlikely to exist. Furthermore, they established that, if such a subgroup did exist, the typical neuropsychological assessment battery would not be able to discriminate any patient, on a case-by-case basis, from those who had fully recovered.

Despite the findings in the most methodologically rigorous studies that indicated no persistent effects of mTBI, many studies that were not included in the previously cited meta-analyses, primarily because of methodological flaws, have reported significant findings. To investigate this issue, Belanger et al. (2005) conducted a meta-analysis, with a portion of the sample including studies that recruited patients at the time of their injury. Belanger et al. found that studies using prospective groups had a chronic symptom (≥3 month) effect size of –0.04 at 3 months postinjury. They contrasted these results with those obtained from studies based on clinical samples. These studies generated a chronic symptom effect size of −0.74. Belanger et al. noted that the clinical samples often had a higher proportion of patients who complained of persistent symptoms. Furthermore, they found that samples of litigating individuals had a cognitive impairment effect size of −0.78. The presence of litigation was consistent with stable cognitive deficits or a worsening of deficits over time. The impact of the sample differences was consistent with the findings of Binder and Rohling (1996), who examined the severity of deficits among subjects with TBI, as well as with those of Rohling et al. (1995), who examined a similarly inclusive sample of injured individuals, although Rohling et al. were assessing the impact of disability in patients with chronic pain rather than TBI. In both samples, effect sizes were influenced by litigation, demonstrating that money matters. Specifically, when examining a slightly different population of patients, those who suffered from chronic pain, Rohling et al. (1995) found that patients who were seeking compensation recovered more slowly, expressed a greater number of complaints, had complaints representing a greater magnitude of dysfunction, and responded less effectively to treatment, despite the fact that they were matched for severity of disorder. Harris, Mulford, Solomon, van Gelder, and Young (2005) reported similar findings for surgical patients who were receiving or seeking disability insurance. They noted, "Compensation status is associated with poor outcome after surgery. This effect is significant, clinically important, and consistent" (p. 1644). Therefore, studies based on samples with litigating subjects routinely have higher effect sizes for persisting symptoms. Consequently, studies using nonprospective subject recruitment and including persons involved in litigation or seeking compensation do not yield results that are representative of the neurocognitive influence of mTBI.

Larrabee, Binder, Rohling, and Ploetz (2013) reported additional evidence related to preexisting neuropsychological differences in persons who had sustained an mTBI. For example, individuals who had experienced an mTBI produced lower scores on measures of premorbid cognitive functioning compared with demographically matched controls. Heitger et al. (2009) found a pre-mTBI effect size using the Wechsler Test of Adult Reading (WTAR; Wechsler, 2001) of −0.75. Similarly, Mathias and Coats (1999) found an effect size of −0.53 with the North American Adult Reading Test (Uttl, 2002) for those with a history of mTBI.

Preexisting psychiatric problems are also predictive of persistent symptoms 3 months postinjury in both mTBI and orthopedic trauma control subjects, whereas for mTBI it was predictive of postconcussive symptoms at 1 week but not at 3 months (Ponsford et al., 2012). In a study of military veterans who sustained an mTBI after discharge, the strongest predictors of post-mTBI outcome were early-life psychiatric difficulties, limited social support, and lower pre-mTBI intelligence as measured by pre–military induction aptitude tests (Luis, Vanderploeg, & Curtiss, 2003). These findings underscore the importance of comparing an orthopedic trauma control group with an mTBI group in research on this topic. Such a control group has similar preexisting psychological and neuropsychological issues that are associated with becoming injured. These preinjury issues may cause differences in individuals' reaction to injury that are due to injury in general, not specific to brain injury.

The importance of including an orthopedic trauma control group extends to neuroimaging investigations. For example, Aoki, Inokuchi, Gunshin, Yahagi, and Suwa (2012) reported an effect size of −0.25 for diffusion tensor imaging (DTI) fractional anisotropy in the corpus callosum of those with a history of mTBI compared with controls, but only one of the 13 studies included in the meta-analysis used an orthopedic trauma control group, and the effect size for this study was −0.07. This was the second smallest effect size reported in the meta-analysis. This particular study also found no DTI differences between those with a history of mTBI who met criteria for postconcussion syndrome and those who did not (Lange, Iverson, Brubacher, Mädler, & Heran, 2012). Lange et al. (2012) noted, "Contrary to the biological explanation, there is very weak evidence from this relatively large study supporting a potent relationship between white matter changes and the postconcussion disorder" (p. 9). Thus, assessment of cognitive functioning is more relevant to determining rate of recovery than are results from neuroimaging, specifically DTI.

Moreover, research by Suhr and Gunstad (2002, 2005) on diagnosis threat showed how perception and awareness of TBI in relation to cognitive function could alter examinees' cognitive test scores. They randomly assigned students with a history of an mTBI to one of two groups. They gave one group neutral instructions before assessment. The other group had attention called to their prior mTBI, suggesting specifically that their mTBI would likely have negative effects on their cognition. The second group obtained significantly lower test scores than the first group. They also rated themselves as putting forth less effort than did the first group, with self-ratings of effort correlating with test performance. However, the second group's scores did not demonstrate any pattern suggestive of feigning, indicating that individuals' expectations influence outcome even without conscious intent.

Finally, Green, Rohling, and colleagues have published a series of studies on the influence of effort or invalid performance on neuropsychological test scores, as well as on cognitive complaints, emotional status, and chronic pain. A seminal article on the topic was published by Green, Rohling, Lees-Haley, and Allen (2001), who found that poor effort accounted for a far greater proportion of cognitive test score variance (25%) than did TBI severity (6%). Furthermore, examinees who failed performance validity tests (PVTs; also known as effort tests; Larrabee, 2012a) complained of more cognitive dysfunction and reported less dysphoric emotion (e.g., depression and anxiety). Rohling, Allen, and Green (2002) replicated these results, demonstrating that the factor structure of a test battery varies significantly depending on whether the examined sample passed or failed PVTs. Rohling and Demakis (2010) reanalyzed data published by Bowden, Shores, and Mathias (2006) and replicated the earlier finding of effort accounting for 25% of cognitive test score variance, whereas TBI severity accounted for just 5% of the variance. Other independent researchers have now replicated these findings several times (e.g., Constantinou, Bauer, Ashendorf, Fisher, & McCaffrey, 2005; Stevens, Friedel, Mehren, & Merten, 2008).

After excluding subjects who failed PVTs, Rohling, Green, Allen, and Iverson (2002) found that depressed mood was unrelated to cognitive test scores, with 0% of the variance in scores accounted for by the variance in measures of depression. However, the variance in cognitive complaints was associated with variance on measures of depression (46%), which was greater than the variance associated with severity of neurological injury (5%). Demakis, Gervais, and Rohling (2008) replicated these findings, but with a sample of patients who complained of posttraumatic stress disorder (PTSD) symptoms and other anxiety disorders rather than depression. Gervais, Rohling, Green, and Ford (2004) further found that cognitive test scores were unrelated to measures of acute or chronic pain. However, measures of pain were associated with measures of depression and cognitive complaints. Green, Rohling, Iverson, and Gervais (2003) demonstrated that the best predictors of cognitive complaints associated with an mTBI were odor identification (i.e., Alberta Smell Test) and mood (i.e., Minnesota Multiphasic Personality Inventory—2 [MMPI–2] Scale 2, Symptom Checklist–90—Revised De, and Beck Depression Inventory). Thus, preexisting conditions, validity tests, and concurrent assessment of emotional status are an important component of the forensic evaluation of mTBI. The issue of odor detection remains open, because there has not been sufficient research replicating this finding to make a recommendation. Nevertheless, clinicians may want to add an assessment of odor detection, particularly during acute stages of recovery, when assessing individuals who have experienced an mTBI, to better categorize the severity of deficits.

More specifically, researchers (e.g., Gargan & Bannister, 1990) have found an association between whiplash and cognitive, emotional, and painful sequelae. However, further examination of the literature, which includes empirical data analysis, does not support the notion that whiplash associated with cervical hyperextension causes brain injury. Hart, Martelli, and Zasler (2000) found that chronic pain often explains cognitive deficits. Similarly, Kessels, Aleman, Verhagen, and van Luijtelaar (2000) conducted a meta-analysis that revealed an association between chronic whiplash and cognitive deficits; however, these authors concluded that the origin of the cognitive deficits could not be determined (Kessels et al., 2000). Obelieniene and colleagues (Obelieniene et al., 1998; Obelieniene, Schrader, Bovim, Miseviciene, & Sand, 1999) conducted a series of studies in Lithuania, a country in which financial incentives for prolonged symptomatology after MVAs do not exist. They demonstrated no association between whiplash injuries and chronic pain or headaches. Alexander (1998) stated there was

> no credible mechanism for clinically meaningful DAI [diffuse axonal injury] in pure whiplash in awake humans who do not report loss of consciousness or amnesia beyond that psychologically appropriate for the acutely stressful time immediately around the accident and injury. (p. 337)

Thus, research has demonstrated that whiplash, much like mTBI, is one of several syndromes in which patients' reports of symptoms often outweigh objective findings of tissue pathology (Barsky & Borus, 1999). Excessive complaints of psychological dysfunction and emotional dysregulation are far more common when litigation or compensation seeking is involved than when it is not, especially when a patient fails validity tests (Green et al., 2001;

Iverson, King, Scott, & Adams, 2001; Lange, Iverson, Brooks, & Rennison, 2010; Rohling, Allen, & Green, 2002; Rohling, Green, et al., 2012).

Postconcussive Syndrome

If symptoms of an mTBI persist beyond expectation, they have frequently been described as postconcussive syndrome (PCS; Gunstad & Suhr, 2004). The PCS triad of physical, cognitive, and emotional symptoms typically includes headaches, irritability, and poor memory. Lees-Haley and Brown (1993) examined the records of 50 nonlitigating medical controls and 170 psychiatric claims litigants. All of the subjects had no neurological claims or injuries. They completed a cognitive symptom checklist, and there were high rates of endorsement of symptoms such as headache (controls = 62%; litigants = 88%), irritability (controls = 38%; litigants = 77%) and poor memory (controls = 20%; litigants = 53%).

Mittenberg, DiGiulio, Perrin, and Bass's (1992) classic article on expectation as etiology might help explain these findings. In their study, non-mTBI participants read vignettes about TBI and were asked to endorse complaints they expected a person with a history of mTBI would endorse. The complaints endorsed by the participants are the same as those commonly endorsed by individuals who have sustained an mTBI and claim to be suffering from persistent symptoms. Suhr and Gunstad (2002, 2005) demonstrated the "good old days" phenomenon, such that persons with an established history of mTBI underestimated the frequency of occurrence of postconcussive symptoms preinjury compared with post-injury. Iverson et al. (2010) found evidence in support of this phenomenon, demonstrating abnormally low retrospective estimates of preconcussive symptoms in people seeking evaluation for financially compensable mTBI; in fact, these examinees as a group reported that they were healthier than were normal uninjured people before the event.

As noted previously, a history of mTBI or its severity does not predict postconcussive symptoms. Rather, preexisting psychiatric disorders are the best predictors of such symptoms. For example, Meares et al. (2011) defined PCS as the presence of three or more concussive-like symptoms. Their study examined both individuals with a TBI history and trauma controls; the controls were involved in an accident but were not head injured. Three months after injury, the presence of so-called postconcussive symptoms, including headaches, dizziness, fatigue, depression, anxiety, noise sensitivity, irritability, and insomnia, was as common in the individuals whose heads were not injured as it was in those who had sustained an mTBI. Of note, a preinjury depressive or anxiety disorder and acute posttraumatic stress at approximately 5 days postinjury were the significant predictors of PCS 3 months later. The authors concluded that non–brain injury factors were the primary cause of the development of these symptoms. Donnell, Kim, Silva, and Vanderploeg (2012) concluded that, when three or more symptoms were used to define the syndrome, an mTBI does not produce symptoms of PCS any more often than do injuries to other body parts. This suggests that PCS is not uniquely related to concussion and is misnamed.

Supporting this assertion, in a sample of veterans only 32% of those who had a history of an mTBI met *Diagnostic and Statistical Manual of Mental Disorders* (4th ed.; American Psychiatric Association, 1994) diagnostic criteria for PCS, as compared with 40% of those diagnosed with PTSD, 50% with generalized anxiety disorder, 57% with major depressive disorder, and 91% with somatization disorder. Dikmen, Machamer, Fann, and Temkin (2010), when considering all degrees of TBI severity, found many symptoms, including headaches and dizziness, occurred more commonly 1 year post-mTBI compared with trauma controls. However, contrary to expectation, patients with a history of mTBI endorsed more postconcussive symptoms than did patients with more severe head injuries. Once again, the best predictor of postconcussive symptoms was preexisting psychiatric problems.

Suhr and Spickard (2012) demonstrated that avoidance or reduced effort occurs in people who fear that a challenging cognitive task will induce or worsen their headaches. Kashluba, Hanks, Casey, and Millis (2008) found that, 3 months postinjury, 58% of persons with a history of mTBI complained of headaches, which is nearly identical to the 59% of controls who complained of headaches. However, ratings of headache pain severity were worse for those with a history of mTBI than for controls. Moreover, complaints of dizziness, irritability, temper outbursts, and light and sound sensitivity were more frequent in the mTBI group compared with the control group. Headache frequency and severity were not associated with head or neck injuries in Lithuania, where opportunity for compensation for symptoms was limited (Stovner, Schrader, Mickevičiene, Surkiene, & Sand, 2009).

Iverson and McCracken (1997) demonstrated the lack of diagnostic specificity of PCS symptoms. They examined healthy controls and patients with chronic pain (Katona et al., 2005) but no history of head injury or concussion. Patients with a history of depression complained of PCS symptoms more frequently than those with no history of depression. Iverson (2006) found that 50% of depressed patients met conservative diagnostic criteria for PCS. In fact, the likelihood of PCS symptoms was greater in individuals who experienced an mTBI and failed tests of effort than after moderate to severe TBI.

Tsanadis et al. (2008) replicated these results, finding that headache, dizziness, and ringing in the ears were more common after an mTBI than after more severe TBI. Ringing in the ears was more than twice as likely in the mTBI group (32%) than in the more severely injured sample (14%). Similarly, those with a history of mTBI were 3 times more likely (40%) to report nausea than more severely injured patients (14%). They were also twice as likely (80%) to report irritability than those who were severely injured (39%), almost twice as likely to report headaches (80% vs. 45%) and depression (71% vs. 39%), and more than twice as likely to report dizziness (50% vs. 22%). The fact that these symptoms are more common after an mTBI than a severe TBI implies a non-neurological basis for these complaints. Even light sensitivity, which is often considered a prototypical symptom of PCS, was better explained by stress and nonorganic factors than by neurological damage (Bengtzen, Woodward, Lynn, Newman, & Biousse, 2008; Goodrich et al., 2014).

Garden and Sullivan (2010) also reported high rates of endorsement of postconcussive symptoms in healthy university students and community volunteers (e.g., headache, 81%; irritability, 78%; memory problems, 56%). Moreover, a subgroup of depressed study participants endorsed very high rates of headache (96%) and memory problems (75%). Iverson and McCracken (1997) noted the similarity of postconcussive symptom ratings between mTBI patients and those with chronic pain. Research on self-reported functioning in groups other than those with mTBI has demonstrated that these symptoms are more strongly associated with patients' mood ratings than with actual objective cognitive performance (e.g., Larrabee & Levin, 1986; Larrabee, West, & Crook, 1991; J. M. Williams, Little, Scates, & Blockman, 1987).

Hänninen et al. (1994) demonstrated the relationship between self-report of cognitive function and somatization. Their findings contradict the recommendation of Gass and Russell (1991), who had developed a correction factor for the MMPI–2 designed to apply to patients suffering from a documented neurological disorder. Gass and Russell reasoned that when neurological patients endorsed these items they were validly reporting their symptoms, rather than it being a consequence of a psychiatric disorder. Their correction factor removed these items from scoring. However, Hänninen et al. found these same items were less associated with GCS and PTA, or cognitive test scores obtained from patients who experienced an mTBI, than they were with scores on the MMPI–2 depression scale (Brulot, Strauss, & Spellacy, 1997; Butcher, Dahlstrom, Graham, Tellegen, & Kaemmer, 1989). The conclusion that one might reach regarding these findings is that PCS has no discriminant or convergent validity, which are the underpinnings of construct validity.

Many PCS symptoms are not specific to TBI, even on an acute basis. For example, Lees-Haley, Fox, and Courtney (2001) found that 67% of the subjects in a sample with mTBI reported being confused and 71% reported feeling dazed at the time of injury, compared with similarly high rates of endorsement of these same symptoms (65% and 52%, respectively) by subjects in the "other-injury" groups. These findings call into question the validity of including the symptoms of feeling dazed and confused in the American Congress of Rehabilitation Medicine definition of mTBI (Mild Traumatic

Brain Injury Committee, 1993), because these symptoms are not specific to mTBI. To increase diagnostic validity, the examiner should rely on objective injury markers, such as LOC, GCS, and PTA, and the results of a mental status exam shortly after injury, rather than patients' subjective complaints weeks, months, or years after an mTBI.

Mittenberg et al. (1992) showed similar rates of endorsement of PCS symptoms by persons asked to imagine they had experienced an mTBI compared with those who had actually experienced an mTBI. They explained these findings as evidence of selective attentional bias, with an overfocus on common internal states, stress, and arousal. Putnam and Millis (1994) and Putnam, Millis, and Adams (1996) provided a similar explanation for the reporting of PCS symptoms. They characterized chronic PCS as a somatoform disorder, drawing parallels between the selective attentional bias in persons with chronic PCS and the self-directed selective attention to bodily sensations in persons with elevated health concerns (see Watson & Pennebaker, 1989, as well as Delis & Wetter, 2007, who proposed a cogniform-type of somatoform pathology). Many individuals who have not had an mTBI experience PCS symptoms in everyday life. This can result in a "perfect storm" in a somatically focused person who subsequently has an mTBI. If a provider diagnoses the somatically focused person's complaints as being the result of an mTBI rather than as also being present before the MBTI, the person may misattribute the symptoms as evidence of a brain injury. It is also possible that such symptoms did not exist before the injury, but developed after it and have no neurological explanation. Under such circumstances, a vicious cycle ensues, as the person's misattribution results in even greater stress and more frequent PCS symptoms.

As demonstrated by the diagnosis threat research of Suhr and Gunstad (2002, 2005), holding the belief that one has sustained a brain injury can have a negative effect on cognitive test performance. This cascade of influences can be considered a form of iatrogenesis or a treatment-caused disorder (Roth & Spencer, 2013). Drawing on Mittenberg's "expectation as etiology" model of PCS, Mittenberg and colleagues (Mittenberg, Tremont, Zielinski, Fichera, & Rayls, 1996; Mittenberg, Zielinski, & Fichera, 1993) developed a cognitive–behavioral treatment model for PCS, with the main component being a presentation of accurate, evidence-based information about recovery and a correction of patients' symptom misattribution.

Outcome of Complicated Mild Traumatic Brain Injury and Multiple Mild Traumatic Brain Injuries

D. H. Williams, Levin, and Eisenberg (1990) were the first to describe individuals who otherwise meet criteria for an mTBI but who have trauma-related abnormalities evident on neuroimaging scans as having a complicated mTBI, for which we propose a new abbreviation, cmTBI. Research has suggested that patients who meet criteria for cmTBI typically experience outcomes that are more similar to those of persons with moderate TBI (e.g., persons with day-of-injury postresuscitation GCS scores of 9–12). Kashluba et al. (2008) also reported similarities between the neuropsychological outcome of persons with cmTBI and those with moderate TBI.

By contrast, Hanlon, Demery, Martinovich, and Kelly (1999) found no differences in cognitive test scores or vocational outcome between mTBI patients with or without positive CT scans at 6 months postinjury. Comparing those with and without abnormalities on MRI scans, Hughes et al. (2004) demonstrated differences at 72 hours. However, at 6 months postinjury the groups did not cognitively differ on measures of return-to-work or symptom complaints. In summary, persons who otherwise meet criteria for an mTBI but who show abnormal CT or MRI on acute radiologic studies may have outcomes more similar to those associated with moderate TBI. Persons with cmTBI may or may not make the full recovery that is characteristic of persons sustaining a single, uncomplicated mTBI. However, this conclusion is not definitive, and more research is needed in this area to guide clinical practice.

Another controversy regarding outcomes exists for patients who have a history of prior mTBIs. There is concern that they may have a different outcome than is common for those who have experienced a single mTBI, with evidence of persisting deficits. However, Belanger et al. (2010) found a nonsignificant overall effect size of −0.06 for athletes who sustained more than one self-reported mTBI compared with those who sustained only one mTBI. Follow-up analyses of specific domains of function showed significant effect sizes for persisting executive functions (−0.24) and delayed memory (−0.16) deficits. Although statistically significant, these values are quite small and may not be of much clinical significance. Furthermore, one pediatric investigation suggested that persons who sustain multiple mTBIs might differ premorbidly from those with no prior history of mTBI. Bijur, Haslum, and Golding (1996) found no evidence for the cumulative effects of mTBI, comparing children with histories of one, two, or three mTBIs with non–head-injured orthopedic trauma controls who had a history of one, two, or three orthopedic injuries. Bijur et al. suggested that cognitive deficits associated with multiple mTBIs were secondary to social and personal factors related to multiple injuries rather than resulting from repeated but minor damage to the head. In addition, in their review of the effects of multiple concussions in athletes and the possibility of a condition termed chronic traumatic encephalopathy, Carone and Bush (2014) concluded that "while [chronic traumatic encephalopathy] may indeed exist, we believe that the available evidence to date suggests a multifactorial etiology rather than a single etiology (e.g., repetitive head/brain trauma)" (p. 318).

Summarizing, existing research is equivocal regarding both persistent effects of cmTBI and cumulative effects of multiple mTBIs. Careful analysis of any individual case showing evidence for either of these clinical histories is required. Individuals with either a history of previous mTBI or a history of mTBI with LOC of 15 minutes, a GCS score of 14, and PTA for less than 24 hours but with a contusion, a subdural hematoma, or a positive neuroimaging scan may or may not experience persisting symptoms or deficits. The vast majority are unlikely to experience symptoms, but a small percentage might. Thus, the neuropsychologist must scrutinize the early medical records for evidence of prolonged confusion, cognitive deficits, or both during the acute and subacute stages of recovery. When a person experiences a rapid resolution of disorientation within 2 hours of an injury, with subsequent return to normal cognition, the predicted pattern of recovery is no different than it is for an uncomplicated mTBI. However, evidence of prolonged cognitive impairment and symptom complaints that extend several days posttrauma is more predictive of TBI with detectable residual impacts. It is important to note that neuropsychologists must gather, examine, and interpret all available close-in-time documentation because relying on examinees' reports several months posttrauma is problematic. The examiner must look for consistent patterns in the data, obtained from multiple sources, across time.

CAUSES FOR INCREASED FORENSIC FOCUS ON MILD TRAUMATIC BRAIN INJURY

mTBI is the most common reason for referral to forensic neuropsychologists related to personal injury (Ruff & Richardson, 1999; Sweet & Meyers, 2012). Clinicians with less experience and knowledge often misdiagnose examinees who have a history of mTBI. An issue of concern is the difficulty in determining the person's actual LOC, PTA, GCS, and close-in-time test results. Too often, examinees' medical records do not include documentation of these data, or the indices collected have low interrater reliability. Many cases diagnosed as having had an mTBI do not have the requisite acute injury data available. If an mTBI is assumed to be the cause of current deficits in the absence of data, or in the presence of data supporting a remote mTBI but an atypical recovery course, the neuropsychologist may not consider alternative diagnoses that can better account for the examinee's complaints and test performance, including evidence of feigning. Moreover, as noted previously, even when the medical records indicate that a person has experienced an mTBI with evidence of contusions on CT or MRI scans (e.g., cmTBI), one should remain cautious about how much variance in current performance is assumed to be caused by the documented mTBI. Consider Dikmen et al.'s (1995) study of residual cognitive deficits after TBI. They included subjects with neuroimaging abnormalities in their mTBI group. The effect size, as indexed by the overall test battery mean (OTBM) for this sample, was not different from zero ($d = -0.02$), based on comparisons with orthopedic controls, with a mean score of 95.1 ($SD = 12.8$).

The forensic neuropsychologist practicing in today's litigious society must be aware of this research. Examining the change in incidence of litigation in the United States related to mTBI, Carone and Bush (2013) used Google Scholar to search case law in both the U.S. state and federal court systems. They documented that during the 10-year period between 1990 and 1999, there were 1,002 cases addressing mild head injury, mild traumatic brain injury, concussion, or concussion syndrome. Using these same terms to search the database for cases over the next decade (i.e., 2000–2009), they located 2,483 cases. Thus, the number of mTBI cases in the legal system had risen nearly 250% since the publication of Rohling et al. (1995), Binder and Rohling (1996), and Binder et al. (1997).

Carone and Bush (2013) also examined the number of state and federal cases that involved the terms *malingering, malingering and neuropsych**, and *mild traumatic brain injury (or head injury)*. For the 10-year period between 1990 and 1999, they found 1,120 cases. In the subsequent decade, between 2000 and 2009, again using the same search terms, they found 3,549 cases. Thus, the rate had risen 317% since Binder, Rohling, and colleagues had published their articles (Binder & Rohling, 1996; Binder et al., 1997; Rohling et al., 1995). In addition, there were 43% more cases related to malingering than there were related to mTBI. Finally, the growth rate for cases focused on malingering rose 27% faster than the growth rate of cases focused on brain injury. Obviously, money is a powerful reinforcer of continued symptoms, and the practicing neuropsychologist must be able to separate organic from nonorganic causes of persistent expression of deficits.

Two historical issues relate directly to the rise in mTBI cases and the increased demand for neuropsychological assessment of such cases. The first relates to investigations into mTBI related to sports concussion. In particular, increased concern has been expressed about the injuries caused by playing contact sports, particularly football and hockey. This concern was initially expressed at the collegiate and professional level but has increasingly trickled down to middle school and high school athletics. The second was U.S. invasions of Afghanistan and Iraq after the terrorist attacks of September 11, 2001. Methods of war have evolved to include improvised explosive devices, or roadside bombs, which have caused many blast-related brain injuries, the vast majority of which have been and continue to be mild in severity. Understanding the impact of the war-related injuries and compensating veterans appropriately for their service-connected disabilities has been and continues to be a driving force behind much of the mTBI research.

Sports Concussion Research and Shifting Revenue Generation

In the mid- to late 1980s, just before the Binder, Rohling, and colleagues' meta-analytic efforts (Binder & Rohling, 1996; Binder et al., 1997; Rohling et al., 1995), Jeffrey Barth, PhD, at the University of Virginia, developed the sports as a laboratory assessment model (Barth et al., 1989) to study mTBI in football. Barth's research eventually led a host of others to investigate the influence of sports concussion on the development of cognitive and emotional disabilities, particularly the potential such concussions have to increase a person's chance of prematurely developing age-related dementia disorders, such as Alzheimer's disease.

Some of those who followed in Barth's shoes were Drs. Rubin Echemendia at Pennsylvania State University in 1995, and Mark Lovell, Mickey Collins, and Joseph Maroon, all of whom were at the University of Pittsburgh Medical Center. The latter three researchers were responsible for the development of the computerized assessment battery titled the Immediate Post-Concussion Assessment and Cognitive Testing (ImPACT) battery. The ImPACT battery (Lovell, Collins, Podell, Powell, & Maroon, 2000) has become the dominant computerized test battery in the field of sports-related concussions. However, many competitors have sprung up since that time, including CogSport (Collie, Darby, & Maruff, 2001); CogState (Westerman, Darby, Maruff, & Collie, 2001); CNS Vital Signs (Gualtieri & Johnson, 2006), now referred to as Concussion

Vital Signs; and Headminder (Erlanger et al., 2003). Drs. Bennet I. Omalu at University of California, Davis (Omalu et al., 2005); Robert C. Cantu (1986); Ann C. McKee (McKee et al., 2009); and Robert A. Stern (Stern et al., 2011) at Boston University have also developed various lines of mTBI research. This confluence of events resulted in a dramatic increase in the number of publications about mTBI appearing in the mid-2000s. Information obtained from sports concussion studies has informed the practice of forensic neuropsychology.

Military Research Associated With Blast-Related Concussions

In the late 1980s and early 1990s, corresponding to the first Gulf War, the Department of Defense and the Department of Veterans Affairs began similar projects in hopes of developing a computerized assessment battery to make return-to-the-field decisions and to determine who might be eligible for Department of Veterans Affairs benefits for service-connected injuries after their service was completed. This research resulted in the development of the Automated Neuropsychological Assessment Metric by Reeves, Kane, Winter, Raynsford, and Pancella (1993), which eventually became the standard test battery used to measure baseline skills and to make return-to-the-field decisions for more than one million soldiers deployed in the Middle East (Bleiberg, Kane, Reeves, Garmoe, & Halpern, 2000). The model of assessment, diagnosis, and treatment developed for the military was quite similar to that used by those involved in sports concussion, and it is noteworthy that neither of these measurement strategies initially included methods to assess examinees on performance validity.

The combination of the military activities in the Middle East and the concern over sports-related concussions caused a dramatic increase in the volume of published research on mTBI. General public concern expanded in conjunction with greater awareness and attention to the topic by scientists, politicians, athletes, and veterans. This, in turn, caused an increase in the number of forensic legal cases, which demanded more expert witness testimony for both plaintiff and defense attorneys. Such an increase has been documented by many, including Carone and Bush (2013), Sweet and Meyers (2012), and Kaufmann and Greiffenstein (2013). In fact, according to data collected by Kaufmann and Greiffenstein, which are quite similar to the data collected by Carone and Bush (2013), the number of cases involving forensic neuropsychology has increased over the 20-year period from 1991 to 2011 by a factor of 12 (i.e., from approximately 250 to more than 3,000).

The Hippocratic Oath: Do No Harm

It has generally been accepted that forensic assessment does not usually result in a therapeutic alliance. Psychotherapists are thought to be more advocates for their clients. However, for the most part, forensic evaluators owe no such duty to their examinees. However, we believe it is important for examiners to keep three perspectives in mind. The first is that the research literature on mTBI has demonstrated that significant and detectable cognitive deficits occur immediately after an mTBI and for days to weeks later (Giza & Hovda, 2001; McCrea et al., 2003). Second, the literature has also definitively shown that one can expect rapid recovery back to baseline. Finally, the research literature has highlighted how resilient human brains and skulls are after these types of injuries.

Nearly all individuals who sustain an mTBI can expect a full recovery from their deficits, typically within 10 to 14 days, and certainly by 3 months. However, when patients get involved in an adversarial system, such as exists in a civil or criminal trial or when applying for disability benefits, the recovery process tends to take longer and is less complete (Binder & Rohling, 1996; Feinstein, Ouchterlony, Somerville, & Jardine, 2001; Paniak et al., 2002; Rohling et al., 1995). To the best of their ability, forensic neuropsychologists should keep in mind the Hippocratic principle of "do no harm," regardless of which side in the legal matter the retaining party represents. Thus, they should remain aware of their fiduciary duty, not as it relates to the specific mTBI case for which they have been hired, but for all cases that they are asked to assess across their career. Whether one initially believes that an mTBI leads people to suffer permanent and disabling deficits or that the majority fully recover in as little as

2 to 4 weeks, an expert's actions should, as much as possible, be updated to consistent with the science in the area. Beliefs and practices need to change across time, so that, to the best of their ability, forensic neuropsychologists do not cause the recovery process to slow or fail to resolve.

GUIDELINES FOR ASSESSMENT OF PERSONS WITH A HISTORY OF MILD TRAUMATIC BRAIN INJURY

The forensic neuropsychological evaluation involves three stages, defined by Greiffenstein and Kaufmann (2012) as the evidentiary tripod. These three stages start with a review of records, followed by a clinical interview, and finally by a direct assessment. We describe each of these stages below. We also present two case examples to demonstrate how each is used in clinical practice.

Medical, Education, Employment, and Criminal Records Review

Before meeting with examinees, the neuropsychologist must thoroughly review the medical records to gather as much information as possible related to the nature and severity of the brain injury, as well as other medical problems and medications that may affect neuropsychological functioning. The forensic examiner attempts to verify these data in interviews with examinees, significant others, and medical staff. It is best that the records reviewed include the emergency medical technicians' (EMTs') report, police reports, and the initial evaluations conducted by medical personnel on arrival to the emergency department (ED). Specifically, the examiner is looking for GCS scores, PTA, and LOC, as well as any signs or symptoms that are associated with the severity of injury (e.g., disorientation, confusion, lethargy, or inability to focus attention).

The neuropsychologist should review the results of any structural neuroimaging scans and pay attention to any abnormalities documented. Granacher (2008) and Nuwer (1997) have shown that abnormal results obtained from procedures such as quantitative electroencephalogram, positron emission tomography scans, and single-photon emission computed tomography scans are not specific to TBI. Thus, the current standard of practice in evaluating mTBI patients does not factor in such imaging methods because they are not accepted as mainstream procedures in such evaluations. DTI imaging remains investigational, with some studies showing no clinically meaningful discrimination of people with mTBI from orthopedic trauma controls (Lange et al., 2012). However, a meta-analysis revealed a small effect size of 0.25 when the data from mTBI samples were compared to normal controls, with high (82%) overlap of DTI values for the two samples (Aoki et al., 2012). Further research on the utility of this imaging technique is warranted.

Transcripts related to an examinee's past educational performance and evidence of prior learning disabilities and placement in special education classes or gifted programs are beneficial, if not essential. These records often include results of standardized achievement tests, such as the Iowa Test of Basic Skills (Hoover, Dunbar, & Frisbie, 2001) or the SAT (College Board, 2011), which can be used to estimate premorbid functioning. The astute neuropsychologist can also use state-specific graduation exam scores or college admission tests, such as the ACT (American College Testing, 2014) or SAT (College Board, 2005), to generate estimates of premorbid cognitive functioning (Koenig, Frey, & Detterman, 2008; Schoenberg, Scott, Duff, & Adams, 2002). Neuropsychologists can use employment records, mental health records, and criminal history to determine the examinee's pre- and postinjury quality of psychosocial adjustment and socioeconomic status. Education and employment records also help practitioners estimate preinjury levels of intellectual functioning, which is valuable in postinjury determinations of impairment. All of these records should be obtained, if possible; however, it is acknowledged that such records are not always available for review.

Initial Clinical and Follow-Up Interviews

During the initial interview, the examiner should ask mostly open-ended questions to determine the examinees' memory and knowledge of the cause, severity, and nature of their injuries as well as their memory for information that might be difficult to recall if they were more severely injured. It is best if these facts are quantified using standardized questionnaires. However, it is important initially to not suggest any signs or symptoms to examinees (Lees-Haley et al., 2001). Rather, as patiently and supportively as possible, the examiner should ask examinees for a chronology of the accident or injury, including how long they remained hospitalized, when they were discharged, how they got home from the hospital, and the circumstances that confronted them once they returned home or to work. A detailed interview of an examinee not only provides information relevant to the assessment of the PTA but also provides evidence for the evaluation of potential PTSD. Specifically, do examinees become aroused and obviously distressed upon describing the event in detail? Can examinees recall, in sequence, the doctors who treated them and their diagnosis? What are their spontaneous complaints? Do they have pain complaints?

The answers to these questions can be quantified by having examinees describe their experience of pain using a 0 to 100 scale, with anchor points at 0 (*no pain at all*) and 100 (*pain so severe they would want to die to escape it*). Examinees are asked to rate their (a) current pain, (b) worst pain, (c) lowest pain, and (d) factors that cause their pain to remit or be more severe. Examinees can also be asked to give frequency estimates for their pain, indicating any daily, weekly, monthly, or seasonal patterns, as well as whether they can predict when they might experience pain. There are several formal rating scales for this purpose as well.

Examinees should also be asked about medication use. What are their current medications? When was the last time they took narcotic analgesics, anxiolytics, and muscle relaxers? A background history is also important to rule out preexisting problems such as attention deficit/hyperactivity disorder, major psychiatric disorders, a history of physical or emotional trauma, or evidence of substance abuse. Family members' educational, social, occupational, and health histories is also important.

The use of a structured interview can be of benefit as well. Several are available, such as the one developed by Levin et al. (1992). There are advantages to moving from open-ended questions in the main interview to more specific questions in the structured interview. The open-ended interview provides the neuropsychologist with the examinees' primary concerns because one can assume that such concerns will be reported freely first in an open-ended interview. The structured interview then provides the examiner with the necessary details and a more comprehensive picture of the situation. Structured interviews, however, sometimes lead to overendorsement of problems not previously mentioned, so some caution is necessary. Examinees who underendorse symptoms might have neurologically based anosognosia if they are more severely injured. However, individuals who have an mTBI that has led to litigation can be often suggestible or exaggerate their deficits. The structured interview, compared with open-ended questions, generally elicits more symptoms. The extent and nature of the difference in symptoms elicited in an open-ended versus a structured interview may aid in differential diagnosis.

Assessment of Cognition, Emotional Stability, Personality, and Pain Complaints

A third component of the forensic evaluation of examinees with a history of mTBI is objective testing. Because the direct testing portion of the examination depends the accuracy of the symptom report and whether the test data accurately represent examinees' actual cognitive ability, validity should be directly assessed using PVTs for cognition (Larrabee, 2012a) and symptom validity tests (SVTs) for emotional stability and pain. PVTs and SVTs are distinct assessment approaches that differ from one another (Van Dyke, Millis, Axelrod, & Hanks, 2013). Accuracy of symptom report can be evaluated by specialized SVT scales on omnibus personality tests, such as the Infrequent Responses, Infrequent Psychopathology Responses, Infrequent Somatic Responses, Symptom Validity, and Response Bias scales of the MMPI–2 Restructured Form (MMPI–2–RF), as well as by patterns of overendorsement on pain scales (Larrabee, 2003a). One can assess whether measurement of an examinee's cognitive ability is valid using freestanding PVTs, such as the Test of Memory Malingering (Tombaugh, 1996), or one can use embedded procedures, derived from score patterns, such as

Reliable Digit Span measure (Greiffenstein, Baker, & Gola, 1994) from various editions of the Wechsler Adult Intelligence Scale (WAIS), the Auditory Verbal Learning Test (Barrash, Suhr, & Manzel, 2004), the Continuous Visual Memory Test (Larrabee, 2009), or the Finger Tapping Test (Arnold et al., 2005). Embedded or derived PVTs identify concerns by means of performances that are atypical in pattern or degree compared with those of patients with bona fide neurological or psychiatric disorders. Concern is further enhanced when the performance patterns captured by these PVTs are typical of performances of noninjured persons simulating (feigning) brain impairment or of individuals identified as probable malingerers by their failure on existing, validated PVTs in the presence of a significant external incentive. These atypical performances can manifest as impaired attention in the context of normal memory (Mittenberg, Azrin, Millsaps, & Heilbronner, 1993), impaired gross motor but preserved fine motor skills (Greiffenstein, Baker, & Gola, 1996), or performance on tests of simple motor function that is worse than that seen in patients with Parkinson's disease or Huntington's disease (Greiffenstein, 2007).

Measures of performance and symptom validity should be spaced throughout the examination to provide continual sampling of the validity of an examinee's test performance (Boone, 2009). Functional areas to be covered in a comprehensive neuropsychological evaluation include language and verbal ability, spatial and perceptual functions, sensorimotor skills, orientation to time, attention, concentration, working memory, processing speed, verbal and visual learning and memory, intellect and problem-solving skills, academic functions, personality testing, and pain scales if pain is a presenting complaint. Larrabee describes such a core battery in Chapter 4 of this handbook.

Interpretation of the test data must integrate the information generated from record review, open-ended and structured interviews, and direct examination. Larrabee (1990, 2012b) previously proposed a consistency model designed to determine whether scores are within the expected range in four different areas. Inconsistency on any of the four following questions should affect the examiner's interpretation of the obtained results. First, did the examinee earn scores in a domain that are higher on more difficult tests than on easier tests? Two, did the examinee show impaired attention but normal memory? Three, did the examinee demonstrate good memory for postinjury history but perform poorly on objective memory tests? Fourth, is the pattern of scores consistent with the known pattern of the claimed neurological disorder, such as with dementia? Even in the presence of inconsistencies, interpretation can occur. For example, if someone has failed multiple PVTs in the context of compensation incentives, consistent with malingering, performance on ability measures, whether in the poor or the normal range, is likely to represent the floor of the examinee's abilities, with actual capabilities at that level or even higher.

Encountering data that has been misadministered or misinterpreted by neuropsychology colleagues, particularly those with relatively little experience, is common. These mistakes include obtaining an impaired Controlled Oral Word Association Test score for an illiterate man who could pass animal naming but, understandably, could not say the alphabet; hence, the Controlled Oral Word Association Test should not have been administered. Another example is invalid MMPI scores for an examinee who reads at the third-grade level and who left school in the eighth grade at age 16; the examinee's reading ability was too low to have been given the MMPI. Finally, misinterpretation is evident when a neuropsychologist diagnoses brain damage on the basis of the examinee's earning a Wechsler Memory Scale—Third Edition (Wechsler, 1987) Attention/Concentration Index of 75 when the examinee also earned a General Memory Index of 129.

The differential diagnosis of mTBI includes non-neurological influences on neuropsychological test data, such as PTSD, anxiety, depression, pain, pain medications, and motivation, as well as preexisting developmental disorders. Malingering is a common phenomenon, occurring in approximately 40% of mTBI cases in litigation (Larrabee, 2003b; Mittenberg, Patton, Canyock, & Condit, 2002).

In Figure 7.3, we present the impairment expected in various reference groups and causally associated with particular neurological conditions using the standardized mean difference effect size. The more negative the effect size, the more impairment is typically demonstrated by the reference group. Such a result causes there to be less overlap in the distribution of scores generated by the two groups (i.e., pathological group vs. normal control group). that reference group typically demonstrates. As shown in Figure 7.3, the effect sizes associated with mental retardation, Alzheimer's disease, moderate to severe TBI, and schizophrenia are the largest. The smallest effect size is for uncomplicated mTBI (Rohling et al., 2011), which is one-10th the magnitude of the effect size for substance abuse, PTSD, and affective disorders. More important, the effect size for uncomplicated mTBI is one-seventh the size of that found for non–brain-injured orthopedic trauma controls or that seen in connection with patients who attribute the reason for their

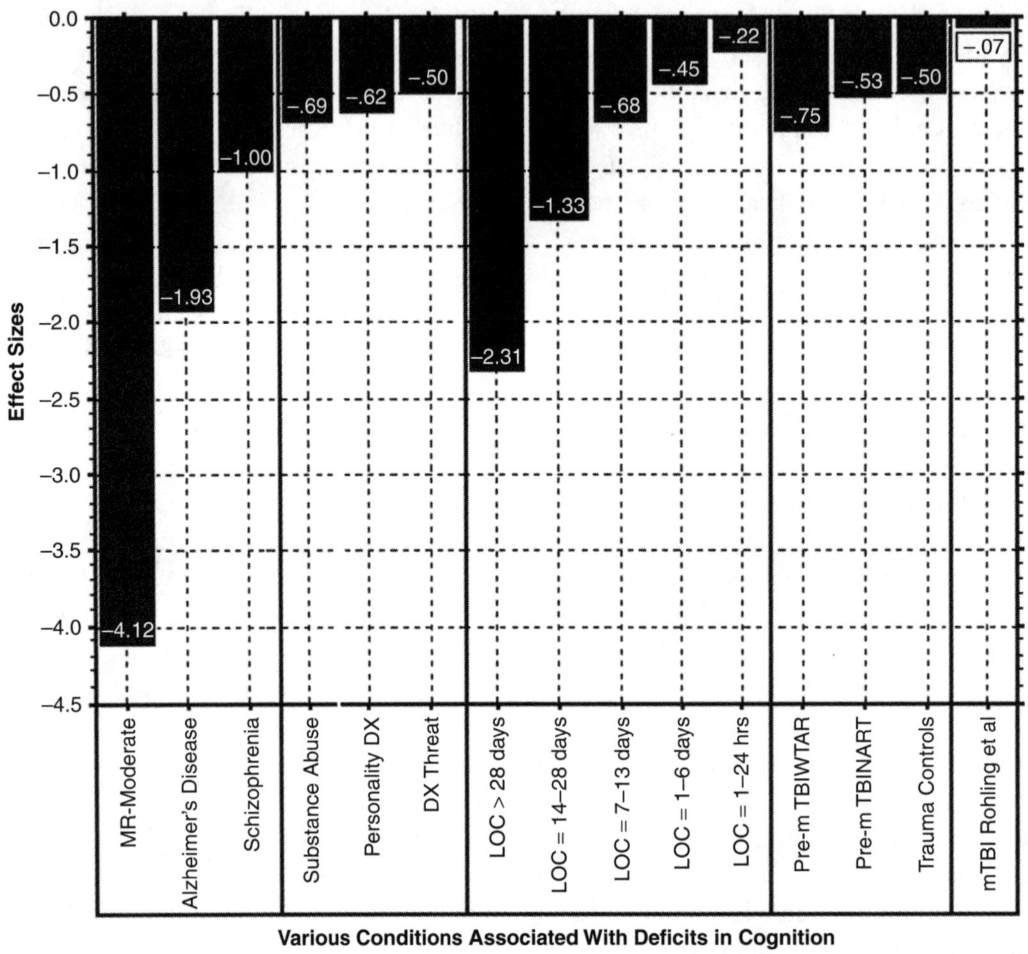

FIGURE 7.3. Effect sizes for various neurological and behavioral conditions associated with cognitive deficits. Effect sizes moderate mental retardation, Alzheimer's disease, and schizophrenia were computed from data reported in the Wechsler Adult Intelligence Scale and Wechsler Memory Scale manuals. Effect sizes for substance abuse, PTSD, affective disorders, personality disorders, and neurosis were calculated from Weiser et al.'s (2004) data. The ffect size for diagnosis threat was generated from Suhr and Gunstad's (2002, 2005) data. Effect sizes for the varying severities of TBI as a function of LOC were calculated from Dikmen et al.'s (1995) data, which Rohling et al. (2011) reanalyzed. Effect sizes for premorbid mTBI differences were calculated using data from Heitger et al. (2009) and Mathias and Coats (1999). The effect size for trauma controls was computed from data published by Dikmen et al. (1995). Last, Rohling et al. (2011) computed effect sizes using data from mTBI patients. dx = diagnosis; LOC = loss of consciousness; MR = mental retardation; mTBI = mild traumatic brain injury; NART = National Adult Reading Test; PTSD = posttraumatic stress disorder; TBI = traumatic brain injury; WTAR = Wechsler Test of Adult Reading.

neuropsychological assessment to a history of mTBI, characterizing the effects of diagnosis threat.

For further contrast, intentional feigning or malingering produces neurocognitive test scores that fall far into the impaired range, with an effect size of −1.43 standard deviations below their estimated true ability (Rohling, Allen, & Green, 2002). Certain tests such as the forced-choice Digit Memory Test show even larger effect sizes equaling or exceeding 2.00 (Vickery, Berry, Inman, Harris, & Orey, 2001). Such effect sizes are of a very large magnitude, in the range obtained by persons with severe TBI or Alzheimer's disease, and are more than 20 times greater than the nonsignificant effects. In conclusion, obtaining results that indicate large deficits in a case involving mTBI should signal the clinician that other factors are the most likely cause of the performance scores. These other factors should be robustly assessed.

MILD TRAUMATIC BRAIN INJURY CASES EXAMPLES

To illustrate the various points we have made about mTBI assessment, we present two example cases that highlight some of the most common issues encountered in a forensic assessment. We demonstrate how a forensic neuropsychologist can follow the recommendations provided by Larrabee and Rohling (2013) through records review. Our intention is to show how these data can be used when available as well as to indicate what can be done when they are not available. We substantiate the importance of administering a comprehensive battery, showing what can go wrong if examiners do not give a sufficient number of tests within a cognitive domain. Another issue we highlight is the importance of using demographically adjusted norms. Finally, we demonstrate ways in which an assessment's validity can be compromised through poor effort, exaggerated symptoms, and intervening variables (i.e., other health conditions) and show the importance of assessing psychiatric and pain complaints. Our examples come from actual cases that the authors assessed in forensic contexts. However, the backgrounds of the examinees, family members, and health care professionals who were involved have been altered to protect their privacy. Details have been changed, added, or deleted, such that it is best to assume that the cases are an amalgam of common cases in mTBI litigation. In this way, we can present fewer cases while covering a large number of relevant issues.

Case Example 1: Motor Vehicle Accident—Review of Tee B. Eyer's Records

Background and demographics of Tee B. Eyer. In this first case example, we refer to the examinee as Tee B. Eyer. At the time of his accident, Mr. Eyer was a 22-year-old African American man. He was raised in a low-income neighborhood in a large urban center on the West Coast of the United States. Mr. Eyer graduated from high school and was attending a community college at the time of his accident. He had enrolled in a technical program to receive training to become a welder. He had a history of substance abuse, having been arrested for driving under the influence and subsequently for possession of cocaine. Both incidents resulted in his accepting a plea bargain that required him to attend an outpatient drug and alcohol rehabilitation program run by the local mental health care agency.

History of trauma experienced by Tee B. Eyer. Late on a Friday afternoon, just before dusk, Mr. Eyer was riding as a passenger in a late-model four-door sedan that was driven by his best friend, Mr. Goody Guy. Police records from the accident scene noted that the tire marks on the road indicated that as Mr. Guy's car approached an intersection, another vehicle unexpectedly passed in front of him. Apparently, the other driver became aware of the impending collision and attempted to stop his car, but it was too late. To avoid the accident, Mr. Guy swerved, and his vehicle careened off the road and hit a light pole.

Both Mr. Guy and Mr. Eyer catapulted through the windshield, because neither was wearing a seat belt. Mr. Guy hit his head on the pole and died instantly. However, Mr. Eyer flew past the pole and landed on the grassy area in front of their vehicle. A pedestrian who was passing by saw the accident and immediately called 911. An ambulance arrived at the scene of the accident approximately 15 minutes later, according to the written report filed by the lead EMT.

The EMTs found Mr. Eyer walking around, alert, but mumbling that he had to get to class. He appeared to be saying that he had missed too many classes in the past for him to miss anymore. He was unaware of his friend's condition and did not realize that he had been in an MVA. Although Mr. Eyer complained of pain in his abdomen and chest, he said that he felt fine and tried to walk away from the scene. When the EMTs tried to place him on a backboard to stabilize his neck, he resisted their efforts and refused to follow any of their instructions.

Acute measures of traumatic brain injury severity and other health problems in Tee B. Eyer. EMT records stated that emergency personnel struggled to get Mr. Eyer strapped to the backboard. He continued to resist but eventually complied. The EMTs recorded his GCS at the scene as a 13, indicating that Mr. Guy was disoriented and not responding to verbal commands. Once they secured Mr. Eyer in the ambulance, he was driven to the ED of the Catholic local trauma hospital, which took about 15 minutes. After arriving at the ED, his GCS was recorded as a 14; he had calmed down and was more cooperative. Records also noted evidence that Mr. Eyer had recently used cocaine and was under the influence of alcohol at the time of the accident. Subsequently, Mr. Guy's pathology report revealed that he had also consumed alcohol, but less than had Mr. Eyer. Mr. Guy's estimated blood alcohol level was below the legal limit of 0.08. However, Mr. Eyer's blood alcohol level at the ED was 0.12. Furthermore, while investigating the accident, police found a vial of crack cocaine and a pipe in the glove compartment of Mr. Guy's automobile.

During Mr. Eyer's hospitalization, multiple CT scans were conducted, with and without contrast. His first CT scan was approximately 3 hours after the accident. Initially, the radiology resident read the scan as being within normal limits. However, the next day, the chief of radiology reread the scan. In her report, she noted that Mr. Eyer had sustained facial fractures, with swelling over his right eye. The type and location of his injuries were consistent with blunt force trauma to both frontal lobes, with evidence of mild damage to the left and right prefrontal cortex.

ED records indicated that during Mr. Eyer's physical examination, he was found to have a distended abdomen, and the attending ED physician became concerned that he was experiencing internal bleeding. It was determined that Mr. Eyer had sustained a lacerated liver of moderate severity. Immediately after his CT scan, Mr. Eyer was sent for surgery to repair his liver. After his surgery, while in the recovery room, Mr. Eyer remained unconscious and required intubation to maintain his respiration. Medical records noted that he remained unconscious for 2 days; he spiked a fever that was thought to be due to an infection after his surgery. Mr. Eyer was prescribed intravenous antibiotics, and his fever remitted after 2 days. He was kept in a barbiturate-induced coma for 2 more days to allow his liver to heal. After being weaned off the barbiturate, the ventilator was removed, and Mr. Eyer regained consciousness a few hours later. After he awoke, his GCS score remained 14 as a result of his memory lapses and continued disorientation. (Table 7.1 lists acute TBI injury severity indices.)

According to the WHO criteria (Cancelliere et al., 2014), Mr. Eyer likely sustained an mTBI with LOC of less than 1 minute, although his CT scan and uncertainty of length of PTA suggested that he sustained a cmTBI (Iverson et al., 2012). His PTA was abnormally long, considering the other TBI severity indicators. It is possible that his internal bleeding and orthopedic injuries caused his PTA to extend beyond what might be expected on the basis of his GCS and LOC, which is common, according to data published by Sherer et al. (2008). Under the circumstances of his surgery and medically induced coma, PTA likely overestimated his severity of brain injury.

Tee B. Eyer's rate of recovery. On the 7th day of his hospitalization, Mr. Eyer was seen by the consulting staff psychologist, Dr. Connie Sultant, who assessed Mr. Eyer with the Cognitive Log (Cog-Log; Novak, 2004). This instrument was developed by the TBI Model Systems program to assess PTA objectively. Similar to the Mini-Mental State Examination, scores for Cog-Log range from a low of 0 (comatose) to a high of 30 (alert, oriented, and without evidence of retrograde or anterograde amnesia).

Mr. Eyer's scores on the multiple administrations of Cog-Log are shown in Figure 7.4. By the 10th day, Mr. Eyer scored a 28 on Cog-Log, which meant that he had cleared PTA. From this point forward, he was encoding, storing, and retrieving new memories into episodic memory. However, he remained hospitalized because of his orthopedic injuries for another 11 days. During his last week of hospitalization, after he was told of Mr. Guy's death, Mr. Eyer began to suffer from depressed mood and symptoms of PTSD. He was prescribed antidepressant and anxiolytic medications and began supportive psychotherapy, which continued on an outpatient basis after his discharge.

Research by Rohling et al. (2011) found that nearly all individuals who experience an uncomplicated mTBI return to their level of premorbid functioning within 3 months. Mr. Eyer's scores on the Cog-Log suggest that he had substantially recovered within 10 days of the accident. Research by Sherer et al. (2008) included 150 TBI patients, of whom 80% had sustained a moderate to severe TBI. When Mr. Eyer's Cog-Log scores were compared with the means drawn from this sample, he was found to be functioning substantially higher than them; as such, his results were inconsistent with having sustained a moderate to severe TBI. This lends support to the conclusion that the severity of his TBI was in the mild range, with evidence of complication. His recovery rate mirrored what that expected for mTBI (High, Levin, & Gary, 1990).

Four months after his MVA, Mr. Eyer was again assessed by Dr. Sultant, who had been providing rehabilitation services and supportive psychotherapy since his discharge. These data were also gathered before Mr. Eyer hired an attorney and filed a personal injury lawsuit. Mr. Eyer's estimate of premorbid general ability (EPGA) and OTBM obtained during this evaluation are presented in Figure 7.5. The analyses presented use the Rohling Interpretive Method (Miller & Rohling, 2001; Rohling et al., 2003, 2011; Rohling, Miller, & Langhinrichsen-Rohling, 2004) to process Dr. Sultant's results. Each bar represents the mean score for the respective cognitive domain. Assignment of scores to domains was based on published factor-analytic research that

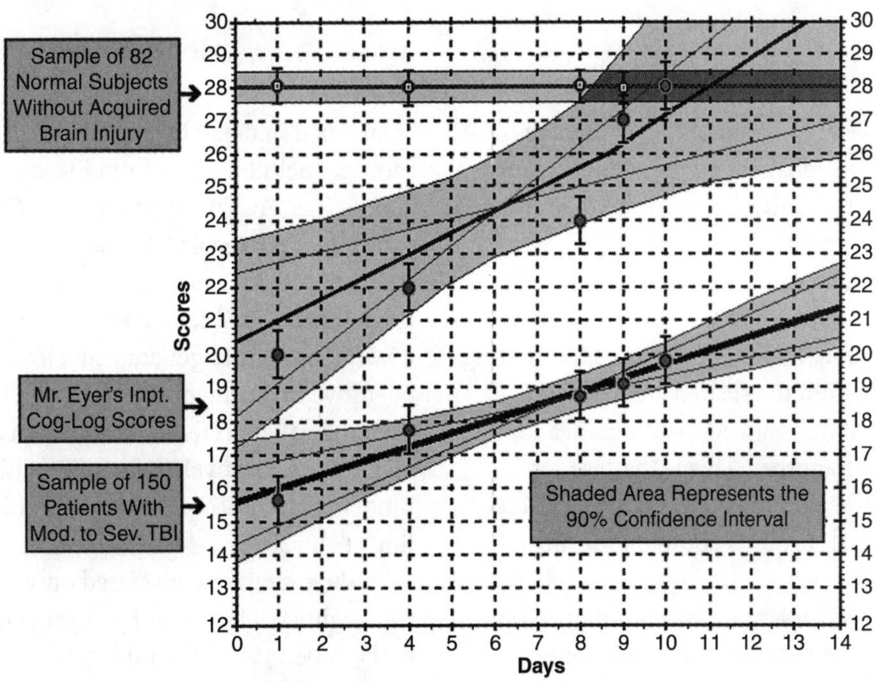

FIGURE 7.4. Cognitive test scores obtained using Cognitive Log (Cog-Log), obtained during Dr. Sultant's assessment of Mr. Eyer during his postaccident hospitalization, showing his expected rate of recovery from mild TBI. TBI = traumatic brain injury.

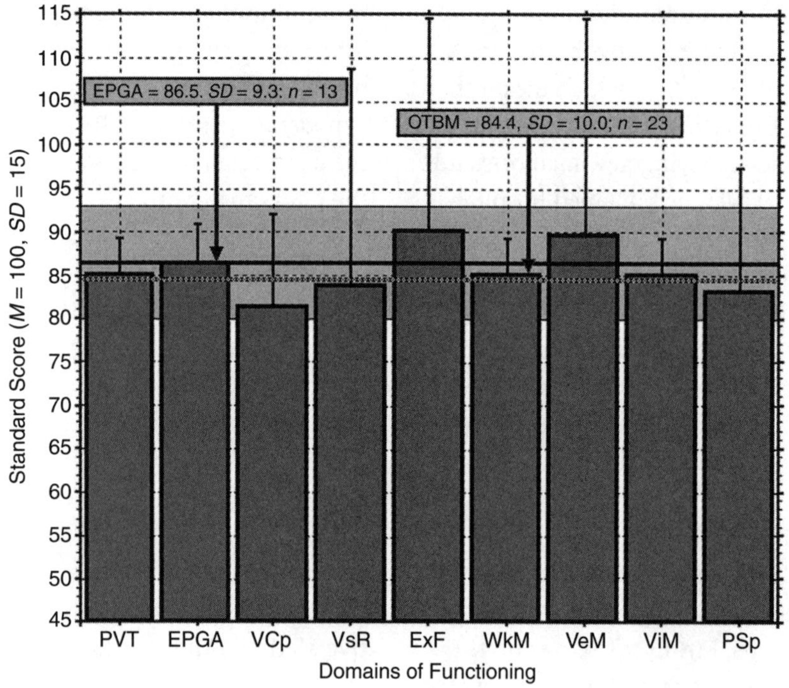

FIGURE 7.5. Tee B. Eyer's scores obtained by Dr. Connie Sultant on an evaluation done 4 months after mTBI. EPGA = estimate of premorbid general ability; ExF = executive functioning; OTBM = overall test battery mean; PSp = processing speed; PVT = performance validity tests; VCp = verbal comprehension; VeM = verbal learning and memory; ViM = visual learning and memory; VsR = visuospatial reasoning; WkM = working memory.

revealed which domain accounted for the most test score variance.

Test scores are assigned to only one domain to retain each of the domain's independence from one another. Figure 7.5 shows a solid dark line at Mr. Eyer's EPGA, and a lighter hatched line represents his OTBM. The shaded area reflects the 90% confidence interval for his EPGA. According to the Rohling Interpretive Method, if the line representing the OTBM falls within the shaded area, the EPGA and OTBM cannot be assumed to be significantly different from one another. This is the case for Mr. Eyer. The scores presented in Figure 7.5 were corrected for age alone, as is common for most published cognitive tests.

Using the 23 dependent measures obtained by Dr. Sultant (i.e., Mini-Mental State Examination, Controlled Oral Word Association Test—FAS, Trail Making Test Parts A and B, Repeatable Battery for the Assessment of Neuropsychological Status, WAIS—Third Edition [WAIS–III], and Wide Range Achievement Test 4 [WRAT4]), Mr. Eyer's age-corrected OTBM was 84.4. His age-corrected EPGA (explained in detail below) included 12 separate indices, including data from his high school transcripts (i.e., ACT Composite, SAT Composite, class rank), reading recognition scores (i.e., WRAT4 Reading, WTAR), and demographic regression predictions. He obtained an age-corrected EPGA of 86.5. These scores generate an effect size of residual cognitive impairment of −0.14, which is within the range of expected recovery from an mTBI. This effect size is relatively consistent with the results of Binder et al. (1997), Rohling et al. (2003), and Rohling et al. (2011).

If the examiner considered only the OTBM, he or she might conclude that Mr. Eyer is mildly impaired, perhaps because of the injury. However, Mr. Eyer's OTBM is not significantly different from his EPGA (p = .56), which suggests that the subaverage performance scores existed before the mTBI. It was thus concluded that Mr. Eyer had sustained an mTBI from which he had reasonably recovered over a 4-month time span. Results indicate that he had returned to his baseline level of performance at the time of the forensic assessment. Although Dr. Sultant administered no freestanding PVTs, scores scores on the recognition portion of the List Learning subtest and Digit Span subtests from the Repeatable Battery for the Assessment of Neuropsychological Status were available to compute the Effort Index (Silverberg, Wertheimer, & Fichtenberg, 2007). Mr. Eyer's Effort Index score of 2 suggests that he exerted adequate but not ideal effort such that his overall cognitive performance scores could be considered reasonably valid. No objective measures of personality or emotional stability were administered, yet, in a progress note written by Dr. Sultant, Mr. Eyer was described as being extremely depressed and suffering from suicidal ideation. No SVTs were administered.

Dikmen et al. (1995) and Rohling et al. (2003) divided TBI patients into six severity groups based on their LOC, shown in the left panel of Figure 7.6. These data show residual cognitive deficits expected by each severity group once maximum neurological recovery has been achieved at least 1 year postinjury. As shown, Mr. Eyer's recovery after his accident was as expected, and he appeared to have fully returned to his premorbid level of cognitive ability 4 months postinjury.

A similar relationship is shown in the right panel of Figure 7.6 using PTA as the severity marker for Mr. Eyer's TBI. The scores shown were generated during Dr. Sultant's evaluation. The figure shows how PTA can be used to predict the range of cognitive impairments an mTBI patient can be expected to incur after a TBI. Alternatively, the association in Figure 7.6 can be used to determine whether maximal neurological recovery has been obtained or to estimate the acute severity of injury. As shown in the figure, Mr. Eyer's OTBM fell in the expected range for neurological recovery based on the assumption that he had sustained either an mTBI or a cmTBI. In fact, based on a liberal estimate of Mr. Eyer's PTA of 9 days, his OTBM is predicted to be between 83 and 104 standard score points. His OTBM, earned during Dr. Sultant's evaluation, equaled an 84.4, which fell at the low end of expectation.

Once litigation was initiated, Mr. Eyer underwent two additional evaluations. One was requested by his attorneys and performed by Dr. Aaron C. Simpler; the other was conducted by Dr. Tessa U. Wells at the request of the defense. In this example, we demonstrate how two experts reached different conclusions and highlight how similar decisions might have been reached if quantitative data, appropriately collected and normed, had been used as the backbone of the derived interpretations.

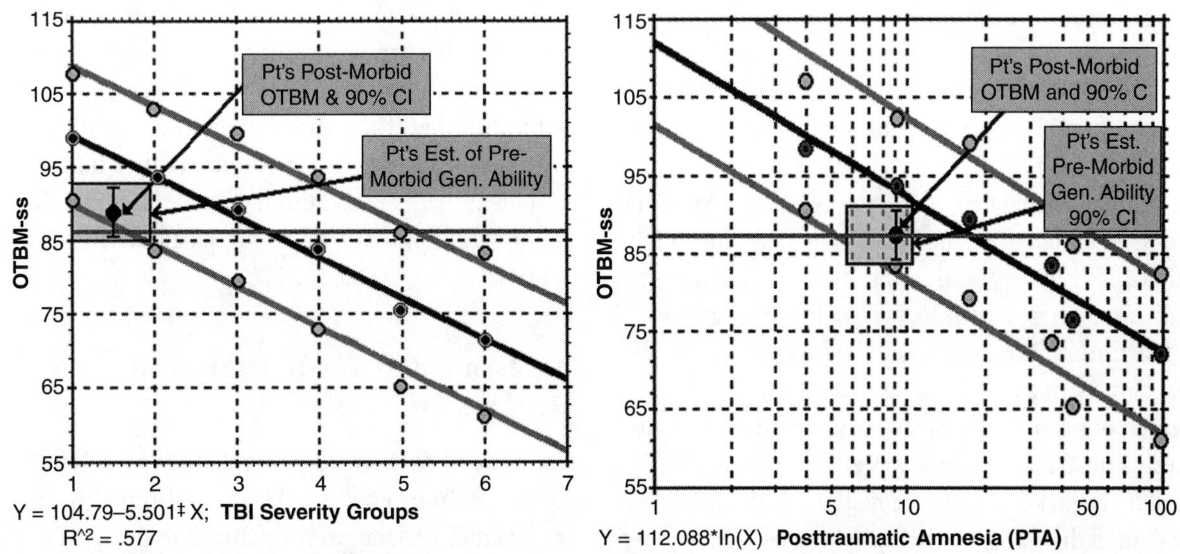

FIGURE 7.6. Tee B. Eyer's overall test battery mean (OTBM; 90% CI) generated using Dr. Sultant's scores. Lines are from regression equations, with the *x*-axis defined by injury severity, using loss of consciousness and posttraumatic amnesia, and the *y*-axis defined by cognitive deficit. Pt. = patient.

Clinical Interview of Tee B. Eyer: Dr. Tessa U. Wells

At 20 months postinjury, Dr. Wells interviewed and assessed Tee B. Eyer in one session that took most of the day to complete. Mr. Eyer drove himself to the appointment and arrived on time, behavior often inconsistent with that of people who have sustained a moderate to severe brain injury. He brought in and recited the names of his medications and all the physicians he had seen, although he could not recall Dr. Sultant's name when asked. He was oriented to person, place, time, and circumstance, although he complained of being fatigued. He believed that the antidepressant he was taking was causing him to be drowsy and stated that he had been sleeping more than usual. He said that he had to fight to stay awake throughout the assessment.

When Dr. Wells asked Mr. Eyer what he recalled about his car accident, he reported having no memory of the events surrounding the accident. He recalled waking up in the hospital, restrained and with tubes running in and out of him. He was suspicious of people who told him that he had been in a car accident because he did not believe that an accident had occurred. However, he was aware that he had undergone surgery to repair his liver. He recalled being discharged from the hospital and returning home. He stated that he had experienced no new serious illnesses or trauma since his discharge. He denied experiencing any seizures, though he knew that he had sustained a TBI. Over the past year, he had two aunts die, whom he described as his favorites. He described one aunt as being "like a mother to me."

Dr. Wells noted that during the assessment Mr. Eyer endorsed a litany of symptoms. He complained of fatigue, low energy, and diffuse pain. He was having daily headaches, which he believed were triggered by frustration. Mr. Eyer rated the severity of his headache pain as moderate to severe. He also complained of blurred vision and double vision. He said that his nose hurt when it was either cold or windy outside. He also said that he had reduced appetite. He denied drinking alcohol or taking any illicit substances. He said that his libido had remained unchanged. His sense of smell was limited, and since starting the antidepressant he thought he heard things that were not there (e.g., a knock at the door or someone calling his name). Mr. Eyer denied visual hallucinations.

Cognitively, Mr. Eyer complained of having trouble staying focused and indicated that his thoughts often appeared to wander. He also complained that his memory was "no good" since his accident. He gave examples of his memory failure, including often leaving the refrigerator door open and forgetting to bring his cell phone with him. Mr. Eyer claimed to have trouble remembering people's names. He also said that he got lost easily, even when he was in a familiar environment. He avoided going places because he was afraid he would get lost. He had lost two jobs since his accident because he could not recall what he had been told to do. Mr. Eyer stated that he was more emotionally reactive, quicker to anger, and more easily frustrated, which had caused him to shut down and withdraw from his social circles. He said he was quite depressed and at times did not want to go on living. However, he had never planned to hurt himself, nor attempted suicide.

Mr. Eyer reported no history of any birth complications, developmental delays, or repeated grades, but he reported having received special education services throughout most of his schooling. He denied any preaccident history of mental illness or chronic health problems. His parents divorced when he was about 9 years old. His mother and aunt were his primary caregivers throughout childhood, although he had remained in frequent contact with his father. He is the youngest of six children. His mother worked as a clerk in an office building, and his father was an auto mechanic. Both are high school graduates but were "not particularly good at school."

Assessment of Tee B. Eyer by Dr. Tessa U. Wells

Estimate of premorbid general ability for Tee B. Eyer. Rohling et al. (2003) demonstrated the importance of accurately quantifying EPGA. They recommended that examiners quantitatively convert data contained in educational records (e.g., high school rank, high school GPA, scores on college entrance exams such as the ACT or SAT; Baade & Schoenberg, 2004) into estimates of premorbid general ability. Furthermore, demographic variables can be used in regression-based prediction models (e.g., Barona, Reynolds, & Chastain, 1984; Holdnack & Drozdick, 2009; Krull, Scott, & Sherer, 1995; Schoenberg et al., 2002). Premorbid estimates are also reasonably valid using standardized reading recognition tests (e.g., WRAT4 [Wilkinson & Robertson, 2006]; Test of Premorbid Functioning [Holdnack & Drozdick, 2009]; North American Adult Reading Test [Uttl, 2002]). For Mr. Eyer, the EPGA generated included three demographic predictions, five reading recognition tests, six scores from college admission tests, and three scores obtained from his high school transcript (i.e., GPA, class rank, and scores on his state high school graduation exam), for a total of 17 different estimates. These measures were used to generate a quantitative EPGA for Mr. Eyer at the time of the assessment.

Specifically, Mr. Eyer's academic records were obtained, which showed that he graduated from a Title I school at the bottom half of his class, at the 34th percentile (standard score [SS] = 94). He had earned an unweighted GPA of 2.76 in special education classes (SS = 92). Other scores listed on his transcript included the results of two college admission tests. For example, his composite score on the SAT placed him at the 13th percentile (SS = 83), and the ACT placed him at the 10th percentile (SS = 80). The ACT composite score has a reported reliability of .96 (American College Testing, 2014, p. 61). The SAT composite score has an internal consistency using coefficient alpha of .91 (Stickler, 2007). High school grade point averages have a split-half interrater reliability of .74 (Cassady& Jerrell, 2001).

Mr. Eyer was also administered two tests of reading recognition. On the WRAT4 (reliability = .98; Wilkinson & Robertson, 2006), he earned a standard score of 88. On the reading recognition portion of the WTAR (reliability = .92), he earned a standard score of 82. Using the WTAR demographic prediction equation, Mr. Eyer earned a score of 84. Again, once all 16 measures were combined and corrected for Eyer's demographic background, his EPGA was 88.3 (*SD* = 10.1), with a minimum score of 63, a maximum score of 100, and a median of 86.0. His EPGA fell at the 22nd percentile, with a 90% confidence interval of ±4.0. Using his own scores, his EPGA composite had a split-half reliability estimate of .97.

Using a cutoff for impairment of 1.0 standard deviation below the mean, seven of the 16 scores included in Mr. Eyer's EPGA fell in the impaired range (44%). These data suggest that, before Mr. Eyer's mTBI, he functioned in the low average range of ability (Wechsler, 2008b). Using Heaton, Miller, Taylor, and Grant's (2004) classification system, Mr. Eyer's EPGA fell in the range of mild impairment. Yet, Dr. Simpler wrote that he was an average student, implying that his EPGA was between 90 and 109, with an expected score of 100, which falls at the 50th percentile. This is inaccurate and is 1.0 standard deviation higher than his actual EPGA. This assumption had a critical impact on the diagnostic conclusion of this case. It is difficult to determine whether persons with a demographic background and performance characteristics similar to Mr. Eyer's are impaired after a TBI or whether their lower scores predate their TBI. If one were to assume that Mr. Eyer was average before his accident, his obtained scores fall well below expectation and indicate impairment. However, a more thorough assessment of Mr. Eyer's premorbid ability indicates that his postinjury performance, before litigation, is most consistent with the conclusion that he has recovered to his preexisting abilities.

Demographic adjustments to Tee B. Eyer's scores. Many neuropsychologists do not adequately adjust examinee's test scores for demographic variables, such as age, sex, quality of education (Manly, Jacobs, Touradji, Small, & Stern, 2002), and ethnicity (Manly, 2005; Manly & Echemendia, 2007). For example, the Halstead Russell Neuropsychological Evaluation System—Revised (Russell & Starkey, 2001) makes no adjustment for ethnicity. This problem can, in part, be addressed by using the Heaton et al.'s (2004) normative system and the more recent versions of the WAIS (third and fourth editions). Heaton et al. oversampled African Americans for their system. Of their 1,212 normative subjects, nearly 48% were African American, and 43% were female.

Other normative systems undersample minorities and females, and their samples are thus not representative of the U.S. population. As a result, error variance is introduced into the diagnostic process. Heaton et al.'s system is more accurate in the assessment of African Americans and women than are other normative systems (e.g., Halstead Russell Neuropsychological Evaluation System—Revised) and is thus strongly recommended when assessing individuals with one or both of these demographic characteristics. Specifically, in the Heaton et al. system the difference between African Americans and Whites across all test scores is −0.46, or nearly 5.0 *T*-score points or 7.0 standard score points. Heaton et al.'s system reports the largest differences in scores between groups for tests that load on the Verbal Comprehension and Verbal Memory domains ($d = -0.62$), whereas, on measures of Sensory Perceptual and Psychomotor skills, score differences by ethnicity are half of those obtained for Verbal skills ($d = -0.26$). Not accounting for demographics when interpreting performance scores can lead to inaccurate conclusions, with important consequences for all involved in the litigation.

In a study that examined the influence of several demographic variables, Manly et al. (2011) found, when testing African American women who were HIV-positive, that age accounted for 14% of test score variance. Years of education accounted for just 4% of test score variance. Race accounted for 3% of test score variance, and reading ability accounted for 12% of test score variance. Reading ability has been considered a proxy for the quality of education, and race has been used as a proxy for acculturation. Manly et al. noted that neuropsychologists should adjust scores for a host of demographic differences. If they do not, there is a substantially higher rate of false positives for subjects with any combination of the above factors.

Residual cognitive deficits and pattern analysis of Tee B. Eyer's scores. Twelve months after his MVA, Mr. Eyer was evaluated by a forensic neuropsychologist, Aaron C. Simpler, who had been hired by Mr. Eyer's attorney. The scores that were obtained by Dr. Simpler are presented in Figure 7.7, and raw scores and standard scores are listed in Appendix 7.1 at the end of this chapter. Dr. Simpler did not quantitatively generate an EPGA, even though he could have had access to 13 of the indices that were used to generate the EPGA presented in this example.

At the time of Dr. Simpler's evaluation, Mr. Eyer was unemployed, not attending school, and living at home with his mother and sister. During Dr. Simpler's assessment, Mr. Eyer passed all 11 of the PVTs that he was administered ($M = 100.4$), suggesting that his resulting cognitive test scores were valid measures of his true abilities. Mr. Eyer obtained lower scores on verbal comprehension measures from various instruments ($M = 81.2$). For example, on the WAIS–III he obtained a Verbal Comprehension Index score equal to 80.0, which was essentially unchanged the score of 82 he obtained 8 months earlier when Dr. Sultant assessed. Mr. Eyer scored better on tests that loaded on the executive function domain (e.g., Booklet Category Test = 95; Animal Naming = 95), obtaining a mean score on measures of executive functioning of 91.3.

Mr. Eyer exhibited similar results on measures of working memory, which had a mean domain score of 90.0 (e.g., Seashore Rhythm = 110; Arithmetic = 95). More specifically, Mr. Eyer earned a WAIS–III Working Memory Index score of 92. Mr. Eyer's obtained some of his lowest scores on measures of verbal learning and memory (79.4), visual learning and memory (81.0), visuospatial reasoning (81.0), and processing speed (82.0). None of the means for these various cognitive domains were significantly different from one another, but executive functioning and working memory were relative strengths for Mr. Eyer.

Mr. Eyer's OTBM, when corrected only for age, was 85.7 ($SD = 10.7$). Based on data published by Meyers and Rohling (2004) and Rohling et al. (2004, 2015), the OTBM has an estimated reliability between .87 and .93; thus, the 90% CI for this composite for Mr. Eyer is ±5.0 points. Dr. Simpler believed, in the absence of a quantitative EPGA, that Mr. Eyer's premorbid ability was at the lower end of the normal range, which is approximately a 95.0. Dr. Simpler then concluded that Mr. Eyer was moderately impaired.

In comparison, using a comprehensive and quantitative EPGA, the conclusion would have been

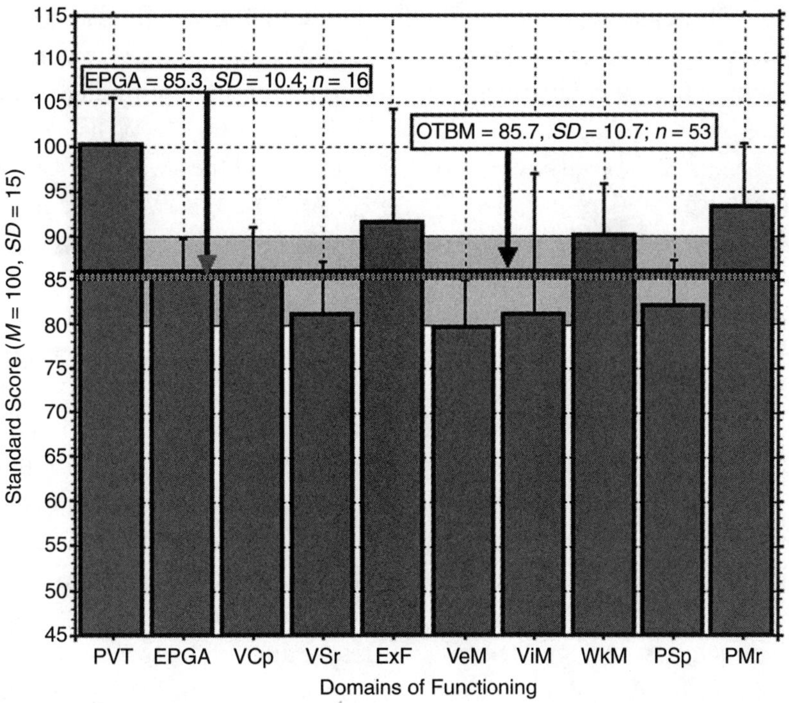

FIGURE 7.7. Tee B. Eyer's scores obtained by Dr. Aaron C. Simpler on an evaluation done 16 months after mild traumatic brain injury. EPGA = estimate of premorbid general ability; ExF = executive functioning; OBTM = overall test battery mean; PMr = psychomotor skills; PSp = processing speed; PVT = performance validity test; VCp = verbal comprehension; VeM = verbal learning and memory; ViM = visual learning and memory; VsR = visuospatial reasoning; WkM = working memory.

that Mr. Eyer had fully recovered to his premorbid level of functioning (EPGA = 86.5). Quickly consulting the tables included in this chapter would have led Dr. Simpler to question his conclusion of substantial impairment post-mTBI. Dr. Simpler's assumptions about Mr. Eyer's premorbid cognitive ability resulted in an estimated postinjury effect size for cognitive deficits of −0.62. The data analyzed by Rohling et al. (2003), and presented in Figure 7.1, indicates that such an effect size is associated with an estimated LOC of 6 to 7 days (but no LOC was noted for Mr. Eyer). Similarly, using the data analysis shown in Figure 7.1, Mr. Eyer's associated PTA would have been estimated to be nearly 630 hours, or 26 days, if this effect size was to be considered accurate. Despite Mr. Eyer's medically induced coma, his actual PTA was considerably less than this estimate and was likely to have been between 6 and 10 days, or 144 to 240 hours. Working backward from the obtained PTA data, the associated residual cognitive deficit experienced by Mr. Eyer should be equal to −0.23. This is within the range of expectation for Mr. Eyer, because the scores from his prelitigation assessment, conducted by Dr. Sultant, generated an effect size of −0.14, with a 90% confidence interval that ranged from 0.00 to −0.28.

The importance of correcting the scores used to generate the OTBM is illustrated next. Dr. Wells took the scores obtained by Mr. Eyer during Dr. Simpler's assessment and adjusted them for age, education, sex, and race using the norms of the WAIS–III, Wechsler Memory Scale—Third Edition, and Heaton et al. (2004) for other neuropsychological tests. It is not clear why Dr. Simpler used the older versions of the Wechsler tests. Mr. Eyer's OTBM differed significantly from that which he would have earned had he been White. Across 53 measures, his OTBM would have been a 79.2 (*SD* = 10.9). However, correcting for his age, education, gender, and race, his OTBM was adjusted to an 85.6 (*SD* = 10.4). The difference between his uncorrected EPGA and uncorrected OTBM was −0.44, which was significant, $t(61) = -2.14$, $p = .037$. However, once the composite scores were corrected for Mr. Eyer's demographic background, the effect size generated was equal to −0.18, which was nonsignificant, $t(61) = 0.69$, $p = .49$.

Again, failure to correct test scores for an examinee's demographics often results in an inaccurate conclusion regarding the examinee's magnitude of impairment. The corrected effect size is in the predicted range on the basis of Dikmen et al. (1995), Binder et al. (1997), Rohling et al. (2003), and Rohling et al. (2011) and is similar to that generated from the examination conducted by Dr. Sultant before the initiation of litigation.

Dr. Tessa U. Wells then went on to conduct her own compulsory medical exam (also known as an independent medical or neuropsychological exam) of Mr. Eyer, after having analyzed all of the available data from Dr. Sultant and Dr. Simpler. The scores obtained from the test battery administered by Dr. Wells are summarized in Figure 7.8. After demographically adjusting scores for age, education, sex, and race, Mr. Eyer's OTBM in this instance increased 5 points, from an 84.4 to an 89.4. Unlike the other assessment results, which were generated prelitigation or by an examiner hired by the plaintiff, during Dr. Wells's assessment Mr. Eyer failed five of the seven PVTs administered to him (72%), earning a PVT domain mean score of 67.0. Across 43 measures, Mr. Eyer obtained an OTBM during this assessment, adjusted for age, education, sex, and ethnicity, of 82.3 (SD = 19.2). This score, although lower, was still not significantly different from his EPGA of 88.3, $t(61) = 1.22$, $p = .23$, with an effect size equal to −0.35. Nearly all of the difference between Dr. Simpler's OTBM and that calculated by Dr. Wells was due to Mr. Eyer's substantially lower scores on the verbal memory measures, with the mean score dropping from 83.8 to a 59.0. These scores are among those that can be most affected by invalid responding (Rohling, Green, et al., 2002), a conclusion supported by Mr. Eyer's scores on the PVTs administered. If the scores from the Verbal Memory domain are excluded, Mr. Eyer's OTBM increases to an 88.3, which is identical to his EPGA. Use of the Rohling Interpretive Method also allows for consideration of the amount of intraindividual variability

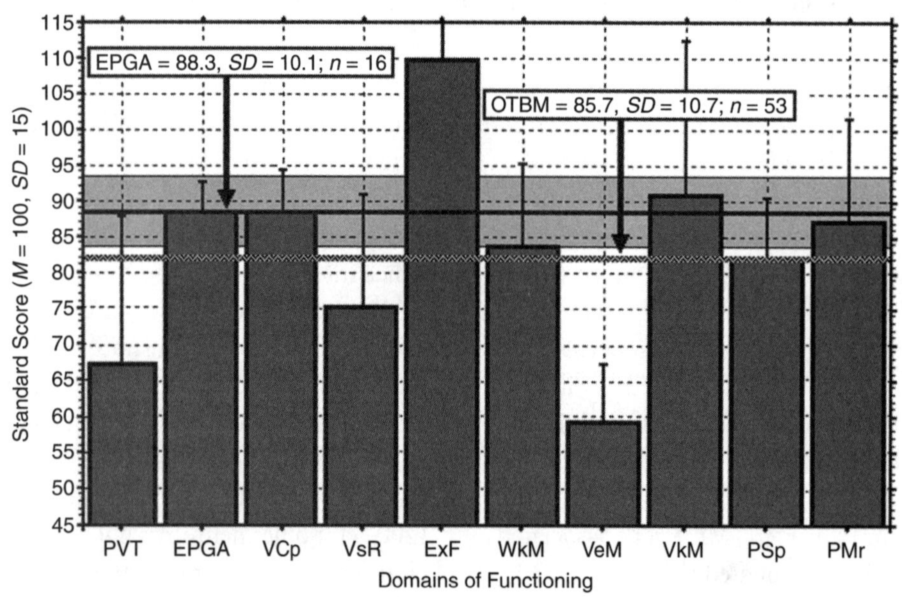

FIGURE 7.8. Tee B. Eyer's scores obtained by Dr. Tessa Wells on an evaluation done 20 months after mild traumatic brain injury. EPGA = estimate of premorbid general ability; ExF = Executive Functioning; OTBM = overall test battery mean; PMr = psychomotor skills; PSp = processing speed; PVT = performance validity test; VCp = verbal comprehension; VeM = verbal learning and memory; ViM = visual learning and memory; VsR = visuospatial reasoning; WkM = working memory.

in the OTBM scores derived from each assessment. The intraindividual variability in the OTBM scores jumped from 8.9 for Dr. Sultant's assessment, to 10.3 for Dr. Simpler's assessment, and finally to 19.2 for Dr. Wells's assessment. Such an increase has been shown by Hill, Rohling, Boettcher, and Meyers (2013) to be associated with invalid performance, substantiating the conclusion that the obtained OTBM of 82.3 is invalid and lower than warranted.

Examining the OTBMs earned by Mr. Eyer across the three outpatient assessments—Dr. Sultant's, conducted 4 months postinjury; Dr. Simpler's, conducted 12 months postinjury; and Dr. Wells', conducted 18 months postinjury—there was a steady decline from 89.4 to 85.5 and finally to 82.3. This drop occurred despite many of the same tests being administered to Mr. Eyer multiple times, which typically results in a practice effect and regression to the mean, both of which lead to higher scores. This drop equaled 7.1 points across 14 months. In fact, using a reliable change score method of predicting scores, Mr. Eyer should have earned an OTBM score of approximately 94.0 on the last assessment, with an estimated 90% CI range of [84.0, 104.0] (±10.0 using a 95% CI). Because Mr. Eyer presented with no evidence of experiencing an intervening neurological injury or disease, such a decrease in OTBM scores across time does not make neurological sense. More likely, the decrease was caused by the influence of litigation, suboptimal effort, diagnosis threat, or all of these.

Finally, returning to the issue of demographic corrections, the average OTBM with only age correction was 79.8. The average OTBM after correcting for age, education, sex, and race was 85.8. The difference between these scores is 6 standard score points, which is consistent with that found in the Heaton et al. (2004) normative system, which was nearly 7 points. It is essential that the forensic neuropsychologist use all available demographic information to generate the most valid scores for the individual in question.

Case Example 2: Work-Related Accident—Review of Will E. Nott's Records

Background and demographics of Will E. Nott. The second example case is also a compilation of various cases we have assessed in our practices. In this second case, we hope to show a different, yet common pattern we have encountered when assessing individuals who allege having experienced an mTBI. We refer to the individual in this case as Will E. Nott. Similar to the first case example, there was no doubt that Mr. Nott was involved in an accident (this time at work) and experienced a head injury that required immediate medical attention. Ms. Hope Fully Moore, employed as a nurse case manager by Preventing Disability Services, referred Mr. Nott to Dr. Faith N. Statts with specific questions regarding his cognitive status, psychiatric symptoms, pain complaints, lack of participation in his rehabilitative treatments, and concern that he was exaggerating his symptoms or was outright feigning. Ms. Moore was also worried that Mr. Nott's complaints might be valid but not the result of the work accident that caused the head injury. Ms. Moore had hoped that Mr. Nott would have returned to gainful employment by the time he was referred, but he had not. Substantial attempts had been made to involve him in the treatment planning process and to get him back to work, but all had failed. By the time Mr. Nott was referred, he had hired an attorney who was assisting him in filing for disability benefits in light of his continued report of subjective pain and cognitive symptoms. Such cases often involve an examinee who may have a premorbid psychiatric disorder that is exacerbated by the accident. Often, these cases evolve into a somatic symptom disorder, or what has been labeled by Delis and Wetter (2007) as *cogniform disorder.* There may also be a component of the "good old days" phenomenon whereby patients minimize any problems experienced before the accident.

At the time of his accident, Will E. Nott was a 47-year-old White man with an 11th-grade education. He believed that his mother experienced no complications during his birth. He thought he had reached all developmental milestones at an age-appropriate time. Mr. Nott had limited information about his parents' health histories. His mother was alive and lived down the block from him. He did not know the highest level of education either of his parents had attained. He assumed that they had not completed high school but was not sure. His father worked as a janitor at a local elementary school, and his mother was employed as an assembly line worker at an automobile plant. However, in 1971, at the age of 41, his father died along with his 11-year-old older brother in a tragic hiking accident. Mr. Nott witnessed the accident but was not seriously injured himself. He was taken to the local hospital; however, his injuries were considered minor, and he was released to his mother's custody that same day.

Regarding Mr. Nott's educational and occupational histories, he dropped out of school in the middle of the 11th grade. His academic transcripts indicated that he was often truant. Nevertheless, he reported no personal or family history of a learning disability or special education. He said that he quit school because he wanted to go to work. He has worked at several different jobs since quitting school. His first job was in the automobile plant where his mother works. He remained employed there for 4 to 5 years as a maintenance worker. After that position, he obtained employment in other unskilled labor and construction positions and had held the most recent position for 4 years before the accident.

Mr. Nott had been married and divorced twice. Before his accident, he and his second wife lived in their own home. He often visited his mother who lived down the street from him. He had a 27-year-old daughter who also lived close by.

Ms. Moore referred Mr. Nott for an independent medical examination pertaining to a head injury he sustained while at work. Employers Claims had contracted with them to aid in the rehabilitation of injured workers from various companies. One year after his accident and 6 months before the referral to Dr. Statts, Mr. Nott hired an attorney. His attorney was helping him file for Workers Compensation benefits, Social Security Disability Insurance, and Supplemental Security Income. Mr. Nott had filed a claim on his own but had received notices of denial, which had prompted him to hire the attorney. He said that his attorney told him that he had a 75% chance of securing benefits because the attorney had experience in successfully filing such appeals in the past.

History of trauma experienced by Will E. Nott. Mr. Nott's medical records noted that he had been employed for several years as a construction worker, primarily engaged in high-rise welding of steel girders. While at a construction site, a steel clamp weighing 6 pounds dropped about 50 feet and struck Mr. Nott on the right forehead. He was wearing a hard hat and safety goggles at the time of the accident, which remained intact, despite the obvious impact the clamp had on his head. Co-workers who witnessed the accident quickly called for an ambulance because of Mr. Nott's facial bleeding. Mr. Nott was taken to a Level I trauma center ED of University Medical Center.

Acute measures of traumatic brain injury severity and other health problems for Will E. Nott. During Dr. Statts's clinical interview, which was conducted 16 months postinjury, Mr. Nott stated that he did not recall being transported by ambulance to the ED. However, records from University Medical Center indicated that he arrived without evidence of LOC. Therefore, although no GCS score was listed in his records, Dr. Statts estimated that Mr. Nott's GCS score at the time of admission was between 13 and 15. Records also noted that after the accident Mr. Nott experienced no retrograde or anterograde amnesia. Thus, his estimated PTA was likely less than a few hours and certainly less than 24 hours. However, during his clinical interview with Dr. Statts, Mr. Nott reported that he did not recall anything that happened in the ED nor subsequently during his hospitalization in the intensive care unit. Although his medical records indicated that during his hospitalization he experienced no anterograde or retrograde amnesia, he claimed that his first memory after the accident was during his discharge from the hospital 4 days later.

While at University Medical Center, Mr. Nott underwent several CT scans. The radiologist who read the scans noted that Mr. Nott had small subarachnoid hemorrhages, multiple skull fractures, a depressed segment of his right temporal bone, and diffuse cerebral edema. Subsequent CT scans revealed mild worsening of the damage located in the right hemisphere, cerebral edema located in the left temporal and right parietotemporal regions, and more evidence of subdural hematomas. One month after his accident, Mr. Nott underwent an open reduction internal fixation of the left maxilla and right orbit due to the facial fractures he sustained during the accident. The surgery was completed without complications, and he was discharged home the next day.

Three months after his surgery, Mr. Nott underwent further outpatient facial surgery for a deviated nasal septum, with chronic maxillary and ethmoid sinusitis. This procedure was also recorded as having no complications. Four months after his accident, Mr. Nott underwent dental surgery, but records of this procedure were not available at the time of his assessment. Mr. Nott had been referred for pain management to Pain Associates and was being followed by a physiatrist, Dr. Bill Tumuch. Mr. Nott's prior health records were not immediately available, and it was difficult to gather a medical history from him during the clinical interview. For example, during the interview, Mr. Nott failed to disclose relevant health-related issues that were subsequently made available to the examiner.

Will E. Nott's rate of recovery. Mr. Nott had experienced substantial neurological recovery by 6 months after his accident but continued to report high levels of acute facial pain that he rated as a 9 on a scale ranging from 1 (*minimal*) to 10 (*excruciating*). He attributed his pain to his accident. Mr. Nott's diagnoses included bilateral hearing loss, which his physicians believed to be due to his long-term history of working in the construction industry, during which he did not wear ear protection. He had in the past also been diagnosed with chronic insomnia and an adjustment disorder with mixed anxiety and depressed mood. Dr. Tumuch's records noted that Mr. Nott was medically difficult to manage because he did not comply with treatment recommendations and appeared to be more interested in pursuing disability benefits than physical recovery (e.g., he refused to attend speech therapy). Furthermore, Mr. Nott was married to his second wife at the time of his accident and rehabilitation, and Dr. Tumuch's records noted that his wife was particularly critical of the rehabilitation treatment plan. Dr. Tumuch wrote that marital stress might be causing Mr. Nott's condition to worsen because his wife told him to discontinue treatment and immediately seek disability benefits. Shortly thereafter, Mr. Nott and his wife divorced.

Clinical Interview of Will E. Nott by Dr. Faith N. Statts

Mr. Nott, a right-handed white man, was 49 years old at the time of Dr. Statts's evaluation, which was completed in 1 day. He drove himself to the appointment, accompanied by his elderly mother. The two lived nearly 200 miles away from the clinic, and they drove to the clinic the night before his appointment, which was scheduled to begin at 9:00 a.m. Mr. Nott arrived on time for his appointment. He had been fitted for a temporary hearing aid to ensure that any problems that he might have adequately hearing the examiner during the evaluation were not due to peripheral hearing loss. Mr. Nott was alert, calm, and cooperative throughout the evaluation. He was oriented to person, place, time, and circumstance, and although he complained of feeling fatigued and experiencing pain, he worked continuously during the evaluation. Other than his complaints, there were no obvious signs of fatigue during the assessment. Mr. Nott ambulated without assistance. Dr. Statts noted no obvious signs of fine-motor or gross-motor impairments in coordination. Mr. Nott's comprehension skills appeared to be within normal limits. His expressive skills appeared unimpaired but indicative of a person of below-average intellect. His vocabulary was simple, and he wrote sentences that had many spelling and grammatical errors. He rarely spontaneously conversed, and he responded to questions in a terse manner. If not asked a direct question, he typically remained silent and motionless in his chair.

At one point during the morning session, Mr. Nott took a break to chew tobacco and use the restroom. He also went out to the parking lot and called his attorney. When he returned, he expressed resistance to continuing the evaluation unless he was given a copy of the report. Dr. Statts explained that she was not able to provide him with feedback regarding his results because the independent medical examination process meant that the insurance company was the client.

During Dr. Statts's interview, Mr. Nott admitted to several symptoms of anxiety and depression. However, she commented that his mood was stable throughout the evaluation. He made eye contact and appeared relaxed as he sat in his chair. Regarding other psychiatric symptoms, Dr. Statts noted that Mr. Nott seemed labile for only a brief period after he had spoken with his attorney, when he seemed suspicious of her and the evaluation process. He responded positively and calmed down after 15 minutes of empathetic conversation with Dr. Statts. Mr. Nott's responses during interview were often delayed, slowly communicated, and were absent of details, which he revealed only after more direct questioning (e.g., "Do you have an attorney representing you?"). As a result, Dr. Statts was concerned that she had not been provided a comprehensive picture of Mr. Nott's health history before his accident.

During the interview with Dr. Statts, Mr. Nott described many medical problems that he believed were caused by his accident. Most significantly, he complained that neck and upper shoulder pain interfered with his attention and ability to remember things. Mr. Nott believed that his experience of pain slowed his thinking, impaired his psychomotor skills, and slowed his mental processing speed. Furthermore, he told Dr. Statts that he had become more irritable, anxious, and frustrated. He had angry outbursts that were directed at his ex-wife, which he said were uncharacteristic of him. In addition, he reported having frequent headaches, blurred vision, hearing loss, and problems with his balance. He said that his medications did not control his symptoms. Furthermore, he reported that he had been having trouble falling asleep, frequently awoke at night, and often had trouble getting back to sleep after he awoke. He claimed to experience little pleasure (anhedonia). Mr. Nott felt excessively fatigued and believed that all of his symptoms were a consequence of the brain injury that resulted from his work-related accident. He initially stated that his symptoms had been worst during the first few months after his accident, but he later said that they had never remitted. Finally, he thought that his injuries were of sufficient severity that he could return neither to his old job nor to any other job.

Regarding other medical disorders, during Dr. Statts's interview Mr. Nott denied any history of high fever, as well as any personal or familial neurological diseases (e.g., Alzheimer's, Huntington's, Parkinson's, or Pick's disease) that are associated with impaired cognition or the experience of pain. When asked by Dr. Statts about any other medical history that he might consider important for her to know about, Mr. Nott denied experiencing any other medical conditions that might influence his cognitive test scores (e.g., diabetes, hepatitis, hypertension, or hypothyroidism). However, he admitted to chronic problems with his hearing and vision. Mr. Nott claimed not to be able to recall what medications he had been taking. However, Dr. Statts noted that during testing that Mr. Nott said he had taken gabapentin (Neurontin) for his pain and duloxetine (Cymbalta) for his mood the morning of the assessment. Records accessed by Dr. Statts indicated that Mr. Nott had been prescribed lisinopril for hypertension. Although he admitted to drinking once in a while, Mr. Nott claimed that he had stopped drinking alcohol since his accident. On direct questioning by Dr. Statts, Mr. Nott denied any history of alcohol abuse before his accident. However, upon further probing by Dr. Statts, Mr. Nott recalled being arrested for driving under the influence at age 27. This resulted in his attending an educational class at the request of the court to avoid harsher legal penalties. He said that he was not a smoker but that he had chewed tobacco since he was 14. He denied any illicit drug use.

Mr. Nott is the younger of two children. He had an older brother (2 years older) who died in a hiking accident 40 years ago. Mr. Nott was 9 years old at the time. He was with his brother and father camping when the accident occurred. His brother had fallen from a cliff into a river, hitting his head and losing consciousness, and his father jumped into the river to rescue him. Unfortunately, his father was swept away by river current and drowned during his rescue attempt. Mr. Nott was not injured, although he was taken to a local hospital and immediately released to his mother's custody. This was a very traumatic experience for him, and he noted that it had affected him his entire life. He felt responsible for his brother's death because he had dared his brother to try to climb the cliff.

Mr. Nott has been married and divorced twice. His first marriage lasted approximately 14 years and resulted in a single child (i.e., daughter who was 27 years old). When asked what led to his divorce from his first wife, he said that they had married when they were both young (i.e., age 18), and they just grew apart. He stated, "We were both too young to really know what we were doing." His second marriage lasted approximately 11 years and had only recently ended. Records indicate that Mr. Nott and his ex-wife often bickered, and his ex-wife was not very encouraging of his participation in rehabilitative therapy.

Since his accident, Mr. Nott has been seen by another psychologist, Dr. Noah A. Little. Dr. Little conducted an assessment, which he followed up with psychotherapy. The assessment was conducted 6 months after Mr. Nott's accident and 1 year before his referral to Dr. Statts. In his report, Dr. Little noted that Mr. Nott had kidney stones, had previously undergone gall bladder surgery, had three cardiac catheterizations, and had two stents implanted. None of these facts were reported by Mr. Nott to Dr. Statts at the time of her assessment.

Finally, Mr. Nott claimed to have lost a filling in a tooth the night before Dr. Statts's evaluation, which caused him to experience even greater pain than he had come to expect. He complained to Dr. Statts that he had trouble eating the day before her assessment and worried that he would not perform well as a result. He rated his pain as 9 on a 10-point scale before the evaluation began and reported that his pain remained relatively high throughout the assessment.

Assessment of Will E. Nott by Dr. Faith N. Statts

Estimate of premorbid general ability for Will E. Nott. Dr. Statts used 12 different methods to estimate Mr. Nott's EPGA. The methods included demographic regression equations (ACS Demographics, Oklahoma Premorbid Intelligence Estimate—III, Barona Index), reading recognition tests (Advanced Clinical Solutions Test of Premorbid Functioning), standardized academic tests (Iowa Test of Basic Skills), and two school-related data points (i.e., GPA and class rank). Averaging across these estimates, Mr. Nott obtained an EPGA of 80.9 ± 5 (90% confidence interval), which is significantly lower than expected for the average person in his community. It fell at approximately the 10th percentile with respect to age, education, sex, and race-matched peers. Of the nine scores, seven were at least 1.0 standard deviation below the mean. His scores ranged from a low of 69 to a high of 106, with a median of 80.

Demographic adjustments to Will E. Nott's scores. As noted previously, Mr. Nott was a 49-year-old White man. English was his primary language, so there was little need to consider cultural diversity or language barriers when examining his test scores. However, because of his limited years of education and dropping out of high school, Mr. Nott's scores were demographically adjusted for age and education. Mr. Nott's had a mean EPGA before adjustment of 80.9 and a mean EPGA after adjustment of 88.3. Similarly, adjusting the scores he earned during Dr. Little's evaluation that were included in the OTBM increased them an average of 6 points.

Residual cognitive deficits and pattern analysis of Will E. Nott's test scores. Records were provided to Dr. Statts by Dr. Noah A. Little, who, as noted earlier, conducted his assessment 6 months after the accident and 1 year before Dr. Statts's assessment. Mr. Nott recalled being assessed by Dr. Little and said that he remembered taking some of the tests that were administered to him during this evaluation. On the basis of available data, Dr. Little could have generated an unadjusted EPGA for Mr. Nott of approximately 80.0, which is close to the 80.9 that was estimated by Dr. Statts during her evaluation. However, Dr. Little did not calculate an EPGA and thus had nothing to compare Mr. Nott's scores with. Using the Wechsler Adult Intelligence Scale—Fourth Edition and WRAT4 data, Mr. Nott obtained an OTBM of 82.4 ± 5 during Dr. Little's evaluation. There was no obvious evidence that Mr. Nott responded in an invalid manner during Dr. Little's evaluation.

Comparing Mr. Nott's scores, obtained by Dr. Little, with those published by Rohling et al. (2004) revealed that Mr. Nott's performance scores fell in the mildly impaired range, with an effect size that was close to zero. However, these scores were consistent with his premorbid abilities. In fact, none of the test scores obtained by Mr. Nott differed significantly from his EPGA. These results suggested that Mr. Nott had not experienced significant residual cognitive deficits from his work-related accident. Unfortunately, in the absence of an EPGA derived from available records,

Dr. Little concluded that Mr. Nott was cognitively impaired as a result of the accident.

Despite valid scores on the cognitive tests, Dr. Little obtained MMPI–2 scores from Mr. Nott that revealed evidence of symptom exaggeration and invalid responding. In particular, scores on several of the MMPI–2 validity indices were extreme, suggesting excessive and invalid complaints of cognitive, psychiatric, and somatic problems. Because of this pattern of invalid responding, no psychiatric diagnosis should have been rendered on the basis of these data. However, Dr. Little listed a diagnosis of traumatic brain injury with resulting borderline intellectual level of functioning as well as situational depression secondary to a general medical condition. Records also showed that Dr. Little believed Mr. Nott was in need of further treatment, yet he suggested that Mr. Nott would experience further spontaneous recovery over the next 18 to 24 months. He gave no basis for either of these opinions in his notes. In his report to Ms. Moore of Preventing Disability Services, Dr. Little wrote that Mr. Nott had "reached maximum medical improvement." He also stated that Mr. Nott was "limited to simple routines, repetitive, one- and two-step tasks." Dr. Little also provided no basis for these statements.

Ms. Moore was not satisfied with Dr. Little's evaluation and opinion and decided to seek a second opinion from Dr. Faith N. Statts. The second evaluation was more comprehensive, particularly in the areas of PVT, assessment of pain complaints, and records review. The resulting scores are presented in Figure 7.9, again using the Rohling Interpretive Method to examine the test scores. Dr. Statts's

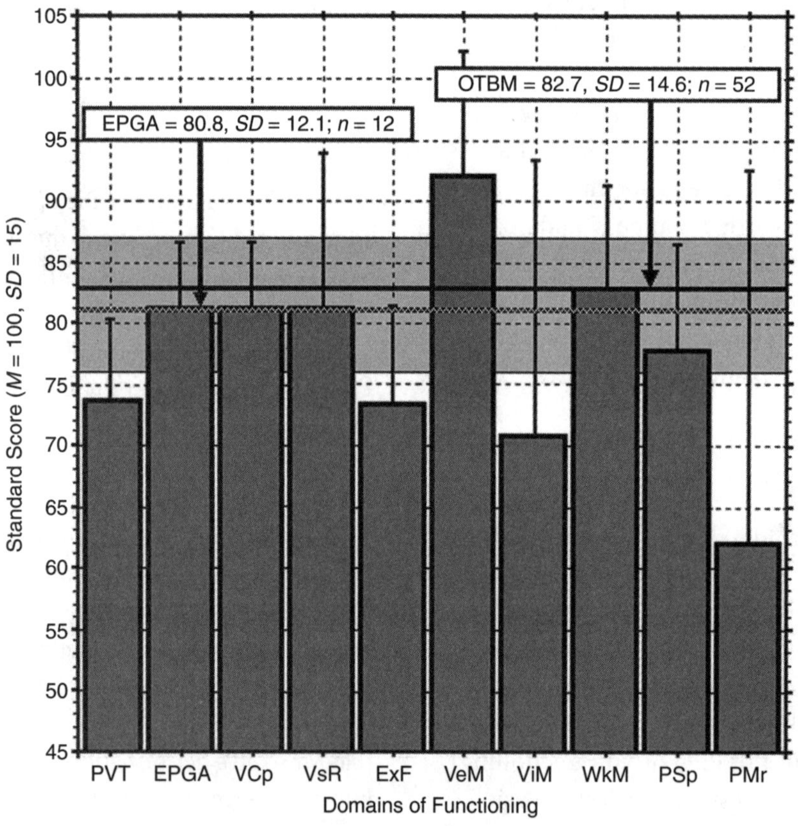

FIGURE 7.9. Will E. Nott's scores obtained by Dr. Faith N. Statts on an evaluation done 18 months after mild traumatic brain injury. EPGA = estimate of premorbid general ability; ExF = executive functioning; OTBM = overall test battery mean; PMr = psychomotor skills; PSp = processing speed; PVT = performance validity test; VCp = verbal comprehension; VeM = verbal learning and memory; ViM = visual learning and memory; VsR = visuospatial reasoning; WkM = working memory.

assessment scores and standard scores are presented in Appendix 7.2 at the end of this chapter. On the basis of Mr. Nott's obtained pattern of scores on the PVTs, as well as his cognitive test scores, Dr. Statts did not believe that Mr. Nott had responded in a valid manner during the assessment. Although he obtained scores above the cutoffs set for most of the cognitive PVTs, his overall average score on the SVTs was 80.5, which fell 1.30 standard deviations below expectation for valid performance. He failed a specific measure related to psychomotor skills, when his finger tapping speed was excessively slow and beyond what might otherwise be expected on the basis of his history (Greiffenstein et al., 1996; Meyers & Volbrecht, 2003). Furthermore, six of 13 cognitive symptom validity scores fell in the impaired range (46%; PVT $M = 73.4$). Such a result is highly improbable for even severely brain-injured patients. For example, moderately to severely brain-injured patients' mean score on these tests is 100, which is 1.77 standard deviations higher than Mr. Nott's mean score.

Furthermore, Mr. Nott's scores on measures of psychiatric SVTs, on which he scored below the cutoff on four of five measures, had a mean score that was 1.81 standard deviations below expectation for valid reporting. In particular, Dr. Statts noted that Mr. Nott's scores on the MMPI–2–RF Infrequent Responses scale ($T = 106$) and the Infrequent Psychopathology scale ($T = 77$) suggested exaggeration of symptoms that was beyond expectation. Even more striking were Mr. Nott's scores on somatic pain validity tests, on which he scored beyond the cutoff on all three measures administered, with a mean score that was 3.13 standard deviations below expectation for valid reporting (Reynolds, Paniak, Toller-Lobe, & Nagy, 2003). In particular, Mr. Nott scored well beyond the cutoff on the Response Bias Scale ($T = 115$), the Infrequent Somatic Responses scale ($T = 88$), and the Symptom Validity scale ($T = 89$). Dr. Statts concluded that all of the scores obtained by Mr. Nott likely underrepresented his true cognitive abilities and overrepresented his experience of psychiatric symptoms and his experience of pain. She had found the same pattern in Mr. Nott's scores obtained during Dr. Little's assessment. In fact, Mr. Nott's SVT scores had worsened over the past year.

Using 52 neurocognitive test scores, Dr. Statts calculated an OTBM for Mr. Nott of 82.7. His mean score placed him at or below the 10th percentile with respect to age-matched peers and fell in the mild range of cognitive impairment. Across the entire test battery, his scores ranged from a low of 52 to a high of 100, with a median of 85. Furthermore, 50% of his scores fell into the impaired range, which is significantly greater than might be expected on the basis of chance alone. Nonetheless, Mr. Nott's OTBM was actually higher than his EPGA of 80.8, with a difference of nearly 2 standard score points. His data were actually consistent with expectations, based on data for a mTBI with an LOC of less than 1 hour (see Dikmen et al., 1995; Rohling et al., 2003). Furthermore, Dr. Statts noted no significant variability in Mr. Nott's test scores, which is associated with an expectation of recovery. This result was unusual considering Dr. Statts's concern about Mr. Nott's level of effort during cognitive testing, but it certainly did not substantiate any deficits due to his injuries. Finally, Mr. Nott's results were virtually identical to those he obtained during Dr. Little's evaluation conducted 1 year earlier, when Mr. Nott obtained an OTBM of 82.0. An estimate of Mr. Nott's actual cognitive skills was likely higher than his test scores suggested, and Dr. Statts estimated them to be around a mean standard score of 85.

Examining Mr. Nott's pattern of test scores, Dr. Statts noted several anomalies in his scores and behaviors during her evaluation. Mr. Nott obtained scores in the Verbal Comprehension domain that were not significantly below his EPGA. His mean Verbal Comprehension score was 77.5, which placed him at the 9th percentile compared with age-matched peers. This score reflects moderate impairment, but is consistent with his pre-injury educational and occupational histories; it is also similar to the scores he obtained during the prior evaluation. Mr. Nott's scores in the Visual Reasoning domain were also not significantly different from his EPGA. His mean visuospatial reasoning score was 81.3, which reflects mild to moderate impairment compared to age-matched peers. Mr. Nott obtained a mean executive functioning domain score of 74.3, reflecting below-average ability in this area, but his score on this domain was also not significantly lower than his EPGA of 80.5. Thus, there is evidence of long-standing deficits rather than injury-specific impairment. Mr. Nott's highest score was on verbal memory, with a mean of 93.1, which was a relative strength and fell in the average range at the 35th percentile with respect to age-matched peers. Only 22% of his scores in this domain fell into the impaired range. Mr. Nott's mean verbal learning and memory score was likely a valid measure of his true ability and stands in contrast to his ongoing complaints of memory impairment. Unfortunately, Dr. Little did not assess Mr. Nott's verbal memory very well, so this second set of scores could not be compared with prior results. Because verbal and memory impairment are the domains of cognition most frequently impaired by TBI, as well as the impairments most frequently complained of after TBI, Dr. Little' failure to assess this function was a critical omission.

Further pattern analysis by Dr. Statts revealed that Mr. Nott's mean score on the processing speed domain was nearly his lowest. He had a mean score on psychomotor tests of 73.5, which fell in the mild to moderate impaired range, at the 4th percentile. However, Dr. Statts considered his scores invalid because he performed worse on simple psychomotor tasks, such as the Finger Tapping Test, and did better on more complex psychomotor tasks, such as the Grooved Pegboard Test. This is an example of the type of inconsistencies one looks for to determine whether the low scores obtained are based on neurological dysfunction, somatic illness disorder, or malingering. It is worth noting that patients who exhibit such excessively low psychomotor skills (fourth percentile) are not likely to be able to drive a car or live independently (Greiffenstein et al., 1996). Furthermore, using a formula generated by Meyers and Volbrecht (2003) on the basis of other speeded tasks administered in the battery, one can predict the probability of Mr. Nott's performance being valid. Mr. Nott's scores were highly improbable, given this pattern and his level of behavioral functioning, and were consistent with symptom exaggeration.

Dr. Statts also noted the similarities between Mr. Nott's current test scores and the scores obtained by Dr. Little 1 year earlier. Dr. Statts stated that Mr. Nott likely did not put forth his best effort during that assessment, but the results obtained from both assessments suggest that he had the requisite cognitive skills to work at the same level of employment he was at before his accident.

Another oddity observed during this evaluation was Mr. Nott's clinical profile on the MMPI–2–RF. He was diagnosed with an adjustment disorder before the accident, and he was taking several prescribed medications for his health symptoms, some of which have a side effect of cognitive impairment. Considering this, Dr. Statts concluded that it was not credible for Mr. Nott to claim that all of his symptoms were due to his accident and none were related to either his lack of premorbid adjustment or the side effects of medication, both of which are equally, if not more, plausible causal agents than his mTBI.

Therefore, with a reasonable degree of medical certainty, Dr. Statts concluded that Mr. Nott was not experiencing cognitive impairment caused by his work-related accident. Rather, she believed that he had experienced full recovery of his cognitive abilities and was functioning as well as he had been before his accident. Dr. Statts remained cautious, however, because Mr. Nott may not have put forth his best effort during testing, making it difficult to know the exact level of his true abilities. Genuine and consistent performance (stable mean and low variance) is necessary for detection of mild cognitive deficits. However, Mr. Nott's failure on PVTs limited Dr. Statts's ability to make an accurate diagnosis.

Dr. Statts also wrote that she did not believe that Mr. Nott's test scores reflected symptoms caused by severe psychopathology. The most likely cause of his emotional, behavioral, and cognitive complaints was one or more of his preexisting conditions. Dr. Statts went on to note that Mr. Nott might have some form of psychiatric dysfunction that predated his accident and was causing him to choose not to return to work or accept rehabilitative therapy. Dr. Statts thought Mr. Nott's failed PVTs were the result of his preoccupation with health concerns and an attempt to present himself as more dysfunctional than might actually be the case. She concluded that his affective presentation was most consistent with a somatic symptom disorder in which he experienced heightened cognitive and physical complaints that were medically unexplained and had strong emotional components at their core. Dr. Statts recommended that health care practitioners provide treatment for Mr. Nott based on objective clinical findings rather than on his subjective symptom complaints. Likewise, she advised mental health treatment explicitly directed to address somatic symptom disorders, using goal-directed and time-limited sessions (eight to 10). The treatment should be evidence based with the primary goal being an expectation of recovery and return to employment.

CONCLUSION

In conclusion, this chapter provided the reader with a review of the relevant literature associated with mTBI. Recapping, we noted the many differing definitions for mTBI and made suggestions as to the most acceptable and comprehensive definitions for the diagnosis of mild, complicated mild, moderate, and severe TBI (Stein, 1996). The criteria we reviewed are detailed in Table 7.1. We also described the varying definitions of mTBI, or concussion, which were developed by the American Congress of Rehabilitation (Kay et al., 1993) and emphasized our concern with the range restrictions in these definitions. These definitions are important because they provide guidelines for the neuropsychologist as to what acute measures of severity should be tracked down in the medical records and discussed with the examinee or significant others to determine the level of TBI severity experienced.

Four main indices are used to determine the severity of injury: (a) LOC; (b) PTA, both retrograde and anterograde; (c) GCS score at the scene of the accident and on presentation to the ED; and (d) the results of any neuroimaging conducted. These indices can then be used to calculate the level of cognitive deficits the examinee can be expected to experience once maximum neurological recovery has been obtained. Such recovery is typically less than 3 months in the case of mTBI, but it might be as long as a year in the case of severe TBI.

When an examinee's level of cognitive deficits is inconsistent with expectations, the examiner must look for the cause of the inconsistency. One common cause is that the severity indices were not well documented, and the neuropsychologist may have overestimated or underestimated the expected cognitive deficits. In either case, the examiner should return to the medical records to see whether a mistake was made in the documentation or in the interpretation of the notes in the record. Second, the examinee may have performed poorly, intentionally (e.g., malingered or feigned deficits) or unintentionally (e.g., somatic symptoms disorder), or there may be an alternative cause, such as an intervening neurological event or a preexisting condition.

To adequately determine the severity of injury, the neuropsychological evaluator must adequately estimate premorbid general ability, which includes not only cognitive functioning, but also psychiatric conditions and physical illnesses, injuries, or developmental disabilities (e.g., dyslexia). Comprehensive review of academic, medical, and employment records is necessary to complete this task competently. This process is analogous to administering a computerized cognitive test battery at baseline (i.e., preseason) in a sports context. The scores are then used to calculate the effect size(s) of cognitive deficits. The tests administered and the resulting scores can be used to examine patterns within the data in an attempt to determine not just the level of functioning but whether any premorbid conditions might better explain the scores rather than assuming they were caused by the event in question.

If another neuropsychologist has previously assessed the examinee, those records should be thoroughly reviewed, and particular attention should be paid to the norms that may have been used to ensure they were appropriate. We recommend that scores be adjusted for demographics, such as age, education, sex, and ethnicity or race. However, the neuropsychologist must correct premorbid scores in the same manner as the postmorbid scores. If no estimates of premorbid functioning are available, it is even more important that the postinjury scores be corrected for demographics.

Once the evaluation has begun, the examiner should expect to spend a fair amount of time conducting a clinical interview and an interview of collateral sources, if available. The interview should start with open-ended questions and move to closed-ended questions or a structured interview to avoid providing leading questions to a more suggestible examinee, who may in turn engage in an overendorsement of symptoms.

When administering assessment instruments, it is important to give a comprehensive battery that includes multiple measures for each of the core cognitive domains. Preferably, at least three tests that are well standardized and normed should be given for each domain. The scores can then be used to generate an OTBM, which is used in generating an effect size of cognitive impairment, using the EPGA as the baseline. Furthermore, both the EPGA and the OTBM must be examined for excessive intraindividual variability, which can be a marker for neurologic dysfunction. When intraindividual variability is excessively large, it is an indication of invalid performance. Scores of this nature across multiple assessments should also be examined, with decreases in deficits and variability expected over the time of recovery. Increases in variability and decreases in ability are suspicious and should lead the examiner to look more deeply into the pattern of performance to try to determine the cause of these trends. Neuropsychologists who engage in all of these activities during an assessment of a person with a history of mTBI can be more confident in the validity of the resulting diagnosis and assist the referral source in appropriate decision making.

APPENDIX 7.1

TEE B. EYER'S SCORES OBTAINED BY DR. TESSA U. WELLS DURING AN EVALUATION DONE 20 MONTHS AFTER MTBI

Var. no.	Instrument or subtest	Type	Domain	Score and type	Scaled	Age-only adjusted	Demographic full adjustment
	Performance validity tests						
1	Medical Symptom Validity Test—Immediate Recognition	Validity	PVT	95%	7	85	85
2	Medical Symptom Validity Test—Delayed Recognition	Validity	PVT	95%	8	90	90
3	Medical Symptom Validity Test—Consistency	Validity	PVT	100%	12	110	110
4	Test of Memory Malingering—Trial 1	Validity	PVT	50 raw	13	116	116
5	Test of Memory Malingering—Trial 2	Validity	PVT	50 raw	11	107	107
6	Test of Memory Malingering—Retention Trial	Validity	PVT	50 raw	11	105	105
7	Reliable Digit Span	Validity	PVT	8 raw	9	95	95
8	California Verbal Learning Test–II—Recognition	Validity	PVT	15 raw	11	106	106
9	Wechsler Memory Test–IV—Logical Memory Recognition	Validity	PVT	75%	12	110	110
10	Wechsler Memory Test–IV—Visual Reproduction Recognition	Validity	PVT	25%	8	90	90
11	Booklet Category Test—Subtest I/II Errors	Validity	PVT	1 raw	8	90	90
	Performance validity tests—*M*	—	—	—	—	100.4	100.4
	Performance validity tests—*SD*	—	—	—	—	10.6	10.6
	Symptom validity tests						
1	Personality Assessment Inventory—Disclosure (X)	Validity	SVT	100 BR	0	45	45
2	Personality Assessment Inventory—Desirability (Y)	Validity	SVT	70 BR	8	92	92
3	Personality Assessment Inventory—Debasement (Z)	Validity	SVT	94 BR	5	77	77
	Symptom validity tests—*M*	—	—	—	—	71.3	71.3
	Symptom validity tests—*SD*	—	—	—	—	24.0	24.0
	Estimate of premorbid general ability						
1	High School Rank—Adjusted	EPGA	EPGA	79/119	9	94	89
2	High School Grade Point Average—Adjusted	EPGA	EPGA	2.76 (30th)	7	92	87
3	Postsecondary Education Readiness (State Graduation Exam)	EPGA	EPGA	99 SS	9	99	102
4	ACT—English	EPGA	EPGA	12 (11th)	5	75	79
5	ACT—Mathematics	EPGA	EPGA	15 (14th)	7	83	87

6	ACT—Critical Reading	EPGA	EPGA	13 (10th)	6	77	81
7	ACT—Science Reasoning	EPGA	EPGA	16 (18th)	7	86	79
	ACT—Composite	Summary	EPGA	14 (10th)	6	80	76
8	Scholastic Aptitude Test (SAT)—Critical Read	EPGA	EPGA	460 (35th)	8	97	92
9	Scholastic Aptitude Test (SAT)—Mathematics	EPGA	EPGA	320 (4th)	9	76	90
10	Scholastic Aptitude Test (SAT)—Writing	EPGA	EPGA	490 (50th)	3	100	67
	Scholastic Aptitude Test (SAT)—Verbal/Math Composite	Summary	EPGA	780 (13th)	7	83	87
11	Wide Range Achievement Test–IV—Reading Recognition	EPGA	EPGA	88 (21st)	6	88	84
12	Wide Range Achievement Test–III—Reading Recognition	EPGA	EPGA	100 (50th)	10	97	99
13	Test of Premorbid Functioning—Raw Score	EPGA	EPGA	82 (11th)	6	82	84
14	Test of Premorbid Functioning—Demographically Predicted	EPGA	EPGA	82 (11th)	8	84	89
15	Oklahoma Premorbid Intelligence Estimate–IV FSIQ	EPGA	EPGA	63 SS	6	63	82
16	Barona Regression Equation—Adjusted FSIQ	EPGA	EPGA	82 SS	7	82	87
	Estimate of premorbid general ability *M*	—	—	—	—	85.3	88.3
	Estimate of premorbid general ability *SD*	—	—	—	—	10.4	10.1
	Overall test battery mean						
1	Wechsler Adult Intelligence Scale–IV—Vocabulary	OTBM	VCp	4 sc	4	61	72
2	Wechsler Adult Intelligence Scale–IV—Similarities	OTBM	VCp	7 sc	7	79	89
3	Wechsler Adult Intelligence Scale–IV—Information	OTBM	VCp	8 sc	8	82	91
4	Wechsler Adult Intelligence Scale–IV—Comprehension	OTBM	VCp	7 sc	7	80	90
	Wechsler Adult Intelligence Scale–IV—Verbal Comprehension Index	Summary	GMs	80 SS	6	70	82
5	Wide Range Achievement Test–IV—Arithmetic	OTBM	VCp	57 raw	7	85	89
6	Wide Range Achievement Test–IV—Spelling	OTBM	VCp	64 raw	9	95	101
7	Boston Naming Test	OTBM	VCp	45 corr	6	73	88
8	Wechsler Adult Intelligence Scale–IV—Block Design	OTBM	VsR	6 sc	6	72	79
9	Wechsler Adult Intelligence Scale–IV—Matrix Reasoning	OTBM	VsR	7 sc	7	74	80
10	Wechsler Adult Intelligence Scale–IV—Picture Completion	OTBM	VsR	7 sc	7	80	86
	Wechsler Adult Intelligence Scale–IV—Perceptual Reasoning Index	Summary	GMs	74 SS	4	64	72
11	Booklet Category Test	OTBM	ExF	45	9	86	92
12	Controlled Oral Word Association—Letter Fluency (FAS)	OTBM	ExF	41	10	94	103
13	Controlled Oral Word Association—Semantic Fluency (Animals)	OTBM	ExF	17 raw	9	82	95
14	Ruff Figural Fluency	OTBM	ExF	86	5	73	80
15	Wechsler Adult Intelligence Scale–IV—Arithmetic	OTBM	WkM	9 sc	9	88	100
16	Wechsler Adult Intelligence Scale–IV—Digit Span	OTBM	WkM	9 sc	9	92	94
17	Wechsler Adult Intelligence Scale–IV—Letter Number Sequence	OTBM	WkM	7 sc	7	80	90
	Wechsler Adult Intelligence Scale–IV—Working Memory Index	Summary	GMs	92 SS	8	84	94
18	Wechsler Memory Scale–IV—Logical Memory I 1st Recall	OTBM	WkM	6 sc	6	74	80
19	California Verbal Learning Test–II—Trial 1	OTBM	WkM	5 raw	7	80	86
20	California Verbal Learning Test–II—List B	OTBM	WkM	3 raw	6	70	76
21	Seashore Rhythm Test	OTBM	WkM	28 corr	12	102	102
22	Speech Sounds Perception Test	OTBM	WkM	7 err	9	86	96
	Wechsler Adult Intelligence Scale–IV—FSIQ	Summary	GMs	77 SS	5	66	79
	Wechsler Adult Intelligence Scale–IV—General Ability Index	Summary	GMs	75 SS	5	66	77
23	Wechsler Memory Scale–IV—Logical Memory I	OTBM	VeM	5 sc	5	72	77
24	Wechsler Memory Scale–IV—Logical Memory %Retention I	OTBM	VeM	8 sc	8	92	97
25	Wechsler Memory Scale–IV—Logical Memory Learning	OTBM	VeM	8 sc	8	92	97
26	Wechsler Memory Scale–IV—Logical Memory II	OTBM	VeM	6 sc	6	78	85
27	Wechsler Memory Scale–IV—Logical Memory %Retention II	OTBM	VeM	8 sc	8	85	91
28	California Verbal Learning Test–II—Total Score	OTBM	VeM	41 raw	5	79	85
29	California Verbal Learning Test–II—Short Delay Free Recall	OTBM	VeM	9 raw	7	85	90
30	California Verbal Learning Test–II—Long Delay Free Recall	OTBM	VeM	6 raw	4	65	75
31	Medical Symptom Validity Test—Paired Associates	OTBM	VeM	70%	6	80	80
32	Medical Symptom Validity Test—Delayed Free Recall	OTBM	VeM	35%	3	62	67
33	Wechsler Memory Scale–IV—Visual Reproduction I	OTBM	ViM	1 sc	1	55	62

(*continues*)

APPENDIX 7.1 (*Continued*)

TEE B. EYER'S SCORES OBTAINED BY DR. TESSA U. WELLS DURING AN EVALUATION DONE 20 MONTHS AFTER MTBI

Var. no.	Instrument or subtest	Type	Domain	Score and type	Scaled	Age-only adjusted	Demographic full adjustment
34	Wechsler Memory Scale–IV—Visual Reproduction II	OTBM	ViM	5 sc	5	70	76
35	Wechsler Memory Scale–IV—Visual Reproduction %Retention	OTBM	ViM	9 sc	9	98	104
36	Tactual Performance Test—Memory	OTBM	ViM	7	9	88	90
37	Tactual Performance Test—Dominant Hand	OTBM	GMs	.93	7	73	81
38	Tactual Performance Test—Nondominant Hand	OTBM	GMs	.98	7	72	74
39	Tactual Performance Test—Both Hands	OTBM	GMs	.70	7	67	73
40	Tactual Performance Test—Location	OTBM	GMs	1	7	74	80
41	Tactual Performance Test—Time	OTBM	GMs	.907	6	68	74
42	Retain Indiana Aphasia Screening Test	OTBM	GMs	3 err	9	97	115
43	Wechsler Adult Intelligence Scale–IV—Coding	OTBM	PSp	5 sc	5	73	79
44	Wechsler Adult Intelligence Scale–IV—Symbol Search	OTBM	PSp	7 sc	7	80	91
	Wechsler Adult Intelligence Scale–IV—Processing Speed Index	Summary	PS	79 SS	5	76	85
45	Trail Making Test—Part A	OTBM	PSp	46 s	6	64	73
46	Trail Making Test—Part B	OTBM	PSp	91 s	8	78	86
47	Finger Tapping Test—Dominant Hand	OTBM	PMr	55 s	11	100	97
48	Finger Tapping Test—Nondominant Hand	OTBM	PMr	48 s	11	97	97
49	Grip Strength—Dominant Hand	OTBM	PMr	41 kg	10	79	79
50	Grip Strength—Nondominant Hand	OTBM	PMr	35 kg	10	79	80
51	Grooved Pegboard—Dominant Hand	OTBM	PMr	103 sec	10	62	70
52	Grooved Pegboard—Nondominant Hand	OTBM	PMr	80 sec	8	80	90
	Overall test battery mean *M*	—	—	—	—	79.5	85.7
	Overall test battery mean *SD*	—	—	—	—	10.9	10.7
	Emotional personality						
1	Million Clinical Multiaxial Inventory–III—Schizoid (1)	Validity	EmP	89 BR	6	82	82
2	Million Clinical Multiaxial Inventory–III—Avoidant (2A)	Validity	EmP	69 BR	8	92	92
3	Million Clinical Multiaxial Inventory–III—Depressive (2B)	Validity	EmP	61 BR	9	96	96
4	Million Clinical Multiaxial Inventory–III—Dependent (3)	Validity	EmP	83 BR	7	86	86
5	Million Clinical Multiaxial Inventory–III—Histrionic (4)	Validity	EmP	12 BR	13	117	117
6	Million Clinical Multiaxial Inventory–III—Narcissistic (5)	Validity	EmP	73 BR	8	91	91
7	Million Clinical Multiaxial Inventory–III—Antisocial (6A)	Validity	EmP	55 BR	10	98	98
8	Million Clinical Multiaxial Inventory–III—Sadistic (6B)	Validity	EmP	70 BR	8	92	92
9	Million Clinical Multiaxial Inventory–III—Compulsive (7)	Validity	EmP	0 BR	19	146	146
10	Million Clinical Multiaxial Inventory–III—Negativistic (8A)	Validity	EmP	95 BR	5	75	75
11	Million Clinical Multiaxial Inventory–III—Masochistic (8B)	Validity	EmP	81 BR	7	87	87
12	Million Clinical Multiaxial Inventory–III—Schizotypal (S)	Validity	EmP	87 BR	7	83	83
13	Million Clinical Multiaxial Inventory–III—Borderline (C)	Validity	EmP	90 BR	6	81	81
14	Million Clinical Multiaxial Inventory–III—Paranoid (P)	Validity	EmP	89 BR	6	82	82
15	Million Clinical Multiaxial Inventory–III—Anxiety (A)	Validity	EmP	101 BR	0	45	45
16	Million Clinical Multiaxial Inventory–III—Somatoform (H)	Validity	EmP	104 BR	0	45	45
17	Million Clinical Multiaxial Inventory–III—Bipolar: Manic (N)	Validity	EmP	69 BR	8	92	92
18	Million Clinical Multiaxial Inventory–III—Dysthymia (D)	Validity	EmP	92 BR	6	79	80
19	Million Clinical Multiaxial Inventory–III—Alcohol "Depend (B)	Validity	EmP	72 BR	8	91	91
20	Million Clinical Multiaxial Inventory–III—Drug Dependence (T)	Validity	EmP	56 BR	9	97	97
21	Million Clinical Multiaxial Inventory–III—PTSD (R)	Validity	EmP	84 BR	7	85	85
	Emotional personality—*M*	—	—	—	—	76.7	76.7
	Emotional personality—*SD*	—	—	—	—	19.5	19.5

APPENDIX 7.2

WILL E. NOTT'S SCORES OBTAINED BY DR. TESSA U. WELLS DURING AN EVALUATION DONE 24 MONTHS AFTER MTBI

Var. no.	Instrument or subtest	Type	Domain	Score and type	Scaled	Age-only adjusted	Demographic full adjustment
	Performance validity tests						
1	Word Memory Test—Immediate Recognition	Validity	PVT	87.5%	4	70	72
2	Word Memory Test—Delayed Recognition	Validity	PVT	80.0%	0	45	47
3	Word Memory Test—Consistency	Validity	PVT	87.5%	5	75	74
4	Rey Fifteen Items Test—Free Recall	Validity	PVT	11 raw	7	85	84
5	Rey Fifteen Items Test—Recognition	Validity	PVT	12 raw	5	75	73
6	Rey Fifteen Items Test—Combined Score	Validity	PVT	23 raw	8	90	88
7	Mittenberg Formula- Vocabulary—Digit Span	Validity	PVT	0 raw	8	90	92
8	Symptom Validity Formula—Finger Tapping	Validity	PVT	30 raw	4	70	70
9	Reliable Digit Span	Validity	PVT	6 raw	7	85	85
10	Advanced Clinical Solutions—Word Recognition	Validity	PVT	65 SS	3	65	65
11	California Verbal Learning Test–II—Recognition	Validity	PVT	10 raw	0	45	45
12	Wisconsin Card Sorting Test—Failure to Maintain Set	Validity	PVT	2 raw	6	80	80
	Performance validity tests—*M*	—	—	—	—	72.9	72.9
	Performance validity tests—*SD*	—	—	—	—	15.3	14.9
	Symptom validity tests						
1	Minnesota Multiphasic Personality Inventory–2–RF—F-r	Validity	SVT	106 T	0	25	25
2	Minnesota Multiphasic Personality Inventory–2–RF—Fp-r	Validity	SVT	77 T	2	60	60
3	Minnesota Multiphasic Personality Inventory–2–RF—Fs	Validity	SVT	42 T	12	110	112
4	Minnesota Multiphasic Personality Inventory–2–RF—FBS-r	Validity	SVT	73 T	3	65	66
5	Minnesota Multiphasic Personality Inventory–2–RF—L-r	Validity	SVT	66 T	5	75	76
6	Minnesota Multiphasic Personality Inventory–2–RF—K-r	Validity	SVT	45 T	8	90	92
7	Minnesota Multiphasic Personality Inventory–2–RF—RBS-r	Validity	SVT	85 T	0	50	48
	Symptom validity tests—*M*	—	—	—	—	60.8	61.0
	Symptom validity tests—*SD*	—	—	—	—	27.8	28.7
	Pain validity tests						
1	Modified Somatic Perceptions Test	Validity	PainV	9 raw	3	65	64
2	Pain Disability Index	Validity	PainV	52 raw	0	25	25
3	McGill Pain Inventory	Validity	PainV	60 raw	4	70	69
	Pain validity tests—*M*	—	—	—	—	61.7	61.0
	Pain validity tests—*SD*	—	—	—	—	10.4	9.8
	Estimate of premorbid general ability						
1	Wide Range Achievement Test–IV—Reading Recognition	EPGA	EPGA	72 SS	5	75	73
2	Oklahoma Premorbid Intelligence Estimate–IV FSIQ	EPGA	EPGA	80 SS	6	80	79
3	Test of Premorbid Functioning—FSIQ Demographically Predicted	EPGA	EPGA	96 SS	9	95	98
4	Test of Premorbid Functioning—FSIQ Ability Predicted	EPGA	EPGA	11 raw	5	75	73
5	Barona Regression Equation—Adjusted FSIQ	EPGA	EPGA	106 SS	11	105	110
6	High School Grade Point Average—Adjusted	EPGA	EPGA	2 %ile	4	70	67
7	High School Rank—Adjusted	EPGA	EPGA	5 %ile	5	75	73
8	ACT—Critical Reading	EPGA	EPGA	14 raw	6	80	79
9	ACT—Mathematics	EPGA	EPGA	16 raw	7	85	86
10	ACT—Social Studies	EPGA	EPGA	14 raw	6	80	79
11	ACT—Science Reasoning	EPGA	EPGA	12 raw	5	75	73
	ACT—Composite	Summary	EPGA	14 raw	6	80	79
	Estimate of premorbid general ability—*M*	—	—	—	—	81.3	80.9
	Estimate of premorbid general ability—*SD*	—	—	—	—	9.8	12.1

(*continues*)

APPENDIX 7.2 (*Continued*)

WILL E. NOTT'S SCORES OBTAINED BY DR. TESSA U. WELLS DURING AN EVALUATION DONE 24 MONTHS AFTER MTBI

Var. no.	Instrument or subtest	Type	Domain	Score and type	Scaled	Age-only adjusted	Demographic full adjustment
	Overall test battery mean						
1	Wide Range Achievement Test–IV—Spelling	OTBM	VCp	75 SS	5	75	73
2	Wide Range Achievement Test–IV—Arithmetic	OTBM	VCp	89 SS	8	90	92
3	Wechsler Adult Intelligence Scale–IV—Similarities	OTBM	VCp	16 raw	6	80	91
4	Wechsler Adult Intelligence Scale–IV—Vocabulary	OTBM	VCp	19 raw	5	75	79
5	Wechsler Adult Intelligence Scale–IV—Information	OTBM	VCp	6 raw	5	75	85
	Wechsler Adult Intelligence Scale–IV—Verbal Comprehension Index	Summary	GMs	18 raw	6	80	79
6	Rey Complex Figure Test—Copy	OTBM	VsR	56 T	3	50	56
7	Wechsler Adult Intelligence Scale–IV—Block Design	OTBM	VsR	32 raw	6	80	92
8	Wechsler Adult Intelligence Scale–IV—Matrix Reasoning	OTBM	VsR	7 raw	6	80	91
9	Wechsler Adult Intelligence Scale–IV—Picture Completion	OTBM	VsR	19 raw	6	80	92
	Wechsler Adult Intelligence Scale–IV—Perceptual Reasoning Index	Summary	GMs	21 raw	7	85	86
10	Wisconsin Card Sorting Test—No. of Perseverative Errors	OTBM	ExF	15 raw	3	65	70
11	Wisconsin Card Sorting Test—No.of Nonperseverative Errors	OTBM	ExF	16 raw	7	85	84
12	Wisconsin Card Sorting Test—No.Categories Completed	OTBM	ExF	3 raw	12	110	110
	Controlled Oral Word Association—Letter Fluency (FAS)	Summary	GMs	24 raw	6	80	79
13	Controlled Oral Word Association—Semantic Fluency (Animals)	OTBM	ExF	11 raw	5	75	68
14	Word Memory Test—Multiple Choice	OTBM	VeM	60.0%	5	75	75
15	Word Memory Test—Paired Associates	OTBM	VeM	65.0%	8	90	90
16	Word Memory Test—Delayed Free Recall	OTBM	VeM	37.5%	6	81	81
17	Word Memory Test—Long Delayed Free Recall	OTBM	VeM	22.5%	4	59	59
18	California Verbal Learning Test–II—Trial 5	OTBM	VeM	13 raw	11	105	107
19	California Verbal Learning Test–II—Total Score	OTBM	VeM	46 raw	9	95	93
20	California Verbal Learning Test–II—Short Delay Free Recall	OTBM	VeM	12 raw	12	110	112
21	California Verbal Learning Test–II—Long Delay Free Recall	OTBM	VeM	14 raw	12	110	120
22	Rey Complex Figure Test—Immediate Recall	OTBM	ViM	39 T	7	85	84
23	Rey Complex Figure Test—Delayed Recall	OTBM	ViM	31 T	4	70	72
24	Rey Complex Figure Test—Recognition	OTBM	ViM	56 T	2	60	56
25	Wechsler Adult Intelligence Scale–IV—Digit Span	OTBM	WkM	18 raw	5	75	80
26	Wechsler Adult Intelligence Scale–IV—Arithmetic	OTBM	WkM	11 raw	9	95	103
27	Wechsler Adult Intelligence Scale–IV—Symbol Search	OTBM	WkM	27 raw	1	55	73
28	Wechsler Adult Intelligence Scale–IV—Letter Number Sequence	OTBM	WkM	7 raw	7	85	91
	Wechsler Adult Intelligence Scale–IV—Working Memory Index	Summary	GMs	16 raw	8	90	92
29	Trail Making Test—Part B	OTBM	WkM	69 sec	10	100	104
30	California Verbal Learning Test–II—Trial 1	OTBM	WkM	4 raw	6	80	76
31	California Verbal Learning Test–II—List B	OTBM	WkM	6 raw	9	95	91
32	Digit Vigilance Test—Total Time	OTBM	WkM	600 sec	4	70	74
33	Digit Vigilance Test—Total Errors	OTBM	WkM	19 raw	5	75	72
34	Rey Complex Figure Test—Time to Copy	OTBM	PSp	40 T	7	85	83
35	Trail Making Test—Part A	OTBM	PSp	48 sec	6	80	74

36	Wechsler Adult Intelligence Scale–IV—Coding	OTBM	PSp	45 raw	1	55	73
37	Wechsler Adult Intelligence Scale–IV—Cancellation	OTBM	PSp	40 raw	3	65	85
	Wechsler Adult Intelligence Scale–IV—Processing Speed Index	Summary	GMs	8 raw	4	70	67
	Wechsler Adult Intelligence Scale–IV—FSIQ	Summary	GMs	75 SS	5	75	73
38	Finger Tapping Test—Dominant Hand	OTBM	PMr	22 raw	1	55	57
39	Finger Tapping Test—Nondominant Hand	OTBM	PMr	38 raw	7	85	79
40	Grip Strength—Dominant Hand	OTBM	PMr	50 kg	12	110	96
41	Grip Strength—Nondominant Hand	OTBM	PMr	54 kg	14	120	110
42	Grooved Pegboard—Dominant Hand	OTBM	PMr	85 sec	6	80	80
43	Grooved Pegboard—Nondominant Hand	OTBM	PMr	107sec	5	75	72
	Overall test battery mean—*M*	—	—	—	—	80.9	80.9
	Overall test battery mean—*SD*	—	—	—	—	16.4	16.4
	Emotional personality						
1	Minnesota Multiphasic Personality Inventory–2–RF—RCd	Valid	EmP	63 T	6	80	80
2	Minnesota Multiphasic Personality Inventory–2–RF—RC1	Valid	EmP	58 T	8	90	88
3	Minnesota Multiphasic Personality Inventory–2–RF—RC2	Valid	EmP	73 T	3	60	60
4	Minnesota Multiphasic Personality Inventory–2–RF—RC3	Valid	EmP	51 T	10	100	102
5	Minnesota Multiphasic Personality Inventory–2–RF—RC4	Valid	EmP	60 T	7	85	85
6	Minnesota Multiphasic Personality Inventory–2–RF—RC6	Valid	EmP	73 T	3	60	60
7	Minnesota Multiphasic Personality Inventory–2–RF—RC7	Valid	EmP	63 T	6	80	80
8	Minnesota Multiphasic Personality Inventory–2–RF—RC8	Valid	EmP	54 T	9	95	95
9	Minnesota Multiphasic Personality Inventory–2–RF—RC9	Valid	EmP	45 T	12	110	110
10	Beck Depression Inventory–II—Total	Valid	EmP	31 T	4	70	72
11	State–Trait Anxiety Inventory—State	Valid	EmP	58 T	8	90	88
12	State–Trait Anxiety Inventory—Trait	Valid	EmP	45 T	12	108	108
	Emotional personality—*M*	—	—	—	—	78.0	78.0
	Emotional personality—*SD*	—	—	—	—	19.8	19.8
	Metacognition						
1	Minnesota Multiphasic Personality Inventory–2–RF—Cognitive	Valid	MCg	82 T	—	—	52
2	Memory Complaints Inventory—General Memory Problems	Valid	MCg	46 T	—	—	106
3	Memory Complaints Inventory—Numeric Information Problems	Valid	MCg	40 T	—	—	115
4	Memory Complaints Inventory—Visuospatial Memory Problems	Valid	MCg	37 T	—	—	120
5	Memory Complaints Inventory—Verbal Memory Problems	Valid	MCg	47 T	—	—	104
6	Memory Complaints Inventory—Pain Interferes with Memory	Valid	MCg	28 T	—	—	133
7	Memory Complaints Inventory—Memory Interferes with Work	Valid	MCg	34 T	—	—	124
8	Memory Complaints Inventory—Impairment of Remote Memory	Valid	MCg	51 T	—	—	98
9	Memory Complaints Inventory—Amnesia for Complex Behavior	Valid	MCg	51 T	—	—	98
10	Memory Complaints Inventory—Amnesia for Antisocial Behavior	Valid	MCg	57 T	—	—	90
	Metacognition—*M*	—	—	—	—	—	86.3
	Metacognition—*SD*	—	—	—	—	—	17.9
	Pain						
1	Minnesota Multiphasic Personality Inventory–2–RF—MLS	Valid	Pain	82 T	—	52	52
2	Minnesota Multiphasic Personality Inventory–2–RF—GIC	Valid	Pain	68 T	—	73	73
3	Minnesota Multiphasic Personality Inventory–2–RF—HPC	Valid	Pain	72 T	—	67	67
4	Minnesota Multiphasic Personality Inventory–2–RF—NUC	Valid	Pain	75 T	—	62	62
	Pain *M*	—	—	—	—	63.6	63.6
	Pain *SD*	—	—	—	—	8.9	8.9

References

Alexander, M. P. (1995). Mild traumatic brain injury: Pathophysiology, natural history, and clinical management. *Neurology*, *45*, 1253–1260. http://dx.doi.org/10.1212/WNL.45.7.1253

Alexander, M. P. (1998). In the pursuit of proof of brain damage after whiplash injury. *Neurology*, *51*, 336–340. http://dx.doi.org/10.1212/WNL.51.2.336

American College Testing. (2014). *ACT technical manual*. Iowa City, IA: Author.

American Psychiatric Association. (1994). *Diagnostic and statistical manual of mental disorders* (4th ed.). Washington, DC: Author.

Aoki, Y., Inokuchi, R., Gunshin, M., Yahagi, N., & Suwa, H. (2012). Diffusion tensor imaging studies of mild traumatic brain injury: A meta-analysis. *Journal of Neurology, Neurosurgery, and Psychiatry*, *83*, 870–876. http://dx.doi.org/10.1136/jnnp-2012-302742

Arnold, G., Boone, K. B., Lu, P., Dean, A., Wen, J., Nitch, S., & McPherson, S. (2005). Sensitivity and specificity of finger tapping test scores for the detection of suspect effort. *Clinical Neuropsychologist*, *19*, 105–120. http://dx.doi.org/10.1080/13854040490888567

Baade, L. E., & Schoenberg, M. R. (2004). A proposed method to estimate premorbid intelligence utilizing group achievement measures from school records. *Archives of Clinical Neuropsychology*, *19*, 227–243. http://dx.doi.org/10.1016/S0887-6177(03)00092-1

Babikian, T., Satz, P., Zaucha, K., Light, R., Lewis, R. S., & Asarnow, R. F. (2011). The UCLA longitudinal study of neurocognitive outcomes following mild pediatric traumatic brain injury. *Journal of the International Neuropsychological Society*, *17*, 886–895. http://dx.doi.org/10.1017/S1355617711000907

Barona, A., Reynolds, C. R., & Chastain, R. (1984). A demographically based index of premorbid intelligence for the WAIS—R. *Journal of Consulting and Clinical Psychology*, *52*, 885–887. http://dx.doi.org/10.1037/0022-006X.52.5.885

Barrash, J., Suhr, J., & Manzel, K. (2004). Detecting poor effort and malingering with an expanded version of the Auditory Verbal Learning Test (AVLTX): Validation with clinical samples. *Journal of Clinical and Experimental Neuropsychology*, *26*, 125–140. http://dx.doi.org/10.1076/jcen.26.1.125.23928

Barsky, A. J., & Borus, J. F. (1999). Functional somatic syndromes. *Annals of Internal Medicine*, *130*, 910–921. http://dx.doi.org/10.7326/0003-4819-130-11-199906010-00016

Barth, J. T., Alves, W. M., Ryan, T. V., Macciocchi, S. N., Rimel, R. W., Jane, J. A., & Nelson, W. E. (1989). Mild head injury in sports: Neuropsychological sequelae and recovery of function. In H. S. Levin, H. M. Eisenberg, & A. L. Benton (Eds.), *Mild head injury* (pp. 257–275). New York, NY: Oxford University Press.

Belanger, H. G., Curtiss, G., Demery, J. A., Lebowitz, B. K., & Vanderploeg, R. D. (2005). Factors moderating neuropsychological outcomes following mild traumatic brain injury: A meta-analysis. *Journal of the International Neuropsychological Society*, *11*, 215–227. http://dx.doi.org/10.1017/S1355617705050277

Belanger, H. G., Spiegel, E., & Vanderploeg, R. D. (2010). Neuropsychological performance following a history of multiple self-reported concussions: A meta-analysis. *Journal of the International Neuropsychological Society*, *16*, 262–267. http://dx.doi.org/10.1017/S1355617709991287

Bengtzen, R., Woodward, M., Lynn, M. J., Newman, N. J., & Biousse, V. (2008). The "sunglasses sign" predicts nonorganic visual loss in neuro-ophthalmologic practice. *Neurology*, *70*, 218–221. http://dx.doi.org/10.1212/01.wnl.0000287090.98555.56

Bijur, P. E., Haslum, M., & Golding, J. (1996). Cognitive outcomes of multiple mild head injuries in children. *Journal of Developmental and Behavioral Pediatrics*, *17*, 143–148. http://dx.doi.org/10.1097/00004703-199606000-00001

Binder, L. M., & Rohling, M. L. (1996). Money matters: A meta-analytic review of the effects of financial incentives on recovery after closed-head injury. *American Journal of Psychiatry*, *153*, 7–10. http://dx.doi.org/10.1176/ajp.153.1.7

Binder, L. M., Rohling, M. L., & Larrabee, G. J. (1997). A review of mild head trauma. Part I: Meta-analytic review of neuropsychological studies. *Journal of Clinical and Experimental Neuropsychology*, *19*, 421–431. http://dx.doi.org/10.1080/01688639708403870

Bleiberg, J., Kane, R. L., Reeves, D. L., Garmoe, W. S., & Halpern, E. (2000). Factor analysis of computerized and traditional tests used in mild brain injury research. *Clinical Neuropsychologist*, *14*, 287–294. http://dx.doi.org/10.1076/1385-4046(200008)14:3;1-P;FT287

Boone, K. B. (2009). The need for continuous and comprehensive sampling of effort/response bias during neuropsychological examinations. *Clinical Neuropsychologist*, *23*, 729–741. http://dx.doi.org/10.1080/13854040802427803

Bowden, S. C., Shores, E. A., & Mathias, J. L. (2006). Does effort suppress cognition after traumatic brain injury? A re-examination of the evidence for the Word Memory Test. *Clinical Neuropsychologist*, *20*, 858–872. http://dx.doi.org/10.1080/13854040500246935

Brulot, M. M., Strauss, E., & Spellacy, F. (1997). Validity of the Minnesota Multiphasic Personality Inventory—2 correction factors for use with patients with suspected head injury. *Clinical Neuropsychologist*, *11*, 391–401. http://dx.doi.org/10.1080/13854049708400468

Butcher, J. N., Dahlstrom, W. G., Graham, J. R., Tellegen, A., & Kaemmer, B. (1989). *The Minnesota Multiphasic Personality Inventory—2 (MMPI–2): Manual for administration and scoring*. Minneapolis: University of Minnesota Press.

Cancelliere, C., Cassidy, J. D., Li, A., Donovan, J., Cote, P., & Hincapie, C. A. (2014). Systematic search and review procedures: Results of the international collaboration on mild traumatic brain injury prognosis. *Archives of Physical Medicine and Rehabilitation, 95*(3, Suppl.), S101–S131. http://dx.doi.org/10.1016/j.apmr.2013.12.001

Cantu, R. C. (1986). Guidelines to return to contact sports after cerebral concussion. *Physician and Sportsmedicine, 14,* 75–83. http://dx.doi.org/10.1080/00913847.1986.11709197

Carone, D. A., & Bush, S. S. (2013). Introduction: Historical perspectives on mild traumatic brain injury, symptom validity assessment, and malingering. In D. A. Carone & S. S. Bush (Eds.), *Mild traumatic brain injury* (pp. 10–11). New York, NY: Springer.

Carone, D. A., & Bush, S. S. (2014). Dementia pugilistica and chronic traumatic encephalopathy. In R. Dean & C. Noggle (Eds.), *Cortical dementias* (pp. 303–326). New York, NY: Springer.

Carroll, L. J., Cassidy, J. D., Holm, L., Kraus, J., & Coronado, V. G. (2004). Methodological issues and research recommendations for mild traumatic brain injury: The WHO Collaborating Centre Task Force on Mild Traumatic Brain Injury. *Journal of Rehabilitation Medicine, 43*(Suppl.), 113–125. http://dx.doi.org/10.1080/16501960410023877

Carroll, L. J., Cassidy, J. D., Peloso, P. M., Borg, J., von Holst, H., Holm, L., . . . Pépin, M. (2004). Prognosis for mild traumatic brain injury: Results of the WHO Collaborating Centre Task Force on Mild Traumatic Brain Injury. *Journal of Rehabilitation Medicine, 43*(Suppl.), 84–105. http://dx.doi.org/10.1080/16501960410023859

Cassady, J. C., & Jerrell, C. (2001). Self-reported GPA and SAT: A methodological note [Special issue]. *Practical Assessment, Research, and Education, 7*(12).

Cassidy, J. D., Carroll, L. J., Peloso, P. M., Borg, J., von Holst, H., Holm, L., . . . Coronado, V. G. (2004). Incidence, risk factors and prevention of mild traumatic brain injury: Results of the WHO Collaborating Centre Task Force on Mild Traumatic Brain Injury. *Journal of Rehabilitation Medicine, 43*(Suppl.), 28–60. http://dx.doi.org/10.1080/16501960410023732

Centers for Disease Control and Prevention. (2003). *Report to Congress on mild traumatic brain injury in the United States: Steps to prevent a serious public health problem.* Atlanta, GA: National Center for Injury Prevention and Control, Division of Unintentional Injury Prevention.

Centers for Disease Control and Prevention. (2015). *Report to Congress on traumatic brain injury in the United States: Epidemiology and rehabilitation.* Atlanta, GA: National Center for Injury Prevention and Control, Division of Unintentional Injury Prevention.

College Board. (2005). *Scholastic Aptitude Test.* Princeton, NJ: Author.

College Board. (2011). *SAT trends 2011.* Princeton, NJ: Author.

Collie, A., Darby, D., & Maruff, P. (2001). Computerised cognitive assessment of athletes with sports related head injury. *British Journal of Sports Medicine, 35,* 297–302. http://dx.doi.org/10.1136/bjsm.35.5.297

Constantinou, M., Bauer, L., Ashendorf, L., Fisher, J. M., & McCaffrey, R. J. (2005). Is poor performance on recognition memory effort measures indicative of generalized poor performance on neuropsychological tests? *Archives of Clinical Neuropsychology, 20,* 191–198.http://dx.doi.org/10.1016/j.acn.2004.06.002

Delis, D. C., & Wetter, S. R. (2007). Cogniform disorder and cogniform condition: Proposed diagnoses for excessive cognitive symptoms. *Archives of Clinical Neuropsychology, 22,* 589–604. http://dx.doi.org/10.1016/j.acn.2007.04.001

Demakis, G. J., Gervais, R. O., & Rohling, M. L. (2008). The effect of failure on cognitive and psychological symptom validity tests in litigants with symptoms of post-traumatic stress disorder. *Clinical Neuropsychologist, 22,* 879–895. http://dx.doi.org/10.1080/13854040701564482

Dikmen, S., Machamer, J., Fann, J. R., & Temkin, N. R. (2010). Rates of symptom reporting following traumatic brain injury. *Journal of the International Neuropsychological Society, 16,* 401–411. http://dx.doi.org/10.1017/S1355617710000196

Dikmen, S. S., Machamer, J. E., Winn, H. R., & Temkin, N. R. (1995). Neuropsychological outcome at 1-year post head injury. *Neuropsychology, 9,* 80–90. http://dx.doi.org/10.1037/0894-4105.9.1.80

Donnell, A. J., Kim, M. S., Silva, M. A., & Vanderploeg, R. D. (2012). Incidence of postconcussion symptoms in psychiatric diagnostic groups, mild traumatic brain injury, and comorbid conditions. *Clinical Neuropsychologist, 26,* 1092–1101. http://dx.doi.org/10.1080/13854046.2012.713984

Erlanger, D., Feldman, D., Kutner, K., Kaushik, T., Kroger, H., Festa, J., . . . Broshek, D. (2003). Development and validation of a Web-based neuropsychological test protocol for sports-related return-to-play decision-making. *Archives of Clinical Neuropsychology, 18,* 293–316. http://dx.doi.org/10.1016/S0887-6177(02)00138-5

Faul, M., Xu, L., Wald, M. M., & Coronado, V. G. (2010). *Traumatic brain injury in the United States: Emergency department visits, hospitalizations, and deaths, 2002–2006*. Atlanta, GA: Centers for Disease Control and Prevention, National Center for Injury and Control.

Feinstein, A., Ouchterlony, D., Somerville, J., & Jardine, A. (2001). The effects of litigation on symptom expression: A prospective study following mild traumatic brain injury. *Medicine, Science, and the Law, 41,* 116–121.

Frencham, K. A. R., Fox, A. M., & Maybery, M. T. (2005). Neuropsychological studies of mild traumatic brain injury: A meta-analytic review of research since 1995. *Journal of Clinical and Experimental Neuropsychology, 27,* 334–351. http://dx.doi.org/10.1080/13803390490520328

Garden, N., & Sullivan, K. A. (2010). An examination of the base rates of post-concussion symptoms: The influence of demographics and depression. *Applied Neuropsychology, 17,* 1–7. http://dx.doi.org/10.1080/09084280903297495

Gargan, M. F., & Bannister, G. C. (1990). Long-term prognosis of soft-tissue injuries of the neck. *Journal of Bone and Joint Surgery (British), 72,* 901–903.

Gass, C. S., & Russell, E. W. (1991). MMPI profiles of patients with closed-head-trauma: Impact of neurologic complaints. *Journal of Clinical Psychology, 47,* 253–260. http://dx.doi.org/10.1002/1097-4679(199103)47:2<253::AID-JCLP2270470210>3.0.CO;2-A

Gervais, R. O., Rohling, M. L., Green, P., & Ford, W. (2004). A comparison of WMT, CARB, and TOMM failure rates in non-head injury disability claimants. *Archives of Clinical Neuropsychology, 19,* 475–487. http://dx.doi.org/10.1016/j.acn.2003.05.001

Giza, C. C., & Hovda, D. A. (2001). The neurometabolic cascade of concussion. *Journal of Athletic Training, 36,* 228–235.

Giza, C. C., Kutcher, J. S., Ashwal, S., Barth, J., Getchius, T. S., Gioia, G. A., . . . Zafonte, R. (2013). Summary of evidence-based guideline update: Evaluation and management of concussion in sports: Report of the Guideline Development Subcommittee of the American Academy of Neurology. *Neurology, 80,* 2250–2257. http://dx.doi.org/10.1212/WNL.0b013e31828d57dd

Goldstein, F. C., & Levin, H. S. (2001). Cognitive outcome after mild and moderate traumatic brain injury in older adults. *Journal of Clinical and Experimental Neuropsychology, 23,* 739–753. http://dx.doi.org/10.1076/jcen.23.6.739.1028

Goodrich, G. L., Martinsen, G. L., Flyg, H. M., Kirby, J., Garvert, D. W., & Tyler, C. W. (2014). Visual function, traumatic brain injury, and posttraumatic stress disorder. *Journal of Rehabilitation Research and Development, 51,* 547–558. http://dx.doi.org/10.1682/JRRD.2013.02.0049

Granacher, R. P., Jr. (2008). Commentary: Applications of functional neuroimaging to civil litigation of mild traumatic brain injury. *Journal of the American Academy of Psychiatry and the Law, 36,* 323–328.

Green, P., Rohling, M. L., Iverson, G. L., & Gervais, R. O. (2003). Relationships between olfactory discrimination and head injury severity. *Brain Injury, 17,* 479–496. http://dx.doi.org/10.1080/0269905031000070242

Green, P., Rohling, M. L., Lees-Haley, P., & Allen, L. M. (2001). Effort has a greater affect on test scores than sever brain injury in compensation claimants. *Brain Injury, 15,* 1045–1060. http://dx.doi.org/10.1080/02699050110088254

Greiffenstein, M. (2007). Motor, sensory and perceptual-motor pseudoabnormalities. In G. J. Larrabee (Ed.), *Assessment of malingered neuropsychological deficits* (pp. 100–130). New York, NY: Oxford University Press.

Greiffenstein, M. F., Baker, W. J., & Gola, J. (1994). Validation of malingered amnesia measures with a large clinical sample. *Psychological Assessment, 6,* 218–224. http://dx.doi.org/10.1037/1040-3590.6.3.218

Greiffenstein, M. F., Baker, W. J., & Gola, T. (1996). Motor dysfunction profiles in traumatic brain injury and postconcussion syndrome. *Journal of the International Neuropsychological Society, 2,* 477–485. http://dx.doi.org/10.1017/S1355617700001648

Greiffenstein, M. F., & Kaufmann, P. M. (2012). Neuropsychology and the law: Principles of productive attorney-neuropsychologist relations. In G. J. Larrabee (Ed.), *Forensic neuropsychology: A scientific approach* (2nd ed., pp. 23–69). New York, NY: Oxford University Press.

Gualtieri, C. T., & Johnson, L. G. (2006). Reliability and validity of a computerized neurocognitive test battery, CNS Vital Signs. *Archives of Clinical Neuropsychology, 21,* 623–643. http://dx.doi.org/10.1016/j.acn.2006.05.007

Guerrero, J. L., Thurman, D. J., & Sniezek, J. E. (2000). Emergency department visits associated with traumatic brain injury: United States, 1995-1996. *Brain Injury, 14,* 181–186. http://dx.doi.org/10.1080/026990500120827

Gunstad, J., & Suhr, J. A. (2004). Cognitive factors in postconcussion syndrome symptom report. *Archives of Clinical Neuropsychology, 19,* 391–405. http://dx.doi.org/10.1016/S0887-6177(03)00073-8

Hanlon, R. E., Demery, J. A., Martinovich, Z., & Kelly, J. P. (1999). Effects of acute injury characteristics on neuropsychological status and vocational outcome following mild traumatic brain injury. *Brain Injury,*

13, 873–887. http://dx.doi.org/10.1080/026990599121070

Hänninen, T., Reinikainen, K. J., Helkala, E. L., Koivisto, K., Mykkänen, L., Laakso, M., . . . Riekkinen, P. J. (1994). Subjective memory complaints and personality traits in normal elderly subjects. *Journal of the American Geriatrics Society*, 42, 1–4. http://dx.doi.org/10.1111/j.1532-5415.1994.tb06064.x

Harris, I., Mulford, J., Solomon, M., van Gelder, J. M., & Young, J. (2005). Association between compensation status and outcome after surgery: A meta-analysis. *JAMA, 293,* 1644–1652. http://dx.doi.org/10.1001/jama.293.13.1644

Hart, R. P., Martelli, M. F., & Zasler, N. D. (2000). Chronic pain and neuropsychological functioning. *Neuropsychology Review, 10,* 131–149. http://dx.doi.org/10.1023/A:1009020914358

Heaton, R. K., Miller, W., Taylor, M. J., & Grant, I. (2004). *Revised comprehensive norms for an expanded Halstead-Reitan Battery: Demographically adjusted neuropsychological norms for African American and Caucasian adults.* Lutz, FL: Psychological Assessment Resources.

Heitger, M. H., Jones, R. D., Macleod, A. D., Snell, D. L., Frampton, C. M., & Anderson, T. J. (2009). Impaired eye movements in post-concussion syndrome indicate suboptimal brain function beyond the influence of depression, malingering or intellectual ability. *Brain: A Journal of Neurology, 132,* 2850–2870. http://dx.doi.org/10.1093/brain/awp181

High, W. M., Jr., Levin, H. S., & Gary, H. E., Jr. (1990). Recovery of orientation following closed-head injury. *Journal of Clinical and Experimental Neuropsychology, 12,* 703–714. http://dx.doi.org/10.1080/01688639008401013

Hill, B. D., Rohling, M. L., Boettcher, A. C., & Meyers, J. E. (2013). Cognitive intra-individual variability has a positive association with traumatic brain injury severity and suboptimal effort. *Archives of Clinical Neuropsychology, 28,* 640–648. http://dx.doi.org/10.1093/arclin/act045

Holdnack, J. A., & Drozdick, L. W. (2009). *Advanced Clinical Solutions: Clinical and interpretive manual.* San Antonio, TX: Pearson.

Holm, L., Cassidy, J. D., Carroll, J., & Borg, J. (2005). Summary of the WHO Collaborative Centre for Neurotrauma Task Force on Mild Traumatic Brain Injury. *Journal of Rehabilitative Medicine, 37,* 137–141. http://dx.doi.org/10.1080/16501970510027321

Hoover, H. D., Dunbar, S. B., & Frisbie, D. A. (2001). *Iowa Tests of Basic Skills.* Rolling Meadows, IL: Riverside.

Hughes, D. G., Jackson, A., Mason, D. L., Berry, E., Hollis, S., & Yates, D. W. (2004). Abnormalities on magnetic resonance imaging seen acutely following mild traumatic brain injury: Correlation with neuropsychological tests and delayed recovery. *Neuroradiology, 46,* 550–558. http://dx.doi.org/10.1007/s00234-004-1227-x

Institute of Medicine. (2006). *Evaluating the HRSA Traumatic Brain Injury Program.* Washington, DC: National Academies Press.

Institute of Medicine. (2009). *Gulf War and Health: Vol. 7. Long-term consequences of traumatic brain injury.* Washington, DC: National Academies Press.

Iverson, G. L. (2006). Misdiagnosis of the persistent postconcussion syndrome in patients with depression. *Archives of Clinical Neuropsychology, 21,* 303–310. http://dx.doi.org/10.1016/j.acn.2005.12.008

Iverson, G. L., King, R. J., Scott, J. G., & Adams, R. L. (2001). Cognitive complaints in litigating patients with head injuries or chronic pain. *Journal of Forensic Neuropsychology*, 2, 19–30. http://dx.doi.org/10.1300/J151v02n01_02

Iverson, G. L., Lange, R. T., Brooks, B. L., & Rennison, V. L. A. (2010). "Good old days" bias following mild traumatic brain injury. *Clinical Neuropsychologist, 24,* 17–37. http://dx.doi.org/10.1080/13854040903190797

Iverson, G. L., Lange, R. T., Wäljas, M., Liimatainen, S., Dastidar, P., Hartikainen, K. M., . . . Ohman, J. (2012). Outcome from complicated versus uncomplicated mild traumatic brain injury. *Rehabilitation Research and Practice, 2012,* 415740.

Iverson, G. L., & McCracken, L. M. (1997). "Postconcussive" symptoms in persons with chronic pain. *Brain Injury, 11,* 783–790. http://dx.doi.org/10.1080/026990597122990

Kashluba, S., Hanks, R. A., Casey, J. E., & Millis, S. R. (2008). Neuropsychologic and functional outcome after complicated mild traumatic brain injury. *Archives of Physical Medicine and Rehabilitation, 89,* 904–911. http://dx.doi.org/10.1016/j.apmr.2007.12.029

Katona, C., Peveler, R., Dowrick, C., Wessely, S., Feinmann, C., Gask, L., . . . Wager, E. (2005). Pain symptoms in depression: Definition and clinical significance. *Clinical Medicine, 5,* 390–395. http://dx.doi.org/10.7861/clinmedicine.5-4-390

Kaufmann, P., & Greiffenstein, M. F. (2013). Forensic neuropsychology: Training, scope of practice, and quality control. *National Academy of Neuropsychology: Newsletter, 27,* 11–14.

Kay, T., Harrington, D. E., Adams, R., Anderson, T., Berrol, S., Cicerone, K., . . . Malec, J. (1993). Definition of mild traumatic brain injury. *Journal of Head Trauma Rehabilitation*, 8, 86–87.

Kessels, R. P. C., Aleman, A., Verhagen, W. I. M., & van Luijtelaar, E. L. J. M. (2000). Cognitive functioning after whiplash injury: A meta-analysis. *Journal of the*

International Neuropsychological Society, *6*, 271–278. http://dx.doi.org/10.1017/S1355617700633027

Koenig, K. A., Frey, M. C., & Detterman, D. K. (2008). ACT and general cognitive ability. *Intelligence*, *36*, 153–160. http://dx.doi.org/10.1016/j.intell.2007.03.005

Krull, K. R., Scott, J. G., & Sherer, M. (1995). Estimation of premorbid intelligence from combined performance and demographic variables (OPIE). *Clinical Neuropsychologist*, *9*, 83–88. http://dx.doi.org/10.1080/13854049508402063

Kushner, D. (1998). Mild traumatic brain injury: Toward understanding manifestations and treatment. *Archives of Internal Medicine*, *158*, 1617–1624. http://dx.doi.org/10.1001/archinte.158.15.1617

Lange, R. T., Iverson, G. L., Brooks, B. L., & Rennison, V. L. A. (2010). Influence of poor effort on self-reported symptoms and neurocognitive test performance following mild traumatic brain injury. *Journal of Clinical and Experimental Neuropsychology*, *32*, 961–972. http://dx.doi.org/10.1080/13803391003645657

Lange, R. T., Iverson, G. L., Brubacher, J. R., Mädler, B., & Heran, M. K. (2012). Diffusion tensor imaging findings are not strongly associated with postconcussional disorder 2 months following mild traumatic brain injury. *Journal of Head Trauma Rehabilitation*, *27*, 188–198. http://dx.doi.org/10.1097/HTR.0b013e318217f0ad

Lange, R. T., Iverson, G. L., & Franzen, M. D. (2009). Neuropsychological functioning following complicated vs. uncomplicated mild traumatic brain injury. *Brain Injury*, *23*, 83–91. http://dx.doi.org/10.1080/02699050802635281

Larrabee, G. J. (1990). Caution on the use of neuropsychological evaluation in legal settings. *Neuropsychology*, *4*, 239–247. http://dx.doi.org/10.1037/0894-4105.4.4.239

Larrabee, G. J. (2003a). Detection of malingering using atypical performance patterns on standard neuropsychological tests. *Clinical Neuropsychologist*, *17*, 410–425. http://dx.doi.org/10.1076/clin.17.3.410.18089

Larrabee, G. J. (2003b). Exaggerated pain report in litigants with malingered neurocognitive dysfunction. *Clinical Neuropsychologist*, *17*, 395–401. http://dx.doi.org/10.1076/clin.17.3.395.18087

Larrabee, G. J. (2009). Malingering scales for the Continuous Recognition Memory Test and the Continuous Visual Memory Test. *Clinical Neuropsychologist*, *23*, 167–180. http://dx.doi.org/10.1080/13854040801968443

Larrabee, G. J. (2012a). Performance validity and symptom validity in neuropsychological assessment. *Journal of the International Neuropsychological Society*, *18*, 625–630. http://dx.doi.org/10.1017/S1355617712000240

Larrabee, G. J. (2012b). A scientific approach to forensic neuropsychology. In G. J. Larrabee (Ed.), *Forensic neuropsychology: A scientific approach* (2nd ed., pp. 3–22). New York, NY: Oxford University Press.

Larrabee, G. J., Binder, L. M., Rohling, M. L., & Ploetz, D. M. (2013). Meta-analytic methods and the importance of non-TBI factors related to outcome in mild traumatic brain injury: Response to Bigler et al. (2013). *Clinical Neuropsychologist*, *27*, 215–237. http://dx.doi.org/10.1080/13854046.2013.769634

Larrabee, G. J., & Levin, H. S. (1986). Memory self-ratings and objective test performance in a normal elderly sample. *Journal of Clinical and Experimental Neuropsychology*, *8*, 275–284. http://dx.doi.org/10.1080/01688638608401318

Larrabee, G. J., & Rohling, M. L. (2013). Neuropsychological differential diagnosis of mild traumatic brain injury. *Behavioral Sciences and the Law*, *31*, 686–701. http://dx.doi.org/10.1002/bsl.2087

Larrabee, G. J., West, R. L., & Crook, T. H. (1991). The association of memory complaint with computer-simulated everyday memory performance. *Journal of Clinical and Experimental Neuropsychology*, *13*, 466–478. http://dx.doi.org/10.1080/01688639108401064

Lees-Haley, P. R., & Brown, R. S. (1993). Neuropsychological complaint base rates of 170 personal injury claimants. *Archives of Clinical Neuropsychology*, *8*, 203–209. http://dx.doi.org/10.1093/arclin/8.3.203

Lees-Haley, P. R., Fox, D. D., & Courtney, J. C. (2001). A comparison of complaints by mild brain injury claimants and other claimants describing subjective experiences immediately following their injury. *Archives of Clinical Neuropsychology*, *16*, 689–695. http://dx.doi.org/10.1093/arclin/16.7.689

Levin, H. S., Benton, A. L., & Grossman, R. G. (1992). *Neurobehavioral consequences of closed head injury*. New York, NY: Oxford University Press.

Levin, H. S., Brown, S. A., Song, J. X., McCauley, S. R., Boake, C., Contant, C. F., . . . Kotrla, K. J. (2001). Depression and posttraumatic stress disorder at three months after mild to moderate traumatic brain injury. *Journal of Clinical and Experimental Neuropsychology*, *23*, 754–769. http://dx.doi.org/10.1076/jcen.23.6.754.1021

Lovell, M. R., Collins, M. W., Podell, K., Powell, J., & Maroon, J. (2000). *ImPACT: Immediate post-concussion assessment and cognitive testing*. Pittsburgh, PA: NeuroHealth Systems.

Luis, C. A., Vanderploeg, R. D., & Curtiss, G. (2003). Predictors of postconcussion symptom complex in community dwelling male veterans. *Journal of the International Neuropsychological Society*, *9*, 1001–1015. http://dx.doi.org/10.1017/S1355617703970044

Manly, J. J. (2005). Advantages and disadvantages of separate norms for African Americans. *Clinical Neuropsychologist, 19,* 270–275. http://dx.doi.org/10.1080/13854040590945346

Manly, J. J., & Echemendia, R. J. (2007). Race-specific norms: Using the model of hypertension to understand issues of race, culture, and education in neuropsychology. *Archives of Clinical Neuropsychology*, 22, 319–325. http://dx.doi.org/10.1016/j.acn.2007.01.006

Manly, J. J., Jacobs, D. M., Touradji, P., Small, S. A., & Stern, Y. (2002). Reading level attenuates differences in neuropsychological test performance between African American and White elders. *Journal of the International Neuropsychological Society*, *8,* 341–348. http://dx.doi.org/10.1017/S1355617702813157

Manly, J. J., Smith, C., Crystal, H. A., Richardson, J., Golub, E. T., Greenblatt, R., . . . Young, M. (2011). Relationship of ethnicity, age, education, and reading level to speed and executive function among HIV+ and HIV− women: The Women's Interagency HIV Study (WIHS) Neurocognitive Substudy. *Journal of Clinical and Experimental Neuropsychology*, *33,* 853–863. http://dx.doi.org/10.1080/13803395.2010.547662

Mathias, J. L., & Coats, J. L. (1999). Emotional and cognitive sequelae to mild traumatic brain injury. *Journal of Clinical and Experimental Neuropsychology*, *21,* 200–215. http://dx.doi.org/10.1076/jcen.21.2.200.930

McCrea, M., Guskiewicz, K. M., Marshall, S. W., Barr, W., Randolph, C., Cantu, R. C., . . . Kelly, J. P. (2003). Acute effects and recovery time following concussion in collegiate football players: The NCAA Concussion Study. *JAMA*, *290,* 2556–2563. http://dx.doi.org/10.1001/jama.290.19.2556

McCrea, M. A. (2008). Challenges in defining and diagnosing MTBI. In M. A. McCrea (Ed.), *Mild traumatic brain injury and postconcussion syndrome* (pp. 13–28). New York, NY: Oxford University Press.

McKee, A. C., Cantu, R. C., Nowinski, C. J., Hedley-Whyte, E. T., Gavett, B. E., Budson, A. E., . . . Stern, R. A. (2009). Chronic traumatic encephalopathy in athletes: Progressive tauopathy after repetitive head injury. *Journal of Neuropathology and Experimental Neurology*, *68,* 709–735. http://dx.doi.org/10.1097/NEN.0b013e3181a9d503

McLean, A., Jr., Temkin, N. R., Dikmen, S., & Wyler, A. R. (1983). The behavioral sequelae of head injury. *Journal of Clinical Neuropsychology*, *5,* 361–376. http://dx.doi.org/10.1080/01688638308401185

Meares, S., Shores, E. A., Taylor, A. J., Batchelor, J., Bryant, R. A., Baguley, I. J., . . . Marosszeky, J. E. (2011). The prospective course of postconcussion syndrome: The role of mild traumatic brain injury. *Neuropsychology*, *25,* 454–465. http://dx.doi.org/10.1037/a0022580

Meyers, J. E., & Rohling, M. L. (2004). Validation of the Meyers Short Battery on mild TBI patients. *Archives of Clinical Neuropsychology*, *19,* 637–651. http://dx.doi.org/10.1016/j.acn.2003.08.007

Meyers, J. E., & Volbrecht, M. E. (2003). A validation of multiple malingering detection methods in a large clinical sample. *Archives of Clinical Neuropsychology*, *18,* 261–276. http://dx.doi.org/10.1093/arclin/18.3.261

Mild Traumatic Brain Injury Committee, American Congress of Rehabilitation Medicine. (1993). Definition of mild traumatic brain injury. *Journal of Head Trauma Rehabilitation*, *8,* 86–87.

Miller, L. S., & Rohling, M. L. (2001). A statistical interpretive method for neuropsychological test data. *Neuropsychology Review*, *11,* 143–169. http://dx.doi.org/10.1023/A:1016602708066

Mittenberg, W., Azrin, R., Millsaps, C., & Heilbronner, R. (1993). Identification of malingered head injury on the Wechsler Memory Scale—Revised. *Psychological Assessment*, *5,* 34–40. http://dx.doi.org/10.1037/1040-3590.5.1.34

Mittenberg, W., DiGiulio, D. V., Perrin, S., & Bass, A. E. (1992). Symptoms following mild head injury: Expectation as aetiology. *Journal of Neurology, Neurosurgery, and Psychiatry*, *55,* 200–204. http://dx.doi.org/10.1136/jnnp.55.3.200

Mittenberg, W., Patton, C., Canyock, E. M., & Condit, D. C. (2002). Base rates of malingering and symptom exaggeration. *Journal of Clinical and Experimental Neuropsychology*, *24,* 1094–1102. http://dx.doi.org/10.1076/jcen.24.8.1094.8379

Mittenberg, W., Tremont, G., Zielinski, R. E., Fichera, S., & Rayls, K. R. (1996). Cognitive-behavioral prevention of postconcussion syndrome. *Archives of Clinical Neuropsychology*, *11,* 139–145. http://dx.doi.org/10.1016/0887-6177(95)00006-2

Mittenberg, W., Zielinski, R., & Fichera, R. (1993). Recovery from mild head injury: A treatment manual for patients. *Psychotherapy in Private Practice*, *12,* 37–52. http://dx.doi.org/10.1300/J294v12n02_03

Novak, T. (2004). *Introduction to the Cognitive Log.* Retrieved from http://www.tbims.org/combi/coglog

Nuwer, M. (1997). Assessment of digital EEG, quantitative EEG, and EEG brain mapping: Report of the American Academy of Neurology and the American Clinical Neurophysiology Society. *Neurology*, *49,* 277–292. http://dx.doi.org/10.1212/WNL.49.1.277

Obelieniene, D., Bovim, G., Schrader, H., Surkiene, D., Mickeviàiene, D., Miseviàiene, I., & Sand, T. (1998). Headache after whiplash: A historical cohort study outside the medico-legal context. *Cephalalgia, 18,* 559–564. http://dx.doi.org/10.1046/j.1468-2982.1998.1808559.x

Obelieniene, D., Schrader, H., Bovim, G., Miseviciene, I., & Sand, T. (1999). Pain after whiplash: A prospective controlled inception cohort study. *Journal of Neurology, Neurosurgery, and Psychiatry, 66,* 279–283. http://dx.doi.org/10.1136/jnnp.66.3.279

Omalu, B. I., DeKosky, S. T., Minster, R. L., Kamboh, M. I., Hamilton, R. L., & Wecht, C. H. (2005). Chronic traumatic encephalopathy in a National Football League player. *Neurosurgery, 57,* 128–134. http://dx.doi.org/10.1227/01.NEU.0000163407.92769.ED

Panayiotou, A., Jackson, M., & Crowe, S. F. (2010). A meta-analytic review of the emotional symptoms associated with mild traumatic brain injury. *Journal of Clinical and Experimental Neuropsychology, 32,* 463–473. http://dx.doi.org/10.1080/13803390903164371

Paniak, C., Reynolds, S., Toller-Lobe, G., Melnyk, A., Nagy, J., & Schmidt, D. (2002). A longitudinal study of the relationship between financial compensation and symptoms after treated mild traumatic brain injury. *Journal of Clinical and Experimental Neuropsychology, 24,* 187–193. http://dx.doi.org/10.1076/jcen.24.2.187.999

Ponsford, J., Cameron, P., Fitzgerald, M., Grant, M., Mikocka-Walus, A., & Schönberger, M. (2012). Predictors of postconcussive symptoms 3 months after mild traumatic brain injury. *Neuropsychology, 26,* 304–313. http://dx.doi.org/10.1037/a0027888

Putnam, S. H., & Millis, S. R. (1994). Psychosocial factors in the development and maintenance of chronic somatic and functional symptoms following mild traumatic brain injury. *Advances in Medical Psychotherapy, 7,* 1–22.

Putnam, S. H., Millis, S. R., & Adams, K. M. (1996). Mild traumatic brain injury: Beyond cognitive assessment. In I. Grant & K. M. Adams (Eds.), *Neuropsychological assessment of neuropsychiatric disorders* (2nd ed., pp. 529–551). New York, NY: Oxford University Press.

Reeves, D., Kane, R., Winter, K., Raynsford, K., & Pancella, T. (1993). *Automated Neuropsychological Assessment Metrics (ANAM): Test administrator's guide. Version 1.0.* St. Louis, MO: Missouri Institute of Mental Health.

Research Advisory Committee on Gulf War Veterans' Illnesses. (2008). *Gulf War illness and the health of Gulf War veterans: Scientific findings and recommendations.* Washington, DC: U.S. Government Printing Office.

Reynolds, S., Paniak, C., Toller-Lobe, G., & Nagy, J. (2003). A longitudinal study of compensation-seeking and return to work in a treated mild traumatic brain injury sample. *Journal of Head Trauma Rehabilitation, 18,* 139–147. http://dx.doi.org/10.1097/00001199-200303000-00005

Rohling, M. L., Allen, L. M., & Green, P. (2002). Who is exaggerating cognitive impairment and who is not? *CNS Spectrums, 7,* 387–395. http://dx.doi.org/10.1017/S1092852900017843

Rohling, M. L., Binder, L. M., Demakis, G. J., Larrabee, G. J., Ploetz, D. M., & Langhinrichsen-Rohling, J. (2011). A meta-analysis of neuropsychological outcome after mild traumatic brain injury: Re-analyses and reconsiderations of Binder et al. (1997), Frencham et al. (2005), and Pertab et al. (2009). *Clinical Neuropsychologist, 25,* 608–623. http://dx.doi.org/10.1080/13854046.2011.565076

Rohling, M. L., Binder, L. M., & Langhinrichsen-Rohling, J. (1995). Money matters: A meta-analytic review of the association between financial compensation and the experience and treatment of chronic pain. *Health Psychology, 14,* 537–547. http://dx.doi.org/10.1037/0278-6133.14.6.537

Rohling, M. L., & Demakis, G. J. (2010). Bowden, Shores, & Mathias (2006): Failure to replicate or just failure to notice. Does effort still account for more variance in neuropsychological test scores than TBI severity? *Clinical Neuropsychologist, 24,* 119–136. http://dx.doi.org/10.1080/13854040903307243

Rohling, M. L., Green, P., Allen, L. M., III, & Iverson, G. L. (2002). Depressive symptoms and neurocognitive test scores in patients passing symptom validity tests. *Archives of Clinical Neuropsychology, 17,* 205–222. http://dx.doi.org/10.1093/arclin/17.3.205

Rohling, M. L., Larrabee, G. J., & Millis, S. R. (2012). The "miserable minority" following mild traumatic brain injury: Who are they and do meta-analyses hide them? *Clinical Neuropsychologist, 26,* 197–213. http://dx.doi.org/10.1080/13854046.2011.647085

Rohling, M. L., Meyers, J. E., & Millis, S. (2003). Neuropsychological impairment following traumatic brain injury: A dose-response analysis. *Clinical Neuropsychologist, 17,* 289–302. http://dx.doi.org/10.1076/clin.17.3.289.18086

Rohling, M. L., Meyers, J. E., Williams, G. R., Kalat, S. S., Williams, S. K., & Keene, J. (2015). Application of the Daubert standards to the Meyers Neuropsychological Battery using the Rohling Interpretive Method. *Psychological Injury and Law, 8,* 252–264. http://dx.doi.org/10.1007/s12207-015-9227-1

Rohling, M. L., Miller, L. S., & Langhinrichsen-Rohling, J. (2004). Rohling's interpretive method for neuropsychological data analysis: A response to critics. *Neuropsychology Review, 14,* 155–169. http://dx.doi.org/10.1023/B:NERV.0000048182.55980.4b

Roth, R. S., & Spencer, R. J. (2013). Iatrogenic risk in the management of mild traumatic brain injury among combat veterans: A case illustration and commentary. *International Journal of Physical Medicine and Rehabilitation, 1,* 2–7.

Ruff, R. M., Camenzuli, L., & Mueller, J. (1996). Miserable minority: Emotional risk factors that influence the outcome of a mild traumatic brain injury. *Brain Injury, 10,* 551–566. http://dx.doi.org/10.1080/026990596124124

Ruff, R. M., Crouch, J. A., Tröster, A. I., Marshall, L. F., Buchsbaum, M. S., Lottenberg, S., & Somers, L. M. (1994). Selected cases of poor outcome following a minor brain trauma: Comparing neuropsychological and positron emission tomography assessment. *Brain Injury, 8,* 297–308. http://dx.doi.org/10.3109/02699059409150981

Ruff, R. M., & Richardson, A. M. (1999). Mild traumatic brain injury. In J. Sweet (Ed.), *Forensic neuropsychology: Fundamentals and practice* (pp. 315–338). Amsterdam, the Netherlands: Swets & Zeitlinger.

Russell, E. W., & Starkey, R. I. (2001). *Halstead Russell Neuropsychological Evaluation System, Revised (HRNES-R).* Los Angeles, CA: Western Psychological Services.

Rutherford, W. H., Merrett, J. D., & McDonald, J. R. (1979). Symptoms at one year following concussion from minor head injuries. *Injury, 10,* 225–230. http://dx.doi.org/10.1016/0020-1383(79)90015-9

Schoenberg, M. R., Scott, J. G., Duff, K., & Adams, R. L. (2002). Estimation of WAIS-III intelligence from combined performance and demographic variables: Development of the OPIE-3. *Clinical Neuropsychologist, 16,* 426–438. http://dx.doi.org/10.1076/clin.16.4.426.13913

Schretlen, D. J., & Shapiro, A. M. (2003). A quantitative review of the effects of traumatic brain injury on cognitive functioning. *International Review of Psychiatry, 15,* 341–349. http://dx.doi.org/10.1080/09540260310001606728

Sherer, M., Struchen, M. A., Yablon, S. A., Wang, Y., & Nick, T. G. (2008). Comparison of indices of traumatic brain injury severity: Glasgow Coma Scale, length of coma and post-traumatic amnesia. *Journal of Neurology, Neurosurgery, and Psychiatry, 79,* 678–685. http://dx.doi.org/10.1136/jnnp.2006.111187

Silverberg, N. D., Wertheimer, J. C., & Fichtenberg, N. L. (2007). An effort index for the Repeatable Battery for the Assessment of Neuropsychological Status (RBANS). *Clinical Neuropsychologist, 21,* 841–854. http://dx.doi.org/10.1080/13854040600850958

Stein, S. C. (1996). Classification of head injury. In R. K. Narayan, J. T. Povishock, & J. E. Wilberger Jr. (Eds.), *Neurotrauma* (pp. 20–21). New York, NY: McGraw-Hill.

Stern, R. A., Riley, D. O., Daneshvar, D. H., Nowinski, C. J., Cantu, R. C., & McKee, A. C. (2011). Long-term consequences of repetitive brain trauma: Chronic traumatic encephalopathy. *PM&R,* 3(10, Suppl. 2), S460–S467. http://dx.doi.org/10.1016/j.pmrj.2011.08.008

Stevens, A., Friedel, E., Mehren, G., & Merten, T. (2008). Malingering and uncooperativeness in psychiatric and psychological assessment: Prevalence and effects in a German sample of claimants. *Psychiatry Research, 157,* 191–200. http://dx.doi.org/10.1016/j.psychres.2007.01.003

Stickler, L. (2007). A critical review of the SAT: Menace or mid-mannered measure? *Journal of Student Scholarship, 9*(April), 1–8.

Stovner, L. J., Schrader, H., Mickevičiene, D., Surkiene, D., & Sand, T. (2009). Headache after concussion. *European Journal of Neurology, 16,* 112–120. http://dx.doi.org/10.1111/j.1468-1331.2008.02363.x

Suhr, J., & Spickard, B. (2012). Pain-related fear is associated with cognitive task avoidance: Exploration of the cogniphobia construct in a recurrent headache sample. *Clinical Neuropsychologist, 26,* 1128–1141. http://dx.doi.org/10.1080/13854046.2012.713121

Suhr, J. A., & Gunstad, J. (2002). "Diagnosis threat": The effect of negative expectations on cognitive performance in head injury. *Journal of Clinical and Experimental Neuropsychology, 24,* 448–457. http://dx.doi.org/10.1076/jcen.24.4.448.1039

Suhr, J. A., & Gunstad, J. (2005). Further exploration of the effect of "diagnosis threat" on cognitive performance in individuals with mild head injury. *Journal of the International Neuropsychological Society, 11,* 23–29. http://dx.doi.org/10.1017/S1355617705050010

Sweet, J. J., & Meyers, D. G. (2012). Trends in forensic practice and research. In G. J. Larrabee (Ed.), *Forensic neuropsychology: A scientific approach* (2nd ed., pp. 501–516). New York, NY: Oxford University Press.

Tombaugh, T. N. (1996). *TOMM: Test of Memory Malingering.* North Tonawanda, NY: Multi-Health Systems.

Tsanadis, J., Montoya, E., Hanks, R. A., Millis, S. R., Fichtenberg, N. L., & Axelrod, B. N. (2008). Brain injury severity, litigation status, and self-report of postconcussive symptoms. *Clinical Neuropsychologist, 22,* 1080–1092. http://dx.doi.org/10.1080/13854040701796928

Uttl, B. (2002). North American Adult Reading Test: Age norms, reliability, and validity. *Journal of Clinical and Experimental Neuropsychology, 24,* 1123–1137. http://dx.doi.org/10.1076/jcen.24.8.1123.8375

Van Dyke, S. A., Millis, S. R., Axelrod, B. N., & Hanks, R. A. (2013). Assessing effort: Differentiating performance and symptom validity. *Clinical Neuropsychologist, 27,* 1234–1246. http://dx.doi.org/10.1080/13854046.2013.835447

Vickery, C. D., Berry, D. T. R., Inman, T. H., Harris, M. J., & Orey, S. A. (2001). Detection of inadequate effort on neuropsychological testing: A meta-analytic review of selected procedures. *Archives of Clinical Neuropsychology, 16,* 45–73.

Watson, D., & Pennebaker, J. W. (1989). Health complaints, stress, and distress: Exploring the central role of negative affectivity. *Psychological Review, 96,* 234–254. http://dx.doi.org/10.1037/0033-295X.96.2.234

Wechsler, D. (1987). *Manual for the Wechsler Memory Scale-Revised.* New York, NY: Psychological Corporation.

Wechsler, D. (1997a). *Manual for the Wechsler Adult Intelligence Scale* (3rd ed.). San Antonio, TX: Psychological Corporation.

Wechsler, D. (1997b). *Manual for the Wechsler Memory Scale* (3rd ed.). San Antonio, TX: Pearson.

Wechsler, D. (2001). *Wechsler Test of Adult Reading.* San Antonio, TX: Psychological Corporation Harcourt Assessment.

Wechsler, D. (2008a). *Manual for the Wechsler Adult Intelligence Scale* (4th ed.). San Antonio, TX: Pearson.

Wechsler, D. (2008b). *Manual for the Wechsler Memory Scale* (4th ed.). San Antonio, TX: Pearson.

Weiser, M., Reichenberg, A., Rabinowitz, J., Knobler, H. Y., Lubin, G., Yazvitzky, R., . . . Davidson, M. (2004). Cognitive performance of male adolescents is lower than controls across psychiatric disorders: A population-based study. *Acta Psychiatrica Scandinavica, 110,* 471–475. http://dx.doi.org/10.1111/j.1600-0447.2004.00385.x

Westerman, R., Darby, D. G., Maruff, P., & Collie, A. (2001). Computer-assisted cognitive function assessment of pilots. *ADF Health, 2*(April), 29–36.

Wilkinson, G. S., & Robertson, G. J. (2006). *Wide Range Achievement Test 4 professional manual.* Lutz, FL: Psychological Assessment Resources.

Williams, D. H., Levin, H. S., & Eisenberg, H. M. (1990). Mild head injury classification. *Neurosurgery, 27,* 422–428. http://dx.doi.org/10.1227/00006123-199009000-00014

Williams, J. M., Little, M. M., Scates, S., & Blockman, N. (1987). Memory complaints and abilities among depressed older adults. *Journal of Consulting and Clinical Psychology, 55,* 595–598. http://dx.doi.org/10.1037/0022-006X.55.4.595

CHAPTER 8

MODERATE TO SEVERE TRAUMATIC BRAIN INJURY

John H. King, Summer N. Rolin, and R. Brock Frost

According to the Centers for Disease Control and Prevention, an estimated 1.7 million people sustained a traumatic brain injury (TBI) annually from 2002 to 2006 in the United States (Faul, Xu, Wald, & Coronado, 2010). The leading causes of TBI were falls (35.2%); motor vehicle accidents and related incidents (17.3%); strikes to or against the head, other than assaults (17.3%); and assaults (10%; Faul et al., 2010). The current epidemiological study did not include injury severity characteristics (Faul et al., 2010), but a previous Centers for Disease Control and Prevention estimate from 1994 to 1995 indicated that moderate to severe injuries accounted for approximately 40% of all patients who were hospitalized with a head injury (Thurman & Guerrero, 1999).

TBI has been defined by the Demographics and Clinical Assessment Working Group of the International and Interagency Initiative toward Common Data Elements for Research on Traumatic Brain Injury and Psychological Health as "an alteration in brain function, or other evidence of brain pathology, caused by an external force" (Menon, Schwab, Wright, & Maas, 2010, p. 1637). Alteration of brain functioning is defined as follows: any period of decreased level of or loss of consciousness (LOC), any loss of memory for events immediately before the injury(retrograde amnesia) or after the injury (anterograde or posttraumatic amnesia [PTA]), neurological deficits, or any alteration in mental state at the time of the injury (Menon et al., 2010). *Other evidence of brain pathology* refers to evidence from diagnostic techniques, such as imaging or laboratory confirmation of brain damage and may also be used to diagnose a TBI, particularly in cases in which a clinical diagnosis is difficult because of a lack of injury characteristics or other confounding factors (Menon et al., 2010, p. 1638). An external force can include

> the head being struck by an object, the head striking an object, the brain undergoing an acceleration/deceleration movement without direct external trauma to the head, a foreign body penetrating the brain, forces generated from events such as blast or explosion, or other force yet to be defined. (Menon et al., 2010, p. 1638)

TBI can result in diffuse axonal injury to the brain. Diffuse axonal injury is nonfocal axonal damage secondary to acceleration or deceleration of the brain that can create cognitive and behavioral deficits proportional to injury severity (Draper & Ponsford, 2008). The effects of TBI on neuropsychological and behavioral functioning are dependent on injury severity, the age of the individual, the site of damage, premorbid personality factors, and the mechanism of injury; however, the similarities in patients' outcome effects on the basis of injury severity have been found to outweigh individual differences because of the previously mentioned factors (Lezak, Howieson, Bigler, & Tranel, 2012, chap. 7). Classification of injury severity is imperative in anticipating expected course or outcome, with TBI severity ranging from mild to severe on the basis of acute injury characteristics (Roebuck-Spencer & Cernich, 2014).

http://dx.doi.org/10.1037/0000032-008
APA Handbook of Forensic Neuropsychology, S. S. Bush (Editor-in-Chief)

INJURY CLASSIFICATION

The Glasgow Coma Scale (GCS) is used to rate the severity of TBI. It is based on a rating scale ranging from 3 to 15, reflecting the degree of altered consciousness on the basis of the patient's eye opening, motor response, and verbal response (Teasdale & Jennett, 1974). TBI severity can be rated on the basis of GCS level as mild, ranging from 13 to 15; moderate, from 9 to 12; and severe (coma), less than 8 (Lezak, Howieson, & Loring, 2004; Rimel, Giordani, Barth, & Jane, 1982). However, GCS score may not be appropriate as a predictor of injury severity for all cases, particularly in situations in which the status of other variables, such as sedation or blood alcohol level, is unknown (Lezak et al., 2004). In addition, the time at which the GCS score is obtained (e.g., at the scene of accident vs. in emergency room after sedation) can influence the determination of TBI severity (Andriessen et al., 2011). GCS score should be evaluated multiple times after injury because assessing it too early can either overestimate or underestimate injury severity, which can be affected by factors such as sedation, intoxication, and developing neurological injury (Roebuck-Spencer & Cernich, 2014). Also, the GCS score should be considered in conjunction with other factors and be used, when possible, in combination with other rating systems. PTA can be considered in conjunction with or in place of the GCS score. PTA estimates for severity of injury are as follows: very mild, less than 5 minutes; mild, 5 to 60 minutes; moderate, 1 to 24 hours; severe, 1 to 7 days; very severe, 1 to 4 weeks; and extremely severe, more than 4 weeks (Bigler, 1990).

The duration of LOC and time to follow commands are often used interchangeably to describe the period of impaired consciousness after TBI (Roebuck-Spencer & Cernich, 2014). The estimate of injury severity for LOC or time to follow commands is classified as follows: 20 minutes or less, mild; more than 20 minutes and 6 hours or less, moderate; and more than 6 hours, severe (Lezak et al., 2004). However, other rating systems have found that LOC of more than 30 minutes best describes an injury considered moderate to severe (Malec et al., 2007). Thus, there are some differences in rating systems for TBI severity. Overall, a moderate to severe TBI can be considered as having a GCS score of 12 or less, a LOC more than 30 minutes, or PTA of more than 24 hours (Malec et al., 2007). Early injury indicators are considered to be good predictors of expected course and outcome for moderate to severe TBI (Andriessen et al., 2011; Teasdale & Jennett, 1974).

Neuroimaging is also considered to be an important factor for injury classification. MRI and computed tomography (CT) scans are common neuroimaging techniques used to identify anatomical indicators of brain injury. CT scans are usually done in the earliest stages of brain injury assessment and identify lesions and bone fractures and fragments, and MRI is commonly done after CT and is sensitive to damage, sometimes even with injuries characterized as mild according to the rating systems previously described (Lezak et al., 2012). Although mild TBI rarely presents with findings on CT or MRI, the presence of positive imaging findings in otherwise mild injuries is often referred to as *complicated mild TBI* (Lezak et al., 2012).

FACTORS AFFECTING OUTCOME

Outcomes after TBI are influenced by many factors, including patient variables, injury characteristics, and postinjury factors (Lingsma et al., 2011). These factors are described in this section.

Patient Characteristics

Patient variables that have consistently been associated with outcome after moderate and severe TBI include patient demographics, socioeconomic factors, and medical comorbidities. The IMPACT database, which as of 2007 contained 9,205 patients who had sustained moderate to severe TBI, has been used to evaluate relationships among these variables and TBI outcomes (Marmarou et al., 2007).

Using the IMPACT dataset, Mushkudiani et al. (2007) demonstrated a positive and generally linear relationship between age at time of injury and unfavorable outcomes after moderate to severe TBI on the basis of the Glasgow Outcome Scale. Despite the generally linear relationship between age and outcome after TBI, this analysis also indicated a slightly increased risk of worse outcomes beginning in the fourth decade of life. Furthermore, McIntyre, Mehta, Aubut, Dijkers, and Teasell (2013) found that individuals older than age 60 years were at significantly greater risk of mortality after a moderate or severe TBI than younger individuals. For those younger than age 55, lower GCS scores are typically associated with greater morbidity and mortality (Husson, Ribbers, Willemse-van Son, Verhagen, & Stam, 2010; Timmons, Bee, Webb, Diaz-Arrastia, & Hesdorffer, 2011). However, for individuals older than age 55 years, lower GCS score was not incrementally associated with greater mortality risk, primarily because of the generalized greater risk of morbidity and mortality after moderate to severe TBI within the geriatric population, regardless of injury severity (McIntyre et al., 2013).

Another patient variable that appears to be associated with outcome after TBI is premorbid educational attainment, theoretically an indicator of cognitive reserve, with higher levels of premorbid education correlated with improved outcomes (Jeon et al., 2008; Jourdan et al., 2013; Sumowski, Chiaravalloti, Krch, Paxton, & Deluca, 2013). Higher premorbid functioning and younger age have both been found to be associated with improved recovery of functioning (R. E. Green et al., 2008). Further evidence for the role of premorbid functioning in outcome after TBI has been derived from a recent study by Rassovsky et al. (2015) that demonstrated that, at a mean of 14 years postinjury, the severity of TBI predicted cognitive, social, and daily functioning outcomes; however, after controlling for injury severity, preinjury intellectual functioning was the most powerful predictor of cognitive status, as well as occupational, social, emotional, and daily functioning.

The IMPACT study also found worse long-term outcomes for African American individuals than for Caucasians (Mushkudiani et al., 2007). The relationship between ethnicity and functional outcomes after TBI, although likely multifaceted and not easily explained, has been found in many studies, with minority groups tending to exhibit worse outcomes than Caucasians (Arango-Lasprilla et al., 2007; Bowman, Martin, Sharar, & Zimmerman, 2007; Egede, Dismuke, & Echols, 2012; Gary, Arango-Lasprilla, & Stevens, 2009; Heffernan et al., 2011). The exception is Asians, who tend to have similar outcomes as Caucasians.

Socioeconomic factors also appear to play a role in outcomes after TBI (Gary et al., 2009), with the relationship between socioeconomic factors and outcome likely mediated by access to care and resources, primarily in the chronic versus acute postinjury phase (Heffernan et al., 2011; Mauritz et al., 2008; McIntyre et al., 2013; Shafi et al., 2007). We should note that although gender has consistently been associated with risk of sustaining a TBI (Frost, Farrer, Primosch, & Hedges, 2013), it has not been associated with outcome of any severity range (i.e., mild, moderate, severe) after TBI (Husson et al., 2010; Mushkudiani et al., 2007). That is, although men are more likely than women to sustain a TBI, the outcomes for men and women are similar for TBI of any severity. Finally, preexisting (e.g., obesity, hypertension, diabetes) and comorbid medical conditions (e.g., seizure, stroke, orthopedic injury) appear to magnify the impact of TBI and increase the risk of poor outcome postinjury (Gardizi, Hanks, Millis, & Figueroa, 2014).

Injury Characteristics

The relationship between injury characteristics and outcomes after TBI has been an area of clinical and research focus for many years. Injury characteristics include injury severity, mechanism of primary injury (e.g., closed vs. penetrating), the presence or absence of structural damage or distortions of the brain, and the presence and extent of secondary insults (Lingsma, Roozenbeek, Steyerberg, Murray, & Maas, 2010).

As noted previously, injury severity has been associated with outcomes after TBI, with greater morbidity and mortality generally correlated with increasing injury severity (Husson et al., 2010; Timmons et al., 2011). Although multiple systems of rating injury severity have been developed, only the GCS, LOC, and PTA are covered here because they are the most widely used indices of injury severity. For a review of other measures (e.g., vocational independence scale, disability rating scale, differential outcomes scale) and their relation to outcomes after TBI, the reader is referred to Cappa, Conger, and Conger (2011).

The GCS is a clinical tool that was developed to standardize the clinical characterization of the "depth and duration of impaired consciousness and coma" after head injury (Teasdale & Jennett, 1974, p. 81). In addition to serving as a metric of injury severity, GCS scores have been demonstrated to predict outcome after TBI (Husson et al., 2010; Timmons et al., 2011). As one might expect, lower GCS scores (more pathological) are associated with worse outcomes, and higher GCS scores (less pathological) are associated with better outcomes. McNett's (2007) review of the literature indicated that GCS scores ranging from 3 to 4 were generally associated with poorer outcomes (moderate or worse disability, persistent vegetative state, or death), and scores ranging from 9 to 15 were generally associated with better outcomes (good recovery or moderate disability outcomes as measured by the Glasgow Outcome Scale). GCS scores ranging between, and sometimes overlapping, these two groups (i.e., 5–8) resulted in mixed findings across studies, suggesting uncertainty in outcomes for seemingly more severe injuries. These studies do not necessarily specify the exact dose–response relationship of GCS scores and morbidity, but it is clear that more severe injuries (i.e., lower GCS scores) generally confer greater risk of death and residual deficits than do less severe injuries (i.e., higher GCS scores).

Another measure, length of coma or time to follow commands (TFC), is a measure of return to conscious arousal that has been shown to predict acute outcome after TBI. TFC can be calculated by examining an individual's performance on the GCS. Specifically, a GCS motor score of 6 equates to the ability to follow commands. Many researchers also specify whether a patient can consistently follow commands, which is generally defined as two consecutive measures of intact motor functioning. In an acute sample of 496 patients who had sustained a moderate to severe TBI, TFC was significantly correlated with functional independence, basic cognitive functioning, and disability status as measured by the FIM, the Disability Rating Scale, and the Rancho Los Amigos Levels of Cognitive Functioning Scale (Whyte, Cifu, Dikmen, & Temkin, 2001). However, the value of TFC may not hold up after accounting for the predictive power of PTA. Perrin et al. (2015) analyzed the relative contribution of admission GCS, TFC, and PTA to FIM scores at discharge in 100 patients who had sustained a TBI. Using hierarchical regression, Perrin et al. found that, after controlling for demographic variables, only PTA provided a unique contribution or added to the prediction of FIM scores at hospital discharge.

In addition to acute outcomes, PTA has also been associated with long-term outcomes after moderate to severe TBI. For example, Walker et al. (2010) found that, at 1 year postinjury follow-up, PTA lasting less than 18 days was most commonly associated with good recovery, PTA lasting between 29 and 49 days was associated with moderate disability, and PTA lasting longer than 80 days was associated with severe disability. At 2-year follow-up, good recovery was associated with PTA of 26 days or less, moderate disability with PTA between 46 and 56 days, and severe disability with PTA of 97 days or longer.

Similarly, Nakase-Richardson et al. (2009) reported on a group of 280 individuals who had sustained moderate to severe TBI who were followed at 1 year postinjury. Nakase-Richardson et al. separated their sample into four groups: those with (a) PTA lasting between zero and 14 days (moderate), PTA lasting between 15 and 28 days (moderate severe), PTA lasting between 29 and 70 days (severe), and PTA lasting longer than 70 days (extremely severe). Overall, at 1-year follow-up only 33% of participants had returned to productivity such as "full- or part-time competitive employment; full- or part-time school enrollment; [and/or] homemaker status as previously defined in TBI Model System outcomes research" (p. 18). However, individuals classified as having moderate TBI showed nearly twice the likelihood of returning to productivity at 1-year follow-up than the overall sample. Furthermore, a severe classification was associated with a one third reduced likelihood of return to productivity. Additional analysis by Nakase-Richardson et al. suggested that the severe and extremely severe TBI categories could be collapsed because of similar outcomes at 1 year postinjury.

Method of brain injury (penetrating vs. closed) is also an important predictor of outcome after TBI, with penetrating injuries generally associated with worse outcomes than closed injuries (Walker et al., 2015). In a review of closed versus penetrating head injuries, Santiago, Oh, Dash, Holcomb, and Wade (2012) described the difference between blunt (closed) and penetrating head injuries:

> In blunt TBI, a concussive mechanical force is imparted to the head through direct contact with a blunt object, an inert broad surface or a rapidly expanding fluid wave. Such a force produces a rapid acceleration and/or deceleration of the head, which may result in scalp lacerations, depressed skull fractures, diffuse brain swelling and intracranial haematomas. Alternatively, penetrating TBI results when a moving projectile or a sharp inanimate object fractures the cranium, perforates the meninges, lacerates and crushes the brain parenchyma along its trajectory and exposes the cranial vault to the external environment. (p. 107)

Using the TBI model systems cohort, Walker et al. (2015) analyzed 7,183 individuals who had sustained at least a moderate TBI and found that, at 2 years postinjury, those with penetrating injuries exhibited significantly lower Glasgow Outcome Scale scores than those with closed-head injury.

Another area of focus regarding injury characteristics is the presence and extent of secondary injuries, which have been defined as "destructive and self-propagating biological changes in cells and tissues that lead to their dysfunction or death over hours to weeks after the initial insult" (Borgens & Liu-Snyder, 2012, p. 89). Secondary injuries such as the presence and extent of subsequently developing intracranial abnormalities (Mata-Mbemba et al., 2014) and complicating medical factors such as hypotension, hypoxia, and hypothermia (Chesnut et al., 1993; McHugh et al., 2007) are significant predictors of outcome after TBI. Thus, both method of injury and presence or absence of secondary injury are important factors to consider when predicting outcome after TBI.

Group-level data have suggested that greatest recovery of functioning occurs within the 1st year after TBI, with the majority of recovery from moderate to severe traumatic brain injury occurring within 2 years of injury and smaller changes observed thereafter (Dikmen, Machamer, Temkin, & McLean, 1990; Ponsford et al., 2014; Ruttan, Martin, Liu, Colella, & Green, 2008; Schretlen & Shapiro, 2003). Data regarding long-term outcomes of cognitive functioning after moderate to severe TBI are limited; however, the available data have indicated that recovery appears to be dependent on injury severity and cognitive domain of interest (Rabinowitz & Levin, 2014). For example, Finnanger et al. (2013) reported on 50 individuals who had sustained moderate to severe TBI who were neuropsychologically evaluated 3 and 12 months postinjury. At 12 months postinjury, those with moderate TBI performed significantly below matched controls only on measures of executive functioning, whereas those with severe TBI performed significantly worse than controls on motor function, processing speed, verbal memory, and executive function. Despite deficits compared with controls, those with moderate or severe injuries showed areas of significantly improved cognitive functioning from 3 to 12 months after TBI (for moderate TBI, in motor functioning, information processing speed, and visual memory; for severe TBI, in information processing speed, visual memory, and executive functioning).

Similarly, in a sample consisting of individuals who had sustained severe TBI, Sigurdardottir et al. (2015) found that 67% exhibited cognitive impairment in at least one of three domains (i.e., executive functioning, processing speed, and memory) at 1 year postinjury. Processing speed was the most common area of weakness, with 58% of individuals exhibiting deficits, and memory deficits were the next most impaired, followed by executive functioning.

Functional Outcome in Moderate to Severe Traumatic Brain Injury

Regarding functional outcomes, Ponsford et al. (2014) reported on patients' self-report of functional recovery at 2, 5, and 10 years after sustaining moderate to severe TBI. In this sample of 141 individuals, "a high proportion" reported some form of persistent cognitive deficit including memory problems, difficulty concentrating, slowed thinking, cognitive fatigue, and word-finding difficulties, as well as "problems with planning, initiative, self-centeredness, and impulsivity" (p. 68). Although most of the sample (95%) reported independence in activities of daily living, upward of 30% required assistance to complete instrumental activities of daily living, with a range between 15% and 30% depending on the specific task. At the 5-year mark, only 50% of the sample had returned to driving independently; however, by the 10-year mark 70% had reinitiated driving. Regarding employment, only a small proportion of the sample had returned to full-time employment at 2, 5, and 10 years after injury (28.4%, 17.6%, and 11.8%, respectively); however, the proportion engaging in part-time employment increased by the end of the 10-year recording period (12.8% at 2 years, 11.1% at 5 years, and 19% at 10 years). Somewhat discouragingly, only 40% of the sample returned to employment in some capacity during the study. Finally, nearly half of the sample reported reduced social functioning, including losing friends, increased social isolation, or both, despite also reporting increased need for support. This finding remained constant over time.

POSTINJURY FACTORS THAT AFFECT RECOVERY AFTER MODERATE TO SEVERE TRAUMATIC BRAIN INJURY

Postinjury factors can negatively impact or complicate recovery trajectory and expected outcome of moderate or severe TBI. Psychiatric symptoms and disorders, anosognosia (impaired awareness), and anger should be considered as factors impacting postinjury presentation and recovery.

Psychiatric Symptoms in Moderate to Severe Traumatic Brain Injury

Psychiatric distress after TBI is common. Individuals frequently experience depression, anxiety, and symptoms of posttraumatic stress disorder (PTSD) that can influence postinjury symptom presentation and recovery (Sanders, Ziegler, & Schmitter-Edgecombe, 2013). Research has supported a biological basis for TBI causing psychiatric illness, specifically major depression, bipolar disorder, and anxiety disorders (van Reekum, Cohen, & Wong, 2000). Researchers have argued that injury in critical areas of the brain can have a negative effect on neuronal and neurotransmitter systems. A dose–response relationship has been established, with increased severity of TBI associated with an increased risk of psychiatric disorder, with the exception of an inverse relationship between TBI severity and PTSD (van Reekum et al., 2000). Furthermore, premorbid psychiatric disorders have also been found to increase the risk of postinjury postconcussional symptoms in patients with TBI, even in moderate cases of TBI (Bombardier et al., 2010; McCauley, Boake, Levin, Contant, & Song, 2001).

When considering psychiatric illness, anxiety and depression are strongly associated with TBI (Griffen & Hanks, 2014; van Reekum et al., 2000); however, research has been inconclusive about the relationship between TBI severity and the development of generalized anxiety disorder (Griffen & Hanks, 2014). Rates of depression after moderate to severe TBI have been found to be 25% to 40% in outpatient populations (Rogers & Read, 2007; van Reekum et al., 2000). In one study, the strongest predictors of mood disturbance up to 3 years after moderate to severe TBI were time since injury, initial discharge destination from the hospital, and cognitive outcome (Valk-Kleibeuker, Heijenbrok-Kal, & Ribbers, 2014). Valk-Kleibeuker and colleagues (2014) found that mood scores stabilized at 18 months postinjury and continued to improve up to 2 years postinjury. The patients in this study also had better mood outcomes if they were discharged directly home from inpatient hospitalization versus discharged to rehabilitation, a nursing home, or another facility. They also had an improvement in mood as cognitive and motor recovery was achieved (Valk-Kleibeuker et al., 2014).

Depression has been found to be the psychiatric disorder most frequently diagnosed in a civilian sample after TBI (Bombardier et al., 2010). Depression after TBI can have a negative impact on functional outcomes (Bombardier et al., 2010), and depression is associated with decreased life satisfaction, family and social functioning, and vocational functioning (Clark, 2014). Effectively managing psychiatric symptoms, such as depression, after TBI has been found to improve disability status (Fann, Uomoto, & Katon, 2001). However, evaluating patients for depression after TBI is complicated by overlapping symptom presentation, with some sequelae of TBI such as "poor concentration, decreased energy, and sleep disturbance" (Clark, 2014, p. 259) similar to what would be expected in depression. Research has found that the most common symptomatology of depression presenting in moderate to severe TBI is fatigue, distractibility, anger and irritability, and rumination (Seel et al., 2003). Screening measures that account for medical comorbidities have been developed and can be used in this population (e.g., the Hospital Anxiety and Depression Scale; Whelan-Goodinson, Ponsford, & Schönberger, 2009).

Although PTSD is common in patients with TBI, it is less likely to occur in moderate to severe TBI as a result of amnesia for the traumatic event or LOC during the event (Belanger, Kretzmer, Yoash-Gantz, Pickett, & Tupler, 2009; Mayou, Bryant, & Duthie, 1993). In addition, there is little evidence to support the incidence of schizophrenia or psychosis after TBI (Griffen & Hanks, 2014; van Reekum et al., 2000).

Impaired Self-Awareness and Anger After Moderate to Severe Traumatic Brain Injury

In addition to emotional difficulties, research has indicated that patients with severe TBI struggle with behavioral difficulties, including apathy and impaired ability to perceive social cues, compared with matched controls (Milders, Fuchs, & Crawford, 2003). TBI can also result in impaired self-awareness or anosognosia (a lack of awareness of or insight into deficits; Sherer, Madison, & Hannay, 2000). Research analyzing self-awareness in patients with moderate to severe TBI and their family members indicated that both groups reported similar preinjury functioning; however, family members reported significantly greater problems than patients after TBI, suggesting that self-awareness of postinjury deficits was impaired in this patient sample (Vanderploeg, Belanger, Duchnick, & Curtiss, 2007). Furthermore, in another study of patients with moderate to severe TBI, patients exhibited moderate levels of anosognosia; however, increased time postinjury was associated with improved levels of awareness (Vanderploeg et al., 2007). Cognitively, dysexecutive functioning has been found to be correlated with anosognosia in patients with severe TBI (Bivona et al., 2008). Patients with better self-awareness of deficits have been found to have better functional outcomes after injury (Noé, Ferri, Caballero, Villode, Sanchez, & Chirivella, 2005; Sherer et al., 2003), less psychiatric symptomatology, and better performance on neuropsychological examination (Noé et al., 2005). Preliminary research has provided early support for treatment models in rehabilitation of persons with moderate to severe TBI injuries suggesting that improvement in self-awareness of deficits after treatment was achieved with intervention (Goverover, Johnston, Toglia, & Deluca, 2007).

Aggression is a common behavioral problem after TBI, with a prevalence rate of around 34% (Tateno, Jorge, & Robinson, 2003). Verbal aggression post-TBI is correlated with the onset of depression, poor social functioning, and dependency on others for activities of daily living (Rao et al., 2009). After moderate to severe TBI, aggression in patients has been found to be most correlated with depression and younger age at injury and can have a negative impact on rehabilitation (Baguley, Cooper, & Felmingham, 2006).

RECOMMENDATIONS FOR ASSESSMENT OF PERSONS WITH MODERATE TO SEVERE TRAUMATIC BRAIN INJURY

When assessing persons with moderate to severe TBI, it is important to consider injury factors, such as the presence of PTA or a state of posttraumatic confusion, which can still be present for several weeks after injury (Stuss et al., 1999). Resolution of PTA and posttraumatic confusion is important to establish before neuropsychological assessment because it can negatively affect the patient's performance. Resolution of PTA and posttraumatic confusion can be ascertained by measuring the patient's ability to demonstrate intact orientation

(Griffen & Hanks, 2014; Roebuck-Spencer & Sherer, 2008) and intact ability to form and retain new memories (Roebuck-Spencer & Sherer, 2008). Orientation can be assessed by measures such as the Orientation Log (Jackson, Novack, & Dowler, 1998) or the Galveston Orientation and Amnesia Test (Levin, O'Donnell, & Grossman, 1979), whereas the Toronto Test of Acute Recovery after TBI (Stuss et al., 1999) can assess the ability to create and retain memories (Roebuck-Spencer & Sherer, 2008).

When selecting cognitive tests, it is important to include tests that tap the domains that are most commonly impaired after moderate to severe TBI, such as attention, processing speed, learning and memory, and executive functioning (Griffen & Hanks, 2014; Roebuck-Spencer & Sherer, 2012). Moreover, measures of premorbid functioning (e.g., word reading tests) are important to establish an estimate of premorbid functioning with which to compare postinjury performance. Although they do not indicate a set neuropsychological battery of tests for moderate to severe TBI, Roebuck-Spencer and Sherer (2012) provided a list of tests used with this population in the research literature from which a battery for a given patient can be derived (see Table 8.1).

Evaluating Symptom and Performance Validity in Moderate to Severe Traumatic Brain Injury

Evaluating symptom and performance validity is an important aspect of neuropsychological test interpretation, and the assessment of validity has become standard practice (Heilbronner, Sweet, Morgan, Larrabee, & Millis, 2009; Sharland & Gfeller, 2007). This is especially true in settings in which external incentives to give suboptimal effort or negative response bias are greater, such as in situations when the examinee is litigating (Boone, 2013; Larrabee, 2012a). *Negative response bias* refers to the reporting of symptoms in excess of what the examinee is actually experiencing, with the goal of appearing more impaired. *Suboptimal effort* refers to the examinee performing poorly on tasks. Suboptimal effort has been found to have a larger impact on response bias than head injury severity (P. Green, Iverson, & Allen, 1999; P. Green, Rohling, Lees-Haley, & Allen, 2001). When test data are not consistent with the natural expected course of recovery from a moderate to severe TBI, the clinician should consider other factors contributing to incomplete effort, such as inadequate effort or negative response bias.

Diagnosing malingered neurocognitive dysfunction. Diagnosing malingering can be a difficult task because of inconsistencies in criteria used to determine malingering and the similarities between malingering and psychiatric disorders that involve invalid symptom reporting (e.g., factitious disorder) or unconscious generation of symptoms (e.g., conversion disorder). The *Diagnostic and Statistical Manual of Mental Disorders* (5th ed.; American Psychiatric Association, 2013) provides limited criteria to aid the clinician. However, Slick, Sherman, and Iverson (1999) developed specific criteria for identifying and diagnosing malingered neurocognitive dysfunction based on levels of diagnostic probability. As an example of one level, definite malingered neurocognitive dysfunction is defined only in the presence of clear exaggeration or feigning of cognitive impairment in the absence of alternative explanations, and certain criteria must be met; for example, the presence of a clear external incentive for giving incomplete effort (such as disability determination or personal injury litigation) must be present at the time of testing. In addition, definite response bias must be present as defined by Criterion B: "below chance performance on one or more forced-choice measure of cognitive functioning" (Slick et al., 1999, p. 553). Probable response bias under Criterion B is defined by poor performance on one or more symptom validity tests (SVTs) designed to measure feigning of cognitive deficits. The base rate of probable malingering or symptom exaggeration in moderate to severe TBI has been reported to be 8.82% among litigating or disability-seeking claimants in past studies (Mittenberg, Patton, Canyock, & Condit, 2002).

Performance validity. Larrabee (2012b) recommended distinguishing between invalid effort on neuropsychological ability measures and invalid responding on psychological tests. Using terminology that reflects these differences and the tests used to assess validity, such as performance validity tests

TABLE 8.1

Examples of Commonly Used Tests for Neuropsychological Assessment of Traumatic Brain Injury by Cognitive Domain

Cognitive domain	Tests used
Orientation	Galveston Orientation and Amnesia Test[a]
Attention/processing speed/flexibility	Paced Auditory Serial Addition Test[b,c]
	Digit Span[a]
	Seashore Rhythm Test[d]
	Stroop Color Word Test[d]
	Trail Making Test, Parts A[a] and B[a,b]
	Symbol Digit Modalities Test
	Digit Symbol[b]
Memory	Rey Complex Figure Test[b]
	Selective Reminding Test[b,d]
	Rey Auditory Verbal Learning Test[a]
	WMS–Logical Memory Test[a,d]
	WMS–Visual Reproduction[d]
	California Verbal Learning Test[c]
Language	Controlled Oral Word Association Test[a,b]
	Token Test[a]
	WAIS–VIQ[d]
Visuospatial skills	Benton Visual Form Discrimination Test[a]
	Block Design Test[a]
	WAIS–PIQ[d]
	Tactile Performance Test[d]
Problem solving/reasoning	Wisconsin Card Sorting Test[a,b]
	Category Test[d]
Motor	Grooved Peg Board Test[a,b]
	Finger Tapping Test[d]
	Namewriting[d]
Behavior	Neurobehavioral Rating Scale[b]
	Neurobehavioral Functioning Inventory[a]

Note. PIQ = Performance IQ; VIQ = Verbal IQ; WAIS = Wechsler Adult Intelligence Scale; WMS = Wechsler Memory Scale. Descriptions of these tests can be found in reference volumes on neuropsychological assessment such as Lezak, Howieson, Bigler, and Tranel (2012) and Spreen and Strauss (1998). From *Forensic Neuropsychology: A Scientific Approach* (2nd ed., p. 267), by G. J. Larrabee (Ed.), 2012, New York, NY: Oxford University Press. Copyright 2012 by Oxford University Press, USA. Reprinted with permission.

[a]Clifton, Hayes, Levin, Michel, and Choi (1992). [b]Traumatic Brain Injury Model Systems National Data Center (1999). [c]Dikmen, Machamer, Winn, and Temkin (1995). [d]Dikmen, Machamer, Powell, and Temkin (2003).

(PVTs) and symptom validity tests, provides clarification when conceptualizing and discussing these issues.

It is both probable and expected that examinees presenting with a history of moderate to severe TBI may have cognitive deficits. Therefore, a false positive error, which refers to the incorrect classification of an examinee with cognitive impairment as exerting poor effort, can occur in the context of moderate to severe TBI because these individuals may have severe cognitive impairment. Therefore, it is important to use PVTs and SVTs that have good classification accuracy and comparisons to similar known groups. PVTs have been designed and validated to maximize specificity and minimize potential false-positive errors to avoid misclassification that can occur among individuals with actual impairment (Heilbronner et al., 2009; Larrabee, 2008).

Research has also suggested that requiring multiple indicators of poor effort lowers the chances of false-positive identification errors in the assessment of performance validity (Greve, Binder, & Bianchini, 2009; Larrabee, 2003, 2008). Larrabee (2003) found that using multiple measures of performance validity improved sensitivity while retaining specificity in a sample with moderate to severe TBI and that using failure on two PVTs or SVTs resulted in a sensitivity of 87.5% and a specificity of 88.9%. Several studies have demonstrated that greater specificity can be achieved with the use of multiple PVTs (Boone & Lu, 2003; Larrabee, 2012a; Vickery et al., 2004; Victor, Boone, Serpa, Buehler, & Ziegler, 2009).

PVTs include a number of measures developed through binomial probability theory that use a forced-choice paradigm. Therefore, if a person performs significantly below chance, it is assumed that he or she must have known the correct answer in order to choose the incorrect one at such an improbable rate. However, significantly below-chance performance is not needed for PVTs that use this paradigm to provide very valuable information regarding effort.

In the supplement to the Computerized Assessment of Response Bias '97 (CARB; Conder, Allen, & Cox, 1992) and Word Memory Test (WMT; P. Green, 2003) manuals, P. Green and Allen (1999) presented normative data for each measure for patients with moderate or severe TBI. In the original sample of 62 participants with severe TBI and 41 participants with moderate TBI, all means and standard deviations for both PVTs were well above the cutoffs. For the WMT, the mean Immediate Recognition score was 95.48 ($SD = 5.05$), the Delayed Recognition mean score was 96.14 ($SD = 3.93$), and the Consistency mean score was 92.76 ($SD = 6.42$). The results from this study indicated that these WMT variables were not related to head injury severity. On the CARB, the overall mean score was 98.32 ($SD = 2.61$).

An additional study (P. Green, Lees-Haley, & Allen, 2003) examined the WMT and CARB in a sample of litigating TBI patients divided into mild and moderate to severe groups. The authors found that compared with patients with mild TBI, those with more severe TBI (moderate to severe) had higher scores on the WMT and CARB, suggesting that injury severity differences between the groups did not account for performance, but effort did. Furthermore, P. Green et al. (2003) found that, similar to previous findings, performance on the WMT was not correlated with variables such as the patients' GCS score, PTA, or LOC. Thus, the WMT has been found to be insensitive to actual cognitive impairment in all but the most impaired samples with moderate to severe TBI (P. Green et al., 1999, 2003).

In populations of patients with severe impairment who fail the commonly used WMT or Medical Symptom Validity Test (MSVT) performance validity variables, the Genuine Memory Impairment Profile—a variable consisting of the pattern of results on certain subtests that is not present in simulation groups—can be considered. Research has established the Genuine Memory Impairment Profile as a measure of true cognitive ability rather than effort, and it has exhibited good specificity (P. Green, 2004, 2008; M. Henry, Merten, Wolf, & Harth, 2010; Singhal, Green, Ashaye, Shankar, & Gill, 2009). Studies that have included the Genuine Memory Impairment Profile have found a 5% false-positive rate in samples with dementia (Howe, Anderson, Kaufman, Sachs, & Loring, 2007; Howe & Loring, 2009) and 98.4% specificity for the WMT and the MSVT (P. Green, Montijo, & Brockhaus, 2011). These results suggest that, even in the presence of more severe types of impairment, these PVTs can distinguish poor effort from genuine impairment with relatively few false positives.

The Test of Memory Malingering (TOMM) has also been found to be insensitive to severity of TBI in all but the most severely impaired persons in numerous research studies (P. Green, 2011; Greve, Bianchini, & Doane, 2006; Locke, Smigielski, Powell, & Stevens, 2008). Patients should score at or above 45 on Trial 2 and the optional retention trial, if used, unless they have serious neurological impairment (Teichner & Wagner, 2004; Tombaugh, 1996, 1997). Greve, Bianchini, and Doane (2006) found that only 6% of a sample with moderate to severe TBI who were classified as having no evidence of malingering on other PVTs failed to achieve a score of 45 or above below on Trial 2 and only 9% failed to achieve that score on the retention trial. They found that, overall, in a sample consisting of individuals with mild TBI, moderate to severe TBI, or memory disorders, the TOMM had a sensitivity of 45% with 95% specificity overall in detecting malingered neurocognitive dysfunction (MND).

P. Green (2011) examined the TOMM and the Nonverbal Medical Symptom Validity Test (NV-MSVT; P. Green, 2008) in litigating patients, including both mild TBI and moderate to severe TBI groups. The moderate to severe TBI group exhibited no failures on the TOMM or the NV-MSVT; in contrast, 10% of the mild TBI group failed the TOMM and 26% failed the NV-MSVT, indicating that injury severity did not affect performance in this sample (P. Green, 2011).

On the Victoria Symptom Validity Test (Slick, Hopp, Strauss, & Thompson, 1997), a score of less than or equal to 7 on either the easy or the hard items or an overall score of less than or equal to 17 is considered invalid and possibly reflective of malingering (Slick et al., 1997). Research has suggested that the Victoria Symptom Validity Test is relatively insensitive to the presence of cognitive impairment (Grote et al., 2000; Slick et al., 2003), and on the basis of research with clinical populations, a score between 16 and 20 correct on the easy or hard items is considered questionable, with a score of 8 to 15 considered probable poor effort (Grote et al., 2000).

The Portland Digit Recognition Test (PDRT; Binder & Willis, 1991) has also been evaluated in TBI populations, and patients with brain damage without financial incentive were found to perform above cutoff scores of 19 correct for the first 36 easy items, 18 correct for the final 36 hard items, and 39 total items correct with 100% specificity. The PDRT has been found to be insensitive to brain damage severity (Binder, 1993), and Binder and Kelly (1996) recommended a more conservative full-scale cutoff score of 46 correct in TBI populations.

Given the PDRT's long administration time (40 minutes), an abbreviated form was developed (Binder, 1993), which includes the first 36 easy items, but only nine of the hard items. A cut score of 19 correct easy items and six (seven, conservatively) of the hard items is recommended, and people failing these criteria are recommended to complete the full 36 hard items (Binder, 1993). Research has supported the use of the abbreviated PDRT in simulation and TBI samples as being as efficacious as the full PDRT (Gunstad & Suhr, 2001, 2004), with use of the aforementioned cutoffs. Gunstad and Suhr (2004) examined the use of the full and abbreviated PDRT in a sample with moderate to severe TBI and, using the abbreviated form, found a conservative cut score of 19 easy and seven hard items produced no false positives. Using a full-scale cutoff of 39 also produced no false positives in the moderate to severe TBI group; however, using a more conservative overall cut off score of 46 produced one false-positive error (Gunstad & Suhr, 2004). Greve and Bianchini (2006) did not find significant differences in the PDRT false-positive error rates in patients with moderate to severe TBI compared with patients with mild TBI, and the specificity of the PDRT was 90% or better, even with less conservative cut scores.

Moore and Donders (2004) evaluated the California Verbal Learning Test—Second Edition (CVLT–II; Delis, Kramer, Kaplan, & Ober, 2000) forced-choice recognition trial and TOMM utility in evaluating performance validity in a mixed TBI sample that included a group with moderate to severe TBI. The forced-choice cutoff recommended by the manual (less than 15 out of 16) was used. Strong agreement was found between the TOMM and the CVLT–II forced-choice trial in detecting invalid performance, with high positive predictive power (95%), and financial and compensation seeking were found to be associated with suboptimal performance.

The Reliable Digit Span (RDS; Greiffenstein, Baker, & Gola, 1994) is an embedded measure originally developed using the Digit Span subtest of the Wechsler Adult Intelligence Scale—Third Edition (Wechsler, 1997) and has been updated for use with the Wechsler Adult Intelligence Scale—Fourth Edition (Wechsler, 2008). Holdnack and Drozdick (2009) included a TBI sample in their RDS study and reported that a cutoff of less than or equal to 6 occurred in 15% or less of their clinical sample. However, specificity was reported to be lower than 90% with a high false-positive rate. A cross-validation study conducted with the RDS found that using a cut score of 6 or less yielded a specificity of 99% across studies with a sample with moderate to severe TBI, but sensitivity rates were low (26%; Schroeder, Twumasi-Ankrah, Baade, & Marshall, 2012).

Reese, Suhr, and Riddle (2012) assessed the predictive accuracy of the RDS derived from the Wechsler Adult Intelligence Scale—Fourth Edition, comparing a simulated impairment group and mild head injury group. They developed an alternate RDS score, calculated by replacing the sum of the length of the number of digits in the longest span correctly recalled on both trials of an item for Digit Span Backward and Digit Span Sequencing, and an enhanced RDS score, which was calculated using the length from the traditional Digit Span Forward and Backward score, combined with the length of Sequencing (Reese et al., 2012). The traditional RDS was found to have a sensitivity of 43% and a specificity of 98% in a TBI group using a cut score of 6, the enhanced RDS had a sensitivity of 59% and a specificity of 94% using a cut score of 11, and the alternate RDS had a sensitivity of 52% and a specificity of 94% using a cut score of 8. The researchers found that the enhanced RDS had the best predictive accuracy compared with the other forms (Reese et al., 2012).

Research analyzing the concordance and predictive accuracy of using multiple PVTs in a group with moderate to severe TBI found the TOMM, MSVT, and CVLT–II forced choice had almost equal discrimination ability individually between patients with moderate to severe TBI and simulators, but the best predictive accuracy was attained by using either the TOMM and CVLT–II forced choice or the MSVT and CVLT–II Forced Choice in conjunction (Bashem et al., 2014).

Research evidence has also supported the utility of embedded indices within screening measures, such as the Repeatable Battery for the Assessment of Neuropsychological Status (RBANS; Randolph, 1998) in detecting effort in TBI samples. Silverberg, Wertheimer, and Fichtenberg (2007) developed the Effort Index using the sum of weighted scores on the Digit Span and List Recognition subtests in the RBANS in a cognitively impaired sample with mixed neurological disorder. When comparing a TBI group with complicated mild to moderate injuries with groups simulating malingering and a clinical malingering group, the researchers identified good specificity (81.3%) and sensitivity (clinical malingering = 66.7%; coached simulating malingering = 75%) using a conservative cut score of 1 (Silverberg et al., 2007). Although no subsequent studies have evaluated the RBANS Effort Index in groups with moderate to severe TBI, research examining the Effort Index's classification accuracy in a known-groups sample with mild TBI and concussion found modest sensitivity (ranging from 53% to 62%) and good specificity (ranging from 92% to 96%) using a cut score greater than or equal to 1 (Armistead-Jehle & Hansen, 2011).

A criticism of the RBANS Effort Index is that it has poor utility in populations with true amnestic disorders. In response to this criticism, the RBANS Effort Scale, which takes into consideration the List Recognition, List Recall, Story Recall, Figure Recall, and Digit Span subtests, was created (Novitski, Steele, Karantzoulis, & Randolph, 2012). Researchers found that the Effort Scale had better sensitivity and specificity than the Effort Index in a group with amnestic mild cognitive impairment and probable Alzheimer's disease (Novitski et al., 2012). However, the Effort Scale has not been evaluated in samples with moderate to severe TBI.

Symptom validity. Well-validated SVTs can be used to determine response or symptom reporting bias. Although there are many examples of SVTs, this chapter focuses on the Minnesota Multiphasic Personality Inventory—2 (MMPI–2; Butcher et al., 2001) and the MMPI–2 Restructured Form (MMPI–2–RF; Ben-Porath & Tellegen, 2008). The MMPI–2 is often cited as the psychological test most often administered as part of a forensic evaluation (Archer, Buffington-Vollum, Stredny, & Handel, 2006; Rabin, Barr, & Burton, 2005).

The MMPI–2 is a self-report personality inventory with multiple validity scales, and it is the SVT most studied with TBI populations (Sweet, Goldman, & Guidotti Breting, 2013). Youngjohn, Davis, and Wolf (1997) observed a paradoxical head injury severity effect when they examined MMPI–2 scale elevations in a TBI sample of both litigants and nonlitigants. They found that the highest clinical scale elevations in the TBI sample occurred in the litigating mild TBI group compared with litigating moderate and severe TBI groups. Furthermore, they found that the lowest incidence of clinical scale elevation occurred in the severe TBI group that was not actively involved in litigation, with the litigating group producing significant elevations on the Hypochondriasis, Hysteria, Schizophrenia, and Health Concerns scales. They also found an inverse relationship between head injury severity and symptom reporting in individuals who were litigating; thus, litigation status, rather than cognitive impairment, was concluded to have affected the manner of responding.

Several subsequent studies found an inverse relationship with MMPI–2 scale elevation and TBI severity when comparing mild TBI groups with moderate to severe TBI groups, suggesting that those with moderate to severe TBI were less likely to have elevations on these scales (P. Green et al., 1999, 2001). Using the Slick et al. (1999) criteria for MND, Greve, Bianchini, Love, Brennan, and Heinly (2006) examined the classification accuracy of the MMPI–2 validity scales in a sample of patients with TBI of mixed severity and found that they had good specificity and sensitivity with regard to the moderate to severe TBI group. The Infrequency, Back Infrequency, and Fake Bad Scale (FBS) had the highest sensitivity in detecting overreporting of psychiatric symptoms in the moderate to severe TBI group compared with the mild TBI group (Greve, Bianchini, et al., 2006).

The FBS, which was developed to identify symptom validity by using items that are correlated with exaggeration of postinjury emotional distress, has shown to be sensitive to litigation status and nonconforming symptom course in TBI litigants. However, it has also been found to correlate with medically documented abnormal neurological signs in patients with moderate to severe TBI. Therefore, for patients with moderate to severe TBI, a more conservative cut score of 24 or higher has been suggested (Greiffenstein, Baker, Gola, Donders, & Miller, 2002).

The MMPI–2–RF is a revised version of the MMPI–2 (Ben-Porath & Tellegen, 2008). The MMPI–2–RF's validity–overreporting scales are Infrequent Responses (F-r), Infrequent Psychopathology (Fp-r), Infrequent Somatic Responses, Symptom Validity (FBS-r), and Response Bias Scale (RBS). The MMPI–2–RF also includes scales designed to assess somatic or cognitive complaints, the Malaise (MLS), Gastrointestinal Complaints, Head Pain Complaints, Neurological Complaints, and Cognitive Complaints scales (Ben-Porath & Tellegen, 2008, 2011). Schroeder, Baade, et al. (2012) examined the frequencies, sensitivity rates, and specificity rates for the MMPI–2–RF validity scales using a sample of clinical groups: (a) patients with TBI who were litigating (19% with moderate to severe TBI) and met criteria for probable malingering (Slick et al., 1999), (b) a litigating TBI group who passed malingering criteria (19% with moderate to severe TBI), (c) a nonlitigating mixed neuropsychological outpatient group who passed malingering criteria, and (d) an epileptic seizure disorder inpatient group. Specificity rates were set at 90% across all nonmalingering clinical groups, and various cut scores were identified for the scales: F-r, $T > 88$; Fp-r, $T > 68$; Fs, $T > 83$; FBS-r, $T > 89$; and RBS, $T > 92$. Using this same specificity rate, F-r had a sensitivity of 38%; Fp-r, 14%; Fs, 43%; FBS-r, 48%; and RBS, 43% in identifying litigating TBI patients who met criteria for probable malingering (Schroeder, Baade, et al., 2012).

Dionysus, Denney, and Halfaker (2011) found that the RBS; Henry–Heilbronner Index, which was developed to be sensitive to pseudosomatic factors (G. K. Henry, Heilbronner, Mittenberg, & Enders, 2006); and the FBS were able to predict probable negative response bias. Bias was ascertained using performance on several performance validity indicators in a sample of litigants with head injuries of varying severity, including moderate to severe injuries, using optimal cutoff scores of higher than 25 for the FBS, higher than 14 for the RBS, and higher than 12 for the Henry–Heilbronner Index. FBS and RBS were found to have excellent discrimination ability in the TBI sample (Dionysus et al., 2011).

The Somatic–Cognitive scales, which according to the manual should be interpreted in conjunction with the Fs and FBS-r scales, indicate, when significantly elevated, that the test taker may have overreported somatic and cognitive symptoms (Ben-Porath & Tellegen, 2008). These scales consist of the MLS scale, which is designed to assess the overall sense of physical debilitation and health; the Gastrointestinal Complaints scale, which assesses symptoms such as nausea, recurring stomach upset, and poor appetite; the Head Pain Complaints scale, which focuses on pain of the head and neck; and the Neurological Complaints scale, which focuses on symptoms of dizziness, weakness, paralysis, and loss of balance (Ben-Porath & Tellegen, 2008).

The Somatic–Cognitive scales have exhibited some utility in predicting effort test failure in TBI samples. Youngjohn, Wershba, Stevenson, Sturgeon, and Thomas (2011) examined the utility of the MMPI–2–RF validity and Somatic–Cognitive scales in detecting suboptimal performance in a sample of litigating mild and moderate to severe TBI groups. MLS was found to have the largest effect size in predicting performance on PVTs compared with the other Somatic–Cognitive scales and with the F-r, Fs, FBS-r, Fp-r, Adjustment Validity, and Uncommon Virtues validity scales (Youngjohn et al., 2011). Of the MMPI–2–RF validity scales and the Somatic–Cognitive scales, MLS was found to be the single best predictor of PVT failure; the MLS had a mean *T* score of 63.36 ($SD = 14.98$) in the moderate to severe TBI group. The Head Pain Complaints scale was found to have an inverse relationship with head injury severity, and all five Somatic–Cognitive scales as a group were better predictors of PVT failure than the MMPI–2–RF validity scales (F-r, Fs, FBS-r, Fp-r, Adjustment Validity, and Uncommon Virtues).

Overall, research has supported the use of the MMPI–2 and MMPI–2–RF as SVTs with persons who have a history of moderate to severe TBI because their validity scales have been found to be relatively insensitive to injury severity in TBI populations (P. Green et al., 1999, 2001; Schroeder, Baade, et al., 2012; Youngjohn et al., 1997, 2011).

Case Studies Examining Performance Validity and Moderate to Severe TBI

Research in the area of malingering and brain injury has largely focused on mild TBI, and there is a dearth of research that has examined cases of moderate to severe TBI. An important consideration in assessing performance validity in mild TBI versus moderate to severe cases is the expected course and outcome. Whereas mild uncomplicated injuries are expected to largely resolve (Dikmen, Machamer, & Temkin, 2001; Draper & Ponsford, 2008; Iverson, 2005; McCrea, 2008), moderate to severe injuries would be expected to result in continued deficits (Griffen & Hanks, 2014; Roebuck-Spencer & Sherer, 2012), which have been found as many as 10 years postinjury (Draper & Ponsford, 2008). Patients with a history of mild TBI have a much greater likelihood of malingering than those with moderate to severe TBI (Sweet et al. 2013); however, patients with moderate to severe injuries have also been known to provide suboptimal effort for a variety of reasons (Bianchini, Greve, & Love, 2003; Boone & Lu, 2003; Paniak, 2009). Bianchini et al. (2003) first provided evidence that definite MND can occur in the presence of moderate to severe TBI. They defined definite MND in terms of the Slick et al. (1999) criteria. All three cases documented met the criteria for moderate to severe injury, were evaluated more than a year after injury, and were actively involved in litigation (Bianchini et al., 2003). However, all three patients performed well below chance on forced-choice PVTs, and despite having injuries that were severe enough to have expected cognitive deficits, their actual deficits could not be accurately ascertained by neuropsychological data because of symptom exaggeration (Bianchini et al., 2003).

Paniak (2009) documented a patient with moderate to severe TBI who produced evidence of probable malingering in the context of litigation while also having persistent neurologically based cognitive deficits. The patient initially produced invalid scores on performance validity indicators during litigation. However, on a follow-up assessment, when the patient had incentive to do well on testing to determine his capacity to manage his own financial affairs, he passed all PVTs. It was determined that he no longer met criteria for probable MND, although his neuropsychological test results were indicative of actual cognitive deficits (Paniak, 2009). This case detailed the crux of evaluating performance validity in patients with moderate to severe TBI; the patient can exaggerate cognitive deficits in the context of having both expected and actual deficits (Paniak, 2009). This situation illustrates the importance of using appropriate validity measures that are insensitive to injury severity in this population. Using PVTs and SVTs is crucial in detailing incidences of suboptimal performance and valid responding, even in the context of patients presenting with probable neuropsychological deficits that occur in moderate to severe TBI.

CONCLUSION

TBI is a relatively common injury in which the brain undergoes an alteration of normal functioning as the result of an external force. TBI severity ranges from mild to severe depending on injury characteristics, with increasingly severe injuries associated with worse outcomes. A variety of preinjury (e.g., age at time of injury, premorbid functioning, access to care) and postinjury (e.g., psychiatric distress, impaired self-awareness, behavioral dyscontrol) variables need to be taken into account when considering expected outcomes. Neuropsychological evaluation after TBI should encompass all cognitive domains, including orientation, attention and concentration, processing speed, working memory, language functioning, learning and memory, visuospatial skills, executive functioning, and motor integrity, as well as performance validity and estimated preinjury functioning. Furthermore, mood and personality functioning, including symptom validity testing, should also be standard elements of neuropsychological evaluation after TBI.

References

American Psychiatric Association. (2013). *Diagnostic and statistical manual of mental disorders* (5th ed.). Washington, DC: Author.

Andriessen, T. M., Horn, J., Franschman, G., van der Naalt, J., Haitsma, I., Jacobs, B., . . . Vos, P. E. (2011). Epidemiology, severity classification, and outcome of moderate and severe traumatic brain injury: A prospective multicenter study. *Journal of Neurotrauma, 28,* 2019–2031. http://dx.doi.org/10.1089/neu.2011.2034

Arango-Lasprilla, J. C., Rosenthal, M., Deluca, J., Komaroff, E., Sherer, M., Cifu, D., & Hanks, R. (2007). Traumatic brain injury and functional outcomes: Does minority status matter? *Brain Injury, 21,* 701–708. http://dx.doi.org/10.1080/02699050701481597

Archer, R. P., Buffington-Vollum, J. K., Stredny, R. V., & Handel, R. W. (2006). A survey of psychological test use patterns among forensic psychologists. *Journal of Personality Assessment, 87,* 84–94. http://dx.doi.org/10.1207/s15327752jpa8701_07

Armistead-Jehle, P., & Hansen, C. L. (2011). Comparison of the Repeatable Battery for the Assessment of Neuropsychological Status Effort Index and standalone symptom validity tests in a military sample. *Archives of Clinical Neuropsychology, 26,* 592–601. http://dx.doi.org/10.1093/arclin/acr049

Baguley, I. J., Cooper, J., & Felmingham, K. (2006). Aggressive behavior following traumatic brain injury: How common is common? *Journal of Head Trauma Rehabilitation, 21,* 45–56. http://dx.doi.org/10.1097/00001199-200601000-00005

Bashem, J. R., Rapport, L. J., Miller, J. B., Hanks, R. A., Axelrod, B. N., & Millis, S. R. (2014). Comparisons of five performance validity indices in bona fide and simulated traumatic brain injury. *Clinical Neuropsychologist, 28,* 851–875. http://dx.doi.org/10.1080/13854046.2014.927927

Belanger, H. G., Kretzmer, T., Yoash-Gantz, R., Pickett, T., & Tupler, L. A. (2009). Cognitive sequelae of blast-related versus other mechanisms of brain trauma. *Journal of the International Neuropsychological Society, 15,* 1–8. http://dx.doi.org/10.1017/S1355617708090036

Ben-Porath, Y. S., & Tellegen, A. (2008). *MMPI–2–RF: Manual for administration, scoring, and interpretation.* Minneapolis: University of Minnesota Press.

Ben-Porath, Y. S., & Tellegen, A. (2011). *MMPI–2–RF manual for administration, scoring, and interpretation: Response Bias Scale supplement.* Minneapolis: University of Minnesota Press.

Bianchini, K. J., Greve, K. W., & Love, J. M. (2003). Definite malingered neurocognitive dysfunction in moderate/severe traumatic brain injury. *Clinical Neuropsychologist, 17,* 574–580. http://dx.doi.org/10.1076/clin.17.4.574.27946

Bigler, E. D. (1990). Neuropathology of traumatic brain injury. In E. D. Bigler (Ed.), *Traumatic brain injury* (pp. 13–49). Austin, TX: Pro-Ed.

Binder, L. M. (1993). Assessment of malingering after mild head trauma with the Portland Digit Recognition Test. *Journal of Clinical and Experimental Neuropsychology, 15,* 170–182. http://dx.doi.org/10.1080/01688639308402555

Binder, L. M., & Kelly, M. (1996). Portland Digit Recognition Test performance by brain dysfunction patients without financial incentives. *Assessment, 3,* 403–409.

Binder, L. M., & Willis, S. C. (1991). Assessment of motivation after financially compensable minor head trauma. *Psychological Assessment*, *3*, 175–181. http://dx.doi.org/10.1037/1040-3590.3.2.175

Bivona, U., Ciurli, P., Barba, C., Onder, G., Azicnuda, E., Silvestro, D., . . . Formisano, R. (2008). Executive function and metacognitive self-awareness after severe traumatic brain injury. *Journal of the International Neuropsychological Society*, *14*, 862–868. http://dx.doi.org/10.1017/S1355617708081125

Bombardier, C. H., Fann, J. R., Temkin, N. R., Esselman, P. C., Barber, J., & Dikmen, S. S. (2010). Rates of major depressive disorder and clinical outcomes following traumatic brain injury. *JAMA*, *303*, 1938–1945. http://dx.doi.org/10.1001/jama.2010.599

Boone, K. B. (2013). *Clinical practice of forensic neuropsychology: An evidence based approach*. New York, NY: Guilford Press.

Boone, K. B., & Lu, P. (2003). Noncredible cognitive performance in the context of severe brain injury. *Clinical Neuropsychologist*, *17*, 244–254. http://dx.doi.org/10.1076/clin.17.2.244.16497

Borgens, R. B., & Liu-Snyder, P. (2012). Understanding secondary injury. *Quarterly Review of Biology*, *87*, 89–127. http://dx.doi.org/10.1086/665457

Bowman, S. M., Martin, D. P., Sharar, S. R., & Zimmerman, F. J. (2007). Racial disparities in outcomes of persons with moderate to severe traumatic brain injury. *Medical Care*, *45*, 686–690. http://dx.doi.org/10.1097/MLR.0b013e31803dcdf3

Butcher, J. N., Graham, J. R., Ben-Porath, Y. S., Tellegen, A., Dahlstrom, W. G., & Kaemmer, B. (2001). *MMPI–2: Manual for administration and scoring* (Rev. ed.). Minneapolis: University of Minnesota Press.

Cappa, K. A., Conger, J. C., & Conger, A. J. (2011). Injury severity and outcome: A meta-analysis of prospective studies on TBI outcome. *Health Psychology*, *30*, 542–560. http://dx.doi.org/10.1037/a0025220

Chesnut, R. M., Marshall, L. F., Klauber, M. R., Blunt, B. A., Baldwin, N., Eisenberg, H. M., . . . Foulkes, M. A. (1993). The role of secondary brain injury in determining outcome from severe head injury. *Journal of Trauma*, *34*, 216–222. http://dx.doi.org/10.1097/00005373-199302000-00006

Clark, A. N. (2014). Emotional distress following traumatic brain injury. In M. Sherer & A. M. Sander (Eds.), *Handbook on the neuropsychology of traumatic brain injury* (pp. 257–269). http://dx.doi.org/10.1007/978-1-4939-0784-7_13

Clifton, G. L., Hayes, R. L., Levin, H. S., Michel, M. E., & Choi, S. C. (1992). Outcome measures for clinical trials involving traumatically brain injured patients: Report of a conference. *Neurosurgery*, *31*, 975–978. http://dx.doi.org/10.1227/00006123-199211000-00028

Conder, R., Allen, L., & Cox, D. (1992). *Computerized Assessment of Response Bias test manual*. Durham, NC: Cognisyst.

Delis, D. C., Kramer, J. H., Kaplan, E., & Ober, B. A. (2000). *CVLT–II: California Verbal Learning Test: Adult version*. San Antonio, TX: Psychological Corporation.

Dikmen, S., Machamer, J., & Temkin, N. (2001). Mild head injury: Facts and artifacts. *Journal of Clinical and Experimental Neuropsychology*, *23*, 729–738. http://dx.doi.org/10.1076/jcen.23.6.729.1019

Dikmen, S., Machamer, J., Temkin, N., & McLean, A. (1990). Neuropsychological recovery in patients with moderate to severe head injury: 2 year follow-up. *Journal of Clinical and Experimental Neuropsychology*, *12*, 507–519. http://dx.doi.org/10.1080/01688639008400997

Dikmen, S. S., Machamer, J. E., Powell, J. M., & Temkin, N. R. (2003). Outcome 3 to 5 years after moderate to severe traumatic brain injury. *Archives of Physical Medicine and Rehabilitation*, *84*, 1449–1457. http://dx.doi.org/10.1016/S0003-9993(03)00287-9

Dikmen, S. S., Machamer, J. E., Winn, H. R., & Temkin, N. R. (1995). Neuropsychological outcome at 1-year post head injury. *Neuropsychology*, *9*, 80–90. http://dx.doi.org/10.1037/0894-4105.9.1.80

Dionysus, K. E., Denney, R. L., & Halfaker, D. A. (2011). Detecting negative response bias with the Fake Bad Scale, Response Bias Scale, and Henry–Heilbronner Index of the Minnesota Multiphasic Personality Inventory—2. *Archives of Clinical Neuropsychology*, *26*, 81–88. http://dx.doi.org/10.1093/arclin/acq096

Draper, K., & Ponsford, J. (2008). Cognitive functioning ten years following traumatic brain injury and rehabilitation. *Neuropsychology*, *22*, 618–625. http://dx.doi.org/10.1037/0894-4105.22.5.618

Egede, L. E., Dismuke, C., & Echols, C. (2012). Racial/ethnic disparities in mortality risk among U.S. veterans with traumatic brain injury. *American Journal of Public Health*, *102*(Suppl. 2), S266–S271. http://dx.doi.org/10.2105/AJPH.2011.300176

Fann, J. R., Uomoto, J. M., & Katon, W. J. (2001). Cognitive improvement with treatment of depression following mild traumatic brain injury. *Psychosomatics*, *42*, 48–54. http://dx.doi.org/10.1176/appi.psy.42.1.48

Faul, M., Xu, L., Wald, M. M., & Coronado, V. (2010). *Traumatic brain injury in the United States: Emergency department visits, hospitalizations, and deaths, 2002–2006*. Atlanta, GA: Centers for Disease Control and Prevention, National Center for Injury Prevention and Control.

Finnanger, T. G., Skandsen, T., Andersson, S., Lydersen, S., Vik, A., & Indredavik, M. (2013). Differentiated patterns of cognitive impairment 12 months after severe and moderate traumatic brain injury. *Brain Injury, 27,* 1606–1616. http://dx.doi.org/10.3109/02699052.2013.831127

Frost, R. B., Farrer, T. J., Primosch, M., & Hedges, D. W. (2013). Prevalence of traumatic brain injury in the general adult population: A meta-analysis. *Neuroepidemiology, 40,* 154–159. http://dx.doi.org/10.1159/000343275

Gardizi, E., Hanks, R. A., Millis, S. R., & Figueroa, M. J. (2014). Comorbidity and insurance as predictors of disability after traumatic brain injury. *Archives of Physical Medicine and Rehabilitation, 95,* 2396–2401. http://dx.doi.org/10.1016/j.apmr.2014.06.004

Gary, K. W., Arango-Lasprilla, J. C., & Stevens, L. F. (2009). Do racial/ethnic differences exist in post-injury outcomes after TBI? A comprehensive review of the literature. *Brain Injury, 23,* 775–789. http://dx.doi.org/10.1080/02699050903200563

Goverover, Y., Johnston, M. V., Toglia, J., & Deluca, J. (2007). Treatment to improve self-awareness in persons with acquired brain injury. *Brain Injury, 21,* 913–923. http://dx.doi.org/10.1080/02699050701553205

Green, P. (2003). *Manual for the Word Memory Test* (Rev. 2005). Edmonton, Alberta, Canada: Green's Publishing.

Green, P. (2004). *Green's Medical Symptom Validity Test (MSVT) for Microsoft Windows: User's manual.* Edmonton, Alberta, Canada: Green's Publishing.

Green, P. (2008). *Manual for the Nonverbal Medical Symptom Validity Test for Windows.* Edmonton, Alberta, Canada: Green's Publishing.

Green, P. (2011). Comparison between the Test of Memory Malingering (TOMM) and the Nonverbal Medical Symptom Validity Test (NV-MSVT) in adults with disability claims. *Applied Neuropsychology, 18,* 18–26. http://dx.doi.org/10.1080/09084282.2010.523365

Green, P., & Allen, L. M. (1999). *Performance of Neurological Patients on the Word Memory Test (WMT) and Computerized Assessment of Response Bias (CARB): Supplement to the Word Memory Test and CARB '97 manuals.* Durham, NC: Cognisyst.

Green, P., Iverson, G. L., & Allen, L. (1999). Detecting malingering in head injury litigation with the Word Memory Test. *Brain Injury, 13,* 813–819. http://dx.doi.org/10.1080/026990599121205

Green, P., Lees-Haley, P., & Allen, L., III. (2003). The Word Memory Test and the validity of neuropsychological test scores. *Journal of Forensic Neuropsychology, 2,* 97–124. http://dx.doi.org/10.1300/J151v02n03_05

Green, P., Montijo, J., & Brockhaus, R. (2011). High specificity of the Word Memory Test and Medical Symptom Validity Test in groups with severe verbal memory impairment. *Applied Neuropsychology, 18,* 86–94. http://dx.doi.org/10.1080/09084282.2010.523389

Green, P., Rohling, M. L., Lees-Haley, P. R., & Allen, L. M., III. (2001). Effort has a greater effect on test scores than severe brain injury in compensation claimants. *Brain Injury, 15,* 1045–1060. http://dx.doi.org/10.1080/02699050110088254

Green, R. E., Colella, B., Christensen, B., Johns, K., Frasca, D., Bayley, M., & Monette, G. (2008). Examining moderators of cognitive recovery trajectories after moderate to severe traumatic brain injury. *Archives of Physical Medicine and Rehabilitation, 89*(12, Suppl.), S16–S24. http://dx.doi.org/10.1016/j.apmr.2008.09.551

Greiffenstein, M. F., Baker, W. J., & Gola, T. (1994). Validation of malingered amnesic measures with a large clinical sample. *Psychological Assessment, 6,* 218–224. http://dx.doi.org/10.1037/1040-3590.6.3.218

Greiffenstein, M. F., Baker, W. J., Gola, T., Donders, J., & Miller, L. (2002). The Fake Bad Scale in atypical and severe closed head injury litigants. *Journal of Clinical Psychology, 58,* 1591–1600. http://dx.doi.org/10.1002/jclp.10077

Greve, K. W., & Bianchini, K. J. (2006). Classification accuracy of the Portland Digit Recognition Test in traumatic brain injury: Results of a known-groups analysis. *Clinical Neuropsychologist, 20,* 816–830. http://dx.doi.org/10.1080/13854040500346610

Greve, K. W., Bianchini, K. J., & Doane, B. M. (2006). Classification accuracy of the test of memory malingering in traumatic brain injury: Results of a known-groups analysis. *Journal of Clinical and Experimental Neuropsychology, 28,* 1176–1190. http://dx.doi.org/10.1080/13803390500263550

Greve, K. W., Bianchini, K. J., Love, J. M., Brennan, A., & Heinly, M. T. (2006). Sensitivity and specificity of MMPI–2 validity scales and indicators to malingered neurocognitive dysfunction in traumatic brain injury. *Clinical Neuropsychologist, 20,* 491–512. http://dx.doi.org/10.1080/13854040590967144

Greve, K. W., Binder, L. M., & Bianchini, K. J. (2009). Rates of below-chance performance in forced-choice symptom validity tests. *Clinical Neuropsychologist, 23,* 534–544. http://dx.doi.org/10.1080/13854040802232690

Griffen, J., & Hanks, R. (2014). Cognitive and behavioral outcomes from traumatic brain injury. In M. Sherer & A. M. Sander (Eds.), *Handbook on the neuropsychology of traumatic brain injury* (pp. 25–48). New York, NY: Springer.

Grote, C. L., Kooker, E. K., Garron, D. C., Nyenhuis, D. L., Smith, C. A., & Mattingly, M. L. (2000). Performance of compensation seeking and non-compensation seeking samples on the Victoria Symptom Validity Test: Cross-validation and extension of a standardization study. *Journal of Clinical and Experimental Neuropsychology, 22,* 709–719. http://dx.doi.org/10.1007/978-1-4939-0784-7_2

Gunstad, J., & Suhr, J. A. (2001). Efficacy of the full and abbreviated forms of the Portland Digit Recognition Test: Vulnerability to coaching. *Clinical Neuropsychologist, 15,* 397–404. http://dx.doi.org/10.1076/clin.15.3.397.10271

Gunstad, J., & Suhr, J. A. (2004). Use of the abbreviated Portland Digit Recognition Test in simulated malingering and neurological groups. *Journal of Forensic Neuropsychology, 4,* 33–47. http://dx.doi.org/10.1300/J151v04n01_02

Heffernan, D. S., Vera, R. M., Monaghan, S. F., Thakkar, R. K., Kozloff, M. S., Connolly, M. D., . . . Cioffi, W. G. (2011). Impact of socioethnic factors on outcomes following traumatic brain injury. *Journal of Trauma and Acute Care Surgery, 70,* 527–534. http://dx.doi.org/10.1097/TA.0b013e31820d0ed7

Heilbronner, R. L., Sweet, J. J., Morgan, J. E., Larrabee, G. J., & Millis, S. R. (2009). American Academy of Clinical Neuropsychology consensus conference statement on the neuropsychological assessment of effort, response bias, and malingering. *Clinical Neuropsychologist, 23,* 1093–1129. http://dx.doi.org/10.1080/13854040903155063

Henry, G. K., Heilbronner, R. L., Mittenberg, W., & Enders, C. (2006). The Henry–Heilbronner Index: A 15-item empirically derived MMPI–2 subscale for identifying probable malingering in personal injury litigants and disability claimants. *Clinical Neuropsychologist, 20,* 786–797. http://dx.doi.org/10.1080/13854040500287749

Henry, M., Merten, T., Wolf, S. A., & Harth, S. (2010). Nonverbal Medical Symptom Validity Test performance of elderly healthy adults and clinical neurology patients. *Journal of Clinical and Experimental Neuropsychology, 32,* 19–27. http://dx.doi.org/10.1080/13803390902791653

Holdnack, J. A., & Drozdick, L. W. (2009). *Advanced clinical solutions for WAIS–IV and WMS–IV: Clinical and interpretive manual.* San Antonio, TX: Pearson.

Howe, L. L., Anderson, A. M., Kaufman, D. A., Sachs, B. C., & Loring, D. W. (2007). Characterization of the Medical Symptom Validity Test in evaluation of clinically referred memory disorders clinic patients. *Archives of Clinical Neuropsychology, 22,* 753–761. http://dx.doi.org/10.1016/j.acn.2007.06.003

Howe, L. L., & Loring, D. W. (2009). Classification accuracy and predictive ability of the Medical Symptom Validity Test's dementia profile and general memory impairment profile. *Clinical Neuropsychologist, 23,* 329–342. http://dx.doi.org/10.1080/13854040801945060

Husson, E. C., Ribbers, G. M., Willemse-van Son, A. H., Verhagen, A. P., & Stam, H. J. (2010). Prognosis of six-month functioning after moderate to severe traumatic brain injury: A systematic review of prospective cohort studies. *Journal of Rehabilitation Medicine, 42,* 425–436. http://dx.doi.org/10.2340/16501977-0566

Iverson, G. L. (2005). Outcome from mild traumatic brain injury. *Current Opinion in Psychiatry, 18,* 301–317. http://dx.doi.org/10.1097/01.yco.0000165601.29047.ae

Jackson, W. T., Novack, T. A., & Dowler, R. N. (1998). Effective serial measurement of cognitive orientation in rehabilitation: The Orientation Log. *Archives of Physical Medicine and Rehabilitation, 79,* 718–721. http://dx.doi.org/10.1016/S0003-9993(98)90051-X

Jeon, I. C., Kim, O. L., Kim, M. S., Kim, S. H., Chang, C. H., & Bai, D. S. (2008). The effect of premorbid demographic factors on the recovery of neurocognitive function in traumatic brain injury patients. *Journal of Korean Neurosurgical Society, 44,* 295–302. http://dx.doi.org/10.3340/jkns.2008.44.5.295

Jourdan, C., Bosserelle, V., Azerad, S., Ghout, I., Bayen, E., Aegerter, P., . . . Azouvi, P. (2013). Predictive factors for 1-year outcome of a cohort of patients with severe traumatic brain injury (TBI): Results from the PariS-TBI study. *Brain Injury, 27,* 1000–1007. http://dx.doi.org/10.3109/02699052.2013.794971

Larrabee, G. J. (2003). Detection of malingering using atypical performance patterns on standard neuropsychological tests. *Clinical Neuropsychologist, 17,* 410–425. http://dx.doi.org/10.1076/clin.17.3.410.18089

Larrabee, G. J. (2008). Aggregation across multiple indicators improves the detection of malingering: Relationship to likelihood ratios. *Clinical Neuropsychologist, 22,* 666–679. http://dx.doi.org/10.1080/13854040701494987

Larrabee, G. L. (Ed.). (2012a). *Forensic neuropsychology: A scientific approach* (2nd ed.). New York, NY: Oxford University Press.

Larrabee, G. J. (2012b). Performance validity and symptom validity in neuropsychological assessment. *Journal of the International Neuropsychological Society, 18,* 625–630. http://dx.doi.org/10.1017/S1355617712000240

Levin, H. S., O'Donnell, V. M., & Grossman, R. G. (1979). The Galveston Orientation and Amnesia Test: A practical scale to assess cognition after head injury. *Journal of Nervous and Mental Disease, 167,*

675–684. http://dx.doi.org/10.1097/00005053-197911000-00004

Lezak, M. D., Howieson, D. B., Bigler, E. D., & Tranel, D. (2012). *Neuropsychological assessment* (5th ed.). New York, NY: Oxford University Press.

Lingsma, H. F., Roozenbeek, B., Li, B., Lu, J., Weir, J., Butcher, I., . . . Steyerberg, E. W. (2011). Large between-center differences in outcome after moderate and severe traumatic brain injury in the International Mission on Prognosis and Clinical Trial design in traumatic brain injury (IMPACT) study. *Neurosurgery, 68,* 601–608. http://dx.doi.org/10.1227/NEU.0b013e318209333b

Lingsma, H. F., Roozenbeek, B., Steyerberg, E. W., Murray, G. D., & Maas, A. I. (2010). Early prognosis in traumatic brain injury: From prophecies to predictions. *Lancet Neurology, 9,* 543–554. http://dx.doi.org/10.1016/S1474-442270065-X

Locke, D. E., Smigielski, J. S., Powell, M. R., & Stevens, S. R. (2008). Effort issues in post-acute outpatient acquired brain injury rehabilitation seekers. *NeuroRehabilitation, 23,* 273–281.

Malec, J. F., Brown, A. W., Leibson, C. L., Flaada, J. T., Mandrekar, J. N., Diehl, N. N., & Perkins, P. K. (2007). The Mayo Classification System for Traumatic Brain Injury Severity. *Journal of Neurotrauma, 24,* 1417–1424. http://dx.doi.org/10.1089/neu.2006.0245

Marmarou, A., Lu, J., Butcher, I., McHugh, G. S., Murray, G. D., Steyerberg, E. W., . . . Maas, A. I. (2007). Prognostic value of the Glasgow Coma Scale and pupil reactivity in traumatic brain injury assessed pre-hospital and on enrollment: An IMPACT analysis. *Journal of Neurotrauma, 24,* 270–280. http://dx.doi.org/10.1089/neu.2006.0029

Mata-Mbemba, D., Mugikura, S., Nakagawa, A., Murata, T., Ishii, K., Li, L., . . . Takahashi, S. (2014). Early CT findings to predict early death in patients with traumatic brain injury: Marshall and Rotterdam CT scoring systems compared in the major academic tertiary care hospital in northeastern Japan. *Academic Radiology, 21,* 605–611. http://dx.doi.org/10.1016/j.acra.2014.01.017

Mauritz, W., Wilbacher, I., Majdan, M., Leitgeb, J., Janciak, I., Brazinova, A., & Rusnak, M. (2008). Epidemiology, treatment and outcome of patients after severe traumatic brain injury in European regions with different economic status. *European Journal of Public Health, 18,* 575–580. http://dx.doi.org/10.1093/eurpub/ckn079

Mayou, R., Bryant, B., & Duthie, R. (1993). Psychiatric consequences of road traffic accidents. *British Medical Journal, 307,* 647–651. http://dx.doi.org/10.1136/bmj.307.6905.647

McCauley, S. R., Boake, C., Levin, H. S., Contant, C. F., & Song, J. X. (2001). Postconcussional disorder following mild to moderate traumatic brain injury: Anxiety, depression, and social support as risk factors and comorbidities. *Journal of Clinical and Experimental Neuropsychology, 23,* 792–808. http://dx.doi.org/10.1076/jcen.23.6.792.1016

McCrea, M. A. (2008). *Mild traumatic brain injury and postconcussive syndrome: The new evidence base for diagnosis and treatment.* New York, NY: Oxford University Press.

McHugh, G. S., Engel, D. C., Butcher, I., Steyerberg, E. W., Lu, J., Mushkudiani, N., . . . Murray, G. D. (2007). Prognostic value of secondary insults in traumatic brain injury: Results from the IMPACT study. *Journal of Neurotrauma, 24,* 287–293. http://dx.doi.org/10.1089/neu.2006.0031

McIntyre, A., Mehta, S., Aubut, J., Dijkers, M., & Teasell, R. W. (2013). Mortality among older adults after a traumatic brain injury: A meta-analysis. *Brain Injury, 27,* 31–40. http://dx.doi.org/10.3109/02699052.2012.700086

McNett, M. (2007). A review of the predictive ability of Glasgow Coma Scale scores in head-injured patients. *Journal of Neuroscience Nursing, 39,* 68–75. http://dx.doi.org/10.1097/01376517-200704000-00002

Menon, D. K., Schwab, K., Wright, D. W., & Maas, A. I. (2010). Position statement: Definition of traumatic brain injury. *Archives of Physical Medicine and Rehabilitation, 91,* 1637–1640. http://dx.doi.org/10.1016/j.apmr.2010.05.017

Milders, M., Fuchs, S., & Crawford, J. R. (2003). Neuropsychological impairments and changes in emotional and social behaviour following severe traumatic brain injury. *Journal of Clinical and Experimental Neuropsychology, 25,* 157–172. http://dx.doi.org/10.1076/jcen.25.2.157.13642

Mittenberg, W., Patton, C., Canyock, E. M., & Condit, D. C. (2002). Base rates of malingering and symptom exaggeration. *Journal of Clinical and Experimental Neuropsychology, 24,* 1094–1102. http://dx.doi.org/10.1076/jcen.24.8.1094.8379

Moore, B. A., & Donders, J. (2004). Predictors of invalid neuropsychological test performance after traumatic brain injury. *Brain Injury, 18,* 975–984. http://dx.doi.org/10.1080/02699050410001672350

Mushkudiani, N. A., Engel, D. C., Steyerberg, E. W., Butcher, I., Lu, J., Marmarou, A., . . . Maas, A. I. (2007). Prognostic value of demographic characteristics in traumatic brain injury: Results from the IMPACT study. *Journal of Neurotrauma, 24,* 259–269. http://dx.doi.org/10.1089/neu.2006.0028

Nakase-Richardson, R., Sepehri, A., Sherer, M., Yablon, S. A., Evans, C., & Mani, T. (2009). Classification schema of posttraumatic amnesia duration-based injury severity relative to 1-year outcome: Analysis of individuals with moderate and severe traumatic brain injury. *Archives of Physical Medicine and Rehabilitation, 90,* 17–19. http://dx.doi.org/10.1016/j.apmr.2008.06.030

Noé, E., Ferri, J., Caballero, M. C., Villodre, R., Sanchez, A., & Chirivella, J. (2005). Self-awareness after acquired brain injury—predictors and rehabilitation. *Journal of Neurology, 252,* 168–175. http://dx.doi.org/10.1007/s00415-005-0625-2

Novitski, J., Steele, S., Karantzoulis, S., & Randolph, C. (2012). The Repeatable Battery for the Assessment of Neuropsychological Status Effort Scale. *Archives of Clinical Neuropsychology, 27,* 190–195. http://dx.doi.org/10.1093/arclin/acr119

Paniak, C. (2009). Moderate to severe traumatic brain injury: Probable malingering . . . and then not. In J. E. Morgan & J. J. Sweet (Eds.), *Neuropsychology of malingering casebook* (pp. 101–120). New York, NY: Psychology Press.

Perrin, P. B., Niemeier, J. P., Mougeot, J.-L., Vannoy, C. H., Hirsch, M. A., Watts, J. A., . . . Whitney, M. P. (2015). Measures of injury severity and prediction of acute traumatic brain injury outcomes. *Journal of Head Trauma Rehabilitation, 30,* 136–142. http://dx.doi.org/10.1097/HTR.0000000000000026

Ponsford, J. L., Downing, M. G., Olver, J., Ponsford, M., Acher, R., Carty, M., & Spitz, G. (2014). Longitudinal follow-up of patients with traumatic brain injury: Outcome at two, five, and ten years post-injury. *Journal of Neurotrauma, 31,* 64–77. http://dx.doi.org/10.1089/neu.2013.2997

Rabin, L. A., Barr, W. B., & Burton, L. A. (2005). Assessment practices of clinical neuropsychologists in the United States and Canada: A survey of INS, NAN, and APA Division 40 members. *Archives of Clinical Neuropsychology, 20,* 33–65. http://dx.doi.org/10.1016/j.acn.2004.02.005

Rabinowitz, A. R., & Levin, H. S. (2014). Cognitive sequelae of traumatic brain injury. *Psychiatric Clinics of North America, 37,* 1–11. http://dx.doi.org/10.1016/j.psc.2013.11.004

Randolph, C. (1998). *RBANS manual.* San Antonio, TX: Psychological Corporation.

Rao, V., Rosenberg, P., Bertrand, M., Salehinia, S., Spiro, J., Vaishnavi, S., . . . Miles, Q. S. (2009). Aggression after traumatic brain injury: Prevalence and correlates. *Journal of Neuropsychiatry and Clinical Neurosciences, 21,* 420–429. http://dx.doi.org/10.1176/jnp.2009.21.4.420

Rassovsky, Y., Levi, Y., Agranov, E., Sela-Kaufman, M., Sverdlik, A., & Vakil, E. (2015). Predicting long-term outcome following traumatic brain injury (TBI). *Journal of Clinical and Experimental Neuropsychology, 39,* 14. http://dx.doi.org/10.1007/s10916-014-0187-x

Reese, C. S., Suhr, J. A., & Riddle, T. L. (2012). Exploration of malingering indices in the Wechsler Adult Intelligence Scale–Fourth Edition Digit Span Subtest. *Archives of Clinical Neuropsychology, 27,* 176–181. http://dx.doi.org/10.1093/arclin/acr117

Rimel, R. W., Giordani, B., Barth, J. T., & Jane, J. A. (1982). Moderate head injury: Completing the clinical spectrum of brain trauma. *Neurosurgery, 11,* 344–351. http://dx.doi.org/10.1227/00006123-198209000-00002

Roebuck-Spencer, T., & Cernich, A. (2014). Epidemiology and societal impact of traumatic brain injury. In M. Sherer & A. Sander (Eds.), *Handbook on the neuropsychology of traumatic brain injury* (p. 3–23). http://dx.doi.org/10.1007/978-1-4939-0784-7_1

Roebuck-Spencer, T., & Sherer, M. (2008). Moderate and severe traumatic brain injury. In J. E. Morgan & J. H. Ricker (Eds.), *Textbook of clinical neuropsychology* (pp. 411–429). New York, NY: Taylor & Francis.

Roebuck-Spencer, T., & Sherer, M. (2012). Moderate and severe traumatic brain injury. In G. J. Larrabee (Ed.), *Forensic neuropsychology: A scientific approach* (2nd ed., pp. 260–280). New York, NY: Oxford University Press.

Rogers, J. M., & Read, C. A. (2007). Psychiatric comorbidity following traumatic brain injury. *Brain Injury, 21,* 1321–1333. http://dx.doi.org/10.1080/02699050701765700

Ruttan, L., Martin, K., Liu, A., Colella, B., & Green, R. E. (2008). Long-term cognitive outcome in moderate to severe traumatic brain injury: A meta-analysis examining timed and untimed tests at 1 and 4.5 or more years after injury. *Archives of Physical Medicine and Rehabilitation, 89*(12, Suppl.), S69–S76. http://dx.doi.org/10.1016/j.apmr.2008.07.007

Sanders, C., Ziegler, E. A., & Schmitter-Edgecombe, M. (2013). Traumatic brain injury and the impact of secondary influences. In P. A. Arnett (Ed.), *Secondary influences on neuropsychological test performance: Research findings and practical applications* (pp. 292–327). New York, NY: Oxford University Press.

Santiago, L. A., Oh, B. C., Dash, P. K., Holcomb, J. B., & Wade, C. E. (2012). A clinical comparison of penetrating and blunt traumatic brain injuries. *Brain Injury, 26,* 107–125. http://dx.doi.org/10.3109/02699052.2011.635363

Schretlen, D. J., & Shapiro, A. M. (2003). A quantitative review of the effects of traumatic brain injury on cognitive functioning. *International Review of Psychiatry, 15,* 341–349. http://dx.doi.org/10.1080/09540260310001606728

Schroeder, R. W., Baade, L. E., Peck, C. P., VonDran, E. J., Brockman, C. J., Webster, B. K., & Heinrichs, R. J. (2012). Validation of MMPI–2–RF validity scales in criterion group neuropsychological samples. *Clinical Neuropsychologist*, 26, 129–146. http://dx.doi.org/10.1080/13854046.2011.639314

Schroeder, R. W., Twumasi-Ankrah, P., Baade, L. E., & Marshall, P. S. (2012). Reliable Digit Span: A systematic review and cross-validation study. *Assessment, 19,* 21–30. http://dx.doi.org/10.1177/1073191111428764

Seel, R. T., Kreutzer, J. S., Rosenthal, M., Hammond, F. M., Corrigan, J. D., & Black, K. (2003). Depression after traumatic brain injury: A National Institute on Disability and Rehabilitation Research Model Systems multicenter investigation. *Archives of Physical Medicine and Rehabilitation, 84,* 177–184. http://dx.doi.org/10.1053/apmr.2003.50106

Shafi, S., Marquez de la Plata, C., Diaz-Arrastia, R., Shipman, K., Carlile, M., Frankel, H., . . . Gentilello, L. M. (2007). Racial disparities in long-term functional outcome after traumatic brain injury. *Journal of Trauma: Injury Infection and Critical Care, 63,* 1263–1270. http://dx.doi.org/10.1097/TA.0b013e31815b8f00

Sharland, M. J., & Gfeller, J. D. (2007). A survey of neuropsychologists' beliefs and practices with respect to the assessment of effort. *Archives of Clinical Neuropsychology*, 22, 213–223. http://dx.doi.org/10.1016/j.acn.2006.12.004

Sherer, M., Hart, T., Nick, T. G., Whyte, J., Thompson, R. N., & Yablon, S. A. (2003). Early impaired self-awareness after traumatic brain injury. *Archives of Physical Medicine and Rehabilitation, 84,* 168–176. http://dx.doi.org/10.1053/apmr.2003.50045

Sherer, M., Madison, C. F., & Hannay, H. J. (2000). A review of outcome after moderate and severe closed head injury with an introduction to life care planning. *Journal of Head Trauma Rehabilitation, 15,* 767–782. http://dx.doi.org/10.1097/00001199-200004000-00002

Sigurdardottir, S., Andelic, N., Wehling, E., Roe, C., Anke, A., Skandsen, T., . . . Schanke, A.-K. (2015). Neuropsychological functioning in a national cohort of severe traumatic brain injury: Demographic and acute injury-related predictors. *Journal of Head Trauma Rehabilitation, 30,* E1–E12. http://dx.doi.org/10.1097/HTR.0000000000000039

Silverberg, N. D., Wertheimer, J. C., & Fichtenberg, N. L. (2007). An effort index for the Repeatable Battery for the Assessment of Neuropsychological Status (RBANS). *Clinical Neuropsychologist*, *21*, 841–854. http://dx.doi.org/10.1080/13854040600850958

Singhal, A., Green, P., Ashaye, K., Shankar, K., & Gill, D. (2009). High specificity of the Medical Symptom Validity Test in patients with very severe memory impairment. *Archives of Clinical Neuropsychology*, 24, 721–728. http://dx.doi.org/10.1093/arclin/acp074

Slick, D., Hopp, G., Strauss, E., & Thompson, G. B. (1997). *Victoria Symptom Validity Test: Professional manual.* Odessa, FL: Psychological Assessment Resources.

Slick, D. J., Sherman, E. M., & Iverson, G. L. (1999). Diagnostic criteria for malingered neurocognitive dysfunction: Proposed standards for clinical practice and research. *Clinical Neuropsychologist, 13,* 545–561. http://dx.doi.org/10.1076/1385-4046(199911)13:04;1-Y;FT545

Slick, D. J., Tan, J. E., Strauss, E., Mateer, C. A., Harnadek, M., & Sherman, E. M. (2003). Victoria Symptom Validity Test scores of patients with profound memory impairment: Nonlitigant case studies. *Clinical Neuropsychologist, 17,* 390–394. http://dx.doi.org/10.1076/clin.17.3.390.18090

Spreen, O., & Strauss, E. (1998). *A compendium of neuropsychological tests: Administration, norms, and commentary*. New York, NY: Oxford University Press.

Stuss, D. T., Binns, M. A., Carruth, F. G., Levine, B., Brandys, C. E., Moulton, R. J., . . . Schwartz, M. L. (1999). The acute period of recovery from traumatic brain injury: Posttraumatic amnesia or posttraumatic confusional state? *Journal of Neurosurgery, 90,* 635–643. http://dx.doi.org/10.3171/jns.1999.90.4.0635

Sumowski, J. F., Chiaravalloti, N., Krch, D., Paxton, J., & Deluca, J. (2013). Education attenuates the negative impact of traumatic brain injury on cognitive status. *Archives of Physical Medicine and Rehabilitation, 94,* 2562–2564. http://dx.doi.org/10.1016/j.apmr.2013.07.023

Sweet, J. J., Goldman, D. J., & Guidotti Breting, L. M. (2013). Traumatic brain injury: Guidance in a forensic context from outcome, dose-response, and response bias research. *Behavioral Sciences and the Law*, *31,* 756–778. http://dx.doi.org/10.1002/bsl.2088

Tateno, A., Jorge, R. E., & Robinson, R. G. (2003). Clinical correlates of aggressive behavior after traumatic brain injury. *Journal of Neuropsychiatry and Clinical Neurosciences, 15,* 155–160. http://dx.doi.org/10.1176/jnp.15.2.155

Teasdale, G., & Jennett, B. (1974). Assessment of coma and impaired consciousness: A practical scale. *Lancet, 304,* 81–84. http://dx.doi.org/10.1016/S0140-6736(74)91639-0

Teichner, G., & Wagner, M. T. (2004). The Test of Memory Malingering (TOMM): Normative data from cognitively intact, cognitively impaired, and elderly patients with dementia. *Archives of Clinical Neuropsychology*, *19,* 455–464. http://dx.doi.org/10.1016/S0887-6177(03)00078-7

Thurman, D., & Guerrero, J. (1999). Trends in hospitalization associated with traumatic brain injury. *JAMA, 282,* 954–957. http://dx.doi.org/10.1001/jama.282.10.954

Timmons, S. D., Bee, T., Webb, S., Diaz-Arrastia, R. R., & Hesdorffer, D. (2011). Using the abbreviated injury severity and Glasgow Coma Scale scores to predict 2-week mortality after traumatic brain injury. *Journal of Trauma and Acute Care Surgery, 71,* 1172–1178. http://dx.doi.org/10.1097/TA.0b013e31822b0f4b

Tombaugh, T. (1996). *Test of Memory Malingering manual.* New York, NY: MultiHealth Systems.

Tombaugh, T. N. (1997). The Test of Memory Malingering (TOMM): Normative data from cognitively intact and cognitively impaired individuals. *Psychological Assessment, 9,* 260–268. http://dx.doi.org/10.1037/1040-3590.9.3.260

Traumatic Brain Injury Model Systems National Data Center. (1999). *National database syllabus.* West Orange, NJ: Author.

Valk-Kleibeuker, L., Heijenbrok-Kal, M. H., & Ribbers, G. M. (2014). Mood after moderate and severe traumatic brain injury: A prospective cohort study. *PLOS ONE, 9,* e87414. http://dx.doi.org/10.1371/journal.pone.0087414

Vanderploeg, R. D., Belanger, H. G., Duchnick, J. D., & Curtiss, G. (2007). Awareness problems following moderate to severe traumatic brain injury: Prevalence, assessment methods, and injury correlates. *Journal of Rehabilitation Research and Development, 44,* 937–950. http://dx.doi.org/10.1682/JRRD.2006.12.0163

van Reekum, R., Cohen, T., & Wong, J. (2000). Can traumatic brain injury cause psychiatric disorders? *Journal of Neuropsychiatry and Clinical Neurosciences, 12,* 316–327. http://dx.doi.org/10.1176/appi.neuropsych.12.3.316

Vickery, C. D., Berry, D. T. R., Dearth, C. S., Vagnini, V. L., Baser, R. E., Cragar, D. E., & Orey, S. A. (2004). Head injury and the ability to feign neuropsychological deficits. *Archives of Clinical Neuropsychology, 19,* 37–48. http://dx.doi.org/10.1016/S0887-6177(02)00170-1

Victor, T. L., Boone, K. B., Serpa, J. G., Buehler, J., & Ziegler, E. A. (2009). Interpreting the meaning of Multiple Symptom Validity Test failure. *Clinical Neuropsychologist, 23,* 297–313. http://dx.doi.org/10.1080/13854040802232682

Walker, W. C., Ketchum, J. M., Marwitz, J. H., Chen, T., Hammond, F., Sherer, M., & Meythaler, J. (2010). A multicentre study on the clinical utility of post-traumatic amnesia duration in predicting global outcome after moderate-severe traumatic brain injury. *Journal of Neurology, Neurosurgery, and Psychiatry, 81,* 87–89. http://dx.doi.org/10.1136/jnnp.2008.161570

Walker, W. C., Ketchum, J. S., III, Marwitz, J. H., Kolakowsky-Hayner, S. A., McClish, D. K., & Bushnik, T. (2015). Global outcome and late seizures after penetrating versus closed traumatic brain injury: A NIDRR TBI Model Systems Study. *Journal of Head Trauma Rehabilitation, 30,* 231–240. http://dx.doi.org/10.1097/HTR.0000000000000127

Wechsler, D. (2008). *Wechsler Adult Intelligence Scale–Fourth Edition: Administration and scoring manual.* San Antonio, TX: NCS Pearson.

Wechsler, D. A. (1997). *Wechsler Adult Intelligence Scale* (3rd ed.). San Antonio, TX: Psychological Corporation.

Whelan-Goodinson, R., Ponsford, J., & Schönberger, M. (2009). Validity of the Hospital Anxiety and Depression Scale to assess depression and anxiety following traumatic brain injury as compared with the Structured Clinical Interview for DSM–IV. *Journal of Affective Disorders, 114,* 94–102. http://dx.doi.org/10.1016/j.jad.2008.06.007

Whyte, J., Cifu, D., Dikmen, S., & Temkin, N. (2001). Prediction of functional outcomes after traumatic brain injury: A comparison of 2 measures of duration of unconsciousness. *Archives of Physical Medicine and Rehabilitation, 82,* 1355–1359. http://dx.doi.org/10.1053/apmr.2001.26091

Youngjohn, J. R., Davis, D., & Wolf, I. (1997). Head injury and the MMPI–2: Paradoxical severity effects and the influence of litigation. *Psychological Assessment, 9,* 177–184. http://dx.doi.org/10.1037/1040-3590.9.3.177

Youngjohn, J. R., Wershba, R., Stevenson, M., Sturgeon, J., & Thomas, M. L. (2011). Independent validation of the MMPI–2–RF Somatic/Cognitive and Validity scales in TBI litigants tested for effort. *Clinical Neuropsychologist, 25,* 463–476. http://dx.doi.org/10.1080/13854046.2011.554444

CHAPTER 9

ASSESSMENT OF PSYCHIATRIC DISORDERS IN FORENSIC NEUROPSYCHOLOGICAL EVALUATIONS

Chriscelyn M. Tussey, Beth Caillouet Arredondo, and Paul M. Richards

The growing prevalence and impact of psychiatric illness spans national and international borders, and the onus is on forensic neuropsychologists to ensure careful assessment of these disorders as part of any evaluation. The first 17 World Mental Health surveys conducted by the World Health Organization indicated that mental disorders commonly occur in all participating countries (Kessler et al., 2009). After combining anxiety, mood, externalizing, and substance use disorders, the interquartile range (25th–75th percentiles) of lifetime *Diagnostic and Statistical Manual of Mental Disorders*, 4th ed., text revision (*DSM–IV–TR;* American Psychiatric Association, 2000) disorder prevalence estimates is 18% to 36%. The interquartile range of 12-month prevalence estimates is 10% to 19%. Prevalence estimates of 12-month serious mental illness are 4% to 7% in one half the countries, 2% to 3% in one fourth, and 1% to 2% in one fourth (Kessler et al., 2009). In the United States in 2014, an estimated 43.6 million adults ages 18 or older had any mental illness in the past year, which represented 18.1% of all U.S. adults at that time (Center for Behavioral Health Statistics and Quality, 2015). The statistics were equally troubling for youth, with slightly more than 20% of children, either currently or at some point during their life, having had a seriously debilitating mental disorder (Merikangas et al., 2010). Furthermore, it is important to emphasize that these data are only estimates and that specific numbers are difficult to obtain for a variety of reasons, such as underreporting and diagnostic differences (e.g., *DSM–IV–TR* vs. *Diagnostic and Statistical Manual of Mental Disorders*, 5th ed. [*DSM–5*; American Psychiatric Association, 2013] vs. *International Classification of Diseases*, 10th revision [World Health Organization, 1992] criteria). Thus, it is conceivable that the rates of mental illness in the United States and globally are far different than current statistics reveal.

Many mental disorders begin in childhood and adolescence and can be (a) preexisting, (b) a single occurrence, or (c) a chronic condition. Psychiatric disorders can, and do, have a profound impact on one's developmental, psychological, social, educational, and employment trajectory. Furthermore, neuropsychological deficits are a cardinal symptom in many psychiatric disorders, such as schizophrenia, bipolar disorder, and depression, and are often at least partially attributable to brain changes associated with these disorders (e.g., Trivedi, 2006). The nature and severity of neuropsychological dysfunction ranges from individual to individual but can impair reasoning and communication; lead to a lack of insight, distractibility, and impulsivity; and result in problems with memory or planning. It is not uncommon for individuals involved in the legal system to be referred for neuropsychological assessment to evaluate the nature and severity of these cognitive difficulties and to assist with prognostic and rehabilitation considerations.

Whether the context is civil litigation or criminal, related to disability or employment law, or otherwise, it is essential that a forensic neuropsychological evaluation include detailed assessment of the examinee's psychiatric history and current status. A forensic neuropsychologist should be able to

http://dx.doi.org/10.1037/0000032-009
APA Handbook of Forensic Neuropsychology, S. S. Bush (Editor-in-Chief)

discuss the potential impact of psychiatric illnesses such as depression or anxiety on cognition and vice versa. Forensic neuropsychologists are often tasked with opining about the relevant psychological or neuropsychological contributions to issues such as causality or intent, which are difficult to address in even the most straightforward of cases.

Although reminders to obtain a thorough psychiatric history may seem unnecessary for the practicing neuropsychologist, the importance of doing so cannot be overemphasized. Indeed, at times psychiatric histories can be overshadowed by the focus on cognitive symptoms. However, a forensic neuropsychologist will best be able to assist a trier of fact if he or she is able to communicate accurately any preexisting and current contexts for a mental illness or cognitive disorder. To this end, just as a neuropsychologist would do in a clinical evaluation, it is prudent to inquire about onset, duration, trajectory, and severity of both cognitive and psychiatric symptoms. Collateral information is essential, though not always available. Careful attention to the longitudinal course of the condition may prove useful when considering causation, and response to treatment may be helpful in evaluating the persistence of impairment, both of which are common questions for forensic neuropsychologists in civil litigation.

This chapter is designed to provide useful information about select psychiatric illnesses, chosen by us for their frequency, in forensic neuropsychological evaluations and the related literature. Depression, anxiety disorders, and trauma and stressor-related disorders are discussed in depth, and brief information is provided about a host of other disorders, including personality disorders, considered relevant for forensic neuropsychological evaluations. This is not an exhaustive review, of course, because any psychiatric disorder could be relevant for a forensic evaluation. Rather, we offer coverage of the disorders about which, at a minimum, any forensic neuropsychologist should be knowledgeable. Contemporary diagnostic considerations, basic neuroanatomical correlates, and evaluation, prognosis, and treatment information are discussed throughout the chapter. Relevant considerations for forensic neuropsychological evaluation related to each specific disorder are explored. Last, relevant psychological assessment measures are discussed, including a brief mention of performance and symptom validity options.

DEPRESSIVE DISORDERS

Depressive disorders are a significant cause of morbidity and mortality in the United States and the rest of the world. The World Health Organization (2004) listed major depressive disorders as one of the most common psychiatric disorders and the leading cause of disability in the United States for individuals ages 15 to 44 years. Greenberg et al. (2003) estimated the vocational cost of depression as approximately $80 billion per year, in conjunction with the adverse consequences of depression after workplace injuries in terms of lost productivity and absenteeism (Ferguson, Iverson, Langenecker, & Young, 2012). The implications of depression in terms of human suffering for patients and their families are immeasurable. In this section, we review diagnostic criteria, pathophysiology, epidemiology, and the necessity for the forensic neuropsychologist to thoroughly evaluate the extent of depression and, if present, to assess the effects it may have had on neuropsychological or cognitive test performance and overall functioning. The provision of forensic neuropsychological opinions as they relate to depression regarding diagnosis, prognosis, causation, permanency, and treatment (duty to mitigate) are discussed.

Diagnostic Considerations

Although an entire issue of the journal *Psychological Injury and Law* (Young, 2013) was devoted to discussing ethical considerations and other problems associated with the use of the *DSM–5* in forensic settings, this diagnostic taxonomy is an important starting point in any discussion of depressive disorders. Even if the forensic neuropsychologist does not use *DSM–5* criteria, opposing experts and previous clinical providers may have, and it is therefore important to understand.

In the *DSM–5*, depressive disorders represent a large category of diagnoses, including disruptive mood dysregulation disorder, major depressive disorder, persistent depressive disorder (dysthymia), premenstrual dysphoric disorder, substance- or medication-induced depressive disorder, depressive disorder due to another medical condition, other specified depressive disorder, and unspecified depressive disorder. In contrast to the *Diagnostic and Statistical Manual of Mental Disorders*, 4th ed. (*DSM–IV*; American Psychiatric Association, 1994), in the *DSM–5* depressive disorders are in a section separate from bipolar and related disorders. The following discussion primarily focuses on major depressive disorder, which is the most common depressive disorder. We use the term *major depressive disorder* synonymously and interchangeably with *major depression* and *major depressive episode*. We further define major depression as moderate to severe depression (as assessed by common psychometric instruments and symptoms elicited on clinical interview discussed elsewhere in this chapter) and differentiate it from bereavement, grief, and adjustment reactions with depressed mood. The specific diagnostic criteria are listed in the *DSM–5*. The criteria consist of the specific symptoms and their impact on daily functioning. The symptoms should not be solely attributable to substances or medical conditions. In addition, severity and code specifiers are available to grade level of depression (mild, moderate, severe) with classifications to specify psychotic features, partial or full remission, and unspecified. Finally, a number of temperamental, environmental, genetic, and physiological risk and prognostic factors related to major depression are described.

There have historically been other ways to classify depression, with distinctions such as psychotic versus neurotic, endogenous (biological) versus reactive, single episode versus recurrent, and unipolar versus bipolar. However, to summarize, the chief diagnostic feature of major depression is a period of at least 2 consecutive weeks during which the person experiences either moderately or severely depressed mood or the loss of interest or pleasure in nearly all activities.

As noted previously, major depressive disorder is associated with high mortality, mostly attributable to suicide. Moreover, depressed persons admitted to nursing homes have a markedly increased likelihood of mortality in the 1st year (American Psychiatric Association, 2013). Major depression is frequently associated with medical conditions such as diabetes, morbid obesity, cardiovascular disease, rheumatoid arthritis, traumatic brain injury (TBI), and chronic pain. TBI is especially important to discuss because it is perhaps the most prevalent condition evaluated by the forensic neuropsychologist. Jorge et al. (2004) studied a large group of individuals with various severities (mild, moderate, and severe) of TBI and found that approximately 33% experienced major depression during the 1st year after sustaining a TBI. Major depression was significantly more frequent among TBI patients than among controls, and those TBI patients with major depression had significantly higher impairment on cognitive tests (especially executive measures) than their nondepressed counterparts. Major depression was also associated with poor social functioning at 6- and 12-month postinjury follow-up evaluations.

Major depression has a high degree of comorbidity with other psychiatric disorders such as anxiety, substance abuse, and posttraumatic stress disorder (PTSD). In any forensic neuropsychological case, the presence of major depression should be viewed as a potential complicating factor that confounds diagnosis and treatment and thereby delays recovery from the underlying event in question (e.g., motor vehicle accident, toxic exposure, fall, sports injury, assault, abuse, criminal act).

The *DSM–5* lists the 12-month prevalence of major depressive disorder in the United States as approximately 7% with marked differences by age group such that the prevalence in 18- to 29-year-old individuals is 3 times higher than the prevalence in individuals age 60 years or older. Females experience a 1.5 to 3 times higher rate of depression than males beginning in early adolescence.

Neuropsychological Functioning

Depression is an important diagnostic consideration for the forensic neuropsychologist for all of the above reasons and because it has long been known that major depression can adversely affect neuropsychological test performance. Many neuropsychological studies of depressed individuals have documented memory (including recognition memory) and learning impairments (verbal and nonverbal) as well as slowed processing speed and attentional deficits (see Howieson, Loring, & Hannay, 2004, for a review). However, as the authors of these studies have noted, research findings are sometimes contradictory, with some studies showing no cognitive impairment associated with depression. These seemingly inconsistent findings likely stem from marked differences on factors such as whether a subject is medicated, severity and length of depression, comorbid conditions, and a host of other research variables. There may not be a prototypic cognitive profile of depression, but when this condition is untreated and moderate to severe, it likely complicates the clinical and forensic presentation of a brain disorder.

When major depression reaches the more severe end of the continuum, it was historically thought to simulate dementia (so-called pseudodementia) and present as organic brain damage (Cavenar, Maltbie, & Austin, 1979; Richards & Ruff, 1989). Sweet (1983) concluded that depression exacerbates neuropsychological findings, leading to misdiagnosis in as many as 40% of studied depressed patients (Newman & Sweet, 1986). Richards and Ruff (1989) found that outpatients meeting diagnostic criteria for major depression of the *Diagnostic and Statistical Manual of Mental Disorders*, 3rd ed. (American Psychiatric Association, 1980) were significantly more impaired on tests of visual–spatial short-term memory and learning and on verbal learning tasks in comparison with a nondepressed control group. Their findings were not attributable to motivational factors; neuropsychological deficits in depressed subjects were discussed in terms of impaired brain functioning. Otto et al. (1994) published norms for depressed patients who were administered the California Verbal Learning Test, a common measure of complex verbal learning and memory. They evaluated 150 outpatients meeting diagnostic criteria for major depression (tested after a drug washout) and found that mean California Verbal Learning Test scores for these patients were between 0.5 and 1 standard deviation below age- and gender-corrected norms for nondepressed populations. Ruff (1994) studied the effects of depression on the 2 and 7 Selective Attention Test, a timed measure that assesses visual–spatial attention, speed, and accuracy. In contrast to the previously described findings, Ruff concluded that "major depression did not for the majority of these patients impair 2 and 7 test performance, particularly if no concurrent motor slowing was present" (p. 63).

Neuroanatomical Correlates

Concurrent with the majority of literature that has indicated that major depression adversely affects neuropsychological findings, neuroimaging data point to a neural substrate of major depression. Sprengelmeyer et al. (2011) used Time 1 weighted magnetic resonance imaging to study the brains of patients with major depressive disorder in comparison with normal controls. Among their findings was reduced insular gray matter volume. They suggested that the insular cortex and the anterior cingulate cortex are key neurocorrelates of symptoms of major depressive disorder. In addition, scores on self-report measures correlated with gray matter volume in these structures.

Beauregard et al. (1998) used functional MRI in an emotional activation paradigm to study major depressive disorder. These researchers found that passive viewing of an emotionally laden film clip produced a significantly greater activation in the left medial prefrontal cortex and in the right cingulate gyrus in depressed patients than in normal controls. Their findings suggest that these two cortical regions are part of an important neural network in the pathophysiology of major depression.

Hercher, Turecki, and Mechawar (2009) reviewed studies examining growth structural changes observed in the brains of patients with major depressive disorders. Their review added additional support to the hypothesis of altered cell plasticity in major depressive disorders that occurs primarily in fronto-limbic areas. They also concluded that morphometric and cell density alterations were region specific, involving multiple neuromodulatory systems, including serotonergic, noradrenergic, GABAergic, and glutamatergic pathways. Rajkowska et al. (1999) used computer-assisted three-dimensional cell counting to examine prefrontal cell pathology in the brains of participants with major depression in comparison with a normal control group. Their findings revealed that "major depression can be distinguished by specific histopathology of both neurons and glial cells in the prefrontal cortex" (p.1085).

Using single-photon emission computed tomography, Mena (2009) documented decreased brain activity in the anterior cingulate when depressed subjects underwent cognitive testing and also found decreased brain activity in the parietal and orbital frontal regions of the brain at rest. Ogura, Morinobu, Kawakatsu, Totsuka, and Komatani (1998) documented decreased brain activity via single-photon emission computed tomography in the left superior frontal, bilateral parietal, and right lateral temporal cortex when the depressed patient was resting and not undergoing cognitive exertion.

Treatment Considerations

The forensic neuropsychologist is often asked to provide opinions regarding permanency and causation in his or her evaluation report and during deposition or trial testimony. Regarding permanency, it should be stressed that major depression is a treatable condition, with a majority of diagnosed individuals experiencing significant improvement in mood, cognition, and day-to-day functioning with treatment. Although it is beyond the scope of this chapter to review the efficacy of antidepressant treatment, suffice it to say that, there are highly effective medications, including selective serotonin reuptake inhibitors and serotonin–norepinephrine reuptake inhibitor, with low side effect profiles that, when combined with evidence-based psychological treatments such as cognitive–behavioral therapy, have been shown to be highly efficacious (e.g., DeRubeis, Siegle, & Hollon, 2008). Even for medication-resistant depressed patients, there are potential mood benefits from electroconvulsive therapy and transcranial magnetic stimulation (Triggs et al., 1999). The prognosis for major depression is typically fair to excellent, and permanency may be difficult to establish in light of the above information. Certainly, it is difficult to conclude that a plaintiff, patient, or defendant will experience lifelong major depression in the absence of multiple and even aggressive treatment trials. Moreover, major depression should ideally be successfully treated to get the most valid picture of any neuropsychological impairments that may be associated with the underlying condition in question.

Implications for Forensic Neuropsychological Evaluations

There are clear-cut, murky, and frankly confusing situations related to establishing causation of major depression as a result of a compensable incident or accident in civil forensic evaluations. For instance, in a plaintiff, patient, or defendant with absolutely no history of depression who then sustains a TBI and afterward develops a major depressive episode, it is straightforward to attribute depression exclusively to the incident in question. However, what if this same person experienced depression that was successfully treated earlier in life, then sustains a TBI and, as a result, develops a major depressive disorder? The neuropsychologist would have to carefully interview and evaluate the patient and comb through pre- and postincident records in an attempt to determine whether the depression represents a new event and therefore was not preexisting. Alternatively, the records and history might clearly indicate that the incident in question exacerbated a prior depressive episode. In some jurisdictions (especially the worker's compensation setting), defendants or employers are liable for damages associated with exacerbation of a preexisting condition with the trier of fact using a "but for" argument ("but for" the accident in question, this patient would have been functioning or working adequately).

To complicate matters further, major depression is often a recurrent and progressive disorder in which depressive episodes are more readily triggered by successively less stressful events throughout an individual's lifetime (Ramasubbu & MacQueen, 2008). These and other authors have offered "stress sensitization" and "kindling" hypotheses to explain this phenomenon. Thus, the forensic neuropsychologist can encounter challenging situations in which, for example, a plaintiff with a history of multiple major depressive episodes is involved in a relatively minor fender bender with no documented injuries but eventually develops major depression with opposing experts opining why or why not a relatively minor motor vehicle accident could result in this significant depressive episode.

The role of depression in criminal forensic evaluations is different, given that causality is not an issue. Although mild to moderate depression alone may not render one incompetent to proceed or offer significant mitigation, depression so severe that psychosis is present can impede trial competence and be a relevant consideration for a range of legal issues (e.g., Cohen, 1996).

In summary, major depression is a complex psychiatric disorder of interactive neuroanatomical, neuropsychological, neurochemical, neuroendocrine, and other factors that, in turn, are influenced by a person's genetic makeup and exposure to environmental stressors. Major depression can be triggered by exposure to life stressors and, alternatively, it can emerge in the absence of stressors or for no apparent reason (Kendler, Hettema, Butera, Gardner, & Prescott, 2003). In civil and criminal forensic settings, major depression can be preexisting and also result in single or recurrent episodes after an event, injury, or disease. In addition to these considerations, major depression can and often does adversely affect neuropsychological test performance and thereby delay recovery from an injury and complicate the clinical and forensic presentation of a case. The forensic neuropsychologist must thoroughly review pre-and postincident medical records and other collateral data, analyze what are often multiple sets of test data (his or her own and the opposing expert's) and conduct careful interviews to provide opinions that hold up to the scrutiny of the expert witness process.

ANXIETY DISORDERS AND TRAUMA- AND STRESSOR-RELATED DISORDERS

Either separately or in combination, the prevalence of anxiety, stress, and trauma in today's society is high and exacts a significant toll. In fact, anxiety disorders are the most common class of psychiatric illness in the general population (Kessler et al., 2009). The estimated lifetime prevalence of any anxiety disorder is more than 15%, and the 12-month prevalence is more than 10% (Kessler et al., 2009). Anxiety disorders tend to be more prevalent in women than in men (McLean, Asnaani, Litz, & Hofmann, 2011). For years, anxiety, stress, and trauma have played a detrimental role in society's physical and mental health. For example, dating back to the 1990s, Greenberg et al. (1999) found that the estimated annual cost of anxiety disorders in the United States was approximately $42.3 billion, most of which was due to nonpsychiatric medical treatment costs. Additionally concerning was that this estimate focused on short-term effects and did not include the effect of outcomes such as the increased risk of other disorders. Also, anxiety disorders have high rates of comorbidity with major depression and alcohol and drug abuse, which can also take staggering tolls on individuals and communities.

Although myriad diagnoses fit under the *DSM–5* (American Psychiatric Association, 2013) categories of anxiety and trauma- and stressor-related disorders, the majority of this section focuses on PTSD, given its popular role in criminal and civil matters (e.g., Berger, McNiel, & Binder, 2012; Sparr & Pitman, 2007). According to *DSM–IV* (American Psychiatric Association, 1994) criteria, in the United States the projected lifetime risk for PTSD, at age 75 years, is 8.7%, with a 12-month prevalence rate among U.S. adults of approximately 3.5%. Similar to anxiety disorders, females have a higher rate of PTSD than males across the life span.

PTSD is particularly appealing in civil litigation because it is considered a diagnosis that can address causality and suggest a victim. Thus, it is desirable in issues related to compensation and claims of personal injury; it is incident specific and therefore it can be easier for attorneys to argue that all of a plaintiff's difficulties emerge from the specific traumatic incident (Rosen & Grunert, 2012). In contrast, diagnoses such as depression or anxiety leave a wide range of possibilities for causation. In the criminal arena, PTSD has been offered as the basis in defenses including insanity, unconsciousness, self-defense, and diminished capacity, as well as in sentence mitigation proceedings (Berger et al., 2012). The ever-expanding definition of PTSD, particular in light of the *DSM–5* criteria change noted below, is leading to "criterion creep" (Rosen, 2004–2005). This can translate to an increase in frequency of this diagnosis and a likely increase in which this diagnosis will be at issue in legal proceedings. For these reasons, it is important that a forensic neuropsychologist be well versed in the nuances of PTSD.

Diagnostic Considerations

The *DSM–5*'s anxiety disorders chapter contains several changes from earlier editions. It no longer includes obsessive–compulsive disorder (OCD; which is now in a separate chapter, "Obsessive–Compulsive and Related Disorders") or PTSD and acute stress disorder (which are included in a separate chapter, "Trauma- and Stressor-Related Disorders"). The anxiety disorder chapter includes separation anxiety disorder, selective mutism, generalized anxiety disorder, agoraphobia, specific phobia, social anxiety disorder, panic disorder, substance- or medication-induced anxiety disorder, anxiety disorder due to another medical condition, other specified anxiety disorder, and unspecified anxiety disorder. It is beyond the scope of this chapter to highlight all of the changes made to each specific diagnosis; however, a few are mentioned. For example, the cumbersome *DSM–IV* (American Psychiatric Association, 1994) terminology for describing various types of panic attacks (i.e., situationally bound or cued, situationally predisposed, and unexpected or uncued) was replaced with the terms *unexpected* and *expected* panic attacks. Also of note, panic attacks function as a marker and prognostic factor for severity of diagnosis, course, and comorbidity associated with multiple disorders, including, but not limited to, those in the anxiety category. Thus, panic attack can be used as a specifier that is applicable to all *DSM–5* disorders. Also, panic disorder and agoraphobia are untethered in *DSM–5*, in contrast to their pairing in *DSM–IV–TR* (panic disorder with agoraphobia, panic disorder without agoraphobia, and agoraphobia without history of panic disorder). Now, there are only two diagnoses, panic disorder and agoraphobia, each with separate criteria.

A significant change to the *DSM–5* is the new chapter, "Trauma- and Stressor-Related Disorders." The rationale for this change was to have PTSD classified with other disorders on the basis of a common etiology (i.e., exposure to a traumatic event), rather than symptoms, which is more consistent with how medical fields label diagnoses (Friedman et al., 2011). As noted earlier, some of the disorders in this chapter were previously listed under anxiety disorders in *DSM–IV–TR*. The disorders included in this section are reactive attachment disorder, disinhibited social engagement disorder, PTSD, acute stress disorder, adjustment disorder, other specified trauma- and stressor- related disorder, and unspecified trauma- and stressor- related disorder. As with anxiety disorders, several modifications have been made in the criteria for these disorders. For instance, adjustment disorders have been reconceptualized in *DSM–5*. In the *DSM–IV–TR*, they were often applied as a residual label when an individual was distressed but insufficiently so to warrant diagnosis with a separate disorder. In the *DSM–5*, adjustment disorders are a diverse collection of stress-response syndromes that occur after exposure to a distressing (traumatic or nontraumatic) event. The subtype characterizations of depressed mood, anxious symptoms, or disturbances in conduct remain the same. Historically, although adjustment disorder diagnoses are seen in forensic neuropsychological contexts, they have not often been as persuasive a mitigating factor compared with other disorders in the same category. This is because adjustment disorders typically have a milder cognitive, emotional, and social impact than other similar diagnoses.

Significant changes were made to the criteria for PTSD in the *DSM–5* (American Psychiatric Association, 2013). First, the stressor criterion (Criterion A) is more explicit with regard to how an individual experienced a traumatic event. Also, the subjective reaction to the traumatic event, Criterion A2, has been eliminated. In *DSM–IV*, there were three symptom clusters (reexperiencing, avoidance–numbing, and arousal). In *DSM–5*, the avoidance–numbing cluster is divided into two distinct clusters—avoidance and persistent negative alterations in cognition and mood—resulting in four major symptom clusters. The latter category, persistent negative alterations in cognition and mood, includes new or reconceptualized symptoms, such as persistent negative emotional states. The final cluster—alterations in arousal and reactivity—adds irritable or aggressive behavior and reckless or self-destructive behavior. In *DSM–5*, the diagnostic thresholds have been lowered to ensure developmental sensitivity, and separate criteria have been added for children age 6 years or younger. Both acute and chronic specifications were omitted from the *DSM–5*. Instead, a diagnosis is given if symptoms last at least 1 month, and no differentiation is made between acute and chronic PTSD. For symptoms that last from 3 days to 1 month after exposure to one or more traumatic events, a diagnosis of acute stress disorder is given. Delayed expression (i.e., *DSM–IV–TR*'s delayed-onset PTSD), which is noted when the criteria for a full diagnosis are not met until at least 6 months after the trauma, remains unchanged in the *DSM–5*. Two subtypes of PTSD have been added, the preschool subtype (PTSD in children younger than age 6 and the dissociative subtype (PTSD with prominent dissociative symptoms).

Differential diagnoses are always relevant to consider, certainly in forensic neuropsychological evaluations in which there is often potential for secondary gain and diagnostic pictures are typically complex. Given the former, symptom validity and malingering must be considered (discussed in a subsequent section). Major depressive disorder is the most common co-occurring disorder in people with PTSD. A well-established causal relationship exists between stressful events and depression, and a prior history of major depressive disorder is predictive of PTSD after exposure to major trauma (Foa, Stein, McFarlane, 2006). Acute stress disorder should be considered if the symptom pattern does not match the severity of PTSD. Other differential diagnoses range from adjustment disorder to psychotic disorders to OCD. The latter may be diagnosed for intrusive thoughts that are recurring but not related to a specific traumatic event. TBI can occur in the context of a traumatic stressor, and TBI and PTSD have many overlapping symptoms. These symptoms are not mutually exclusive, and the focus should be on identifying symptoms that are distinct to each presentation.

Additionally, although the *DSM–5* does not recognize complex traumatic stress, given its increasing presence in the literature, and the possibility of encountering individuals with such experiences, a brief discussion seems relevant (Courtois & Ford, 2009). Individuals who have experienced multiple traumas, ranging from prolonged and repeated trauma during childhood to repetitive trauma in the context of significant interpersonal relationships, are at increased risk for complex traumatic stress (Herman, 1992). These individuals have usually developed individual, unique reactions to trauma (Herman, 1992). Often, the symptoms of complex trauma do not entirely match PTSD criteria, and the severity and impact of complex trauma can exceed that of PTSD (Courtois & Ford, 2009). Forensic neuropsychological experts are encouraged to review the current literature on this topic if it arises in work on a case.

Last, in-depth coverage of measures to assess PTSD and anxiety disorders is outside the scope of this chapter. However, brief mention of a few PTSD-specific measures is indicated, and broader coverage of measures of psychological functioning is included later. Self-report measures (e.g., the Beck Anxiety Inventory) and objective measures of personality described below can be useful in assessing anxiety and trauma and stressor-related disorders (as well as other areas of psychological functioning). Many checklists and semistructured interviews have been developed to assess PTSD. One, the Posttraumatic Stress Disorder Checklist (Weathers et al., 2013), a 30-question structured interview considered the gold standard for PTSD assessment, was recently revised to accommodate the *DSM–5* diagnostic criteria. Research has indicated that it is a psychometrically sound measure of *DSM–5* PTSD symptoms that is useful for identifying provisional PTSD diagnostic status, quantifying PTSD symptom severity, and detecting clinical change over time in PTSD symptoms among service members seeking treatment (Wortmann et al., 2016). Several other measures have been updated to assess PTSD with the new *DSM–5* criteria, including the Clinician-Administered PTSD Scale for DSM–5–Child/Adolescent Version, Dissociative Subtype of PTSD Scale, PTSD Checklist for DSM–5, and Life Events Checklist for DSM–5. The Primary Care PTSD Screen, which will also be available in Spanish, is still being revised.

A unique measure of PTSD that is less known is the Morel Emotional Numbing Test (MENT; Morel, 1998), which was specifically designed to identify feigned PTSD. Among the symptoms of PTSD, it focuses on emotional numbing. Contrary to what might be expected on first sight, most adults can easily complete the MENT tasks accurately, with the possible exception of some of the types of individuals that forensic neuropsychologists may be asked to evaluate (e.g., those with severe cognitive deficits). The MENT has demonstrated its usefulness in a number of studies, which have recently been summarized by Morel and Shepherd (2008). The estimated sensitivity of the MENT over five published studies is between 63% and 92%, with a pooled sensitivity estimate of 79%. Specificity estimates ranged from 77% to 100%, with a pooled estimate of 96%. Two major test modifications have been made, although they have yet not achieved widespread use or a solid body of validation literature (e.g., Messer & Fremouw, 2007).

Neuropsychological Functioning

Of the disorders mentioned earlier, perhaps the largest body of empirical literature exists for the effects of PTSD on cognitive functioning. Associations between PTSD and deficits on neuropsychological tasks have been well documented and include attentional deficits (Jenkins, Langlais, Delis, & Cohen, 2000), difficulty learning and recalling new information (Schuitevoerder et al., 2013), working memory deficits (Leskin & White, 2007), and impaired cognitive inhibition (Swick, Honzel, Larsen, Ashley, & Justus, 2012). A recent meta-analysis has supported these findings, with the largest effect sizes for learning new verbal information and processing speed (Scott et al., 2015). These cognitive deficits likely contribute to the functional impairments that are common in individuals with PTSD (Rodriguez, Holowka, & Marx, 2012) and adversely affect quality of life (Schnurr, Lunney, Bovin, & Marx, 2009).

For example, memory dysfunction has been found to accurately predict social and occupational functioning in veterans with PTSD (Geuze, Vermetten, de Kloet, Hijman, & Westenberg, 2009). Moreover, recognizing that most PTSD research has focused on retrospective memory, McFarland et al. (2016) examined event-based prospective memory among veterans and the role of PTSD in their ability to execute intentional behavior. Results suggested that elevated PTSD symptoms were associated with more difficulty completing tasks requiring prospective memory. Difficulty with both retrospective and prospective memory can create significant barriers for day-to-day functioning and warrants consideration in evaluations.

Given that the astute forensic neuropsychologist will be knowledgeable and able to discuss current literature on the stand should the need arise, it is worth noting that most research conducted on PTSD is in the context of mild to severe TBI and has been done with a veteran population. As such, it can be difficult to discern the etiological effects of TBI from those of PTSD and other comorbidities. Research from Pineau, Marchand, and Guay (2014) has underscored this point. They characterized the neuropsychological profile in individuals with PTSD and mild TBI (mTBI) using objective measures of attention, memory, and executive functions. The authors examined four groups: those with PTSD; those with mTBI; those with two formal diagnoses, PTSD and mTBI; and controls ($n = 25$). Confounding variables, such as medical, developmental, or neurological antecedents, were controlled, and measures of comorbid conditions, such as depression and anxiety, were examined for potential interaction effects. The PTSD and mTBI–PTSD groups reported more anxiety and depressive symptoms and evidenced more cognitive deficits than the mTBI group. Because the two PTSD groups differed in severity of PTSD symptoms but not in severity of depression and anxiety symptoms, the PTSD condition could not be considered as the unique factor. These findings highlight the complexities of research and diagnosis in this population and the importance of controlling for confounding medical and psychological comorbidities in the evaluation and treatment of PTSD populations. This is especially true when a concomitant mTBI is also suspected.

Neuroanatomical Correlates

Structural and functional imagining have revealed that the amygdala is essential in modulating fear and anxiety, and individuals with anxiety disorders often evidence heightened amygdala response to anxiety cues (Keeton, Kolos, &Walkup, 2009). Because of the connection between the amygdala and other limbic structures and the prefrontal cortex, hyperresponsivity of the amygdala may result in reduced activation thresholds in response to threats (Keeton et al., 2009). Interestingly, prefrontal–limbic activation abnormalities have been shown to reverse with clinical response to psychological or pharmacological interventions.

The previously referenced neuropsychological deficits in inattention, verbal learning and memory, working memory, cognitive inhibition, and processing speed reflect the underlying neural abnormalities associated with PTSD, including dysfunction within limbic and paralimbic circuits involving the prefrontal cortex, hippocampus, and amygdala (Rauch, Shin, & Phelps, 2006). For additional information, reviews by Rauch et al. (2006), Yehuda and LeDoux (2007), and Liberzon and Sripada (2007) are comprehensive and useful. A critical issue is determining whether particular anatomical or functional differences that have been associated with PTSD existed before the trauma exposure or arose afterward (Botteron, 2008). Preexisting differences may indicate risk or vulnerability factors, whereas differences that arise after exposure are more likely to be consequences of the traumatic event or the development of PTSD.

Treatment Considerations

Effective interventions have been identified to treat anxiety as well as stress and trauma-related disorders. Regarding the former, therapy, at times in conjunction with medication, has typically proven helpful (National Institute of Mental Health, 2016). With respect to the latter group of disorders, and PTSD specifically, it is important to highlight that most individuals who have experienced or are exposed to life-threatening trauma do not develop PTSD. Among those who meet criteria for PTSD, approximately two thirds recover in 3 months (Kessler, Sonnega, Bromet, Hughes, & Nelson, 1995). Given the frequency with which PTSD emerges in legal cases, particularly those involving causation and permanency, it is important to briefly note that several effective treatments have been identified. Cognitive–behavioral therapies have been found effective in a range of randomized controlled studies (e.g., Foa, Keane, Friedman, & Cohen, 2009). These therapies include exposure-based methods that include prolonged exposure, cognitive-oriented techniques, and combinations of exposure with anxiety management, cognitive restructuring, or both. Variants of cognitive–behavioral techniques, such as eye movement desensitization and reprocessing, are gaining increasing attention. However, research has demonstrated that in eye movement desensitization and reprocessing, unique, but often unnecessary, elements are included that do not add incrementally to the efficacy of traditional techniques (Rosen & Davison, 2003).

Recent research by Metcalf et al. (2016) noted multiple interventions, largely derived from a mind–body philosophy (such as yoga and acupuncture), are among the novel emerging treatment options. Similar to eye movement desensitization and reprocessing, the active components of these interventions does not seem to differ substantially from established treatments, and additional research is needed to determine their efficacy.

Research has indicated that treatment can result in longitudinal changes that have the potential to alter the trajectory of the illness (e.g., Foa et al., 2009). Achieving a better understanding of the possible interactions between PTSD and TBI, among other disorders, is of utmost clinical importance. If areas implicated in PTSD or their interconnecting pathways have been injured, symptom severity, response to treatment, or both may be altered accordingly.

Implications for Forensic Neuropsychological Evaluations

The previous pages have highlighted the role that anxiety, stress, and trauma play in an individual's functioning and the potential salience of any or all of these factors for the forensic neuropsychologist. Again, homing in on PTSD with the *DSM–5* diagnostic criteria in mind, the implications for forensic neuropsychological evaluations seem considerable. Indeed, per Dr. Alan Stone (1993),

> No diagnosis in the history of American psychiatry has had a more dramatic and pervasive impact on law and social justice than PTSD. . . . The diagnosis of

> PTSD has also provided a new credibility to a variety of victims who come before the courts either as defendants or plaintiffs. (pp. 23–24)

As previously noted, PTSD has been an influential factor in a range of criminal defense strategies, and the expanded criteria of the *DSM–5* as well as the newly added symptoms are likely to increase the use of PTSD diagnoses by defendants. From the civil perspective, categorizing PTSD as it is currently—a trauma- and stressor-related disorder—may strengthen the perception of direct causation, despite evidence that predisposing factors and posttrauma experiences often play an important role in the development of PTSD (Vogt, King, & King, 2007).

Levin, Kleinman, and Adler (2014) provided an excellent review of forensic considerations related to PTSD and the *DSM–5*. Forensic neuropsychologists will be faced with typical tasks inherent in evaluations in which there is potential for secondary gain, whether it is monetary or related to one's freedom. It will be essential to assess for effort and the possibility of malingering, and collateral information will, as always, be crucial. Although there will almost always be benefit to open-ended questioning in forensic interviews, the *DSM–5* changes to the PTSD criteria broaden it such that evaluators may want a checklist or structured interview to ensure that all important areas are assessed.

Levin et al. (2014) also noted concern about the language of specific stressors. For instance, sexual violence, new to *DSM–5*, is vaguely defined with no prior benchmarks, leaving it open to interpretation. Imagine an employment litigation case in which a forensic neuropsychologist has been hired to evaluate an employee for potential cognitive deficits that "must have" contributed to his "out-of-character noncontact sexual abuse" toward a coworker. The coworker is claiming that this behavior is the precipitant for the alleged PTSD from which he is now suffering. In this case, the forensic neuropsychologist will have to grapple with this vague definition while evaluating the neuropsychological functioning of the alleged perpetrator. It seems likely that expert and legal scholars will struggle to reach consensus about what constitutes stressor-qualifying sexual violence. Also, although thus far it is thought that removal of *DSM–IV–TR* A2 criteria (that the individual experience intense fear, helplessness, or horror at the time of the traumatic event criteria) will not affect the prevalence of PTSD, Levin et al. pointed out that this change is counterintuitive and may increase the potential for malingering. For instance, although a plaintiff could claim PTSD with no emotional response at the time of the traumatic event, per the *DSM–5* definition the forensic neuropsychologist hired by the plaintiff could reasonably be asked how the plaintiff could develop PTSD if he or she did not initially experience any of those emotional reactions to the traumatic event.

Additional examples of *DSM–5* and PTSD considerations for forensic neuropsychologists include the often difficult task of distinguishing PTSD-based recklessness and aggression from the effects of other contributors to violence such as substance abuse and depression or psychosocial factors, which are highly comorbid with PTSD. This distinction can be particularly relevant, for example, in the evaluation of diminished capacity or mitigation in the criminal process. Indeed, Donley et al. (2012) demonstrated in a low-income, urban, civilian population that exposure to trauma and a diagnosis of PTSD increased risk of involvement in the criminal justice system. Furthermore, individuals with PTSD were more likely than those without PTSD to have been charged for violent offenses.

The new emphasis on dissociation adds another consideration for criminal defense strategy. Although dissociation is not a novel construct, and it is present in other conditions, now that the specific dissociative subtype is explicitly listed in the *DSM–5*, it is possible that defendants and plaintiffs will target more of their focus on this as a potential legal strategy (e.g., claiming that they do not recall the alleged crime because of dissociation). Although this could be a valid tactic, all involved parties will need to remain mindful that dissociation does not equate to a break in reality. Similarly, extended flashbacks may be relevant when considering criminal responsibility and one's ability to understand the nature and quality or the wrongfulness of one's actions. However, these factors will need to be considered in the context of all of the relevant pretraumatic, peritraumatic, and posttraumatic factors that must be taken into account. Last, there is the question of how subthreshold disorders (compared with PTSD), such as adjustment disorder or unspecified trauma- and stressor-related disorder, may be used. The *DSM–5* language will permit plaintiffs to include the term *trauma* when describing potential damages, without clear enumeration of specific necessary symptoms. This could lead to overuse of this diagnosis.

Broadly, as is the case with any forensic neuropsychological evaluation, it is essential to consider relevant cultural components when evaluating anxiety and trauma-related disorders. Although research is limited across cultures, PTSD has been observed in Southeast Asian, South American, Middle Eastern, and Native American survivors (Osterman & de Jong, 2007; Wilson & Tang, 2007). As Stamm and Friedman (2000) emphasized, however, simply observing PTSD does not mean that it is the "best conceptual tool for characterizing post-traumatic distress among non-Western individuals" (p. 73). In fact, many cross-cultural trauma-related symptoms do not fit the *DSM–5* criteria. The expert must be knowledgeable about these issues as they relate to the specific examinee and be able to articulate these considerations.

Although it is not possible to predict exactly how attorneys or courts will respond to the new PTSD criteria in the *DSM–5*, we hypothesize that due to the expansion of the definition, there will be an increase in use, or attempted use, of this diagnosis. Practically speaking, this increase could result in new civil claims or novel criminal defense approaches, as well as increased disability claims. In the courtroom, the response of triers of fact will be determined by the forensic neuropsychologist's ability to articulate his or her findings. Levin et al. (2014) pointed out that the concept of trauma and PTSD has become more accepted and understood as a result of the September 11, 2001, terrorist attacks and their aftermath and the return of veterans with PTSD. Levin et al. (2014) proposed that the combination of increased public acceptance of PTSD, and the broader diagnostic criteria, could have a long-lasting impact.

OTHER DISORDERS OF INTEREST

In addition to depression, anxiety, and trauma- and stressor-related disorders, many other psychiatric conditions warrant attention. Although all of these cannot be included in this chapter, in this section we review select disorders with brief diagnostic considerations, information about neuropsychological functioning, and implications for forensic neuropsychological evaluations.

Schizophrenia Spectrum and Other Psychotic Disorders

Diagnostic considerations. Schizophrenia spectrum and other psychotic disorders are characterized by the presence of delusions, hallucinations, disorganization in thought and behavior, and negative symptoms, according to the *DSM–5* and vary with regard to severity of symptoms, presence or absence of depression or manic symptoms, and timeline. *DSM–5* includes the following diagnoses in this category: schizotypal personality disorder, delusional disorder, catatonia, brief psychotic disorder, schizophreniform disorder, schizophrenia, schizoaffective disorder, substance- or medication-induced psychotic disorder, psychotic disorder due to another medical condition, and other specified and unspecified schizophrenia spectrum and other psychotic disorders. As with all diagnoses, the symptoms must correspond with deficits in functioning in major areas, such as employment, interpersonal relationships, or ability to care for self. Typical age of onset is between the late teens and early adulthood, with a slightly earlier peak onset for males. Differential diagnostic considerations include major depressive or bipolar disorders with psychotic or catatonic features, OCD and body dysmorphic disorder, PTSD, and autism spectrum disorder or communication disorders. Schizophrenia spectrum and other psychotic disorders are frequently associated with comorbid substance-related disorders and, to a lesser degree, anxiety disorders, OCD, and panic disorder. Individuals with schizophrenia and other psychotic spectrum disorders are also at risk for comorbid medical conditions and poor health, including weight gain, diabetes, metabolic syndrome, and cardiovascular and coronary disease.

Neuropsychological functioning. Individuals with schizophrenia display a range of cognitive deficits that correlate with significant functional impairment (see Marcopulos & Kurtz, 2012, for a review). Although there is great heterogeneity, cognitive deficits in schizophrenia include impairment in overall IQ and general functioning that predate the onset of other symptoms, with particular deficits in attention and working memory, executive functioning, episodic memory (verbal and nonverbal), language, processing speed, and social cognition (Kurtz & Marcopulos, 2012). Negative symptoms of schizophrenia correlate with neuropsychological test performance, including verbal fluency, verbal memory, and IQ, with disorganization relating to problems with attention and visual memory. Positive symptoms correlate with processing speed but have a lesser impact on performance than negative symptoms or disorganization.

Implications for forensic neuropsychological evaluations. Individuals with schizophrenia and other psychotic spectrum disorders pose a unique challenge in civil forensic settings because cognitive deficits often predate the onset of other symptoms of psychosis. Examiners should carefully establish a baseline of deficits before the incident in question to determine whether the current reported symptoms are beyond expectations on the basis of the individual's history. TBI in young adults poses a particular challenge, given that the typical onset of psychotic symptoms is in adolescence and young adulthood, and this age group is also at higher risk for brain injury (Roebuck-Spencer & Sherer, 2008). Recent meta-analyses have suggested a complex relationship between TBI and development of schizophrenia, with a higher risk of schizophrenia symptoms after TBI in relatives of individuals with schizophrenia but also an increased incidence of TBI in that group compared with controls (Molloy, Conroy, Cotter, & Cannon, 2011). Collateral information from preinjury records or discussion with third parties can help to differentiate new-onset cognitive concerns from long-standing deficits.

In criminal forensic settings, neuropsychologists can be especially helpful in describing deficits related to cognitive symptoms of schizophrenia in a way that is useful to answering the psycholegal question. Individuals diagnosed with a psychotic disorder are more likely to be found incompetent to stand trial than those without such a diagnosis (Pirelli, Gottdiener, & Zapf, 2011), and cognitive deficits are associated with incompetence to stand trial (Nestor, Daggett, Haycock, & Price, 1999; Ryba & Zapf, 2011). A thorough neuropsychological assessment can help to illustrate situations in which a person's psychiatric symptoms are well controlled but the person remains incompetent because of cognitive difficulties that affect his or her ability to understand or apply legal knowledge.

Bipolar Disorder

Diagnostic considerations. *DSM–5* bipolar and related disorders include bipolar I disorder, bipolar II disorder, cyclothymic disorder, substance- or medication-induced bipolar and related disorder, bipolar and related disorder due to another medical condition, other specified bipolar and related disorder, and unspecified bipolar and related disorder, with distinctions made on the basis of symptom severity. Manic symptoms include mood changes and increased energy, along with (a) grandiosity, (b) reduced need for sleep, (c) increased talking, (d) racing thoughts, (e) distractibility, (f) increased goal-directed activity, and (g) participation in activities with likely negative outcomes. Typical age of onset is approximately age 18, although onset can range from childhood to later adulthood. Differential diagnostic considerations include major depressive disorder, anxiety disorders, attention deficit/hyperactivity disorder, personality disorders, and disorders with prominent irritability. Bipolar I disorder is also associated with substance use disorders, associated medical conditions (e.g., metabolic syndrome, migraine), anxiety disorders, attention deficit/hyperactivity disorder, or other impulse control disorders.

Neuropsychological functioning. Cognitive deficits associated with bipolar disorder include processing speed, executive functioning, and learning and memory (Langenecker, Lee, & Bieliauskas, 2009). These deficits can be disabling, although they are typically not as severe as the deficits found in schizophrenia and other psychotic spectrum disorders (Bortolato, Miskowiak, Köhler, Vieta, & Carvalho, 2015). Deficits associated with bipolar disorder are naturally more severe when the individual is experiencing manic symptoms or symptoms of depression but persist even in euthymic states.

Implications for forensic neuropsychological evaluations. In civil forensic settings, the symptoms of bipolar disorder should be carefully differentiated from symptoms related to the incident in question (e.g., distractibility due to mania vs. impaired attention due to TBI). Individuals with bipolar disorder often come to the attention of the criminal justice system during a manic episode. If an individual is in an active manic phase, testing should be postponed until those symptoms have abated to provide for the best opportunity to establish a person's functioning when euthymic.

Personality Disorders

Diagnostic considerations. A personality disorder is a persisting approach to life and interactions with others that falls outside of social and cultural norms and causes functional impairments (*DSM–5*). Cluster A personality disorders include paranoid personality disorder, schizoid personality disorder, and schizotypal personality disorder. Cluster B includes antisocial personality disorder, borderline personality disorder, histrionic personality disorder, and narcissistic personality disorder. Cluster C includes avoidant personality disorder, dependent personality disorder, and obsessive–compulsive personality disorder. Additional diagnoses include personality change due to another medical condition and other specified personality disorder and unspecified personality disorder. Differential diagnostic considerations include other mental disorders and personality traits, psychotic disorder, anxiety and depressive disorders, PTSD, substance use disorders, and personality change due to another medical condition.

Neuropsychological functioning. With regard to cognitive functioning, schizotypal personality disorder is associated with deficits in attention, working memory, and executive functioning (Rosell, Futterman, McMaster, & Siever, 2014). One study suggested problems in vocational functioning in schizotypal and paranoid personality disorder, even when cognitive functioning was controlled (McGurk et al., 2013). However, limited information was available regarding cognitive deficits in paranoid personality disorder or schizoid personality disorder. Regarding Cluster B disorders, individuals with borderline personality disorder exhibit deficits in executive functioning, processing speed, attention, visuospatial skills, learning and memory, and verbal intelligence (Ruocco, 2005; Unoka & Richman, 2016), with larger deficits associated with greater psychiatric comorbidities and smaller deficits associated with higher education of the individuals and their parents.

Research regarding cognition and antisocial personality disorder has largely focused on deficits in executive functioning, with mixed results (Morgan & Lilienfeld, 2000), and available studies have conflated antisocial personality disorder with criminal or violent behavior and psychopathy. Limited information is available regarding cognition and histrionic personality disorder or narcissistic personality disorder. Regarding Cluster C disorders, obsessive–compulsive personality disorder is associated with executive functioning deficits (Aycicegi-Dinn, Dinn, & Caldwell-Harris, 2009; Fineberg et al., 2015; García-Villamisar & Dattilo, 2015). Little information is available regarding potential cognitive deficits in avoidant or dependent personality disorder, but one study suggested line bisection deficits in dependent personality disorder (Wang et al., 2003). Another study of Cluster B and Cluster C personality disorders did not indicate significant differences from controls on a measure of executive functioning (Ruocco, McCloskey, Lee, & Coccaro, 2009).

Implications for forensic neuropsychological evaluations. In civil forensic settings, individuals with schizotypal and borderline personality disorder may provide the greatest difficulty for examiners in teasing apart possible cognitive deficits from new-onset difficulties resulting from the incident in question; premorbid records and collateral information will be useful in making this determination. In civil and criminal forensic settings, as in clinical settings, personality pathology can pose a significant barrier to accurate assessment. Examiners should maintain adequate boundaries and provide sufficient explanation about the evaluation process. Examiners should assess for emotional distress within the evaluation session, taking breaks as needed. The battery should be targeted, with limited extra tests, to allow for maximum assessment in case the emotional toll is overwhelming and the person refuses to complete testing. In criminal forensic settings, particularly inpatient ones, care should be taken to work with treatment teams to intervene if the emotional toll of testing leads to self-injurious or aggressive behaviors.

Dissociative Disorders

Diagnostic considerations. In *DSM–5*, dissociative disorders include dissociative identity disorder, dissociative amnesia, depersonalization–derealization disorder, other specified dissociative disorder, and unspecified dissociative disorder and are defined by interruption in the typical experience of awareness, memory, and other characteristics of human experience. The onset of dissociative disorders is often associated with the experience of trauma. Differential diagnostic considerations include mood disorder, PTSD, psychotic disorders, substance- or medication-induced disorders, personality disorders, conversion disorder, neurological disorders (e.g., seizure, TBI), factitious disorder, and malingering.

Neuropsychological functioning. Cognitive deficits associated with dissociative disorders are controversial and typically include amnesia for autobiographical information (Markowitsch & Staniloiu, 2013; Staniloiu & Markowitsch, 2014). This type of memory deficit is not typical of neurologically based memory impairment in the absence of other cognitive deficits (i.e., global amnesia after severe TBI), raising questions regarding the validity of dissociative amnesia as a genuine amnestic disorder (Giesbrecht, Lynn, Lilienfeld, & Merckelbach, 2008; Marcopulos, Hedjar, & Arredondo, 2016). A review of the literature did not indicate particular cognitive profiles associated with dissociative disorders beyond minor deficits in memory and cognition related to the dissociative process (Giesbrecht et al., 2008; Rossini, Schwartz, & Braun, 1996).

Implications for forensic neuropsychological evaluations. Examiners in civil and criminal forensic settings should carefully verify and validate reported memory concerns by obtaining collateral information, when possible, about the individual's knowledge of autobiographical information. Denney (2008) described a process of creating two-alternative forced-choice options to assess for accuracy of claimed amnesia for the circumstances of a crime in criminal cases, and this process could be modified to assess for claimed autobiographical amnesia, using information gathered from records or collateral informants.

Somatic Symptom Disorders

Diagnostic considerations. In *DSM–5*, somatic symptom and related disorders include somatic symptom disorder, illness anxiety disorder, conversion disorder (functional neurological symptom disorder), psychological factors affecting other medical conditions, factitious disorder, other specified somatic symptom and related disorder, and unspecified somatic symptom and related disorder. These diagnoses are characterized by significant physical concerns. Differential diagnostic considerations include other medical conditions, panic disorder and other anxiety disorders, depressive disorders, delusional disorder or other psychotic disorder, neurological disorder, body dysmorphic disorder, OCD, dissociative disorders, and malingering.

Neuropsychological functioning. Cognitive deficits associated with somatic symptom disorders are difficult to characterize because the presentation of deficits depends on the presentation of psychiatric symptoms, and these disorders can co-occur with medical illness associated with cognitive deficits. For example, an individual with conversion disorder related to physical symptoms may not have any cognitive deficits (Ali et al., 2015). A person presenting with psychogenic nonepileptic spells might demonstrate cognitive deficits similar to those of a person with epilepsy (Dickinson & Looper, 2012) or may have a combination of psychogenic nonepileptic spells and epileptic seizures, which can be associated with cognitive deficits. A person with functional cognitive disorder or medically unexplained symptoms may present with significant deficits on testing without a clear cause or report significant difficulties in daily life (Binder & Campbell, 2004; Pennington, Newson, Hayre, & Coulthard, 2015).

Implications for forensic neuropsychological evaluations. In civil forensic settings, examiners should rely on previous medical records to assess for the presence of somatic symptomatology before the incident in question. Care should be given to validate or verify self-report with observer report or documented changes in functioning. Individuals with somatic symptom and related disorders often present to primary medical settings before or instead of mental health settings, and a careful review of medical records may help to differentiate a long-standing pattern of somatic concerns from new onset symptom report following an event. In criminal cases, examiners should consider that somatic symptoms can present as functionally identical to physical illness. For example, individuals experiencing a psychogenic nonepileptic event may not be aware of their actions, and if they experience comorbid psychogenic nonepileptic spells and epilepsy, it may not be possible to distinguish between event types.

ASSESSMENT MEASURES

A more detailed accounting of the process and considerations in selecting assessment measures can be found in other chapters of this handbook and are not recounted here. Examiners are encouraged to approach the cognitive assessment in forensic evaluations carefully, choosing tests that address the areas of interest in a reliable and valid way. As noted in the American Academy of Clinical Neuropsychology amicus brief in *Baxter v. Temple* (2008), the process of evaluation is not dramatically different in clinical and forensic contexts because examiners should always "strive for objectivity and accuracy" (p. 4), regardless of the practice setting. However, neuropsychologists providing services to the court should be aware of the particular jurisdiction's admissibility standards to ensure to the best of their ability that the testimony they plan to provide is based on procedures that will be admissible in court (*Frye v. United States,* 1923; *Daubert v. Merrell Dow Pharmaceuticals,* 1993). Although it is ultimately the judge's decision whether to allow testimony, examiners are encouraged to use well-established measures and procedures with support in the literature to increase confidence in responding to admissibility challenges should they arise.

The following discussion is intended to assist practitioners in considering the impact of psychological and emotional functioning on frequently used tests of performance and symptom validity and symptom validity scales within frequently used measures of personality and emotional functioning. Table 9.1 provides a quick reference regarding effects of some of the psychiatric diagnoses discussed in this chapter on performance validity tests (PVTs) and cognitive testing.

Practice reviews of neuropsychologists suggest that use of a flexible battery approach is most common (82%) and that more than half of neuropsychologists participate in some forensic practice (Sweet, Benson, Nelson, & Moberg, 2015). Assessment of performance and symptom validity (Larrabee, 2012c) is an integral part of any neuropsychological evaluation, and such assessment is particularly important in civil and criminal forensic settings, given the strong opportunity for secondary gain. Research has suggested estimated base rates of definite malingering of 10% in civil neuropsychological settings (Slick, Tan, Strauss, & Hultsch, 2004) and of probable malingering ranging from 19% to 54% in criminal forensic settings (Ardolf, Denney, & Houston, 2007; Marcopulos et al., 2014; Mittenberg, Patton, Canyock, & Condit, 2002). Major neuropsychological professional organizations have acknowledged the importance of validity assessment in practice guidelines and policy papers (Board of Directors, 2007; Bush et al., 2005; Heilbronner, Sweet, Morgan, Larrabee, & Millis, 2009). Because this chapter focuses on psychiatric disorders and Chapter 5 of this handbook focuses on validity assessment, this chapter places greater emphasis on the assessment of symptom validity than on performance validity.

TABLE 9.1

Effects of Psychiatric Diagnoses on Performance Validity Tests and Cognitive Testing

Diagnostic category	PVT	SVT	Intellectual functioning	Attention	Processing speed	Language	Visuospatial functioning	Learning and memory	Executive functioning
Depression	—	—	—	R	R	—	—	R	—
PTSD/anxiety	—	—	—	R	R	—	—	R	R
Schizophrenia spectrum	C	C	R	R	R	R	—	R	R
Bipolar disorder	—	—	—	—	R	—	—	R	R
Paranoid PD	—	—	—	—	—	—	—	—	—
Schizoid PD	—	—	—	—	—	—	—	—	—
Schizotypal PD	—	—	—	R	—	—	—	—	R
Antisocial PD	—	—	—	—	—	—	—	—	R
Borderline PD	—	—	—	R	R	—	R	R	R
Histrionic PD	—	—	—	—	—	—	—	—	—
Narcissistic PD	—	—	—	—	—	—	—	—	—
Avoidant PD	—	—	—	—	—	—	—	—	—
Dependent PD	—	—	—	—	—	—	R	—	—
O-C PD	—	—	—	—	—	—	—	—	R
Dissociative	—	C	—	—	—	—	—	R	—
Somatic symptom disorders[a]	—	C	—	—	—	—	—	—	—

Note. C = use caution when interpreting; — = no known effect; O-C = obsessive–compulsive; PD = personality disorder; PTSD = posttraumatic stress disorder; PVT = Performance Validity Test; R = reduced performance relative to controls; SVT = Symptom Validity Test.

[a]Somatic symptom disorders related to neurological concerns (e.g., psychogenic nonepileptic spells) may affect cognitive testing. Use caution when interpreting PVTs and SVTs in individuals with limited intellectual abilities or cognitive disorders.

Performance Validity Measures

A recent survey of general neuropsychological practice indicated that almost all (92%) respondents used PVTs (Martin, Schroeder, & Odland, 2015).[1] The most frequently used stand-alone PVTs were the TOMM (78%) and WMT (58%). A previous survey of civil forensic neuropsychological practice indicated that the TOMM (71%), FIT (75%), RMT (50%), and WMT (50%) were most used (Slick et al., 2004). A meta-analysis of the VSVT, TOMM, WMT, LMT, and MSVT found large effect sizes across tests, studies, and practice areas, suggesting that these tests are useful in assessing performance validity (Sollman & Berry, 2011). Goldberg, Back-Madruga, and Boone (2007) reviewed existing literature on PVT performance and common psychiatric disorders and concluded that depression, OCD, anxiety disorders, and somatoform disorders did not have a significant effect on a range of PVTs, including forced-choice and performance-based stand-alone measures and embedded measures. Limited research has suggested that neuropsychological evaluation can be useful in assessing the validity of reported memory impairment in dissociative disorders (Marcopulos et al., 2016; Peters, van Oorsouw, Jelicic, & Merckelbach, 2013) and in assessing performance validity in borderline personality disorder (Ruocco, 2016). More research is needed on other diagnostic categories, but it is likely that positive findings for PVTs are suggestive of

[1]PVTs include, but are not limited to, the Test of Memory Malingering (TOMM; Tombaugh, 1996), Word Memory Test (WMT; P. Green, 2003), Rey 15-item Test (FIT; Strauss, Sherman, & Spreen, 2006), Recognition Memory Test (RMT; Warrington, 1984), Victoria Symptom Validity Test (VSVT; Slick, Hopp, Strauss, & Spellacy, 1996), Letter Memory Test (LMT; Inman et al., 1998), and Medical Symptom Validity Test (MSVT; P. Green, 2004).

reduced engagement in individuals with most major psychiatric diagnoses rather than genuine cognitive impairment.

Examiners should exercise caution when evaluating performance validity with individuals with schizophrenia spectrum and other psychotic disorders and in individuals with low intellectual functioning because the rate of false positive findings with these individuals using established cut scores may be higher (Marcopulos et al., 2014; Ruocco, 2016; Victor & Boone, 2007). Regardless of the diagnosis, performance at below-chance levels, failure of multiple PVTs, and use of additional criteria for determining reduced engagement or malingering can limit false-positive errors (Boone, 2007; Larrabee, 2012a, 2014; Slick, Sherman, & Iverson, 1999; Victor, Boone, Serpa, Buehler, & Ziegler, 2009).

Symptom Validity Measures

The Structured Inventory of Reported Symptoms (SIRS; Rogers, 1992) is the most studied stand-alone symptom validity measure (Kane & Dvoskin, 2011; Melton et al., 2007). It is designed as a structured interview with 172 items to assess endorsement of uncommon symptoms and exaggeration of symptoms with eight primary scales: Rare Symptoms, Symptom Combinations, Improbable and Absurd Symptoms, Reported Versus Observed Symptoms, Blatant Symptoms, Subtle Symptoms, Selectivity of Symptoms, and Severity of Symptoms. Research has suggested its utility in assessing symptom validity in civil and criminal forensic cases (Kane & Dvoskin, 2011; Rogers, 2008; Rogers, Payne, Berry, & Granacher, 2009), with caution recommended in use with individuals with limited intellectual abilities, cognitive dysfunction, and dissociative identity disorder. Meta-analysis indicated increased sensitivity but lower specificity in the literature than in the initial studies (D. Green & Rosenfeld, 2011).

The second edition of the SIRS was published in 2010 (Rogers, Sewell, & Gillard, 2010), and validation research outside of the initial studies has suggested high specificity but significantly reduced sensitivity (D. Green, Rosenfeld, & Belfi, 2013). Examiners should take into account the SIRS's limited utility in evaluating cognitive symptom exaggeration. The SIRS also takes up to 40 minutes to administer, which may be prohibitive in an already lengthy evaluation setting, particularly if the primary questions relate to cognitive concerns.

In a prolonged neuropsychological evaluation, the use of screening measures allows the examiner to determine whether further evaluation of symptom validity is needed. The Miller Forensic Assessment of Symptoms Test (Miller, 2001) is a screening measure with 25 items in a structured interview format that takes between 5 and 10 minutes to administer. Scales include Reported versus Observed Symptoms, Extreme Symptomatology, Rare Combinations, Unusual Hallucinations, Unusual Symptom Course, Negative Image, and Suggestibility. Studies have suggested utility as a screening measure in correctional settings using the total scale (Vitacco & Rogers, 2010) and in civil settings (Alwes, Clark, Berry, & Granacher, 2008). Similar to the SIRS, the Miller Forensic Assessment of Symptoms Test focuses primarily on psychiatric symptoms rather than cognitive symptoms, which limits its usefulness in screening for overreporting of cognitive symptoms. The Structured Inventory of Malingered Symptomatology (Widows & Smith, 2005) is a 75-item true–false questionnaire written at a fifth-grade reading level with an approximate 15-minute administration time. Scales include Low Intelligence, Affective Disorders, Neurological Impairment, Psychosis, and Amnesia. Studies have suggested its utility as a screening measure for psychiatric symptoms in criminal and civil forensic settings (Alwes et al., 2008; Vitacco & Rogers, 2010). A recent meta-analysis indicated that the Structured Inventory of Malingered Symptomatology is useful for screening but may overestimate feigning in populations with schizophrenia, intellectual disability, and psychogenic nonepileptic spells (van Impelen, Merckelbach, Jelicic, & Merten, 2014).

Personality and Emotional Functioning

Practice surveys of forensic psychologists and neuropsychologists have suggested that the Minnesota Multiphasic Personality Inventory (MMPI) and the MMPI–2; Butcher et al., 2001) is the instrument most frequently used to assess personality and emotional functioning (Archer, Buffington-Vollum, Stredny, & Handel, 2006; Rabin, Barr, & Burton,

2005). Responders in the Archer at al. (2006) study also rated the Personality Assessment Inventory (PAI; Morey, 1991) and the Millon Clinical Multiaxial Inventory (MCMI; Millon, 1997) as commonly used in forensic evaluations; a subset of responders in this study had neuropsychology experience.

Minnesota Multiphasic Personality Inventory. The MMPI is the most studied objective measure of personality and emotional functioning, with decades of research in a variety of settings (see Boone, 2012; Butcher, Hass, Greene, & Nelson, 2015; Larrabee, 2012b; Sweet & Goldman, 2015). The most current iteration of this test is the Minnesota Multiphasic Personality Inventory—2 Restructured Form (MMPI–2–RF; Ben-Porath & Tellegen, 2008), a 338-item, true–false questionnaire based on the MMPI–2 test items and a normative sample. The MMPI–2–RF takes between 35 and 50 minutes to administer and has a 4.5- to 5th-grade reading level. Comparison groups for scoring include civil and criminal forensic populations, and validity scales were created to assess for psychiatric symptom validity and cognitive and medical symptom validity. Validity scales include Cannot Say, Variable Response Inconsistency, True Response Inconsistency, Infrequent Responses, Infrequent Psychopathology Responses, Infrequent Somatic Responses, Symptom Validity, Response Bias Scale, Uncommon Virtues, and Adjustment Validity. Research has indicated that the newer scales are comparable to the MMPI–2 validity scales (Hoelzle, Nelson, & Arbisi, 2012) and are effective in civil forensic settings (Rogers, Gillard, Berry, & Granacher, 2011; Tarescavage, Wygant, Gervais, & Ben-Porath, 2013; Wygant et al., 2009) and criminal forensic settings (Sellbom, Toomey, Wygant, Kucharski, & Duncan, 2010), including assessment of cognitive concerns (Gervais, Wygant, Sellbom, & Ben-Porath, 2011). Many of the available studies of the MMPI–2–RF were completed by a handful of researchers with ties to the test. This is not necessarily negative, but examiners should assess the literature with this in mind. Studies from outside researchers have also suggested its utility (Rogers et al., 2011; Schroeder et al., 2012; Youngjohn, Wershba, Stevenson, Sturgeon, & Thomas, 2011). An additional benefit to using clinical measures with symptom validity scales is that the tests provide useful clinical information if the response style is valid, justifying the lengthy administration time.

Personality Assessment Inventory. The PAI (Morey, 1991) is a 344-item, multiple-choice measure that takes approximately 50 to 60 minutes to administer. It has a fourth-grade reading level. Validity scales include Inconsistency, Infrequency, Negative Impression Management, and Positive Impression Management; additional validity scales include the Malingering Index (Morey, 1996) and the Rogers Discriminant Function (Rogers, Sewell, Morey, & Ulstad, 1996). Research has suggested the PAI's utility for assessing overreporting, particularly in individuals with schizophrenia spectrum disorders (Hawes & Boccaccini, 2009) or PTSD (Rogers, Gillard, Wooley, & Ross, 2012; Wooley & Rogers, 2015), with mixed results when assessing feigned TBI (Keiski, Shore, Hamilton, & Malec, 2015; Whiteside, Galbreath, Brown, & Turnbull, 2012) and dissociative disorders (Stadnik, Brand, & Savoca, 2013). It is used in civil and criminal forensic settings (Edens, Cruise, & Buffington-Vollum, 2001) but may have a high false-positive rate (Bender, 2008; Sellbom & Bagby, 2008). For these reasons, Kane and Dvoskin (2009, citing Sellbom & Bagby, 2008) cautioned that the PAI may be more effective at "screening out malingering" than "screening in" (p. 136).

Millon Clinical Multiaxial Inventory. The MCMI (Millon, Grossman, & Millon, 2015), currently in its fourth edition (MCMI–IV), is a 195-item, true–false questionnaire that takes 25 to 30 minutes to administer. The reading level for the MCMI–IV is not clearly stated, but previous versions were at the 8th grade level. Researchers have expressed concerns about the use of the MCMI in forensic settings because the normative sample included only clinical populations, raising the possibility of overpathologizing nonclinical responders, and because of the limited research on response-style scales (Kane & Dvoskin, 2011). The MCMI–IV is not recommended for forensic use until independent validity research is published.

Disorder-Specific Measures

At times, examiners may want more detailed and specific information regarding the presence of a particular disorder (such as the PTSD-specific measures discussed above), or their evaluation may be limited by time constraints or the low reading level of the examinee. The most commonly used disorder-specific questionnaires in forensic evaluations include the Beck Depression Inventory, Second Edition (Beck, Steer, & Brown, 1996) and the Beck Anxiety Inventory (Archer et al., 2006; Beck & Steer, 1990). Questionnaires exist for almost all of the diagnoses discussed in this chapter (see Kane & Dvoskin, 2011, for additional measures), but the examiner is cautioned to avoid relying heavily on responses to these questionnaires because they are often face valid and lack symptom validity scales.

CONCLUSION

Because of their unique knowledge of the brain, behavior, and psychopathology, forensic neuropsychologists are often called on to assist triers of fact in making a legal decision. As part of the forensic assessment process, evaluators must ensure that in addition to the traditional focus on cognition, they conduct a thorough investigation into the individual's psychiatric history and present mental health functioning, as well as his or her family history of such difficulties.

Although this chapter does not exhaustively cover all psychiatric conditions, we have discussed some of those most salient to forensic work. Although it can be difficult, if not impossible, to discern the etiology of the cognitive deficits (e.g., are scores decreased because of untreated depression, because of a head injury sustained several weeks ago, or because of related symptoms of PTSD?), the prudent forensic neuropsychologist must be able to effectively evaluate, and articulate to a judge or jury, the potential impact of psychiatric conditions on cognitive functioning and vice versa. A forensic neuropsychologist can accomplish this goal by taking into account the psychiatric diagnostic considerations and forensic implications discussed throughout this chapter, as well as by staying abreast of emerging literature in the field, including base rates of relevant conditions, and by making dedicated efforts to obtain collateral information. Forensic neuropsychologists are uniquely poised to assess, address, and educate those in the legal system about the interplay of psychiatric illness and cognitive dysfunction and to translate this to real-world considerations for the examinee, court, and society. Conscientious, comprehensive, and effective work in this area is likely to ensure continued proliferation of work for forensic neuropsychologists.

References

Ali, S., Jabeen, S., Pate, R. J., Shahid, M., Chinala, S., Nathani, M., & Shah, R. (2015). Conversion disorder—mind versus body: A review. *Innovations in Clinical Neuroscience, 12,* 27–33.

Alwes, Y. R., Clark, J. A., Berry, D. T. R., & Granacher, R. P. (2008). Screening for feigning in a civil forensic setting. *Journal of Clinical and Experimental Neuropsychology, 30,* 133–140. http://dx.doi.org/10.1080/13803390701260363

American Academy of Clinical Neuropsychology. (2007). *Amicus brief in support of flexible battery use: State of New Hampshire Supreme Court.* Retrieved from https://theaacn.org/wp-content/uploads/2015/10/baxter_v_temple.pdf

American Psychiatric Association. (1980). *Diagnostic and statistical manual of mental disorders* (3rd ed.). Washington, DC: Author.

American Psychiatric Association. (1994). *Diagnostic and statistical manual of mental disorders* (4th ed.). Washington, DC: Author.

American Psychiatric Association. (2000). *Diagnostic and statistical manual of mental disorders* (4th ed., text revision). Washington, DC: Author.

American Psychiatric Association. (2013). *Diagnostic and statistical manual of mental disorders* (5th ed.). Washington, DC: Author.

Archer, R. P., Buffington-Vollum, J. K., Stredny, R. V., & Handel, R. W. (2006). A survey of psychological test use patterns among forensic psychologists. *Journal of Personality Assessment, 87,* 84–94. http://dx.doi.org/10.1207/s15327752jpa8701_07

Ardolf, B. R., Denney, R. L., & Houston, C. M. (2007). Base rates of negative response bias and malingered neurocognitive dysfunction among criminal defendants referred for neuropsychological evaluation. *Clinical Neuropsychologist, 21,* 899–916. http://dx.doi.org/10.1080/13825580600966391

Aycicegi-Dinn, A., Dinn, W. M., & Caldwell-Harris, C. L. (2009). Obsessive-compulsive personality traits: Compensatory response to executive function deficit?

International Journal of Neuroscience, 119, 600–608. http://dx.doi.org/10.1080/00207450802543783

Baxter v. Temple, 157 N.H. 280, 949 A.2d 167 (2008).

Beauregard, M., Leroux, J. M., Bergman, S., Arzoumanian, Y., Beaudoin, G., Bourgouin, P., & Stip, E. (1998). The functional neuroanatomy of major depression: An fMRI study using an emotional activation paradigm. *Neuroreport, 9,* 3253–3258. http://dx.doi.org/10.1097/00001756-199810050-00022

Beck, A. T., & Steer, R. A. (1990). *Beck Anxiety Inventory manual.* San Antonio, TX: Psychological Corporation.

Beck, A. T., Steer, R. A., & Brown, G. (1996). *Beck Depression Inventory manual* (2nd ed.). San Antonio, TX: Psychological Corporation.

Bender, S. D. (2008). Malingered traumatic brain injury. In R. Rogers (Ed.), *Clinical assessment of malingering and deception* (3rd ed., pp. 69–86). New York, NY: Guilford Press.

Ben-Porath, Y. S., & Tellegen, A. (2008). *MMPI–2–RF (Minnesota Multiphasic Personality Inventory—2 Restructured Form): Manual for administration, scoring, and interpretation.* Minneapolis: University of Minnesota Press.

Berger, O., McNiel, D. E., & Binder, R. L. (2012). PTSD as a criminal defense: A review of case law. *Journal of the American Academy of Psychiatry and the Law, 40,* 509–521.

Binder, L. M., & Campbell, K. A. (2004). Medically unexplained symptoms and neuropsychological assessment. *Journal of Clinical and Experimental Neuropsychology, 26,* 369–392. http://dx.doi.org/10.1080/13803390490510095

Board of Directors. (2007). American Academy of Clinical Neuropsychology (AACN) practice guidelines for neuropsychological assessment and consultation. *Clinical Neuropsychologist, 21,* 209–231. http://dx.doi.org/10.1080/13825580601025932

Boone, K. B. (Ed.). (2007). *Assessment of feigned cognitive impairment: A neuropsychological perspective.* New York, NY: Guilford Press.

Boone, K. B. (Ed.). (2012). *Clinical practice of forensic neuropsychology: An evidence-based approach.* New York, NY: Guilford Press.

Bortolato, B., Miskowiak, K. W., Köhler, C. A., Vieta, E., & Carvalho, A. F. (2015). Cognitive dysfunction in bipolar disorder and schizophrenia: A systematic review of meta-analyses. *Neuropsychiatric Disease and Treatment, 11,* 3111–3125.

Botteron, K. N. (2008). Regional specificity of traumatic stress-related cortical reduction: Further evidence from a twin study of post-traumatic stress disorder. *Biological Psychiatry, 63,* 539–541. http://dx.doi.org/10.1016/j.biopsych.2008.01.015

Bush, S. S., Ruff, R. M., Tröster, A. I., Barth, J. T., Koffler, S. P., Pliskin, N. H., . . . Silver, C. H. (2005). Symptom validity assessment: Practice issues and medical necessity. *Archives of Clinical Neuropsychology, 20,* 419–426. http://dx.doi.org/10.1016/j.acn.2005.02.002

Butcher, J. N., Graham, J. R., Ben-Porath, Y. S., Tellegen, A., Dahlstrom, W. G., & Kaemmer, B. (2001). *Minnesota Multiphasic Personality Inventory—2 (MMPI–2): Manual for administration, scoring, and interpretation* (Rev. ed.). http://dx.doi.org/10.1016/B0-08-043076-7/01294-8

Butcher, J. N., Hass, G. A., Greene, R. L., & Nelson, L. D. (2015). *Using the MMPI–2 in forensic assessment.* http://dx.doi.org/10.1037/14571-000

Cavenar, J. O., Maltbie, A. A., & Austin, L. (1979). Depression simulating organic brain disease. *American Journal of Psychiatry, 136,* 521–523.

Center for Behavioral Health Statistics and Quality. (2015). *Behavioral health trends in the United States: Results from the 2014 National Survey on Drug Use and Health.* Retrieved from https://www.samhsa.gov/data/sites/default/files/NSDUH-FRR1-2014/NSDUH-FRR1-2014.htm

Cohen, F. (1996). Offenders with mental disorders in the criminal justice-correctional process. In B. D. Sales & D. W. Shuman (Eds.), *Law, mental health, and mental disorder* (pp. 397–413). Pacific Grove, CA: Brooks/Cole.

Courtois, C. A., & Ford, J. D. (Eds.). (2009). *Treating complex traumatic stress disorders: An evidence-based guide.* New York, NY: Guilford Press.

Daubert v. Merrell Dow Pharmaceuticals, Inc., 509 U.S. 579 (1993).

Denney, R. L. (2008). Negative response bias and malingering during neuropsychological assessment in criminal forensic settings. In R. L. Denney & J. P. Sullivan (Eds.), *Clinical neuropsychology in the criminal forensic setting* (pp. 91–134). New York, NY: Guilford Press.

DeRubeis, R. J., Siegle, G. J., & Hollon, S. D. (2008). Cognitive therapy versus medication for depression: Treatment outcomes and neural mechanisms. *Nature Reviews Neuroscience, 9,* 788–796. http://dx.doi.org/10.1038/nrn2345

Dickinson, P., & Looper, K. J. (2012). Psychogenic nonepileptic seizures: A current overview. *Epilepsia, 53,* 1679–1689. http://dx.doi.org/10.1111/j.1528-1167.2012.03606.x

Donley, S., Habib, L., Jovanovic, T., Kamkwalala, A., Evces, M., Egan, G., . . . Ressler, K. J. (2012). Civilian PTSD symptoms and risk for involvement in the criminal justice system. *Journal of the American Academy of Psychiatry and the Law, 40,* 522–529.

Edens, J. F., Cruise, K. R., & Buffington-Vollum, J. K. (2001). Forensic and correctional applications of the Personality Assessment Inventory. *Behavioral Sciences and the Law, 19,* 519–543. http://dx.doi.org/10.1002/bsl.457

Ferguson, K. E., Iverson, G. L., Langenecker, S. A., & Young, A. H. (2012). Depression in the context of workplace injury. In S. S. Bush & G. L. Iverson (Eds.), *Neuropsychological assessment of work-related injuries* (pp. 187–242). New York, NY: Guilford Press.

Fineberg, N. A., Day, G. A., de Koenigswarter, N., Reghunandanan, S., Kolli, S., Jefferies-Sewell, K., . . . Laws, K. R. (2015). The neuropsychology of obsessive-compulsive personality disorder: A new analysis. *CNS Spectrums, 20,* 490–499. http://dx.doi.org/10.1017/S1092852914000662

Foa, E. B., Keane, T. M., Friedman, M. J., & Cohen, J. A. (Eds.). (2009). *Effective treatments for PTSD: Practice guidelines from the International Society for Traumatic Stress studies* (2nd ed.). New York, NY: Guilford Press.

Foa, E. B., Stein, D. J., & McFarlane, A. C. (2006). Symptomatology and psychopathology of mental health problems after disaster. *Journal of Clinical Psychiatry, 67*(Suppl. 2), 15–25.

Friedman, M. J., Resick, P. A., Bryant, R. A., Strain, J., Horowitz, M., & Spiegel, D. (2011). Classification of trauma and stressor-related disorders in *DSM–5*. *Depression and Anxiety, 28,* 737–749. http://dx.doi.org/10.1002/da.20845

Frye v. United States, 293 F. 1013, 34 ALR 145 (D.C. Cir. 1923)

García-Villamisar, D., & Dattilo, J. (2015). Executive functioning in people with obsessive-compulsive personality traits: Evidence of modest impairment. *Journal of Personality Disorders, 29,* 418–430. http://dx.doi.org/10.1521/pedi_2013_27_101

Gervais, R. O., Wygant, D. B., Sellbom, M., & Ben-Porath, Y. S. (2011). Associations between symptom validity test failure and scores on the MMPI–2–RF validity and substantive scales. *Journal of Personality Assessment, 93,* 508–517. http://dx.doi.org/10.1080/00223891.2011.594132

Geuze, E., Vermetten, E., de Kloet, C. S., Hijman, R., & Westenberg, H. G. (2009). Neuropsychological performance is related to current social and occupational functioning in veterans with posttraumatic stress disorder. *Depression and Anxiety, 26,* 7–15. http://dx.doi.org/10.1002/da.20476

Giesbrecht, T., Lynn, S. J., Lilienfeld, S. O., & Merckelbach, H. (2008). Cognitive processes in dissociation: An analysis of core theoretical assumptions. *Psychological Bulletin, 134,* 617–647. http://dx.doi.org/10.1037/0033-2909.134.5.617

Goldberg, H. E., Back-Madruga, C., & Boone, K. B. (2007). The impact of psychiatric disorders on cognitive symptom validity test scores. In K. B. Boone (Ed.), *Assessment of feigned cognitive impairment: A neuropsychological perspective* (pp. 281–309). New York, NY: Guilford Press.

Green, D., & Rosenfeld, B. (2011). Evaluating the gold standard: A review and meta-analysis of the Structured Interview of Reported Symptoms. *Psychological Assessment, 23,* 95–107. http://dx.doi.org/10.1037/a0021149

Green, D., Rosenfeld, B., & Belfi, B. (2013). New and improved? A comparison of the original and revised versions of the Structured Interview of Reported Symptoms. *Assessment, 20,* 210–218. http://dx.doi.org/10.1177/1073191112464389

Green, P. (2003). *Green's Word Memory Test for Microsoft Windows*. Edmonton, Alberta, Canada: Green's.

Green, P. (2004). *Medical Symptom Validity Test for Windows: User's manual and program*. Edmonton, Alberta, Canada: Green's.

Greenberg, P. E., Kessler, R. C., Birnbaum, H. G., Leong, S. A., Lowe, S. W., Berglund, P. A., & Corey-Lisle, P. K. (2003). The economic burden of depression in the United States: How did it change between 1990 and 2000? *Journal of Clinical Psychiatry, 64,* 1465–1475. http://dx.doi.org/10.4088/JCP.v64n1211

Greenberg, P. E., Sisitsky, T., Kessler, R. C., Finkelstein, S. N., Berndt, E. R., Davidson, J. R., . . . Fyer, A. J. (1999). The economic burden of anxiety disorders in the 1990s. *Journal of Clinical Psychiatry, 60,* 427–435. http://dx.doi.org/10.4088/JCP.v60n0702

Hawes, S. W., & Boccaccini, M. T. (2009). Detection of overreporting of psychopathology on the Personality Assessment Inventory: A meta-analytic review. *Psychological Assessment, 21,* 112–124. http://dx.doi.org/10.1037/a0015036

Heilbronner, R. L., Sweet, J. J., Morgan, J. E., Larrabee, G. J., & Millis, S. R. (2009). American Academy of Clinical Neuropsychology Consensus Conference Statement on the neuropsychological assessment of effort, response bias, and malingering. *Clinical Neuropsychologist, 23,* 1093–1129. http://dx.doi.org/10.1080/13854040903155063

Hercher, C., Turecki, G., & Mechawar, N. (2009). Through the looking glass: Examining neuroanatomical evidence for cellular alterations in major depression. *Journal of Psychiatric Research, 43,* 947–961. http://dx.doi.org/10.1016/j.jpsychires.2009.01.006

Herman, J. L. (1992). *Trauma and recovery*. New York, NY: Basic Books.

Hoelzle, J. B., Nelson, N. W., & Arbisi, P. A. (2012). MMPI–2 and MMPI–2 Restructured Form validity scales: Complementary approaches to evaluate response validity. *Psychological Injury and Law, 5,* 174–191. http://dx.doi.org/10.1007/s12207-012-9139-2

Howieson, D. B., Loring, D. W., & Hannay, H. J. (2004). Neurobehavioral variables and diagnostic issues. In M. D. Lezak, D. B. Howieson, & D. W. Loring (Eds.), *Neuropsychological assessment* (4th ed., pp. 286–334). New York, NY: Oxford University Press.

Inman, T. H., Vickery, C. D., Berry, D. T. R., Lamb, D. G., Edwards, C. L., & Smith, G. T. (1998). Development and initial validation of a new procedure for evaluating adequacy of effort given during neuropsychological testing: The Letter Memory Test. *Psychological Assessment, 10,* 128–139. http://dx.doi.org/10.1037/1040-3590.10.2.128

Jenkins, M. A., Langlais, P. J., Delis, D. A., & Cohen, R. A. (2000). Attentional dysfunction associated with posttraumatic stress disorder among rape survivors. *Clinical Neuropsychologist, 14,* 7–12. http://dx.doi.org/10.1076/1385-4046(200002)14:1;1-8;FT007

Jorge, R. E., Robinson, R. G., Moser, D., Tateno, A., Crespo-Facorro, B., & Arndt, S. (2004). Major depression following traumatic brain injury. *Archives of General Psychiatry, 61,* 42–50. http://dx.doi.org/10.1001/archpsyc.61.1.42

Kane, A. W., & Dvoskin, J. A. (2011). *Evaluation for personal injury claims.* http://dx.doi.org/10.1093/med:psych/9780195326079.001.0001

Keeton, C. P., Kolos, A. C., & Walkup, J. T. (2009). Pediatric generalized anxiety disorder: Epidemiology, diagnosis, and management. *Paediatric Drugs, 11,* 171–183. http://dx.doi.org/10.2165/00148581-200911030-00003

Keiski, M. A., Shore, D. L., Hamilton, J. M., & Malec, J. F. (2015). Simulation of traumatic brain injury symptoms on the Personality Assessment Inventory: An analogue study. *Assessment, 22,* 233–247. http://dx.doi.org/10.1177/1073191114539380

Kendler, K. S., Hettema, J. M., Butera, F., Gardner, C. O., & Prescott, C. A. (2003). Life event dimensions of loss, humiliation, entrapment, and danger in the prediction of onsets of major depression and generalized anxiety. *Archives of General Psychiatry, 60,* 789–796. http://dx.doi.org/10.1001/archpsyc.60.8.789

Kessler, R. C., Aguilar-Gaxiola, S., Alonso, J., Chatterji, S., Lee, S., Ormel, J., . . . Wang, P. S. (2009). The global burden of mental disorders: An update from the WHO World Mental Health (WMH) surveys. *Epidemiologia e Psichiatria Sociale, 18,* 23–33. http://dx.doi.org/10.1017/S1121189X00001421

Kessler, R. C., Sonnega, A., Bromet, E., Hughes, M., & Nelson, C. B. (1995). Posttraumatic stress disorder in the National Comorbidity Survey. *Archives of General Psychiatry, 52,* 1048–1060. http://dx.doi.org/10.1001/archpsyc.1995.03950240066012

Kurtz, M. M., & Marcopulos, B. A. (2012). Cognition in schizophrenia. In B. A. Marcopulos & M. M. Kurtz (Eds.), *Clinical neuropsychological foundations of schizophrenia* (pp. 1–25). New York, NY: Psychology Press.

Langenecker, S. C., Lee, H. J., & Bieliauskas, L. A. (2009). Neuropsychology of depression and related mood disorders. In I. Grant & K. Adams (Eds.), *Neuropsychological assessment of neuropsychiatric and neuromedical disorders* (pp. 523–559). Oxford, England: Oxford University Press.

Larrabee, G. J. (2012a). Assessment of malingering. In G. J. Larrabee (Ed.), *Forensic neuropsychology: A scientific approach* (pp. 116–159). New York, NY: Oxford University Press.

Larrabee, G. J. (Ed.). (2012b). *Forensic neuropsychology: A scientific approach* (2nd ed.). New York, NY: Oxford University Press.

Larrabee, G. J. (2012c). Performance validity and symptom validity in neuropsychological assessment. *Journal of the International Neuropsychological Society, 18,* 625–630. http://dx.doi.org/10.1017/S1355617712000240

Larrabee, G. J. (2014). False-positive rates associated with the use of multiple performance and symptom validity tests. *Archives of Clinical Neuropsychology, 29,* 364–373. http://dx.doi.org/10.1093/arclin/acu019

Leskin, L. P., & White, P. M. (2007). Attentional networks reveal executive function deficits in posttraumatic stress disorder. *Neuropsychology, 21,* 275–284. http://dx.doi.org/10.1037/0894-4105.21.3.275

Levin, A. P., Kleinman, S. B., & Adler, J. S. (2014). *DSM–5* and posttraumatic stress disorder. *Journal of the American Academy of Psychiatry and the Law, 42,* 146–158.

Liberzon, I., & Sripada, C. S. (2007). The functional neuroanatomy of PTSD: A critical review. *Progress in Brain Research, 167,* 151–169. http://dx.doi.org/10.1016/S0079-6123(07)67011-3

Marcopulos, B. A., Caillouet, B., Bailey, C., Tussey, C., Kent, J. A., & Frederick, R. (2014). Clinical decision making in response to PVT failure in a psychiatric setting. *Clinical Neuropsychologist, 28,* 633–652. http://dx.doi.org/10.1080/13854046.2014.896416

Marcopulos, B. A., Hedjar, L., & Arredondo, B. (2016). Dissociative amnesia or malingered amnesia? *Journal of Forensic Psychology Practice, 16,* 106–117.

Marcopulos, B. A., & Kurtz, M. M. (Eds.). (2012). *Clinical neuropsychological foundations of schizophrenia.* New York, NY: Psychology Press.

Markowitsch, H. J., & Staniloiu, A. (2013). The impairment of recollection in functional amnesic states. *Cortex, 49,* 1494–1510. http://dx.doi.org/10.1016/j.cortex.2012.05.020

Martin, P. K., Schroeder, R. W., & Odland, A. P. (2015). Neuropsychologists' validity testing beliefs and practices: A survey of North American professionals. *Clinical Neuropsychologist, 29,* 741–776. http://dx.doi.org/10.1080/13854046.2015.1087597

McFarland, C. P., Clark, J. B., Lee, L. O., Grande, L. J., Marx, B. P., & Vasterling, J. J. (2016). Event-based prospective memory among veterans: The role of posttraumatic stress disorder symptom severity in executing intentions. *Journal of Clinical and Experimental Neuropsychology, 38,* 251–260. http://dx.doi.org/10.1080/13803395.2015.1102203

McGurk, S. R., Mueser, K. T., Mischel, R., Adams, R., Harvey, P. D., McClure, M. M., . . . Siever, L. J. (2013). Vocational functioning in schizotypal and paranoid personality disorders. *Psychiatry Research, 210,* 498–504. http://dx.doi.org/10.1016/j.psychres.2013.06.019

McLean, C. P., Asnaani, A., Litz, B. T., & Hofmann, S. G. (2011). Gender differences in anxiety disorders: Prevalence, course of illness, comorbidity and burden of illness. *Journal of Psychiatric Research, 45,* 1027–1035. http://dx.doi.org/10.1016/j.jpsychires.2011.03.006

Melton, G. B., Petrila, J., Poythress, N. G., Slobogin, C., Lyons, P. M., Jr., & Otto, R. K. (2007). *Psychological evaluations for the courts: A handbook for mental health professionals and lawyers* (3rd ed.). New York, NY: Guilford Press.

Mena, I. (2009). Basal and frontal activation neuroSPECT demonstrates functional brain changes in major depression. *Alasbimn Journal, 11,* 1–12.

Merikangas, K. R., He, J. P., Burstein, M., Swanson, S. A., Avenevoli, S., Cui, L., . . . Swendsen, J. (2010). Lifetime prevalence of mental disorders in U.S. adolescents: Results from the National Comorbidity Survey Replication—Adolescent Supplement (NCS–A). *Journal of the American Academy of Child and Adolescent Psychiatry, 49,* 980–989. http://dx.doi.org/10.1016/j.jaac.2010.05.017

Messer, J., & Fremouw, W. J. (2007). Detecting malingered posttraumatic stress disorder using the Morel Emotional Numbing Test-Revised (MENT-R) and the Miller Forensic Assessment of Symptoms Test (M-FAST). *Journal of Forensic Psychology Practice, 7,* 33–57. http://dx.doi.org/10.1300/J158v07n03_02

Metcalf, O., Varker, T., Forbes, D., Phelps, A., Dell, L., DiBattista, A., . . . O'Donnell, M. (2016). Efficacy of fifteen emerging interventions for the treatment of posttraumatic stress disorder: A systematic review. *Journal of Traumatic Stress, 29,* 88–92. http://dx.doi.org/10.1002/jts.22070

Miller, H. A. (2001). *M-FAST: Miller Forensic Assessment of Symptoms Test professional manual.* Odessa, FL: Psychological Assessment Resources.

Millon, T. (1997). *Millon Clinical Multiaxial Inventory—III manual* (3rd ed.). Minneapolis, MN: NCS Pearson.

Millon, T., Grossman, S., & Millon, C. (2015). *Millon Clinical Multiaxial Inventory—IV* (4th ed.). Minneapolis, MN: NCS Pearson.

Mittenberg, W., Patton, C., Canyock, E. M., & Condit, D. C. (2002). Base rates of malingering and symptom exaggeration. *Journal of Clinical and Experimental Neuropsychology, 24,* 1094–1102. http://dx.doi.org/10.1076/jcen.24.8.1094.8379

Molloy, C., Conroy, R. M., Cotter, D. R., & Cannon, M. (2011). Is traumatic brain injury a risk factor for schizophrenia? A meta-analysis of case-controlled population-based studies. *Schizophrenia Bulletin, 37,* 1104–1110. http://dx.doi.org/10.1093/schbul/sbr091

Morel, K. R. (1998). Development and preliminary validation of a forced-choice test of response bias for posttraumatic stress disorder. *Journal of Personality Assessment, 70,* 299–314. http://dx.doi.org/10.1207/s15327752jpa7002_8

Morel, K. R., & Shepherd, B. E. (2008). Developing a symptom validity test for posttraumatic stress disorder: Application of the binomial distribution. *Journal of Anxiety Disorders, 22,* 1297–1302. http://dx.doi.org/10.1016/j.janxdis.2008.01.011

Morey, L. C. (1991). *The Personality Assessment Inventory professional manual.* Odessa, FL: Psychological Assessment Resources.

Morey, L. C. (1996). *An interpretive guide to the Personality Assessment Inventory (PAI).* Odessa, FL: Psychological Assessment Resources.

Morgan, A. B., & Lilienfeld, S. O. (2000). A meta-analytic review of the relation between antisocial behavior and neuropsychological measures of executive function. *Clinical Psychology Review, 20,* 113–136. http://dx.doi.org/10.1016/S0272-7358(98)00096-8

National Institute of Mental Health. (2016). *Anxiety disorders.* Retrieved from http://www.nimh.nih.gov/health/topics/anxiety-disorders/index.shtml#part_145337

Nestor, P. G., Daggett, D., Haycock, J., & Price, M. (1999). Competence to stand trial: A neuropsychological inquiry. *Law and Human Behavior, 23,* 397–412. http://dx.doi.org/10.1023/A:1022339130582

Newman, P. J., & Sweet, J. (1986). The effects of clinical depression on the Luria–Nebraska Neuropsychological Battery. *International Journal of Clinical Neuropsychology, 8,* 109–114.

Ogura, A., Morinobu, S., Kawakatsu, S., Totsuka, S., & Komatani, A. (1998). Changes in regional brain activity in major depression after successful treatment with antidepressant drugs. *Acta Psychiatrica Scandinavica, 98,* 54–59. http://dx.doi.org/10.1111/j.1600-0447.1998.tb10042.x

Osterman, J. E., & de Jong, J. T. V. M. (2007). Cultural issues and trauma. In M. J. Friedman, T. M. Keane, & P. A. Resick (Eds.), *Handbook of PTSD: Science and practice* (pp. 425–446). New York, NY: Guilford Press.

Otto, M. W., Bruder, G. E., Fava, M., Delis, D. C., Quitkin, F. M., & Rosenbaum, J. F. (1994). Norms for depressed patients for the California Verbal Learning Test: Associations with depression severity and self-report of cognitive difficulties. *Archives of Clinical Neuropsychology, 9,* 81–88. http://dx.doi.org/10.1093/arclin/9.1.81

Pennington, C., Newson, M., Hayre, A., & Coulthard, E. (2015). Functional cognitive disorder: What is it and what to do about it? *Practical Neurology, 15,* 436–444. http://dx.doi.org/10.1136/practneurol-2015-001127

Peters, M. J. V., van Oorsouw, K. I. M., Jelicic, M., & Merckelbach, H. (2013). Let's use those tests! Evaluations of crime-related amnesia claims. *Memory, 21,* 599–607. http://dx.doi.org/10.1080/09658211.2013.771672

Pineau, H., Marchand, A., & Guay, S. (2014). Objective neuropsychological deficits in post-traumatic stress disorder and mild traumatic brain injury: What remains beyond symptom similarity? *Behavioral Science, 4,* 471–486. http://dx.doi.org/10.3390/bs4040471

Pirelli, G., Gottdiener, W. H., & Zapf, P. A. (2011). A meta-analytic review of competency to stand trial research. *Psychology, Public Policy, and Law, 17,* 1–53. http://dx.doi.org/10.1037/a0021713

Rabin, L. A., Barr, W. B., & Burton, L. A. (2005). Assessment practices of clinical neuropsychologists in the United States and Canada: A survey of INS, NAN, and APA Division 40 members. *Archives of Clinical Neuropsychology, 20,* 33–65. http://dx.doi.org/10.1016/j.acn.2004.02.005

Rajkowska, G., Miguel-Hidalgo, J. J., Wei, J., Dilley, G., Pittman, S. D., Meltzer, H. Y., . . . Stockmeier, C. A. (1999). Morphometric evidence for neuronal and glial prefrontal cell pathology in major depression. *Biological Psychiatry, 45,* 1085–1098. http://dx.doi.org/10.1016/S0006-3223(99)00041-4

Ramasubbu, R., & MacQueen, G. (2008). Alterations in neural structures as risk factors for depression. In K. S. Dobson & D. J. A. Dozois (Eds.), *Risk factors in depression* (pp. 37–61). http://dx.doi.org/10.1016/B978-0-08-045078-0.00003-4

Rauch, S. L., Shin, L. M., & Phelps, E. A. (2006). Neurocircuitry models of posttraumatic stress disorder and extinction: Human neuroimaging research—past, present, and future. *Biological Psychiatry, 60,* 376–382. http://dx.doi.org/10.1016/j.biopsych.2006.06.004

Richards, P. M., & Ruff, R. M. (1989). Motivational effects on neuropsychological functioning: Comparison of depressed versus nondepressed individuals. *Journal of Consulting and Clinical Psychology, 57,* 396–402. http://dx.doi.org/10.1037/0022-006X.57.3.396

Rodriguez, P., Holowka, D. W., & Marx, B. P. (2012). Assessment of posttraumatic stress disorder-related functional impairment: A review. *Journal of Rehabilitation Research and Development, 49,* 649–665. http://dx.doi.org/10.1682/JRRD.2011.09.0162

Roebuck-Spencer, T., & Sherer, M. (2008). Moderate and severe traumatic brain injury. In J. E. Morgan & J. H. Ricker (Eds.), *Textbook of clinical neuropsychology* (pp. 411–429). New York, NY: Taylor & Francis.

Rogers, R. (1992). *Structured Interview of Reported Symptoms.* Odessa, FL: Psychological Assessment Resources.

Rogers, R. (2008). Structured interviews and dissimulation. In R. Rogers (Ed.), *Clinical assessment of malingering and deception* (3rd ed., pp. 301–323). New York, NY: Guilford Press.

Rogers, R., Gillard, N. D., Berry, D. T. R., & Granacher, R. P. (2011). Effectiveness of the MMPI–2–RF validity scales for feigned mental disorders and cognitive impairment: A known-groups study. *Journal of Psychopathology and Behavioral Assessment, 33,* 355–367. http://dx.doi.org/10.1007/s10862-011-9222-0

Rogers, R., Gillard, N. D., Wooley, C. N., & Ross, C. A. (2012). The detection of feigned disabilities: The effectiveness of the Personality Assessment Inventory in a traumatized inpatient sample. *Assessment, 19,* 77–88. http://dx.doi.org/10.1177/1073191111422031

Rogers, R., Payne, J. W., Berry, D. T. R., & Granacher, R. P., Jr. (2009). Use of the SIRS in compensation cases: An examination of its validity and generalizability. *Law and Human Behavior, 33,* 213–224. http://dx.doi.org/10.1007/s10979-008-9145-9

Rogers, R., Sewell, K. W., & Gillard, N. D. (2010). *SIRS-2: Structured Interview of Reported Symptoms: Professional manual.* Odessa, FL: Psychological Assessment Resources.

Rogers, R., Sewell, K. W., Morey, L. C., & Ulstad, K. L. (1996). Detection of feigned mental disorders on the Personality Assessment Inventory: A discriminant analysis. *Journal of Personality Assessment, 67,* 629–640. http://dx.doi.org/10.1207/s15327752jpa6703_15

Rosell, D. R., Futterman, S. E., McMaster, A., & Siever, L. J. (2014). Schizotypal personality disorder: A current review. *Current Psychiatry Reports, 16,* 452. http://dx.doi.org/10.1007/s11920-014-0452-1

Rosen, G. M. (2004–2005). Traumatic events, criterion creep, and the creation of pretraumatic stress disorder. *Scientific Review of Mental Health Practice, 3,* 39–42.

Rosen, G. M., & Davison, G. C. (2003). Psychology should list empirically supported principles of change (ESPs) and not credential trademarked therapies or other treatment packages. *Behavior Modification, 27,* 300–312. http://dx.doi.org/10.1177/0145445503027003003

Rosen, G. M., & Grunert, B. C. (2012). Posttraumatic stress disorder in the workplace. In G. L. Iverson & S. S. Bush (Eds.), *Neuropsychological injury in the workplace* (pp. 163–186). New York, NY: Guilford Press.

Rossini, E. D., Schwartz, D. R., & Braun, B. G. (1996). Intellectual functioning of inpatients with dissociative identity disorder and dissociative disorder not otherwise specified: Cognitive and neuropsychological aspects. *Journal of Nervous and Mental Disease, 184,* 289–294. http://dx.doi.org/10.1097/00005053-199605000-00004

Ruff, R. M. (1994). What role does depression play on the performance of the Ruff 2 and 7 Selective Attention Test? *Perceptual and Motor Skills, 78,* 63–66. http://dx.doi.org/10.2466/pms.1994.78.1.63

Ruocco, A. C. (2005). The neuropsychology of borderline personality disorder: A meta-analysis and review. *Psychiatry Research, 137,* 191–202. http://dx.doi.org/10.1016/j.psychres.2005.07.004

Ruocco, A. C. (2016). Compliance on neuropsychological performance validity testing in patients with borderline personality disorder. *Psychological Assessment, 28,* 345–350. http://dx.doi.org/0.1037/a0039481

Ruocco, A. C., McCloskey, M. S., Lee, R., & Coccaro, E. F. (2009). Indices of orbitofrontal and prefrontal function in Cluster B and Cluster C personality disorders. *Psychiatry Research, 170,* 282–285. http://dx.doi.org/10.1016/j.psychres.2008.12.003

Ryba, N. L., & Zapf, P. A. (2011). The influence of psychiatric symptoms and cognitive abilities on competence-related abilities. *International Journal of Forensic Mental Health, 10,* 29–40. http://dx.doi.org/10.1080/14999013.2010.550982

Schnurr, P. P., Lunney, C. A., Bovin, M. J., & Marx, B. P. (2009). Posttraumatic stress disorder and quality of life: Extension of findings to veterans of the wars in Iraq and Afghanistan. *Clinical Psychology Review, 29,* 727–735. http://dx.doi.org/10.1016/j.cpr.2009.08.006

Schroeder, R. W., Baade, L. E., Peck, C. P., VonDran, E. J., Brockman, C. J., Webster, B. K., & Heinrichs, R. J. (2012). Validation of MMPI–2–RF validity scales in criterion group neuropsychological samples. *Clinical Neuropsychologist, 26,* 129–146. http://dx.doi.org/10.1080/13854046.2011.639314

Schuitevoerder, S., Rosen, J. W., Twamley, E.W., Ayers, C.R., Sones, H., Lohr, J.B., . . . Thorp, S. R. (2013). A meta-analysis of cognitive functioning in older adults with PTSD. *Journal of Anxiety Disorders, 27,* 550–558. http://dx.doi.org/10.1016/j.janxdis.2013.01.001

Scott, J. C., Matt, G. E., Wrocklage, K. M., Crnich, C., Jordan, J., Southwick, S. M., . . . Schweinsburg, B. C. (2015). A quantitative meta-analysis of neurocognitive functioning in posttraumatic stress disorder. *Psychological Bulletin, 141,* 105–140. http://dx.doi.org/10.1037/a0038039

Sellbom, M., & Bagby, R. M. (2008). Response styles on multiscale inventories. In R. Rogers (Ed.), *Clinical assessment of malingering and deception* (3rd ed., pp. 69–86). New York, NY: Guilford Press.

Sellbom, M., Toomey, J. A., Wygant, D. B., Kucharski, L. T., & Duncan, S. (2010). Utility of the MMPI–2–RF (Restructured Form) validity scales in detecting malingering in a criminal forensic setting: A known-groups design. *Psychological Assessment, 22,* 22–31. http://dx.doi.org/10.1037/a0018222

Slick, D. J., Hopp, G., Strauss, E., & Spellacy, F. J. (1996). Victoria Symptom Validity Test: Efficiency for detecting feigned memory impairment and relationship to neuropsychological tests and MMPI–2 validity scales. *Journal of Clinical and Experimental Neuropsychology, 18,* 911–922. http://dx.doi.org/10.1080/01688639608408313

Slick, D. J., Sherman, E. M. S., & Iverson, G. L. (1999). Diagnostic criteria for malingered neurocognitive dysfunction: Proposed standards for clinical practice and research. *Clinical Neuropsychologist, 13,* 545–561. http://dx.doi.org/10.1076/1385-4046(199911)13:04;1-Y;FT545

Slick, D. J., Tan, J. E., Strauss, E. H., & Hultsch, D. F. (2004). Detecting malingering: A survey of experts' practices. *Archives of Clinical Neuropsychology, 19,* 465–473. http://dx.doi.org/10.1016/j.acn.2003.04.001

Sollman, M. J., & Berry, D. T. R. (2011). Detection of inadequate effort on neuropsychological testing: A meta-analytic update and extension. *Archives of Clinical Neuropsychology, 26,* 774–789. http://dx.doi.org/10.1093/arclin/acr066

Sparr, L. F., & Pitman, R. K. (2007). PTSD and the law. In M. J. Friedman, T. M. Keane, & P. Resick (Eds.), *Handbook of PTSD: Science and practice* (pp. 449–468). New York, NY: Guilford Press.

Sprengelmeyer, R., Steele, J. D., Mwangi, B., Kumar, P., Christmas, D., Milders, M., & Matthews, K. (2011). The insular cortex and the neuroanatomy of major depression. *Journal of Affective Disorders, 133,* 120–127. http://dx.doi.org/10.1016/j.jad.2011.04.004

Stadnik, R. D., Brand, B., & Savoca, A. (2013). Personality Assessment Inventory profile and predictors of elevations among dissociative disorder patients. *Journal of Trauma and Dissociation, 14,* 546–561. http://dx.doi.org/10.1080/15299732.2013.792310

Stamm, B. H., & Friedman, M. J. (2000). Cultural diversity in the appraisal and expression of traumatic exposure. In A. Shalev, R. Yehuda, & A. McFarlane (Eds.), *International handbook of human response to trauma* (pp. 69–85). http://dx.doi.org/10.1007/978-1-4615-4177-6_5

Staniloiu, A., & Markowitsch, H. J. (2014). Dissociative amnesia. *Lancet Psychiatry, 1,* 226–241. http://dx.doi.org/10.1016/S2215-0366(14)70279-2

Stone, A. A. (1993). Post-traumatic stress disorder and the law: Critical review of the new frontier. *Bulletin of the American Academy of Psychiatry and the Law, 21,* 23–36.

Strauss, E., Sherman, E. M. S., & Spreen, O. (2006). *A compendium of neuropsychological tests: Administration, norms, and commentary* (3rd ed.). New York, NY: Oxford University Press.

Sweet, J. (1983). Confounding effects of depression on neuropsychological testing: Five illustrative cases. *Clinical Neuropsychology, 5,* 103–109.

Sweet, J. J., Benson, L. M., Nelson, N. W., & Moberg, P. J. (2015). The American Academy of Clinical Neuropsychology, National Academy of Neuropsychology, and Society for Clinical Neuropsychology (APA Division 40) 2015 TCN Professional Practice and "Salary Survey": Professional practices, beliefs, and incomes of U.S. neuropsychologists. *Clinical Neuropsychologist, 29,* 1069–1162. http://dx.doi.org/10.1080/13854046.2016.1140228

Sweet, J. J., & Goldman, D. J. (2015). Forensic neuropsychology: Annual review. In S. Koffler, J. Morgan, B. Marcopulos, & M. F. Greiffenstein (Eds.), *Neuropsychology: A review of science and practice* (2nd ed., pp. 70–96). New York, NY: Oxford University Press.

Swick, D., Honzel, N., Larsen, J., Ashley, V., & Justus, T. (2012). Impaired response inhibition in veterans with post-traumatic stress disorder and mild traumatic brain injury. *Journal of the International Neuropsychological Society*, 18, 917–926. http://dx.doi.org/10.1017/S1355617712000458

Tarescavage, A. M., Wygant, D. B., Gervais, R. O., & Ben-Porath, Y. S. (2013). Association between the MMPI–2 Restructured Form (MMPI–2–RF) and malingered neurocognitive dysfunction among non-head injury disability claimants. *Clinical Neuropsychologist, 27,* 313–335. http://dx.doi.org/10.1080/13854046.2012.744099

Tombaugh, T. N. (1996). *TOMM: Test of Memory Malingering.* North Tonawanda, NY: Multi-Health Systems.

Triggs, W. J., McCoy, K. J., Greer, R., Rossi, F., Bowers, D., Kortenkamp, S., . . . Goodman, W. K. (1999). Effects of left frontal transcranial magnetic stimulation on depressed mood, cognition, and corticomotor threshold. *Biological Psychiatry, 45,* 1440–1446.

Trivedi, J. K. (2006). Cognitive deficits in psychiatric disorders: Current status. *Indian Journal of Psychiatry, 48,* 10–20. http://dx.doi.org/10.4103/0019-5545.31613

Unoka, Z., & Richman, M. J. (2016). Neuropsychological deficits in BPD patients and the moderator effects of co-occurring mental disorders: A meta-analysis. *Clinical Psychology Review, 44,* 1–12. http://dx.doi.org/10.1016/j.cpr.2015.11.009

van Impelen, A., Merckelbach, H., Jelicic, M., & Merten, T. (2014). The Structured Inventory of Malingered Symptomatology (SIMS): A systematic review and meta-analysis. *Clinical Neuropsychologist, 28,* 1336–1365. http://dx.doi.org/10.1080/13854046.2014.984763

Victor, T. L., & Boone, K. B. (2007). Identification of feigned mental retardation. In K. B. Boone (Ed.), *Assessment of feigned cognitive impairment: A neuropsychological perspective* (pp. 310–345). New York, NY: Guilford Press.

Victor, T. L., Boone, K. B., Serpa, J. G., Buehler, J., & Ziegler, E. A. (2009). Interpreting the meaning of multiple symptom validity test failure. *Clinical Neuropsychologist, 23,* 297–313. http://dx.doi.org/10.1080/13854040802232682

Vitacco, M. J., & Rogers, R. (2010). Assessment of malingering in correctional settings. In C. L. Scott & J. B. Gerbasi (Eds.), *Handbook of correctional mental health* (2nd ed., pp. 255–276). Washington, DC: American Psychiatric Association.

Vogt, D. S., King, D. W., & King, L. A. (2007). Risk pathways for PTSD: Making sense of the literature. In M. J. Friedman, T. M. Keane, & P. A. Resick (Eds.), *Handbook of PTSD: Science and practice* (pp. 99–115). New York, NY: Guilford Press.

Wang, W., Wang, Y., Gu, J., Drake, R. A., Livesley, W. J., & Jang, K. L. (2003). Line bisection performance in patients with personality disorders. *Cognitive Neuropsychiatry, 8,* 273–285. http://dx.doi.org/10.1080/13546800344000048

Warrington, E. K. (1984). *Recognition Memory Test: Manual.* Berkshire, England: NFER-Nelson.

Weathers, F. W., Litz, B. T., Keane, T. M., Palmieri, P. A., Marx, B. P., & Schnurr, P. P. (2013). *The PTSD*

Checklist for DSM–5 (PCL–5). Retrieved from http://www.ptsd.va.gov/professional/assessment/adult-sr/ptsd-checklist.asp

Whiteside, D. M., Galbreath, J., Brown, M., & Turnbull, J. (2012). Differential response patterns on the Personality Assessment Inventory (PAI) in compensation-seeking and non-compensation-seeking mild traumatic brain injury patients. *Journal of Clinical and Experimental Neuropsychology, 34,* 172–182. http://dx.doi.org/10.1080/13803395.2011.630648

Widows, M., & Smith, G. P. (2005). *Structured Inventory of Malingered Symptomatology (SIMS) and professional manual*. Odessa, FL: Psychological Assessment Resources.

Wilson, J. P., & Tang, C. (Eds.). (2007). *Cross-cultural assessment of PTSD and related stress disorders*. New York, NY: Springer SBM.

Wooley, C. N., & Rogers, R. (2015). The effectiveness of the Personality Assessment Inventory with feigned PTSD: An initial investigation of Resnick's model of malingering. *Assessment, 22,* 449–458. http://dx.doi.org/10.1177/1073191114552076

World Health Organization. (1992). *The ICD–10 classification of mental and behavioural disorders: Clinical descriptions and diagnostic guidelines*. Geneva, Switzerland: Author.

World Health Organization. (2004). Annex Table 3: Burden of disease in DALYs by cause, sex, and mortality stratum in WHO regions, estimates for 2002. In *The world health report 2004: Changing history* (pp. 126–131). Geneva, Switzerland: Author.

Wortmann, J. H., Jordan, A. H., Weathers, F. W., Resick, P. A., Dondanville, K. A., & Hall-Clark, B., . . . Litz, B. T. (2016). Psychometric analysis of the PTSD Checklist—5 (PCL–5) among treatment-seeking military service members. *Psychological Assessment, 28,* 1392–1403.

Wygant, D. B., Ben-Porath, Y. S., Arbisi, P. A., Berry, D. T. R., Freeman, D. B., & Heilbronner, R. L. (2009). Examination of the MMPI–2 Restructured Form (MMPI–2–RF) validity scales in civil forensic settings: Findings from simulation and known group samples. *Archives of Clinical Neuropsychology, 24,* 671–680. http://dx.doi.org/10.1093/arclin/acp073

Yehuda, R., & LeDoux, J. (2007). Response variation following trauma: A translational neuroscience approach to understanding PTSD. *Neuron, 56,* 19–32. http://dx.doi.org/10.1016/j.neuron.2007.09.006

Young, G. (Ed.). (2013). *DSM–5* [Special issue]. *Psychological Injury and Law, 6*(4).

Youngjohn, J. R., Wershba, R., Stevenson, M., Sturgeon, J., & Thomas, M. L. (2011). Independent validation of the MMPI–2–RF somatic/cognitive and validity scales in TBI litigants tested for effort. *Clinical Neuropsychologist, 25,* 463–476. http://dx.doi.org/10.1080/13854046.2011.554444

CHAPTER 10

EVOLUTION, FORENSIC IMPLICATIONS, AND FUTURE OF SOMATIC SYMPTOM DISORDERS

David E. Hartman

People presenting for forensic neuropsychological evaluations may present with symptoms that are qualitatively different from or more extreme than would be expected on the basis of an objectively established or suspected injury or illness. Helping litigants, triers of fact, and other involved parties understand the nature of such presentations can be a valuable neuropsychological service. These types of unusual presentations can result from or be conceptualized according to various clinical conditions, including somatization.

Somatization may be unique among psychodiagnostic concepts in its combination of flawed origin, general acceptance, forensic ubiquity, and utter ambiguity. What is somatization? It depends whom you ask. The term *somatization* is attributed to Wilhelm Stekel (1943), one of Freud's first students, who described it as a diversion of psychological symptoms into body organs, equivalent to Freud's conversion disorder. However, this "neurotic" version of somatization is only one of many definitions.

Merskey (2000) submitted that clinicians and researchers commonly interpret the term *somatization* in at least seven ways: (a) the label of *somatization disorder;* (b) conversion symptoms; (c) hypochondriasis; (d) hyperawareness of body states that respond to reassurance, examination, and investigation; (e) psychophysical expression of anxiety or depression; (f) schizophrenic body delusions; and (g) any of these combined with symptoms of an actual physical disease. Gureje, Simon, Ustun, and Goldberg (1997) also included high levels of medically unexplained symptoms and somatic presentation of a psychiatric disorder. Angel and Guarnaccia (1989) implied that somatization occurs when personal perception of poor health is discrepant from physician assessment. Evens, Vendetta, Krebs, and Herath (2015) suggested inclusion of not just unexplained symptoms but also symptoms that are "not compatible with known anatomic and physiologic principles" (p. 1059). It is this writer's experience that *somatization* is often used casually by nonpsychiatric physicians, who append the term to a physical diagnosis when symptoms include complaints of nonspecific pain, headache, or soft tissue discomfort.

These definitions are then considered with somatic expressions of other problems such as pain, fatigue, weakness, cognitive dysfunction, motor or sensory limitation, and virtually any subjective complaint involving any organ system. Symptoms may be discrete, combined, unconnected to actual physical problems, or magnified extensions of verified physical disorder. Problems labeled by physicians as somatization range from annoying to multiyear litigated assertion of complete disability. With definition, cause, presentation, severity, and aim free to vary, defining somatization makes the parable of the blind men and the elephant (in which each blindfolded wise man touches a different part of the animal and attempts to describe the whole) seem trivial by comparison. In describing somatization, it can be argued that psychologists are not just blindly examining different parts of the elephant, but also have different beliefs about what constitutes an elephant, use different methods to examine the

http://dx.doi.org/10.1037/0000032-010
APA Handbook of Forensic Neuropsychology, S. S. Bush (Editor-in-Chief)

elephant, and are sometimes examining a different animal but calling it an elephant. It is hardly surprising, then, to find that estimates of somatization among primary care patients (using criteria of the fourth edition of the *Diagnostic and Statistical Manual of Mental Disorders* [*DSM*] and the 10th version of the *International Classification of Diseases*) range from 0.8% to 49% (Haller, Cramer, Lauche, & Dobos, 2015), depending on the diagnostic criteria, and that even then such disorders may be underdiagnosed (Wilhelm, Finch, Davenport, & Hickie, 2008). In neurology specifically, patients tend to meet diagnostic criteria for somatoform disorders approximately 30% of the time, compared with primary care settings in which approximately 20% of patients tend to meet full or abridged criteria (Lamberty, 2008). With the publication of the fifth edition of the *DSM* (*DSM–5*; American Psychiatric Association, 2013), the prevalence of what is now termed *somatic symptom disorder* (SSD) is reportedly unknown but is estimated to be approximately 5% to 7% in the general adult population.

HISTORY

Various incarnations of somatization are as old as recorded medical text, filtered through prevailing theories of nonbodily phenomena. Philosophers, inquisitors, and barristers (attorneys) have labeled, and in many cases continue to label, mentally influenced physical symptom complaint through prisms of gender, demonic possession, moral stature, cultural norms, premorbid psychopathology, and prevarication. That psychologically produced physical symptoms could be malingered is as early an explanation as the rest. Issues of disability and credibility were engraved, literally, into the early history of somatization.

Understanding of somatization has changed over time, filtered through "the vicissitudes of psychiatry as it passed through phases of medicalization, demedicalization and remedicalization" (Menninger & Nemiah, 2000, p. 74). Southard (1912–1913) examined the autopsied brains of patients with "somatic delusions." He described a set of gravely ill patients presenting with unusual somatic symptom complaints; it was unclear from his description whether their somatic complaints were colorful metaphor or actually delusional. Southard chose 38 patients whose eventual autopsy did not reveal (to a physician working in that period) obvious brain lesions. Southard reported results from eight of these cases, whose disorders included tuberculosis, dementia, and cancer, all disorders now considered to have cognitive and somatic symptoms. He found it understandably difficult to make strong connections between symptom content, disease state, and psychological influence. He allowed that hereditary and acquired dispositions can contribute to unexplained correlations and that even ancestry could influence the character of psychosomatic complaint. In an insight that presages current research that has demonstrated the relationship between childhood abuse and adult somatization, Southard suggested that understanding of critically important, though perhaps forgotten, emotional past experiences might better explain or even prevent some delusional conditions. Southard characterized one patient whose somatic complaint was of "bees in the skull" as a "phenomenal liar" (p. 338).

The vast subterranean steam engine of psychoanalysis soon interposed a much more complex theory of somatization. According to this theory, psychosomatic symptoms were produced when drives were diverted from their preferred aim and converted into physical symptoms. Citing Freud, London (1946) explained that psychic conflicts in hysteria were converted into bodily symptoms through somatization of the libido. This diversion of psychology into physiology came at a time when very little was known about more subtle neurological phenomena. When Charcot proposed a psychological mechanism of hysteria, subtle epileptic phenomena and the neuropathology of closed-head injury, which were likely responsible for some early cases attributed to hysteria, were unknown. Webster (2003) noted that Charcot's most famous "traumatic hysteria" patient "Le Log" developed symptoms after he

> was hit from the side by a carriage which was being driven at great speed . . . spun through the air and landed on the ground. He was picked up completely

> unconscious. . . . He remained unconscious for five or six days. Six months later he was transferred to La Salpêtrière. By this time the lower extremities of his body were almost completely paralysed, there was a twitching or tremor in the corner of his mouth, he had a permanent headache and there were "blank spaces in the tablet of his memory". In particular he could not remember the accident itself. But, because there had never been any signs of external injury, Charcot decided that Le Log . . . was a victim of traumatic hysteria and that his symptoms had arisen as a result of the psychological trauma he had suffered. ("Freud and Charcot," para. 7)

Many of Freud's classic hysterical patients with somaticized physical symptoms would now be understood as suffering from neurological disorders. These patients include Emmy von N., whose convulsive head movements, clicking tongue sounds, and involuntary speech now suggest Tourette syndrome, or Lucy R., who had recurrent olfactory hallucinations now thought to be characteristic of temporal lobe epilepsy. Freud's theory that explained somatization was buttressed by his initial assertion that he had cured or partially cured these neurotic patients, a claim that was later found to be false (Webster, 2003).

It might be expected that a diagnosis based to some extent on a flawed or fraudulent representation of symptoms and their cures would eventually reveal large-scale misdiagnosis of medical illness being diagnosed as hysteria or conversion. The extent of likely misdiagnosis was marked, with Slater (1965) suggesting that at least one third of medically ill patients were diagnosed instead with psychologically somaticized symptoms. Slater characterized the diagnosis of hysteria as a delusion and a snare. Stone et al. (2005) reviewed more recently available studies and concluded that misdiagnosis had declined since Slater's publication, to about 4% currently, but most of the reviewed studies involved inpatient evaluations rather than evaluations performed in outpatient psychiatric or primary care contexts.

London's (1946) use of the term *somatization* appears to have been the first English-language journal citation of *somatization*. However, between Stekel's 1943 coinage and London's 1946 discussion, the term had been already adopted by the U.S. Army in 1945 as a disability diagnosis. In the *Bulletin of the U.S. Army Medical Department* (Office of the Surgeon General, 1946) an attempt was made to estimate the incidence of somatization reactions in patients with psychoneurotic disorders. The term *somatization reaction* is footnoted and explained as follows:

> This term has been adopted by the U.S. Army (TB MED 203, 19 October 1945) in preference to "psychosomatic reactions" since the latter term refers to a point of view on the discipline of medicine as a whole rather than to certain specific conditions. Somatization reactions probably result from the channeling of impulses originating from anxiety through the autonomic nervous system into the viscera where they cause some dysfunction. It includes the so-called "organ neurosis." (pp. 383–384)

The 1946 Army bulletin noted that in its survey many of the diagnosed "were men who had been evacuated from overseas for neuropsychiatric disorders" (p. 383). It seems reasonable to conclude, given the range of organs thought to suffer from neurotic damage and the high rates of misdiagnoses revealed by subsequent surveys, that many of these patients with gastrointestinal, cardiovascular, genitourinary, allergic, skin, asthenic, and other somatization reactions were actually physically ill. The majority of these patients were diagnosed with some degree of organ dysfunction. In data from 585 cases, "the psychoneurotic disorder manifested itself by some organ dysfunction in 159 cases (27%)," with an additional 229 cases (39%) showing "some organ dysfunction," for a total of 66% showing "some psychogenic somatic disturbance of clinical importance" (p. 383).

The earliest federal court citation of the term *somatization* was a disability claim. In *John H.*

Frederick v. United States (1960), the plaintiff, an Army major in the Dental Corps, was found physically fit for service but "came out of the service in 1945 a sick and disabled man" with a mental illness. The Army contended that the plaintiff's illness was neither incurred nor aggravated by Army service. The plaintiff's disability was described in various ways, including an "emotional instability reaction" that at times resembled the following: "manic depressive reaction, recurrent depression, psychasthenia, hysteria and somatization reaction" (para. 21 and 22).

Somatization as a civil claim for disability dates at least to the 1960s. In 1965, in *Mark v. Celebrezze* (1965), a case was filed for disability benefits related to chronic psychogenic headaches. Mr. Mark asserted that he suffered from continuing severe headaches to the point of all but total disability. There was debate as to whether the appellant's chronic middle ear infection was related to the headache claim, a claim that the examiner rejected.

An examining psychiatrist, Dr. Games, opined that the headaches were psychogenic in origin and would become worse if he tried to work.

> I think that the most certain statement that can be made with regard to ***[appellant] is that it is likely he would get worse were he to do work, in that under conditions of his attempting to do even a very minimal amount of work he has shown greatly increased somatization. Thus, the net result is that through a combination of his personality defect and his somatizing tendency he is impaired from a full gainful employment. At the same time there is no evidence of psychosis and also there is no evidence of undue tension at this particular time when he is not employed. (para. 13)

SOMATIZATION IN AND OUT OF THE *DSM*

As might be expected for a diagnosis describing everything from discomfort to disability, the American Psychiatric Association has, in its *DSM*, struggled to produce and develop a rational, reliable, diagnostic category for somatization. The original *DSM* (American Psychiatric Association, 1952) accepted somatization not as another intrapsychic neurosis but rather as a medical disorder capable of inflicting actual damage to the designated organ or organ system. In doing so, the *DSM* avoided the label of *somatization* entirely, preferring the more medical-sounding *psychophysiologic autonomic and visceral disorder* to describe what it termed *visceral expressions of affect*. Psychophysiologic autonomic and visceral disorder was preferred to *psychosomatic disorders* and *somatization reactions* and was considered a separate grouping between psychotic and psychoneurotic reactions that could allow more accurate accumulation of data about etiology, course, and relation to other mental disorders. Symptoms were deemed *organ neuroses* rather than *psychoneuroses*. The *DSM* tailored its diagnostic categories in the apparent expectation that they would encourage study of psychosomatic injury to specific organ systems, such as musculoskeletal, gastrointestinal, and nervous system reactions.

The second edition of the *DSM* (American Psychiatric Association, 1968) allowed for psychosomatic symptoms under psychological disorders such as involutional melancholia and within several neuroses including hypochondriacal, hysterical, and neurasthenic neurosis (weakness, fatigue, exhaustion). The latter two also occurred in more completely developed personality patterns (hysterical personality, asthenic personality). There was an attempt to retain the original *DSM* psychophysical form of somatization as well. The *psychophysiologic disorders* category features psychosomatic symptoms of neurological causation, with a more parsimonious, autonomic basis for somatization. This disorder was characterized by physical symptoms that were caused by emotional factors and affected only a single organ system. The physical symptoms were similar to those that typically accompany emotional disorders but were more intense and sustained, and the patient may have been unaware of the emotional state. The psychophysiologic disorders were then coded under 305 as physical disorders of presumably psychogenic origin and were again listed according to the organ system involved.

Somatization finally merited a diagnostic identity in the third edition of the *DSM* (*DSM–III*; American Psychiatric Association, 1980), in which it was classified as one of the somatoform disorders. Somatoform disorders as a group were considered to be not under voluntary control and without objective medical basis. The subcategory of somatization disorder included hysteria or Briquet's syndrome and was characterized by recurrent somatic complaints of several years' duration that did not appear to result from a physical disorder. The disorder was said to occur in approximately 1% of females and even more rarely in males. It was considered to be chronic, beginning before age 30, with a fluctuating course. There could be complaints of pain, conversion symptoms, and gastrointestinal distress, but there was no longer an attempt to classify symptoms organ by organ. Sexual indifference, dizziness, or physical-sounding complaints without an objective medical basis were also included. Although malingering and factitious disorder, which are considered under voluntary control, were not grouped under this category, *DSM–III* listed features of somatization that would now be considered highly comorbid with malingering, such as the presence of antisocial personality disorder and odd symptoms suggesting malingered psychosis. There was no discussion as to whether the context of symptom presentation (e.g., civil or criminal proceedings) and associated secondary gains for the production of symptoms should be considered in the diagnosis.

The fourth edition, text revision, of the *DSM* (American Psychiatric Association, 2000) continued to describe somatization disorder as a subtype of somatoform disorder and as synonymous with hysteria or Briquet's syndrome. In a subtle change of focus, the criteria shifted from being physical symptoms without a medical basis to multiple symptoms that could not be fully explained by a known medical condition or the direct effects of a substance. Lifetime prevalence was then reported to be 0.2% to 2% in women and less than 0.2% in men. Cultural expressions of symptoms were acknowledged as an influence on prevalence.

DSM–5 (American Psychiatric Association, 2013) provides the most radical attempt to redefine somatization. The term itself once again disappears and in its place are a heterogeneous group of what are called *somatic symptom and related disorders*. Rather than attempting to separate out psychological complaints by organ system, as in the first or second editions of the *DSM*, or known versus unknown medical causation, as in the third and fourth editions, the *DSM–5* suggests that these issues are irrelevant, cannot be appropriately demonstrated, are too difficult to use, or have no diagnostic boundaries. *DSM–5* proposes that centrality of known-versus-unknown medical causation is pejorative because it reinforces mind–body dualism and because it implies to patients that their symptoms are not real. Instead of diagnoses being based on the absence of a medical explanation, *DSM–5* requires diagnoses to be made on the basis of positive signs and symptoms, such as distressing somatic symptoms plus abnormal thoughts, feelings, and behaviors in response to the symptoms. A distinctive feature of this disorder is the patient's presentation and interpretation of the somatic symptoms rather than the presence of the symptoms themselves.

DSM–5's radical reworking of this diagnostic cluster has its critics. Rather than throwing the baby out with the bathwater, *DSM–5* has been criticized as having thrown the entire nursery into the same communal bath. The new category

> summarizes very heterogeneous conditions. Patients suffering from the former somatization disorder will receive this diagnosis, but similarly, this diagnosis will be used for most (yet not all) patients suffering from hypochondriasis, chronic pain conditions, patients worrying about the prognosis of a serious medical condition (e.g., diabetes, cancer), and many others. (Rief, 2013, p. 584)

Hauser and Wolfe (2013) suggested that distressing somatic symptoms are common to both medically ill and mentally ill persons and that adoption of SSD elevates the risk of giving medically ill patients a mental illness diagnosis. They noted that there are no clear criteria for what constitutes a "disproportionate" symptom. One clinician's disproportionate may be another's expectation. As of this writing, the diagnosis turns on a professional's subjective estimate, which Dimsdale and Levenson (2013) reminded is not unique to this diagnosis. However, their sample suggestion, asking the patient "Do you worry far more than you think you should about the recurrence of your cancer?" (p. 588) does not appear very helpful.

DSM–5 not only abandons the attempt to find a neurological or neurotic cause of somatization but also permits SSD to be diagnosed regardless of whether a symptom is caused by genetics, early trauma, learning, or cultural norms and differences. How this will work in subsequent studies of SSD is unclear; it seems unlikely *prima facie* that adult presentation of childhood sexual abuse as SSD is the same diagnosis as SSD symptoms expressed by an anxious cancer patient.

The reliance on self-report for somatic symptom disorders is problematic from a number of perspectives. First, self-report, particularly in the context of potential secondary gain, is perilous because malingerers can accurately simulate self-report symptoms (Martin, Hayes, & Gouvier, 1996). Patients may shape their self-reported symptom pattern and causation to fit the claimed cause, diagnosis, and degree of disability. In one pain patient sample, 80% of subjects pursuing compensation claims had undisclosed past pain history or serious comorbidities (e.g., drug or alcohol abuse) that they denied in the context of their litigated claim (Carragee, 2008). Mental disorder claims as a group have been noted by the Social Security Administration to be highly susceptible to fraud (U.S. General Accounting Office, 1999), and even naïve subjects can accurately simulate psychological and psychosomatic disorders (Lees-Haley & Dunn, 1994).

MEDICALLY UNEXPLAINED SYMPTOMS

Medically unexplained symptoms and disorders are characterized by greater symptoms, disability, and suffering than objective medical findings and pathology would indicate (Binder & Campbell, 2004). Exposure to trauma is associated with the development of medically unexplained physical symptoms, as well as substance use and various psychological disorders, including somatoform disorder (Binder & Campbell, 2004). In the United States, medically unexplained symptoms are the fifth most common reason for visiting a doctor, resulting in 60 million visits annually (Creed, Henningsen, & Fink, 2011) and annual medical costs of approximately $256 billion per year (Evens et al., 2015). In European neurology clinics, annual prevalence rates for medically unexplained symptoms range from 26% to 45% (Creed et al., 2011), with only a tiny fraction (0.4%) later being found to have an organic disease that was plausibly the cause of the presenting problems (Stone et al., 2009). Forensic neuropsychologists at times encounter examinees who have self-reported problems or evaluation findings that are atypical and can be difficult to understand from a medical perspective (see Chapter 7, this handbook, for a case example). The neuropsychological evaluation can help triers of fact and other legal and administrative decision makers arrive at just determinations.

EFFORTS TO EXPLAIN THE PREVIOUSLY UNEXPLAINED

Valiant efforts have been made to help practitioners understand and explain previously unexplained neuropsychological symptoms. Cognitive condition and disorder and neurocognitive hypochondriasis are examples of such efforts.

Cogniform Condition and Disorder

Delis and Wetter (2007) proposed two new diagnoses, cogniform disorder and cogniform condition, that are similar to SSDs but are limited to cognitive symptoms. The diagnoses are intended to "encompass cases of excessive cognitive complaints and inadequate test-taking effort in the absence of sufficient evidence to diagnose malingering" (p. 589). Cogniform condition, which is the less severe form, is characterized by a pattern of cognitive complaints or low scores on psychometric cognitive tests that cannot be fully explained by a neurological disorder, mental disorder, medical condition, effects of a psychoactive substance, or other factors known to affect cognitive functioning such as fatigue. Cogniform disorder includes these same criteria as well as significant manifestations of cognitive dysfunction in multiple areas of everyday life.

Cogniform condition and disorder can involve behavioral and test-based evidence of noncompliance, including failure on performance validity measures. The specifier "with evidence of external incentive" is applied when secondary gain is present but there is insufficient evidence of conscious intent to deceive. These diagnoses, although very relevant to the practice of forensic neuropsychology and reflecting efforts to improve the understanding of examinees who do not easily fit into existing diagnostic categories, are not without limitations involving validity and applicability (Binder, 2007; Boone, 2007; Larrabee, 2007). Among the limitations are a lack of specific criteria for determining whether there is insufficient evidence of a conscious intent to deceive and incompatibility with the Slick, Sherman, and Iverson (1999) criteria for malingered neurocognitive disorder. Slick and Sherman (2013) concluded, "Given these issues, our view is that a cogniform diagnosis should not normally be considered in cases where an examinee meets criteria for probable or definite malingering" (p. 69). Despite the intuitively appealing aspects of the proposed diagnoses of cogniform disorder and cogniform condition, their use does not seem to have become widely adopted in the 10 years since they were proposed by Delis and Wetter (2007).

Neurocognitive Hypochondriasis

Boone (2009) proposed a variant of hypochondriasis (i.e., preoccupation with the body and disease states) that is relevant for neuropsychological practice and is termed *neurocognitive hypochondriasis*. Neurocognitive hypochondriasis involves a fixed belief that one has neurologically based cognitive impairment in the absence of objective evidence of such impairment. This condition, which typically develops in the context of other psychiatric problems and problematic interpersonal relationships, is characterized by hypervigilance to minor cognitive difficulties and failures and is often precipitated by a real illness or injury to which the difficulties continue to be attributed. Diagnosis requires a lack of objective evidence of real or feigned impairment (i.e., performance validity test scores fall within normal limits). Iatrogenic effects of being told by treating clinicians that a single, uncomplicated, mild traumatic brain injury alone has caused severe or permanent cognitive deficits can contribute to the development of this condition.

FORENSIC APPLICATIONS

Forensically, *DSM–5* does nothing to help clarify the uneasy relationship between exaggeration and somatization. In *Carradine v. Barnhart* (2004), a slip-and-fall claimant pursued disability benefits because of chronic pain and fibromyalgia, and her claim was initially rejected for intentional symptom magnification. Judge Posner ruled that somaticized exaggeration of pain was not malingering and that psychogenic pain exaggeration was different from intentionally falsified symptom production. More recent scientific study has indicated that that malingered pain disorder is diagnostically distinct from pain symptoms with psychiatric overlay (e.g., Greve, Etherton, Ord, Bianchini, & Curtis, 2009). While accepting that pain may cause magnified symptoms and that magnification is not automatically malingering, Greve, Ord, Bianchini, and Curtis (2009) nevertheless estimated actual malingering among those asserting pain-related disability as between 20% and 40%.

In *Harrington v. Secretary of Health and Human Services* (1986), the Sixth Circuit affirmed denial of disability because a patient diagnosed with conversion disorder or somatization had "no clear medical basis" for his pain. Flatt (2010) noted that "if the claimant's impairments had been evaluated with a decreased emphasis on the physical evidence requirement, as has become more common in recent years, the court may have come to a very different conclusion" (p. 1417). However, with *DSM–5*'s reliance on subjective symptom distress or severity over whether the claimant has a medically documented malady, it now seems likely that favorable judgments of disability will increase.

If *DSM–5*'s reliance on somatic symptom self-report does loosen the basis for awarding disability, this will increase an already high burden on health care systems. Medical utilization costs under the older somatization standard of medically unexplained symptoms were estimated at $265 billion a year (Evens et al., 2015). In England, somaticizing patients incur an estimated 10% (£3 billion) of the National Healthcare Service budget for the working-age population (Bermingham, Cohen, Hague, & Parsonage, 2010). Finally, by grouping plausible physical symptom complaints with subjective pain complaints with unprovable somaticized stress complaints, the *DSM–5* widens the "imperfect fit" between questions of law and diagnosis to an unbridgeable chasm.

DSM–5 acknowledges that because impairments, abilities, and disabilities vary considerably within diagnostic categories, assignment of a diagnosis does not equate to or necessarily imply functional impairment or disability. However, the *DSM–5* does not address essential questions, such as what combination of historical, psychopathological, symptomatic, and learned factors is sufficient for diagnosis and at what level of severity and at what point do combinations of culture, learning, history, and so forth become a disability? Will the diagnosis be helpful from a treatment standpoint and better than somatization disorder? If somatization disorder was considered pejorative because it implied the disorder is all in one's head, does SSD communicate to the patient "it's all in your body" and iatrogenically encourage the reality of a physical abnormality? Physicians are often reluctant to tell their patients they have a psychogenic illness, perceiving that a psychogenic illness, perhaps because it is out of their treatment purview, "provides invalidation and erects barriers" to patient rapport. Finding a medical condition, by contrast, tells patients that their illness is genuine and significant, and even if the diagnosis does not alter the course of the patient's condition or improve the outcome it can provide psychological comfort (Thomas, 2012). This appears to be a rationalization for medicalizing psychological distress, iatrogenically shaping patient concerns to sustain medical attention and medical treatment. It is an as-yet unanswered empirical question whether a focus on the somatic symptom's reality will assist or impede the treatment of somaticizing patients.

NEUROPSYCHOLOGICAL EVALUATIONS

The presence of neurologically unexplained cognitive symptoms provides a rationale for a neuropsychological evaluation. However, there is no single test or approach to the assessment of somatization. The same comprehensive evaluation used by a neuropsychologist to address most forensic neuropsychological questions is likely to be useful with somatization. The evaluation should include a thorough psychological assessment, which may lead to a psychological understanding of the cognitive symptoms. As Lamberty (2008) noted, "Complaints about cognitive difficulties are rather common and are most often associated with distress in a generic sense.. . . People who feel unwell—for all manner of reasons—also tend to feel like their cognitive functioning is poor" (pp. 48–49). A forensic neuropsychological evaluation can help put subjective cognitive problems in proper context.

DIAGNOSIS

Despite efforts to move from a diagnosis of exclusion to a positive diagnosis (e.g., American Psychiatric Association, 2013; Evens et al., 2015), in practice diagnosing cognitive somatization remains largely a process of eliminating other identifiable (e.g., neurological) causes of cognitive problems. A somatic symptom disorder must be considered when medical, neuropsychological, and background information do not fully explain the presenting symptoms. Of course, the science is far from resolving all questions about neurological functioning, so there may be unidentified medical or neurological explanations for currently unexplained symptoms. However, diagnosis requires considering probabilities, and in any given case of unusual cognitive symptoms, neuropsychologists must consider whether there is a greater probability of a SSD than of a true unidentified neurological disorder.

In addition to consideration of a SSD, the presence of atypical or excessive neuropsychological symptoms should raise the possibility of a factitious disorder or malingering, both of which require conscious intent to deceive. Although in a factitious disorder the intent is to obtain attention and caring from health care professionals, the presence of secondary gain (e.g., disability benefits, financial award, avoidance of unpleasant circumstances) reflects malingering. Neuropsychologists need to keep in mind that diagnostic possibilities do not only consist of the identified neurological injury versus no neurological injury; alternative or additional neurological insults or illnesses may exist and coexist with psychiatric disorders and incentive.

CONCLUSION

Traumatic events, including litigated injuries, can trigger a stress reaction whereby the stress is manifest through new onset or perpetuation of previous physical (including cognitive) symptoms rather than overt emotional distress. Depending on the nature of the symptoms and the definitions considered, such problems have been termed *conversion disorders, pain disorders, somatization,* and *SSDs* (previously *somatoform disorders*). Neuropsychologists in forensic contexts are often challenged to identify and explain cognitive symptoms that are atypical or excessive given an identified injury or illness.

In the interregnum between *DSM–5* and the sixth edition of the *DSM,* additional research and diagnostic utilization may make it clearer whether somatization (now SSD) has overcome its unsavory past and has become a useful diagnosis with respect to validity, treatment choice, and outcome. Beginning as it did with misunderstood neurological symptoms, and probably erroneous psychoanalytic explanations, it remains unclear whether somatization disorder or SSD actually exists as a distinct entity rather than being simply a set of physical complaints made by patients with separate disorders and for different reasons. *DSM–5*'s grand unification theory and laudable attempt to include so many variables compressed into a subjectively derived diagnosis may simply explode under the pressure of complexity. In that case, somatization may disappear once again, subsumed as features of more commonly agreed-on mental disorders. In either case, mental health and legal professionals will continue to struggle to make sense of this quixotic concept, and forensic neuropsychologists will work to present a complex interaction of factors to triers of fact and other involved parties.

References

American Psychiatric Association. (1952). *Diagnostic and statistical manual of mental disorders*. Washington, DC: Author.

American Psychiatric Association. (1968). *Diagnostic and statistical manual of mental disorders* (2nd ed.). Washington, DC: Author.

American Psychiatric Association. (1980). *Diagnostic and statistical manual of mental disorders* (3rd ed.). Washington, DC: Author.

American Psychiatric Association. (2000). *Diagnostic and statistical manual of mental disorders* (4th ed., text revision). Washington, DC: Author.

American Psychiatric Association. (2013). *Diagnostic and statistical manual of mental disorders* (5th ed.). Washington, DC: Author.

Angel, R., & Guarnaccia, P. J. (1989). Mind, body, and culture: Somatization among Hispanics. *Social Science and Medicine, 28,* 1229–1238. http://dx.doi.org/10.1016/0277-9536(89)90341-9

Bermingham, S. L., Cohen, A., Hague, J., & Parsonage, M. (2010). The cost of somatisation among the working-age population in England for the year 2008–2009. *Mental Health in Family Medicine, 7,* 71–84.

Binder, L. M. (2007). Comment on cogniform disorder and cogniform condition: Proposed diagnoses for excessive cognitive symptoms. *Archives of Clinical Neuropsychology, 22,* 681–682. http://dx.doi.org/10.1016/j.acn.2007.07.006

Binder, L. M., & Campbell, K. A. (2004). Medically unexplained symptoms and neuropsychological assessment. *Journal of Clinical and Experimental Neuropsychology, 26,* 369–392. http://dx.doi.org/10.1080/13803390490510095

Boone, K. B. (2007). Commentary on "Cogniform disorder and cogniform condition: Proposed diagnoses for excessive cognitive symptoms" by Dean C. Delis and Spencer R. Wetter. *Archives of Clinical Neuropsychology, 22,* 675–679. http://dx.doi.org/10.1016/j.acn.2007.07.005

Boone, K. B. (2009). Fixed belief in cognitive dysfunction despite normal neuropsychological scores: Neurocognitive hypochondriasis? *Clinical Neuropsychologist, 23,* 1016–1036. http://dx.doi.org/10.1080/13854040802441135

Carradine v. Barnhart, 360 F.3d 751 (6th Cir. 2004).

Carragee, E. J. (2008). Validity of self-reported history in patients with acute back or neck pain after motor vehicle accidents. *Spine Journal, 8,* 311–319. http://dx.doi.org/10.1016/j.spinee.2007.04.008

Creed, F., Henningsen, P., & Fink, P. (Eds.). (2011). *Medically unexplained symptoms, somatisation, and bodily distress.* http://dx.doi.org/10.1017/CBO9780511977862

Delis, D. C., & Wetter, S. R. (2007). Cogniform disorder and cogniform condition: Proposed diagnoses for excessive cognitive symptoms. *Archives of Clinical*

Neuropsychology, *22*, 589–604. http://dx.doi.org/10.1016/j.acn.2007.04.001

Dimsdale, J. E., & Levenson, J. (2013). Diagnosis of somatic symptom disorder requires clinical judgment [Letter to the editor]. *Journal of Psychosomatic Research*, *75*, 588.

Evens, A., Vendetta, L., Krebs, K., & Herath, P. (2015). Medically unexplained neurologic symptoms: A primer for physicians who make the initial encounter. *American Journal of Medicine*, *128*, 1059–1064. http://dx.doi.org/10.1016/j.amjmed.2015.03.030

Flatt, G. C. (2010). All in your head: A comprehensive approach to somatoform disorders in adult disability claims. *Washington University Law Review*, *87*, 1397–1427.

Greve, K. W., Etherton, J. L., Ord, J., Bianchini, K. J., & Curtis, K. L. (2009). Detecting malingered pain-related disability: Classification accuracy of the test of memory malingering. *Clinical Neuropsychologist*, *23*, 1250–1271. http://dx.doi.org/10.1080/13854040902828272

Greve, K. W., Ord, J. S., Bianchini, K. J., & Curtis, K. L. (2009). Prevalence of malingering in patients with chronic pain referred for psychologic evaluation in a medico-legal context. *Archives of Physical Medicine and Rehabilitation*, *90*, 1117–1126. http://dx.doi.org/10.1016/j.apmr.2009.01.018

Gureje, O., Simon, G. E., Ustun, T. B., & Goldberg, D. P. (1997). Somatization in cross-cultural perspective: A World Health Organization study in primary care. *American Journal of Psychiatry*, *154*, 989–995. http://dx.doi.org/10.1176/ajp.154.7.989

Haller, H., Cramer, H., Lauche, R., & Dobos, G. (2015). Somatoform disorders and medically unexplained symptoms in primary care: A systematic review and meta-analysis of prevalence. *Deutsches Ärzteblatt International*, *112*, 279–287.

Harrington v. Secretary of Health and Human Services, No. 85-4069, 1986 WL 18406, at *1 (6th Cir. Nov. 18, 1986).

Hauser, W., & Wolfe, F. (2013). The somatic symptom disorder in *DSM–5* risks mislabeling people with major medical diseases as mentally ill [Letter to the editor]. *Journal of Psychosomatic Research*, *75*, 586–587.

John H. Frederick v. United States, 280 F.2d 844 (Ct. Cl. 1960).

Lamberty, G. J. (2008). *Understanding somatization in the practice of clinical neuropsychology*. New York, NY: Oxford University Press.

Larrabee, G. J. (2007). Commentary on Delis and Wetter, "Cogniform disorder and cogniform condition: Proposed diagnoses for excessive cognitive symptoms." *Archives of Clinical Neuropsychology*, *22*, 683–687. http://dx.doi.org/10.1016/j.acn.2007.07.007

Lees-Haley, P. R., & Dunn, J. T. (1994). The ability of naive subjects to report symptoms of mild brain injury, post-traumatic stress disorder, major depression, and generalized anxiety disorder. *Journal of Clinical Psychology*, *50*, 252–256. http://dx.doi.org/10.1002/1097-4679(199403)50:2<252::AID-JCLP2270500217>3.0.CO;2-T

London, L. S. (1946). *Libido and delusion* (enlarged 2nd ed.). Washington, DC: Mental Therapy.

Mark v. Celebrezze, 348 F.2d 289 (9th Cir. 1965).

Martin, R. C., Hayes, J. S., & Gouvier, W. D. (1996). Differential vulnerability between postconcussion self-report and objective malingering tests in identifying simulated mild head injury. *Journal of Clinical and Experimental Neuropsychology*, *18*, 265–275. http://dx.doi.org/10.1080/01688639608408281

Menninger, R. W., & Nemiah, J. C. (2000). *Postwar growth of clinical psychiatry*. Washington, DC: American Psychiatric Press.

Merskey, H. (2000). Beware somatization. *European Journal of Pain*, *4*, 3–4. http://dx.doi.org/10.1053/eujp.2000.0164

Office of the Surgeon General. (1946). News and comment: Incidence of somatization reactions in psychoneurotic disorders. *Bulletin of the U.S. Army*, *5*, 383–384.

Rief, W. (2013). A commentary on: Somatic symptom disorder: An important change in *DSM*. *Journal of Psychosomatic Research*, *75*, 584. http://dx.doi.org/10.1016/j.jpsychores.2013.10.012

Slater, E. (1965). Diagnosis of "hysteria." *British Medical Journal*, *1*, 1395–1399. http://dx.doi.org/10.1136/bmj.1.5447.1395

Slick, D. J., Sherman, E. M., & Iverson, G. L. (1999). Diagnostic criteria for malingered neurocognitive dysfunction: Proposed standards for clinical practice and research. *Clinical Neuropsychologist*, *13*, 545–561. http://dx.doi.org/10.1076/1385-4046(199911)13:04;1-Y;FT545

Slick, D. J., & Sherman, E. M. S. (2013). Differential diagnosis of malingering. In D. A. Carone & S. S. Bush (Eds.), *Mild traumatic brain injury: Symptom validity assessment and malingering* (pp. 57–72). New York, NY: Springer.

Southard, E. E. (1912–1913). On the somatic sources of somatic delusions. *Journal of Abnormal Psychology*, *7*, 326–339. http://dx.doi.org/10.1037/h0070895

Stekel, W. (1943). *The interpretation of dreams: New developments and technique*. New York, NY: Liveright.

Stone, J., Carson, A., Duncan, R., Coleman, R., Roberts, R., Warlow, C., . . . Sharpe, M. (2009). Symptoms "unexplained by organic disease" in 1144 new neurology out-patients: How often does the diagnosis change at follow-up? *Brain*, *132*, 2878–2888. http://dx.doi.org/10.1093/brain/awp220

Stone, J., Smyth, R., Carson, A., Lewis, S., Prescott, R., Warlow, C., & Sharpe, M. (2005). Systematic review of misdiagnosis of conversion symptoms and "hysteria." *BMJ*, *331*, 989–991. http://dx.doi.org/10.1136/bmj.38628.466898.55

Thomas, L. E. (2012). Are your patient's medically unexplained symptoms really "all in her head"? *Medical Hypotheses*, *78*, 542–547. http://dx.doi.org/10.1016/j.mehy.2012.01.031

U.S. General Accounting Office. (1999). *Supplemental Security Income: Additional actions needed to reduce program vulnerability to fraud and abuse*. Retrieved from http://gao.gov/archive/1999/he99151.pdf

Webster, R. (2003). *Freud, Charcot, and hysteria: Lost in the labyrinth*. Retrieved from http://www.richardwebster.net/freudandcharcot.html

Wilhelm, K. A., Finch, A. W., Davenport, T. A., & Hickie, I. B. (2008). What can alert the general practitioner to people whose common mental health problems are unrecognised? *Medical Journal of Australia*, *188*(Suppl.), S114–S118.

CHAPTER 11

CHRONIC PAIN AND NEUROPSYCHOLOGICAL ASSESSMENT

John E. Meyers

Chronic pain is a prevalent condition in society and commonly co-occurs with cognitive complaints (Iverson, King, Scott, & Adams, 2001). Because chronic pain and cognitive deficits can each be a focus of damages in litigation or a reason for pursuing disability benefits, they are relevant for forensic neuropsychology. Neuropsychologists must understand the relationship between chronic pain and cognitive functioning to make accurate diagnoses and provide opinions that are of value to courts and other decision makers.

A series of authors have looked at the incidence of chronic pain and found that between 19% and 22% of the population experience pain on a chronic basis at any point in time (e.g., Breivik, Collett, Ventafridda, Cohen, & Gallacher, 2006; Eriksen, Jensen, Sjøgren, Ekholm, & Rasmussen, 2003). To better understand the prevalence of pain in 15 European countries and Israel, Breivik et al. (2006) conducted a large-scale survey via telephone. The total number of survey respondents ages 18 years and older who endorsed pain at the initial screening was 46,394. The investigators found that approximately 65% of those respondents rated their pain severity as 5 to 7 out of 10, and 34% rated their pain severity as 8 to 10 out of 10. Investigators with the World Health Organization examined the prevalence of chronic pain on a more global scale in a survey of 31,000 individuals across Asia, Africa, and the Americas and found that the prevalence of pain lasting 6 months or more was 22% and ranged from a low of 5.5% to a high of 33.0% (Gureje, Von Korff, Simon, & Gater, 1998). From these studies, it can be determined that the prevalence of chronic pain is universal and affects approximately 22% of the world's population.

Bruns (2014) noted, "Despite pain's subjective nature, litigation for pain and suffering has been recognized by the courts for centuries, and currently accounts for the majority of damages awarded in medical malpractice cases" (p. 279). Because many persons presenting for forensic neuropsychological evaluation have been injured in accidents of various kinds and are experiencing and claiming disability or damages for pain, the potential impact of pain on cognitive and emotional functioning is of considerable importance. Understanding the relationship between pain and neuropsychological performance helps forensic neuropsychologists make accurate diagnoses, prognoses, and disability determinations.

Despite the prevalence of chronic pain and its relevance for forensic neuropsychology, relatively little systematic attention has been paid to the interface between pain and neuropsychological functioning (McCracken & Thompson, 2012). Rather, these authors stated, "The clinical management of chronic pain and neuropsychological problems seems fraught with assumptions and a distinct nonuniformity in theory and method" (p. 243). Thus, continued advances in the understanding of the interplay of chronic pain and its associated issues, such as pain medications, poor sleep, and litigation, on cognitive and emotional functioning will better prepare forensic neuropsychologists to make accurate diagnoses and statements about causality,

http://dx.doi.org/10.1037/0000032-011
APA Handbook of Forensic Neuropsychology, S. S. Bush (Editor-in-Chief)

prognosis, and disability status, thus allowing triers of fact and other decision makers to come to appropriate determinations. This chapter strives to contribute to such advancement. However, worthy of note here is that, in their meta-analysis of the effect of compensation on the experience and treatment of chronic pain, Rohling, Binder, and Langhinrichsen-Rohling (1995) found that being in a state of compensation or seeking compensation results in more complaints, increased ratings of pain, slower recovery, and worse response to treatment. This occurred despite the use of similar objective measures of physical injury or disease with the compensation and noncompensation samples. This suggests that invalid responding should be explored in most cases, particularly whenever secondary gain issues are well known.

CHRONIC PAIN, EMOTIONAL STATE, AND FUNCTIONING

Between 30% and 50% of chronic pain patients report depressive symptoms that would warrant a diagnosis of depression (Banks & Kerns, 1996). In a Canadian sample, Currie and Wang (2004) found that those with chronic pain complaints were 3 times more likely to be depressed than those without such complaints. McWilliams, Cox, and Enns (2003) reported finding that 35.1% of persons suffering from chronic pain also suffered from anxiety. Demyttenaere et al. (2007) found in their sample of 85,000 people that those with chronic pain had higher rates of depressive diagnoses, anxiety disorders, posttraumatic stress disorder, agoraphobia, and panic disorder.

Patients who report chronic pain also report more functional limitations (Breivik et al., 2006). Using a 4-point rating scale, Gureje et al. (1998) found that of those persons who claimed to be experiencing chronic pain, 31% claimed to be moderate to severely impaired, whereas only 13% of those without chronic pain reported the same level of impairment. On average, people who do not complain of chronic pain rate themselves as living at 94% of their maximum functional capacity, whereas patients who report experiencing chronic pain rate themselves as living at 77% of their maximum functional capacity (Von Korff et al., 2005).

CHRONIC PAIN AND COGNITION

Neuropsychological symptoms and chronic pain commonly co-occur. Nearly 60% of persons with a history of TBI experience chronic pain (Nampiaparampil, 2008). In addition, patients who are reporting chronic pain also report cognitive difficulties (Dick, Eccleston, & Crombez, 2002; Moriarty, McGuire, & Finn, 2011; Park, Glass, Minear, & Crofford, 2001). Between 40% and 60% of patients who are pursuing treatment for chronic pain report difficulty with cognitive functioning (Iverson & McCracken, 1997; McCracken & Thompson, 2012). These difficulties often include deficits in working memory. Working memory is described as the memory storage needed to hold information in mind long enough to perform a task (Baddeley, 2003; Pribram, Miller, & Galanter, 1960). The relationship between chronic pain and working memory difficulties has been reported by several authors (Antepohl, Kiviloog, Andersson, & Gerdle, 2003; Apkarian, Hashmi, & Baliki, 2011; Eccleston & Crombez, 1999; Hart, Martelli, & Zasler, 2000; Iezzi, Duckworth, Vuong, Archibald, & Klinck, 2004; Moore, Keogh, & Eccleston, 2012).

Researchers have proposed at least three different mechanisms to explain the effect of pain on working memory. One mechanism is that hypervigilance to the pain sensation draws a person's attention from the task at hand and results in an excessive focus on nociception (Legrain, Iannetti, Plaghki, & Mouraux, 2011). A second mechanism is that cerebral networks become accustomed to processing nociceptive input and prioritize such input at the expense of other types of stimuli, leaving fewer cognitive resources available to process other information (Ashendorf, Constantinou, & McCaffrey, 2004; Maljkovic & Nakayama, 1994). A third mechanism is that nociception disrupts inhibitory cognitive processes and deactivation of brain areas such that nociception is prioritized over most other types of input, resulting in pain patients attending to nociceptive stimuli to the exclusion of other sensory and cognitive signals (Baliki, Geha, Apkarian, & Chialvo, 2008).

A large-scale factor analysis of the effects of pain on cognition was conducted by Berryman et al. (2013). In their initial sample of the literature, they examined 1,436 articles, yet only 23 of those articles had sufficient methodological rigor and data collection standards to meet their inclusion criteria. In analyzing the 23 studies, the authors concluded that controls consistently performed better cognitively than chronic pain patients. Several important findings were generated by their meta-analysis, one example of which is that electroencephalograph "results demonstrated no difference between chronic pain patients and controls" (p. 1191). Because each study differed methodologically, Berryman et al. stated that "cognitive impairment in people with chronic pain needs to be investigated in a standardized and targeted manner" (p. 1191). Furthermore, they indicated that a new paradigm should be developed to conceptualize the physiological and behavioral deficits associated with chronic pain. A major weakness of many of the neuropsychological studies was that they did not include performance validity measures (PVMs), making it impossible to determine the influence of feigning or secondary gain.

In 2000, Hart et al. provided a summary of 23 studies. These authors wanted to determine which neuropsychological tests were the most sensitive to the effects of chronic pain. Despite their original goal, their results were inconsistent and did not converge on any particular domain of functioning. As an example, Gimse, Bjorgen, Tjell, Tyssedal, and Bo (1997) found that the Rey Auditory Verbal Learning Test and Paced Serial Addition Test were sensitive to the impairing effects of chronic pain. However, Grace, Berg, and Nielson (1995) found these same two measures to be insensitive to the effects of chronic pain. Many of the subjects in these studies were involved in litigation, and only a few of the studies included normal control subjects for comparative purposes.

In another example of the inconsistency among studies of neuropsychology and pain, Kaplan, Meadows, Vincent, Logigian, and Steere (1992) found that pain patients performed similarly on memory tests to patients with depression. Yet, Landro, Stiles, and Sletvold (1997) found that patients' ratings of pain intensity were not associated with memory test scores. Such inconsistencies led the authors to conclude that much more systematic research was needed to examine the effects of pain on cognition. One of the major limitations of these early studies was their failure to include PVMs in the test battery to control for exaggeration or fabrication of problems, which occurs with some frequency in the secondary gain contexts in which many persons with pain are evaluated. In defense of these early researchers, most PVMs have been developed over the past 20 years, with widespread use occurring more recently, and most of the early studies were conducted before their development and widespread use. However, Gervais, Rohling, Green, and Ford (2004) found that neither chronic nor acute pain had an influence on cognitive performance once subjects who had failed a PVM were excluded from the sample.

Guéz, Brännström, Nyberg, Toolanen, and Hildingsson (2005) examined 42 chronic pain patients, 21 whiplash trauma patients, and 21 noninjured subjects. Whiplash patients reported more forgetfulness and more concentration difficulties than the two other groups. Yet, the two patient groups did not differ from one another, nor did they differ from normal controls, on scores obtained from objective cognitive measures. On the Minnesota Multiphasic Personality Inventory—2, pain patients and whiplash patients did differ from normal controls. The authors concluded that subjective complaints of cognitive difficulty in patients with chronic neck pain are likely related to somatization and inadequate emotional coping skills.

Bell, Primeau, Sweet, and Lofland (1999) examined 60 subjects with migraine headaches, nonheadache chronic pain, or mild traumatic brain injury (mTBI). They found that headache and pain patients did not differ on memory performance, and that TBI patients were more impaired on memory tasks. They concluded that their data did not support the hypothesis of a link between migraine headaches and cognitive impairment.

The Meyers Neuropsychological Battery (MNB) is a specific core battery of tests that have been found to be able to discriminate between various diagnostic groups (Meyers, Miller, & Tuita, 2014). The MNB has been favorably compared with computed tomography and MRI data (Meyers & Rohling, 2009) and has been found to be sensitive not only to the presence of cognitive impairment but also to the degree of impairment (Rohling, Meyers, & Millis, 2003). The MNB has also been found to be sensitive to emotional distress (Meyers, Grills, Zellinger, & Miller, 2014). Thus, the MNB was thought to be a valid and reliable core battery of tests that would be expected to be able to differentiate between groups of patients with similar complaints. The MNB uses a pattern-matching approach. A specific patient's data can be directly compared with those of various groups. Also, various neural networks and discriminant functions are used in conjunction with the pattern-matching approach to help the clinician arrive at a reliable and valid diagnosis.

To better understand the neuropsychology of chronic pain, MNB data from a sample of 403 individuals were examined and are presented here for the first time. These data were originally collected as part of the MNB dataset. To be included in the analyses, the individuals selected from the database must have completed the MNB, including the Minnesota Multiphasic Personality Inventory—2 Restructured Form (MMPI–2–RF), have a clear diagnosis identified in their medical records, and have passed all 19 internal MNB PVMs (Meyers, 2009). The demographic makeup of the groups is described in Table 11.1. The subjects were divided into five groups: mTBI, depression, chronic pain, anxiety, and normal controls.

The 73 subjects in the mTBI group reported a history of mTBI; all had a brief loss of consciousness or change in awareness at the time of the injury. Of these, 63% had documented evidence in their medical records at the time of the injury event that substantiated their experience of an mTBI. The remainder did not immediately seek medical treatment at the time of injury but did complain of cognitive impairments at the time of the assessment. For those with medical records from the injury, the mean amount of time from injury to evaluation was 23.0 months ($SD = 38.8$). Forty of these individuals were involved in litigation. An independent-samples t test indicated that overall performance between the litigating group and the reported non–compensation-seeking group was not significantly different ($p = .25$). So, the litigating and the non–compensation-seeking individuals were combined. The cognitive and psychological test scores for all groups are detailed in Tables 11.2 and 11.3, respectively.

Those in the depression group were all currently being treated for depression as their primary diagnosis. All were treated with various antidepressant medications and psychotherapy, and all were seen for neuropsychological assessment because of their cognitive complaints. The level of depression reported on the MMPI–2–RF is presented in Table 11.3. None of the 116 individuals were involved in litigation or disability proceedings.

All subjects in the chronic pain group reported constant pain at a 7 out of 10 or higher (i.e., higher numbers reflect greater complaints). All subjects also complained of impaired cognition. In this group, 53 were involved in litigation, and 32 were not. An independent-samples t test indicated that the litigating and non–compensation-seeking subjects were not significantly different from one another in their overall test battery mean ($p = .36$), so the litigating and non–compensation-seeking chronic pain groups were combined as well.

The "normal" group consisted of 49 individuals who were hospitalized for treatment for minor medical issues (i.e., ingrown toenail, hemorrhoids) and not for any neurological or psychiatric issues. These individuals agreed to undergo a neuropsychological assessment and have their data stored for use in future studies. All of the control subjects were living independently in the community.

The anxiety group was composed of individuals who had a primary diagnosis of anxiety or posttraumatic stress disorder. The severity of behavior health issues is presented in Table 11.3. Of these patients, 24 were involved with or pursuing disability and 56 were not. An independent-samples t test found no significant differences ($p = .15$) in cognitive test scores.

A one-way analysis of variance found that the overall test battery mean was significantly different between the groups, $F(4, 398) = 31.63$, $p < .001$. A series of correlations were computed and are presented in Table 11.4. The results indicate that individuals who report chronic pain, a history of

TABLE 11.1

Demographic Description of Groups

		Age	Education	Handed	Ethnic	Gender
TBI (mild; *N* = 73)	*M* *SD*	33.15 10.852	12.90 1.945	Right = 65 Left = 8	African American = 1(1%) Caucasian = 65(89%) Hispanic = 5(6%) Pacific Islander = 2(2%)	Female = 17 Male = 56
Depression (*N* = 116)	*M* *SD*	39.91 12.497	13.60 2.384	Right = 108 Left = 8	Other = 2(1%) African American = 2(1%) Caucasian = 108 (93%) Hispanic = 4 (3%)	Female = 50 Male = 66
Pain (*N* = 85)	*M* *SD*	43.00 10.785	12.29 2.103	Right = 82 Left = 3	African American = 5(5%) Caucasian = 75 (88%) Asian = 1 (1%) Native American = 2 (2%) Hispanic = 2(2%)	Female = 36 Male = 49
Normals (*N* = 49)	*M* *SD*	31.53 8.249	13.33 2.014	Right = 45 Left = 4	African American = 4 (8%) Caucasian = 35 (71%) Native American = 2 (4%) Hispanic = 6 (12%) Pacific Islander = 2 (4%)	Female = 7 Male = 42
Anxiety (*N* = 80)	*M* *SD* *SD*	34.58 11.620 10.174	12.99 2.090 2.499	Right = 74 Left = 6	Other = 2(2%) African American = 9 (11%) Caucasian = 55 (68%) Asian = 3 (3%) Native American = 1 (1%) Hispanic = 6 (7%) Pacific Islander = 4 (5%)	Female = 26 Male = 54
Total (*N* = 403)	*M* *SD*	37.26 11.926	13.04 2.190	Right = 374 Left = 29	Other = 4 (<1%) African American = 21 (5%) Caucasian = 338 (83%) Asian = 4 (<1%) Native American = 5 (1%) Hispanic = 23 (5%) Pacific Islander = 8 (1%)	Female = 136 Male = 267

Note. TBI = traumatic brain injury.

mTBI, depression, or anxiety tend to report similar behavioral health issues as measured by the MMPI–2–RF. However, the correlations with the cognitive test scores from the assessment indicate differences in the pattern and level of performance among the groups. To further examine these pattern differences among the groups, a series of stepwise discriminant analyses were conducted, which included scores from the MNB and the MMPI–2–RF. The results of these analyses are presented in Table 11.5. The analyses showed better than an 80% correct classification rate for each of the discriminant results (80.6%–96.1%). These results indicate that a pattern-matching approach, such as that used with the MNB, is capable of differentiating the groups examined. Thus, a forensic examiner can use these results to aid with diagnosis when chronic pain is a suspected condition. These results also reinforce the usefulness of neuropsychological assessment with chronic pain patients. A more accurate diagnosis will likely be the result, which in turn will mean that patients will receive more appropriate treatment. For example, if an individual reporting chronic pain is evaluated according to this approach and the results indicate that the pattern is

TABLE 11.2

Descriptive Statistics of Neuropsychological Data for Each Meyers Neuropsychological Battery Study Group

Test name	TBI (mild)		Depression		Pain		Normal		Anxiety	
	M	*SD*	*M*	*SD*	*M*	*SD*	*M*	*SD*	*M*	*SD*
WAIS										
PC	50.0	8.8	51.7	9.1	49.2	9.3	54.8	9.3	51.9	8.7
CD	42.0	7.9	49.3	9.2	47.0	9.3	50.2	11.1	48.6	8.7
SI	46.6	8.2	51.1	10.0	46.6	6.8	52.3	7.9	49.9	5.8
BD	51.0	8.6	52.0	9.2	47.9	9.2	54.4	9.7	53.9	8.0
AR	48.7	8.5	51.5	8.6	46.5	7.8	53.6	7.8	47.5	8.5
DS	48.5	7.2	51.1	8.3	48.9	6.9	52.6	8.4	49.0	7.2
IN	46.9	7.1	53.1	8.2	44.3	9.0	54.6	9.1	50.3	7.0
Forced choice	41.5	12.0	49.4	9.9	45.2	10.1	51.4	7.8	45.3	11.0
Animals	48.0	9.9	53.7	10.5	54.4	10.1	51.7	9.2	49.5	8.8
COWA–FAS	42.4	8.4	46.2	9.9	46.4	9.7	48.7	7.4	48.6	8.7
Dich										
Lsn, L	39.8	11.3	47.9	8.2	45.4	8.6	47.4	7.0	46.1	8.5
Lsn, R	45.1	9.7	50.3	7.6	49.9	8.3	51.6	5.0	50.1	6.1
Lsn, B	40.0	13.3	50.1	9.7	47.1	10.8	50.1	8.0	48.6	10.0
Sent. Rep.	43.0	10.5	49.2	11.4	43.5	10.7	54.7	13.0	43.0	10.5
JLO	52.7	7.4	54.2	6.9	53.5	7.4	54.7	5.4	55.0	6.1
BNT	39.6	8.6	46.4	7.0	43.8	8.8	47.0	5.8	44.4	8.5
FTT										
Dom	42.9	6.5	47.8	7.2	46.7	6.5	48.9	7.4	48.7	6.8
Ndom	45.1	10.7	48.7	7.1	47.2	7.6	50.4	6.6	51.2	7.2
FLOC										
Dom	55.2	3.5	55.4	5.5	53.2	5.7	56.5	2.5	55.7	3.8
Ndom	50.2	9.1	51.9	5.0	50.9	6.4	52.6	3.1	52.0	3.3
Trails A	45.2	9.9	47.3	9.9	48.8	9.4	52.2	10.4	50.5	9.8
Trails B	47.2	10.9	49.0	9.7	51.1	8.6	54.5	9.0	54.1	9.9
Token Test	52.7	5.8	54.5	4.4	53.0	4.7	55.6	3.3	52.9	6.0
Category Test (Victoria version)	45.2	11.3	46.3	10.5	41.1	8.5	53.6	11.7	52.0	11.3
RAVLT										
Tr1	44.9	11.1	50.4	12.0	46.0	10.2	53.7	10.8	44.9	8.3
Total	40.0	11.5	51.8	10.2	42.4	11.5	56.1	9.2	47.0	10.0
Im FR	41.9	11.8	51.5	10.4	41.0	11.8	57.4	6.4	51.3	10.1
Del FR	39.3	11.4	49.9	10.5	39.8	11.9	55.3	8.1	48.8	10.0
Rgn	45.6	8.6	51.6	5.2	47.9	7.4	49.7	7.3	49.8	6.4
RCFT										
Copy	40.3	15.6	44.5	12.3	40.0	14.2	45.7	10.3	45.4	10.8
Im FR	46.2	15.0	53.2	11.7	45.1	12.6	56.0	11.6	55.5	13.7
Del FR	44.8	15.0	52.6	11.5	44.3	12.7	54.0	10.8	52.5	13.4
Rgn	50.2	12.4	52.2	11.3	49.7	10.8	55.3	12.0	56.5	10.7

Note. Animals = Animal Naming; AR = Arithmetic; B = both ears; BD = Block Design; BNT = Boston Naming Test; CD = Coding; COWA–FAS = Controlled Oral Word Association Test; Del FR = Delayed Free Recall; Dich = Dichotic; Dom = dominant hand; DS = Digit Span; FLOC = Finger Localization; FTT = Finger Tapping Test; Im FR = Immediate Free Recall; IN = Information; JLO = Judgment of Line Orientation; L = left ear; Lsn = Listening; Ndom = nondominant hand; PC = Picture Completion; R = right ear; RAVLT = Rey Auditory Verbal Learning Test; RCFT = Rey Complex Figure Test; Rgn = Recognition; Sent. Rep. = Sentence Repetition; SI = Similarities; TBI = traumatic brain injury; Trails A = Trail Making Test—Part A; Trails B = Trail Making Test—Part B; Tr1 = trial 1; WAIS = Wechsler Adult Intelligence Scale (3rd or 4th ed.).

TABLE 11.3

MMPI–2–RF Scores for Each Group in the Meyers Neuropsychological Battery Study

Subscale	mTBI (mild)		Depression		Pain		Normal		Anxiety	
	M	*SD*	*M*	*SD*	*M*	*SD*	*M*	*SD*	*M*	*SD*
VRIN-r	50.0	8.8	51.7	9.1	49.2	9.3	54.8	9.3	51.9	8.7
TRIN-r	42.0	7.9	49.3	9.2	47.0	9.3	50.2	11.1	48.6	8.7
F-r	46.6	8.2	51.1	10.0	46.6	6.8	52.3	7.9	49.9	5.8
Fp-r	51.0	8.6	52.0	9.2	47.9	9.2	54.4	9.7	53.9	8.0
Fs	48.7	8.5	51.5	8.6	46.5	7.8	53.6	7.8	47.5	8.5
FBS-r	48.5	7.2	51.1	8.3	48.9	6.9	52.6	8.4	49.0	7.2
RBS-r	45.1	10.7	48.7	7.1	47.2	7.6	50.4	6.6	51.2	7.2
L-r	46.9	7.1	53.1	8.2	44.3	9.0	54.6	9.1	50.3	7.0
K-r	41.5	12.0	49.4	9.9	45.2	10.1	51.4	7.8	45.3	11.0
EID	48.0	9.9	53.7	10.5	54.4	10.1	51.7	9.2	49.5	8.8
THD	42.4	8.4	46.2	9.9	46.4	9.7	48.7	7.4	48.6	8.7
BXD	39.8	11.3	47.9	8.2	45.4	8.6	47.4	7.0	46.1	8.5
RCd	45.1	9.7	50.3	7.6	49.9	8.3	51.6	5.0	50.1	6.1
RC1	40.0	13.3	50.1	9.7	47.1	10.8	50.1	8.0	48.6	10.0
RC2	43.0	10.5	49.2	11.4	43.5	10.7	54.7	13.0	43.0	10.5
RC3	52.7	7.4	54.2	6.9	53.5	7.4	54.7	5.4	55.0	6.1
RC4	39.6	8.6	46.4	7.0	43.8	8.8	47.0	5.8	44.4	8.5
RC6	42.9	6.5	47.8	7.2	46.7	6.5	48.9	7.4	48.7	6.8
RC7	45.1	10.7	48.7	7.1	47.2	7.6	50.4	6.6	51.2	7.2
RC8	55.2	3.5	55.4	5.5	53.2	5.7	56.5	2.5	55.7	3.8
RC9	50.2	9.1	51.9	5.0	50.9	6.4	52.6	3.1	52.0	3.3
MLS	45.2	9.9	47.3	9.9	48.8	9.4	52.2	10.4	50.5	9.8
GIC	47.2	10.9	49.0	9.7	51.1	8.6	54.5	9.0	54.1	9.9
HPC	52.7	5.8	54.5	4.4	53.0	4.7	55.6	3.3	52.9	6.0
NUC	45.2	11.3	46.3	10.5	41.1	8.5	53.6	11.7	52.0	11.3
COG	44.9	11.1	50.4	12.0	46.0	10.2	53.7	10.8	44.9	8.3
SUI	40.0	11.5	51.8	10.2	42.4	11.5	56.1	9.2	47.0	10.0
HLP	41.9	11.8	51.5	10.4	41.0	11.8	57.4	6.4	51.3	10.1
SFD	39.3	11.4	49.9	10.5	39.8	11.9	55.3	8.1	48.8	10.0
NFC	45.6	8.6	51.6	5.2	47.9	7.4	49.7	7.3	49.8	6.4
STW	40.3	15.6	44.5	12.3	40.0	14.2	45.7	10.3	45.4	10.8
AXY	46.2	15.0	53.2	11.7	45.1	12.6	56.0	11.6	55.5	13.7
ANP	44.8	15.0	52.6	11.5	44.3	12.7	54.0	10.8	52.5	13.4
BRF	50.2	12.4	52.2	11.3	49.7	10.8	55.3	12.0	56.5	10.7
MSF	50.0	8.8	51.7	9.1	49.2	9.3	54.8	9.3	51.9	8.7
JCP	42.0	7.9	49.3	9.2	47.0	9.3	50.2	11.1	48.6	8.7
SUB	46.6	8.2	51.1	10.0	46.6	6.8	52.3	7.9	49.9	5.8
AGG	51.0	8.6	52.0	9.2	47.9	9.2	54.4	9.7	53.9	8.0
ACT	48.7	8.5	51.5	8.6	46.5	7.8	53.6	7.8	47.5	8.5
FML	48.5	7.2	51.1	8.3	48.9	6.9	52.6	8.4	49.0	7.2
IPP	46.9	7.1	53.1	8.2	44.3	9.0	54.6	9.1	50.3	7.0
SAV	41.5	12.0	49.4	9.9	45.2	10.1	51.4	7.8	45.3	11.0
SHY	48.0	9.9	53.7	10.5	54.4	10.1	51.7	9.2	49.5	8.8
DSF	42.4	8.4	46.2	9.9	46.4	9.7	48.7	7.4	48.6	8.7
AES	39.8	11.3	47.9	8.2	45.4	8.6	47.4	7.0	46.1	8.5
MEC	45.1	9.7	50.3	7.6	49.9	8.3	51.6	5.0	50.1	6.1
AGGR-r	40.0	13.3	50.1	9.7	47.1	10.8	50.1	8.0	48.6	10.0
PSYC-r	43.0	10.5	49.2	11.4	43.5	10.7	54.7	13.0	43.0	10.5

(*continues*)

TABLE 11.3 (*Continued*)

MMPI–2–RF Scores for Each Group in the Meyers Neuropsychological Battery Study

Subscale	mTBI (mild)		Depression		Pain		Normal		Anxiety	
	M	*SD*	*M*	*SD*	*M*	*SD*	*M*	*SD*	*M*	*SD*
DISC-r	52.7	7.4	54.2	6.9	53.5	7.4	54.7	5.4	55.0	6.1
NEGE-r	39.6	8.6	46.4	7.0	43.8	8.8	47.0	5.8	44.4	8.5
INTR-r	42.9	6.5	47.8	7.2	46.7	6.5	48.9	7.4	48.7	6.8

Note. ACT = Activation; AES = Aesthetic-Literary Interests; AGG = Aggression; AGGR = Aggressiveness; ANP = Anger Proneness; AXY = Anxiety; BRF = Behavior Restricting Fears; BXD = Behavioral/Externalizing Dysfunction; COG = Cognitive Complaints; DISC = Disconstraint; DSF = Disaffiliativeness; EID = Emotional/Internalizing Dysfunction; F = Infrequent Responses; FBS = Symptom Validity; FML = Family Problems; Fp = Infrequent Psychopathology Responses; Fs = Infrequent Somatic Responses; GIC = Gastrointestinal Complaints; HLP = Helplessness/Hopelessness; HPC = Head Pain Complaints; INTR = Introversion/Low Positive Emotionality; IPP = Interpersonal Passivity; JCP = Juvenile Conduct Problems; K = Adjustment Validity; L = Uncommon Virtues; MEC = Mechanical-Physical Interests; MLS = Malaise; MMPI–2–RF = Minnesota Multiphasic Personality Inventory—2 Restructured Form; MSF = Multiple Specific Fears; mTBI = mild traumatic brain injury; NEGE = Negative Emotionality/Neuroticism; NFC = Inefficacy; NUC = Neurological Complaints; PSYC = Psychoticism; r = revised; RBS = Response Bias Scale; RCd = Demoralization; RC1 = Somatic Complaints; RC2 = Low Positive Emotions; RC3 = Cynicism; RC4 = Antisocial Behavior; RC6 = Ideas of Persecution; RC7 = Dysfunctional Negative Emotions; RC8 = Aberrant Experiences; RC9 = Hypomanic Activation; SAV = Social Avoidance; SFD = Self-Doubt; SHY = Shyness; STW = Stress/Worry; SUB = Substance Abuse; SUI = Suicidal/Death Ideation; THD = Thought Dysfunction; TRIN = True Response Inconsistency; VRIN = Variable Response Inconsistency.

TABLE 11.4

Overall Correlations for Each Group in the Meyers Neuropsychological Battery Study

Group	Cognitive *r*	MMPI–2–RF *r*
Pain	—	—
Depression	.53	.89
Anxiety	.50	.84
TBI	.75	.86
Normal controls	.13	.56

Note. MMPI–2–RF = Minnesota Multiphasic Personality Inventory—2 Restructured Form; TBI = traumatic brain injury.

more consistent with depression rather than chronic pain, this would lead to a recommendation for treatment of depression, with less of an emphasis on chronic pain. Even if the individual is not complaining of depression, depression treatment may be a better approach to treating the pain complaint.

More specifically, between eight and 14 variables are used to discriminate between the various groups when pairwise comparisons are made. The more similar the samples are to one another, the more variables are needed to adequately separate them from one another. The common variables that exist in two or more pairwise comparisons were Infrequent Responses–revised, Malaise, and Stress/Worry from the MMPI–2–RF, as well as Information and Block Design from the Wechsler Adult Intelligence Scale, Animal Naming, the Category Test, Sentence Repetition, and the Token Test. Additional scores are needed to increase the accuracy of classification, but these additional tests are unique to the comparison being made, depending on the samples included in the analyses. The easiest discrimination was between pain patients and normals, followed by pain patients and anxiety sufferers. The most difficult discrimination was between pain patients and mTBI subjects. To some degree, this reinforces the assumption that pain patients are most similar to mTBI patients than they are to those suffering from anxiety or who have experienced depression.

TABLE 11.5

Stepwise Canonical Discriminant Function Coefficients for Meyers Neuropsychological Battery Study

Pain vs. normal function[a]		**Pain vs. TBI function**[b]		**Pain vs.depression function**[c]		**Pain vs. anxiety function**[d]	
< 0 = pain > = 0 Normal		**< 0 = TBI > 0 = Pain**		**< 0 = Pain > = 0 depression**		**< 0 = Pain > = 0 = anxiety**	
Measure	**B**	**Measure**	**B**	**Measure**	**B**	**Measure**	**B**
MLS	−.028	WAIS CD	.063	WAIS IN	.057	WAIS BD	.045
WAIS IN	.041	WAIS BD	−.065	Sent Rep	.020	WAIS AR	−.048
Sent Rep	.025	Animal	.033	Trails B	−.021	WAIS IN	.052
Animal	−.029	Dich Lis L	.026	Token	.049	Animal	−.069
Cat Test	.029	BNT	.032	AVLT Total	.035	COWA	.033
AVLT FR	.032	Cat Test	−.035	VRIN-r	.032	Token	−.067
ANP	.011	MLS	.034	F-r	.050	Cat Test	.069
SUI	−.033	ANP	−.034	RC1	−.043	F-r	.020
(Constant)	−.915	(Constant)	−2.85	RC2	−.041	K-r	−.023
				MLS	−.044	MLS	−.026
				STW	−.016	HPC	−.019
				SHY	.019	STW	.021
				AGGR-r	−.042	(Constant)	1.609
				RBS	.025		
				(Constant)	−3.185		

Note. For all computations, *T* scores were used. Unstandardized beta weights are shown. AGGR = Aggression; Animals = Animal Naming; ANP = Anger Problems; AR = Arithmetic; AVLT = Rey Auditory Verbal Learning Test; BD = Block Design; BNT = Boston Naming Test; Cat. Test = Victoria Version of the Category Test; CD = Coding; COWA = Controlled Oral Word Association Test; Dich Lis L = Dichotic Listening Left ear; F = Infrequency; FR = Free Recall (Immediate recall); HPC = Head Pain Complaints; IN = Information; K = Adjustment Validity; MLS = Malaise; r = revised; RBS = Response Bias Scale; RC1 = Somatic Complaints; RC2 = Low Positive Emotions; Sent. Rep. = Sentence Repetition; SHY = Shyness; STW = Stress/Worry; SUI = Suicidal/Death Ideation; TBI = traumatic brain injury; Token = Token Test; Trails B = Trail Making Test B; VRIN-r = Variable Response Inconsistency; WAIS = Wechsler Adult Intelligence Scale.

[a]Eigenvalue = 2.235, canonical r = .831, Wilks' λ = .309, $\chi2(8)$ = 144.4, $p < .001$, OAC% = 96.1. [b]Eigenvalue = .835, canonical r = .675, Wilks' λ = .545, $\chi^2(8)$ = 89.3, $p < .001$, OAC% = 80.6. [c]Eigenvalue = 1.702, canonical r = .794, Wilks' λ = .370, $\chi^2(14)$ = 186.9, $p < .001$, OAC% = 88.1. [d]Eigenvalue = 1.513, canonical r = .776, Wilks' λ = .398, $\chi^2(12)$ = 139.1, $p < .001$, OAC% = 89.4.

CHRONIC PAIN AND PERFORMANCE VALIDITY

Pain-related disability is a complex and multifaceted problem that can result in exaggeration or fabrication of cognitive and emotional problems and functional limitations. Dissimulation can occur in different and sometimes multiple domains (Bianchini, Greve, & Glynn, 2005), including cognitive domains. PVMs are the current best-practice approach to assessing the validity of cognitive performance during forensic neuropsychological evaluations (Bush et al., 2005; Heilbronner, Sweet, Morgan, Larrabee, & Millis, 2009). Some authors have used the terms *performance validity tests* (PVTs) or *symptom validity tests* (SVTs) rather than PVMs (Larrabee, 2012). The preference here is to do as Larrabee (2012) suggested and use *performance validity* as meaning the validity of actual test performance ability and *symptom validity* to refer to the validity of symptomatic self-report complaints.

The use of PVMs with a variety of disorders has been studied by numerous authors. Rees, Tombaugh, and Boulay (2001) found that depression did not negatively affect performance on PVMs. Likewise, the combination of depression and anxiety had no significant effect on PVM scores (Ashendorf et al., 2004), nor did the combination of chronic pain and depression (Iverson, Le Page, Koehler, Shojania, & Badii, 2007). Even direct application of pain (cold pressor) had no significant impact on PVM performance (Etherton, Bianchini, Ciota, & Greve, 2005; Etherton, Bianchini, Greve, & Ciota, 2005). Using a known-groups design, the Reliable Digit Span was found to adequately identify those malingering with pain-related disability from those not classified as such (Greve et al., 2010).

In an earlier study, Meyers and Volbrecht (2003) presented the number of PVMs failed in a chronic pain sample. They found that 13% of pain patients not in litigation at the time of the assessment failed only one of the nine PVMs used (the remaining 87% failed none of them). In contrast, of those pain patients who were involved in litigation, 51% failed one or more PVMs. These findings illustrate the need for the use of PVMs when assessing patients with chronic pain complaints, even if they are not involved in current litigation (Meyers, Volbrecht, Axelrod, & Reinsch-Boothby, 2011). This is one of the major limitations of many of the prior studies of pain effects on neuropsychological testing. Simply stated, unless the data were adequately screened for valid performance, the findings of these studies cannot be relied on (Meyers & Volbrecht, 2003).

Larrabee (2008) provided an important contribution to this research by "chaining" different PVMs to provide a probability that the data would be invalid. This chaining process was expanded by Meyers, Miller, Thompson, et al. (2014). To the four PVMs and one SVT presented by Larrabee, Meyers, Miller, Thompson, et al. added 10 more PVMs and one SVT. The two studies used similar assumptions and showed that PVMs with different sensitivities and specificities can be combined to provide probability statements for nonvalid data sets. Some may suggest that those in litigation may be more stressed or that being seen by the neuropsychologist for the other side may be more stressful than being evaluated by one's treating clinician and that this is why there are PVM failures. This idea was investigated by Meyers, Reinsch-Boothby, Miller, Rohling, and Axelrod (2011), who found that there was no difference between PVM failures on the basis of referral source. Although early research involving patients with chronic pain and neuropsychological assessment is limited in its application to current patients' assessment because it did not use PVMs, other more recent research has found that many of the standard PVMs can be successfully used with litigants who are reporting pain. Similar to the Slick, Sherman, and Iverson (1999) criteria for determining malingered neurocognitive dysfunction, Bianchini et al. (2005) offered a structured framework for diagnosing malingered pain-related disability that some neuropsychologists may find quite valuable in the context of forensic evaluations.

PAIN MEDICATIONS AND COGNITION

Opioid analgesic medications can be effective for the treatment of noncancer pain in carefully selected and monitored patients (Chou et al., 2009). Therefore, some neuropsychological examinees with chronic pain will currently be using or have a history of using such medications to help control pain. However, the effects of opioid analgesic medications on cognition are far from straightforward and may be extremely difficult to determine for a given examinee. Some research has found that these medications have the potential to adversely affect a wide range of cognitive abilities, including some combination of the following: attention and concentration, memory, visuospatial skills, psychomotor speed, and hand–eye coordination (Gruber, Silveri, & Yurgelun-Todd, 2007; Sjøgren, Thomsen, & Olsen, 2000). Other research found little to no effect of opioid analgesic medications on cognition (Ersek, Cherrier, Overman, & Irving, 2004; Raja et al., 2002). In contrast, some research has indicated that such medications have a positive effect on cognitive performance (Rowbotham et al., 2003), presumably by alleviating the distracting effects of the pain. Differences in research findings may reflect, at least in part, differences among study participants. Forensic neuropsychologists should strive to understand the cognitive effects of recent or chronic use of pain medications for each examinee.

ASSESSMENT OF PAIN

Understanding the location, nature, frequency, and intensity of pain can be an important part of a forensic neuropsychological evaluation. "Advances in technology notwithstanding, the experience of pain cannot be objectively assessed and must instead be assessed by psychological methods" (Bruns, 2014, p. 297). A number of procedures and measures exist to facilitate the understanding of an examinee's pain. These procedures range from basic rating scales such as the Wong–Baker FACES Pain Rating Scale (Wong–Baker FACES Foundation, 2015), numeric pain rating scales (McCaffrey & Pasero, 1999), and pain location drawings (Melzack, 1975) to more comprehensive measures that typically include symptom validity scales, such as the Brief Battery for Health Improvement 2 (Disorbio & Bruns, 2002), Millon Behavioral Medicine Diagnostic (Millon, Antoni, Millon, Meagher, & Grossman, 2001), and the MMPI–2–RF in forensic contexts (Aguerrevere, Greve, & Bianchini, 2013). Of note, neither the Personality Assessment Inventory nor the Millon Clinical Multiaxial Inventory—III has medical norms.

In Chapter 4 of this handbook, Larrabee, in his description of recommended tests, notes that in his forensic evaluations, he typically administers three self-report pain scales: the McGill Pain Questionnaire (Melzack, 1975), Pain Disability Index (Tait, Chibnall, & Krause, 1990), and Modified Somatic Perception Questionnaire (Main, 1983). He further explained, citing his earlier work (Larrabee, 2003), that he established SVT cutoffs for all three of these scales, with Bianchini et al. (2014) (a) replicating his findings for the Pain Disability Index and Modified Somatic Perception Questionnaire, (b) refining the cutoff scores, and (c) demonstrating that item endorsement on the Pain Disability Index and Modified Somatic Perception Questionnaire is not related to the degree of actual physical pathology. Ultimately, having considered the science and common practices, the manner in which pain is assessed in a given case is left to the neuropsychologist's judgment.

PAIN IN THE *DIAGNOSTIC AND STATISTICAL MANUAL OF MENTAL DISORDERS*

Because of the subjective nature of pain and the close relationship between pain and psychological issues, chronic pain disorders are commonly listed among psychiatric disorders in diagnostic manuals, including the *Diagnostic and Statistical Manual of Mental Disorders* (*DSM*; Bruns, 2014). Despite its prevalence and significant impact on so many persons encountered in forensic neuropsychological evaluations, the term *chronic pain* was basically dropped from the *DSM* in its most recent (i.e., fifth) edition (*DSM–5*; American Psychiatric Association, 2013). The *DSM–5* mentions the term *chronic pain* only a few times, such as when it states, "Some individuals with chronic pain would be appropriately diagnosed as having a somatic symptom disorder, with predominant pain. For others, psychological factors affecting other medical conditions or an adjustment disorder would be more appropriate" (p. 813). The complex biopsychosocial nature of chronic pain must be understood for appropriate evaluations to be performed, accurate diagnoses to be made, and helpful recommendations to be offered. This complexity may or may not be adequately captured by the *DSM* or other diagnostic systems. Therefore, in forensic neuropsychological reports, qualitative descriptions may be needed instead of or in addition to the available diagnostic nomenclature.

CONCLUSION

Questions of neuropsychological impairment confronting courts and those making determinations about disability benefits can be complicated by the chronic pain that often co-occurs with neurocognitive disorders. The complex biopsychosocial nature of chronic pain contributes to questions about the effects of chronic pain on neuropsychological functioning. Forensic neuropsychologists strive to understand the relationship between pain and neuropsychological performance for each examinee, using appropriate methods and measures to clarify and quantify pain levels, psychological status, cognitive abilities, and symptom and performance validity. Test data are interpreted in the context of the examinee's presentation and additional related sources of information. Neuropsychological evaluations, with their scientific evidence base, have much to offer triers of fact and other decision makers in their efforts to understand persons who report both cognitive deficits and chronic pain. Yet, conclusions should be offered with cautionary statements when the complexity of a case limits the confidence that can be placed in determinations about diagnosis, prognosis, causality, and disability status.

References

Aguerrevere, L., Greve, K., & Bianchini, K. (2013). Multivariate cluster analysis of the MMPI–2–RF in pain patients with financial compensation: Characterization of subgroups based on demographics, medico-legal and predictive outcome variables. *Journal of Pain, 14*(4, Suppl.), S22. http://dx.doi.org/10.1016/j.jpain.2013.01.099

American Psychiatric Association. (2013). *Diagnostic and statistical manual of mental disorders* (5th ed.). Washington, DC: Author.

Antepohl, W., Kiviloog, L., Andersson, J., & Gerdle, B. (2003). Cognitive impairment in patients with chronic whiplash-associated disorder—A matched control study. *NeuroRehabilitation, 18,* 307–315.

Apkarian, A. V., Hashmi, J. A., & Baliki, M. N. (2011). Pain and the brain: Specificity and plasticity of the brain in clinical chronic pain. *Pain, 152*(Suppl.), S49–S64. http://dx.doi.org/10.1016/j.pain.2010.11.010

Ashendorf, L., Constantinou, M., & McCaffrey, R. J. (2004). The effect of depression and anxiety on the TOMM in community-dwelling older adults. *Archives of Clinical Neuropsychology, 19,* 125–130. http://dx.doi.org/10.1093/arclin/19.1.125

Baddeley, A. (2003). Working memory: Looking back and looking forward. *Nature Reviews Neuroscience, 4,* 829–839. http://dx.doi.org/10.1038/nrn1201

Baliki, M. N., Geha, P. Y., Apkarian, A. V., & Chialvo, D. R. (2008). Beyond feeling: Chronic pain hurts the brain, disrupting the default-mode network dynamics. *Journal of Neuroscience, 28,* 1398–1403. http://dx.doi.org/10.1523/JNEUROSCI.4123-07.2008

Banks, S. M., & Kerns, R. D. (1996). Explaining high rates of depression and chronic pain: A diathesis-stress framework. *Psychological Bulletin, 119,* 95–110. http://dx.doi.org/10.1037/0033-2909.119.1.95

Bell, B. D., Primeau, M., Sweet, J. J., & Lofland, K. R. (1999). Neuropsychological functioning in migraine headache, nonheadache chronic pain, and mild traumatic brain injury patients. *Archives of Clinical Neuropsychology, 14,* 389–399. http://dx.doi.org/10.1016/S0887-6177(98)00020-1

Berryman, C., Stanton, T. R., Bowering, J. K., Tabor, A., McFarlane, A., & Moseley, L. G. (2013). Evidence for working memory deficits in chronic pain: A systematic review and meta-analysis. *Pain, 154,* 1181–1196. http://dx.doi.org/10.1016/j.pain.2013.03.002

Bianchini, K. J., Aguerrevere, L. E., Guise, B. J., Ord, J. S., Etherton, J. L., Meyers, J. E., . . . Bui, J. (2014). Accuracy of the Modified Somatic Perception Questionnaire and Pain Disability Index in the detection of malingered pain-related disability in chronic pain. *Clinical Neuropsychologist, 28,* 1376–1394. http://dx.doi.org/10.1080/13854046.2014.986199

Bianchini, K. J., Greve, K. W., & Glynn, G. (2005). On the diagnosis of malingered pain-related disability: Lessons from cognitive malingering research. *Spine Journal, 5,* 404–417. http://dx.doi.org/10.1016/j.spinee.2004.11.016

Breivik, H., Collett, B., Ventafridda, V., Cohen, R., & Gallacher, D. (2006). Survey of chronic pain in Europe: Prevalence, impact on daily life, and treatment. *European Journal of Pain, 10,* 287–333. http://dx.doi.org/10.1016/j.ejpain.2005.06.009

Bruns, D. (2014). Clinical and forensic standards for the psychological assessment of patients with chronic pain. *Psychological Injury and Law, 7,* 297–316. http://dx.doi.org/10.1007/s12207-014-9211-1

Bush, S. S., Ruff, R. M., Tröster, A. I., Barth, J. T., Koffler, S. P., Pliskin, N. H., . . . Silver, C. H. (2005). Symptom validity assessment: Practice issues and medical necessity. *Archives of Clinical Neuropsychology, 20,* 419–426. http://dx.doi.org/10.1016/j.acn.2005.02.002

Chou, R., Fanciullo, G. J., Fine, P. G., Adler, J. A., Ballantyne, J. C., Davies, P., . . . Miaskowski, C. (2009). Clinical guidelines for the use of opioids therapy in chronic non-cancer pain. *Journal of Pain, 10,* 113–130. http://dx.doi.org/10.1016/j.jpain.2008.10.008

Currie, S. R., & Wang, J. (2004). Chronic back pain and major depression in the general Canadian population. *Pain, 107,* 54–60. http://dx.doi.org/10.1016/j.pain.2003.09.015

Demyttenaere, K., Bruffaerts, R., Lee, S., Posada-Villa, J., Kovess, V., Angermeyer, M. C., . . . Von Korff, M. (2007). Mental disorders among persons with chronic back or neck pain: Results from the World Mental Health Surveys. *Pain, 129,* 332–342. http://dx.doi.org/10.1016/j.pain.2007.01.022

Dick, B., Eccleston, C., & Crombez, G. (2002). Attentional functioning in fibromyalgia, rheumatoid arthritis, and musculoskeletal pain patients. *Arthritis and Rheumatism, 47,* 639–644. http://dx.doi.org/10.1002/art.10800

Disorbio, J. M., & Bruns, D. (2002). *Brief Battery for Health Improvement 2.* San Antonio, TX: Pearson.

Eccleston, C., & Crombez, G. (1999). Pain demands attention: A cognitive-affective model of the interruptive function of pain. *Psychological Bulletin, 125,* 356–366. http://dx.doi.org/10.1037/0033-2909.125.3.356

Eriksen, J., Jensen, M. K., Sjøgren, P., Ekholm, O., & Rasmussen, N. K. (2003). Epidemiology of chronic non-malignant pain in Denmark. *Pain, 106,* 221–228. http://dx.doi.org/10.1016/S0304-3959(03)00225-2

Ersek, M., Cherrier, M. M., Overman, S. S., & Irving, G. A. (2004). The cognitive effects of opioids. *Pain Management Nursing, 5,* 75–93. http://dx.doi.org/10.1016/j.pmn.2003.11.002

Etherton, J. L., Bianchini, K. J., Ciota, M. A., & Greve, K. W. (2005). Reliable Digit Span is unaffected by laboratory-induced pain: Implications for clinical use. *Assessment, 12,* 101–106. http://dx.doi.org/10.1177/1073191104270789

Etherton, J. L., Bianchini, K. J., Greve, K. W., & Ciota, M. A. (2005). Test of Memory Malingering Performance is unaffected by laboratory-induced pain: Implications for clinical use. *Archives of Clinical Neuropsychology, 20,* 375–384. http://dx.doi.org/10.1016/j.acn.2004.09.007

Gervais, R. O., Rohling, M. L., Green, P., & Ford, W. (2004). A comparison of WMT, CARB, and TOMM failure rates in non-head injury disability claimants. *Archives of Clinical Neuropsychology, 19,* 475–487. http://dx.doi.org/10.1016/j.acn.2003.05.001

Gimse, R., Bjorgen, I. A., Tjell, C., Tyssedal, J. S., & Bo, K. (1997). Reduced cognitive functions in a group of whiplash patients with demonstrated disturbance in the posture control system. *Journal of Clinical and Experimental Neuropsychology, 19,* 838–849. http://dx.doi.org/10.1080/01688639708403764

Grace, G. M., Berg, M. A., & Nielson, W. (1995). Assessment of attention, concentration, and memory in patients with fibromyalgia. *Journal of the International Neuropsychological Society, 1,* 137–148.

Greve, K. W., Bianchini, K. J., Etherton, J. L., Meyers, J. E., Curtis, K. L., & Ord, J. S. (2010). The Reliable Digit Span test in chronic pain: Classification accuracy in detecting malingered pain-related disability. *Clinical Neuropsychologist, 24,* 137–152. http://dx.doi.org/10.1080/13854040902927546

Gruber, S. A., Silveri, M. M., & Yurgelun-Todd, D. A. (2007). Neuropsychological consequences of opiate use. *Neuropsychology Review, 17,* 299–315. http://dx.doi.org/10.1007/s11065-007-9041-y

Guéz, M., Brännström, R., Nyberg, L., Toolanen, G., & Hildingsson, C. (2005). Neuropsychological functioning and MMPI–2 profiles in chronic neck pain: A comparison of whiplash and non-traumatic groups. *Journal of Clinical and Experimental Neuropsychology, 27,* 151–163. http://dx.doi.org/10.1080/13803390490515487

Gureje, O., Von Korff, M., Simon, G. E., & Gater, R. (1998). Persistent pain and well-being: A World Health Organization Study in Primary Care. *JAMA, 280,* 147–151. http://dx.doi.org/10.1001/jama.280.2.147

Hart, R. P., Martelli, M. F., & Zasler, N. D. (2000). Chronic pain and neuropsychological functioning. *Neuropsychology Review, 10,* 131–149. http://dx.doi.org/10.1023/A:1009020914358

Heilbronner, R. L., Sweet, J. J., Morgan, J. E., Larrabee, G. J., & Millis, S. R. (2009). American Academy of Clinical Neuropsychology Consensus Conference Statement on the neuropsychological assessment of effort, response bias, and malingering. *Clinical Neuropsychologist, 23,* 1093–1129. http://dx.doi.org/10.1080/13854040903155063

Iezzi, T., Duckworth, M. P., Vuong, L. N., Archibald, Y. M., & Klinck, A. (2004). Predictors of neurocognitive performance in chronic pain patients. *International Journal of Behavioral Medicine, 11,* 56–61. http://dx.doi.org/10.1207/s15327558ijbm1101_7

Iverson, G. L., King, R. J., Scott, J. G., & Adams, R. L. (2001). Cognitive complaints in litigating patients with head injuries or chronic pain. *Journal of Forensic Neuropsychology, 2,* 19–30. http://dx.doi.org/10.1300/J151v02n01_02

Iverson, G. L., Le Page, J., Koehler, B. E., Shojania, K., & Badii, M. (2007). Test of Memory Malingering (TOMM) scores are not affected by chronic pain or depression in patients with fibromyalgia. *Clinical Neuropsychologist, 21,* 532–546. http://dx.doi.org/10.1080/13854040600611392

Iverson, G. L., & McCracken, L. M. (1997). "Postconcussive" symptoms in persons with chronic pain. *Brain Injury, 11,* 783–790. http://dx.doi.org/10.1080/026990597122990

Kaplan, R., Meadows, M., Vincent, L., Logigian, E., & Steere, A. (1992). Memory impairment and depression in patients with Lyme encephalopathy: Comparison with fibromyalgia and nonpsychotically depressed patients. *Neurology, 42,* 1263–1267. http://dx.doi.org/10.1212/WNL.42.7.1263

Landro, N. I., Stiles, T. C., & Sletvold, H. (1997). Memory functioning in patients with primary fibromyalgia and major depression and healthy controls. *Journal of Psychosomatic Research, 42,* 297–306. http://dx.doi.org/10.1016/S0022-3999(96)00301-7

Larrabee, G. J. (2003). Exaggerated pain report in litigants with malingered neurocognitive dysfunction. *Clinical Neuropsychologist, 17,* 395–401. http://dx.doi.org/10.1076/clin.17.3.395.18087

Larrabee, G. J. (2008). Aggregation across multiple indicators improves the detection of malingering: Relationship to likelihood ratios. *Clinical Neuropsychologist, 22,* 666–679. http://dx.doi.org/10.1080/13854040701494987

Larrabee, G. J. (2012). Assessment of malingering. In G. L. Larrabee (Ed.), *Forensic neuropsychology: A scientific approach* (2nd ed., pp. 116–159). New York, NY: Oxford University Press.

Legrain, V., Iannetti, G. D., Plaghki, L., & Mouraux, A. (2011). The pain matrix reloaded: A salience detection system for the body. *Progress in Neurobiology, 93,* 111–124. http://dx.doi.org/10.1016/j.pneurobio.2010.10.005

Main, C. J. (1983). The Modified Somatic Perception Questionnaire (MSPQ). *Journal of Psychosomatic Research, 27,* 503–514. http://dx.doi.org/10.1016/0022-3999(83)90040-5

Maljkovic, V., & Nakayama, K. (1994). Priming of pop-out: I. Role of features. *Memory and Cognition, 22,* 657–672. http://dx.doi.org/10.3758/BF03209251

McCaffrey, M., & Pasero, C. (1999). *Pain: Clinical manual* (2nd ed.). St. Louis, MO: Mosby.

McCracken, L. M., & Thompson, M. (2012). Neuropsychological aspects of chronic pain. In S. S. Bush & G. L. Iverson (Eds.), *Neuropsychological assessment of work-related injuries* (pp. 243–262). New York, NY: Guilford Press.

McWilliams, L. A., Cox, B. J., & Enns, M. W. (2003). Mood and anxiety disorders associated with chronic pain: An examination in a nationally representative sample. *Pain, 106,* 127–133. http://dx.doi.org/10.1016/S0304-3959(03)00301-4

Melzack, R. (1975). The McGill Pain Questionnaire: Major properties and scoring methods. *Pain, 1,* 277–299. http://dx.doi.org/10.1016/0304-3959(75)90044-5

Meyers, J., Reinsch-Boothby, L., Miller, R., Rohling, M., & Axelrod, B. (2011). Does the source of a forensic referral affect neuropsychological test performance on a standardized battery of tests? *Clinical Neuropsychologist, 25,* 477–487. http://dx.doi.org/10.1080/13854046.2011.554442

Meyers, J. E. (2009). *Meyers Neuropsychological Battery online help file.* Retrieved from http://www.meyersneuropsychological.com

Meyers, J. E., Grills, C. E., Zellinger, M. M., & Miller, R. M. (2014). Emotional distress affects attention and concentration: The difference between mountains and valleys. *Applied Neuropsychology: Adult, 21,* 28–35. http://dx.doi.org/10.1080/09084282.2012.721148

Meyers, J. E., Miller, R. M., Thompson, L. M., Scalese, A. M., Allred, B. C., Rupp, Z. W., . . . Junghyun Lee, A. (2014). Using likelihood ratios to detect invalid performance with performance validity measures. *Archives of Clinical Neuropsychology, 29,* 224–235. http://dx.doi.org/10.1093/arclin/acu001

Meyers, J. E., Miller, R. M., & Tuita, A. R. R. (2014). Using pattern analysis matching to differentiate TBI and PTSD in a military sample. *Applied Neuropsychology: Adult, 21,* 60–68. http://dx.doi.org/10.1080/09084282.2012.737881

Meyers, J. E., & Rohling, M. L. (2009). CT and MRI correlations with neuropsychological tests. *Applied Neuropsychology, 16,* 237–253. http://dx.doi.org/10.1080/09084280903098752

Meyers, J. E., Volbrecht, M., Axelrod, B. N., & Reinsch-Boothby, L. (2011). Embedded symptom validity tests and overall neuropsychological test performance. *Archives of Clinical Neuropsychology, 26,* 8–15. http://dx.doi.org/10.1093/arclin/acq083

Meyers, J. E., & Volbrecht, M. E. (2003). A validation of multiple malingering detection methods in a large clinical sample. *Archives of Clinical Neuropsychology, 18,* 261–276. http://dx.doi.org/10.1093/arclin/18.3.261

Millon, T., Antoni, M., Millon, C., Meagher, S., & Grossman, S. (2001). *Millon Behavioral Medicine diagnostic manual.* Minneapolis, MN: Pearson Assessments.

Moore, D. J., Keogh, E., & Eccleston, C. (2012). The interruptive effect of pain on attention. *Quarterly Journal of Experimental Psychology, 65,* 565–586. http://dx.doi.org/10.1080/17470218.2011.626865

Moriarty, O., McGuire, B. E., & Finn, D. P. (2011). The effect of pain on cognitive function: A review of clinical and preclinical research. *Progress in Neurobiology, 93,* 385–404. http://dx.doi.org/10.1016/j.pneurobio.2011.01.002

Nampiaparampil, D. E. (2008). Prevalence of chronic pain after traumatic brain injury: A systematic review. *JAMA, 300,* 711–719. http://dx.doi.org/10.1001/jama.300.6.711

Park, D. C., Glass, J. M., Minear, M., & Crofford, L. J. (2001). Cognitive function in fibromyalgia patients. *Arthritis and Rheumatism, 44,* 2125–2133. http://dx.doi.org/10.1002/1529-0131(200109)44:9<2125::AID-ART365>3.0.CO;2-1

Pribram, K. H., Miller, G. A., & Galanter, E. (1960). *Plans and the structure of behavior.* New York, NY: Holt, Rinehart & Winston.

Raja, S. N., Haythornthwaite, J. A., Pappagallo, M., Clark, M. R., Travison, T. G., Sabeen, S., . . . Max, M. B. (2002). Opioids versus antidepressants in postherpetic neuralgia: A randomized, placebo-controlled trial. *Neurology, 59,* 1015–1021. http://dx.doi.org/10.1212/WNL.59.7.1015

Rees, L. M., Tombaugh, T. N., & Boulay, L. (2001). Depression and the Test of Memory Malingering. *Archives of Clinical Neuropsychology, 16,* 501–506. http://dx.doi.org/10.1093/arclin/16.5.501

Rohling, M. L., Binder, L. M., & Langhinrichsen-Rohling, J. (1995). Money matters: A meta-analytic review of the association between financial compensation and the experience and treatment of chronic pain. *Health Psychology, 14,* 537–547. http://dx.doi.org/10.1037/0278-6133.14.6.537

Rohling, M. L., Meyers, J. E., & Millis, S. R. (2003). Neuropsychological impairment following traumatic brain injury: A dose-response analysis. *Clinical Neuropsychologist, 17,* 289–302. http://dx.doi.org/10.1076/clin.17.3.289.18086

Rowbotham, M. C., Twilling, L., Davies, P. S., Reisner, L., Taylor, K., & Mohr, D. (2003). Oral opioid therapy for chronic peripheral and central neuropathic pain. *New England Journal of Medicine, 348,* 1223–1232. http://dx.doi.org/10.1056/NEJMoa021420

Sjøgren, P., Thomsen, A. B., & Olsen, A. K. (2000). Impaired neuropsychological performance in chronic nonmalignant pain patients receiving long-term oral opioid therapy. *Journal of Pain and Symptom Management, 19,* 100–108. http://dx.doi.org/10.1016/S0885-3924(99)00143-8

Slick, D. J., Sherman, E. M. S., & Iverson, G. L. (1999). Diagnostic criteria for malingered neurocognitive dysfunction: Proposed standards for clinical practice and research. *Clinical Neuropsychologist, 13,* 545–561. http://dx.doi.org/10.1076/1385-4046(199911)13:04;1-Y;FT545

Tait, R. C., Chibnall, J. T., & Krause, S. (1990). The Pain Disability Index: Psychometric properties. *Pain, 40,* 171–182. http://dx.doi.org/10.1016/0304-3959(90)90068-O

Von Korff, M., Crane, P., Lane, M., Miglioretti, D. L., Simon, G., Saunders, K., . . . Kessler, R. (2005). Chronic spinal pain and physical-mental comorbidity in the United States: Results from the National Comorbidity Survey Replication. *Pain, 113,* 331–339. http://dx.doi.org/10.1016/j.pain.2004.11.010

Wong–Baker FACES Foundation. (2015). *Wong–Baker FACES Pain Rating Scale.* Retrieved from http://www.wongbakerfaces.org

Part IV

SPECIAL TOPICS AND POPULATIONS

CHAPTER 12

VETERAN'S DISABILITY EXAMINATION: CONSIDERATIONS FOR NEUROPSYCHOLOGISTS

Joshua E. Caron

The U.S. Department of Veterans Affairs (VA) provides disability benefits to veterans. To obtain these benefits, veterans must often go through a disability examination. Neuropsychologists perform such exams when their expertise is relevant to the claimed disability, and the information from these exams is used by adjudicators to help determine the need for, and appropriate amount of, benefits. Although the VA disability exam has the same ethical and practice considerations as other types of disability exams, it also has other considerations that are unique to the VA.

Neuropsychologists who are new to the VA have a bit of a learning curve when it comes to understanding the other considerations that are unique to it. Whether one is an experienced forensic psychologist or not, there is much to learn about VA's examination process, including navigation of the various electronic record systems and correctly filling out the VA's report templates. There is also much to learn about working with veterans and the federal regulations that guide the VA disability process. Regarding the latter, the most important regulations are Parts 3 and 4 of Title 38 of U.S. Code of Federal Regulations (C.F.R.), which can be reviewed at http://www.ecfr.gov/cgi-bin/searchECFR. The point is, being competent in forensics or neuropsychology is necessary but not enough to be a good provider of VA disability examinations. Once one is familiar with the VA process, however, it becomes much easier to provide useful examinations.

One way to better understand the process that the VA uses is to become familiar with the history and evolution of VA disability benefits and adjudication. In-depth review of this history is beyond the scope of this chapter, but there are several excellent resources on this topic (e.g., Economic Systems Inc., 2004; Ridgway, 2011, 2013; Russo, 2013, 2014; Worthen & Moering, 2011). Briefly put, political and public pressures have shaped the bureaucratic nature of the adjudication process over the years, and there have been key transition periods in which the disability model fundamentally changed. Perhaps the most important of these transition periods was in 1917 when the disability benefits model changed from a gratuity model to the current indemnity model as part of amendments that were made to the War Risk Insurance Act of 1914 (Economic Systems Inc., 2004). As explained by Worthen and Moering (2011), the indemnity model means the VA only compensates for losses related to the disability and does not provide a gratuity payment for a service injury. This means disability benefits adjudicators must understand two things: whether the claimed condition exists and the level of impairment associated with it. The need for this information is what makes the disability examination so important.

This chapter and the opinions stated herein do not reflect the opinions or beliefs of the U.S. Department of Veterans Affairs or the U.S. government. The opinions expressed in this chapter are mine alone. I thank James Atkinson, Christine Ramsay, Brad Roper, and Keith Stabler for their constructive feedback. For Dr. Timothy Fjordbak (1951–2015).

http://dx.doi.org/10.1037/0000032-012
APA Handbook of Forensic Neuropsychology, S. S. Bush (Editor-in-Chief)

BASIC INFORMATION ABOUT VA AND VA DISABILITY

The VA is made up of three branches, and each one provides an important service to veterans. The Veterans Benefits Administration (VBA) is the branch responsible for benefits, including disability benefits, and it is tasked with the adjudication process. The other two branches are the Veterans Health Administration (VHA) and the National Cemetery Administration. The VHA typically provides the examiners for the disability examination, although sometimes contract agencies or fee-based providers are used because of the large demand for examinations. As such, neuropsychologists performing these exams are usually employed by the VHA, but their role is to inform adjudicators within the VBA. Although not a perfect analogy, the VBA may be thought of as the judge in this process and VHA disability examiners the expert witness.

Disability examinations in VA are called *compensation and pension exams,* commonly referred to as "C&P." Many people think of C&P as a singular concept or entitlement, but it actually represents two different benefits. On one hand, compensation is the reimbursement for lost earning capacity due to a service-connected disability. Pension, on the other hand, is a needs-based benefit for veterans who are disabled from a non–service-connected disability. The latter is available to veterans who served during a wartime period, as long as the non–service-connected condition was not the result of their own willful misconduct. Extensive information on C&P benefits and eligibility is located at http://www.benefits.va.gov/benefits/.

When there is a disability, the VA will reimburse the veteran for the average impairment of earning capacity, reflecting the indemnity model. The average loss of earnings is determined by the degree of disability on a scale ranging from 0% to 100% (Title 38 C.F.R. Part 4, Schedule for Rating Disabilities). It is not uncommon to hear veterans refer to themselves as a percentage, for example, "I'm 50%." What they are describing is their disability rating from VBA.

It is important for new examiners to understand that the VA disability claims process is nonadversarial and *ex parte* (Latin meaning "for one party"). It is overtly designed to favor veterans' claims. The VA will even assist veterans with developing their disability claims as part of the Veterans Claims Assistance Act of 2000 ("Department of Veterans Affairs Assistance," 2008). As Riley (2010) has summarized, the

> VA disability benefits system is distinctive from other legal systems and government agencies in its nonadversarial and pro-claimant nature, its lack of a statute of limitations for bringing compensation claims, and its application of a more favorable burden of proof. (p. 16)

Regarding that burden of proof, the main evidentiary standard in VA disability is *equipoise* (*Gilbert v. Derwinski*, 1990), which means benefit of the doubt is given to the veteran in cases in which evidence for and against is balanced evenly or is considered "at least as likely as not" supportive of the condition ("Reasonable Doubt," 2001; Ridgeway, 2012, p. 84). An often-cited analogy from *Gilbert v. Derwinski* is "the tie goes to the runner" (Riley, 2010, p. 15). Sometimes, the burden of evidence can be even further relaxed to ensure no unnecessary barriers are in the way of obtaining benefits. For example, when posttraumatic stress disorder (PTSD) is related to a combat stressor, there does not need to be documentation of the specific stressor cited by the veteran as long as PTSD can be diagnosed symptomatically and there is some indication the stressor event could have happened the way it was claimed (e.g., the veteran was awarded a Combat Action Badge). Although learning how to adhere to presumptions and relaxed standards for VA disability examinations may seem complicated at first, the adjustment is not too difficult because just as in any other forensic setting, there still needs to be supporting evidence for the claim, and diagnoses are still based on established professional diagnostic standards.

Operating in an *ex parte* environment with considerable public and political pressures to ensure veterans receive what they are owed can be a challenge when trying to balance objectivity and professional standards against those pressures. VA disability examiners learn quickly that it is incumbent on them to ensure standards of assessment are met during examinations. The VA offers very little guidance on or oversight of neuropsychology-specific practice standards for C&P exams. Moreover, C&P department managers are often administrators from VA's Business Service Line who have no clinical background or awareness of the possible ethical dilemmas facing examiners seeking to balance VA's demands with ethical practice. In most cases, it is up to individual examiners to ensure all standards are met.

THE CLAIMS PROCESS AND ROLES

Claimants filing for C&P benefits begin the process by contacting the VBA; however, most veterans will first seek the assistance of a Veterans Service Organization (VSO). VSOs are not part of the VA—they are veteran advocate groups whose job is to help veterans receive as much VA (disability) benefits as possible. If the VSO is a VA-recognized organization, it can legally represent the claimant as the veteran's power of attorney and file all paperwork on behalf of that veteran. The VBA's website (http://www.va.gov/vso) contains more information on VSOs, as well as a list of VA-recognized VSOs.

Perhaps because their names are so similar, and perhaps because they have slightly overlapping goals, VSOs and Veterans Service Representatives (VSRs) are sometimes confused. VSRs are VBA employees dedicated to helping claimants develop disability claims. Their job is essentially to help the VA conform to the aforementioned Veterans Claims Assistance Act of 2000. They assist with locating relevant military records and other sources of evidence needed for disability claims. They are also adjudicators in certain cases and may provide decisions on monetary award actions, dependency changes, determining character of service, and other solely administrative issues (K. Stabler, personal communication, February 27, 2015). Most rating adjudication, however, is reserved for rating veterans service representatives (RVSRs).

Once the claims paperwork has been submitted to the VBA, VSRs start the claims process by organizing evidence into a claims file (C-file). The C-file is then reviewed by disability examiners as part of the exam process and by adjudicators during the claims review process. The adjudicators making rating decisions are typically RVSRs, but they could also be decision review officers if, for example, there is an appeal. If the review of a C-file by an RVSR suggests the claim has merit but lacks sufficient information to accurately rate the claim, then she or he will request an examination to obtain the needed information. The RVSR is not a health care expert, so there will often be a need for a qualified expert to explain the condition in ways that will help the RVSR make the rating decision. This is where disability examiners come into the process. Once the RVST has sufficient information from records and the examination, she or he RVSR will make a rating.

Notification and Appeal

Once a rating decision has been made, the VBA will notify the claimant. If the veteran is dissatisfied with the rating, he or she can write a Notice of Disagreement within 1 year of the decision, and a decision review officer will perform a second review of the case. The local regional office will then send legal information about the original rating decision and forms for submitting an appeal of that decision. The VA's appeals process is complex, and it has multiple (sometimes nonlinear) stages. When a rating decision is appealed, however, the next stage is often a hearing with the Board of Veterans Appeals, which will conduct a *de novo* review of the case and decide whether to allow or deny the appeal. Sometimes, however, the Board of Veterans Appeals will determine that there is not enough information and send the case back to VBA to gather more information in a process called *remand*. Examiners will often have to perform an evaluation for remand cases, creating a situation in which repeat testing is involved. In this situation, neuropsychological examiners need to be careful because repeat testing can introduce practice effects and other sources of variance into the test results. This risk can be mitigated, however, if the examiner takes certain information into account and modifies interpretations accordingly (Calamia, Markon, & Tranel, 2012, 2013; Heilbronner et al., 2010).

The Client

The client for the disability exam is the RVSR. The report, however, is not only located in the C-file, it is often visible in the veteran's electronic medical records as well, so the audience reading the report will frequently be quite a diverse group, including the veteran, the veteran's treatment providers, attorneys and judges during appeals, and perhaps even other C&P examiners. It is important to keep this in mind when writing the examination report, while not forgetting that the primary purpose of the exam is to provide the RVSR with the requisite information needed to make a rating decision.

Although the RVSR is always the primary client for any C&P evaluation, situations can occur in which there is more than one client. This happens when other C&P examiners who are not neuropsychologists request neuropsychological examinations to help inform their own examination of the veteran. When the exam request is generated by another examiner, the neuropsychologist should strive to accommodate the needs of both the RVSR and the other examiner. C&P examiners evaluating traumatic brain injury (TBI) are those who most frequently request neuropsychological examination (they are not neuropsychologists), but other C&P psychologists can as well if they believe such testing would be necessary and is beyond their scope of practice.

Neuropsychologists Provide Mental Disorder Exams, Not Traumatic Brain Injury Exams

The VA does not use neuropsychologists as the primary examiner in C&P TBI evaluations because the VA requires the initial diagnosis of TBI (for C&P purposes) to be made by a psychiatrist, neurologist, physiatrist, or neurosurgeon (the "core four"). In cases in which a TBI diagnosis has already been made by one of the core four, then the evaluation of TBI can be conducted by any kind of general medical examiner as long as she or he is certified by the VA to conduct TBI C&P exams. The main point here is that TBI exams are conducted by professionals trained in medicine, not psychology, presumably because the TBI examination includes a physical examination, and it assesses conditions such as headache, vertigo, hearing, and more. Although the VA mandates that medical examiners perform the official TBI examination, it also recognizes the importance of neuropsychological testing in that examination. In fact, the VA's TBI exam report template (explained later) explicitly instructs examiners to request neuropsychological testing (when not already available) so that they can better describe neurocognitive and neurobehavioral effects.

When the TBI examiner requests neuropsychological testing to inform her or his examination, the C&P office will put in a request to a neuropsychologist for a mental disorders exam or a PTSD exam (if PTSD is also being claimed). There is no "neuropsychology exam," although such may be specifically requested as part of a mental disorders exam. When asked for such, the RVSR will often also ask for an opinion on what symptoms might be related to TBI versus some other mental disorder (e.g., depression, PTSD, or insomnia). When PTSD is also being claimed along with TBI, a PTSD examination will usually be requested. When PTSD is not part of the claim, or it has already been assessed by another examiner, then the request will be for a mental disorders exam.

When asked to perform a mental disorders evaluation to assist with the adjudication of benefits for TBI, neuropsychologists need to be clear about their role. RSVRs will never ask neuropsychologists to decide whether there was a TBI or not, so neuropsychologists should refrain from overstepping their bounds on this issue. The VBA considers it the role of the TBI examiner to determine whether there has been a TBI. The neuropsychologist's job is to evaluate the neurocognitive or neurobehavioral outcome of the diagnosed TBI. Put another way, neuropsychologists are asked to identify whether there is a neurocognitive disorder associated with TBI diagnosis (made by the TBI examiner) and, if so, to describe the symptoms and impairment associated with it. If during the course of a mental disorders examination a neuropsychologist determines that the possibility of TBI is questionable at best, based on the history and the absence of impairment, then it is perfectly reasonable for that neuropsychologist to explain why it is not possible to diagnose a neurocognitive disorder on the basis of those conditions.

The neuropsychologist should not, however, make statements about the absence of TBI. This is a subtle distinction, but an important one.

C&P EXAMINER COMPETENCIES

Although the VA's disability process is unique, it is still a forensic exam because it is used for adjudicating benefits, not for treatment. Therefore, neuropsychologists performing C&P exams should possess the prerequisite professional and ethical competencies relevant to forensic psychology and clinical neuropsychology.

Basic Competencies

At a bare minimum, examiners should have a working familiarity with the American Psychological Association's (APA's; 2002a) Ethics Code, the *Specialty Guidelines for Forensic Psychology* (APA, 2013), the American Academy of Psychiatry and the Law's *Practice Guideline for the Forensic Evaluation of Psychiatric Disability* (Gold et al., 2008), and the American Academy of Clinical Neuropsychology's (2007) *Practice Guidelines for Neuropsychological Assessment and Consultation.* A very useful online resource listing prominent literature relevant to many of these general ethical competencies is located on the American Academy of Clinical Neuropsychology's web page, and is appropriately titled *Neuropsychology-Related Ethics References* (Bush, 2014). Bush and his colleagues have published work on ethics in forensics and neuropsychology that are also valuable for reference (e.g., Bush, 2005; Bush, Connell, & Denney, 2006; Bush & Drexler, 2002).

Special Competencies

Beyond the basic forensic and neuropsychological competencies, all C&P examiners should possess knowledge in at least three specialized areas. The first involves familiarity with federal regulations, the second involves knowledge of VA processes, and the third is competence in military culture. The first two are discussed throughout this chapter; the third is discussed here in more detail.

Although cultural competency as a whole should be considered a core competency in every aspect of psychology, insightful knowledge of military culture is absolutely necessary for C&P work. Obtaining this competency is also necessary from an ethical standpoint. APA's (2002b) *Guidelines on Multicultural Education, Training, Research, Practice, and Organizational Change for Psychologists* emphasize practicing from a culturally informed vantage point, which is stressed throughout APA's (2002a) Ethics Code (see Standards 9.06, Interpreting Assessment Results; Standards 2.01b and 2.01c, Boundaries of Competence; and Standard 3.01, Unfair Discrimination).

Military culture is fairly complex and diverse, and this point should not be lost in the following review of some basic concepts. It is important to recognize that there are many subcultures based on branches, specialties within those branches, and rank. It is also important to recognize that there are unique challenges facing certain groups within the military (and later in VA), such as female veterans (L. K. Hall, 2008, p. 69; Slone & Friedman, 2008, p. 215) and lesbian, gay, bisexual, and transgender veterans (De Angelis, Sandhoff, Bonner, & Segal, 2013; Elders, Brown, Coleman, Kolditz, & Steinman, 2015; Moradi, 2009). Perhaps less intuitively, other groups such as reservists being called to active duty also face unique challenges related to the delicate balance of their civilian and military lives (Slone & Friedman, 2008, p. 214; Tucker, 2008). Thus, military culture is as complex and intricate as any other, with much to consider and learn. It is not possible to adequately review all areas of military culture or subcultures, so readers are strongly encouraged to review the resources provided in Appendix 12.1. The literature presented there is hardly exhaustive, but it should make up for the brevity of this chapter and provide a solid foundation of knowledge for anyone interested in learning more.

Moore (2011) and Reger, Etherage, Reger, and Gahm (2008) have previously discussed how competence in military culture involves understanding its norms, values, language, class structure, and customs. For example, one common value in military culture pertains to collectivism. In the military, concern for one's individual achievement over the group is viewed as a negative trait and considered a sign of poor character. The collectivistic approach is valued because it increases the chance of a successful mission (and survival). Collaboration tends to reduce dysfunction within a unit and create cohesion. The stresses of war combined with the collectivistic nature of the culture often galvanizes bonds among service members, and the examiner who is unaware of just how strong these bonds can be may fail to fully appreciate how emerging from combat physically unscathed (when others did not) could contribute to a mental disorder.

It is also helpful for examiners to understand the social class system (Moore, 2011), based on rank, that is well accepted by the military community. The social class hierarchy in the military is accepted because it makes roles and responsibilities transparent. It minimizes inefficiencies and reduces diffusion of responsibility. As an examiner, recognizing the highest rank (social class) of a veteran can be very informative in estimating premorbid functioning, and it can help explain certain observed communication styles and mannerisms that may differ depending on whether the veteran was a high-ranking officer or enlisted personnel (Moore, 2013).

Understanding the language often used by military personnel and veterans is very important because the expansive lexicon of acronyms and colorful euphemisms used by veterans will make it difficult for inexperienced examiners to keep up with the history being provided during interviews. For example, when a veteran is asked to describe events leading to a possible TBI, the response could include a barrage of terms such as *155s, contact, the TC, Hajis, MRAP, doc, bird, FOB, TMC,* and *MACE,* and that is just for starters. The examiner who does not understand this language will miss critical pieces of history, so it is important to clarify unfamiliar terms to avoid missing out on important information. However, excessively seeking clarification may also create barriers: It will introduce intolerable inefficiency, and it will often create doubt in the veteran's mind about the examiner's ability to be objective and fair because it will be quite apparent that the examiner has no conception of the world being described. As such, it is highly advisable to become proficient with common military terms (see Appendix 12.1).

On a related note, when coming to a C&P examination many veterans assume they will be entering an adversarial environment, and they imagine that they will be negatively judged by a civilian with little ability to understand their experience. As such, many veterans will be (understandably) a little on edge. A culturally competent examiner, however, can do a lot to alleviate the veteran's concerns and reduce barriers to building rapport. Such steps can greatly improve the exam's reliability and validity, and they are yet another reason why becoming competent in military culture is so important.

THE C&P EXAM: CONSIDERATIONS AND PROCEDURES

The official C&P reference guide is the *Procedure Guide 1601E.01: C&P Disability Evaluations* (U.S. Department of Veterans Affairs, 2014), and examiners should familiarize themselves with this resource. There is also an unofficial (non-VA) guide that every mental health examiner should read: Mark Worthen and Robert Moering's 2011 article "A Practical Guide to Conducting VA Compensation and Pension Exams for PTSD and Other Mental Disorders." The article does an excellent job of explaining C&P concepts and federal regulations, and it expertly details the core features of a C&P exam by mental health professionals. Such features include the records review, history gathering, test considerations, and writing sufficient reports. Of course, these core steps are also reviewed here, but from more of a neuropsychological perspective.

The Process Begins With the Records Review

Moering (2011) has provided expert guidance on how to review C-files effectively and competently. As Moering pointed out, the first record to review should be VA Form 21-2507 (commonly referred to as the "2507"), the Request for Examination form sent by VBA to VHA. Understanding the 2507 is vital to understanding the purpose of the exam and the information needed by the RVSR to adjudicate the claim. In addition to the referral question, the 2507 contains other useful information such as the examination priority (whether it is an initial exam or review exam), the kind of examination needed (i.e., PTSD or mental disorders), and whether a medical opinion is needed for the condition. If the 2507 is ever unclear, and sometimes it will be, examiners should contact the RVSR who sent the exam request. The RVSR's contact information will always be provided on the 2507.

2507 request for medical opinion. Neuropsychologists often receive 2507s requesting a medical opinion, and it is not a mistake. VA uses the term *medical opinion* quite liberally, and it simply means the RVSR needs an expert opinion on some aspect of the claimed condition. The medical opinion that is provided must use legally recognized language (e.g., *at least as likely as not, more likely than not, is due to*) or it will not be sufficient for VBA's purposes and might be returned. This language is intended to reflect the examiner's opinion about the probability of the condition or contention in question (Ridgeway, 2012, pp. 82–84; U.S. Department of Veterans Affairs, 2014; Worthen & Moering, 2011, p. 188).

Reviewing the rest of the C-file. After reviewing the 2507 and understanding the reason for the referral, the next step is to review the contents of the C-file. C-files are now mostly electronic, although paper charts still exist. All remaining paper C-files, however, are currently in the process of being converted to PDFs, and eventually all C-files will be electronic. This conversion process started in 2012, but it will take years of scanning before the paper C-files become obsolete. Electronic C-files are located in the Veterans Benefits Management System, a secure web-based system that requires some VA security clearance. More information about the Veterans Benefits Management System is located on VA's intranet site (http://vbaw.vba.va.gov/vbms).

Whether the C-file is electronic or paper, it will contain several different kinds of records. The Service Treatment Records, sometimes called Service Medical Records, are the medical records from the veteran's time in military service and are often the key to linking the claimed condition to military service (Moering, 2011). Other important documents to review include the DD-214 (discharge form), military performance evaluations, private-sector medical records, and VA medical records. Sometimes there may be prior C&P examinations or medical board evaluations (when there has been a medical discharge) that are relevant to the condition of interest. Often the RVSR will be kind enough to bookmark some relevant documents for the examiner, which makes locating them much easier. This will not always be the case, however, and even when it is it does not mean the examiner can skip the rest of the C-file or assume there is nothing else important to review.

Finally, the only records that should be reviewed are the ones contained within the C-file or VA's Computerized Medical Records System. Examiners do not peruse social media outlets for additional information on veterans, and information from such (as tempting as it might be) should never be used as part of the records review or examination process. The VA does not condone searching for claimants online as a way of gathering more information about their social functioning. Information discovered on the Internet or through social media is always considered unverified and insufficient. For more information about reviewable evidence, VA employees are referred to the VA's intranet site (http://vaww.demo.va.gov); this site, and some of the other intranet sites that may be referenced here, may not be accessible to those outside of the VA system.

In-Person Exam

After reviewing the C-file, the next step is to evaluate the veteran. To meet neuropsychology's professional and ethical standards, the evaluation should include a discussion that informs the veteran about the examination process before proceeding with history gathering, behavioral observations, and administration of appropriate tests. The VA has no standardized in-person exam procedure. This has its advantages and disadvantages, but the take-away message is that it is solely up the examiner to ensure the examination meets professional standards. The following outline of in-person exam procedures and considerations is by no means comprehensive, but if reasonably followed, it should help ensure basic standards are met.

Informed consent. Obtaining informed consent at the outset of an evaluation is an important ethical practice in psychology, including assessment (APA [2002a] Ethics Code Standards 3.10, Informed Consent, and 9.03, Informed Consent in Assessments). For veterans examined in C&P contexts, however, participation in the exam process is required, and their consent is not, if they want to continue pursuing benefits. Although it is still advisable to obtain consent, their failure to submit to an exam without good cause could subject them to negative rating decisions. It is permissible to proceed with a C&P examination without formally obtaining a veteran's consent in this situation (Standard 3.10a and b, Informed Consent), but examiners are still expected to provide sufficient information about the exam in a manner consistent with the Ethics Code (see Standards 3.07, Third-Party Requests for Services; 3.10c, Informed Consent; and 3.11, Psychological Services Delivered to or Through Organizations) and obtain the veteran's assent. Examiners should take care to explain the nature and objectives of the exam. They should also explain who is the recipient of the exam information, who is the client, the examiner's role and relationship with all parties, the uses of the information, and the limits of confidentiality (Ethics Code Standards 3.11, Psychological Services Delivered to or Through Organizations, and 4.02, Discussing the Limits of Confidentiality).

Worthen and Moering (2011) discussed the VA's lack of formal guidance for examiners on the process of informing veterans about relevant C&P exam information. As such, the burden falls on examiners to make sure this important information is shared with veterans. Fortunately, in their article, Worthen and Moering also provided an informed consent template (p. 198) that is tailormade for C&P psychological exams. Russo (2014, p. 188) also provided an informed consent template for neuropsychologists working in VA. Both templates can be adapted to suit individual needs, and it is recommended that examiners create their own template to follow and perhaps have the veteran sign it as proof that the information was appropriately shared. The process of discussing exam information and limits to confidentiality should also be documented in the report. Having such documentation can be very useful if an ethics complaint is made.

Interview. With regard to history gathering and diagnostic interviewing, personal experience and discussion with colleagues suggests that most neuropsychological C&P examiners spend about 45 minutes on this task, depending on the complexity of the history. During this time, the examiner collects very detailed information about the claimed condition and its effects on social and occupational functioning. Other relevant history is also collected and reported, including medical, psychiatric, substance use, legal, and developmental history. The VA's exam report template has individual history sections dedicated to these areas (more on this later), so documenting the relevant history is fairly straightforward. Many examiners follow the report template's history structure when interviewing to improve efficiency during the writing process.

Testing. There is no standard test battery or norm selection process for C&P exams. Neuropsychologists create test batteries on the basis of the referral question and their knowledge of tests and norms. Consistent with APA's (2002a) Ethics Code Standard 9.02 (Use of Assessments), the "perfect battery" for any C&P exam is the one that is most useful and informative. Examiners should also refrain from using obsolete tests, while being mindful that the newest version of a test may not yet have demonstrated the strongest psychometric properties for a given patient population (Bush, 2010). For test creation and norm selection refreshers, the reader is referred to classic texts such as Lezak, Howieson, Bigler, and Tranel (2012), Mitrushina, Boone, Razani, and D'Elia (2005), and Strauss, Sherman, and Spreen (2006). There are also classic position papers on the debate over fixed versus flexible battery approaches (Bigler, 2007; Hom, 2003; Russell, Russell, & Hill, 2005). In general, it is advisable to select tests that have substantial research support and select norms that are not only large, but representative (Boone, 2013).

The elephant in the room. Veterans undergoing C&P exams have an inherent monetary incentive to perform poorly, and this kind of motivation can undermine the validity of test results. As of March 2015, veterans rated at 100% receive about $3,000 a month (tax free) in addition to other benefits such as free health care and travel reimbursement for medical appointments (see http://www.benefits.va.gov/COMPENSATION/resources_comp01.asp). Because motivational factors can greatly influence test results (Green, Rohling, Lees-Haley, & Allen, 2001), assessing the credibility of C&P exam results is important. Base rates of suboptimal effort are often greater than 30% in disability exams (Chafetz, 2008; Larrabee, 2003; Mittenberg, Patton, Canyock, & Condit, 2002; Russo, 2012), and C&P is no different. The need to evaluate credibility in this context should not be surprising because it is standard practice in forensic evaluation to use performance validity tests and symptom validity tests (Armistead-Jehle, 2010; Bush et al., 2005; Heilbronner, Sweet, Morgan, Larrabee, & Millis, 2009; Mittenberg et al., 2002). In fact, not including them in this context is ethically questionable (Ethics Code Standards 9.02, Use of Assessments, and 9.06, Interpreting Assessment Results). At the same time, it is equally as important to recognize that some aspects of military culture (e.g., honor, integrity, drive, and machismo) can lead some veterans to underreport their symptomatology. Thus, C&P examiners must thoroughly examine both sides of the response bias coin in every examination.

Neuropsychologists are good at identifying noncredible performances when they appropriately assess for such (Larrabee, 2012), but identifying the cause of the noncredible performance is difficult unless the person has a significantly below-chance performance on forced-choice tests (Slick, Sherman, & Iverson, 1999). Thus, examiners need to be cautious and not assume that the underlying explanation is monetary incentive. Veterans often present with several beliefs or issues that could explain evidence of suboptimal effort. For example, some veterans view higher ratings as validation of their military experience (McNally & Frueh, 2013). Compensation neurosis (R. C. W. Hall & Hall, 2012) and cogniform disorder (Delis & Wetter, 2007) are related concepts that could also influence test result credibility and are not malingering. Psychiatric comorbidities and chronic pain (Heilbronner et al., 2009, pp. 1108–1117) are highly prevalent in veterans seeking disability benefits, and each could also potentially affect the reliability of test results. Thus, there are numerous threats to test validity during the C&P examination beyond simple malingering. Regardless of the underlying cause, however, identifying noncredible data is important to avoid misdiagnosis or misrepresentation of the condition.

There is general agreement that noncredible performance is best identified through converging evidence (Larrabee, 2003; Meyers & Volbrecht, 2003; Victor, Boone, Serpa, Buehler, & Ziegler, 2009), including both quantitative and qualitative indicators such as (observed) mental status or medical history that is inconsistent with test results, unexplainable intertest and intratest variability, and positive indications from several performance validity tests (Heilbronner et al., 2009, p. 1103). Continuous assessment of effort using a variety of methods is also helpful, and this approach has considerable support in the literature (Boone, 2009; Chafetz, 2011; Heilbronner et al., 2009; Slick et al., 1999). Other important validity testing considerations are reviewed and highlighted in the spirited debates by Larrabee (2012) and Bigler (2012).

Completing the Disability Benefits Questionnaire

The report template for C&P exams is called the Disability Benefits Questionnaire (DBQ). It may be helpful to view a DBQ before reading this section; examples can be found at http://www.benefits.va.gov/compensation/dbq_ListByDBQFormName.asp. Recall that neuropsychologists are asked to perform mental disorders and PTSD exams, so look for those specifically. The DBQs located on the website are fairly identical to the ones used by VA examiners, but C&P examiners do not use these particular DBQs. Instead, they complete electronic DBQs that are located in the VA's Automated Medical Information Exchange (AMIE; Office of Enterprise Development Management and Financial Systems, 1995) system. Once the DBQ in AMIE has been completed, the examiner signs it electronically, which instantly releases it to the VBA for adjudication.

The DBQ's structure is often confusing to new examiners because it was not designed for examiners. It was designed to help RVSRs quickly locate pertinent information needed for rating decisions and to force examiners to use the required regulatory language by templating this language for them. Therefore, the DBQ is sometimes less than intuitive, at least from a psychologist's perspective. For example, there is no test results section (at least at this time, but it is always being updated so this may not be true in the future), and it was almost 2014 before the DBQ included a behavioral observations section. Although the DBQ may not include sections for pertinent information, there is never an excuse for leaving relevant information out of the report. The burden falls on the examiner to find creative ways to include relevant information in the DBQ.

Mental disorders DBQs and PTSD DBQs are almost identical. The main difference is that the PTSD DBQ includes an additional section for reporting stressors and PTSD symptoms. Both are essentially divided into two sections. The first section is dedicated to establishing the diagnosis and differentiating the symptoms and impairment associated with each diagnosis. In fact, the very first question asked on the DBQ is whether the claimant has a diagnosis or not. When there is a diagnosis, it needs to conform to the *Diagnostic and Statistical Manual of Mental Disorders* (5th ed.; American Psychiatric Association, 2013). Each diagnosis must be definite and defendable, and it is not permissible to call a diagnosis a "differential" or "rule out" when uncertain.

The second section of the DBQ is devoted to documenting history and specifying symptoms, but it contains a few other sections that do not fit neatly anywhere else. These subsections include places for examiners to verify that they reviewed the C-file, describe behavioral observations, and state whether the claimant has capacity to manage VA finances. The end of the DBQ includes a "Remarks" section. This section is important because it is where neuropsychologists can include all the relevant information that could not be included anywhere else. Many examiners use this section to document the informed consent process if they included one (or at least that limits of confidentiality were reviewed and other relevant information), as well as assessment procedures, test results, and interpretation.

Documenting symptoms is self-evident in the DBQ because it has specified areas to do this, and some are as simple as checking boxes. Sometimes, however, confusion can result regarding how to document overlapping symptoms from multiple diagnoses. If the veteran has more than one diagnosis, the RVSR will need to know how symptoms relate to each diagnosis in order to provide appropriate ratings for each diagnosis. RSVRs always ask examiners to explicitly separate symptoms for them because they are not medical or psychological experts and do not have the authority to make assumptions about symptoms. Separating overlapping symptoms associated with multiple mental disorders is often easier said than done, but it is often helpful to consider the onset and course when seeking clues and to cite those factors in the rationale. When it is not possible to separate symptoms for some reason, examiners must provide the rationale for why it is not possible and use the regulatory language "without resorting to mere speculation" in their explanation.

Another part of the DBQ that examiners sometimes feel uneasy about answering is the question about whether the veteran is capable of managing his or her financial affairs. This question is asked because it is another source of information about the presence and severity of the condition being adjudicated and because it helps identify when it is in the best interests of the veteran to have a fiduciary. It is very difficult to have the determination reversed once it set in motion, so examiners need to be absolutely certain the veteran is truly incapable of managing his or her finances before endorsing this question. They need to be confident there has been a prolonged departure from normal behavior compared with social standards (Office of Enterprise Development Management and Financial Systems, 1995, p. 26). When thinking about how to answer this question, examiners may find it helpful to refer to Section 3.353(a) of the C.F.R.'s Title 38, which says, "A mentally incompetent person is one who . . . lacks the mental capacity to contract or to manage his or her own affairs, including disbursement of funds without limitation." Consideration should be paid to the veteran's ability to communicate, understand relevant financial information, appreciate potential outcomes of financial decisions or actions, and apply an appropriate rationale (Appelbaum & Grisso, 1988).

Once the DBQ is fully completed, the examiner signs it, which transfers it electronically to the VBA. Expectations for how many DBQs examiners will complete in a given day, or week, can vary considerably by region. The turnaround time for most general mental health DBQs is 3 days after the examination. Depending on the regional office, neuropsychological exams may be given some latitude on this because of the time-intense nature of these exams. The bottom line is that the time allowed to complete a DBQ depends on each regional office and there is considerable variability, so it is important for examiners to verify the expectation of their local regional office to avoid insufficient performance.

CONCLUSION

Neuropsychologists working for the VA have the distinct honor of working with veterans. To ensure they do their job properly, neuropsychologists should possess the basic competencies for forensic psychology and neuropsychology, as well as specialized competencies for working in the VA system and with veterans. Ethical examiners value the integrity of their work and uphold professional standards. It should be clear from this chapter that Parts 3 and 4 of Title 38 of the C.F.R. dictate much of the VA's disability process. The C.F.R. provides significant guidance on how claims are adjudicated, but it says little about how to balance the VA's adjudication needs with forensic psychology's professional standards. It is up to individual neuropsychologists to ensure that their exams live up to both requirements. Neuropsychological examiners should appreciate that veterans are a diverse group of people while also understanding that most have been influenced in some way by military culture. Understanding this culture is essential for competent C&P work. A basic familiarity with all the unique tools and processes used in the examination, from the VA's records systems to the DBQ, will also be important. Readers are strongly encouraged to review the works and resources cited in this chapter to improve their mastery of key concepts.

APPENDIX 12.1. MILITARY CULTURE RESOURCES

Books

Bush, S. S. (Ed.). (2012). *Neuropsychological practice with veterans*. New York, NY: Springer.

Bush, S. S. (Ed.). (2014). *Psychological assessment of veterans*. New York, NY: Oxford University Press.

Higbee, D. (2010). *Military culture and education*. Surrey, England: Ashgate.

Kennedy, C. H., & Williams, T. J. (2010). *Military neuropsychology*. New York, NY: Springer.

Mathews, M. (2009). The soldier's mind: Motivation, mindset, and attitude. In S. Morgillo-Freeman, B. A. Moore, & A. Freeman (Eds.), *Living and surviving in harm's way: A psychological treatment handbook for pre-postdeployment of military personnel* (pp. 9–26). New York, NY: Taylor & Francis.

Moore, B. (2011). Understanding and working within the military culture. In B. A. Moore & W. E. Penk (Eds.), *Treating PTSD in military personnel: A clinical handbook* (pp. 9–22). New York, NY: Guilford Press.

Journal Articles and Other Publications

Greene-Shortridge, T., Britt T., & Andrew, C. (2007). The stigma of mental health problems in the military. *Military Medicine, 172,* 157–161.

Reger, M., Etherage, J., Reger, G., & Gahm G. (2008). Civilian psychologists in an Army culture: The ethical challenge of cultural competence. *Military Psychology, 20,* 21–35.

Shaw, M., & Hector, M. (2010). Listening to military members returning from Iraq and/or Afghanistan: A phenomenological investigation. *Professional Psychology: Research and Practice, 41,* 128–134.

U.S. Department of the Army. (2007). *The soldier's guide: The complete guide to U.S. Army traditions, training, duties, and responsibilities*. New York, NY: Skyhoarse.

Web Resources

http://www.deploymentpsych.org

http://www.mentalhealth.va.gov/communityproviders/military_culture.asp#sthash.vE8KQh2Q.dpbs

http://www.militaryacronyms.net/s

http://www.militarywords.com

http://www.samhsa.gov/sites/default/files/military_white_paper_final.pdf

References

American Academy of Clinical Neuropsychology. (2007). American Academy of Clinical Neuropsychology (AACN) practice guidelines for neuropsychological assessment and consultation. *Clinical Neuropsychologist, 21,* 209–231. http://dx.doi.org/10.1080/13825580601025932

American Psychiatric Association. (2013). *Diagnostic and statistical manual of mental disorders* (5th ed.). Washington, DC: Author.

American Psychological Association. (2002a). Ethical principles of psychologists and code of conduct. *American Psychologist,* 57, 1060–1073. http://dx.doi.org/10.1037/0003-066X.57.12.1060

American Psychological Association. (2002b). *Guidelines on multicultural education, training, research, practice, and organizational change for psychologists.* Retrieved from http://www.apa.org/pi/oema/resources/policy/multicultural-guidelines.aspx

American Psychological Association. (2013). Specialty guidelines for forensic psychology. *American Psychologist, 68,* 7–19. http://dx.doi.org/10.1037/a0029889

Appelbaum, P. S., & Grisso, T. (1988). Assessing patients' capacities to consent to treatment. *New England Journal of Medicine, 319,* 1635–1638. http://dx.doi.org/10.1056/NEJM198812223192504

Armistead-Jehle, P. (2010). Symptom validity test performance in U.S. veterans referred for evaluation of mild TBI. *Applied Neuropsychology,* 17, 52–59. http://dx.doi.org/10.1080/09084280903526182

Bigler, E. D. (2007). A motion to exclude and the "fixed" versus "flexible" battery in "forensic" neuropsychology: Challenges to the practice of clinical neuropsychology. *Archives of Clinical Neuropsychology,* 22, 45–51. http://dx.doi.org/10.1016/j.acn.2006.06.019

Bigler, E. D. (2012). Symptom validity testing, effort, and neuropsychological assessment. *Journal of the International Neuropsychological Society, 18,* 632–640. http://dx.doi.org/10.1017/S1355617712000252

Boone, K. B. (2009). The need for continuous and comprehensive sampling of effort/response bias during neuropsychological examinations. *Clinical Neuropsychologist, 23,* 729–741. http://dx.doi.org/10.1080/13854040802427803

Boone, K. B. (2013). *Clinical practice of forensic neuropsychology: An evidence-based approach.* New York, NY: Guilford Press.

Bush, S. S. (Ed.). (2005). *A casebook of ethical challenges in neuropsychology.* New York, NY: Psychology Press.

Bush, S. S. (2010). Determining whether or when to adopt new versions of psychological and neuropsychological tests: Ethical and professional considerations. *Clinical Neuropsychologist, 24,* 7–16. http://dx.doi.org/10.1080/13854040903313589

Bush, S. S. (2014). *Neuropsychology-related ethics references.* Retrieved from http://www.theaacn.org/positionpapers.aspx

Bush, S. S., Connell, M. A., & Denney, R. L. (2006). *Ethical practice in forensic psychology: A systematic model for decision-making.* http://dx.doi.org/10.1037/11469-000

Bush, S. S., & Drexler, M. L. (Eds.). (2002). *Ethical issues in clinical neuropsychology.* Lisse, the Netherlands: Swets & Zeitlinger.

Bush, S. S., Ruff, R. M., Tröster, A. I., Barth, J. T., Koffler, S. P., Pliskin, N. H., . . . Silver, C. H. (2005). Symptom validity assessment: Practice issues and medical necessity. *Archives of Clinical Neuropsychology, 20,* 419–426. http://dx.doi.org/10.1016/j.acn.2005.02.002

Calamia, M., Markon, K., & Tranel, D. (2012). Scoring higher the second time around: Meta-analyses of practice effects in neuropsychological assessment. *Clinical Neuropsychologist, 26,* 543–570. http://dx.doi.org/10.1080/13854046.2012.680913

Calamia, M., Markon, K., & Tranel, D. (2013). The robust reliability of neuropsychological measures: Meta-analyses of test-retest correlations. *Clinical Neuropsychologist, 27,* 1077–1105. http://dx.doi.org/10.1080/13854046.2013.809795

Chafetz, M. (2011). Reducing the probability of false positives in malingering detection of Social Security disability claimants. *Clinical Neuropsychologist, 25,* 1239–1252. http://dx.doi.org/10.1080/13854046.2011.586785

Chafetz, M. D. (2008). Malingering on the Social Security disability consultative exam: Predictors and base rates. *Clinical Neuropsychologist, 22,* 529–546. http://dx.doi.org/10.1080/13854040701346104

De Angelis, K., Sandhoff, M., Bonner, K., & Segal, D. R. (2013). Sexuality in the military. In A. K. Baumle (Ed.), *International handbook on the demography of sexuality* (pp. 363–381). http://dx.doi.org/10.1007/978-94-007-5512-3_18

Delis, D. C., & Wetter, S. R. (2007). Cogniform disorder and cogniform condition: Proposed diagnoses for excessive cognitive symptoms. *Archives of Clinical Neuropsychology, 22,* 589–604. http://dx.doi.org/10.1016/j.acn.2007.04.001

Department of Veterans Affairs assistance in developing claims, 38 C.F.R. §3.159 (2008).

Economic Systems Inc. (2004). *VA disability compensation program: Legislative history.* Washington, DC: VA Office of Policy, Planning, and Preparedness.

Elders, M. J., Brown, G. R., Coleman, E., Kolditz, T. A., & Steinman, A. M. (2015). Medical aspects of transgender military service. *Armed Forces and Society*, *41*, 199–220. http://dx.doi.org/10.1177/0095327X14545625

Gilbert v. Derwinski, 1 Vet. App. 49 (1990).

Gold, L. H., Anfang, S. A., Drukteinis, A. M., Metzner, J. L., Price, M., Wall, B. W., . . . Zonana, H. V. (2008). AAPL practice guideline for the forensic evaluation of psychiatric disability. *Journal of the American Academy of Psychiatry and the Law, 36*(4, Suppl.), S3–S50.

Green, P., Rohling, M. L., Lees-Haley, P. R., & Allen, L. M., III. (2001). Effort has a greater effect on test scores than severe brain injury in compensation claimants. *Brain Injury*, *15,* 1045–1060. http://dx.doi.org/10.1080/02699050110088254

Hall, L. K. (2008). *Counseling military families: What mental health professionals need to know*. New York, NY: Taylor & Francis.

Hall, R. C. W., & Hall, R. C. W. (2012). Compensation neurosis: A too quickly forgotten concept? *Journal of the American Academy of Psychiatry and the Law*, *40,* 390–398.

Heilbronner, R. L., Sweet, J. J., Attix, D. K., Krull, K. R., Henry, G. K., & Hart, R. P. (2010). Official position of the American Academy of Clinical Neuropsychology on serial neuropsychological assessments: The utility and challenges of repeat test administrations in clinical and forensic contexts. *Clinical Neuropsychologist*, *24,* 1267–1278. http://dx.doi.org/10.1080/13854046.2010.526785

Heilbronner, R. L., Sweet, J. J., Morgan, J. E., Larrabee, G. J., & Millis, S. R. (2009). American Academy of Clinical Neuropsychology Consensus Conference Statement on the neuropsychological assessment of effort, response bias, and malingering. *Clinical Neuropsychologist*, *23,* 1093–1129. http://dx.doi.org/10.1080/13854040903155063

Hom, J. (2003). Forensic neuropsychology: Are we there yet? *Archives of Clinical Neuropsychology*, *18,* 827–845. http://dx.doi.org/10.1016/S0887-6177(03)00076-3

Larrabee, G. J. (2003). Detection of malingering using atypical performance patterns on standard neuropsychological tests. *Clinical Neuropsychologist*, *17,* 410–425. http://dx.doi.org/10.1076/clin.17.3.410.18089

Larrabee, G. J. (2012). Performance validity and symptom validity in neuropsychological assessment. *Journal of the International Neuropsychological Society*, *18,* 625–630. http://dx.doi.org/10.1017/S1355617712000240

Lezak, M. D., Howieson, D. B., Bigler, E. D., & Tranel, D. (2012). *Neuropsychological assessment* (5th ed.). New York, NY: Oxford University Press.

McNally, R. J., & Frueh, B. C. (2013). Why are Iraq and Afghanistan War veterans seeking PTSD disability compensation at unprecedented rates? *Journal of Anxiety Disorders*, *27,* 520–526. http://dx.doi.org/10.1016/j.janxdis.2013.07.002

Meyers, J. E., & Volbrecht, M. E. (2003). A validation of multiple malingering detection methods in a large clinical sample. *Archives of Clinical Neuropsychology*, *18,* 261–276. http://dx.doi.org/10.1093/arclin/18.3.261

Mitrushina, M., Boone, K. B., Razani, J., & D'Elia, L. F. (2005). *Handbook of normative data for neuropsychological assessment* (2nd ed.). New York, NY: Oxford University Press.

Mittenberg, W., Patton, C., Canyock, E. M., & Condit, D. C. (2002). A national survey of symptom exaggeration and malingering base rates [Abstract]. *Journal of the International Neuropsychological Society*, *8,* 247.

Moering, R. G. (2011). Military service records: Searching for the truth. *Psychological Injury and Law*, *4,* 217–234. http://dx.doi.org/10.1007/s12207-011-9114-3

Moore, B. (2011). Understanding and working within the military culture. In B. A. Moore & W. E. Penk (Eds.), *Treating PTSD in military personnel: A clinical handbook* (pp. 9–22). New York, NY: Guilford Press.

Moradi, B. (2009). Sexual orientation disclosure, concealment, harassment, and military cohesion: Perceptions of LGBT military veterans. *Military Psychology*, *21,* 513–533. http://dx.doi.org/10.1080/08995600903206453

Office of Enterprise Development Management and Financial Systems. (1995). *Automated Medical Information Exchange (AMIE) V. 2.7/Medical Administration Service (MAS) user manual* (rev. 2016). Retrieved from http://www.va.gov/vdl/documents/Financial_Admin/Auto_Medical_Info_Exchg_(AMIE)/masus.pdf

Reasonable doubt, 38 C.F.R. §3.102 (2001).

Reger, M., Etherage, J., Reger, G., & Gahm, G. (2008). Civilian psychologists in an Army culture: The ethical challenge of cultural competence. *Military Psychology*, *20,* 21–35. http://dx.doi.org/10.1080/08995600701753144

Ridgway, J. (2011). The splendid isolation revisited: Lessons from the history of veterans' benefits before judicial review. *Veterans Law Review*, *3,* 135–219.

Ridgway, J. (2012). Mind reading and the art of drafting medical questions in veterans benefits claims. *Psychological Injury and Law*, *5,* 72–87. http://dx.doi.org/10.1007/s12207-012-9119-6

Ridgway, J. (2013). Recovering an institutional memory: The origins of the modern veterans benefits system, 1914 to 1958. *Veterans Law Review*, *5,* 1–55.

Riley, R. (2010). The importance of preserving the pro-claimant policy underlying the Veterans' Benefits Scheme: A comparative analysis of the administrative structure of the Department of Veterans Affairs disability benefits system. *Veterans Law Review, 2,* 1–40.

Russell, E. W., Russell, S. L., & Hill, B. D. (2005). The fundamental psychometric status of neuropsychological batteries. *Archives of Clinical Neuropsychology, 20,* 785–794. http://dx.doi.org/10.1016/j.acn.2005.05.001

Russo, A. (2012). Consistency of self reported memory functioning and symptom validity test performance of OEF/OIF veterans with positive VA comprehensive TBI evaluations. *Archives of Clinical Psychology, 27,* 840–848.

Russo, A. (2013). Ethical, legal and risk management considerations in the neuropsychological assessment of veterans. *Psychological Injury and Law, 6,* 21–30. http://dx.doi.org/10.1007/s12207-013-9145-z

Russo, A. (2014). Assessing veteran symptom validity. *Psychological Injury and Law, 7,* 178–190. http://dx.doi.org/10.1007/s12207-014-9190-2

Slick, D. J., Sherman, E. M., & Iverson, G. L. (1999). Diagnostic criteria for malingered neurocognitive dysfunction: Proposed standards for clinical practice and research. *Clinical Neuropsychologist, 13,* 545–561. http://dx.doi.org/10.1076/1385-4046(199911)13:04;1-Y;FT545

Slone, L. B., & Friedman, M. J. (2008). *After the war zone: A practical guide for troops and their families.* New York, NY: Da Capo Books.

Strauss, E., Sherman, E. M. S., & Spreen, O. (2006). *A compendium of neuropsychological tests: Administration, norms, and commentary.* New York, NY: Oxford University Press.

Title 38 Code of Federal Regulations. Retrieved from http://www.ecfr.gov/cgi-bin/text-idx?SID=20a43ce2d1055f2a4351050cfb835818&tpl=/ecfrbrowse/Title38/38cfrv1_02.tpl#0

Tucker, L. L. (2008). *Army reserve culture: A critical part of transformation.* Carlisle, PA: U.S. Army War College, Carlisle Barracks. Retrieved from http://oai.dtic.mil/oai/oai?verb=getRecord&metadataPrefix=html&identifier=ADA478526

U.S. Department of Veterans Affairs. (2014). *Procedure guide 1601E.01: C&P disability evaluations.* Washington, DC: Author.

Veterans Claims Assistance Act of 2000, Pub. L. No. 106-475, 114 Stat. 2096.

Victor, T. L., Boone, K. B., Serpa, J. G., Buehler, J., & Ziegler, E. A. (2009). Interpreting the meaning of multiple symptom validity test failure. *Clinical Neuropsychologist, 23,* 297–313. http://dx.doi.org/10.1080/13854040802232682

Worthen, M. D., & Moering, R. G. (2011). A practical guide to conducting VA compensation and pension exams for PTSD and other mental disorders. *Psychological Injury and Law, 4,* 187–216. http://dx.doi.org/10.1007/s12207-011-9115-2

CHAPTER 13

NEUROPSYCHOLOGICAL EVALUATIONS IN DISABILITY DETERMINATIONS

Robert L. Heilbronner and Shane S. Bush

Case example: Mr. Claimant is a 44-year-old, right-handed, Caucasian man with 19 years of formal education. He previously worked as an attorney but resigned in August 2014 after developing symptoms of severe depression and anxiety that reportedly rendered him unable to carry out the duties and responsibilities of his job. He has been receiving disability benefits from A-1 Insurance Company since December 2014. The present neuropsychological evaluation is for the purpose of examining Mr. Claimant's current cognitive functioning and emotional status; the results will be used to assist in the determination of his capacity to return to work.

The application of neuropsychological knowledge and procedures to forensic questions, including disability determinations, has increased substantially over the past couple of decades as neuropsychology's unique contributions to understanding questions relevant to disability status have become more widely understood (Heilbronner, 2004; Kaufmann, 2009; Sweet, King, Malina, Bergman, & Simmons, 2002). More than other health providers, neuropsychologists are able to determine, quantify, and explain complex issues involving cognitive, sensory-motor, linguistic, psychiatric, and behavioral problems associated with illness or injuries that affect a person's capacity to work. In addition, with an understanding of the psychological and neuropsychological research on issues of effort, response bias, and malingering (Heilbronner, Sweet, Morgan, Larrabee, & Millis, 2009), neuropsychologists are well positioned to address questions of symptom exaggeration and fabrication with a multimethod approach that includes empirically based tests and questionnaires.

DISABILITY DETERMINATION PROCESS

A neuropsychological disability examination (NDE), also commonly referred to as the more generic *independent medical examination* (IME), is requested by a third party, such as a disability insurance carrier or the Social Security Administration, to authenticate the level of function or dysfunction of an individual claiming disability. The goal of the examiner (be it a physician or neuropsychologist) is to address the central question "Does the claimant have the ability to perform the occupation outlined?"

The definitional concept of "disability" differs across settings. For instance, the definition used to determine disability may differ across private and public entities. Moreover, it is possible for a private entity to offer multiple contracts, each with a different definition of disability. More important, because disability represents a contractual or legal concept, it is rarely established by the medical or psychological specialist. Instead, the specialist serves as a source of information for those seeking to determine disability. Neuropsychologists are increasingly recognized as essential for making determinations of impairment, limitations, and restrictions as they

http://dx.doi.org/10.1037/0000032-013
APA Handbook of Forensic Neuropsychology, S. S. Bush (Editor-in-Chief)

apply to behavioral health disability (Lovejoy & Oakes, 2012; Oakes, Lovejoy, & Bush, 2017). Although opinions regarding disability status, including degree of disability, are requested from neuropsychologists in some contexts, such requests are typically not made, and are in fact discouraged, in evaluations performed for disability insurance carriers.

Claims for disability benefits related to behavioral and neuropsychological health conditions are often viewed as challenging for those attempting to adjudicate them (Waldron, 2003). In addition to the difficulties associated with understanding how multiple factors interact to predict a general picture of disability, some have noted that the often subjective nature of neuropsychological complaints (e.g., forgetting things, trouble concentrating) also contributes to the overall challenge in evaluating such claims. There are no clear empirically based guidelines or models for reliably establishing the degree of occupational impairment associated with behavioral health or neuropsychological conditions (Lovejoy & Oakes, 2012). At present, a comprehensive neuropsychological evaluation is considered the most comprehensive method for clarifying the complex and multifactorial presentations of individuals reporting work-related impairments or disability secondary to neuropsychological conditions. The broad goal of such assessments is to examine the variables identified as important clinical and contextual contributors to the experience of work-related impairment and disability (e.g., variables related to symptom constellations, symptom severity, motivation, work setting, economic circumstances, and job satisfaction).

DeBofsky (2009) identified two recent court rulings that demonstrate the value of neuropsychological testing in disability cases. In *Smith v. Reliance Standard Life Insurance Company* (2004), the plaintiff alleged disability because of chronic fatigue syndrome. It was argued that the claimant's condition resulted in a "substantial reduction in previous levels of occupational, educational, social, or personal activities." Because no known diagnostic laboratory tests exist for chronic fatigue syndrome, and because the insurer alleged that it could not assess the insured's self-reports of fatigue, the disability determination was based on the severity of the claimant's claimed cognitive impairment allegedly associated with the physical condition. The plaintiff submitted a detailed neuropsychological report that the insurer had a psychiatrist review. The court determined that the psychiatrist completely overlooked many of the findings made by the neuropsychologist and offered no rebuttal to some of the neuropsychologist's test results and interpretation. Because of the deficiencies in the insurer's review and consideration of the neuropsychological evidence, the court ordered benefits to be paid.

In another case, *Hunter v. Federal Express Corporation* (2004), an employee of Federal Express became disabled after a stroke. Although disability benefits were subsequently paid for a period of time, Federal Express terminated benefits after concluding that the claimant had sufficiently recovered to be able to work at an occupation. The court overruled the determination, based in substantial part on a neuropsychological evaluation that correlated with an MRI of the brain showing the stroke. The court relied on the neuropsychological test results, which demonstrated significant deficits in visual perceptual and visuospatial reasoning, judging relationships, reasoning in visuospatial terms, reduced mental speed and flexibility, and so forth. Thus, on the basis of the objective evidence of cognitive impairment, the court ordered that benefits be reinstated with interest and also found the insurer's actions "culpable" and awarded attorneys' fees.

DIFFERENCES BETWEEN CLINICAL EVALUATIONS AND NEUROPSYCHOLOGICAL DISABILITY EVALUATIONS

In clinical contexts, the person who undergoes a neuropsychological evaluation is referred to as the *patient* or *client;* in disability evaluation contexts, the person is referred to as the *examinee, insured,* or *claimant.* Using different terms to describe persons who undergo neuropsychological evaluations in these different contexts helps all parties to remain clear about the nature of the roles and relationships of those involved. More specifically, describing someone as an examinee promotes an understanding that the usual doctor–patient relationship does not exist in forensic contexts (Bush, Barth, et al., 2005).

In addition, in clinical contexts neuropsychologists often accept patient self-reports as accurate, whereas neuropsychologists performing NDEs tend to view patient self-reports more skeptically because of the well-established higher prevalence of dissimulation in forensic contexts. Questions and methods may differ on the basis of the type or context of the evaluation. The roles and responsibilities of treating clinicians versus experts also differ in important ways as described in detail elsewhere (e.g., American Psychological Association [APA], 2013; Greenberg & Shuman, 1997; Lamberty, 2012).

DIFFERENCES BETWEEN DIFFERENT TYPES OF NEUROPSYCHOLOGICAL DISABILITIES EXAMINATIONS

Disability evaluations can vary according to the specific referral questions and resources (records, reimbursement) provided by the referral source. For example, some disability insurance carriers request very thorough evaluations to address a wide range of complex questions about diagnosis, neurocognitive and functional capacities, emotional states and personality traits, and symptom validity. In contrast, the needs of some governmental agencies (e.g., Social Security Administration) are satisfied with more circumscribed evaluations, with corresponding limitations in reimbursement for services. Neuropsychologists are responsible for selecting methods and procedures needed to address the specific referral questions posed for a particular evaluation, being aware that the peer review present in adversarial contexts such as disability determinations allows inadequate evaluations to be exposed.

In disability contexts, neuropsychologists, like doctors from other medical specialties, are usually retained by, and on behalf of, a party other than the person being evaluated (e.g., the disability insurance company). Because they do not have clinical, emotional, or financial obligations to the person being examined, the neuropsychologists in such forensic contexts are often referred to as *independent;* this term is often applied to the examiner as well as the examination (e.g., IME, independent neuropsychological examination). The term *independent* is typically not applied to examinations performed by experts who are retained by a third party who represents or is otherwise working on behalf of the examinee, such as an attorney. Regardless of the retaining party, neuropsychologists retained by either side should have the same commitment to objectivity and independence in decision making. (For a more extended description of neuropsychological IMEs, please refer to Bush & Heilbronner, 2012; Oakes et al., 2017.)

NEUROPSYCHOLOGICAL DISABILITY EVALUATION PROCESS

The neuropsychological disability evaluation is not a single event; it is a process that begins well before face-to-face contact with the examinee and continues after the examinee has left the office. Understanding the process and attending to its various components positions the neuropsychologist to provide services that are beneficial to decision makers in a manner that is clear and agreed upon by all the parties involved.

Preparation

Preparation for an NDE begins well before a neuropsychologist is contacted by a referral source; it begins with establishing competence to perform this type of evaluation. Professional competence for performing NDEs involves a skill set that is often not obtained during clinical training. Except for the rare neuropsychologist who completes a forensic postdoctoral residency, clinicians interested in performing NDEs typically obtain their knowledge and skills through self-study, continuing education courses, formal supervision, consultation, and working with a mentor. Because NDEs can vary in their nature, scope, and examinee populations, competent neuropsychologists prepare for the specific types of NDEs that they are likely to perform (see Bush & Heilbronner, 2012). To that end, neuropsychologists should make efforts to educate themselves about the particulars involved in disability determinations, including their role and the goals and intentions of the various involved parties (e.g., claimant, disability carrier, disability attorney).

Communication With the Retaining Party

Referrals for NDEs typically come from a variety of sources, including attorneys, government agencies, and disability insurance carriers, either directly or via companies or vendors that contract with the disability insurance carrier. Contact persons representing such referral sources often vary widely in their understanding of the nature and role of neuropsychology. As a result, neuropsychologists commonly need to educate the retaining party about the nature of the evaluation in the context in which a given NDE is requested. Some retaining parties use or contract with neuropsychology consultants to help clarify the need for evaluations, generate referral questions, and identify other neuropsychologists to perform NDEs. Such peer-to-peer interaction often facilitates the NDE process. However, when third parties use inexperienced or unqualified psychologist consultants to serve those roles or to review the work of independent neuropsychologists, the process can become frustrating and less productive for all parties.

Establishing the Parameters of the Neuropsychological Disability Evaluation

It is important for neuropsychologists who perform NDEs to establish protocols that cover the logistics of performing such evaluations. Such protocols cover (a) fees, (b) expected time requirements, (c) informed consent issues, (d) methods and tests to be used, (e) questions about third-party observers or recording devices, (f) possible conflicts of interest, and (g) use and retention of records. On the basis of established protocol, the parameters of the evaluation are conveyed to the retaining party and agreed upon at the outset of the neuropsychologist's involvement. Likewise, retaining parties often provide parameters to which neuropsychologists are asked to adhere. Such parameters often include (a) fees and payment schedule, (b) time frame for completion of the report, (c) informed consent issues, (d) use of specific tests or types of tests, and (e) specific referral questions to be addressed.

Sometimes disagreements exist between the clinician and the retaining party about the parameters of the evaluation. It is always best to work out such problems before the day of the evaluation. Discussion and negotiations between the neuropsychologist and the retaining party often resolve conflicting expectations or practices. It is beneficial to have the parameters outlined in writing and signed by the neuropsychologist and the retaining party. The retaining party typically conveys to examinees or their representatives aspects of the parameters that directly affect the examinees, such as anticipated time needed for the evaluation and issues involving third-party observers or recording devices. When the established parameters of an NDE are challenged by an examinee or the examinee's representative, the neuropsychologist should strive to resolve the matter by explaining the reasons for parameters and, if needed, contacting the disability insurance carrier or other retaining party before performing the evaluation.

Review of Records

Examinee self-report is, intentionally or unintentionally, often unreliable for both biographical and injury-related information (Gunstad & Suhr, 2001; Mittenberg, DiGuilio, Perrin, & Bass, 1992), and this is especially common in forensic contexts. As a result, police accident reports, emergency medical personnel records, and emergency department records are particularly informative for verifying and providing the context for examinees' self-reported experiences.

The reports of neuropsychological evaluations performed before the NDE provide important information for making diagnostic determinations and judgments regarding functional impairment. Given recovery or deterioration trajectories for many disorders, comparing current results with previous test results can help with diagnostic clarification and expectations for future functioning. Reviewing previous neuropsychological test data for scoring accuracy can help determine whether prior conclusions were faulty, particularly when the results do not seem to make neuropsychological sense. Such review is often done by the in-house or consulting neuropsychologist who uses that information to determine whether an NDE needs to be done.

Medical and mental health records can also reveal a history of significant injuries, illnesses, and problems that predate the current illness or injury and can influence functioning in the workplace. Because of the greater tendency for forensic examinees as a group to misrepresent their background, the opportunity to review educational, vocational, military, and other biographical records can be particularly informative for confirming examinee self-report or determining correct information. As Heilbronner et al. (2009) stated, "No examiner in any discipline is required to simply accept self-reported facts and history of examinees. The validity of *self-reported* disability and symptoms needs to be evaluated, especially when such complaints occur in a forensic context" (p. 1102). It is often helpful to review records before meeting with the examinee because the information contained in the records can help guide the clinical interview and avoid use of inappropriate measures or data sets. For example, because examinees commonly overreport education level (Greiffenstein, Baker, & Johnson-Greene, 2002), obtaining objective evidence of educational achievement can help ensure the selection of correct normative data. When records are not initially provided by the retaining party, neuropsychologists can, and often should, request that the retaining party provide relevant records before offering conclusions or completing a report.

Evaluation

The methods and procedures used in NDEs and the focus of reports vary depending on the goals and nature of the NDE and the training and preferences of the clinician. Compared with other types of forensic evaluations that focus more on diagnosis and causality of deficits or impairment, the focus of most NDEs is on the presence or degree of neuropsychological impairment and how it may pose limitations to or restrictions on the claimant's capacity to work (whether it be "own occupation" or "any occupation"). Neuropsychologists emphasize examinees' functional activities and abilities and often do not directly address disability status, given that disability status is typically based on the insurance policy and other sources of information that are the purview of the disability insurance carrier.

Describing the parameters of the neuropsychological disability examination: Informed consent.

> Mr. Claimant was informed of the parameters associated with the present evaluation; that is, who the retaining party was, the limits of confidentiality, the importance of honesty and good effort, who the report would be directed to, that a treating doctor–patient relationship did not apply to the current circumstances, and that treatment would not be provided. He indicated that he understood, and he agreed to participate.

At the beginning of NDEs, neuropsychologists typically confirm the examinee's identity via photo identification. The neuropsychologist also discusses with the examinee the parameters of the evaluation as established with the retaining party. Logistics such as the estimated length of time of the evaluation, the neuropsychologist's commitment to the examinee's physical comfort in terms of issues such as room temperature and breaks, and the importance of turning off phones or other electronic devices are reviewed. Neuropsychologists often ask examinees whether they have been coached about how to respond or perform during the NDE, and they often inform examinees that specific measures of effort and honesty will be used. Neuropsychologists often ask examinees to sign a written consent form or other documentation detailing the nature and parameters of the NDE and the examinee's willingness to participate (see Bush, Barth, et al., 2005, for a sample consent form).

Clinical interview.

> Mr. Claimant was previously a self-employed attorney who engaged in real estate and trust litigation. In December 2013, he began experiencing marked work- and family-related stress that resulted in symptoms of depression and anxiety. He also reportedly struck his head in August 2013, prompting a visit to the emergency department at a local hospital. However, there are no records documenting this visit. Mr. Claimant's symptoms of prominent anxiety and depression led to his seeking psychiatric treatment, and it was recommended that he participate in a day treatment program

> at a local medical center, which he did from March to July 2014. Because his emotional status reportedly rendered him unable to carry out the duties and responsibilities of his job, he consequently applied for and was awarded disability benefits from A-1 Insurance Company and has been receiving $8,700 per month since July 2014 (onset of disability: March 2014). Emotionally, Mr. Claimant reported that his mood has improved over time, although he continues to experience some symptoms of depression and anxiety. He currently participates in weekly psychotherapy, and his psychotropic medications are being managed by a psychiatrist. Historically, Mr. Claimant had never received any psychiatric or psychotherapeutic treatment before March 2014.
>
> Cognitively, Mr. Claimant reports that he has been experiencing problems related to his memory and attention beginning around January 2014. He said that his short-term memory adversely affected him when he was at work and at home (e.g., he forgets details of conversations). He described himself as an inattentive and disorganized individual who has problems with multitasking and gross concept formation (i.e., he does not grasp the big picture). Often, he avoids doing tasks altogether, particularly if they are perceived as overwhelming or causing conflict for him. Although it is no longer a common occurrence, Mr. Claimant has also experienced lapses in his memory in which he has no recollection of activities performed over several hours. Because of these symptoms, he was referred to Dr. Neuropsyche for a neuropsychological evaluation in early 2014 (comparison of test results discussed later). His psychiatrist included a diagnosis of attention deficit/hyperactivity disorder (ADHD) and added amphetamine and dextroamphetamine (Adderall) to the medication regimen. Although Mr. Claimant demonstrated rapid, pressured speech throughout the present evaluation and acknowledged a history of manic-like symptoms (i.e., heightened energy, self-confidence, hyperactivity, decreased need for sleep, racing thoughts, and excessive spending), he said that a diagnosis of bipolar disorder has never been considered. Mr. Claimant's previous medical history is unremarkable, and he also denied current or past substance use. Current prescription medications include citalopram, aripiprazole (Abilify), and Adderall.

Interviews provide an opportunity to gather and clarify background information; details about the illness or injury and the examinee's experience of the illness or injury; subsequent symptoms and changes in functioning; treatments; and, for those who are not working, plans regarding return to work. Neuropsychologists interview the examinee and may interview significant others, employers, health care providers, and others who have information about the examinee's history and neuropsychological and functional status before and after the work-related injury. In addition to information commonly obtained in other types of clinical and forensic neuropsychological evaluations, an emphasis is placed on functioning, particularly in the workplace. Questions cover (a) work history and status, (b) work-related stressors, (c) financial stressors while working and since ceasing to work, (d) difficulties performing work-related tasks, (e) use of assistive devices, (f) past and current daily activities, and (g) plans to return to work or other productive activities, such as volunteer activities.

Individuals involved in an examinee's life and who can describe daily activities and changes or similarities before and after the onset of an examinee's neuropsychological problems can be valuable sources of information. Interviews with such collateral sources of information can help clarify information provided by an examinee or found in records. However, persons who have a financial stake in the outcome of the case or a personal investment in helping the examinee may be motivated to provide selective or inaccurate information that they believe supports the case. At the outset of an interview of a collateral source, it is incumbent on the examiner to advise the spouse, employer, treating doctor, or other person that the information he or she conveys will not be held in confidence but will be included in the neuropsychological report. Collateral sources must also be informed that the conversation does not imply the existence of a treating relationship. The clinical interview of the examinee occurs before test administration because information gained from the interview helps inform test selection and the need for subsequent interviews or to determine that additional interviews or testing are not needed. Although the clinical interview may be sufficient for answering the referral questions in some contexts, testing is typically a necessary component of the NDE.

Observations.

> Mr. Claimant arrived alone and on time, having commuted by train from his home in the suburbs. He was casually dressed and appropriately groomed. Attention was adequate for testing purposes. There were no gross or fine motor abnormalities observed, and his gait was normal. No problems with vision or hearing were noted or reported. His ability to understand language was adequate for questions and instructions. He exhibited rapid and pressured speech, which was particularly evident during his lengthy elaborations to questions posed during the clinical interview; frequent redirection was necessary. Thought processes were mildly tangential but were otherwise goal directed, organized, and without evidence of psychotic thinking. Regarding his mood, Mr. Claimant appeared anxious, although an appropriate range of affect was displayed; this was notable in his frequent requests for repetition and clarification of task instructions. Overall, Mr. Claimant was cooperative and responsive to questions. He did not appear unduly fatigued either during or on completion of formal testing. Social comportment was intact. No situational factors that could affect test performance (e.g., intoxication, significant pain, environmental distractions) were present. On the basis of his observable behavior and his results on several measures of effort (i.e., Word Memory Test, Reliable Digit Span, California Verbal Learning Test—Second Edition Forced Choice recognition), his performances across measures are considered a valid representation of his current neuropsychological functioning.

Observations of examinees during NDEs provide valuable information that contributes to determinations regarding diagnosis and functional status. In addition to the usual observations made in clinical contexts, observations of behaviors outside of the one-to-one evaluation of the examinee (e.g., in waiting areas or parking lots) are more likely to occur in NDEs. In addition, NDE referral sources sometimes provide secretive surveillance recordings of examinees in the community. Such materials provide views of examinees engaged in daily activities when they are not aware that they are being observed, which may confirm or refute information reported by examinees or observed during the evaluation. Neuropsychologists consider such materials to the extent that they facilitate the goals of the NDE. Neuropsychologists consider whether observations, history, and test results combine to provide converging information that promotes diagnostic decision making or result in discrepancies that raise questions about the accuracy or validity of one or more of the sources of information.

It is sometimes requested that a third party, typically an attorney or an attorney's representative, be permitted to observe or record a NDE. The purposes of such requests include wanting to (a) ensure the integrity of the evaluation process, (b) gather information to be used to oppose evaluation results if needed, (c) comfort the examinee, and, in some cases, (d) intimidate examiners. In some jurisdictions, having a third party present during the NDE is the examinee's legal right. When considering such requests, neuropsychologists must clarify whether the request is for the clinical interview, test administration, or both. Neuropsychologists may choose, at their discretion, to permit a quiet and unobtrusive third party to be present during the clinical interview because such a presence does not affect test security or neurocognitive performance and should not affect the examinee's responses or behavioral presentation. When examinees exercise their right to record clinical interviews, it is advantageous for the neuropsychologist to also record the interview so that evidence exists to challenge any edited or altered examinee recording.

With few exceptions, it is the position of neuropsychology as a profession that requests for third parties to observe neuropsychological testing be denied (American Academy of Clinical Neuropsychology, 2001; National Academy of Neuropsychology Policy and Planning Committee, 2000). Despite the right granted examinees in some jurisdictions to have a third party present during the testing component of NDEs or to record test administration, neuropsychologists do not have to work under conditions that knowingly compromise the validity of the results (see McCaffrey, 2005, for a review). When requests are made to observe or record (audio or video) the test administration component of a neuropsychological NDE, neuropsychologists can educate all involved parties about the inherent problems with such procedures and provide supporting professional literature, which often suffices. However, when the requesting parties do not relent, or if a judge orders the evaluation to proceed with the third party present, it is entirely appropriate and typically advisable for the neuropsychologist to decline the referral. The knowledge or belief that a local colleague will perform the NDE with a third party present is not sufficient reason to compromise one's assessment practices.

Selecting measures. Consistent with professional ethics (APA, 2017), neuropsychologists base their conclusions and opinions, whether in reports, testimony, or other statements, on information and techniques sufficient to substantiate their findings (Ethical Standard 9.01a). The goals of neuropsychological NDEs typically require a comprehensive, systematic, multimethod evaluation approach (Bush, Connell, & Denney, 2006). Depending on jurisdiction, admissibility in court proceedings requires test methods to be generally accepted within the profession and, often, to have an established scientific foundation (see, e.g., *Daubert v. Merrell Dow Pharmaceuticals, Inc.*, 1993; *Frye v. U.S.*, 1923). Commercially available psychological and neuropsychological tests typically satisfy such criteria.

Surveys have revealed that most neuropsychologists use a flexible battery assessment approach in which multiple individual measures are combined into a core battery that is used relatively consistently by the neuropsychologist, with tests added or removed as needed for a given examinee (Rabin, Barr, & Burton, 2005; Sweet, Moberg, & Suchy, 2000). Bush and Heilbronner (2012) provided a sample NDE test battery that is based on such an approach. For a more extended review of the particulars associated with establishing and implementing a test battery that is generally accepted as reasonable among neuropsychology peers, the reader is referred to the American Academy of Clinical Neuropsychology (2007) Practice Guidelines for Neuropsychological Assessment and Consultation.

Interpretation, diagnosis, and determinations. The first step in the test data interpretation process involves making a determination about the validity of the examinee's presentation, including effort on tests and honesty in responding to questions. Neuropsychologists look for consistencies among the examinee's complaints, test results, information in the medical records, and reports of collateral sources. Inconsistencies raise questions about symptom or performance validity, with greater inconsistencies providing increasing evidence of an invalid presentation. When an examinee's approach to a NDE is determined to be invalid, the findings are described as not reliable or valid or, at most, representing the examinee's minimum ability level, and the differential diagnosis typically involves a somatic symptom disorder (unintentional) versus malingering (intentional), using probabilistic language (e.g., Slick, Sherman, & Iverson, 1999). Having a well-documented neurological injury or illness and valid deficits does not preclude an examinee from exaggerating problems or fabricating additional problems. Compared with clinical contexts in which some neuropsychologists discontinue test administration when there is strong evidence of invalid performance, the customary practice in NDEs is to complete the test administration.

With valid test data, the interpretive process in NDEs is similar to that in clinical evaluations. The level of impairment (e.g., 1.5 or 2 standard deviations below the mean) is selected a priori, the examinee's level of performance is compared with estimated preinjury levels and appropriate normative data, base rates of low scores are considered, patterns of strengths and weaknesses are compared with established patterns for various psychiatric and neurological disorders, and determinations about underlying brain integrity and functional abilities are generated (Bush & Heilbronner, 2012). Diagnosis, causality, prognosis, and, if requested, recommendations are addressed. Compared with other types of neuropsychological evaluations, in NDEs an emphasis is often placed on the examinee's ability to perform essential work-related functions, in the prior or current occupation or in any occupation. In the interpretive process, neuropsychologists consider the difference among test results, diagnosis, and functioning and, as Larrabee (2012) so concisely stated, "Everything must make 'neuropsychological sense'" (p. 9).

The report: Summary and conclusions.

> Mr. Claimant is a man of high average to superior intelligence who has been suffering from symptoms of depression and anxiety since March 2014. The present objective test results revealed generally average to above average performances across cognitive domains, with a pattern of strengths and relative weaknesses. His observable behavior and results on several measures of effort suggest that the current scores accurately represent his current neuropsychological abilities. Working memory was a particular strength for Mr. Claimant, with his performance falling in the superior range. Verbal comprehension, perceptual reasoning, and processing speed were all in the high average range. His ability to learn and retain both visual and verbal information were both well above average. Language, attention, executive functions, and visuospatial skills were all within normal limits.
>
> Emotionally, Mr. Claimant does not currently endorse clinically significant symptoms of depression or anxiety on the Beck Depression Inventory–II and the Beck Anxiety Inventory; this was also reflected in his responses to the items of the Minnesota Multiphasic Personality Inventory–2. The only significant clinical scale elevation was on Scale 3 (Hysteria), although he endorsed a number of items related to depression and low positive emotions. Thus, the profile does not reflect symptoms of prominent and pervasive depression and anxiety at this time. Clearly, he seems to have improved, at least in term of his reporting of symptoms at the time he first began receiving disability benefits (March 2014). Regarding ADHD symptomatology, his responses on several self-report inventories are not indicative of such a history.
>
> Overall, Mr. Claimant demonstrated a solidly average to above-average neuropsychological profile, and there was no evidence to suggest impairments related to memory or attention, both of which are his primary cognitive concerns. Compared with the prior neuropsychological test results (1 year ago), the present data indicate that his cognitive status has remained the same and, in some instances, has improved. For example, visual memory and processing speed are now average and high average, respectively. Emotionally, Mr. Claimant also appears to have improved, with his depression and anxiety having become less severe since he has obtained adequate treatment for those symptoms. Regarding a history of possible ADHD, Mr. Claimant

> did not endorse clinically significant symptoms of either current or childhood attention difficulties, and he does not show objective attention difficulties. Presently, Mr. Claimant meets criteria for a diagnosis of major depressive disorder, recurrent, in partial remission. He would benefit from ongoing participation in weekly psychotherapy and should remain appropriately compliant with his medication regimen. From a neuropsychological perspective, the overall results of this evaluation do not suggest impairment in essential work-related abilities.

NDE reports differ in important ways from clinical reports in their strong emphasis on the examinee's functional daily activities (e.g., capacity to manage hygiene, finances) and ability to perform activities in a work setting. Sources of information (e.g., examinee report, report of a collateral source) are clearly described in NDE reports, rather than stating the information as fact. Also, NDE referral sources frequently provide specific questions, the answers to which are often provided in place of a summary or conclusions section.

Statements about functional capabilities should be based on objective evidence and data to the extent possible. Citations from the scientific literature can help substantiate conclusions, although inclusion of extensive references can distract readers and detract from the conclusions. Standardized scores for the tests administered are typically appended to the report or included in the body of the report. Limitations of the data (e.g., invalid performance, impact of situational factors) or significant reservations about the findings (e.g., need for additional information) are described. Neuropsychologists are commonly asked by disability insurance carriers not to comment on whether the insured is disabled per se because such determination of disability status is a process that requires the application of contractual language to the medical data. In other disability evaluation contexts, neuropsychologists may be asked to address presence or degree of disability specifically. All parties are well served when such issues are clarified in advance.

NDE reports, once submitted to a referral source such as disability insurance carriers or NDE vendors, may be reviewed by their neuropsychology consultants or employees who may request clarification or offer edits or comments to consider. Whether the feedback or request offered by the reviewing neuropsychologist is accepted or rejected, the independent neuropsychologist remains responsible for his or her work product.

Symptoms, deficits, diagnosis, and function. Subjective symptoms of memory loss or concentration problems do not necessarily reflect objective deficits with those abilities, and neither symptoms nor deficits necessarily reflect a compromised ability to perform activities in the home or work setting. Many individuals can overcome or compensate for symptoms and deficits, allowing them to engage in productive or social activities. In contrast, some people with mild symptoms or deficits are not able to perform tasks that require high levels of proficiency. It is important in NDE reports to distinguish among symptoms, deficits, and function. Linking symptoms and objective evidence of impairment to limitations in functioning is of particular value to disability decision makers.

Having a psychiatric or neurocognitive disorder is not synonymous with an inability to perform personal, social, or productive activities. Rather, it is the examinee's specific deficits, rather than the diagnosis, in the context of the work-related tasks to be performed that determines whether the examinee's neuropsychological deficits pose functional limitations.

Feedback to examinees. Despite the wishes of some examinees, NDEs do not include feedback sessions. This parameter of the evaluation is explained to examinees as part of the informed consent process. Examinees are informed that copies of the report may be available from the referring party (e.g., disability carrier), often via the examinee's attorney, if one has been retained.

Financial Arrangements and Managing Records

Billing practices vary among neuropsychologists and retaining parties. Whether to bill hourly or flat fees and to require prepayment are decisions for neuropsychologists to make and discuss with retaining parties. A fee schedule that lists basic examination fees, no-show or late cancellation fees, and fees for additional services helps clarify the billing parameters for all parties. The fee schedule should be dated to avoid confusion about which fees are in effect for a given NDE and, once agreed on, should be signed by the retaining party in advance of the NDE. The APA (2017) *Ethical Principles of Psychologists and Code of Conduct* (Standard 6.04, Fees and Financial Arrangements) requires that billing arrangements be established as early as possible in the professional relationship (see Appendix 13.1).

Jurisdictional laws, professional ethics, and related guidelines (e.g., APA, 2007) govern the retention and release of records. However, authoritative sources often do not differentiate between records generated and obtained as part of clinical and forensic (e.g., NDE) evaluations, resulting in a lack of clarity in the context of NDEs about which records to keep and how long to keep them. For the record review aspect of NDEs, neuropsychologists commonly receive extensive records, and additional records are typically generated in the course of a comprehensive NDE, all of which can be a burden to retain for an extended period. Some referral sources only request that records be retained for a number of months or until a determination has been made about the case. Such time frames are typically shorter than the requirements posed by state law or professional organizations. The APA has recognized the "inherent tensions" that practitioners experience in their decisions about when to dispose of records. The APA has encouraged practitioners to carefully weigh the advantages and disadvantages of retention and disposal when making such decisions.

Maintaining records in an electronic format addresses some of the logistical problems with storage, although appropriate care must be taken to ensure the security and confidentiality of electronic records (Ethical Standard 6.02, Maintenance, Dissemination, and Disposal of Confidential Records of Professional and Scientific Work; APA, 2017; see also Bush, Naugle, & Johnson-Greene, 2002). The *Specialty Guidelines for Forensic Psychology* (APA, 2013) state,

> Forensic practitioners strive to inform the retaining party of the limits of record keeping times. If requested to do so, forensic practitioners consider maintaining such records until notified that all appeals in the matter have been exhausted, or sending a copy of any unique components/aspects of the record in their care and control to the retaining party before destruction of the record. (Guideline 10.08, Record Keeping, p. 16)

In the context of NDEs, neuropsychologists inform examinees during the informed consent process that the report will be released only to the retaining party or its representatives rather than to the examinee or the examinee's representatives. Retaining parties commonly request that neuropsychologists who perform NDEs provide copies of raw test data to their neuropsychologist consultants or employees. Neuropsychologists release raw test data to appropriate colleagues on request and to others in a manner consistent with ethical and professional guidelines (APA, 2013; Bush, Rapp, & Ferber, 2009).

Challenges Encountered in Neuropsychological Disability Examinations

Awareness of some of the common challenges encountered in disability determination contexts allows neuropsychologists who perform, or who are considering performing, NDEs to provide competent and beneficial services. For a more extended review of some of the pitfalls that can arise during the course of doing IMEs in general, the reader is referred to Bush and Heilbronner (2012).

The practice of all health care specialties, including neuropsychology, evolves over time, requiring practitioners to remain current with advances in their fields. Failure to remain abreast of evidence-based changes interferes with the competent practice of neuropsychology and the value that NDEs offer decision makers. For example, empirically based symptom and performance validity assessment is now a standard of practice in neuropsychology (Bush, Heilbronner, & Ruff, 2014; Bush, Ruff, et al., 2005; Heilbronner et al., 2009), with multiple empirically based validity measures being expected in a comprehensive neuropsychological NDE.

NDEs differ from many non-neuropsychological disability evaluations by the inclusion of multiple objective measures of the constructs of interest. The data from such measures, when compared with appropriate normative groups, offer NDEs a distinct advantage that is appealing to decision makers. Use of empirically based measures of cognition and psychological status allows for more objective decisions than can be obtained without the use of such measures.

Compassion can lead to a desire to advocate on behalf of others who seem to be suffering. However, statements of advocacy in NDEs cross the line into the treating doctor role and threaten to bias results and result in unjust disability determinations. Neuropsychologists in NDE contexts strive to maintain the independent examiner role by avoiding biased statements, such as advocating for or against the allotment of benefits to the examinee.

In NDE contexts in which orthopedic injuries or other medical problems seem to be adversely affecting the examinee's functioning, neuropsychologists may be tempted to base conclusions about functional status on such problems. However, decisions based on orthopedic or other problems outside the neuropsychologist's areas of expertise should be deferred to the appropriate specialist.

CONCLUSION

Neuropsychologists commonly perform independent evaluations to help determine whether disability benefits should be provided or continued. The NDE parameters, process, and work product differ in important ways from neuropsychological evaluations of individuals encountered in clinical contexts. NDEs also differ from the IMEs of other health care professionals and from those in civil litigation, offering a more objective and evidence-based approach than is typically offered by some specialties. The results of NDEs can help decision makers determine disability status and allocation of benefits and monetary awards. Understanding the differences between clinical neuropsychological evaluations and NDEs allows neuropsychologists to provide competent, ethical services in support of the critically important disability determination process.

APPENDIX 13.1. NEUROPSYCHOLOGICAL DISABILITY EVALUATION FEE SCHEDULE

---

1. Neuropsychological examination (full day) $________
   - Includes clinical interview; behavioral observations; test administration, scoring, interpretation, and report; and record review (up to 1 hour)
   - Additional record review (per hour) $________
   - Consultation/discussion with attorney or insurance carrier (per hour) $________
   - No show/cancellation less than 5 business days $________
2. Case review or peer review, with report (per hour) $________
   - Retainer amount established on the basis of amount of records and estimated time requirement

I, ________, on behalf of ________, certify that the above fees are acceptable.

____

Signature Date

References

American Academy of Clinical Neuropsychology. (2001). Policy statement on the presence of third party observers in neuropsychological assessments. *Clinical Neuropsychologist, 15,* 433–439. http://dx.doi.org/10.1076/clin.15.4.433.1888

American Academy of Clinical Neuropsychology. (2007). Practice guidelines for neuropsychological assessment and consultation. *Clinical Neuropsychologist, 21,* 209–231. http://dx.doi.org/10.1080/13825580601025932

American Psychological Association. (2007). Record keeping guidelines. *American Psychologist, 62,* 993–1004. http://dx.doi.org/10.1037/0003-066X.62.9.993

American Psychological Association. (2013). Specialty guidelines for forensic psychology. *American Psychologist, 68,* 7–19. http://dx.doi.org/10.1037/a0029889

American Psychological Association. (2017). *Ethical principles of psychologists and code of conduct* (2002, Amended June 1, 2010 and January 1, 2017). Retrieved from http://www.apa.org/ethics/code/index.aspx

Bush, S., Naugle, R., & Johnson-Greene, D. (2002). Interface of information technology and neuropsychology: Ethical issues and recommendations. *Clinical Neuropsychologist, 16,* 536–547. http://dx.doi.org/10.1076/clin.16.4.536.13911

Bush, S. S., Barth, J. T., Pliskin, N. H., Arffa, S., Axelrod, B. N., & Blackburn, L. A. (2005). Independent and court-ordered forensic neuropsychological examinations: Official statement of the National Academy of Neuropsychology. *Archives of Clinical Neuropsychology, 20,* 997–1007. http://dx.doi.org/10.1016/j.acn.2005.06.003

Bush, S. S., Connell, M. A., & Denney, R. L. (2006). *Ethical practice in forensic psychology: A systematic model for decision making.* http://dx.doi.org/10.1037/11469-000

Bush, S. S., & Heilbronner, R. L. (2012). The neuropsychological IME. In S. S. Bush & G. L. Iverson (Eds.), *Neuropsychological assessment of work-related injuries* (pp. 280–302). New York, NY: Guilford Press.

Bush, S. S., Heilbronner, R. L., & Ruff, R. M. (2014). Psychological assessment of symptom and performance validity, response bias, and malingering: Official position of the Association for Psychological Advancement in Psychological Injury and Law. *Psychological Injury and Law, 7,* 197–205. http://dx.doi.org/10.1007/s12207-014-9198-7

Bush, S. S., Rapp, D. L., & Ferber, P. S. (2009). Maximizing test security in forensic neuropsychology. In A. M. Horton, Jr., & L. C. Hartlage (Eds.), *Handbook of forensic neuropsychology* (2nd ed., pp. 177–195). New York, NY: Springer.

Bush, S. S., Ruff, R. M., Tröster, A. I., Barth, J. T., Koffler, S. P., Pliskin, N. H., . . . Silver, C. H. (2005). Symptom validity assessment: Practice issues and medical necessity. *Archives of Clinical Neuropsychology, 20,* 419–426. http://dx.doi.org/10.1016/j.acn.2005.02.002

Daubert v. Merrell Dow Pharmaceuticals, Inc., 509 U.S. 579 (1993).

DeBofsky, M. D. (2009). Disability benefits adjudication: Attorney representing disability claimants. In J. E. Morgan & J. J. Sweet (Eds.), *Neuropsychology of malingering casebook* (pp. 476–487). New York, NY: Psychology Press.

Frye v. U.S., 293 F. 1013 (D.C. Cir. 1923).

Greenberg, S. A., & Shuman, D. W. (1997). Irreconcilable conflict between therapeutic and forensic roles. *Professional Psychology: Research and Practice, 28,* 50–57. http://dx.doi.org/10.1037/0735-7028.28.1.50

Greiffenstein, M. F., Baker, W. J., & Johnson-Greene, D. (2002). Actual versus self-reported scholastic achievement of litigating postconcussion and severe closed head injury claimants. *Psychological Assessment, 14,* 202–208. http://dx.doi.org/10.1037/1040-3590.14.2.202

Gunstad, J., & Suhr, J. A. (2001). "Expectation as etiology" versus "the good old days": Postconcussion syndrome symptom reporting in athletes, headache sufferers, and depressed individuals. *Journal of the International Neuropsychological Society, 7,* 323–333. http://dx.doi.org/10.1017/S1355617701733061

Heilbronner, R. L. (2004). A status report on the practice of forensic neuropsychology. *Clinical Neuropsychologist, 18,* 312–326. http://dx.doi.org/10.1080/13854040490501574

Heilbronner, R. L., Sweet, J. J., Morgan, J. E., Larrabee, G. J., & Millis, S. R. (2009). American Academy of Clinical Neuropsychology Consensus Conference Statement on the neuropsychological assessment of effort, response bias, and malingering. *Clinical Neuropsychologist, 23,* 1093–1129. http://dx.doi.org/10.1080/13854040903155063

Hunter v. Federal Express Corporation, U.S. Dist. LEXIS 328, Mo. Ct. App. (2004).

Kaufmann, P. M. (2009). Protecting raw data and psychological tests from wrongful disclosure: A primer on law and other persuasive strategies. *Clinical Neuropsychologist,* 23, 1130–1159.

Lamberty, G. J. (2012). Neuropsychological evaluation and treatment: The clinician's perspective. In S. S. Bush & G. L. Iverson (Eds.), *Neuropsychological assessment of work-related injuries* (pp. 265–279). New York, NY: Guilford Press.

Larrabee, G. J. (2012). A scientific approach to forensic neuropsychology. In G. J. Larrabee (Ed.), *Forensic neuropsychology: A scientific approach* (2nd ed., pp. 3–22). New York, NY: Oxford University Press.

Lovejoy, D. W., & Oakes, H. J. (2012). The behavioral health provider as a participant in the disability determination process: Evaluations, terminology, and systems. In S. S. Bush & G. L. Iverson (Eds.), *Neuropsychological assessment of work-related injuries* (pp. 321–343). New York, NY: Guilford Press.

McCaffrey, R. J. (Ed.). (2005). Third party observers [Special issue]. *Journal of Forensic Neuropsychology, 4*(2).

Mittenberg, W., DiGiulio, D. V., Perrin, S., & Bass, A. E. (1992). Symptoms following mild head injury: Expectation as aetiology. *Journal of Neurology, Neurosurgery, and Psychiatry, 55,* 200–204. http://dx.doi.org/10.1136/jnnp.55.3.200

National Academy of Neuropsychology Policy and Planning Committee. (2000). Presence of third party observers during neuropsychological testing: Official statement of the National Academy of Neuropsychology. *Archives of Clinical Neuropsychology, 15,* 379–380. http://dx.doi.org/10.1093/arclin/15.5.379

Oakes, H., Lovejoy, D., & Bush, S. S. (2017). *The independent neuropsychological evaluation.* New York, NY: Oxford University Press.

Rabin, L. A., Barr, W. B., & Burton, L. A. (2005). Assessment practices of clinical neuropsychologists in the United States and Canada: A survey of INS, NAN, and APA Division 40 members. *Archives of Clinical Neuropsychology, 20,* 33–65. http://dx.doi.org/10.1016/j.acn.2004.02.005

Slick, D. J., Sherman, E. M. S., & Iverson, G. L. (1999). Diagnostic criteria for malingered neurocognitive dysfunction: Proposed standards for clinical practice and research. *Clinical Neuropsychologist, 13,* 545–561. http://dx.doi.org/10.1076/1385-4046(199911)13:04;1-Y;FT545

Smith v. Reliance Standard Life Insurance Company, 332 F.Supp.2d 1168, 1177 (D. Colo. 2004).

Sweet, J. J., King, J. H., Malina, A. C., Bergman, M. A., & Simmons, A. (2002). Documenting the prominence of forensic neuropsychology at national meetings and in relevant professional journals from 1990 to 2000. *Clinical Neuropsychologist, 16,* 481–494. http://dx.doi.org/10.1076/clin.16.4.481.13914

Sweet, J. J., Moberg, P. J., & Suchy, Y. (2000). Ten-year follow-up survey of clinical neuropsychologists: Part I. Practices and beliefs. *Clinical Neuropsychologist, 14,* 18–37. http://dx.doi.org/10.1076/1385-4046(200002)14:1;1-8;FT018

Waldron, C. (2003). Trends in morbidity: Pricing and reserving individual disability insurance is no walk in the park. *Actuary, 37,* 7–8.

Chapter 14

CIVIL CAPACITIES

George J. Demakis and Eric G. Mart

Clinical psychologists—and clinical neuropsychologists in particular—are uniquely trained and experienced to evaluate civil capacity issues. Examples of capacity-related referral questions may include whether a man with severe and persistent mental illness can refuse psychotropic medication, an elderly woman with possible dementia can change her power of attorney and her will, or a young adult who suffered a traumatic brain injury can manage a large financial settlement. These cases require a careful assessment of cognitive and psychological functioning, medical issues, and family dynamics, sometimes in the context of family conflict and an unwilling examinee. If in a legal context, familiarity with state statutes, case law, and local practices and customs is paramount. Although capacity evaluations are obviously not confined to older adults, such issues are more likely in this population given the increased likelihood of dementing conditions with their attendant effect on cognitive, psychological, and behavioral functioning. Capacity issues and evaluations are also likely to be more prevalent now given the increase in blended families—with their divided loyalties and conflict—and the huge expected intergenerational transfer of wealth (see Demakis, 2012a, for review). Not surprisingly, financial issues are sometimes prominent in such cases; Gunther (2011) estimated that financial exploitation in Utah in 2009 cost older residents, businesses, and government as much as $52 million. More than 70% of the perpetrators in these cases were family members.

This chapter is designed to address financial, health care, and testamentary capacity because these are the three most common capacity issues researched in the psychological literature. Other civil capacities are clearly important, such as the ability to enter into contracts, to make a gift or donation, and to convey real estate, as well as domestic issues such as the capacity to engage in sexual relations, marry, divorce, and adopt (for a review of mostly case law, see Perlin, Champine, Dlugacz, & Connell, 2008) but are beyond the scope of this chapter, primarily because there is relatively little if any psychological literature on the topic. We do, however, address sexual consent capacity in some detail as an area worthy of further investigation.

Moreover, this chapter does not address capacity issues that may emerge in criminal cases and have been well studied, such as the capacity to stand trial, to waive Miranda rights, or even to be executed (see Denney, 2012). Our focus, rather, is to first provide relevant background and contextual information on capacity evaluations and then address practical issues likely to be of clinical use such as a conceptual framework for these evaluations, guidance in report writing, and common ethical issues. We conclude with a summary of important future directions for research.

TWO EVALUATION CONTEXTS AND SEVERAL KEY ISSUES

At the outset, it is important to differentiate the two settings—clinical and legal—in which capacity

http://dx.doi.org/10.1037/0000032-014
APA Handbook of Forensic Neuropsychology, S. S. Bush (Editor-in-Chief)

issues are addressed. In the clinical setting, a referral is made regarding the capacity of an examinee to perform a particular task, such as driving, changing a will, managing finances, or making health care decisions. The referral source is typically another health care provider (although a lawyer may make such referrals, too) who is seeking specific information about the particular issue; the resultant feedback is used to provide for patient care, management, and perhaps even treatment planning. More important, this feedback may be on a continuum, because an opinion about financial capacity may include strengths and weaknesses or perhaps areas of retained ability. In these cases, the psychologist's opinion is based on clinical findings and may be tied to observed or reported functional abilities or level of impairment on testing. For instance, a psychologist may opine that an examinee who recently had a stroke and has right hemiplegia and expressive aphasia is unable to drive or that an examinee with a recent moderate to severe traumatic brain injury with concomitant severe neuropsychological impairment with poor insight and judgment is unable to manage her finances. In some cases, a psychologist may use the elements of capacity that Grisso and Appelbaum (1998a) developed on the basis of their review of the literature and case law to guide the examination. These elements include the ability to express a choice, to understand information, to appreciate the significance of this information for one's own situation, and to reason with this information. Although these elements were initially developed in the context of the capacity to consent to treatment, they have been applied to other capacities as well (e.g., Marson & Huthwaite, 2005). To our knowledge, these elements have not been incorporated into state statutes but are present and developed in case law.

Mental health professionals, including neuropsychologists, have much to offer in such evaluations and are already quite involved. For instance, in an informal online survey of practicing neuropsychologists, capacity issues were reported to arise in up to 75% of cases (Moberg & Kniele, 2006), with such issues being much more common in dementia versus learning disorder or attention deficit/hyperactivity disorder evaluations. These participants considered executive functioning to be the most important cognitive domain for determining capacity. A more recent survey of consultation–liaison psychiatrists—likely relevant for some hospital-based neuropsychological services—found that almost 20% of all referrals were for decision-making capacity assessments (Seyfried, Ryan, & Kim, 2013). According to these psychiatrists, the most common diagnoses of referred patients were dementia and delirium. In the hospital setting, it is not surprising that capacity evaluations are common regarding the patients' capacity to sign out against medical advice or refuse treatment (e.g., Kornfeld, Muskin, & Tahil, 2009) or to provide informed consent or return home (Farnsworth, 1990). In the Farnsworth (1990) study, most referrals were from medicine, and "organic mental disorder" was the most common diagnosis. In the clinical cases described previously, the court system is not involved, at least not initially, and the consumer of the examination is the referral source. Of course, findings from these evaluations may be available for the neuropsychologist in a court-ordered evaluation and may even be used by the trier of fact, but these evaluations are not specifically designed to address a specific psycholegal question, nor do they tie their opinion to relevant laws. The evaluation is designed, again, to assist the referral source in making decisions about patient care and disposition.

Although legal evaluations share some similarities with the clinically based evaluation—both typically focus on cognitive functioning and activities of daily living—they have notable differences. In legal cases, the referral source is typically an attorney or judge seeking assistance with a specific psycholegal question—for our purposes, whether the individual meets statutorily defined criteria for incapacity or incompetency. The criteria vary by state (Demakis, 2013; Sabatino & Basinger, 2000), but a core of many states' definitions is that an individual is unable to manage his or her own affairs, make decisions independently, or meet essential needs because of some disabling condition (see Table 14.1, which lists three states with varying terminology and criteria). As such, these evaluations evaluate capacity more broadly than the clinical evaluation. In addition to statutes, there is also related case law interpreting and fleshing out these statutes that can

TABLE 14.1

Examples of Statutes Governing Incompetency/Incapacity in Three States

State	Statute
Minnesota	"Incapacitated person" means an individual who, for reasons other than being a minor, is impaired to the extent of lacking sufficient understanding or capacity to make or communicate responsible personal decisions, and who has demonstrated deficits in behavior which evidence an inability to meet personal needs for medical care, nutrition, clothing, shelter, or safety, even with appropriate technological assistance. Minn. Stat. Ann. § 524.5-102-Subd 6.
North Carolina	"Incompetent adult" means an adult or emancipated minor who lacks sufficient capacity to manage the adult's own affairs or to make or communicate important decisions concerning the adult's person, family, or property whether the lack of capacity is due to mental illness, mental retardation, epilepsy, cerebral palsy, autism, inebriety, senility, disease, injury, or any similar cause or condition. N.C. Gen. Stat. § 35A-1101 (7).
New Mexico	"Incapacitated person" means any person who demonstrates over time either partial or complete functional impairment by reason of mental illness, mental deficiency, physical illness or disability, chronic use of drugs, chronic intoxication or other cause, except minority, to the extent that the person is unable to manage the person's personal affairs or the person is unable to manage the person's estate or financial affairs or both; "inability to manage the person's personal care" means the inability, as evidenced by recent behavior, to meet one's needs for medical care, nutrition, clothing, shelter, hygiene or safety so that physical injury, illness or disease has occurred or is likely to occur in the near future; "inability to manage the person's estate or financial affairs or both" means gross mismanagement, as evidenced by recent behavior, of one's income and resources or medical inability to manage one's income and resources that has led or is likely in the near future to lead to financial vulnerability. N.M. Stat. Ann. § 45-5-101 F-H.

Note. From "State Statutory Definitions of Incompetency/Incapacity: Issues for Psychologists," by G. J. Demakis, 2013, *Psychology, Public Policy, and Law, 19*, pp. 333–335. Copyright 2013 by the American Psychological Association.

be particularly important because the statutes tend to be vague (Demakis, 2013).

The court, after a hearing or series of hearings and perhaps with aid of a psychological evaluation, ultimately makes the final decision about the examinee's legal status. If the examinee is adjudicated incapacitated or incompetent, the court assigns a guardian or conservator to care for, manage, and make decisions for the individual. Again, the terminology varies by state, but some states such as California use the term *conservator* to refer to only financial and estate-related decision making. The decider or trier of fact in such cases may be a judge or jury, and the decision is typically all-or-none (i.e., the individual either does or does not possess capacity), although there has been a move to reduce such plenary or full guardianships in favor of limited guardianships (Moye & Naik, 2011; Moye, Wood, Edelstein, Wood, et al., 2007). The latter are designed to preserve the rights of individuals facing guardianship to the extent possible and to ensure that, while still protected, they can maintain some degree of autonomy and dignity. Jurisdictions have provisions for capacity restoration that are particularly relevant in acute or changing conditions, such severe traumatic brain injury, in which an individual regains some functioning after the acute effects of the injury. Although necessary to protect vulnerable individuals who need assistance and perhaps protection, Gibson and Ferrini (2010) noted that the process in such legal cases can be adversarial, slow, expensive, and lacking flexibility to deal with complex and sometimes changing individuals. Again, the procedures governing these court-related capacity evaluations are designed to address the psycholegal question of incompetency or incapacity as defined by specific state statutes and case law.

Several points are warranted regarding these two types of evaluations. First, in some cases they may overlap, such as when a neuropsychological report generated by a clinical concern (e.g., does this person possess capacity to refuse this medical treatment?) is later reviewed by the court to make a legal capacity decision. In conducting almost exclusively court-ordered evaluations, one of us (Demakis) occasionally reviews such evaluations and incorporates them into his evaluation. In addition, findings from a court-ordered evaluation may include treatment recommendations or prognostic information to the court and guardian ad litem or attorney. Although the key issue in such reports is whether the individual is competent, who should serve as guardian, or both, clinical questions or issues are occasionally raised and may need to be addressed.

Second, at least historically, different terms were used in clinical and legal settings: *Capacity* or *incapacity* was used clinically, and *competency* or *incompetency* was used forensically. In other words, *lacking capacity* was (and still is) used clinically, but an individual who was deemed to have not met the relevant state statutes was adjudicated incompetent. This distinction, however, has diminished; a majority of states now prefer the term *incapacitated* rather than *incompetent* to refer to these individuals because the former is considered to be less pejorative and seemingly more amenable to restoration (Demakis, 2013). As such, although we use the term *capacity* or *incapacity* throughout this chapter for both legal and clinical contexts, we occasionally use the term *competency* or *incompetency* if that is the preferred term in the reviewed research or state statutes. In either case, the context for whatever term is used will be clear.

A final relevant issue is that capacity evaluations, whether legal or clinical, can be challenging. In Seyfried et al.'s (2013) survey of experienced consultation psychiatrists, approximately 60% judged capacity assessments to be both more challenging and more time consuming than other types of assessments. Ethical issues and patients in the gray area between capacity and incapacity were judged to be the most challenging aspects of such cases. Given that gray-area examinees or those for whom capacity issues are not obvious (e.g., an individual with mild dementia) are more likely to be referred for evaluation, it is not surprising that research has demonstrated that clinicians vary in their conceptualization of and decision making about capacity issues.

Marson, McInturff, Hawkins, Bartolucci, and Harrell (1997) found that neurologists and geriatricians demonstrated little agreement (56%) in decision making about capacity to consent to medical treatment in patients with mild Alzheimer's disease (AD). In contrast, agreement was 98% for elderly control participants, although these patients are not likely to be the type referred for evaluation. In this study, capacity judgments were based on a videotaped standardized consent capacity interview, as well as a brief clinical vignette and Mini-Mental State Examination score. Some improvement was evidenced in a later, similar type of study by Marson, Earnst, Jamil, Bartolucci, and Harrell (2000) after participant physicians underwent training, including review of a videotape and practice competency judgments. Another difference between these two studies is that the latter included some participants with moderate dementia (the former included only participants with mild dementia), which made the capacity judgments easier.

Kim et al. (2011) also found significant variability in consulting psychiatrists' capacity judgments of Alzheimer's patients regarding consent to research and appointing a research proxy. A significant source of variability was that the judges varied in how strict they were in applying different capacity thresholds. Although the research cited earlier is based on clinical criteria, not legal capacity criteria, we see no reason why such variability would not exist for legal cases as well.

INFLUENCES ON CONCEPTUAL AND EMPIRICAL WORK ON CAPACITY ISSUES

There have been multiple influences on our current understanding of capacity issues (Moye, Marson, & Edelstein, 2013). First, demographic changes and the increase in age-related dementia have stimulated attention and research in this area. Such increases will continue apace. Second, the Guardianship Reform movement in the United States—particularly motivated by various legal and geriatric advocacy groups—has sought to improve the procedural protections and due process rights of alleged incompetent individuals. Improvements include, among others, the opportunity to be present at one's own competency–guardianship hearings and to cross-examine witnesses, enhanced focus on behavioral and cognitive functioning versus a reliance on diagnoses to determine competency, increased use of limited versus full or plenary guardianships, and enhanced certification and monitoring of guardians. Improvements such as these are summarized yearly by the Commission on Law and Aging of the American Bar Association (2014). These improvements were clearly needed because abuses, lack of procedural protections, and poor court oversight of guardianships have been documented (Quinn, 2005). A seminal Associated Press report (Bayles & McCartney, 1987) of guardianship practices across the United States demonstrated that, for example, 44% of alleged incompetent individuals were not represented by an attorney and 49% were not at their own hearing, and about 34% of the files did not include supporting medical evidence. This movement can be viewed in the broader context of the patient and disability rights movements, as well as the deinstitutionalization of people with mental illness (Moye et al., 2013).

More important for our purposes, much of the influence on current capacity work has emerged from the evolution of state statutes and related case law, as well as a maturation of capacity science and theory. Early writing and conceptualization of both civil and criminal capacity issues were developed in English case law, which continues to influence the U.S. legal system (see Perlin et al., 2008, for extensive review). *Banks vs. Goodfellow* (1869–1870) is a particularly well-known case that influenced subsequent case law and research on testamentary capacity (Reed, 1979). In this case involving a contested will of a mentally ill man, the court ruled that a testator (person making a will) must understand the nature of the act of making a will and the nature and extent of his or her property and comprehend and appreciate the claims that he "ought to give effect." Moreover, though the testator may be mentally ill, he or she needs to be free of an "insane delusion" that may affect the disposal of the will (see later in the chapter for a full description of these criteria). Subsequent case law has demonstrated that a will may be invalidated if it was made on the basis of a delusion or if it was the product of undue influence (Perlin et al., 2008).

Unfortunately, relatively little empirical work has been done on testamentary capacity, and extant research is based on small samples. Roked and Patel (2008), for instance, found that AD severity was related to testamentary capacity as determined by clinicians, such that 63% of those with mild AD, 35% with moderate AD, and only 3% with severe AD were judged to possess testamentary capacity. In contrast, in a case study from Australia, a woman with severe aphasia was judged to possess testamentary capacity (Ferguson et al., 2003). Promising conceptual work by Marson, Hebert, and Solomon (2012) is partially based on case law and hypothesized that cognitive constructs, assessable in a neuropsychological evaluation, are related to testamentary capacity criteria in predictable ways. For instance, language skills such as semantic memory, verbal abstraction, and comprehension are proposed to be key to the understanding of a will and more important than abstraction. Although they have yet to be tested, Marson, Hebert, and Solomon's (2012) hypotheses provide a roadmap for empirically linking psycholegal criteria to cognitive functioning.

Much of the actual research on capacity issues emerges from psychology, particularly forensic psychology and neuropsychology. Such research, for instance, seeks to define a particular capacity, sometimes with help from statutes or case law as noted previously, develop a model of that capacity, operationalize it via a specific measure, and then examine that measure empirically. An excellent example of such work is the MacArthur Treatment Competence Study that operationalized decision making about medical treatment as the ability to communicate a choice, understand relevant information, appreciate the nature of the situation and likely consequences, and rationally manipulate information (Appelbaum & Grisso, 1995). These standards emerged from case law and legal precedent. The semistructured interview measure Appelbaum and Grisso (1995) developed to assess these standards—the MacArthur Competence Assessment Tool for Treatment (MacCAT-T)—is designed to assess these abilities regarding the examinee's medical issues. The measure has acceptable interrater reliability (Grisso, Appelbaum, & Hill-Fotouhi, 1997) and can be administered in about 15 to 20 minutes. Early work demonstrated, for instance, that patients with mental illness such as schizophrenia and depression perform worse than age-matched controls and medically ill patients (Grisso & Appelbaum, 1995) in all areas. Deficits were more pronounced in patients with schizophrenia. More recently, Raymont et al. (2004) examined the MacCAT-T in hospitalized medically ill patients with a wide variety of conditions and found that approximately 40% lacked medical decision-making capacity. Increasing age and cognitive impairment were associated with incapacity.

A more recent and excellent example of programmatic capacity research is Marson's work on financial capacity (see Marson, Triebel, & Knight, 2012, for review) that demonstrates a robust theoretical and empirical approach. In this approach, financial capacity is conceptualized to consist of three broad levels—specific, general, and overall or global capacity—that can be assessed on a measure he and colleagues developed, the Financial Capacity Instrument (FCI). The 18 FCI items range from the simple, such as naming and counting coins, to the complex, ranging from managing a bank statement and preparing bills to investment decision making. Research has indicated that the FCI is able to distinguish individuals with moderately severe AD from those with mild AD and nondemented elderly control participants (Marson, Sawrie, et al., 2000). Those with moderate AD were deemed "incapable" (as defined by the researchers and not a court) of performing essentially all financial tasks, whereas participants with mild AD were incapable of only the most complex tasks. Longitudinally, individuals with mild AD declined over a one-year period in both simple and complex financial domains (Martin et al., 2008) whereas elderly healthy controls did not decline.

The above findings on financial and testamentary capacity—and other similar work in medical decision making (see Palmer, Savla, & Harmell, 2012, for review)—address capacity as a clinical construct and on a continuum. Such findings are particularly relevant for clinical work, although they may be applied to court-ordered work as well. An important caveat, however, is that performance on such measures does not directly map onto the related legal constructs, nor does it predict ultimate incapacity adjudications. The development of capacity tests, however, seems to reify the underlying capacity and to "pull" for such legal either–or categorizations. An excessive focus on test results, without an understanding of test performance in broad clinical context, may result in automatic and reflexive use of such measures (Demakis, 2012a). Kapp and Mossman (1996) detailed cautions about a fictional "capacimeter" including, as suggested previously, a misconception about the nature of capacity and core conceptual problems such as where cutoffs would be set and whether sensitivity or specificity would be preferred.

Another concern is that such a test—and the quantification and categorization of capacity—may misdirect the psychologist from what the examinee needs to assist and improve autonomy. These concerns are in the context of capacity to make medical decisions, but they are applicable to other capacities as well. Kapp and Mossman (1996) concluded that clinical guidelines or practice parameters rather than simply capacity tests are needed to provide guidance for a broader and more nuanced examination. The detailed and useful publications resulting from collaborations between the American Bar Association (ABA) and American Psychological Association (APA) have produced such a helpful framework for such evaluations of older adults (ABA & APA Assessment of Capacity in Older Adults Project Working Group, 2008). Separate handbooks are designed for attorneys, psychologist, and judges, and they address some of the key questions Kapp and Mossman (1996) raised at the end of their article on the capacity examination.

In contrast to the work previously described, relatively little research has been done on capacity issues in the court setting. Much of this work has been descriptive. For instance, a high rate of individuals are found to be incapacitated (Dudley & Goins, 2003) and, despite attempts to improve protections for alleged incompetent individuals, limited guardianships are infrequently used (Moye, Wood, Edelstein, Armesto, et al., 2007). Similarly, this latter group of researchers concluded that the majority of written testimony in these cases was lacking because many did not address key issues such as diagnosis, prognosis, cognitive or psychiatric symptoms, functional abilities, values or preferences, and social system. The lack of such information would presumably affect the quality of the court's ultimate capacity decision. To our knowledge, only one study examined how well cognitive and functional variables predict actual court adjudications (Quickel & Demakis, 2013). Not surprisingly, it found that individuals adjudicated incompetent—they had a variety of psychiatric and neurological diagnoses—performed more poorly than those adjudicated competent on a range of neuropsychological and functional tests. These functional measures (select subtests of the Independent Living Scales) better predicted incompetency adjudications than cognitive tests such as the Mini-Mental State Examination or the Trail-Making Tests. This study was unique because competency decisions are public in this jurisdiction (North Carolina), thus allowing a unique opportunity to determine the factors that best predict such decisions.

EXPERT KNOWLEDGE AND FRAMEWORK FOR CAPACITY ASSESSMENT

The U.S. Supreme Court defined an expert witness as follows:

> If scientific, technical, or other specialized knowledge will assist the trier of fact to understand the evidence or determine a fact in issue, a witness qualified as an expert by knowledge, skill, expertise, training, or education, may testify thereto in the form of an opinion or otherwise if (a) the testimony is based upon sufficient facts or data, (b) the testimony is the product of reliable principles and methods, and (c) with this has applied the principles and methods reliably to the facts of the case. (*Federal Rules of Evidence,* 2010, Rule 702)

Rule 702 makes it clear that the role of the psychologist serving as a witness is to provide the court with scientific or technical information that the average nonpsychologist does not know. The psychologist must demonstrate that he or she has the appropriate training and experience to provide the court with reliable information, and the information must be relevant. This is a very different role from that of an attorney in the same case whose job it is to vigorously advocate for the position of the individual who retained his or her services. It is also a very different role from that of the judge, whose job it is to make a legal decision about the matter at issue. In the area of civil capacities, the trier of fact arrives at legal conclusions on the basis of the testimony of experts such as evaluating psychologists, psychiatrists, and health providers as well as nontechnical testimony from lay witnesses (nonexperts) who are familiar with the case. This legal determination is referred to as the ultimate issue. In most jurisdictions, a psychologist is permitted to state his or her opinion regarding the ultimate issue (e.g., the examinee lacked testamentary capacity at the time a will was signed or had sufficient understanding of a medical condition to be considered to possess capacity to make treatment decisions).

It should be noted that there is some controversy about whether psychologists or other experts should directly provide opinions regarding the ultimate issue in their testimony and reports. Some authors (e.g., Melton, Petrila, Poythress, & Slobogin, 2007) have contended that it is inappropriate for clinicians to express an opinion regarding the ultimate issue. Their rationale is that although conclusions regarding matters such as diagnosis and the relationship of diagnosis to behavior relevant to the current issue are based on scientific principles, conclusions regarding legal constructs such as testamentary capacity are primarily moral and are under the purview of the judge or jury. They have also stated that when psychologists directly address the ultimate issue, they are confusing the court by disguising what are basically commonsense opinions as scientific testimony. Grisso (2003, pp. 36–38) shares this opinion and suggested that although legal capacity constructs are often vaguely defined, practitioners should avoid opining regarding the ultimate issue. He suggested that, as the best way to assist the court, the psychologist should describe the examinee's abilities in detail, particularly in terms of incongruity between situation-specific demands (e.g., handling one's financial affairs, entering into a contract).

Other authorities have argued that it is not problematic for expert witnesses to proffer opinions regarding the ultimate issue. For example, Frolik (1999) stated that more latitude should be given to expert witnesses in probate matters because the court only needs to weigh the probative value of the testimony while reserving the ultimate legal decision to itself. Other authorities have suggested avoiding this issue by changing the terms used by psychologists in their reports and testimony regarding civil capacities. For example, *Assessment of Older Adults With Diminished Capacity: A Handbook for Psychologists* (ABA & APA Assessment of Capacity in Older Adults Project Working Group, 2008) suggested that confusion regarding the terms *competency*, which they regard as a legal term, and *capacity*, which refers to clinical observations and conclusions, could be avoided by adopting the phrases *legal capacity* and *clinical capacity* in describing conclusions reached in probate-related matters. Other authors have arrived at similar conclusions, suggesting that the expert's opinion regarding the ultimate issue in cases involving civil capacities is one piece of information that the court weighs in whatever manner seems appropriate and that expressing such an opinion does not necessarily usurp the prerogatives of the court (Mart & Alban, 2011). In the final analysis, the decision of whether to opine regarding the ultimate issue is a matter of personal and professional choice.

In keeping with the principle that an expert witness is an individual with specialized knowledge not readily available to the court, it is important that psychologists perform and describe their assessments in a manner that provides the court with a clear idea of the conceptual underpinnings of their methodology. The difficulties courts have in assessing the utility of expert opinions was clearly expressed by the New Hampshire Supreme Court (*State of New Hampshire v. Wayne Cressey*, 1993). In this case, a psychologist testified that the drawings of children suspected of having been sexually abused, along with the presence of repetitive dreams and dissociative symptoms, indicated that abuse had likely occurred. The court found this testimony problematic for a number of reasons, but the main issue was that the psychologist's reliance on the data was without a logical nexus between conclusions and the data relied on in reaching those conclusions. In the absence of an explicit nexus between these two elements of the psychologist's testimony, the court could not follow her reasoning to make an independent judgment about how such conclusions were reached. Although there are clearly important differences between child sexual abuse cases and the assessment of civil capacities, the concern of the New Hampshire Supreme Court that conclusions be logically related to data are relevant. For this reason, it is important that psychologists performing civil capacity assessments rely on an explicit methodology. In addition, the use of such a methodology facilitates performing assessments and providing testimony in an organized manner.

One widely used conceptual–methodological framework has been articulated by Grisso (2003), who included five components in a capacity assessment. The first of these is the functional component. In the assessment phase, the psychologist gathers data regarding the individual's ability to perform relevant activities associated with specific capacity. Examples of this type of data include the ability to manage medications, perform basic activities of living, manage finances, or enter into a contract. The functional assessment also examines whether the individual has the cognitive skills to understand the implications of choices and decisions associated with specific capacities. Examples of this include understanding the implications of undergoing or refusing a medical procedure or deciding whether one can afford to take out a loan at a specific interest rate.

It is important to note that this process is very different from a purely diagnostic assessment. The focus in the functional component of this methodology is what the examinee can or cannot do or understand rather than the presence or absence of a specific neuropsychological condition. Greenberg, Shuman, and Meyer (2004) noted that a diagnosis provides very little information to the court about an individual's functional abilities and may actually be misleading. For example, in an evaluation of an individual's competency to stand trial in a criminal case, an opinion to the court that the defendant has a mild intellectual impairment conveys essentially nothing about whether he or she understands the process of standing trial, has a reasonable grasp of the roles of trial participants, or is able to effectively consult with counsel. In the same way, in a case involving the determination of the presence or absence of testamentary capacity, a diagnosis of mild dementia in a testator provides the court with little information regarding that individual's grasp of the process of making a will. Furthermore, providing a diagnosis without functional assessment risks misleading the court because the judge may not be aware that many individuals with a similar condition have sufficient capacity to make a will or modify estate planning documents.

The second component of Grisso's (2003) methodology is the causal component, in which the psychologist provides the court with information that explains the underlying causes of observed functional limitations. This component of the assessment is important for several reasons. The first of these is that, as Grisso noted, the language of many statutes associated with civil capacities prescribe a two-step analysis. The statutes frequently require that "inability to care for oneself or one's property" must be "because of" or "as a result of" mental, developmental, or physical disability, to meet the standard for legal incompetence (Sabatino & Basinger, 2000, pp. 123–125). Grisso raised the question of why the law is concerned about the underlying cause of observed functional deficits. With regard to civil capacities, such an assessment is important because some functional deficits may be temporary or caused by transient circumstances or conditions. A classic example is delirium in an elderly individual caused by a urinary tract infection that quickly resolves with treatment. It is important to note that courts have traditionally considered the loss of personal liberty associated with the imposition of a guardian or conservator very seriously. For this reason, the legal system seeks reassurance that such loss of liberty and self-determination is likely to be required for a substantial amount of time or even permanently.

Grisso (2003) referred to the next component of his methodology as the interactive component. This component focuses on the individual's ability to perform specific functions in the context in which they are needed. In this component of the methodology, there is a recognition that individuals with similar levels of impairment may function adequately or inadequately depending on the situation. For example, Testator A with mild dementia may have the capacity to execute a will in which the issues are not complex. This individual may have a house that is paid off, money in savings, a life insurance policy, and two automobiles. He wishes to leave all of his possessions to his wife and, if she predeceases him, to his son and daughter in equal shares. Testator B, who has a similar level of mild dementia as Testator A, has very different circumstances. He has a large estate that includes interests in several businesses, multiple properties, a large portfolio of stocks and securities, and children from two marriages. Although his basic cognitive capacity is the same as that of Testator A, a psychologist may opine that he does not have the capacity to make changes in his estate planning because of the interaction between the complexity of the estate and his diminished cognitive ability.

Given that all civil capacities take place in a situational context, it is incumbent on the psychologist to carefully examine the interaction between the individual's cognitive abilities and what it is the individual is being required to do, whether it involves making a will, managing finances, or making decisions about medical treatment. Clearly, this requires analysis beyond a simple cutoff score on a test measuring a particular cognitive ability or functional skill.

Grisso (2003) referred to the final elements of his methodology as the judgmental and dispositional components. He defined these elements as follows:

> Legal competence constructs require a *judgment* that person-context incongruity is of a sufficient magnitude to warrant a finding of legal incompetence. Part of that judgment is based on the fact that when the judgment is made, law prescribes certain *dispositional* consequences. The competence decision sets a disposition in motion, and in that sense, the disposition is part of the legal competence construct.

> The interactive component, as described above, addresses questions of the degree to which a functional ability exists, how much is demanded by the situation, and how much of a discrepancy exists between the two. The judgmental component then addresses the ultimate question: *How much incongruity is enough toward a finding of incompetence?* (Grisso, 2003, p. 36)

Grisso stated that mental health professionals performing evaluations of civil capacities should address but not answer the question of whether the examinee retains enough functional ability to be considered legally competent. This task is achieved by describing the examinee's strengths and deficits in a manner that allows the fact-finder to apply his or her view of the legal standard to the data and to come to a legal conclusion regarding competence. Grisso reiterated his view that conclusions regarding the ultimate issue are moral or social judgments, but he also noted that many mental health professionals find that distinguishing between providing statements regarding the ultimate issue versus a description of the degree of ability and context demand is a distinction without a difference.

It has been our experience that not providing the court with an opinion regarding the ultimate issue is problematic for several reasons. The first is that this clinical and legal capacity–competence distinction is frequently lost on the court, just as it is with mental health professionals. For example, a statement that an examinee is experiencing significant difficulties with basic computation and that memory problems make it impossible for him or her to remember to pay bills in a timely fashion is generally seen as a statement that the individual is incompetent to manage his or her finances. A second problem is that courts have come to expect opinions regarding competence from psychologists and typically ask for this opinion directly if it is not provided in reports or testimony. Consequently, it is recommended that such opinions be provided, along with a statement that the final opinions regarding the ultimate issue rest with the court.

SPECIFIC CAPACITIES

Psychologists are uniquely suited to evaluate the specific capacities described below—testamentary capacity, health care decision-making capacity, and financial decision-making capacity—because these have developed research literatures and practice recommendations. These are not the only capacities that may be the focus of concern, but they are among the most common referral questions for clinical neuropsychologists.

Testamentary Capacity

Testamentary capacity refers to an individual's ability to make a valid will. The exact statutory language describing what abilities must be present in the testator varies from jurisdiction to jurisdiction but almost always follows what has been referred to as the *Goodfellow criteria. Banks v. Goodfellow* (1869–1870) defined testamentary capacity as follows:

> It is essential to the exercise of such a power that a testator [a] shall understand the nature of the act and its effects; [b] shall understand the extent of the property of which he is disposing; [c] shall be able to comprehend and appreciate the claims to which he ought to give effect; and with a view to the latter object, that no disorder of the mind shall poison his affections, pervert his sense of right, or prevent the exercise of his natural faculties—that no insane delusion shall influence his will and disposing of his property and bring about a disposal of it which, if the mind had been sound, would not have been made.

Similar language has been adopted in nearly all states. Consequently, when a neuropsychologist undertakes to assist the court in the determination of whether a testator had testamentary capacity at the time a will was executed, four functional abilities must be considered: (a) whether the testator understood the purpose of the document he or she was signing, (b) whether the testator had a general understanding of the property he or she intends to distribute, (c) whether the testator recalled the natural objects of his or her bounty (i.e., the people who would generally be expected to be beneficiaries such as spouses or children), and (d) whether or not a desire to leave property to persons other than natural objects was reasonable or whether it was the result of an "insane delusion." An insane delusion has been defined in various ways in different jurisdictions, but it is generally considered to be present when the testator harbors irrational or delusional perceptions of a person who would normally have been included in the will but is now excluded on the basis of that delusion. Examples of this would be a testator who has enjoyed a close relationship with his sons, but as a result of psychosis concludes they are minions of Satan and disinherits them, or a testator who disinherited his son because of a delusional belief that his son was an imposter, as might be seen in Capgras syndrome. These may be a basis for invalidating a will.

Psychologists may be requested to perform assessments of testamentary capacity in a number of contexts. One increasingly common situation is when an individual wishes to amend or make a new will and is concerned that there are parties who are likely to contest the will on the basis of lack of capacity. In these situations, attorneys for the testator may make a video record of an evaluation of the testator by the psychologist to be able to show, at a later date, that the testator understood the issues involved in making a will and was rational during the process. The existence of such a recording discourages unnecessary and expensive probate litigation when it is obvious that the testator possessed testamentary capacity.

A second context in which psychological evaluations are requested occurs when there is already a challenge to a will based on an allegation that the testator lacked capacity when the will was signed. In these situations, the general assessment techniques that were previously discussed should be used. The psychologist should obtain and review all relevant documents, including financial and medical records. If there were previous wills, they should also be reviewed so that the testator can be questioned regarding his or her reasons for making changes. It is also important to obtain the information necessary to determine whether the testator is providing accurate answers during the examination. For example, it is not possible to know whether the testator has a reasonable knowledge of his or her assets if the psychologist does not know what these assets actually are, and the same applies to knowledge of family members, financial transactions, and personal history. Medical records may document conditions such as dementia, delirium, stroke, or depression that may have an impact on the testator's cognitive abilities. It is also important to review medications that have been prescribed because a wide variety of medications can cause cognitive impairment, including benzodiazepines, antipsychotics, opiates, anticholinergics, and certain antihypertensives (Gray, Lai, & Larson, 1999). In addition, medical records may provide information as to whether the testator's mental state is declining gradually, as in most forms of dementia, or is fluctuating because of delirium. In the latter case, more information will have to be gathered to determine whether the will was executed during a lucid interval. A lucid interval is generally defined as a period of clarity or temporary improvement in mental state that may be sufficient so that a testator possesses capacity to execute a will or perform other related functions (Peisah & Shulman, 2012).

Once relevant documentation has been reviewed, the psychologist can commence the assessment proper. Although there are no empirically supported instruments available to assess testamentary capacity, a semistructured approach can be used to ensure that all relevant information is addressed. The Semi-Structured Interview for the Assessment of Testamentary Capacity is one example of this approach (Mart & Alban, 2011). Using this interview guide, the psychologist carefully questions the examinee in areas directly relevant to the legal criteria for testamentary capacity. Exhibit 14.1 presents the areas to be explored.

If there are no indications that the testator has deficits in any of these areas, it may not be necessary to proceed further. However, if the testator provides responses that are questionable or suggest incapacity, formal testing should be undertaken. Moreover, Peisah and Shulman (2012) reviewed the links between the legal criteria for testamentary capacity and the

Exhibit 14.1
Areas to Be Explored in Testamentary Capacity Evaluations

(a) Current living situation
(b) Financial situation
  (i) How supported?
  (ii) Assets
    (1) Checking accounts
    (2) Savings accounts
    (3) IRAs, pensions, Social Security, etc.
    (4) Properties
    (5) Businesses
    (6) Vehicles
    (7) Other assets
    (8) Indebtedness
  (iii) Understanding of purpose of will or trust
    (1) What is a will?
    (2) Why do people have them?
    (3) Do you have one?
    (4) Did you have one before the latest will?
    (5) How is the new one different from the last one?
    (6) Why are you making these changes?
    (7) With whom did you discuss these changes?
    (8) Do you have any misgivings about these changes? (Why or why not?)
  (iv) Natural objects of testator's bounty
    (1) Who do people usually leave their money to?
    (2) Why is that?
    (3) Questions regarding testator's decisions in relation to changes in will/trust.

Note. IRA = individual retirement account. From *The Practical Assessment of Testamentary Capacity and Undue Influence in the Elderly* (Supplementary materials CD, Semi-Structured Interview for the Assessment of Testamentary Capacity [SSIATC], pp. 1–8), by E. G. Mart and A. D. Alban, 2011, Sarasota, FL: Professional Resource Press. Copyright 2011 by Professional Resource Press. Adapted with permission.

underlying associated cognitive functions for these criteria. As examples, they suggested that crystallized semantic knowledge is required to fulfill the first criteria regarding understanding the nature of the will-making act and its effects. For understanding the extent of one's property, they submitted that the following cognitive abilities are required: (a) long-term semantic and autobiographical memory regarding assets; (b) recent episodic and working memory if there have been recent changes to the estate; (c) verbal learning; (d) assuming the testator had been informed about his or her estate; and (e) mathematical ability.

Many neuropsychological instruments can be used to assess the core cognitive abilities involved with testamentary decisional capacity. In some cases, the administration of a comprehensive intelligence test such as the Wechsler Adult Intelligence Scale—Fourth Edition may be indicated, because some of the functions indicated previously are evaluated by this test. In other cases, briefer instruments such as the Reynolds Intellectual Assessment Scales or the Wechsler Abbreviated Scale of Intelligence—Second Edition can be used, particularly when the examinee is likely to be fatigued by longer test administration. The Wechsler Memory Scale—Fourth Edition and other memory batteries such as the California Verbal Learning Test—Second Edition or the Rivermead Behavioural Memory Test can be used to explore various aspects of memory. Language can be assessed by means of instruments such as the Boston Diagnostic Aphasia Examination, and executive functions can be addressed through tests such as the Delis-Kaplan Executive Function System.

One test battery that is particularly useful in this context is the Neuropsychological Assessment Battery. This comprehensive neuropsychological test battery includes a screening module that provides normative scores for attention, memory, language, spatial, and executive domains. This screening module is particularly useful because the authors have calculated upper and lower cutoffs for each domain. Should the examinee score below these cutoffs, the full module for these domains need not be given because it is highly unlikely that further useful information will be elicited through more comprehensive testing. Using this testing approach with moderately or severely impaired examinees saves time and reduces the chances of false-positive results that might occur because of overtesting and fatigue. In other cases in which initial screening with instruments such as the Mini-Mental State Examination or the Montreal Cognitive Assessment indicates significant cognitive impairment, more detailed batteries such as the Repeatable Battery for the Assessment of Neuropsychological Status or the Dementia Rating Scale—2 can provide additional information about general neuropsychological functioning.

In cases in which psychiatric issues such as psychosis or mood disorders may have an effect on capacity, objective psychological tests can be used. The Minnesota Multiphasic Personality Inventory–2, Minnesota Multiphasic Personality Inventory–2 Restructured Form, or the Personality Assessment Inventory can be used, assuming the examinee can tolerate longer tests and has sufficient attentional and language resources to understand test content. The Minnesota Multiphasic Personality Inventory–2 Restructured Form may be superior in this context because it is briefer. In situations in which such lengthy testing is not practical, tests such as the Symptom Checklist–90 or Brief Symptom Inventory may be appropriate, although they do not include validity scales.

Another source of information that can be very important in these types of assessments is instruments completed about the testator by individuals who know him or her well. These instruments include adaptive behavior scales such as the Vineland Adaptive Behavior Scales, Second Edition, and the Adaptive Behavior Assessment System, Third Edition, that provide a detailed view of the examinee's ability to perform activities of daily living. A large number of dementia rating scales can also be used in this manner. For the assessment of emotional status, Achenbach's Adult Behavior Checklist (18–59 years) and Older Adult Behavior Checklist (60–90-plus years) can be completed by an informant. However, as noted previously, will contests occur because those close to the examinee are engaged in conflict over the will, and they may provide wildly different views of the individual's functioning. More objective and accurate ratings of behavior and cognitive and emotional status are generally obtained from individuals who do not have a stake in the outcome of the court proceedings.

One unusual feature of evaluations for determinations of testamentary capacity is that they are sometimes retrospective. In many cases, there is no challenge to the will until the testator is deceased and unavailable for direct evaluation. Obviously, in such situations there is no contemporaneous interview or testing. When this occurs, record review and information obtained from collateral informants may be the only available sources of information. Psychologists performing retrospective assessments should carefully review and document information that will provide the court with relevant information concerning the testator's cognitive, emotional, and behavioral functioning around the time a will was executed. There are situations in which a will was drawn up months or even years before it was executed, during a time when the testator clearly had capacity, but it should not be assumed that the testator had the same preferences and desires for the distribution of his or her estate at a later period of time. Testators must have capacity at the time the will is actually signed.

One area of retrospective assessment of testamentary capacity that has received recent attention is the issue of deathbed wills (Peisah et al., 2014). Peisah et al. (2014) noted that although clinicians are sometimes asked to proffer opinions about a dying testator's capacity at the time the will was written or executed, very little research has been done on the subject. However, they pointed out that many conditions present near death that affect cognitive functioning are commonly missed by medical personnel. For example, delirium is very common but infrequently assessed. In addition, the cognitive abilities of dying patients may be clouded by fatigue, severe pain, medications such as opiates and benzodiazepines, and depression and anxiety. The presence or absence of these factors should be explored thoroughly when wills are written or signed close to the testator's death.

Health Care Decision-Making Capacity

All jurisdictions in the United States require that absent incapacity, adult medical patients must voluntarily agree to undergo a procedure or treatment before such service is provided. This is referred to as informed consent and has been defined as "the requirement that a patient be apprised of the nature and risks of a medical procedure before the physician can validly claim exemption from liability for battery or from responsibility for medical complications" (Gifis, 2010, p. 269). As noted previously, one generally accepted view of the functional elements of the ability to provide consent to medical treatment includes the ability to express a choice, understand information regarding the treatment, appreciate treatment-related information, and make rational decisions.

An individual's ability to meet the four criteria previously noted can break down on a number of levels. Obviously, an individual who is comatose and unresponsive cannot give informed consent to any type of medical procedure. The same is true of patients with severely impaired cognition such as those with moderate to severe dementia or acute delirium. Other conditions such as severe depression may render a patient either unresponsive or apathetic, making it difficult or impossible for the patient to express a choice regarding treatment options or to comprehend provided information. However, it is possible for a patient to be able to express a choice and to fully understand the information provided to him or her and still not have the ability to provide informed consent. Examples of this would be a patient with bipolar disorder who is capable of expressing a choice and fully understands the information being provided about the treatment of that condition. However, because of the effects of this condition on judgment and reality testing, the patient may simply refuse to accept the fact that he or she has the disorder. In the same vein, a patient may fully appreciate his or her medical situation but vacillate about whether to have a certain procedure and be unable to settle on a course of action. In both of these situations, the patient would likely be considered to lack the capacity to provide informed consent.

Health care providers have an obligation to be reasonably sure that adult patients have the capacity to provide informed consent before applying diagnostic procedures or treatments. All jurisdictions have mechanisms for providing substitute judgments if a patient lacks the capacity to consent to treatment. For example, many individuals appoint a family member or other person as their health care agent through a durable power of attorney for health care. If the patient lacks capacity to give informed consent, this individual is empowered to make medical decisions in the patient's place.

The psychological assessment of ability to consent to medical procedures involves using a variety of techniques designed to provide information regarding the patient's functional abilities associated with health care choices, as well as the underlying causes of observed incapacity and the possibility of remediation of any deficits. As with other civil capacities, such assessments use a variety of techniques and instruments to make these determinations. As noted earlier, these include record review, clinical interview of the patient, collateral interviews with health care providers and family members, neuropsychological tests, and instruments specifically designed to address functional capacity and the underlying causes of observed deficits.

Because informed consent issues emerge so frequently in medical settings, many instruments have been developed to assist in the assessment of this issue. The MacCAT-T has been discussed previously and is one of the best-researched instruments of this type. However, there are others that use varying methods to obtain this information. One such instrument is the Hopemont Capacity Assessment Interview (Edelstein, 1999). The Hopemont is a semistructured interview designed to assess both the ability to give informed consent for medical procedures and financial capacity. The psychologist begins the interview by explaining that examinees have the right to make decisions about financial and medical matters. In the section related to capacity to make medical decisions, the psychologist explains that a physician should explain the benefits of a particular testing procedure as well the attendant risks. The idea that the choice involves making a decision about doing one of two or more things is also explained. After this general orientation, examinees are provided with a number of short stories about a friend asking them for advice about a medical decision, including the potential benefits and risks of two courses of action (e.g., taking or not taking prescribed medication and signing an advance directive that CPR should or should not be used in the event of a heart attack). Examinees are then questioned about the risks and benefits of these choices, how they would advise their friend, and their rationale for doing so. The use of the Hopemont provides information about where the process of providing informed consent may be impaired. In some cases, examinees simply cannot remember the available choices. Others may be unable to make a reasoned decision or may make their decisions on the basis of irrelevant information. Finally, some examinees may simply not be able to express a choice or decision.

In cases in which the ability to provide informed consent is impaired or absent, it is important for the psychologist to determine whether capacity can be enhanced. On one hand, if the underlying deficits are static or likely to worsen over time, as in long-standing traumatic brain injury or dementia, it is unlikely that remediation will be successful. On the other hand, in situations in which the level of impairment fluctuates, as in dementia caused by medications or infections, it may be possible to delay treatment until the acute confusion has resolved. It is also important for individuals who have regained capacity to have an in-depth discussion with their physician and family members to create advance directives consistent with their wishes and values if they become incapacitated in the future.

Financial Decision-Making Capacity

Financial capacity determinations emerge in a number of different psycholegal contexts. Financial capacity has been defined as "decision making regarding a number of financial tasks, such as general financial management of assets and debts, writing checks, paying bills, knowing and using currency and coin, making contracts, [and] writing wills" (ABA & APA Assessment of Capacity in Older Adults Project Working Group, 2008, p. 153). Assessment of financial capacity may be performed as part of a broader guardianship evaluation or may be undertaken as part of a more limited request for conservatorship (i.e., management of financial and estate-related matters only). Because financial transactions are one of the more complex civil competencies, there is a general recognition that there are individuals who have difficulty adequately managing their finances but can otherwise live independently. In such cases, a conservator may be appointed with the limited responsibility of paying bills, managing investments, and providing money for incidental expenses.

Although financial capacity has in the past been viewed as a set of abilities that an individual either did or did not possess, there has been a growing recognition that there are different levels of financial capacity. For example, some individuals with dementia cannot perform basic functions associated with managing their finances. Problems may include dyscalculia, loss of ability to understand basic financial concepts, or deficits in memory and cognition that interfere with tasks such as bill paying and bank statement management. In other cases, individuals maintain basic finance-related skills but lack the judgment necessary to manage investments or prevent themselves from being defrauded. For instance, Marson, Triebel, and Knight's (2012) conceptual model of financial capacity includes a range of skills ranging from basic monetary skills such as identifying and counting coins and currency to asset or estate knowledge and investment decision making. Other skills include checkbook and bank statement management and financial judgment to detect and avoid mail and telephone fraud.

As with other civil capacities, evaluation of financial capacity begins with a thorough assessment including a clinical interview. When the focus of the assessment is on financial capacity, the examinee should be questioned regarding understanding of financial issues generally and his or her own financial status specifically. It is also important to determine whether the examinee simply has little or no experience with financial matters. It is not uncommon for one member of a married couple or domestic partnership to have taken responsibility for managing the couple's finances. In these situations, a surviving spouse may have the potential for financial capacity but has never paid bills or managed finances.

A number of tests and procedures can provide information about financial capacity. These instruments use a number of approaches to obtain this information. One approach is to use the structured observations of others who know the examinee well to provide information about financial capacity. Adaptive behavior scales such as the Vineland Adaptive Behavior Scales, Second Edition, and the Adaptive Behavior Assessment System, Third Edition, cover a wide range of adaptive behaviors, including the ability to manage one's finances. One potential drawback of these instruments is that they rely on third parties to obtain this information, and the accuracy of the respondent's judgment may be affected by how well he or she knows the examinee as well as potential biases.

A second method of obtaining information about financial capacity is to use performance-based assessment techniques. One of these instruments is the Independent Living Scales (ILS), which contains a battery of subtests that use direct questions and performance on specific tasks to measure an individual's performance of activities of daily living. Domains include Memory/Orientation, Managing Money, Managing Home and Transportation, Health and Safety, and Social Adjustment. The Managing Money domain includes questions about the individual's financial status, ability to make change, steps taken to guard against fraud, and why bills must be paid. The examinee is also asked to perform tasks such as counting out a specific amount of money from a pile of change and calculating the copay on a medical bill. The performance-based items are particularly helpful in assessments of financial capacity because the examinee is required to complete tasks very similar to those that are required in daily life. The Language Module of the Neuropsychological Assessment Battery also includes a Bill Payment subtest that uses facsimiles of a bill, check, and check registry in a similar manner and also requires the examinee to fill out an envelope so that the check is sent to the correct address for payment.

As with other areas of civil capacity, psychological testing with traditional neuropsychological tests can be helpful in establishing the causes of deficits. With financial capacity, direct assessment of mathematical abilities and quantitative concepts is particularly important because an individual with impairments in these areas is unlikely to be able to perform the basic operations involved in managing finances. The Arithmetic subtest of the Wechsler Adult Intelligence Scale—Fourth Edition and the Math Computation subtest of the Wide Range Achievement Test 4 can both provide useful information. One newer IQ test that may be especially useful is the Reynolds Adaptable Intelligence Test. In addition to subtests that measure crystallized and fluid intelligence, it provides a Quantitative Intelligence Index. This index is composed of the Quantitative Knowledge and Quantitative Reasoning subtests. The Quantitative Knowledge subtest measures the ability to perform basic mathematical operations using both word problems and computational problems. The Quantitative Reasoning subtest requires numerical reasoning with less emphasis on formal mathematical calculation. Although the test was recently published and it has relatively little supporting research, it has the potential to provide information relevant to the assessment of financial capacity.

CAPACITY EXAMINATION

Although each of the capacities discussed in this chapter have different aspects and require specific assessment of these unique features, there is also a good deal of commonality in how they are assessed. A good psychological evaluation of a particular civil capacity should always include a number of features. Many of these features are also included in diagnostic assessments, but the emphasis in evaluations of civil capacities is often different.

A thorough record review is an essential feature of assessments of civil capacities. Psychologists performing such evaluations should obtain and review documentation from a variety of sources. These sources include relevant legal documents, because they help define the facts at issue and the positions of the parties. Such documents are useful in developing hypotheses that can be pursued with other techniques. They are also useful in providing context for any current disputes regarding the examinee's abilities and clearly define the issues that the court has identified as referral questions.

A review of the individual's medical records can be very important in cases involving civil capacities. There is sometimes an extensive record containing information about office visits and hospitalizations, which may provide information about an individual's neurological and psychiatric condition both leading up to and contemporaneous with the capacity issue. The information in these records can be helpful from a diagnostic viewpoint and also from the standpoint of functional assessment, particularly if the individual was hospitalized. Most hospitals have ongoing assessment of a patient's ability to perform activities of daily living, fall risk, and to some extent cognitive status. However, the psychologist should be cautious when reviewing these records, for several reasons.

In most medical examinations, whether they take place in the doctor's office or in a hospital, the physician performs a history and a physical. This includes checking vital signs as well as examination of respiratory, cardiac, abdominal, visual, and other systems. Some assessment of the neurological system is included, and a brief psychiatric screening is sometimes performed. The records from these examinations summarize the findings of the physician under the heading "physical examination." The neurological section of the examination generally contains some form of mental status examination. A formal mental status examination can be quite comprehensive and cover a wide variety of areas of mental function including mood and affect, thought processes, thought content, judgment, and insight. However, when examinations are performed in a medical context in which the patient's mental state is not the main focus, the mental status examination performed by the physician can be quite cursory. It is very common that the only notation regarding mental status will be a statement such as "Patient awake and alert, oriented x3, remote memory intact." Although such orientation information may be useful when reviewing records, it may also be misleading for several reasons. Similar to many brief tests of cognition, assessing orientation is a highly sensitive measure but may have deficient specificity. Put simply, if an individual is not fully oriented, there is a very high likelihood of some type of cognitive problem, whereas being fully oriented is not a reliable sign that the individual has no deficits that would affect civil capacity. Consequently, disorientation is likely to be very probative of cognitive deficiencies, but being fully oriented provides less useful information.

Another problem with this type of brief mental status examination is that it will sometimes miss delirium, which is quite common in elderly people with serious physical illnesses. It is estimated that anywhere from 15% to 60% of elderly patients experience delirium before or during hospitalization, but this diagnosis is missed by physicians 70% of the time and is often not suspected by family members or attorneys (Peisah et al., 2014). Although there are highly accurate tests for delirium such as the Confusion Assessment Method (Inouye et al., 1990), they are infrequently used in medical settings.

Other types of records can be helpful in assessing an individual's capacity in relation to specific civil competencies. For example, an examination of the individual's financial records provides information as to whether the examinee was managing his or her finances before the capacity issue being raised. A review of such documentation provides the psychologist with data regarding whether the individual was paying bills, keeping a checkbook, and accurately maintaining the check ledger. It is, however, important to note that an individual may be physically unable to perform such tasks because of physical infirmity but is able to direct another person to do so. A number of authors have referred to this distinction between what they term *decisional capacity,* which is the ability to make a reasonable decision, and *executional capacity* which is the ability to act on a choice (Collopy, 1988, as cited in ABA & APA Assessment of Capacity in Older Adults Project Working Group, 2008). Some civil capacities, such as the capacity to make health care decisions, involve only decisional capacity, and others, such as the capacity to drive, involve both decisional and executional capacities.

Depending on the type of assessment, other forms of documentation may be helpful. Education records provide a baseline that can be compared with current performance. Occupational records, if available, can also provide information regarding an individual's premorbid functioning. However, it is usually not necessary to review large volumes of prior records because most assessments of civil capacity deal with the individual's current level of functioning.

As previously noted, collateral interviews may also be an important source of information. Potential sources of information may include physicians, nurses, and other caregivers, and a face-to-face or phone interview may provide a depth of information unavailable in a record review. Statements from neighbors may also be useful, and it may also be important to speak to police officers who may have responded if the examinee has had acute episodes of confusion or agitation. Generally, it is useful to speak to anyone who has in-depth knowledge of an individual's functioning in a variety of settings. Interviewing individuals who have interacted with the examinee in different contexts can be important because some conditions may cause capacity to wax and wane. Examples of these types of conditions include delirium, metabolic encephalopathy, and sundowning. In addition, a variety of conditions can limit an individual's ability to accurately describe symptoms or history. Conditions such as depression or other mood disorders can mimic or coexist with organic conditions, and treating these may improve an individual's functioning such that he or she may eventually possess the capacity under consideration. In some cases, others who know the individual well may be able to provide a history that is helpful in making a differential diagnosis and obtaining treatment.

Family members can be useful sources of information, but caution must also be exercised. Family members may have an agenda that affects their objectivity or leads to actual misrepresentation of the examinee's capacities. This is particularly true in evaluations involving testamentary capacity or allegations of undue influence because conflict between the family members may have originally led to the referral. Another factor that can lead to unreliability in family reports is the frequent contact some family members may have with the individual. This may seem paradoxical, but because some forms of cognitive impairment progress gradually, family members may fail to notice signs of decline. When questioned closely, they may report that an elderly relative sometimes gets lost driving to their home, has a refrigerator full of spoiled food, neglects personal appearance, or misplaces keys or wallet, but instead of viewing these as indicative of cognitive decline, they will say, "That is just Uncle Jim." Consequently, it is important to ask detailed questions about specific activities and abilities in addition to allowing a relative to provide a narrative about the examinee's abilities.

Behavioral observations of individuals being assessed for civil capacities are essential. These occur contemporaneously with other activities and consist of the psychologist's observations of the examinee's appearance, mood, affect, speech and language, thought processes and content, cognition, insight, and judgment. All of these observations can help generate hypotheses that can be further assessed through psychometric testing. For example, an observation that the patient is apathetic should raise the possibility of depression or psychosis, whereas word-finding difficulty may suggest aphasia or dementia.

There is no substitute for a detailed, formal mental status evaluation, which should not be confused with a few simple questions that allow the examiner to note that the examinee is awake, alert, and oriented. A formal mental status examination also goes beyond the simple tests of orientation, registration, memory, speech, and praxis that make up instruments such as the Mini-Mental State Examination; the examination should contain these elements, but they make up only a portion of the entire examination. The mental status examination is analogous to the physical examination in medicine because it seeks to elicit objective signs of cognitive or emotional problems, as opposed to the clinical interview and history, which are methods of eliciting the examinee's experience and memory (Trzepacz & Baker, 1993).

Another essential component of civil capacity examinations is the clinical interview and history. Obtaining a good history can provide important information that bears directly on the referral questions and will typically include, for example, education and occupation history, medical and psychiatric history, activities of daily living, and the forensic issue that led to the referral (e.g., testamentary or financial capacity). It may also be helpful to use a structured or semistructured interview when eliciting this type of information. In his book on interviewing, Rogers (2001) stated that the semistructured or structured interview is helpful in psychological evaluations. He noted that the use of such interviews is superior to freewheeling, unstructured interviewing in that it ensures that the psychologist will remember to question the examinee on all important areas. In addition, standardized interviews have established reliability and validity (see Garb, 2005).

Because of the type of cases involving civil capacities, situations will often occur in which it is clear that the examinee is an unreliable reporter. For example, individuals with dementia may not recall some of the information the psychologist is attempting to elicit or may confabulate responses. This is, of course, important information in and of itself. When this occurs, the psychologist will have to rely more heavily on records and collateral sources of information.

Formal psychological and cognitive testing generally occurs subsequent to the clinical interview. Tests are performed in these types of assessments to provide information regarding both the functional and the causal components of Grisso's (2003) methodology. Two broad types of psychological tests are commonly used in civil capacity assessments. The first type consists of instruments designed to be similar to the capacities being assessed, and the second includes traditional neuropsychological tests. A wide variety of the former have been developed, but a typical example, as earlier noted, is the MacCAT-T (Grisso & Appelbaum, 1998b), which was developed to assist in the assessment of health care decision making. Grisso and Appelbaum (1998b) noted that the four functional abilities necessary for competence to consent to treatment are the ability to express a choice, to understand information relevant to treatment decision making, to appreciate the significance of that information for one's own health, and to reason with relevant information to weigh treatment options (Grisso & Appelbaum, 1998a).

The MacCAT-T is designed to address capacity to make health care decisions in a fixed sequence. The psychologist first explains that treatment providers have become concerned about the examinee's ability to make treatment decisions. He or she then provides the patient with an explanation of his or her condition, the nature of the proposed treatment, and the risks and benefits of that treatment. Once this has been accomplished, the psychologist then asks the patient to explain what was just learned about the condition and whether he or she agrees or disagrees with the information. This part of the MacCAT-T is designed to provide information regarding the examinee's understanding of his or her medical situation. Similar procedures are used to determine whether the patient understands the risks and benefits of the offered treatment options, and the patient is asked what he or she has decided to do and why. This type of direct functional assessment is typical of instruments designed to measure civil capacities, with the individual asked about understanding of the current situation, grasp of the available choices, and rationale for making a particular choice. These types of tests tend to have good ecological validity because they either directly assess the relevant capacity or use analogous scenarios to achieve the same result.

More traditional neuropsychological tests are also useful for addressing the causal component of Grisso's (2003) methodology. However, in general practice it is unusual for neuropsychologists to perform extensive test batteries in situations involving civil competencies. There are a number of reasons for this. One of these is that the bar for possessing capacity to make a will, manage one's finances, or make decisions regarding medical care is relatively low, and subtle problems in memory, language, attention, or executive function are unlikely to render an individual incapacitated. Consequently, the types of fine-grained diagnostic assessments that a neuropsychologist might perform for other types of referral questions are generally not required. Another factor is that some individuals assessed for civil capacity are elderly and may become fatigued by extensive testing, even if spread over several days.

For this reason, brief screening batteries or combinations of short standalone tests are often sufficient in this context. Examples of screening batteries that are useful include the Repeatable Battery for the Assessment of Neuropsychological Status, the screening module of the Neuropsychological Assessment Battery, and the Dementia Rating Scale—2. These screening batteries may be supplemented with other tests as appropriate. There may be occasions when modifications of standard assessment procedures or more extensive testing may be appropriate. For example, an individual with expressive language problems may be capable of expressing choices and rationales for decisions involving finances or health care in writing or using assistive technology, but not orally (Mart, 2012).

REPORT WRITING

Generally speaking, writing reports related to assessments of civil capacities is no different than writing any other type of forensic psychological report. Certain well-known components should be part of the report such as, for example, the reason for the referral, evaluation techniques, behavioral observations, clinical interview, and test results. The level of detail included in the reports is a matter of professional judgment. The APA (2017) *Ethical Principles of Psychologists and Code of Conduct* (hereinafter referred to as the Ethics Code) states the following in Standard 4.04 (Minimizing Intrusions on Privacy): "Psychologists include in written and oral reports and consultations, only information germane to the purpose for which the communication is made" (p. 7).

Although a thorough clinical interview and history is an essential component of any psychological assessment, information will be elicited that has no direct bearing on the referral questions. As such, it is important that sufficient information be included to provide the court with an accurate picture of the individual's past and present functioning while avoiding the inclusion of irrelevant, embarrassing, or potentially damaging personal information.

It is also important to note that forensic psychological reports are written for and consumed by nonpsychologists. The format and use of terms of art should be designed to be understandable and useful to the court while still providing the type of technical information that would allow another psychologist to understand the results of the assessment and testing in more detail. The latter goal can be achieved by the use of an appendix that includes scores, percentiles, and confidence intervals for each test administered. However, overly technical explanations in the actual report may confuse the reader unless steps are taken to prevent this. Wherever possible, jargon should be avoided, and the results should be described in plain English. One approach is to clarify the meaning of a potentially confusing term in the text. For example, an examinee may have significant deficits in working memory and a *T* score of 25 on a test of working memory. This could be clarified by adding a statement such as "*Working memory* refers to the ability to hold information in short-term memory and manipulate it to solve problems. Mr. Smith's *T* score of 25 indicates that his level of working memory is below the 1st percentile of individuals in his age group." Another way of making reports more understandable to nonpsychologists is to describe what the individual is and is not able to do when faced with various tasks. Stating "When Mr. Jones was asked to tell me about his health over the last year, he correctly stated that he had suffered from heart failure but did not mention that he was being treated for gout, glaucoma, and thyroid problems, even when prompted" helps the court understand the impact of the examinee's diminished capacity on daily functioning.

Retrospective reports such as those done on a deceased testator present a unique challenge. The Ethics Code makes it clear that when it is not possible to have a face-to-face interview with the examinee, the psychologist is obliged to mention this and to acknowledge the limitations of not having performed such an interview. One way of doing this is to cite the actual section of the Code and then provide a brief discussion of why it was still possible to provide the court with an opinion. Doing so both satisfies the ethical requirement to supply this information and also prevents any appearance that the psychologist was attempting to obscure these limitations.

ETHICAL ISSUES

As in any area of clinical practice, sensitivity to ethical issues is important in capacity evaluations. For psychologists, APA's (2017) Ethics Code provides an overarching ethical framework for clinical practice, and the Specialty Guidelines for Forensic Psychology (APA, 2013) provide more specific coverage of forensic issues. The fact that the forensic guidelines are the only guidelines promulgated by APA for a specialty practice area speaks to the unique issues that may arise in forensic practice. Though we briefly touched on ethical issues previously, in this section we focus on these issues and first review select generic ethical issues most relevant for capacity issues and then focus on more specific capacity-based issues. The reader is referred to the following sources for more in-depth examination of ethical issues as applied to capacity issues (Kontos, Freudenreich, & Querques, 2013; Moberg & Shah, 2012) and clinical neuropsychology more broadly (Bush, 2007). We note the number of each Ethics Code standard addressed below.

Relevant Generic Issues

Competence (Standard 2.01). Competence—of the practitioner, that is—is an essential ethical ingredient of a successful capacity evaluation. In other words, the psychologist should possess the necessary skills, training, and experience to accurately address the referral question. Such skills will typically encompass several areas of clinical psychology and clinical neuropsychology (in the case of an examinee with neurological issues), including clinical interviewing, psychological assessment (including cognitive, functional, and emotional functioning), psychopathology, substance abuse, and family systems and dynamics. A strong grounding in medical issues and medications, their effects on cognition and psychological functioning, and possible side effects is paramount. In addition to these explicit psychological issues, knowledge and understanding of relevant state statutes, case law, and local practices and customs regarding capacity issues is particularly important in legal cases. In our view, neuropsychologists are uniquely suited to conduct these evaluations and, should they desire additional training, this chapter and its references are good places to start. Of course, consultation with a colleague experienced in such evaluations would be appropriate as well.

Bases for and use of assessments (Standards 9.01–9.02). As previously described, an important consideration in any capacity evaluation is a proper framework to guide one's work as well as use of the proper assessment techniques (e.g., interviews and tests). As articulated in the Ethics Code, a proper framework with appropriate techniques will ensure that the basis for the examination is "sufficient to substantiate their findings" (Standard 9.01a; APA, 2017, p. 12) and that techniques are "appropriate in light of the research on or evidence of the usefulness and proper application of the techniques" (Standard 9.02a; APA, 2017, p. 12). The framework should be guided by the referral question and informed by relevant conceptual and theoretical work. Two often-cited frameworks are those provided by Grisso (2003; detailed above) and the ABA and APA Assessment of Capacity in Older Adults Project Working Group (2008) collaboration on capacity evaluations. The ABA and APA document includes the following "pillars of capacity": medical condition, cognition, everyday functioning, values and preferences, and the risk of harm or level of supervision needed. In addition, many sources now detail both an approach for selecting appropriate tests (Sullivan, 2012) and specific recommendations for which tests to use in various domains. As previously noted, an important caveat is that performance on any one test does not equate to capacity because there is no "capacimeter"; rather, test results need to be integrated into the broader contours of the evaluation such as medical records, collateral interviews, and behavioral observations.

Relevant Capacity-Specific Issues

Respect for people's rights and dignity (Principle E). According to the Ethics Code, "Psychologists respect the dignity and worth of all people, and rights of individuals to privacy, confidentiality, and self-determination" (APA, 2017, p. 4). Although all of these issues are important for capacity evaluations, the respect for self-determination or autonomy is particularly relevant. Respect for autonomy is one of the four bioethical principles or common moral norms described by Beauchamp and Childress (2009)—the others are nonmaleficence, beneficence, and justice—and a key component of the Patient Self-Determination Act enacted by Congress in 1990 that focused on health care decision making (part of the Omnibus Budget Reconciliation Act of 1990). Autonomy presupposes adequate receipt and understanding of information, again particularly relevant in health care decision making, as well as voluntariness or the ability to make decisions without manipulation, coercion, or undue influence. These latter issues can sometimes be problematic in capacity assessments (Quinn, 2002). Respect for autonomy is contrasted with paternalism, which tends to arise when an individual with capacity makes a decision considered unwise by another or that does not conform to societal expectations. This, however, does not necessarily reflect a lack of capacity—individuals are free to make apparently bad or poor decisions; the criteria for capacity is not the quality of the decision per se. This respect for autonomy and the examinee's wishes and desires is critical in capacity evaluations because the recommendation or outcomes of these evaluations can meaningfully restrict rights and freedom.

For instance, the clinical capacity evaluation may provide a recommendation to provide unwanted (but perhaps medically necessary) treatments or procedures or, in a different context, provide part of the rationale by which an examinee may lose driving privileges. Even though not a legal judgment per se, Marson, Savage, and Phillips (2006) asserted that the clinician's findings have "adjudicative significance, as they are accepted by client and family members, and usually result in actual restrictions on autonomy" (p. 86). Even more troubling, a legal capacity evaluation may provide a recommendation that strips the examinee of essentially all rights and assigns a guardian to make decisions for the examinee. This loss of freedom, autonomy, and decision making can be devastating. Because examinees have so much to lose in such cases, most states have a high bar for meeting incapacity criteria—"clear, cogent, and convincing"—is a common one. Nonetheless, psychologists should not fail to make appropriate incapacity recommendations because of the fear of violating examinees' rights and dignity. As described earlier, psychologists are on solid footing when they are sufficiently competent to make such decisions and complete a thorough and appropriate examination.

It is important to note that, when involved, the psychologist does not restrict the rights of examinees per se. Attending clinicians, family members, judges, juries—among others—do this by virtue of their respective roles or responsibilities. What is clear, however, at least in the legal setting, is that the trier of fact tends to follows the recommendation of the clinician. This has been found repeatedly in competency to stand trial decisions. For instance, Zapf, Hubbard, Cooper, Wheeles, and Ronan (2004) found only one case of judge–clinician disagreement in 300 cases of defendants referred for competency-to-stand trial evaluations in Alabama. To our knowledge, only one study (Quickel & Demakis, 2013) examined this issue in civil capacity evaluations and found 92% judge–psychologist capacity agreement across individuals with a variety of clinical diagnoses in North Carolina. There is simply no such data on clinical cases, though we would expect the same dynamic between clinicians and family members, with the latter following the psychologist's recommendations. In any case, the psychologist's opinion tends to have a meaningful impact on the ultimate disposition of the case.

The other side of this focus on self-determination and autonomy is the next sentence in the Ethics Code: "Psychologists are aware that special safeguards may be necessary to protect the rights and welfare of persons or communities whose vulnerabilities impair autonomous decision making" (APA, 2017, p. 4). If it can be reasonably concluded that an individual is at risk and in danger because of incapacity—perhaps an elderly person living alone with significant difficulties with activities of daily living or an individual with a severe traumatic brain injury who is spending money recklessly—psychologists take appropriate steps to protect such individuals. Ruchinskas (2012) described the challenges in judging and managing risk in capacity assessments and made two key points. First, as risk increases, so too does the need for higher levels of decision-making capacity. For instance, the reasoning necessary to make a decision about life or death treatment is different than that for an optional medical procedure. Such a determination demands a careful analysis of the examinee's abilities, as well as environmental supports and challenges. Second, in some cases it may be more beneficial to alter the environment of or the demands on the examinee (e.g., safety proofing a home) rather than engaging in these sometimes difficult risk estimations. Overall, this dynamic—preserving the rights of examinees while also protecting them—requires a careful and nuanced perspective that is at the heart of the capacity evaluation. Of course, where to draw this line in an individual case is not easy, particularly in the case of an examinee whose psychiatric stability may fluctuate or an individual post–traumatic brain injury who is still improving.

Multiple relationships (Standard 3.05). Psychologists refrain from multiple relationships when they "could reasonably be expected to impair the psychologist's objectivity, competence, or effectiveness in performing his or her functions as a psychologist, or otherwise risks exploitation or harm to the person" (APA, 2017, p. 6) who is being evaluated. These relationships may occur in capacity evaluations when a psychologist is asked to evaluate the capacity of a client he or she is treating in psychotherapy or, alternatively, when asked to treat a patient that the psychologist has already evaluated. Much has been written about how the therapeutic and forensic roles differ and, in fact, may conflict (Greenberg & Shuman, 1997), although there is some disagreement about aspects of the distinction (e.g., Bush, 2005; Bush, Connell, & Denney, 2006). Briefly, a therapist is supportive, accepting, establishes an alliance with the client, and seeks benefit for the patient via assessment or therapy. In contrast, in a forensic evaluation, the psychologist adopts a neutral and objective stance toward the examinee, advocates for his or her opinion rather than for the examinee, and supplements information from the client with records and collateral sources as opposed to sole reliance on the client. Moreover, in a legal capacity evaluation, the client is the court—assuming the examinee has been court referred—and the psychologist works to assist the court in answering a particular psychologal question. Attorneys may also be clients as well; clinically, the psychologist works for the client, a more traditional and well-understood role. Keeping these professional roles separate is particularly important in a capacity evaluation referred by the court (Packer, 2008).

In the experience of one the authors (Demakis), capacity evaluations conducted by treating physicians who blur these roles are not particularly useful. These professionals tend to (a) uncritically accept the examinee's position or one side of the family's position even in the context of family conflict, (b) rely on relatively little and sometimes biased information to formulate an opinion, and (c) not know the state statutes governing legal capacity. In fact, their opinions tend to be brief, sometimes only a paragraph, and to advocate for their patient even though the court needs a thorough and objective assessment. Again, in Demakis's experience, such opinions are generally not perceived as particularly informative by the court and, even in the case of several such opinions, a more thorough capacity evaluation may be requested.

Informed consent for decisionally impaired persons (Standards 3.10 and 9.03). Perhaps one of the most vexing ethical issues in capacity evaluations is how to obtain informed consent—a key ethical feature of psychological practice—from those individuals who may not possess the capacity to provide such consent. A relevant section from the Ethics Code on informed consent addresses this apparent paradox:

> For persons who are legally incapable of giving informed consent, psychologists nevertheless (1) provide an appropriate explanation, (2) seek the individual's assent, (3) consider such person's preferences and best interests, and (4) obtain appropriate permission from a legally

> authorized person, if such substitute consent is permitted or required by law. When consent by a legally authorized person is not permitted or required by law, psychologists take reasonable steps to protect the individual's rights and welfare. (APA, 2017, pp. 6–7)

A related section on providing informed consent in assessment from Standard 9.03, informed consent in assessments, states the following:

> Psychologists inform persons with questionable capacity to consent or for whom testing is mandated by law or governmental regulations about the nature and purpose of the proposed assessment services, using language that is reasonably understandable to the person being assessed. (APA, 2017, p. 12)

A bit of context is important to understand this issue (see Gottlieb & Coleman, 2012, for a fuller discussion). First, whether the examinee can reasonably provide informed consent is unknown—the same cognitive abilities necessary to provide this are likely to be similar to those questioned in an evaluation regarding, for instance, an examinee's ability to consent to a medical procedure or to make financial decisions. At the outset of the evaluation, the capacity to provide informed consent is not known, but at least some difficulties with decision making would not be unexpected. However, if it becomes clear that the examinee lacks capacity to consent, the key issue becomes one of obtaining assent or agreement to participate rather than informed consent per se to participation, because the individual does not have capacity to provide informed consent. If the individual cannot provide informed consent, assent should be obtained, and the psychologist should, according to Johnson-Greene (2005), (a) explain the nature and purpose of the evaluation, (b) use language that is reasonably understandable, (c) consider the examinee's preferences and best interests, (d) take reasonable steps to protect the examinee's rights and welfare, (e) obtain substitute consent when permitted or required by law, and (f) document the written or oral assent. In addition, information about where and to whom the report will be sent is appropriate for discussion, and the examinee should have an opportunity to ask questions. If appropriate, the examinee's family or attorney—if he or she has one—can become part of the process of informing the examinee. Overall, Moberg and Shah (2012) provided good advice to the psychologists in such cases: "Because of cognitive impairment, poor health literacy, and individuals coming from culturally and linguistically disadvantaged backgrounds, the vocabulary used in this discussion should be simple and avoid any medical jargon" (p. 269).

This information is relevant for an individual presumed to have capacity and not under guardianship. Should the examinee have a guardian, the guardian is required to provide informed consent, and it would presumably be done in a manner consistent with the values and preferences of the examinee. In the case of a capacity evaluation that is ordered by the court, the examinee cannot truly provide informed consent, because, at least theoretically, failure to comply with this request could result in a contempt of court charge. Realizing the sensitivity of such an issue in civil capacity examination, there is no provision in North Carolina state statute to compel presence at a capacity evaluation for an individual who refuses, nor is there apparently any legal penalty for failure to appear.

CONCLUSION

Clinical neuropsychologists have much to offer referral sources when capacity issues are raised, and they made significant contributions to the conceptual and empirical study of various capacity issues. More empirical work, however, is needed. We predict such issues will increase in the future given the aging of our society, and there will be increased emphasis on patient autonomy and decision making even in the face of serious medical and psychiatric illness, as well as greater access to life-extending technology (Kontos et al., 2013). Research is needed in the two types of assessments previously noted, legal and clinical. Demakis (2012b) broadly reviewed the literature and provided several areas for future research. Although there was some research in each area of capacity assessment, it was fairly sparse and without broad applicability. Here we provide several key unanswered questions in each domain and provide illustrative references that may help provide direction for future research.

- *Practice patterns (Moye, Wood, Edelstein, Armesto, et al., 2007).* What psychological tests do neuropsychologists routinely use to make capacity recommendations? How do they incorporate the resulting findings into capacity decisions? How do they incorporate (or not) state statutes into recommendations? What is the format of capacity reports?
- *Psychological tests (Sullivan, 2012).* Which psychological tests best assess each type of capacity (testamentary, financial, and medical decision making)? Is there a preferred format (self-report vs. performance based)? What are the normative data and psychometric characteristics of these tests? Which tests best predict the ultimate court capacity decision in court-based cases?
- *Trier of fact* (see Chapter 20, this handbook). How does the trier of fact (typically a judge, but a jury in some states) use findings and recommendations from psychological reports? How are these data best weighed relative to other data sources such as behavioral observations, medical records, family testimony, and the like?
- *Multicultural considerations (Blackhall, Murphy, Frank, Michel, & Azen, 1995).* How do racial and cultural differences affect capacity issues such as cognitive performance, trier of fact decision making, and subsequent guardianship? More broadly, are there ethnic differences in attitudes toward autonomy and independence that may affect whether a family pursues guardianship?
- *Testamentary capacity (Mart & Alban, 2011; Shulman, Cohen, Kirsh, Hull, & Champine, 2007).* How can this capacity—arguably the least studied empirically—best be modeled and evaluated? How is this capacity related to state statute and case law on testamentary capacity?
- *Family conflict (Peisah, Brodaty, & Quadrio, 2006; Quinn, 2002).* How do undue influence and family conflict influence the presentation and adjudication of capacity issues? More important, what are the key indicators of undue influence? What are the best ways to prevent, intervene, and manage undue influence?

Two additional areas would benefit from additional research—basic data on the prevalence, nature, and disposition of competency cases across the United States and sexual consent capacity. In contrast to research on adjudicative competency or competency to stand trial (e.g., Denney, 2012; Pirelli, Gottdiener, & Zapf, 2011), relatively little is known—even the basics—about court-based competency evaluations (e.g., see Uekert & Schauffler, 2008). For instance, how many individuals have been adjudicated incompetent and are under guardianship in the United States is not known, nor is much known about the demographics, diagnoses, family context, and dynamics of such evaluation or the nature, extent, and quality of subsequent guardianships. There are a few examples of work in this area such as that of Quickel and Demakis (2013) in North Carolina and Moye, Wood, Edelstein, Wood, et al. (2007) in Colorado, Pennsylvania, and Massachusetts. These studies were unique because by publicly examining available court files they were able to provide information about allegedly incompetent individuals and how incompetency decisions are made by the courts. These studies, then, provide a slice of capacity issues across the United States, and the question of how they generalize to other states remains salient. Yet, such information is important for determining the future judicial, legal, and mental health resources necessary to properly adjudicate capacity cases. This is especially important considering that the U.S. population continues to age and capacity cases are likely to increase. From a psychological perspective, Moye, Wood, Edelstein, Armesto, et al.'s (2007) work is particularly valuable in demonstrating the quality (or lack thereof) of competency reports, which can be used as a starting point for training, and Quickel and Demakis (2013) demonstrated the value of functional measures for predicting judicial adjudications. Both of these studies can help guide clinical practice and research.

Two additional points regarding the recommendation for additional research are important. First, there is some research on competency and guardianship practices in various states, but it has been survey based (Karp & Wood, 2007; Uekert, 2010) with lower than desired response rates. Unfortunately, very little, if any, information regarding competency and guardianship data is available in any systematic way from the states because technological applications and innovations in this area lag, though there are select exceptions (for examples, see Uekert & Schauffler, 2008). Naturally, this research also provides little information or guidance for clinical practice, but it may have impact at the policy level, which is why it remains important. Another issue, as previously noted, is that the competency and guardianship process is under control of the states and not the federal government. As such, there is variability in state terminology and definitions of an individual in need of guardianship (Demakis, 2013), competency restoration standards and processes (Cassidy, 2013), and provisions for clinical evaluations (Mayhew, 2005). Moreover, as of 2011, Moye and Naik documented that more than 272 bills had been voted into law reworking capacity and guardianship issues within the past 20 years across all 50 states. Such variability in state statutes and the fact that these cases are sometimes moving targets adds to the complexity of conducting research in this area.

Sexual consent capacity is a topic that needs further conceptual and empirical refinement—of the little published work on this, the following vivid case study provides a sense of the contours of this work. Marson and Huthwaite (2005) detailed a case in which a 76-year-old woman with dementia, residing in a nursing home, engaged in sexual relations with the middle-aged son of another resident. This occurred after the man removed her from the nursing home without the knowledge or consent of the nursing home or her family. The man alleged that the sex was consensual. Marson was retained by the plaintiff's attorney in a civil case against the nursing home and, on the basis of his evaluation, concluded that she lacked capacity to consent to sexual relations, using the criteria previously described—the ability to make a choice as well as the ability to understand, reason about, and appreciate the consequences of her choice. Interestingly, Marson was consulted after the woman had died; his retrospective evaluation included a review of medical and neuropsychological records, interviews of collateral sources of information, and review of a videotape of the woman the day after the alleged rape in which the family asked her about the events (she did not recall them). The case against the nursing home was settled out of court, and the man was eventually convicted of kidnapping, sexual assault, and rape and, at the time of this publication, was serving a 10-year prison sentence.

Although this case is illustrative in some ways, it differs from other cases involving sexual consent capacity, particularly when it arises in a longer-term relationship: Does a wife with moderate dementia living in a nursing home possess capacity to consent to sexual relations with her husband? If so, how and by whom should such consent be determined? Should the husband have a role in deciding this—an obvious conflict of interest—if he is her guardian? Can two adults with intellectual disabilities engage in sexual relations? Can an adult with intellectual disability consent to sexual relations with an individual who does not have cognitive impairment? How is potential coercion or undue influence factored into the latter scenario?

In addressing these and related questions, it is important to note first that there has been a movement to protect and promote the sexual rights of individuals with possible capacity issues (Lyden, 2007). There has been a concomitant increase in the recognition that sex may confer a variety of positive health and psychosocial benefits (see White, 2010, for review). The past was marked by paternalism and repression for many of these individuals, including, at the most extreme, sterilization. It is further important to note that sexual issues differ from other capacity issues in key ways. First, sexual issues are particularly difficult for some individuals (of all ages) to address in an open and forthright manner. This is especially true if other family members became involved—adult children for the elderly patient with dementia and parents of those with intellectual disabilities—in decision making. Second, decisions about sex, in some cases at least, need to be made on the spot and perhaps with little time to reason through the risks and benefits (Mona et al., 2010). In contrast, more lead time is typically available to make decisions about health care and finances, allowing for consideration of pros and cons of a particular action.

In this context, it is thus not surprising that there is relatively little empirical work in this area, although there has been some relevant case law and state statutes that have helped shape thinking (Christopher & Pinals, 2010; Lyden, 2007). What is known empirically? Work by Kennedy (2003) and Bogacki, Armstrong, and Stuempfle (2004) is representative of the little research in the area; both of these studies examined the cognitive correlates of sexual consent capacity in middle-aged adults with mental retardation. Kennedy defined capacity based on an assessment tool designed to assess issues such as understanding of the nature of sexual contact and the ability to resist coercion. Using well-known neuropsychological measures such as the California Verbal Learning Test and Wisconsin Card Sorting Test, she found—not surprisingly—that most measures discriminated between groups deemed competent versus not competent to consent to sex. Paralleling these findings, Bogacki et al. found that institutionalized adults with mental retardation who scored low on a measure the authors created—Social Sexual Awareness Scale—also had low levels of intelligence and adaptive functioning. Participants with low scores were also more likely to be under guardianship than participants who with higher scores. These two studies highlight the importance of cognitive functioning in sexual consent capacity.

To our knowledge, there is only one measure—a structured interview for nursing home residents—designed to assess sexual consent capacity in these individuals, although these questions certainly apply to other types of patients as well. Lichtenberg and Strzepek's (1990) instrument includes the following three broad domains with representative questions:

- Patient's awareness of the relationship: Is the patient aware of who is initiating sexual contact? Does the patient believe that the other person is a spouse and thus acquiesce out of a delusional belief, or is the patient cognizant of the other's identity and intent? Can the patient state what level of sexual intimacy he or she would be comfortable with?
- Patient's ability to avoid exploitation: Is the behavior consistent with formerly held beliefs or values? Does the patient have capacity to say no to any uninvited sexual contact?
- Patient's awareness of potential risks: Does the patient realize that this relationship may be time limited (e.g., if placement on the unit is temporary)? Can the patient describe how he or she will react when the relationship ends?

This instrument was designed to be administered in two parts—an initial interview of the patient with a same-sex professional and then review by an interdisciplinary team who provided feedback that "supported or contradicted the patients' responses" (Lichtenberg & Strzepek, 1990, p. 119). Competency decisions were then made. The authors detailed that over the course of a year on a dementia unit, the instrument was used five times and judged a success. Although based on limited data, they found that patients deemed competent performed better on the Mini-Mental State Examination than those found not competent.

Despite this latter finding, this measure has not been subject to much empirical examination, but such research would be welcome. Understanding the specific cognitive correlates of sexual consent capacity in elderly adults would help in better understanding what constitutes this capacity and would allow for prediction of patients at high risk for sexual exploitation. Such work has already been done with health care consent capacity (e.g., Palmer & Savla, 2007). Of course, a more thorough understanding of related (a) emotional and psychological issues, (b) interpersonal and family dynamics, and (c) cultural issues, including spiritual and religious beliefs, would also be valuable because they are likely to have a key role in sexual consent as well.

Finally, it is important to note that some statutes address this capacity and, as with other capacities, the states vary (Lyden, 2007). For example, in New York an individual must be capable of understanding the social mores of sexual behavior—an arguably high standard—along with the nature and possible consequences of sexual behavior. New Jersey only requires that the individual voluntarily engage in sexual relations and understand the sexual nature of the act. At the very least, application of the empirical findings must be sensitive to state statutes and the related case law.

References

American Bar Association & American Psychological Association Assessment of Capacity in Older Adults Project Working Group. (2008). *Assessment of older adults with diminished capacity: A handbook for psychologists*. Retrieved from http://www.apa.org/pi/aging/programs/assessment/capacity-psychologist-handbook.pdf

American Psychological Association. (2013). Specialty guidelines for forensic psychology. *American Psychologist, 68,* 7–19. http://dx.doi.org/10.1037/a0029889

American Psychological Association. (2017). *Ethical principles of psychologists and code of conduct* (2002, Amended June 1, 2010 and January 1, 2017). Retrieved from http://www.apa.org/ethics/code/index.aspx

Appelbaum, P. S., & Grisso, T. (1995). The MacArthur Treatment Competence Study. I: Mental illness and competence to consent to treatment. *Law and Human Behavior, 19,* 105–126. http://dx.doi.org/10.1007/BF01499321

Banks v. Goodfellow (1869–1870 L.R. 5 Q.B. 549).

Bayles, F., & McCartney, S. (1987). *Guardians of the elderly: An ailing system, part I*. Retrieved from http://www.apnewsarchive.com/1987/Guardians-of-the-Elderly-An-Ailing-System-Part-I-Declared-Legally-Dead-by-a-Troubled-System/id-1198f64bb05d9c1ec690035983c02f9f

Beauchamp, T. L., & Childress, J. F. (2009). *Principles of biomedical ethics* (6th ed.). New York, NY: Oxford University Press.

Blackhall, L. J., Murphy, S. T., Frank, G., Michel, V., & Azen, S. (1995). Ethnicity and attitudes toward patient autonomy. *JAMA, 274,* 820–825. http://dx.doi.org/10.1001/jama.1995.03530100060035

Bogacki, D. F., Armstrong, D. J., & Stuempfle, P. (2004). The Social Sexual Awareness Scale (SSAS): Development and validation of an instrument to measure capacity to consent to high risk sexual behavior. *American Journal of Forensic Psychology, 22,* 5–38.

Bush, S. S. (2005). Introduction to ethical challenges in forensic neuropsychology. In S. S. Bush (Ed.), *A casebook of ethical challenges in neuropsychology* (pp. 10–14). New York, NY: Psychology Press.

Bush, S. S. (2007). *Ethical decision making in clinical neuropsychology*. New York, NY: Oxford University Press.

Bush, S. S., Connell, M. A., & Denney, R. L. (2006). *Ethical issues in forensic psychology: A systematic model for decision making*. http://dx.doi.org/10.1037/11469-000

Cassidy, J. (2013). State statutory authority for restoration of rights in termination of adult guardianship. *Bifocal, 34,* 123–128.

Christopher, P. P., & Pinals, D. A. (2010). Capacity to consent to sexual acts: Understanding the nature of sexual conduct. *Journal of the American Academy of Psychiatry and the Law, 38,* 417–420.

Commission on Law and Aging, American Bar Association. (2014). *State adult guardianship legislation: Directions of reform—2014*. Retrieved from http://www.flprobatelitigation.com/files/2015/01/2014_final_guardianship_legislative_update.authcheckdam.pdf

Demakis, G. J. (2012a). Introduction to basic issues in civil capacities. In G. J. Demakis (Ed.), *Civil capacities in clinical neuropsychology: Research findings and practical applications* (pp. 3–16). New York, NY: Oxford University Press.

Demakis, G. J. (2012b). Looking ahead: Directions for future research in civil capacities. In G. J. Demakis (Ed.), *Civil capacities in clinical neuropsychology: Research findings and practical applications* (pp. 310–315). New York, NY: Oxford University Press.

Demakis, G. J. (2013). State statutory definitions of incompetency/incapacity: Issues for psychologists. *Psychology, Public Policy, and Law, 19,* 331–342. http://dx.doi.org/10.1037/a0032827

Denney, R. L. (2012). Criminal forensic neuropsychology and assessment of competency. In G. J. Larrabee (Ed.), *Forensic neuropsychology: A scientific approach* (2nd ed., pp. 438–500). New York, NY: Oxford University Press.

Dudley, K. C., & Goins, R. T. (2003). Guardianship capacity evaluations of older adults: Comparing current practice to legal standards in two states. *Journal of Aging and Social Policy, 15,* 97–115. http://dx.doi.org/10.1300/J031v15n01_06

Edelstein, B. (1999). *Hopemont Capacity Assessment Interview manual and scoring guide*. Morgantown: West Virginia University.

Farnsworth, M. G. (1990). Competency evaluations in a general hospital. *Psychosomatics, 31,* 60–66. http://dx.doi.org/10.1016/S0033-3182(90)72218-9

Federal rules of evidence. (2010). Washington, DC: U.S. Government Printing Office.

Ferguson, A., Worrall, L., McPhee, J., Buskell, R., Armstrong, E., & Togher, L. (2003). Testamentary capacity and aphasia: A descriptive case report with implication for clinical practice. *Aphasiology*,

17, 965–980. http://dx.doi.org/10.1080/02687030344000337

Frolik, L. (1999). Science, common sense, and the determination of mental capacity. *Psychology, Public Policy, and Law, 5,* 41–58. http://dx.doi.org/10.1037/1076-8971.5.1.41

Garb, H. N. (2005). Clinical judgment and decision making. *Annual Review of Clinical Psychology, 1,* 67–89. http://dx.doi.org/10.1146/annurev.clinpsy.1.102803.143810

Gibson, R. M., & Ferrini, R. (2010). You let them do what??!! Decision-making capacity and the exercise of patient autonomy in long-term care. *Annals of Long-Term Care: Clinical Care and Aging, 18,* 25–30.

Gifis, S. H. (2010). *Law dictionary* (6th ed.). Hauppauge, NY: Barron's Educational Series.

Gottlieb, M. C., & Coleman, A. (2012). Ethical challenges in forensic psychology practice. In S. J. Knapp, M. C. Gottlieb, M. M. Handelsman, & L. D. VandeCreek (Eds.), *APA handbook of ethics in psychology: Vol. 2. Practice, teaching, and research* (pp. 91–123). http://dx.doi.org/10.1037/13272-006.

Gray, S., Lai, K., & Larson, E. (1999). Drug-induced cognition disorders in the elderly: Incidence, prevention and management. *Drug Safety, 21,* 101–122.

Greenberg, S. A., & Shuman, D. W. (1997). Irreconcilable conflict between therapeutic and forensic roles. *Professional Psychology: Research and Practice, 28,* 50–57. http://dx.doi.org/10.1037/0735-7028.28.1.50

Greenberg, S. A., Shuman, D. W., & Meyer, R. G. (2004). Unmasking forensic diagnosis. *International Journal of Law and Psychiatry, 27,* 1–15. http://dx.doi.org/10.1016/j.ijlp.2004.01.001

Grisso, T. (2003). *Evaluating competencies: Forensic assessments and instruments* (2nd ed.). New York, NY: Kluwer Academic/Plenum Press.

Grisso, T., & Appelbaum, P. S. (1995). The MacArthur Treatment Competence Study III: Abilities of patients to consent to psychiatric and medical treatments. *Law and Human Behavior, 19,* 149–174. http://dx.doi.org/10.1007/BF01499323

Grisso, T., & Appelbaum, P. S. (1998a). *Assessing competency to consent to treatment: A guide for physicians and other health professionals.* New York, NY: Oxford University Press.

Grisso, T., & Appelbaum, P. S. (1998b). *MacArthur Competence Assessment Tool for Treatment (MacCAT-T).* Sarasota, FL: Professional Resource Press.

Grisso, T., Appelbaum, P. S., & Hill-Fotouhi, C. (1997). The MacCAT-T: A clinical tool to assess patients' capacities to make treatment decisions. *Psychiatric Services, 48,* 1415–1419. http://dx.doi.org/10.1176/ps.48.11.1415

Gunther, J. (2011). The Utah cost of financial exploitation. *Bifocal, 32,* 45–56.

Inouye, S. K., van Dyck, C. H., Alessi, C. A., Balkin, S., Siegal, A. P., & Horwitz, R. I. (1990). Clarifying confusion: The confusion assessment method. A new method for detection of delirium. *Annals of Internal Medicine, 113,* 941–948. http://dx.doi.org/10.7326/0003-4819-113-12-941

Johnson-Greene, D., & NAN Policy and Planning Committee. (2005). Informed consent in clinical neuropsychology practice: Official statement of the National Academy of Neuropsychology. *Archives of Clinical Neuropsychology, 20,* 335–340. http://dx.doi.org/10.1016/j.acn.2004.08.003

Kapp, M. B., & Mossman, D. (1996). Measuring decisional capacity: Cautions of the construction of a "capacimeter." *Psychology, Public Policy, and Law, 2,* 73–95. http://dx.doi.org/10.1037/1076-8971.2.1.73

Karp, N., & Wood, E. F. (2007). Guardianship monitoring: A national survey of court practices. *Stetson Law Review, 37,* 183–192.

Kennedy, C. H. (2003). Legal and psychological implications in the assessment of sexual consent in the cognitively impaired population. *Assessment, 10,* 352–358. http://dx.doi.org/10.1177/1073191103258592

Kim, S. Y. H., Appelbaum, P. S., Kim, H. M., Wall, I. F., Bourgeois, J. A., Frankel, B., . . . Karlawish, J. H. (2011). Variability of judgments of capacity: Experience of capacity evaluators in a study of research consent capacity. *Psychosomatics, 52,* 346–353. http://dx.doi.org/10.1016/j.psym.2011.01.012

Kontos, N., Freudenreich, O., & Querques, J. (2013). Beyond capacity: Identifying ethical dilemmas underlying capacity evaluation requests. *Psychosomatics, 54,* 103–110. http://dx.doi.org/10.1016/j.psym.2012.06.003

Kornfeld, D. S., Muskin, P. R., & Tahil, F. A. (2009). Psychiatric evaluation of mental capacity in the general hospital: A significant teaching opportunity. *Psychosomatics, 50,* 468–473. http://dx.doi.org/10.1016/S0033-3182(09)70839-4

Lichtenberg, P. A., & Strzepek, D. M. (1990). Assessments of institutionalized dementia patients' competencies to participate in intimate relationships. *Gerontologist, 30,* 117–120. http://dx.doi.org/10.1093/geront/30.1.117

Lyden, M. (2007). Assessment of sexual consent capacity. *Sexuality and Disability, 25,* 3–20. http://dx.doi.org/10.1007/s11195-006-9028-2

Marson, D. C., Earnst, K. S., Jamil, F., Bartolucci, A., & Harrell, L. E. (2000). Consistency of physicians' legal standard and personal judgments of competency in patients with Alzheimer's disease. *Journal of the*

American Geriatrics Society, *48*, 911–918. http://dx.doi.org/10.1111/j.1532-5415.2000.tb06887.x

Marson, D. C., Hebert, K., & Solomon, A. C. (2012). Assessing civil competencies in older adults with dementia. In G. J. Larrabee (Ed.), *Forensic neuropsychology: A scientific approach* (2nd ed., pp. 401–437). New York, NY: Oxford University Press.

Marson, D. C., & Huthwaite, J. S. (2005). An unexpected excursion: Sexual consent capacity in a nursing home patient with Alzheimer's disease. In R. L. Heilbronner (Ed.), *Forensic neuropsychology casebook* (pp. 146–164). New York, NY: Guilford Press.

Marson, D. C., McInturff, B., Hawkins, L., Bartolucci, A., & Harrell, L. E. (1997). Consistency of physician judgments of capacity to consent in mild Alzheimer's disease. *Journal of the American Geriatrics Society*, *45*, 453–457. http://dx.doi.org/10.1111/j.1532-5415.1997.tb05170.x

Marson, D. C., Savage, R., & Phillips, J. (2006). Financial capacity in persons with schizophrenia and serious mental illness: Clinical and research ethics aspects. *Schizophrenia Bulletin*, *32*, 81–91. http://dx.doi.org/10.1093/schbul/sbj027

Marson, D. C., Sawrie, S. M., Snyder, S., McInturff, B., Stalvey, T., Boothe, A., . . . Harrell, L. E. (2000). Assessing financial capacity in patients with Alzheimer disease: A conceptual model and prototype instrument. *Archives of Neurology*, *57*, 877–884. http://dx.doi.org/10.1001/archneur.57.6.877

Marson, D. C., Triebel, K., & Knight, A. (2012). Financial capacity. In G. J. Demakis (Ed.), *Civil capacities in clinical neuropsychology: Research findings and practical applications* (pp. 3–16). New York, NY: Oxford University Press.

Mart, E. G. (2012). Case study: The assessment of an intestate ward with anomic aphasia to determine testamentary capacity. *Open Access Journal of Forensic Psychology*, *4*, 81–90.

Mart, E. G., & Alban, A. D. (2011). *The practical assessment of testamentary capacity and undue influence in the elderly*. Sarasota, FL: Professional Resource Press.

Martin, R., Griffith, H. R., Belue, K., Harrell, L., Zamrini, E., Anderson, B., . . . Marson, D. (2008). Declining financial capacity in patients with mild Alzheimer disease: A one-year longitudinal study. *American Journal of Geriatric Psychiatry*, *16*, 209–219. http://dx.doi.org/10.1097/JGP.0b013e318157cb00

Mayhew, M. (2005). Survey of state guardianship laws: Statutory provision for clinical evaluations. *Bifocal*, *27*, 12–19.

Melton, G., Petrila, J., Poythress, N. G., & Slobogin, C. (2007). *Psychological evaluations for the courts: A handbook for mental health professionals and lawyers* (3rd ed.). New York, NY: Guilford Press.

Minn. Stat. Ann. § 524.5-102-Subd 6. (2016).

Moberg, P. J., & Kniele, K. (2006). Evaluation of competency: Ethical considerations for neuropsychologists. *Applied Neuropsychology*, *13*, 101–114. http://dx.doi.org/10.1207/s15324826an1302_5

Moberg, P. J., & Shah, S. (2012). Ethical issues in capacity and competency evaluations. In G. J. Demakis (Ed.), *Civil capacities in clinical neuropsychology: Research findings and practical applications* (pp. 264–289). New York, NY: Oxford University Press.

Mona, L. R., Goldwaser, G., Syme, M. L., Cameron, R. P., Clemency, C., . . . Ballan, M. S. (2010). Assessment and conceptualization of sexuality among older adults. In P. A. Lichtenberg (Ed.), *Handbook of assessment in clinical gerontology* (pp. 331–355). New York, NY: Elsevier.

Moye, J., Marson, D. C., & Edelstein, B. (2013). Assessment of capacity in an aging society. *American Psychologist*, *68*, 158–171. http://dx.doi.org/10.1037/a0032159

Moye, J., & Naik, A. D. (2011). Preserving rights for individuals facing guardianship. *JAMA*, *305*, 936–937. http://dx.doi.org/10.1001/jama.2011.247

Moye, J., Wood, E., Edelstein, B., Wood, S., Bower, E. H., Harrison, J. A., & Armesto, J. C. (2007). Statutory reform is associated with improved court practice: Results of a tri-state comparison. *Behavioral Sciences and the Law*, *25*, 425–436. http://dx.doi.org/10.1002/bsl.762

Moye, J., Wood, S., Edelstein, B., Armesto, J. C., Bower, E. H., Harrison, J. A., & Wood, E. (2007). Clinical evidence in guardianship of older adults is inadequate: Findings from a tri-state study. *Gerontologist*, *47*, 604–612. http://dx.doi.org/10.1093/geront/47.5.604

N.C. Gen. Stat. § 35A-1101 (7) (2016).

N.M. Stat. Ann. § 45-5-101 F-H. (2011).

Omnibus Budget Reconciliation Act of 1990, Pub. L. No. 101-508, 104 Stat. 1388.

Packer, I. K. (2008). Specialized practice in forensic psychology: Opportunities and obstacles. *Professional Psychology: Research and Practice*, *39*, 245–249. http://dx.doi.org/10.1037/0735-7028.39.2.245

Palmer, B. W., & Savla, G. N. (2007). The association of specific neuropsychological deficits with capacity to consent to research or treatment. *Journal of the International Neuropsychological Society*, *13*, 1047–1059. http://dx.doi.org/10.1017/S1355617707071299

Palmer, B. W., Savla, G. N., & Harmell, A. L. (2012). Healthcare decision-making capacity. In

G. J. Demakis (Ed.), *Civil capacities in clinical neuropsychology: Research findings and practical applications* (pp. 69–94). New York, NY: Oxford University Press.

Peisah, C., Brodaty, H., & Quadrio, C. (2006). Family conflict in dementia: Prodigal sons and black sheep. *International Journal of Geriatric Psychiatry, 21,* 485–492. http://dx.doi.org/10.1002/gps.1501

Peisah, C., Luxenberg, J., Liptzin, B., Wand, A. P., Shulman, K., & Finkel, S. (2014). Deathbed wills: Assessing testamentary capacity in the dying patient. *International Psychogeriatrics, 26,* 209–216. http://dx.doi.org/10.1017/S1041610213001774

Peisah, C., & Shulman, K. (2012). Testamentary capacity. In G. J. Demakis (Ed.), *Civil competencies in clinical neuropsychology: Research findings and practical applications* (pp. 95–120). New York, NY: Oxford University Press.

Perlin, M. L., Champine, P. R., Dlugacz, H. A., & Connell, M. A. (2008). *Competence in the law: From legal theory to clinical application.* http://dx.doi.org/10.1002/9781118269916

Pirelli, G., Gottdiener, W. H., & Zapf, P. A. (2011). A meta-analytic review of competency to stand trial research. *Psychology, Public Policy, and Law, 17,* 1–53. http://dx.doi.org/10.1037/a0021713

Quickel, E. J. W., & Demakis, G. J. (2013). The Independent Living Scales in civil competency evaluations: Initial findings and prediction of competency adjudication. *Law and Human Behavior, 37,* 155–162. http://dx.doi.org/10.1037/lhb0000009

Quinn, M. J. (2002). Undue influence and elder abuse: Recognition and intervention strategies. *Geriatric Nursing, 23,* 11–17. http://dx.doi.org/10.1067/mgn.2002.122560

Quinn, M. J. (2005). *Guardianship of adults: Achieving justice, autonomy, and safety.* New York, NY: Springer.

Raymont, V., Bingley, W., Buchanan, A., David, A. S., Hayward, P., Wessely, S., & Hotopf, M. (2004). Prevalence of mental incapacity in medical inpatients and associated risk factors: Cross-sectional study. *Lancet, 364,* 1421–1427. http://dx.doi.org/10.1016/S0140-6736(04)17224-3

Reed, T. J. (1979). The stolen birthright—An examination of the psychology of testation and an analysis of the law of testamentary capacity—a modest proposal. *Western New England Law Review, 1,* 429–533.

Rogers, R. (2001). *Handbook of diagnostic and structured interviewing.* New York, NY: Guilford Press.

Roked, F., & Patel, A. (2008). Which aspects of cognitive function are best associated with testamentary capacity in patients with Alzheimer's disease? *International Journal of Geriatric Psychiatry, 23,* 552–553. http://dx.doi.org/10.1002/gps.1947

Ruchinskas, R. (2012). Other aspects of data collection in capacity evaluations. In G. J. Demakis (Ed.), *Civil capacities in clinical neuropsychology: Research findings and practical applications* (pp. 228–241). New York, NY: Oxford University Press.

Sabatino, C. P., & Basinger, S. L. (2000). Competency: Reforming our legal fictions. *Journal of Mental Health and Aging, 6,* 119–144.

Seyfried, L., Ryan, K. A., & Kim, S. Y. H. (2013). Assessment of decision-making capacity: Views and experiences of consultation psychiatrists. *Psychosomatics, 54,* 115–123. http://dx.doi.org/10.1016/j.psym.2012.08.001

Shulman, K. I., Cohen, C. A., Kirsh, F. C., Hull, I. M., & Champine, P. R. (2007). Assessment of testamentary capacity and vulnerability to undue influence. *American Journal of Psychiatry, 164,* 722–727. http://dx.doi.org/10.1176/ajp.2007.164.5.722

State of New Hampshire v. Wayne Cressey. (1993). Retrieved from http://nh.findacase.com/research/wfrmDocViewer.aspx/xq/fac.19930715_0002.NH.htm/qx

Sullivan, K. A. (2012). Civil capacity instruments: Research trends and recommendations for future research. In G. J. Demakis (Ed.), *Civil capacities in clinical neuropsychology: Research findings and practical applications* (pp. 206–227). New York, NY: Oxford University Press.

Trzepacz, P., & Baker, R. (1993). The psychiatric mental status examination. New York, NY: Oxford University Press.

Uekert, B., & Schauffler, R. Y. (2008, November). The need for improved adult guardianship data. *Caseload Highlights.* Retrieved from http://www.courtstatistics.org/~/media/Microsites/Files/CSP/Highlights/15_2_Adult_Guardianship_Data.ashx

Uekert, B. K. (2010). *Adult guardianship court data and issues: Results from an online survey.* Retrieved from http://www.guardianship.org/reports/Guardianship_Survey_Report.pdf

White, M. C. (2010). The eternal flame: Capacity to consent to sexual behavior among nursing home residents with dementia. *Elder Law Journal, 18,* 139–161.

Zapf, P. A., Hubbard, K. L., Cooper, V. G., Wheeles, M. C., & Ronan, K. A. (2004). Have the courts abdicated their responsibility for determinations of competency to stand trial to clinicians. *Journal of Forensic Psychology Practice, 4,* 27–44. http://dx.doi.org/10.1300/J158v04n01_02

CHAPTER 15

COMPETENCY TO STAND TRIAL AND CRIMINAL RESPONSIBILITY IN FORENSIC NEUROPSYCHOLOGY PRACTICE

Loren E. Mallory and Michelle R. Guyton

Competency-to-stand-trial (CST) evaluations are the backbone of criminal forensic psychology practice. CST evaluations may be the most common criminal forensic psychology evaluation (Zapf & Roesch, 2009). Criminal responsibility (CR) defenses are relatively rare, used in only about 1 in 1,000 felony cases (Melton, Petrila, Poythress, & Slobogin, 2007; Packer, 2009). The number of CR evaluations completed is unknown but is likely significantly greater than the number of CR defenses actually taken to trial. The forensic psychology literature has many excellent reviews of CST and CR (e.g., Hall, 2008; Weiner & Hess, 2006). Although forensic neuropsychologists are more likely to practice in civil court, they play a growing role in criminal court as well, including CST and CR evaluations. In fact, neuropsychology is likely underused in CST and CR cases, even when brain disorder or neurocognitive deficits are suspected.

This chapter provides an introduction to the concepts of CST and CR and reviews the landmark cases, precedents, and concepts involved in each. A review of the literature and legal cases specifically for neuropsychology and CST and CR is provided. True to the identity of this volume as a practical handbook, we emphasize practical issues and recommendations for conducting forensic neuropsychological CST and CR evaluations.

Although *CST* and *CR* are used throughout this chapter, there are many alternate names. CR refers primarily to insanity and may be termed *not guilty by reason of insanity* or *guilty except for insanity*. The focus of a CR evaluation is the defendant's capacity to have understood, at the time of the offense, that the conduct was wrong. There are closely related issues as well, such as questions of extreme emotional disturbance (EED) or diminished capacity.

CST is also known as *adjudicative competency, trial competency*, or *fitness to proceed*. Defendants found incompetent are known as *incompetent to stand trial* (IST). An evaluator may assess many specific competencies: to (a) waive Miranda rights, (b) confess, (c) waive counsel, (d) represent oneself, (e) make a plea, and so forth. For a discussion of these specific competencies in forensic neuropsychology see Horton and Hartlage (2010). As used in this chapter, CST refers to whether the defendant (a) has a factual and rational understanding of the legal proceedings against defendant, (b) is able to assist the attorney, and (c) is able to participate in the defense. These three concepts are often referred to the "three prongs" of CST.

PRIMER ON THE LEGAL CONCEPTS OF COMPETENCE TO STAND TRIAL AND CRIMINAL RESPONSIBILITY

Both CST and CR have long social and legal histories. In the sections that follow, we provide brief historical outlines of these concepts, intended to assist in developing an understanding of their use in today's court systems.

Legal Development: Competence to Stand Trial

The concept of CST dates far back to the 13th century in Anglo-Saxon law. In legal proceedings at that

http://dx.doi.org/10.1037/0000032-015
APA Handbook of Forensic Neuropsychology, S. S. Bush (Editor-in-Chief)

time, defendants were required to enter a plea as part of the process. However, some defendants did not speak, and courts sought to distinguish those who were "mute by visitation of God" from those who stood "mute by malice." The former group was seen as afflicted in some manner, and punishing these individuals was viewed as unfair for multiple reasons. First, punishing such individuals was considered an exercise of "extreme inhumanity and cruelty" (Roesch, Zapf, Golding, & Skeem, 1999, p. 331). Second, individuals so disordered would be unable to defend themselves in an adversarial process, which would violate one of the basic tenets of Anglo-Saxon jurisprudence.

These same ideals were brought into the development of early American law. In *Youtsey v. United States* (1899), Youtsey was a criminal defendant with epilepsy. His trial was delayed for several months because of his claims that his condition impaired his memory and ability to communicate with his attorney. He was eventually tried and convicted, but the Court of Appeals overturned this conviction. The court doubted that Youtsey could appreciate his legal situation or communicate relevantly with his attorney, establishing the premise in American law that defendants must be aware of their legal situation and able to defend themselves against charges.

The due process clause of the 14th Amendment guarantees that states cannot deprive citizens of the rights guaranteed to them in the Bill of Rights, including those held in the Sixth Amendment. The U.S. Constitution guarantees criminal defendants a variety of rights, such as the right to (a) a speedy and public trial, (b) confront accusers, (c) an impartial jury, (d) be informed of the charges, and (e) assistance of counsel. Although it is not specifically laid out in the text, the Sixth Amendment is interpreted to mean that a defendant must be able to understand and participate in the criminal court process. Defendants who are unable to appreciate the criminal proceedings against them cannot effectively confront accusers or assist counsel. Ensuring that defendants are competent has two functions: protecting the defendant and protecting the court's interest in a fair proceeding (Bonnie, 1992).

Although CST has a long legal history, there was little guidance for centuries about how to define this construct. One of the first such attempts was in the *Dusky v. United States* (1960) case. In this less-than-full-page decision, the Supreme Court opined,

> It is not enough for the district judge to find that 'the defendant [is] oriented to time and place and [has] some recollection of events,' but that the 'test must be whether he has sufficient present ability to consult with his lawyer with a reasonable degree of rational understanding—and whether he has a rational as well as factual understanding of the proceedings against him. (p. 1)

The *Dusky* case forms the basis for American criminal law with regard to CST. Competency includes two components, often referred to as *prongs:* (a) factual and rational understanding and (b) the ability to rationally consult with an attorney. The first prong covers static knowledge such as the accusations, the range of potential punishments, and knowledge of how the legal system functions. However, such factual knowledge is not enough; the defendant must be able to apply that knowledge to the legal case and work with the defense attorney. Although fundamental in setting the competency standard, *Dusky* provided little guidance in how to determine how much legal knowledge a defendant must possess or how well a defendant must work with the attorney.

Kruh and Grisso (2009) distilled several important points from the *Dusky* decision. First, the words *sufficient* and *reasonable* are important. *Sufficient understanding* means that a defendant does not need to be a legal expert or remember every detail about the case. Rather, he or she must retain enough information to proceed through the case. Next, *reasonable understanding* implies that the level of knowledge is related to the complexity of the case. This latter point makes intuitive sense: A murder case is likely more complicated than a drug possession case and would require more from the defendant. Kruh and Grisso also noted that the focus is on present functioning, which acknowledges that competency can fluctuate in response to treatment or other factors. A competent defendant can deteriorate and become incompetent at later points, which could cause the process to halt until the defendant has regained sufficient capacity. Finally, use of the terms *factual* and *rational* means that mere legal knowledge is insufficient; the defendant must be able to apply that knowledge to the case.

In 1975, the Supreme Court expanded the definition of competency in the *Drope v. Missouri* case. In *Drope,* the Court opined that a defendant must be able to "assist in preparing his defense." Richard Bonnie (1992), a noted legal scholar, interpreted *Drope* to add a third prong to the foundation laid out by *Dusky*. Not only must a defendant be able to demonstrate factual and rational understanding, the defendant must be able to assist counsel in preparing the defense strategy.

In the U.S. District Court decision *Wieter v. Settle* (1961), the judge expanded on *Dusky* and outlined eight functional abilities. Defendants must (a) demonstrate the mental capacity to appreciate their presence in relation to time, place, and things and understand (b) that they are before the court as a result of criminal charges; (c) the role of the judge; (d) the role of the prosecutor; (e) the role of the defense attorney; (f) the ability to tell the defense attorney about the alleged offense; (g) that a jury may decide on their guilt, and (h) that they have sufficient memory to recall the events. The *Wilson v. United States* (1968) case further expands on the latter *Wieter* item to include six factors considered when a defendant lacks memory for recalling pertinent case-related events. The *Wilson* factors require the court to consider (a) how amnesia affects the defendant's ability to consult with counsel, (b) how amnesia affects the defendant's ability to testify, (c) evidence relating to the crime or potential alibis, (d) how the government assisted the defendant and defense counsel in reconstructing the evidence, (e) the strength of the prosecutor's case, and (f) any other facts and circumstances that would indicate whether the defendant had a fair trial.

Whereas CST is the main focus of many cases, competency is a construct that runs throughout the defendant's contact with the judicial system. At the beginning of the process, suspects must be competent to confess and, toward the end in the most serious of cases, convicted offenders must be competent to be executed. There is case law that defines these benchmarks, but it is notable that they are separate yet related constructs.

One question that originally sparked considerable controversy was whether the test for CST was the same as for competency to proceed without an attorney (frequently referred to as proceeding *pro se*). This question was addressed in the Supreme Court decision of *Godinez v. Moran* (1993). During the course of a robbery, Richard Moran shot and killed a bartender and a patron; 9 days later, he shot his ex-wife to death and attempted suicide by shooting himself. He also tried cutting his wrists. Moran summoned police to the hospital and confessed to the murders. His CST was evaluated by two psychiatrists who agreed that although depressed, Moran was competent. At his trial 3 months later, he discharged his public defender, pled guilty to all three counts, and refused to allow any mitigating evidence to be presented. He was sentenced to death. Moran appealed his death sentence, asserting that he was mentally incompetent to defend himself. His appeal was rejected by the Nevada Supreme Court and a habeas corpus appeal was denied by the Federal District Court. In the Court of Appeals, his appeal was upheld, and the district court's findings were set aside. The Court of Appeals cited the trial court's error in not considering that Moran's competency to waive counsel required a higher level of functioning than described in *Dusky*. This court noted that a defendant who waives counsel or pleads guilty must be able to demonstrate "capacity for reasoned choice among those choices available" (p. 394). However, in a writ of certiorari (an action by a superior court to review a lower court's findings), the Supreme Court disagreed and in a 7–2 decision decreed that these various competencies (i.e., to stand trial, plead guilty, waive counsel) were the same; a defendant competent to stand trial is also competent to waive counsel.

Golding (2008) argued that *Godinez* should be interpreted as meaning that "any significant change in the context in which a defendant was evaluated may trigger the need for a reevaluation" (p. 78). That is, any change in the defendant's circumstances (including mental status), legal circumstances, or case issues may create new demands on the defendant and necessitate a new competency evaluation. In the *Godinez* case, Moran was evaluated before he decided to waive counsel. Applying the *Pate v. Robinson* (1966) decision that all officers of the court have a responsibility to raise and resolve the issue of competency at any and all points during a criminal proceeding, Golding argued that Moran's context changed significantly once he waived counsel, and his competency should have been reassessed at that time.

A more recent case suggested a different course of reasoning by the Supreme Court. In Indiana, Ahmad Edwards was arrested for stealing a pair of shoes and subsequently shooting three people: an FBI agent, a security officer, and a bystander (*Indiana v. Edwards*, 2008). Edwards was found incompetent for the first 5 years after his arrest but was eventually determined to be competent to stand trial. His first trial resulted in a hung jury; before the second, Edwards requested to waive counsel. This was initially granted, but Edwards's ability to conduct the defense was poor, as noted by his filing of documents that contained disorganized and unrelated content. The trial court then overturned the earlier decision to allow him to waive counsel. He was again represented and convicted on all counts. Edwards appealed, citing the *Godinez* case and *Faretta v. California* (1975), which cited a defendant's right to self-representation when that choice is made knowingly and intelligently. The Indiana Supreme Court agreed with Edwards, but the U.S. Supreme Court did not, deciding that the right to waive counsel can be limited if the defendant does not have sufficient mental capacity to conduct the trial by himself.

The Court thus made it clear that competency to waive counsel includes different functional abilities than CST. A defendant competent to stand trial may not be competent to waive counsel. The *Edwards* decision did not comment explicitly on how competency to waive counsel should be assessed, thus leaving this question for evaluators and trial judges. A joint brief submitted by the American Psychiatric Association and American Association for Psychiatry and Law to the Supreme Court (Taranto, 2007) advocated for a functional assessment of the defendant's abilities within the expanded context of proceeding *pro se*. For example, communication and decision-making abilities are already assessed in CST evaluations, but self-representation requires greater abilities in these areas and should be further assessed in such cases. It remains to be seen how future courts will interpret the *Edwards* decision and if more specific guidance is needed about the factors that courts will use to determine competency to waive counsel.

Legal Development: Criminal Responsibility

Similar to CST, the legal history of insanity or CR has long roots that date back to ancient civilizations. The concept of insanity as a defense to criminal charges is rooted in English common and case law. Courts found it inhumane to punish an individual who "lacked understanding and memory as to not know what he is doing any more than an infant, a brute, or a wild beast" (*Rex v. Arnold*, 1724). In England, kings pardoned individuals who were "mad" at the time of their crime. In the 16th and 17th centuries, legal scholars and judges wrote about excusing the conduct of individuals who could not tell the difference between right and wrong.

This concept of insanity as the inability to distinguish right from wrong became cemented in English common law in the *M'Naghten* (1843) case. Daniel M'Naghten developed delusional beliefs about the ruling Tory Party in England and believed that they were following and trying to murder him. M'Naghten traveled to London to shoot the Prime Minister, Sir Robert Peel, to end this persecution. He ended up killing the prime minister's secretary, Edward Drummond. His attorneys used an insanity defense because of his delusional beliefs. He was found insane by the court and subsequently committed to a mental hospital for the remainder of his life. The court explained insanity:

> It must be clearly proved that, at the time of the committing of the act, the party accused was laboring under such a defect of reason, from disease of the mind, as not to know the nature and quality of the act he was doing; or, if he did know it, that he did not know he was doing what was wrong. (*M'Naghten*, 1843, p. 722)

This decision was heavily criticized on all sides. Public and official outcry, including from Queen Victoria, raised concerns about defendants avoiding responsibility for their actions. Others criticized the standard as being too strict, noting that an exclusive focus on the cognitive aspect (knowing right from wrong) was incomplete and did not account for defendants' ability to control their behavior.

In the United States, the *M'Naghten* standard was adopted in a widespread manner. However, concerns about the standard being too narrowly focused on cognition led to a supplemental test for insanity. Called the *irresistible impulse test,* this standard required that as a result of mental disease or defect, a defendant was unable to control his or her actions and resist the impulse to commit a crime. The irresistible impulse test added a volitional prong to insanity statutes that broadened the scope of insanity.

In response to dissatisfaction that both of these standards were too strict, the District of Columbia Court of Appeals developed the "product test" for insanity. This standard had existed for several decades in New Hampshire but had received little support. The product test was defined as follows: "An accused is not criminally responsible if his unlawful act was the product of mental disease or defect" (*Durham v. United States,* 1954). The concept behind this test was to allow mental health professionals to provide broader information to the courts and to "humanize" the criminal justice system (Bazelon, 1988). However, other courts were concerned that the product test was overbroad and that it was difficult to define how behavior was a product of mental illness. How much did a person's mental illness have to contribute to his or her criminal act to be considered a product of it? Few states adopted the product test, and those that did soon abolished it in favor of the American Law Institute (ALI; 1962) standard.

The ALI released its proposed standard for insanity in 1962 after many years of legal study and analysis. It included both cognitive and volitional prongs:

> A person is not responsible for criminal conduct if at the time of such conduct as a result of mental disease or defect he lacks substantial capacity either to appreciate the criminality [wrongfulness] of his conduct or to conform his conduct to the requirements of the law. (ALI, 1962, § 4.01[1])

The ALI standard was adopted by a majority of jurisdictions, including the federal courts.

The ALI standard was applied to John Hinckley, who attempted to assassinate President Reagan. Hinckley had suffered from depression for many years and had developed an erotomanic fixation on actress Jodie Foster. His assassination plot was designed to ensure his place in history books, which he felt would impress Ms. Foster and get her to notice him. In this assassination attempt, Hinckley wounded the president and three others. In 1983, Hinckley was found not guilty by reason of insanity in federal court of the attempted assassination of Ronald Reagan.

Public outcry over the Hinckley insanity finding was immense. Even though Hinckley would be hospitalized or under supervision and monitoring for the remainder of his life, many were outraged at the notion that he avoided punishment for trying to kill the president. In response, three states abolished the insanity defense, and Congress took up the issue and ultimately passed the Insanity Defense Reform Act in 1984. The act limited the scope of the insanity standard to the cognitive prong: "As a result of a severe mental disease or defect, he was unable to appreciate the nature and quality or wrongfulness of his act" (p. 201). However, the Insanity Defense Reform Act applies only to federal cases and the minority of states that adopted the language.

Other Criminal Responsibility Defenses

In addition to the insanity standard, other criminal defenses have developed that focus on the defendant's mental capacity at the time of the crime. The diminished capacity defense is a partial defense that focuses on the defendant's *mens rea,* or intent to commit the crime. This defense requires that some type of mental impairment reduced the defendant's ability to form the required intent that is an element of the crime charged (Packer, 2009). A diminished capacity defense argues that the defendant's mental state was such that the requisite intent for that crime could not have been developed. A successful diminished capacity defense results in a conviction for a general-intent crime with a lower criminal sanction (i.e., manslaughter) rather than a specific-intent crime (i.e., murder) that typically carries a higher criminal punishment (Melton et al., 2007).

In California, the diminished capacity defense served as a "mini-insanity defense" in which mentally impaired defendants ineligible for the formal insanity statute could have their sentences reduced because of their impaired mental state. Although conceptualized by psychiatrist Bernard Diamond (1994) as a way for psychiatry to positively influence the law, the diminished capacity defense was abolished in 1981 in part because of the case of Dan White. White killed San Francisco Mayor George Moscone and City Supervisor Harvey Milk. White had been a city supervisor who was fired from his position. He blamed both men and plotted to kill them. He avoided metal detectors by climbing through a window in City Hall, packed extra bullets, and shot each man multiple times. White's attorneys argued that he was depressed over losing his job. One defense expert linked White's high consumption of junk food with a chemical imbalance that resulted in depression. Although it was unclear how influential this testimony was, it was picked up in the media as the "Twinkie defense." White was convicted of voluntary manslaughter, the least serious homicide charge, as a result of the diminished capacity defense. Because of subsequent public outrage, the diminished capacity defense was eliminated in California the following year.

Diminished capacity defenses still exist in various jurisdictions. Experts may opine about how the defendant's mental condition affected the ability to form the requisite intent for a particular crime. Some states have starkly limited the ability of mental health professionals to offer expert testimony regarding mental state (see *Clark v. Arizona*, 2006).

EED is another partial defense against criminal charges. An EED defense is an extension of the provocation defense, the latter of which applies to a defendant who reacted in the heat of passion to a situation that would ordinarily make most individuals lose control. A prototypical scenario involves an individual who discovers his or her spouse engaged in infidelity and assaults the spouse's lover. The provocation defense assumes an objective "reasonable person" standard: a situation that would inflame an ordinary person to the extent that he or she would lose control. EED broadens the provocation defense to allow a more subjective evaluation of the defendant's mental state (Packer, 2009). Specifically, the ALI (1962) Model Penal Code states that the crime of murder would be reduced to manslaughter if the person was under the influence of extreme mental or emotional disturbance for which there was reasonable explanation or excuse. The reasonableness of such explanation or excuse would be determined from the viewpoint of "a person in the actor's situation under the circumstances as he believes them to be" (ALI, 1985, § 210.3[1][b]).

The EED defense is different from the insanity defense in that the person could clearly understand that the actions were wrong at the time. EED typically involves less severe mental impairments than an insanity defense, and the individual is still criminally sanctioned. The EED defense differs from diminished capacity in that it does not focus on the ability to form the intent. A successful EED might involve an individual who fully intended to harm the victim, but the defendant's reasons for doing so involved circumstances that a reasonable person might find to be an excuse.

Forensic Assessment Instruments

Clinicians have traditionally relied on clinical interviews to assess a defendant's competence. An important aspect of the interview is to determine the defendant's current mental state and diagnosis. The examiner queries about prior psychiatric history but focuses on current symptoms and functioning. Traditional psychological tests may also be used to assess intelligence, cognitive skills, and mental health symptoms. Assessment of mental health condition is imperative because the presence of psychotic symptoms is one of the strongest predictors of incompetence (Pirelli, Gottdiener, & Zapf, 2011). However, traditional psychological tests provide limited information regarding the assessment of competence to stand trial. Presence of mental health symptoms or intellectual deficit does not necessarily equate to impaired competence. Rather, symptoms or cognitive limitations must be explicitly linked to the functional abilities required in a competence assessment. This is commonly referred to as the *nexus* between symptoms and psycholegal abilities; establishing this nexus is a critical piece of the forensic examiner's job.

To assess the functional capacities of competency, an interview with the defendant is typically performed. In such interviews, defendants are asked about their knowledge of the legal system and their specific case and how they work with their attorney. Forensic interviews should also assess the individual's decision-making abilities. More specifically, the interview should include an assessment of the extent to which symptoms affect how the person makes decisions about the case. For example, a defendant wanting to fire a defense attorney because of paranoid delusional beliefs about the attorney suggests impairment in the defendant's ability to cooperate with counsel. The interview data may yield definitive data about the examinee's level of competence. The nature of these interviews is as varied as the range of clinicians who perform them, and there is no one preferred method or gold standard to assess competence.

Grisso (2003) enumerated advantages of using forensic assessment instruments (FAIs) in competency evaluations. FAIs provide structure and guidance to the examiner and enhance communication with legal professionals. Use of FAIs also increases reliability among different examiners (Melton et al., 2007). These instruments aid examiners in directly addressing the specific psycholegal constructs that traditional psychological tests do not. Forensic examiners' opinions of competency have a history of unreliability (Skeem & Golding, 1998). To increase the reliability and subsequent validity of these assessments, checklists and other tools were developed. Despite the encouragement of experts to use FAIs in competency cases, they are not frequently used. Archer, Buffington-Vollum, Stredny, and Handel (2006) surveyed 123 forensic psychologists about their use of various assessment instruments in a forensic context. Of those surveyed who had ever used them, 55% of those surveyed had never used the Evaluation of Competence to Stand Trial—Revised (ECST–R), 20% had never used the MacArthur Competence Assessment Tool for Criminal Adjudication (MacCAT–CA), and 36% had never used the Competence Assessment for Standing Trial for Defendants With Mental Retardation (CAST–MR). Only 9% used the ECST–R in 50% or more of their cases; 17% used the MacCAT–CA and 5% used the CAST–MR with similar frequency. Clearly, there is room for more widespread adoption.

A comprehensive review of these various methods is beyond the scope of this chapter; instead, four tools that are often used in current practice are discussed.

Evaluation of Competence to Stand Trial—Revised. The ECST–R (Rogers, Tillbrook, & Sewell, 2004) was developed along the *Dusky* standard. The measure focuses primarily on CST but also contains items that assess a defendant's competency to plead guilty and waive counsel. Taking about 30 minutes to administer, the ECST–R contains a total of 18 items that are both structured and semistructured and focus on case-specific information and relationship with counsel. The 18 items are grouped into three individual scales: Factual Understanding of the Courtroom Proceedings, Rational Understanding of the Courtroom Proceedings, and Consult with Counsel. The latter two scales are grouped into an Overall Rational Ability score. An added benefit of the ECST–R is its inclusion of five response-style scales, termed the Atypical Presentation Scales, for feigned incompetency. The ECST–R is based on a normative sample of 200 competency referrals, 128 jail inmates, and 78 feigners from simulation research. The ECST–R produces *T* scores for each of the scales.

Studies of the ECST–R since its development have been sparse, and the existing publications tend to focus on the response-style scales. Vitacco, Rogers, and Gabel (2009) found good interrater reliability (intraclass correlations ranged from .97 to 1.00) and internal reliability (alpha coefficients ranged from .85 to .95) for the competency scales. The Atypical Presentation Scales also differentiated between probable feigners and genuine responders. In a college student simulation sample, Norton and Ryba (2010) found that the four competency scales were significantly different between coached feigners and genuine responders. All of the genuine responders fell in the normal to mild impairment category, and all would likely be deemed competent on this basis. However, more than half of the coached feigners also fell in the normal to mild impairment category. Three of the Atypical Presentation Scales correctly classified 92% of the feigning and genuine responders.

MacArthur Competence Assessment Tool for Criminal Adjudication. Another assessment tool was developed by researchers funded by the MacArthur Foundation. This network of scholars sought to improve the reliability of competency evaluations by providing a framework for inquiring about and rating a defendant's psycholegal abilities. The MacCAT–CA (Hoge, Bonnie, Poythress, & Monahan, 1999) contains 22 items across three independent scales: Understanding, Reasoning, and Appreciation. It takes about 30 minutes to administer. The Understanding and Reasoning sections are based on the defendant's answers to a hypothetical situation; the third is specific to the defendant's case. Each item is rated on a 3-point scale for amount of demonstrated knowledge or skill. Hoge et al. (1999) stressed that the MacCAT–CA is not a competency assessment but rather a tool that provides additional information to be considered in rendering an opinion about competency. In other words, an individual is neither competent nor incompetent on the basis of the test scores. Rather, test scores contribute to an overall understanding of the defendant's functional abilities. This warning applies to all tests but especially the MacCAT–CA because of its reliance on a vignette that is unlikely to approximate a particular defendant's circumstance.

Studies have demonstrated the adequacy of the tool's psychometric properties (Poythress, Bonnie, Monahan, Otto, & Hoge, 2002). Otto et al. (1998) found Cronbach's alpha coefficients for the three scales ranged from .81 to .88 and interrater reliability ranged from .75 to .90 in the normative sample. The MacCAT–CA easily distinguished between jail inmates and hospitalized incompetent defendants with large effect sizes. In another study, Viljoen, Zapf, and Roesch (2004) used the MacCAT–CA and Fitness Interview Test—Revised to compare the scores of psychotic and nonpsychotic defendants. Participants with a psychotic disorder showed more impairment on the appreciation domain than the Understanding and Reasoning sections of the MacCAT–CA. Psychotic symptoms also demonstrated a strong inverse relationship with scores on the three MacCAT–CA scales. Whereas hallucinations were generally unrelated to MacCAT–CA scale scores, conceptual disorganization was strongly related. Experiencing unusual thoughts was moderately correlated with reasoning and strongly correlated with appreciation. Confirmatory factor analysis supports the three-factor model presented in the test manual (Jacobs, Ryba, & Zapf, 2008).

Competence Assessment for Standing Trial for Defendants With Mental Retardation. The CAST–MR (Everington & Luckasson, 1992) was developed to aid forensic mental health professionals in assessing competence in defendants with intellectual limitations. Poythress et al. (2002) proscribed the MacCAT–CA's use with individuals with intellectual deficits, and the ECST–R is not to be used with individuals with IQ scores below 60. However, individuals with intellectual disabilities come into contact with the legal system, and assessment of their competence to stand trial is often required. The CAST–MR was thus designed to help fulfill this need. CAST–MR has 50 items grouped into three sections. The first section, Basic Legal Concepts, contains 25 multiple-choice questions addressing the defendant's knowledge of legal terminology and roles of courtroom personnel. Skills to Assist Defense, the second section, contains 15 multiple-choice items that provide brief scenarios about working with a defense attorney. The final section, Understanding Case Events, uses 10 open-ended items to assess the defendant's knowledge of the facts of the legal case. Items in this third section are scored 0, 0.5, or 1 point on the basis of the quality of the information provided. Each of the three sections is scored separately, and the three are then summed for a total score. As with the other tools, Everington and Luckasson (1992) emphasized that the CAST–MR should be used along with other data sources to develop an opinion about a defendant's competency.

Two studies examined the psychometric properties of the CAST–MR. Estimates of interrater reliability were between .80 and .87 for the third section (Everington & Dunn, 1995). Internal consistency of the total score was estimated to be .93 (Everington, 1990). Overall, the CAST–MR has a high level of homogeneity across several estimates of internal consistency reliability (Everington & Dunn, 1995).

Despite these psychometric data, the CAST–MR has been criticized for being overly simplistic and a poor measure of the psycholegal skills a defendant needs to proceed through the adjudication process. In a study of 113 female and male prison inmates with intellectual disability, low agreement was between scores on the CAST–MR and MacCAT–CA (Jurecska, Peterson, & Millkey, 2012). Participants with intellectual disability produced substantially lower scores on all three scales of the MacCAT–CA compared with normative data. However, on the CAST–MR, these same inmates produced scores that would suggest competence in greater numbers. Logically, this creates a situation in which defendants with intellectual disability who are assessed with the CAST–MR may have a lower bar for competence than intellectually intact defendants assessed with the MacCAT–CA. This is concerning. Jurecska et al. (2012) questioned whether the CAST–MR sets a disproportionately low bar for competence in defendants with intellectual disability.

In addition, the CAST–MR has no measures of response style, and it may be vulnerable to malingering. In a dissimulation study, both intellectually disabled and intellectually typical defendants instructed to feign incompetence showed significantly lower scores on the CAST–MR than the normative sample (Everington, Notario-Smull, & Horton, 2007). No appreciable difference was found between the scores of intellectually disabled and intellectually typical feigners. Everington et al. (2007) concluded that defendants with intellectual disability may be able to feign incompetence in certain circumstances.

Rogers Criminal Responsibility Assessment Scales. The Rogers Criminal Responsibility Assessment Scales (RCRAS) is the only FAI specifically developed to assess insanity (Rogers, 1984). Rogers (1984) set out to quantify the psychological (i.e., symptoms of mental illness) and situational (i.e., planning for the crime, defendant's reported loss of self-control) variables that related to the crime and to offer a structured method for making decisions about an individual's CR. The RCRAS was presented as an empirical approach to collecting relevant data related to insanity evaluations. The RCRAS has 30 variables that are rated by the examiner on a scale ranging from 0 to 6, with 0 indicating no information available, 1 indicating no symptom, and scores from 2 to 6 indicating the degree to which the symptom is present. The first 25 variables can be combined into six summary psycholegal criteria. The scores of these criteria are then fed into a decision-tree model that results in one of three outcomes: sane, insane, or no opinion.

The RCRAS has demonstrated good interrater reliability across several of the items and domains (Rogers & Shuman, 2000). Borum (2003) noted the instrument's good internal validity. Few indicators of its external validity are available, in large part because of the difficulty of finding an adequate test or outcome to compare it with. In the test manual, Rogers (1984) described one study of 112 cases in which the RCRAS was performed, but the specific test results were not reported to the court. Overall, there was an 88% agreement between the final outcome on the RCRAS and the legal outcome of the case. The false-positive rate was 26.7%, and the false-negative rate was 4.8%. Agreement was highest in cases in which the defendant exhibited either very little or significant psychopathology. There was less agreement at more moderate levels of symptom severity.

Melton et al. (2007) outlined concerns that the RCRAS "promises more than it delivers in terms of the scientific rigor" (p. 255). The ratings of each of the variables are ordinal, and the manual provides no instruction on how to measure each of the constructs. In essence, the assignment of ordinal ratings to relevant psycholegal constructs differs very little from the process of clinical decision making and does not deliver an empirical answer to the question of insanity. Rather, the RCRAS can serve as a tool for structuring the assessment of insanity by ensuring that examiners ask about each of the relevant domains. Clinicians must then determine the weight given to each of the variables and how the RCRAS data fits into their opinion. However, it appears that few clinicians actually do. In the Archer et al. (2006) survey, 57% of participants reported never using the RCRAS, and only 9% used it in at least 50% of their insanity cases.

NEUROPSYCHOLOGICAL EVALUATION OF COMPETENCE TO STAND TRIAL AND CRIMINAL RESPONSIBILITY

Neuropsychology is a relatively new profession. Questions concerning the applicability of neuropsychological techniques to the forensic arena and the admissibility of neuropsychological testimony are still being answered.

Relevant Legal Cases

According to Kaufmann (2008), the admissibility of psychologist's testimony regarding mental defect or organic injury was first addressed in an appeal in *Jenkins v. United States* (1962). The appellate court determined that "some psychologists are qualified to render expert testimony" (p. 647). In *Simmons v. Mullen* (1974), it was concluded that a psychologist was competent to testify as an expert on brain injury. More recently, courts have upheld the usefulness of neuropsychological testing (*In re Elmore,* 2007). In *Elmore,* the court found neuropsychological testing to be an accepted method for evaluating functional deficits.

Since *Frye v. United States* (1923), the standard for the acceptance of scientific evidence to be admitted in court, including expert testimony, has been that the scientific information was "sufficiently established to have gained general acceptance in the particular field in which it belongs" (p. 1). The weakness in this test is clear: A potential expert's opinion about any subject, however erroneous, such as astrology or phrenology, may be generally accepted by practitioners in that particular field. In *Daubert v. Merrell Dow Pharmaceuticals* (1993), this standard was tightened considerably. In *Daubert,* the court relied on Rule 702 of the *Federal Rules of Evidence* (2011) and opined that a witness must be qualified as an expert by knowledge, skill, experience, training, or education in order to present an opinion regarding the issue in court. Under *Daubert,* potential testimony may be judged on (a) whether the information has been empirically tested, (b) whether it has been subjected to peer review, (c) whether there is a known error rate, (d) the existence of standards and controls regarding the information, and (e) the degree to which the theory or technique is generally accepted in the scientific community.

Daubert helped to eliminate much pseudoscientific and poorly founded expert testimony. It also caused a rush of hearings regarding the admissibility of different scientists, practitioners, and scientific information in court. These were sometimes referred to as "702 hearings."

Neuropsychological testing, evaluations, and testimony have most often been found to meet *Daubert* standards for admissibility. Sweet, Ecklund-Johnson, and Malina (2009) identified 47 court cases in which the admissibility of neuropsychological testimony under *Daubert* was considered. Of the 47 cases, 31 rulings (66%) were in favor of admitting or upheld the admittance of neuropsychological information. Sweet et al. reported,

> Neuropsychologists do not appear to have fared worse than other experts.. . . Mainstream scientist-practitioner neuropsychologists have never been threatened by the need to provide empirical justification for their work and should applaud such standards, as they target witnesses from fields without a firm grounding in science. (p. 871)

Although becoming generally accepted, neuropsychology is still gaining ground in terms of acceptance by various attorneys and court systems. On the basis of case law to date, several points can be made. A neuropsychological examination is not mandatory for a CST evaluation, even in cases involving possible brain disorder. For example, in *State v. Serra* (2002), the defendant had a history of learning disabilities and brain injury. The defendant was evaluated by a clinical psychologist, who found him IST, and a neuropsychiatrist, who found him CST. He was found CST in a legal hearing, and his court case proceeded. On appeal, the defense argued that the defense was inadequate because a neuropsychological evaluation was not completed. The finding of CST was upheld, and the court stated that the defendant's rights of equal protection and due process were not violated because neuropsychological testing was not performed. Similar findings were obtained in other cases (*Allen v. Mullin,* 2004; *Jefferson v. Hall,* 2009; *State v. Zachery W,* 2014). In *Reese v. State* (2009), the Florida Supreme Court opined that the defense cannot be considered ineffective for failing to obtain a neuropsychological evaluation.

In contrast, failure to obtain a neuropsychological evaluation has been found at the appeals level to have indicated ineffective counsel in some cases (*Commonwealth v. Gaboriault,* 2001; *Jones v. Ryan,* 2009; *Porter v. McCollum,* 2009). At times, the court has clearly expected a defense attorney to follow through on a neuropsychological evaluation and ensure that an adequate evaluation was completed (*Fautenberry v. Mitchell,* 2008). In *Fautenberry v. Mitchell* (2008), the court stated that the defense should zealously pursue evidence of neuropsychological impairment.

Neuropsychological Research

A review of the literature reveals a modest literature specifically for neuropsychology and CST and CR evaluations. Early work focused on neuropsychology and civil forensic practice. Over time, a greater emphasis on criminal forensic practice has developed. In 1992, Martell argued that the role of forensic neuropsychology "has evolved almost exclusively in the realm of the civil law, given its relevance to issues in disability determination, workman's compensation, and personal injury cases" (p. 313). Martell noted little focus in the literature to that date in neuropsychology and criminal law.

Early research identified a positive correlation between low intelligence and incompetency, particularly for verbal intelligence (Rogers, Ustad, Sewell, & Reinhart, 1996; Steadman, Monahan, Hartstone, Davis, & Robbins, 1982). However, this relationship exists only at the lowest levels of intelligence, and mild intellectual impairments do not seem to correlate with incompetency (Nicholson & Kugler, 1991). The relationship between specific neurocognitive domains and competency has been studied far less (Grandjean, 2004).

One of the earliest research articles in neuropsychology and criminal forensics was Nestor and Haycock (1997). These authors compared the neuropsychological characteristics of 28 murder defendants who were found not guilty by reason of insanity with those of murderers found guilty. They found those in the group who were not guilty by reason of insanity were more likely to have been psychotic at the time of the murder and were more likely to have killed a family member, especially a parent. Murderers found guilty were more likely to have used alcohol during the offense and to have killed a spouse or lover. However, Nestor and Haycock found no neuropsychological tests or characteristics that differentiated the defendants who were not guilty by reason of insanity and those found guilty in this early study.

Nestor, Daggett, Haycock, and Marilyn (1999), studied 181 men charged with serious felonies who underwent competency evaluations at Bridgewater State Hospital; 128 were found by evaluation to be competent, and 53 were found to be incompetent. Nestor et al. found that defendants deemed competent scored higher on intelligence, memory, and attention and concentration measures. Measures of academic achievement and executive functions did not differentiate between those found competent or incompetent. Incompetent defendants recalled fewer details in episodic memory tasks, suggesting that the ability to remember episodes and events may be an essential part of competence. They concluded that limitations of semantic knowledge are rarely roadblocks to competency.

Nestor et al. (1999) opined that declarative memory is particularly important in competence and that episodic and semantic memory, each a unique aspect of declarative memory, play unique and different roles in competence. Episodic memory (i.e., the ability to recollect personal events related to the crime in question) may influence the defendant's ability to assist counsel. Semantic knowledge (i.e., overall level of preexisting knowledge) provides a baseline against which the competency-related concepts of factual and rational knowledge can be compared; however, semantic knowledge was not considered to have a direct bearing on the legal question of competence.

Nestor et al. (1999) also opined that social abilities play an important role in CST. Competence may require an understanding of social situations and customs that underlie communication and one's working relationship with an attorney. They noted that competency may be viewed as a transactional construct lying between the attorney and the client. Social behaviors such as attachment and affiliation, they argued, may be mediated in part by common brain circuits involving limbic and brain stem regions. The adaptive importance of social intelligence may affect a defendant's ability to assist council. Nestor et al. indicated that the Comprehension and Picture Arrangement subtests from the Wechsler intelligence tests may be helpful in evaluating the interpersonal aspects of competence.

In a more recent study, Grandjean (2004) studied 55 defendants with mental disorders charged with crimes that resulted in bodily injury. The defendants were in a competency evaluation unit at a maximum security forensic state hospital. Of the 55 participants, seven were found to be malingering and were excluded; 18 were found competent on the basis of evaluation, and 30 were found to be incompetent. Grandjean found competent and incompetent participants did not differ in attention, visuospatial skills, or nonverbal memory. However, competent defendants performed better on measures of verbal comprehension, verbal memory, social judgment, and executive functions.

Kirkish and Sreenivasan (1999) completed a separate analysis regarding the application of neuropsychological concepts to CST. These authors divided cognitive functional capacity into four broad skill areas that are essential to trial competence: language, memory, auditory attentional, and reasoning. They suggested a process approach to evaluating these domains by (a) observations, (b) assessment with the Mini-Mental State Examination, and (c) further testing if needed. They also recommended a focus on the possibility of malingering. Denney (2012), in a book chapter on the assessment of competency, integrated the Nestor et al. (1999) and Grandjean (2004) data and concluded that "functional domains of intellect, attention, verbal learning/memory, and social judgment are important areas of focus" (p. 463).

Conducting Forensic Neuropsychological Competency-to-Stand-Trial and Criminal Responsibility Evaluations

Forensic neuropsychology has been defined as "the application of the science of brain-behavior relationships to legal decision making" (Horton & Hartlage, 2010, p. 5). The legal arena is a new and different place for many neuropsychologists who want to develop forensic expertise. These differences can be both challenging (Horton, 2010) and rewarding (Hartlage & Stern, 2010). As Horton (2010) pointed out, differences include the fact that the evaluator must take an objective and neutral stance rather than advocate for patients, as is commonly done with clinical cases. In fact, it is important to remember that defendants in forensic evaluations are not patients, and a doctor–patient or therapist–patient relationship does not exist. The legal setting is an adversarial one, and neuropsychological reports and opinions are used as weapons to fight a case (Zillmer & King, 2013). The evaluator must maintain emotional and practical distance from these factors and maintain professional objectivity. The evaluator must learn to have close working relationships with attorneys but maintain a professional distance and objectivity. More extensive performance validity assessment is needed in forensic cases compared with routine clinical cases. Communicating neuropsychological concepts, testing procedures, and results to a legal audience, either in report writing or during depositions and testimony, can be challenging. Even the neuropsychologist experienced in civil court proceedings may find criminal court different and challenging.

Neuropsychologists in court. LaDuke, DeMatteo, Heilbrun, and Swirsky-Sacchetti (2012) explored the experiences, training, and practices of neuropsychologists with experience in forensic neuropsychology. This study did not focus on CST or CR evaluations specifically. The vast majority of forensic neuropsychologists reported experience in civil court (98%); a smaller percentage (34%) reported experience in criminal court. Participants reported receiving training in neuropsychology while in graduate school and internships, but most developed expertise in forensic psychology later, while in professional practice, through continuing education and supervision. Most (80%) were board certified.

Neuropsychologists are performing forensic neuropsychological evaluations in growing numbers (Boake, 2008; Heilbronner, 2004). The use of neuropsychologists in court has been increasing faster than the use of other forensic mental health professionals in court (Kaufmann, 2008), and neuropsychology may be the predominant mental health specialty in court in the future (Sweet, King, Malina, Bergman, & Simmons, 2002). Attorneys may be the largest referral source for neuropsychologists (Sweet, Moberg, & Suchy, 2000). However, these data do not differentiate civil from criminal law.

A WestlawNext search completed in April 2015 revealed 526 cases in which *competency to stand trial* and *brain damage* were searched, using the syntax "(competency to stand trial) & (brain damage)." The search revealed 200 cases in which *competency to stand trial* and *dementia* were searched, 803 cases in which *insanity* and *brain damage* were searched, and 761 cases in which *insanity* and *dementia* were searched. However, when *competency to stand trial* and the root word *neuropsycholog* were searched, only 27 cases were found; only 21 were found for *insanity* and *neuropsycholog*. These findings also did not differentiate a case in which neuropsychology was only mentioned from a case in which a qualified neuropsychologist actually conducted a neuropsychological evaluation. Although these data are only suggestive, it appears that neuropsychology plays a role in a relatively small number of competency and sanity cases in which brain damage or dementia are considered. This trend may be reversing. Forensic neuropsychologists are placing a greater emphasis on criminal cases (Horton & Hartlage, 2010), to some degree because of the high number of reported head injuries in criminal cases (Denney & Wynkoop, 2000; Martell, 1992).

A forensic neuropsychologist may address a variety of issues and evaluations in a criminal setting. However, forensic psychologists and neuropsychologists are more likely to become involved in CST evaluations than CR evaluations, simply because there are many more of them. As of 2000, an estimated 60,000 competency evaluations were conducted annually in the United States (Bonnie & Grisso, 2000). About 2% to 8% of felony defendants are referred for CST evaluations (Bonnie, 1992; Golding, 1993; Hoge, Bonnie, Poythress, & Monahan, 1992), and rates of CST evaluations are also growing each year (Zapf & Roesch, 2006). Alternatively, insanity defenses are fairly rare (Cirincione, Steadman, & McGreevy, 1995).

Specialized knowledge. What differentiates a neuropsychologist from other psychologists is not the tests used but specialized knowledge. This is true in court as well. What neuropsychologists have to offer is specialized knowledge in the measurement of cognition, neuroanatomy, neuropathology, diagnosis of neurological conditions, and brain–behavior relationships. In addition, neuropsychologists bring advanced knowledge and techniques for identifying malingering (Boone, 2007, 2013; Larrabee, 2007; Rogers, 1997; Slick, Sherman, & Iverson, 1999). Neuropsychologists are often used because of their adherence to a scientific approach that meets judicial standards for expert testimony (Kaufmann, 2008).

Multidata source model. Psychological and neuropsychological testing are not necessary for many CST or CR evaluations (Marcopulos, Caillouet, & Tussey, 2013). In fact, a fairly conservative approach to testing is the rule in criminal forensic psychology (Heilbrun, 1992). The belief is that decisions about competency and responsibility are fundamentally issues of practical, functional skills, and testing does not necessarily assess these skills. However, in many circumstances neuropsychological testing data can be helpful. Heilbrun (1992) recommended that tests be carefully selected on the basis of the following factors: (a) commercial availability, (b) citations in at least two sources, (c) reliability of .80 or higher, (d) relevance to the legal issue or psychological construct being measured, and (e) standardization.

Neuropsychological testing data should be thought of as one source of information in an evaluation that should include multiple sources of data (Denney, 2012; Denney & Wynkoop, 2000). Forensic evaluations, compared with clinical evaluations, typically require broader sources of data (Denney, 2012).

A CST evaluation focuses on the present. Historical information that is included in a CST evaluation is included only as it helps to understand present capacities. A CR evaluation, however, necessitates a comprehensive review of personal history, present functioning, and mental state at the time of the offense. In this regard, the focus of a CST evaluation is the present, and the focus of a CR evaluation is some point in the past.

As a result, the more sources of data the better, particularly for a CR evaluation. Such sources include the following: medical, mental health, and substance use or treatment records; previous evaluations and psycholegal opinions; educational, military service, and other vocational records; legal history and records related to current legal circumstances and charges; witness statements, private investigator reports, attorney observations, and confessions; family interviews or statements; reports of parole or probation officers; clinical interview and mental status; psychological and neuropsychological testing; performance and validity measures; and FAI tests. For CR evaluations, the following are particularly valuable: the defendant's account of the offense; the defendant's understanding of his or her mental condition at the time of the offense; the defendant's interpretations of why it happened; any accounts by others of the defendant's behavior leading up to, during, and immediately after the offense; and any other available information. It is important to identify convergence among multiple sources of data to make a final CST or CR recommendation.

Neuropsychological testing. Evaluators who are employed by a state hospital, prison, or other facility may have the luxury of completing their evaluations in their own office or in a testing room. However, this is not true for many forensic psychologists. Many forensic neuropsychologists working in criminal contexts must be ready to travel to different jails or prisons, private attorneys' offices, public defenders' or district attorneys' offices, or other locations to complete evaluations. Although one must be careful to ensure basic testing conditions are adequate, such as privacy, forensic practice requires a great deal of flexibility in the application of interview and testing skills. The first author (Loren E. Mallory) once completed a CST evaluation sitting on the tailgate of his pickup truck because the defendant was too paranoid and anxious to go inside. Luckily, this was a rural setting, and there was adequate privacy.

In general, a lean and flexible approach to neuropsychological testing is indicated for CST and CR evaluations, although more time and resources may be spent on a CR evaluation. Long and comprehensive batteries are not the rule. It is important to understand that neuropsychological tests should be chosen to rule out significant abnormalities or deficits. Forensic neuropsychological evaluators working in criminal contexts are not interested in subtle, mild weaknesses or fine discriminations between the above-average and superior range. They are interested in identifying or ruling out significant neurocognitive deficits that have a functional impact on the defendant's CST or CR.

Individual neuropsychological screening tests are not recommended even though they are commonly used. As many as 50% of psychologists who perform forensic criminal evaluations use some level of neuropsychological testing (Borum & Grisso, 1995). Neuropsychological screening tests in forensic evaluations are sometimes used, in theory, to rule out the presence of neurocognitive deficits or identify the need for a full neuropsychological evaluation. Screening tests harken back to a time in which the concept of "organicity" was in vogue—an overarching condition or deficit that could differentiate something "organic" from something "functional." This is no longer current thought in neuropsychology. Lezak, Howieson, Bigler, and Tranel (2012) recommended caution in the interpretation of screening tests and suggested a symptom pattern analysis approach instead. That is, instead of a specific test with a cutoff score, the evaluator chooses tests to help understand the client's cognitive functioning and makes determinations on the basis of history and patterns of symptoms.

Theoretically, a screening test rules out deficits in a broad array of cognitive domains (Smith, Ivnik, & Lucas, 2008). In this regard, a screening test has high sensitivity and low specificity. The screening test emphasizes negative predictive power over positive predictive power; it should accurately identify those not in need of further neuropsychological evaluation, at the cost of identifying some for further neuropsychological evaluation in error. Put another way, the evaluator should feel certain about the cases ruled out for further neuropsychological evaluation. Few tests actually meet these expectations, and the identification of appropriate cutoff scores is difficult (Lezak et al., 2012).

Neuropsychological screening tests may be misunderstood and misused in a court proceeding or a legal process. The danger is that the court system will assume that the defendant has had his or her chance at a neuropsychological evaluation if he or she has been given a screening test.

In *Johnson v. State* (2012), the defendant, referred to as a "movant" in this context, had been found guilty of murder and other charges by a jury in Missouri and sentenced to death. His sentence had been upheld at the appellate level. One previous psychological evaluation indicated that the movant "does have an organic brain syndrome combined with significant psychiatric disorders and those are permanent conditions" (p. 6). This first psychologist's report was not used in the defense. Three psychologists or psychiatrists evaluated Johnson for the case, and all suspected brain damage. Two of them recommended to the defense attorney that a forensic neuropsychological evaluation be conducted. However, the defense did not obtain a forensic evaluation by a qualified neuropsychologist. Postconviction relief was sought at the Supreme Court level. Johnson claimed that the defense had been inadequate because an evaluation by a qualified neuropsychologist had not been included in the defense. To quote the opinion,

> Movant believes that had counsel consulted with a neuropsychologist, counsel would have discovered that his brain damage and neuropsychological impairments affected his ability to think, problem solve, act rationally, and deal with stress. Further, had the jury been presented this evidence, there was a reasonable probability that it would not have found that Movant deliberated and would have imposed a life sentence. (p. 5)

The Supreme Court denied Johnson's request for relief, citing, "One of the evaluations contained some neuropsychological testing, and it did not reveal results that would be suggestive of significant neuropsychological impairment" (*Johnson v. State*, 2012, p. 8). Exactly what "some" neuropsychological testing meant is not clear, but it is clear that the psychologist was not considered a neuropsychologist. Of course, it cannot be known how a qualified forensic neuropsychological evaluation may have affected this case.

Rather than neuropsychological screening tests, a thorough clinical interview is recommended to better identify cases in which a neuropsychological evaluation is needed. A clinical interview has less chance of being misunderstood or misused later in the legal process. For a list of historical issues and conditions typically explored in such an interview, see Exhibit 15.1.

Cognitive screening tests such as the Mini-Mental State Examination (Folstein, Folstein, & McHugh, 1975; Folstein, Folstein, McHugh, & Fanjiang, 2001) or the Montreal Cognitive Assessment (1996) are too brief and rely too heavily on face validity (are too easily exaggerated or malingered) for regular use. However, they are helpful when time or access is limited or when the evaluator needs to document blatantly poor orientation or severe neuropsychological deficits in a very impaired defendant. The Montreal Cognitive Assessment is recommended over the Mini-Mental State Examination because it has specifically been studied in competency cases (Najolia, Dunning, Smith, Knopp, & Zolnikov, 2014) and found to be helpful, along with other factors, in the evaluation of CST. The Montreal Cognitive Assessment has good support and research behind it, and is easily downloaded.

The approach advocated for forensic neuropsychological testing in CST and CR cases is a flexible, brief battery, hypothesis-testing, process approach. This is similar to the hypothesis-testing approach suggested by Lezak et al. (2012) or the scientific approach to forensic neuropsychology recommended by Larrabee (2012). The first step of the process is developing hypotheses, followed by testing and refining these hypotheses.

This hypothesis-testing approach can be extended to the psycholegal question at hand. The evaluator may have a hypothesis, based on all of the

Exhibit 15.1
Typical Historical Items and Conditions Queried in a Forensic Neuropsychological Background Interview

Items to be questioned about

Pregnancy and birth resulting in defendant and defendant's health at birth
Developmental history
History of childhood diseases and accidents
Life history of serious accidents and illnesses
For every head trauma, concussion, or traumatic brain injury reported, ask about loss of consciousness, posttraumatic confusion or amnesia, retrograde amnesia, emergency responders and emergency treatment, rehabilitation services, course of recovery, any reported permanent symptoms
Heart disease
Stroke and transient ischemic attacks
Blood pressure
Cholesterol levels
Poisoning or exposure to toxic chemicals
Anoxia
Seizures and seizurelike episodes, syncope, or loss of consciousness without cause
History of all surgeries
Current health and an current illnesses or conditions
Current medications, vitamins, over the counter, substances, and naturopathic remedies taken
Substance abuse
Family/genetic history of dementia

information available beforehand, that the defendant is likely IST because of psychosis (e.g., the defendant was described as paranoid and unable to work with his attorney). From the first interactions with the defendant, this hypothesis is tested (e.g., does he speak logically? Is there any paranoia or delusional material apparent? Is there another explanation?). Alternative possibilities are explored (e.g., maybe the defendant is not paranoid, maybe he is disoriented because of substance abuse or has such severe memory problems he appears disoriented and is easily irritated; the defendant is older, dementia should be ruled out). Procedures are guided by the hypotheses (e.g., add more questions about orientation and give additional memory testing). The evaluator should include hypotheses specifically about the prongs of the CST test (e.g., given a history of stroke, this defendant has a gross communication disorder, he probably has a fluent aphasia, and he could have difficulty understanding or expressing himself to his attorney; he may be incompetent if he cannot communicate with his attorney; better add some language tests and discuss a legal vignette with him to see how well he can communicate about legal issues).

Regarding testing per se, the evaluator should begin with a flexible brief battery and, as hypotheses about neurocognitive functioning develop, choose specific tests to explore those hypotheses further. The flexible battery should include not only neuropsychological tests, but performance and symptom validity measures, tests of personality traits and emotional states, and specific forensic assessment instruments.

Instruments such as the Repeatable Battery for the Assessment of Neuropsychological Status (Randolph, 2003) and the Neuropsychological Assessment Battery, Screening Module (NAB–SM; Stern & White, 2003), are brief neuropsychological batteries. Instead of focusing on a single test or score to identify the presence or absence of brain disorder (as occurs with measures such as the Mini-Mental State Examination), brief batteries are designed to provide a quick but broad survey of neurocognitive domains. These brief batteries are a good beginning point for a forensic neuropsychological evaluation.

Alternatively, evaluators can develop their own brief batteries of well-designed and normed tests for different primary cognitive domains or begin with a few selected subtests from a comprehensive measure such as the Wechsler Adult Intelligence Scale—Fourth Edition and generate hypotheses from there.

Generally speaking, tests that can be given on a laptop computer are acceptable, although sometimes permission to bring a laptop into a jail or prison is needed ahead of time. However, testing procedures that require an online connection or Internet access will typically not work because an Internet connection is usually not allowed.

The primary cognitive domains of interest in a CST and CR evaluation are intelligence, language and communication, social judgement, auditory attention, memory, and reasoning skills (Denney, 2012; Kirkish & Sreenivasan, 1999; Nestor et al., 1999). Tests that explore these domains should be included in the additional tests that the evaluator has with him or her during all evaluations.

Specific forensic assessment instruments such as the MacCAT–CA are best used during clinical interview. That is, they are used much as a structured interview. For neuropsychological testing, the first author (Loren E. Mallory) typically begins with the Word Memory Test (WMT; Green, 1994) on a laptop computer. During the 30-minute delay for the WMT, an intellectual screening test will be administered, such as the Reynolds Intellectual Screening Test or the Reynolds Intellectual Assessment Scales, depending on time and clinical case issues. The NAB–SM is begun but not continued as far as the memory tests (so as not to interfere with the WMT or throw off the timing of the NAB–SM memory tests). Then the delayed portion of the WMT is administered. After that, the NAB–SM is continued, including the memory tests, and completed. Then the Word Reading subtest from the Wide Range Achievement Test 4 is administered. The defendant will work on a Psychological Assessment Inventory or Minnesota Multiphasic Personality Inventory—Second Edition, or the Minnesota Multiphasic Personality Inventory—Second Edition Restructured Form, for a few minutes, during which time the WMT and NAB–SM are scored on the computer. Digits from the NAB–SM are used to produce a Reliable Digit Span score. The WMT and NAB–SM work together nicely and provide a list-learning memory test, a story-learning memory test, and a spatial memory test. After that, specific tests from the NAB may be chosen for administration, depending on the neurocognitive hypotheses generated so far. Then personality testing is completed.

Although this may be a basic testing strategy, the battery is always adjusted for specific circumstances. A comprehensive intellectual abilities test (i.e., Wechsler Adult Intelligence Scale—Fourth Edition) is administered when there is an indication of intellectual disability. An Adaptive Behavior Assessment System–Second Edition is added if a more thorough analysis of functional life skills is needed. If memory is a specific issue, or if dementia is a specific concern, the NAB–SM may be given without the screening memory tests, and the full NAB Memory Module will be given. The NAB provides the ability to select different co-normed tests from different domains as needed. In particular, the NAB Memory Module Daily Living Memory Scales and NAB Language Module Daily Living Scales have been helpful additional tests, and they have the added virtue of demonstrated ecological validity (Temple et al., 2009; Zgaljardic, Yancy, Temple, Watford, & Miller, 2011).

An outline for competency-to-stand-trial and criminal responsibility reports. There are many forms and styles of evaluation reports. Reports by different evaluators are divided into different sections. However, good reports by experienced forensic psychologists and neuropsychologists generally contain the same information. It is helpful for the novice forensic neuropsychologist to begin by reading different reports produced in their jurisdiction. The reports produced at the state hospital or state facility in one's jurisdiction may provide a general outline of what is expected. A senior forensic psychologist or neuropsychologist may be able to share some redacted reports. Examples of CST and CR report outlines flexibly used by Loren E. Mallory are provided (see Tables 15.1 and 15.2). The exact report is adjusted to meet the specific circumstances of each evaluation.

TABLE 15.1

An Example Report Outline for a Forensic Neuropsychological Competency-to-Stand-Trial (CST) Evaluation

Content item	Notes
Identification	
Summary statement	Clearly set apart in some way
Referral and specific referral questions	
Legal precedent	Include appropriate statute here
Legal circumstances and legal history	Include a knowledge test and any forensic assessment instruments here
Review of background documents	For CST, include all appropriate medical, educational, and vocational records and carefully selected legal records if thought to be pertinent to present capacity
Medical, mental health, and substance abuse history	Include neurological history and questioning about all head traumas, etc.
Education, military service, and vocational history	
Family, relationship, and social history	
Mental status and behavioral observations	Be comprehensive here—a CST evaluation is about present functioning
Integrated interpretation of psychological and neuropsychological testing	Include a clear statement of whether this is a normal or abnormal cognitive profile
Analysis of the potential for malingering	
Diagnosis	
Psycholegal analysis	Analyze case vis-a-vis appropriate statute, possibly on a prong-by-prong basis
Psycholegal opinion	Carefully worded
If found incompetent, a discussion of what treatment may rehabilitate defendant to competency	
If appropriate, an opinion of whether defendant is safe to be rehabilitated in the community	
Further discussion and treatment recommendations	May be omitted—this is not necessary, but often appreciated
Appendix A: Cognitive and neuropsychological testing scores	
Appendix B: Psychological or personality testing scores	

The Nexus

The point at which forensic neuropsychology and statutory requirements for CST or CR come together in a specific case is called the *nexus*. The evaluator must analyze how to integrate and understand the interplay of psychological and neurocognitive factors, testing results, and the defendant's history and conditions as they affect the statutory definition of CST or CR. The evaluator considers questions such as the following:

1. Does a neurocognitive disorder based on head trauma affect the defendant's ability to communicate and assist his or her attorney?
2. Do poor testing scores translate into real functional limitations in the context of CST?
3. Does memory loss due to dementia cause the defendant to be unable to remember or know his or her legal circumstances?
4. Did paranoid delusions resulting from a psychotic disorder make the defendant unable to appreciate the wrongfulness of his or her actions at the time of an offense?

It is important to connect psychiatric and cognitive symptoms to functional behaviors that have an impact on CST or CR. This step is often missed by the novice evaluator. It is not adequate to state that a defendant has dementia and is therefore incompetent to stand trial. Rather, the evaluator must identify how a specific symptom or deficit affects a particular psycholegal construct or functional ability.

TABLE 15.2

An Example Report Outline for a Forensic Neuropsychological Criminal Responsibility (CR) Evaluation

Content item	Notes
Identification	
Summary statement	Clearly set apart in some way
Referral and specific referral questions	
Legal precedent	Include statute here
Legal circumstances and legal history	Include a comprehensive interview of the client's understanding of his charges, what he is alleged to have done, what he says happened, his understanding of why it happened, an analysis of his state of mind at the time, etc.
Review of background documents	For CR, include all appropriate medical, educational and vocational records, and a comprehensive review of all legal records pertaining to the crime, especially outlining any information or descriptions of the defendant informative to the defendant's state of mind at the time of the offense
Medical, mental health, and substance abuse history	Include neurological history and questioning about all head traumas etc.
Education, military service, and vocational history	
Family, relationship and social history	
Mental status and behavioral observations	
Integrated interpretation of psychological and neuropsychological testing	Include clear statement of whether this is a normal or abnormal cognitive profile
Analysis of the potential for malingering	
Diagnosis	
Psycholegal analysis	Analyze case vis-a-vis appropriate statute, possibly on a prong-by-prong basis
Psycholegal opinion	Carefully worded
Further discussion and treatment recommendations	May be omitted—this is not necessary, but often appreciated
Appendix A: Cognitive/neuropsychological testing scores	
Appendix B: Psychological or personality testing scores	

The evaluator provides important information to the court about how the defendant's mental state affects the legal question at hand. For example, a defendant with dementia may have trouble recalling case-related information or be unable to appreciate the adversarial nature of the legal system. A defendant's paranoid delusions may extend to the defense attorney, resulting in an unwillingness to share important information. In a CR case, a defendant with command auditory hallucinations may have been unable to understand the wrongfulness of the conduct.

In these cases, it is important not only to identify those mental conditions that impair psycholegal abilities but also identify those that do not. For example, one defendant with bipolar disorder may be unable to make rational decisions about his case as a result of thought disorganization and grandiosity. However, another defendant with bipolar disorder may be better able to make a decision about his case but have difficulty communicating relevantly about it. In each case, the evaluator must explain how the defendant's mental state does and does not impair psycholegal functioning or, in a CR case, does or does not meet established criteria for insanity.

The nexus in competency to stand trial. The evaluator must fashion the evaluation around the appropriate statute for the court that has jurisdiction in the case. This is generally the appropriate state statute or, if a federal case, the federal statute. The federal CST language ("Offenders With Mental Disease or Defect," 2006) reads "presently suffering from a mental disease or defect rendering him mentally incompetent to the extent that he is unable to understand the nature and consequences of the proceedings against him or to assist properly in his defense" (p. 4241).

In the jurisdiction in which both authors practice most often, Oregon, the statute for CST reads,

> (2)A defendant may be found incapacitated if, as a result of mental disease or defect, the defendant is unable: (a) To understand the nature of the proceedings against the defendant; or (b) To assist and cooperate with the counsel of the defendant; or (c) To participate in the defense of the defendant. (Oregon Revised Statutes, 2016, Title 16, Chap. 161.360)

Most state statutes about CST relate in some way to *Dusky v. United States* (1960). The Oregon language "to understand the nature of the proceedings against the defendant" relates fairly directly to the *Dusky* "rational as well as factual understanding of the proceedings against him" ("Offenders With Mental Disease or Defect," 2006, p. 4241) prong. The Oregon "assist and cooperate with the counsel" language is an outgrowth of the *Dusky* "consult with his lawyer with a reasonable degree of rational understanding" ("Offenders With Mental Disease or Defect," 2006, p. 4241) prong. Finally, the Oregon "participate in the defense" language relates to the *Drope* "assist in preparing his defense" ("Offenders With Mental Disease or Defect," 2006, p. 4241) language. Different state statutes vary in how they translate these concepts into state law.

It is noteworthy that in most jurisdictions some sort of mental disease or defect (i.e., a diagnosis) is necessary to trigger the application of the statute. Usually, diagnoses such as a personality disorder or voluntary substance use do not meet the statutory definition. In these jurisdictions, a forensic evaluator must first establish a diagnosis and then analyze related functional abilities as they relate to the statute. However, in a few jurisdictions, a diagnosis is not required. In such jurisdictions, all that is required is a functional incapacity to assist one's counsel. In Washington, the statute simply states, "No incompetent person shall be tried, convicted, or sentenced for the commission of an offense so long as such incapacity continues" (Revised Code of Washington, 1974, Title 10, Chap. 77, § 050).

Competency to stand trial: Knowledge and the nexus. The factual and rational understanding requirement for competency is often referred to as the "knowledge test." That is, does the defendant possess adequate general knowledge (semantic memory) about the legal process, and does the defendant possess adequate specific knowledge of the case (episodic memory) to understand what is happening? Defendants are typically interviewed about the facts of their specific legal case, the roles of the players in a trial, and the possible outcomes of their case. The use of forensic assessment instruments is helpful here. Verbal intelligence tests or subtests such as the Information scale from Wechsler Adult Intelligence Scale—Fourth Edition may be helpful in understanding the defendant's semantic memory abilities. When deficits in factual knowledge cause incapacity, an educational or rehabilitation approach may be appropriate.

The ability to simply state a fact does not necessarily imply an understanding of that fact—there is a requirement for rational understanding as well as factual understanding. Further inquiry is required to ensure the individual is not simply parroting the information. Instead of asking only what the charges are, it is helpful to ask questions such as the following: What do the charges mean? What is the defendant alleged to have done? Why is that wrong in the eyes of the law? Instead of asking only the name of the attorney, ask the defendant what the attorney's role is in the case. What is the attorney's job? Is the attorney on the defendant's side? Although the standard should not be understood as requiring a very deep or advanced level of rational understanding, some level of basic rational understanding should be present to participate in the defense. As stated previously, the requirement is that sufficient factual and rational information to proceed in a specific case is required. Language and communication skills, auditory attention, episodic memory, and reasoning skills are all important.

In a CST evaluation, however, the evaluator should be careful about asking specifically what the defendant did during the alleged offense or whether the defendant is guilty. First, it is usually unnecessary. CST is about the defendant's present ability to assist counsel; it is not about the defendant's mental state at the time of the alleged offense. Second, it is important to ensure that a CST report does not become a confession, deposition, or fact-finding tool. There is an art to evaluating the defendant's ability to understand his or her legal circumstances without eliciting a confession or potentially damaging information. The use of hypothetical questions and legal scenarios can be helpful. Forensic assessment instruments are also helpful. Some evaluators reason that they should ask questions about the offense and just not include that information in the report. However, there is the danger of being questioned in deposition or during testimony. The evaluator will be compelled to answer in those circumstances.

Competency to stand trial: Ability to assist counsel and the nexus. The ability to assist counsel requires the defendant to establish some sort of basic working relationship with the attorney, have a basic level of trust in the attorney, listen to and understand what the attorney is saying, convey information to the attorney, learn and remember information about the case, reason through options such as plea bargains or legal strategies, and plan with the attorney. Intelligence, social cognition, receptive and expressive language and communication skills, auditory attention and memory, reasoning, and planning are all important. Attorney feedback about the defendant can be helpful, and at times, it is even helpful to observe the defendant with the attorney.

Competency to stand trial: Ability to participate in the defense and the nexus. This requirement is far less defined or discussed in legal and psychological sources. In *Drope v. Missouri* (1975), the defendant attempted suicide during the trial. The trial court, believing that the defendant had voluntarily shot himself to avoid trial, denied an appeal for reevaluation of the defendant's CST and continued the proceedings while the defendant was hospitalized and not present in court. The defendant was found guilty of rape and attempted murder and sentenced to life in prison. The defense appealed to the Missouri Supreme Court and the Missouri Court of Appeals, without success. The case was then heard by the U.S. Supreme Court. The Court found this was a violation of the defendant's due process rights and overturned the finding. The Supreme Court opined that the correct action would have been to suspend the trial until a reevaluation of the defendant's CST could be conducted. The language of the finding included the statement that the defendant has the right to be able to "assist in preparing his defense."

Bonnie (1992), relying in part on the *Drope* case, identified two related but separate constructs important in CST. The first is competence to assist counsel, and the second is "a contextualized concept of decisional competence" (p. 294). This idea of decisional competence is a logical outgrowth of the defendant's right to be competent to assist in preparing the defense.

Bonnie (1992) noted that 90% of cases do not end in a trial. The capacity to assist counsel and decisional competence to make decisions required to resolve the case without going to trial are in most cases more important than trial competency per se. Bonnie noted that defendants are required to make certain decisions autonomously, including (a) accepting or rejecting a plea, (b) whether the case should be tried in front of a jury, and (c) whether the defendant will testify. Decisions such as these "are committed, by law, to the defendant and not to the attorney" (p. 296). Decisional competence relies on psychological capacities that overlap with, but extend beyond, the capacities necessary to assist counsel: (a) the ability to communicate a preference, (b) the ability to understand relevant information about a particular decision, and (c) the ability to appreciate the significance of that information.

Although little scholarship has been conducted on the relationship between neuropsychology and decisional competence, some initial thoughts are appropriate. As with the ability to assist counsel, interpersonal skills, expressive and receptive language skills, and verbal intelligence are important. However, the ability to understand multiple choices in a complex and emotionally laden decision would seem to place a heavy burden on executive functions. The ability to understand the pluses and minuses of multiple options, the fluidity of thought necessary to identify and smoothly move back and forth between choices, the ability to place the appropriate level of importance on the decision, the complex attention and self-direction of attentional resources necessary for the task, and the planning and forethought necessary all indicate the importance of executive functions. Perhaps scholarship will explore this relationship further in the future.

The nexus in criminal responsibility. The federal statute regarding insanity ("Insanity Defense," 18 U.S.C. § 17, 1986) states:

> It is an affirmative defense to a prosecution under any Federal statute that, at the time of the commission of the acts constituting the offense, the defendant, as a result of a severe mental disease or defect, was unable to appreciate the nature and quality or the wrongfulness of his acts. Mental disease or defect does not otherwise constitute a defense. (p. 114)

To continue using Oregon as an example, the statute regarding CR reads,

> A person is guilty except for insanity if, as a result of mental disease or defect at the time of the engaging in criminal conduct, the person lacks substantial capacity either to appreciate the criminality of the conduct or to conform the conduct to the requirements of the law. (Oregon Revised Statutes, 2016, Title 16, Chap. 161.295)

In Oregon, mental disease or defect cannot mean solely a personality disorder, antisocial conduct, or substance abuse. The appreciation prong—the capacity to appreciate or understand the wrongfulness of one's action—is present in all jurisdictions. In some jurisdictions, as in Oregon, the conform prong (the ability to conform one's behavior to the requirement of the law or control one's behavior) is present.

In a CR or insanity evaluation, the primary question explored by the evaluator is whether, at the time of the offense, as a result of mental disease or defect, the defendant was unable to understand the wrongfulness of the behavior that underlies the charges. In practicality, a blatant psychosis or severe neurocognitive disorder such as dementia is required to meet the appreciation prong. It is a very difficult standard to meet. This is why insanity defenses are rare, and success is even rarer. Cirincione et al. (1995) found that in the United States, the insanity defense is attempted in about .85% of criminal cases and, of that small number of cases, about 28% are successful. An interesting aspect to this study was that in states in which more insanity defenses are attempted, fewer of them succeed, so that the volume of defendants found insane remains consistent across different jurisdictions. The authors commented, "This relationship may suggest that there is some acceptable range of acquittals such that a high volume of pleas is offset by a relatively low acquittal rate and vice versa" (p. 399).

In jurisdictions in which the conform prong exists, an argument can be made that an overwhelming impulse to act was present at the time of the offense. A manic disorder with psychosis or a delusional disorder may be pertinent here, for example. The first author (Loren E. Mallory) once argued that serious frontal lobe damage with pseudopsychopathy caused an uncontrollable impulse to act, but the judge found this too high a standard for an insanity defense. Again, these standards are very difficult to meet.

It is more common for an attorney to use any diminished capacity or EED defense available in the relevant jurisdiction. In practice, the threat of an insanity defense is used more often to move the case forward to some sort of alternative dispensation. The arguments and cross examinations for an insanity case can be rather surreal if not comical. Loren E. Mallory can recall a case in which a defendant with schizophrenia believed that the people in his family had been replaced by Martians and were going to eat his brain. The prosecution attempted to make the case that even if he felt endangered by Martians, he knew that attacking a Martian would be wrong.

SPECIAL ISSUES AND RECOMMENDATIONS

Loren E. Mallory asked questions of several legal professionals, who were chosen because they read and use many CST and CR evaluations. The informal sample included 25 or more defense attorneys, two judges, and one district attorney. They were asked about how they read an evaluation report, what they find helpful, and what they find frustrating. These were informal conversations, not a scientific questionnaire; however, consistent feedback was identified. Much of the information provided below was informed by this process.

Findings From the Informal Survey

Know the statute. Consumers of CST and CR reports are frustrated when the evaluation, discussion, and results do not pertain to the appropriate statute. A competent CST or CR evaluation should be planned and executed around the appropriate statute for the jurisdiction in which it is intended. Reports should be written in an organized way that begins with the statute, presents findings to address the statute, perhaps addresses the prongs individually, and ends with a conclusion about the statute. The statute should be included in the report, most often in a section titled "Legal Precedents" or something similar. A final opinion should be included that answers the ultimate question in the context of the statute (e.g., is the person competent to stand trial?)

The evaluator should get to know the relevant statutes very well and memorize their numbers. On occasion, evaluators have been observed during testimony who could not identify the correct statute and requirements for their decisions. The court is not likely to take the evaluator seriously in this case.

In addition, it is important to obtain a working knowledge of how these statutes are understood and applied in the jurisdiction in which the evaluation is performed. This knowledge only comes with experience. Some neuropsychologists may receive some of this experience during training. However, most neuropsychologists focus on neuropsychology rather than forensic psychology during training. For practicing neuropsychologists who are developing forensic skills, it is important to work with forensic psychologists or forensic neuropsychologists experienced in the jurisdiction. Depending on the clinical context, it may be possible to work with a more experienced psychologist in one's practice setting, or formal supervision may need to be arranged until professional competency is established. There is also a growing tendency for jurisdictions to require certification to engage in forensic psychology practice. Neuropsychologists should determine whether there is such a requirement in their jurisdiction and become certified if needed.

Write to the consumer. The consumers of CST and CR reports are for the most part attorneys and judges. It has been said that psychologists, especially early-career psychologists, often write in a voice that is appropriate for other psychologists or even to their former supervisors. Yet it is important to write in a voice that nonpsychologists can understand and not to use jargon that would be understood only by another neuropsychologist. If a scientific name or statement is needed, add a brief explanation so that nonpsychologists will know what was meant.

Judges and attorneys have their own concerns and needs from the report. They want to be able to quickly understand the opinion about CST or CR as it relates to the appropriate statute. They do not want to wade through a lot of jargon or loosely related esoteric information.

Be concise and clear. Evaluations should be complete, make a good case, and be well organized, but they do not have to be very long. CST evaluations can be fairly brief. CR evaluations may be significantly longer because of their greater analysis of the defendant's thoughts and behaviors relating to the alleged crime; a comprehensive review of legal, medical, substance use, and mental health records; and a more complicated analysis and opinion. The type and scope of neuropsychological testing will also have an impact on the length of the report. Neuropsychologists should ensure that every section and paragraph in the report adds to the analysis of the referral question.

Loren E. Mallory provides a testing score sheet in an appendix to the report. In the body of the report, an integrated interpretation of the testing results is provided. A clear statement about whether this is a normal or abnormal neurocognitive profile is given. It is not recommended that a test-by-test or score-by-score analysis be provided in these evaluations. Such information is not helpful to the consumer.

The summary is key. A judge who was interviewed stated that she reads the introduction and summary of an evaluation. She will then see what both attorneys—the prosecutor and defense attorney—think about the case. If they agree, she will not read the rest of the report. If there is conflict and likely to be a hearing, then she will read the report in its entirety. This idea that the summary is all that is read was very consistent across our interviews of both attorneys and judges. One attorney from a large public defense organization who reads many reports explained that the summary is the end product of the evaluation. It is akin to the legal opinion or finding in a legal document. The rest of the report is like the footnotes—simply the data on which the opinion (summary) is based.

It is important to provide a clearly labeled and easily found summary. The summary must provide a concise statement of the evaluator's opinion and clearly state why he or she came to that conclusion, including a brief statement about whether the defendant does or does not meet statutory requirements for the relevant question. The summary is not an afterthought; it may be the most important portion of the report and should be allotted time accordingly when writing the report. The summary can be at the beginning or ending of the report.

The Cart Before the Horse

Attitudes differ among evaluators about whether it is appropriate to complete a CR evaluation with an incompetent defendant. We believe it is best practice in most circumstances not to do so. The reason is twofold: First, a CR evaluation includes questioning about the crime that could be used against the defendant. Because the defendant is incompetent, he or she is not able to make a knowing and rational decision to share that information. It is true in some jurisdictions, technically, that information identified in a CST evaluation is not supposed to be used against the defendant; however, experience has indicated that this is not always the case. Second, if the defendant is not competent then he or she should not be choosing to engage in legal strategies or whether to participate in a CR evaluation process.

There is an assumption that a defendant referred for a CR evaluation is competent to choose to participate, has discussed the evaluation with the defense attorney, and is able to decide to share and discuss potentially damaging information with the evaluator. In practice, evaluators should always do a CST evaluation before a CR evaluation, if only for themselves. It is possible at times to be certain a defendant is competent on the basis of only a brief conversation. The issue may never be mentioned in the CR report. However, a skilled evaluator always makes sure that a defendant has no current competency issues before proceeding with a CR evaluation.

Referral sources often request what is essentially a hybrid report by asking the evaluator to complete both CST and CR evaluations and, perhaps, consider other possibilities (i.e., EED or diminished capacity). Generally, the CST evaluation should be done first and, if the defendant is determined to be competent, then the evaluator can move forward to complete the CR evaluation. The evaluator can produce separate reports for each issue. Alternatively, a single report with two sections may be produced that addresses the CST issue before moving on to the CR issue. If the evaluator believes the defendant is incompetent, then the evaluation should be stopped, and the evaluator should produce findings only about CST. If the defendant is treated and later found to be competent, or even if the issue is adjudicated and the defendant is found competent, then the evaluator should resume the evaluation.

The Issue of the Ultimate Issue

The *ultimate issue* refers to whether the defendant meets the statutory requirements, for example, to be found incompetent or not or insane or not. Some evaluators believe that an evaluation should include all information necessary for the decision but not an ultimate opinion (Grisso, 1986, 1988). The basis for this is a philosophical belief that it is not the evaluator's place to make such decisions; it is the purview of the trier of fact (judge or jury). Those who argue that it is best to provide an opinion on the ultimate issue (Rogers & Ewing, 1989) believe that the court benefits from clearly knowing the evaluator's opinion and that the trier of fact will make the final decision anyway. It is better to provide a direct opinion than to leave the consumer of the report guessing about or inferring what the evaluator believes.

It is very important to word an ultimate opinion carefully. It is never appropriate to say "the defendant is incompetent," for example; this is clearly the decision of a judge, not an evaluator. It is best to say something such as "In this evaluator's professional opinion, defendant meets the requirements to be found incompetent to stand trial as stated in [statute]."

On the basis of an informal review of psychologists on several national professional email distribution groups, most psychologists do in fact provide their ultimate opinion. However this issue appears to be a long-standing and sometimes emotional point of contention among forensic psychologists, with experienced and competent psychologists on both sides.

Some Special Considerations About Memory

Forensic neuropsychologists encounter defendants who report memory loss. About 30% of criminal defendants report amnesia for the crime (Cima, Nijman, Merckelbach, Kremer, & Hollnack, 2004; Guðjónsson, Pétursson, Skúlason, & Sigurðardóttir, 1989, Taylor & Kopelman, 1984). In most circumstances, failure to remember an alleged crime, or amnesia for the event, does not render the defendant IST. If the individual is presently able to consider the facts of the case, understand and reason about them, make decisions about the case, and work with the defense attorney, CST is retained. This is sometimes the case in crimes that occurred during alcohol or other substance intoxication, in which the individual may have amnesia for the event but can presently consider the facts about what happened and understand them and participate in his or her legal defense. In *Price v. Thurmer* (2011), the Court of Appeals found that the test of competence is the ability to assist one's lawyer rather than memory of the crime.

In *Wilson v. U.S.* (1968), the defendant, the getaway driver in a bank robbery, experienced a car accident immediately after the crime. He experienced a substantial brain injury and had no memory for the crime as a result of retrograde amnesia. His CST was questioned. If he could not remember the offense, how could he assist his attorney in his case? The case was ultimately argued in the D.C. Circuit Court of Appeals. The finding was that memory for the offense is not necessary to put on an adequate defense and to be competent to stand trial. However in a case in which an alibi is possible, the alibi must be presumed to exist, even if not remembered, and in this instance the person may be considered incompetent because of an inability to assist counsel in pursuing the alibi as a defense.

Memory in CR cases is even more complicated. A large number of defendants, especially in murder or serious violent crimes, claim not to remember the offense (Bourget & Whitehurst, 2007). It is often difficult to know what to make of this. There are multiple possible causes of reported amnesia: "organic disease, dissociative amnesia, amnesia due to a psychotic episode, or malingered amnesia" (p. 469). It is not uncommon for a defendant to experience a blow to the head during the crime, which may cause amnesia. Often, alcohol or drug use during the incident may be the best explanation.

Experienced evaluators tend to be skeptical, or at least conservative, about claims of amnesia. Often, these claims make little sense. A defendant may claim that as the result of a head trauma years ago, he has no memory of the offense. However, he remembers his life, graduated from high school, and was gainfully employed during the years between the childhood head trauma and the alleged offense and seems to remember from soon after the incident to the present. This is not a sensible pattern of amnesia resulting from a head trauma. Another implausible pattern of reported amnesia that often occurs is when the defendant initially claims no memory of the offense but then later gives details about that time period.

At times, amnesia for the event does make sense. For example, consider an individual who allegedly shot someone during a gang-related fight and was struck on the head with a baseball bat afterward. He reports no memory of the gang violence, the few hours before the violence, and several days afterward, during which time he was recuperating in a hospital. This is a sensible pattern of memory loss resulting from a moderately severe traumatic brain injury.

Regardless of the reason for or the veracity of reported amnesia for an event, it makes completion of a CR evaluation difficult and sometimes impossible. The evaluator can make every attempt to understand the mental or neurological condition of the defendant: review all descriptions of the defendant's behavior leading up to, during, and after the offense; and take all historical information into account to see whether it is possible to make a determination about whether the defendant understood the wrongfulness of his or her behavior at the time of the offense. Sometimes, however, the evaluator simply has to admit he or she does not know.

It should also be noted that amnesia for a specific event in the past is different than a present neurocognitive disorder that may include memory deficits. Current neurocognitive disorders, including amnestic disorder, may be far more pertinent in a legal case, especially a CST evaluation.

Developing Expertise

Forensic psychology is a complex and challenging specialty. The neuropsychologist who wants to develop criminal forensic skills should not take the task lightly. A strategic plan of reading appropriate sources of information is important, in both forensic neuropsychology and forensic psychology. As an introduction to forensic psychology, Weiner and Hess (2006) is an excellent resource, but there are many fine volumes related to forensic psychology. Those still in training may have the opportunity to take classes or practicums specifically in forensic psychology, but most neuropsychologists who develop skills in forensic neuropsychology do so with continuing education and supervision. Conferences held by the American Academy of Forensic Psychology, the American Academy of Clinical Neuropsychology (AACN), the National Academy of Neuropsychology, and the American Psychology-Law Society are excellent places to gain additional information. It is also possible to become an associate member or professional member of these organizations. Although not required, board certification is available in forensic psychology and neuropsychology, and completion of such reasonably rigorous peer-reviewed processes demonstrates general competence in a specialty.

It is important that the early-career neuropsychologist, or the practicing neuropsychologist who wants to develop forensic skills, seeks out supervision from an experienced forensic psychologist or forensic neuropsychologist in the legal jurisdiction in which forensic practice will occur. Because criminal forensic cases can be very complex and the legal forum often feels like a new world to the novice practitioner, supervision is the only way to learn the skills one specifically needs in the jurisdiction in which services will be provided. How much supervision is needed and for how long differs on the basis of the evaluator. In our opinion, the licensed practicing neuropsychologist developing new forensic skills in CST and CR evaluations should count on using supervision for up to the first dozen or so cases he or she takes on and then having supervision available as needed for at least a couple of years in early forensic practice. Supervision is especially important for CR evaluations, which tend to be more complicated. Furthermore, collegial support and peer consultation is necessary throughout one's career, and developing these contacts is an important aspect of career development.

What's in a Name?

In most states and federal court, there is no definition of who is and is not a neuropsychologist. However, "courts must evaluate expert qualifications, and determine the relevance of the expert opinions to the issue at bar" (Kaufmann, 2012, p. 72). Board certification in neuropsychology by (a) the American Board of Professional Psychology/American Board of Clinical Neuropsychology, (b) the American Board of Professional Neuropsychology, or (c) the American Board of Pediatric Neuropsychology is the best way to demonstrate to the court that one is a qualified neuropsychologist. However, many qualified neuropsychologists have chosen not to complete board certification. Exhibiting to the court that one meets the definition of a neuropsychologist adopted by the National Academy of Neuropsychology (2001) is also an acceptable way to demonstrate neuropsychological expertise. The definition includes a doctoral degree in psychology from an accredited university, an internship or its equivalent in a clinically relevant area of professional practice, 2 years of training experience in neuropsychology with 1 year at the postdoctoral level, and licensure to practice psychology or neuropsychology.

Malingering

Malingering is not the focus of this chapter, and we cannot provide thorough coverage of this complex and sometimes controversial topic. However, malingering is such an important issue that it must be discussed at least briefly. The concept and evaluation of malingering in neuropsychology has been addressed in several fine books and many articles (Boone, 2007, 2013; Larrabee, 2007; Rogers, 1997; Slick et al., 1999). As noted by Demakis et al. (2001) "If effort is fully applied throughout testing, the resulting test data can be considered valid, but if incompletely or insufficiently applied (whether because of psychopathology, malingering, or some other cause), test data may be invalid" (p. 240). Both the AACN (Heilbronner, Sweet, Morgan, Larrabee, & Millis, 2009) and the National Academy of Neuropsychology (Bush et al. 2005) released position papers in support of the use of performance validity measures during neuropsychological testing.

As defined by Slick et al. (1999) malingering is "the volitional exaggeration or fabrication of cognitive dysfunction for the purpose of obtaining substantial material gain, or avoiding or escaping formal duty or responsibility" (p. 552). Although performance validity measures may provide information about the validity of the assessment results, the decision about malingering is based on much more than performance validity tests. Slick et al. recommended an approach in which malingering is divided into three classifications—possible, probable, and definite malingering—on the basis of the presence of an external motivation to malinger, negative response bias on testing, and behaviors suggestive of malingering (p. 552). Best practices suggest caution when considering using the term *malingering* in a report. It may be better to provide a discussion of invalid assessment results instead, unless there is a clear and convincing case based on multiple data points and the Slick criteria that malingering exists.

Best standards in forensic neuropsychology include a comprehensive assessment of performance validity and possible malingering using (a) a clinical analysis of the motivation for malingering, (b) review of historical documents, (c) clinical interview and observations, (d) analysis of testing results, (e) use of multiple free-standing and embedded performance validity measures, (f) use of standardized personality measures with validity scales, and (g) use of specific psychiatric tests of malingering (e.g., the Structured Interview of Malingered Symptoms or Structured Interview of Reported Symptoms).

To avoid evaluator bias, a helpful exercise is to compare how often the evaluator suspects or finds malingering compared with established base rates. In a criminal population, base rates of suspected malingering of psychiatric conditions range from 20% (Rogers, 1986) to 31% (Lewis, Simcox, & Berry, 2002). For the malingering of neurocognitive disorders in a criminal setting, some researchers (Mittenberg, Patton, Canyock, & Condit, 2002) had initially estimated a range of 19% to 23%, but more recent estimates of probable and definite malingered of neurocognitive dysfunction have been as high as 54% (Denney & Sullivan, 2008). If the evaluator's findings of suspected malingering are significantly inconsistent with expectations, the process by which performance validity and malingering are evaluated should be reconsidered.

Third-Party Observers

Whether to allow third-party observers (TPOs) in an evaluation is another complex issue that has been covered in multiple books and articles (Greiffenstein & Kaufmann, 2012). Both the AACN (2001) and National Academy of Neuropsychology (1999) have produced position papers on this issue. To summarize, an audience may affect the evaluation process and testing results and should be avoided whenever possible. It is best not to have TPOs present during any of the evaluation process; however, in forensic practice, this is not always possible.

We have allowed TPOs during the interview process at times, but not during neuropsychological testing. If an attorney or representative insists on being present, then an agreement should be obtained beforehand. The agreement should include at least an understanding that the evaluation process is not a deposition and the attorney is not there to help the defendant answer questions. The evaluator should ask for any limitations on the interview process beforehand so that the attorney has no need to interrupt. The observer should sit behind and out of view of the defendant if possible. If the observer wishes to take notes, then it should be done quietly. The same stance applies to audio recording—allow it if necessary during interview but not during testing. When audio recording is initiated by one party, the neuropsychologist is wise to also record the interview so that any edited or incomplete recordings can be detected and challenged. If the evaluation is conducted in a jail or prison, this issue is often moot because most jails and prisons will not allow recording devices. We believe that video recording affects the defendant's behavior too much and recommend avoiding it during all aspects of the evaluation process whenever possible.

The evaluator should be ready to decline the referral if the conditions are not conducive to an adequate evaluation process. In one case, the prosecuting attorney, two defense attorneys, and a hired expert requested that they all be allowed to observe the evaluation. The referral was politely declined.

CASE EXAMPLES

Example 1

The defendant was a man in his 60s who was charged with capital murder and several other crimes. The defense attorney contacted the neuropsychologist and told him he had a defendant with brain damage and referred him for a CST evaluation. Attorney stated that the defendant's mind wandered, his memory was problematic, and he had a history of posttraumatic disorder (PTSD), alcoholism, and a gunshot wound to the head. The defendant's angry and uncooperative behavior was difficult for the attorney to deal with. The defendant had been found guilty except for insanity once previously for a charge of menacing. He had multiple previous arrests for disorderly conduct. The defendant was evaluated in a county jail.

The defendant stated that he had a penetrating head injury. In his 30s, he attempted suicide by shooting himself with a small-caliber pistol. He stated that the bullet's trajectory was from below his chin upward and to the right, up the right behind his face, "right behind my face and out above my right eye." He added that it took "out my tongue, palate, sinus, and nasal bones." He was hospitalized for 6 weeks after emergency surgery and spent several months in a rehabilitation facility. He stated that he had brain scans that showed no actual brain damage. He did indeed have scars that would support this injury. Medical records were found that referred to this occurrence, but medical records of the event itself were not available. The defendant also had hypertension and did not receive medication or regular health care.

The defendant began drinking alcohol by age 12. His alcohol use escalated quickly, and by high school he was a heavy and regular drinker. He reported drinking about 12 beers daily throughout most of his life, except when incarcerated or hospitalized. He used marijuana occasionally. He had completed residential alcohol treatment without success. He admitted that drinking had caused him to be unable to hold down employment for very long.

The defendant spent 4 years in military service and 18 months in combat. He was diagnosed with PTSD as a result of his military experience. He declined to share his military experience with the neuropsychologist. He received a partial disability pension because of PTSD.

The defendant was raised in a strict, authoritarian, and possibly abusive environment. He dropped out of school in the 12th grade, completed a GED, and entered the military. He was trained in engineering during his military career.

After the defendant left the service, he married and joined the laborer's union. He held multiple jobs in construction and labor, which he tended to keep for a few months to a year at a time. The marriage was tumultuous and lasted less than 10 years. He left his wife with three children, has had no real contact with them since, and has not paid child support. Since then, he has engaged in a series of short-term and intense relationships, often living with a woman. He has not held steady employment, doing periodic jobs with payment off the books, and is often supported by whomever he is living with. His alcohol consumption has been out of control, and he has spent short periods of time homeless.

The defendant has a long history of involvement with gangs and antisocial characters, illegal activities and trouble with the law, brief and violent

Exhibit 15.2
Neuropsychological Testing Score Sheet for Case 1

Reynolds Intellectual Screening Test (RIST)			
Scale	**Standard score**	**Percent**	**Interpretation**
RIST Index	118	89	Above average
Wide Range Achievement Test—Fourth Edition			
Scale	**Standard score**	**Percent**	**Interpretation**
Word Reading	112	79	Average
Word Memory Test			
Scale		**Percent**	
Immediate Recognition		100	
Delayed Recognition		95	
Consistency		95	
Multiple Choice		85	
Paired Associate Recall		90	
Free Recall		63	
Neuropsychological Assessment Battery			
Module	**Standard score**	**Percent**	**Interpretation**
Attention	110	75	Above average
Language	111	77	Above average
Memory	99	47	Average
Spatial	114	82	Above average
Executive	100	50	Average
Total Index	111	77	Above average
Reliable Digit Span = 6 + 5 = 11			

relationships, fighting and violence, living off of others, children with no relationship or history of supporting them, and underachievement in academic and vocational pursuits. He has a moderate legal history. These factors all began before his gunshot wound.

The defendant was evaluated several years earlier by a different evaluator who obtained a superior IQ on the basis of the Wechsler Adult Intelligence Scale—Third Edition and a normal performance on the Repeatable Battery for the Assessment of Neuropsychological Status.

The defendant did not describe symptoms of PTSD presently. He sleeps well without nightmares, does not experience flashbacks or reliving of any traumatic experiences, and does not exhibit anxiety, hyperarousal, or hyperstartle. In fact, the presence of these symptoms in the past was unclear.

A neuropsychological data sheet for the defendant's testing is provided (see Exhibit 15.2). Defendant functioned in the above-average range intellectually according to a brief intelligence test; however, previous testing with a full Wechsler Adult Intelligence Scale—Third Edition indicated superior intelligence. His vocabulary was in the above-average range. His Word Memory Test scores suggested adequate effort with intact memory. Reliable Digit Span and embedded measures on the Wisconsin Card Sorting Test also indicated adequate effort. All module scores on the NAB were in the average or above-average range. Further inquiry about executive functioning with the Wisconsin Card Sorting Test was in the average range.

The defendant produced a valid Psychological Assessment Inventory profile indicative of moderate depression, alcohol dependence, and antisocial and borderline characteristics. He produced a valid Structured Interview of Malingered Symptomatology profile.

The diagnoses for defendant were PTSD by history, depressive disorder not otherwise specified, alcohol dependence, and antisocial and borderline personality disorders.

The statute in Oregon for competency includes one requirement and three prongs. A mental disease or defect is required for the CST statute to be triggered, and this cannot be solely a personality disorder, antisocial conduct, or substance abuse. The defendant suffers from moderate depression and, historically at least, PTSD. These disorders were adequate to trigger consideration of the statute. The three prongs of competency in Oregon are the ability to understand his legal circumstances, assist his counsel, and participate in his defense.

The defendant clearly understood his charges, the possible consequences, who his attorney was, the roles of all the players in a trial, and so forth. He clearly passed the knowledge test. He showed the ability to reason about his case and to understand possible plea bargains and different outcomes of his case. He appeared to be able to participate in his own defense and to make decisions independently. The problems found were in the "ability to assist counsel" prong of the CST requirements. He was angry, belligerent, and uncooperative with his counsel. He did not trust his attorney. However, although the defendant had difficulty cooperating with his attorney, this was apparently due to his personality disorder. Because of this, his difficulty getting along with his attorney would not be considered adequate to cause the defendant to be considered incompetent per Oregon statutes. It is interesting to note that if these difficulties in working with his attorney were caused by paranoid schizophrenia, for example, then it might have met the statutorial requirements to be found IST.

The opinion about the ultimate question was that the defendant does not meet the statutory requirements to be found IST and is therefore competent. A defendant is legally competent until a judge rules otherwise.

This case demonstrated a common difficulty in forensic neuropsychological evaluations: the inability to obtain all medical records. The evaluator should make a reasonable attempt to do so, but it is often impossible. The evaluator must make the best interpretations possible with whatever background information has been obtained.

This case also highlights two errors commonly made by novice evaluators: equating cause and effect and the tendency to assume or overinterpret neurocognitive disorder. Equating cause and effect is the tendency to talk about an injury or event as if it was a condition. It is common for novice evaluators to say something in court such as "the defendant has brain injury" as though this is explanatory and may jump from this brain injury to incompetency as though the connection is apparent. Brain injury is a cause, not a condition or symptom. Not all people who experience a brain injury develop a neurocognitive disorder. The correct statement would be "the defendant experienced a head injury that could possibly be the cause of brain damage and neurocognitive disorder. However in this case, the defendant does not appear to have a neurocognitive disorder." In this case example, mild depression and a somewhat questionable history of PTSD would not be adequate to cause the defendant to be considered incompetent.

Example 2

Defendant was a married man in his 70s. He was charged with attempted murder, kidnapping, menacing, and attempted assault. He had no legal history or history of violence, nor did he have a mental health history. He was referred for evaluation by his defense attorney, who simply wanted to understand him.

The defendant reported that he graduated from high school and worked in construction throughout his life. He had a successful working career. He was in his second marriage, which had lasted for 31 years. He had several children from his current marriage and one from his first marriage.

The defendant reported having sustained a concussion when he was a child after falling down and hitting a rock, but he was unsure whether he lost consciousness. He reported a stroke some 5 to 6 years before the crime. He was remodeling a house he was selling when his speech began to slur. He spent a night in the hospital and was released. He was told he had a stroke. He does not remember what treatment he received. Records were not available for review. Neither the defendant nor the defendant's family felt that the stroke was the start of any sort of cognitive decline. He had taken an 81-millgram aspirin daily since the stroke. Before that, the defendant had a history of heart disease, heart attack, heart surgery, and hypertension that was poorly controlled most of his life.

The defendant began acting strangely on an airplane during a trip abroad. He believed that he was being spied on and that the government was watching him through electronic devices. During this trip, he became increasingly irritable and agitated and ended up pushing his wife and pulling her hair. His wife demanded they cut the trip short and fly home. At home, he continued to be paranoid and agitated. He was frightening to his wife. After a few months of this, his adult children attempted to separate them by having the father move out of the home until things improved. The wife eventually filed for divorce, but the defendant became obsessed with seeing his wife.

The instant offense occurred one afternoon as he drove by his home, in violation of his restraining order, and saw his estranged wife outside. He ended up grabbing his wife by the neck and forcing her back into the home with him. This was charged as kidnapping and assault. He verbally threatened to kill her while he had his hands on her throat, which was charged as attempted murder. He caused his wife to feel threatened and afraid, which was charged as menacing. Once there, he forced her to sit down with him and opened a bottle of wine so they could talk. He said that this is all he wanted. Scared, his wife kept him talking for an hour or so until she could talk him into calling one of their children. She let her daughter know what was happening while making the conversation sound normal to keep the defendant calm. Their daughter called the police, who broke into the home believing it to be a kidnapping and maybe a murder.

The defendant was initially evaluated regarding CST. He was confused and moderately disoriented, and he did not understand who his attorney was, or even why he had one. He had an understanding that he was facing charges, but not exactly what they were or what he was said to have done. His memory for legal facts was limited and confused, and his understanding of his legal circumstances seemed unrealistic. He did not understand that he was in jeopardy of serious consequences. He seemed to just want his wife back. He was not able to reason to any degree about his legal situation and was not able to make reasonable decisions. He was not able to assist his attorney and participate in his defense.

The neuropsychologist initially reported that defendant met the statutory definition to be found IST. This issue was adjudicated and, against the neuropsychologist's recommendation, defendant was found competent, and the legal case proceeded.

A follow-up CR interview was conducted. When questioned about the alleged offense by the neuropsychologist, the defendant was confused and had very little insight into his behavior at the time of the incident. He did not understand why he was not allowed to talk to his wife. He was cooperative and made an attempt to answer all questions, but there was a paucity of content. His answers were short and shallow. He did not appear to understand that what he had done was wrong, even thought when asked theoretical questions about whether violence was right or wrong, he provided the correct answer. In his mind, he had simply asked his wife to sit down and talk.

The defendant was tested and found to have a pattern of marked behavior change including impulsive, erratic, and violent behavior; a remarkable lack of insight into his current problems (anosognosia); delusions; moderate attention and executive deficits; slowed cognition; and significant memory deficits (see Exhibit 15.3). A neurological consultation was obtained, and an MRI of the brain revealed multiple old strokes and damage to the left basal ganglia. Diffuse brain atrophy was noted, along with more prominent atrophy of the basal forebrain and frontal lobes. The neurologist diagnosed him with a vascular dementia with delusions and personality change resulting from vascular disease. The neuropsychological diagnosis was dementia with mixed etiology: vascular disease and frontal-temporal degeneration.

The defendant's right to a jury trial was waived, and the case was argued to a judge. The neuropsychologist testified at the trial that the defendant suffered from dementia. Because of his dementia, at the time of the offense he was in a delusional state, lacked insight into his behavior, did not understand

Exhibit 15.3
Neuropsychological Testing Score Sheet for Case 2

Reynolds Intellectual Screening Test

Scale	Standard score	Percent	Interpretation
RIST Index	102	55	Average

Word Memory Test

Scale	Percent
Immediate Recognition	83
Delayed Recognition	90
Consistency	73
Multiple Choice	60
Paired Associates	60
Free Recall	25

Note. Easy–hard difference = 33.

Neuropsychological Assessment Battery—Screening Module

Domain	Standard score	Percent	Interpretation
Attention	75	5	Mildly to moderately impaired
Language	108	70	Above average
Memory	—		
Spatial	92	30	Average
Executive	84	14	Mildly impaired

Neuropsychological Assessment Battery

Module	Standard score	Percent	Interpretation
Memory	72	3	Mildly to moderately impaired

Psychological Assessment Inventory—Invalid

Scale or index	*T* score
Inconsistency	82
Infrequent Responses	44
Negative Impression Management	66
Defensiveness Index	38
Cashel Discriminant Function	37
Malingering Index	57
Rogers Discriminant Function	37

his behavior to be threatening or violent, and did not understand that his behavior was wrong. An expert for the prosecution testified that defendant was antisocial and violent and belonged in jail. The judge found defendant to be guilty except for insanity and placed him into a geriatric unit of the state hospital. He resided there for more than a year, but then the staff of the hospital felt he had stabilized enough to be released. He was released to live with one of his children who lived in another state, away from his ex-wife. The neuropsychologist was informed he did well there initially, but additional information was not received over the course of the following years.

CONCLUSION

The forensic neuropsychological evaluation of CST and CR is a challenging and rewarding area of practice that requires specialized knowledge and career development. Neuropsychology is likely underused even in appropriate criminal cases. Depending on the appropriate jurisdiction, CST can be divided into three prongs: (a) factual and rational understanding of the legal circumstances, (b) the ability to assist the attorney, and (c) the ability to participate in the defense. CR can be divided into two prongs: (a) the ability to appreciate or understand the wrongfulness of the conduct and (b) the ability to conform or control one's behavior to the requirements of the law. Understanding the statutory requirements for CST and CR for the appropriate jurisdiction is absolutely necessary. Evaluations should be organized and written to address the appropriate statute and give a clear recommendation regarding the issue at hand. A flexible neuropsychological testing style is recommended. Careful consideration of malingering and the use of multiple data points is necessary to form an opinion about a defendant's CST or CR.

References

Allen v. Mullin, 368 F.3d 1220 (10th Cir. 2004).

American Academy of Clinical Neuropsychology. (2001). Policy statement on the presence of third party observers in neuropsychological assessments. *Clinical Neuropsychologist, 15,* 433–439. http://dx.doi.org/10.1076/clin.15.4.433.1888

American Law Institute. (1962). *Model penal code.* Retrieved from https://www.ali.org/publications/show/model-penal-code

American Law Institute (1985). *Model penal code and annotations.* Retrieved from https://www.ali.org/publications/show/model-penal-code

Archer, R. P., Buffington-Vollum, J. K., Stredny, R. V., & Handel, R. W. (2006). A survey of psychological test use patterns among forensic psychologists. *Journal of Personality Assessment, 87,* 84–94. http://dx.doi.org/10.1207/s15327752jpa8701_07

Bazelon, D. L. (1988). *Questioning authority: Justice and criminal law.* New York, NY: Knopf.

Boake, C. (2008). Clinical neuropsychology. *Professional Psychology: Research and Practice, 39,* 234–239. http://dx.doi.org/10.1037/0735-7028.39.2.234

Bonnie, R. J. (1992). The competence of criminal defendants: A theoretical reformulation. *Behavioral Sciences and the Law, 10,* 291–316. http://dx.doi.org/10.1002/bsl.2370100303

Bonnie, R. J., & Grisso, T. (2000). Adjudicative competence and youthful offenders. In T. Grisso & R. G. Schwartz (Eds.), *Youth on trial: A developmental perspective on criminal justice* (pp. 73–104). Chicago, IL: University of Chicago Press.

Boone, K. B. (2007). *Assessment of feigned cognitive impairment: A neuropsychological perspective.* New York, NY: Guilford Press.

Boone, K. B. (2013). *Clinical practice of forensic neuropsychology: An evidence-based approach.* New York, NY: Guilford Press.

Borum, R. (2003). Insanity defense. In T. Grisso (Ed.), *Evaluating competencies: Forensic assessments and instruments* (2nd ed., pp. 193–228). New York, NY: Kluwer Academic/Plenum Press.

Borum, R., & Grisso, T. (1995). Psychological test use in criminal forensic evaluations. *Professional Psychology: Research and Practice, 26,* 465–473. http://dx.doi.org/10.1037/0735-7028.26.5.465

Bourget, D., & Whitehurst, L. (2007). Amnesia and crime. *Journal of the American Academy of Psychiatry and the Law, 35,* 469–480.

Bush, S. S., Ruff, R. M., Tröster, A. I., Barth, J. T., Koffler, S. P., Pliskin, N. H., . . . Silver, C. H. (2005). Symptom validity assessment: Practice issues and medical necessity. *Archives of Clinical Neuropsychology, 20,* 419–426. http://dx.doi.org/10.1016/j.acn.2005.02.002

Cima, M., Nijman, H., Merckelbach, H., Kremer, K., & Hollnack, S. (2004). Claims of crime-related amnesia in forensic patients. *International Journal of Law and Psychiatry, 27,* 215–221. http://dx.doi.org/10.1016/j.ijlp.2004.03.007

Cirincione, C., Steadman, H. J., & McGreevy, M. A. (1995). Rates of insanity acquittals and the factors associated with successful insanity pleas. *Bulletin of the American Academy of Psychiatry and the Law, 23,* 399–409.

Clark v. Arizona, 126 S.Ct. 2709 (2006).

Commonwealth v. Gaboriault, Criminal No. 9673CR290A-B, WL 410345 (Mass. Cmmw. 2001). http://dx.doi.org/10.1037/1040-3590.13.2.240

Daubert v. Merrell Dow Pharmaceuticals, Inc., 509 U.S. 579, 589 (1993).

Demakis, G. J., Sweet, J. J., Sawyer, T. P., Moulthrop, M., Nies, K., & Clingerman, S. (2001). Discrepancy between predicted and obtained WAIS–R IQ scores discriminates between traumatic brain injury and insufficient effort. *Psychological Assessment, 13,* 240–248.

Denney, R. L. (2012). Criminal forensic neuropsychology and assessment of competency. In G. J. Larrabee (Ed.), *Forensic neuropsychology: A scientific approach* (2nd ed., pp. 438–472). New York, NY: Oxford University Press.

Denney, R. L., & Sullivan, J. P. (2008). *Clinical neuropsychology in the criminal forensic setting.* New York, NY: Guilford Press.

Denney, R. L., & Wynkoop, T. F. (2000). Clinical neuropsychology in the criminal forensic setting. *Journal of Head Trauma Rehabilitation, 15,* 804–828. http://dx.doi.org/10.1097/00001199-200004000-00005

Diamond, B. L. (1994). *The psychiatrist in the courtroom: Selected papers of Bernard L. Diamond, M.D.* Hillsdale, NJ: Analytic Press.

Drope v. Missouri, No. 73-6038, 420 U.S. 162, 95 S.Ct. 896 (1975).

Durham v. United States, 214 F. 2d 862 (1954).

Dusky v. United States, 362 U.S. 402 (1960).

Everington, C. T. (1990). The Competence Assessment for Standing Trial for Defendants With Mental Retardation (CAST–MR): A validation study. *Criminal Justice and Behavior, 17,* 147–168. http://dx.doi.org/10.1177/0093854890017002001

Everington, C. T., & Dunn, C. (1995). A second validation study of the Competence Assessment for Standing Trial for Defendants With Mental Retardation (CAST–MR). *Criminal Justice and Behavior, 22,* 44–59. http://dx.doi.org/10.1177/0093854895022001004

Everington, C. T., & Luckasson, R. (1992). *Competency assessment for standing trial for defendants with mental retardation.* Columbus, OH: IDS.

Everington, C., Notario-Smull, H., & Horton, M. L. (2007). Can defendants with mental retardation successfully fake their performance on a test of competence to stand trial? *Behavioral Sciences and the Law, 25,* 545–560. http://dx.doi.org/10.1002/bsl.735

Faretta v. California, 422 U.S. 806 (1975).

Fautenberry v. Mitchell, No. 05-3568 (6th Cir. 2008).

Federal rules of evidence. (2011). Washington, DC: U.S. Government Printing Office.

Folstein, M. F., Folstein, S. E., & McHugh, P. R. (1975). "Mini-mental state": A practical method for grading the cognitive state of patients for the clinician. *Journal of Psychiatric Research, 12,* 189–198. http://dx.doi.org/10.1016/0022-3956(75)90026-6

Folstein, M. F., Folstein, S. E., McHugh, P. R., & Fanjiang, G. (2001). *Mini-Mental State Examination: User's guide.* Lutz, FL: Psychological Assessment Resources.

Frye v. United States, 293 F. 1013 (D.C. Cir. 1923)

Godinez v. Moran, No. 92-725, 509 U.S. 389, 113 S.Ct. 2680 (1993).

Golding, S. L. (1993). *Interdisciplinary Fitness Interview—Revised: A training manual.* Salt Lake City: University of Utah.

Golding, S. L. (2008). Evaluations of adult adjudicative competency. In R. Jackson (Ed.), *Learning forensic assessment* (pp. 75–108). New York, NY: Routledge/Taylor & Francis.

Grandjean, N. R. (2004). *Neuropsychological predictors of incompetency to stand trial in defendants referred for competency restoration* (Unpublished doctoral dissertation). University of North Texas, Denton. Retrieved from http://digital.library.unt.edu/ark:/67531/metadc4705/m2/1/high_res_d/dissertation.pdf

Green, P. (1994). *Word Memory Test.* Retrieved from http://wordmemorytest.com/word-memory-test

Greiffenstein, M. F., & Kaufmann, P. M. (2012). Neuropsychology and the law: Principles of productive attorney-neuropsychologist relations. In G. J. Larrabee (Ed.), *Forensic neuropsychology: A scientific approach* (pp. 23-69). New York, NY: Oxford University Press.

Grisso, T. (1986). *Evaluating competencies: Forensic assessments and instruments.* http://dx.doi.org/10.1007/978-1-4899-5046-8

Grisso, T. (1988). *Competency to stand trial evaluations: A manual for practice.* Sarasota, FL: Professional Resource Exchange.

Grisso, T. (2003). *Evaluating competencies: Forensic assessments and instruments* (3rd ed.). New York, NY: Kluwer Academic/Plenum Press.

Guðjónsson, G. H., Pétursson, H., Skúlason, S., & Sigurðardóttir, H. (1989). Psychiatric evidence: A study of psychological issues. *Acta Psychiatrica Scandivanica, 80,* 165–169. http://dx.doi.org/10.1111/j.1600-0447.1989.tb01321.x

Hall, H. V. (2008). *Forensic psychology and neuropsychology for criminal and civil cases.* Boca Raton, FL: CRC Press.

Hartlage, L. C., & Stern, B. H. (2010). Neuropsychology in the courtroom. In A. M. Horton & L. C. Hartlage (Eds.), *Handbook of forensic neuropsychology* (pp. 291–308). New York, NY: Springer.

Heilbronner, R. L., Sweet, J. J., Morgan, J. E., Larrabee, G. J., & Millis, S. R. (2009). American Academy of Clinical Neuropsychology Consensus Conference Statement on the neuropsychological assessment of effort, response bias, and malingering. *Clinical Neuropsychologist, 23,* 1093–1129. http://dx.doi.org/10.1080/13854040903155063

Heilbronner, R. L. (2004). A status report on the practice of forensic neuropsychology. *Clinical Neuropsychologist, 18,* 312–326. http://dx.doi.org/10.1080/13854040490501574

Heilbrun, K. (1992). The role of psychological testing in forensic assessment. *Law and Human Behavior, 16,* 257–272. http://dx.doi.org/10.1007/BF01044769

Hoge, S. K., Bonnie, R. J., Poythress, N., & Monahan, J. (1992). Attorney-client decision-making in criminal cases: Client competence and participation as perceived by their attorneys. *Behavioral Sciences and the Law, 10,* 385–394. http://dx.doi.org/10.1002/bsl.2370100308

Hoge, S. K., Bonnie, R. J., Poythress, N., & Monahan, J. (1999). *The MacArthur Competence Assessment Tool–Criminal Adjudication.* Odessa, FL: Psychological Assessment Resources.

Horton, A. M. (2010). Overview of forensic neuropsychology. In A. M. Horton (Ed.), *Handbook of forensic neuropsychology* (2nd ed., pp. 3–10). New York, NY: Springer.

Horton, A. M., & Hartlage, L. C. (2010). *Handbook of forensic neuropsychology* (2nd ed.). New York, NY: Springer.

Indiana v. Edwards, 554 U.S. 164 (2008).

In re Elmore, No. 70233-1, 162 Wash.2d 236, 172 P.3d 335 (2007).

Insanity defense, 18 U.S.C. § 17, 114–119 (1986).

Insanity Defense Reform Act of 1984, 18 U.S.C. § 17.

Jacobs, M. S., Ryba, N. L., & Zapf, P. A. (2008). Competence-related abilities and psychiatric symptoms: An analysis of the underlying structure and correlates of the MacCAT–CA and the BPRS. *Law and Human Behavior, 32,* 64–77. http://dx.doi.org/10.1007/s10979-007-9086-8

Jefferson v. Hall, No. 07-12502 (11th Cir. 2009).

Jenkins v. United States, 307 F. 2d 637 (D.C. Cir. 1962).

Johnson v. State, 388 S.W.3d 159, WL 5921199 SC91787 (November 20, 2012).

Jones v. Ryan, No. 07-99000, 583 F.3d 626, WL 3152396 (9th Cir. October 2, 2009).

Jurecska, D. E., Peterson, M. A., & Millkey, A. (2012). Comparative study of the MacCAT–CA and CAST–MR for individuals with intellectual disabilities. *American Journal of Forensic Psychology, 3,* 67–89.

Kaufmann, P. M. (2008). Admissibility of neuropsychological evidence in criminal cases. In R. L. Denney & J. P. Sullivan (Eds.), *Clinical neuropsychology in the criminal forensic setting* (pp. 55–90). New York, NY: Guilford Press.

Kaufmann, P. M. (2012). Admissibility of expert opinions based on neuropsychological evidence. In G. J. Larrabee (Ed.), *Forensic neuropsychology: A scientific approach* (2nd ed., pp. 70–100). New York, NY: Oxford University Press.

Kirkish, P., & Sreenivasan, S. (1999). Neuropsychological assessment of competency to stand trial evaluations: A practical conceptual model. *Journal of the American Academy of Psychiatry and the Law, 27,* 101–113.

Kruh, I., & Grisso, T. (2009). *Evaluations of juveniles' competence to stand trial.* New York, NY: Oxford University Press.

LaDuke, C., DeMatteo, D., Heilbrun, K., & Swirsky-Sacchetti, T. (2012). Clinical neuropsychology in forensic contexts: Practitioners' experience, training, and practice. *Professional Psychology: Research and Practice, 43,* 503–509. http://dx.doi.org/10.1037/a0028161

Larrabee, G. L. (2007). *Assessment of malingered neuropsychological deficits.* New York, NY: Oxford University Press.

Larrabee, G. J. (2012). A scientific approach to forensic neuropsychology. In G. J. Larrabee (Ed.), *Forensic neuropsychology: A scientific approach* (pp. 3–22). New York, NY: Oxford University Press.

Lewis, J. L., Simcox, A. M., & Berry, D. T. R. (2002). Screening for feigned psychiatric symptoms in a forensic sample by using the MMPI–2 and the structured inventory of malingered symptomatology. *Psychological Assessment, 14,* 170–176. http://dx.doi.org/10.1037/1040-3590.14.2.170

Lezak, M. D., Howieson, D. B., Bigler, E. D., & Tranel, D. W. (2012). *Neuropsychological assessment* (5th ed.). New York, NY: Oxford University Press.

Marcopulos, B. A., Caillouet, B. A., & Tussey, C. (2013). The role of neuropsychology in competency to stand trial evaluations. *National Academy of Neuropsychology Bulletin, 27,* 20–23.

Martell, D. A. (1992). Forensic neuropsychology and the criminal law. *Law and Human Behavior, 16,* 313–336. http://dx.doi.org/10.1007/BF01044772

Melton, G. G. B., Petrila, J., Poythress, N. G., & Slobogin, C. (2007). *Psychological evaluations for the courts.* New York, NY: Guilford Press.

Mittenberg, W., Patton, C., Canyock, E. M., & Condit, D. C. (2002). Base rates of malingering and symptom exaggeration. *Journal of Clinical and Experimental Neuropsychology, 24,* 1094–1102. http://dx.doi.org/10.1076/jcen.24.8.1094.8379

M'Naghten Case 8 Eng. Rep. 718 (1843).

Montreal Cognitive Assessment. (1996). Retrieved from http://www.mocatest.org

Najolia, G. M., Dunning, C., Smith, L., Knopp, P., & Zolnikov, B. (2014). Use of the Montreal Cognitive Assessment in evaluations of adjudicative competency. *Journal of Forensic Psychology Practice, 14,* 342–354. http://dx.doi.org/10.1080/15228932.2014.954892

National Academy of Neuropsychology. (1999). Presence of third party observes during neuropsychological testing: Official statement of the National Academy of Neuropsychology. *Archives of Clinical Neuropsychology, 15,* 379–380.

National Academy of Neuropsychology. (2001). *NAN definition of a clinician neuropsychologist*. Retrieved from https://www.nanonline.org/docs/PAIC/PDFs/NANPositionDefNeuro.pdf

Nestor, P. G., Daggett, D., Haycock, J., & Price, M. (1999). Competence to stand trial: A neuropsychological inquiry. *Law and Human Behavior, 23,* 397–412. http://dx.doi.org/10.1023/A:1022339130582

Nestor, P. G., & Haycock, J. (1997). Not guilty by reason of insanity of murder: Clinical and neuropsychological characteristics. *Journal of the American Academy of Psychiatry and the Law, 25,* 161–171.

Nicholson, R. A., & Kugler, K. E. (1991). Competent and incompetent criminal defendants: A quantitative review of comparative research. *Psychological Bulletin, 109,* 355–370. http://dx.doi.org/10.1037/0033-2909.109.3.355

Norton, K. A., & Ryba, N. L. (2010). An investigation of the ECST–R as a measure of competence and feigning. *Journal of Forensic Psychology Practice, 10,* 91–106. http://dx.doi.org/10.1080/15228930903446625

Offenders with mental disease or defect, 18 U.S.C. Chap. III, § 313, 4241–4248 (2006).

Oregon Revised Statutes, Title 16, Chap. 161 (2016). Retrieved from https://www.oregonlegislature.gov/bills_laws/ors/ors161.html

Otto, R. K., Poythress, N. G., Nicholson, R. A., Edens, J. F., Monahan, J., Bonnie, R. J., . . . Eisenberg, M. (1998). Psychometric properties of the MacArthur Competence Assessment Tool–Criminal Adjudication. *Psychological Assessment, 10,* 435–443. http://dx.doi.org/10.1037/1040-3590.10.4.435

Packer, I. (2009). *Evaluation of criminal responsibility*. http://dx.doi.org/10.1093/med:psych/9780195324853.001.0001

Pate v. Robinson, 383 U.S. 375 (1966).

Pirelli, G., Gottdiener, W. H., & Zapf, P. A. (2011). A meta-analytic review of competency to stand trial research. *Psychology, Public Policy, and Law, 17,* 1–53. http://dx.doi.org/10.1037/a0021713

Porter v. McCollum, No. 08-10537, 558 U.S. 30, 130 S.Ct. 447 (November 30, 2009).

Poythress, N. G., Bonnie, R. J., Monahan, J., Otto, R. K., & Hoge, S. K. (2002). *Adjudicative competence: The MacArthur studies*. http://dx.doi.org/10.1007/978-1-4419-8493-7

Price v. Thurmer, No. 09-3851, 637 F.3d 831, WL 1458694 (7th Cir. April 18, 2011).

Randolph, C. (2003). *Repeatable Battery for the Assessment of Neuropsychological Status update*. San Antonio, TX: Pearson.

Reese v. State, No. SC07-1309, 14 So.3d 913, 2009 WL 775393 (March 26, 2009).

Revised Code of Washington, Title 10, Chap. 77, § 050 (1974). Retrieved from https://app.leg.wa.gov/rcw/default.aspx?cite=10.77.050

Rex v. Arnold, 16 How. St. Tr. 695 (1724).

Roesch, R., Zapf, P., Golding, S. L., & Skeem, J. (1999). Defining and assessing competency to stand trial. In I. B. Weiner & A. K. Hess (Eds.), *Handbook of forensic psychology* (2nd ed., pp. 327–349). New York, NY: Wiley.

Rogers, R. (1984). *Rogers Criminal Responsibility Assessment Scales (RCRAS) and test manual*. Odessa, FL: Psychological Assessment Resources.

Rogers, R. (1986). *Conducting insanity evaluations*. New York, NY: Van Nostrand Reinhold.

Rogers, R. (1997). *Clinical assessment of malingering and deception* (2nd ed.). New York, NY: Guilford Press.

Rogers, R., & Ewing, C. P. (1989). Ultimate opinion prescriptions: A cosmetic fix and plea for empiricism. *Law and Human Behavior, 13,* 357–374. http://dx.doi.org/10.1007/BF01056408

Rogers, R., & Shuman, D. (2000). *Conducting insanity evaluations*. New York, NY: Guilford Press.

Rogers, R., Tillbrook, C. E., & Sewell, K. W. (2004). *Evaluation of competency to stand trial—Revised professional manual*. Lutz, FL: Psychological Assessment Resources.

Rogers, R., Ustad, K. L., Sewell, K. W., & Reinhardt, V. (1996). Dimensions of incompetency: A factor analytic study of the Georgia Court Competency Test. *Behavioral Sciences and the Law, 14,* 323–330. http://dx.doi.org/10.1002/(SICI)1099-0798(199622)14:3<323::AID-BSL243>3.0.CO;2-Z

Simmons v. Mullen, 231 Pa. Superior Court 199, 331 A.2d 892 (1974).

Skeem, J. L., & Golding, S. L. (1998). Community examiners' evaluations of competence to stand trial: Common problems and suggestions for improvement. *Professional Psychology: Research and Practice, 29,* 357–367. http://dx.doi.org/10.1037/0735-7028.29.4.357

Slick, D. J., Sherman, E. M. S., & Iverson, G. L. (1999). Diagnostic criteria for malingered neurocognitive dysfunction: Proposed standards for clinical practice and research. *Clinical Neuropsychologist, 13,* 545–561. http://dx.doi.org/10.1076/1385-4046(199911)13:04;1-Y;FT545

Smith, G. E., Ivnik, R. J., & Lucas, J. (2008). Assessment techniques: Tests, test batteries, norms, and methodological approaches. In J. E. Morgan & J. H. Ricker (Eds.), *Textbook of clinical neuropsychology* (pp. 38–57). New York, NY: Taylor & Francis.

State v. Serra, Del. Super. (2002).

State v. Zachery W., No. 13-1177, WL 4662486. (September 19, 2014).

Steadman, H. J., Monahan, J., Hartstone, E., Davis, S., & Robbins, P. (1982). Mentally disordered offenders: A national survey of patients and facilities. *Law and Human Behavior, 6,* 31–38. http://dx.doi.org/10.1007/BF01049311

Stern, R. A., & White, T. (2003). *Neuropsychological Assessment Battery (NAB): Administration, scoring, and interpretation manual.* Lutz, FL: Psychological Assessment Resources.

Sweet, J. J., Ecklund-Johnson, E., & Malina, A. (2009). Forensic neuropsychology: An overview of issues and directions. In J. Morgan & J. Ricker (Eds.), *Textbook of clinical neuropsychology* (pp. 869–890). New York, NY: Taylor & Francis.

Sweet, J. J., King, J. H., Malina, A. C., Bergman, M. A., & Simmons, A. (2002). Documenting the prominence of forensic neuropsychology at national meetings and in relevant professional journals from 1990 to 2000. *Clinical Neuropsychologist, 16,* 481–494. http://dx.doi.org/10.1076/clin.16.4.481.13914

Sweet, J. J., Moberg, P. J., & Suchy, Y. (2000). Ten-year follow-up survey of clinical neuropsychologists: Part II. Private practice and economics. *Clinical Neuropsychologist, 14,* 479–495. http://dx.doi.org/10.1076/clin.14.4.479.7201

Taranto, J. (2007). *State of Indiana v. Ahmad Edwards: Brief for the American Psychiatric Association and American Academy of Psychiatry and the Law amici curiae in support of neither party.* Retrieved from http://www.aapl.org/docs/pdf/Amicus%20Briefs%20Edwards.pdf

Taylor, P. J., & Kopelman, M. D. (1984). Amnesia for criminal offences. *Psychological Medicine, 14,* 581–588. http://dx.doi.org/10.1017/S003329170001518X

Temple, R. O., Zgaljardic, D. J., Abreu, B. C., Seale, G. S., Ostir, G. V., & Ottenbacher, K. J. (2009). Ecological validity of the neuropsychological assessment battery screening module in post-acute brain injury rehabilitation. *Brain Injury, 23,* 45–50. http://dx.doi.org/10.1080/02699050802590361

Viljoen, J. L., Zapf, P. A., & Roesch, R. (2004). Diagnosis, current symptomatology, and the ability to stand trial. *Journal of Forensic Psychology Practice, 3,* 23–37. http://dx.doi.org/10.1300/J158v03n04_02

Vitacco, M. J., Rogers, R., & Gabel, J. (2009). An investigation of the ECST–R in male pretrial patients: Evaluating the effects of feigning on competency evaluations. *Assessment, 16,* 249–257. http://dx.doi.org/10.1177/1073191108325057

Weiner, I. B., & Hess, A. K. (Eds.). (2006). *The handbook of forensic psychology* (3rd ed.). Hoboken, NJ: Wiley.

Wieter v. Settle, 193 F. Supp. 318 (W. D. Mo. 1961).

Wilson v. United States, 97 F. 937 (1968).

Youtsey v. United States, 97 F. 937 (6th Cir. 1899).

Zapf, P. A., & Roesch, R. (2006). Competency to stand trial: A guide for evaluators. In I. B. Weiner & A. K. Hess (Eds.), *The handbook of forensic psychology* (3rd ed., pp. 305–331). Hoboken, NJ: Wiley.

Zapf, P. A., & Roesch, R. (2009). *Evaluation of competency to stand trial (best practices in forensic mental health assessment).* New York, NY: Oxford University Press.

Zgaljardic, D. J., Yancy, S., Temple, R. O., Watford, M. F., & Miller, R. (2011). Ecological validity of the screening module and the daily living tests of the Neuropsychological Assessment Battery using the Mayo–Portland Adaptability Inventory—4 in postacute brain injury rehabilitation. *Rehabilitation Psychology, 56,* 359–365. http://dx.doi.org/10.1037/a0025466

Zillmer, E. A., & King, C. M. (2013). Forensic neuropsychological assessment. In R. P. Archer & E. M. A. Wheeler (Eds.), *Forensic uses of clinical assessment instruments* (pp. 291–310). Mahwah, NJ: Erlbaum.

CHAPTER 16

DIVERSITY CONSIDERATIONS IN FORENSIC NEUROPSYCHOLOGY

Shelley Peery, Desiree A. Byrd, and Adriana M. Strutt

With the expanding diversity within U.S. society, the forensic neuropsychologist is ethically obligated to approach each case with an ever more sophisticated appreciation of the impact of sociodemographic variables on standardized neuropsychological and psychological test performance (Ethical Standard 9.02, Use of Assessments; American Psychological Association [APA], 2017). Cultural differences (Burton, Vilar-López, & Puente, 2012), race or ethnicity, language, educational experiences, and socioeconomic status (Manly, Jacobs, Touradji, Small, & Stern, 2002) have well-documented impacts on neuropsychological test performance. Thus, as society diversifies, neuropsychologists must adapt their practices accordingly.

Theories underpinning cross-cultural assessment span two ends of a spectrum akin to nature versus nurture. *Universality* is the assumption that people are essentially the same (i.e., nature) and thus methods and procedures need not differ for clients from different cultures. *Radical environmentalism* proposes the opposite (i.e., nurture) and is reflective of Aristotle's tabula rasa in that all knowledge is assumed to be culture-bound and people's behavior stems from their environment. Assessment decisions based on radical environmentalism favor methods specific to the backgrounds of diverse clients. In a professional specialty whose name is a concatenation of neurology and psychology, it should come as no surprise that the field is made up of elements that are biological in nature as well as those that are culture-bound (i.e., nature and nurture).

Currently, there is greater appreciation of the influence of sociocultural factors on performance differences. Because many neuropsychologists operate largely within their own culture, it is easy to forget which aspects of a neuropsychologist's process are culture-bound (Ardila, 2005) and to assume that people of other backgrounds should perform as well as members of the majority culture. For example, many believe that visuospatial measures may be culture-fair (Rosselli & Ardila, 2003), but the literature has illustrated that nonverbal measures are just as affected by culture as verbal measures (Boone, Victor, Wen, Razani, & Pontón, 2007; Jacobs et al., 1997; Manly et al., 1998; Rosselli & Ardila, 2003).

Consideration of sociodemographic variables is essential when conducting forensic assessments with diverse examinees to preserve the construct validity of measures and to ensure that misdiagnosis does not result. A well-known example is the case of Larry P. (*Larry P. v. Riles,* 1974). The litigation involved a California student, one of many African American children placed in a classroom setting for "educable mentally retarded" on the basis of IQ scores "designed to evaluate white middle-class students, not black children" (Wade, 1980, p. 1195). Indeed, whenever examining individuals of backgrounds that differ from the normative sample, the neuropsychologist must carefully consider whether tests actually measure the intended construct and adjust the interpretation for known threats to validity. Spurious deflation or inflation of scores resulting from differences between the examinee and the normative group alters the sensitivity and specificity

http://dx.doi.org/10.1037/0000032-016
APA Handbook of Forensic Neuropsychology, S. S. Bush (Editor-in-Chief)

of tests, thus obscuring diagnostic patterns (Manly et al., 2002).

Neuropsychologists have developed a science around measuring feigning, malingering, over- and underreporting of impairments, and the effect of the presence of secondary gain. Identifying and understanding these possibilities is more complicated in cross-cultural evaluations. Discrepancies in neuropsychological test performance due to sociodemographic variables attenuate the specificity of neuropsychological measures in general. Accounting for these differences is important to pass a *Daubert* challenge (*Daubert v. Merrell Dow Pharmaceuticals, Inc.*, 1993), which addresses the reliability (i.e., validity in scientific terms) of neuropsychological tests and whether the practitioner reliably applied the principles and methods of cross-cultural neuropsychology to draw valid conclusions. This chapter provides an overview of these principles and methods with an emphasis on American ethnic minorities, although an extension can be made to forensic examinees from other countries. It also offers an update regarding ways to limit the threats to test validity that are inherent in cross-cultural assessments, including suggestions for the use of interpreters and test translations.

DIVERSITY IN NEUROPSYCHOLOGICAL ASSESSMENT

Broadly defined, diversity includes differences in ethnic or racial backgrounds; culture; gender; language dominance, including degrees of bilingualism; educational quantity and quality; disability status; and age, among other factors. Although a full treatment of cross-cultural assessment is beyond the scope of this chapter, we emphasize ethnic, cultural, linguistic, and educational diversity because these characteristics have the strongest and most researched impact on neuropsychological test performance and, thus, are most relevant to forensic assessments.

Ethnicity

Research regarding variability in neuropsychological functioning across ethnic groups is fraught with controversy. Even among neurologically normal adults from different racial/ethnic backgrounds, significant group-level performance differences exist. By attributing racial or ethnic differences in cognitive test performance to underlying genetic or biological differences, such tests were historically used to justify institutionalized racism (Durodoye, 2003; Gould, 1981; Guthrie, 1998; Helms, 2012; Manly, 2006). Today, however, race is widely recognized to be a social construct (Helms, Jernigan, & Mascher, 2005; Romero et al., 2009; Smedley & Smedley, 2005), and these differences have been found to stem largely from differences in proxy variables, such as quality of education, reading level, acculturation, English fluency, stereotype threat, socioeconomic status, and early life experiences (Boone et al., 2007; Rivera Mindt et al., 2008; Romero et al., 2009; Thames et al., 2013). For example, differences in neuropsychological test performance between ethnic groups are no longer significant after controlling for education (Dotson, Kitner-Triolo, Evans, & Zonderman, 2009; Manly et al., 2002; Manly, Byrd, Touradji, & Stern, 2004; Sisco et al., 2015). Despite the fact that many of these variables are correlated, consideration of each factor is imperative.

A primary problem when assessing ethnic minorities is that normative reference groups for many neuropsychological tests are composed primarily of Caucasians. When applying these normative standards to ethnic minorities, there is an inherent disadvantage because of the baseline between-group differences that exist between neurologically healthy ethnic groups and the related risk for false-positive errors in the detection of impairment (Heaton, Taylor, & Manly, 2003). One proposed solution to this problem is the development and use of ethnicity-specific normative data, which significantly reduces the rate of false-positive errors. It is also in alignment with the APA (2017) ethical principles for use of assessments that are appropriate to the individual (Ethical Standard 9.02). This has been accomplished for some tests—mostly for African American adults (Heaton, Miller, Taylor, & Grant, 2004; Lucas et al., 2005; Norman et al., 2011; Peña-Casanova et al., 2009), Spanish speakers (Cherner et al., 2007; Strutt, Burton, Resendiz, & Peery, 2016), and Cantonese and Mandarin speakers (Lee & Wang, 2010; Lee, Yuen, & Chan, 2002), but few norms exist for other groups (Boone et al., 2007; Ferraro, 2002; Fujii, 2011).

Acculturation

Acculturation refers to the extent to which an individual is integrated into the dominant culture in terms of language, popular culture (e.g., television, music), everyday institutions of school and work, and the cultural background of his or her friends. Acculturation may be measured formally via self-report questionnaires or informally through an interview. Formal measures have been developed and validated for use with specific ethnic groups, non–English speakers, and deaf populations, among other types of cultural minorities (Zea, Asner-Self, Birman, & Buki, 2003).

Research has demonstrated that scores on these acculturation measures can account for a significant proportion of variance in cognitive test performance and, in some instances, diminish differences between members of minority and majority cultures. The inclusion of acculturation measures in forensic assessments can assist the examiner in gaining insight into the examinees' cultural orientation, which cannot be inferred from ethnicity alone. Unacculturated persons might require more attention to corrections for education and other proxy variables. When examinees are primarily acculturated to their native culture (and not to the majority culture), the validity of standard neuropsychological methods becomes questionable, thus requiring interpretive caveats. For example, although neuropsychologists understand the importance of maintaining standardized testing practices, nonacculturated examinees may struggle with the formality of the assessment process. Forensic practitioners working with certain diverse examinees may benefit from providing them with an explanation of this procedure, in particular when working with examinees who have low levels of acculturation, education, or test wiseness. In such cases, forensic practitioners are encouraged to explain the standardized testing process clearly; the examinee should be advised to expect the formal presentation of instructions and stimuli with little explanation and limited casual interaction once testing has begun. Ensuring that the examinee understands the task by providing examples and explanation of exemplars when appropriate (i.e., not invalidating the standardized task) is highly recommended. A brief discussion regarding the balance between speed and accuracy of performance is also important because cultural practices may negatively affect performance on speeded measures (Ardila, 2005; Strutt et al., 2016). Accurate communication is a vital component of a valid assessment because poor interactions between the examiner and examinee may lead to inaccurate diagnoses and inappropriate statements regarding causality, degree of disability, decision-making capacity, or other issues addressed by the evaluation (Ardila, 2005; Robbins, Schuler, Ferrett, & Strutt, 2016).

Language

An examinee self-reporting his or her preferred language is not always the best indicator of the language most suitable for testing (Artiola i Fortuny & Mullaney, 1997) because of social pressure for linguistic minorities to demonstrate adequate English fluency. All individuals have lexicons used at home, in the community, at work, and at school that differ from person to person and are often specific to the setting. An individual may feel more fluent in the language spoken at home (Spanish, e.g.), but the language spoken at school (English) may still be more accurate for the assessment of cognitive skills. The language spoken at school during high school, if attended, is often a useful indicator, especially considering that many neuropsychological instruments assess skills and knowledge acquired at school. Artiola i Fortuny (2008) recommended administering verbal measures (e.g., semantic fluency, confrontation naming, vocabulary) in both languages to identify the bilingual examinee's dominant language empirically. A more in-depth procedure to assess proficiency in both languages is available for English–Spanish bilinguals using the Woodcock-Muñoz Language Survey—Revised (Woodcock, Muñoz-Sandoval, Ruef, & Alvarado, 2005). Riverside Publishing also offers the Bilingual Verbal Abilities Test to assess proficiency in 17 languages, with matching forms in English for comparison (Alvarado, 2014).

Once language dominance is determined, neuropsychologists must consider their own level of proficiency in the examinee's dominant language.

Recommendations by practicing neuropsychologists have included that bilingual examiners characterize their language skills according to the guidelines for proficiency developed by the American Council on the Teaching of Foreign Languages (2012), with classifications of advanced or better being suggested as adequate for neuropsychological evaluation (Rivera Mindt, 2009). Artiola i Fortuny and Mullaney (1998) proposed that neuropsychologists should ask themselves whether they could successfully engage in all academic activities (reading, writing, listening, and thinking) at an advanced level if they were to enroll in a foreign university's graduate or professional program. They argued that linguistic proficiency should be at the level of one who has completed advanced studies in the target language. Although the proficiency standards proposed by these authors are admirable, most neuropsychologists currently practicing in the United States do not possess such a degree of proficiency, according to self-ratings (Echemendía, Harris, Congett, Diaz, & Puente, 1997; Renteria, 2010). In these cases, referral to a neuropsychologist fluent in the language is preferred (Judd et al., 2009). However, when this is not reasonable (e.g., the only neuropsychologist that speaks a given language in the area lacks forensic experience, works with a different age group than the examinee, or lacks experience with the diagnosis in question), then collaboration with a bilingual psychologist or psychometrist are better solutions than using an interpreter, an option that should be reserved for uncommon languages (Artiola i Fortuny & Mullaney, 1998).

Although several advances have been made in the neurocognitive assessment of African Americans and Spanish speakers, the same cannot be said of many other races, cultures, or linguistic groups (Robbins et al., 2016). Suggestions for working with interpreters when that is necessary are offered later in this chapter.

Education

The influence of education is one of the variables with the most impact on neuropsychological test performance, especially among individuals with a relatively low quantity or quality of education. Number of years in an education system alone is often not a good proxy for premorbid IQ or functioning level in the targeted groups because disparities exist in curriculum quality, school resources and policies, quality of teacher training and subsequent instruction, and impact of parental levels of education on the examinee (Wechsler Intelligence Scale for Children—Fourth Edition in Spanish; Wechsler, 2005). For example, Manly and others have found that correcting for education quality with reading level removes much of the neuropsychological differences between racial groups (Manly et al., 2002, 2004; Rohit et al., 2007). These investigators demonstrated that the number of years of education completed does not take the quality of education into account.

Quality of education must be considered when interpreting the neuropsychological test performance of ethnically diverse individuals. In native English speakers without suspicion of a reading disability, performance on reading recognition tests such as the Wide Range Achievement Test 4 corresponds to education quality (Sayegh, Arentoft, Thaler, Dean, & Thames, 2014). Education-adjusted normative data are available for the Wechsler Adult Intelligence Scale, Fourth Edition (Wechsler, 2008), and Wechsler Memory Scale (Wechsler, 2009b) for individuals with 8 years of education or less, or age 18 years or older, from the Advanced Clinical Solutions package (Wechsler, 2009a). Thus, we recommend examination of reading level and, when the grade-equivalent score is lower than the achieved education level, using the former as an interpretive basis. This process is a more precise method to improve construct validity in cross-cultural assessment than use of ethnicity-specific norms and is generalizable to more ethnic groups.

Normative Data

When assembling test batteries for assessments of diverse examinees, preferentially selecting tests that have ethnicity-based normative data is one way to increase specificity, better prepare for a *Daubert* challenge, and increase confidence that conclusions are valid. However, this option is not available for all tests and certainly not for all ethnic minority groups, making it impractical for many cross-cultural assessments. Furthermore, this method is not without its critics, even for the extant tests and groups they address.

One major critique of ethnicity-specific norms is that they can give the impression that race or ethnicity alone explains the variability between groups rather than correlating with factors such as education quality, language status, or other sociodemographic variables that underlie performance differences (Manly, 2005). As a social construct, ethnicity naturally varies across time and geography, which brings into question which specific norms might be best suited for any particular examinee. This point is especially relevant for persons who have multiple ethnic identities. In some cases, such as when the referral question is about functioning relative to the general population, applying standard norms to an ethnic minority examinee may be appropriate.

An alternative to the use of ethnicity-specific normative data in the assessment of ethnic minorities is to adjust the interpretation of test scores in light of sociodemographic variables that have been demonstrated to influence neuropsychological test performance (Manly, 2005). For example, as mentioned previously, quality of education can be measured by examining the grade equivalent of a reading test (e.g., Wide Range Achievement Test 4 Reading). Because quality of education explains much of the variance attributed to race/ethnicity, this is recommended to inform interpretation of test data from individual examinees.

Another consideration when selecting norms for a cross-cultural evaluation is the consistency of demographic corrections across the tests in the battery. Impairment estimates can be falsely inflated or deflated as a direct result of the application of normative standards that are derived from vastly different samples and offer corrections for different demographic factors. This risk extends beyond ethnicity considerations and is a challenge for the discipline at large. However, it deserves special attention in assessments of diverse examinees. For example, when examiners use instruments that have norms for their examinees' ethnicity and supplement these tests with others using traditional Caucasian norms, resulting patterns may vary as a result of comparison with different norms and not as a reflection of the examinee's cognitive strengths and weaknesses. Therefore, although the use of disparate norms is often necessary, neuropsychologists are responsible for clearly reporting the source of normative data and describing the limitations when making comparisons between tests that differ in their normative samples and the demographic corrections they use. For examinees whose dominant language is not English, adaptation of tests to other cultures and languages, test translation, and use of interpreters are discussed later in this chapter.

FORENSIC CONSIDERATIONS

This section covers diversity considerations for two aspects of forensic neuropsychology: the assessment of civil capacities and the diagnosis of malingered neurocognitive dysfunction.

Civil Capacities

Evaluation of legal competencies requires an appreciation of "the environment or social context in which the examinee will be expected to function" (Grisso, 2003, p. 35). Thus, culture is critical to the assessment of functional capacity in forensic evaluations of civil capacities. For the culturally diverse examinee, neuropsychologists must consider both the interpretation of formal test results and the impressions of functional status through a cultural lens. Very poor test performance may or may not be consistent with reports of diminished functional capacity depending on the relevance of the task to the examinee's everyday functioning. For example, if someone does not typically use a checkbook, relying on questions about checkbook use will not provide information about functional changes or impairment. Thus, the interviews with the examinee and collateral sources must be tailored to the examinee's specific instrumental activities of daily living.

Assessment of the individual's capacity to live at home alone safely or to make health care and financial decisions typically includes interviews with questions specific to the tasks at issue. Through careful interview and by querying the examinee and informants about the changes observed in the examinee's functioning, the neuropsychologist may assess novel problem solving through hypotheticals that may arise in that individual's situation. Throughout the process, the neuropsychologist must be careful to consider the various manners in which individuals can adapt to life's demands and how they can differ vastly across subcultures.

Malingered Neurocognitive Dysfunction

Slick, Sherman, and Iverson (1999) developed criteria for identification of malingering based on several factors and requiring consideration of multiple sources of information (see also Heilbronner, Sweet, Morgan, Larrabee, & Millis, 2009). The criteria include (a) formal symptom and performance validity tests (PVTs) and related measures that are free-standing or embedded within measures of other abilities, (b) record review, (c) clinical interview, (d) interviews of collateral sources, and (e) behavioral observations in the context of the examinee's sociodemographic background and potential for secondary gain. After data collection, malingered neurocognitive dysfunction is diagnosed by ruling out psychiatric or neurological explanations for invalid performance. Following is a discussion of (a) the ways in which race/ethnicity, education, and language may be considered when measuring performance validity; (b) the need for greater reliance on collateral interviews and behavioral observations in cross-cultural evaluations; and (c) diversity considerations in psychiatric diagnoses.

Performance validity. The administration of PVTs is straightforward, and the stimuli are typically culturally neutral, although the possibility of ethnic performance differences exists. Nevertheless, only scant research has been conducted on this issue. Objective measures of effort are a relatively new addition to the neuropsychology toolkit and do not benefit from the same amount of research as other cognitive tests. The dearth of research limits conclusions about cultural background's influence on performance on these tests. Several studies have supported the use of standard PVTs and their established cutoffs without any need for special consideration in the context of cross-cultural evaluations. For example, Burton et al. (2012) evaluated three PVTs (Dot Counting, Rey 15-Item Memory Test, and Test of Memory Malingering) in Spanish speakers across three settings—capital murder cases, other forensic cases, and clinical controls—and found that established cutoffs yielded failure rates comparable to expectations among English speakers. Although this study did not establish the specificity of the measures in Spanish speakers, it is useful to know that failure rates were similar across the two cultural groups. Yet work by Salazar, Lu, Wen, and Boone (2007) indicated that the utility of established cutoffs for specific PVTs varied depending on the ethnic group under investigation. For instance, these authors found that for African Americans, standard cutoffs for Reliable Digit Span and the Dot Counting Test yielded adequate specificity, but the Rey Osterrieth effort equation and Rey Auditory Verbal Learning Test effort equation and recognition cutoffs all required significant adjustment to achieve adequate specificity in this group.

Other investigators also uncovered performance differences that warrant special group-specific interpretive consideration. Yang et al. (2012) explored the utility of the Reliable Digit Span as an indicator of suboptimal performance in a Taiwanese sample. This study determined that healthy Taiwanese produced baseline recall strings that were significantly longer than the U.S. norms, leading to poorer discriminability of the Reliable Digit Span when applying standard cutoffs to these Taiwanese adults.

Examiners must also adjust their thresholds for identifying response bias by considering differences in sensitivity and specificity cutoffs that vary with education and language (Salazar et al., 2007), especially for low-education groups (e.g., less than a third-grade reading level for Green's Word Memory Test; Green & Flaro, 2003). Data have suggested that the appropriateness of standard effort measures in Spanish speakers varies by education level. A literature review by Salazar et al. (2007) on the effects of language or race on malingering yielded only 12 studies: Seven examined cognitive malingering among native Chinese speakers, and five addressed malingering among those of Latin descent, yet most of these explored issues of malingered psychiatric symptoms. Given the limited research, the authors concluded that practitioners are often left to infer the appropriateness of common validity assessment instruments when used in cross-cultural evaluations.

Regarding PVTs that have not been validated across diverse samples, some basic tenets apply across all sociodemographic groups because of statistical principles. On forced-choice instruments, significantly and consistently below-chance performance reflects suboptimal performance regardless of cultural background, except in severely impaired individuals (e.g., those with severe dementia or delirium). Chance performance on forced-choice instruments with two options is 50% regardless of sociodemographic background, and performing significantly below chance requires knowledge of the answers. By the same token, perfect performance (i.e., 100% accuracy) is consistent with good effort regardless of background. Although the specificity of many PVTs across cultures has not yet been determined, failure on multiple PVTs increases the likelihood of noncredible effort, particularly when failure involves performance that is not significantly different from or below statistical chance levels of responding.

In summary, the limited available literature is mixed and, at best, has suggested that clinicians should choose and interpret effort indices with greater scrutiny when evaluating diverse examinees. Additional research is needed to establish the cross-cultural validity of available measures and indices as well as critical examination of the diversity of normative samples for existing effort measures.

Behavioral observations and interviews of informants. A structured decision-making process to assist in case conceptualization of minority examinees using a systematic approach to collecting background information (e.g., medical and mental health, lifestyle and cultural practices, academic and vocational experience, exposure to Westernized practices) is recommended. When noting behavioral observations of ethnic minorities and when obtaining collateral information, a holistic approach, unveiling details regarding culture, traditional values and expectations and lifestyle practices, is imperative in better understanding the examinee and the reported medical and mental health issues (Robbins et al., 2016). The use of such an approach in a forensic setting affords the examiner an increased capacity to understand the interplay between neurocognitive functioning and sociodemographic influences. In light of the diversity that exists between individuals who share sociodemographic similarities, forensic evaluators should inquire about the examinee's unique life experiences and practices. Assumptions regarding sociodemographic factors should not be made solely on the basis of commonalities within regions or countries of origin because differences may exist that are unfamiliar to the examiner, resulting in unknown confounds (Ardila, 2005; Strutt et al., 2016).

The value of detailed behavioral observations and the use of informants should be emphasized in a cross-cultural forensic examination. Forensic neuropsychologists must carefully rule out plausible alternative explanations for invalid performance, regardless of the examinee's background. However, for examinees with diverse backgrounds, what constitutes plausible alternative explanations can be quite distinct from those considered reasonable for examinees of a mainstream background. Test-wiseness is how familiar an individual is with the expectations of performance on tests and informs speed–accuracy trade-offs (Ardila, 2005), but sometimes slow performance is mistaken for evidence of malingering. Differences in comprehension of stimuli can arise from lack of language mastery (e.g., symptom report may be vague partly because of poor ability to articulate challenges in individuals with low education) or lack of familiarity with Western culture (e.g., the picture of an igloo could just as easily be a clay oven). The presence of atypical or unusual symptoms or symptom combinations (e.g., delusions or hallucinations that only arise in specific settings) raises suspicion of symptom fabrication (Heilbronner et al., 2009) regardless of sociodemographic factors, but one must be aware of various culturally appropriate expressions of distress so as not to overpathologize. Significant deviations between reported history and records must be explored, but peculiar omissions or inconsistent ability to recall information (e.g., good for the details related to an accident but poor for how everyday functions are accomplished) is not expected regardless of sociodemographic differences. Behavioral observations can aid the examiner in contextualizing test results to appreciate the impact of sociodemographic differences versus poor effort or malingering.

Informants can provide examples of the impact of loss of cognitive functioning on an examinee's everyday life that may not be part of an examiner's typical interview (e.g., role in family or community, quality of work on hobbies, or particular talents). However, clinical utility of informants may vary depending on cultural practices and beliefs. The process by which information is obtained should be described in the report. When the opportunity arises, it may be of benefit to conduct collateral interviews without the presence of the examinee, because informants are likely to feel more at ease in reporting sensitive information. A hierarchy in the relationship of the examinee and the collateral source may be present, and the possibility of a biased report should be investigated. Moreover, although family members usually serve as informants, the reliability of the provided information should be considered. For example, many Hispanic and Asian adult children of older adults feel that it is disrespectful to highlight their elders' shortcomings and as such may minimize or dismiss noted declines. Some research has shown that African American informants may be more likely to underreport declines in cognition and functional skills, and non-Hispanic White sources may be likely to overreport (Rivera Mindt, Arentoft, Coulehan, & Byrd, 2013).

The use of informants will likely be of greater benefit when test instruments are not published that have validity data for samples with the examinee's demographic background and when performance on standardized outcome measures seems questionable (O'Bryant, 2008; Potter et al., 2009). Because the conclusions of neuropsychological evaluations stem from the integration of test results with other sources of data, information from a reliable collateral may carry more weight than poor performance on validity measures when the data all converge (i.e., the collateral reports are similar to test results).

Rule out psychiatric disorders. Idioms of distress include variants of psychiatric disorders as expressed in other cultures (Draguns & Tanaka-Matsumi, 2003). For example, some Native Americans refer to a darkness hanging over them, a metaphor for distress, but they can describe it in terms that can lead a clinician to consider it a visual hallucination. Talking to ghosts can be a culturally normative form of bereavement (Asociación Psiquiátrica de América Latina, 2004) that should be distinguished from auditory and visual hallucinations via careful exploration of the phenomena. The *Diagnostic and Statistical Manual of Mental Disorders* (5th ed.; American Psychiatric Association, 2013) and its analog in Latin America, the *Guía Latino Americana de Diagnostico Psiquiátrico* (Asociación Psiquiátrica de América Latina, 2004), both list a number of culturally specific psychiatric manifestations of distress, especially depression and posttraumatic stress disorder, that could be mistaken for exaggeration or somatoform disorders. These must be considered when making or ruling out psychiatric diagnoses and determining the impact of psychological distress on neurocognitive functioning.

Generally speaking, the communication and interpersonal styles of a minority examinee may differ from those of dominant-culture examinees concerning personal disclosure and rapport, expression of physical and mental distress, locus of control, and role expectations. Moreover, because neurocognitive and psychological assessments are data-driven procedures, the nonverbal conventions of an examinee (i.e., pace of exchange, eye contact, interpersonal distance, touch, and gestures) are important in the examiner's overall understanding of the examinee and his or her clinical interpretation and diagnostic impression (Judd & Beggs, 2005). The neuropsychologist is responsible for understanding the culture of the examinee and recognizing variations in expression of emotions and psychiatric symptoms to avoid overpathologizing or missing symptoms (e.g., because of a culture of reserved emotional expression).

Working With Interpreters

Delivery of culturally and linguistically appropriate neuropsychological services for individuals with no or limited English proficiency is among the major challenges facing forensic neuropsychology because the number of bilingual neuropsychologists pales in comparison to the present demand (Casas et al., 2012). Under ideal circumstances, the examiner should communicate with the examinee in the examinee's native language rather than through an interpreter. Some scholars have argued that it is almost obligatory (Artiola i Fortuny & Mullaney, 1997), citing various standards of APA's (2017) *Ethical Principles of Psychologists and Code of Conduct*. For example, Ethical Standard 9.02(c) (Use of Assessments) states, "Psychologists use assessment methods that are appropriate to an individual's language preference and competence" (APA, 2017). However, this document does not specify whether the use of interpreters constitutes an appropriate, albeit alternative, method for providing psychological services that are consistent with an examinee's language preference. The *Guidelines for Providers of Psychological Services to Ethnic, Linguistic, and Culturally Diverse Populations* (APA, 1993) offer more specificity, stating, "Psychologists interact in the language requested by the client, and, if this is not feasible, make an appropriate referral" (p. 47). In addition, an educational paper from the National Academy of Neuropsychology asserted that, "ideally, the examinee is evaluated in his or her preferred and/or best language" (Judd et al., 2009, p. 128). However, there is still ambiguity. Ethical Standard 2.02 states that psychologists "can provide services to individuals for whom other mental health services are not available and for which psychologists have not obtained the necessary training. Psychologists may provide such services in order to ensure that services are not denied" (APA, 2017). Given this flexibility in the standards, examiners must decide whether their clinical acumen allows them to provide an appropriate service after making an effort to refer out or identify a bilingual psychologist or psychometrist with whom to collaborate (Artiola i Fortuny & Mullaney, 1998).

If an individual is dominant in a language other than English, testing in English because he or she speaks "well enough" can spuriously deflate the individual's test performance by a standard deviation or more (Roberts, Garcia, Desrochers, & Hernandez, 2002). If the appropriate resources are not available for the examinee, then several caveats are required (Ethical Standards 9.01, Bases for Assessments, and 9.06, Interpreting Assessment Results; APA, 2017).

A bicultural interpreter facilitates an understanding of the examinee's nonverbal behaviors including kinesics, paralanguage, eye contact, touch, and proxemics (personal and social space) and provides a holistic understanding of the examinee. Unfortunately, neuropsychologically trained bicultural interpreters can be difficult to find, and most interpreters have been grandfathered into their careers without formal language training.

Caution when using an interpreter is no idle concern. Research revealed that 80% of practicing neuropsychologists have relied on interpreters without any formal psychological or neuropsychological training (Echemendía et al., 1997). Subsequent professional guidelines and neuropsychology literature (Rivera Mindt, Byrd, Saez, & Manly, 2010; U.S. Department of Health and Human Services, 2001) highlighted the need to appropriately prepare for non–English-speaking minority clients. Recommendations included the need for examiners and interpreters to be sociolinguistically competent and professionally trained in the realm of neurocognitive and psychological assessment (Judd et al., 2009; Paradis, 2008; Rivera Mindt et al., 2008).

Although this was the beginning of a movement to address health disparities, more than a decade later follow-up research revealed the lack of compliance with these recommendations by a large number of professionals. Inappropriate clinical practices continued, and research has revealed a tendency for poor clinical practices when working with non–English speakers. Renteria (2010) reported that 25% of neuropsychologists "never" referred their clients to providers who could provide services to them in their native language. This practice underscores a vast disservice in the field of neuropsychology and one that may be vulnerable to a *Daubert* challenge. To mitigate threats to validity, understanding the limitations faced by examiners who cannot communicate with an examinee in his or her dominant language is imperative, as is implementation of strategies to improve the validity of neuropsychological evaluations conducted with interpreters.

Practical considerations. The use of nonprofessional interpreters has its own set of potentially undesirable consequences, including potential secondary motivations to aid or hinder the examinee's performance. Such influences of interpreters on examinee performance can occur in the case of family or friends who have a personal stake in the case or of a stranger who becomes emotionally connected to the examinee. Nonprofessional interpreters may have a poor grasp of the language or dialect despite purporting to be proficient, or they may be reticent to interpret sensitive material, among many other potential weaknesses (Paradis, 2008; Strutt et al., 2016). Whenever possible, neuropsychologists should avoid using persons known to the client as interpreters, unless circumstances dictate and permit such use (APA, 2017).

Once an interpreter has been identified, a practice run is recommended to gauge the ability of the neuropsychologist and interpreter to work together and follow standardized procedures. The neuropsychologist should attempt to work with the same interpreter because continuous work together will refine both their skills. Proposing a practice run to the referral source may not be permissible because the referral source covers the cost of the interpreter and in most cases will pay the interpreter directly. However, a brief training session (including cost of this session in the overall fee) is of benefit to all parties involved.

Of ultimate importance is the need to ascertain and clarify with all parties the limits of confidentiality. The interpreter must explain to the examinee that the neuropsychologist in a forensic setting is not establishing a doctor–patient relationship and that all information provided will be discoverable given the forensic nature of the assessment. The examinee may share sensitive information, and thus interpreters should be well trained regarding their role in the delivery of such information to the examiner. The interpreter should also refrain from inquiring directly of the examinee without the direction of the examiner.

When working with an interpreter, the accuracy of the interpretation is maximized when the neuropsychologist limits utterances to the working memory limitations of the interpreter (i.e., a sentence or two). The test instructions and all stimuli should be translated before the testing session to reduce error that can occur when it is done spontaneously during the evaluation. Educating the interpreter regarding standardized testing practices is essential to ensure the interpreter is not inadvertently assisting the examinee. More important, the interpreter should be asked to provide a literal interpretation of the examinee's verbal output, meaning that the examinee's language should not be corrected or altered. If poor grammar or language errors are made, the interpreter should inform the examiner of such errors and provide exact responses, even if they are incorrect or do not make sense. Omitting or paraphrasing information may lead to invalid results.

The examiner should review a basic behavioral observations template with the interpreter and ask that the interpreter make note of verbal and nonverbal cues that may be of importance. The behavioral observations template should be reviewed a few times throughout the testing session so that the examiner is aware of what the interpreter has considered noteworthy and that the examiner may also be able to witness. Behavioral observations noted by the interpreter should be presented as such. The quality of the interaction between the examinee and the interpreter and between the examinee and examiner via the interpreter should be described. Possible sources of error or confounding variables should be mentioned.

Although a court-credentialed or professional interpreter is suggested, a bilingual psychometrist would be more appropriate for those who service non–English-speaking minorities often, because these trained individuals have experience with examiner–examinee interactions and an appreciation of the importance of standardized testing procedures. The interpreter should be identified by name in the examiner's report, and the individual's qualifications and assessment experience should be included.

Test translations. It is imperative to use published translations of outcome measures to ensure correct translation and construct validity. Site translations are strongly discouraged because of the variability introduced in the translation that reduces standardization and because errors in translation cannot be corrected or, if they are spontaneously corrected, can result in multiple exposures to the stimuli or simply confuse the examinee. Published adaptations or direct translations of some tests are available for some languages (e.g., Spanish, Cantonese/Mandarin, Taiwanese, Russian, German, Japanese, and Vietnamese). Guidelines for test adaptation have been published (International Test Commission, 2005). Adaptation is intended to improve construct validity over direct translation because a string of words in one language may successfully be translated into another language and back again without error but also without fidelity of meaning. For example, although "feeling blue" may be easily translated, the connotation related to sadness is lost in translation. Artiola i Fortuny and Mullaney (1997) offer several examples of the pitfalls of test translation. Similarly, the psychometrics of a test may be altered by translation (e.g., word length, word frequency, item difficulty). When no published adaptation or translation is available, translating the test in advance permits addressing such threats to validity. A formal translation involves native-speaking psychologists of both languages agreeing that the meaning is preserved through harmonization (International Test Commission, 2005).

CONCLUSION

In this chapter, we described issues for neuropsychologists to consider in the forensic evaluation of examinees from diverse racial, cultural, and linguistic backgrounds and offered suggestions for how to improve the validity of cross-cultural assessments. The suggestions include accounting for education quality, measuring acculturation, accounting for differences in language dominance in testing, and using ethnicity-specific normative data, when available. Several guidelines have been established in the field of cross-cultural neuropsychological assessment that mitigate threats to validity of tests used across cultures. These guidelines include considerations for working responsibly with interpreters and carefully considering neurobehavioral observations and information obtained from informants. Satisfactory validity is achieved when these procedures are followed in a sensible manner. Although caveats regarding limitations in test validity are still necessary, these recommendations foster convergent validity of conclusions that would likely pass a *Daubert* challenge.

Neuropsychologists who conduct evaluations with minority clients are ethically responsible for ensuring that they are adequately trained to conduct such evaluations. Cross-cultural forensic neuropsychological assessments require a knowledge base and skill set similar to that for clinical evaluations plus an appreciation for the impact of the previously discussed sociodemographics. Despite the fact that cross-cultural neuropsychological assessment has made significant gains, ongoing research is needed to fully delineate the mechanisms by which culture interacts with other factors to influence test performance, symptom validity, and clinical presentations in forensic evaluations.

References

Alvarado, C. G. (2014). *Bilingual special education evaluation of culturally and linguistically diverse individuals using Woodcock tests.* Retrieved from http://educationeval.com/yahoo_site_admin/assets/docs/BilingualSpEdEvalofCLDIndividualsUsingWoodcockTests.11182740.pdf

American Council on the Teaching of Foreign Languages. (2012). *American Council on the Teaching of Foreign Languages proficiency guidelines* (3rd ed.). Alexandria, VA: Author.

American Psychiatric Association. (2013). *Diagnostic and statistical manual of mental disorders* (5th ed.). Washington, DC: Author.

American Psychological Association. (1993). Guidelines for providers of psychological services to ethnic, linguistic, and culturally diverse populations. *American Psychologist, 48,* 45–48. http://dx.doi.org/10.1037/0003-066X.48.1.45

American Psychological Association. (2017). *Ethical principles of psychologists and code of conduct* (2002, Amended June 1, 2010 and January 1, 2017). Retrieved from http://www.apa.org/ethics/code/index.aspx

Ardila, A. (2005). Cultural values underlying psychometric cognitive testing. *Neuropsychology Review, 15,* 185–195. http://dx.doi.org/10.1007/s11065-005-9180-y

Artiola i Fortuny, L. (2008). Research and practice: Ethical issues with immigrant adults and children. In J. Morgan & J. Ricker (Eds.), *Textbook of clinical neuropsychology* (pp. 960–981). New York, NY: Psychology Press.

Artiola i Fortuny, L., & Mullaney, H. A. (1997). Neuropsychology with Spanish speakers: Language use and proficiency issues for test development. *Journal of Clinical and Experimental Neuropsychology, 19,* 615–622. http://dx.doi.org/10.1080/01688639708403747

Artiola i Fortuny, L., & Mullaney, H. A. (1998). Assessing patients whose language you do not know: Can the absurd be ethical? *Clinical Neuropsychologist, 12,* 113–126. http://dx.doi.org/10.1076/clin.12.1.113.1727

Asociación Psiquiátrica de América Latina, Sección de Diagnostico y Clasificación. (2004). *Guía Latinoamericana de diagnostico psiquiátrico (GLAD–P)* [Latin American guide for psychiatric diagnosis]. Guadalajara, Mexico: Author.

Boone, K. B., Victor, T. L., Wen, J., Razani, J., & Pontón, M. (2007). The association between neuropsychological scores and ethnicity, language, and acculturation variables in a large patient population. *Archives of Clinical Neuropsychology, 22,* 355–365. http://dx.doi.org/10.1016/j.acn.2007.01.010

Burton, V., Vilar-López, R., & Puente, A. E. (2012). Measuring effort in neuropsychological evaluations of forensic cases of Spanish speakers. *Archives of Clinical Neuropsychology, 27,* 262–267. http://dx.doi.org/10.1093/arclin/acs026

Casas, R., Guzmán-Vélez, E., Cardona-Rodriguez, J., Rodriguez, N., Quiñones, G., Izaguirre, B., & Tranel, D. (2012). Interpreter-mediated neuropsychological testing of monolingual Spanish speakers. *Clinical Neuropsychologist, 26,* 88–101. http://dx.doi.org/10.1080/13854046.2011.640641

Cherner, M., Suarez, P., Lazzaretto, D., Fortuny, L. A., Mindt, M. R., Dawes, S., . . . Heaton, R. (2007). Demographically corrected norms for the Brief Visuospatial Memory Test—Revised and Hopkins Verbal Learning Test—Revised in monolingual Spanish speakers from the U.S.–Mexico border region. *Archives of Clinical Neuropsychology, 22,* 343–353. http://dx.doi.org/10.1016/j.acn.2007.01.009

Daubert v. Merrell Dow Pharmaceuticals, Inc., 509 U.S. 579 (1993).

Dotson, V. M., Kitner-Triolo, M. H., Evans, M. K., & Zonderman, A. B. (2009). Effects of race and socioeconomic status on the relative influence of education and literacy on cognitive functioning. *Journal of the International Neuropsychological Society, 15,* 580–589. http://dx.doi.org/10.1017/S1355617709090821

Draguns, J. G., & Tanaka-Matsumi, J. (2003). Assessment of psychopathology across and within cultures: Issues and findings. *Behaviour Research and Therapy, 41,* 755–776. http://dx.doi.org/10.1016/S0005-7967(02)00190-0

Durodoye, B. A. (2003). The science of race in education. *Multicultural Perspectives, 5,* 10–16. http://dx.doi.org/10.1207/S15327892MCP0502_3

Echemendía, R. J., Harris, J. G., Congett, S. M., Diaz, M. L., & Puente, A. E. (1997). Neuropsychological training and practices with Hispanics: A national survey. *Clinical Neuropsychologist, 11,* 229–243. http://dx.doi.org/10.1080/13854049708400451

Ferraro, F. R. (2002). *Minority and cross-cultural aspects of neuropsychological assessment.* Lisse, the Netherlands: Swets & Zeitlinger.

Fujii, D. E. M. (2011). *The neuropsychology of Asian Americans.* New York, NY: Taylor & Francis.

Gould, S. J. (1981). *The mismeasure of man.* New York, NY: Norton.

Green, P., & Flaro, L. (2003). Word Memory Test performance in children. *Child Neuropsychology, 9,* 189–207. http://dx.doi.org/10.1076/chin.9.3.189.16460

Grisso, T. (2003). Legally relevant assessments for legal competencies. In T. Grisso (Ed.), *Evaluating competencies: Forensic assessments and instruments* (pp. 21–40). New York, NY: Kluwer Academic/Plenum Press.

Guthrie, R. V. (1998). *Even the rat was white: A historical view of psychology.* Boston, MA: Allyn & Bacon.

Heaton, R. K., Miller, S. W., Taylor, M. J., & Grant, I. (2004). *Revised comprehensive norms for an expanded Halstead–Reitan battery: Demographically adjusted neuropsychological norms for African American and Caucasian adults.* Lutz, FL: Psychological Assessment Resources.

Heaton, R. K., Taylor, M. J., & Manly, J. (2003). Demographic effects and use of demographically corrected norms with the WAIS–III and WMS–III. In D. S. Tulsky, D. H. Saklofske, R. K. Heaton, R. Bornstein, M. F. Ledbetter, G. J. Chelune, . . . Prifitera, A. (Eds.), *Practical resources for the mental health professional: Clinical interpretation of the WAIS–III and WMS–III* (pp. 181–210). http://dx.doi.org/10.1016/B978-012703570-3/50010-9

Heilbronner, R. L., Sweet, J. J., Morgan, J. E., Larrabee, G. J., & Millis, S. R. (2009). American Academy of Clinical Neuropsychology consensus conference statement on the neuropsychological assessment of effort, response bias, and malingering. *Clinical Neuropsychologist, 23,* 1093–1129. http://dx.doi.org/10.1080/13854040903155063

Helms, J. E. (2012). A legacy of eugenics underlies racial-group comparisons in intelligence testing. *Industrial and Organizational Psychology: Perspectives on Science and Practice, 5,* 176–179. http://dx.doi.org/10.1111/j.1754-9434.2012.01426.x

Helms, J. E., Jernigan, M., & Mascher, J. (2005). The meaning of race in psychology and how to change it: A methodological perspective. *American Psychologist, 60*, 27–36. http://dx.doi.org/10.1037/0003-066X.60.1.27

International Test Commission. (2005). *International guidelines on test adaptation.* Retrieved from https://www.intestcom.org/files/guideline_test_adaptation.pdf

Jacobs, D. M., Sano, M., Albert, S., Schofield, P., Dooneief, G., & Stern, Y. (1997). Cross-cultural neuropsychological assessment: A comparison of randomly selected, demographically matched cohorts of English- and Spanish-speaking older adults. *Journal of Clinical and Experimental Neuropsychology, 19*, 331–339. http://dx.doi.org/10.1080/01688639708403862

Judd, T., & Beggs, B. (2005). Cross-cultural forensic neuropsychological assessment. In K. Barrett & W. H. George (Eds.), *Race, culture, psychology and law* (pp. 141–162). http://dx.doi.org/10.4135/9781452233536.n10

Judd, T., Capetillo, D., Carrión-Baralt, J., Mármol, L. M., Miguel-Montes, L. S., Navarrete, M. G., . . . Valdés, J. (2009). Professional considerations for improving the neuropsychological evaluation of Hispanics: A National Academy of Neuropsychology education paper. *Archives of Clinical Neuropsychology, 24*, 127–135. http://dx.doi.org/10.1093/arclin/acp016

Larry P. v. Riles, 502 F.2d 963 (9th Cir. 1974).

Lee, T. M. C., & Wang, K. (2010). *Neuropsychological measures: Normative data for Chinese.* Hong Kong, China: Laboratory of Neuropsychology, University of Hong Kong.

Lee, T. M. C., Yuen, K. S. L., & Chan, C. C. H. (2002). Normative data for neuropsychological measures of fluency, attention, and memory measures for Hong Kong Chinese. *Journal of Clinical and Experimental Neuropsychology, 24*, 615–632. http://dx.doi.org/10.1076/jcen.24.5.615.1001

Lucas, J. A., Ivnik, R. J., Smith, G. E., Ferman, T. J., Willis, F. B., Petersen, R. C., & Graff-Radford, N. R. (2005). Mayo's Older African Americans Normative Studies: Norms for Boston Naming Test, Controlled Oral Word Association, Category Fluency, Animal Naming, Token Test, WRAT–3 Reading, Trail Making Test, Stroop Test, and Judgment of Line Orientation. *Clinical Neuropsychologist, 19*, 243–269. http://dx.doi.org/10.1080/13854040590945337

Manly, J. J. (2005). Advantages and disadvantages of separate norms for African Americans. *Clinical Neuropsychologist, 19*, 270–275. http://dx.doi.org/10.1080/13854040590945346

Manly, J. J. (2006). Deconstructing race and ethnicity: Implications for measurement of health outcomes. *Medical Care, 44*(Suppl. 3), S10–S16. http://dx.doi.org/10.1097/01.mlr.0000245427.22788.be

Manly, J. J., Byrd, D. A., Touradji, P., & Stern, Y. (2004). Acculturation, reading level, and neuropsychological test performance among African American elders. *Applied Neuropsychology, 11*, 37–46. http://dx.doi.org/10.1207/s15324826an1101_5

Manly, J. J., Jacobs, D. M., Sano, M., Bell, K., Merchant, C. A., Small, S. A., & Stern, Y. (1998). Cognitive test performance among nondemented elderly African Americans and whites. *Neurology, 50*, 1238–1245. http://dx.doi.org/10.1212/WNL.50.5.1238

Manly, J. J., Jacobs, D. M., Touradji, P., Small, S. A., & Stern, Y. (2002). Reading level attenuates differences in neuropsychological test performance between African American and White elders. *Journal of the International Neuropsychological Society, 8*, 341–348. http://dx.doi.org/10.1017/S1355617702813157

Norman, M. A., Moore, D. J., Taylor, M., Franklin, D., Jr., Cysique, L., Ake, C., . . . Heaton, R. K. (2011). Demographically corrected norms for African Americans and Caucasians on the Hopkins Verbal Learning Test–Revised, Brief Visuospatial Memory Test–Revised, Stroop Color and Word Test, and Wisconsin Card Sorting Test 64-Card Version. *Journal of Clinical and Experimental Neuropsychology, 33*, 793–804. http://dx.doi.org/10.1080/13803395.2011.559157

O'Bryant, S. (2008). Exploring the relationship between culture and cognition. *Journal of Clinical and Experimental Neuropsychology, 30*, 967–970. http://dx.doi.org/10.1080/13803390801937175

Paradis, M. (2008). Language and communication disorders in multilinguals. In B. Stemmer & H. A. Whitaker (Eds.), *Handbook of the neuroscience of language* (pp. 341–349). http://dx.doi.org/10.1016/B978-008045352-1.00033-1

Peña-Casanova, J., Blesa, R., Aguilar, M., Gramunt-Fombuena, N., Gómez-Ansón, B., Oliva, R., . . . Sol, J. M. (2009). Spanish Multicenter Normative Studies (NEURONORMA Project): Methods and sample characteristics. *Archives of Clinical Neuropsychology, 24*, 307–319. http://dx.doi.org/10.1093/arclin/acp027

Potter, G. G., Plassman, B. L., Burke, J. R., Kabeto, M. U., Langa, K. M., Llewellyn, D. J., . . . Steffens, D. C. (2009). Cognitive performance and informant reports in the diagnosis of cognitive impairment and dementia in African Americans and whites. *Alzheimer's and Dementia, 5*, 445–453. http://dx.doi.org/10.1016/j.jalz.2009.04.1234

Renteria, L. (2010, February). *Current practices survey on the neuropsychological assessment of Hispanics in the U.S.* Paper presented at the first meeting of the

Hispanic Neuropsychological Society, Acapulco, Mexico.

Rivera Mindt, M. (2009, June). *Sociocultural issues in neuropsychology: Theoretical, empirical, and practical considerations.* Paper presented at the annual meeting of the American Academy of Clinical Neuropsychology, San Diego, CA.

Rivera Mindt, M., Arentoft, A., Kubo Germano, K., D'Aquila, E., Scheiner, D., Pizzirusso, M., . . . Gollan, T. H. (2008). Neuropsychological, cognitive, and theoretical considerations for evaluation of bilingual individuals. *Neuropsychology Review, 18,* 255–268. http://dx.doi.org/10.1007/s11065-008-9069-7

Rivera Mindt, M. R., Arentoft, A., Coulehan, K., & Byrd, D. (2013). Considerations for the neuropsychological evaluation of older ethnic minority populations. In L. D. Ravdin & H. L. Katzen (Eds.), *Handbook on the neuropsychology of aging and dementia* (pp. 25–41). http://dx.doi.org/10.1007/978-1-4614-3106-0_3

Rivera Mindt, M. R., Byrd, D., Saez, P., & Manly, J. (2010). Increasing culturally competent neuropsychological services for ethnic minority populations: A call to action. *Clinical Neuropsychologist, 24,* 429–453. http://dx.doi.org/10.1080/13854040903058960

Robbins, R. N., Schuler, M., Ferrett, H. L., & Strutt, A. M. (2016). Operationalizing a standard and ethical approach to neuropsychological assessment across diverse cultures. In R. F. Ferraro (Ed.), *Minority and cross-cultural aspects of neuropsychological assessment: Enduring and emerging trends* (2nd ed., pp. 411–435). New York, NY: Taylor & Francis.

Roberts, P. M., Garcia, L. J., Desrochers, A., & Hernandez, D. (2002). English performance of proficient bilingual adults on the Boston Naming Test. *Aphasiology, 16,* 635–645. http://dx.doi.org/10.1080/02687030244000220

Rohit, M., Levine, A., Hinkin, C., Abramyan, S., Saxton, E., Valdes-Sueiras, M., & Singer, E. (2007). Education correction using years in school or reading grade-level equivalent? Comparing the accuracy of two methods in diagnosing HIV-associated neurocognitive impairment. *Journal of the International Neuropsychological Society, 13,* 462–470. http://dx.doi.org/10.1017/S1355617707070506

Romero, H. R., Lageman, S. K., Kamath, V., Irani, F., Sim, A., Suarez, P., . . . Attix, D. K. (2009). Challenges in the neuropsychological assessment of ethnic minorities: Summit proceedings. *Clinical Neuropsychologist, 23,* 761–779. http://dx.doi.org/10.1080/13854040902881958

Rosselli, M., & Ardila, A. (2003). The impact of culture and education on non-verbal neuropsychological measurements: A critical review. *Brain and Cognition, 52,* 326–333. http://dx.doi.org/10.1016/S0278-2626(03)00170-2

Salazar, X. F., Lu, P. H., Wen, J., & Boone, K. B. (2007). The use of effort tests in ethnic minorities and in non-English-speaking and English as a second language populations. In K. B. Boone (Ed.), *Assessment of feigned cognitive impairment: A neuropsychological perspective* (pp. 405–427). New York, NY: Guilford Press.

Sayegh, P., Arentoft, A., Thaler, N. S., Dean, A. C., & Thames, A. D. (2014). Quality of education predicts performance on the Wide Range Achievement Test-4th Edition Word Reading subtest. *Archives of Clinical Neuropsychology, 29,* 731–736. http://dx.doi.org/10.1093/arclin/acu059

Sisco, S., Gross, A. L., Shih, R. A., Sachs, B. C., Glymour, M. M., Bangen, K. J., . . . Manly, J. J. (2015). The role of early-life educational quality and literacy in explaining racial disparities in cognition in late life. *Journals of Gerontology, Series B: Psychological Sciences and Social Sciences, 70,* 557–567. http://dx.doi.org/10.1093/geronb/gbt133

Slick, D. J., Sherman, E. M., & Iverson, G. L. (1999). Diagnostic criteria for malingered neurocognitive dysfunction: Proposed standards for clinical practice and research. *Clinical Neuropsychologist, 13,* 545–561. http://dx.doi.org/10.1076/1385-4046(199911)13:04;1-Y;FT545

Smedley, A., & Smedley, B. D. (2005). Race as biology is fiction, racism as a social problem is real: Anthropological and historical perspectives on the social construction of race. *American Psychologist, 60,* 16–26. http://dx.doi.org/10.1037/0003-066X.60.1.16

Strutt, A. M., Burton, V. J., Resendiz, C. V., & Peery, S. (2016). Neurocognitive assessment of Hispanic individuals residing in the U.S.: Current issues and potential solutions. In R. F. Ferraro (Ed.), *Minority and cross-cultural aspects of neuropsychological assessment: Enduring and emerging trends* (2nd ed., pp. 201–228). New York, NY: Taylor & Francis.

Thames, A. D., Hinkin, C. H., Byrd, D. A., Bilder, R. M., Duff, K. J., Mindt, M. R., . . . Streiff, V. (2013). Effects of stereotype threat, perceived discrimination, and examiner race on neuropsychological performance: Simple as black and white? *Journal of the International Neuropsychological Society, 19,* 583–593. http://dx.doi.org/10.1017/S1355617713000076

U.S. Department of Health and Human Services, Office of Minority Health. (2001). *National standards for culturally and linguistically appropriate services in health care: Final report.* Washington, DC: Author.

Wade, D. L. (1980). Racial discrimination in IQ testing—Larry P. v. Riles. *DePaul Law Review, 29,* 1193–1214. Retrieved from http://via.library.depaul.edu/law-review/vol29/iss4/12

Wechsler, D. (2005). *Wechsler Intelligence Scale for Children, Fourth Edition—Spanish.* San Antonio, TX: Psychological Corporation.

Wechsler, D. (2008). *Wechsler Adult Intelligence Scale, Fourth Edition.* San Antonio, TX: Pearson.

Wechsler, D. (2009a). Overview of Advanced Clinical Solutions for WAIS–IV and WMS–IV. In D. Wechsler (Ed.), *Advanced clinical solutions for WAIS–IV and WMS–IV* (pp. 1–14). San Antonio, TX: Pearson.

Wechsler, D. (2009b). *Wechsler Memory Scale* (4th ed.). San Antonio, TX: Pearson.

Woodcock, R. W., Muñoz-Sandoval, A. F., Ruef, M. L., & Alvarado, C. G. (2005). *Woodcock–Munoz language survey—Revised.* Itasca, IL: Riverside.

Yang, C. C., Kao, C. J., Cheng, T. W., Yang, C. C., Wang, W. H., Yu, R. L., . . . Hua, M. S. (2012). Cross-cultural effect on suboptimal effort detection: An example of the Digit Span subtest of the WAIS–III in Taiwan. *Archives of Clinical Neuropsychology*, 27, 869–878. http://dx.doi.org/10.1093/arclin/acs081

Zea, M. C., Asner-Self, K. K., Birman, D., & Buki, L. P. (2003). The Abbreviated Multidimensional Acculturation Scale: Empirical validation with two Latino/Latina samples. *Cultural Diversity and Ethnic Minority Psychology*, *9*, 107–126. http://dx.doi.org/10.1037/1099-9809.9.2.107

Part V

NEUROPSYCHOLOGY IN THE COURTROOM

CHAPTER 17

FORENSIC NEUROPSYCHOLOGICAL REPORTS

Stephen S. Meharg

Neuropsychologists are uniquely trained in the objective measurement of brain–behavior relationships. Given the relevance of these relationships and related functions to many types of legal questions (decision-making capacity, impact of brain injury, etc.), neuropsychological evidence has played an increasing role in the justice system (Heilbronner, 2005; Kaufmann, 2009; Sweet, Peck, Abramowitz, & Etzweiler, 2002). Apart from oral testimony, neuropsychologists generally provide information related to legal issues in the form of a written report. Such documents summarize the neuropsychologist's approach and reasoning in support of findings and opinions. These reports typically represent the neuropsychologist's primary work product. The quality of these reports has an impact on the reputation and usefulness of neuropsychology within the justice system.

Despite the centrality of report writing to the neuropsychologist's professional activity, there are few standards or quality measures regarding what constitutes essential style, format, and elements in these critical documents. The reasons for this are varied. Although principles of neuropsychology may be taught in the classroom, the practice of neuropsychology remains a craft learned through apprenticeship. Clinical and forensic trainees learn to style their writing largely to gain the approval of their mentors. These mentors learned to write reports in the same fashion, thus creating a rich and varied heritage of formats and styles.

Once independent, early-career forensic neuropsychologists tend to hold on to the familiar elements of reporting established in training, making adaptations on the basis of growing trial-and-error experience, continuing education, case consultation, and the demands and sometimes painful feedback from those who retain their services. Forensic work is neither a particularly accommodating nor forgiving endeavor.

With a few notable text and online exceptions (e.g., Griffith, Stankovic, & Baranoski, 2010; Lichtenberger, Mather, Kaufman, & Kaufman, 2004; Wanlass, 2012), there are few if any practical guides for writing reports and no scientific literature addressing the issue of forensic neuropsychological report writing beyond basic statistics on time spent conducting assessments. Survey-based research has tended to confirm that forensic neuropsychologists generally conduct longer assessments and produce longer reports than their clinical counterparts, the latter of whom tend to believe their reports are rarely or only partially read (Sweet et al., 2002). No information has been provided on the extent to which forensic practitioners believe their reports are actually read by the intended recipient. Perhaps the more pertinent issue is the extent to which forensic neuropsychological reports are actually understood by the intended reader.

Further contributing to the variety of reporting methods is that many neuropsychologists see their work product not merely as a technical document but also as a labor of personal creative expression. Neuropsychologists must grapple with and clearly explain human behavior and mental processes to audiences who rarely understand these complexities

http://dx.doi.org/10.1037/0000032-017
APA Handbook of Forensic Neuropsychology, S. S. Bush (Editor-in-Chief)

and who may want to artificially simplify, amplify, or otherwise distort them to conform to a specific agenda and desired outcome. Forensic neuropsychologists are often placed in the position of explaining complex issues in simple terms without sacrificing either breadth or objectivity. This is a task ill suited to mechanical or scripted check-the-box styles of reporting. Such reports are rarely rewarding to produce or to read. Rather, creativity is required.

As noted by Griffith and colleagues (Griffith & Baranoski, 2007; Griffith et al., 2010), writers of forensic reports try to create a narrative story or artistic portrait of the case expressed in their own voices. Because creativity is characterized by divergence, originality, and expressiveness, variation in the basic structure and format of neuropsychological reports is both expected and valued. There is also a need to remain mindful that the forensic report must function effectively within the justice system and thus requires balancing creative expression with the demand for precision, clarity, and comprehensiveness.

The goal of this chapter is not to stifle creativity by outlining strict rules and formulas of forensic reports but rather to promote creativity expressed within the bounds of the highest standards of professional, literary, and scientific integrity. Commitment to these standards enhances the quality of neuropsychological evaluations and assists the trier of fact by offering credible, meaningful, and relevant information about the examinee to promote an appropriate outcome to the case.

DIFFERENCES BETWEEN CLINICAL AND FORENSIC REPORTS

A neuropsychological report most often communicates symptomatic complaints, patient history, review of archival or third-party information, and the assessment method, as well as conclusions. The basic goals of clinical and forensic reports are very similar. There are also some important practical and conceptual differences between the two reports (see Melton, Petrila, Poythress, & Slobogin, 2007). Despite sharing such common elements, the nature of forensic work affects the extent to which these elements are relied on and used.

Forensic reports have distinctly different purposes and require a different approach. This approach is based in a skill set informed by knowledge of relevant legal principles, experience interacting with legal professionals, and appreciation of their unique culture and expectations. These differences, of course, do not imply one type of report is more careful, scientific, or superior to the other. Both clinical and forensic examinees deserve the highest quality services and scientific rigor.

A review of contrasts between clinical and forensic reporting allows for increased clarity when approaching a forensic examination and provides a basis for discussing essential elements of the forensic report. Attention to such elements communicates (a) an understanding of the needs of the legal system; (b) the way in which the forensic context shapes what elements are and are not included and how and when reports are released and to whom; and (c) under what circumstances reports may be modified on the basis of feedback from the examinee or retaining party.

Identity of the Client

Many practicing forensic neuropsychologists begin this work as clinicians, who—by choice, necessity, or accident—become drawn in to the legal arena by way of their expertise in diagnostic assessment. It is easy for clinicians trained in typical professional values to lose sight of the fact that their client is not the examinee but rather the referring person or agency. Forensic examinees are not patients, nor should they be referred to as such within the report. This topic is addressed in more detail later in the chapter.

Clinical reports routinely identify the referral source and the reason for the evaluation. Forensic reports also make a special effort in the introductory paragraph to clearly identify the referral source. This allows the reader to understand the source of the evaluation and the relationships of the parties. It is generally assumed that the referring source is also responsible for payment. Any other arrangement should be made clear. Precisely how the referral source is described in the opening sentences of the report will naturally vary on the basis of the referral context and the author's style. However, essential elements of who is referred and by whom should be clear.

> *Example:* William Black is a 36-year-old man referred for neuropsychological examination by his attorney, Michael White.

This example is obviously a bare-bones statement in need of elaboration. The "for what" issue of the referral is addressed in the next section of this chapter.

The neuropsychological report is likely to become one of many documents presented to the court. Reviewers of these documents benefit from clear identifying information on each page of the report. It is therefore prudent to provide a header (or footer) on each page of the report that provides basic information such as identity of the examinee and examiner, type of examination (i.e., "Neuropsychological Evaluation"), and date and page of the document. In clinical reports, examinees are traditionally identified by name and date of birth. A medical record number may also be appropriate. Forensic reports may also include name and date of birth and an identifying number issued by the court, such as a case, cause, or docket number. The identity of the examiner should include not only name and degree but also the examiner's professional title and state license or registration number (e.g., "Licensed Psychologist, NV# PY9999"). This information allows the reviewer to clearly identify, properly order, and reference the report.

Scope of the Evaluation

Forensic reports identify as early as possible not only the source of referral but also the scope of the referral question. Clinical reports may specify the main symptom or question prompting the referral but may otherwise leave the neuropsychologist free to address broad issues. Forensic reports address narrowly defined events and causal interactions, making it important not to subvert the examination by venturing into irrelevant matters. Clearly stating and sticking to very specific referral questions is the best way to maintain focus, avoid more critical exposure than is necessary, and resist pressures to contort findings and opinions to meet the biases of the parties or become entrapped by interrogations going well beyond what can reasonably be addressed. Most experienced forensic neuropsychologists appreciate the relief felt when deflecting an invitation to venture "into the weeds" by pointing out that the questions or issues they are being asked to address are beyond the scope of their evaluation, expertise, or both. The safety net of a clearly defined scope of evaluation is much easier to land in when it is already securely in place.

As noted by Wanlass (2012), the source of the referral should be explicitly provided early in the introductory statement of the report, as should a summary of the referral question. This makes clear who is referring the examinee, as noted previously, but also for what purpose. When well crafted, such statements establish the scope of the evaluation. The issue is especially important because referring sources may attempt to broaden the scope of the evaluation beyond what a neuropsychologist can rightly address. The more tightly the examination scope can be defined, the less likely it is that the neuropsychologist will be led astray.

> *Example 1:* William Black was referred for neuropsychological examination by his attorney, Ms. White, to determine the presence, nature, and severity of neurocognitive impairment and—if impairment is documented—the degree to which such impairment may be confidently attributed to injuries sustained in the motor vehicle accident on April 25, 2015.
>
> *Example 2:* Mrs. French is an 86-year-old woman and alleged incapacitated person referred to my office by the guardian ad litem assigned to her case, Mr. Deutsch, for neuropsychological examination as it pertains to the petition for guardianship filed in her case. Specifically, I have been asked to provide an objective assessment of Mrs. French's cognitive functioning as this relates to her capacity to make decisions regarding her estate and/or medical care.

Use of Terminology to Identify the Examinee

As noted previously, forensic neuropsychological reports strictly avoid suggesting that there is a therapeutic relationship between examiner and examinee. The examinee may be referred to by his or her name or other appropriate designator, such as *examinee, claimant, plaintiff,* or *defendant.* Other descriptors such as *alleged incapacitated person* may be accurate, but persistent use of lengthy terms becomes fatiguing to the reader.

In some contexts, it may be acceptable to use an examinee's given name (e.g., *William* or *Bill*). This may be more appropriate in pediatric cases or in some jurisdictions with a more relaxed sense of formality. It is preferable to maintain a formal stance unless one is sure about this. Such formal language demonstrates respect both for the examinee and the judicial process.

Informed Consent

Informing the examinee of the nature and purpose of the evaluation and obtaining the examinee's willingness to participate in an evaluation is ethically important regardless of type of services performed. Forensic examinees frequently assume they have the same rights of confidentiality, entitlement of advocacy, ability to bill insurance, and access to their record as when they see other doctors. The opening statements of the report should comment on how issues of informed consent or notification of purpose were presented and consent or assent was obtained before the examination began. As noted by Wanlass (2012), legal statues and professional ethics often dictate the need for this, and informed examinees are more likely to cooperate if they understand the nature and purpose of the evaluation.

Typically, forensic neuropsychologists develop detailed written informed consent statements that the examinee is asked to review and sign before being seen. Various examples of these exist (see Boone, 2013; Bush et al., 2005). Documentation of this process within the narrative report need not be extensive and may reflect a brief summary of major points contained within more extensive written materials. Such document can be later produced on request.

Depending on the forensic context, several elements of consent should be present in the report, including mention that informed consent was obtained before the examination began, how the purpose and scope of the evaluation was clarified, how confidentiality was clarified and managed, and the identity of the recipient of the information. The specific nature of the examination may necessitate inclusion of other elements, such expectation of honest and sincere effort, intentions to verify effort with direct and indirect measures, potential consequences of inadequate cooperation or effort, and general discussion of potential benefits and risks to the examinee (see Bush & NAN Policy and Planning Committee, 2005, and Bush, Heilbronner, & Ruff, 2014, for sample consent forms). Apart from more basic issues of physical or emotional discomfort during the exam, a documented discussion of the risks and benefits principally confirms that the examinee understands the neuropsychological report could either aid or thwart their interests. Inclusion of such statement is prudent to remind the examinee the neuropsychologist is committed to objectivity and is neither their advocate nor a tool of the examinee's attorney.

Notation of informed consent may also include the extent to which the examinee communicated agreement to proceed with the examination under the conditions outlined. When assessing very impaired or incapacitated persons, there are times when the ability to obtain consent may be absent or questionable. It is nonetheless wise to at least document assent to the process. Examples of relevant text regarding informed consent follow.

> *Example 1:* Before the interview began, the claimant received explanation as to the nature and scope of the examination as an effort to provide the Department of Disability Determination Services (DDS) with information useful in the evaluation of possible incapacity or disability. The claimant was informed that all information discussed and collected would be made available to DDS and that honest and maximum effort was expected on measures of emotional functioning and mental capacity. The claimant was informed that effort would be assessed throughout the examination and that evidence of noncooperation, dishonesty, or suboptimal effort could have an adverse

impact on his claim. The claimant clearly understood and agreed to take part in the examination under these conditions.

Example 2: Before the examination, Mr. X received both written and oral information about the examiner's qualifications and the nature, purpose, and scope of the examination. Mr. X was reminded that this was not a treatment relationship and that no treatment or advocacy would be provided. Limits of confidentiality were reviewed, as were arrangements of fees and payment. Potential risks of the examination were also discussed, including how the outcome could aid or impede his case. Mr. X was informed that maximum and honest effort was expected on all tests and that effort would be assessed by different methods throughout the testing. Mr. X expressed an understanding of these issues and agreed to proceed with the examination.

Attention to Records

Clinical workups often include a review of relevant medical records. Forensic reports require extensive analysis of documents from many different sources. The manner in which examinees tell their stories and describe their symptoms is heavily influenced by myriad factors, including perspective and motivation. Records review is an important tool in establishing examinee credibility and also in guarding against bias and detecting signs of symptom invalidity.

Comprehensive review of archived information is a demanding and often tedious task, requiring the neuropsychologist to manage considerable and seemingly unimportant details buried deep in the record. This process may involve endless hours of digging for only an occasional nugget of relevant information. Information can be derived from education, medical, military, legal, and vocational records. Ignorance of such data may discredit the report, weakening its conclusions, and prove embarrassing on the witness stand.

Careful review of established records allows the neuropsychologist to reach more valid conclusions regarding the context of the examinee's reported cognitive symptoms and reduce the vulnerability of the conclusions to critique. A critical element and distinguishing feature of forensic reporting is the breadth and depth of records review. It may not be unusual for this to be the longest section of the report. In some cases (e.g., postmortem examinations regarding testamentary capacity), records may be among the few sources of useful information.

Reliance on Self-Report

Directly paralleling the careful review of records is how examinees' and collateral informants' reports are managed. As noted previously, examinees and other parties in the case have unique motives and perspectives. Neuropsychologists must be constantly vigilant for these motives and perspectives and accurately attribute statements to the source of the information. The value and potential sketchiness of self-report is not lost on clinicians but they may provide leeway in an effort to relieve, rather than scrutinize, a patient's self-reported distress.

In court settings, statements of presumed fact are heavily scrutinized and open for debate. Thus, when the examinee or collateral informants provide information that cannot be readily verified (e.g., "Mr. X was highly skilled in graphic arts before his injury"), it is wise to move the burden of proof away from the examiner and on to the person reporting the information (e.g., "According to Mr. X's spouse, Mr. X was highly skilled in graphic arts before his injury"). Failure to provide clear attributions increases ambiguity and perceived bias. Carefully stating where and from whom information was derived clarifies the source, allows for accountability, reduces bias, and thus enhances credibility.

Consumer Sophistication

Requests for a forensic neuropsychological examination can originate from many sources. Consumers of such reports include attorneys, judges, nurse case managers, claims adjusters, guardians ad litem, and workers' or disability compensation case managers. Concepts and procedures that neuropsychologists take for granted are often completely foreign to consumers of their reports.

Clinical reports are often written with the expectation that the reader understands anatomy, medical terminology and abbreviations, medication usages, and basic descriptive statistics. The reader is also assumed to have at least a working knowledge of psychiatric and neuropsychological principles and procedures. In reality, how neuropsychologists define and assess complex cognitive processes and statistical minutia are often poorly understood, even by medically trained persons.

Assisting consumers in accurately understanding neuropsychological concepts, methods, and conclusions is particularly important in forensic settings. Highly educated legal professionals often have no more understanding of neuropsychology than does the lay public, making it especially important to adopt an educative stance when describing concepts and procedures. This is among the most important roles neuropsychologists can play in the legal system. When writing forensic reports, it may be useful to view the reader as a highly intelligent person who happens to have little idea what a neuropsychologist is or does. Proceeding with this approach presents a unique opportunity to establish public awareness of the value of neuropsychology as a profession and has direct consequences for the format and style of the report. Examples are provided.

Defining terms. Neuropsychologists conceive of and operationally define executive functioning in specific ways. This and similar terms are used as a form of shorthand when communicating to other neuropsychologists about the domain and are often foreign to non-neuropsychologists. Yet, when they are provided with a concrete description and behavioral correlates of the domain, legal professionals are quick to see the relevance of issues related to judgment, impulse control, decision making, insight, and organizational ability.

Similarly, symptom validity is a well-worn issue in professional neuropsychology, but readers of forensic reports are unlikely to know how neuropsychologists approach this issue. Providing helpful distinctions regarding symptom and performance validities and how these are assessed require the neuropsychologist to further parse the subject in ways the reader understands and recognizes as meaningful.

Describing tests. Adopting an educative stance within the report requires the neuropsychologist not only to be intimately knowledgeable about procedures and tests he or she uses but also to be able to describe them in ways that make sense. These descriptions serve several important purposes. One of these purposes is procedural. When presenting a neuropsychologist's report during a hearing or trial, it is common for a lawyer to ask the neuropsychologist to walk through the examination step by step, including asking about each test used, what the test involves, what it measures, and how the results should be interpreted. This is a common way to present evidence, and it can become quite tedious when the protocol extends into dozens of tests, scales, and related subscales. Furthermore, test procedures and exactly what is measured by many venerated and standard neuropsychological measures (e.g., the Trail Making Tests, Category Test) are difficult to describe to a lay audience. Some examples follow.

> *Example:* The two-part Trail Making Test was used as a measure of visual tracking and processing speed, as well as more complex skills relating to divided attention and mental flexibility. Part A of the measure is essentially a connect-the-dots task requiring the examinee to use a pencil to connect in proper order 25 circled numbers randomly arranged on a page. This relatively simple task requires good visual scanning and motor quickness. Part B is more demanding and involves connecting a series of 25 circled numbers and letters in alternating numerical and alphabetical order (i.e., 1–A, 2–B, 3–C). This task relies on the same visual search and speed elements as Part A but adds the element of divided attention and being able to efficiently switch from one mental set to another. Part B taps these types of multitasking skills and correlates well with other measures of focused attention, processing speed, and mental flexibility. The Trail Making Test is sensitive to many types of neurocognitive

> disorder. Part B performance also shows good predictive validity in vocational and everyday functioning, with better performance usually associated with better work outcomes, benefit from rehabilitation efforts, and independent self-care, as well as driving safety.

Note that the inclusion of at least some individual test descriptions will significantly lengthen the report and may be why forensic reports tend to be longer than their clinical counterparts (McCaffrey, Williams, Fisher, & Laing, 1993). It is sensible to maintain a set of scientific references to support statements of reliability and validity contained within the descriptions. Such references are often available in the test's technical manual and also in larger reference texts (e.g., Lezak, Howieson, Bigler, & Tranel, 2012; Strauss, Sherman, & Spreen, 2006) and the general neuropsychological scientific literature. These references could be listed as footnotes within the report, but should at least be held in reserve to buttress claims if requested or challenged on the stand.

Descriptions of disorders. The neuropsychologist may also educate the reader about the particular disorder in question (e.g., dementia, postconcussive syndrome, stroke). Offering a brief, nontechnical description of the disorder and how it might be expected to affect behavior and mental capacity promotes accurate understanding of the examinee among readers unfamiliar with the shorthand of diagnostic categorization. In some cases, pointing out implausible and nonphysiological symptom reporting requires the reader to understand how certain injuries normally present. Although clinical reports may abbreviate terms and procedures without significant compromise to the goal of diagnosis and treatment planning, the usefulness of forensic reports is improved when reader naiveté is assumed and accommodated by paying careful attention to explaining a medical or neurological condition, including both typical and atypical expressions of the condition.

Categorizing performance and use of normative data. As noted previously, clinical neuropsychologists may assume their readers have some understanding of descriptive statistics, but statistics and psychometrics tend not be among the core studies of legal professionals. Providing the reader with an isolated numerical score (e.g., "Mrs. France obtained a WAIS–IV PRI of 64") or citing multivariate base rates does little to ensure correct understanding and how the information relates to the legal question. Even adding that this constitutes a moderate level of deficit may not help much when the court is faced with making often dichotomous decisions, such as whether or not Mrs. France maintains sufficient mental capacity to alter her existing will. Complicating matters further is the general lack of consensus in the field regarding what is meant by *mild*, *moderate*, *severe*, and other descriptions of ability or deficit severity (Guilmette, Hagan, & Giuliano, 2008).

Authors of forensic reports consider the reader's lack of sophistication and include information that helps him or her make sense of scores, impairment categories, and how they were derived. This information may also note which normative databases were used, which helps the reader to understand that test scores and their interpretation are not simply concocted but rather have a scientific origin and are empirically based. Although scores on many standardized test batteries (e.g., the Wechsler scales) are assumed to be derived from technical manuals, many free-standing tests may have multiple sets of norms used in multiple contexts and produced by different authors (e.g., Mitrushina, Boone, Razani, & D'Elia, 2005). Clarifying which normative sets were used in scoring enhances not only credibility but also accountability and allows scores to be checked for accuracy by other neuropsychologists. As with scientific references supporting test descriptions, the neuropsychologist may use his or her discretion as to whether to include normative references. Specific norms used may be presented in an addendum, in a table of test data, or omitted altogether, but the neuropsychologist should be ready to produce these on request.

Neuropsychologists who include accessible and relatively jargon-free descriptions of constructs, testing methods, and relevant medical conditions may preempt the need to be deposed in detailed fashion, although this is unlikely. Such descriptions also provide the neuropsychologist with a handy reference tool during testimony. Because basic factual information about terms, tests, and disorders change little over time, neuropsychologists may want to develop adaptable templates that can easily be inserted in the report.

Furthermore, many forensic cases never reach the point of requiring in-court expert testimony. Providing the reader with a detailed, step-by-step description of the examination often satisfies procedural requirements for testimony, allowing the report to speak for itself and effectively contributing to pretrial resolution of the case.

Therapeutic Versus Legal Purpose

Clinical reports emphasize accurate diagnosis for the purpose of treatment planning. Proximate cause of the disorder and level of impairment are commonly mentioned, but the focus is on treatment. Depending on the referral question, forensic reports focus on determining whether impairment is present, the proximate cause (when possible), and the nature, extent, course, and implications of this dysfunction on relevant functional capacities. Treatment planning is not the priority of forensic assessment, although it may be addressed in cases in which rehabilitation planning is an aspect of the legal questions, such as specifying which resources need to be allocated to improve an impairment or whether treatment is likely to restore relevant functional capacities.

Premorbid Emphasis

Neuropsychological assessment offers a detailed snapshot of current functioning, but such information does not necessarily address whether the symptomatic picture represents change over time. Such issues are very relevant to many clinical cases, especially in suspected progressive dementias and other acquired brain syndromes. Consideration of premorbid functioning is similar in clinical and forensic examinations, although the latter tend to require special attention. This is particularly important when the alleged neurocognitive injury is presumed to be tied to a specific event. Although a description how a premorbid estimation performed is beyond the scope of this chapter (see Lezak et al., 2012; McCaffery & Vanderslice-Barr, 2010; and Strauss et al., 2006, for reviews), it is important to point out that a solid review of the issue is an essential element of forensic reports when a change from a previous level of functioning is relevant to the case. Furthermore, this issue deserves the same type of commonsense description as those previously outlined.

Assumption of Expertise

Clinical examinations are typically performed at the request of health care colleagues. These colleagues assume expertise on the part of the neuropsychologist and tend to value the resulting report. This is why they refer. In contrast, forensic audiences are engaged in an adversarial system. This leaves the parties free to vigorously question the neuropsychologist's expertise and to scrutinize and criticize neuropsychological methods despite limited knowledge of or perspective on the field. Opposing counsel may have an incentive to prove the neuropsychologist's report both shoddy and wrong. Retaining counsel may grumble that certain goals of their case are not highlighted enough, not supported with sufficient fervor, or perhaps even controverted by the findings. Clinical reports typically assist and thereby please the reader. Forensic reports rarely please anybody and are certain to disgruntle some.

Recognition and Management of Bias

The problem of bias or prejudiced consideration by the examiner is commonly understood, but not always recognized (van Gorp & McMullen, 1997). Examiner bias may be intentional or unintentional, but in either case it influences the way in which a neuropsychologist manages information, interprets test data, and renders opinions. Clinicians also remain aware of the need for objectivity but maintain a warm and accommodating approach to the patient to promote trust and alliance. Unless blatantly obvious or a threat to accurate diagnosis, clinicians generally do not take time in a clinical report to wrestle with issues of bias. In contrast, forensic examiners may view this as among the most significant threats to their work product, and—when appropriate—document how such issues were considered, accommodated, and may potentially have influenced test outcome and interpretation.

Some biases may be minor and relatively harmless when properly recognized and accounted for. Harmful biases are commonly rooted in an attitude of advocacy. Considerable pressure may be placed by retaining parties for certain outcomes. Experts may also be influenced by financial incentives, the desire to create a good impression, and which records they are, and are not, provided. Neuropsychologists are nonetheless solely responsible for the constructive control of bias. As pointed out by van Gorp and McMullen (1997), ethical standards and objectivity are upheld to the extent that experts are mindful of sources of bias in forensic evaluations and highlight conditions and behaviors that should be avoided. Methods for recognizing and controlling for bias have been outlined (Heilbronner, 2005; Sweet & Moulthrop, 1999).

Bias may be addressed in the forensic report in several ways. Among the most obvious is the general manner in which the neuropsychologist conveys objectivity and fidelity to the examination process rather than to the agenda of the retaining party or an impulse to advocate on behalf of the examinee. Explanations regarding objectivity and neutrality to outcome detailed within the section on informed consent set the stage for accomplishing this goal. Forensic neuropsychologists may also be careful to point out within the report any possible perception of conflict of interest in the case. Consistent with established guidelines, neuropsychologists should disclose the nature of the relationship between him- or herself and the retaining party and the examinee, explain how such a relationship might be perceived as representing a potential conflict of interest, and note how the examinee was assured that continued adherence to professional ethics was upheld (Bush et al., 2005).

Emphasis on Validity

Validity is a broad-reaching topic, extending beyond considerations of simple feigning to the integrity and accuracy of the assessment procedure as a whole. Obviously, clinical examinations deserve no less consideration of such issues, but forensic examinations include vigorous efforts to identify, report, and reconcile any threats to the validity of testing procedure and document these efforts in the body of the report.

For example, forensic examinations may occur in less-than-ideal conditions (e.g., prisons, noisy nursing homes) and with individuals with sometimes severe sensory, communication, and motor deficits. These conditions bear little resemblance to the more pristine environments and healthy, cooperative subjects used to norm most tests. Threats to test accuracy also include violation of standardized test procedures, extracting subtests from larger batteries, and using tests despite examinee physical limitations that may impede performance. To provide remotely meaningful assessments in difficult situations, neuropsychologists may engage in "off-label" use of tests (e.g., using impromptu tasks or using tests designed for children on an elderly examinee for qualitative assessment of performance). Other examples may include testing in an unavoidably distracting environment, providing written rather than oral instructions to individuals with hearing impairment, giving a graphomotor test to a person with substantial motor tremor, or using a test with a 91-year-old examinee when available norms go only to age 89. Neuropsychologists in the field are sometimes faced with having to adapt their assessment in response to environmental and examinee characteristics. Forensic reports place special emphasis on describing threats to test validity and reliability, the rationale for proceeding in the manner taken, how the modifications could alter test results, and in what ways the resulting data need to be qualified when rendering an opinion.

As with many distinctions, the emphasis on establishing credibility of symptom reporting in clinical and forensic reports may be a matter of degree. Symptom and performance validity tests are standard aspects of both clinical and forensic examinations (American Academy of Clinical Neuropsychology, 2007; Bush et al., 2005; Heilbronner, Sweet, Morgan, Larrabee, & Millis, 2009). For both ethical and practical reasons, neuropsychologists who perform forensic examinations need to be very familiar with the use and limitations of current procedures for assessing response bias and be ready to explain in detail the rationale for validity assessment, the multiple ways in which it was assessed, resulting findings of each measure, and how the individual, integrated, and aggregated results of validity assessment influence the overall findings of the examination. Proper use, interpretation, and description of these measures improve accuracy and the likelihood of appropriate case outcome.

ESSENTIAL ELEMENTS OF FORENSIC REPORTS

As noted previously, specific elements of both clinical and forensic reports are based on tradition and usually learned through mentoring. Little literature exists on what are considered critical elements of forensic neuropsychological reports, although commentary noting flaws or weaknesses in such reports exists. For example, Boone (2013) outlined the following seven common flaws in forensic neuropsychological reports: (a) failure to assess appropriately for response bias, (b) use of inappropriate tests or norms, (c) failure to draw conclusions consistent with published research, (d) failure to consider all possible etiologies, (e) overinterpretation of low scores, (f) claims that low cognitive scores document brain injury, and (g) misinterpretation of the Minnesota Multiphasic Personality Inventory, Second Edition, or the Minnesota Multiphasic Personality Inventory, Second Edition, Restructured Form.

Neuropsychologists have flexibility in the manner in which they choose to craft their reports and present their findings. The elements recommended here are not meant as a strict format to which all forensic examinations must adhere but rather as a comment on traditional elements of clinical report writing that may be expanded to include specific issues within the forensic context.

Identification of Examinee and Client or Retaining Party

Language used to describe the examinee is appropriate and generally formal and does not imply a therapeutic relationship. Review any potential conflicts of interest and how they are managed to preserve objectivity.

Scope of the Evaluation

A clear and concise description of what questions and issues will be addressed and, when indicated, what issues remain outside the scope of evaluation.

Documentation of Informed Consent

Summarize the issues covered and include a statement of the examinee's consent or assent to undergo the examination.

Examinee Self-Report and Collateral Reports

Sometimes termed "Chief Complaints" or "History of Presenting Problem," this section largely summarizes recollections and symptomatic descriptions of the examinee and collateral informants. Such statements are directly attributed to the source and not assumed to be factual unless independently verified. If collateral informants are used extensively, it may be useful to organize them under distinct subheadings within the section to allow easy recognition and provide a reference point for the reader.

Review of Relevant Records

Keeping in mind the reader's presumed lack of medical sophistication, the neuropsychologist may take the opportunity to clarify aspects of and educate the reader regarding information obtained from school, vocational, and medical records. The explanations may include relevant diagnostic procedures, medical abbreviations, diagnosed conditions, and the typical neurobehavioral consequences of these conditions. Descriptions of inconsistencies between records can also be informative.

Assessment Procedures

In summary form, this section describes persons interviewed, records obtained and reviewed, and all tests administered. The author may also wish to include a rationale for why specific tests were selected and how the normative bases applied are appropriate for the examinee within the context of the examination.

Behavioral Observations and Mental Status

Clinical examinees are typically known to the referee, as in the case of a physician referring his or her patient for memory testing. Recipients of forensic reports may not have extended contact with the examinee and are not likely present during the examination, and many eventual consumers of the report may not ever have personally met the examinee.

The goal of this section is to provide the reader with a reasonable sense of the way in which the examinee presents by describing behaviors observed during the interview and testing sessions. Common elements include descriptions of appearance, level of consciousness and alertness, orientation, speech and motor activity, mood and affect, immediate memory, thinking and perceptual styles, insight, and level of cooperation. The scope of the evaluation may lead some of these to be more emphasized than others.

A detailed and objective review of these behaviors helps to establish that the neuropsychologist's impressions and case formulation are based on multiple sources of information and rooted in careful observation of behavior. Effort accounts for a considerable degree of variance in test scores (Green, Rohling, Lees-Haley, & Allen, 2001). In conjunction with direct symptom validity testing, behavioral observation of effort serves as a basis on which a neuropsychologist drives confidence, or lack thereof, in the accuracy of test scores. These observations allow comparison of the examinee's self-report with actual behavior as a means of assessing congruency and credibility. For example, an examinee reporting profound depression and dense amnesia yet presenting as neatly coiffed, buoyant, and a detailed historian should raise suspicion.

Assessment Results

In this section, estimation of premorbid functioning is considered, evidence regarding response bias is thoroughly and repeatedly addressed, and neurobehavioral functions assessed within the examination are systematically reviewed. This section is traditionally organized by domain-specific subheadings, but there is latitude in this approach. Maintaining an educative stance, this section may include concrete descriptions of neuropsychological constructs (e.g., memory, attention, executive functioning), specific tests used, resulting test data, rationale of categorization, and normative data bases used. This section should also include any caveats such as threats to test score validity other than response bias (e.g., inadequate norms, nonstandard administration), how these were accommodated, and what impact they have on interpretation.

Summary and Conclusions

In this section, the referral question and scope of evaluation is restated, along with a summary of the examinee's situation and self-report. Professional opinions are rendered regarding the referral question or questions. These opinions are supported by evidence obtained from the examinee, records, other informants, and pool of test data. Test interpretations and conclusions should be consistent with published research and consistent with the cognitive profile of the claimed condition as demonstrated in published literature. Alternative etiologies are presented. Consideration of premorbid functioning and normal variability is demonstrated. Low scores are not overinterpreted or automatically considered to represent brain injury. This section is commonly the most challenging section of the report to write.

The order of these elements is subject to personal discretion while keeping in mind the need for logical connections between basic elements. Although some of the outer elements may remain fixed (how the report is started and concluded), the inner elements may be ordered differently without disrupting the usefulness or flow of the document. For example, after establishing the identity of the parties, some forensic practitioners prefer to immediately notate all assessment procedures before proceeding with records review or the examinee's presenting recollections and complaints. There is merit in this approach because it is common during courtroom testimony for expert to be sequentially asked (a) who they are, (b) what they did, and (c) what they found. Reciting all assessment procedures before proceeding to the findings and conclusions is consistent with the way in which courts prefer to hear expert testimony.

Some examiners may prefer to review records before describing the examinee's self-report. This may serve to establish an objective record on which to later gauge the veracity of the self-report. Similarly, neuropsychologists may want to begin the discussion of the test results with an analysis of symptom and performance validity. If validity threats are evident, it may be both appropriate and necessary to warn the reader ahead of time that tests results about to be discussed should be considered invalid rather than waiting until the end and surprising them with this fact. Some referral sources provide specific questions that they want restated and addressed in the report, either in addition to or instead of the usual summary and conclusions section. When such questions are outside the scope of neuropsychology practice, answers are deferred to appropriate specialists.

CONTENT TO AVOID PUTTING INTO FORENSIC NEUROPSYCHOLOGICAL REPORTS

Forensic reports are designed to be relatively comprehensive and include data from many types of sources. However, in striving for completeness, forensic practitioners sometimes include content that is irrelevant, obscuring, discrediting, biased, prohibited, or just plain ignorant. Inclusion of certain content may also significantly increase the neuropsychologist's exposure to criticism, dismissal as lacking credibility, and perhaps even chances of ethical charges.

Matters Beyond the Scope of the Evaluation

Content irrelevant to the referral question, esoteric treatises, personal diatribes, and using obscure or pseudoscientific literature to justify an opinion should be avoided. Content and opinions straying from the established scope of the evaluation, perhaps driven by hubris or a naïve assumption that more is better, tend only to distract and open room for more questions than answers. Such content tends only to add fuel to the adversarial fire of the legal process.

Forensic reports do not typically include treatment recommendations, unless they are specifically requested or part of the purpose of the forensic referral. However, under the principle of due diligence, if the neuropsychologist discovers a critical and unrecognized health condition in the examinee during the course of examination, the neuropsychologist is responsible for instructing the examinee to seek appropriate medical care. In any such case, the neuropsychologist should document within his or her forensic report the details of the matter, what action was taken and the rationale for doing so, and how these events influenced the validity of the eventual test findings and opinions.

Topics Prohibited by Statute or Regulation

Neuropsychologists need to research and be keenly aware of procedural and evidentiary regulations pertaining to the specific types of evaluations they perform. In some cases, certain questions and content may be prohibited by the nature of the evaluation and jurisdictions, such as probing the examinee in a criminal case for information that may be self-incriminating.

Value-Laden Descriptors

As noted previously, many forensic practitioners were steeped in clinical training and instinctually attempt to engage the forensic examinee with a warm and supportive approach. The importance of the forensic neuropsychologist's adopting a respectful and thoughtful stance toward an examinee should not be underestimated. However, concerns about bias and diminished objectivity are introduced to the extent the practitioner displays overfamiliarity, advocacy, or a derisive stance toward an examinee, which may be indicated by use of value-laden terms such as *likeable, delightful, talented, beautiful, tragic, wronged, heartbreaking, two-faced,* or *money grubbing*. Although the neuropsychologist may want to note when and how third-party informants use similar terms, the examining neuropsychologist should not be the source of such material.

Unprofessional Verbiage

Similar to value-laden descriptors, slang terms, obscure colloquialisms, sarcasm, sexism, callousness, judgmentalism, obscenities, and other potentially offensive remarks have no place in professional reports. Such content quickly discredits the author and the credibility of his or her opinions, demonstrates disrespect for the judicial system, and tarnishes the reputation of the field as a whole.

RELEASING PRELIMINARY REPORTS

Forensic neuropsychologists may be asked to release a draft version of a report, share test data and conclusions, or chat about the examination results for clinical or other purposes. It is not uncommon for such requests to come from the retaining party, who, out of curiosity or for strategic reasons, may want a sneak peek at the data and the neuropsychologist's developing conclusions. Retaining parties are within their right to ask for this, and it is up to the neuropsychologist's discretion how much to provide while remaining mindful of the persistent threats of influence and introduction of bias.

Such requests may also come from examinees, their families, doctors, or lawyers. Unlike clinical referrals, where patients maintain the right to access, review, and amend their records, forensic reports are released only to the retaining party and not to anyone else without the permission of the retaining party. There are exceptions to what is otherwise a strict rule. As noted by Bush et al. (2005), the neuropsychologist maintains overlapping professional and ethical responsibility that encompasses both the retaining party and the examinee. The most notable example includes examinees voicing suicidal or homicidal ideation, in which case sufficient information about the examinee must be shared with appropriate authorities to protect the safety and welfare of the examinee and those around him or her.

Some neuropsychologists who perform evaluations for clinical purposes in medicolegal contexts label their clinical reports *preliminary* or *initial,* which implies that a forensic report may be available, for a fee, to an attorney who desires a more thorough report or evaluation for the purposes of litigation. Such a practice is inviting a dual relationship and may reflect examiner bias. Any report that has been submitted for a given purpose should be considered complete or final for that purpose, with exceptions as noted in the next section.

MODIFYING OR REVISING REPORTS

With forensic assessments, retaining parties should never be considered unbiased, accommodating, or even friendly to the neuropsychologist. These individuals have a specific task and are obliged not to science but rather to outcomes that are in their client's favor, which can result in attempts to sway experts' opinions. If the resulting neuropsychological report is not congruent with or contains threats to these interests, retaining parties may ask for a revision or reconsideration before the final document is submitted. Such actions are rarely requested in clinical reports and are more often generated by the patient who wants to set the record straight than by the referral source. Neuropsychologists must remain vigilant at all times regarding the introduction of bias and are obliged to decline requests that lead to the perception of being influenced to alter opinions, circumvent or counter established scientific literature, or go beyond what can be reasonably addressed by the available data. Certain types of revisions or modifications, discussed next, may be considered when bias is not introduced, and improved clarity may be achieved without compromising professional standards.

Typographical Errors

Correcting typographical errors improves professionalism and credibility.

> *Example*: Although spell checked, Dr. V's report contained numerous accidental word substitutions. The parties wonder what else Dr. V might be careless about.

Factual Errors

Factual accuracy supports correct conclusions. Even when trivial, such errors also detract from credibility and can sometimes have a significant impact on opinions.

> *Example:* Misreading her handwritten notes, Dr. X accidently describes the examinee as experiencing 10 hours of loss of consciousness after a mild head injury, rather than 10 minutes as reported by the examinee and the emergency room records.

Apparent Contradictions

Like typos, accidental word omissions or reversals are inevitable while writing detailed and technical documents. Readers may detect apparent contradictions and rightly ask for clarification.

> *Example:* Dr. Y inadvertently writes "The examinee reports history of substance abuse" when meaning to write "The examinee reports no history of substance abuse."

The initial statement contradicts known facts and Dr. Y's statements in other sections.

Ambiguities

The retaining party may request that statements be reworded to improve clarity or to meet certain statutory requirements. While being mindful of potential manipulation, a neuropsychologist may agree to rephrase sections or statements as long as he or she determines that doing so will improve clarity and not substantively compromise the meaning of the statement or change the resulting conclusions.

> *Example 1:* Dr. X opines that deficits in psychomotor processing speed and working memory are severe and definite signs of disabling brain injury. The reader has no idea what this means and asks for further clarification on how these deficits would be expected to affect decision-making capacity in specific, real-life situations. The paragraph is reworded to accommodate these requests.
>
> *Example 2:* In the same report, Dr. X asserts that on the basis of low test scores, the examinee is incompetent to make financial decisions. The retaining party reminds Dr. X that competency is a judicial, not a clinical, decision and requests his statements be omitted or rephrased accordingly.

Provision of New Records

At the time of evaluation, the neuropsychologist cannot possibly know whether he or she had been provided with all relevant records. Records may surface that deserve consideration and may alter the conclusions of the report.

> *Example:* Told that academic records were destroyed, Dr. A relies on examinee self-report and standard reading and regression-based formulas to estimate premorbid cognitive functioning in an examinee referred for evaluation after being struck by a car in a crosswalk. She concludes that the observed patterns of persistently low test scores likely represent acquired neurocognitive impairments. Academic records then surface and reveal near-failing grades and a history of special education services based on borderline IQ and multiple learning disabilities.

When considering requests for modifications of reports, the neuropsychologist must assess for the intrusion of bias and the degree to which the requested changes either enhance or detract from the goals of accuracy, clarity, meaning, and relevance to the scope of the evaluation. Such decisions are made in consultation with ethical guidelines and, when possible, consultation with trusted colleagues. Correcting the report and resubmitting it in final form may be suitable when the corrections are minor. More substantial revisions or those that involve alterations of the conclusions are best communicated in the form of an addendum or secondary document that clearly describes changes made, the rationale for doing so, and the implications for the final opinions expressed.

CONCLUSION

The usefulness and credibility of the forensic neuropsychological report is derived from a summation of the various elements contained in it and by the creative and adaptive manner in which these elements are presented. A neuropsychologist could possibly be so clear, thorough, and compelling that nothing else would need to be said and further testimony would be averted. This is the type of report neuropsychologists aspire to write. At the very least, such a report might assist in reaching an appropriate resolution of cases before trial is needed. Each of the potential purposes for providing this level of detail remains subservient to the primary goal of helping the reader to accurately understand the examination and, thus, the examinee.

References

American Academy of Clinical Neuropsychology. (2007). Practice guidelines for neuropsychological assessment and consultation. *Clinical Neuropsychologist, 21,* 209–231. http://dx.doi.org/10.1080/13825580601025932

Boone, K. B. (2013). *Clinical practice of forensic neuropsychology: An evidence-based approach.* New York, NY: Guilford Press.

Bush, S. S., & NAN Policy and Planning Committee. (2005). Independent and court-ordered forensic neuropsychological examinations: Official statement of the National Academy of Neuropsychology. *Archives of Clinical Neuropsychology, 20,* 997–1007. http://dx.doi.org/10.1016/j.acn.2005.06.003

Bush, S. S., Heilbronner, R. L., & Ruff, R. M. (2014). Psychological assessment of symptom and performance validity, response bias, and malingering: Official position of the Association for Psychological Advancement in Psychological Injury and Law. *Psychological Injury and Law, 7,* 197–205. http://dx.doi.org/10.1007/s12207-014-9198-7

Bush, S. S., Ruff, R. M., Tröster, A. I., Barth, J. T., Koffler, S. P., Pliskin, N. H., . . . Silver, C. H. (2005). Symptom validity assessment: Practice issues and medical necessity. *Archives of Clinical Neuropsychology, 20,* 419–426. http://dx.doi.org/10.1016/j.acn.2005.02.002

Green, P., Rohling, M. L., Lees-Haley, P. R., & Allen, L. M., III. (2001). Effort has a greater effect on test scores than severe brain injury in compensation claimants. *Brain Injury, 15,* 1045–1060. http://dx.doi.org/10.1080/02699050110088254

Griffith, E. E., & Baranoski, M. V. (2007). The place of performative writing in forensic psychiatry. *Journal of the American Academy of Psychiatry and the Law, 35,* 27–31.

Griffith, E. E. H., Stankovic, A., & Baranoski, M. (2010). Conceptualizing the forensic psychiatry report as performative narrative. *Journal of the American Academy of Psychiatry and the Law, 38,* 32–42.

Guilmette, T. J., Hagan, L. D., & Giuliano, A. J. (2008). Assigning qualitative descriptions to test scores in neuropsychology: Forensic implications. *Clinical Neuropsychologist, 22,* 122–139. http://dx.doi.org/10.1080/13854040601064559

Heilbronner, R. L. (2005). *Forensic neuropsychology casebook.* New York, NY: Guilford Press.

Heilbronner, R. L., Sweet, J. J., Morgan, J. E., Larrabee, G. J., & Millis, S. R. (2009). American Academy of Clinical Neuropsychology Consensus Conference Statement on the neuropsychological assessment of effort, response bias, and malingering. *Clinical Neuropsychologist, 23,* 1093–1129. http://dx.doi.org/10.1080/13854040903155063

Kaufmann, P. M. (2009). Protecting raw data and psychological tests from wrongful disclosure: A primer on the law and other persuasive strategies. *Clinical Neuropsychologist, 23,* 1130–1159. http://dx.doi.org/10.1080/13854040903107809

Lezak, M. D., Howieson, D. B., Bigler, E. D., & Tranel, D. (2012). *Neuropsychological assessment* (5th ed.). New York, NY: Oxford University Press.

Lichtenberger, E. O., Mather, N., Kaufman, N., & Kaufman, A. S. (2004). *Essentials of assessment report writing.* Hoboken, NJ: Wiley.

McCaffrey, R. J., & Vanderslice-Barr, J. L. (2010). Estimation of premorbid IQ. In A. M. Horton Jr. & L. C. Hartlage (Eds.), *Handbook of forensic neuropsychology* (2nd ed., pp. 365–379). New York, NY: Springer.

McCaffrey, R. J., Williams, A. D., Fisher, J. M., & Laing, L. C. (1993). Forensic issues in mild head injury. *Journal of Head Trauma Rehabilitation, 8,* 38–47. http://dx.doi.org/10.1097/00001199-199309000-00006

Melton, G. B., Petrila, J., Poythress, N. G., & Slobogin, C. (2007). *Psychological evaluations for the courts: A handbook for mental health professionals and lawyers* (3rd ed.). New York, NY: Guilford Press.

Mitrushina, M., Boone, K. B., Razani, J., & D'Elia, L. F. (2005). *Handbook of normative data for neuropsychological assessment* (2nd ed.). New York, NY: Oxford University Press.

Strauss, E., Sherman, E. M. S., & Spreen, O. (2006). *A compendium of neuropsychological tests.* New York, NY: Oxford University Press.

Sweet, J. J., & Moulthrop, M. A. (1999). Self-examination questions as a means of identifying bias in adversarial assessments. *Journal of Forensic Neuropsychology, 1,* 73–88. http://dx.doi.org/10.1300/J151v01n01_06

Sweet, J. J., Peck, E. A., III, Abramowitz, C., & Etzweiler, S. (2002). National Academy of Neuropsychology/Division 40 of the American Psychological Association practice survey of clinical neuropsychology in the United States, Part I: Practitioner and practice characteristics, professional activities, and time requirements. *Clinical Neuropsychologist, 16,* 109–127. http://dx.doi.org/10.1076/clin.16.2.109.13237

van Gorp, W., & McMullen, W. (1997). Potential sources of bias in forensic neuropsychological evaluations. *Clinical Neuropsychologist, 11,* 180–187. http://dx.doi.org/10.1080/13854049708407048

Wanlass, R. L. (2012). *The neuropsychology toolkit: Guidelines, formats, and language.* http://dx.doi.org/10.1007/978-1-4614-1882-5

CHAPTER 18

ADMISSIBILITY OF NEUROPSYCHOLOGICAL EVIDENCE

Gerald Young

The set of criteria for admissibility of evidence to court defines the legal bar for proper neuropsychological assessment and testimony to the court, given its scientific basis and evidentiary standards. This chapter reviews the dynamic changes in evidence law over the past few decades, including moving away from general acceptance, as described in *Frye v. United States* (1923), toward a more contemporary understanding of good compared with bad, poor, or "junk" science (the *Daubert* trilogy, e.g., *Daubert v. Merrell Dow Pharmaceuticals,* 1993; *General Electric v. Joiner,* 1997; *Kumho Tire Company v. Carmichael,* 1999). The chapter reviews relevant federal rules of evidence (FREs) and their relationship to these cases. Also, it considers the evolution of acceptance of neuropsychological testimony to the court, according to 12 major topics: expert qualifications and competence, fixed versus flexible batteries, symptom and performance validity testing, clinical experience, data, observers, causation, malingering, criminal responsibility and the insanity defense or mitigation in sentencing, level of certainty, addressing the ultimate issue, and bias. Generally, in reaching standards of admissibility, forensic neuropsychological evidence proffered to the trier of fact in court (and related venues) needs to be relevant to the case at hand, of assistance to the trier of fact, and more probative than prejudicial and not invade the province of the trier of fact. In the end, it needs to be based on methods that are reliable and valid, as defined by psychology, regardless of the conclusions offered in the testimony or a written report. Therefore, to meet evidentiary standards, neuropsychologists need to (a) stay current in their knowledge of the scientific literature regarding psychometrics, instruments, and interpretations; (b) conduct assessments that are comprehensive, scientifically informed, and impartial; and (c) answer the referral question according to the parameters of the jurisdiction involved, including with respect to the applicable evidence laws as well as according to relevant professional regulations and ethical codes and statements by the relevant professional associations.

LAW, ADMISSIBILITY, AND NEUROPSYCHOLOGY

Much of the present section concerns the implications and applications of U.S. Supreme Court rulings on evidence law, referred to as the *Daubert* trilogy. Also, the present section examines other issues related to neuropsychological work for court, such as FREs. In the end, to meet admissibility requirements for court, the evidence proferred should be relevant, reliable, and valid, being helpful and probative more than prejudicial and reflective of junk or poor science.

Admissibility

Admissibility of neuropsychological evidence to the court and related venues is governed by relevant federal and state laws, as well as the rules of evidence based on them, and case law (i.e., prior rulings). FREs owe their current iteration to the *Daubert* trilogy of U.S. Supreme Court rulings.

http://dx.doi.org/10.1037/0000032-018
APA Handbook of Forensic Neuropsychology, S. S. Bush (Editor-in-Chief)

This chapter reviews these rulings and rules while considering the major areas to which they apply in forensic neuropsychological evidence. The chapter begins with a focus on the legal side of the relationship between law and neuropsychology, including addressing the *Frye v. United States* (1923) general evidence criterion for admissibility of evidence to court, the *Daubert* trilogy (e.g., *Daubert v. Merrell Dow Pharmaceuticals*, 1993), and the FREs. Then, the 12 areas relevant to the question of forensic neuropsychological evidence and its admissibility to the court are addressed. These topics involve (a) the needed expert qualifications and competence; (b) five aspects of the assessment proper (fixed vs. flexible batteries, symptom and performance validity testing, clinical experience, data, observers); (c) five aspects related to interpretation (causation, malingering, criminal responsibility and the insanity defense or mitigation in sentencing, level of certainty, addressing the ultimate issue); and (d) the role of bias. The chapter concludes with a discussion of the preparation of forensic neuropsychological evidence so that it is accepted by the court and survives any legal challenge to admissibility. Much of the chapter is based on a thorough review of past and recent relevant published articles and book chapters, as well as case law.

Neuropsychology

Greiffenstein and Kaufmann (2012) defined forensic neuropsychology as the application of neuropsychology evidence for the purpose of informing legal questions. E. L. Leonard (2015) noted that forensic neuropsychology uses assessment and methodological practices that are relevant to questions stemming from the legal system.

Kaufmann (2013) reviewed the neuropsychological evidence and standards regarding admissibility. Using methods and tests aimed at determining brain–behavior relationships in known or suspected neurological disease, injury, or both, neuropsychologists must have the skill set to properly assess, diagnose (rule in or rule out and differentially diagnose), and treat individuals with valid conditions. Moreover, they must have the skill set to deal with legally contentious conditions, such as mild traumatic brain injury (TBI), persistent postconcussive syndrome, their comorbidities, and the claimed impairments and disabilities associated with them. Furthermore, neuropsychologists entering the forensic legal arena must have additional skill sets. For example, for criminal cases they need to be able to assess, when possible, the mental state of the alleged perpetrator at the moment of the crime in question. Civilly, they need to determine whether those cases that are valid to begin with, that is, not malingered, are causally related to the event at issue.

Kaufmann (2013) noted the rapid rise of neuropsychological evidence in the courts. Historically, expert testimony was treated with skepticism by the court (e.g., *Winnans v. N.Y. & Erie Railroad Co.*, 1859). Gradually, psychologists were deemed experts who could assist the trier of fact (*People v. Hawthorne*, 1940). Clinical psychologists were recognized for their expertise in *Jenkins v. United States* (1962) and neuropsychologists in *Simmons v. Mullins* (1975). Kaufmann concluded that expert testimony must be reliable (or valid in psychological terminology), relevant (to the case at issue), and helpful (or of assistance, i.e., more probative than prejudicial) to the trier of fact.

Legal Matters

Law. Criminal cases are taken to appropriate courts dealing with these matters and are prosecuted and defended, with neuropsychologists retained as experts for one side or the other, or both. The adversarial divide is defined by the two sides of a case. Typically, the first neuropsychological expert involved receives a referral from an attorney, which more often than not comes from the defense attorney in a criminal case and the plaintiff's attorney in a civil case. The opposition is defined as the neuropsychological expert who is retained by the opposing legal side, specifically the prosecution in a criminal case and the defense attorney in a civil case (Young, 2014a).

Finch, Guthrie, and Henderson (2008) noted that psychological injury claims are contested either in civil lawsuits or in administrative proceedings. The former involves adjudicating judges, and the latter involves administrative law judges, who are not judges in the conventional sense, although they have experience in resolving these types of claims. To a large degree, for civil lawsuits most U.S. states are informed by *Daubert* (1993) and its progeny. In those states that still consider evidence according to *Frye* (1923) or its equivalent, the states involved might stick to the spirit of *Daubert*, but not obligatorily so.

Finch et al. (2008) went on to say that any one locale (town, county, state, provincial, federal) has a multiplicity of courts and that their designations vary. For example, in Florida, a state court is a circuit court and appeals of its decisions go to a district court. At the federal level, the first judicial level is a district court and the appellate court is called a circuit court! The Federal Rules of Civil Procedure (2017), or their state equivalents, apply to almost all these various courts, which helps manage in their understanding and procedures.

Chin (2014) named some states that still adhere to *Frye* (1923) instead of *Daubert* (1993), some of which are the largest ones (e.g., California, New York, Michigan). He added that some states use only part of the *Daubert* trilogy (typically *Daubert* and *Joiner* [1997], not *Kumho* [1999]; see Bernstein & Jackson, 2004). Chin noted that the *Daubert* trilogy is binding in Canada as much as it is in the United States (*R v. JLJ*, 2000; *R v. Mohan*, 1994; see Goudge, 2008). For overseas jurisdictions, O'Brien, Daeid, and Black (2015) noted that, in England and Wales, the approach to admissibility of evidence is "somewhat laissez-faire" (p. 2). Forensic evidence is rarely determined as inadmissible. They concluded that this system is "fundamentally flawed" (p. 2) compared to the American reliance on *Daubert* criteria.

Case type. Neuropsychologists are called on to present evidence to the court in both criminal and civil proceedings. The major criminal and civil questions in court relate to the following: In criminal cases, the alleged perpetrator must be shown to have committed the crime at the level of beyond a reasonable doubt. The neuropsychologist might be involved in an insanity defense, to mitigate the sentence if the party was considered guilty, and so on.

Regarding civil cases, Drogin, Hagan, Guilmette, and Piechowski (2015) noted that, in personal injury tort cases, four basic elements need to be satisfied by the plaintiff:

1. Duty: Did the defendant have an affirmative responsibility of omission or commission?
2. Breech: Did the defendant fail to meet the obligation required?
3. Harm: Did an identifiable injury result?
4. Causality: Was the wrongful behavior involved truly the source of said injury?

The latter element refers to proximate cause, which has bedeviled the courts for centuries. Drogin et al. contended that harm does not refer to a diagnosis per se but to any functional impacts of the injury.

Science. For an excellent discussion of the nature of science from the perspective of forensic neuropsychology, see Larrabee (2012). Essentially, the scientific method allows for falsifiability or testability while ruling in the theory, model, concept, or hypothesis that fits the best evidence at hand. In contrast, pseudoscience seeks evidence only in support of its suspect idea and ignores disconfirming data.

Law and science. Greiffenstein and Kaufmann (2012) described the conflicting epistemologies that are constituted by law and science. First, they have conflicting agendas (e.g., advocacy vs. objectivity). Also, they have different evidentiary standards and time frames (the law is less conservative and needs to resolve cases in the short time frame, for example).

In addition, forensic neuropsychologists face other types of conflicts. First, because they work in the adversarial divide (e.g., plaintiff, defense), they must negotiate referral source pressures to proffer testimony that is advantageous to the referral source. Second, they need to adopt a professional stance that is different than the clinical one that they might also adopt in other cases in their professional work with patients.

DECISIONS AND RULES AND CHALLENGES

This section examines in depth the *Daubert* trilogy and FREs. It considers admissibility challenges that arise from this legal framework and whether *Daubert* factors are even considered by the judges who have the gatekeeping function of the court.

Evidence Law Decisions

Kaufmann (2012) reviewed the evolution of standards by the court in evaluating experts and their evidence. According to *Frye* (1923, p. 1), evidence that requires "special experience or special knowledge" from experts who are "skilled" in a "particular science" (or trade, or art) for the question at issue is admissible as evidence to the court. The proffered evidence needs to gain "standing and scientific recognition" among the relevant "authorities" involved. Kaufmann went on to say that evidence from the time of *Frye* (1923) until the passage of *Daubert* (1993) had been admitted to court only if the relevant "scientific community" involved had "generally accepted" it (*Frye*, 1923, p. 3).

Greiffenstein (2008) took excerpts from *Frye* (1923) that further elucidate its nature. He noted that for *Frye*, expert testimony is "deduced from a well-recognized scientific principle or discovery" that "must be sufficiently established to have gained general acceptance" within the "particular field" at issue (*Frye*, 1923, p. 1).

Greiffenstein (2008) summarized the specific criteria of admissibility according to *Daubert* (1993), which focused on evidence related to scientific principles or assessment methods. The criteria involved add four new ones to the *Frye* (1923) one of general acceptance. First, *falsifiability* refers to the scientific canon that theory cannot be proved; it only fail to be disproved. Second, *peer review* refers to the vetting process in accepting submissions for publication in journals (or scholarly books). Third, the principle or technique at issue needs to have a known or potential error rate. This refers to the validity of the technique and its detection accuracy for a conclusion at issue (e.g., moderate brain injury, malingering) or to the validity of a classification (e.g., according to an extant nosological system, such as the 5th edition of the *Diagnostic and Statistical Manual of Mental Disorders* [*DSM–5;* American Psychiatric Association, 2013]). Greiffenstein summarized error rate as possibly referring to a study of zero-order validity (or its absence) or to errors in diagnostic classification (or their absence). Fourth, the principle or technique at issue is generally accepted, as per *Frye*. Fifth, the principle or technique is controlled operationally, for example, with a manual.

According to Kaufmann (2012), the court addressed the scope of *Daubert* (1993) in *Joiner* (1997) and in *Kumho* (1999). In *Joiner*, the court held that a trial court's decision on admissibility of expert evidence cannot be reversed by an appellate court unless the judge involved had committed a clear abuse of discretion. As for *Kumho* (1999), the court ruled that *Daubert* applied not only to scientific testimony but also to other experts who are not scientists. Scientific knowledge is not the only basis for admitting evidence in that experts' "skill, experience, and other specialized knowledge" (Kaufmann, 2012, p. 88) are acceptable factors to consider.

For Greiffenstein (2008), *Kumho* (1999) helped specify that the five *Daubert* (1993) factors are not exhaustive, nor do they all have to be met for any one technique or procedure. However, Stern (2001) maintained that all or most of the *Daubert* criteria must be supported, or the evidence involved will be barred from court. Greiffenstein also said that *Daubert* had given authority to the judge as gatekeeper of these criteria. *Joiner* (1997) reinforced the gatekeeping function of the trial judge for proffered scientific evidence.

However, Greiffenstein (2008) described that judges rarely consider more than general acceptance in admissibility challenges (Groscup, Penrod, Studebaker, Huss, & O'Neil, 2002). The same happens for mental health evidence (Dahir et al., 2005).

Greiffenstein and Kaufmann (2012) noted that admissibility and weight have different implications for evidence submitted to the court. The former concerns a judge's decision on the probative value or relevance to a case at hand, whereas the latter concerns the relative importance and believability of the evidence as perceived by the jury once it is admitted by a judge. For example, for the former, psychological tests with different levels of validity bear equal standing, which is not the case for the latter in that tests with better validity would be given more weight, everything else being equal.

Rules of Evidence

FREs are standards that govern the proffering of evidence to court and the basis for contesting its admissibility. They are based, in part, on federal Supreme Court rulings, especially the *Daubert* trilogy (*Daubert*, 1993; *Joiner*, 1997; *Kumho*, 1999). These FREs have state counterparts. In addition, states have rulings equivalent to *Daubert*, but a minority are still more consistent with *Frye* (1923), as mentioned previously.

Greiffenstein (2008) noted that FREs were codified federally in 1975 (FRE, 1975). The 400 series concerns rules relating to proffered evidence and the legal issues in litigation. The 700 series serves to define witnesses who present the evidence. FRE 401 concerns relevance, which involves the potential impact of evidence on legal decisions. FRE 402 adds that evidence needs to be probative and not overly prejudicial. FRE 701 defines a lay or fact witness, for example, a treating compared with an expert forensic psychologist. FRE 702 defines an expert witness as having specialized knowledge that can help the trier of fact. FRE 703 allows for hearsay evidence, which is important for the expert neuropsychologist who must use evidence related to brain scans, reports, verbal interview behavior, and so forth. FRE 704 concerns the boundaries of expert opinion, for example, testifying on ultimate issues. For example, a neuropsychologist can testify whether an event at issue is causally related to permanent neurocognitive deficits in civil matters but not on the impact of neuropsychological deficits on criminal culpability.

Kaufmann (2013) noted that FRE 702 was amended in 2002 and now reads as follows:

> If scientific, technical, or other specialized knowledge will assist the trier of fact to understand the evidence or to determine a fact in issue, a witness qualified as an expert by knowledge, skill, experience, training, or education, may testify thereto in the form of an opinion or otherwise, if (1) the testimony is based upon sufficient facts or data, (2) the testimony is the product of reliable principles and methods, and (3) the witness has applied the principles and methods reliably to the facts of the case. (p. 743)

As presently constituted, Rule 702 addresses expert competence, the comprehensive nature of the assessment required, and the care required in achieving reliability (validity in psychological terms). I would add that neuropsychological evidence can arrive at this bar by adopting a science-first and impartial stance in the comprehensive forensic assessments purposes (Young, 2014a). The next section considers challenges to admissibility of evidence proffered to the court along these lines.

Admissibility Challenges

Fradella, Forgarty, and O'Neill (2003) analyzed 73 cases with behavioral science admissibility challenges according to *Daubert* (1993). The issues involved expert qualifications, whether there was adherence to established protocols, addressing ultimate issues, and invading the province of the trier of fact or a lack of assistance to same. Of 11 cases involving emotional distress, only two were excluded. They involved experts who had used unorthodox methods or who had testified in areas outside of their competence.

Johnson (2000) described that expert testimony is most often excluded for reasons of lack of relevance and not being of assistance to the court. The specific *Daubert* (1993) factors of reliability, peer review, and falsifiability were rarely at issue. Shapiro (2012) described different cases with much the same pattern. Drogin et al. (2015) noted that a survey of forensic neuropsychologists found that their testimony to court was infrequently challenged. Moreover, the challenges were about specific aspects of a case rather than testimony as a whole (LaDuke, DeMatteo, Heilbrun, & Swirsky-Sachetti, 2012).

Shapiro, Mixon, Jackson, and Shook (2015) reported their research on 97 criminal and civil cases that they had analyzed for admissibility decisions. They used the search engine LexisNexis, focusing on appellate court decisions. They found that reliability and helpfulness to the trier of fact were most often factors in admissibility determinations, along with relevance and qualifications. The decisions were about evenly split between denying and accepting into court the proffered evidence. The four major specific *Daubert* (1993) scientific factors (the first four) were rarely used in the decisions. Shapiro et al. indicated that their results were consistent with those of Faust, Grimm, Ahern, and Sokolik (2010). For example, in *United States v. Simmons* (2006), expert qualifications were more relevant for admissibility decisions than the *Daubert* factors.

Chin (2014) found that judges, attorneys, and jurors have difficulty in understanding and applying the *Daubert* (1993) criteria (as per McAuliff & Groscup, 2009). Judges have the most difficulty with understanding the concepts of testability and error rate (Gatowski et al., 2001). Finch et al. (2008) noted that judges might lack understanding of the meaning of core *Daubert* scientific criteria, such as falsifiability (Dobbin et al., 2002). Moreover, they are obligated to consider legal precedents, some of which might be poor or wrong interpretations.

Chin (2014) noted that states adopting *Daubert* (1993) criteria did not manifest an effect on evidence admissibility rates (as per Groscup et al., 2002). Bernstein and Lasker (2015) showed that many jurisdictions or judges do not properly discharge their gatekeeping functions. They either ignore FRE 702 or incorrectly reinterpret it to avoid its provisions. FRE 702 standardizes the *Daubert* trilogy on reliability of expert evidence proffered to the court. The result of resisting the *Daubert* factors in judges' gatekeeping is that expert testimony survives admissibility challenges more often than it should. This undermines the court's gatekeeping function, thereby allowing unsupported evidence into court. In response to these matters, Bernstein and Lasker (2015) recommended a tightening of the wording for FRE 702.

FORENSIC NEUROPSYCHOLOGICAL ADMISSIBILITY ISSUES IN COURT

Having presented the federal court decisions involving the admissibility of evidence to court and the federal rules based on them, the chapter turns to 12 issues that are relevant to neuropsychological evidence presented to the court. They range from qualifications to issues in testimony and reports and the bias that influences experts.

Qualification of Experts

For Kaufmann (2013), FREs pertaining to expert qualifications include FRE 104 on preliminary questions in this regard and FRE 403, which addresses relevance and to which FRE 104 refers. Part a of FRE 104 expresses that the court must determine the preliminary questions of witness qualifications, aside from evidence admissibility. Part b of FRE 104 expresses that relevance involves sufficient proof of the existence of a fact; the reference to FRE 403 clarifies that evidence is relevant when its probative value outweighs by a large degree any bias or prejudice that its admission to court could generate (or confuse, mislead, cause undue delay, etc.).

Kaufmann (2012) reminded that the *Daubert* trilogy of cases was used to amend FRE 702, which now says that experts can qualify to admit evidence and testify to the court, whether through an opinion or otherwise, assuming that they possess the requisite specialized knowledge (scientific, technical, or other) through their skill, experience, training, or education. Aside from competence issues, the expert's knowledge must help the trier of fact to either understand the proffered evidence or determine a fact at issue. The evidence must help the trier of fact beyond what information a fact witness might provide the court. The testimony that is proffered must be based on evidentiary standards that reach acceptable thresholds of reliability (validity) for methodology and principle, as well as the application, so that data or facts are acceptable (sufficient).

These standards of expert competence and good practice comport with expectations of licensing boards and practice guidelines, as well as ethics codes. They dictate that neuropsychologists who want their evidence accepted in court need to have the requisite competence, for example, for assessment skills considered broadly. In particular, they need to fairly apply skills in their evaluations such that the eventual testimony, report, or other manner of presenting evidence to court (e.g., affidavit, in discovery) meets the threshold of evidential admissibility (i.e., good as opposed to poor or junk science).

Tests are crucial to good assessment practice, but so is good clinical skill. The next four issues relate to admissibility issues of these components of assessment, as well as how data should be gathered and disseminated.

Conducting the Assessment

Fixed versus flexible batteries. In their assessments, neuropsychologists use either fixed batteries that have standard tests applied universally to cases, or they use flexible ones that tailor the tests included to each case (Kaufmann, 2012). Neuropsychologists have for the most part been gravitating to using flexible batteries, and both types have been subject to court decisions (Kaufmann, 2012). Hom (2003) stated that the Halstead–Reitan fixed neuropsychological test battery fulfills evidentiary standards for court. Kaufmann (2012) noted that the flexible approach is, generally, supported (e.g., *Chapple v. Ganger,* 1994; *Minner v. American Mortgage & Guaranty Co.,* 2000). In this regard, *Baxter v. Temple* (2005) is a newer case in which a particular flexible approach (the Boston Process Approach) was criticized in court because it had not met the basic *Daubert* (1993) factors for good science. However, on appeal, the New Hampshire Supreme Court reversed the lower court (McCrystal, 2012), arguing that the Boston Process Approach met all but one of the *Daubert* factors and that each of the tests of the battery meets the relevant *Daubert* factors.

Rohling et al. (2015) demonstrated that the Meyers Neuropsychological Battery (MNB; Meyers, 2014) used in conjunction with the Rohling Interpretative Method (RIM; e.g., Rohling, Miller, & Langhinrichsen-Rohling, 2004) meets the *Daubert* (1993) criteria for admissibility of evidence. The MNB contains components that are both fixed and flexible, and the RIM is a systematic approach to flexible battery interpretation that can be applied to other batteries, too. The MNB is constituted of preexisting tests, including more than 50% of those ranked among the top 30 frequently used neuropsychological instruments. It takes only 3 hours to administer, which is less than 50% of the typical time taken for other batteries and is a major advantage. The RIM is statistically rigorous, using a linear combination of scores. It gives as a primary outcome measure the overall test battery mean. Together, this neuropsychological approach is referred to as MNB–RIM (Meyers & Rohling, 2004).

As for the *Daubert* (1993) criteria in relation to the MNB–RIM neuropsychological approach, falsifiability has been interpreted as testability. According to Rohling et al. (2015), the research has shown that both the MNB and the RIM have been tested for scientific accuracy. With respect to the *Daubert* criteria of peer-reviewed publication, the MNB–RIM approach has increasingly been researched and reviewed. Rohling et al. noted it has been examined in 65 publications, including by researchers independent of them. Positive reviews have been written, for example by Carone and Bush (2013). Also, it has demonstrated sensitivity to different causes of cognitive dysfunction (Miller, Fichtenberg, & Millis, 2010). In reviewing the MNB, Russell (2012) referred to its diagnostic accuracy (93% sensitivity, 90% specificity, 92% overall predictive power).

In terms of the *Daubert* (1993) factor of error rate, Rohling et al. (2015) considered this as reliability and, more important, as internal and external validity. For the former, the MNB–RIM includes 11 internal performance validity tests (PVTs); their sensitivity to invalid responding was .83, their specificity was 1.00, and their overall correct classification was 95% (Meyers, 2014). For the RIM, Rohling, Williamson, Miller, and Adams (2003) found that duration of loss of consciousness in patients with TBI was related to the overall test battery mean, which is a measure of the degree of cognitive impairment. Also, Rohling et al. found that the MNB–RIM normative system was highly correlated with two other normative systems, both in referred cases and in a control undergraduate student sample. Other results have linked the MNB–RIM with brain scan results in brain-lesioned patients (Meyers & Rohling, 2009). The measure is generally accepted; examiners are increasingly using the test, and its positive reviews proliferate. Regarding the *Daubert* factor of whether there is a method for controlling its use, the MNB manual constitutes such a method (for each of the areas of administration, scoring, and interpreting).

Are there recent decisions that preclude use of flexible or fixed batteries? The recent *White v. Dozier-Clemons et al.* (2015) case reaffirmed that scientific testimony based on the fixed Halstead-Russell Neuropsychological Evaluation System—Revised did not meet the *Daubert* (1993) standards for admissibility. The decision in this case referred to the article by Rohling et al. (2015) just summarized, and that this article was published in *Psychological Injury and Law*.

Performance validity tests and symptom validity tests. Larrabee (2015) noted that PVTs indicate whether the evaluee is providing a measure that accurately assesses actual ability (e.g., the Test of Memory Malingering; Tombaugh, 1996). In contrast, symptom validity tests (SVTs) measure the degree to which the evaluee provides an accurate report of his or her symptoms (e.g., the Minnesota Multiphasic Personality Inventory—2 Restructured Form [MMPI–2–RF] validity scales; Ben-Porath & Tellegen, 2008/2011).

Kaufmann (2012) noted that SVTs have been challenged for their admissibility in court, but he maintained that they are here to stay. Professional neuropsychological organizations have published position papers on them (e.g., Bush et al., 2005; Heilbronner, Sweet, Morgan, Larrabee, & Millis, 2009). Several peer-reviewed journal articles have also addressed these issues (e.g., see Bush, Heilbronner, & Ruff, 2014; Young, 2014b). The authors of these position papers and journal articles have indicated the need to use PVTs and SVTs in forensic and related evaluations. Seegmiller (2015) also referred to society position statements when stating that PVTs should be used in neuropsychological disability evaluations.

A major focus in forensic cases, when evidence is proffered from the MMPI–2 or MMPI–2–RF (Butcher et al., 2001), has been on the validity of the Fake Bad Scale (FBS; Lees-Haley, English, & Glenn, 1991). The FBS has been incorporated into the scoring programs of both the MMPI–2 and the MMPI–2–RF. However, its name was changed to the Symptom Validity Scale for the MMPI–2–RF. Butcher and colleagues (e.g., Butcher, Arbisi, Atlis, & McNulty, 2003; Gass & Odland, 2012) have argued that the FBS is more probative to the trier of fact than prejudicial. The arguments put forth by Butcher and colleagues have been substantially challenged and well addressed by Ben-Porath and colleagues (e.g., Ben-Porath, Greve, Bianchini, & Kaufmann, 2009; Nelson, Hoelzle, Sweet, Arbisi, & Demakis, 2010). A Florida judge ruled the FBS was too prejudicial because of the "faking bad" label (*Williams v. CSX Transportation Inc.*, 2007). However, most Florida judges have not supported this decision (e.g., *Nason v. Shafranski*, 2008). In general, the science of SVT is routinely admitted to court despite isolated Florida cases (e.g., *United States v. Bitton*, 2008; *Jackson v. Mason*, 2009; *Johnson v. Rockwell Automation*, 2009). That being said, implications of test results for the question of malingering have been disallowed in some cases (e.g., *Nason v. Shafranski*, 2008).

For Kaufmann (2013), the question of malingering can be addressed by a comprehensive assessment and examination. Rogers and Fiduccia (2015) noted that measures requiring open-ended responses to questions might negatively affect respondents' ability to feign (Rogers, Boals, & Drogin, 2011).

To conclude, malingering should be attributed only when a full set of reliable data in a case overwhelmingly supports this conclusion, or else different language about the problematic presentation and performance should be used (Young, 2014a). As for the base rate of malingering, a recent literature review indicated that the dominant view in forensic disability and related contexts is that the rate of malingering is about 40% +/– 10%, especially for persistent postconcussive syndrome after mild TBI (Larrabee, Millis, & Meyers, 2009). However, in some types of cases that are not related to persistent postconcussive syndrome after mild TBI, this figure may be too high. For example, Young's (2015b) extensive literature review found that the prevalence rate together for malingering and problematic presentations or feigning together could be this high, but not outright malingering alone.

Clinical experience. Greiffenstein and Kaufmann (2012) noted that each case has unique legal aspects that have not been tested nomothetically in the population so that they can be considered only through clinical judgment, which they refer to as a process of extrapolation and logic. I would add that scientific reasoning needs to be used in the latter process so that, for any one legal case, scientific empirical findings and conceptual underpinnings are used for each aspect of the case. The need to use a scientific approach even in clinical skill application in assessment is consistent with the principles behind the approach to this type of work of forensic mental health assessment (Heilbrun & LaDuke, 2015).

For some, clinical judgment is an insufficient basis by itself for proffering valid evidence to court, and it risks admissibility challenges (Campbell & Lorandos, 2008, 2015). However, Shapiro (2012) noted that, as per *Canavan* (2000), clinical experience could constitute the basis of admissible expert testimony. That is, reliability analysis can be applied to clinical experience. Moreover, clinical (personal) observations informed by experience constitute evidence that is considered scientific technique, although, according to Shapiro (2012), not in the same way as implied in *Daubert* (1993).

Greiffenstein and Kaufmann (2012) correctly noted that the logical pathway from idiographic data (observations) and (scientific) literature to conclusions offered in evidence must be clearly transparent, as per *Joiner* (1997). It is often stated that *Daubert* (1993) and its progeny refer only to the scientific basis of the methodology used by experts, such as neuropsychologists. However, the logical pathway followed from methods and data to conclusions must be as valid as the methods themselves (i.e., in terms of scientific reasoning, as per forensic mental health assessment) for the conclusions deriving from them to be valid.

Heilbrun and LaDuke (2015) described that, in forensic mental health assessment, data interpretation should consider response style, ideographic and nomothetic data, and scientific reasoning in attempting to causally connect clinical condition and functional abilities. The findings and limits of the testimony should be described in a way so that they can withstand ("change little") under cross-examination. Note that Heilbrun and LaDuke (2015) referred to clinical condition and functional impairments and did not mention diagnosis. Hagan and Guilmette (2015) evaluated the *DSM–5* for court, indicating its forensic limitations. The *DSM–5* cautions in its preface that it provides an imperfect fit between legal needs and diagnoses. One example relevant to neuropsychologists involves neurocognitive disorder related to TBI. The *DSM–5* has mild and major categories of TBI but not a moderate category, even though the disorder exists on a continuum. Also, the distinction between mild and moderate neurocognitive disorder is acknowledged as arbitrary.

Hagan and Guilmette (2015) noted that in a U.S. Supreme Court case, Justice Scalia pointed out that the *DSM–5*'s authors "change their minds" on diagnoses (p. 18) and they advised not using *DSM–5* diagnoses in forensic neuropsychology work. They instead recommended that assessments focus on functional impact of the condition. The task is quintessentially clinical, yet it should be based on scientific reasoning. There are no appropriate forensic neuropsychological tests of functionality, per se.

Raw data. Greiffenstein and Kaufmann (2012) discussed how to manage the assessment procedure and outcome conflicts. For example, for access to raw data, after a comprehensive analysis of the relevant ethics code (e.g., American Psychological Association, 2017) and case law (e.g., *Detroit Edison Co. v. NLRB*, 1979; *Lumsden v. United States*, 2010), they advised that maintaining test security for psychology manuals and stimuli constitutes best practice policy.

Note that although test security is paramount in releasing test data to the court, this does not preclude releasing appropriate screened test responses, subject to the necessary signed releases, laws, or court orders (Grote & Pyykkonen, 2012). Proprietary factors relate to the test items and not the responses, although it is acknowledged that the responses might at times give information about the test items.

Third-Party Observers

Eastvold, Belanger, and Vanderploeg (2012, as cited in Shindell, McCaffrey, & Silk-Eglit, 2014) noted in their meta-analysis of the research that a third-party observer affects neuropsychological performance. In particular, they affect delayed recall, learning and memory, attention and processing speed, and intellectual and academic ability test performance.

In the research conducted by Eastvold et al. (2012, as cited in Shindell, McCaffrey, & Silk-Eglit, 2014), the statistical effects for the first domain listed were adverse and large, but they were minimal, not adverse, or absent for the remaining five domains. In their article, Greiffenstein and Kaufmann (2012) recommended against permitting third-party observers during the testing phase of an assessment, and the variability of third-party observer effects on neuropsychological performance found in Eastvold et al. reinforces this conclusion. The approach taken by Greiffenstein and Kaufmann (2012) is consistent with position papers of major neuropsychology organizations, such as the American Academy of Clinical Neuropsychology (2001).

That being said, Greiffenstein and Kaufmann (2012) noted that third-party observation is still contested in court. In general, Kaufmann (2012) noted that wrongful disclosure of psychological tests is taking place and a group has been formed to help protect test integrity (the Group Protecting the Integrity of Psychological Examinations).

Interpretation of Assessments

This section considers issues related to the admissibility of neuropsychological evidence to court in terms of interpretation and conclusion. These factors are contentious because they get to the heart of the relevance of neuropsychological evidence and its admissibility to the court.

Causation. Greiffenstein (2008) noted the useful distinction between general causation (generally, e.g., about average brain functions in people) and specific causation (e.g., about the particular effects of a motor vehicle accident on the brain of any one individual motor vehicle accident survivor). Young and Shore (2007) noted that general causation refers to nomothetic understanding and specific causation to idiographic understanding.

Finch et al. (2008) maintained that expert testimony concerning the causes of psychological injury is problematic. For example, *DSM* diagnoses do not usually address etiology. Typically, causal mechanisms in such cases are complex and not linear. *Ephedra Products Liability Litigation* (2005) held that the experts involved could testify about causation only if they acknowledged that their conclusions were not scientifically definitive. Greiffenstein (2008) noted that *Hutchison v. American Family Mutual Insurance* (1994) determined that causation refers to the physical state of the brain (e.g., in brain injury) and causation to altered brain state, with most courts generally allowing such causation testimony.

Kaufmann (2012) reviewed the multiple cases in which opinions on causation were ruled as admissible to the court or not. Most legal decisions have favored allowing neuropsychologists to testify about causation (e.g., *Wiles v. Department of Education,* 2008), although some have not (e.g., *Louderback v. Orkin Exterminating Co.,* 1998). The latter case typifies the nature of the decisions disallowing testimony on causation—they concerned toxic exposure or untested or unproven technologies, such as quantitative electroencephalography (*John v. Im,* 2002). However, even more recent cases have excluded causation testimony related to physical or medical causation of brain damage, for example, *Grenitz v. Tomlian* (2003). In this case, the neuropsychologist was not allowed to testify that oxygen deprivation was the cause of the brain damage, although the brain damage at issue was accepted as the etiological source of the atypical behaviors evaluated.

Causation testimony for neuropsychologists refers not only to impacts on the brain but also to disability. Greiffenstein (2008) noted that the American Psychological Association was involved in reversing a lower North Carolina court's workers compensation decision on the matter as initially supported in *Horne v. Goodson Logging Co.* (1986).

Dillon v. Auto-Owners Insurance Company (2015) is a case that illustrates two salient points about causality testimony. First, the admissibility challenge was denied even though the neuropsychologist's testimony about causation was subject to question. That is, despite the doubts expressed, her evidence was deemed admissible because the scientific methodology behind the conclusions was sufficiently reliable. Second, denying admissibility is not the preferred way to challenge opinion in this type of case; rather, the court opined that the flaws in the opinions offered pertaining to the weight or value of the evidence presented by conflicting (opposing) expert testimony could be challenged in court.

In terms of the assessment of causality, Kaufmann (2013) noted that there are no psychological tests for causation, per se. Therefore, conclusions offered in this regard must be based on assessing the multifactorial causal factors in a case as adduced from the interview, mental status evaluation, psychometric testing, documentation and record review, and collateral information from secondary sources.

Gholizadeh and Malcarne (2015) added the professional and ethical challenges in undertaking causality determinations related to psychological disability. They focused on the California workers compensation system. Not only is it difficult to determine whether an event at issue is predominant (i.e., in this context, it equals 51% of the causal nexus), it is also even more difficult to assign specific percentages for each of the various causal factors that might be at play, and multicausality is involved more often than not.

Gholizadeh and Malcarne (2015) referred to Young's (2007) concept of a biopsychosocial approach to causality, which is also forensic. They referred to Young's (2008) inventory of 25 possible causal factors, including malingering. They concluded that, as yet, there are no reliable and valid measures to aid in causal determinations and that, when guidelines become developed, they should be culturally informed. A 5-point scale of causality apportionment has been developed that might be helpful (Young, 2007, 2008).

Young (2015a) noted that a difference in civil and criminal cases relates to the threshold for attributing causality. As per the U.S. Supreme Court decision in *Burrage v. United States* (2014), causality in the criminal context compared with the civil one is more stringent than simply finding that a contributing factor is involved. In the civil arena, causality simply involves determining whether a factor at issue is a material or substantive contributor to the effects at issue within a multifactorial array of causal factors, including preexisting ones. However, in the criminal context, the standard must reach the "but-for" threshold (because of, based on, or results from an actual cause or cause in fact), such that the effect of the crime at issue clearly could not have happened if the alleged perpetrated action had not happened (and this must be sufficiently demonstrated to the court).

When dealing with causality, a complicating issue is whether the obtained testing is valid. Malingering in the criminal context typically refers to feigning to avoid being found guilty or to have the sentence reduced. In the civil sphere, it typically involves exaggerating symptoms for financial gain. In both cases, the stance taken is conscious (Young, 2014a).

Malingering. Taylor (2009) argued that malingering appears to be the most dominant litigating issue in civil trials. Its impact was recognized in *Kelley v. John R. Daily Co.* (1919), and juries are especially sensitive to it (*Southwire Co. v. George,* 1996). Most courts permit testimony about malingering (*Rose v. Figgie International Inc.*, 1997). The appeal of the *Means v. Gates* (2001) case underscored that malingering determinations are critical to testimony and should not be disallowed. For both civil and criminal cases, Greiffenstein (2008) described rulings in which SVT and PVT measures were considered admissible to the court (*Coe v. State,* 2000; *Villalba v. Consolidated Freightways Corp.*, 2000).

To conclude, as shown above, neuropsychologists are increasingly obligated to use PVTs and SVTs, according to various professional guidelines and statements, and the role of these instruments is to help in malingering determinations. Malingering should not be diagnosed, unless there is incontrovertible evidence, for example, in testing or in gross inconsistencies in the full set of reliable data gathered (e.g., Young, 2014a).

Criminal context. For Kaufmann (2013), the critical issue encountered in the criminal area, which is not dealt with as much as the civil area in reviews on admissibility of neuropsychological evidence, relates to criminal responsibility, the insanity defense, and sentence mitigation due to neurological injury or disease and its attendant neuropsychological effects. The ultimate issue of guilt should be scrupulously avoided in proffered evidence, especially for possible murder convictions.

Kaufmann (2012) addressed the differences in neuropsychological admissibility questions between the criminal and the civil arenas. First, the burden of proof in civil proceedings typically involves the plaintiff proving that the matter at issue is at the threshold of "more likely than not" or in terms of the preponderance of the evidence. In contrast, in criminal cases, the state must prove guilt beyond a reasonable doubt. Second, the neuropsychologist in criminal cases can help the trier of fact in multiple ways that are distinct from civil cases, such as, for example, evaluating the following issues in the perpetrator: competence, legal insanity, aspects of related culpability, and mitigation of the sentence if guilty. The Insanity Defense Reform Act of 1984 specifies that, in an insanity pleading, the criminal defendant must show that he or she could not appreciate the nature and quality or the wrongfulness of the alleged criminal conduct at issue because of a severe degree of mental disease or defect at the time of the event at issue. In contrast, competency relates to the full sequence of criminal proceedings subsequent to the act at issue, for example, with respect to issuance of Miranda warnings, plea entry, waiver of counsel, the trial proceedings itself (standing trial), and, where applicable, sentencing and punishment.

Neuroimaging data are increasingly being presented to the court in the criminal context. Denno (2015) reviewed 800 criminal cases involving neuroscientific evidence. The concern has been that neuroscience has been used either to inappropriately absolve guilt or to inappropriately brand defendants as posing a continuing danger to society. Denno found, rather, that in criminal cases neuroscience is typically used to mitigate the death penalty phase in first-degree murder convictions.

Another neuroscientific issue relates to determining the truth of statements in court. Kaufmann (2012) noted that functional MRI lie detection methods have failed to meet admissibility standards. This has happened in both *Frye* (e.g., New York) and *Daubert* (e.g., Tennessee) jurisdictions (e.g., *Wilson v. Corestaff Services,* 2010; *United States v. Semrau,* 2010).

In a case related to neuropsychological evidence (*United States v. Santos-Bueno,* 2006), the judge queried whether a brain injury 6 months before the index crime caused persistent and significant cognitive deficits. The neuropsychologist involved was found to have used "reliable reasoning and methodology" (p. 24) in arriving at his conclusions, and so his evidence was not excluded according to a *Daubert* analysis. Nevertheless, the judge did not allow admission of testimony related to "difficulty in exercising judgment" and appreciation of the "consequences of his actions" (p. 27) or evidence about the effect of the injury on the enhancement of "vulnerability to suggestion" (p. 10). Kaufmann (2012) concluded that, ultimately, the neuropsychologist's evidence was admitted because it was sufficiently reliable and relevant for the major issues addressed.

Brooks (2014) added that neurobiological findings that suggest diminished capacity do not equate with lessened criminal culpability. Morse (2015) referred to neurolaw in criminal court in terms of both legal exuberance and scientific exuberance. Neurolaw in court should avoid "brain overclaim syndrome" to have relevance to law.

At the civil level, Grey (2014) further noted that neuroscientific findings can be used to justify emotional harm claims. In this regard, Jones, Buckholtz, Schall, and Marois (2015) noted that brain scans have been admitted in civil (motor vehicle accident) and criminal (incompetency to stand trial) cases (*Fini v. General Motors Corp.*, 2003; *United States v. Kasim,* 2008).

Level of certainty. A complication in arriving at conclusions in court relates to the different bars set in criminal and civil cases for the degree of certainty required in the court's deliberations and conclusions. As has been shown above, the terms *reasonable certainty* and *more likely than not* are used in the civil context. Lewin (1998) noted that these terms might mean more than the typical ±50% probability level assigned. Furthermore, the National Commission on Forensic Science (2015a, 2015b) argued that the term *reasonable scientific certainty* has no place in court (e.g., *State v. DeLeon,* 2014). Expert opinion only needs to be reasonable and deduced from the proffered evidence (Kaye, Bernstein, & Mnookin, 2011; D. P. Leonard, Imwinkelreid, Kaye, Bernstein, & Mnookin, 2015).

Ultimate Issue

The ultimate issue concerns matters on which the trier of fact must decide, such as culpability in the criminal context and disability in the civil one. Although guidelines for addressing the ultimate issue are well known in the criminal context for neuropsychologists, the matter is not that clear on the civil side. For example, questions of causation and malingering might be beyond the province of the neuropsychologist in some cases of evidence proffered to the court.

The neuropsychologist should consult the laws in the jurisdiction involved and the attorney for the case at hand. For Heilbrun and LaDuke (2015), the ultimate issue should be assessed carefully. It should be addressed only in jurisdictions that allow it (e.g., positive for some issues: *Tennessee Code Annotated,* 1995, compared with *Michigan Statute Annotated,* 1954).

The last issue that relates to the admissibility of neuropsychological evidence to court considered in this chapter concerns the biases that could undermine the evidence presented and lead to admissibility challenges. Neuropsychologists need to adopt an impartial stance in their work related to court and a good understanding of biases can help in this regard.

Bias

Aside from the scientific credibility of proffered evidence, expert credibility stands as a cardinal issue. Neal and Brodsky (2016) referred to forensic psychologists having a bias blind spot. Richards, Geiger, and Tussey (2015) noted the "dirty dozen" sources of bias in forensic neuropsychology that could undermine testimony. The first four are deemed logistical and administrative: (a) In role bias, the expert conflates clinical and forensic roles; (b) in financial and payment bias, practices such as contingency payments are arranged; (c) in referral source bias, the neuropsychologist succumbs to retaining attorney pressure; and (d) in self-report bias, the evaluee's narrative is taken at face value without corroborative evidence. The next two biases are statistical in nature: (a) First, the neuropsychologist underuses base rates and (b) next, he or she ignores normal variance in test scores. For the former, base rate knowledge will increase diagnostic and prognostic accuracy. For the latter, not all abnormal scores indicate brain dysfunction. Also, an abnormal score does not necessarily reflect an acquired brain injury.

The next six biases in forensic neuropsychology are cognitive, personal, and attributional biases (Richards et al., 2015). They include not only the well-known confirmation bias and overconfidence bias, but also biases related to diagnostic momentum and the "good old days." The first refers to suppressing evidence that does not fit prior diagnoses and the last to the evaluee's tendency to minimize preevent negatives in symptoms or functioning. Finally, in personal or political bias, personal life histories, political tendencies, and the like can influence the neuropsychologist. In group attribution error, the evaluator believes that an evaluee's traits represent those of a whole group. Richards et al. (2015) concluded that neuropsychologists need to use appropriate checks of these and other biases for effective admissible testimony or evidence in court. They offer the requisite advice in these regards.

Murrie and colleagues (Murrie & Boccaccini, 2015; Murrie, Boccaccini, Guarnera, & Rufino, 2013) referred to the bias that is expressed by experts in court as *adversarial allegiance.* Opinions drift toward the presumed expectations of the retaining party due to unconscious heuristics and cognitive biases. For example, in offender cases, DeMatteo, Edens, Galloway, Cox, Smith, Koller, and Bersoff (2014) and DeMatteo, Edens, Galloway, Smith, and Formon (2014) found higher scores on relevant risk measure tests that were assigned by prosecution evaluators compared with defense evaluators.

Murrie et al. (2013) conducted an experimental study that confirmed this finding. They paid 108 forensic psychologists and psychiatrists to review offender case files. Some of the reviewers were made to believe that they were consulting for the defense, and others, who reviewed the same files, that they were consulting for the prosecution. The research participants had to score two common risk assessment instruments, the Psychopathy Checklist—Revised (Hare, 2003) and the Static-99R (Helmus, Thornton, Hanson, & Babchishin, 2012). Participants who believed that they were working as consultants for the prosecution, compared with the defense, assigned higher scores on the risk measures to the offenders in the cases, especially for the Psychopathy Checklist—Revised, which requires more subjective clinical judgment in scoring than the more straightforward Static-99R. To explain the results, Murrie and Boccaccini (2015) referred to the unconscious heuristics of "our side" mentality, cognitive factors such as confirmatory bias, and outright financial incentives.

Neal and Grisso (2014) referred to the biases that might affect forensic experts as representative, availability, and anchoring biases. The first includes base rate neglect, the second confirmation bias, and the third framing by first information or context, respectively.

Drogin et al. (2015) reported that there are numerous published court cases in which mental health experts were accused of showing bias (Edens et al., 2012). They recommended not working as an expert below expected benchmarks. Also, plaintiffs' biased, self-serving narratives should be treated with caution. According to Drogin et al., however, attorneys are not necessarily seeking experts who provide objective, evidence-based testimony because they have their own biases. Finally, passing through the whole legal and assessment system can lead plaintiffs to experience litigation distress.

These observations are consistent with Young (2010), who described the multiple sources of bias operating in tort and related legal contexts. In this regard, Lamberty, Nelson, and Yamada (2013) argued that litigation itself is involved in a psychological injury. For example, litigation served as a significant moderator in the late stage of a concussive injury (Belanger, Curtiss, Demery, Lebowitz, & Vanderploeg, 2005).

In the end, mental health experts have their evidence admitted when it is based on scientific reliability and validity (Campbell & Lorandos, 2008, 2015). Young (2008) argued that experts must maintain their objectivity. They have to be wary of being co-opted, submitting to pressures, and not advocating for anything but the full data set gathered, the truth in the case, and the court. Neal and Brodsky (2016) listed the debiasing techniques reported by forensic psychologists. They identified explicit didactic training and education about objectivity and decision making, in particular, as effective in debiasing.

CONCLUSION

This chapter explored the nature of admissibility of forensic neuropsychological evidence, according to federal rulings and rules of evidence, as well as the primary issues in these regards. The *Frye* (1923) federal ruling governed the admissibility of evidence for 70 years until *Daubert* (1993) and its progeny narrowed the scope of proffered evidence in some jurisdictions by having it meet not only the standard of general acceptance but also scientific criteria for good as opposed to bad, poor, or junk science. FREs have codified *Daubert* factors of acceptable evidence in the 400 and 700 series, in particular. Ultimately, scientific evidence must be based on methods that are reliable and valid from a psychological point of view or reliable (i.e., psychologically valid) and relevant from a legal one.

Challenges to forensic neuropsychological evidence consider most major issues with which neuropsychologists must deal, such as being competent for the task; following psychological standards for conducting assessments; considering both clinical and interview and test data in appropriate ways in arriving at conclusions; understanding the differences in criminal and civil cases; addressing the topics of causation, malingering, and its testing and the ultimate issue; and being aware of relevant legal thresholds such as level of certainty.

The forensic neuropsychologist who wants to have evidence admitted to court and have it survive admissibility challenges needs to be aware of the range of biases that can affect her or his work, which includes not only those acting on the self but also those acting on the evaluee through the attorney. By adhering to the best professional practice, legal, and ethical guidelines and standards expected in preparing forensic neuropsychological evidence (e.g., American Psychological Association, 2002, 2013, 2017), such as being scientific, comprehensive, and impartial in dealing with referral sources, evaluees, and court, the neuropsychologist is best positioned to function effectively in court and meet all evidence admissibility challenges.

Moreover, forensic neuropsychologists need to approach the presentation of evidence to court not as a passive enterprise but as an educational and instructive one. They represent a profession that some consider tarnished by examples of either poor science or bias in court. They need to use only the best scientific research, methods, and reasoning. If they conduct litigation-driven science, it must reach the same standards of excellence expected of neuropsychological research in general. Forensic neuropsychology is not just about the application of neuropsychological evidence for the purposes of informing legal questions; it is also about the creation and dissemination at a level of excellence of the research involved as well as the untarnished application of the standards and ethics of the profession to practice.

References

American Academy of Clinical Neuropsychology. (2001). Policy statement on the presence of third party observers in neuropsychological assessments. *Clinical Neuropsychologist, 15,* 433–439. http://dx.doi.org/10.1076/clin.15.4.433.1888

American Psychiatric Association. (2013). *Diagnostic and statistical manual of mental disorders* (5th ed.). Washington, DC: Author.

American Psychological Association. (2002). Ethical principles of psychologists and code of conduct. *American Psychologist, 57,* 1060–1073. http://dx.doi.org/10.1037/0003-066X.57.12.1060

American Psychological Association. (2013). Specialty guidelines for forensic psychology. *American Psychologist, 68,* 7–19. http://dx.doi.org/10.1037/a0029889

American Psychological Association. (2017). *Ethical principles of psychologists and code of conduct* (2002, Amended June 1, 2010 and January 1, 2017). Retrieved from http://www.apa.org/ethics/code/index.aspx

Baxter v. Temple, 949 A.2d 167 (N. H. Sup. Ct. 2005).

Belanger, H. G., Curtiss, G., Demery, J. A., Lebowitz, B. K., & Vanderploeg, R. D. (2005). Factors moderating neuropsychological outcomes following mild traumatic brain injury: A meta-analysis. *Journal of the International Neuropsychological Society, 11,* 215–227. http://dx.doi.org/10.1017/S1355617705050277

Ben-Porath, Y. S., Greve, K. W., Bianchini, K. J., & Kaufmann, P. M. (2009). The MMPI–2 Symptom Validity Scale (FBS) is an empirically-validated measure of overreporting in personal injury litigants and claimants: Reply to Butcher et al. (2008). *Psychological Injury and Law, 2,* 62–85. http://dx.doi.org/10.1007/s12207-009-9037-4

Ben-Porath, Y. S., & Tellegen, A. (2011). *MMPI–2–RF: Manual for administration, scoring, and interpretation.* Minneapolis: University of Minnesota Press. (Original work published 2008)

Bernstein, D. E., & Jackson, J. D. (2004). The *Daubert* trilogy in the states. *Jurimetrics, 4,* 351–368.

Bernstein, D. E., & Lasker, E. G. (2015). Defending *Daubert*: It's time to amend federal rules of evidence 702. *William and Mary Law Review, 57,* 1–48.

Brooks, J. D. (2014). "What any parent knows" but the Supreme Court misunderstands: Reassessing neuroscience's role in diminished capacity jurisprudence. *New Criminal Law Review, 17,* 442–501.

Burrage v. United States, 571 U.S. _____ (2014).

Bush, S. S., Heilbronner, R. L., & Ruff, R. M. (2014). Psychological assessment of symptom and performance validity, response bias, and malingering: Official position of the Association of Psychological Advancement in Psychological Injury and Law. *Psychological Injury and Law, 7,* 197–205. http://dx.doi.org/10.1007/s12207-014-9198-7

Bush, S. S., Ruff, R. M., Tröster, A. I., Barth, J. T., Koffler, S. P., Pliskin, N. H., . . . Silver, C. H. (2005). Symptom validity assessment: Practice issues and medical necessity. *Archives of Clinical Neuropsychology, 20,* 419–426. http://dx.doi.org/10.1016/j.acn.2005.02.002

Butcher, J. N., Arbisi, P. A., Atlis, M. M., & McNulty, J. L. (2003). The construct validity of the Lees-Haley Fake Bad Scale. Does this scale measure somatic malingering and feigned emotional distress? *Archives of Clinical Neuropsychology, 18,* 473–485.

Butcher, J. N., Graham, J. R., Ben-Porath, Y. S., Tellegen, A., Dahlstrom, W. G., & Kaemmer, B. (2001). *MMPI–2: Manual for administration, scoring, and interpretation* (Rev. ed.). Minneapolis: University of Minnesota Press.

Campbell, T. W., & Lorandos, D. (2008). *Cross-examining experts in the behavioral sciences.* St. Paul, MN: Thomson-West.

Campbell, T. W., & Lorandos, D. (2015). *Cross-examining experts in the behavioral sciences.* Eagan, MN: Thomson-Reuters.

Canavan, 733 N.E. 2d (2000).

Carone, A. C., & Bush, S. S. (2013). *Mild traumatic brain injury: Symptom validity assessment and malingering.* New York, NY: Springer.

Chapple v. Ganger, 851 F. Supp. 1481 (E.D. Wash. 1994).

Chin, J. M. (2014). Psychological science's replicability crisis and what it means for science in the courtroom. *Psychology, Public Policy, and Law, 20,* 225–238. http://dx.doi.org/10.1037/law0000012

Coe v. State, 17 S.W. 3d 193 (Tenn. 2000).

Dahir, V. B., Richardson, J. T., Ginsburg, G. P., Gatowski, S. I., Dobbin, S. A., & Merlino, M. L. (2005). Judicial application of *Daubert* to psychological syndrome and profile evidence: A research note. *Psychology, Public Policy, and Law, 11,* 62–82. http://dx.doi.org/10.1037/1076-8971.11.1.62

Daubert v. Merrell Dow Pharmaceuticals, Inc., 509 U.S. 579, 113 S. Ct. 2786 (1993).

DeMatteo, D., Edens, J. F., Galloway, M., Cox, J., Smith, S. T., & Formon, D. (2014). The role and reliability of the Psychopathy Checklist—Revised in U.S. sexually violent predator evaluations: A case law survey. *Law and Human Behavior, 38,* 248–255. http://dx.doi.org/10.1037/lhb0000059

DeMatteo, D., Edens, J. F., Galloway, M., Cox, J., Smith, S. T., Koller, J. P., & Bersoff, B. (2014). Investigating the role of the Psychopathy Checklist—Revised in United States case law. *Psychology, Public Policy, and Law, 20,* 96–107. http://dx.doi.org/10.1037/a0035452

Denno, D. W. (2015). The myth of the double-edged sword: An empirical study of neuroscience evidence in criminal cases. *Boston College Law Review, 56,* 493–551.

Detroit Edison Co. v. NLRB, 440 U.S. 301 (1979).

Dillon v. Auto-Owners Insurance Company, 14-cv-00246-LTB-MJW (2015).

Dobbin, S. A., Gatowski, S. I., Richardson, J. T., Ginsburg, G. P., Merlino, M. L., & Dahir, V. (2002). Applying *Daubert*: How well do judges understand science and scientific method? *Judicature, 85,* 244–247.

Drogin, E. Y., Hagan, L. D., Guilmette, T. J., & Piechowski, L. D. (2015). Personal injury and other tort matters. In B. L. Cutler & P. A. Zapf (Eds.), *APA handbook of forensic psychology: Vol. 1. Individual and situational influences in criminal and civil contexts* (pp. 471–509). http://dx.doi.org/10.1037/14461-014

Edens, J. F., Smith, S. T., Magyar, M. S., Mullen, K., Pitta, A., & Petrila, J. (2012). "Hired guns," "charlatans," and their "voodoo psychobabble": Case law references to various forms of perceived bias among mental health expert witnesses. *Psychological Services, 9,* 259–271. http://dx.doi.org/10.1037/a0028264

Ephedra Products Liability Litigation, 393 F.Supp.2d 181, 187 (S.D. N.Y. 2005).

Faust, D., Grimm, P. W., Ahern, D. C., & Sokolik, M. (2010). The admissibility of behavioral science evidence in the courtroom: The translation of legal to scientific concepts and back. *Annual Review of Clinical Psychology, 6,* 49–77. http://dx.doi.org/10.1146/annurev.clinpsy.3.022806.091523

Federal rules of civil procedure. (2017). Grand Rapids: Michigan Legal Publishing.

Federal rules of evidence for United States courts and magistrates. (1975). St. Paul, MN: West.

Finch, M., Guthrie, C., & Henderson, C. (2008). Expert testimony on psychological injury: Procedural and evidentiary issues. *Psychological Injury and Law, 1,* 20–35. http://dx.doi.org/10.1007/s12207-007-9001-0

Fini v. General Motors Corp., WL 18161025 (Mich. App. 2003).

Fradella, H. F., Forgarty, A., & O'Neill, L. (2003). The impact of *Daubert* on the admissibility of behavioral science testimony. *Pepperdine Law Review, 30,* 403–444.

Frye v. United States, 293 F. 1013, 34 ALR 145 (D.C. Cir. 1923).

Gass, C. S., & Odland, A. P. (2012). Minnesota Multiphasic Personality Inventory—2 Revised Form Symptom Validity Scale—Revised (MMPI–2–RF FBS–r; also known as Fake Bad Scale): Psychometric characteristics in a nonlitigation neuropsychological setting. *Journal of Clinical and Experimental Neuropsychology, 34,* 561–570. http://dx.doi.org/10.1080/13803395.2012.666228

Gatowski, S. I., Dobbin, S. A., Richardson, J. T., Ginsburg, G. P., Merlino, M. L., & Dahir, V. (2001). Asking the gatekeepers: A national survey of judges on judging expert evidence in a post-*Daubert* world. *Law and Human Behavior, 25,* 433–458. http://dx.doi.org/10.1023/A:1012899030937

General Electric v. Joiner, 522 U.S. 136 (1997).

Gholizadeh, S., & Malcarne, V. L. (2015). Professional and ethical challenges in determinations of causality of psychological disability. *Psychological Injury and Law, 8,* 334–347. http://dx.doi.org/10.1007/s12207-015-9237-z

Goudge, S. T. (2008). *Inquiry into pediatric forensic pathology in Ontario.* Retrieved from https://www.attorneygeneral.jus.gov.on.ca/inquiries/goudge/report/v1_en_pdf/Vol_1_Eng.pdf

Greiffenstein, M. F. (2008). Basics of forensic neuropsychology. In J. E. Morgan & J. Richter (Eds.), *Textbook of clinical neuropsychology* (pp. 905–941). New York, NY: Guilford Press.

Greiffenstein, M. F., & Kaufmann, P. M. (2012). Neuropsychology and the law: Principles of productive attorney–neuropsychologist relations. In G. J. Larrabee (Ed.), *Forensic neuropsychology: A scientific approach* (2nd ed., pp. 23–69). New York, NY: Oxford University Press.

Grenitz v. Tomlian, 858 So.2d 999 (Fla. 2003).

Grey, B. J. (2014). The future of emotional harm. *Fordham Law Review, 83,* 2605–2653.

Groscup, J. L., Penrod, S. D., Studebaker, C. A., Huss, M. T., & O'Neil, K. M. (2002). The effects of *Daubert* on the admissibility of expert testimony in state and federal criminal cases. *Psychology, Public Policy, and Law, 8,* 339–372. http://dx.doi.org/10.1037/1076-8971.8.4.339

Grote, C. L., & Pyykkonen, B. A. (2012). Ethical practice of forensic neuropsychology. In G. J. Larrabee (Ed.), *Forensic neuropsychology: A scientific approach* (2nd ed., pp. 101–115). New York, NY: Oxford University Press.

Hagan, L. D., & Guilmette, T. J. (2015). *DSM–5:* Challenging diagnostic testimony. *International Journal of Law and Psychiatry, 42–43,* 128–134. http://dx.doi.org/10.1016/j.ijlp.2015.08.017

Hare, R. D. (2003). *The Hare Psychopathy Checklist—Revised: Technical manual* (2nd ed.). Toronto, Ontario, Canada: Multi-Health Systems.

Heilbronner, R. L., Sweet, J. J., Morgan, J. E., Larrabee, G. J., & Millis, S. R. (2009). American Academy of Clinical Neuropsychology Consensus Conference Statement on the neuropsychological assessment of effort, response bias, and malingering. *Clinical Neuropsychologist, 23,* 1093–1129. http://dx.doi.org/10.1080/13854040903155063

Heilbrun, K., & LaDuke, C. D. (2015). Foundational aspects of forensic mental health assessment. In B. L. Cutler & P. A. Zapf (Eds.), *APA handbook of forensic psychology: Vol. 1. Individual and situational influences in criminal and civil contexts* (pp. 3–18). http://dx.doi.org/10.1037/14461-001

Helmus, L., Thornton, D., Hanson, R. K., & Babchishin, K. M. (2012). Improving the predictive accuracy of Static-99 and Static-2002 with older sex offenders: Revised age weights. *Sex Abuse, 24,* 64–101. http://dx.doi.org/10.1177/1079063211409951

Hom, J. (2003). Forensic neuropsychology: Are we there yet? *Archives of Clinical Neuropsychology, 18,* 827–845. http://dx.doi.org/10.1016/S0887-6177(03)00076-3

Horne v. Goodson Logging Co., 349 S.E.2d 293 (1986).

Hutchison v. American Family Mutual Insurance, 514 N.W.2d 882 (Iowa 1994).

Insanity Defense Reform Act of 1984, Pub. L. No. 98-473, Title II, Chap. IV, 98 Stat. 2057, 18 U.S.C. 4241 et seq.

Jackson v. Mason, Case No. 5:08-cv-5267-JLH (W.D.Ark 2009).

Jenkins v. United States, 307 F.2d 637 (D.C. Cir. 1962).

John v. Im, 559 S.E.2d 697 (Va. 2002).

Johnson, M. T. (2000). *Expert testimony in federal civil trials: A preliminary analysis.* Washington, DC: Federal Judicial Center.

Johnson v. Rockwell Automation, Inc., U. S. Dist. LEXIS 57450 (E.D.Ark. 2009).

Jones, O. D., Buckholtz, J. W., Schall, J. D., & Marois, R. (2015). Brain imaging for judges: An introduction to law and neuroscience. *Court Review, 50,* 44–51.

Kaufmann, P. M. (2012). Admissibility of expert opinions based on neuropsychological evidence. In G. J. Larrabee (Ed.), *Forensic neuropsychology: A scientific approach* (2nd ed., pp. 70–100). New York, NY: Oxford University Press.

Kaufmann, P. M. (2013). Neuropsychologist experts and neurolaw: Cases, controversies, and admissibility challenges. *Behavioral Sciences and the Law, 31,* 739–755. http://dx.doi.org/10.1002/bsl.2085

Kaye, D. H., Bernstein, D. A., & Mnookin, J. L. (2011). *The new Wigmore on evidence: Expert evidence* (2nd ed.). New York, NY: Wolters Kluwer.

Kelley v. John R. Daily Co. 181 P.326 (Mont. 1919).

Kumho Tire Company v. Carmichael, 526 U.S. 137 (1999).

LaDuke, C., DeMatteo, D., Heilbrun, K., & Swirsky-Sacchetti, T. (2012). Clinical neuropsychology in forensic contexts: Practitioners' experience, training, and practice. *Professional Psychology: Research and Practice, 43,* 503–509. http://dx.doi.org/10.1037/a0028161

Lamberty, G. J., Nelson, N. W., & Yamada, T. (2013). Effects and outcomes in civilian and military traumatic brain injury: Similarities, differences, and forensic implications. *Behavioral Sciences and the Law, 31,* 814–832. http://dx.doi.org/10.1002/bsl.2091

Larrabee, G. J. (2012). A scientific approach to forensic neuropsychology. In G. J. Larrabee (Ed.), *Forensic neuropsychology: A scientific approach* (2nd ed., pp. 3–22). New York, NY: Oxford University Press.

Larrabee, G. J. (2015). The multiple validities of neuropsychological assessment. *American Psychologist, 70,* 779–788. http://dx.doi.org/10.1037/a0039835

Larrabee, G. J., Millis, S. R., & Meyers, J. E. (2009). 40 plus or minus 10, a new magical number: Reply to Russell. *Clinical Neuropsychologist, 23,* 841–849. http://dx.doi.org/10.1080/13854040902796735

Lees-Haley, P. R., English, L. T., & Glenn, W. J. (1991). A Fake Bad Scale on the MMPI–2 for personal injury claimants. *Psychological Reports, 68,* 203–210. http://dx.doi.org/10.2466/pr0.1991.68.1.203

Leonard, D. P., Imwinkelreid, E. J., Kaye, D. H., Bernstein, D. E., & Mnookin, J. L. (2015). *The new Wigmore: A treatise on evidence* (2nd ed.). New York, NY: Wolters Kluwer.

Leonard, E. L. (2015). Forensic neuropsychology and expert witness testimony: An overview of forensic practice. *International Journal of Law and Psychiatry, 42–43,* 177–182. http://dx.doi.org/10.1016/j.ijlp.2015.08.023

Lewin, J. L. (1998). The genesis and evolution of reasonable uncertainty about "reasonable medical certainty." *Maryland Law Review, 57,* 380–504.

Louderback v. Orkin Exterminating Co., 26 F.Supp.2d 1298 (D. Kan. 1998).

Lumsden v. United States, No. 7:06-CV-60-F (E. Dist. N.C. 2010).

McAuliff, B. D., & Groscup, J. L. (2009). *Daubert* and psychological science in court. In J. L. Skeem, K. S. Douglas, & S. O. Lilienfeld (Eds.), *Psychological science in the courtroom: Consensus and controversy* (pp. 25–53). New York, NY: Guilford Press.

McCrystal, L. (2012, September 23). 11 years on, verdict in lead case. *Concord Monitor.* Retrieved from http://www.concordmonitor.com/new/4304579-95/lead-caseseufert-shelby

Means v. Gates, 558 S.E.2d 921 (S.C. Ct. App. 2001).

Meyers, J. E. (2014). *Manual for the Meyers Neuropsychological Battery (MNB).* Retrieved from http://www.meyersneuropsychological.com

Meyers, J. E., & Rohling, M. L. (2004). Validation of the Meyers short battery on mild TBI patients. *Archives of Clinical Neuropsychology, 19,* 637–651. http://dx.doi.org/10.1016/j.acn.2003.08.007

Meyers, J. E., & Rohling, M. L. (2009). CT and MRI correlations with neuropsychological tests. *Applied Neuropsychology, 16,* 237–253. http://dx.doi.org/10.1080/09084280903098752

Michigan Statute Annotated, 28.1043, 20a(6)(c) (1954).

Miller, J. B., Fichtenberg, N. L., & Millis, S. R. (2010). Diagnostic efficiency of an ability-focused battery. *Clinical Neuropsychologist, 24,* 678–688. http://dx.doi.org/10.1080/13854041003601493

Minner v. American Mortgage & Guaranty Co., 791 A.2d 826 (Del. Super. Ct. 2000).

Morse, S. J. (2015). The status of neurolaw: A plea for current modesty and future, cautious optimism. *Court Review, 50,* 94–103.

Murrie, D. C., & Boccaccini, M. T. (2015). Adversarial allegiance among expert witnesses. *Annual Review of Law and Social Science, 11,* 37–55. http://dx.doi.org/10.1146/annurev-lawsocsci-120814-121714

Murrie, D. C., Boccaccini, M. T., Guarnera, L. A., & Rufino, K. A. (2013). Are forensic experts biased by the side that retained them? *Psychological Science, 24,* 1889–1897. http://dx.doi.org/10.1177/0956797613481812

Nason v. Shafranski, Florida 19th Circuit, St. Lucie Country (Sept. 11, 2008, Ruling).

National Commission on Forensic Science. (2015a). *Presentation of expert testimony policy recommendations.* Gaithersburg, MD: National Institute of Standards and Technology, Department of Justice. Retrieved from http://www.ascld.org/wp-content/uploads/2015/09/draft_on_expert_testimony.pdf

National Commission on Forensic Science. (2015b). *Testimony using the term "reasonable scientific certainty."* Gaithersburg, MD: National Institute of Standards and Technology, Department of Justice. Retrieved from http://www.justice.gov/ncfs/file/641331/download

Neal, T. M. S., & Brodsky, S. L. (2016). Forensic psychologists' perceptions of bias and potential correction strategies in forensic mental health evaluations. *Psychology, Public Policy, and Law, 22,* 58–76. http://dx.doi.org/10.1037/law0000077

Neal, T. M. S., & Grisso, T. (2014). The cognitive underpinnings of bias in forensic mental health evaluations. *Psychology, Public Policy, and Law, 20,* 200–211. http://dx.doi.org/10.1037/a0035824

Nelson, N. W., Hoelzle, J. B., Sweet, J. J., Arbisi, P. A., & Demakis, G. J. (2010). Updated meta-analysis of the MMPI–2 symptom validity scale (FBS): Verified utility in forensic practice. *Clinical Neuropsychologist, 24,* 701–724. http://dx.doi.org/10.1080/13854040903482863

O'Brien, E., Daeid, N. N., & Black, S. (2015). Science in the court: Pitfalls, challenges and solutions. *Philosophical Transactions of the Royal Society B: Biological Sciences, 370,* 20150062. http://dx.doi.org/10.1098/rstb.2015.0062

People v. Hawthorne, 291 N. W. 205, 208 (Mich. 1940).

R v. JLJ, 2 SCR 600 (2000).

R v. Mohan, 2 SCR 9 (1994).

Richards, P. M., Geiger, J. A., & Tussey, C. M. (2015). The dirty dozen: 12 sources of bias in forensic neuropsychology with ways to mitigate. *Psychological Injury and Law, 8,* 265–280. http://dx.doi.org/10.1007/s12207-015-9235-1

Rogers, R., Boals, A., & Drogin, E. Y. (2011). Applying cognitive models of deception to national security investigations: Considerations of psychological research, law, and ethical practice. *Journal of Psychiatry and Law, 39,* 339–364. http://dx.doi.org/10.1177/009318531103900209

Rogers, R., & Fiduccia, C. E. (2015). Forensic assessment instruments. In B. L. Cutler & P. A. Zapf (Eds.), *APA handbook of forensic psychology: Vol. 1. Individual and situational influences in criminal and civil contexts* (pp. 19–34). http://dx.doi.org/10.1037/14461-002

Rohling, M. L., Meyers, J. E., Williams, G. R., Kalat, S. S., Williams, S. K., & Keene, J. (2015). Application of the *Daubert* standards to the Meyers Neuropsychological Battery using the Rohling Interpretative Method. *Psychological Injury and Law, 8,* 252–264. http://dx.doi.org/10.1007/s12207-015-9227-1

Rohling, M. L., Miller, L. S., & Langhinrichsen-Rohling, J. (2004). Rohling's interpretive method for neuropsychological case data: A response to critics. *Neuropsychology Review, 14,* 155–169. http://dx.doi.org/10.1023/B:NERV.0000048182.55980.4b

Rohling, M. L., Williamson, D. J., Miller, L. S., & Adams, R. L. (2003). Using the Halstead–Reitan Battery to diagnose brain damage: A comparison of the predictive power of traditional techniques to Rohling's Interpretive Method. *Clinical Neuropsychologist, 17,* 531–543. http://dx.doi.org/10.1076/clin.17.4.531.27938

Rose v. Figgie International Inc., 495 S.E.2d 77 (Ga. App. 1997).

Russell, E. W. (2012). *Scientific foundations of neuropsychological assessment with application to forensic evaluation.* Waltham, MA: Elsevier.

Seegmiller, R. A. (2015). Challenges in assessing and assisting military personnel with mild traumatic brain injuries. *University of Miami National Security and Armed Conflict Law Review, 5,* 66–80.

Shapiro, D. L. (2012). What is all the fuss about *Daubert*? A re-analysis. *Psychological Injury and Law, 5,* 202–207. http://dx.doi.org/10.1007/s12207-012-9136-5

Shapiro, D. L., Mixon, L., Jackson, M., & Shook, J. (2015). Psychological expert witness testimony and judicial decision making trends. *International Journal of Law and Psychiatry, 42–43,* 149–153. http://dx.doi.org/10.1016/j.ijlp.2015.08.020

Shindell, M. R., McCaffrey, R. J., & Silk-Eglit, G. M. (2014). Third-party observer impact on neuropsychological exams in litigation. *Trial Evidence, 23,* 31–38.

Simmons v. Mullins, 331 A.2d 892 (Pa. Super. Ct. 1975).

Southwire Co. v. George, 470 S.E.2d 865 (Ga. 1996).

State v. DeLeon, 319 P.3d 382, 403 (Haw. 2014).

Stern, B. H. (2001). Admissibility of neuropsychological testimony after *Daubert* and *Kumho*. *NeuroRehabilitation, 16,* 93–101.

Taylor, J. S. (2009). Personal injury court: Plaintiff attorney. In J. E. Morgan & J. J. Sweet (Eds.), *Neuropsychology of malingering casebook* (pp. 494–507). New York, NY: Psychology Press.

Tennessee Code Annotated, 39-11-501 (1995).

Tombaugh, T. N. (1996). *TOMM: The Test of Memory Malingering manual.* North Tonawanda, NY: Multi-Health Systems.

United States v. Bitton, Case No. 2:05-CR-661 TS. U.S. District Court of Utah, Central Division (July 1, 2008, Memorandum Decision and Order).

United States v. Kasim, 2008 WL 4822291 (N.D. Ind. 2008).

United States v. Santos-Bueno, Criminal No. 04-40023-FDS, 2006 U.S. Lexis 6275 (D. Mass. Jan. 5, 2006).

United States v. Semrau, No. 07-10074 MI/ P (W.D. Tenn. June 1, 2010).

United States v. Simmons, No. 05-4725 (4th Cir. 2006).

Villalba v. Consolidated Freightways Corp., Case No. 98 C 5347 (N.D. Illinois, Eastern Division, 2000).

White v. Dozier-Clemons et al., 502013CA005412AA (2015).

Wiles v. Department of Education, U.S. Dist. LEXIS 110037 (D. Haw. 2008).

Williams v. CSX Transportation, Inc., Case 04-CA-008892 (Fla. 2007).

Wilson v. Corestaff Services, N.Y. Mixc. LEXIS 1044 (N.Y. Sup.Ct. 2010).

Winnans v. N.Y. & Erie Railroad Co., 62 U.S. 88 (U.S. 1859).

Young, G. (2007). Causality: Concepts, issues, and recommendations. In G. Young, A. W. Kane, & K. Nicholson (Eds.), *Causality of psychological injury: Presenting evidence in court* (pp. 49–86). New York, NY: Springer Science+Business Media.

Young, G. (2008). Causality and causation in law, medicine, psychiatry, and psychology: Progression or regression? *Psychological Injury and Law, 1,* 161–181. http://dx.doi.org/10.1007/s12207-008-9017-0

Young, G. (2010). Trends in psychological/psychiatric injury and law: Continuing education, practice comments, recommendations. *Psychological Injury and Law, 3,* 323–355. http://dx.doi.org/10.1007/s12207-010-9092-x

Young, G. (2014a). *Malingering, feigning, and response bias in psychiatric/psychological injury: Implications for practice and court.* Dordrecht, the Netherlands: Springer Science+Business Media.

Young, G. (2014b). Resource material for ethical psychological assessment of symptom and performance validity, including malingering. *Psychological Injury and Law, 7,* 206–235. http://dx.doi.org/10.1007/s12207-014-9202-2

Young, G. (2015a). Causality in criminal forensic and in civil disability cases: Legal and psychological comparison. *International Journal of Law and Psychiatry*, 42–43, 114–120. http://dx.doi.org/10.1016/j.ijlp.2015.08.015

Young, G. (2015b). Malingering in forensic disability-related assessments: Prevalence 15 ± 15%. *Psychological Injury and Law*, *8*, 188–199. http://dx.doi.org/10.1007/s12207-015-9232-4

Young, G., & Shore, Y. (2007). Dictionary of terms related to causality, causation, law, and psychology. In G. Young, A. W. Kane, & K. Nicholson (Eds.), *Causality of psychological injury: Presenting evidence in court* (pp. 87–135). http://dx.doi.org/10.1007/978-0-387-36445-2_4

CHAPTER 19

NEUROPSYCHOLOGICAL TESTIMONY

Robert L. Heilbronner

This chapter is designed to help the reader become aware of some of the particular issues and challenges that arise when testifying as a neuropsychological expert, either in court or during a deposition. It is hoped that through an examination of some of the critical issues involved in neuropsychological testimony, the reader will gain an understanding of some of the principles involved so that he or she can convey some rather complex clinical and scientific information in a logical and easy-to-understand way to the trier-of-fact (e.g., judge, jury).

"Do you swear that the testimony you are about to give in this case, is the truth, the whole truth, and nothing but the truth, so help you God?"

If you say "Yes" to the preceding question (and I think virtually everyone does) and mean it, then the rest of your testimony should go fairly smoothly. In fact, that sort of sums up this chapter in a nutshell. Just be honest and present your opinions in an objective and nonbiased manner (to the best degree possible), and your goal of providing effective neuropsychological testimony is essentially done. Seems simple, right?

Of course, there is more to be covered, and an attempt is made to do so in the following pages, but it is important to emphasize this point: If you testify honestly, provide a factual basis for your opinions, and are willing to concede the limits of your testimony, then you should not lose too much sleep about having to go to court and testify. Why, then, do so many qualified professionals get so anxious about testifying? What is it about the process that seems to make it so arduous? I suspect that there are a variety of reasons why individuals find it difficult to testify in court or during a deposition, but I hope that this chapter will help to make what is unknown known so that the process goes more smoothly. This information is based on my 25-plus years of experience working as a clinical neuropsychologist, with a significant portion of my practice devoted to forensic neuropsychological activities. If someone else had been invited to write this chapter, I suspect that he or she would highlight other things, and there could certainly be reasonable differences of opinion with what I have written. However, I was invited to write this chapter, so you're getting my points of view.

A multitude of books, articles, Internet sites, and so forth have been devoted to helping people cope with testifying in court (Babitsky & Mangraviti, 2003; Barsky, 2012; Brodsky, 2004; Lubet, 1998). In addition, many excellent resources on forensic psychological (Melton, Petrila, Poythress, & Slobogin, 2007) and neuropsychological issues are available (Denney & Sullivan, 2008; Heilbronner, 2005, 2008; Larrabee, 2012; Sweet, 1999), with a few of them even including chapters that have portions devoted specifically to neuropsychological testimony (Boone, 2012; Bush, 2008; Greiffenstein, 2008; Hartlage & Williams, 2010). The reader is referred to these resources for a more extended discussion of relevant forensic psychological and neuropsychological issues (e.g., deposition basics, differences between clinical and forensic assessments, threats to validity, and admissibility of evidence). This chapter describes the various phases (e.g., preparation, voir dire, direct testimony, and

http://dx.doi.org/10.1037/0000032-019
APA Handbook of Forensic Neuropsychology, S. S. Bush (Editor-in-Chief)

cross-examination) associated with neuropsychological testimony and how the expert can best cope with the stress and demands associated with each of these phases.

Before venturing into the specifics of providing neuropsychological testimony, it is necessary to point out a few important facts. The legal arena is different from the clinical realm, and the education and training of psychologists and neuropsychologists is vastly different than that of their legal peers. Thus, the main conflict between the two disciplines is partisanship versus objectivity. According to Greiffenstein (2008), various structural conflicts exist between the law and neuropsychology. Whereas attorneys are partisan and represent their clients with zealous advocacy, neuropsychologists are supposed to be objective and unconcerned with the legal outcome. The goal for the attorney is winning the case; for the neuropsychologist, the goal is truth over justice and finding the best-fitting neuropsychological theory to explain the results and his or her opinions. In the courtroom, the attorney's goal is persuasion through emotional impact; for the neuropsychologist, it is persuasion by means of logic, facts, and supportable theory. The reader is referred to Table 45.1 in Greiffenstein (2008, p. 908) for a more detailed discussion of the various structural conflicts between law and neuropsychology.

Attorneys play an adversarial role, have no affirmative obligation to the complete truth, and strive to ignore or minimize evidence inconvenient to their medical–legal theories. In contrast, neuropsychologists operate under the ethos of objectivity, choosing clinical theories that best fit the facts irrespective of the social or financial implications of their conclusions. In civil legal cases, a preponderance-of-evidence model is applied (e.g., at least 51% of the evidence in its favor), whereas in criminal cases, the evidentiary threshold is beyond a reasonable doubt (e.g., a 90% confidence level in many states). In contrast, neuropsychologists use instruments derived from quasi-experimental research, showing that findings associated with 95% to 99% confidence group differences are most likely not due to chance. Despite the inherent differences between the two worlds, the evidence (Kaufmann, 2009) has suggested that neuropsychologists have over the years been relied on as experts by attorneys with increasing frequency. There may be several reasons for this, not the least of which is neuropsychologists' familiarity with disciplined scrutiny (i.e., peer review), use of clinical procedures emphasizing data-based decision making (i.e., accountability), and a hypothesis-testing approach (i.e., differential diagnosis) to answer questions (Sweet, 1999).

Apart from a limited few well-known examples, neuropsychologists are not attorneys. Thus, except for the laws governing their practice, it is not their job to know the law, interpret the law, and so forth. That is the responsibility of lawyers and judges who are involved in the case. However, neuropsychologists should have at least some basic knowledge and understanding of the environment into which they have been invited (either voluntarily or under duress). Greiffenstein (2008) wrote, "Neuropsychologists anticipating involvement in adjudicated cases need to have a core forensic knowledge database" (p. 909) that both supports an understanding of the legal process and promotes productive interactions with the retaining attorney. Knowledge of one's state's admissibility standards (e.g., *Daubert v. Merrell Dow Pharmaceuticals*, 1993; *Frye v. United States*, 1923), which are the rules that govern admission and disqualification of evidence, is important as well. At the very least, neuropsychologists should be familiar with three broad legal issues: (a) competence to testify, (b) scope of testimony, and (c) the specific methodologies relied on by neuropsychologists who are expert witnesses. Indeed, it is incumbent on the testifying neuropsychologist to understand the process and procedures associated with testimony so that he or she can anticipate some of the pitfalls that invariably occur. Indeed, even the most seasoned neuropsychological experts can run into trouble if they deviate from their role as an impartial, unbiased examiner of the facts. (The reader is referred to Greiffenstein, 2008, and Greiffenstein & Cohen, 2012, for a more extended discussion of some of these issues.)

PREPARATION

It should go without saying that preparing in advance for your intended testimony (whether it be for a deposition or court appearance) is a must. Like any athlete, performer, or speaker, it pays to practice and to be able to anticipate the coming event. There is no right or wrong way to prepare to testify in a neuropsychological case, but I do not recommend winging it (e.g., testifying without adequate preparation). At the very least, the following should occur in advance of testifying:

1. Review your neuropsychological report; if an evaluation was not done or allowed, at least review your opinions, which have likely been presented in a formal legal document (e.g., a 213 Interrogatory in Illinois, which requires a party to state the subject matter of each expert's testimony, the expert's conclusions and opinions, the bases for them, and the expert's qualifications).
2. Review relevant records that support or contrast with your opinions.
3. Review the opinions of the opposing experts.
4. Review your discovery deposition transcript (if there is one).

It is often wise to schedule a time to meet with the attorney who retained you in advance of giving your deposition. That way, you have an idea or understanding of the direction in which the attorney wants to proceed during the direct exam. If the attorney chooses not to take the time to meet with you or does not want to spend the money to cover the associated time, then the attorney increases the risk that he or she may receive undesirable answers to his or her questions. Should that be the case, the responsibility is on the attorney, not you. It is the attorney's case to win or lose.

VOIR DIRE

Voir dire is the first stage of testimony: It consists of an examination by the attorneys (and perhaps the judge) designed to determine the qualifications of the witness. As an expert, the witness may offer inferences, conclusions, and opinions regarding matters in his or her field of expertise. The voir dire establishes the extent and limits of this expertise (Melton et al., 2007). When a witness's credentials are particularly impressive, or at least are known to be sufficient, the side proffering the witness wants to put them on display; in contrast, the opposing side attempts to downplay them and may stipulate (e.g., make an express demand or arrangement as a condition of agreement) to the expert's qualifications in an effort to avoid the psychological impact his or her expertise may have on the judge or jury.

During voir dire, the attorney who calls the witness (retaining side) initially leads the witness through a fairly predictable series of questions designed to elicit the expert's education history, professional training, and clinical experience. If asked, the expert should be prepared to present his or her credentials, emphasizing substantive areas of expertise (e.g., traumatic brain injury, posttraumatic stress disorder) if asked. Brodsky and Poythress (1985) suggested reviewing a few areas before testifying (e.g., formal educational background, practical experience, professional certification and licensure, membership in professional organizations, professional publications, and prior court experience). Most experts are quite familiar with their own professional experiences (occasionally updating a curriculum vitae certainly helps) or have at least had to recite them during previous depositions, so this task is not all that arduous.

Here is how the typical qualification process might proceed for someone with previous forensic experience. In this example, the attorney represents the plaintiff and the doctor has been retained by the plaintiff's attorney in an alleged mild traumatic brain injury case.

Attorney: Doctor, have you given a deposition before?

Doctor: Yes.

Attorney: So you know the ground rules?

Doctor: Yes.

Attorney: The most important one is if, at any time today, I or opposing counsel asks you a question that you do not understand, please tell us you don't understand them, okay?

Doctor: Sure.

Attorney: Anytime you answer a question, we will assume that you've understood the question asked and that's the answer you intended to give. Okay?

Doctor: Okay.

Attorney: I have a 23-page CV for you that was attached to the plaintiff's answers or 213 disclosures. Is this your most current and up-to-date CV?

Doctor: May I see it, please? It looks pretty up to date. There may be one or two publications that were in press at the time that have now appeared in print, and they would have a volume, page number, and all that. But, beyond that, it appears pretty similar to what the current iteration is.

The attorney may then progress to inquiring about other issues (e.g., postdoctoral training, board certification, hospital appointments, licenses in other states, what is clinical neuropsychology, how does it differ from clinical psychology). As the qualifying progresses, issues related to previous forensic work typically arise. Again, the purpose of this is to establish the expert's credentials, as a means to demonstrate credibility and expertise related to the particular psycholegal issue at hand. (The reader is referred to Heilbronner, 2008, for additional questions related to credentials or qualifications of neuropsychological experts.)

Attorney: Doctor, in your practice, do you still see patients?

Doctor: Yes.

Attorney: Can you give me a breakdown as to what percentage of your work is seeing your own patients, as opposed to doing medical–legal work?

Doctor: Sure. It's varied over the years. Some years I am more prominently involved in medical–legal cases, other years less so. In the past 2 to 3 years, my practice has been more clinically focused, and the forensic work has been a little less than in the past. I would say that for the current year, forensic work has been about 20% to 25% of my practice, which includes civil, criminal, and administrative types of law.

Attorney: So, you would say that about 20% to 25% of your time in the past year has been spent on these medical–legal cases?

Doctor: That's a rough estimate, yes.

Attorney: Now, if you were to break down that 20% to 25%, what is the percentage in which it's civil litigation and what is the percentage in which it's criminal litigation?

Doctor: Lately, it has been more criminal work. Over the past year or 2, it's been roughly equivalent, about 50/50.

Attorney: Now, in the civil cases you do, for what percentage have you been hired—retained—by the plaintiff as opposed to the defendant?

Doctor: A rough estimate would be about 65% to 70% defense, and the remaining would be plaintiff.

Attorney: Have you ever received a case from my law firm before?

Doctor: No.

Attorney: Doctor, how much money have you made over the past 5 years doing medical–legal consulting?

Doctor: I don't keep those kinds of records, but I can provide you with a best estimate.

Attorney: Okay. Let me ask it this way. What percentage of your income over the past 5 years has been from forensic work?

Doctor: The percentage of my income from doing forensic work, which includes review of records, consultation, formal evaluations, and testimony, over the past 5 years has ranged from 30% to 50%. Again, this includes civil, criminal, and administrative types of cases.

Attorney: What percentage of the forensic work is strictly medical–legal?

Doctor: Probably about 60%.

After this rather direct line of questioning, the opposing attorney may focus on what the expert is not.

Attorney: Doctor, you are not a medical doctor are you?

Attorney: Doctor, you do not prescribe medications do you?

Attorney: Doctor, you only saw the patient one time right? Wouldn't you defer to the opinion of his treating psychologist, who has followed him over the course of 8 months?

Attorney: Doctor, how much money have you billed on this case to date? Are these your usual and customary fees? Why do you charge more for forensic work than you do for clinical work?

And so on.

The aforementioned example is fairly representative of how things often proceed in the voir dire phase of testimony. Suffice it to say that things can become much more contentious. In some cases, opposing counsel may request copies of your 1099 forms, as a means by which to obtain concrete evidence of the income you have made doing forensic work. In fact, it is becoming increasingly common for attorneys to request 1099s or even income tax returns, which are used to attack your credibility (Note: You are not required to release this information, but you should probably consult with your own attorney—not the one who retained you—about how to proceed in this instance.) The goal of the opposing attorney is to challenge the expertise of the witness and to expose biases, all in an effort to damage the potential expert witness's credibility. The opposing attorney wants to demonstrate to the trier of fact that you are a hired gun and that your opinions can be bought. However, if this is done too aggressively, especially in front of a jury, it can backfire. This is especially true if the expert is court appointed and has not been retained by either side: He or she is essentially a neutral party providing expertise to the judge or jury. Attacking the expert will make the attorney look bad, potentially alienating him or her from the jury.

DIRECT TESTIMONY

Once you have been qualified as an expert in the substantive area in which you are about to testify, the direct exam proceeds. This is the portion of the testimony in which the expert is examined by the attorney who has retained him or her (either opposing counsel or the retaining attorney). Lubet (1998) described the direct exam as "the intersection of credibility and preparation" (p. 51). The expert has done her or his work diligently and thoroughly, the research is finished, the documents have been reviewed and assimilated, the literature has been studied, and the report has been written. As far as the expert knows, there are no unturned stones. With careful preparation, the direct examination is usually the smoothest stage of testimony; however, some (Lubet, 1998) regard it as generally more important and frequently more complex and demanding than cross-examination. Typically, open-ended kinds of questions are asked that allow for considerable latitude in the expert's response. An effective direct examination must sort through and organize a large amount of information, paring it down to the essential elements and presenting it in an interesting and easy-to-understand manner. For the uninitiated (and even the most seasoned experts), this can be difficult.

Direct testimony usually entails describing the evaluation procedures, the data obtained, and the opinions of the expert; it may also include questions related to the literature on a topic relevant to the case at hand (e.g., concussion or mild traumatic brain injury). A number of approaches can be taken to structure the testimony, and attorneys usually have their own preferred style for conducting a direct examination. Melton et al. (2007) described an inverted pyramid model, in which the expert begins by describing the evaluation procedures (e.g., interview, administration of neuropsychological tests) and the subsequent findings, then proceeds to inferences, and ends with the peak of the pyramid, which is the summary and conclusions. The reader is referred to Barsky (2012) who provides a list of rules (e.g., convey professionalism and genuineness; speak slowly, loudly, and without hesitation; provide clear, concise answers; maintain eye contact, etc.) for direct examination.

Often, the expert neuropsychologist will be asked to discuss the validity of the test results and to describe the method of test development. As a profession, clinical neuropsychology is well positioned to address validity issues (Heilbronner, Sweet, Morgan, Larrabee, & Millis, 2009). Nevertheless, describing measurement issues, such as construct development, standardization, normative sampling, standard errors of measurement, postpredictive validity, and confidence intervals can be quite challenging for even the best of communicators. I have rarely been asked to describe these psychometric details (e.g., the standard error of measurement of the Wisconsin Card Sorting Test; test–retest reliabilities of the California Verbal Learning Test—Second Edition) to judges or juries. In fact, I believe that doing so would essentially result in your losing your audience. However, the expert should be prepared for this possibility. A reasonable response might be

> I do not know the answer to your question. In fact, in my opinion, very few competent clinical neuropsychologists would be able to give you an answer to your question off the top of their heads. However, the test manual contains the information you seek. I can provide the manual to you at the conclusion of my testimony, if you formally request in writing that I do so.

The key to effective direct examination is the expert's theory. No direct examination will succeed (and no cross-examination would be necessary) if the witness simply spits out a number of facts, details, technicalities, or statistics. The meaning of the information must come forth; for example, what do all of these data mean? What are your opinions? Can it be of use to assist the trier of fact in the effort to answer the psycholegal issue at hand (e.g., whether or not the motor vehicle accident was the proximate cause of the plaintiff's alleged disability)? Below is an excerpt of a direct examination of a neuropsychologist retained by the defense.

Attorney: Doctor, after reviewing all of the records, including your report and the report of Dr. Smith, the expert who was retained by the plaintiff, do you have an opinion as to whether or not Mr. Quince has sustained any neuropsychological injuries?

Doctor: Yes.

Attorney: What is your opinion?

Doctor: The objective evidence suggests that Mr. Quince does not have any objective problems in any neuropsychological domain, at least as measured by the battery of tests that was administered by me and by Dr. Smith. In other words, his performance was at the level one would expect for individuals his age and with his educational background.

Attorney: Doctor, did you find any evidence that suggests that the May 12, 2009, motor vehicle accident caused problems with memory as the plaintiff alleges?

Doctor: No.

Attorney: Doctor, do you hold these opinions to a reasonable degree of neuropsychological certainty?

Doctor: Yes.

An expert witness has considerable latitude in framing his or her responses to questions on direct examination. Of course, the answers must be responsive to the questions, they must be relevant to issues associated with the case, and they must consist of admissible evidence. Beyond that, the content, structure, organization, and length of the answer are in the witness's control. The goal is provide the court with clarity of view in a credible manner; to ensure that the judge or jury understands your testimony, and to provide it in a manner that is objective, nonpartisan, and based on the facts of the case.

CROSS-EXAMINATION

After the retaining attorney's direct examination, the expert will be tendered to opposing counsel for cross-examination. Although not required, cross-examination is almost always done, and for this reason, the expert must be prepared to respond to a fairly direct, and at times aggressive or hostile, line of questioning. The opposing attorney's goal is almost always, and whenever possible, to minimize the expert's impact and show his or her biases with an eye toward damaging his or her credibility or the credibility of his or her testimony. Gone are the friendly, understanding expressions of the attorney who led the direct testimony. Yet, the expert's objective (and demeanor) should remain the same as it was during the direct examination—to teach and provide expert opinions in a manner that can assist the trier of fact in his or her effort to come to some resolution concerning the matters at hand.

The objective of cross-examination is to challenge the credibility and competency of the expert and the logical basis of the expert's opinions. There are a number of general principles for coping with cross-examination. According to Greiffenstein (2008), the overriding principles are (a) preparation, (b) acknowledging weaknesses in one's approach or conclusions when confronted with genuine issues, and (c) maintaining the mental set that the neuropsychologist is there to educate the judge or jury in general principles of neuropsychology and the basis for one's opinion. Not all cross-examination questions are genuine efforts to understand the expert's position. Some questions are designed to undermine credibility; others, to manufacture pseudoissues, blur important distinctions, or create misimpressions. A general feature is the use of ambiguity and imprecision to impeach previous testimony. Questions may be worded slightly differently, or your previous testimony may be slightly rephrased in a way to convey a meaning different than originally intended. Coping with cross-examination undoubtedly requires attentive listening for imprecision or ambiguity and being prepared for some of the more common approaches that attorneys use as a means by which to raise the expert's anxiety (see Greiffenstein, 2008, pp. 927–929 for some common cross-examination gambits).

As part of an attempt to undermine the credibility of an expert, attorneys sometimes present a scientific or professional publication; this is referred to as a *learned treatise,* and its content typically contradicts the experts' knowledge, methods, or conclusions. The key step is asking whether the expert will accept the author or journal or book as a recognized or authoritative source of professional knowledge. When the author is nationally known or the book is a frequently used text, the unsuspecting witness may agree. The expert may be confronted with a quote or section from the source that explicitly differs from an important part of the witness's own testimony. The witness then must try to reconcile the differences. It is hard to look good when one of the lead researchers in your field is quoted as saying that the approach you have taken to the testing is unreliable, invalid, without dependable norms, and idiosyncratic to the individual clinician.

How does one respond to the learned treatise gambit? One option is to decline absolutely all such acknowledgments of others' expertise unless you have a thorough, ready mastery of the documents or the writings of the expert and do indeed agree with everything in them—a highly unlikely proposition. Consider the following example: The incredulous attorney asks, "You mean to tell this court that you think you know more about the neuropsychology of malingering than Glenn Larrabee?" Such refusals to accept these sources or distinguished figures as expert require a calm demeanor and a willingness not to accept the party line. Indeed, a response affirming your opinions and integrity are in order. A response to the question might include "I cannot speak at all for the writings, experiences, and knowledge of Dr. Larrabee." If the attorney persists, which is common, the expert may come across as evasive or out of touch with the literature and with important scholars. For that reason, the expert should be prepared to address his or her own key issues and sources.

I previously addressed the learned treatise issue with three colleagues in the field (Heilbronner, 2005), asking each of them how they would respond to the question, "Doctor, do you consider [insert any text here] to be an 'authoritative text' in clinical neuropsychology?" (p. 340). Here are their answers:

> *Jerry Sweet:* "The answer to this often-asked query depends upon the particular book. For example, there are a small number of books for which the answer might be 'No, I do not consider that book authoritative.' Alternatively, there are some books for which the answer is 'I am not familiar with that text.' Finally, among the more likely titles that will be brought up by attorneys, most will be familiar and well-known in the field. In that case, a reasonable answer to the question is, 'I am familiar with that book and, in fact, have a copy on my shelf. It is considered generally authoritative, which as you know does not mean that all facts and opinions stated within it are correct or accepted by my peers or by me."

> *Manfred Greiffenstein:* "I agree with Brodsky's advice to always turn down the learned treatise gambit. Any agreement that a text has blanket authority means that every statement in it is beyond dispute. A prudent answer may be, 'I consider this book [paper/pamphlet] an important contribution to the field, but I don't agree with everything that is written in there.' Always ask for a copy of the document or book rather than accept what the cross-examining attorney says about it."

The final expert response to the learned treatise question about whether any named text was considered an authoritative text was offered by Paul Less-Haley. His reply, in its entirety, was "No."

During the course of cross-examination, especially during a deposition, opposing counsel may adopt a hostile, challenging, or confrontational demeanor to observe how the expert reacts. This can be of use to the opposing counsel should the case proceed to trial; they want to have a sense in advance of how the expert responds to pressure and confrontation. Cross-examination might also proceed in a friendly, relaxed manner, to enhance the possibility that the expert may become equally relaxed and thus be freed up to make extraneous comments or mistakes. Often, the opposing attorney will attempt to emphasize that whatever was done during the evaluation was insufficient, inadequate, or not in keeping with acceptable standards in the field. For this reason, a useful approach for coping with cross-examination (particularly during a discovery deposition) is to answer the questions but not reveal more information than is necessary. In other words, tell the truth but do not elaborate beyond the question asked. Going beyond the question asked puts the expert in the position of having his or her testimony impeached (e.g., stricken), because he or she may have said things that are different than, or even contrary to, the testimony he or she provided during the direct examination. Keep it short and simple. Answer simply "yes" or "no."

However, if opposing counsel is asking leading questions in which your responses are always "yes," then you have fallen into a trap, and you are being controlled or boxed in with little room to move. From the attorney's perspective, a successful cross-examination is one during which the expert responds yes or no (in a manner that is supportive of the attorney's case); a failed cross-examination is one in which the expert has been given an opportunity to explain in greater detail why the cross-examining attorney's case is not valid. In addition, when questions are asked for which there is no good yes-or-no answer, the expert should not feel compelled to stay boxed in, despite instruction from the attorney to respond only yes or no. A response such as the following may allow the expert to explain the issue rather than respond directly to an otherwise misleading question: "That question cannot be accurately answered with yes or no, and I want to be as accurate as possible with my answers."

The most important way of coping with cross-examination is careful preparation (Melton et al., 2007), which begins at the outset of the case and includes conducting a careful evaluation, becoming familiar with the reliability and validity of the tests used, going over depositions, and consulting with the retaining attorney. It is okay (even preferred) to acknowledge differences of opinion with the other experts and to acknowledge controversial points and concede minor or indefensible ones, but not at the expense of a balanced presentation that includes positive support for one's position. From the witness's perspective, the goal remains (as it did during direct examination) to teach and explain. To do so, the expert must be as cooperative as the cross-examiner will allow. Do not be adversarial, and do not take any attacks personally; an adversarial and uncooperative witness tends to diminish his or her own credibility. Remember, you are not representing the other side of the case, and it is not your goal to defeat the cross examiner. You are there to simply represent the facts of the case from a neuropsychological perspective. It may help to remember that the cross-examining attorney is not really the intended recipient of the information; it is the judge or jury who are the primary recipients; the lawyer is only incidental to the process.

When I am preparing to testify, particularly during the cross-examination process, I try to anticipate the questions that will be asked of me, as though another well-trained expert, as qualified as I am, was providing the attorney with the questions. I try to anticipate the questions that will likely follow in sequence. Invariably, the cross-examining attorney does not always ask me the next logical question I am expecting. Then, I say to myself, "Oh, you [the attorney] should have asked thus and so." When he or she does not, it increases my confidence and leads me to believe that perhaps the attorney does not have someone equally as qualified and experienced as I, which in turn lowers my anxiety. Cross-examinations tend to go smoothly when the opposing attorney tries to don the hat of a neuropsychologist: He or she does not stand much of a chance when querying someone who is much more experienced in brain–behavior relationships. If it becomes clear that the questions posed during cross-examination were prepared by another neuropsychologist, then I regard it as a healthy interchange between myself and someone else with whom I might disagree, but with whom I am having a logical dispute of the facts.

Here is an excerpt of what a cross-examination of a defense expert might sound like:

Attorney: Doctor, the interpretation of the test results, is there a subjective element to that?

Doctor: That's a good point. It is true that there's some element of subjectivity, but the scores are what they are. Two independent neuropsychologists who examine the same set of scores may differ in their interpretations, depending on a number of factors.

Attorney: What are some of those factors, Doctor?

Doctor: Their years of education and experience, their background and training, their familiarity with the particular condition in question. In this case, which is one of a mild traumatic brain injury, their own biases, the scoring system they relied on, whether they use 1 standard deviation or 1.5 standard deviations to describe impairment—all can make a difference. These are the kinds of things that are important for neuropsychologists to be vigilant about, so they can be as objective as possible in developing conclusions.

Attorney: Is it fair to say that the main thrust of your opinion in this case is that the testing my client underwent was essentially invalid because of the effort she put forth or the intentional and purposeful wrong answers she gave in the questions?

Doctor: I'm not sure I follow.

Attorney: Let me try again. The main thrust of your opinions is that the tests you administered to my client are useless because my client wasn't trying on them. Fair to say?

Doctor: No, that's not fair to say. I would say that, based on the pattern of performance provided by your client during my assessment, which included scores so low on measures of performance validity that they raised my concern about the validity of her other complaints and symptoms—so much so, that the test results, in the context of all the records I have reviewed, led me to doubt the veracity of her complaints and symptoms, which she suggests are all caused by her alleged concussion. So, my opinion is based on more than just a performance validity test. Specifically, the accumulated evidence of her entire case has led me to question the overall reliability and validity of her complaints.

For me, the key to effectively responding to cross-examination questions (as in all phases of testimony) is to be honest. This includes responding to the question in the best manner possible, but also remaining aware of what you previously testified to during direct examination. It means being upfront about how certain biases may potentially have affected your opinions. It is the expert's responsibility to be vigilant about the effects of bias in all phases of the process, beginning from the moment the attorney calls you to discuss the case, all the way through your appearance on the witness stand. The reader is referred to Sweet and Moulthrop (1999) and van Gorp and McMullen (1997) for a more complete discussion the role of bias in forensic neuropsychology and ways to combat the effects of bias.

CONCLUSION

In his chapter on neuropsychological testimony, Bush (2008) concluded the following:

> Expert testimony is a complex and highly demanding intellectual and psychological task. Under considerable pressure, we are required to succinctly and clearly explain complicated ideas, which often involve sophisticated and arcane technical material, to laypeople who likely have little interest and knowledge about the subject matter of our field. Moreover, expert disagreements often turn on long-standing professional and scientific controversies, which remain largely unresolved after years of debate and study by learned people who are passionate about the issues. Efficacy in this stressful and challenging role requires . . . integrity, composure, knowledge, grit, finesse, and communication skill. (p. 222)

In my opinion, Bush (2008) adequately summed up the process of providing neuropsychological testimony. It is important, though, to remember that testifying in court or during a deposition is a process that requires attention, vigilance to detail, a commitment to objectivity and empiricism, and a willingness to acknowledge one's weaknesses and limitations. As with any skill or exercise, it requires practice and experience. A solid foundation in empiricism and brain–behavior relationships, combined with a commitment to the provision of honest and objective neuropsychological opinions, will be instrumental in helping judges and juries in their effort to answer some very important legal questions.

References

Babitsky, S., & Mangraviti, J. J. (2003). *How to excel during depositions: Techniques that work.* Falmouth, MA: SEAK.

Barsky, A. E. (2012). *Clinicians in court: A guide to subpoenas, depositions, testifying, and everything else you need to know* (2nd ed.). New York, NY: Guilford Press.

Boone, K. (2012). *Clinical practice of forensic neuropsychology: An evidence-based approach.* New York, NY: Guilford Press.

Brodsky, S. L. (2004). *Coping with cross-examination and other effective pathways to effective testimony.* http://dx.doi.org/10.1037/10748-000

Brodsky, S. L., & Poythress, N. (1985). Expertise on the witness stand: A practitioner's guide. In C. Ewing (Ed.), *Psychology, psychiatry, and the law: A clinical and forensic handbook* (pp. 389–411). Sarasota, FL: Professional Resource Press.

Bush, D. S. (2008). Through the looking glass: Commentary on neuropsychological testimony. In R. L. Heilbronner (Ed.), *Neuropsychology in the courtroom: Expert analysis of reports and testimony* (pp. 199–224). New York, NY: Guilford Press.

Daubert v. Merrell Dow Pharmaceuticals, Inc., 509 U.S. 579, 113 S. Ct. 2786 (1993).

Denney, R. L., & Sullivan, J. P. (2008). *Clinical neuropsychology in the criminal setting.* New York, NY: Guilford Press.

Frye v. United States, 293 F. 1013, 34 ALR 145 (D.C. Cir. 1923).

Greiffenstein, M. F. (2008). Basics of forensic neuropsychology. In J. E. Morgan & J. H. Ricker (Eds.), *Textbook of clinical neuropsychology* (pp. 905–941). New York, NY: Psychology Press.

Greiffenstein, M. F., & Cohen, L. (2012). Principles of productive neuropsychologist-attorney interactions. In G. L. Larrabee (Ed.), *Forensic neuropsychology: Scientific foundations* (2nd ed., pp. 23–69). New York, NY: Oxford University Press.

Hartlage, L. C., & Williams, B. L. (2010). Depositions. In A. M. Horton & L. C. Hartlage (Eds.), *Handbook of forensic neuropsychology* (pp. 277–290). New York, NY: Springer.

Heilbronner, R. L. (2005). *Forensic neuropsychology handbook.* New York, NY: Guilford Press.

Heilbronner, R. L. (2008). *Neuropsychology in the courtroom: Expert analysis of reports and testimony.* New York, NY: Guilford Press.

Heilbronner, R. L., Sweet, J. J., Morgan, J. E., Larrabee, G. J., & Millis, S. R. (2009). American Academy of Clinical Neuropsychology Consensus Conference Statement on the neuropsychological assessment of effort, response bias, and malingering. *Clinical Neuropsychologist, 23,* 1093–1129. http://dx.doi.org/10.1080/13854040903155063

Kaufmann, P. M. (2009). Protecting raw data and psychological tests from wrongful disclosure: A primer on the law and other persuasive strategies.

Clinical Neuropsychologist, 23, 1130–1159. http://dx.doi.org/10.1080/13854040903107809

Larrabee, G. J. (2012). *Forensic neuropsychology: A scientific approach.* New York, NY: Oxford University Press.

Lubet, S. (1998). *Expert testimony: A guide for expert witnesses and the lawyers who examine them.* Boston, MA: LexisNexis/National Institute for Trial Advocacy.

Melton, G. B., Petrila, J., Poythress, N. G., & Slobogin, C. (2007). *Psychological evaluations for the courts: A handbook for mental health professionals and lawyers* (3rd ed.). New York, NY: Guilford Press.

Sweet, J. J. (1999). *Forensic neuropsychology: Fundamentals and practice.* Lisse, the Netherlands: Swets & Zeitlinger.

Sweet, J. J., & Moulthrop, M. (1999). Self-examination questions as a means of identifying bias in adversarial cases. *Journal of Forensic Neuropsychology, 1,* 73–88. http://dx.doi.org/10.1300/J151v01n01_06

van Gorp, W., & McMullen, W. (1997). Potential sources of bias in forensic neuropsychological evaluations. *Clinical Neuropsychologist, 11,* 180–187. http://dx.doi.org/10.1080/13854049708407048

CHAPTER 20

FORENSIC NEUROPSYCHOLOGY AND THE LEGAL CONSUMER

Emalee J. W. Quickel and George J. Demakis

Forensic neuropsychology, once described as a "hybrid, combining neuropsychological science and practice with forensic science and practice" (Heilbronner, 2004, p. 313), is a growing field in which neuropsychologists are tasked with assisting the courts in both civil and criminal cases. Forensic neuropsychologists, along with practitioners in overlapping areas such as clinical psychology and psychiatry, are often asked for expert testimony on the science or literature behind certain psychological constructs, the assessments used to evaluate those constructs, or both. In addition to this general expert testimony, forensic neuropsychologists also provide testimony on specific cases in which they have conducted neuropsychological evaluations. Much of neuropsychologists' unique expertise focuses on brain functioning and how different disorders or diagnoses manifest behaviorally, cognitively, and functionally.

Neuropsychological testimony is increasingly used in court to assist the trier of fact (e.g., judges, juries, clerks of the court) in arriving at a legal decision. This assistance is expanding. Kaufmann and Greiffenstein (2013) documented an exponential increase in the number of state and federal cases that contained search terms such as *neuropsycholo!* and *forensic psycholo!*[1] every 5 years from 1981 to 2011 (p. 11). Forensic neuropsychological testimony is requested in both civil and criminal cases (see Greiffenstein & Kaufmann, 2012, Table 2.3). Civil cases that forensic neuropsychologists are likely to assist with include global civil competency or the ability to manage one's own affairs; specific aspects of civil competency such as the ability to make financial decisions or consent to treatment; workers' compensation and other personal injury cases; disability evaluations; and civil commitment evaluations (i.e., dangerousness to self and others; for a review of civil capacities, see Chapter 14, this handbook). Criminal cases that may require expert testimony include competency to stand trial (CST), criminal responsibility (i.e., the insanity defense), competency to waive one's *Miranda* rights, and competency to be executed (see Chapter 15, this handbook).

In general, how the courts perceive, consume, and ultimately use neuropsychological—or, even more generally, psychological—testimony is not well understood. This remains true despite the fact that certain areas of practice (e.g., CST) have received considerable scholarly attention. In most aspects of daily living, the decisions that individuals make and whether they believe they have made them accurately have relatively innocuous consequences (e.g., what one chooses to eat for lunch). However, in some contexts it seems to be extraordinarily important that decisions be made optimally and without bias. The legal system is one of these contexts. The purpose of this chapter is to describe how legal consumers use psychological and

[1]Search terms containing an exclamation point allow the root word to be searched with any possible ending (e.g., *neuropsycholo!* would return searches for *neuropsychology, neuropsychologist,* and *neuropsychological*).

http://dx.doi.org/10.1037/0000032-020
APA Handbook of Forensic Neuropsychology, S. S. Bush (Editor-in-Chief)

neuropsychological testimony with an emphasis on the background of forensic assessment, legal issues surrounding admissibility of clinical expert testimony, current research and methodological issues in psychology and neuropsychology and the law, a brief review of debates in the literature, and directions for future research and clinical practice.

TYPES OF FORENSIC ASSESSMENT

As mentioned previously, forensic neuropsychologists are called on to complete a diverse range of assessments to assist the courts. There is a great deal of variability in what is included in the assessment process, and the typical assessment has changed over time. In Petrella and Poythress's (1983) examination of thoroughness and quality in both CST and criminal responsibility reports, psychological testing is only briefly mentioned as an indicator of possible thoroughness. More common indicators included activities such as record review and obtaining interview data from collateral sources. In the past 30 years, however, there has been an increasing emphasis on the psychometric characteristics of tests, particularly reliability and validity. This emphasis has changed what the components of a thorough or high-quality neuropsychological evaluation and report might include.

The first generation of forensic assessment instruments (FAIs) emerged in the early 1970s in the area of CST (Borum & Otto, 2000). Borum and Otto (2000) argued that although great strides had been made in adjudicative competence and violence risk assessment during the 30 years before their review, FAIs in domains such as competency restoration, criminal responsibility, and civil competency areas have not seen as much growth. Borum and Otto, in their introduction to the special issue of *Law and Human Behavior* that focused on advances in assessment and treatment of forensic populations, encouraged readers to view forensic psychology as a realm in which clinicians inform research and researchers inform subsequent clinical decisions. This symbiotic relationship is important for the ongoing advancement of forensic evaluation.

Despite the growth of FAIs in select areas, forensic neuropsychologists have the difficult task of choosing which instruments to use in various assessments. In 2003, Lally measured opinions of diplomates in forensic psychology in the use and acceptability of various available instruments; acceptability is an important domain because of its relevance for expert admissibility standards (i.e., *Daubert v. Merrell Dow Pharmaceuticals,* 1993, criteria). He found that in six different areas of criminal forensic assessment, the Wechsler Adult Intelligence Scale—Third Edition and the Minnesota Multiphasic Personality Inventory–2 (MMPI–2) were universally rated as "at least" acceptable (and, in most cases, as acceptable and recommended). FAIs specific to a unique criminal construct (e.g., violence risk assessment) also fared well, with all areas except criminal responsibility judged as having acceptable and recommended FAIs available for use (Lally, 2003).

In their meta-analysis of CST research, Pirelli, Gottdiener, and Zapf (2011) compared five FAIs specific to CST (i.e., Competency Screening Test, Georgia Court Competency Test, Fitness Interview Test, Metropolitan Toronto Forensic Service Fitness Questionnaire, Mosley Forensic Competency Scale) with three traditional psychological measures (i.e., MMPI and MMPI–2, the Wechsler intelligence measures, and the Brief Psychiatric Rating Scale) in their ability to discriminate between competent and incompetent defendants. Similar to Lally's (2003) findings (i.e., psychologists deem both traditional measures and FAIs acceptable in various domains), Pirelli et al. (2011) determined that although CST FAIs had larger effect sizes than traditional measures, the evidence to support the superiority of FAIs over traditional assessment tools was inadequate. It appears from these studies that neuropsychologists regularly use FAIs related to a specific construct; however, there also appears to be a reliance on more traditional or general measures of intellectual or personality functioning. In addition, professionals do not agree on a standard neuropsychological battery. Lees-Haley, Smith, Williams, and Dunn (1996) assessed the reports of 100 experts in personal injury evaluations and found that no two evaluators chose the same battery, with the exception of a handful of assessors who used only a few tests. It is unclear to what extent these broad inclusion criteria for instrument choice affect legal consumers who are tasked with evaluating such evidence for both utility and admissibility.

Despite the demonstrated value of standardized, reliable, and valid assessment instruments, researchers have documented variability in their use. Borum and Grisso (1996) found that approximately 19% of forensic psychologists and psychiatrists rated psychological testing as essential for CST and insanity defense evaluations, and only 11 of the 66 CST reports reviewed by Robbins, Waters, and Herbert (1997) included "at least one procedure outside of the interview" (p. 476), which included testing or record review. Ryba, Cooper, and Zapf (2003) found that 44% of psychologists rated psychological testing as essential and only 29% of the same sample rated forensic testing as essential for juvenile CST reports. Of the more than 5,000 insanity defense cases reviewed by Warren, Murrie, Chauhan, Dietz, and Morris (2004), 22% of psychologists and only 6% of psychiatrists used psychological testing; only 10% of psychologists and 2% of psychiatrists used neuropsychological testing.

Similarly, it is not clear that the courts value the additional standardization, reliability, and validity that assessment instruments offer. On the basis of a hypothetical insanity defense case, Redding, Floyd, and Hawk (2001) surveyed 59 judges and 72 attorneys in Virginia and found that both judges and attorneys found more probative value in descriptive or clinical evidence than in statistical or actuarial evidence. This echoed findings from two decades earlier, in which 30 judges from Michigan preferred testimony related to descriptive information, the ultimate issue, and the clinical interpretation of the legal standard in question (Poythress, 1981, as cited in Redding et al., 2001). Even when clinical testimony is based on highly scientific or actuarial evidence, the courts were uninterested in hearing about those details, making it impossible to determine what information is valid or reliable. Mock jurors, too, appear to find expert testimony based on clinical evidence more influential in capital sentencing cases than expert testimony based on actuarial evidence (Krauss & Sales, 2001). Two hundred eight undergraduates in Arizona rated how influential expert testimony was in a mock trial. Ratings of dangerousness changed more dramatically after hearing clinical evidence than after hearing actuarial evidence, indicating a greater degree of influence in decision making. Their perceptions of how influential the testimony was corresponded with these ratings as well (Krauss & Sales, 2001). Thus, in criminal contexts, it appears that legal decision makers value clinical information to a higher degree than the scientific underpinnings of those clinical recommendations.

More recently, Quickel, Demakis, and Reeve (in press) objectively examined civil competency decisions using a methodology called *policy capturing*. This methodology, described in more detail later, allows researchers to uncover which factors decision makers use to make decisions without reliance on their self-report. They found that legal decision makers were no more likely to use psychological testimony in forming civil competency determinations when that testimony was based on psychological test data than when it was based on a clinical interview alone. The addition of psychological test data did not interact with the recommendation of the psychologist, rendering psychological recommendations no more influential when they contained objective information than when they only contained that psychologist's interview. This study, however, did not ask participants about their preference for information or their perceptions of how influential the testimony was when it contained varying degrees of psychological rigor (i.e., test data vs. a clinical interview alone). Even though there has been a shift in psychological research and professional practice guidelines to base evaluations on assessment instruments with demonstrated psychometric properties, the actual practices of clinical evaluators and preferences of the courts have not reliably mirrored this growth despite significant changes in the laws governing the admissibility of expert evidence.

ADMISSIBILITY OF NEUROPSYCHOLOGICAL EVIDENCE

Since 1923, expert evidence was admissible in court if the evidence was based on a technique that was considered generally accepted by the scientific field

(*Frye v. United States,* 1923). This evidentiary standard did not require that judges or other legal decision makers possess specialized scientific knowledge; admissibility was determined by the judge on the basis of the acceptance of the scientific community alone. Over the next 70 years, 45 states adopted *Frye* or articulated a *Frye*-like standard for the admissibility of evidence (Hamilton, 1998). During that time, Rule 702 of the Federal Rules of Evidence (1975) pronounced that expert evidence was admissible if that evidence would assist the trier of fact and if the expert was qualified to testify on the basis of his or her "knowledge, skill, experience, training, or education" (p. 14). These rules ignored *Frye,* which left jurisdictions unclear about how to negotiate these competing standards (Hamilton, 1998).

Finally, in 1993, the U.S. Supreme Court further articulated admissibility standards with the decision in *Daubert v. Merrell Dow Pharmaceuticals, Inc.* In this ruling, the court clarified that the Federal Rules of Evidence replaced the original *Frye* ruling and that judges were effectively placed in a gatekeeping role in deciding what evidence to admit. Judges were instructed to base their admissibility judgments on the following criteria: whether the evidence is based on scientific methods that are falsifiable, peer reviewed, contain information about possible or known error rates, are relevant to the court proceedings, and have a high degree of scientific reliability. Thirty states have implemented *Daubert* standards, seven states have explicitly rejected *Daubert,* and the remaining 13 are uncertain (see Kaufman, 2006, for a review of admissibility decisions by state). As previously reviewed, however, research has indicated that legal decision makers still have a preference for clinical information, despite the increased focus on scientific findings and methodologies associated with the *Daubert* criteria.

When judges are asked about admissibility laws, however, a different picture emerges. Gatowski et al. (2001) surveyed 400 judges across the United States about *Daubert* (1993) and their purported role as the gatekeepers of scientific evidence. Whereas 91% of judges reported that the gatekeeper role was judicially appropriate, only 52% felt prepared by their training and education to fully enact this role given the diversity of scientific evidence that appears in court. This discrepancy worsened when the judges were asked to demonstrate knowledge of the criteria set forth in *Daubert* by providing operational definitions of the constructs it contains. Only 6% of judges were able to define falsifiability correctly, and only 4% were able to articulate a conceptual understanding of error rate. Judges fared much better when defining the process of peer review (71%) and general acceptance (82%; Gatowski et al., 2001). In a different type of study, when methodological quality of psychological research was manipulated by Kovera and McAuliff (2000) in a sexual harassment case, judges were not sensitive to these differences, rating study quality consistently across levels of quality manipulation. This inability to distinguish valid from invalid scientific research extends to both attorneys and jurors in hostile work environment cases (see Kovera, Russano, & McAuliff, 2002, for a review).

This observed difficulty with the articulation and application of *Daubert* (1993) criteria is a relevant consideration for how legal consumers use neuropsychological testimony. The same standards that forensic neuropsychologists are encouraged to use when selecting assessments may not translate into the preferences or utility of those assessments in court. For example, although a neuropsychologist may select a particular test because of its psychometric properties, legal decision makers may prefer tests that have a higher degree of face validity because they can readily apply them to the context at hand. Nicholson and Norwood (2000) eloquently reviewed the promises of forensic psychological assessment as it maps onto the current practices of the field and concluded that the field has far to go to live up to its intentions. If one adds the courts into the symbiotic relationship between clinicians and research described by Borum and Otto (2000), one can see that symbiosis might be even further off than one thinks.

HOW LEGAL DECISION MAKERS USE NEUROPSYCHOLOGICAL FINDINGS

Researchers have long been interested in how legal decision makers use neuropsychological or psychological findings to inform their decisions, and this general inquiry has been approached in myriad ways. One of the most common ways to link psychological assessment and legal decisions is to elicit legal opinions of assessment reports. Wettstein (2005) reviewed four studies[2] in which judges and attorneys were sent either actual case reports or mock reports in a vignette format. Diverse findings were discovered: Judges were satisfied with reports in New York, attorneys desired more information regarding the basis for the legal recommendations in Oklahoma, and both judges and attorneys preferred reports that included clinical information rather than statistical information in Virginia. Moreover, a national sample of judges was unable to evaluate scientific concepts (i.e., error rate) contained in reports. Across these four studies, these legally informed participants were only able to review the report, which is limited because it is only a "window into the evaluation itself" (Wettstein, 2005, p. 167). Thus, although one can learn what aspects of the neuropsychological report are considered legally useful or valuable to the courts, what aspects of the neuropsychological evaluation are most effective for assisting the trier of fact remain unknown. There are no known studies that observe neuropsychological evaluations in an attempt to link the evaluation itself (e.g., behaviors of the evaluator, whether tests are given in optimal ways) with any legal outcome; researchers rely solely on the reports that follow an evaluation, which only represent the conclusions and interpretations gleaned from the evaluative context (Wettstein, 2005).

Another approach to linking psychological assessment and legal decisions is to investigate the admissibility of expert evidence in court (e.g., Gatowski et al., 2001) to see what information legal decision makers permit to be used in various legal domains. However, this line of inquiry has not yet sought to extend the investigation to the understanding of how the information is used by the courts once it is deemed admissible (i.e., how does neuropsychological testimony compare with other types of information at judges' disposal?) How legal decision makers use the findings of forensic neuropsychological assessment, and which information matters, remains unclear. Because very few researchers have explicitly asked this question, we can only begin to amalgamate pieces of the puzzle from the few direct and many more indirect ways in which this important question has been examined. A review of research that can inform this discussion follows.

Links Between Psychological Recommendations and Legal Decisions

Research linking psychological recommendations with ultimate legal decisions has demonstrated high rates of agreement in both criminal and civil competency areas. Zapf et al. (2004) reviewed CST cases in Alabama and found almost perfect agreement between mental health evaluators and judges. They used a retrospective analysis of 328 cases in which a CST evaluation was conducted by a mental health professional and the subsequent court decision was available for review. In 327 of those cases, the court decision and the mental health evaluator agreed (Zapf et al., 2004). As a follow-up to these findings, Zapf et al. (2004) consulted the legal decision makers to help explain and understand this near-perfect agreement. On the basis of several qualitative interviews, they reported that the general attitude of the judges was deference to the mental health professional as more of an expert in matters of competency, even though adjudicative competency is a legal, not a psychological, construct.

Other studies have found high rates of agreement as well. Gowensmith, Murrie, and Boccaccini (2012) investigated clinical–legal agreement in CST cases in Hawaii, a state that requires three independent evaluations during CST proceedings. When all three clinicians agreed, the courts agreed with those recommendations 97.7% of the time; the courts agreed with the majority recommendations in 78.3% of nonunanimous cases (Gowensmith et al., 2012). In North Carolina, Quickel and Demakis (2013) documented a clinician–court agreement rate of 92.3% in civil competency cases. It appears that this tendency for courts to agree with the recommendations of

[2]To review the original articles regarding these studies, see Redding, Floyd, and Hawk (2001); Owens, Rosner, and Harmon (1985); LaFortune and Nicholson (1995); and Dahir et al. (2005), as cited in Wettstein (2005).

the mental health evaluator spans criminal and civil contexts and across multiple states with different statutes and diverse court proceedings. Some scholars (e.g., Perlin, 2004; Zapf et al., 2004) have raised concerns that such high rates of agreement reflect a tendency of the courts to default to the opinion of the evaluator instead of thoughtfully and independently considering and weighing the evidence.

In the different domain of predisposition juvenile assessment, Hecker and Steinberg (2002) also found high rates of acceptance of psychological recommendations among judges in Pennsylvania, regardless of report quality. Out of 86 assessment reports, only five contained recommendations that were fully rejected by the courts; this high rate of acceptance occurred even though expert coders rated the sufficiency of eight different content areas (e.g., mental health history, cognitive functioning) with an average of only 33% of reports containing sufficient or better information across the content domains. The highest rated content area was family history (63% of reports rated sufficient or better), and the lowest rated content area was mental health history (only 10% of reports rated sufficient or better; Hecker & Steinberg, 2002). Thus, there is mounting evidence across diverse legal contexts that indicates that legal decision makers accept or agree with the recommendations of clinical testimony, regardless of quality.

Quickel et al. (in press) recently empirically investigated this apparent concern by asking legal decision makers in North Carolina to respond to vignettes depicting prototypical civil competency case information. These vignettes varied on five factors: diagnosis (schizophrenia vs. Alzheimer's disease), spousal testimony (competent vs. incompetent), medical records (competent vs. incompetent), psychologist opinion (competent vs. incompetent), and basis for the psychologist's opinion (clinical interview alone vs. clinical interview plus psychological test data). Using a unique methodology called *policy capturing*, objective factor weights were derived that compared the influence of these factors in ultimate competency decisions made by legal decision makers. Once a participant renders competency decisions for all possible vignettes, his or her individual data are entered into a separate database, and a regression analysis is performed; unstandardized regression coefficients are then entered as data into a subsequent database that combines the individual decisional weights of each participant. We found that participants relied most heavily on the recommendation of the psychologist when making competency determinations, regardless of the methods used by the psychologist to make that recommendation (i.e., psychological test data or a clinical interview alone). However, participants also strongly and significantly relied on the information provided by medical records and the wife of the respondent. Although this information was not weighted as heavily as the psychological testimony, it suggests that legal decision makers do not simply default to the opinion of the mental health evaluator; rather, multiple pieces of information are considered in their decisions about civil competency.

Source of the Testimony

Some studies have attempted to isolate the specific type of mental health testimony provided, including the professional who delivers the testimony. Historically, legal decision makers preferred testimony proffered by a psychiatrist versus a nonmedical mental health professional (e.g., Perlin, 1977, as cited by Petrella & Poythress, 1983). As with the utility and admissibility of FAIs, the literature contains contradictory findings that seem to indirectly point to a trend of abandoning these historical beliefs in favor of psychologists as the preferred expert witness. As early as 1983, researchers documented a stated preference by judges and attorneys for testimony provided by doctoral-level psychologists than by psychiatrists in both CST and criminal responsibility cases (Petrella & Poythress, 1983). Shortly after, Swenson, Nash, and Roos (1984) also found that expert information provided by a clinical psychologist was preferable to jury-eligible undergraduate students assessing a mock child custody case, compared with psychiatric testimony. Similarly and more recently, in a vignette-based study of the impact of a traumatic brain injury on a criminal trial, Gresham and Brodie (2012) found that a majority of jury-eligible participants rated expert testimony from a neuropsychologist as more credible than expert testimony from a psychiatrist. This is the only known study that compared evidentiary preference for a neuropsychologist; most reviewed research only used the psychology–psychiatry distinction and did not specify subspecialties of the psychologist.

In contrast to the above findings, Redding et al. (2001) found that judges, prosecutors, and defense attorneys prefer that forensic evaluations of criminal responsibility be conducted by psychiatrists, but doctoral-level psychologists were preferred as a close second. Master's-level psychologists, nonpsychiatric physicians, social workers, and other mental health providers trailed behind in terms of preference (Redding et al., 2001). In a recent study, Quickel et al. (in press) hypothesized that legal decision makers in North Carolina might use psychological and medical testimony differently such that physicians might have more influence on civil competency decisions in people with Alzheimer's disease, whereas psychologists might have more influence on these decisions in cases of schizophrenia; perhaps the discrepancy seen in the aforementioned literature is due to differential evaluation of relative expertise depending on case information. However, this hypothesis was not supported, and participants did not use expert information in different ways across diagnostic categories. Thus, the reasons why certain sources of testimony may be preferred over others, and what personal or contextual factors predict these preferences, remain unknown.

CURRENT AND HISTORICAL RESEARCH METHODS IN PSYCHOLEGAL DECISION MAKING

Similar to other areas of psychological research, questions surrounding forensic neuropsychology and, specifically, how legal decision makers construe neuropsychological information can be investigated in a variety of ways. To understand the current state of the literature, it is important to understand the challenges that researchers of legal decision making face. Different types of research methodologies possess advantages and disadvantages, and when a variety of methods arrive at similar conclusions, one naturally has an increased level of confidence in those conclusions. One of the most fundamental distinctions is whether a study will be retrospective or prospective.

Retrospective studies (e.g., Gowensmith et al., 2012, Quickel & Demakis, 2013; Zapf et al., 2004) typically use actual case information that has previously occurred, which allows researchers to observe what transpired but does not allow interpretations of how those decisions arose. These researchers find their variables of interest in case files, often coding content and analyzing diverse cases through one set of criteria. For example, Quickel and Demakis (2013) analyzed 71 cases from an urban county in North Carolina, coding for variables such as diagnosis, performance on functional and neuropsychological tests, and the ultimate court adjudication of civil competency. One main advantage to this type of methodology is ecological validity, or the extent to which the research context maps onto the real world. When actual case files are used, researchers can be confident that they are obtaining a glimpse into the real-world variables at play. Other practical advantages include the ability to include a large quantity of data because variables are not actively linked to human participants, who can be difficult to recruit and incentivize. For example, Warren et al. (2006) reviewed 8,416 CST evaluations from Virginia in an attempt to better understand how clinicians form opinions related to adjudicative capacity. It would be difficult, if not impossible, to survey that many individuals who were currently participating in these types of trials. Working with case files thus allows researchers an advantage in participant recruitment and data collection.

One major disadvantage of retrospective research methodologies is that the researcher has little experimental control over the variables in question. Experimental research in the psychological sciences is largely built on the premise that isolating and manipulating one variable at time is the best way to observe the causal impact of that variable. Because retrospective cases have already occurred, researchers cannot isolate variables in this way. Quickel and Demakis (2013) noted this as a weakness; although they found that a functional instrument (i.e., the Independent Living Scales; Loeb, 1996) was the most accurate predictor of court competency determinations, the determinations themselves were not independent of the clinician recommendation, which relied heavily on the information gleaned from the Independent Living Scales. The variable of functional assessment information could not be isolated or manipulated to observe subsequent changes in court adjudication. Thus, a criterion contamination problem occurs. These types of circular and confounding problems are often unavoidable in retrospective research, in which outcomes cannot naturally be untangled from other case information. This impairs researchers' ability to understand which information matters to legal decision makers because their decisions cannot be separated from the factors that might influence them.

Prospective research, however, presents participants with decision-making scenarios and asks them to respond to questions of capacity, competency, or some other construct in question. For example, Kovera and McAuliff (2000) asked judges to rate descriptions of expert testimony as to whether that expert's research would be admissible in court. Consistent with *Daubert* (1993) criteria, the peer-review status and the internal validity of the research in question were manipulated. In general, there were low admissibility rates across these manipulations, such that judges were no more likely to admit peer-reviewed research than non–peer-reviewed research, and they were no more likely to admit valid research than they were to admit research without a control, with a confound, or with the presence of experimenter bias (Kovera & McAuliff, 2000). Although these findings are discouraging in relation to the gatekeeping role judges embody in a post-*Daubert* court, the ability of researchers to isolate causal variables (e.g., peer-review status) and test the impact of their variations on a particular outcome (e.g., admissibility) demonstrates a clear strength of prospective research. However, prospective studies tend to lack ecological validity and do not always map nicely onto real-world contexts. For example, Kovera and McAuliff (2000) compared the low levels of reported admissibility found in one study with a "highly publicized hostile work environment case tried in the Florida courts (*Robinson v. Jacksonville Shipyard, Inc., 1991)*" (p. 580) that did admit gender-stereotyping evidence similar to that in question. Another criticism of prospective studies, which often rely on simulated contexts versus the real environment, is that the same consequences are not attached to the outcomes; getting it wrong in a study is arguably an outcome with much lower risk than getting it wrong in an actual court trial.

In addition to the distinction between retrospective and prospective research methodologies, legal decision-making research also falls into two main categories: self-report (i.e., subjective) and empirically derived (i.e., objective). This distinction is particularly important for questions of why or how legal decisions are made. A large body of psychological research has documented the biases in judgment and decision making, starting with Tversky and Kahneman's (1974) seminal piece about heuristics. In the past 40 years, research has continued to document biased decision making in a variety of populations, contexts, and arenas, including forensic evaluation (Neal & Grisso, 2014). Motivation toward accuracy does not lead to higher rates of unbiased decisions than what is found in the general population (e.g., Shamir, 1998). Moreover, higher degrees of cognitive ability do not seem to attenuate the susceptibility to these heuristics (e.g., West, Meserve, & Stanovich, 2012). Not only are more intelligent individuals equally as biased as their less intelligent counterparts, they also have a tendency to judge themselves to be more accurate, a phenomenon known as the "bias blind spot" (West et al., 2012). These biases also extend to individuals who have expertise in a particular field. In a review of the literature on expert clinical decision makers, Dawes, Faust, and Meehl (1989) demonstrated that decision makers who use clinical (i.e., subjective) methods were less accurate than those who based their judgments on actuarial methods. For example, Dawes et al. outlined research on the Goldberg Rule for MMPI diagnosis, an actuarial method for distinguishing neuroses from psychosis, and found this actuarial approach had a 70% accuracy rate, whereas the accuracy of the average human judge was 62% (p. 1669).

Although no gold standard exists for accuracy in legal contexts (i.e., the concepts found in these contexts are entirely socially constructed; there is not a right or wrong answer apart from what the courts decide), Dawes et al. (1989) established that actuarial models derived from clinical decision makers consistently outperform the clinical decision makers themselves because of increased reliability. Even when clinical decision makers were provided with the actuarial information, they incorrectly modified the information at higher rates than they correctly modified it and thereby achieved lower overall accuracy rates than if they relied on the actuarial methods alone (Dawes et al., 1989).

It should be noted that in most psychological contexts, including forensic ones, neuropsychologists do not receive feedback on the accuracy of their opinions (Garb & Schramke, 1996). Psychologists may not know the outcome of the case and, if they do, they do not know whether the courts reached an "accurate" decision or how the decision was made. Even if one assumes that there are "right" and "wrong" answers to questions of legal competencies or other legal standards, the socially constructed nature of these concepts make it impossible to evaluate decisional accuracy beyond the decisions themselves. In addition, Garb and Schramke (1996) noted that neuropsychologists are subject to the same cognitive biases as laypeople and other psychologists and encouraged researchers to systematically investigate these biases in the future. A growing body of research in the area of decisional science is discrediting the assumption that either clinical evaluators or legal decision-makers weigh and integrate all relevant information to form recommendations or ultimate legal decisions (Goodman-Delahunty & Dhami, 2013).

Forensic neuropsychologists and legal decision makers are not exempt from these aforementioned biases. Neal and Grisso (2014) outlined how these traditional heuristics and biases first posited by Tversky and Kahneman (1974) continue to apply to forensic evaluators. It seems logical that legal decision makers would also be subject to biased decision making given that they make similar judgments as the evaluators discussed by Neal and Grisso (2014). Specifically, Neal and Grisso provided reasoning and support for how the heuristics of availability, representativeness, and anchoring are applicable to the forensic setting. One example they used is the representativeness heuristic that Tversky and Kahneman (1974) originally defined as "when A is highly representative of B, the probability that A originates from B is judged to be high" (p. 1124). Individuals use the representativeness heuristic when they ignore simple probabilities that may provide a more accurate prediction. The example Neal and Grisso provided describes a man as shy, withdrawn, helpful, structured, and detailed; on the basis of this description, one can predict whether this man's occupation is librarian or farmer. Tversky and Kahneman (1974) indicated that the fact that there are many more farmers than librarians should be an important consideration, yet individuals tend to make predictions on the basis of how representative the description is of a stereotypical librarian, ignoring this useful base-rate information.

Neal and Grisso (2014) described how this heuristic can lead to clinicians ignoring base rates of the constructs they are assessing that can cause them to overemphasize case-specific information in a similar way. For example, they recounted an instance from the John Hinckley trial in which a forensic psychiatrist used widened sulci in the brain to support a diagnosis of schizophrenia, stating that one in three of individuals diagnosed with schizophrenia had this brain abnormality compared with only one in 50 of the general population. However, because of the low base rate of schizophrenia (< 1%), the probability was actually higher that Mr. Hinckley represented one of the one in 50 cases seen in the general population (Neal & Grisso, 2014). This seems to echo the recommendations of Garb and Schramke (1996), who urged neuropsychologists to attend to both local and national base rates and even to use computerized assessment procedures and statistical decision-making rules to improve predictions. Goodman-Delahunty and Dhami (2013) also recommended the use of decision aids in legal contexts.

It seems likely that both forensic neuropsychologists and legal decision makers display the same biases as the general population. Yet, society continues to expect these professionals to make important decisions based on their own expertise (i.e., clinical methods). Subjective research, which asks individuals to identify their reasons for why and how they make decisions, can also be influenced by these biases. For decades, research in social psychology has documented this issue. Nisbett and Wilson (1977) even concluded that the "accuracy of subjective reports is so poor as to suggest that any introspective access that may exist is not sufficient to produce generally correct or reliable reports" (p. 233). Forensic psychologists have echoed these same concerns when investigating what factors might influence how jurors view expert testimony in hostile work environment trials (Kovera et al., 2002).

Objective, or empirically derived, research allows researchers to determine which factors influence a participant's decision without asking the participant to self-report these reasons. One particular type of objective methodology that has had some success in explaining legal decision making is policy capturing (see Aiman-Smith, Scullen, & Barr, 2002, for a review and tutorial). Policy capturing is a methodological tool in which researchers vary several influential factors to create a set of vignettes to which participants respond. As briefly explained earlier, each of their responses to a different vignette is treated as a separate piece of data. Once the participant has provided responses to all vignettes, a regression is conducted on each individual's responses to uncover that participant's decision-making policy by deriving regression coefficients for each of the varied vignette factors; this occurs separately for each participant. Then, these regression coefficients can be combined into a new database with other participants. This process allows researchers to answer questions about variability in decision making or differences in decision-making patterns across groups.

Policy capturing, though originally developed for organizational science research, has been applied to forensic psychological science for more than two decades, though those applications remain limited in scope. Dhami and Ayton (2001) used this methodology to investigate bail decision making among magistrates in England and Wales. They discovered that despite extremely high levels of confidence in self-reported cue use (i.e., which pieces of information individuals explicitly report using in the decision-making process), most magistrates' empirically derived decisions were incongruent with their subjective report. Most bail decisions were made using only one of nine possible cues (e.g., previous convictions), which indicated an incomplete assessment of relevant information. In addition, the most salient cue used differed dramatically between magistrates, with fewer than one quarter of the sample using any given piece of information (Dhami & Ayton, 2001). This research supports the idea that using subjective self-report methods to understand decision making might lead to inaccurate conclusions.

Similarly, Sensibaugh and Allgeier (1996) used this methodology to investigate judges' decisions regarding judicial bypass in juvenile abortion cases (i.e., allowing minors to receive abortions without parental consent) in Ohio. A few years earlier, the Ohio Supreme Court had ruled against implementing more concrete criteria for judges' use in this process under the assumption that juvenile court judges were already using these criteria; however, Sensibaugh and Allgeier found that judges used fewer factors in their judgments than what was outlined in the aforementioned court case, as well as fewer factors than the judges had predicted on the basis of subjective ratings. Specifically, of the six possible pieces of information, judges reported that they had equally considered all pieces of information. In reality, only one or two factors (e.g., age of the juvenile) were highly rated, the maximum number of factors that explained variance in judicial decisions was four, and the factors used varied from judge to judge (Sensibaugh & Allgeier, 1996). This study demonstrates that in a juvenile bypass context, both judges' and policymakers' assumptions about how legal decisions are made were inaccurate, overly confident, and inconsistent with optimal decision-making procedures (i.e., carefully considering all available information).

However, not all policy-capturing studies identify suboptimal decision making. York (1992) used policy capturing in sexual harassment cases and demonstrated that not only are judges consistent in their determinations, but they made their judgments in ways that were fundamentally congruent with published guidelines for sexual harassment cases. The Equal Employment Opportunity Commission (1980, as cited in York, 1992) put forth *Guidelines on Sexual Harassment* that defined sexual harassment according to degrees of coercion, the form of the harassment, and the victim's reaction, all of which were salient decision-making cues in York's (1992) study. On the basis of data from actual and hypothetical cases, using both judges and Equal Employment Opportunity officers, he concluded that individuals were making decisions about sexual harassment in the ways that they ought to be (York, 1992). In this case, he used policy capturing to infer that the legal system was functioning in an optimal way (i.e., consistent, on the basis of guidelines), unlike the other studies described in this section. This research continues to support the utility of this type of methodology in confirming the adequacy of a decision-making process.

In many ways, objective studies are preferable to subjective (i.e., self-report) studies because they remove the aforementioned component of bias in individual reporting. However, some practical constraints make objective research difficult. For example, in Quickel et al. (in press), participants read and responded to 36 vignettes; fewer than one third of the participants completed the entire study, possibly as a result of the lack of compensating incentive given the amount of work the participation required. Research in psycholegal decision making is continuing to evolve, and researchers are finding increasingly new and creative ways to answer important questions in this domain. In addition to methodological considerations, debate among legal scholars also furthers the literature through discourse by experts. One debate in the consideration of how legal decision makers use neuropsychological testimony is the question of the ultimate issue.

THE ULTIMATE ISSUE

One important debate throughout psycholegal literature is whether various courts permit or even encourage forensic neuropsychologists to opine on the ultimate issue—the legal standards by which the defendant or respondent meets legal criteria for the construct in question. This issue is relevant for the understanding of legal decision making because the testimony that a forensic neuropsychologist gives, either via report writing or orally in court, is the way in which psychological information is disseminated to the legal decision makers. Thus, debate about the form of that information is highly relevant here. Historically, this type of testimony has been considered inadmissible under the Federal Rule of Evidence 704(b), introduced as an amendment to the original rules in 1984 (Buchanan, 2006). In this rule, opinions about mental state are specifically addressed and excluded from admissibility; however, this rule has been applied inconsistently and with greater tolerance in civil (e.g., competency to execute a will) versus criminal (e.g., insanity defense pleas) contexts (Buchanan, 2006). In a compelling discussion of the advantages and disadvantages of this type of testimony, Tillbrook, Mumley, and Grisso (2003) illustrated their conclusions with a vignette that demonstrates that legal boundaries are infringed when a clinician opines on statutory definitions. However, despite the widespread opinion of many legal scholars that experts should not give testimony on the ultimate issue, many legal decision makers appreciate and encourage such testimony. Varying degrees of this form of evidence are also found throughout case law examples (Slovenko, 2006). In a review of seven studies conducted from 1994 to 1998, Nicholson and Norwood (2000) concluded that "the overwhelming majority of reports from each state included an ultimate opinion" (p. 17) about CST. Perhaps the prevalence of this type of testimony speaks to the controversy often seen between what is and what ought to be.

Slovenko (2006) concluded that Federal Rule of Evidence 704(b) is unnecessary because of the other evidentiary standards that judges can use at their discretion to determine admissibility of evidence. Moreover, he summarized that Rule 704(b) "promotes indirect and incomplete testimony" (p. 25). In their instructions to clinicians regarding what to include in a report on civil capacity, Benson and Romano (2012) reminded them that this decision is court specific and that some courts actually expect these types of conclusions from psychological experts. Thus, it appears as though the imbalance between what some legal scholars recommend versus the actions of courts and the psychologists who assist them currently co-exists in a philosophical draw. This ambiguity can be confusing to forensic neuropsychologists who seek to stay within the scope of practice while also being as helpful as possible to the trier of fact. Neuropsychologists who conduct evaluations in legal contexts are recommended to initiate discussions with court personnel about legal expectations of ultimate-issue testimony. Additional recommendations for readers currently in practice are outlined in the following section.

RECOMMENDATIONS FOR FORENSIC NEUROPSYCHOLOGY EVALUATORS

In light of the limited research on how the trier of fact incorporates and uses neuropsychological testimony, we offer a few recommendations for forensic neuropsychologists conducting these evaluations. It is important for clinicians to clarify their role and conduct their evaluations in ethically and culturally sensitive ways that also optimize communications with the courts. Hebben and Milberg (2009) made a distinction between traditional neuropsychology and forensic neuropsychology in the relative roles of the clinician; that is, "treater" and "expert," respectively (p. 199). They subsequently described that forensic neuropsychologists are consultants whose allegiance is to the facts of the case rather than a treating clinician whose primary responsibility is to advocate for appropriate treatment. There are distinctions that exist in the details (e.g., neuropsychologists typically provide feedback to clients via a face-to-face meeting, whereas forensic neuropsychologists typically provide feedback to the referral source via written report), and distinctions that exist in the broad scope of one's practice (e.g., forensic neuropsychologists' assessments may be held to a higher scientific standard because their assessment instruments sometimes pass courtroom standards of admissibility of evidence).

This distinction echoes a sentiment discussed by Appelbaum (2008) that forensic practitioners have two ethical principles under consideration: "truth-telling and respect for persons" (p. 196). Appelbaum argued that forensic experts are bound by their duty to testify truthfully in court, regardless of whether that truth is helpful to the party who retained them. Moreover, those truths should be based on the available scientific data regarding the construct in question. Respect for persons is explained as forensic evaluators taking care to not exploit, invade, or otherwise deceive those individuals with whom they are working; these two ethical guidelines are known as the *Standard Position* (Appelbaum, 2008). This is consistent with the *Ethical Principles of Psychologists and Code of Conduct* (American Psychological Association, 2017) that includes respect for people's rights and dignity as one of its foundational guiding principles and that also states that "psychologists base the opinions contained in their recommendations, reports, and diagnostic or evaluative statements, including forensic testimony, on information and techniques sufficient to substantiate their findings" (p. 12). This assumes that psychologists will use assessment information is an unbiased way, which, as previously noted, may be an unfounded assumption. Yet, the degree to which clinicians are aware of the possibility of bias is likely to ameliorate the negative impact such biases will have. Once the literature is able to provide increased insight into the process of legal decision making, additional recommendations are likely to emerge.

FUTURE DIRECTIONS IN RESEARCH AND CLINICAL PRACTICE

It is clear that additional research is needed to investigate how legal decision makers use neuropsychological testimony and test data to inform their legal judgments. Researchers are tasked with the challenge of designing creative and methodologically rigorous studies that capture unbiased decision making in ecologically valid ways. Admittedly, this is not an easy trade-off to make. However, once studies begin to accumulate that examine this topic from differing perspectives, future researchers will be able to fit together the puzzle pieces of this literature to address this difficult yet vitally important question. Researchers are encouraged to use a variety of methodologies, in a variety of jurisdictions, with a variety of case types to create the most representative body of literature possible.

Clinically, the challenge is different. Clinicians are encouraged to develop relationships with the triers of fact in their jurisdictions and find out how they can be optimally helpful to them, as required by the Federal Rules of Evidence (outlined above). For example, one author (Demakis) of this chapter regularly solicits feedback from the clerks of the court (who decide civil competency and guardianship cases in North Carolina) in the county he predominantly serves; because of this feedback, he has been able to modify his report writing. This exchange of information also gives him the opportunity to educate the legal decision makers on matters related to neuropsychological testing and research. This dialogue most closely approximates the symbiotic relationship described by Borum and Otto (2000), in which research and practice inform each other to advance both fields. Legal scholars are also calling for enhanced dialogue among law professors, practicing attorneys, and judges by encouraging law professors to participate in engaged scholarship that is written for a broad and inclusive audience (i.e., not just an academic audience; Hricik & Salzmann, 2005). Including the interests and voices of all parties involved (e.g., clinician, attorney, decision maker, researcher), as well as marketing relevant research to all parties, will strengthen this relationship and the results it provides. Perhaps one day, in the not-too-distant future, the promises and practices of forensic assessment (Nicholson & Norwood, 2000) will not have such a wide gulf between them. Understanding more about how legal consumers use information from forensic neuropsychologists will certainly be one way to narrow this gap and lead to more optimal psychological practice.

References

Aiman-Smith, L., Scullen, S. E., & Barr, S. H. (2002). Conducting studies of decision making in organizational contexts: A tutorial for policy-capturing and other regression-based techniques. *Organizational Research Methods, 5,* 388–414. http://dx.doi.org/10.1177/109442802237117

American Psychological Association. (2017). *Ethical principles of psychologists and code of conduct* (2002, Amended June 1, 2010 and January 1, 2017). Retrieved from http://www.apa.org/ethics/code/index.aspx

Appelbaum, P. S. (2008). Ethics and forensic psychiatry: Translating principles into practice. *Journal of the American Academy of Psychiatry and the Law, 36,* 195–200.

Benson, F. R., & Romano, J. (2012). A legal consumer's perspective on competency evaluations. In G. J. Demakis (Ed.), *Civil capacities in clinical neuropsychology: Research findings and practical applications* (pp. 293–309). New York, NY: Oxford University Press.

Borum, R., & Grisso, T. (1996). Establishing standards for criminal forensic reports: An empirical analysis. *Bulletin of the American Academy of Psychiatry and the Law, 24,* 297–317.

Borum, R., & Otto, R. (2000). Advances in forensic assessment and treatment: An overview and introduction to the special issue. *Law and Human Behavior, 24,* 1–7. http://dx.doi.org/10.1023/A:1005480018608

Buchanan, A. (2006). Psychiatric evidence on the ultimate issue. *Journal of the American Academy of Psychiatry and the Law, 34,* 14–21.

Daubert v. Merrell Dow Pharmaceuticals, Inc., 509 U.S. 579, 113 S. Ct. 2786 (1993).

Dawes, R. M., Faust, D., & Meehl, P. E. (1989). Clinical versus actuarial judgment. *Science, 243,* 1668–1674. http://dx.doi.org/10.1126/science.2648573

Dhami, M. K., & Ayton, P. (2001). Bailing and jailing the fast and frugal way. *Journal of Behavioral Decision Making, 14,* 141–168. http://dx.doi.org/10.1002/bdm.371

Federal Rules of Evidence, 28 U.S.C. (West 1975).

Frye v. United States, 54 App. D.C. 46, 293 F. 1013 (1923).

Garb, H. N., & Schramke, C. J. (1996). Judgement research and neuropsychological assessment: A narrative review and meta-analyses. *Psychological Bulletin, 120,* 140–153. http://dx.doi.org/10.1037/0033-2909.120.1.140

Gatowski, S. I., Dobbin, S. A., Richardson, J. T., Ginsburg, G. P., Merlino, M. L., & Dahir, V. (2001). Asking the gatekeepers: A national survey of judges on judging expert evidence in a post-*Daubert* world. *Law and Human Behavior, 25,* 433–458. http://dx.doi.org/10.1023/A:1012899030937

Goodman-Delahunty, J., & Dhami, M. K. (2013). A forensic examination of court reports. *Australian Psychologist, 48,* 32–40. http://dx.doi.org/10.1111/j.1742-9544.2012.00082.x

Gowensmith, W. N., Murrie, D. C., & Boccaccini, M. T. (2012). Field reliability of competence to stand trial opinions: How often do evaluators agree, and what do judges decide when evaluators disagree? *Law and Human Behavior, 36,* 130–139. http://dx.doi.org/10.1037/h0093958

Greiffenstein, M. F., & Kaufmann, P. M. (2012). Neuropsychology and the law: Principles of productive attorney-neuropsychologist relations. In G. J. Larrabee (Ed.), *Forensic neuropsychology: A scientific approach* (2nd ed., pp. 23–69). New York, NY: Oxford University Press.

Gresham, V. J., & Brodie, L. A. (2012). Perspectives on neuropsychological testimony. *World Academy of Science, Engineering and Technology, 6,* 792–795.

Hamilton, H. G. (1998). The movement from *Frye* to *Daubert:* Where do the states stand? *Jurimetrics Journal, 38,* 201–213.

Hebben, N., & Milberg, W. (2009). *Essentials of neuropsychological assessment* (2nd ed.). Hoboken, NJ: Wiley.

Hecker, T., & Steinberg, L. (2002). Psychological evaluation at juvenile court disposition. *Professional Psychology: Research and Practice, 33,* 300–306. http://dx.doi.org/10.1037/0735-7028.33.3.300

Heilbronner, R. L. (2004). A status report on the practice of forensic neuropsychology. *Clinical Neuropsychologist, 18,* 312–326. http://dx.doi.org/10.1080/13854040490501574

Hricik, D., & Salzmann, V. S. (2005). Why there should be fewer articles like this one: Law professors should write more for legal decision-makers and less for themselves. *Suffolk University Law Review, 38,* 761–787.

Kaufman, M. S. (2006). *The status of* Daubert *in state courts.* Retrieved from http://www.atlanticlegal.org/daubertreport.pdf

Kaufmann, P. M., & Greiffenstein, M. F. (2013). Forensic neuropsychology: Training, scope of practice, and quality control. *National Academy of Neuropsychology Bulletin, 27,* 11–15.

Kovera, M. B., & McAuliff, B. D. (2000). The effects of peer review and evidence quality on judge evaluations of psychological science: Are judges effective gatekeepers? *Journal of Applied Psychology, 85,* 574–586. http://dx.doi.org/10.1037/0021-9010.85.4.574

Kovera, M. B., Russano, M. B., & McAuliff, B. D. (2002). Assessment of the commonsense psychology underlying *Daubert*: Legal decision-makers' abilities to evaluate expert evidence in hostile work environment cases. *Psychology, Public Policy, and Law, 8,* 180–200. http://dx.doi.org/10.1037/1076-8971.8.2.180

Krauss, D., & Sales, B. D. (2001). The effects of clinical and scientific expert testimony on juror decision making in capital sentencing. *Psychology, Public Policy, and Law, 7,* 267–310. http://dx.doi.org/10.1037/1076-8971.7.2.267

Lally, S. J. (2003). What tests are acceptable for use in forensic evaluations? A survey of experts. *Professional Psychology: Research and Practice, 34,* 491–498. http://dx.doi.org/10.1037/0735-7028.34.5.491

Lees-Haley, P. R., Smith, H. H., Williams, C. W., & Dunn, J. T. (1996). Forensic neuropsychological test usage: An empirical survey. *Archives of Clinical Neuropsychology, 11,* 45–51. http://dx.doi.org/10.1093/arclin/11.1.45

Loeb, P. A. (1996). *Independent Living Scales manual.* San Antonio, TX: Psychological Corporation.

Neal, T. M. S., & Grisso, T. (2014). The cognitive underpinnings of bias in forensic mental health evaluations. *Psychology, Public Policy, and Law, 20,* 200–211. http://dx.doi.org/10.1037/a0035824

Nicholson, R. A., & Norwood, S. (2000). The quality of forensic psychological assessments, reports, and testimony: Acknowledging the gap between promise and practice. *Law and Human Behavior, 24,* 9–44. http://dx.doi.org/10.1023/A:1005422702678

Nisbett, R. E., & Wilson, T. D. (1977). Telling more than we can know: Verbal reports on mental processes. *Psychological Review, 84,* 231–259. http://dx.doi.org/10.1037/0033-295X.84.3.231

Perlin, M. L. (2004). Everything's a little upside down, as a matter of fact the wheels have stopped: The fraudulence of the incompetency evaluation process. *Houston Journal of Health Law and Policy, 4,* 239–253.

Petrella, R. C., & Poythress, N. G., Jr. (1983). The quality of forensic evaluations: An interdisciplinary study. *Journal of Consulting and Clinical Psychology, 51,* 76–85. http://dx.doi.org/10.1037/0022-006X.51.1.76

Pirelli, G., Gottdiener, W. H., & Zapf, P. A. (2011). A meta-analytic review of competency to stand trial research. *Psychology, Public Policy, and Law, 17,* 1–53. http://dx.doi.org/10.1037/a0021713

Quickel, E. J. W., & Demakis, G. J. (2013). The Independent Living Scales in civil competency evaluations: Initial findings and prediction of competency adjudication. *Law and Human Behavior, 37,* 155–162. http://dx.doi.org/10.1037/lhb0000009

Quickel, E. J. W., Demakis, G. J., & Reeve, C. L. (in press). Which information matters? Using policy capturing to understand civil competency decisions. *Journal of Forensic Psychology Practice.*

Redding, R. E., Floyd, M. Y., & Hawk, G. L. (2001). What judges and lawyers think about the testimony of mental health experts: A survey of the courts and bar. *Behavioral Sciences and the Law, 19,* 583–594. http://dx.doi.org/10.1002/bsl.455

Robbins, E., Waters, J., & Herbert, P. (1997). Competency to stand trial evaluations: A study of actual practice in two states. *Journal of the American Academy of Psychiatry and the Law, 25,* 469–483.

Ryba, N. L., Cooper, V. G., & Zapf, P. A. (2003). Juvenile competence to stand trial evaluations: A survey of current practices and test usage among psychologists. *Professional Psychology: Research and Practice, 34,* 499–507. http://dx.doi.org/10.1037/0735-7028.34.5.499

Sensibaugh, C. C., & Allgeier, E. R. (1996). Factors considered by Ohio juvenile court judges in judicial bypass judgments: A policy-capturing approach. *Politics and the Life Sciences, 15,* 35–47.

Shamir, J. (1998). Motivation and accuracy in estimating opinion distributions: A survey experiment. *International Journal of Public Opinion Research, 10,* 91–108. http://dx.doi.org/10.1093/ijpor/10.2.91

Slovenko, R. (2006). Commentary: Deceptions to the rule on ultimate issue testimony. *Journal of the American Academy of Psychiatry and the Law, 34,* 22–25.

Swenson, R. A., Nash, D. L., & Roos, D. C. (1984). Source credibility and perceived expertness of testimony in a simulated child-custody case. *Professional Psychology: Research and Practice, 15,* 891–898. http://dx.doi.org/10.1037/0735-7028.15.6.891

Tillbrook, C., Mumley, D., & Grisso, T. (2003). Avoiding expert opinions on the ultimate legal question: The case for integrity. *Journal of Forensic Psychology Practice,* 3, 77–87. http://dx.doi.org/10.1300/J158v03n03_05

Tversky, A., & Kahneman, D. (1974). Judgment under uncertainty: Heuristics and biases. *Science, 185,* 1124–1131. http://dx.doi.org/10.1126/science.185.4157.1124

Warren, J. I., Murrie, D. C., Chauhan, P., Dietz, P. E., & Morris, J. (2004). Opinion formation in evaluating sanity at the time of the offense: An examination of 5175 pre-trial evaluations. *Behavioral Sciences and the Law, 22,* 171–186. http://dx.doi.org/10.1002/bsl.559

Warren, J. I., Murrie, D. C., Stejskal, W., Colwell, L. H., Morris, J., Chauhan, P., & Dietz, P. (2006). Opinion formation in evaluating the adjudicative competence and restorability of criminal defendants: A review of 8,000 evaluations. *Behavioral Sciences and the Law, 24,* 113–132. http://dx.doi.org/10.1002/bsl.699

West, R. F., Meserve, R. J., & Stanovich, K. E. (2012). Cognitive sophistication does not attenuate the bias blind spot. *Journal of Personality and Social Psychology, 103,* 506–519. http://dx.doi.org/10.1037/a0028857

Wettstein, R. M. (2005). Quality and quality improvement in forensic mental health evaluations. *Journal of the American Academy of Psychiatry and the Law, 33,* 158–175.

York, K. M. (1992). A policy capturing analysis of federal district and appellate court sexual harassment cases. *Employee Responsibilities and Rights Journal, 5,* 173–184. http://dx.doi.org/10.1007/BF01384735

Zapf, P. A., Hubbard, K. L., Cooper, V. G., Wheeles, M. C., & Ronan, K. A. (2004). Have the courts abdicated their responsibility for determinations of competency to stand trial to clinicians? *Journal of Forensic Psychology Practice, 4,* 27–44. http://dx.doi.org/10.1300/J158v04n01_02

Part VI

FUTURE DIRECTIONS

CHAPTER 21

TECHNOLOGY AND COMPUTERIZED ASSESSMENTS: CURRENT STATE AND FUTURE DIRECTIONS

Dustin Wahlstrom

In 2013, 75% of U.S. families had some sort of mobile device in the home, up from 52% just 2 years earlier (Rideout & Saphir, 2013). Similarly, the number of children between the ages of 0 and 8 years who had used a mobile device doubled, from 38% in 2011 to 72% in 2013. This number will only increase in the years to come and speaks to how ubiquitous technology has become in people's everyday lives. A child assessed today with the Wechsler Primary and Preschool Scale of Intelligence—Fourth Edition will never know a world without the iPad, and even teenagers being evaluated with the Wechsler Adult Intelligence Scale—Fourth Edition (WAIS–IV) will hardly remember a world without the iPod. These changes are beginning to transform the field of neuropsychology as well. Although various forms of computerized testing and scoring have been used for years, especially in research, the advent of mobile technology has resulted in a proliferation of new products, many of which are intended primarily for clinicians.

This chapter summarizes the current state of assessment-based technology in neuropsychology and discusses how the future of the field may benefit from the digital revolution that is currently underway. It begins with a summary of the major types of assessment technologies currently available to practicing neuropsychologists, followed by a discussion of considerations related to the use of digital systems. Data summarizing the impact of digital test administration are reviewed, with a focus on the implications for the interpretation of test data. Finally, future implications for the field of neuropsychology are discussed. It is hoped that this chapter will inform clinicians and forensic practitioners who are making decisions regarding technology adoption, whether it be a conservative move to online scoring or a more comprehensive transition to a completely paperless office, and excite them about the future of a technology-based field of clinical and forensic neuropsychology.

REVIEW OF CURRENT TECHNOLOGY

Neuropsychologists have historically relied on pencil-and-paper testing, with only 10% of practitioners using any form of technology in their practice as recently as 2000 (Camara, Nathan, & Puente, 2000). Few options existed at that time, with the exception of scoring software and a few stand-alone test administration programs, but recent years have seen an explosion of systems that leverage web-based and mobile technology to improve the assessment workflow. In general, most technologies currently available to neuropsychologists fall into one of the following categories:

1. Scoring systems: These systems score tests that have been administered on paper and yield either comprehensive scoring output or narrative interpretive reports. Historically, they took the form of software programs that were stored locally on a user's hard drive, but today most if not all are web based.
2. Administration systems: These systems support the administration of a wide range of

http://dx.doi.org/10.1037/0000032-021
APA Handbook of Forensic Neuropsychology, S. S. Bush (Editor-in-Chief)

tests, including both questionnaires that can be completed by the examinee alone and performance tests that require the examiner to be present.
3. Stand-alone neuropsychological tests: These are similar to administration systems, but different in that they are a single test or suite of tests, as opposed to a general system in which various types of tests can be placed.

A full review of all the tests in each category is beyond the scope of this chapter. Rather, examples are discussed in the text, with tables summarizing a wider range of available options.

Scoring Systems

Scoring software has been available to neuropsychologists for decades, although historically it was relatively inconvenient to use. Software had to be downloaded locally on to hard drives, which made frequent updating difficult, and software packages were sometimes developed for each test individually, meaning any individual clinician might have several different programs that had to be used for a single client. Programs did not always work on both Windows and Mac and became outdated quickly because they were not always updated to be compatible with the newest operating systems. Fortunately, nearly all of the major test publishers have converted their local scoring programs to web-based systems. These include Pearson's Q-global, Multi-Health Systems's Online Assessment Center, and PAR's PARiConnect, each of which hosts the scoring of multiple tests published by each company (see Table 21.1). In addition, many tests that are not supported by a larger system, such as the Woodcock–Johnson IV, have also moved to web-based systems. These scoring systems typically result in two different kinds of output: (a) an in-depth score report that contains a detailed breakdown of scores and (b) narrative interpretive reports. Interpretive reports may be a relatively simple description of test scores, such as that generated for the WAIS–IV, or a much more detailed interpretive report, such as that generated for personality tests such as the Minnesota Multiphasic Personality Inventory.

Administration Systems

The same platforms that are used for scoring (e.g., Q-global, Online Assessment Center, and PARiConnect) are also being used to support on-screen test administration. These systems provide a common interface through which dozens of tests, many of them widely used in the paper world, can be administered. The types of tests that are administered fall into one of two primary categories. First, some web-based measures are questionnaire-based tests that do not need to be administered or proctored by an examiner, which includes tests such as the Behavior Rating Inventory of Executive Function on PARiConnect; the Behavior Assessment System for Children—Second Edition on Q-Global; and the Connors Continuous Performance Test—Third Edition on the Online Assessment Center. Table 21.1 lists some of the more widely used tests that can be administered using digital systems. One attractive feature of web-based testing is that tests can be administered via email links that take parents, teachers, or caregivers to secure portals where the questionnaire can be completed. This has the potential to significantly change the assessment workflow because it is much easier to get information from reporters who will not be present at the assessment session, and the systems synthesize these data into a single dashboard (and, sometimes, combined reports). As a result, examiners can have more data about an examinee before testing that informs hypothesis formulation and test battery creation and results in a more targeted, efficient assessment plan.

These same systems are also beginning to support the administration of performance-based cognitive tests, such as the Reynolds Adaptable Intelligence Test, Peabody Picture Vocabulary Test—Fourth Edition, and the General Ability Measure for Adults. In general, these tests are administered on a computer screen or mobile device and require relatively simple responses on the part of the examinee, which are made with a mouse or by touching the screen. Although the examiner is typically present to answer questions and ensure the validity of the assessment, these tests are for the most part self-guided. Instructions are shown on screen, and logic programmed into the system

TABLE 21.1

Examples of Traditional Paper-and-Pencil Tests That Can Be Scored or Administered Using Web- or Application-Based Systems

Test	System	Online scoring	Digital administration
	Intelligence		
Kaufman Assessment Battery for Children—Second Edition	Q-global	✓	
Reynolds Adaptable Intelligence Test	PARiConnect	✓	✓
Wechsler Adult Intelligence Scale—Fourth Edition	Q-global or Q-interactive	✓	✓
Wechsler Intelligence Scale for Children—Fifth Edition	Q-global or Q-interactive	✓	✓
Wechsler Preschool and Primary Scale of Intelligence—Fourth Edition	Q-global or Q-interactive	✓	✓
Woodcock–Johnson IV Tests of Cognitive Abilities	WJ Online Scoring and Reporting System	✓	
	Achievement and language		
Clinical Evaluation of Language Fundamentals—Fifth Edition	Q-global or Q-interactive	✓	✓
Wechsler Individual Achievement Test—Third Edition	Q-global or Q-interactive	✓	✓
Woodcock–Johnson IV Tests of Achievement	WJ Online Scoring and Reporting System	✓	
Woodcock–Johnson IV Tests of Oral Language	WJ Online Scoring and Reporting System	✓	
	Executive functioning and memory		
Behavior Rating Inventory of Executive Function	PARiConnect	✓	✓
California Verbal Learning Test—Second Edition and California Verbal Learning Test—Children's Version	Q-interactive		✓
Comprehensive Executive Function Inventory	Online Assessment Center	✓	✓
Delis-Rating of Executive Function	Q-global	✓	✓
Wechsler Memory Scale—Fourth Edition	Q-global or Q-interactive	✓	✓
	Behavior, emotion, and personality		
Autism Spectrum Rating Scale	Online Assessment Center	✓	✓
Beck Depression Inventory–II	Q-global	✓	✓
Behavior Assessment System for Children—Second Edition	Q-global	✓	✓
Children's Depression Inventory–2	Online Assessment Center	✓	✓
Clinical Assessment of Depression	PARiConnect	✓	✓
Connors Continuous Performance Test—Third Edition	Online Assessment Center	✓	✓
Millon Clinical Multiaxial Inventory–III	Q-global	✓	✓
Minnesota Multiphasic Personality Inventory–2	Q-global	✓	✓
Multidimensional Anxiety Scale for Children—Second Edition	Online Assessment Center	✓	✓
NEO Personality Inventory–3	PARiConnect	✓	✓
Personality Assessment Inventory	PARiConnect	✓	✓
Trauma Symptom Inventory–2	PARiConnect	✓	✓

governs the flow of administration (e.g., start points, discontinue rules). One impact of this technology moving forward is that it has the potential to enable group administration, which could be used to screen for individuals who need more in-depth assessment. Similarly, it could support the growing trend of tele-assessment, in which tests can be given over long distances via the Internet.

These web-based systems are not well suited for the individually administered assessments that make up the bulk of a neuropsychologist's practice. Conversely, Q-interactive is a unique system intended specifically for the administration of tests such as the Wechsler Intelligence Scale for Children—Fifth Edition (WISC–V) and Delis-Kaplan Executive Function System. It leverages two iPads connected via Bluetooth, one belonging to the clinician and the other to the client. The clinician uses his or her device to show images to the client, read instructions, time performance, and record and score responses. The client responds on his or her device or, in the case of some tests such as WISC–V Comprehension, does not use a device at all. The system automatically tracks start points, reversals, and discontinue rules (all can be overridden for limit testing or other clinical reasons), and all scoring occurs automatically once the clinician enters item raw scores. Relative to other digital assessment products, Q-interactive is unique in the emphasis placed on clinical rapport. Whereas many of the systems discussed in this chapter use a single device and require minimal intervention on the part of the examiner, Q-interactive aims to enhance the interaction between clinician and client by simplifying the number of materials to manage, automating some of the mundane aspects of test administration (e.g., tracking discontinue points), and providing the clinician more time and energy for observation.

Q-interactive is unique among digitally administered tests in that it is a system for the administration of tests that have historically been administered on paper. More common are stand-alone digital systems that were developed specifically for computerized testing and are intended to assess more specific cognitive domains. Examples include MicroCog and Cogstate. Both are computer-administered tests that cover a multitude of cognitive areas such as attention, memory, and reaction time and have research demonstrating their utility in cognitive assessment (Elwood, 2001; Maruff et al., 2009). Another example is CANTAB, which has a long history of use in the research community (De Luca et al., 2003; Robbins et al., 1994) and has spawned a clinically focused dementia screener called CANTAB Mobile. It consists of a short paired-associates learning test, as well as a depression screener and activities of daily living questionnaire. The test is designed for use by medical and mental health professionals and is intended to help identify early onset of dementia.

In 2013, National Institutes of Health (NIH) researchers unveiled the NIH Toolbox for Assessment of Neurological and Behavioral Function (NIH Toolbox), a computerized battery of neurological and behavioral tests with normative information that spans ages 3 to 85 years (Hodes, Insel, & Landis, 2013). Supported by the NIH Blueprint for Neuroscience Research and more than 250 researchers, the toolbox is intended to provide a comprehensive set of validated measures that can provide a standardized metric for neurocognitive research. The toolbox measures four high-level domains: cognition, emotion, motor, and sensation (Gershon et al., 2013). The cognitive domain is of most interest to neuropsychologists and consists of executive function (Dimensional Change Card Sort Test, Flanker Inhibitory Control and Attention Test), episodic memory (Picture Sequence Memory Test, Auditory Verbal Learning Test), language (Oral Reading Recognition Test, Picture Vocabulary Test), processing speed (Pattern Comparison Processing Speed Test, Oral Symbol Digit Test), attention (Flanker Inhibitory Control and Attention Test), and working memory (List Sorting Working Memory Test) subdomains (Weintraub et al., 2013). All tests are administered and scored automatically by the system, and instructions are shown on screen. The examiner is required to be present to provide instructions orally and to monitor the examinee for compliance and other validity threats. All tests have been normed using preliminary validation samples and exhibit good reliability and concurrent validity. Although intended as a research-based measure at this time, as additional normative and clinical data are collected, it is possible that the NIH Toolbox could be used in clinical and forensic settings in the future.

Stand-Alone Administration Systems

As opposed to general systems that are used to assess a wide cross-section of abilities, there are several testing systems intended for a specific cognitive domain. The most widely used are continuous performance tests (CPTs), tests of sustained and selective attention that have long been part of the neuropsychologist's testing library. A number of CPT tests are currently on the market, with the most common being the Connors Continuous Performance Test—Third Edition, Test of Variables of Attention, and the Integrated Visual and Auditory CPT. They vary in subtle ways, but all follow a similar format. The examinee must respond to stimuli that repeat at regular intervals for a sustained period of time (e.g., letters or shapes that repeat every second for 15 minutes total). In one condition, typically referred to as *low stimulation,* the examinee is asked to respond to the infrequent stimuli and withhold responses to frequent stimuli (e.g., "Respond when you see a square and do not respond to any other shapes," with the square appearing only once every five shapes). This pulls primarily for attentional vigilance (i.e., whether the examinee can maintain focus for the duration of the task), which is measured by errors of omission, or failing to respond to the square when it appears. The opposite condition, referred to as *high stimulation,* requires the examinee to respond to a frequently occurring stimulus and withhold responses to other stimuli (e.g., "Respond when you see the square and do not respond to any other shapes," with other shapes appearing only once every five shapes). This condition is aimed at measuring inhibitory control, which is measured by errors of commission (e.g., whether the examinee can withhold from responding to the other shapes when they appear, even though he or she is in the habit of responding to the square).

Although widely used, the research support for CPTs is somewhat mixed. On the one hand, data have historically suggested good sensitivity for attention deficit/hyperactivity disorder (ADHD; Conners, 1985; Greenberg & Waldman, 1993) and adequate split-half and test–retest reliability (Conners, 2008). On the other hand, correlations with parent and teacher rating scales are modest (Forbes, 1998), and the false-positive rate is suspect (Forbes, 1998; A. M. Schatz, Ballantyne, & Trauner, 2001). Given these data, it is clear that CPT tests are best used as a single data point in a more comprehensive evaluation. Interestingly, two new systems, QbTest and Quotient, pair CPTs with unique motion-tracking hardware to enhance their effectiveness in identifying symptoms related to ADHD. Both QbTest and Quotient use a procedure whereby cameras record the examinee's motion during the CPT via a reflective device that he or she wears. These movement data are combined with cognitive data to generate reports that tie them into different aspects of inattention, hyperactivity, and impulsivity. These tests are not intended to be sole sources for identifying ADHD, but a growing research base has suggested that they are effective in discriminating individuals with ADHD from healthy controls (Brocki, Tillman, & Bohlin, 2010; Heiser et al., 2004; Teicher, Lowen, Polcari, Foley, & McGreenery, 2004).

EFFECTS OF DIGITAL ADMINISTRATION ON TEST PERFORMANCE

Adapting tests into a digital format is accompanied by a number of psychometric questions: Does it change test-taking behavior? Are the digital tests reliable? Do subtle changes in how stimuli are displayed change the construct being measured? Clinicians using digital tests are obliged to understand these issues, and professional organizations have developed detailed guidelines for test publishers who adapt tests into a computerized format. For example, digital tests should have documented reliability and validity information if normed digitally, demonstrate raw and construct equivalence to paper parallel forms when appropriate, be accessible by individuals with disability when possible, and be developed with deep knowledge of user experience factors to ensure that the digital administration modality does not introduce construct-irrelevant variance into task performance (American Educational Research Association, American Psychological Association, & National Council on Measurement in Education, 2014; International Test Commission, 2005).

Fortunately, a growing literature has examined the psychometric properties of digital tests and how they compare with traditional paper-based tests. A full discussion of this literature is beyond the scope of this chapter, but readers are encouraged to consult recent reviews for more details (Noyes & Garland, 2008; Wild, Howieson, Webbe, Seelye, & Kaye, 2008). With respect to questionnaire-based tests, some evidence exists that respondents self-disclose differential rates of both positive and negative behaviors if the tests are administered via a secure Internet portal rather than paper (Knapp Whittier, Seeley, & St. Lawrence, 2004; Mangunkusumo et al., 2005). However, a recent evaluation of the Computerized Adaptive Minnesota Multiphasic Personality Inventory—Second Edition indicated comparable reliability and validity to the paper version despite the fact that the computerized version leverages computerized adaptive testing algorithms and administered items via audio files (Forbey, Ben-Porath, & Arbisi, 2012). Other studies have similarly found no difference between computer- and paper-administered questionnaires (Vaughn Sarrazin, Hall, Richards, & Carswell, 2002).

Data regarding the adaptation of cognitive tests have been similarly mixed. Adaptations of the Wisconsin Card Sorting Test, in which the computer shows stimuli and provides feedback, reveal several issues preventing the interchangeable use of norms. Although the digital versions are reliable, examinees make more errors on them, and error variances on the digital version are larger than those on the standard manual administration (Steinmetz, Brunner, Loarer, & Houssemand, 2010; Tien et al., 1996). Some adaptations of the Tower of Hanoi task have suggested no differences between computer- and paper-administered versions (D. J. Williams & Noyes, 2007), whereas others have indicated higher overall scores and longer completion time, which would result in nonequivalence of scores (Noyes & Garland, 2003). Adaptations of basic perceptual speed tasks using touch-screen monitors have indicated that paper and digital versions demonstrate comparable reliability and similar correlations with validity measures (Ackerman & Beier, 2007), and a computerized version of the Raven's Standard Progressive Matrices test was equivalent to a paper version as measured in a sample of healthy young adults (J. E. Williams & McCord, 2006). Thus, as this small cross-section of the data indicates, data vary across studies on different types of tasks and, as seen with the Tower of Hanoi, sometimes even across studies on the same test.

Pearson has published a series of nine non–peer-reviewed technical reports for Q-interactive that assesses the equivalence of scores obtained from paper- and tablet-administered versions of their tests. In general, data across the reports have indicated raw score equivalence between paper and Q-interactive for tests such as the WISC–V, WAIS–IV, and Wechsler Memory Scale—Fourth Edition as evidenced by format effect sizes below an a priori standard of .20 (Daniel, 2012a, 2012b, 2013a, 2013b; Daniel, Wahlstrom, & Zhang, 2014). In the WISC–IV equivalence study (Daniel, 2012b), which was a randomly assigned equivalent groups design ($N = 344$), Matrix Reasoning and Picture Concepts had effect sizes that slightly exceeded the equivalence threshold (.27 and .21, respectively). These results were not replicated in the WISC–V equivalence study (Daniel et al., 2014), in which both subtests had effect sizes below the .20 threshold. One important point about these studies is that the samples consisted of healthy controls, which was an intentional decision to focus on the basic question of whether anything in the digital interface affected test performance. Additional data describing how Q-interactive affects select clinical subgroups are now being released. The first technical report (Raiford, Holdnack, Drozdick, & Zhang, 2014) focused on children with mild intellectual disability and intellectual giftedness and found that their patterns of performance were similar across formats. Because the impact of digital format on clinical group performance is a topic of great interest, it is likely that additional studies of this type will be released in the future.

It is difficult to make broad generalizations regarding the reliability, validity, or equivalence of digital tests because study methodology varies wildly between studies. Samples range in size, include examinees at various points in the life span, and focus on both typically and atypically developing individuals. In addition, the research questions differ slightly (e.g., whether raw scores from paper and digital tests are equivalent, whether this digital test yields similar reliability, and so on), and the psychometric methodologies and standards to address these questions are inconsistent. Perhaps most important, there is considerable variation in how the tests are adapted. For example, Forbey et al. (2012) leveraged technological features when adapting the Minnesota Multiphasic Personality Inventory—Second Edition to administer items via a computer-based audio format and use computerized adaptive testing to limit item sets, both of which had the potential to have a significant impact on scores yielded from the digital version. Alternatively, the adaptation of tests by Q-interactive is purposefully conservative to maintain raw score equivalence; items are still read by examiners, and manipulatives such as Block Design blocks are still used even though one could imagine the test being completed on screen.

The difference between these two adaptations illustrates the pitfalls when attempting to make general conclusions about digital tests. What does this mean for clinicians working in forensic settings, who may find their assessment procedures under greater scrutiny relative to the average provider? The Specialty Guidelines for Forensic Psychology state that

> forensic practitioners use assessment instruments whose validity and reliability have been established for use with members of the population assessed. When such validity and reliability have not been established, forensic practitioners consider and describe the strengths and limitations of their findings. (American Psychological Association, 2013, p. 15)

Clinicians who use a computerized test should determine on a test-by-test and patient-by-patient basis whether the psychometric data collected on it supports its use. In cases in which a test was developed specifically for a digital platform, this means determining whether the reliability and validity evidence meet the same standards required of paper tests, including data specific to the population being assessed by the practitioner. In the case of digital tests that leverage paper norms, clinicians should evaluate whether sufficient evidence has been collected that demonstrates raw score equivalence between the paper and digital versions, to ensure that the previously collected psychometric data can be applied to the digital version of the test.

PRACTICAL, ETHICAL, AND LEGAL IMPLICATIONS OF TECHNOLOGY USE

Technology use is accompanied by significant changes to nearly all aspects of a clinician's practice. Test administration, data storage and retention, communication with other providers, and purchasing all change in a digital medium, and along with these changes comes a responsibility to assess the benefits and risks. This is especially the case for forensic neuropsychologists, who are required to meet unique requirements given their subspecialty. One area affected by digital testing is the accuracy of scores, which is especially relevant in forensic settings, which are characterized by an increased risk of examiner bias and examinees motivated to present themselves in a certain way to obtain some sort of benefit (Bush & Lees-Haley, 2005).

A number of studies on paper test protocols have suggested that examiners are prone to myriad administration errors such as failing to record information or implementing discontinue rules and start points incorrectly (Loe, Kadlubek, & Marks, 2007). Furthermore, although less common than administration errors, clerical scoring errors (e.g., summing item scores incorrectly, using the wrong look-up tables in the manual) also occur relatively frequently and have a much greater impact on scores (Belk, LoBello, Ray, & Zachar, 2002; Hopwood & Richard, 2005). To the extent that digital scoring and administration systems automate these basic processes, related examiner errors can be drastically reduced or eliminated altogether. Given this fact, it is not surprising that comparisons of digital and paper neuropsychological tests such as the Wisconsin Card Sorting Test and Tower of Hanoi suggest that the digital versions boast reliability that is as high or better than that of their paper counterparts (Mataix-Cols & Bartrés-Faz, 2002; P. Schatz & Browndyke, 2002; Tien et al., 1996). Of course, digital testing is unable to remove all sources of examiner error, especially in the cases of scoring software (when tests are administered on paper) or examiner-driven systems such as Q-interactive. Furthermore, technology may introduce new types of errors because examiners are unfamiliar with digital interfaces, which means proper training on digital products requires practice with both test content and the hardware and software used to deliver it.

To the extent that computerized assessments change set-up, administration, and scoring procedures, they can both introduce efficiencies and create new types of overhead for practitioners to manage. In general, computerized test setup is fast and convenient, digital batteries are easy to use (Fillit, Simon, Doniger, & Cummings, 2008), and automated scoring outputs can easily be incorporated into written reports. More important, components of digital systems such as computerized adaptive testing algorithms promise to significantly reduce the number of items that have to be administered to achieve adequate construct measurement (Gibbons et al., 2008). This can decrease testing time and allow for greater construct coverage in a shorter period of time. Although administration time promises to decrease in a digital world, automated scoring can provide similar efficiency gains. Historically, hand-scoring protocols or entering raw data into software programs (e.g., entering lists into the California Verbal Learning Test software) can take a significant amount of time depending on the size of the assessment battery. To the extent that these procedures can be automated and removed from the practitioner workflow, significant time savings can be achieved. Alternatively, digital products are also associated with their own setup inconveniences. Software needs to be updated frequently, and if hardware becomes outdated it might not be able to support newer versions of software packages. Software programs sometimes contain glitches that can interfere with testing procedures, especially for clinicians who are not skilled at troubleshooting technology. Practitioners using digital products should develop good habits related to updating devices, stay apprised of changes in the software field, and plan ahead to make sure that updates or changes to software will not interfere with their assessment session.

Digital testing may have both positive and negative impacts on examinee behavior. On the positive side, technology has the ability to increase engagement and cooperation during administration for some examinees. Technology is ubiquitous at home and school, and so it is not surprising that children report that they prefer taking tests on tablets as opposed to paper if given the choice (Castro, Viezel, Dumont, & Guiney, 2015). Boredom, fatigue, and distractibility are all threats to test validity, so to the extent that digital administration is engaging to examinees, it can increase examiner confidence in test results, especially in forensic settings in which there is intensified scrutiny of examinee effort. On the flip side, technology might be perceived as intimidating to those with low computer familiarity, which is supported by evidence suggesting that less exposure to computers is related to decreased performance on digital assessments (Iverson, Brooks, Ashton, Johnson, & Gualtieri, 2009; Tun & Lachman, 2010; but see Salthouse, Berish, & Miles, 2002, for evidence of no relationship between experience and test performance). This may be especially true for older individuals, who are one of the fastest growing groups of digital adopters (Hart, Chaparro, & Halcomb, 2008) but who still have less computer exposure than younger examinees. The same can be said of individuals from impoverished backgrounds, who also have less computer experience than the typical test taker. The Specialty Guidelines for Forensic Psychologists (American Psychological Association, 2013) state that "forensic practitioners consider the . . . various test factors, test-taking abilities, and other characteristics of the person being assessed, such as situational, personal, linguistic, and cultural differences that might affect their judgments or reduce the accuracy of their interpretations" (p. 15). This suggests that practitioners choosing to use digital testing systems need to use their clinical judgment to identify cases in which computerized testing may not be appropriate, whether because of computer familiarity, physical limitations that prevent interactions with digital interfaces, or anxiety. In addition, practitioners should stay apprised of trends in technology adoption, which change rapidly as more and more cohorts gain access to digital devices.

Data security is also an important consideration when selecting a testing format. Testing with digital systems opens up myriad questions, such as how and where data are stored, who can access patient data stored in third-party digital systems, and what additional consent requirements, if any, are required if computerized testing systems are being used. In the United States, federals laws such as the Health Insurance Portability and Accountability Act (1996) and Health Information Technology for Economic and Clinical Health Act (2009) and state laws regulate the protection of patient health information, including security standards and the release of health information. In addition, the American Academy of Clinical Neuropsychology and the National Academy of Neuropsychology issued a joint position addressing a number of professional ethics issues that includes security (Bauer et al., 2012). Practitioners should be familiar with these documents, as well as with any state statutes, psychology board regulations, and local and organizational policies that legislate patient privacy, when making the decision to incorporate technology into their practice.

Computerized testing requires practitioners to be familiar with new policies and change their practice accordingly, but there are positives to this shift as well. In many ways, the server-based models of data storage that many publishers use is more secure than paper-based or low-tech options such as flash drive storage. Human error is the primary cause of data breaches (Lewis, 2003; Liginlal, Sim, & Khansa, 2009) despite the fact that the vast majority of media attention focuses on large-scale breaches caused by hackers. Lost flash drives, score reports left on a common printer, unlocked file cabinets or storage closets, and laptop theft are all more likely to result in a patient data breach than unauthorized access to a third-party server. The implications are twofold. First, practitioners should be confident in the storage of electronic data because computerized testing products must meet high security standards. Second, they should be aware of how their own behavior can place patient data at risk, given the multitude of ways they interact with it on a daily basis.

What does digital data storage mean for forensic neuropsychologists, who are frequently asked to release raw data for discovery purposes and obligated to maintain all data that form the basis of their evidence (Committee on Ethical Guidelines for Forensic Psychologists, 1991)? There are two potential implications. First, it is essential that potential users of technology evaluate the data output from digital tests to ensure that they can output the raw examinee responses required. If a test does not output such responses, instead yielding only summary scores, for example, it may not be appropriate for forensic use. Second, as with paper tests, clinicians using digital tests need to balance disclosure requirements against potential misuse of data by unqualified professionals and the need to protect the intellectual property of test publishers. Technology may offer some relief for clinicians attempting to protect test content because many tests, such as the Minnesota Multiphasic Personality Inventory–2, dissociate examinee responses (e.g., true–false) from the related test questions. Presumably, this allows responses to be released without also releasing the item content associated with it. Of course, any release of examinee responses without the appropriate context increases the likelihood of misinterpretation (Rapp & Ferber, 2003), so practitioners must balance these risks before releasing any data (see Bush & Lees-Haley, 2005, for an in-depth discussion of this issue).

Finally, the incorporation of technology into forensic evaluations also has implications for third-party observation. A well-established literature has demonstrated the impact of third-party observation on test results, with complex cognitive skills most likely to be negatively affected (Howe & McCaffrey, 2010; McCaffrey, Lynch, & Yantz, 2005). Not surprisingly, organizations such as the American Academy of Neuropsychology and the National Academy of Neuropsychology discourage the use of third-party observation in forensics cases (American Academy of Neuropsychology, 2001; Axelrod et al., 2000), although the American Psychological Association's statement offered suggestions for less invasive types of observation (e.g., audio or video recording) in cases in which some type of third-party observation was required (Committee on Psychological Tests and Assessment, 2007). Advancements in mobile technology have made it easy for these types of audio and video data to be collected, and although audio recording has numerous benefits (e.g., accuracy, research, training graduate students), forensic neuropsychologists should proceed carefully. Data have suggested that even audio and video recording can have a negative impact on scores on some types of neuropsychological measures (Constantinou, Ashendorf, & McCaffrey, 2002, 2005), and those methodologies do not remove other concerns raised by third-party observers (security of intellectual property, etc.).

FUTURE DIRECTIONS

Digital testing affords numerous benefits in its current form, but the true promise of technology lies in what is ahead. Right now, many of the digital applications available to clinicians are adaptations of a test that was originally developed for paper, which constrains test developers because of a need to maintain construct validity. Although that is not true in all cases (e.g., CPT tasks are a good illustration of a test that has been available for a long time and can only be administered digitally because of the detailed response-time data and rapid stimulus presentation), for the most part digitally administered intelligence, memory, and other neuropsychological tests are measuring very similar constructs to what has historically been measured with paper tests. As more and more tests are developed and normed digitally, clinicians should have access to a new set of reliable and valid tests that measure cognitive processes in ways never before possible in a paper world. One need look no further than the innovative tasks being used in cognitive neuroscience research over the past decade, such as tasks of affective and social decision making (Güroğlu, van den Bos, & Crone, 2009; Kerr & Zelazo, 2004), delayed discounting (Olson et al., 2009), and reward processing (Galvan et al., 2006; Van Leijenhorst et al., 2010). As digital testing becomes more ubiquitous in clinical settings, will tasks such as these become a part of the clinician's assessment toolbox? They may not any time soon, because many of these tasks do not have the necessary reliability and validity research to support their use as clinical measures. However, digital testing, combined with rapid increases in the use of electronic health records (Patel, Jamoom, Hsiao, Furukawa, & Buntin, 2013), promises to make obtaining these data easier by pushing psychology into the age of big data that is already transforming other industries.

Initiatives like the NIH Toolbox are taking the first step by having a common set of tasks that the research community can use, allowing for a common currency that can be used to communicate findings and a standardized set of data that could potentially be aggregated. Similarly, the server-based scoring and administration systems adopted by test publishers allow them to interact with clinicians to obtain real-time data that can be leveraged to create unique clinical group norms or other types of scores, which can in turn be used by practitioners. The aggregation of these data should allow for more informative data sets, which will, one hopes, result in better assessment results and improved outcomes for the individuals and forensic clients served by neuropsychologists. Readers are encouraged to reference one of several available commentaries on the opportunities and challenges that big data present for health care (e.g., Murdoch & Detsky, 2013; Roski, Bo-Linn, & Andrews, 2014).

Big data is not the only thing that has exploded in recent years. The gaming industry has seen similar growth, fueled by advances in hardware, software, and integration with other systems via the Internet. A simple search of math and reading games in the Apple App Store yields thousands of results, and gamification techniques (e.g., the use of gaming mechanics in nongame contexts to increase engagement and meaning) are being embedded throughout the educational experience to make learning more fun and effective (Kapp, 2012). This technique has obvious applications to the field of assessment, especially because tests are implemented digitally to take easy advantage of gaming principles. As in education, gaming applications have the potential to make assessments more engaging and less anxiety provoking than traditional tests, which should have a positive impact on examinee cooperation and ensure that maximal performance is being achieved. There are a host of psychometric issues to be sorted out; any assessment influenced by gaming concepts must demonstrate reliability and validity data on par with or better than traditional tests, and thus any gaming components that are incorporated must not introduce any construct-irrelevant variance. GlassLab is a nonprofit group that is helping to lead the exploration into game-based assessment; its white paper regarding the psychometric considerations required for this type of testing is a good reference for those interested (Mislevy et al., 2014).

Much of the technology discussed in this chapter is intended to be a replacement for paper materials in traditional assessment setting. However, advancements in technology will someday go farther, perhaps replacing the typical assessment session with something more effective. Some of this work has already started with the implementation of virtual reality- (VR-) based assessments, which are being used for the assessment of attention (Parsons, Courtney, Arizmendi, & Dawson, 2011), memory (Knight & Titov, 2009), and executive functioning (Parsons et al., 2012). VR is appealing because it allows for the controlled simulation of ecologically valid tasks and activities in a real-world environment, rather than the contrived experimental settings that are typically used today. Although the standardization, reliability, and validity of these paradigms require intense study, data collected thus far suggest that VR assessments have promise. As with all technology, VR systems are likely to improve and become more cost-effective over time, and as they do their practical applications in the field of psychology, including forensic neuropsychology, will likely expand.

CONCLUSION

After decades of incremental technological advancements, neuropsychology is beginning to see a rapid expansion of digital applications available to clinicians. In the short term, these applications promise to replace paper materials and will make testing more efficient, accurate, and engaging for both the examinee and the examiner. In the long term, technology will likely revolutionize the practice of forensic neuropsychology similarly to how it has other industries, whether through advanced data analytics, the creation of new tests that change the constructs used to understand examinees, or completely new environments that replace the traditional testing setting. Although the exact nature of these changes is impossible to predict, it promises an exciting future for the field, one that will benefit both practitioners and those using forensic neuropsychological services.

References

Ackerman, P. L., & Beier, M. E. (2007). Further explorations of perceptual speed abilities in the context of assessment methods, cognitive abilities, and individual differences during skill acquisition. *Journal of Experimental Psychology: Applied, 13,* 249–272. http://dx.doi.org/10.1037/1076-898X.13.4.249

American Academy of Clinical Neuropsychology. (2001). Policy statement on the presence of third party observers in neuropsychological assessments. *Clinical Neuropsychologist, 15,* 435–439.

American Educational Research Association, American Psychological Association, & National Council on Measurement in Education. (2014). *Standards for educational and psychological testing*. Washington, DC: Author.

American Psychological Association. (2013). Specialty guidelines for forensic psychology. *American Psychologist, 68,* 7–19. http://dx.doi.org/10.1037/a0029889

Axelrod, B., Barth, J., Faust, D., Fisher, J., Heilbronner, R., Larrabee, G., . . . Silver, C. (2000). Presence of third party observers during neuropsychological testing: Official statement of the National Academy of Neuropsychology. *Archives of Clinical Neuropsychology, 15,* 379–380. http://dx.doi.org/10.1093/arclin/15.5.379

Bauer, R. M., Iverson, G. L., Cernich, A. N., Binder, L. M., Ruff, R. M., & Naugle, R. I. (2012). Computerized neuropsychological assessment devices: Joint position paper of the American Academy of Clinical Neuropsychology and the National Academy of Neuropsychology. *Archives of Clinical Neuropsychology, 27,* 362–373. http://dx.doi.org/10.1093/arclin/acs027

Belk, M. S., LoBello, S. G., Ray, G. E., & Zachar, P. (2002). WISC–III administration, clerical, and scoring errors made by student examiners. *Journal of Psychoeducational Assessment, 20,* 290–300. http://dx.doi.org/10.1177/073428290202000305

Brocki, K. C., Tillman, C. M., & Bohlin, G. (2010). CPT performance, motor activity, and continuous relations to ADHD symptom domains: A developmental study. *European Journal of Developmental Psychology, 7,* 178–197. http://dx.doi.org/10.1080/17405620801937764

Bush, S. S., & Lees-Haley, P. R. (2005). Threats to the validity of forensic neuropsychological data: Ethical considerations. *Journal of Forensic Neuropsychology, 4,* 45–66. http://dx.doi.org/10.1300/J151v04n03_04

Camara, W. J., Nathan, J. S., & Puente, A. E. (2000). Psychological test usage: Implications in professional psychology. *Professional Psychology: Research and Practice, 31,* 141–154.

Castro, C. J., Viezel, K. D., Dumont, R. D., & Guiney, M. C. (2015, February). *Comparing test behavior using Q-interactive WISC–IV versus paper-pencil WISV–IV.* Poster presented at the Annual Meeting of the National Association of School Psychologists, Orlando, FL.

Committee on Ethical Guidelines for Forensic Psychologists. (1991). Specialty guidelines for forensic psychologists. *Law and Human Behavior, 15,* 655–665. http://dx.doi.org/10.1007/BF01065858

Committee on Psychological Tests and Assessment, American Psychological Association. (2007). *Statement on third party observers in psychological testing and assessment: A framework for decision making.* Retrieved from http://www.apa.org/science/programs/testing/third-party-observers.pdf

Conners, C. K. (1985). Issues in the study of adolescent ADD-H/hyperactivity. *Psychopharmacology Bulletin, 21,* 243–250.

Conners, C. K. (2008). *Conners Continuous Performance Test—Third Edition.* Toronto, Ontario, Canada: Multi-Health Systems.

Constantinou, M., Ashendorf, L., & McCaffrey, R. J. (2002). When the third party observer of a neuropsychological evaluation is an audio-recorder. *Clinical Neuropsychologist, 16,* 407–412. http://dx.doi.org/10.1076/clin.16.3.407.13853

Constantinou, M., Ashendorf, L., & McCaffrey, R. J. (2005). Effects of a third party observer during neuropsychological assessment: When the observer is a video camera. *Journal of Forensic Neuropsychology, 4,* 39–47. http://dx.doi.org/10.1300/J151v04n02_04

Daniel, M. H. (2012a). *Equivalence of Q-interactive-administered cognitive tasks: WAIS–IV* (Q-interactive Tech. Rep. No. 1). Bloomington, MN: Pearson.

Daniel, M. H. (2012b). *Equivalence of Q-interactive-administered cognitive tasks: WISC–IV* (Q-interactive Tech. Rep. No. 2). Bloomington, MN: Pearson.

Daniel, M. H. (2013a). *Equivalence of Q-interactive and paper administration of WMS–IV cognitive tasks* (Q-interactive Tech. Rep. No. 6). Bloomington, MN: Pearson.

Daniel, M. H. (2013b). *Equivalence of Q-interactive and paper scoring of academic tasks: Selected WIAT–III subtests* (Q-interactive Tech. Rep. No. 5). Bloomington, MN: Pearson.

Daniel, M. H., Wahlstrom, D., & Zhang, O. (2014). *Equivalence of Q-interactive and paper administrations of cognitive tasks: WISC–V* (Q-interactive Tech. Rep. No. 8). Bloomington, MN: Pearson.

De Luca, C. R., Wood, S. J., Anderson, V., Buchanan, J. A., Proffitt, T. M., Mahony, K., & Pantelis, C. (2003). Normative data from the CANTAB. I: Development of executive function over the lifespan. *Journal of Clinical and Experimental Neuropsychology, 25,* 242–254. http://dx.doi.org/10.1076/jcen.25.2.242.13639

Elwood, R. W. (2001). MicroCog: Assessment of cognitive functioning. *Neuropsychology Review, 11,* 89–100. http://dx.doi.org/10.1023/A:1016671201211

Fillit, H. M., Simon, E. S., Doniger, G. M., & Cummings, J. L. (2008). Practicality of a computerized system for cognitive assessment in the elderly. *Alzheimer's and Dementia, 4,* 14–21. http://dx.doi.org/10.1016/j.jalz.2007.09.008

Forbes, G. B. (1998). Clinical utility of the Test of Variables of Attention (TOVA) in the diagnosis of attention-deficit/hyperactivity disorder. *Journal of Clinical Psychology, 54,* 461–476. http://dx.doi.org/10.1002/(SICI)1097-4679(199806)54:4<461::AID-JCLP8>3.0.CO;2-Q

Forbey, J. D., Ben-Porath, Y. S., & Arbisi, P. A. (2012). The MMPI–2 computerized adaptive version (MMPI–2–CA) in a Veterans Administration medical outpatient facility. *Psychological Assessment, 24,* 628–639. http://dx.doi.org/10.1037/a0026509

Galvan, A., Hare, T. A., Parra, C. E., Penn, J., Voss, H., Glover, G., & Casey, B. J. (2006). Earlier development of the accumbens relative to orbitofrontal cortex might underlie risk-taking behavior in adolescents. *Journal of Neuroscience, 26,* 6885–6892. http://dx.doi.org/10.1523/JNEUROSCI.1062-06.2006

Gershon, R. C., Wagster, M. V., Hendrie, H. C., Fox, N. A., Cook, K. F., & Nowinski, C. J. (2013). NIH toolbox for assessment of neurological and behavioral function. *Neurology, 80*(Suppl. 3), S2–S6. http://dx.doi.org/10.1212/WNL.0b013e3182872e5f

Gibbons, R. D., Weiss, D. J., Kupfer, D. J., Frank, E., Fagiolini, A., Grochocinski, V. J., . . . Immekus, J. C. (2008). Using computerized adaptive testing to reduce the burden of mental health assessment. *Psychiatric Services, 59,* 361–368. http://dx.doi.org/10.1176/ps.2008.59.4.361

Greenberg, L. M., & Waldmant, I. D. (1993). Developmental normative data on the Test of Variables of Attention (TOVA). *Journal of Child Psychology and Psychiatry, and Allied Disciplines, 34,* 1019–1030. http://dx.doi.org/10.1111/j.1469-7610.1993.tb01105.x

Güroğlu, B., van den Bos, W., & Crone, E. A. (2009). Neural correlates of social decision making and relationships: A developmental perspective. *Annals of the New York Academy of Sciences, 1167,* 197–206. http://dx.doi.org/10.1111/j.1749-6632.2009.04502.x

Hart, T., Chaparro, B., & Halcomb, C. (2008). Evaluating websites for older adults: Adherence to senior-friendly guidelines and end-user performance. *Behaviour and Information Technology, 27,* 191–199. http://dx.doi.org/10.1080/01449290600802031

Health Information Technology for Economic and Clinical Health Act, Pub. L. No. 111-5, Div. A, Title XII, Div. B, Title IV, 123 Stat. 226, 467, 42 U.S.C. 300jj et seq.; 17901 et seq. (2009).

Health Insurance Portability and Accountability Act, Pub. L. No. 104-191, 42 U.S.C. § 300gg, 29 U.S.C. § 1181–1183, and 42 U.S.C. § 1320d1–1320d9 (1996).

Heiser, P., Frey, J., Smidt, J., Sommerlad, C., Wehmeier, P. M., Hebebrand, J., & Remschmidt, H. (2004). Objective measurement of hyperactivity, impulsivity, and inattention in children with hyperkinetic disorders before and after treatment with methylphenidate. *European Child and Adolescent Psychiatry, 13,* 100–104. http://dx.doi.org/10.1007/s00787-004-0365-3

Hodes, R. J., Insel, T. R., & Landis, S. C. (2013). The NIH toolbox: Setting a standard for biomedical research. *Neurology, 80*(Suppl. 3), S1. http://dx.doi.org/10.1212/WNL.0b013e3182872e90

Hopwood, C. J., & Richard, D. C. S. (2005). Graduate student WAIS–III scoring accuracy is a function of full scale IQ and complexity of examiner tasks. *Assessment, 12,* 445–454. http://dx.doi.org/10.1177/1073191105281072

Howe, L. L. S., & McCaffrey, R. J. (2010). Third party observation during neuropsychological evaluation: An update on the literature, practical advice for practitioners, and future directions. *Clinical Neuropsychologist, 24,* 518–537. http://dx.doi.org/10.1080/13854041003775347

International Test Commission. (2005). *International guidelines on computer-based and internet-delivered testing (Version 1.0).* Retrieved from https://www.intestcom.org/files/guideline_computer_based_testing.pdf

Iverson, G. L., Brooks, B. L., Ashton, V. L., Johnson, L. G., & Gualtieri, C. T. (2009). Does familiarity with computers affect computerized neuropsychological test performance? *Journal of Clinical and Experimental Neuropsychology, 31,* 594–604. http://dx.doi.org/10.1080/13803390802372125

Kapp, K. M. (2012). *The gamification of learning and instruction: Game-based methods and strategies for training and education.* San Francisco, CA: Wiley.

Kerr, A., & Zelazo, P. D. (2004). Development of "hot" executive function: The children's gambling task. *Brain and Cognition, 55,* 148–157. http://dx.doi.org/10.1016/S0278-2626(03)00275-6

Knapp Whittier, D., Seeley, S., & St. Lawrence, J. S. (2004). A comparison of web- with paper-based surveys of gay and bisexual men who vacationed in a gay resort community. *AIDS Education and Prevention, 16,* 476–485.

Knight, R. G., & Titov, N. (2009). Use of virtual reality tasks to assess prospective memory: Applicability and evidence. *Brain Impairment, 10,* 3–13. http://dx.doi.org/10.1375/brim.10.1.3

Lewis, J. (2003). Cyber terror: Missing in action. *Knowledge, Technology, and Policy, 16,* 34–41. http://dx.doi.org/10.1007/s12130-003-1024-6

Liginlal, D., Sim, I., & Khansa, L. (2009). How significant is human error as a cause of privacy breaches? An empirical study and a framework for error management. *Computers and Security, 28,* 215–228. http://dx.doi.org/10.1016/j.cose.2008.11.003

Loe, S. A., Kadlubek, R. M., & Marks, W. J. (2007). Administration and scoring errors on the WISC–IV among graduate student examiners. *Journal of Psychoeducational Assessment, 25,* 237–247. http://dx.doi.org/10.1177/0734282906296505

Mangunkusumo, R. T., Moorman, P. W., Van Den Berg-de Ruiter, A. E., Van Der Lei, J., De Koning, H. J., & Raat, H. (2005). Internet-administered adolescent health questionnaires compared with a paper version in a randomized study. *Journal of Adolescent Health, 36,* 70.e1–70.e6. http://dx.doi.org/10.1016/j.jadohealth.2004.02.020

Maruff, P., Thomas, E., Cysique, L., Brew, B., Collie, A., Snyder, P., & Pietrzak, R. H. (2009). Validity of the CogState brief battery: Relationship to standardized tests and sensitivity to cognitive impairment in mild traumatic brain injury, schizophrenia, and AIDS dementia complex. *Archives of Clinical Neuropsychology, 24,* 165–178. http://dx.doi.org/10.1093/arclin/acp010

Mataix-Cols, D., & Bartrés-Faz, D. (2002). Is the use of the wooden and computerized versions of the Tower of Hanoi puzzle equivalent? *Applied Neuropsychology, 9,* 117–120. http://dx.doi.org/10.1207/S15324826AN0902_8

McCaffrey, R. J., Lynch, J. K., & Yantz, C. L. (2005). Third party observers: Why all the fuss? *Journal of Forensic Neuropsychology, 4,* 1–15. http://dx.doi.org/10.1300/J151v04n02_01

Mislevy, R. J., Andreas, O., Bauer, M. I., von Davier, A. A., Hao, J., Corrigan, S., . . . John, M. (2014). *Psychometric considerations in game-based assessment.* Redwood City, CA: GlassLab Research.

Murdoch, T. B., & Detsky, A. S. (2013). The inevitable application of big data to health care. *JAMA, 309,* 1351–1352. http://dx.doi.org/10.1001/jama.2013.393

Noyes, J. M., & Garland, K. J. (2003). Solving the Tower of Hanoi: Does mode of presentation matter? *Computers in Human Behavior, 19,* 579–592. http://dx.doi.org/10.1016/S0747-5632(03)00002-5

Noyes, J. M., & Garland, K. J. (2008). Computer- vs. paper-based tasks: Are they equivalent? *Ergonomics, 51,* 1352–1375. http://dx.doi.org/10.1080/00140130802170387

Olson, E. A., Collins, P. F., Hooper, C. J., Muetzel, R., Lim, K. O., & Luciana, M. (2009). White matter integrity predicts delay discounting behavior in 9- to 23-year-olds: A diffusion tensor imaging study. *Journal of Cognitive Neuroscience, 21,* 1406–1421. http://dx.doi.org/10.1162/jocn.2009.21107

Parsons, T. D., Courtney, C., Rizzo, A. A., Armstrong, C., Edwards, J., & Reger, G. (2012). Virtual reality paced serial assessment test for neuropsychological assessment of a military cohort. *Studies in Health Technology and Informatics, 173,* 331–337.

Parsons, T. D., Courtney, C. G., Arizmendi, B., & Dawson, M. (2011). Virtual reality Stroop task for neurocognitive assessment. *Studies in Health Technology and Informatics, 163,* 433–439.

Patel, V., Jamoom, E., Hsiao, C. J., Furukawa, M. F., & Buntin, M. (2013). Variation in electronic health record adoption and readiness for meaningful use: 2008-2011. *Journal of General Internal Medicine, 28,* 957–964. http://dx.doi.org/10.1007/s11606-012-2324-x

Raiford, S. E., Holdnack, J., Drozdick, L., & Zhang, O. (2014). *Q–interactive special group studies: The WISC–V and children with intellectual giftedness and intellectual disability* (Q-interactive Tech. Rep. No. 9). Bloomington, MN: Pearson.

Rapp, D. L., & Ferber, P. S. (2003). To release, or not to release raw test data, that is the question. In A. M. Horton, Jr., & L. C. Hartlage (Eds.), *Handbook of forensic neuropsychology* (pp. 337–368). New York, NY: Springer.

Rideout, V., & Saphir, M. (2013). *Zero to eight: Children's media use in America 2013.* San Francisco, CA: Common Sense Media.

Robbins, T. W., James, M., Owen, A. M., Sahakian, B. J., McInnes, L., & Rabbitt, P. (1994). Cambridge Neuropsychological Test Automated Battery (CANTAB): A factor analytic study of a large sample of normal elderly volunteers. *Dementia and Geriatric Cognitive Disorders, 5,* 266–281. http://dx.doi.org/10.1159/000106735

Roski, J., Bo-Linn, G. W., & Andrews, T. A. (2014). Creating value in health care through big data: Opportunities and policy implications. *Health Affairs, 33,* 1115–1122. http://dx.doi.org/10.1377/hlthaff.2014.0147

Salthouse, T. A., Berish, D. E., & Miles, J. D. (2002). The role of cognitive stimulation on the relations between age and cognitive functioning. *Psychology and Aging, 17,* 548–557. http://dx.doi.org/10.1037/0882-7974.17.4.548

Schatz, A. M., Ballantyne, A. O., & Trauner, D. A. (2001). Sensitivity and specificity of a computerized test of attention in the diagnosis of attention-deficit/hyperactivity disorder. *Assessment, 8,* 357–365. http://dx.doi.org/10.1177/107319110100800401

Schatz, P., & Browndyke, J. (2002). Applications of computer-based neuropsychological assessment. *Journal of Head Trauma Rehabilitation, 17,* 395–410. http://dx.doi.org/10.1097/00001199-200210000-00003

Steinmetz, J. P., Brunner, M., Loarer, E., & Houssemand, C. (2010). Incomplete psychometric equivalence of scores obtained on the manual and the computer version of the Wisconsin Card Sorting Test? *Psychological Assessment, 22,* 199–202. http://dx.doi.org/10.1037/a0017661

Teicher, M. H., Lowen, S. B., Polcari, A., Foley, M., & McGreenery, C. E. (2004). Novel strategy for the analysis of CPT data provides new insight into the effects of methylphenidate on attentional states in children with ADHD. *Journal of Child and Adolescent Psychopharmacology, 14,* 219–232. http://dx.doi.org/10.1089/1044546041648995

Tien, A. Y., Spevack, T. V., Jones, D. W., Pearlson, G. D., Schlaepfer, T. E., & Strauss, M. E. (1996). Computerized Wisconsin Card Sorting Test: Comparison with manual administration. *Kaohsiung Journal of Medical Sciences, 12,* 479–485.

Tun, P. A., & Lachman, M. E. (2010). The association between computer use and cognition across adulthood: Use it so you won't lose it? *Psychology and Aging, 25,* 560–568. http://dx.doi.org/10.1037/a0019543

Van Leijenhorst, L., Zanolie, K., Van Meel, C. S., Westenberg, P. M., Rombouts, S. A., & Crone, E. A. (2010). What motivates the adolescent? Brain regions mediating reward sensitivity across adolescence. *Cerebral Cortex, 20,* 61–69. http://dx.doi.org/10.1093/cercor/bhp078

Vaughn Sarrazin, M. S., Hall, J. A., Richards, C., & Carswell, C. (2002). A comparison of computer-based versus pencil-and-paper assessment of drug use. *Research on Social Work Practice, 12,* 669–683. http://dx.doi.org/10.1177/1049731502012005006

Weintraub, S., Dikmen, S. S., Heaton, R. K., Tulsky, D. S., Zelazo, P. D., Bauer, P. J., . . . Gershon, R. C. (2013). Cognition assessment using the NIH Toolbox. *Neurology, 80*(Suppl. 3), S54–S64. http://dx.doi.org/10.1212/WNL.0b013e3182872ded

Wild, K., Howieson, D., Webbe, F., Seelye, A., & Kaye, J. (2008). Status of computerized cognitive testing in aging: A systematic review. *Alzheimer's and Dementia, 4,* 428–437. http://dx.doi.org/10.1016/j.jalz.2008.07.003

Williams, D. J., & Noyes, J. M. (2007). Effect of experience and mode of presentation on problem solving. *Computers in Human Behavior, 23,* 258–274. http://dx.doi.org/10.1016/j.chb.2004.10.011

Williams, J. E., & McCord, D. M. (2006). Equivalence of standard and computerized versions of the Raven Progressive Matrices Test. *Computers in Human Behavior, 22,* 791–800. http://dx.doi.org/10.1016/j.chb.2004.03.005

Chapter 22

EDUCATION AND TRAINING IN FORENSIC NEUROPSYCHOLOGY

Michelle Hoy-Watkins, Shane S. Bush, and Joseph J. Sesta

The goal of education and training is to establish competence to perform a given task or service. Competence in psychology is an ethical mandate (Ethical Standard 2; American Psychological Association [APA], 2017), established to promote the provision of beneficial services and just decisions. Competent practice of forensic neuropsychology requires unique knowledge and skills obtained through education, training, and experience in the recognized specialty areas of both neuropsychology and forensic psychology. Because the interface of psychology, neuropsychology, and the law continues to expand at a rapid rate (Kaufmann, 2009), the need for competent practitioners of forensic neuropsychology is greater than ever before.

MODELS OF EDUCATION AND TRAINING

The Houston Conference (HC) policy statement on specialty education and training in neuropsychology provides a benchmark for standards of education, training, and practice in clinical neuropsychology (Bieliauskas, 1998; Hannay et al., 1998). The HC model is based on a scientist–practitioner model (Belar & Perry, 1992). The policy statement suggests, in part, that

> all aspects of general neuropsychology and professional education and training should be integrated; this is the "horizontal" dimension of education and training. Integration should begin with doctoral education and should continue through internship and residency education and training; this is the "vertical" dimension of education and training. (Bieliauskas, 1998, p. 160).

More specifically, according to the HC model,

> specialization in clinical neuropsychology begins at the doctoral level which provides the generic psychology and clinical core. In addition, it includes foundations for the study of brain-behavior relations and the practice of clinical neuropsychology. . . . The purpose of the internship is to complete training in the general practice of professional psychology and extend specialty preparation in science and professional practice in clinical neuropsychology. . . . Residency education and training is designed to provide clinical, didactic and academic training to produce an advanced level of competence in the specialty of clinical neuropsychology and to complete the education and training necessary for independent practice in the specialty. . . . The expected period of residency extends for the equivalent of two years of full-time education and training. All specialists in clinical neuropsychology are expected to engage in annual continuing education. (Bieliauskas, 1998, pp. 163–164)

A survey on the influence of the HC on the practice of neuropsychology revealed that

http://dx.doi.org/10.1037/0000032-022
APA Handbook of Forensic Neuropsychology, S. S. Bush (Editor-in-Chief)

> the HC guidelines appear to have been widely adopted by training programs, in that a large proportion of younger practitioners endorsed having had HC-adherent training; and . . . HC-adherent training is associated with a higher frequency endorsement of being well prepared to engage in key professional activities subsequent to the completion of training when compared with those not having HC-adherent training. Overall, the [Inter-Organization Summit on Education and Training] Steering Committee has concluded that the HC guidelines have been widely adopted and that trainees associate participation in HC-adherent training as advantageous. (Sweet, Perry, Ruff, Shear, & Guidotti Breting, 2012, p. 1055)

The HC model makes no reference to forensic practice.

As with neuropsychology, models for education and training exist for forensic psychology (DeMatteo, Marczyk, Krauss, & Burl, 2009). However, as DeMatteo et al. (2009) noted, "Despite the increased availability of forensic psychology training programs, there is little consensus regarding the core substantive components of these programs" (p. 184). That is, among the nearly 50 graduate programs available in forensic psychology (American Psychology–Law Society, 2008), little agreement exists among programs on appropriate training models, curricula, and training goals (DeMatteo et al., 2009). Such diversity is problematic because of the wide variability in forensic psychology knowledge and skills possessed by graduates of the various programs, which can be confusing to both practitioners and retaining parties because of the uncertainty about what is required for competent practice of forensic psychology. However, an appealing aspect of the diversity in education and training programs is that it offers students and trainees opportunities to pursue those components of professional development that are of greatest interest to them.

DeMatteo et al. (2009) described three broad models for doctoral-level psychology and forensic psychology education and training: the scientist–practitioner (Boulder) model, the practitioner–scientist model, and the scientist–scholar model. They offered a forensic psychology doctoral curriculum consisting of education and training in the following seven areas: (a) substantive psychology, (b) research–design methodology and statistics, (c) conducting research, (d) legal knowledge, (e) integrative law-psychology knowledge, (f) ethics and professional issues, and (g) clinical forensic training. Citing Otto and Heilbrun (2002), they also noted that most specialty training in forensic psychology occurs at the doctoral level. DeMatteo et al. concluded,

> Just as traditional PhD programs in clinical psychology (at least those that adhere to the Boulder model) prepare students to function in a variety of roles (e.g., researcher, clinician, academic), it is essential that forensic psychology training programs prepare students to assume several different roles. Rather than creating specialists, forensic psychology training programs would be better advised to provide students with a foundational level of competence in a variety of core component areas, which is consistent with the guidelines promulgated by the APA's Committee on Accreditation (2008) in terms of preparing students for entry-level practice in professional psychology. Specialization in a particular area of forensic psychology would seem to be best achieved at the postdoctoral level after the student has obtained a core set of competencies. (p. 190)

There are no education and training guidelines specific to forensic neuropsychology, leaving educators and training directors, informed by the models provided for forensic psychology and neuropsychology, to integrate components of both specialties. In addition to the references previously described, key resources, among the many that exist, include the *Specialty Competencies in Clinical Neuropsychology* (Lamberty & Nelson, 2012), *Specialty Competencies in Forensic Psychology* (Packer & Grisso, 2011), and *Specialty Guidelines for Forensic Psychology* (APA, 2013).

Rodolfa et al. (2005) provided a conceptual framework model for competency development in psychology. Their cube model covers both foundational (knowledge, skills, attitudes, and values) and functional (professional activities) competencies. Foundational competencies include the following: "(a) reflective practice—self-assessment, (b) scientific knowledge and methods, (c) relationships, (d) individual and cultural diversity, (e) ethical and legal standards—policy issues, and (f) interdisciplinary systems" (p. 350). Functional competencies include the following: "(a) assessment–diagnosis–case conceptualization, (b) intervention, (c) consultation, (d) research—evaluation, (e) supervision—training, and (f) management—administration" (p. 351; see also Fouad et al., 2009). Educators and supervisors also model respectful and ethical professional behavior, addressing only those aspects of practice in which they possess specific training or competence, delegating to colleagues topics for which their competence is lacking.

Once the content to be covered has been selected, general theories of learning can be applied. Mintz (2015) summarized the lessons learned from such theories as follows: (a) Information that is relevant and meaningful is easier to remember than information that is not, (b) practice or rehearsal makes it easier to retain an idea, (c) prior knowledge or preconceptions can advance or hinder future learning, (d) memory is improved when a learner categorizes ideas or concepts (e.g., by using mnemonics), and (e) memory is context dependent (i.e., it is easiest to remember an idea in a particular context than outside of that context). For more information on translating learning principles into effective learning experiences, the reader is referred to Mintz (2015).

EDUCATION AND TRAINING PROGRAMS IN FORENSIC NEUROPSYCHOLOGY

A Google search revealed very few programs in the United States that offer graduate-level coursework specific to forensic neuropsychology, and we are aware of relatively few psychology training programs that provide didactic, experiential, or research opportunities in this subspecialty. In addition, between the time this chapter was initally written and the time this handbook went to press, some of the programs changed or were discontinued.

Educational Opportunities in Forensic Neuropsychology

Boston University has a PhD program in behavioral neuroscience that offers a course in forensic practice in neuropsychology and neuroscience. The course description indicates that the program focuses on "the delineation and analysis of perceptual, cognitive, linguistic, affective, and behavioral disorders observed in neurological disease, as these disorders contribute to an understanding of normal brain function and its modification by pathology" (Boston University, n.d., para. 4) both structural and metabolic. The course addresses neuropsychology, psychiatry, and behavioral neurology and their intersection with the law and judicial process. The course also addresses forensic-related issues including malingering, criminal competencies, and criminal responsibility, among others. The course is taught by a multidisciplinary group including, but not limited to, psychologists, judges, attorneys, neuroscientists, and physicians.

Fielding Graduate University offers a PhD program in clinical psychology that has been accredited by the American Psychological Association since 1991. The program offers a concentration in forensic psychology that offers an elective course titled Forensic Neuropsychological Assessment, which is an advanced course worth two semester credits that includes a 1-day face-to-face lab. To be eligible to take the course, students must complete the prerequisite Forensic Psychology course. The latter course provides "an overview of the field of forensic psychology" and integrates "psychological art and science to legal and quasi-legal problems" (Fielding Graduate University, 2016).

Regent University has offered a continuing education workshop titled Forensic Neuropsychology in Civil Competency (http://www.regent.edu/

events/calendar/event_details.cfm?event_id=1986). The course addressed issues related to known and suspected neurocognitive deficits that may affect examinee competence. Psychological assessment, ethical considerations, and functional capacities were also addressed. An online version of the workshop had been mentioned on the university's website, but it was no longer there as this handbook went to press.

Structuring a Forensic Neuropsychology Educational Program

A forensic neuropsychology specialty concentration could be offered within a clinical psychology doctoral program that houses forensic psychology or neuropsychology tracts. Such a program could be designed to include core clinical psychology courses as recommended by APA. The program would also offer both core and elective courses in forensic psychology and neuropsychology. To that end, all students in the program would receive didactic and experiential training in broad and general clinical psychology foundational courses consistent with APA guidelines for doctoral training in psychology.

The neuropsychology and forensic psychology aspects of the concentration would be developed in accordance with the training models and guidelines described previously in this chapter. After completing prerequisite coursework required of all clinical psychology doctoral students, those in the forensic neuropsychology concentration would receive specialized training through a three-course sequence: Clinical Neuropsychology, Forensic Psychology, and Applied Forensic Neuropsychology. The Clinical Neuropsychology course would be the foundation course for the neuropsychology concentration and build on students' earlier coursework in biological bases of behavior, psychological assessment, statistics, and other core courses. This course would introduce students to the structural and functional organization of the brain, review the basics of various neurodiagnostic and neuroimaging procedures (e.g., MRI, functional MRI, single-photon emission computed tomography, positron emission tomography, electroencephalography), and cover brain disorders.

Next, in the Forensic Psychology course, students would be introduced to theories, principles, and techniques of practice in various forensic contexts. In the final course in the specialty concentration sequence, Applied Forensic Neuropsychology, students would learn to integrate the knowledge and skills acquired in the neuropsychology and forensic psychology components of the program. Throughout the sequence of courses, students would obtain an overview of the forensic neuropsychological examination process from referral through assessment, scoring, interpretation, report writing, and expert testimony. Special issues in forensic neuropsychology may be covered, including (a) symptom and performance validity assessment for both neurocognitive and psychological complaints, (b) neuropsychological evaluation of sexually violent predators, (c) disorders that are likely to be encountered in the forensic arenas (e.g., traumatic brain injury, neurotoxicity), (d) pediatric forensic neuropsychology, and (e) neuropsychological evaluation of competency to proceed to trial and criminal responsibility and mental state at the time of the offense. Professors would integrate their forensic practice experiences into their instruction. Ethical issues, challenges, and solutions would be covered throughout.

In addition to coursework, predoctoral clinical training experiences would be intended to establish broad clinical skills, with elective rotations in forensic neuropsychology contexts. Efforts could be made to assist graduates in obtaining more specialized postdoctoral experiences in settings that integrate both neuropsychology and forensic psychology.

CONTINUING EDUCATION AND CREDENTIALING

With the rapidly expanding science underlying the practice of forensic neuropsychology, effective practitioners must remain abreast of advances and changes in the field. Practitioners who fail to do so risk providing harmful services, offering inaccurate diagnoses and forensic opinions, and providing information that is not helpful or is misleading to triers of fact or other decision makers. Such practice

is inconsistent with ethical requirements (Ethical Standard 2.03, Maintaining Competence; APA, 2017) and guidelines (Guideline 2.02, Gaining and Maintaining Competence; APA, 2013). Continuing education workshops on various aspects of neuropsychology and forensic psychology, as well as specific to forensic neuropsychology, are available from numerous professional organizations. Self-study, consultation with colleagues, and participation in relevant online groups provide ways to supplement more formal education and contribute to a broad approach to the maintenance of professional competence. Many states require continuing education for maintenance of licensure.

Formal peer review through a reasonably rigorous board certification process provides evidence of the specialized knowledge and skill required for competent practice of a specialty, including neuropsychology and forensic psychology. The board certification credential provides consumers a means of identifying qualified practitioners. For forensic practitioners in particular, board certification often (a) makes practitioners more appealing to retaining parties, (b) facilitates the credential review aspect of testimony, and (c) facilitates temporary or permanent credentialing outside of one's primary jurisdiction of practice. Of course, board certification in a specialty does not necessarily imply competence in all aspects of that specialty. For example, a practitioner who specializes in criminal evaluations of adults' mental state at the time of the offense may not be qualified to provide civil forensic neuropsychological evaluations of children who have sustained a traumatic brain injury in a motor vehicle collision. Board-certified clinicians, like all psychologists, have an ethical obligation to practice only within their areas of competence or take steps to expand areas of competence. For board-certifying bodies offering subspecialty credentials, certification in forensic neuropsychology may become an option for practitioners. Regarding maintenance of competence, it has become common for board-certifying organizations to require evidence of continuing education in the specialty, which is particularly valuable in jurisdictions in which continuing education is not required by the licensing board.

CONCLUSION

Forensic neuropsychology continues to gain recognition as a subspecialty within both forensic psychology and neuropsychology, and this recognition gains in importance as the demand for forensic neuropsychology practitioners grows. The Commission for the Recognition of Specialties and Proficiencies in Professional Psychology recognizes both clinical neuropsychology and forensic psychology as specialty areas in professional psychology. Several professional organizations in neuropsychology and forensic psychology offer cross-disciplinary continuing education in forensic neuropsychology and related topics needed for competent practice in the specialty.

Although APA currently only accredits doctoral training programs in four psychological specialties (clinical, counseling, school, and combined), the specialty of forensic psychology has developed such that it contains a body of literature, instruments, and procedures and requires knowledge and skills distinct from clinical, counseling, or school psychology. As such, specialized training programs that integrate forensic psychology and neuropsychology can help meet the growing demand for neuropsychological expertise in forensic matters. The information presented in this chapter may inform the development of future programs invested in providing quality education and training for the next generation of forensic neuropsychologists.

References

American Psychological Association. (2013). Specialty guidelines for forensic psychology. *American Psychologist, 68,* 7–19. http://dx.doi.org/10.1037/a0029889

American Psychological Association. (2017). *Ethical principles of psychologists and code of conduct* (2002, Amended June 1, 2010 and January 1, 2017). Retrieved from http://www.apa.org/ethics/code/index.aspx

American Psychology–Law Society. (2008). *Guide to graduate programs in forensic and legal psychology (2007–2008).* Southport, NC: Author.

Belar, C. D., & Perry, N. W. (1992). National Conference on Scientist-Practitioner Education and Training for the Professional Practice of Psychology. *American Psychologist, 47,* 71–75. http://dx.doi.org/10.1037/0003-066X.47.1.71

is inconsistent with ethical requirements (Ethical Standard 2.03, Maintaining Competence; APA, 2017) and guidelines (Guideline 2.02, Gaining and Maintaining Competence; APA, 2013). Continuing education workshops on various aspects of neuropsychology and forensic psychology, as well as specific to forensic neuropsychology, are available from numerous professional organizations. Self-study, consultation with colleagues, and participation in relevant online groups provide ways to supplement more formal education and contribute to a broad approach to the maintenance of professional competence. Many states require continuing education for maintenance of licensure.

Formal peer review through a reasonably rigorous board certification process provides evidence of the specialized knowledge and skill required for competent practice of a specialty, including neuropsychology and forensic psychology. The board certification credential provides consumers a means of identifying qualified practitioners. For forensic practitioners in particular, board certification often (a) makes practitioners more appealing to retaining parties, (b) facilitates the credential review aspect of testimony, and (c) facilitates temporary or permanent credentialing outside of one's primary jurisdiction of practice. Of course, board certification in a specialty does not necessarily imply competence in all aspects of that specialty. For example, a practitioner who specializes in criminal evaluations of adults' mental state at the time of the offense may not be qualified to provide civil forensic neuropsychological evaluations of children who have sustained a traumatic brain injury in a motor vehicle collision. Board-certified clinicians, like all psychologists, have an ethical obligation to practice only within their areas of competence or take steps to expand areas of competence. For board-certifying bodies offering subspecialty credentials, certification in forensic neuropsychology may become an option for practitioners. Regarding maintenance of competence, it has become common for board-certifying organizations to require evidence of continuing education in the specialty, which is particularly valuable in jurisdictions in which continuing education is not required by the licensing board.

CONCLUSION

Forensic neuropsychology continues to gain recognition as a subspecialty within both forensic psychology and neuropsychology, and this recognition gains in importance as the demand for forensic neuropsychology practitioners grows. The Commission for the Recognition of Specialties and Proficiencies in Professional Psychology recognizes both clinical neuropsychology and forensic psychology as specialty areas in professional psychology. Several professional organizations in neuropsychology and forensic psychology offer cross-disciplinary continuing education in forensic neuropsychology and related topics needed for competent practice in the specialty.

Although APA currently only accredits doctoral training programs in four psychological specialties (clinical, counseling, school, and combined), the specialty of forensic psychology has developed such that it contains a body of literature, instruments, and procedures and requires knowledge and skills distinct from clinical, counseling, or school psychology. As such, specialized training programs that integrate forensic psychology and neuropsychology can help meet the growing demand for neuropsychological expertise in forensic matters. The information presented in this chapter may inform the development of future programs invested in providing quality education and training for the next generation of forensic neuropsychologists.

References

American Psychological Association. (2013). Specialty guidelines for forensic psychology. *American Psychologist, 68*, 7–19. http://dx.doi.org/10.1037/a0029889

American Psychological Association. (2017). *Ethical principles of psychologists and code of conduct* (2002, Amended June 1, 2010 and January 1, 2017). Retrieved from http://www.apa.org/ethics/code/index.aspx

American Psychology–Law Society. (2008). *Guide to graduate programs in forensic and legal psychology (2007–2008)*. Southport, NC: Author.

Belar, C. D., & Perry, N. W. (1992). National Conference on Scientist-Practitioner Education and Training for the Professional Practice of Psychology. *American Psychologist, 47*, 71–75. http://dx.doi.org/10.1037/0003-066X.47.1.71

is inconsistent with ethical requirements (Ethical Standard 2.03, Maintaining Competence; APA, 2017) and guidelines (Guideline 2.02, Gaining and Maintaining Competence; APA, 2013). Continuing education workshops on various aspects of neuropsychology and forensic psychology, as well as specific to forensic neuropsychology, are available from numerous professional organizations. Self-study, consultation with colleagues, and participation in relevant online groups provide ways to supplement more formal education and contribute to a broad approach to the maintenance of professional competence. Many states require continuing education for maintenance of licensure.

Formal peer review through a reasonably rigorous board certification process provides evidence of the specialized knowledge and skill required for competent practice of a specialty, including neuropsychology and forensic psychology. The board certification credential provides consumers a means of identifying qualified practitioners. For forensic practitioners in particular, board certification often (a) makes practitioners more appealing to retaining parties, (b) facilitates the credential review aspect of testimony, and (c) facilitates temporary or permanent credentialing outside of one's primary jurisdiction of practice. Of course, board certification in a specialty does not necessarily imply competence in all aspects of that specialty. For example, a practitioner who specializes in criminal evaluations of adults' mental state at the time of the offense may not be qualified to provide civil forensic neuropsychological evaluations of children who have sustained a traumatic brain injury in a motor vehicle collision. Board-certified clinicians, like all psychologists, have an ethical obligation to practice only within their areas of competence or take steps to expand areas of competence. For board-certifying bodies offering subspecialty credentials, certification in forensic neuropsychology may become an option for practitioners. Regarding maintenance of competence, it has become common for board-certifying organizations to require evidence of continuing education in the specialty, which is particularly valuable in jurisdictions in which continuing education is not required by the licensing board.

CONCLUSION

Forensic neuropsychology continues to gain recognition as a subspecialty within both forensic psychology and neuropsychology, and this recognition gains in importance as the demand for forensic neuropsychology practitioners grows. The Commission for the Recognition of Specialties and Proficiencies in Professional Psychology recognizes both clinical neuropsychology and forensic psychology as specialty areas in professional psychology. Several professional organizations in neuropsychology and forensic psychology offer cross-disciplinary continuing education in forensic neuropsychology and related topics needed for competent practice in the specialty.

Although APA currently only accredits doctoral training programs in four psychological specialties (clinical, counseling, school, and combined), the specialty of forensic psychology has developed such that it contains a body of literature, instruments, and procedures and requires knowledge and skills distinct from clinical, counseling, or school psychology. As such, specialized training programs that integrate forensic psychology and neuropsychology can help meet the growing demand for neuropsychological expertise in forensic matters. The information presented in this chapter may inform the development of future programs invested in providing quality education and training for the next generation of forensic neuropsychologists.

References

American Psychological Association. (2013). Specialty guidelines for forensic psychology. *American Psychologist, 68,* 7–19. http://dx.doi.org/10.1037/a0029889

American Psychological Association. (2017). *Ethical principles of psychologists and code of conduct* (2002, Amended June 1, 2010 and January 1, 2017). Retrieved from http://www.apa.org/ethics/code/index.aspx

American Psychology–Law Society. (2008). *Guide to graduate programs in forensic and legal psychology (2007–2008).* Southport, NC: Author.

Belar, C. D., & Perry, N. W. (1992). National Conference on Scientist-Practitioner Education and Training for the Professional Practice of Psychology. *American Psychologist, 47,* 71–75. http://dx.doi.org/10.1037/0003-066X.47.1.71

Bieliauskas, L. A. (1998). The Houston conference on specialty education and training in clinical neuropsychology: Policy statement. *Archives of Clinical Neuropsychology, 13*, 160–166. http://dx.doi.org/10.1093/arclin/13.2.160

Boston University. (n.d.). *PhD in behavioral neuroscience.* Retrieved from http://www.bu.edu/academics/gms/programs/behavioral-neuroscience

DeMatteo, D., Marczyk, G., Krauss, D. A., & Burl, J. (2009). Educational and training models in forensic psychology. *Training and Education in Professional Psychology, 3,* 184–191. http://dx.doi.org/10.1037/a0014582

Fielding Graduate University. (2016). *Psychology with an emphasis in clinical psychology, PhD (with optional concentrations).* Retrieved from http://catalog.fielding.edu/preview_program.php?catoid=3&poid=154&returnto=113

Fouad, N. A., Grus, C. L., Hatcher, R. L., Kaslow, N. J., Hutchings, P. S., Madson, M. B., . . . Crossman, R. E. (2009). Competency benchmarks: A model for understanding and measuring competence in professional psychology across training levels. *Training and Education in Professional Psychology,* 3(4, Suppl.), S5–S26. http://dx.doi.org/10.1037/a0015832

Hannay, H. J., Bieliauskas, L. A., Crosson, B. A., Hammeke, T. A., Hamsher, K. deS., & Koffler, S. P. (1998). Proceedings: The Houston conference on specialty education and training in clinical neuropsychology. *Archives of Clinical Neuropsychology, 13,* 157–158.

Kaufmann, P. M. (2009). Protecting raw data and psychological tests from wrongful disclosure: A primer on the law and other persuasive strategies. *Clinical Neuropsychologist, 23,* 1130–1159. http://dx.doi.org/10.1080/13854040903107809

Lamberty, G. J., & Nelson, N. W. (2012). *Specialty competencies in clinical neuropsychology.* http://dx.doi.org/10.1093/med:psych/9780195387445.001.0001

Mintz, S. (2015). *The fundamentals of college and university teaching.* Retrieved from http://gsas.columbia.edu/sites/default/files/GSAS_fundamentals_handbook.pdf

Otto, R. K., & Heilbrun, K. (2002). The practice of forensic psychology: A look toward the future in light of the past. *American Psychologist, 57,* 5–18. http://dx.doi.org/10.1037/0003-066X.57.1.5

Packer, I. K., & Grisso, T. (2011). *Specialty competencies in forensic psychology.* http://dx.doi.org/10.1093/med:psych/9780195390834.001.0001

Rodolfa, E., Bent, R., Eisman, E., Nelson, P., Rehm, L., & Ritchie, P. (2005). A cube model for competency development: Implications for psychology educators and regulators. *Professional Psychology: Research and Practice, 36,* 347–354. http://dx.doi.org/10.1037/0735-7028.36.4.347

Sweet, J. J., Perry, W., Ruff, R. M., Shear, P. K., & Guidotti Breting, L. M. (2012). The Inter-Organizational Summit on Education and Training (ISET) 2010 survey on the influence of the Houston Conference training guidelines. *Clinical Neuropsychologist, 26,* 1055–1076. http://dx.doi.org/10.1080/13854046.2012.705565

Index